W9-AAD-929

Case Studies in Finance
Managing for Corporate Value Creation

Case Studies in Finance
Managing for Corporate Value Creation

Third Edition

Robert F. Bruner

Boston   Burr Ridge, IL   Dubuque, IA   Madison, WI
New York   San Francisco   St. Louis   Bangkok   Bogotá   Caracas   Lisbon
London   Madrid   Mexico City   Milan   New Delhi   Seoul   Singapore   Sydney   Taipei   Toronto

IRWIN/McGraw-Hill

*A Division of The **McGraw·Hill** Companies*

CASE STUDIES IN FINANCE: MANAGING FOR CORPORATE VALUE CREATION
Copyright © 1999 by The McGraw-Hill Companies, Inc. All rights reserved. Previous editions ©
1990 and 1994, by Richard D. Irwin, a Times Mirror Higher Education Group, Inc., company.
Printed in the United States of America. Except as permitted under the United States Copyright
Act of 1976, no part of this publication may be reproduced or distributed in any form or by any
means, or stored in a data base or retrieval system, without the prior written permission of the
publisher.

This book is printed on acid-free paper.

4 5 6 7 8 9 0 DOC/DOC 9 3 2 1

ISBN 0-256-16698-6

Vice president and editorial director: *Michael W. Junior*
Publisher: *Craig S. Beytien*
Editorial coordinator: *Paula M. Krauza*
Senior marketing manager: *Katie Rose-Matthews*
Senior project manager: *Gladys True*
Production supervisor: *Michael R. McCormick*
Freelance design coordinator: *Laurie J. Entringer*
Supplement coordinator: *Cathy L. Tepper*
Compositor: *Carlisle Communications, Ltd.*
Typeface: *10/12 Times Roman*
Printer: *R. R. Donnelley & Sons Company*

Library of Congress Cataloging-in-Publication Data

Bruner, Robert F. (date)
   Case studies in finance : managing for corporate value creation /
   Robert F. Bruner. — 3rd ed.
      p.   cm.
   ISBN 0-256-16698-6
   1. Corporations—Finance—Case studies. 2. International business
enterprises—Finance—Case studies. 3. Decision-making—Case
studies. 4. Women executives. I. Title.
HG4015.5.B78 1999
   658.15—dc21   98-23633
http://www.mhhe.com

THE IRWIN/MCGRAW-HILL SERIES IN FINANCE, INSURANCE AND REAL ESTATE

Stephen A. Ross
Franco Modigliani Professor of Financial Economics
Sloan School of Management
Massachusetts Institute of Technology
Consulting Editor

Financial Management

Benninga and Sarig
Corporate Finance:
A Valuation Approach

Block and Hirt
Foundations of Financial
Management
Eighth Edition

Brealey and Myers
Principles of Corporate
Finance
Fifth Edition

Brealey, Myers and Marcus
Fundamentals of Corporate
Finance
Second Edition

Brooks
PC FinGame: The Financial
Management Decision Game
Version 2.0 -
DOS and Windows

Bruner
Case Studies in Finance:
Managing for Corporate
Value Creation
Third Edition

Bruner, Eades and Harris
Finance Interactive:
Pre-MBA Series 2000

Chew
The New Corporate Finance:
Where Theory Meets
Practice
Second Edition

Grinblatt and Titman
Financial Markets and
Corporate Strategy

Helfert
Techniques of Financial
Analysis: A Modern
Approach
Ninth Edition

Higgins
Analysis for Financial
Management
Fifth Edition

Hite
A Programmed Learning
Guide to Finance

Kester, Fruhan, Piper
and Ruback
Case Problems in Finance
Eleventh Edition

Nunnally and Plath
Cases in Finance
Second Edition

Parker and Beaver
Risk Management:
Challenges and Solutions

Ross, Westerfield and Jaffe
Corporate Finance
Fifth Edition

Ross, Westerfield and Jordan
Essentials of
Corporate Finance
Second Edition

Ross, Westerfield and Jordan
Fundamentals of
Corporate Finance
Fourth Edition

Schall and Haley
Introduction to Financial
Management
Sixth Edition

Smith
The Modern Theory of
Corporate Finance
Second Edition

White
Financial Analysis with an
Electronic Calculator
Third Edition

Investments

Ball and Kothari
Financial Statement Analysis

Bodie, Kane and Marcus
Essentials of Investments
Third Edition

Bodie, Kane and Marcus
Investments
Fourth Edition

Cohen, Zinbarg and Zeikel
Investment Analysis and
Portfolio Management
Fifth Edition

Farrell
Portfolio Management:
Theory and Applications
Second Edition

Hirt and Block
Fundamentals of Investment
Management
Sixth Edition

Jarrow
Modelling Fixed Income Securities and Interest Rate Options
Morningstar, Inc., and Remaley
U.S. Equities OnFloppy Educational Version
Annual Edition
Shimko
The Innovative Investor
Excel Version

Financial Institutions and Markets

Cornett and Saunders
Fundamentals of Financial Institutions Management
Flannery and Flood
Flannery and Flood's ProBanker: A Financial Services Simulation
Johnson
Financial Institutions and Markets: A Global Perspective
Rose
Commercial Bank Management
Third Edition
Rose
Money and Capital Markets: Financial Institutions and Instruments in a Global Marketplace
Sixth Edition
Rose and Kolari
Financial Institutions: Understanding and Managing Financial Services
Fifth Edition
Santomero and Babbel
Financial Markets, Instruments, and Institutions

Saunders
Financial Institutions Management: A Modern Perspective
Second Edition

International Finance

Eun and Resnick
International Financial Management
Kester and Luehrman
Case Problems in International Finance
Second Edition
Levi
International Finance
Third Edition
Levich
International Financial Markets: Prices and Policies
Stonehill and Eiteman
Finance: An International Perspective

Real Estate

Berston
California Real Estate Principles
Seventh Edition
Brueggeman and Fisher
Real Estate Finance and Investments
Tenth Edition
Corgel, Smith and Ling
Real Estate Perspectives: An Introduction to Real Estate
Third Edition
Lusht
Real Estate Valuation: Principles and Applications
Sirmans
Real Estate Finance

Second Edition

Financial Planning and Insurance

Allen, Melone, Rosenbloom and VanDerhei
Pension Planning: Pension, Profit-Sharing, and Other Deferred Compensation Plans
Eighth Edition
Crawford
Life and Health Insurance Law
Eighth Edition (LOMA)
Harrington and Niehaus
Risk Management and Insurance
Hirsch
Casualty Claim Practice
Sixth Edition
Kapoor, Dlabay and Hughes
Personal Finance
Fifth Edition
Kellison
Theory of Interest
Second Edition
Lang
Strategy for Personal Finance
Fifth Edition
Skipper
International Risk and Insurance: An Environmental-Managerial Approach
Williams, Smith and Young
Risk Management and Insurance
Eighth Edition

In dedication to my wife,

Bobbie

Love . . . is an ever-fixèd mark
That looks on tempests and is never shaken;
It is the star to every wand'ring bark,
Whose worth's unknown, although his height be taken.

William Shakespeare, from Sonnet 116

About the Author

Robert F. Bruner is Distinguished Professor of Business Administration at the Darden Graduate School of Business Administration, University of Virginia. His work has been published in journals such as *Financial Management, Journal of Accounting and Economics, Journal of Applied Corporate Finance, Journal of Financial Economics, Journal of Financial and Quantitative Analysis,* and *Journal of Money, Credit, and Banking.* His research has concentrated in corporate finance, particularly mergers, restructurings, and corporate financing policies. He is the co-author of *Finance Interactive,* multimedia tutorial software in finance, and of *The Portable MBA.* He has received numerous awards for teaching and casewriting in the United States and Europe. *Business Week* magazine has cited him as one of the "Masters of the MBA classroom." Industrial corporations, financial institutions, and government agencies have retained him for counsel and training. He has served the Darden School and community organizations in various positions of leadership.

Foreword

by Michael C. Jensen
Jesse Isidor Straus Professor
Harvard Business School

The case literature in Finance has changed dramatically in the last 20 years. On one hand, this mirrors the revolutionary transformation in markets and organization we have seen in the business world. And on the other hand, it reflects the many major advances in Finance theory and empirical research. Since case studies are an important avenue along which scholars, students, and practitioners communicate, it is very important that this literature grow along with practice and the theoretical and large sample empirical scholarship in finance.

Bob Bruner has contributed significantly to the growth and change of the Finance case literature. First, his cases link managerial decisions to capital markets and the expectations of investors. At the core of almost all of his cases is a valuation task that requires the student to look to financial markets for guidance in resolving the case problem. Second, he has brought into the literature a wide range of contemporary problems of interest to scholars and practitioners, including cases in real and financial options, agency conflicts, financial innovation, investing in emerging markets, and corporate control. Bruner's case on Volvo/Renault is an example of the marriage of clinical research articles with the preparation of teaching cases—as the literature continues to mature, we should look for more of this kind of presentation of clinical research. At the same time, he has presented sharp redefinitions of classic problems in Finance, including dividend policy, the mix of debt and equity, the estimation of future financial requirements, and the choice between mutually exclusive investments. Third, his cases invite the student to apply modern information technology (in the form of computers and Internet) to the analysis of managerial decisions. Instructors in Finance need to be able to serve up case problems that invite students to harness technology that they will use in the workplace and that can help them penetrate to key insights effectively.

The third edition of Case Studies in Finance: Managing for Corporate Value Creation extends the many contributions to the literature offered in the first two editions. The collection covers a very broad range of issues that are important to instructors in corporate finance. Above all, the cases exercise the perspective of financial markets in the problem-solving of corporate managers and investors. This is a book which will provide a valuable resource to instructors, students, and practitioners, and which further advances the case literature in Finance.

June 1998

Preface

The inexplicable is all around us. So is the incomprehensible. So is the unintelligible. Interviewing Babe Ruth[1] in 1928, I put it to him, "People come and ask what's your system for hitting home runs— that so?" "Yes," said the Babe, " and all I can tell 'em is I pick a good one and sock it. I get back to the dugout and they ask me what it was I hit and I tell 'em I don't know except it looked good."

Carl Sandburg[2]

Managers are not confronted with problems that are independent of each other, but with dynamic situations that consist of complex systems of changing problems that interact with each other. I call such situations messes . . . Managers do not solve problems: they manage messes.

Russell Ackoff[3]

ORIENTATION OF THE BOOK

Practitioners tell us that much in finance is inexplicable, incomprehensible, and unintelligible. Like Babe Ruth, their explanations for their actions often amount to "I pick a good one and sock it." Fortunately for a rising generation of practitioners, tools and concepts of modern finance provide a language and approach for excellent performance. The aim of this book is to illustrate and exercise the application of these tools and concepts in a messy world.

Focus on Value. The subtitle of this third edition remains *Managing for Corporate Value Creation*. Economics teaches us that value creation should be an enduring focus of concern because value is the foundation of survival and prosperity of the enterprise. The focus on

---

[1]George Herman "Babe" Ruth (1895–1948) was one of the most famous players in the history of American baseball, leading the league in home runs for 10 straight seasons, setting a record of 60 home runs in one season, and hitting 714 home runs in his career. Ruth was also known as the "Sultan of the Swat."

[2]Carl Sandburg, "Notes for Preface," in *Harvest Poems* (New York: Harcourt Brace Jovanovich, 1960), p. 11.

[3]Russell Ackoff, "The Future of Operational Research Is Past," *Journal of Operational Research Society,* 30, no. 1 (Pergamon Press, Ltd., 1979), 93–104.

value also helps managers understand the impact of the firm on the world around it. These cases harness and exercise this economic view of the firm. It is the special province of finance to highlight value as a legitimate concern for managers. The cases in this book exercise valuation analysis over a wide range of assets, debt, equities, and options, and a wide range of perspectives, such as investor, creditor, manager, and government.

Linkage to Capital Markets.   An important premise of these cases is that managers should take cues from the capital markets. The cases in this volume help the student learn to look at the capital markets in four ways. First, they illustrate important players in the capital markets (such as the new cases on Warren Buffett, Jeanne Mockard, and the Fidelity Magellan Fund). Second, they exercise the students' abilities to interpret capital market conditions. Third, they explore the design of financial securities, and rationalize the use of exotic securities in support of corporate policy. Finally, they help students understand the implications of transparency of the firm to investors, and the impact of news about the firm in an efficient market.

Respect for the Administrative Point of View.   The real world is messy. Information is incomplete, arrives late, or is reported with error. The motivations of counterparties are ambiguous. Resources often fall short. These cases illustrate the immense practicality of finance theory in sorting out the issues facing managers, assessing alternatives, and illuminating the effects of any particular choice. A number of the cases in this book present practical ethical dilemmas or moral hazards facing managers. Most of the cases (and teaching plans in the associated instructor's manual) call for *action plans* rather than mere analyses or descriptions of a problem.

Contemporaneity.   All cases in this book are set in the 1990s. The mix of cases reflects the global business environment: 50 percent of the cases in this book are set outside the United States or have strong cross-border elements. Finally, the blend of cases continues to reflect the growing role of women in managerial ranks: 42 percent of the cases present women as key protagonists and decision makers. Generally, these cases reflect the increasingly diverse world of business participants.

PLAN OF THE BOOK

The cases may be taught in many different combinations. The sequence indicated by the table of contents corresponds to course designs used at Darden. Each cluster of cases in the table of contents suggests a concept module, with a particular orientation.

I. Setting Some Themes.   The cases in Part I introduce basic concepts of value creation, assessment of performance against a capital market benchmark, and capital market efficiency that reappear throughout a case course. The numerical analysis required of the student is relatively light. The synthesis of case facts into an important framework or perspective is the main challenge. The new case "Warren E. Buffet, 1995" sets the nearly universal theme of this volume: the need to think like an investor. The case about Federal Express and UPS uses "economic profit" (or EVA$^{®}$) to explore the origins of value creation and destruction, and its competitive implications for the future.

II. Financial Analysis and Forecasting.   In this section, students are introduced to the crucial skills of financial-statement analysis, break-even analysis, ratio analysis, and financial statement forecasting. One case ("The Body Shop") takes the student step-by-step through the preparation of forecasts, both by hand and with the aid of a computer-spreadsheet program. Other cases address issues in the analysis of working-capital management and credit analysis.

III. Estimating the Cost of Capital.   This module begins with a new discussion of "best practices" among leading firms. The cases exercise skills in estimating the cost of capital for firms and their business segments. The cases aim to exercise and solidify students' mastery of the capital asset pricing model, the dividend-growth model, and the weighted-average cost of capital formula. A new case, "Teletech Corporation, 1996," explores the implications of mean-variance analysis to business segments within a firm, and gives a useful foundation for discussing value-additivity.

IV. Capital Budgeting and Resource Allocation.   The focus of these cases is the evaluation of investment opportunities and entire capital budgets. The analytical challenges range from simple time-value-of-money problems to setting the entire capital budget for a resource-constrained firm. Key issues in this module include the estimation of free cash flows; the comparison of various investment criteria (NPV, IRR, payback, and equivalent annuities); the treatment of issues in mutually exclusive investments; and capital budgeting under rationing. A new case, "Astral Records," explores the economics of waiting to invest (i.e., rather than investing now), and exercises a range of financial skills.

V. Management of Shareholders' Equity.   This module seeks to develop practical principles about dividend policy and share issues by drawing on concepts about dividend irrelevance, signaling, investor clienteles, bonding, and agency costs. "Northboro Machine Tools" explores a dividend decision through the lenses of a range of theoretical concepts, including signaling, clientele effects, and residual policies. The new case, "Donaldson, Lufkin, and Jenrette, 1995," considers numerous issues in initial public offerings, including underpricing, choice of comparables, and underwriter risk.

VI. Management of the Corporate Capital Structure.   The problem of setting capital structure targets is introduced in this module. Prominent issues are the use and creation of debt tax shields, the role of industry economics and technology, the influence of corporate competitive strategy, the trade-offs between debt policy, dividend policy, and investment goals, and the avoidance of costs of distress. This module includes four new cases. "Polaroid Corporation, 1996" addresses the classic trade-off between optimizing the capital structure optimality and providing financial flexibility. "MCI Communications Corp." assesses the value of debt tax shields. "Planet Cópias & Imagem" considers the trade-offs between debt and equity financing for the rapidly growing firm.

VII. Analysis of Financing Tactics: Leases, Options, and Foreign Currency.   While the preceding module is concerned with setting debt targets, this module addresses a range of tactics a firm might use to pursue those targets, hedge risk, and exploit market opportunities. Included are domestic and international debt offerings, swaps of various types, recapitalizations, warrants, and convertibles. With these cases, students will exercise techniques in securities valuation, including the use of option-pricing theory. This module includes three new cases. "Burlington Northern Railroad" gives a lucid exercise in the analysis of leases. "Boston Chicken" presents an introduction to the valuation of convertible bonds. And the case "General Motors: 1991 Equity Financing" provides an opportunity to evaluate an innovation in security design.

VIII. Valuing the Enterprise: Acquisitions, Buyouts, Restructurings, and Projects.
This module exercises students' skills in valuing the firm. The focus includes valuation using DCF and multiples, techniques of valuing highly leveraged firms, reallocation of value in financial distress, and distribution of joint value in merger negotiations. This module features four new cases, including a new bilateral merger negotiation exercise between AT&T and McCaw Cellular Communications.

IX. Cross-Border Investments into Emerging Markets.
This module is new to the third edition and considers issues faced by investors in entering emerging markets. Here, students confront adjustments for political risk, currency, and country risk. Larger issues of interpreting macroeconomic trends and cultural differences figure importantly in the managerial decision making. "Procter & Gamble" surveys issues in hedging currency exposure in emerging markets. "Paginas Amarelas" exercises skills in estimating costs of capital for investments in Argentina, Brazil, and Chile. "Continental Cablevision" invites an analysis of a joint venture in Argentina, and "Westmoreland Energy" invites student analysis of a project in China.

X. Setting Corporate Financial Policy.
This module gives comprehensive problems in corporate financial policy and tactics. The students must address three sets of questions: (1) What is the firm's financing requirement, and how do the chief executive officer's vision and strategy drive that requirement? (2) Are the firm's securities valued fairly in the capital markets? If not, why? What should be done about this? (3) What should be the firm's financial policy in the future? And what specific actions should be taken to meet the financing need? A technical note on structuring corporate financial policy helps motivate the work of students with these cases. The module features a new case, "Massive Power Design Corporation," which considers the problem of financing a turnaround. These cases are excellent vehicles for end-of-course classes, student term papers, and/or presentations by teams of students.

SUMMARY OF CHANGES FROM THE SECOND EDITION

The third edition represents a substantial change from the second edition. The changes may be summarized as follows:

- New cases in this edition amount to 54 percent of the total number.
- The cases are set in the 1990s. Time marches on. In the interest of presenting a fresh and contemporary collection, older cases have been updated and/or replaced with new case situations. Several of the most favorite "classic" cases from the first two editions are given in the instructor's manual, from which instructors who adopt this edition may copy them for classroom use.
- This edition features a new module: Cross-Border Investments into Emerging Markets.
- All cases and teaching notes have been edited to sharpen the opportunities for student analysis.

The book continues with a strong international aspect (half of the cases are set outside the United States or feature significant cross-border issues). Also, the collection continues to feature women decision makers and protagonists prominently (42 percent of the cases).

SUPPLEMENTS

The case studies in this volume are supported by various resources that help make student engagement a success:

- Spreadsheet files in Excel support student and instructor preparation of the cases.
- A guide to the novice on case preparation, "Note to the Student: How to Study and Discuss Cases," appears in this volume.
- Eight cases in the instructor's manual provide counterparty roles for two negotiation exercises or present detailed discussions of case outcomes (i.e., the "B" case to cases appearing in this volume). These supplemental cases can significantly extend student learning and expand the opportunities for classroom discussion.
- An instructor's manual of over 1,200 pages contains teaching notes for each case. Each teaching note includes suggested assignment questions, a hypothetical teaching plan, and a prototypical finished case analysis.
- Web-site addresses are given in many of the teaching notes. These provide a convenient avenue for updates on the performance of undisguised companies appearing in the book.
- The instructor's manual contains notes on how to design a case method course, on using computers with cases, and on preparing to teach a case.
- Seven "classic" cases and their associated teaching notes are given in the instructor's manual. These cases were among the most popular and durable cases in the first two editions of *Case Studies in Finance*. They are offered here to round out an instructor's selection of favorite cases. Instructors adopting this volume for classroom use have permission to reproduce these "classic" cases for their courses.

ACKNOWLEDGMENTS

This book would not be possible without the contributions of many other people. Colleagues at Darden who have taught, contributed to, or commented on these cases are Yiorgos Allayannis, Karl-Adam Bonnier, Susan Chaplinsky, John Colley, Bob Conroy, Ken Eades, Mark Eaker, Bob Fair, Jim Freeland, Sherwood Frey, Bob Harris, Mark Haskins, Charles Meiburg, Jud Reis, William Sihler, and Robert Spekman. I am grateful for their collegiality, and for the support of the Darden School Foundation, the Citicorp Global Scholars Program, and INSEAD for my casewriting efforts.

Colleagues at other schools whose work appears here include Herwig Langohr (INSEAD) and Lee Remmers (INSEAD). I am delighted to give their excellent work exposure in this collection.

Colleagues at other schools provided worthy insights and encouragement toward the development of the three editions of *Case Studies in Finance*. I am grateful to the following persons (listed with the schools with which they were associated at the time of my correspondence or work with them):

Raj Aggarwal	*John Carroll*	Wesley Marple	*Northeastern*
Ed Altman	*NYU*	Felicia Marston	*UVA (McIntire)*
James Ang	*Florida State*	John Martin	*Texas*
Paul Asquith	*M.I.T.*	Ronald Masulis	*Vanderbilt*
Geert Bekaert	*Stanford*	John McConnell	*Purdue*
Michael Berry	*James Madison*	Catherine McDonough	*Babson*
Randy Billingsley	*VPI&SU*	Richard McEnally	*North Carolina*
John Boquist	*Indiana*	Wayne Mikkelson	*Oregon*
Michael Brennan	*UCLA*	Michael Moffett	*Thunderbird*
Ed Burmeister	*Duke*	Nancy Mohan	*Dayton*
Kirt Butler	*Michigan State*	Ed Moses	*Rollins*
Don Chance	*VPI&SU*	Charles Moyer	*Wake Forest*
Andrew Chen	*Southern Methodist*	David Mullins	*Harvard*
C. Roland Christensen	*Harvard*	James T. Murphy	*Tulane*
Thomas E. Copeland	*McKinsey*	Chris Muscarella	*Penn State*
Jean Dermine	*INSEAD*	Robert Nachtmann	*Pittsburgh*
Michael Dooley	*UVA Law*	Ben Nunnally	*UNC-Charlotte*
Peter Eisemann	*Georgia State*	Robert Parrino	*Texas (Austin)*
Ben Esty	*Harvard*	Pamela Peterson	*Florida State*
Thomas H. Eyssell	*Missouri*	Larry Pettit	*Virginia (McIntire)*
Pablo Fernandez	*IESE*	Tom Piper	*Harvard*
Kenneth Ferris	*Thunderbird*	John Pringle	*North Carolina*
John Finnerty	*Fordham*	Ahmad Rahnema	*IESE*
Joseph Finnerty	*Illinois*	Al Rappaport	*Northwestern*
Steve Foerster	*Western Ontario*	Allen Rappaport	*Northern Iowa*
Günther Franke	*Konstanz*	David Ravenscraft	*North Carolina*
Dan Galai	*Jerusalem*	Henry B. Reiling	*Harvard*
Jim Gentry	*llinois*	Lee Remmers	*INSEAD*
Robert Glauber	*Harvard*	Jay Ritter	*Florida*
Mustafa Gultekin	*North Carolina*	Richard Ruback	*Harvard*
Benton Gup	*Alabama*	Art Selander	*Southern Methodist*
Jim Haltiner	*William & Mary*	Israel Shaked	*Boston*
Rob Hansen	*PI&SU*	Dennis Sheehan	*Penn State*
Philippe Haspeslagh	*INSEAD*	J. B. Silvers	*Case Western*
Pekka Hietala	*INSEAD*	Luke Sparvero	*Texas*
Rocky Higgins	*Washington*	Richard Stapleton	*Lancaster*
Pierre Hillion	*INSEAD*	Laura Starks	*Texas*
Laurie Simon Hodrick	*Columbia*	Jerry Stevens	*Richmond*
John Hund	*Texas*	John Strong	*William & Mary*
Daniel Indro	*Kent State*	Marti Subrahmanyam	*NYU*
Thomas Jackson	*UVA Law*	Anant Sundaram	*Thunderbird*
Pradeep Jalan	*Regina*	Rick Swasey	*Northeastern*
Michael Jensen	*Harvard*	Bob Taggart	*Boston College*
Sreeni Kamma	*Indiana*	Anjan Thakor	*Indiana*
Steven Kaplan	*Chicago*	James G. Tompkins	*Kenesaw State*
Andrew Karolyi	*Western Ontario*	Walter Torous	*UCLA*
Kathryn Kelm	*Emporia State*	Nick Travlos	*Boston College*
Carl Kester	*Harvard*	Lenos Trigeorgis	*Cyprus*
Dan Laughhunn	*Duke*	George Tsetsekos	*Drexel*
Ken Lehn	*Pittsburgh*	Peter Tufano	*Harvard*
Saul Levmore	*UVA Law*	James Van Horne	*Stanford*
Wilbur Lewellen	*Purdue*	Nick Varaiya	*San Diego State*
Scott Linn	*Oklahoma*	Theo Vermaelen	*INSEAD*
Dennis Logue	*Dartmouth*	Michael Vetsuypens	*Southern Methodist*
Paul Malatesta	*Washington*	Claude Viallet	*INSEAD*

Ingo Walter	*NYU*	Fred Yeager	*St. Louis*
J. F. Weston	*UCLA*	Betty Yobaccio	*Framingham State*
Peter Williamson	*Dartmouth*	Marc Zenner	*North Carolina*
Brent Wilson	*Brigham Young*		

I am also grateful to the following practitioners (listed here with affiliated companies at the time of my work with them):

Norm Bartczak	*Center for Financial Strategy*	John Newcomb	*BankBoston*
Bo Brookby	*First Wachovia*	Ralph Norwood	*Polaroid*
W. L. Lyons Brown	*Brown-Forman*	Marni Gislason Obernauer	*J. P. Morgan*
Bliss Williams Browne	*First Chicago*	Michael Pearson	*McKinsey*
George Bruns	*BankBoston*	Nancy Preis	*Kleinwort Benson*
Ned Case	*General Motors*	Joe Prendergast	*First Wachovia*
Daniel Cohrs	*Marriott*	Luis Quartin-Bastos	*Planet*
David Crosby	*Johnson & Johnson*	Jack Rader	*FMA*
Jinx Dennett	*BankBoston*	Christopher Reilly	*S. G. Warburg*
Ty Eggemeyer	*McKinsey*	Gerry Rooney	*NationsBank*
Geoffrey Elliott	*Morgan Stanley*	Emilio Rottoli	*Glaxo*
Catherine Friedman	*Morgan Stanley*	Barry Sabloff	*First Chicago*
James Gelly	*General Motors*	Linda Scheuplein	*J. P. Morgan*
Ed Giera	*General Motors*	Keith Shaughnessy	*BankBoston*
Charles Griffith	*AlliedSignal*	Jack Sheehan	*Johnstown*
Ian Harvey	*BankBoston*	Katrina Sherrerd	*AIMR*
Betsy Hatfield	*BankBoston*	John Smetanka	*Security Pacific*
Christopher Howe	*Kleinwort Benson*	John Smith	*General Motors*
Paul Hunn	*Manufacturers Hanover*	Rick Spangler	*First Wachovia*
Thomas Jasper	*Salomon Brothers*	Kirsten Spector	*BankBoston*
Andrew Kalotay	*Salomon Brothers*	Martin Steinmeyer	*MediMedia*
Mary Lou Kelley	*McKinsey*	Stephanie Summers	*Lehman Brothers*
Francesco Kestenholz	*UBS*	Sven-Ivan Sundqvist	*Dagens Nyheter*
Eric Linnes	*Kleinwort Benson*	Peter Thorpe	*Citicorp.*
Peter Lynch	*Fidelity Investments*	Katherine Updike	*Excelsior*
Frank McTigue	*McTigue Associates*	Tom Verdoorn	*Land O' Lakes*
Jean McTighe	*BankBoston*	David Wake Walker	*Kleinwort Benson*
Michael Melloy	*Planet*	Frank Ward Corp.	*Performance Systems*
David Meyer	*J. P. Morgan*	Ulrich Wiechmann	*UWINC*
Jeanne Mockard	*Putnam Investments*	Scott Williams	*McKinsey*
Pascal Montiero de Barros	*Planet*	Harry You	*Salomon Brothers*
Lin Morison	*BankBoston*		

Research assistants working under my direction have helped gather data and prepare drafts: Darren Berry, Anne Campbell, David Eichler, Jerry Halpin, Peter Hennessy, Casey Opitz, Katarina Paddack, Thien Pham, Michael Schill, John Sherwood, Jane Sommers-Kelly, Carla Stiassni, Sanjay Vakharia, Larry Weatherford, and Steve Wilus. I have supervised numerous others in the development of individual cases—those worthy contributors are recognized in the first footnote of each case.

A busy professor soon learns the wisdom in the adage "Many hands make light work." I am very grateful to the staff of the Darden School for its support in this project. Excellent editorial assistance at Darden was provided by Kathleen Jump (the nonpareil lead editor for this edition) and Stephen Smith. Superior production support at Darden was given by Valerie Redd, Dot Govoruhk, Cassandra Truzy, Pat Hall, Debbie Quarles, and Betty Sprouse. Strong archival and copying support were given by Donald Aielli, Barbara Goldman, Michael Hamm, and Ann Morris. Outstanding library research support was given by Henry Wingate and Karen Marsh. The patience, care, and dedication of these people are richly appreciated.

At Irwin/McGraw-Hill, Craig Beytien, Publisher, also served as Sponsoring Editor and Development Editor on this edition. Mike Junior, now Vice President, recruited me into this project years ago; the legacy of our early vision-setting continues in this edition. Cathy Tepper was supplements coordinator; Gladys True was production editor; and Paula Krauza served as editorial assistant on this edition.

Of all the contributors, my wife, Barbara McTigue Bruner, and two sons, Jonathan and Alexander, have endured great sacrifices to see this book appear. As Milton said, "They also serve who only stand and wait." Development of this third edition would not have been possible without their fond patience.

All these acknowledgments notwithstanding, responsibility for these materials is mine. I welcome suggestions for their enhancement. Please let me know of your experience with these cases, either through Irwin or at the address given below.

Robert F. Bruner
Distinguished Professor of Business Administration

Darden Graduate School of Business
University of Virginia
P.O. Box 6550
Charlottesville, Virginia 22906
Web site: http://faculty.darden.edu/brunerb/

Individual copies of all the Darden cases in this and previous editions may be obtained promptly from Irwin/McGraw-Hill or from Darden Educational Materials Services (804-982-2192). Proceeds from these case sales support casewriting efforts. Please respect the copyrights on these materials.

Contents

PART IX
Cross-Border Investments into Emerging Markets

PART X
Setting Corporate Financial Policy

Note to the Student: How to Study and Discuss Cases

The credit belongs to the man[1] who is actually in the arena—whose face is marred by dust and sweat and blood . . . who knows the great enthusiasms, the great devotions—and spends himself in a worthy cause—who at best if he wins knows the thrills of high achievement—and if he fails, at least fails while daring greatly so that his place shall never be with those cold and timid souls who know neither victory nor defeat.

Theodore Roosevelt

Good judgment comes from experience. Experience comes from bad judgment.

Walter Wriston

The lessons most worth learning all come from taking a stand. From that truth flows the educative force of the case method. In the typical case, the student is projected into the position of an executive who must do something in response to a problem. It is this choice of what to do that constitutes the executive's "stand."[2] Over the course of a career, an executive who takes stands gains wisdom. If the stand provides an effective resolution of the problem, so much the better for all concerned. If it does not, however, the wise executive analyzes the reasons for the failure and may learn even more than from a success. As Wriston suggests, wisdom can grow out of error. In case method education, this process of years is collapsed into months. The extent to which a student learns the case lessons depends on how the case study is approached. What can one do to gain the maximum from the study of these cases?

1. READING THE CASE

The very first time you read any case, look for the forest, not the trees. This requires that your first reading be quick. Do not begin taking notes on the first round; instead, read the case like a magazine article. The first few paragraphs of a well-constructed case usually say something about the problem—read those carefully. Then quickly read the rest of the

---

[1]Today, a statement such as this would surely recognize women as well.
[2]Even deciding not to decide, is to decide, as Napoleon once observed.

case, seeking mainly a sense of the scope of the problems and what information the case contains to help resolve them. Leaf through the exhibits, looking for what information they hold rather than for any analytical insights. At the conclusion of the first pass, read any supporting articles or notes that your instructor may have recommended.

2. GETTING INTO THE CASE SITUATION: DEVELOP YOUR "AWARENESS"

With the broader perspective in mind, the second and more detailed reading will be more productive. The reason is that, as you now encounter details, your mind will be able to organize them in some useful fashion rather than inventorying them randomly. Making linkages among case details is necessary toward solving the case. At this point you can take the notes that will set up your analysis.

The most successful students project themselves into the position of the decision maker, because this perspective helps them link case details as well as develop a stand on the case problem. Assignment questions may help you do this, but it is a good idea to get into the habit of doing it yourself. Here are the kinds of questions you might try to answer in preparing every case:

1. Who are the protagonists in the case? Who must take action on the problem? What do they have at stake? What pressures are they under?
2. In what business is the company? What is the nature of its product? What is the nature of demand for that product? What is the firm's distinctive competence? With whom does it compete?[3] What is the structure of the industry? Is the firm comparatively strong or weak? In what ways?
3. What are the goals of the firm? What is the firm's strategy in pursuit of these goals? (The goals and strategy might be explicitly stated, or they may be implicit in the way the firm does business.) What are the firm's apparent functional policies in marketing (e.g., push versus pull strategy); production (e.g., in labor relations, use of new technology, distributed production versus centralized); and finance (e.g., the use of debt financing, payment of dividends)? Financial and business strategies can be inferred from analysis of financial ratios and a sources-and-uses-of-funds statement.
4. How well has the firm performed in pursuit of its goals? (The answer to this question calls for simple analysis using financial ratios, such as the Du Pont system, compound growth rates, and measures of value creation.)

The larger point of this phase of your case preparation is to broaden your awareness of issues. Perhaps the most successful investor in history, Warren Buffett (see Case 1), said, "Any player unaware of the fool in the market, probably is the fool in the market." Awareness is an important attribute of successful managers.

---

[3]Think broadly about competitors. Mark Twain wrote, in *A Connecticut Yankee in King Arthur's Court,* "The best swordsman in the world doesn't need to fear the second best swordsman in the world; no, the person for him to be afraid of is some ignorant antagonist who has never had a sword in his hand before; he doesn't do the thing he ought to do, and so the expert isn't prepared for him; he does the thing he ought not to do; and it often catches the expert out and ends him on the spot."

3. DEFINING THE PROBLEM

A common trap for many executives is to assume that the issue at hand is the real problem most worthy of their time, rather than a symptom of some larger problem that *really* deserves their time. For instance, a lender is often asked to advance funds to help tide a firm over a cash shortfall. Careful study may reveal that the key problem is not a cash shortfall but rather product obsolescence, unexpected competition, or careless cost management. Even in cases where the decision is fairly narrowly defined (such as in a capital expenditure choice), the "problem" generally turns out to be the believability of certain key assumptions. Students who are new to the case method tend to focus narrowly in defining problems and often overlook the influence which the larger setting has on the problem. In doing this the student develops narrow specialist habits, never achieving the general manager perspective. It is useful and important for you to define the problem yourself and, in the process, validate the problem as suggested by the protagonist in the case.

4. ANALYSIS: RUN THE NUMBERS AND GO TO THE HEART OF THE MATTER

Virtually all finance cases require numerical analysis. This is good because figure work lends rigor and structure to your thinking. But some cases, reflecting reality, invite you to explore blind alleys. If you are new to finance, even these explorations will help you learn.[4] The best case students develop an instinct for where to devote their analysis. Economy of effort is desirable. If you have invested wisely in problem definition, economical analysis tends to follow. For instance, a student might assume that a particular case is meant to exercise financial forecasting skills and will spend two or more hours preparing a detailed forecast, instead of preparing a simpler forecast in one hour and conducting a sensitivity analysis based on key assumptions in the next hour. An executive rarely thinks of a situation as having to do with a forecasting method or discounting or any other technique, but rather thinks of it as a problem of judgment, deciding on which people or concepts or environmental conditions to bet. The best case analyses get down to the *key bets* on which the executive is wagering the prosperity of the firm, and his or her career. Get to the business issues quickly, and avoid a lengthy churning through of relatively unimportant calculations.

5. PREPARE TO PARTICIPATE: TAKE A STAND

To develop analytical insights without making recommendations is useless to executives and drains the case-study experience of some of its learning power. A stand means having

---

[4]Case analysis is often iterative: an understanding of the big issues invites an analysis of details—then the details may restructure the big issues and invite the analysis of other details. In some cases, getting to the "heart of the matter" will mean just such iteration.

a point of view about the problem, a recommendation, and an analysis to back up both of them. To prepare to take a stand, remember the words of Walt Disney: "Get a good idea and stay with it. Dog it and work at it until it's done, and done right."

6. IN CLASS: PARTICIPATE ACTIVELY IN SUPPORT OF YOUR CONCLUSIONS, BUT BE OPEN TO NEW INSIGHTS AS THEY EMERGE

Of course, one can have a stand without the world being any wiser. To take a stand in case discussions means to participate actively in the discussion and to advocate your stand until new facts or analysis emerge to warrant a change.[5] Learning by the case method is not a spectator sport. A classic error many students make is to bring into the case method classroom the habits of the lecture hall (i.e., passively absorbing what other people say). These habits fail miserably in the case method classroom because they only guarantee that one absorbs the truths and fallacies uttered by others. The purpose of case study is to develop and exercise *one's own* skills and judgment. This takes practice and participation, just as in a sport. Here are two good general suggestions: (1) defer significant note-taking until after class and (2) strive to contribute to every case discussion.

7. TRUST THE PROCESS

The learnings from a case-method course are impressive. They arrive cumulatively over time. In many cases, the learnings continue well after the course has finished. Occasionally these learnings hit you with the force of a tsunami. But generally the learnings creep in quietly, yet powerfully, like the tide. After the case course, you will look back and see that your thinking, mastery, and appreciation for finance have changed dramatically. The key point is that you should not measure the success of your progress on the basis of any single case discussion. Trust that in the cumulative work over many cases you will gain the mastery you seek.

CONCLUSION: FOCUS ON PROCESS, AND RESULTS WILL FOLLOW

View the case method experience as a series of opportunities to test your mastery of techniques and your business judgment. If you seek a list of axioms to be etched in stone, you are bound to disappoint yourself. As in real life, there are virtually no "right" answers to these cases in the sense that a scientific or engineering problem has an exact solution. Jeff Milman has said, "The answers worth getting are never found in the back of the book." What matters is that you obtain a way of thinking about business situations that you can carry from one job (or career) to the next. In the case method it is largely true that *how you learn is what you learn.*[6]

---

[5]There is a difference between taking a stand and being pigheaded. Nothing is served by clinging to your stand to the bitter end in the face of better analysis or common sense. Good managers recognize new facts and arguments as they come to light, and adapt.

[6]In describing the work of case teachers, John H. McArthur has said, "How we teach is what we teach."

Part I

Setting Some Themes

Case 1

Warren E. Buffett, 1995

On August 25, 1995, Warren Buffett, the CEO of Berkshire Hathaway, announced that his firm would acquire the 49.6 percent of GEICO Corporation that it did not already own. The $2.3 billion deal would give GEICO shareholders $70.00 per share, up from the $55.75 per share market price before the announcement. Observers were astonished at the 26 percent premium that Berkshire Hathaway would pay, particularly since Buffett proposed to change nothing about GEICO, and there were no apparent synergies in the combination of the two firms. At the announcement, Berkshire Hathaway's shares closed up 2.4 percent for the day, for a gain in market value of $718 million.[1] That day, the Standard & Poor's 500 index closed up 0.5 percent.

The acquisition of GEICO renewed public interest in its architect, Warren Buffett. In many ways he was an anomaly. One of the richest individuals in the world (with an estimated net worth of about $7 billion), he was also respected and even beloved. Though he had accumulated perhaps the best investment record in history (a compound annual increase in wealth of 28 percent from 1965 to 1994),[2] Berkshire Hathaway paid him only $100,000 per year to serve as its CEO. Buffett and other insiders controlled 47.9 percent of the company, yet Buffett ran the company in the interests of all shareholders. He was the subject of numerous laudatory articles and three biographies,[3] yet he remained an intensely private individual. Though acclaimed by many as an intellectual genius, he shunned the company of intellectuals and preferred to affect the manner of a down-home

---

[1] The change in Berkshire Hathaway's share price at the date of the announcement was $609.60. The company had outstanding 1,177,750 shares.

[2] Buffett's initial cost per share in Berkshire Hathaway in 1965 was about $17.578. On August 25, 1995, the price per share closed at $25,400.

[3] Robert G. Hagstrom, Jr., *The Warren Buffett Way* (New York: John Wiley & Sons, 1994); Andrew Kilpatrick, *Of Permanent Value: The Story of Warren Buffett* (Birmingham: AKPE, 1994); and Roger Lowenstein, *Buffett: The Making of an American Capitalist* (New York: Random House, 1995).

This case was prepared by Professor Robert F. Bruner as the basis for classroom discussion rather than to illustrate effective or ineffective handling of an administrative situation. Copyright © 1996 by the University of Virginia Darden School Foundation, Charlottesville, VA. All rights reserved. *No part of this publication may be reproduced, stored in a retrieval system, used in a spreadsheet, or transmitted in any form or by any means— electronic, mechanical, photocopying, recording, or otherwise—without the permission of the Darden Foundation. For inquiries, please send an e-mail to dardencases@virginia.edu.* Rev. 5/98. Version 1.5.

Nebraskan (he lived in Omaha), and a tough-minded investor. In contrast to other investment "stars," Buffett acknowledged his investment failures quickly and publicly. Though he held an MBA from Columbia University and credited his mentor, Professor Benjamin Graham, with developing the philosophy of value-based investing that guided Buffett to his success, he chided business schools for the irrelevance of their theories of finance and investing.

Numerous writers sought to distill the essence of Buffett's success. What were the key principles that guided Buffett? Could these be applied broadly in the late 1990s and into the 21st century, or were they unique to Buffett and his time? From an understanding of these principles, analysts hoped to illuminate Berkshire Hathaway's acquisition of GEICO. Under what assumptions would this acquisition make sense? What were Buffett's probable motives in the acquisition? Would the acquisition of GEICO prove to be a success? How would it compare to the firm's other recent investments in Salomon Brothers, USAir, and Champion International?

BERKSHIRE HATHAWAY, INC.

The company was incorporated in 1889 as Berkshire Cotton Manufacturing, and eventually grew to become one of New England's biggest textile producers, accounting for 25 percent of the country's cotton textile production. In 1955, Berkshire merged with Hathaway Manufacturing and began a secular decline due to inflation, technological change, and intensifying competition from foreign competitors. In 1965 Buffett and some partners acquired control of Berkshire Hathaway, believing that the decline could be reversed. Over the next 20 years it became apparent that large capital investments would be required to remain competitive and that even then the financial returns would be mediocre. In 1985, Berkshire Hathaway exited the textile business. Fortunately, the textile group generated enough cash in the initial years to permit the firm to purchase two insurance companies headquartered in Omaha: National Indemnity Company and National Fire & Marine Insurance Company. Acquisitions of other businesses followed in the 1970s and 1980s.

The investment performance of a share in Berkshire Hathaway had astonished most observers. In 1977 the firm's year-end closing share price was $89. On August 25, 1995, the firm's closing share price was $25,400. In comparison, the annual average total return on all large stocks from 1977 to the end of 1994 was 14.3 percent.[4] Over the same period, the Standard & Poor's 500 index grew from 107 to 560. Some observers called for Buffett to split the firm's share price, to make it more accessible to the individual investor. He steadfastly refused.

In 1994, Berkshire Hathaway described itself as "a holding company owning subsidiaries engaged in a number of diverse business activities."[5] Exhibit 1 gives a summary of revenues, operating profits, capital expenditures, depreciation, and assets for the various segments. By 1994, Berkshire's portfolio of businesses included the following:

---

[4]Reported in *Stocks, Bonds, Bills, and Inflation, 1994* (Chicago: Ibbotson Associates), p. 10.
[5]Berkshire Hathaway, Inc., annual report, 1994, p. 6.

Share Price of Berkshire Hathaway versus S&P 500 Index

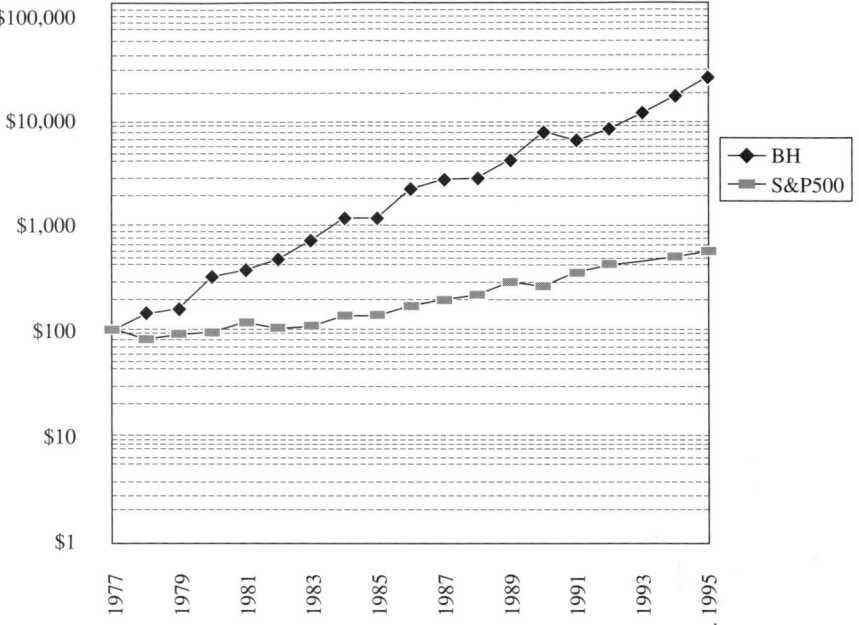

- *Insurance Group.* The largest component of Berkshire's portfolio focused on property and casualty insurance, on both a direct and a reinsurance basis. The investment portfolios of the Insurance Group included meaningful equity interests in 10 other publicly traded companies. The equity interests are summarized in Exhibit 2, along with Berkshire's share of undistributed operating earnings in these companies. Because the earnings in some of these companies could not be consolidated with Berkshire's under generally accepted accounting principles (GAAP), Buffett published Berkshire's "look-through" earnings[6]—as shown in Exhibit 2, the share of undistributed earnings of major investees accounted for 40–50 percent of Berkshire's total "look-through" earnings. Exhibit 3 summarizes investments in convertible preferred[7] stocks that Berkshire Hathaway had made in recent years, serving as a "white squire" to major corporations—each of these firms had been the target of actual or rumored takeover attempts.
- *Buffalo News.* A daily and Sunday newspaper in upstate New York.
- *Fechheimer.* A manufacturer and distributor of uniforms.

---

[6]"Look-through" earnings was calculated as the sum of Berkshire's operating earnings reported in its income statement, plus the retained operating earnings of major investees not reflected in Berkshire's profits, less tax on what would be paid by Berkshire if these earnings had been distributed to Berkshire. (The presentation used a 14 percent tax rate, the rate Berkshire paid on dividends it received.)

[7]Convertible preferred stock is preferred stock that carries the right to be exchanged by the investor for common stock. The exchange, or "conversion," right is like a call option on the common stock of the issuer. The terms of the convertible preferred state the price at which common shares can be acquired in exchange for the principal value of the convertible preferred stock.

- *Kirby.* A manufacturer and marketer of home cleaning systems and accessories.
- *Nebraska Furniture.* A retailer of home furnishings.
- *See's Candies.* A manufacturer and distributor of boxed chocolates and other confectionery products.
- *Childcraft and World Book.* A publisher and distributor of encyclopedias and related educational and instructional materials.
- *Campbell Hausfeld.* A manufacturer and distributor of air compressors, air tools, and painting systems.
- *H. H. Brown Shoe Company; Lowell Shoe, Inc.; and Dexter Shoe Company.* Companies involved in the manufacture, import, and distribution of footwear.

In addition to these businesses, Berkshire owned an assortment of smaller businesses[8] generating about $400 million in revenues.

BERKSHIRE HATHAWAY'S ACQUISITION POLICY

The GEICO announcement renewed general interest in Buffett's approach to acquisitions. Exhibit 4 gives the formal statement of acquisition criteria contained in Berkshire Hathaway's 1994 annual report. In general, the policy expressed a tightly disciplined strategy that refused to reward others for actions that Berkshire Hathaway might just as easily take on its own. Therefore, analysts scrutinized the criteria to assess where they might offer winning ideas to Buffett.

One prominent example to which Buffett referred was Berkshire Hathaway's investment in Scott & Fetzer in 1986. The managers of Scott & Fetzer had attempted a leveraged buyout of the company in the face of rumored hostile takeover attempt. When the Labor Department objected to the company's use of an employee stock ownership plan to assist in the financing, the deal fell apart. Soon the company attracted unsolicited proposals to purchase the company, including one from Ivan F. Boesky, the arbitrageur. Buffett offered to buy the company for $315 million (which compared to its book value of $172.6 million). Following the acquisition, Scott & Fetzer paid Berkshire Hathaway dividends of $125 million, even though it earned only $40.3 million that year. In addition, Scott & Fetzer was conservatively financed, going from modest debt at the acquisition to virtually no debt by 1994. Exhibit 5 gives the earnings and dividends for Scott & Fetzer from 1986 to 1994. Buffett noted that in terms of return on book value of equity, Scott & Fetzer would have easily beaten the Fortune 500 firms.[9] The annual average total return on large company stocks from 1986 to 1994 was 12.6 percent.[10]

---

[8]These included companies in conduit fittings, marketing motivational services, retailing fine jewelry, air compressors, sun and shade control products, appliance controls, zinc die cast fittings, automotive compounds, pressure and flow measurement devices, fractional horsepower motors, boat winches, cutlery, truck bodies, furnace burners, compressed gas fittings, and molded plastic components.

[9]This exempts from the comparison firms emerging from bankruptcy in recent years. Buffett's observation was made in Berkshire Hathaway's 1994 annual report.

[10]Reported in *Stocks, Bonds, Bills, and Inflation, 1994.*

BUFFETT'S INVESTMENT PHILOSOPHY

Warren Buffett was first exposed to formal training in investing at Columbia University, where he studied under Professor Benjamin Graham. The coauthor of a classic text, *Security Analysis,* Graham developed a method of identifying undervalued stocks (i.e., stocks whose price was less than "intrinsic value"). This became the cornerstone of the modern approach of "value investing." Graham's approach was to focus on the value of assets such as cash, net working capital, and physical assets. Eventually, Buffett modified that approach to focus also on valuable franchises that were not recognized by the market.

Over the years, Buffett had expounded his philosophy of investing in his CEO's letter to shareholders in Berkshire Hathaway's annual report. By 1995, these lengthy letters had accumulated a broad following because of their wisdom and their humorous, self-deprecating tone. The letters emphasized the following elements:

1. *Economic reality, not accounting reality.* Financial statements prepared by accountants conformed to rules that might not adequately represent the *economic* reality of a business. Buffett wrote:

> Because of the limitations of conventional accounting, consolidated reported earnings may reveal relatively little about our true economic performance. Charlie and I, both as owners and managers, virtually ignore such consolidated numbers . . . Accounting consequences do not influence our operating or capital-allocation process.[11]

Accounting reality was conservative, backward-looking, and governed by generally accepted accounting principles (GAAP). Investment decisions, on the other hand, should be based on the economic reality of a business. In economic reality, intangible assets such as patents, trademarks, special managerial know-how, and reputation might be very valuable, yet under GAAP they would be carried at little or no value. GAAP measured results in terms of net profit; in economic reality, the results of a business were its *flows of cash.*

A key feature of Buffett's approach defined economic reality at the level of the business itself, not the market, the economy, or the security—he was a *fundamental analyst* of a business. His analysis sought to judge the simplicity of the business, the consistency of its operating history, the attractiveness of its long-term prospects, the quality of management, and the firm's capacity to create value.

2. *The cost of the lost opportunity.* Buffett compared an investment opportunity against the next best alternative, the so-called lost opportunity. In his business decisions, he demonstrated a tendency to frame his choices as "either/or" decisions rather than "yes/no" decisions. Thus, an important standard of comparison in testing the attractiveness of an acquisition was the potential rate of return from investing in common stocks of other companies. Buffett held that were was no fundamental difference between buying a business outright and buying a few shares of that business in the equity market. Thus, for him, the comparison of an investment against other returns available in the market was an important benchmark of performance.

3. *Value creation: time is money.* Buffett assessed intrinsic value as the present value of future expected performance.

---

[11]Berkshire Hathaway, Inc., annual report, 1994, p. 2.

[All other methods fall short in determining whether] an investor is indeed buying something for what it is worth and is therefore truly operating on the principle of obtaining value for his investments . . . Irrespective of whether a business grows or doesn't, displays volatility or smoothness in earnings, or carries a high price or low in relation to its current earnings and book value, the investment shown by the discounted-flows-of-cash calculation to be the cheapest is the one that the investor should purchase.[12]

Enlarging on his discussion of "intrinsic value," Buffett used an educational example:

We define intrinsic value as the discounted value of the cash that can be taken out of a business during its remaining life. Anyone calculating intrinsic value necessarily comes up with a highly subjective figure that will change both as estimates of future cash flows are revised and as interest rates move. Despite its fuzziness, however, intrinsic value is all-important and is the only logical way to evaluate the relative attractiveness of investments and businesses.

To see how historical input (book value) and future output (intrinsic value) can diverge, let's look at another form of investment, a college education. Think of the education's cost as its "book value." If it is to be accurate, the cost should include the earnings that were foregone by the student because he chose college rather than a job. For this exercise, we will ignore the important noneconomic benefits of an education and focus strictly on its economic value. First, we must estimate the earnings that the graduate will receive over his lifetime and subtract from that figure an estimate of what he would have earned had he lacked his education. That gives us an excess earnings figure, which must then be discounted, at an appropriate interest rate, back to graduation day. The dollar result equals the intrinsic economic value of the education. Some graduates will find that the book value of their education exceeds its intrinsic value, which means that whoever paid for the education didn't get his money's worth. In other cases, the intrinsic value of an education will far exceed its book value, a result that proves capital was wisely deployed. In all cases, what is clear is that book value is meaningless as an indicator of intrinsic value.[13]

To illustrate the mechanics of this example, consider the hypothetical case presented in Exhibit 6. Suppose an individual has the opportunity to invest $50 million in a business—this is its "cost" or "book value." This business will throw off cash at the rate of 20 percent of its investment base each year. Suppose that instead of receiving any dividends, the owner decides to reinvest all cash flow back into the business—at this rate the book value of the business will grow at 20 percent per year. Suppose that the investor plans to sell the business for its book value at the end of the fifth year. Does this investment create value for the individual? One determines this by discounting the future cash flows to the present at a cost of equity of 15 percent—suppose that this is the investor's opportunity cost, the required return that could have been earned elsewhere at comparable risk. Dividing the present value of future cash flows (i.e., Buffett's "intrinsic value") by the cost of the investment (i.e., Buffett's "book value") indicates that every dollar invested buys securities worth $1.23. Value is created.

Consider an opposing case, summarized in Exhibit 7. The example is similar in all respects except for one key difference: the annual return on the investment is 10 percent. The result is that every dollar invested buys securities worth $0.80. Value is destroyed.

---

[12]Berkshire Hathaway, Inc., annual report, 1992, p. 14.
[13]Berkshire Hathaway, Inc., annual report, 1994, p. 7.

Comparing the two cases in Exhibits 6 and 7, the difference in value creation and destruction is driven entirely by the relationship between the expected returns and the discount rate: in the first case, the spread is positive; in the second case, it is negative. Only in the instance where expected returns equal the discount rate will book value equal intrinsic value. In short, book value or the investment outlay may not reflect economic reality: One needs to focus on the prospective rates of return, and how they compare to the required rate of return.

4. *Measure performance by gain in intrinsic value, not accounting profit.* Buffett wrote:

> Our long-term economic goal . . . is to maximize the average annual rate of gain in intrinsic business value on a per-share basis. We do not measure the economic significance or performance of Berkshire by its size; we measure by per-share progress.[14]

The gain in intrinsic value could be modeled as the value added by a business above and beyond a charge for the use of capital in that business. The gain in intrinsic value was analogous to "economic profit" and "market value added," measures used by analysts in leading corporations to assess financial performance. Those measures focus on the ability to earn returns in excess of the cost of capital.

5. *Risk and discount rates.* Conventional academic and practitioner thinking held that the more risk one took, the more one should get paid. Thus, discount rates used in determining intrinsic values should be determined by the risk of the cash flows being valued. The conventional model for estimating discount rates was the capital asset pricing model (CAPM), which added a risk premium to the long-term risk-free rate of return (such as the U.S. Treasury bond yield).

Buffett departed from conventional thinking, by using the rate of return on the long-term (e.g., 30-year) U.S. Treasury bond to discount cash flows.[15] Defending this practice, Buffett argued that he avoided risk, and therefore should use a "risk-free" discount rate. His firm used almost no debt financing. He focused on companies with predictable and stable earnings. He or his vice chairman, Charlie Munger, sat on the boards of directors where they obtained a candid, inside view of the company and could intervene in decisions of management if necessary. Buffett wrote:

> I put a heavy weight on certainty. If you do that, the whole idea of a risk factor doesn't make sense to me. Risk comes from not knowing what you're doing.[16]

> We define risk, using dictionary terms, as "the possibility of loss or injury." Academics, however, like to define "risk" differently, averring that it is the relative volatility of a stock or a portfolio of stocks—that is, the volatility as compared to that of a large universe of stocks. Employing data bases and statistical skills, these academics compute with precision the "beta" of a stock—its relative volatility in the past—and then build arcane investment and capital allocation theories around this calculation. In their hunger for a single statistic to measure risk, however, they forget a fundamental principle: It is better to be approximately right than precisely wrong.[17]

---

[14]Ibid., p. 2.

[15]The yield on the 30-year U.S. Treasury bond on August 25, 1995, was 6.86 percent. The beta of Berkshire Hathaway was 0.95.

[16]Quoted in Jim Rasmussen, "Buffett Talks Strategy with Students," *Omaha World-Herald,* January 2, 1994, p. 26.

[17]Berkshire Hathaway annual report, 1993, and republished in Andrew Kilpatrick, *Of Permanent Value: The Story of Warren Buffett* (Birmingham: AKPE, 1994), p. 574.

6. *Diversification.* Buffett disagreed with conventional wisdom that investors should hold a broad portfolio of stocks in order to shed company-specific risk. In his view, investors typically purchased far too many stocks rather than waiting for the one exceptional company. Buffett said,

> Figure businesses out that you understand, and concentrate. Diversification is protection against ignorance, but if you don't feel ignorant, the need for it goes down drastically.[18]

7. *Investing behavior should be driven by information, analysis, and self-discipline, not by emotion or "hunch."* Buffett repeatedly emphasized "awareness" and information as the foundation for investing. He said, "Anyone not aware of the fool in the market probably is the fool in the market."[19] Buffett was fond of repeating a parable told him by Benjamin Graham:

> There was a small private business and one of the owners was a man named Market. Every day Mr. Market had a new opinion of what the business was worth, and at that price stood ready to buy your interest or sell you his. As excitable as he was opinionated, Mr. Market presented a constant distraction to his fellow owners. "What does he know?" they would wonder, as he bid them an extraordinarily high price or a depressingly low one. Actually, the gentleman knew little or nothing. You may be happy to sell out to him when he quotes you a ridiculously high price, and equally happy to buy from him when his price is low. But the rest of the time you will be wiser to form your own ideas of the value of your holdings, based on full reports from the company about its operations and financial position.[20]

Buffett used this allegory to illustrate the irrationality of stock prices as compared to true intrinsic value. Graham believed that an investor's worst enemy was not the stock market, but oneself. Superior training could not compensate for the absence of the requisite temperament for investing. Over the long term, stock prices should have a strong relationship with the economic progress of the business. But daily market quotations were heavily influenced by momentary greed or fear and were an unreliable measure of intrinsic value. Buffett said,

> As far as I am concerned, the stock market doesn't exist. It is there only as a reference to see if anybody is offering to do anything foolish. When we invest in stocks, we invest in businesses. You simply have to behave according to what is rational rather than according to what is fashionable.[21]

Accordingly, Buffett did not try to "time the market" (i.e., trade stocks based on expectations of changes in the market cycle)—his was a strategy of patient, long-term investing. As if in contrast to "Mr. Market," Buffett expressed more contrarian goals: "We simply attempt to be fearful when others are greedy and to be greedy only when others are fearful."[22] Buffett also said, "Lethargy bordering on sloth remains the cornerstone of our investment style,"[23] and, "The market, like the Lord, helps those who help themselves. But unlike the Lord, the market does not forgive those who know not what they do."[24]

---

[18]Quoted in *Forbes,* October 19, 1993, and republished in Andrew Kilpatrick, *Of Permanent Value: The Story of Warren Buffett,* p. 574.

[19]Quoted in Michael Lewis, *Liar's Poker* (New York: Norton, 1989), p. 35.

[20]Originally published in Berkshire Hathaway, Inc., annual report, 1987. This quotation was paraphrased from James Grant, *Minding Mr. Market* (New York: Times Books, 1993), p. xxi.

[21]Peter Lynch, *One Up on Wall Street* (New York: Penguin Books, 1990), p. 78.

[22]Berkshire Hathaway, Inc., annual report, 1986, p. 16.

[23]Berkshire Hathaway, Inc., annual report, 1990, p. 15.

[24]Berkshire Hathaway, Inc., *Letters to Shareholders,* 1977–1983, p. 53.

Buffett scorned the academic theory of capital market efficiency. The efficient markets hypothesis (EMH) held that publicly known information was rapidly impounded into share prices, and that as a result, stock prices were "fair" in reflecting what was known about a company. Under EMH, there were no bargains to be had and trying to outperform the market would be futile. "It has been helpful to me to have tens of thousands turned out of business schools taught that it didn't do any good to think," Buffett said.[25]

> I think it's fascinating how the ruling orthodoxy can cause a lot of people to think the earth is flat. Investing in a market where people believe in efficiency is like playing bridge with someone who's been told it doesn't do any good to look at the cards.[26]

8. *Alignment of agents and owners.* Explaining his significant ownership interest in Berkshire Hathaway, Buffett said, "I am a better businessman because I am an investor. And I am a better investor because I am a businessman."[27]

As if to illustrate this sentiment, he said,

> A managerial "wish list" will not be filled at shareholder expense. We will not diversify by purchasing entire businesses at control prices that ignore long-term economic consequences to our shareholders. We will only do with your money what we would do with our own, weighing fully the values you can obtain by diversifying your own portfolios through direct purchases in the stock market.[28]

For four of Berkshire's six directors, over 50 percent of their family net worth was represented by shares in Berkshire Hathaway. The senior managers of Berkshire Hathaway subsidiaries held shares in the company, or were compensated under incentive plans that imitated the potential returns from an equity interest in their business unit, or both.

GEICO CORPORATION

Berkshire Hathaway began purchasing shares in GEICO in 1976, and by 1980 had accumulated a 33 percent interest (34.25 million shares) for $45.7 million. During the period from 1976 to 1980, GEICO's share price had been hammered by double-digit inflation, higher accident rates, and high damage awards that raised the costs of its business more rapidly than premiums could be increased. By August 1995, that stake had grown to 50.4 percent of the firm's shares (because GEICO had repurchased some of its own shares while Berkshire had maintained its holdings) and the original stake of $45.7 million had grown in value to $1.9 billion.[29] Also, GEICO had paid an increasing dividend each year (see Exhibit 8). From 1976 to 1994, the average annual total return on large company stocks was 13.5 percent.[30]

In explaining the decision to acquire the rest of the shares in GEICO, Buffett noted:

- The firm was the seventh largest auto insurer in the United States, underwriting policies for 3.7 million cars.

---

[25]Quoted in Kilpatrick, *Of Permanent Value,* p. 353.

[26]Quoted in L. J. Davis, "Buffett Takes Stock," *New York Times,* April 1, 1990, p. 16.

[27]Quoted in *Forbes,* October 19, 1993, and republished in Kilpatrick, *Of Permanent Value,* p. 574.

[28]"Owner-Related Business Principles" in Berkshire Hathaway, Inc., annual report, 1994, p. 3.

[29]This assumes the pre-announcement GEICO share price of $55.75.

[30]Reported in *Stocks, Bonds, Bills, and Inflation, 1994,* p. 10.

- The firm's senior managers were "extraordinary" and had an investment style similar to Buffett's. These managers would add depth to Berkshire Hathaway's senior management bench and provide continuity in case anything happened to Buffett (age 65) or Munger (age 72).
- The firm was the lowest-cost insurance provider in the industry.

Some analysts sought to test the suitability of Buffett's $70 per share offer for GEICO using the discounted cash flow approach. On July 7, 1995, Value Line published a forecast of GEICO's dividends[31] and future stock price within a range of possible outcomes:

Value Line Forecast Information

Forecasted Dividends	*Low End of Range*	*High End of Range*
1996	$1.16	$1.16
1997	$1.25	$1.34
1998	$1.34	$1.55
1999	$1.44	$1.79
2000	$1.55	$2.07
Forecasted stock price in 2000	$90.00	$125.00

Value Line also presented evidence consistent with a cost of equity for GEICO of 11 percent.[32] GEICO had outstanding 67,889,574 shares as of April 30, 1995.

Analysts noted that the timing of Berkshire Hathaway's bid followed closely Walt Disney Company's bid to buy Capital Cities/ABC for $19 billion. Since some of the proceeds would be in cash, Berkshire Hathaway would need to reinvest the funds elsewhere.

CONCLUSION

Conventional thinking held that it would be difficult for Warren Buffett to maintain his record of 28 percent annual growth in shareholder wealth. Buffett acknowledged, "A fat wallet is the enemy of superior investment results."[33] He stated that it was the firm's goal to meet a 15 percent annual growth rate in intrinsic value. Would the GEICO acquisition serve the long-term goals of Berkshire Hathaway? Was the bid price appropriate? What might account for the share price increase for Berkshire Hathaway at the announcement?

---

[31]GEICO paid dividends quarterly, though Value Line presented only an annual forecast. Annual figures are given here for simplicity.

[32]Analysts used the capital asset pricing model to estimate GEICO's cost of equity. Value Line estimated GEICO's beta at 0.75. (In comparison, Berkshire Hathaway's beta was 0.95.) The equity market risk premium was about 5.5 percent. And the risk-free rate estimated by the yield on the 30-year U.S. Treasury bond was 6.86 percent.

[33]Quoted in Garth Alexander, "Buffett Spends $2bn on Return to His Roots," Times Newspapers Ltd., August 17, 1995.

EXHIBIT 1 Business Segment Information, Berkshire Hathaway, Inc. (dollars in millions)

Segment	Revenues		Pretax Operating Profit*		Capital Expenditures		Depreciation		Identifiable Assets	
	1994	1993	1994	1993	1994	1993	1994	1993	1994	1993
Insurance	$1,437	$1,591	$639	$ 961	$ 0.9	$ 1.2	$ 0.9	$ 0.8	$18,494	$16,127
Candy	216	201	47	40	4.1	4.3	4.1	4.1	69	70
Encyclopedias	191	199	24	19	0.1	0.7	1.4	1.5	76	75
Home-cleaning systems	207	193	44	41	1.0	1.5	4.2	5.3	42	49
Home furnishings	245	209	17	21	22.6	5.3	6.2	2.7	128	101
Newspaper	151	145	54	50	5.2	3.6	2.2	1.9	48	45
Shoes	609	370	76	40	17.9	4.4	10.2	5.2	673	642
Uniforms	151	122	14	13	4.6	1.0	2.5	1.8	95	88
Other	639	568	†(192)	60	10.7	13.0	18.0	17.3	1,712	2,324
Total	$3,847	$3,599	$722	$1,246	$67.1	$35.0	$49.6	$40.5	$21,338	$19,520

*Before interest expense.
†Includes pretax charge of $269 representing an other-than-temporary decline in value of investment in USAir Group, Inc. preferred stock.
N.B. Columns may not sum to the total because of rounding.

Source: Berkshire Hathaway, Inc., annual report, 1994.

EXHIBIT 2 Major Investees of Berkshire Hathaway, and "Look-Through" Earnings (dollars in millions)

Berkshire's Major Investees	Berkshire's Approximate Ownership at Year-end		Berkshire's Share of Undistributed Operating Earnings (in millions)	
	1994	1993	1994	1993
American Express Co.	5.5%	2.4%	$ 25	$ 16
Capital Cities/ABC	13.0	13.0	85	83
Coca-Cola	7.8	7.2	116	94
Federal Home Loan Mortgage	6.3	6.8	47	41
Gannett	4.9	—	4	—
GEICO	50.2	48.4	63	76
Gillette	10.8	10.9	51	44
PNC Bank	8.3	—	10	—
Washington Post	15.2	14.8	18	15
Wells Fargo	13.3%	12.2%	73	53
Berkshire's share of undistributed earnings			$ 492	$422
Hypothetical tax on these earnings			(68)	(59)
Reported operating earnings of Berkshire			606	478
Total "look-through" earnings of Berkshire			$1,030	$841

Source: Berkshire Hathaway, Inc., annual report, 1994, p. 13.

EXHIBIT 3   Berkshire's Investments in Private Purchases of Convertible Preferred Stocks

	Dividend Rate	Year of Purchase	Cost (in millions)	Market Value (in millions, at Dec. 1995)
Champion International Corp.[a]	9.25%	1989	$300	$ 388
First Empire State Corp.[b]	9.00	1991	40	110
The Gillette Company[c]	8.75	1989	600	2,502
Salomon Inc.[d]	9.00	1987	700	728
USAir Group, Inc.[e]	9.25	1989	358	215

[a]The Champion International issue could be converted into common shares at $38.00 per share. At August 25, 1995, Champion International's common share price was $57.50. By December 31, 1995, Champion's share price had fallen to $42.75.

[b]The First Empire issue could be converted into common shares at a conversion price of $78.91 per share. First Empire has the right to redeem the issue beginning in 1996. At August 25, 1995, First Empire's common share price was $184.50.

[c]The Gillette issue could be converted into common stock at $25.00 per share, and carried a mandatory redemption by Gillette after 10 years. In February 1991, following the highly successful introduction of the Sensor razor, Gillette announced that it would redeem the issue at $31.75, which effectively forced Berkshire to convert its holding into common stock. Berkshire converted, and received 12 million common shares, or 11 percent of Gillette's total shares outstanding. At August 25, 1995, Gillette's share price was $43.00.

[d]The Salomon issue could be converted into common stock at $38.00 per share. If Berkshire did not convert the preferred stock, Salomon would redeem it over five years, beginning October 1995. At August 25, 1995, Salomon's common share price was $37.125.

[e]The USAir issue could be converted into common shares at $60 per share. If Berkshire did not convert the series into common stock, USAir would have to redeem the preferred in 10 years. At August 25, 1995, the USAir common share price was $8.50.

Source: Berkshire Hathaway, annual report, 1995, p. 16.

EXHIBIT 4   Berkshire Hathaway Acquisition Criteria

We are eager to hear about businesses that meet all of the following criteria:

1. Large purchases (at least $10 million of after-tax earnings).
2. Demonstrated consistent earning power (future projections are of no interest to us, nor are "turnaround" situations).
3. Businesses earning good returns on equity while employing little or no debt.
4. Management in place (we can't supply it).
5. Simple businesses (if there's lots of technology, we won't understand it).
6. An offering price (we don't want to waste our time or that of the seller by talking, even preliminarily, about a transaction when the price is unknown).

The larger the company, the greater will be our interest: We would like to make an acquisition in the $2–$3 billion range.

We will not engage in unfriendly takeovers. We can promise complete confidentiality and a very fast answer—customarily within five minutes—as to whether we're interested. We prefer to buy for cash, but will consider issuing stock when we receive as much in intrinsic business value as we give.

Our favorite form of purchase is one fitting the pattern through which we acquired Nebraska Furniture Mart, Fechheimer's, Borsheim's, and Central States Indemnity. In cases like these, the company's owner-managers wish to generate significant amounts of cash, sometimes for themselves, but often for their families or inactive shareholders. At the same time, these managers wish to remain significant owners who continue to run their companies just as they have in the past. We think we offer a particularly good fit for owners with such objectives and we invite potential sellers to check us out by contacting people with whom we have done business in the past.

Charlie and I frequently get approached about acquisitions that don't come close to meeting our tests: We've found that if you advertise an interest in buying collies, a lot of people will call hoping to sell you their cocker spaniels. A line from a country song expresses our feeling about new ventures, turnarounds, or auction-like sales: "When the phone don't ring, you'll know it's me."

Besides being interested in the purchase of businesses as described above, we are also interested in the negotiated purchase of large, but not controlling, blocks of stock comparable to those we hold in Capital Cities, Salomon, Gillette, USAir, and Champion. *We are not interested, however, in receiving suggestions about purchases we might make in the general stock market.*

Source: Berkshire Hathaway, Inc., annual report, 1994, p. 21.

EXHIBIT 5   Scott & Fetzer, Book Value of Equity, Earnings, and Dividends, 1986–1994

	Beginning Book Value	Earnings	Dividends	Ending Book Value
1986	$172.6	$40.3	$125.0	$ 87.9
1987	87.9	48.6	41.0	95.5
1988	95.5	58.0	35.0	118.5
1989	118.5	58.5	71.5	105.5
1990	105.5	61.3	33.5	133.3
1991	133.3	61.4	74.0	120.7
1992	120.7	70.5	80.0	111.2
1993	111.2	77.5	98.0	90.7
1994	$ 90.7	$79.3	$ 76.0	$ 94.0

Source: Berkshire Hathaway, Inc., annual report, 1994, p. 7.

EXHIBIT 6   Hypothetical Example of Value Creation

Assume:

- A five-year investment horizon, when you liquidate at "book" or accumulated investment value.
- An initial investment of $50 million.
- No dividends paid; all cash flows reinvested.
- ROE = 20%.
- Cost of equity = 15%.

	Year					
	0	*1*	*2*	*3*	*4*	*5*
Investment, or book equity, value	50	60	72	86	104	124

Market value (or "intrinsic value") = PV @ 15% of 124 = $61.65

Market/book = $61.65/50.00 = 1.23

Value created: $1.00 invested becomes $1.23 in market value.

Source: Casewriter analysis.

EXHIBIT 7   Hypothetical Example of Value Destruction

Assume:

- A five-year investment horizon, when you liquidate at "book" or accumulated investment value.
- An initial investment of $50 million.
- No dividends are paid; all cash flows are reinvested.
- ROE = 10%.
- Cost of equity = 15%.

	Year					
	0	*1*	*2*	*3*	*4*	*5*
Investment, or book equity, value	*50*	*55*	*60*	*67*	*73*	*81*

Market value (or "intrinsic value") = PV @ 15% of $81 = $40.30

Market/book = $40.30/50.00 = 0.80

Value destroyed: $1.00 invested becomes $0.80 in market value.

Source: Casewriter analysis.

EXHIBIT 8 GEICO Dividend Payment History (dollars in millions, except per-share figures)

Year	GEICO Dividend Per Share	Total Dividends to Berkshire Hathaway*
1976	$0.00	$ 0.00
1977	0.01	0.34
1978	0.04	1.37
1979	0.07	2.40
1980	0.09	3.08
1981	0.10	3.43
1982	0.11	3.77
1983	0.14	4.80
1984	0.18	6.17
1985	0.20	6.85
1986	0.22	7.54
1987	0.27	9.25
1988	0.33	11.30
1989	0.36	12.33
1990	0.40	13.70
1991	0.46	15.76
1992	0.60	20.55
1993	0.68	23.29
1994	$1.00	$34.25

*Total dividends to Berkshire were estimated by multiplying the per share dividend times 34.25 million shares, Berkshire's holdings in GEICO. This presentation assumes that all of Berkshire's shares in GEICO were acquired in 1976.

Source of annual dividends per share: Value Line Investment Survey.

The Fidelity Magellan Fund, 1995

1988: *The only thing that sets him apart is this: For 10 years now, he has been the best mutual fund manager alive . . . "Around Fidelity," says one former marketing aide, "Peter Lynch is God."*[1]

1991: *Morris Smith does things his way at Fidelity Magellan—but he gets the same old stellar results.*[2]

1993: *If young Jeff Vinik keeps up his torrid performance as manager of Fidelity's Magellan Fund, his shareholders might soon forget there ever was a Peter Lynch . . . Vinik is now the hero*[3].

In the autumn of 1995, investors in the Magellan Fund of Fidelity Management & Research Company (FMR) could look back on a remarkable record of performance: an average annual total return of 22.7 percent per year over the previous 15 years, which surpassed the return on the Standard & Poor's 500 (S&P 500) index by 7.77 percent per year. In addition, the fund beat the broad market average for the previous 10, 5, and 3 years— results that Fidelity advertised in soliciting new investors to the fund. These results stood in stark contrast to the historical performance of equally ambitious and talented managers

---

[1]Joseph Nocera, "The Ga-Ga Years," *Esquire,* February 1988, p. 87.

[2]Geoffrey Smith, "Peter Lynch? Why's Peter Lynch?" *Business Week,* May 20, 1991, p. 118.

[3]"Who Needs Peter Lynch? Upstart Magellan Manager Scores Big," *Barron's,* June 21, 1993, p. 36.

This case was written by Professor Robert F. Bruner. This case was written as a basis for class discussion rather than to illustrate effective or ineffective handling of an administrative situation. Copyright © 1995 by the University of Virginia Darden School Foundation, Charlottesville, VA. All rights reserved. *No part of this publication may be reproduced, stored in a retrieval system, used in a spreadsheet or transmitted in any form or by any means—electronic, mechanical, photocopying, recording or otherwise—without the permission of the Darden Foundation. For inquiries, please send an e-mail to dardencases@virginia.edu.* Rev. 11/97. Version 1.5.

of other mutual funds. Furthermore, the results contrasted with conventional theories suggesting that in markets characterized by high competition, easy entry, and informational efficiency, it would be extremely difficult to "beat the market" on a sustained basis. Observers wondered what might explain Magellan's performance.

Of special note was that the fund had delivered superior performance despite turnover in its management. The fund's longstanding and highly successful manager, Peter Lynch, retired in 1990 at the age of 46. His replacement was Morris Smith, who retired in 1992 at the age of 34. *His* replacement was the present manager, Jeffrey Vinik, now 36. The financial press noted that all three managers "beat the market" during their tenure.

The Magellan Fund was the largest equity mutual fund in the world, with nearly $51 billion in net assets in late 1995. FMR, the parent of Fidelity Investments, which provided management and advisory services to the fund's shareholders, was a privately held company, managing 223 funds. Fidelity's revenue in 1992 was $1.84 billion; net income was $94 million.[4] Fidelity's assets under management in 1995 were nearly $390 billion. Wide acknowledgment placed Fidelity among the most innovative—and aggressive—mutual fund advisers in the industry.

THE U.S. EQUITY MARKET

Institutional investors, or "money managers," who managed pension funds and mutual funds on behalf of individual investors dominated the market for common stocks in the United States in the mid-1990s. While statistics still revealed that households, life insurance companies, personal trusts (i.e., those managed by bank trust departments), and non-profit institutions held the majority of shares of common stock, the percentage had been declining over the previous 30 years. Indeed, at the end of 1994, equity mutual funds owned only 13 percent of the almost $6 trillion of market value of American common stock—private pension funds owned slightly more than 13 percent.

But the aggregate figures somewhat masked the explosive growth of mutual funds from 1979 to 1995. Over this period, assets of all mutual funds grew from $95 billion to $2.6 trillion. Moreover, the percentage of individual investors who owned mutual fund shares rose from 15.8 percent to about 33 percent between 1981 and 1995.

More important, the sheer dominance of money managers appeared not in assets held but in their trading muscle—their ability to move huge sums of money into and out of stocks on short notice. Accordingly, money managers were the principal price setters (or "lead steers") in the stock market. Approximately 90 percent of all trades on the New York Stock Exchange (NYSE) involved institutional investors. The rising dominance of institutional investors resulted in the growth of trading volume, average trade size, and especially in block trading (i.e., individual trades of more than 10,000 shares) which was virtually nonexistent 30 years ago but by 1986 accounted for about half of the trading volume.

---

[4]Alyssa A. Lappen, "Fidelity Grapples with Gigantism," *Institutional Investor,* September 1995, p. 90.

MUTUAL FUND INDUSTRY

Mutual funds served several economic functions for investors. First, they afforded the individual investor the opportunity to diversify his or her portfolio efficiently (i.e., own many different stocks) without having to invest the sizable amount of capital usually necessary to achieve efficiency. Efficiency was also reflected in the ability of mutual funds to exploit scale economies in trading and transactions costs, economies unavailable to the typical individual investor. Second, in theory, mutual funds provided the individual investor the professional expertise necessary to earn abnormal returns through successful securities analysis.

A third view was that the mutual fund industry provided "an insulating layer between the individual investor and the painful vicissitudes of the marketplace":

> This service, after all, allows individuals to go about their daily lives without spending too much time on the aggravating subject of what to buy and sell and when, and it spares them the even greater aggravation of kicking themselves for making the wrong decision . . . Thus, the money management industry is really selling "more peace of mind" and "less worry," though it rarely bothers to say so.[5]

In the 10 years from 1985 to 1995, the number of mutual funds grew from 1,528 to 6,683.[6] This total included many different kinds of funds, each pursuing a specific investment focus and categorized into several acknowledged segments of the industry: aggressive growth (i.e., capital appreciation oriented), equity-income, growth, growth and income, international, option, specialty, small-company, balanced, and a variety of bond or fixed-income funds.[7] Funds whose principal focus of investing was common stocks comprised the largest sector of the industry.

To some extent, the growth in number and types of mutual funds reflected the increased liquidity in the market and the demand by investors for equity. But more important, it reflected the effort by mutual fund organizations to segment the market; that is, to identify the specialized and changing needs of investors, and to create products to meet those needs. One important result was a broader customer base for the mutual fund industry as well as deeper penetration of the total market for financial services.

Another important result of this development was that it added a degree of complexity to the marketplace that altered the investment behavior of some equity investors. In particular, this tended to encourage fund switching, especially from one type of fund to another within a family of funds. This reflected the greater range of mutual funds from which to choose, the increased volatility in the market, and the increased trend toward timing-oriented investment strategies. In short, as the mutual fund industry grew, mutual fund money became "hotter," tending to turn over faster.

The performance of a mutual fund could be evaluated in terms of its total returns to investors as calculated by:

---

[5]Contrarious, "Good News and Bad News," *Personal Investing,* August 26, 1987, p. 128.

[6]"The Seismic Shift in American Finance," *The Economist,* October 21, 1995, p. 75; Morningstar Mutual Funds, September 29, 1995.

[7]Aggressive growth funds seek to maximize capital gains. Current income is of little concern. Growth funds invest in more well-known companies with steadier track records. Growth and income funds invest in companies with longer track records that are expected to increase in value and provide a steady income stream. International funds invest in foreign companies. Option funds seek to maximize current returns by investing in dividend-paying stocks on which call options are traded. Balanced funds attempt to conserve principal while earning both current income and capital gains.

$$\text{Annual total return} = \frac{\text{Change in net asset value} + \text{Dividends} + \text{Capital gain distributions}}{\text{Net asset value (at the beginning of the year)}}$$

Net asset value (NAV) was computed as total assets, less liabilities, and divided by the number of mutual fund shares outstanding. Computing the annual total return in this manner took into account annual management fees, and did not take into account front-end or back-end "loads."

Mutual fund advisers received compensation under various schemes that featured variations on two components:

Initial payments: Nearly three-quarters of all mutual funds were sold under some kind of commission, sales fee, or "load." The load could be as large as 8.5 percent of the investor's principal. Back-end loads (i.e., redemption fees) were also possible.

Annual fees: Annual management fees ranged from under 0.5 to over 2 percent of fund assets. Some funds also charged a separate fee for marketing and promotion expenses, which could run up to 2 percent of assets.

The net effect of these payments on shareholder returns could be dramatic.[8] Another drag on returns to shareholders was the tendency of funds to keep 10 percent of assets in cash—5 percent to meet redemptions and 5 percent to meet unexpected bargains. In comparison, Magellan carried only 1.4 percent in cash before the stock market crash in October 1987, ultimately forcing Peter Lynch to dump $1 billion worth of shares in the market in order to meet unexpectedly high redemptions.[9]

PERFORMANCE OF THE MUTUAL FUND INDUSTRY

Exhibit 1 reveals that the average return on 1,841 domestic equity funds over the 1-, 5-, and 10-year periods was below that of the Wilshire 5000 index of common stocks, and barely exceeded the S&P 500 over the 3- and 5-year range. Indexes such as the Wilshire, S&P 500, Dow Jones, and Value Line were each measures of the investment performance of hypothetical portfolios of stock.[10] In each of the recent years, only about one-quarter of all equity mutual funds provided returns (before fees and expenses) greater than the S&P 500. The performance of pension funds was similar.

---

[8]For instance, suppose that you invested $10,000 in a fund that would appreciate at 10 percent annually, and that you sold out after three years. Also suppose that the advisory firm charged annual fees of 2 percent and a redemption fee of 4 percent. The fees would cut pretax profit by 35 percent—from $3,310 to $2,162.

[9]One industry observer, economist Henry Kaufman, warned that a sudden economywide shock from interest rates or commodities prices could spook investors into panic-style redemptions from mutual funds, who themselves would liquidate investments and send securities prices into a tailspin. Unlike the banking industry, which enjoys the liquidity afforded by the Federal Reserve System to respond to the effects of panic by depositors, the mutual fund industry enjoys no such government-backed reserve.

[10]The Dow Jones indexes of industrial companies, transportation companies, and utilities reflected the stocks of a small number (e.g., 30) of large "blue-chip" companies, all traded on the New York Stock Exchange. The S&P 500 was an index of shares of the 500 largest companies, traded on both the New York and American Stock Exchanges. The Value Line reflected 1,400 different companies. The Wilshire was the broadest index, and covered 5,000 companies—virtually the entire universe of regularly traded shares. As the index sample became larger, it reflected a greater weighting of smaller, high-growth companies.

The two most frequently used measures of performance were (*a*) the percentage annual growth rate of net asset value assuming reinvestment (i.e., total return on investment), and (*b*) the absolute dollar value today of an investment made at some time in the past. These measures were then compared to the performance of a benchmark portfolio such as the Wilshire 5000 or the S&P 500. However, academicians criticized these approaches because of their failure to adjust for the riskiness of the mutual fund. Over long periods, as Exhibit 2 shows, different types of securities yielded different levels of total return. But Exhibit 3 shows that each of these different types of securities was associated with different degrees of risk (measured as the standard deviation of returns). The relationship between risk and return was reliable on average and over time. For instance, it should be expected that a conservatively managed mutual fund would yield a lower return—precisely because it took fewer risks.

After adjusting for the riskiness of the fund, academic studies reported that mutual funds were able to perform up to the market on a gross returns basis; however, when expenses were factored in, they underperformed the market. For instance, Michael Jensen, in a paper published in 1968, reported that gross risk-adjusted returns were −0.4 percent and that net risk-adjusted returns (i.e., net of expenses) were −1.1 percent. In 1977, Main updated the study and found that for a sample of 70 mutual funds, net risk-adjusted returns were essentially zero. Some analysts attributed this general result to the average 1.3 percent expense ratio of mutual funds and their desire to hold cash.[11]

Most mutual fund managers relied on some variation of two classic schools of securities analysis:

Technical analysis: This involved the identification of profitable investment opportunities based on trends in stock prices, volume, market sentiment, Fibonacci numbers, and so on.[12]

Fundamental analysis: This approach relied on insights afforded by an analysis of the economic fundamentals of a company and its industry: demand and supply, costs, growth prospects, and so on.

While variations on these approaches often produced supernormal returns in certain years, there was no guarantee that they would produce such returns consistently over time. Burton Malkiel, an academic researcher, concluded that a passive buy-and-hold strategy (of a large diversified portfolio) would do as well for the investor as the average mutual fund:

> Even a dart-throwing chimpanzee can select a portfolio that performs as well as one carefully selected by the experts. This, in essence, is the practical application of the theory of efficient markets . . . The theory holds that the market appears to adjust so quickly to information about individual stocks and the economy as a whole, that no technique of selecting a portfolio—neither technical nor fundamental analysis—can consistently outperform a strategy of simply buying and holding a diversified group of securities such as those that make up the popular market averages . . . One has to be impressed with the substantial volume of evidence suggesting that stock prices display a remarkable degree of efficiency . . . If some degree of mispricing exists, it does not persist for long. "True value will always out" in the stock market.[13]

---

[11]Jeffrey M. Laderman, "The Best Mutual Funds," *Business Week,* February 22, 1988, p. 64.

[12]The sequence, named for Leonard Fibonacci (1175–1240) consisted of the numbers 1, 1, 2, 3, 5, 8, 13, and so on. Each number after the first two equals the sum of the two numbers before it. No academic research associates this sequence with a consistent ability to earn supernormal returns from investing in the market.

[13]From *A Random Walk Down Wall Street* by Burton G. Milkiel. Copyright © 1990, 1985, 1981, 1975, 1973 by W. W. Norton & Company, Inc. Reprinted by permission of W. W. Norton & Company, Inc.

Many academicians accepted this view. They argued that the stock market followed a "random walk," where the price movements of tomorrow were essentially uncorrelated with the price movements of today. In essence, this denied the possibility that there could be momentum in the movement of common stock prices. According to this view, technical analysis was the modern-day equivalent of alchemy. Fundamental analysis, too, had its academic detractors. They argued that capital markets were informationally efficient and that the insights available to any one fundamental analyst were bound to be impounded quickly into share prices.

By implication, these academic theories were highly critical of the services provided by active mutual fund managers. Paul Samuelson, the Nobel Prize–winning economist said:

> [E]xisting stock prices already have discounted in them an allowance for their future prospects. Hence . . . one stock [is] about as good or bad a buy as another. To [the] passive investor, chance alone would be as good a method of selection as anything else.[14]

Various popular tests of this thinking seemed to support it. For instance, *Forbes* magazine chose 28 stocks by throwing darts in June 1967 and invested $1,000 in each. By 1984, the $28,000 investment was worth $131,697.61, for a 9.5 percent compound rate of return. This beat the broad market averages and almost all mutual funds. *Forbes* concluded, "It would seem that a combination of luck and sloth beats brains."[15]

Yet the nagging problem remained that there were still *some* superstar money managers—like Peter Lynch, Morris Smith, and Jeffrey Vinik—who, over long periods of time, greatly outperformed the market. In reply, Professor Burton Malkiel suggested that beating the market was much like participating in a coin-tossing contest where those who consistently flip heads are the winners.[16] At the first flip, half of the contestants are eliminated. At the second flip, half of the surviving contestants are eliminated. And so on until on the seventh flip only eight contestants remain. To the naive observer the ability to flip heads consistently looks like extraordinary skill. By analogy, Professor Malkiel suggested that the success of a few superstar portfolio managers could be explained as luck.

As might be expected, the community of money managers received the academic theories with great hostility. And even in the ranks of academicians, dissension appeared in the form of the "investment behaviorists" who suggested that greed, fear, and panic are much more significant factors in the setting of stock prices than the mainstream theory admits. For instance, the stock market crash of October 1987 seemed to many to be totally inconsistent with the view of markets as fundamentally rational and efficient. Professor Lawrence Summers of Harvard argued that the crash was a "clear gap with the theory. If anyone did seriously believe that price movements are determined by changes in information about economic fundamentals, they've got to be disabused of that notion by [the] 500-point drop."[17] Professor Robert Shiller of Yale said, "The efficient market hypothesis is the most remarkable error in the history of economic theory. This is just another nail in its coffin."[18]

---

[14]Ibid., p. 182.
[15]Ibid., p. 164.
[16]Ibid., pp. 175–76.
[17]B. Donnelly, "Efficient-Market Theorists Are Puzzled by Recent Gyrations in Stock Market," *Wall Street Journal,* October 23, 1987, p. 7.
[18]Ibid.

Academic research exposed other inconsistencies with the efficient-market hypothesis. These included apparently predictable stock price patterns indicating reliably abnormally positive returns in early January of each year (the "January effect"), and a "blue Monday" effect where average stock returns are negative from the close of trading on Friday to the close of trading on Monday. Other evidence suggested that stocks with low price/earnings multiples tended to outperform those with high price/earnings multiples. Finally, some evidence emerged for positive serial correlation (i.e., "momentum") in stock returns from week to week or month to month. These results were inconsistent with a random walk of prices and returns. Yet, despite the existence of these anomalies, the efficient-markets hypothesis remained the dominant paradigm in the academic community.

FIDELITY MAGELLAN FUND

Exhibit 4 presents a summary of the Magellan Fund as it stood in mid-1995 and of its performance over the previous 15 years. Morningstar Mutual Funds, a well-known statistical service reporting on mutual fund performance, gave Magellan a five-star rating, its highest for investment performance. Exhibit 5 gives a comparison of Magellan's return versus other "growth-stock oriented" mutual funds. The long-term performance results suggested that Magellan tended to outperform the market in bull markets and underperform the market in bear markets.[19] This was attributed to the fund managers' conscious strategy of staying fully invested at all times rather than attempting to time the extent of market investments.

The other striking fact about Magellan's recent financial results was its sheer rate of growth. As early as 1988, one journalist wrote:

> Because of its enormous size, Magellan can no longer beat the market the way it once could. Lynch himself advises people looking for big gains to try another fund. But they won't.[20]

Yet, despite its size, the fund continued to outperform the broad market averages. In 1995, however, one pension fund consultant said,

> The fewer stocks in a portfolio, the more stock selection drives performance. The more names, the more performance is driven by [industry] sectors. And funds [like Magellan] that were built as stock selection vehicles become far less so as time goes on. Magellan in the early 1980s had eye-popping numbers that just cannot be repeated, even with big sector bets.[21]

One popular explanation for the fund's performance was the unusual skill of its managers. Peter Lynch was an adherent of the fundamental analysis approach to investing. In his book on equity investing, he wrote:

> It seemed to me that most of what I learned at Wharton, which was supposed to help you succeed in the investment business, could only help you fail . . . Quantitative analysis taught me that the things I saw happening at Fidelity couldn't really be happening. I also found it difficult to inte-

---

[19]A "bull market" was a period of time in which stock prices were generally rising. A "bear market" was a period of time in which stock prices were generally declining.

[20]Nocera, "The Ga-Ga Years," p. 88.

[21]Reprinted with permission from *One Up on Wall Street,* Peter Lynch with John Rothchild (New York: Simon & Schuster, 1989).

grate the efficient-market hypothesis . . . with the random walk hypothesis . . . Already I'd seen enough odd fluctuations to doubt the rational part, and the success of the great Fidelity fund managers was hardly unpredictable. It also was obvious that Wharton professors who believed in quantum analysis and random walk weren't doing nearly as well as my new colleagues at Fidelity, so between theory and practice, I cast my lot with the practitioners.[22]

The following are Lynch's "favorable attributes" of stocks to invest in:

1. It sounds dull—or even better, ridiculous.
2. It does something dull.
3. It does something disagreeable.
4. It's a spinoff.
5. The institutions don't own it, and the analysts don't follow it.
6. The rumors about it: It's involved with toxic waste and/or the Mafia.
7. There's something depressing about it.
8. It's a no-growth industry.
9. It's got a niche.
10. People have to keep buying it.
11. It's a user of technology.
12. The insiders are buyers.
13. The company is buying back shares.[23]

In summary, Peter Lynch said, "I continue to think like an amateur as frequently as possible." After accumulating an impressive performance record, Peter Lynch retired on May 31, 1990, at the age of 46. He confessed to being burned out by 80-hour weeks that left him without enough time for his wife and three daughters, and noted that his father had died of cancer at the age of 46.

Morris Smith assumed the helm of the Magellan Fund just months before the market slump beginning in late 1990. At the time, Magellan's assets were $13 billion. Smith had been hired by Fidelity in 1982, and rose to manage its OTC Portfolio Fund, which posted an outstanding performance record during his tenure. In contrasting his investing strategy with Peter Lynch's, Smith said,

> I've never been married to one strategy, and I always try to interpret the market as it is. Peter and I are both bottom-up types of investors . . . visiting companies, a lot of hands-on research . . . [I]t's difficult for me to analyze what the differences are.[24]

Still, investors were skeptical that Peter Lynch's performance would be maintained: "The probabilities aren't in favor of anyone doing as well as Peter Lynch," wrote Charlie Hooper, editor of *Mutual Fund Strategist.*[25] Indeed, the *Boston Globe* instituted a "Morris Watch" column in its Sunday business section, tracking Magellan's performance each week, looking for the stumble that would differentiate him from Peter Lynch.

---

[22]Reprinted with permission from *One Up on Wall Street,* Peter Lynch with John Rothchild (New York: Simon & Schuster, 1989).

[23]Ibid., pp. 122–36.

[24]Sharon Harvey, "Mr. Smith Goes to Magellan," *Institutional Investor,* March 1991, pp. 131–32.

[25]John Waggoner, "Magellan's New Star," *USA Today,* April 5, 1991, p. 1B.

The stumble never occurred. Smith configured Magellan's investments conservatively, and successfully rode out the market decline of 1990–91. Indeed, in 1991 he beat the S&P 500 by 10.5 percent. Then in April 1992, Smith stunned the investment community with the announcement that he would retire from the fund. The 34-year-old manager, an Orthodox Jew, planned to move to Israel to spend more time with his wife and children and study the Talmud. He claimed not to have had the time to read a book for leisure since 1982.

Smith's successor, Jeffrey Vinik, joined Fidelity in 1987, having graduated from Duke University and Harvard Business School. Within two years he became an assistant to Peter Lynch, and then won appointments to be the manager of increasingly prominent Fidelity funds, including Contrafund and Growth & Income Fund. When Vinik, age 32, assumed responsibility for the Magellan Fund, its assets had risen to $22 billion. One observer said, "If you're running a $22-billion fund, you're basically buying the market,"[26] implying that investors would be better off allocating their wealth to an index fund that closely mirrored the performance of the S&P 500, and doing so with lower costs. In reply, Vinik said flatly, "My goal is to beat the S&P."[27] He had allocated the fund's assets to nearly 500 issues of common stock, but had concentrated almost half of the fund in the technology sector. One observer called Vinik a "manic" trader, pointing to the very high turnover rates of previous portfolios he had managed—for the year to August 1995 the turnover rate for the fund was 120 percent, indicating that Vinik had executed nearly $60 billion of trades so far that year. Notwithstanding the complexity of his portfolio and his high trading volume, Vinik said that he would continue leaving the office at 5:30 PM, limiting workweeks to 60–65 hours: "My family was the first thing I thought about when I was approached about the job. I feel like I can handle it—stress is part of the job."[28] Vinik was reported to own at least 30,000 shares in FMR, worth about $100 apiece, and to earn more than $1 million per year.[29]

In part, Magellan's remarkable growth in assets was due to its superior investment performance—supported by a deep talent pool of portfolio managers and a research staff over 100 strong. Internal research was supplemented with research purchased from numerous external analysts. But industry observers also credited the growth, in part, to aggressive marketing by FMR, the parent company. Roger Servison, an FMR executive said, "We want to own [the financial consumer's] brain. We want them to think of us as their primary financial provider."[30] FMR's chief executive officer, Ned Johnson, said,

> Oh, [growth] isn't an end. It's every day—the challenge of running and improving the businesses, being rewarded, and also providing something of value to others. It's like collecting or like playing a professional sport. It's a desire to win, yes, but it's also the desire to produce something that has value to many people.[31]

---

[26]Quotation of Sheldon Jacobs, editor of *No-Load Fund Investor,* in Thomas Watterson, "Jeffrey Vinik's Nest Egg," *Boston Globe,* January 17, 1993.

[27]Ibid.

[28]Geoffrey Smith, "Morris We Hardly Knew Ye," *Business Week,* May 11, 1992, p. 40.

[29]Lappen, "Fidelity Grapples with Gigantism," p. 86.

[30]Ibid., p. 78.

[31]Ibid., p. 80.

Nevertheless, other observers saw FMR as a company driven toward aggressive growth, with a highly competitive internal culture, that might lead to the firm's ultimate downfall. One journalist wrote:

> As the assets of the chief Fidelity funds swell . . . their portfolio managers may well feel compelled, in the ultracompetitive Fidelity climate, to take added risks to sustain their impressive, growth-fund-style returns. "The more money you manage and the more fields you are in," notes the marketing head of a major competitor, "the greater the chances that you will be on the playground when a big mortar hits."[32]

CONCLUSION

Judged from almost any perspective, the performance of the Magellan Fund was remarkable. Its long-run, market-beating performance defied conventional academic theories. And its ability to achieve this performance in the face of the fund's staggering size challenged most pragmatists who believed that the fund would eventually become a clone of the broad market.

Investors, academicians, and market observers wondered about the sources of Magellan's superior performance, and about its sustainability into the future. As of mid-1995, was it rational for the equity investor to buy shares in Magellan?

---

[32]Ibid., p. 82.

EXHIBIT 1   Morningstar Comparison of Performance of Mutual Fund Categories and Broad Market Indexes

Performance Close-Ups

Benchmark Performance

No. of Funds	Objective	TR% YTD 09-08-95	1Mo	3Mo	6Mo	1Yr	Annualized 3Yr	5Yr	10Yr	1987	1988	1989	1990	1991	1992	1993	1994
1841	**Domestic Stock**	27.14	0.97	10.14	18.43	20.45	14.77	15.53	13.25	1.20	15.78	25.25	-5.74	37.02	9.32	12.86	-1.54
93	Aggressive Growth	33.77	1.24	16.11	23.96	26.86	19.45	18.79	14.36	-2.97	15.42	27.17	-8.29	53.59	8.49	19.49	-3.56
132	Equity-Income	20.38	0.99	4.60	12.65	13.91	11.18	12.99	11.53	-2.23	16.05	21.35	-5.78	26.70	9.19	13.20	-1.73
811	Growth	27.85	0.81	10.35	18.93	20.31	14.47	15.37	13.59	2.82	14.82	27.55	-4.52	37.36	8.30	11.61	-1.86
460	Growth and Income	24.03	0.61	6.21	15.40	16.98	12.50	13.58	12.49	2.22	15.11	23.66	-4.55	28.84	8.25	10.99	-1.15
345	Small Company	30.35	1.74	15.47	22.06	25.98	19.30	19.38	13.98	-2.32	19.91	22.81	-10.1	49.21	14.09	16.94	-0.69
656	**International Stock**	6.85	-1.64	3.74	11.79	-2.22	12.29	7.99	14.06	11.23	15.76	23.22	-11.5	14.94	-3.53	38.98	-2.99
54	Diversified Emerging Market	-0.01	-2.05	1.71	12.03	-15.71	13.73	11.00	11.21	0.23	10.50	28.11	-9.74	18.10	0.26	72.16	-9.60
41	Europe Stock	15.18	-2.88	3.32	12.39	8.39	10.55	4.99	12.52	15.95	7.00	25.69	-5.37	7.28	-7.93	26.45	2.55
310	Foreign Stock	4.81	-1.58	3.63	11.33	-3.89	11.67	7.62	14.82	8.25	16.97	21.92	-11.6	12.57	-4.43	37.94	-2.20
89	Pacific Stock	0.93	-2.00	1.13	8.11	-8.99	13.89	6.07	15.50	32.42	22.66	27.70	-19.8	13.68	-3.98	57.82	-8.17
162	World Stock	14.12	-1.10	6.18	14.43	5.15	13.04	10.39	12.77	5.68	13.64	22.54	-9.81	19.21	-0.38	31.61	-2.27
284	**Specialty Stock**	20.35	1.25	7.69	16.76	14.78	14.99	13.18	11.93	7.55	6.87	27.38	-9.38	24.78	5.24	30.65	-4.13
15	Communication	23.52	1.81	12.80	20.46	16.83	22.22	21.40	16.39	6.59	21.89	45.01	-13.1	29.61	16.16	32.11	-1.98
16	Financial	31.71	4.18	11.43	20.70	17.72	21.36	26.21	13.14	-11.4	19.03	24.84	-15.7	58.98	35.08	16.75	-2.78
18	Health	27.46	2.07	13.04	17.34	24.99	13.02	16.78	17.71	0.27	11.61	38.50	14.99	63.76	-4.69	3.76	4.26
38	Natural Resources	16.20	0.23	3.29	14.58	7.14	10.31	6.61	8.46	9.33	9.80	29.41	-8.60	6.26	2.89	21.86	-2.64
42	Precious Metals	7.93	1.15	5.53	18.37	-1.69	14.15	3.48	5.95	36.79	-17.7	25.65	-23.8	-3.89	-15.2	84.97	-11.7
32	Real Estate	7.80	0.96	5.53	9.77	5.03	10.79	10.92	—	-7.68	15.60	10.57	-16.6	33.11	12.74	22.63	-4.34
27	Technology	52.83	1.43	24.09	41.13	58.36	33.23	26.61	15.71	2.92	2.36	22.20	-2.57	47.46	12.57	20.91	15.23
80	Utilities	14.94	1.18	2.92	9.33	10.34	7.29	11.41	9.92	-7.00	11.61	26.95	-0.45	20.81	9.31	14.39	-8.87
16	Unaligned	26.06	0.13	9.50	17.70	15.62	15.97	16.32	15.37	-4.99	24.24	23.63	-9.19	33.54	10.60	21.48	-5.84
498	**Hybrid**	17.95	0.71	4.74	12.15	13.19	9.88	11.78	11.19	3.50	11.12	17.85	-0.14	23.58	7.36	12.46	-2.74
166	Asset Allocation	18.40	0.66	4.74	12.16	14.49	10.35	11.95	9.93	2.44	9.73	15.97	1.19	21.96	8.14	11.98	-1.76
278	Balanced	18.86	0.88	5.03	12.44	13.92	9.91	12.25	11.70	1.70	12.61	19.12	-0.43	26.22	7.41	11.17	-2.82
54	Multiasset Global	12.28	0.05	3.19	10.64	6.75	8.69	9.52	10.11	15.14	7.28	17.32	-2.06	16.60	5.16	20.36	-4.56
381	**Specialty Bond**	12.09	-0.10	1.81	9.23	10.00	8.00	11.94	9.80	3.02	11.39	4.26	-2.67	28.19	11.38	17.00	-4.94
42	Convertible Bond	17.31	0.76	6.58	13.14	11.56	11.78	13.65	10.90	-3.96	11.92	14.47	-6.04	28.55	13.81	15.50	-4.58
131	Corp Bond–High Yield	12.20	0.16	2.26	8.07	10.46	9.44	13.56	9.70	2.02	12.82	-0.48	-9.96	36.58	17.39	18.84	-3.71
58	Multisector Bond	11.76	0.35	1.67	8.38	9.80	6.74	10.58	9.81	1.40	13.05	6.88	1.40	24.39	8.31	14.65	-5.03
150	World Bond	10.69	-0.75	0.15	9.47	9.26	5.10	7.72	8.79	15.97	5.12	6.16	13.46	13.22	2.60	16.38	-6.21
642	**Corporate Bond**	10.27	0.99	1.50	6.64	8.87	5.48	8.55	9.14	2.14	8.02	10.98	7.09	14.84	6.19	9.26	-3.00
390	Corp Bond–General	11.30	1.10	1.55	7.26	9.69	6.21	9.27	9.45	2.20	8.66	10.82	6.27	16.39	7.39	10.30	-3.50
211	Corp Bond–High Quality	9.54	0.94	1.43	6.02	8.64	5.56	8.20	8.73	2.41	7.14	11.65	7.63	14.25	6.35	8.33	-2.05
211	Corp Bond–High Quality	9.54	0.94	1.43	6.02	8.64	5.56	8.20	8.73	2.41	7.14	11.65	7.63	14.25	6.35	8.33	-2.05
41	Short-Term World Income	4.57	0.26	1.43	4.06	2.78	1.45	3.74	—	-9.26	10.15	-14.3	13.43	7.99	-0.73	6.33	-2.93
646	**Government Bond**	9.78	0.96	1.25	5.94	8.17	4.68	8.13	8.72	1.46	7.37	12.59	8.34	14.30	6.02	7.68	-3.50
67	Govt Bond–Adj-Rate Mortgage	3.25	0.46	0.33	2.44	1.12	1.47	5.90	—	-1.24	5.91	12.33	8.27	10.53	4.68	3.90	-2.77
378	Govt Bond–General	10.14	1.01	1.31	6.16	8.62	4.90	7.89	8.12	1.50	6.64	11.93	8.38	14.01	6.05	8.00	-3.58
134	Govt Bond–Mortgage	10.92	0.96	1.52	6.36	9.42	4.98	8.06	8.38	2.16	7.68	12.92	9.39	14.64	6.43	7.10	-3.40
67	Govt Bond–Treasury	11.77	1.14	1.36	7.41	10.59	6.33	9.50	11.86	-0.03	9.86	14.44	6.50	15.41	6.20	10.86	-4.11
1735	**Municipal Bond**	10.89	1.04	0.73	4.56	7.08	6.05	7.99	8.29	-1.00	10.85	9.44	6.11	11.44	8.63	11.84	-5.88
164	Muni Bond–California	11.47	1.08	0.37	4.46	6.89	5.98	7.98	8.18	-2.41	10.95	9.68	6.58	11.01	8.42	12.12	-6.77
502	Muni Bond–National	10.33	0.99	0.93	4.61	7.06	5.95	7.90	8.38	-0.18	10.38	9.28	6.12	11.35	8.42	11.25	-5.07
126	Muni Bond–New York	10.99	1.09	0.65	4.68	6.73	5.94	8.19	8.18	-1.76	10.64	9.32	5.21	12.93	9.42	12.27	-6.56
943	Muni Bond–Single State	11.07	1.05	0.70	4.53	7.18	6.16	8.04	8.17	-1.38	11.43	9.56	6.20	11.28	8.65	12.10	-6.09
6683	**Total Fund Average**	15.77	0.66	4.39	10.76	11.17	9.76	11.33	11.34	1.95	12.07	17.28	-0.42	23.11	7.37	14.69	-3.51
	S&P 500 Index	26.87	0.25	5.97	16.79	21.42	13.83	15.10	15.19	5.26	16.61	31.68	-3.12	30.48	7.62	10.06	1.32
	Lehman Bros Aggregate	—	1.21	1.72	7.79	11.30	6.75	9.61	9.95	2.76	7.89	14.53	8.96	16.01	7.40	9.75	-2.92
	U.S. 90-Day Treasury Bill	—	0.44	1.34	2.75	5.47	4.02	4.45	5.63	5.83	6.67	8.11	7.51	5.41	3.46	3.02	4.27

Index Performance

Index	1Mo	3Mo	6Mo	1Yr	Annualized 3Yr	5Yr	10Yr	Index	1Mo	3Mo	6Mo	1Yr	Annualized 3Yr	5Yr	10Yr
Domestic Stock								**Government and Corporate**							
Wilshire 5000	0.98	8.49	17.98	21.95	14.80	15.93	14.53	Lehman Bros Corp	1.61	2.07	9.58	13.48	7.96	10.79	10.71
Wilshire 4500	2.33	13.57	20.15	22.42	16.93	17.73	13.14	Lehman Bros Govt	1.17	1.57	7.72	10.90	6.74	9.56	9.62
Russell 2000	2.07	13.55	20.09	20.79	19.23	19.00	11.86	Lehman Bros ARM	0.61	1.39	4.62	8.22	—	—	—
S&P MidCap 400	1.85	11.52	18.51	20.48	16.18	19.66	16.47	Lehman Bros Mortgage	1.04	1.79	6.99	10.94	6.14	9.07	10.11
International Stock								**Municipal Bond**							
MSCI EAFE	-3.81	0.38	9.33	U.49	12.17	7.01	15.34	Lehman Bros Muni	1.27	1.34	5.91	8.34	6.78	8.64	9.42
MSCI World	-2.25	2.56	12.13	8.24	12.51	9.65	14.06	Lehman Bros CA Muni	1.26	0.86	5.57	8.42	—	—	—
MSCI Europe	-3.87	2.10	12.61	10.65	12.19	9.15	16.00	Lehman Bros NY Muni	1.40	1.34	6.10	7.74	—	—	—
MSCI Pacific	-3.77	-1.20	6.47	-7.57	12.25	5.15	14.81	**Specialty Bond**							
MSCI Latin America	0.90	5.13	17.76	-27.13	10.62	25.73	—	First Boston High Yield	0.28	2.51	8.95	13.21	10.74	15.51	—
MSCI Emerging Markets	-3.42	-2.50	3.71	-18.27	15.58	13.70	—	Salomon Bros World Govt	-5.72	-4.75	8.27	16.67	9.64	13.41	14.84

Morningstar Comparison of Performance of Mutual Fund Categories and Broad Market Indexes, MORNINGSTAR, 1995.

EXHIBIT 2   Long-Term Cumulative Returns on Major Asset Categories

**Wealth Indices of
Investments in the
U.S. Capital Markets**

Year-End 1925 = $1.00

From 1925 to 1994

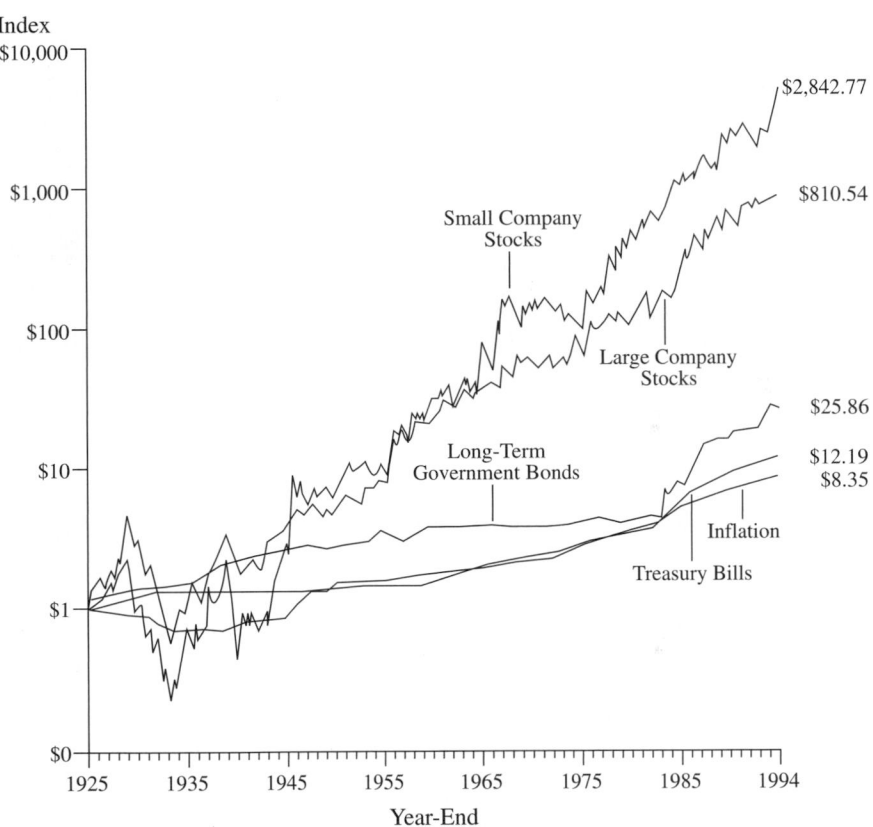

Source: Ibbotson Associates. Used with permission. © 1998 Ibbotson Associates, Inc. All rights reserved. [Certain portions of this work were derived from copyrighted works of Roger G. Ibbotson and Rex Sinquefield.]

EXHIBIT 3   Mean Returns and Standard Deviation of Returns by Major Asset Categories

Basic Series:
Summary Statistics of
Annual Total Returns

From 1926 to 1994

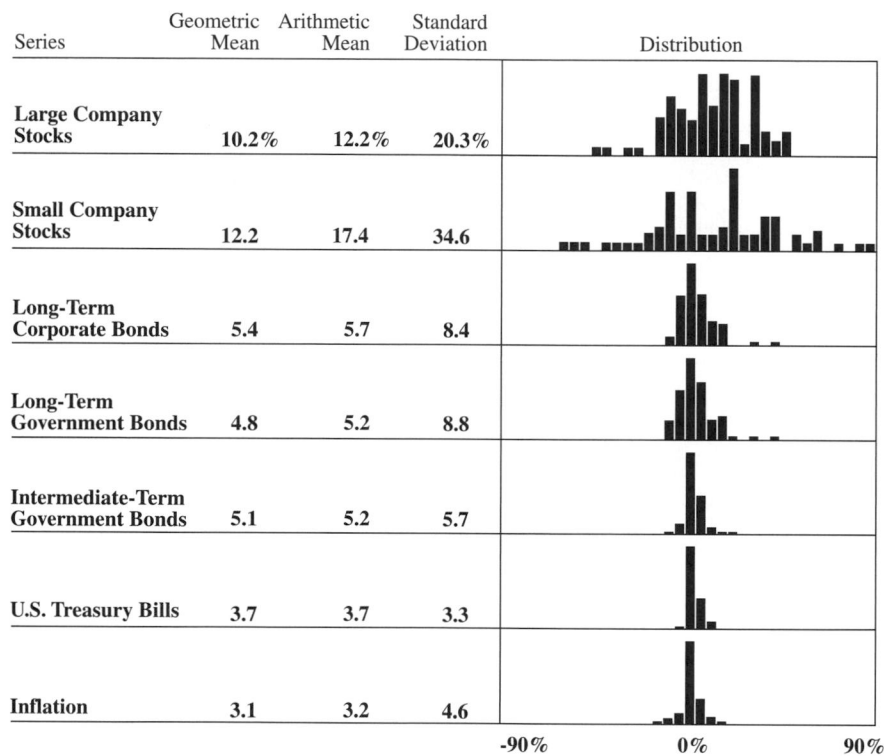

Series	Geometric Mean	Arithmetic Mean	Standard Deviation	Distribution
Large Company Stocks	10.2%	12.2%	20.3%	
Small Company Stocks	12.2	17.4	34.6	
Long-Term Corporate Bonds	5.4	5.7	8.4	
Long-Term Government Bonds	4.8	5.2	8.8	
Intermediate-Term Government Bonds	5.1	5.2	5.7	
U.S. Treasury Bills	3.7	3.7	3.3	
Inflation	3.1	3.2	4.6	

-90%   0%   90%

*The 1933 Small Company Stock Total Return was 142.9 percent.

Used with permission. © 1995 Ibbotson Associates, Inc. All rights reserved. [Certain portions of this work were derived from copyrighted works of Roger G. Ibbotson and Rex Sinquefield.]

EXHIBIT 4 Morningstar Report on Fidelity Magellan Fund

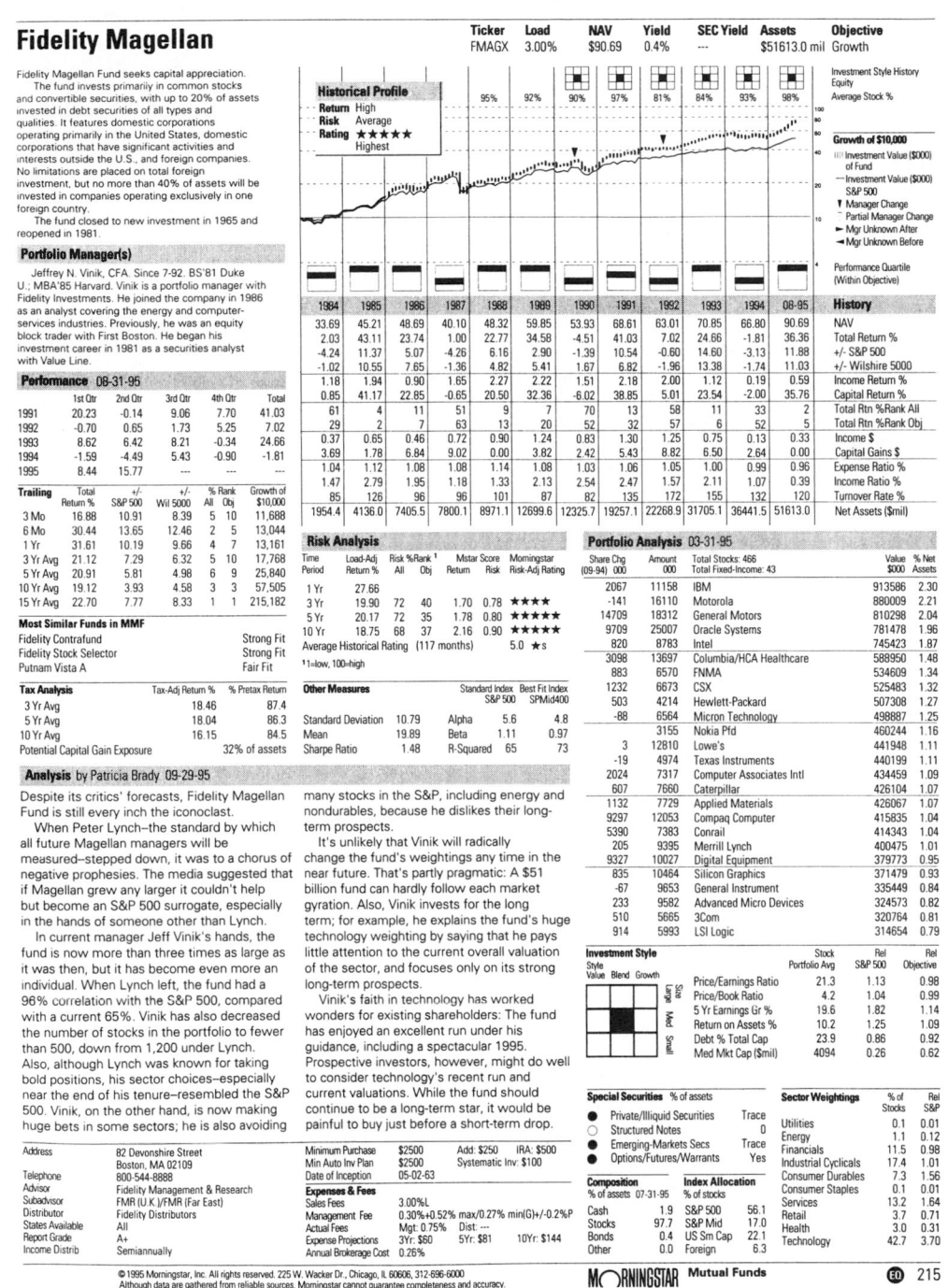

"The Fidelity Magellan Fund, 1995, Morningstar Report on FMF," MORNINGSTAR, 1995.

EXHIBIT 5   Performance Comparison of Fidelity Magellan Fund versus Other Growth Funds

Fund Size (total assets in millions on Sept. 30, 1995)	*Number of Funds in Category*	*Total Assets (in millions on Sept. 30, 1995)*	*Total Reinvested Performance (percentage increase in initial investment value from inception to Sept. 30, 1995)*			
			10 Years	*5 Years*	*1 Year*	*Year to Date*
$250–$500	51	$ 18,697	306.0%	129.6%	26.8%	28.8%
$500–$750	17	10,742	318.7	144.1	27.3	27.7
$750–$1,000	19	16,517	328.6	155.9	29.1	30.6
$1,000–$2,000	36	48,519	321.9	145.5	26.9	28.7
$2,000+	23*	134,793	390.8	162.7	29.6	30.4
Fidelity Magellan Fund	1	$ 46,653†	514.5%	181.0%	37.6%	38.9%

*The category of funds larger than $2 billion includes the results of Fidelity Magellan Fund in its performance statistics.†This is the reported balance in May 1995. As the case text notes, the assets under management in the fall of 1995 were closer to $51 billion.

Source: "Performance Comparison of Fidelity Magellan Fund versus Other Growth Funds," LIPPER MUTUAL FUND PERFORMANCE ANALYSIS, September 1995, Lipper Analytical Services, Inc.

Jeanne Mockard At Putnam Investments

On May 29, 1996, Jeanne Mockard considered three pairwise choices among possible investments for the two preferred stock mutual funds she managed for Putnam Investments. Institutional salespersons at other firms called her daily with offers to sell her preferred stocks. From various calls that day, she had culled six potential investments— but she limited her action to buying only three of these, to concentrate her buying power and to avoid unnecessary redundancy. The reality was that these investment opportunities might remain open only for a few hours. Other investors were almost certainly considering these opportunities. Competing with other institutional investors, she sought to improve the return on her fund within strict investment guidelines set by Putnam. Current capital market conditions were buoyant (see Exhibit 1). The yield curve[1] was moderately sloped but had risen since the beginning of 1996, reflecting analysts' expectations of inflation as the U.S. economy completed its fifth year of expansion. And there were rumors of a change in the tax code that would affect the tax advantages enjoyed by corporate investors in preferred stocks. Mockard needed to decide quickly what action to take on these six investment opportunities.

———————

[1]A yield curve was simply a graph of the market yields on U.S. Treasury securities by maturity. An example is given in Exhibit 1. A steeply rising curve would indicate that yields on debt instruments would vary significantly with maturity. A relatively flat yield curve would indicate that yields were relatively insensitive to maturity. The slope and height of the curve change with variations in market conditions.

This case was prepared by Professors Yiorgos Allayannis and Robert Bruner from field interviews. The case was written as a basis for class discussion rather than to illustrate effective or ineffective handling of an administrative situation. Copyright © 1997 by the University of Virginia Darden School Foundation, Charlottesville, VA. All rights reserved. *No part of this publication may be reproduced, stored in retrieval system, used in a spreadsheet, or transmitted in any form or by any means— electronic, mechanical, photocopying, recording, or otherwise— without the permission of the Darden School Foundation. For inquiries, please send an e-mail to dardencases@virginia.edu.* Rev. 11/97. Version 1.0.

PUTNAM INVESTMENTS

Mockard worked for a large, well-known investment management company located in Boston, Massachusetts. Owned by Marsh & McLennan, Putnam offered a family of 41 mutual funds available for investment by the general public. Putnam also managed funds for specific clients in the United States and globally, such as pension trusts, 401(k) plans, and charitable institutions that were not open for investment by the public. Putnam's public funds were grouped into four investment categories and had assets of $147 billion.

1. *Growth funds* included 14 funds focusing on investing in fast-growing companies and sought to maximize the value of investment over time. These funds were segmented by region (e.g., United States, Asia, Europe), industry (e.g., health, natural resources), and size of company (e.g., small emerging companies, large established growth companies).
2. *Growth and income funds,* as the name suggests, balanced their emphasis on growth and income investing. These included eight funds with specialties ranging from a balanced blend of stocks and bonds, to a particular industry (e.g., utilities), to a focus on particular securities (e.g., convertible securities).
3. *Tax-free funds* included seven funds aimed at investing in bonds and money-market instruments issued by states and municipalities in the United States. Income from these was exempt from federal income tax in the United States, and from certain state and local taxes.
4. *Income funds* sought to offer a regular stream of income through investing in bonds and dividend-paying stocks. These included 12 funds emphasizing current income (rather than growth) and varying among U.S. government debt securities, corporate debt, and corporate preferred stocks.

The two funds that Jeanne Mockard managed were classified as income funds.

Putnam was known in the financial community for its highly disciplined approach to investing. In recent years, the public had learned that prominent managers at other fund companies were pursuing investment strategies that deviated sharply from their advertised fund objectives. For example, one equity growth fund manager had deployed a significant portion of the fund's assets into U.S. government securities in the expectation of sharp interest rate changes. In another instance, equity funds had invested in interest-rate swaps and options. In a third case, a conservative equity fund was revealed to hold 10 percent of its assets in Mexican bonds. Fund investors were outraged, because these mutual funds had advertised that they would invest in growth stocks. Putnam funds were not involved in these unhappy incidents. Indeed, the company prided itself on the clarity of investment focus achieved at each fund, largely through careful delineation of excluded types of investments, and of investment concentration limits. The Putnam approach required managers who were disciplined "team players," not the solo "superstar" managers who had been lionized by the press in recent years.

Some money-management companies aimed to offer the highest returns in any investment category. Skeptics believed that this goal motivated fund managers to take unusual risks, since returns were largely determined by risks. Putnam, however, aimed more conservatively to rank in the top half of an investment category *consistently over time*.

PUTNAM PREFERRED-INCOME FUND AND PUTNAM DIVIDEND-INCOME FUND

The two funds that Mockard managed focused on investing in corporate preferred stocks. The Putnam Preferred-Income Fund was an open-ended fund with assets of about $121 million.[2] The Putnam Dividend-Income Fund was a closed-ended fund with assets of about $115 million.[3] Each fund held 70 to 90 separate issues of securities. The investment strategy of one of these funds was described as follows:

> The fund seeks to achieve its objective by investing at least 80 percent of its total assets (taken at current value) in investment-grade adjustable-rate preferred stock[4] and . . . common or preferred stocks, which pay dividends that are generally higher than the average dividend paid by the stocks included in the Standard & Poor's 500 Composite Stock Price Index. Under normal market conditions, the fund will invest at least 65 percent of its total assets in preferred stock. The fund may also invest up to 20 percent of its total assets in government and investment-grade corporate debt securities and high-quality, short-term money market instruments.[5]

The 65 percent limit was an absolute minimum; 80 percent was the target minimum. Mockard could not invest in securities rated less than Baa or BBB at the time of investment, nor could her funds hold more than 5 percent of their assets in any one issuer.

The Putnam Dividend-Income Fund currently held a three-star rating from Morningstar Mutual Funds, indicating average return and risk within its fund category. Exhibit 2 presents the Morningstar report on Putnam Dividend-Income Fund at mid-1996. (The Putnam Preferred-Income Fund was not covered by Morningstar.)

PREFERRED STOCK

Preferred stock differed from common stock in having preference over the common in dividend payments and in distribution of assets in the event of liquidation of the firm. Because preferred stock was viewed legally as *equity,* it held no special right to draw the firm into bankruptcy proceedings. Preferred dividends were typically *cumulative,* meaning that if a preferred dividend payment were missed, the obligation to pay that dividend would remain, and would take precedence before any common dividends could be paid. Preferred stockholders usually had rights to elect some directors to the firm's board in the event that preferred dividends were not paid. Otherwise, preferred stockholders had no

---

[2]An open-ended fund has a variable number of shares outstanding, depending on the inflows into the fund by investors. Transactions in fund shares are between investors and the fund. The assets under management may vary due to changes in market value of fund assets and variations in the number of shares outstanding.

[3]A closed-ended fund has a fixed number of shares outstanding. Transactions in fund shares are between investors. The assets under management are relatively fixed as a result (i.e., except for changes in market values of fund assets).

[4]The dividend rates on adjustable-rate preferred stocks are adjusted every 90 days to reflect any changes in benchmark interest rates, such as the yields on U.S. Treasury securities.

[5]Source: Putnam Preferred-Income Fund PROSPECTUS, April 1, 1996, p. 8.

voting privileges. Preferred shares typically carried a stated liquidation value, such as $25 per share. The dividend on the preferred stock could either be expressed in dollar terms per share, or as a "coupon rate" or "dividend yield of stated value" equaling the dollar dividend divided by the liquidation value. Because the market values of preferred stock typically fluctuated, preferred stock returns could also be quoted as "strip yields."[6]

A paradox was that preferred-stock dividend yields were often at or below yields on bonds of similar risk—even though preferreds were subordinate to bonds. If market returns are determined by risk, preferred yields should be higher. This paradox might be explained by an unusual tax feature of preferred stocks. Dividends from preferred stocks were subject to a "dividends received deduction" (DRD) of 70 percent when the owner of the shares was another corporation. This meant that 70 cents of every dollar of preferred dividends received by corporations would not be taxed. To compare the yields on preferred stock with other securities, it would be necessary to "gross up" the preferred stock yield to a pretax equivalent.[7] Thus, a preferred stock bearing a dividend yield of 7 percent would have a pretax equivalent yield to a corporate investor of 9.6 percent (where the corporate investor had a marginal tax rate of 35 percent). If the DRD were reduced to 50 percent, the pretax equivalent yield in this example would fall to 8.9 percent; if DRD were reduced to 20 percent, the pretax equivalent yield would fall to 7.8 percent. In comparison, Exhibit 1 gives pretax yields on corporate bonds.

The comparison of standard preferred stocks to bonds was not completely inappropriate: Both were regarded as fixed-income securities, and investors in either participated in the growth in value of the enterprise. The value of preferred stocks was sensitive to changes in interest rates. Finally, like debt, preferred stocks often could be redeemed (or "called") before maturity at the option of the issuer. But preferred stock usually ranked behind debt in priority in liquidation of the firm. Furthermore, the dividends paid on preferred stock were not deductible from income for purposes of computing corporate tax— unlike interest payments, which were deductible.

Given the similarities of preferred stock to debt, and yet the disadvantages of preferred compared to debt, many observers wondered what might motivate corporations to issue preferred stock. The range of answers suggested that preferred stock resolved difficult trade-offs in *managing the corporate capital structure.* For instance, preferred stock looked like equity to creditors (and therefore was thought to expand the borrowing base of the firm), but looked like a liability to common stockholders (and therefore increased the financial leverage of the firm). This hybrid-like nature of preferred stock was of special interest to firms facing a nontrivial risk of bankruptcy: Accumulated unpaid dividends were not debts of a corporation and thus could not trigger bankruptcy proceedings. Preferred stock was equity, and yet it did not carry votes; it did not dilute the voting control of common stockholders. Finally, in regulated industries (such as electric power generation) it might be possible to pass the tax disadvantage of preferred dividends on to customers—electric utilities were large issuers of preferred stock.

---

[6]Strip yield was calculated as

$$\text{Dollar dividend}/(\text{Current price} - \text{Accumulated dividends})$$

[7]The estimate of a pretax equivalent yield of preferred stock assumes that in an efficient market securities of equivalent risk will offer the same return after taxes. Thus, the dividend yield of preferred stock (PDY) should have the following relationship to the pretax yields (YTM) of other securities that are not subject to the DRD:

$$(\%\text{DRD} \times \text{PDY}) + [(1 - \%\text{DRD}) \times (1 - t) \times \text{PDY}] = \text{YTM} \times (1 - t)$$

Yield on an Adjustable-Rate Preferred Stock (ARPS)

With Collar at 4% and 10%

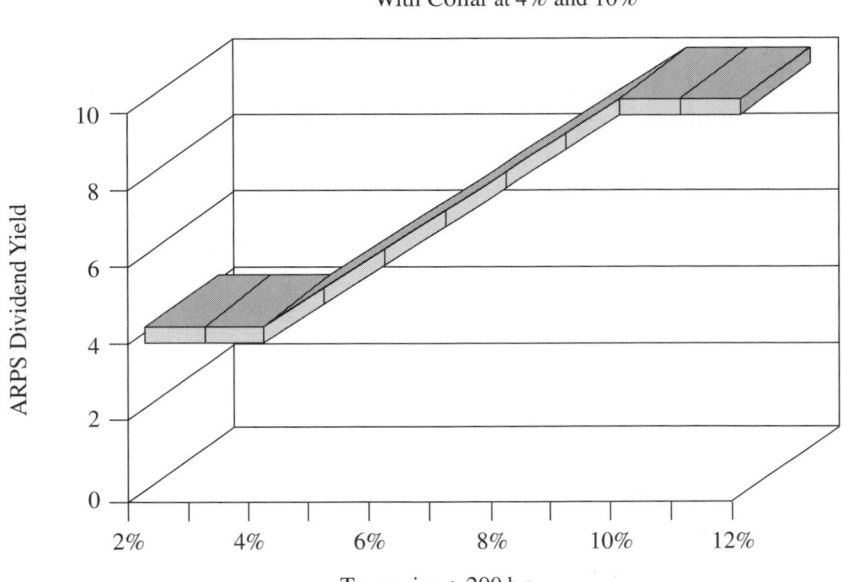

In the spring of 1996, rumors circulated that the Clinton administration was considering reducing the dividends received deduction from 70 percent to 50 percent. This would have the effect of somewhat lowering the attractiveness of preferred stock as an investment medium for corporations.

Adjustable-Rate Preferred Stock

A special variety of preferred stock featured a coupon rate that would reset every 90 days to float at a target level above some benchmark rate such as the market yield on U.S. Treasury securities. Adjustable-rate preferred stock (ARPS) was attractive to corporate treasurers looking for an investment in which to place a firm's excess cash balance for a period of time. Because the yield varied, the market value of the investment would remain relatively fixed,[8] ensuring that the treasurer would not have to explain extraordinary gains or losses in securities to her board of directors. In addition, the yields on ARPS offered a premium return compared to yields on U.S. Treasury instruments or other short-term money market instruments. For a corporate investor, this yield would be augmented by the 70 percent dividends received deduction.

---

[8]The exception to this rule was when the market yields varied above the collar maximum or below the minimum.

Typically, the dividend yield on ARPS would be allowed to vary within a set range, between a minimum and maximum. The upper and lower bounds formed a "collar." The accompanying figure gives a graph of the possible yields offered an investor by a collar set at 4 percent and at 10 percent. Suppose that within the collar, yields would be set to equal the yield on a specific U.S. Treasury security plus 200 basis points. The floor would protect the investor against an unusually low yield; the ceiling would protect the issuer against an unusually high yield. The width of the collar was a matter of choice to the issuer at the time the ARPS was originally issued. In general, a wider collar meant that the investor bore more uncertainty about the return to be received at the next reset date; a narrower collar meant less uncertainty.

JEANNE MOCKARD

Mockard joined Putnam Investments in 1990 upon completion of her MBA degree. Initially, she worked as a securities analyst. She assumed responsibility for the two funds in 1993. In May 1996, she held the title of senior vice president. Mockard described her work this way:

> I compete for securities, for good investments. There are only a couple of other funds with a specific focus on preferred stock like mine. However there are a large number of mutual funds with at least a little appetite for preferred stocks. In addition, I compete with large corporations like IBM and Disney who invest their excess cash directly into preferred stocks.
>
> On the other side, I compete for investors to buy shares in my funds. A few of the investors are private individuals, but most are corporations. The smaller firms that invest in the funds consider me their cash management/investment officer. We offer them a chance to diversify their risk and gain ready access to market dealers who bring me their investment ideas.
>
> The size of my fund is a competitive advantage in this market. To make money here, you have to be a big player. People come to me when they want to do a deal. I network a lot so that preferred stock traders call me; and so that I know whom to call. The market in preferred stocks is different from common equities where you have up-to-the-minute electronic information. Information about preferreds is exchanged more by word of mouth. Information is simply less available. Also, the market in preferreds is not as liquid as the market for common—I simply can't buy every issue that's out there. When an opportunity to invest does come along, I have to think carefully and strategically, since the opportunity may not reappear for a while.
>
> Though my focus is preferred stocks, I have to have an opinion on where interest rates are headed. Preferreds are income securities, and thus affected by changes in the interest rate environment. You need a real appreciation of the yield curve. Adjustable-rate preferreds trade off of the short end of the curve, because they are reset every 90 days against the short-term Treasury rate. Perpetual preferreds trade more in relation to the long end of the yield curve.
>
> I'm like a brand manager: I have a clear idea of my customer and the market segment I'm trying to serve. I can't be all things to all people. My goal is to invest mainly in perpetual preferred stocks, balanced with some adjustable-rate preferreds and sinking fund preferreds to dampen the swings in value as interest rates move. I have to practice a strategy of "disciplined opportunism." I want to serve the investor and the mission of the fund. I also want to beat the Merrill Lynch preferred stock index—the benchmark for "the market" in the preferred stock arena; I aim to wind up in the top half of the league tables in my segment.
>
> I spend 50 percent of my time traveling. I talk to companies to assess investment risk, and to anticipate the private actions of corporate executives beforehand. I go to conferences to get a

sense of industry trends. The content of this work always surprises me. I love what I do. You have to be interested in everything. No two days are alike. It's not an orderly job. Market developments constantly require you to decide how to manage your time best.

Quotes from Jeanne Mockard, senior vice president at Putnam Investment, 1996.

PUTNAM'S ECONOMIC AND MARKET OUTLOOK

Dr. Robert Goodman, managing director and senior economic advisor at Putnam described the company's outlook on the economy in the following way in his Summer 1996 *Commentary*:

As we enter the second half of 1996, confusion and uncertainty about economic prospects abound. The confusion has manifested itself in a rise in long-term government bond yields to more than 7 percent and an equity market that has been stuck in a broad trading range for most of the year. While traders in both bonds and stocks are at risk in such environment, history suggests that investors with long-term horizons can take advantage of these circumstances.

Chief among the uncertainties currently facing investors is the prospect of increased inflation as we go forward. Anxiety about accelerating inflation stems from a rise in commodity prices, such as the recent spurt in gasoline prices, and the possibility of wage increases if economic growth should reaccelerate. In my view, both of these concerns have been exaggerated in the media and on Wall Street.

Since 1979, the bond market, battered by brutal experience, has imposed a very real and severe constraint on the ability of the Fed to pursue an inflationary monetary policy. The bond market vigilantes, as these defenders of price stability have been called, have been responsible for the downtrend in interest rates and inflation that took place throughout the 1980s and continues today. Should the Fed embark upon a policy deemed to be inflationary by bond market participants, bonds would be sold in anticipation of that inflation and long-term interest rates would rise.

. . . What we are likely to experience going forward are shifts in relative prices among commodities, reflecting supply and demand conditions in the marketplace. But these price changes should not be translated into a generalized inflation spiral.

Nevertheless, until investors accept this analysis, the bond market will be buffeted by fears of renewed inflationary pressure. It is quite possible, therefore, that for a time interest rates may rise to levels exceeding long-term equilibrium. In my opinion, long-term bond yields above 7 percent are not sustainable and, when they are available, represent good value relative to the average rate of inflation we are likely to experience over the longer run.

THE SIX INVESTMENT OPPORTUNITIES

Exhibit 3 presents data summarizing the three pairwise choices that Mockard needed to decide on soon. The exhibit gives information that she used to make buy-or-sell decisions quickly. This information included the credit ratings of the issues determined by Moody and S&P. (Exhibit 4 gives the rating definitions of these categories.) The "ex date" was the next date in 1996 after which purchase of the security would not entitle the investor to the next quarterly dividend. The strip yield was calculated simply as the annual dividend of the security divided by the current price less accrued dividends. The "spread versus 30-year" was the difference between the strip yield and the yield on the 30-year U.S. Treasury bond. YTC stands for *yield to call,* the preferred's internal rate of return yield calculated as if the issuer were to redeem the issue at the earliest possible date, indicated by "call date." These data were drawn by Mockard's assistant from a Bloomberg terminal.

- *Decision A:* An institutional salesperson at R.W. Baird had called to say that two pre-ferred issues from Georgia Power had come on the market. These issues were perpetual preferreds and were similar in many respects. The Series Q carried a coupon of $1.9875 per share, while the Series R carried a coupon of $1.9375 per share.
- *Decision B:* An institutional salesperson at Salomon Brothers called to offer perpetual preferred issues on two different companies: Travelers Insurance and Merrill Lynch. The Travelers issue carried a coupon rate of 9.25 percent, whereas the Merrill Lynch issue carried a coupon rate of 9.00 percent.
- *Decision C:* An institutional salesperson at Lehman Brothers offered Mockard two dif-ferent issues of adjustable-rate preferreds. One, issued by Texas Utilities, held a current coupon rate of 6.5 percent, and a collar that would permit coupon rates between 6.5 and 13 percent. The other issue, from Puget Sound, offered a current coupon of 6.31 percent and a collar that would permit coupon rates to vary between 4 and 10 percent.

Mockard needed to decide quickly between the alternatives within each pair of opportunities. As she turned to the data, she reflected on the possible impact of changes in the environment. Interest rates had been rising all spring; how would Putnam's interest-rate outlook affect the three decisions? Also, the Clinton administration might lower the dividends received deduc-tion. How, if at all, should this possible change influence her thinking?

EXHIBIT 1   Capital Market Conditions (May 29, 1996)

U.S. Treasury Obligations	*Yield*
90-day bills	5.18%
1-year notes	5.74
2-year notes	6.24
5-year notes	6.63
10-year bonds	6.85
30-year bonds	6.92

Long-Term Corporate Debt Obligations	
AAA	7.63%
AA	7.73
A	7.99
BBB	8.26
BB+	8.60
BB/BB−	10.34
B	10.38

Other Instruments	
Prime rate loans	8.25%
Federal Reserve Bank discount rate	5.00
Certificates of deposit (90-day)	5.36
Commercial paper (6 months)	5.42

U.S. Treasury Yield Curve

Sources: *Bloomberg Business News; Standard & Poor's Current Statistics.*

EXHIBIT 2 Morningstar Report

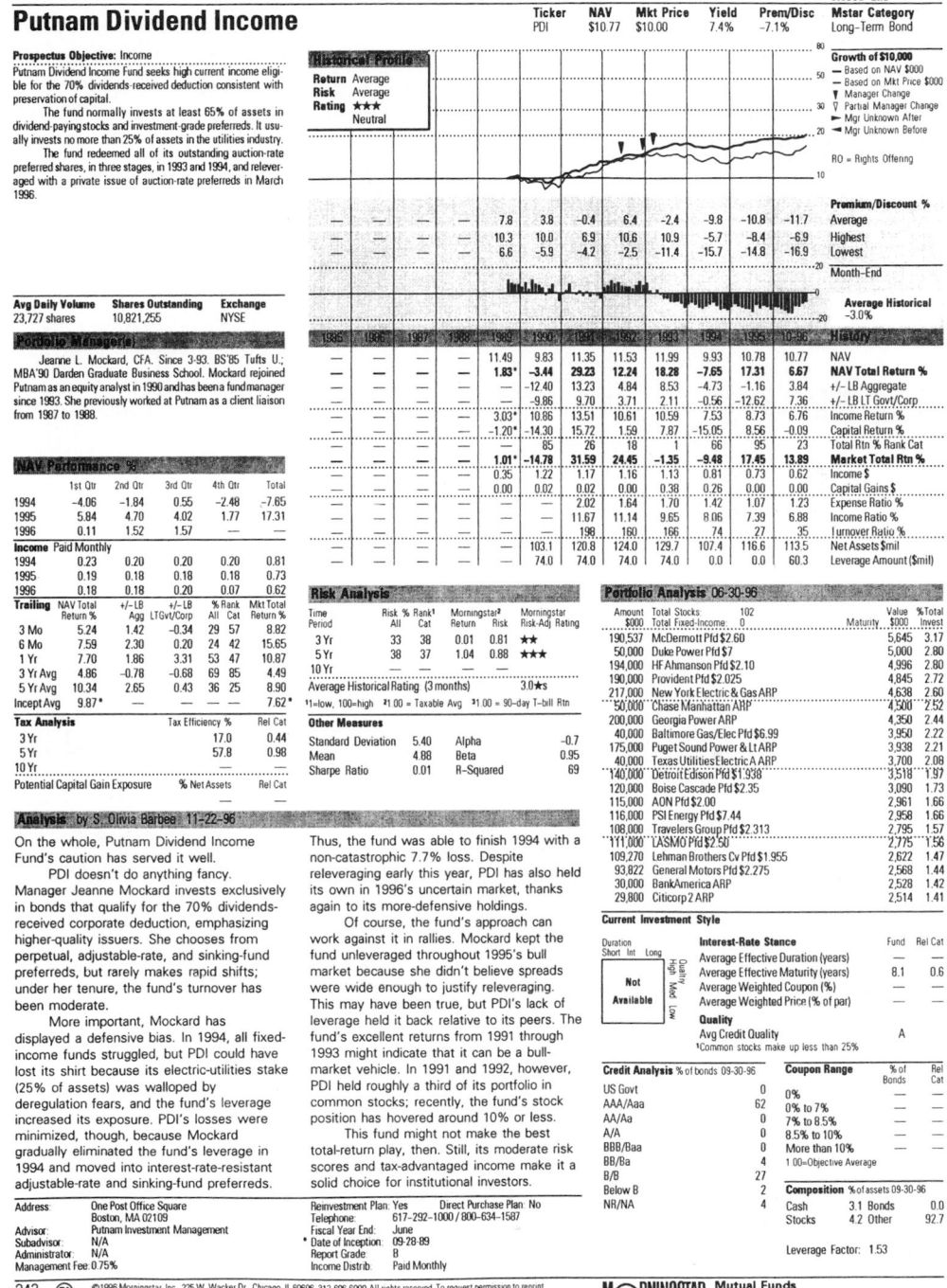

Putnam Dividend Income

	Ticker	NAV	Mkt Price	Yield	Prem/Disc	Closed–End Mstar Category
	PDI	$10.77	$10.00	7.4%	–7.1%	Long-Term Bond

Prospectus Objective: Income

Putnam Dividend Income Fund seeks high current income eligible for the 70% dividends-received deduction consistent with preservation of capital.

The fund normally invests at least 65% of assets in dividend-paying stocks and investment-grade preferreds. It usually invests no more than 25% of assets in the utilities industry.

The fund redeemed all of its outstanding auction-rate preferred shares, in three stages, in 1993 and 1994, and releveraged with a private issue of auction-rate preferreds in March 1996.

Historical Profile

Return	Average	
Risk	Average	
Rating	★★★	
	Neutral	

Growth of $10,000
- Based on NAV $000
- Based on Mkt Price $000
- Manager Change
- Partial Manager Change
- Mgr Unknown After
- Mgr Unknown Before

RO = Rights Offering

Avg Daily Volume	Shares Outstanding	Exchange
23,727 shares	10,821,255	NYSE

Portfolio Manager(s)

Jeanne L. Mockard, CFA. Since 3-93. BS'85 Tufts U.; MBA'90 Darden Graduate Business School. Mockard rejoined Putnam as an equity analyst in 1990 and has been a fund manager since 1993. She previously worked at Putnam as a client liaison from 1987 to 1988.

Premium/Discount %

7.8	3.8	-0.4	6.4	-2.4	-9.8	-10.8	-11.7	Average
10.3	10.0	6.9	10.6	-5.7	-8.4	-6.9	Highest
6.6	-5.9	-4.2	-2.5	-11.4	-15.7	-14.8	-16.9	Lowest

Month–End

Average Historical –3.0%

History

1985	1986	1987	1988	1989	1990	1991	1992	1993	1994	1995	10-96	
—	—	—	—	11.49	9.83	11.35	11.53	11.99	9.93	10.78	10.77	NAV
—	—	—	—	1.83*	-3.44	29.23	12.24	18.28	-7.65	17.31	6.67	NAV Total Return %
—	—	—	—	-12.40	13.23	4.84	8.53	-4.73	-1.16	3.84	+/- LB Aggregate
—	—	—	—	-9.86	9.70	3.71	2.11	-0.56	-12.62	7.36	+/- LB LT Govt/Corp
—	—	—	3.03*	10.86	13.51	10.61	10.59	7.53	8.73	6.76	Income Return %
—	—	—	-1.20*	-14.30	15.72	1.59	7.87	-15.05	8.56	-0.09	Capital Return %
—	—	—	85	26	18	1	66	95	23	Total Rtn % Rank Cat
—	—	—	1.01*	-14.78	31.59	24.45	-1.35	-9.48	17.45	13.89	Market Total Rtn %
—	—	—	0.35	1.22	1.17	1.16	1.13	0.81	0.73	0.62	Income $
—	—	—	0.00	0.02	0.02	0.00	0.38	0.26	0.00	0.00	Capital Gains $
—	—	—		2.02	1.64	1.70	1.42	1.07	1.23	Expense Ratio %
—	—	—		11.67	11.14	9.65	8.06	7.39	6.88	Income Ratio %
—	—	—		198	160	166	74	27	35	Turnover Ratio %
—	—	—	103.1	120.8	124.0	129.7	107.4	116.6	113.5	Net Assets $mil
—	—	—	74.0	74.0	74.0	74.0	0.0	0.0	60.3	Leverage Amount ($mil)

NAV Performance %

	1st Qtr	2nd Qtr	3rd Qtr	4th Qtr	Total
1994	-4.06	-1.84	0.55	-2.48	-7.65
1995	5.84	4.70	4.02	1.77	17.31
1996	0.11	1.52	1.57	—	—

Income Paid Monthly

	1st Qtr	2nd Qtr	3rd Qtr	4th Qtr	Total
1994	0.23	0.20	0.20	0.20	0.81
1995	0.19	0.18	0.18	0.18	0.73
1996	0.18	0.18	0.20	0.07	0.62

Trailing

	NAV Total Return %	+/- LB Agg	+/- LB LTGvt/Corp	% Rank All	% Rank Cat	Mkt Total Return %
3 Mo	5.24	1.42	-0.34	29	57	8.82
6 Mo	7.59	2.30	0.20	24	42	15.65
1 Yr	7.70	1.86	3.31	53	47	10.87
3 Yr Avg	4.86	-0.78	-0.68	69	85	4.49
5 Yr Avg	10.34	2.65	0.43	36	25	8.90
Incept Avg	9.87*	—	—	—	—	7.62*

Tax Analysis

	Tax Efficiency %	Rel Cat
3 Yr	17.0	0.44
5 Yr	57.8	0.98
10 Yr	—	—
Potential Capital Gain Exposure	% Net Assets	Rel Cat

Risk Analysis

Time Period	Risk % Rank[1] All	Cat	Morningstar[2] Return	Morningstar Risk	Morningstar Risk-Adj Rating
3 Yr	33	38	0.81	0.81	★★
5 Yr	38	37	1.04	0.88	★★★
10 Yr	—	—	—	—	
Average Historical Rating (3 months)				3.0★s	

[1]=low, 100=high [2]1.00 = Taxable Avg [3]1.00 = 90-day T-bill Rtn

Other Measures

Standard Deviation	5.40	Alpha	-0.7
Mean	4.88	Beta	0.95
Sharpe Ratio	0.01	R-Squared	69

Portfolio Analysis 06-30-96

Amount $000	Total Stocks: 102 Total Fixed-Income: 0	Maturity	Value $000	%Total Invest
190,537	McDermott Pfd $2.60		5,645	3.17
50,000	Duke Power Pfd $7		5,000	2.80
194,000	HF Ahmanson Pfd $2.10		4,996	2.80
190,000	Provident Pfd $2.025		4,845	2.72
217,000	New York Electric & Gas ARP		4,638	2.60
50,000	Chase Manhattan ARP		4,500	2.52
200,000	Georgia Power ARP		4,350	2.44
40,000	Baltimore Gas/Elec Pfd $6.99		3,950	2.22
175,000	Puget Sound Power & Lt ARP		3,938	2.21
40,000	Texas Utilities Electric A ARP		3,700	2.08
140,000	Detroit Edison Pfd $1.938		3,518	1.97
120,000	Boise Cascade Pfd $2.35		3,090	1.73
115,000	AON Pfd $2.00		2,961	1.66
116,000	PSI Energy Pfd $7.44		2,958	1.66
108,000	Travelers Group Pfd $2.313		2,795	1.57
111,000	LASMO Pfd $2.50		2,775	1.56
109,270	Lehman Brothers Cv Pfd $1.955		2,622	1.47
93,822	General Motors Pfd $2.275		2,568	1.44
30,000	BankAmerica ARP		2,528	1.42
29,800	Citicorp 2 ARP		2,514	1.41

Current Investment Style

Duration Short Int Long	Quality High Med Low	Interest-Rate Stance	Fund	Rel Cat
	Not Available	Average Effective Duration (years)	—	—
		Average Effective Maturity (years)	8.1	0.6
		Average Weighted Coupon (%)	—	—
		Average Weighted Price (% of par)	—	—
		Quality		
		Avg Credit Quality	A	
		[1]Common stocks make up less than 25%		

Credit Analysis % of bonds 09-30-96

	%
US Govt	0
AAA/Aaa	62
AA/Aa	0
A/A	0
BBB/Baa	0
BB/Ba	4
B/B	27
Below B	2
NR/NA	4

Coupon Range

	% of Bonds	Rel Cat
0%	—	—
0% to 7%	—	—
7% to 8.5%	—	—
8.5% to 10%	—	—
More than 10%	—	—
1.00=Objective Average		

Composition % of assets 09-30-96

Cash	3.1	Bonds	0.0
Stocks	4.2	Other	92.7

Leverage Factor: 1.53

Analysis by S. Olivia Barbee 11-22-96

On the whole, Putnam Dividend Income Fund's caution has served it well.

PDI doesn't do anything fancy. Manager Jeanne Mockard invests exclusively in bonds that qualify for the 70% dividends-received corporate deduction, emphasizing higher-quality issuers. She chooses from perpetual, adjustable-rate, and sinking-fund preferreds, but rarely makes rapid shifts; under her tenure, the fund's turnover has been moderate.

More important, Mockard has displayed a defensive bias. In 1994, all fixed-income funds struggled, but PDI could have lost its shirt because its electric-utilities stake (25% of assets) was walloped by deregulation fears, and the fund's leverage increased its exposure. PDI's losses were minimized, though, because Mockard gradually eliminated the fund's leverage in 1994 and moved into interest-rate-resistant adjustable-rate and sinking-fund preferreds.

Thus, the fund was able to finish 1994 with a non-catastrophic 7.7% loss. Despite releveraging early this year, PDI has also held its own in 1996's uncertain market, thanks again to its more-defensive holdings.

Of course, the fund's approach can work against it in rallies. Mockard kept the fund unleveraged throughout 1995's bull market because she didn't believe spreads were wide enough to justify releveraging. This may have been true, but PDI's lack of leverage held it back relative to its peers. The fund's excellent returns from 1991 through 1993 might indicate that it can be a bull-market vehicle. In 1991 and 1992, however, PDI held roughly a third of its portfolio in common stocks; recently, the fund's stock position has hovered around 10% or less.

This fund might not make the best total-return play, then. Still, its moderate risk scores and tax-advantaged income make it a solid choice for institutional investors.

Address:	One Post Office Square Boston, MA 02109	Reinvestment Plan: Yes	Direct Purchase Plan: No
Advisor:	Putnam Investment Management	Telephone:	617-292-1000 / 800-634-1587
Subadvisor:	N/A	Fiscal Year End:	June
Administrator:	N/A	* Date of Inception:	09-28-89
Management Fee:	0.75%	Report Grade:	B
		Income Distrib:	Paid Monthly

342 (FI) ©1996 Morningstar, Inc. 225 W Wacker Dr, Chicago, IL 60606, 312-696-6000 All rights reserved. To request permission to reprint please call 312-696-6100 Although data are gathered from reliable sources, Morningstar cannot guarantee completeness and accuracy

MORNINGSTAR Mutual Funds

Morningstar Report on Putnam Dividend Income, 1996.

EXHIBIT 3 Summary of Investment Opportunities

Decision	Broker	Security	Number of Shares	Moody Rating	S&P Rating	Ex Date	Asking Price	Spread Strip Yield (%)	vs.30-Year (b.p.)	YTC	YTC Spread (b.p.)	Call Date	Call Price	30-Year Bond Yield
A	Baird	Georgia Power Series Q, $1.9875 coupon	13,500	A2	A	6/13	$25.60	7.88	+96	6.68	+117	6/2/97	$25.00	6.92
	Baird	Georgia Power Series R $1.9375 coupon	11,300	A2	A	6/13	$25.55	7.69	+77	6.73	+117	7/2/97	$25.00	6.92
B	Salomon	Travelers Series D, 9.25% coupon	212,500	A1	A	5/29	$25.80	8.96	+204	5.49	−14	7/1/97	$25.00	6.92
	Salomon	Merrill Lynch Series A 9.0% coupon	189,870	A1	A−	6/13	$28.875	7.92	+100	6.84	+26	12/30/04	$25.00	6.92
C	Lehman	Texas Util. Series A, ARPS, collar: 6.5–13%, current coupon = 6.5%	50,000	Baa3	BBB	7/10	$92.18	7.12	+20[a]	—	—	—	—	6.92
	Lehman	Puget Sound Series B, ARPS, Collar: 4–10%, current coupon = 6.31%	200,000	Baa1[b]	BBB+	7/18	$22.50	6.41	−51[c]	—	—	—	—	6.92

[a]The Texas Utilities ARPS yield was 103 percent of the 30-year Treasury bond yield (7.12/6.92).
[b]Puget Sound was listed for a possible downgrade by Moody's.
[c]The Puget Sound ARPS yield was 93 percent of the 30-year Treasury bond yield (6.41/6.92).

EXHIBIT 4   Standard & Poor's Risk Rating Definitions

AAA	Preferred stock rated AAA has the highest rating assigned by S&P. Capacity to pay dividends and meet redemption requirements is extremely strong.
AA	Preferred stock rated AA has a very strong capacity to pay dividends and meet redemption requirements and differs from the higher rated issues only in small degree.
A	Preferred stock rated A has a strong capacity to pay dividends and meet redemption requirements, although it is somewhat more susceptible to the adverse effects of changes in circumstances and economic conditions than preferred stock in higher rated categories.
BBB	Preferred stock rated BBB is regarded as having an adequate capacity to pay dividends and meet redemption requirements. Whereas it normally exhibits adequate protection parameters, adverse economic conditions or changing circumstances are more likely to weaken the capacity to pay dividends and meet redemption requirements for preferred stock in this category than in higher rated categories.
BB, B, CCC, CC, C	Preferred stock rated BBB, B, CCC, CC, or C is regarded, on balance, as predominantly speculative with respect to capacity to pay dividends and redemption requirements in accordance with the terms of the obligation. BB indicates the lowest degree of speculation and C the highest degree of speculation. While such preferred stock will likely have some quality and protective characteristics, these are outweighed by large uncertainties or major risk exposure to adverse conditions.

Source: Paraphrased from Standard & Poor's *Bond Guide.*

The Battle for Value: Federal Express Corporation versus United Parcel Service of America, Inc. (Abridged)

We will produce outstanding financial returns by providing totally reliable, competitively superior global air-ground transportation of high-priority goods and documents that require rapid, time-certain delivery.

Federal Express Mission Statement

Federal Express is a leader of the pack in developing information systems aimed at keeping its customers informed and serving them better.

Tom Peters, *Liberation Management*

Clearly, the competencies that are most valuable are those that represent a gateway to a wide variety of potential product markets. To take a financial analogy, investing in core competencies is like investing in options. A core competence leader possesses an option on participation in the range of end-product markets that rely on that core competence . . . A core competence is a bundle of skills and technologies that enables a company to provide a particular benefit to customers . . . At Federal Express the benefit is on-time delivery, and the core competence, at a very high level is logistics management.

Gary Hamel and C. K. Pralahad, *Competing for the Future*

[We will] maintain a financially strong, manager-owned company earning a reasonable profit, providing long-term competitive returns to our shareowners.

United Parcel Service Mission Statement

This is probably one of the three or four defining moments for this company.

John Alden, UPS Senior Vice President, referring to a major reengineering effort announced May 23, 1995[1]

Then one day the company looked out upon its business and saw that times had changed. The practices had become "inoperative" because the strategies had become outdated. The strategies had become outdated because smaller upstart rivals and old foes had become more competitive. Profits declined. So UPS examined what its customers wanted, sought ideas from its employees, swallowed hard, and decided it had better start doing business differently—or there might not be any more business to do. So it did. Now UPS is living happily ever after once again. For now.[2]

On July 10, 1995, J. C. Penney announced the award to United Parcel Service (UPS) of a $1 billion, five-year contract for delivery services. This was the largest distribution contract ever awarded and represented a dramatic concentration of Penney's business with one carrier. "They're stealing business from each other. The question is, who can do it at the lowest cost?"[3] said one analyst. A J. C. Penney spokesperson confirmed that the additional UPS business was coming at the expense of other carriers—Penney's previously standing agreement with UPS had entailed shipments worth $160 million over three years. At the announcement, the stock price of Federal Express Corporation (FedEx) fell 2.33 percent; FedEx's total market value of equity declined by $85 million.

The contract announcement surprised many observers. Federal Express had virtually invented customer logistical management and was widely perceived as innovative, entrepreneurial, and an operational leader. Business pundits applauded the company for its outstanding operational practices. In 1990, FedEx received the crowning acknowledgment of excellence by winning the coveted Malcolm Baldrige award for quality. As Chairman Fred Smith explained: "Quality was really part of the culture from the outset. I think it came from the fundamental recognition that in providing time-definite transportation, quality was really all that we were selling."[4] So good was FedEx at this that they were generally credited with redefining the product.

UPS had also garnered awards and recognitions. But historically it had the reputation as a big, bureaucratic industry follower. However, UPS was shedding this image as it became an innovator and an increasingly tenacious adversary. UPS's transition had involved some rude awakenings, however, about the customer expectations that had changed. The

---

[1]Robert Frank, "Efficient UPS Tries to Increase Efficiency," *The Wall Street Journal,* May 24, 1995, p. B1.

[2]Charles R. Day, "Shape Up and Ship Out," *Industry Week,* February 6, 1995.

[3]"UPS Gets $1 billion, 5-Year Contract from J. C. Penney," *Bloomberg Business News,* July 11, 1995.

[4]Virtually all of Federal Express's business activities were in the air-express segment of the package delivery industry. But UPS had roughly 27 percent of its revenues derived from air express.

This case was written by Professor Robert F. Bruner and Derick Bulkley as a basis for class discussion rather than to illustrate effective or ineffective handling of an administrative situation. Copyright © 1995 by the University of Virginia Darden School Foundation, Charlettesville, VA. All rights reserved. *No part of this publication may be reproduced, stored in a retrieval system, used in a spreadsheet, or transmitted in any form or by any means—electronic, mechanical, photocopying, recording, or otherwise—without the permission of the Darden School Foundation. For inquiries, please send an e-mail to dardencases@virginia.edu.* Rev. 11/97. Version 2.2.

announcement by J. C. Penney seemed to suggest that UPS was successfully making the transition into the new world of air-express package delivery.

The competition between FedEx and UPS for dominance of the $19 billion air-express delivery market foreshadowed an unusually challenging future:[5]

- Intensifying efforts at product innovation, customer focus, quality management, and reengineering.
- High and rising investment in the business. According to Fred Smith, the CEO of FedEx: "Anyone who's unwilling to spend on quality is really mapping a blueprint for liquidation."[6] For the future, analysts forecast large investment outlays as each firm attempted to gain the upper hand through efficient, modern technology and infrastructure.
- Shifting market shares. FedEx's dominance of the overnight express package market was high; growth in that segment was slowing as the market matured. The new intensive battleground was in the market for two- and three-day delivery.

Against the backdrop of the J. C. Penney announcement, industry observers wondered how this titanic struggle would resolve itself, particularly for investors in those two firms. Was the performance of the firms in recent years an indication of the future?

FEDERAL EXPRESS CORPORATION

At the end of 1994, FedEx had nearly $6 billion in assets and net income of $204 million, on revenues of about $8.5 billion. FedEx had survived the lean years of 1991–93, and by 1994 the firm's financial ratios indicated an improvement (see Exhibit 1).

FedEx first took form as Fred Smith's term paper in a Yale economics course. Smith's strategy dictated that FedEx would actually acquire the planes for transport, whereas all other competitors used the cargo space on commercial airlines. In addition to using his own planes, Smith's key innovation was to apply a hub-and-spoke distribution pattern, which permitted cheaper and faster service to more locations than his competitors. Smith invested his $4 million inheritance and raised $91 million in venture capital to launch the firm—this was the largest venture capital start-up in memory. In the early years FedEx experienced losses, and Smith would have been ousted from his chairmanship were it not for improved results and the support of his president. By 1976 FedEx finally saw a modest profit, though, of $3.6 million on an average daily volume of 19,000 packages. Through the rest of the 1970s FedEx continued to grow by expanding services, acquiring more trucks and aircraft, and raising capital. The formula was successful; in 1981 FedEx generated more revenue than any other U.S. air-delivery company.

By 1981 competition in the industry had started to rise. Emery Air Freight began to imitate FedEx's hub system and to acquire airplanes. UPS began to move into the overnight

---

[5]Virtually all of Federal Express's business activities were in the air-express segment of the package-delivery industry. But UPS had roughly 27 percent of its revenues derived from air express.

[6] "Federal Express" UVA-OM-0721 Darden Educational Materials Services, Charlottesville, VA.

air market. The U.S. Postal Service (USPS) positioned its overnight letter at half the price of FedEx's, but quality problems and FedEx's now immortal "absolutely positively overnight" ad campaign quelled any potential threat from that quarter. In 1983 FedEx had reached $1 billion in revenues and seemed poised to own the market.

In 1990, FedEx received the prestigious Malcolm Baldrige National Quality Award from U.S. President George Bush. FedEx was the first service firm to win the award. FedEx had won 194 other awards for operational excellence since 1973. Part of this success could be attributed to deregulation and to operational strategy, but credit could also be given to FedEx's philosophy of "people–service–profit," which reflected an emphasis on customer focus, total quality management, and employee participation. In explaining its philosophy, the company's 1994 annual report stated: "We believe that by working as a team, we can produce exemplary service for our customers, which in turn will provide outstanding long-term financial returns for our stockholders." Extensive attitude surveying, a promote-from-within policy, effective grievance procedures that sometimes resulted in a chat with Fred Smith himself, and a high emphasis on personal responsibility and initiative not only earned FedEx the reputation as a great place to work but also helped to keep the firm largely union-free.

FedEx's entire history was set against a background of fundamental changes in the business environment. The first was deregulation in transportation. For instance, government deregulation of the airline industry in 1978 permitted larger planes to replace smaller planes, reducing the number of trips between cities—this permitted FedEx to purchase several Boeing 727s, which helped reduce its unit costs. Deregulation of the trucking industry in 1994 permitted FedEx to establish an integrated regional trucking system that would lower its unit costs further on short-haul trips, and to compete more effectively with UPS. And trade deregulation in the Asia-Pacific region permitted FedEx to establish a new base of operations there. The second major change was induced by inflation and rising global competitiveness—these forces compelled manufacturers to manage their inventories closely and to emulate "just-in-time" supply programs of the Japanese. This created a demand for rapid and carefully monitored movement of components. The third major force was technological innovation, which afforded advances in customer ordering, package tracking, and process monitoring.

UNITED PARCEL SERVICE, INC.

Founded in 1907, manager-owned UPS was the largest transportation company in America. Consolidated parcel delivery, both on-ground and through the air, was the primary business of the company. Service was offered to and from every address in the United States and Western Europe, and many addresses in other countries—it was the only express delivery company to service all areas of the United States (except Northern Alaska). The company delivered between 10 and 20 million packages a day, 20 times the amount delivered by the U.S. Post Office. This translated into an estimated 80–90 percent market share of the entire domestic small-package delivery market. UPS employed 303,000 people, and owned 221 aircraft and 135,000 ground vehicles. UPS stock was owned by UPS managers or their families, by former employees, or by charitable foundations owned by UPS. The company acted as the market-maker in its own shares, buying or selling shares at a "fair market value"[7] determined by the board of directors each quarter.

The key to UPS's success was efficiency. According to *Business Week* reporter Todd Vogel, "Every route is timed down to the traffic light. Each vehicle was engineered to exacting specifications. And the drivers, all 62,000 of them, endure a daily routing calibrated down to the minute."[8] But this demand for machinelike precision met with resistance by UPS's unionized labor force. Of those demands, UPS driver Mark Dray said:

> Drivers are expected to keep precise schedules (hours broken down into hundredths) that do not allow for variables such as weather, traffic conditions, and package volume. If they're behind, they're reprimanded, and if they're ahead of schedule, their routes are lengthened. Drivers make 100 to 120 deliveries a day.[9]

In its quest for efficiency, UPS experienced several strikes resulting from changes in labor practices and driver requirements.

More aggressive and more vocal than ever before, the new UPS of 1995 was the product of extensive reengineering efforts and a revitalized business focus. UPS was girding itself for battle. UPS, although much larger than FedEx, had not chosen to compete directly in the overnight delivery market until 1982. According to observers, such a late entry typified the slow, plodding nature of the heavily unionized UPS.

In 1994, *Fortune* magazine ranked UPS as the 10th most-admired company in the United States—the magazine had ranked UPS as the most-admired transportation company for each of the preceding 10 years. The survey particularly cited UPS for its successful record as a long-term investment, and for its innovations in package-tracking capabilities with cellular technology.[10] Traditionally, the company had been the industry's low-cost provider. In recent years, the company had been investing heavily in information technology, aircraft, and facilities to support service innovations, maintain quality, and reduce costs.

At year-end 1994, UPS reported assets, revenues, and profits of $11.1 billion, $19.6 billion, and $943 million, respectively (see Exhibit 2 for various financial ratios about the firm). The company's financial conservatism was reflected in its AAA bond rating.

---

[7]In setting its share price, the board considered a variety of factors including past and current earnings, earnings estimates, the ratio of UPS common stock to debt of UPS, the business and outlook of UPS, and the general economic climate. The opinions of outside advisers were sometimes considered. The stock price had never decreased in value. The employee stock purchases were often financed with Stock Hypothecation Loans from commercial banks. As the shares provided collateral for these loans, the assessment by the outside lenders provided some external validation for the share price.

[8]Todd Vogel and Chuck Hawkins, "Can UPS Deliver the Goods in a New World?" *Business Week,* June 4, 1990.

[9]Jill Hodges, "Driving Negotiations: Teamsters Survey Says UPS Drivers among Nation's Most Stressed Workers," *Star Tribune,* March 1994, p. 43.

[10]In 1994, UPS introduced electronic clipboards which communicated with cellular technology to a communications center in New Jersey. From there, delivery information could be forwarded to customers. As more manufacturers used express delivery companies to move inventory on a just-in-time basis, package-tracking capabilities became important. Reprinted with permission of the *Star Tribune,* Minneapolis-St. Paul.

COMPETITION IN THE EXPRESS DELIVERY MARKET, 1982–95

Exhibit 3 gives a detailed summary of the major events marking the competitive rivalry between FedEx and UPS. Significant dimensions of this rivalry included increased customer focus, price competition, and business process reengineering with an emphasis on quality of service (see Exhibit 4). However, three dimensions of competition drew particular attention.

1. *Globalization.* In 1984, FedEx entered the international delivery market with its first acquisition, Gelco Express, that delivered to 84 countries—this was followed quickly with acquisitions in Britain, the Netherlands, and United Arab Emirates. In 1985, it established an airport hub in Brussels, aiming to build an intra-Europe delivery system, much as it had built in Memphis in the United States. In 1989 FedEx bought Tiger International for $883 million—the acquisition proved to be one of FedEx's costliest investments, augmenting the company's debt by 250 percent to $2.1 billion. FedEx bought Tiger only three weeks after learning it was for sale, claiming that it hurried the transaction to prevent UPS's purchase. UPS insisted that it had contemplated, but rejected, the purchase after deciding that it would not be profitable. An international delivery service, Tiger represented FedEx's hope to acquire an immediate (and profitable) presence in Europe—FedEx wanted Tiger's existing delivery routes and landing privileges for access to Europe, East Asia, and South America. The acquisition had given FedEx a 7 percent international market share. However, Tiger's fleet consumed enormous sums for extensive modifications to meet FAA standards and by 1991 international losses at FedEx amounted to $194 million. Then in 1992, with European demand remaining only a tiny fraction of the U.S. overnight demand, FedEx relinquished its hub in Europe by selling the Brussels operation to DHL. Analysts estimated that FedEx had lost $1 billion in Europe since its entry there. FedEx would continue to deliver to Europe, but rely on local partners. In total, between 1982 and 1994, FedEx had invested about $2.5 billion in its overseas operations.

UPS did not break into the European market in earnest until 1988, with the acquisition of 10 European courier services. To enhance its international delivery systems, UPS created a system that coded and tracked packages, and automatically billed customers for customs duties and taxes. Throughout the 1988–92 period, UPS seemed to announce the acquisition of local and regional distributors as rapidly as FedEx. Also, UPS expanded to Asia, using its own planes and canceling a contract previously held with Tiger International. Unfortunately, the company had not earned a profit on its international services; Kent Nelson speculated that UPS would not turn its first international profit until 1998, but said,

> We could have had great difficulties sustaining the losses we had in international operations if we were a public company. It would have taken a lot of dancing and a lot of explaining, and somebody could have replaced me and dramatically cut our losses overnight by bailing out. If I were going after short-term profits, I might have chosen another course. But international is going to be one of our winners.[11]

---

[11]"The Wizard Is Oz," *Chief Executive,* March 1994, p. 42.

UPS hoped that its international service would account for one-third of total revenue by the year 2000. Donald Layden, UPS's international operations manager, commented, "The overall strategy is for us to be the leading provider of package distribution services world-wide.[12] In May 1995, UPS announced that it would spend more than $1 billion to expand its European operations during the next five years. UPS noted that its first-quarter pretax international losses narrowed to $47 million from $77 million a year earlier.

Exhibit 5 presents segment data decomposing revenues, operating profit, and assets for both firms by domestic and foreign orientation. However, analysts noted that allocations between these segments were often a matter of judgment—for instance, how was a sorting facility to be allocated if it served both domestic and foreign routes?

2. *Information technology.* Every package handled by FedEx was logged by a central computer system, Customer, Operations, Service, Master On-line System (COSMOS). This global computer network transmitted data from package movements, customer pick-ups, invoices, and deliveries to a central database at the Memphis headquarters. At every transition in the delivery cycle, the bar-coded data on each package were scanned and processed, allowing package movements to be tracked precisely. In 1992 COSMOS performed 250,000 of these transactions—each day. In 1993, FedEx introduced Powership 3, a desktop shipping system given to customers who shipped three or more packages a day. This system stored frequently used addresses, printed labels, requested a courier without a telephone, traced packages, and was connected directly to FedEx. Also in 1993, FedEx announced the introduction of three other technology systems aimed at more efficient handling or better control.

UPS had much catching up to do, according to Francis Erbrick, vice president of information systems: "If you went into our information services facility in 1985, you went into 1975 in terms of technology."[13] To catch up, UPS invested in an $80 million central data facility in New Jersey to link all of UPS's computers worldwide. From there, investment in information technology grew exponentially—by 1992, the cumulative total investment was $1.4 billion. "Nineteen ninety-two was the first year we spent more on computers than on vehicles," said UPS CEO Kent Nelson. "Initially that scared me, but information is just as important as packages." UPS planned on spending an additional $3.2 billion on information technology by 1996, including a worldwide computer network known as PRISM to handle customer requests, billing, and package tracing internationally. Later UPS introduced the Delivery Information Acquisition Device (DIAD), which scanned package bar codes and recorded customer signatures. These handheld units were carried by the drivers and, once back in the truck, would connect with the central computer system by a Motorola cellular modem. Other technological improvements at UPS included the creation of optical character recognition equipment that could translate address labels or other documents to be saved directly on the computer without hand typing.

3. *Service expansion and new service introduction.* FedEx launched Zapmail in 1984 at a cost of $100 million. Designed to capture the growing fax market before the machines were priced low enough to be universal, technical problems and the meteoric plunge in facsimile machine prices caused the service to fail and then close just two years later. The cumulative

---

[12]"UPS Optimistic about Shipping Its Strategy Worldwide," *Los Angeles Times,* July 4, 1992, p. D2.
[13]Resa W. King, "UPS Gets a Big Package—of Computers," *Business Week,* July 25, 1988.

write-off on Zapmail was about $400 million.[14] FedEx responded to UPS's price competition by guaranteeing delivery by 10:30 AM instead of noon, as it had previously. The new competition from UPS spurred FedEx to further expand its geographic service to 95 percent of the United States, from 74 percent. Throughout the 1980s FedEx, armed with volume discounts and superb quality, went after big clients that had previously used UPS without thought. At the same time, FedEx continued to find new markets such as contract warehousing services for mission-critical inventory that could be delivered anywhere at a moment's notice.

This competition forced UPS to revise its strategy. The company began to copy FedEx's customer interfaces, such as installing 11,500 drop-off boxes to compete with FedEx's 12,000 boxes, 165 drive-through stations, and 371 express-delivery stores. Further, UPS began to pick up packages on the same day that the order was received, a service that FedEx had always offered—wherever and whenever a customer called. As UPS tried to enter FedEx's business, so too did FedEx enter UPS's. In 1990 FedEx entered UPS's core business: the two-day ground-delivery market. At the same time, UPS began to offer modest discounts to volume shippers. In 1993 UPS added a new and cheaper three-day delivery service to undercut FedEx's more expensive two-day service. Up until the summer of 1995, the race seemed to be one of how quickly each competitor could transform itself into the other. UPS had begun Saturday pickups and deliveries to match FedEx. FedEx bought $200 million in ground vehicles to match UPS. In January 1995 UPS bought SonicAir, a *same-day* delivery company, for $60 million.

The largest recent innovations entailed offering integrated logistics services to large corporate clients. These services were aimed at providing total inventory control, and included purchase orders, receipt of goods, order entry and warehousing, inventory accounting, shipping, and accounts receivable. For instance, the London design company Laura Ashley retained FedEx to store, track, and ship products quickly to individual stores worldwide. Similarly, Dell Computer retained UPS to manage its total inbound and outbound shipping.

One measurable impact of this competition between FedEx and UPS—investment spending—is given in Exhibit 6. Through 1989 net cash used for investment rose at an annualized rate of 27 percent at Federal Express and 17 percent at UPS. By 1994 UPS had outspent FedEx by a factor of nearly two to one. After the U.S. Congress deregulated intrastate trucking in October 1994, FedEx announced that it would augment its ground service with the purchase of 4,000 new trucks and an investment of $200 million in ground vehicles. Greg Smith, an analyst with the research consulting firm Colography Group commented, "The more you can do with trucks, the more FedEx will buy and the more they'll become like UPS."[15]

Fred Smith, CEO of FedEx, argued that his company had compelled UPS to deliver packages faster. "UPS has had to adapt to all the innovations we have offered," he said. "The middle ground (two- and three-day delivery) is the battleground. In the next century, people will find it absurd not to move things by express. How many people go by bus today?"[16]

---

[14]When FedEx announced the establishment of Zapmail in 1984, its stock price fell nearly $10 from the mid-$40s to the mid-$30s. Later, when Zapmail was terminated, FedEx's stock price rose $8 per share.

[15]Quoted in Joan Feldman, "The Price of Success: FedEx Is Solidly No. 1 in Express Shipping and Is Relying on Technology to Stay There Despite the Pressures of Rising Costs," *Air Transport World,* September 1994, p. 46.

[16]Richard Weintraub, "Delivering a Revolution: The Fierce Rivalry between FedEx and UPS Remakes Global Commerce," *Washington Post,* August 28, 1994.

TABLE 1   Express Delivery Market Shares

	1987	1991			1994		
	Air Overnight Package and Letter	Air Overnight Letter	Air Overnight Package	Air Deferred Packages and Letters	Air Overnight Letter	Air Overnight Package	Air Deferred Packages and Letters*
Federal Express	52.80%	56.80%	28.40%	35.10%	58.30%	29.40%	36.60%
Airborne	6.60	15.90	18.70	10.00	15.10	19.80	19.40
UPS	13.20	10.20	35.40	63.20	12.70	41.50	42.60
U.S. Postal Service	8.00	13.00	4.90	—	9.60	3.40	—
DHL	2.50	NA	8.50	—	2.90	2.70	—
Others	16.90	4.10	4.10	1.70	1.40	3.20	1.40
Total	100.00%	100.00%	100.00%	100.00%	100.00%	100.00%	100.00%

*1994 market share for deferred packages and letters reflects the research of the Colography Group, which indicated that some delivery services sold by UPS as "air delivery" actually traveled by truck and rail. In 1994 (but not 1991) that volume has been removed. This adjustment should be taken into consideration when comparing UPS's market share in the "Deferred Packages and Letters" category.

Source: Greg Smith of the Colography Group; and *Business Week,* March 30, 1987.

SHARES OF MARKET

Reflecting this competitive turbulence, the market shares of FedEx and UPS had changed over the preceding seven years as illustrated in Table 1.

PERFORMANCE ASSESSMENT

Virtually all interested observers—customers, suppliers, investors, and employees—watched the competitive struggle of these two firms for hints about the next steps in the drama. The conventional wisdom was that if a firm were operationally excellent, strong financial performance would follow. Indeed, FedEx had set a goal of "producing outstanding financial returns," while UPS targeted "competitive returns to shareholders." Had the two firms achieved their goals? Moreover, did the trends in financial performance suggest whether strong performance could be achieved in the future? In pursuit of these questions, the exhibits afford several possible avenues of analysis.

- *Earnings per share, market values, and returns.* Exhibit 7 presents the share prices, earnings per share, and price/earnings ratios for the two firms. Also included is the annual total return from holding each share (percent gain in share price, plus dividend yield). Some analysts questioned the appropriateness of using UPS's "fair market value" share price because it was set by the board of directors rather than in an open market.
- *Ratio analysis.* Exhibits 1 and 2 present a variety of analytical ratios computed from the financial statements of each firm.

• *Economic profit analysis.* Also known as Economic Value Added™ (EVA™). EVA computed the value created or destroyed each year by deducting a charge for capital from the firm's net operating profit after taxes (NOPAT).

$$EVA = \text{Operating profits} - \text{A capital charge}$$
$$= \text{NOPAT} - (K \times \text{Capital})$$

The capital charge was determined by multiplying the weighted average cost of capital, K, by the capital employed in the business or operation.

Estimating Capital.   Included in capital are near-capital items that represent economic value employed on behalf of the firm such as the present value of operating leases, amortized goodwill, and losses. The rationale for including losses and write-offs in continuing capital is that such losses represent unproductive assets, or failed investment. Were they excluded from the capital equation, the sum would only count successful efforts, and not accurately reflect the performance of the firm.

Estimating NOPAT.   Net operating profit after taxes (NOPAT) is calculated with a similar regard for losses and write-offs. Here the aim is to arrive at the actual cash generated by the concern. To do so, the estimates add increases in deferred taxes back into income because it is not a cash expense, and calculate the interest expense of the leased operating assets as if they were leased capital assets.

Estimating Cost of Capital.   The capital charge applied against NOPAT should be based on a blend of the costs of all the types of capital the firm employs, or the weighted average cost of capital. The cost of debt (used for both debt and leases) is the annual rate consistent with each firm's bond rating (BBB for FedEx, and AAA for UPS). The cost of equity may be estimated in a variety of ways—in the analysis here, the capital asset pricing model was employed.[17] FedEx's beta and cost of equity are used in estimating FedEx's cost of capital. Since UPS's beta was unobservable, the analysis that follows uses the average beta each year of FedEx, Roadway Package Services, and Airborne Express, UPS's publicly held peer firms.

Estimating EVA and MVA.   In Exhibits 8 and 9 the stock of capital and the flow of NOPAT are used to calculate the actual return and, with the introduction of the WACC, the EVA. These exhibits present the EVA calculated each year, and cumulatively through time. The panel at the bottom of each exhibit estimates the market value created or destroyed (or market value added [MVA]) over the observation period. MVA is calculated as the difference between the current market value of the company and its investment base. The market value created could be compared with cumulative economic value added. In theory, the following relationships would hold:

$$MVA = \text{Present value of all future EVA}$$
$$MVA = \text{Market value of debt and equity minus capital}$$

---

[17]The capital asset pricing model describes the cost of equity as the sum of the risk-free rate of return and a risk premium. The risk premium is the average risk premium for a large portfolio of stocks times the risk factor (or "beta") for the company. A beta equal to 1.0 suggests that the company is just as risky as the market portfolio; less than 1.0 suggests lower risk; greater than 1.0 implies greater risk. In July 1995, FedEx's beta was 1.13.

Thus,

$$\text{Market value} = \text{Capital plus present value of all future EVA}$$

In other words, maximizing the present value of EVA amounted to maximizing the market value of the firm.

OUTLOOK FOR FEDERAL EXPRESS IN MID-1995

About 75 percent of FedEx's common shares were held by institutional investors, who, it could be assumed, were instrumental in setting the prices for the company's shares.[18] Typically, these investors absorbed the thinking of the several securities analysts and analytical services who followed Federal Express in 1995. The following excerpts indicate the outlook held by these analysts:

> *As noted, the recent weakness in FDX stock appears, to us, more an indication of general concerns about the health of the economy and the implications for the air express market, and, relatedly, renewed worries that Federal might not be able to reverse its domestic earnings declines by boosting prices. The added recent concern about its being vulnerable to U.S.–Japan trade tensions might have added one too many worries for some holders. The stock has . . . underperformed the market. We continue our market performance rating on the stock.*

> P. R. Schlesinger, Donaldson, Lufkin & Jenrette Securities, May 26, 1995

> *The domestic operations have been suffering margin erosion. Federal is working to trim costs and get rid of less profitable business, and we expect fiscal 1996 will bring some relief . . . Meanwhile, the international segment is running strong. Brisk traffic continues to lift revenues and margins, and the air courier is now tapping into the huge market in Asia to keep the momentum going . . . This neutrally ranked stock is interesting for its 3- to 5-year appreciation potential, based on the increasing globalization of Federal's network. Indeed, foreign operations should provide the lion's share of profits by early next century.*

> M. M. Royce, Value Line, June 23,1995

> *The domestic business was a disappointment. Although volume growth remained robust (up 20.1%), cost per domestic package fell only 2.6% versus a revenue per package yield decline of 5.9%. Thus, the domestic operating margin was squeezed to 4.2% from last year's 6.7% level. The business mix shift toward lower-yielding deferred delivery products requires a more rapid reduction in the cost base than the company was able to achieve during the quarter . . . We are raising our estimates for the remainder of the fiscal year and beyond. The international performance was spectacular, and we expect it to continue to offset the deterioration in domestic operating income. Given the outlook, we continue to rate the common shares "buy."*

> H. P. Boyle, Jr., Alex, Brown & Sons, March 14, 1995

---

[18]Officers, directors, and employees of FedEx owned 10 percent of the shares. The remainder, about 15 percent, were owned by individual investors not affiliated with the company.

Federal Express paid no common stock dividend, which meant that returns to investors would derive entirely from capital gains.

CONCLUSION

Observers of the air-express package delivery industry pondered the recent performance of the two leading firms and their prospects. What had been the impact of the intense competition between the two firms? Which firm was doing better? The announcement about the J. C. Penney contract might contain clues about the prospects for competition in the future.

EXHIBIT 1   Analytical Financial Ratios, Federal Express Corporation

	1985	1986	1987	1988	1989	1990
Activity Analysis						
Average days outstanding	47.43	47.83	44.92	43.43	46.41	47.73
Working capital turnover	22.59	17.89	34.34	125.84	149.90	162.81
Fixed assets turnover	164	178	186	190	182	200
Total asset turnover	1.18	1.23	1.33	1.41	1.24	1.28
Liquidity Analysis						
Current ratio	1.34	1.42	1.01	1.10	1.01	1.06
Cash ratio	0.04	0.43	0.04	0.10	0.14	0.08
Cash from operations ratio			0.92	1.08	1.17	0.47
Defensive interval			1.11	1.51	3.28	1.96
Long-term Debt and Solvency Analysis						
Debt/equity ratio	0.75	0.51	0.69	0.63	1.43	1.30
Times interest earned	5.58	8.87	7.81	5.65	3.68	2.06
Fixed change coverage ratio	4.78	3.71	1.73	1.55	1.47	0.46
Capital expenditure ratio			0.60	0.93	0.55	0.87
Cash from operations-debt ratio			0.53	0.65	0.31	0.24
Profitability Analysis						
Margin before interest and tax	12.83%	13.37%	11.48%	9.77%	8.21%	5.52%
Net profit margin	3.77	5.12	(2.06)	4.83	3.57	1.65
Return on assets	5.98	6.74	(1.27)	7.29	5.73	4.08
Return on total equity	9.90	13.82	(6.04)	15.58	13.07	7.37
Financial leverage effect	29.42	38.32	(17.98)	49.47	43.48	29.89

	1984–85	1985–86	1986–87	1987–88	1988–89	1989–90
Growth						
Sales		27.65%	23.51%	22.17%	33.07%	35.77%
Total adjusted capital	41.19%	38.80	13.69	19.47	62.66	8.47
Book assets	20.98	15.29	19.95	19.90	53.76	3.92
Net income before unusual (gain) loss		38.87	N.M.F.	N.M.F.	(11.33)	(30.45)
Adjusted NOPAT		14.94	4.37	5.21	22.28	16.10
Net income		73.30	N.M.F.	N.M.F.	(1.69)	(37.27)
Operating income		33.02	6.02	4.03	11.85	(8.74)

Source: Federal Express annual report.

EXHIBIT 1   *(concluded)*

1991	1992	1993	1994	
47.28	45.79	44.08	43.23	365/ Receivables turnover
(233.91)	(47.22)	(82.89)	78 .62	Sales/Average net working capital
214	215	227	245	Sales/Average net fixed assets
1.36	1.36	1.39	1.44	Sales/ Average total assets
0.90	0.87	0.99	1.15	Current assets/Current liabilities
0.08	0.06	0.11	0.26	(Cash + Mkt securities)/Current liabilities
0.63	0.37	0.52	0.53	Cash from operations/Current liabilities
2.38	3.20	2.54	3.18	(Cash + AR + Cash taxes)/(Rents + Gross CAPEX)
1.09	1.14	1.13	0.85	Total debt/Total equity
1.39	0.14	2.34	3.73	EBIT/Interest expense
(0.36)	(0.93)	0.27	0.49	Earnings before fixed changes and taxes/Fixed changes
1.02	1.04	0.91	1.95	Cash from operations/CAPEX
0.43	0.29	0.39	0.47	Cash from operations/Total debt
3.28%	0.30%	4.83%	6.26%	EBIT/Sales
.08	(1.51)	0.69	2.41	Net income/Sales
2.04	(0.08)	2.40	4.17	(Net income + After-tax interest costs)/Average total assets
0.36	(7.01)	3.31	11.37	Net income/Average total equity
2.34	(495.42)	14.28	38.51	Net income/Operating income

1990–91	1991–92	1992–93	1993–94	*Compound Annual Growth Rate*	
9.60%	(1.80)%	3.42%	8.60%	17.31%	(85–94)
1.71	2.15	7.57	8.46	18.11	(84–94)
1.62	(5.87)	1.90	(0.78)	11.98	(84–94)
(94.91)	N.M.F.	N.M.F.	86.11	4.40	(85–94)
(36.43)	(8.76)	21.42	35.74	11.61	(85–94)
(94.91)	N.M.F.	N.M.F.	279.40	11.61	(85–94)
(34.91)	(90.89)	154.24	40.69	8.31	(85–94)

EXHIBIT 2   Financial Ratios, United Parcel Service

	1985	1986	1987	1988	1989	1990
Activity Analysis						
Average days outstanding	16.31	14.80	10.63	9.40	16.42	21.23
Working capital turnover	175.90	382.90	77.65	(109.36)	(112.44)	101.75
Fixed asset turnover	3.28	3.26	2.84	2.53	2.42	2.44
Total asset turnover	1.83	1.70	1.59	1.52	1.51	1.54
Liquidity Analysis						
Current ratio	1.01	1.03	1.16	0.78	1.11	1.04
Cash ratio	0.31	0.30	0.40	0.22	0.26	0.08
Cash from operations ratio		1.00	1.12	1.36	0.60	0.60
Defensive interval		1.40	0.81	0.62	1.31	1.13
Long-term Debt and Solvency Analysis						
Debt/equity ratio	0.07	0.05	0.10	0.04	0.24	0.24
Times interest earned	288.82	134.44	259.96	197.54	81.93	14.61
Fixed change coverage ratio	10.38	22.66	13.57	16.76	(0.04)	(7.49)
Capital expenditure ratio		1.62	1.14	1.34	0.98	0.94
Cash from operations to debt ratio		10.38	4.80	13.54	1.33	1.28
Profitability Analysis						
Margin before interest and tax	10.66%	13.44%	10.03%	9.75%	9.83%	7.73%
Net profit margin	6.97	7.76	8.10	6.88	5.61	4.39
Return on assets	16.13	19.83	19.10	16.17	12.43	9.06
Return on total equity	25.99	29.76	28.53	24.44	20.49	16.59
Financial leverage effect	65.40	57.75	80.78	70.56	57.06	56.72

	1984–85	1985–86	1986–87	1987–88	1988–89	1989–90
Growth						
Sales	12.50%	12.14%	12.33%	13.94%	12.02%	10.10%
Total adjusted capital	27.58	21.19	23.19	5.02	33.74	5.71
Book assets	39.12	18.22	37.60	21.52	13.30	5.03
Net income before unusual (gain) loss	19.12	17.85	(6.61)	21.45	(8.61)	(13.94)
Adjusted NOPAT	—	1.93	(3.33)	10.94	0.89	(9.41)
Net income	—	40.39	17.22	(3.24)	(8.61)	(13.94)
Operating income	—	58.98	(16.20)	10.77	13.02	(13.42)

Source: United Parcel Services annual report.

EXHIBIT 2   *(concluded)*

1991	1992	1993	1994	
22.23	23.13	23.11	25.66	365/Receivables turnover
124.67	140.99	543.54	313.87	Sales/Average net working capital
2.54	2.64	2.71	2.69	Sales/Average net fixed assets
1.60	1.68	1.78	1.71	Sales/Average total assets
1.08	1.03	1.00	1.04	Current assets/Current liabilities
0.14	0.06	0.12	0.09	(Cash + Mkt. securities)/Current liabilities
0.85	0.69	0.83	0.68	Cash from operations/Current liabilities
1.58	1.71	1.83	1.50	(Cash + AR + Cash taxes)/(Rents + Gross CAPEX)
0.21	0.23	0.22	0.24	Total debt/Total equity
24.61	30.48	42.87	53.27	EBIT/Interest expense
2.18	3.23	14.90	13.16	Earnings before fixed changes and taxes/Fixed changes
1.53	1.56	1.60	0.96	Cash from operations/CAPEX
1.92	1.68	2.06	1.43	Cash from operations/Total debt
8.33%	7.74%	8.20%	7.95%	EBIT/Sales
4.66	3.12	4.55	4.82	Net income/Sales
9.91	6.77	10.24	11.03	(Net income + After-tax interest cost)/Average total assets
18.72	13.59	21.13	21.96	Net income/Average total equity
55.96	40.40	55.54	60.63	Net income/Operating income

1990–91	1991–92	1992–93	1993–94	*Compound Annual Growth Rate*	
10.39%	9.98%	7.65%	10.08%	11.10%	(84–94)
8.55	6.69	3.62	13.90	14.48	(84–94)
7.51	3.92	6.15	14.84	16.12	(84–94)
17.33	9.27	5.82	16.51	7.07	(84–94)
(2.16)	12.26	3.03	9.89	2.44	(85–94)
17.33	(26.28)	56.86	16.51	7.88	(85–94)
18.92	2.12	14.08	6.74	8.01	(85–94)

EXHIBIT 3 Time Line of Competitive Developments

FedEx		UPS
Offers 10:30 AM delivery	1982	Enters overnight package delivery
Increases service area from 74% to 94% Later cutoff times Introduces technology to link services	1983	
Acquires Gelco: access to 83 countries	1984	
Sets up Brussels hub	1985	Begins making significant IT investment
Warehouse for IBM, National Semiconductor, Laura Ashley	1987	TV advertising; lower rates
	1988	Offers automated customs service
Announces standard overnight service Announces reduced corporate rate Buys Tiger International International acquisitions	1989	Offers same-day pickup Invests $80 million in computer and telecommunications center International acquisitions
	1990	Offers delivery by 10:30 AM
	1991	Raises rates—32% for commercial, 16% for residential Launches DIAD system
Exits from Europe Offers two-day delivery	1992	Offers Saturday delivery
Introduces PowerShip software Introduces business logistics services Allies with IBM, Kinko's, Claris, Radio Shack, Sam's, Connect Soft	1993	Offers HAZMAT shipping Offers logistics service Offers prepaid letter Offers Saturday pickup Offers three-day service New ad campaign
Persuades UPS catalog customers to defect from UPS Buys 4,000 trucks Offers service through Internet	1994	DIAD fully functional Raises rates 3.9% Offers heavy package delivery Offers early AM service Offers service on Internet
	1995	Acquires SonicAir Offers same-day delivery Exclusive contract with J. C. Penney, $1 billion over five years

EXHIBIT 4   Comparative Pricing of Major Overnight Carriers: 1993, 1995 (two-pound package, Baltimore to Los Angeles)

Company	Same-Day 1995	Next AM 1993	Next AM 1995	Two-Day 1993	Two-Day 1995
Federal Express					
Price	$159	$24.25	$24.25	$14.00	$14.00
Commitment		10:30 AM	10:30 AM	4:30 PM	4:30 PM
Airborne					
Price	$155	N/A	$25.00	$9.00	$9.00
Commitment			12:00 noon	3:00 PM	3:00 PM
United Parcel Service					
Price	$159	$18.50	$16.75	$10.50	$5.25
Commitment		10:30 AM	10:30 AM	4:00 PM	4:00 PM
U.S. Postal Service					
Price	N/A	$13.95	$15.00	N/A	N/A
Commitment		3:00 PM	3:00 PM		
DHL					
Price	$159	$24.25	$24.25	N/A	N/A
Commitment		12:00 noon	12:00 noon		
Price premium of FedEx over UPS		31.08%	44.78%	33.33%	93.10%

Source: Telephone Survey: 1995, Alex Brown & Sons, Inc., 1993 and 1995. "Federal Express Corporation: Profile of a Maturing Company," by H. Perry Boyle, Jr., BT Alex Brown Inc., December 6, 1993, p.p. 17–18. Reprinted with permission.

EXHIBIT 5 Segment Information (in thousands of dollars)

	1986	1987	1988	1989	1990	1991	1992	1993	1994
United Parcel Service									
Domestic									
Revenue						$13,694,728	$14,721,686	$15,822,558	$17,297,843
Income before income taxes						1,470,645	1,545,484	1,698,299	1,902,140
Identifiable assets						7,982,237	7,873,398	8,359,395	9,886,634
Foreign									
Revenue						1,325,102	1,796,935	1,959,795	2,277,847
Loss before income taxes						(253,580)	(276,189)	(266,602)	(326,764)
Identifiable assets						876,174	1,164,419	1,214,436	1,295,770
Consolidated									
Revenue						15,019,830	16,518,621	17,782,353	19,575,690
Income before income taxes						1,217,065	1,269,295	1,431,697	1,575,376
Identifiable assets						8,858,561	9,037,817	9,573,831	11,182,404
Federal Express									
Domestic									
Revenues	$2,456,832	$2,924,742	$3,459,427	$4,144,827	4,784,887	5,057,831	5,194,684	5,667,964	6,199,940
Operating income (loss)	358,267	393,876	409,977	467,143	608,069	671,186	635,872	559,140	559,629
Identifiable assets				3,007,348	3,798,364	4,032,361	3,941,022	4,432,578	4,883,644
Foreign									
Revenues	116,397	253,566	423,390	1,022,140	2,230,182	2,630,465	2,355,376	2,140,179	2,279,516
Operating income (loss)	$ (14,246)	$ (29,144)	$ (30,525)	(42,708)	(194,490)	(391,393)	(612,905)	(181,967)	(28,997)
Identifiable assets				$2,286,074	$1,876,709	$1,640,100	$1,522,164	$1,360,486	$ 1,108,854
Consolidated									
Revenues	2,573,229	3,178,308	3,882,817	5,166,967	7,015,069	7,688,296	7,550,060	7,808,043	8,479,456
Operating income (loss)	$ 344,021	$ 364,743	$ 379,452	424,435	413,579	279,793	377,173	22,967	530,632
Identifiable assets				$5,293,422	$5,675,073	$5,672,461	$5,463,186	5,793,064	5,992,498

Source: United Parcel Service reports to shareholders and Federal Express annual reports, S.E.C., 10–K reports.

EXHIBIT 6   Comparative Capital Investment Information

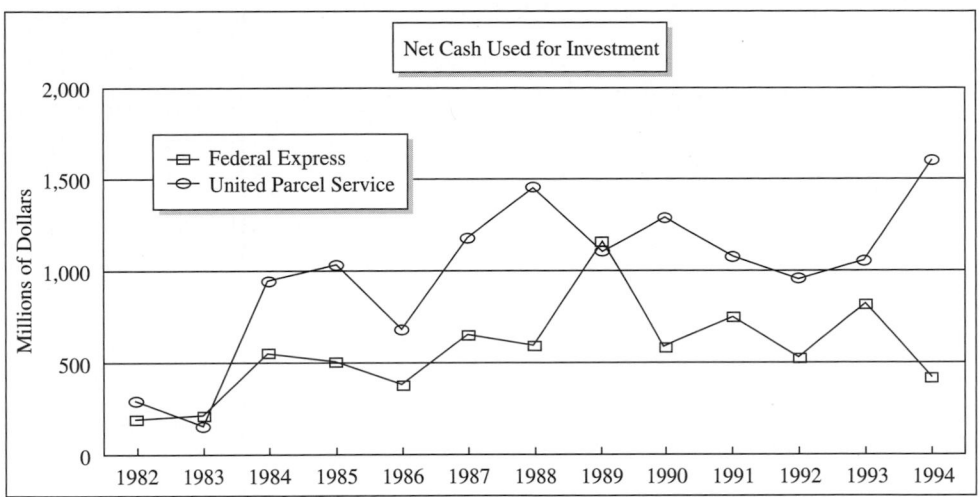

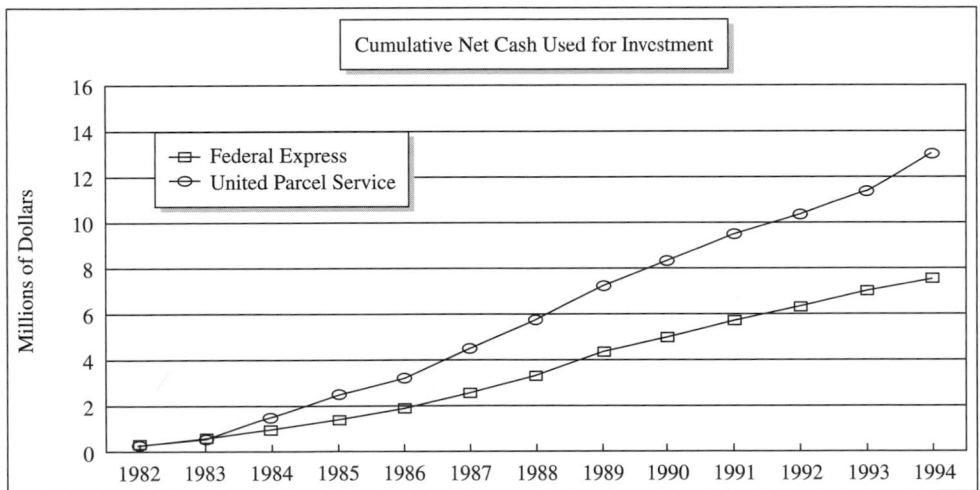

Source: Casewriter analysis of annual reports.

EXHIBIT 7 Equity Returns and Prices

	1981	1982	1983	1984	1985	1986	1987	1988	1989	1990	1991	1992	1993	1994	1995, Q2
Federal Express															
Stock price, December 31st	$31.25	$37.13	$23.13	$34.50	$60.63	$63.13	$39.88	$50.63	$45.75	$33.88	$38.75	$54.50	$70.88	$60.25	60.75
Earnings per share	1.85	2.03	2.52	1.61	2.64	2.65	(1.26)	3.56	3.53	2.18	0.11	(2.11)	0.98	3.65	5.27
Price/Earnings multiple	16.89	18.29	9.18	21.43	22.96	23.86	n.m.f	14.20	12.96	15.56	350.51	n.m.f	72.00	16.51	11.53
Total capital appreciation return		18.80%	(37.71)%	49.19%	75.72%	4.12%	(36.83)%	26.96%	(9.63)%	(25.96)%	14.39%	40.65%	30.05%	(14.99)%	0.83%
Cumulative compound annual return		18.80%	(26.00)%	10.40%	94.00%	102.00%	27.60%	62.00%	46.40%	8.40%	24.00%	74.40%	126.80%	92.80%	94.40%
United Parcel Service															
Fair market value, December 31st	$1.69	$2.31	$4.13	$6.25	$8.25	$10.25	$12.00	$13.38	$14.50	$15.25	$16.00	$18.50	$20.75	$23.50	$24.50
Earnings per share	0.49	0.49	0.73	0.71	0.84	0.99	1.16	1.12	1.07	0.95	1.14	0.87	1.40	1.63	—
Implied Price/Earnings multiple	3.48	4.70	5.69	8.87	9.82	10.34	10.33	11.90	13.54	15.98	14.08	21.33	14.86	14.45	—
Dividends per share	0.10	0.16	0.35	0.34	0.38	0.39	0.41	0.43	0.46	0.47	0.47	0.49	0.49	0.54	—
Capital appreciation return		37.04%	78.38%	51.52%	32.00%	24.24%	17.07%	11.46%	8.41%	5.17%	4.92%	15.63%	12.16%	13.25%	4.26%
Income return		24.63%	22.52%	13.59%	11.59%	10.71%	10.44%	8.86%	7.68%	6.41%	7.27%	5.03%	7.11%	7.35%	—
Total annual return		61.66%	100.90%	65.11%	43.59%	34.96%	27.52%	20.32%	16.10%	11.59%	12.19%	20.65%	19.28%	20.60%	4.26%
Cumulative compound annual return		61.66%	224.78%	436.24%	669.96%	939.11%	1225.03%	1494.24%	1750.84%	1965.29%	2217.10%	2695.67%	3234.54%	3921.60%	4092.73%
Standard & Poor's 500 Index Return, with Reinvestment															
Annual	(4.91)%	21.41%	22.51%	6.27%	32.16%	18.47%	5.23%	16.81%	31.49%	(3.17)%	30.55%	7.67%	9.99%	1.31%	20.22%
Cumulative		21.41%	48.74%	58.07%	108.90%	147.48%	160.43%	204.20%	300.00%	287.32%	405.64%	444.43%	498.81%	506.63%	629.28%
Cumulative Compound Annual Returns, Net of the Standard & Poor's 500															
Federal Express		(2.61)%	(74.74)%	(47.67)%	(14.90)%	(45.48)%	(132.83)%	(142.20)%	(253.60)%	(278.92)%	(381.64)%	(370.03)%	(372.01)%	(413.83)%	(534.88)%
United Parcel Service		40.25%	176.04%	378.17%	561.06%	791.63%	1064.60%	1290.04%	1450.84%	1677.97%	1811.46%	2251.25%	2735.73%	3414.96%	3463.45%

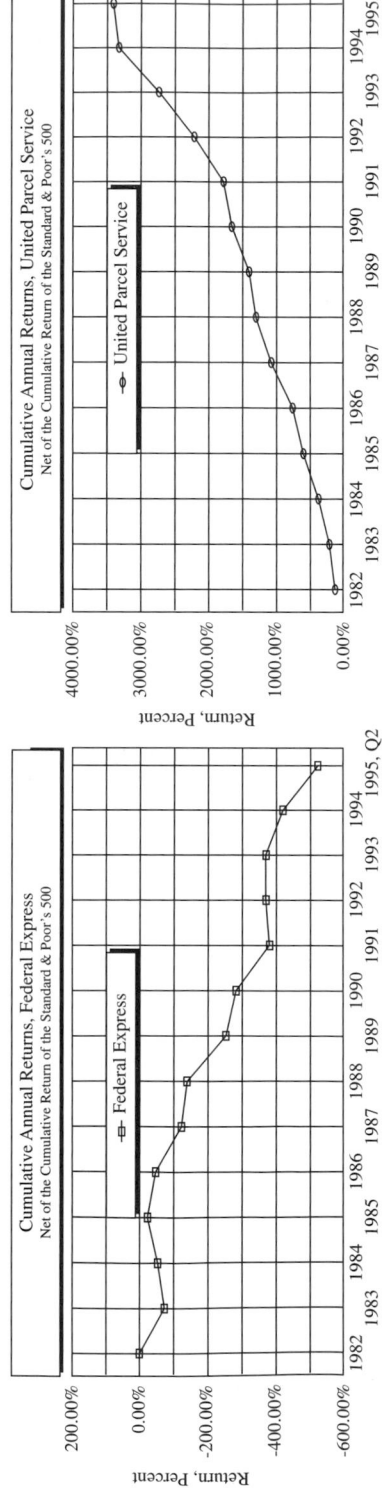

Cumulative Annual Returns, United Parcel Service
Net of the Cumulative Return of the Standard & Poor's 500

Cumulative Annual Returns, Federal Express
Net of the Cumulative Return of the Standard & Poor's 500

EXHIBIT 8 EVA™ Estimation, FedEx

	1985	1986	1987	1988	1989	1990	1991	1992	1993	1994
NOPAT	$ 235,029	$ 270,140	$ 281,950	$ 296,642	$ 362,744	$ 421,152	$ 267,728	$ 244,280	$ 296,612	$ 402,621
Beginning capital	$1,403,280	$1,981,285	$2,551,826	$2,901,126	$3,465,870	$5,637,746	$6,115,501	$6,220,035	$6,353,969	$6,834,676
Rate of return	16.75%	13.63%	11.05%	10.23%	10.47%	7.47%	4.38%	3.93%	4.67%	5.89%
WACC										
Long-term debt	$ 607,508	$ 561,716	$ 744,914	$ 838,730	$2,138,940	$2,148,142	$1,826,781	$1,797,844	$1,882,279	$1,632,202
PV noncapitalized operating leases	$ 111,384	$ 291,264	$ 510,900	$ 488,929	$ 604,217	$ 996,153	$1,214,342	$1,246,275	$1,334,481	$1,567,249
PV of capital leases	$ 295,075	$ 299,228	$ 321,310	$ 319,165	$ 512,079	$ 467,755	$ 239,254	$ 225,800	$ 221,740	$ 199,004
Total	$1,013,967	$1,152,208	$1,577,124	$1,646,824	$3,255,236	$3,612,050	$3,280,377	$3,269,919	$3,438,500	$3,398,455
Average shares outstanding	46,970	49,840	51,905	52,670	52,272	53,161	53,350	53,961	54,719	56,012
Share price	$ 58.00	$ 66.00	$ 44.00	$ 49.00	$ 45.00	$ 34.00	$ 33.00	$ 55.00	$ 70.00	$ 57.00
Market value of equity	$2,724,260	$3,289,440	$2,283,820	$2,580,830	$2,352,240	$1,807,474	$1,760,550	$2,967,855	$3,830,330	$3,192,684
Tax rate	46.00%	46.00%	34.00%	34.00%	34.00%	34.00%	34.00%	34.00%	35.00%	35.00%
Long-term USG bonds	10.74%	8.14%	8.76%	9.11%	8.62%	8.81%	8.24%	7.61%	6.46%	7.43%
Yield of senior BBB	12.19%	10.37%	10.55%	10.75%	10.35%	10.86%	10.12%	9.18%	8.55%	8.91%
Beta	1.35	1.30	1.15	1.10	1.10	1.05	1.05	1.15	1.20	1.25
Cost of equity	18.03%	15.16%	14.97%	15.05%	14.56%	14.48%	13.91%	13.82%	12.94%	14.18%
Cost of capital	14.93%	12.68%	11.70%	11.95%	10.07%	9.61%	9.20%	9.75%	9.45%	9.86%
EVA™										
NOPAT/Beginning capital	16.75%	13.63%	11.05%	10.23%	10.47%	7.47%	4.38%	3.93%	4.67%	5.89%
WACC	14.93%	12.68%	11.70%	11.95%	10.07%	9.61%	9.20%	9.75%	9.45%	9.86%
Spread	1.82%	0.95%	-0.65%	-1.73%	0.39%	-2.14%	-4.83%	-5.82%	-4.78%	-3.96%
× Beginning capital	$1,403,280	$1,981,285	$2,551,826	$2,901,126	$3,465,870	$5,637,746	$6,115,501	$6,220,035	$6,353,969	$6,834,676
Annual economic value added	$ 25,583	$ 18,914	($ 16,596)	($ 50,079)	$ 13,620	($ 120,431)	($ 295,178)	($ 362,265)	($ 303,694)	($ 270,959)
Cumulative annual EVA™	$ 25,583	$ 44,497	$ 27,901	($ 22,178)	($ 8,557)	($ 128,988)	($ 424,166)	($ 786,431)	($1,090,125)	($1,361,084)

FedEx: Measures of Value Creation (billions)

	1985	1994	Change
Cumulative EVA™	0.026	(1.361)	(1.387)
Analysis of market value added			
Book value of equity	0.815	1.925	1.109
Interest-bearing debt and equivalents	1.014	3.398	2.384
Capital (book value)	1.829	5.323	3.494
Market value of equity	2.724	3.193	0.468
Interest-bearing debt and equivalents	1.014	3.398	2.384
Capital (market value)	3.738	6.591	2.853
Market value added	1.909	1.268	(0.641)

Source: Casewriter analysis of annual reports.

EXHIBIT 9 Economic Profit Estimation, UPS

	1985	1986	1987	1988	1989	1990	1991	1992	1993	1994
NOPAT	$ 831,562	$ 847,624	$ 819,396	$ 909,046	$ 917,178	$ 830,912	$ 812,968	$ 912,629	$ 940,269	$ 1,033,291
Beginning capital	$2,333,765	$2,977,489	$3,608,550	$4,445,420	$4,668,509	$6,243,546	$6,599,950	$7,164,016	$7,642,932	$7,919,479
Rate of return	35.63%	28.47%	22.71%	20.45%	19.65%	13.31%	12.32%	12.74%	12.30%	13.05%
WACC										
Long-term debt	$ 150,950	$ 113,882	$ 293,825	$ 140,009	$ 848,036	$ 854,687	$ 830,634	$ 862,378	$ 852,266	$ 1,127,405
PV noncapitalized operating leases	—	—	—	—	—	$ 334,593	$ 451,534	$ 562,073	$ 621,874	$ 635,233
PV of capital leases	385,935	341,656	344,608	345,383	345,265	342,122	333,074	320,616	289,838	233,639
Total	536,885	455,538	638,433	485,392	$1,193,301	$1,531,402	$1,615,242	$1,745,067	$1,763,978	$1,996,277
Average shares outstanding	675,746	675,000	675,000	675,000	647,481	625,481	616,000	595,000	580,000	580,000
Share price	$ 8.25	$ 10.25	$ 12.00	$ 13.38	$ 14.50	$ 15.25	$ 16.00	$ 18.50	$ 20.75	$ 23.50
Market value of equity	$5,574,908	$6,918,750	$8,100,000	$9,028,125	$9,388,477	$9,538,588	$9,856,000	$11,007,500	$12,035,000	$13,630,000
Tax rate	46.00%	46.00%	34.00%	34.00%	34.00%	34.00%	34.00%	34.00%	35.00%	35.00%
U.S. treasury bond yield (30-yr.)	10.74%	8.14%	8.76%	9.11%	8.62%	8.81%	8.24%	7.61%	6.46%	7.43%
Cost of debt (AAA-rated)	10.93%	9.02%	9.32%	9.55%	9.16%	9.34%	8.69%	8.27%	7.16%	7.80%
Beta	1.10	1.01	0.97	0.97	0.96	1.02	1.02	0.94	1.07	1.05
Cost of equity	16.66%	13.59%	14.00%	14.34%	13.82%	14.34%	13.75%	12.68%	12.21%	13.11%
Cost of capital	15.72%	13.05%	13.42%	13.93%	12.94%	13.20%	12.62%	11.69%	11.25%	12.08%
EVA™										
NOPAT/Beginning capital	35.63%	28.47%	22.71%	20.45%	19.65%	13.31%	12.32%	12.74%	12.30%	13.05%
WACC	15.72%	13.05%	13.42%	13.93%	12.94%	13.20%	12.62%	11.69%	11.25%	12.08%
Spread	19.92%	15.41%	9.28%	6.52%	6.70%	0.10%	-0.30%	1.05%	1.06%	0.97%
× Beginning capital	$2,333,765	$2,977,489	$3,608,550	$4,445,420	$4,668,509	$6,243,546	$6,599,950	$7,164,016	$7,642,932	$7,919,479
Annual economic value added	$ 464,804	$ 458,971	$ 334,978	$ 289,955	$ 313,001	$ 6,469	$ (19,902)	$ 75,258	$ 80,720	$ 76,463
Cumulative annual EVA™	$ 464,804	$ 923,775	$1,258,753	$1,548,708	$1,861,710	$1,868,179	$1,848,277	$1,923,534	$2,004,255	$2,080,718

UPS: Measures of Value Creation (billions)

	1985	1994	Change
Cumulative EVA™	0.465	2.081	1.616
Analysis of market value added			
Book value of equity	2.026	4.647	2.621
Interest-bearing debt and equivalents	0.537	1.996	1.459
Capital (book value)	2.563	6.644	4.080
Market value of equity	5.575	13.630	8.055
Interest-bearing debt and equivalents	0.537	1.996	1.459
Capital (market value)	6.112	15.626	9.514
Market value added	3.548	8.983	5.434

Source: Casewriter Analysis of Annual Reports

Part II

Financial Analysis and Forecasting

The Financial Detective, 1996

Financial characteristics of companies vary for many reasons. The two most prominent drivers are industry economics and firm strategy.

Each industry has a financial norm around which companies within the industry tend to operate. An airline, for example, would naturally be expected to have a high proportion of fixed assets (airplanes), while a consulting firm would not. A steel manufacturer would be expected to have a lower gross margin than a pharmaceutical manufacturer, because commodity products like steel are subject to strong price competition, while highly differentiated products like patented drugs enjoy much more pricing freedom. Because of unique economic features of each industry, average financial statements will vary from one industry to the next.

Similarly, companies within industries have different financial characteristics, in part because of varied strategies. Executives choose strategies that will position their company favorably in the competitive jockeying within an industry. Strategies typically entail making important choices in how a product is made (e.g., capital intensive versus labor intensive), how it is marketed (e.g., direct sales versus use of distributors), and how the company is financed (e.g., the use of debt or equity). Strategies among companies in the same industry can differ dramatically. Different strategies can produce arresting differences in financial results for firms in the same industry.

The following paragraphs describe two participants in a number of different industries. Their strategies and market niches provide clues to the financial condition and perfor-

This case was prepared by Mark S. Bonney under the direction of Professor Robert F. Bruner at the Darden Graduate School of Business Administration. This case was written as a basis for class discussion rather than to illustrate effective or ineffective handling of an administrative situation. Copyright © 1996 by the University of Virginia Darden School Foundation, Charlottesville, VA. All rights reserved. *No part of this publication may be reproduced, stored in a retrieval system, used in a spreadsheet, or transmitted in any form or by any means—electronic, mechanical, photocopying, recording, or otherwise—without the permission of the Darden Foundation. For inquiries, please send an e-mail to dardencases@ virginia.edu.* Revised 2/98. Version 1.2.

mance one would expect of them. The companies' common-sized financial statements and operating data as of early 1996 have been presented in a standardized format in Exhibit 1. It is up to you to match the financial data with the company descriptions. Also, try to explain the differences in financial results *across* industries.

HEALTH PRODUCTS

Companies A and B manufacture and market health care products. One firm develops, manufactures, and distributes ethical drugs (pharmaceuticals) to doctors and hospitals through a direct sales force. This firm holds a substantial number of patents on original research. Also it owns shares in joint ventures and small biotech firms as part of a strategy of tapping new research breakthroughs.

The other firm manufactures and nationally mass-markets a broad line of over-the-counter remedies (i.e., nonprescription drugs), name-brand toiletries, and consumer baby care products. Its products are sold to retailers and distributors, from where they are sold directly to consumers. Brand development and management is a major element of this firm's mass-market-oriented strategy.

HOUSEHOLD APPLIANCES

The two home-appliance manufacturers are companies C and D. One focuses on manufacturing and marketing high-quality washers, dryers, dishwashers, and refrigerators under its own brand name. The strategy of this first company is to be the quality leader in the industry, and to charge commensurate prices.

The other company attempts to segment the market for the same products by selling under its own and three private-label brand names. In particular, this second firm is a captive supplier of private-label appliances on a large multiyear contract with one of the leading retailers in the United States.

COMPUTERS

Companies E and F sell computers and related equipment. One company is a mail-order seller of personal computers primarily to the consumer market. This firm is located in modest facilities in a rural region, and it outsources important elements of its manufacturing. The key strategy of this firm is to keep costs low, charge low prices, and achieve high unit sales volumes.

The other company sells its computers through dealers and a sales force. Many of this company's sales are to the business market. This firm has a leading brand name. More of this firm's manufacturing is internal (i.e., rather than outsourced). The key strategy of this firm is to be the quality and service leader in the industry, and to offer a broad product line in its segment.

RETAILING

Companies G and H are two retailers with different marketing emphases. One company is a large, national chain of department stores. This company sells, largely on credit, everything from automotive equipment and services to clothing and household items. Its properties are primarily leased.

The other firm is a rapidly growing chain of consumer home-improvement stores offering a large selection of home-improvement items at low prices. The firm has been called a category killer by virtue of its strategy to underprice the competition, advertise heavily, and enjoy large market share and unit sales volumes. This firm's stores are in a "warehouse" format and are all leased.

HOTELS

Companies I and J are both operators of large hotel/motel chains. One of these two companies owns one of the largest food-service contractors in the country. This firm finances its hotels via off-balance-sheet limited partnerships. The company has significant assets in the form of food service and hotel management contracts. The key strategy of this firm is to manage, not own, its hotels.

The other firm operates a worldwide chain of high-quality hotels and motels in addition to a smaller line of casinos. The key strategy of this firm is to concentrate in the lodging and entertainment businesses, and to own its properties.

NEWSPAPERS

Companies K and L own newspapers. One has a large flagship newspaper that is sold around the country and around the world. Because the company is centered largely around one product, it has strong central controls. Competition for subscribers and advertising revenues in this firm's chosen segment is fierce.

The other firm owns a number of newspapers in relatively smaller communities throughout the Midwest. Some analysts view this firm as holding a portfolio of small local monopolies in newspaper publishing. This company has a significant amount of goodwill on its balance sheet stemming from acquisitions. Key to this firm's operating success is a strategy of decentralized decision making and administration.

BEER

Of the beer companies, M and N, one is a national brewer of mass-market consumer beers under a variety of brand names. This company also owns several theme parks.

The other company is one of a group of "microbrewers" with smaller production volume and higher prices. This company outsources much of its brewing activity and has recently completed a successful initial public offering (IPO) of its stock.

STEEL

Companies O and P manufacture and sell steel. One of the steel companies is a "mini-mill." This company serves a specific segment of the steel market that is not as vulnerable to foreign competition. Being smaller, the firm can fill smaller production orders profitably. Not being as unionized as the rest of the industry, the firm enjoys lower labor costs. The key strategic emphases of this firm are low costs, low prices, and nimble service.

The other company is a large integrated steel producer able to provide a full range of products. While it has higher costs (mainly in labor) it aims to offset this with long production runs in the fulfillment of large contracts.

EXHIBIT 1   Common-Sized Financial Data and Ratios

	Health Products		Appliances		Computers	
	A	B	C	D	E	F
Assets						
Cash and equivalents	7.6	7.5	6.7	1.9	9.5	15.1
Receivables	16.3	10.6	19.6	27.1	40.2	36.1
Inventories	12.7	5.8	12.5	13.2	27.6	20.0
Other current assets	7.8	4.8	4.0	3.2	6.2	5.9
Total current assets	44.4	28.7	42.8	45.4	83.5	77.1
Net fixed assets	29.1	29.4	33.0	22.8	14.2	15.1
Other assets	26.5	41.9	24.2	31.8	2.3	7.8
Total assets	100.0	100.0	100.0	100.0	100.0	100.0
Liabilities and equity						
Accounts payable	9.0	7.1	6.7	12.5	17.7	20.9
Other ST liabilities	15.6	27.4	10.5	36.6	16.6	25.8
Total current liabilities	24.6	34.5	17.2	49.1	34.3	46.7
Long-term debt	11.8	18.0	25.3	12.6	3.8	1.0
Other liabilities	13.0	9.8	27.5	11.9	2.9	2.9
Total liabilities	49.4	62.3	70.0	73.6	41.0	50.6
Equity	50.6	37.7	30.0	26.4	59.0	49.4
Total liabilities and equity	100.0	100.0	100.0	100.0	100.0	100.0
Sales	100.0	100.0	100.0	100.0	100.0	100.0
Cost of goods sold (CGS)	33.1	27.9	74.0	75.6	77.0	83.3
Gross profit	66.9	72.1	26.0	24.4	23.0	16.7
Selling, general and administrative (SG&A)	48.3	42.8	16.5	19.6	14.3	10.0
Loss / (Gain)	0.2	(1.0)	5.8	(0.7)	0.6	(0.4)
Earnings before interest and taxes (EBIT)	18.4	30.3	3.7	5.5	8.1	7.1
Interest expense	0.8	4.2	1.7	1.7	0.0	0.0
Pretax income	17.6	26.1	2.0	3.8	8.1	7.1
Income taxes	4.9	6.8	2.5	1.2	2.7	2.4
Income before minority and extraordinary	12.7	19.3	(0.5)	2.6	5.4	4.7
Minority interests and extraordinary items	0.0	(14.6)	0.2	0.1	0.0	0.0
Net income / (loss)	12.7	33.9	(0.7)	2.5	5.4	4.7
Market data						
Beta	1.10	1.10	1.25	1.55	1.46	1.55
P/E ratio	23.0	24.5	13.7	19.0	17.2	11.2
Market / Book	6.1	5.7	3.4	2.1	2.9	3.3
Dividend payout ratio	34.4%	32.6%	NMF	48.0%	0.0%	0.0%
Liquidity						
Current ratio	1.8	0.8	2.5	0.9	2.4	1.7
Quick ratio	0.3	0.2	0.4	0.0	1.5	0.3
Asset management						
Inventory turnover	2.8	2.1	6.9	6.8	2.7	17.7
Receivables turnover	6.9	4.4	6.2	4.2	5.4	11.2
(Net) fixed asset turnover	3.7	1.6	4.2	5.2	14.4	28.3
Debt management						
Debt to assets	13.6%	31.2%	25.4%	38.2%	3.8%	2.2%
(LT) debt to equity	23.3%	47.7%	84.2%	52.4%	6.5%	2.0%
Times interest earned	24.2	7.2	2.2	3.2	NMF	NMF
DuPont analysis						
Profit margin (1)	12.7%	19.3%	-0.5%	2.6%	5.4%	4.7%
Asset turnover (2)	112.4	46.8	131.3	115.5	211.0	388.1
Return on assets (1) × (2)	14.3%	9.0%	-0.7%	3.0%	11.4%	18.2%

*NMF = Not meaningful.

Retail		Hotels		Newspapers		Beer		Steel	
G	*H*	*I*	*J*	*K*	*L*	*M*	*N*	*O*	*P*
1.8	1.4	13.3	5.5	1.9	2.7	0.9	47.7	7.5	8.8
60.7	4.4	7.0	18.0	10.2	8.2	5.1	21.0	13.7	12.3
12.2	29.7	0.4	4.5	3.3	1.3	5.5	12.1	13.0	13.4
5.1	0.8	2.7	6.3	3.3	1.5	2.7	4.3	1.3	1.7
79.8	36.3	23.4	34.3	18.7	13.7	14.2	85.1	35.5	36.2
15.3	60.7	55.4	20.7	19.3	37.8	63.9	8.0	45.0	63.8
4.9	3.0	21.2	45.0	62.0	48.5	21.9	6.9	19.5	0.0
100.0	100.0	100.0	100.0	100.0	100.0	100.0	100.0	100.0	100.0
18.5	11.2	10.0	20.0	4.3	4.6	6.4	11.2	8.8	9.3
25.6	8.0	7.5	18.0	16.5	10.7	5.3	14.9	9.3	10.1
44.1	19.2	17.5	38.0	20.8	15.3	11.7	26.1	18.1	19.4
30.3	9.8	34.9	20.1	13.5	18.9	30.9	2.4	22.1	4.7
8.5	2.1	6.6	15.7	10.2	18.0	15.5	0.0	37.8	6.1
82.9	31.1	59.0	73.8	44.5	52.2	58.1	28.5	78.0	30.2
17.1	68.9	41.0	26.2	55.5	47.8	41.9	71.5	22.0	69.8
100.0	100.0	100.0	100.0	100.0	100.0	100.0	100.0	100.0	100.0
100.0	100.0	100.0	100.0	100.0	100.0	100.0	100.0	100.0	100.0
65.5	72.3	44.4	21.9	40.3	54.1	65.7	48.8	87.5	83.8
34.5	27.7	55.6	80.1	59.7	45.9	34.3	51.2	12.5	16.2
25.7	19.8	44.1	72.6	35.9	36.4	17.0	45.0	5.6	3.8
(0.1)	0.2	(15.1)	0.3	0.0	(2.0)	1.0	(0.8)	0.4	(0.3)
8.9	7.7	26.6	5.2	23.8	11.5	16.3	7.0	6.5	12.7
3.9	0.0	7.5	0.6	2.7	2.0	2.2	0.2	1.5	0.3
5.0	7.7	19.1	4.6	21.1	9.5	14.1	6.8	5.0	12.4
2.0	3.0	7.0	1.8	8.0	3.9	5.5	(1.5)	1.9	4.5
3.0	4.7	12.1	2.8	13.1	5.6	8.6	8.3	3.1	7.9
(2.2)		0.3	0.0	0.0	0.0	2.4	0.0	0.0	0.0
5.2	4.7	11.8	2.8	13.1	5.6	6.2	8.3	3.1	7.9
1.32	1.40	1.20	1.30	0.80	1.00	1.00	NMF*	1.15	1.20
15.5	32.3	25.8	24.9	19.1	21.2	19.4	56.0	9.2	18.2
3.8	4.7	2.4	1.8	3.4	1.8	3.8	6.8	1.6	3.6
26.4%	12.3%	33.5%	14.1%	34.7%	39.9%	66.8%	0.0%	6.5%	9.0%
1.8	1.9	1.3	0.9	0.9	0.9	1.2	3.3	2.0	1.9
0.0	0.1	0.8	0.1	0.1	0.2	0.1	1.8	0.4	0.5
5.7	5.7	48.0	51.2	27.6	35.6	12.2	8.7	9.4	10.6
1.8	51.8	7.1	13.0	8.4	9.2	18.1	11.6	9.6	12.8
7.5	3.9	0.9	11.0	4.6	2.0	1.6	31.2	3.0	2.5
51.7%	9.8%	42.0%	20.1%	22.1%	19.0%	30.9%	2.5%	25.0%	4.7%
247.4%	14.4%	85.3%	76.5%	24.3%	39.6%	73.8%	3.4%	100.6%	7.7%
2.3	289.2	3.6	8.8	9.0	5.7	7.5	42.5	4.3	47.6
3.0%	4.7%	12.1%	2.8%	13.4%	5.6%	8.6%	8.3%	3.1%	7.9%
99.2	235.6	48.9	248.1	84.1	74.0	97.8	279.0	128.4	161.1
3.0%	11.1%	5.9%	6.9%	11.3%	4.1%	8.4%	23.2%	4.0%	12.7%

Oracle Systems Corporation

The company has experienced phenomenal growth, having doubled in size, year after year, for most of its 13-year history. Lawrence J. Ellison is known for his almost fanatical aggressiveness and take-no-prisoners attitude regarding competitors. "It is not sufficient that I succeed; all others must fail," he once said, paraphrasing Genghis Khan. But now the picture could be changing.[1]

Until 1990 Oracle Systems Corporation had logged a nearly unparalleled record of sustained rapid growth: 118 percent compound annual sales growth from 1982 to 1989. Competitors, investors, and customers had searched the financial results of the company for clues to its success. These searches, however, tended to generate more questions than answers. Now, in the first half of 1990, the company had disclosed unsettling news that triggered a 66 percent drop in the company's share price. This event renewed efforts of outsiders to understand the company: Was the company healthy now in late September 1990? Had management made the right choices in running the company? Was management doing a good job? What represented the real source of value in this company? Investors also wondered what, exactly, was happening in the company that warranted such a dizzying drop in share price.

THE COMPANY

Oracle Systems Corporation was founded in 1979 by Lawrence J. Ellison to commercialize an innovative database management system (DBMS) that he had just developed for an American intelligence agency. The company produced a broad product line of systems,

---

[1]Quoted from Andrew Pollack, "Fast Growth Oracle Systems Confronts the First Downturn," *New York Times,* September 10, 1990. Copyright ©1990 by The New York Times Company. Reprinted by permission.

This case was prepared by Professor Robert F. Bruner from public information with the assistance of Fadi Micaelian. The case was written as a basis for class discussion rather than to illustrate effective or ineffective handling of an administrative situation. Copyright © 1992 by the University of Virginia Darden School Foundation, Charlottesville, VA. All rights reserved. *No part of this publication may be reproduced, stored in a retrieval system, used in a spreadsheet, or transmitted in any form or by any means—electronic, mechanical, photocopying, recording, or otherwise—without the permission of the Darden School Foundation. For inquiries, please send an e-mail to dardencases@virginia.edu.* Rev. 11/97. Version 1.5.

tools, and applications, which by 1990 were portable across all major computing platforms, from personal computer to mainframe. Under Ellison's aggressive leadership, Oracle more than doubled its sales every year from 1980 to 1989; it became the fastest growing software company in the world, and with sales of $971 million in the fiscal year (FY) ended May 31, 1990, was the dominant software producer in its specialty. Exhibits 1, 2, and 3 present the firm's income statements, balance sheets, and financial ratios for 1985–90.

An extremely aggressive business strategy distinguished Oracle from its peers. Outside observers cited four main elements to this strategy:

- *Sell aggressively.* Oracle distributed its products through a proprietary sales force and had 44 offices in the United States alone. This approach allowed close management and control of the field sales force. Sales representatives were given ambitious objectives each quarter. Typically, a quota almost doubled on a yearly basis, while the representative's territory often was reduced. The firm was particularly generous to representatives who achieved or exceeded their objectives. Those who fell short of their quotas were summarily fired. Sales representatives, perceived by some as arrogant and aggressive, often sold Oracle software that was not yet available in order to achieve their quotas. Outsiders attributed the company's marketing style to its founder.
- *Maintain technology and product leadership.* Oracle's current technological leadership benefited from an early lucky decision to use the SQL computer language. Eventually adopted by IBM, this language became the industry standard. Continued development efforts had widened the use of Oracle's software to virtually all types and brands of computer systems. Oracle was the first to offer networking capabilities with its database, and Oracle had aggressively expanded its range of products.

  To maintain its leadership, Oracle recruited aggressively from what it believed were the top five computer schools in the United States (Harvard, the Massachusetts Institute of Technology, Stanford, the University of California at Berkeley, and Carnegie Mellon). Engineers in research and development enjoyed flexible work schedules, higher salaries than the industry average, sizable bonuses, and stock-purchase plans. In 1990 the company built a large headquarters complex in Belmont, California, that included the largest and most modern corporate gymnasium in northern California.
- *Diversify into related fields.* The company had expanded out of the production of software and into computer consulting services and then into the area of systems integration. As the range of Oracle's product line expanded, these compatible services expanded as well.
- *Expand internationally.* Oracle had established subsidiaries and close exclusive distributors in more than 70 countries around the world. Oracle ranked among the top 50 U.S. exporters.

Oracle Systems went public on March 12, 1986, at an issue price of $2.00. Four years later, the share price peaked at $28.375.

THE SOFTWARE INDUSTRY

The broad business sector referred to as computing had, until the 1980s, been dominated by equipment manufacturers. With the advent of personal computers and the increasing competition among hardware vendors, however, the software vendors had become significant players in the computing sector. In the 1980s, customers increasingly made hardware decisions based on software availability. This trend drove the hardware manufacturers to integrate forward into software development, a step with comparatively low capital requirements.

By 1990 the DBMS segment of the software industry included three types of competitors: (1) hardware producers that had integrated forward (e.g., IBM, DEC); (2) specialized database vendors (e.g., Oracle, Ingres, Informix, Sybase, Ashton Tate, Gupta Technologies) whose software could work on a variety of hardware platforms; and (3) many small software houses providing highly specialized DBMS products. One analyst estimated that the market demand for DBMS exceeded \$10 billion.[2] The major buying segment of this market consisted of large corporations that had heterogeneous computing environments. Oracle permitted these firms to link their machines together and share the data. Exhibit 4 reveals that IBM and Oracle dominated the DBMS market. Oracle's revenues had grown faster than IBM's because of Oracle's multiple-platform operating ability.

DISCLOSURES IN MARCH 1990

On March 20, Oracle reported quarter earnings essentially unchanged from the same quarter a year earlier. The company attributed the zero-growth results to the disallowal by auditors of about \$15 million in sales. Many Oracle software contracts were sold on a trial basis, which raised questions about when revenue could be recognized.[3] For the first time, the auditors opined that some of these "sales" would never actually be realized. This surprise triggered rumors about declining product quality, increases in accounts receivable (and doubtful accounts), and reports of sales representatives leaving the company. Upon this revelation, the company's stock price plunged 31 percent from its all-time high of \$28.375 per share (achieved just days before the announcement). Journalists reported the following comments by securities analysts:

---

[2]S. M. Smith et al., "Oracle Systems," Donaldson, Lufkin and Jenrette, 1991.

[3]Accountants acknowledge that *when* revenue can be recognized is a matter of some judgment. Typically, revenues represent not only cash sales but also credit sales. The key point of judgment is when revenue has been earned, or "realized." Once it has been realized, it can be "recognized" in the income statement. Realization depends on (*a*) management's being able to *measure* the revenue (i.e., knowing with fair certainty how much revenue has been earned) and (*b*) the occurrence of a *critical event* at which there is fair certainty that the revenue-generating transaction will be completed. For instance, consider at which moment revenue should be recognized: the "handshake" deal, receipt of a formal order, shipment of the order, receipt of cash? The crucial phrase here is "fair certainty," and it is an important focus of the auditor's work. There are many revenue-recognition methods. Special industries (e.g., consulting, project management, contracting, mining and petroleum, land sales, franchising, and entertainment) have unique recognition techniques.

One prominent accounting textbook states:

A misconception about reported numbers is that they are exact or precise. In spite of the best efforts of managers and internal and external auditors, this is rarely if ever the case. There are many reasons for the lack of precision in accounting measures; some may be attributed to necessarily arbitrary cost allocations or alternative reporting procedures, while others may be a function of the intentional manipulation of reported accounting numbers. [E. R. Brownlee, II; K. R. Ferris; and M. E. Haskins, *Corporate Financial Reporting* (Homewood, IL: Richard D. Irwin, 1990), pp. 80–81.]

There is a credibility issue on the part of management . . . are these random and fragmentary items constrained to this one quarter, or are they symbolic of a longer-term problem? [David Readermann, analyst with Shearson Lehman Hutton]

Management is stretching harder and harder to make their growth objectives. The disallowal of some sales by auditors tells you that the growth is not sustainable; that the business is just not there. [Rick Sherlund, analyst with Goldman, Sachs]

There is a lot of controversy still swirling around Oracle. Most people would consider the first bit of bad news a big red flag and stand clear. I'm still a big fan of the strategy and how well they've done to date. [Mark Findlay, analyst with Soundview Financial Group][4]

Following the announcement and price drop, 20 lawsuits were filed against Oracle. Essentially, these suits alleged fraud and misrepresentation. Investors vented more outrage when it was disclosed that six Oracle officers profited by selling 645,000 shares before the March earnings disclosure. The company denied any wrongdoing.

ANNOUNCEMENT IN SEPTEMBER 1990

On September 25, 1990, Oracle announced its first-ever quarterly loss, $36 million (versus a profit of $11.7 million for the same quarter a year earlier). Ellison told investors that the loss came mainly from a $45 million shortfall in U.S. sales, plus a $25 million write-down resulting from a restructuring of the firm. Oracle's U.S. finance department, which was responsible for the faulty third- and fourth-quarter 1990 financial statements, was merged into the corporate finance department to ensure strict accounting standards. The company also announced that 10 percent of its domestic workforce (about 400 persons) would be laid off. Ellison said,

Oracle is shifting its strategy to emphasize profitability and product quality, instead of market share and sales growth, to meet demands in the maturing market for database applications . . . Implementation of the reorganization just took too long. Several managers responsible for the restructuring have been fired.[5]

Oracle also indicated that its revenue growth for the first fiscal quarter would be only 30 percent, rather than the 50 percent the company had projected. Finally, the company reduced its growth projections for the rest of the year from 50 percent to 25 percent.

At this September announcement, the company's stock price dropped to $8.125. One journalist commented,

Investors had been becoming increasingly wary of Oracle, if only because it was inevitable that the company's breakneck growth would have to slow eventually. Some analysts have also said the company had angered customers, in part by promising more product features than it could deliver in its rush for sales . . . If the suspicions are correct, it would indicate that the company's problems run deeper. . . But Oracle paints a rosier picture, saying it continues to gain market share. "As we adjust to a more conventional growth rate, our company will be stronger than ever," Mr. Ellison said. Some other providers of database software have also seen some softening of business.[6]

---

[4]All quotations are from Lawrence M. Fisher, "Surprise Hurts Oracle Systems," *New York Times,* April 5, 1990.

[5]Quoted from Reuters financial report, September 25, 1990. Copyright ©1990 by The New York Times Company. Reprinted by permission.

[6]Andrew Pollack, "Fast-Growth Oracle Systems Confronts First Downturn," *New York Times,* September 10, 1990.

CONCLUSION

About $2 billion in Oracle Systems' market value of equity evaporated between the end of February and the end of September 1990. Analysts wondered whether this change in value was in fact associated with changes in financial performance in the recent past. The company's share-price performance had been outstanding (as shown in Exhibit 5). What had changed? What was the rate of change? Was the company *unhealthy?* For comparison purposes, Exhibit 6 gives financial ratios for a portfolio of other software companies, and Exhibit 7 presents comparative financial ratio information on the 11 leading producers of relational DBMSs.

EXHIBIT 1 Income Statements, 1984–90 (in thousands except per share amounts)

	Fiscal Year Ended May 31							1990 Quarter Ended	
	1984	1985	1986	1987	1988	1989	1990	Aug. 31	Feb. 28
Revenues									
Licenses	$12,282	$21,902	$44,657	$101,264	$205,435	$417,825	$689,898	$214,799	$245,561
Services	433	1,257	10,726	30,007	76,678	165,848	280,946		
Total revenues	12,715	23,159	55,383	131,271	282,113	583,673	970,844		
Operating expenses									
Sales and marketing	6,431	14,542	27,171	65,651	124,148	272,812	465,074		
Cost of services	—	—	5,644	18,661	51,241	100,987	160,426		
Research and development	2,009	3,886	7,478	9,949	25,708	52,570	88,291	20,615	21,685
General and administrative	1,673	1,989	4,248	8,603	17,121	34,344	67,258	230,187	174,673
Total operating expenses	10,113	20,417	44,541	102,864	218,218	460,713	781,049		
Operating income	2,602	2,742	10,842	28,407	63,895	122,960	189,795	(36,003)	49,203
Other income (expense)	(305)	(157)	(367)	(509)	1,084	(2,715)	(17,135)	7,516	5,342
Income before taxes	2,297	2,585	10,475	27,898	64,979	120,245	172,660		
Taxes	908	1,034	4,579	12,275	22,093	38,479	55,250	(14,796)	14,035
Net income	1,389	1,551	5,896	15,623	42,886	81,766	117,410	$(28,723)	$ 29,826
Earnings per share	$0.11	$0.12	$0.11	$0.12	$0.32	$0.61	$0.86		
Number of shares outstanding	12,340	12,770	54,864	125,028	132,950	135,066	136,826		

Source: Company annual reports.

EXHIBIT 2 Balance Sheets, 1985–90 (in thousands)

| Assets | Fiscal Year Ended May 31 | | | | | | Quarter Ended |
	1985	1986	1987	1988	1989	1990	Aug. 31, 1990
Current assets							
Cash and cash equivalents	$ 599	$12,524	$ 37,557	$ 48,610	$ 49,393	$ 49,828	$ 50,198
Trade receivables	9,032	26,554	65,205	129,999	261,989	468,071	394,648
Other current assets	331	2,393	6,376	13,218	25,551	51,358	76,428
Total current assets	9,962	41,471	109,138	191,827	336,933	569,257	521,274
Property, net	4,491	14,152	26,896	47,554	94,455	171,945	203,887
Computer software development	0	0	4,818	6,920	13,942	33,396	41,707
Other assets	1,010	1,805	2,940	3,267	14,879	12,649	12,245
Total assets	$15,463	$57,428	$143,792	$249,568	$460,209	$787,247	$779,113
Liabilities and stockholders' equity							
Current liabilities							
Notes payable	$ 694	$ 3,164	$ 5,196	$ 6,507	$ 23,334	$ 42,501	$ 34,970
Accounts payable	1,432	4,835	10,645	23,502	51,582	64,922	57,281
Accrued expenses	3,360	11,301	28,737	62,627	88,014	134,028	82,135
Customer advances	897	2,993	3,847	9,547	15,403	42,121	70,011
Total current liabilities	6,383	22,293	48,425	102,183	178,333	283,572	244,397
Long-term debt	1,373	5,641	9,025	5,363	39,208	94,065	165,643
Deferred income taxes	340	843	3,686	7,379	12,114	22,025	10,397
Stockholders' equity	7,367	28,651	82,656	134,643	230,554	387,585	358,676
Total liabilities and stockholders' equity	$15,463	$57,428	$143,792	$249,568	$460,209	$787,247	$779,113

Note: Accounts receivable (A/R) are net of these allowances for doubtful accounts:

		% of A/R	% of A/R (Restated)
1987	$ 6,628,000	10.2	
1988	$10,102,000	7.8	
1989	$16,829,000	6.4	
1990	$28,445,000	6.1	14.2

The 1990 allowance for doubtful accounts was restated to $66,445,000.

Source: Company annual reports.

EXHIBIT 3   Analytical Financial Ratios, 1985–90

	Fiscal Year Ended May 31					
	1985	*1986*	*1987*	*1988*	*1989*	*1990*
Current ratio	1.56	1.86	2.25	1.88	1.89	2.01
Quick ratio	1.51	1.75	2.12	1.75	1.75	1.83
Debt/Total assets	13.37%	15.33%	9.89%	4.76%	13.59%	17.35%
Days' sales outstanding	142	175	181	168	164	176
Debt/Equity	0.28	0.31	0.17	0.09	0.27	0.35
Times interest earned	17.46	29.54	55.81	58.94	45.29	11.08
Inventory turnover	69.97	23.14	20.59	21.34	22.84	18.90
Asset turnover	1.50	0.96	0.91	1.13	1.27	1.23
Operating profit margin	11.84%	19.58%	21.64%	22.65%	21.07%	19.55%
Net profit margin	6.70%	10.65%	11.90%	15.20%	14.01%	12.09%
Return on total assets	10.03%	10.27%	10.86%	17.18%	17.77%	14.91%
Return on equity	21.05%	20.58%	18.90%	31.85%	35.47%	30.29%

Source: Company annual reports.

EXHIBIT 4 Percentage Shares of Market for Database Management Systems Expected in 1991

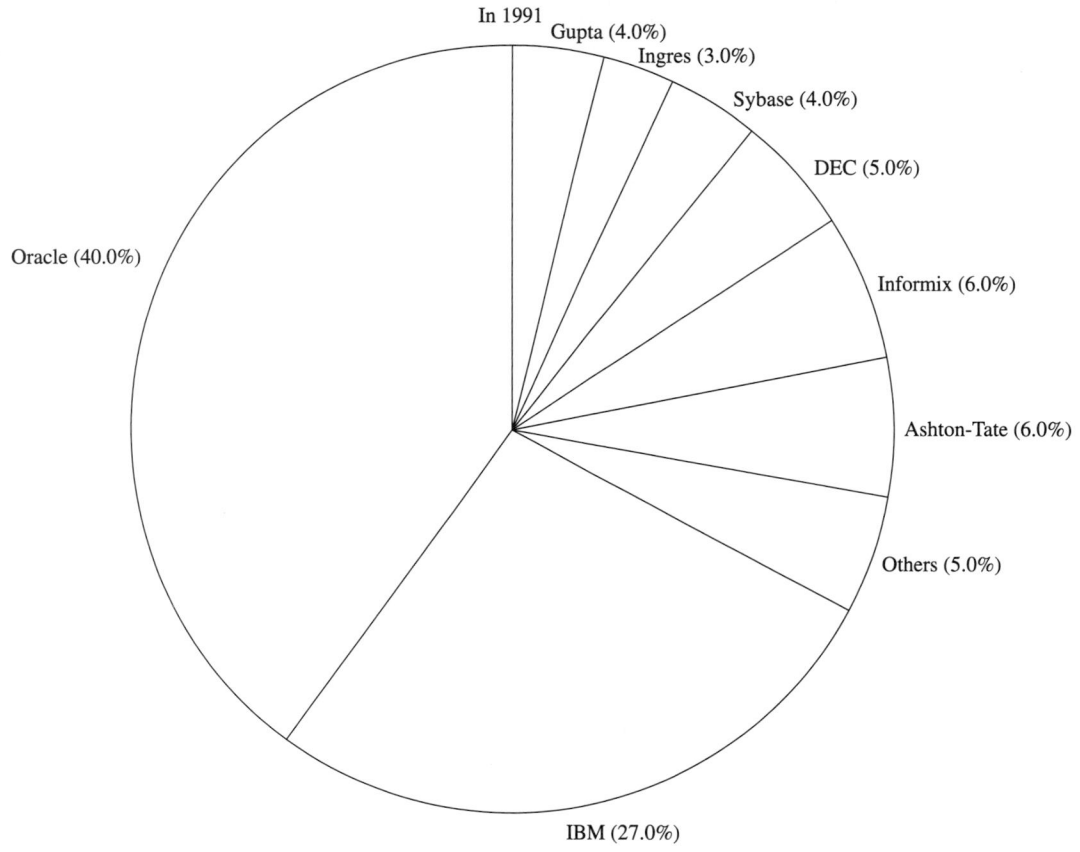

Expected Worldwide Market Share in DBMS

In 1991

Gupta (4.0%)

Ingres (3.0%)

Sybase (4.0%)

DEC (5.0%)

Informix (6.0%)

Oracle (40.0%)

Ashton-Tate (6.0%)

Others (5.0%)

IBM (27.0%)

Source of market share estimates: Datamation.

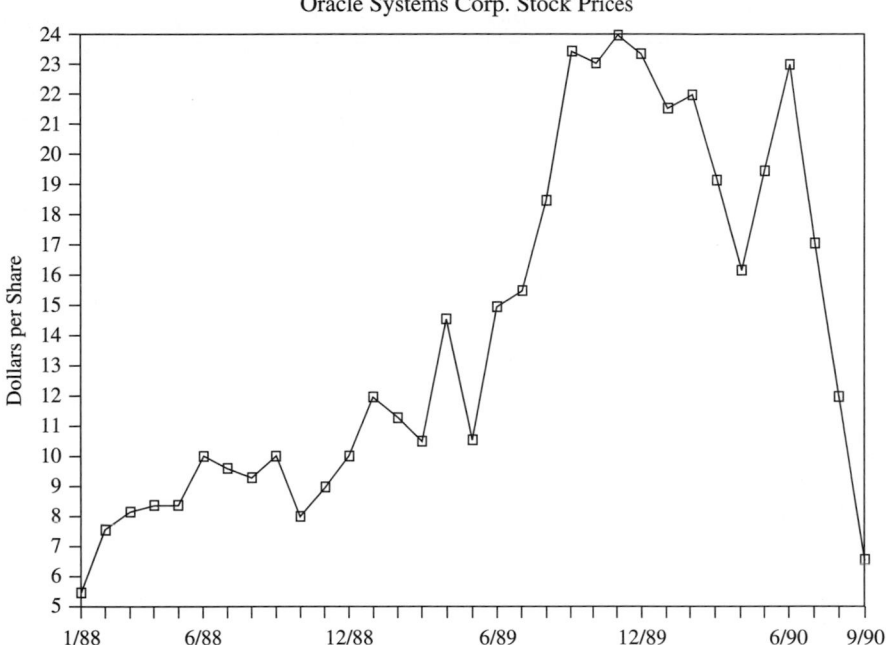

EXHIBIT 5   Oracle Systems Month-End Share Prices, Adjusted for Stock Splits

Note: This graph presents Oracle share prices at month-ends. The all-time high share price, $28.375, occurred in mid-month, March 1990.

Source of data: *Daily Stock Price Record: Over-the-Counter,* New York: Standard & Poor's Corporation, quarterly volumes from Q1 1998 to Q3 1990.

"Reprinted by permission of Standard & Poor's, a division of The McGraw Hill Companies."

EXHIBIT 6   Common-Sized Financial Statements of Computer-Software Producers' Averages, 1986–90
(in percentages)

	1986	1987	1988	1989	1990
Income statement					
Sales	100.0	100.0	100.0	100.0	100.0
Costs and expenses	80.6	79.9	79.0	78.9	82.3
Operating income	19.4	20.1	21.0	21.1	17.7
Depreciation	6.1	6.1	5.9	5.3	5.2
Interest	1.0	1.1	0.8	1.0	1.1
Special items	0.9	−0.7	0.0	0.0	0.0
Income taxes	4.9	5.4	5.2	4.7	4.1
Net income	6.5	8.2	9.1	10.1	7.3
Common dividends	1.6	1.2	1.1	1.5	1.3
Balance sheet: Assets					
Cash and equivalents	28.8	24.2	20.1	17.2	19.2
Receivables	22.9	26.0	27.9	32.4	31.8
Inventories	1.3	1.7	1.7	1.7	1.5
Other current assets	6.1	4.3	3.3	3.7	3.5
Total current assets	59.2	56.2	53.0	55.0	55.9
Net property, plant, and equipment	26.8	19.5	20.0	19.1	17.5
Intangibles	9.7	8.5	9.2	10.0	9.1
Other assets	4.3	15.9	17.7	15.8	17.5
Total assets	100.0	100.0	100.0	100.0	100.0
Balance sheet: Liabilities and equity					
Notes payable	0.8	0.8	0.8	0.9	3.3
Current long-term debt	1.4	1.4	1.4	0.7	0.9
Accounts payable	3.3	3.8	3.8	4.5	3.9
Taxes payable	6.6	6.2	5.7	5.9	5.7
Accrued expenses	5.1	3.7	3.2	5.0	5.8
Other current liabilities	8.5	9.2	9.8	9.0	9.8
Total current liabilities	25.7	24.6	24.6	26.1	29.4
Long-term debt	18.7	12.2	11.0	11.2	5.8
Deferred taxes	1.4	2.6	3.7	3.4	3.5
Investment tax credit	0.9	0.0	0.0	0.0	0.0
Other liabilities	2.4	2.3	1.8	1.9	1.7
Common stock	1.1	1.0	0.9	2.1	2.0
Capital surplus	12.0	23.1	22.8	19.4	19.0
Retained earnings	38.6	37.6	41.0	43.9	46.6
Less treasury stock	−0.8	−3.3	−5.8	−8.0	−8.1
Total liabilities and equity	100.0	100.0	100.0	100.0	100.0

Note: The companies on which this exhibit is based include Autodesk, Automatic Data, Computer Associates, Computer Sciences, Lotus Development, Novell, Oracle, Shared Medical Systems, and Cullinet.

Source: Standard & Poor's Corporation, *Industry Surveys 1,* July 1992.
"Reprinted by permission of Standard & Poor's, a division of The McGraw Hill Companies."

EXHIBIT 7 Financial Ratios for Competitors in Database Management Software

	Ask Computer (FY 6/90)	BMC Software (FY 3/90)	Borland International (FY 3/90)	Computer Associates (FY 3/90)	Informix Corp. (12/89)	Lotus Development (12/89)	Microsoft Corp. (FY 6/90)	Oracle Systems (FY 5/90)	Platinum Technology (12/89)	Progress Software (11/89)	Software Publisher (FY 9/90)	Sybase, Inc. (12/89)
Business focus	DBMS	DBMS	Broad line	Broad line	DBMS	Broad line	Broad line	DBMS	DBMS	DBMS	Broad line	DBMS
Previous four quarters' sales	$112 mm	$110 mm	$262 mm	$1.25 bn	$14.9 mm	$652 mm	$1.3 bn	$980 mm	$11.1 mm	$26.9 mm	$140 mm	$89 mm
Liquidity ratios												
Quick ratio	1.88	2.97	2.54	2.13	2.68	3.39	3.37	1.51	1.99	1.54	3.64	2.00
Current ratio	2.01	3.26	2.92	2.20	2.94	3.73	3.85	1.75	1.99	1.67	3.95	2.07
Sales/Cash	0.35	1.66	8.79	11.32	5.76	2.02	2.63	18.39	12.93	3.61	1.78	3.43
Activity ratios												
Receivables turnover	3.42	9.53	27.20	2.11	2.00	5.69	6.54	2.18	2.57	4.24	7.38	2.23
Days' sales outstanding	105	38	13.23	170	180	63	55	165	140	85	48.8	161
Inventory turnover	53.6	NA	290	49.16	27.46	24	21.3	NA	NA	46.23	73.4	NA
Days' inventory outstanding	6.67	NA	1.24	7.32	13.11	15	16.9	NA	NA	7.8	4.9	NA
Sales/Net working capital	40.5	1.86	8.87	3.14	2.05	1.85	2.22	3.90	4.32	4.5	1.77	2.54
Sales/Plant and equipment	20.18	4.64	18.63	3.90	6.68	3.55	3.64	5.33	37.7	9.62	11.83	4.79
Sales/Current assets	2.03	1.29	5.78	1.72	1.35	1.36	1.64	1.68	2.15	1.80	1.32	1.31
Sales/Assets	1.25	1.00	4.36	0.86	1.01	0.92	1.07	1.20	2.03	1.48	1.17	1.01
Sales/Employees	220,028	205,396	649,407	180,348	122,570	198,583	210,017	134,546	NA	NA	214,033	105,385
Leverage ratios												
Liabilities/Assets	0.32	0.34	0.38	0.32	0.48	0.54	0.17	0.56	0.48	0.54	0.25	0.49
Liabilities/Capital	0.47	0.52	0.51	0.46	0.86	0.68	0.20	1.00	0.90	1.08	0.34	0.97
Liabilities/Equity	0.47	0.52	0.61	0.47	0.93	1.17	0.20	1.27	33.47	1.15	0.34	0.97
Times interest earned	37.8	NA	NA	NA	NA	NA	NA	10.77	NA	31.66	NA	7.76
Total debt/Equity	0.01	NA	0.19	0.03	NA	0.73	NA	0.30	NA	0.11	NA	NA
Assets/Equity	1.47	1.52	1.61	1.47	1.93	2.17	1.20	2.27	1.90	2.15	1.34	1.97
Profitability ratios												
Net income/Sales	0.02	0.19	−0.04	0.10	0.04	0.12	0.24	0.09	0.06	0.09	0.14	0.06
Net income/Assets	0.03	1.19	−0.19	0.08	0.04	0.11	0.25	0.11	0.12	0.13	0.16	0.06
Net income/Capital	0.04	0.29	−0.26	0.12	0.08	0.14	0.30	0.19	0.23	0.25	0.22	0.12
Net income/Equity	0.04	0.29	−0.31	0.12	0.09	0.24	0.30	0.24	8.66	0.27	0.22	0.12

Source: *Disclosure Database* (Bethesda, MD: Disclosure Incorporated, 1990).

The Body Shop International PLC: An Introduction to Financial Modeling

Finance bored the pants off me; I fell asleep more times than not.[1]

Anita Roddick, founder and managing director,
The Body Shop International

Roddick, as self-righteous as she is ambitious, professes to be unconcerned [with financial results] . . . "Our business is about two things: social change and action, and skin care," she snaps. "Social change and action come first. You money-conscious people . . . just don't understand." Well, maybe we don't but we sure know this: Roddick is one hell of a promoter . . . She and her husband, Gordon, own shares worth not far from $300 million. Now that's social action.[2]

In the late 1980s and early 1990s, The Body Shop International PLC was one of the fastest growing manufacturer-retailers in the world. Focusing on the production and sales of naturally based skin and hair care products, the company boasted 1,102 outlets spread across Europe, North America, and Japan. The Body Shop was headquartered in Britain. In the fiscal years ended February 28, 1991 and 1992, the sales of The Body Shop grew by 37 and 28 percent, respectively. This dramatic success notwithstanding, some analysts worried that

---

[1] Anita Roddick, *Body and Soul* (London: Ebury Press, 1991), p. 105.
[2] Jean Sherman Chatzky, "Changing the World," *Forbes,* March 2, 1992, p. 87.

This case was written by Susan Shank and John Vaccaro under the direction of Professors Robert Bruner and Robert Conroy as a basis for class discussion rather than to illustrate effective or ineffective handling of an administrative situation. Copyright © 1996 by the University of Virginia Darden School Foundation, Charlottesville, VA. All rights reserved. *No part of this publication may be reproduced, stored in a retrieval system, used in a spreadsheet, or transmitted in any form or by any means—electronic, mechanical, photocopying, recording, or otherwise—without the permission of the Darden School Foundation. For inquiries, please send an e-mail to dardencases@virginia.edu.* Rev. 10/97. Version 2.1.

large retailers would successfully imitate the firm's products and merchandising format and that the decline in sales growth in 1992 was an early indication of future competition. In the face of these concerns, Anita Roddick lent iconoclastic leadership to the company and a deep commitment to quality natural products, customer satisfaction, and social activism. She seemed to disavow any interest in the financial performance of the firm.

Suppose that Roddick came to you in the spring of 1992 for assistance in near-term and long-range planning for The Body Shop. As a foundation for this work you will need to estimate The Body Shop's future earnings and financial needs. The challenge of this advisory work should not be underestimated: Anita Roddick is a talented manager with little taste for finance and financial jargon. Your projections must not only be technically correct, but they must also yield practical insights and be straightforward. What you have to say and how you say it are equally important.

AN OVERVIEW OF FINANCIAL FORECASTING

In seeking to respond to Roddick's request, you can draw on at least two classical forecasting methods and a variety of hybrids that use some of each method. The two methods are

T-account forecasting. This method starts with a base year of financial statements (e.g., last year). Entries through double-entry bookkeeping determine how each account will change and what the resulting new balances will be. While exactly true to the mechanics of how funds flow through the firm, this method is cumbersome and may require a degree of forecast information about transactions unavailable to many analysts outside (and even inside) a firm.

Percent-of-sales forecasting. This method starts with a forecast of sales and then estimates other financial statement accounts based on some presumed relationship between sales and that account. While simple to execute, this technique is easily misused. For instance, some naive analysts may assume that operational capacity can increase in fractional amounts with increases in sales—but can an airline company really buy only half a jumbo jet? Operational capacity usually increases in "lumps" rather than by smooth amounts. The lesson here is that when you use this technique, you should scrutinize the percent-of-sales relationships for their reasonableness.

The most widely used approach is a hybrid of these two. For instance, T-accounts are used to estimate shareholders' equity and fixed assets. Percent-of-sales is used to estimate income statements, current assets, and current liabilities, because the latter items may credibly vary with sales. Other items will vary as a percentage of accounts other than sales: Tax expense will usually be a percentage of pretax income, dividends will vary with after-tax income, and depreciation will usually vary with gross fixed assets.

A FORECAST WITH PENCIL AND PAPER

Prepare a pro forma (or projected) income statement and balance sheet for The Body Shop for 1993 (income statement for the entire year; balance sheet for year-end). All values should be in pounds sterling. Use the following assumptions as a guide:

Sales	£191,673,000 (a 30 percent increase over 1992)
Cost of goods sold (COGS)	44 percent of sales
Distribution and administration (D&A) expense	36 percent of sales
Interest expense	10 percent of debt (about the current interest rate)
Profit before tax	Sales − COGS − D&A − Interest
Tax	35 percent of profit before tax (the going corporate tax rate in Britain)
Dividends	19 percent of profit after tax
Earnings retained	Profit after tax − Dividends
Current assets	42 percent of sales
Fixed assets	£58,657,000
Total assets	Current assets + Fixed assets
Current liabilities	35 percent of sales
Debt	Total assets − Current liabilities − Shareholders' equity
Common equity	£74,360,000 plus retentions to earnings

Income statement. Begin with sales, and use it to estimate COGS and D&A. For the time being, leave interest expense at zero since we do not yet know the amount of debt. Estimate profit before tax, tax expense, profit after tax, dividends, and earnings retained.

Balance sheet. Estimate current assets (42 percent of sales) and add that to £58,657,000 to get an estimate for total assets. Next, estimate current liabilities (35 percent of sales) and common equity. Debt becomes the "plug" figure that makes the two sides of the balance sheet balance. This amount is your estimate of the external financing The Body Shop will need by year-end 1993. Estimate the plug by subtracting the amounts for current liabilities and common equity from total assets.

Iterate. Initially, you entered an interest expense of zero on the income statement. But this cannot be correct if debt is outstanding. This is a classic problem in finance arising from the dependence of the income statement and balance sheet on each other: Interest expense is necessary to estimate retained earnings, which is necessary to estimate debt. Let's call this the problem of circularity. The way to deal with this problem is to insert your best estimate of interest expense in the income statement (using 10 percent times debt), then reestimate the plug figure, then reestimate interest expense, and so on. By *iterating* through the two statements four or five times, you will come to estimates of interest expense and debt that do not change very much further. Stop iterating when changes get to be small.

A FORECAST WITH A SPREADSHEET MODEL

Fortunately, the tedium of iterating can be eliminated with the aid of a computer and spreadsheet software such as Lotus, Excel, and Quattro Pro. The specific commands reviewed here relate to Lotus v. 4 and Excel v. 5. (These commands will appear in table form within the text. The Lotus commands will be in the left column, and the Excel commands will be in the right column.) The adaptation to other spreadsheet programs should be straightforward. Try the same forecast for The Body Shop using a computer spreadsheet.

Setup. Start with a clean spreadsheet. Set the recalculation mode to MANUAL so that the model will iterate only when you press CALC [F9]. The commands here are:

Lotus	*Excel*
/WGRM	Choose the Tools menu and then the Options menu item Then choose the Calculations tab and select the button next to Manual.

Use the format in Exhibit 1 as a guide to plan your worksheet. To facilitate sensitivity analysis, it is generally best to place the "Input Data" at the top of the worksheet. You may wish to widen column A at this point. A width of 20 is usually enough.

Lotus	*Excel*
/WCS	Select column A by clicking the top of the column on the letter A. Choose the Format menu and then the Column menu item, and then the Width submenu item. Enter the width (20) and choose OK.

Viewing. You may find splitting the screen handy so that you can see the different sections of the worksheet simultaneously. The [F6] key will move your cursor to either side of the window.

Lotus	*Excel*
Place the cursor at the point where you want to split and enter /WWH.	Place the cursor at the point where you want to split and choose the Window menu, and then the Split menu item.
To remove the split, enter /WWC.	To remove the split, choose the Window menu, and then the Remove Split item.

Saving. As you develop your model, be sure to save it onto a disk every five minutes or so just for insurance.

Lotus	*Excel*
/FS	Choose the File menu, and then the Save menu item.

Format. Next, develop the income statement just as you did by pencil and paper. Use Exhibit 2 as a guide. Be sure to tie the cells to the proper percentage rate in the Input Data section. (It is probably best to "point" with the cursor the first several times.) The first time through, enter 0 for interest. We will return to it later.

Now do the balance sheet. Again, be sure to tie the balance sheet together by formulas. Don't forget to tie starting equity to earnings retained (see Exhibit 2, lines 13, 25, and 35.)

With the basic format laid out, go back and enter the formula to calculate interest as "interest rate times debt." Press the [F9] key and you should see the worksheet change. (In order to watch, split your worksheet again.) You should be able to press the [F9] key several more times until the numbers stop changing, which means the model has converged to a solution. You should have interest as exactly 10 percent of long-term liabilities and a balance sheet that balances.

Once you have seen how this works, you may want to have the model converge without having to press CALC several times. In order to do this, you must set the number of iterations you wish the spreadsheet to perform. In this case, 4 or 5 should do.

Lotus	*Excel*
Enter/WGRI, and then 4 or 5.	Choose the Tools menu, and then the Options menu item. Then choose the Calculations tab and check the box next to Iterations. Enter the number of iterations (4 or 5).

Your worksheet should now look like Exhibit 3.

PROJECTING FARTHER

So far you have managed to project The Body Shop's financial statements through 1993. Now extend your projection to 1994 and 1995. A simple way to do this is to copy your model for the two additional years.

Lotus	*Excel*
It will be easiest to copy the entire range of your data by entering /C, and then pointing to the data.	Select the range of your data by highlighting it in the worksheet. Choose the Edit menu and then the Copy menu item.
Press <Enter> and then move the cursor to the cell where you want the upper left hand of the copy to begin (C17). Press <Enter>again.	Highlight the cells where you want the copy to go (C17 and D17). Choose the Edit menu and then the Paste menu item.

Note that you will have to change the equity formula for 1994 and 1995. For 1994, enter 1993's equity, +B35, and add 1994's additions to retained earnings. Also, you should make sales grow by compounding. To do this, multiply 1993's sales, +B17, times 1994's expected sales growth rate (say, 28 percent). As you enter these changes, you should see the effect ripple through your model. Next, make sure that if you've referenced cells B3 through B13 anywhere in cells B17 through B36, the references are absolute references as opposed to relative references. (An absolute reference means that when you copy cells B17 through B36 to other parts of your spreadsheet, the cells are still linked back to the originals, for example, B5. Otherwise, the program assumes that the cells should be linked to new cells, for example, C5. To make a reference absolute, put in dollar signs—B3 instead of B3.)

WHEN DEBT IS NEGATIVE

Now modify the model to deal with the situation where the plug for debt is negative—this can happen routinely for firms with seasonal or cyclical sales patterns. Negative debt can be interpreted as excess cash. But this is an odd way to show cash; a nonfinancial manager (like Anita Roddick) might not appreciate this type of presentation. The solution is to add a line for "excess cash" on the assets side of the balance sheet and then set up three new lines below the last entry in the balance sheet:

Name	*Formula*
Trial assets	Current assets + Fixed assets
Trial liabilities and equity	Current liabilities + Equity
Plug	Trial assets − Trial liabilities

Now enter the formula for excess cash:

Lotus	*Excel*
@IF(PLUG<0,−PLUG,0)	=IF(PLUG<0,−PLUG,0)

Instead of the word "PLUG" you should use the cell address for the actual plug number. The formula for DEBT is:

Lotus	*Excel*
@IF(PLUG>0,+PLUG,0)	=IF(PLUG>0,+PLUG,0)

See Exhibit 4 for an example of how your spreadsheet should look. To see how these modifications really work, change your COGS/SALES assumption to 0.60 and press [F9].

With excess cash, you might want to add the interest you would draw on marketable securities. Add a new input, INTEREST ON MARKETABLE SECURITIES, and a new line to the income statement. Enter the formula to calculate the amount and fix the total formulas to account for the new line. (This is optional, and not shown in Exhibit 5.)

An example of finished results appears in Exhibit 5.

EXPLORE SENSITIVITIES

After your model replicates the exhibit, you are ready to conduct a sensitivity analysis on the pro forma years by seeing how variations in the forecast assumptions will affect the financing requirements. Try the following variations one at a time (then, later, in combination).

- Suppose sales in 1993 will be £250 million.
- Suppose COGS runs at 55 percent of sales.

- Suppose dividends are increased to 50 percent of net income.
- Suppose that The Body Shop must double its manufacturing capacity by adding a new £60 million facility in 1993.
- Assume inventories run higher than expected (model this by increasing current assets to 55 percent of sales).
- Assume that accounts receivable collections improve so that current assets run at 40 percent of sales.
- Assume that distribution and administration expense increases faster than sales.

What happens to the plug value (i.e., debt) under these different circumstances? In general, which assumptions in the Input Data section of your spreadsheet seem to have the biggest effect on future borrowing needs?

The "Data Table" is an invaluable tool for conducting a sensitivity analysis. It automatically calculates debt (or whatever else you want to focus on) as it varies across different values for a particular assumption, such as growth rates. In Lotus 1-2-3 and Excel, you can create a data table in a two-step process illustrated in the following examples. Suppose that you want to estimate The Body Shop's debt required and excess cash generated at COGS/SALES ratios of .45, .55, .65, .66, .67, .70, and .75.

1. *Set up the table.* Move to a clean part of the spreadsheet and type the COGS/SALES ratios in a column. At the top of the next column enter the location value to be estimated, debt, or +B34. In the next column type the cell location for excess cash, +B28. Your data table should be formatted as in Exhibit 6.
2. *Set the program to iterate automatically.* Rather than pressing [F9] continually, tell the computer to do it for you. If you want it to iterate automatically 5 times, then type the following commands:

Lotus	*Excel*
/WGRI5	Choose the Tools menu and then the Options menu item. Then choose the Calculations tab and check the box next to Iterations. Enter the number of iterations (5).

3. *Enter the data table commands.*

Lotus	*Excel*
Type/DT1.	Highlight cells C9 to E16.
The program will ask you to identify the range of the table; using the pointer, highlight the entire area of the table, from C9 to E16.	Choose the Data menu and then the Table menu item.
Press <Enter>.	
The program will ask you to specify where the COGS/SALES assumption is in your analysis. Using the arrow keys, point to B5 or simply type it in. Press <Enter>.	In the Column Input Cell box, enter the cell where your COGS/SALES assumption is (B5).
The computer will fill in the table.	The computer will fill in the table.

The result should look like Exhibit 7.

The data table in Exhibit 7 reveals that at COGS/SALES ratios higher than 66 percent, the firm will need to borrow. This should trigger questions in your mind about what might cause that to happen, such as a price war or a surge in materials costs. Your spreadsheet format can tell you about more sophisticated data-table formats. No financial analyst can afford to ignore this valuable tool.

MS. RODDICK WANTS TO KNOW . . .

Now that you have completed a simplified forecast, prepare a forecast based on the full range of accounts as actually reported by The Body Shop in 1992. Exhibit 8 presents the results for the past three years. Please forecast all of the accounts individually for the next three years: You will see many familiar accounts, as well as some unusual accounts like minority interests. [3] Also, please make "overdrafts" (i.e., short-term bank loans) the plug figure, and base interest expense (at 10 percent) on both the long-term liabilities and overdrafts. You should get a very different forecast of financing needs than was derived on the preceding pages of this note. The reason is that in the preceding example, overdrafts were bundled with all other current liabilities; therefore, interest on overdrafts was ignored. Use your knowledge about the basic mechanics of forecasting to generate this more detailed forecast.

The average expectation of securities analysts was that The Body Shop's revenues would grow at the rate of 28 percent per year over this period, although the growth estimates ranged from a high of 75 percent to a low of 10 percent. Make other assumptions as needed. Prepare to report to Roddick your answers to the following questions:

- How did you derive your forecast? Why did you choose the "base case" assumptions that you did?
- Based on your pro forma projections, how much additional financing will The Body Shop need during this period?
- What are the three or four most important assumptions ("key drivers") in this forecast? What is the effect on financing need of varying each of these assumptions up or down from the base case? Intuitively, *why* are these assumptions so important?
- Why are your findings relevant to a general manager like Roddick? What are the implications of these findings for her? What action should she take based on your analysis?

In discussing your analysis with Roddick, do not permit yourself to get mired in forecast technicalities or financial jargon. Focus your comments on your results; state them as simply and intuitively as you can. Do not be satisfied with simply presenting results. Link your findings to recommendations: key factors to manage; opportunities to enhance results; issues warranting careful analysis. Remember that Roddick plainly admits she finds finance boring; whenever possible, try to express your analysis in terms that she finds interesting: people, customers, quality natural products, and the health and dynamism of her business. Good luck!

---

[3] Minority interests arise where The Body Shop owns less than 100 percent of an asset (i.e., shares ownership with a minority owner) and yet consolidates 100 percent of the earnings and asset values into the financial statements. The minority interest entries in the income statement and balance sheet in effect adjust for The Body Shop's less than full ownership.

EXHIBIT 1   Format for Developing a Spreadsheet Model

	A	B
1		
2		
3	Input Data	
4	SALES	191,673
5	COGS/SALES	.44
6	D&A/SALES	.36
7	INTEREST RATE	.10
8	TAX RATE	.35
9	DIVIDENDS/NET PROFITS	.19
10	CURR. ASSETS/SALES	.42
11	CURR. LIABS./SALES	.35
12	FIXED ASSETS	58,657
13	STARTING EQUITY	74,360
14		
15	INCOME STATEMENT	**1993**
16		
17	SALES	
18	COGS	
19	D&A	
20	INTEREST EXPENSE (INCOME)	
21	PROFIT BEFORE TAX	
22	TAX	
23	PROFIT AFTER TAX	
24	DIVIDENDS	
25	EARNINGS RETAINED	
26		
27	BALANCE SHEET	**1993**
28		
29	CURRENT ASSETS	
30	FIXED ASSETS	
31	TOTAL ASSETS	
32		
33	CURRENT LIABILITIES	
34	DEBT	
35	EQUITY	
36	TOTAL LIAB. & NET WORTH	

EXHIBIT 2 Spreadsheet Formulas

	A	B
1		
2		
3	Input Data	
4	SALES	191,673
5	COGS/SALES	.44
6	D&A/SALES	.36
7	INTEREST RATE	.10
8	TAX RATE	.35
9	DIVIDENDS/NET PROFITS	.19
10	CURR. ASSETS/SALES	.42
11	CURR. LIABS./SALES	.35
12	FIXED ASSETS	58,657
13	STARTING EQUITY	74,360
14		
15	INCOME STATEMENT	**1993**
16		
17	SALES	+B4
18	COGS	+B5*B17
19	D&A	+B6*B17
20	INTEREST EXPENSE (INCOME)	+B7*B34
21	PROFIT BEFORE TAX	+B17-B18-B19-B20
22	TAX	+B8*B21
23	PROFIT AFTER TAX	+B21-B22
24	DIVIDENDS	+B9*B23
25	EARNINGS RETAINED	+B23-B24
26		
27	BALANCE SHEET	**1993**
28		
29	CURRENT ASSETS	+B10*B17
30	FIXED ASSETS	+B12
31	TOTAL ASSETS	+B29+B30
32		
33	CURRENT LIABILITIES	+B11*B17
34	DEBT	+B31-B33-B35
35	EQUITY	+B13+B25
36	TOTAL LIAB. & NET WORTH	+B33+B34+B35

EXHIBIT 3 Basic Forecasting Results for 1993.

	A	B
1		
2		
3	Input Data	
4	SALES	191,673
5	COGS/SALES	.44
6	D&A/SALES	.36
7	INTEREST RATE	.10
8	TAX RATE	.35
9	DIVIDENDS/NET PROFITS	.19
10	CURR. ASSETS/SALES	.42
11	CURR. LIABS./SALES	.35
12	FIXED ASSETS	58,657
13	STARTING EQUITY	74,360
14		
15	INCOME STATEMENT	**1993**
16		
17	SALES	191,673
18	COGS	84,336
19	D&A	69,002
20	INTEREST EXPENSE (INCOME)	(2,372)
21	PROFIT BEFORE TAX	40,706
22	TAX	14,247
23	PROFIT AFTER TAX	26,459
24	DIVIDENDS	5,027
25	EARNINGS RETAINED	21,432
26		
27	BALANCE SHEET	**1993**
28		
29	CURRENT ASSETS	80,503
30	FIXED ASSETS	58,657
31	TOTAL ASSETS	139,160
32		
33	CURRENT LIABILITIES	67,086
34	DEBT	(23,718)
35	EQUITY	95,792
36	TOTAL LIAB. & NET WORTH	139,160

EXHIBIT 4 Adjusting to Reflect Excess Cash

	A	B
1		
2		
3	Input Data	
4	SALES	191,673
5	COGS/SALES	.44
6	D&A/SALES	.36
7	INTEREST RATE	.10
8	TAX RATE	.35
9	DIVIDENDS/NET PROFITS	.19
10	CURR. ASSETS/SALES	.42
11	CURR. LIABS./SALES	.35
12	FIXED ASSETS	58,657
13	STARTING EQUITY	74,360
14		
15	INCOME STATEMENT	**1993**
16		
17	SALES	191,673
18	COGS	84,336
19	D&A	69,002
20	INTEREST EXPENSE (INCOME)	+(B7*B34)-(B7*B28)
21	PROFIT BEFORE TAX	40,706
22	TAX	14,247
23	PROFIT AFTER TAX	26,459
24	DIVIDENDS	5,027
25	EARNINGS RETAINED	21,432
26		
27	BALANCE SHEET	**1993**
28	EXCESS CASH	@IF(B40<0,-B40,0) ◄───
29	CURRENT ASSETS	80,503
30	FIXED ASSETS	58,657
31	TOTAL ASSETS	+B29+B30+B28
32		
33	CURRENT LIABILITIES	67,086
34	DEBT	@IF(B40>0,+B40,0) ◄───
35	EQUITY	95,792
36	TOTAL LIAB. & NET WORTH	+B33+B34+B35
37		
38	TRIAL ASSETS	+B29+B30
39	TRIAL LIABILITIES AND EQUITY	+B33+B35
40	PLUG: DEBT (EXCESS CASH)	+B38-B39
41		
42	**Important note: The boxed formulas are in Lotus format. In Excel:**	
43		
44	B28	=IF(B40<0,-B40,0)
45	B34	=IF(B40>0,+B40,0)

EXHIBIT 5   Finished Results

	A	B
1		
2		
3	Input Data	
4	SALES	191,673
5	COGS/SALES	.44
6	D&A/SALES	.36
7	INTEREST RATE	.10
8	TAX RATE	.35
9	DIVIDENDS/NET PROFITS	.19
10	CURR. ASSETS/SALES	.42
11	CURR. LIABS./SALES	.35
12	FIXED ASSETS	58,657
13	STARTING EQUITY	74,360
14		
15	INCOME STATEMENT	**1993**
16		
17	SALES	191,673
18	COGS	84,336
19	D&A	69,002
20	INTEREST EXPENSE (INCOME)	(2,372)
21	PROFIT BEFORE TAX	40,706
22	TAX	14,247
23	PROFIT AFTER TAX	26,459
24	DIVIDENDS	5,027
25	EARNINGS RETAINED	21,432
26		
27	BALANCE SHEET	**1993**
28	EXCESS CASH	23,718
29	CURRENT ASSETS	80,503
30	FIXED ASSETS	58,657
31	TOTAL ASSETS	162,877
32		
33	CURRENT LIABILITIES	67,086
34	DEBT	0
35	EQUITY	95,792
36	TOTAL LIAB. & NET WORTH	162,877
37		
38	TRIAL ASSETS	139,160
39	TRIAL LIABILITIES AND EQUITY	162,877
40	PLUG: DEBT (EXCESS CASH)	(23,718)

EXHIBIT 6   Setup for a Data Table

	A	B	C	D	E
1					
2					
3	Input Data				
4	SALES	191,673	Sensitivity Analysis		
5	COGS/SALES	.44	Debt and Excess Cash		
6	D&A SALES	.36	By COGS/SALES		
7	INTEREST RATE .	.10			
8	TAX RATE	.35	COGS/SALES	DEBT	Ex. CASH
9	DIVIDENDS/NET PROFITS	.19		+B34	+B28
10	CURR. ASSETS/SALES	.42	.75		
11	CURR. LIABS./SALES	.35	.70		
12	FIXED ASSETS	58,657	.67		
13	STARTING EQUITY	74,360	.66		
14			.65		
15	INCOME STATEMENT	**1993**	.55		
16			.45		
17	SALES	191,673			
18	COGS	84,336			
19	D&A	69,002			
20	INTEREST EXPENSE (INCOME)	(2,372)			
21	PROFIT BEFORE TAX	40,706			
22	TAX	14,247			
23	PROFIT AFTER TAX	26,459			
24	DIVIDENDS	5,027			
25	EARNINGS RETAINED	21,432			
26					
27	BALANCE SHEET	**1993**			
28	EXCESS CASH	23,718			
29	CURRENT ASSETS	80,503			
30	FIXED ASSETS	58,657			
31	TOTAL ASSETS	162,877			
32					
33	CURRENT LIABILITIES	67,086			
34	DEBT	0			
35	EQUITY	95,792			
36	TOTAL LIAB. & NET WORTH	162,877			
37					
38	TRIAL ASSETS	139,160			
39	TRIAL LIABILITIES AND EQUITY	162,877			
40	PLUG: DEBT (EXCESS CASH)	(23,718)			

EXHIBIT 7 A Finished Data Table

	A	B	C	D	E
1					
2					
3	Input Data				
4	SALES	191,673	Sensitivity Analysis		
5	COGS/SALES	.44	Debt and Excess Cash		
6	D&A SALES	.36	By COGS/SALES		
7	INTEREST RATE .	.10			
8	TAX RATE	.35	COGS/SALES	DEBT	Ex. CASH
9	DIVIDENDS/NET PROFITS	.19		+B34	+B28
10	CURR. ASSETS/SALES	.42	.75	9,305	0
11	CURR. LIABS./SALES	.35	.70	3,979	0
12	FIXED ASSETS	58,657	.67	783	0
13	STARTING EQUITY	74,360	.66	0	282
14			.65	0	1,348
15	INCOME STATEMENT	**1993**	.55	0	12,000
16			.45	0	22,653
17	SALES	191,673			
18	COGS	84,336			
19	D&A	69,002			
20	INTEREST EXPENSE (INCOME)	(2,372)			
21	PROFIT BEFORE TAX	40,706			
22	TAX	14,247			
23	PROFIT AFTER TAX	26,459			
24	DIVIDENDS	5,027			
25	EARNINGS RETAINED	21,432			
26					
27	BALANCE SHEET	**1993**			
28	EXCESS CASH	23,718			
29	CURRENT ASSETS	80,503			
30	FIXED ASSETS	58,657			
31	TOTAL ASSETS	162,877			
32					
33	CURRENT LIABILITIES	67,086			
34	DEBT	0			
35	EQUITY	95,792			
36	TOTAL LIAB. & NET WORTH	162,877			
37					
38	TRIAL ASSETS	139,160			
39	TRIAL LIABILITIES AND EQUITY	162,877			
40	PLUG: DEBT (EXCESS CASH	(23,718)			

EXHIBIT 8 Historical Financial Statements (in £ thousands)

	1990 (£)	1990 (% Sales)	1991 (£)	1991 (% Sales)	1992 (£)	1992 (% Sales)
			Fiscal Year Ended February 28			
Income statement						
Turnover	84,480	100.0	115,599	100.0	147,441	100.0
Cost of sales	36,831	43.6	50,393	43.6	68,210	46.3
Gross profit	47,649	56.4	65,206	56.4	79,231	53.7
Distribution expense	19,767	23.4	27,494	23.8	32,021	21.7
Administrative expense	11,008	13.0	15,725	13.6	19,335	13.1
Net interest expense	2,366	2.8	1,950	1.7	2,672	1.8
Profit before tax	14,508	17.2	20,037	17.3	25,203	17.1
Tax expense	5,519	6.5	7,311	6.3	8,688	5.9
Profit after tax	8,989	10.6	12,726	11.0	16,515	11.2
Minority interest	454	0.5	623	0.5	120	0.1
Ordinary dividends	1,558	1.8	2,261	2.0	2,995	2.0
Profit retained	6,977	8.3	9,842	8.5	13,400	9.1
Assets						
Cash	239	0.3	344	0.3	483	0.3
Accounts receivable	9,358	11.1	18,298	15.8	26,485	18.0
Inventories	23,360	27.7	33,484	29.0	38,457	26.1
Other current assets	6,981	8.3	8,597	7.4	9,576	6.5
Net fixed assets	31,442	37.2	45,598	39.4	58,657	39.8
Total assets	71,380	84.5	106,321	92.0	133,658	90.7
Liabilities and equity						
Accounts payable	8,577	10.2	9,307	8.1	10,112	6.9
Taxes payable	5,351	6.3	7,002	6.1	6,157	4.2
Accruals	2,369	2.8	2,752	2.4	3,356	2.3
Overdrafts	19,404	23.0	12,708	11.0	29,748	20.2
Other current liabilities	2,722	3.2	4,374	3.8	4,687	3.2
Long-term liabilities	5,991	7.1	3,480	3.0	5,128	3.5
Minority interests	974	1.2	1,552	1.3	292	0.2
Shareholders' equity	25,992	30.8	65,149	56.4	74,178	50.3
Total liabilities and equity	71,380	84.5	106,324	92.0	133,658	90.7

Padgett Paper
Products Company

Negotiations with Padgett Paper Products Company had been going on for almost a year. Francis Libris hoped the time had come when they could be pushed to a mutually satisfactory conclusion. If not, Padgett might seek another bank as its source of funds. Alternatively, Libris would be subject to criticism by his superiors for failing to deliver on his commitment to manage and structure the relationship properly. Libris was vice president of the Caslon Trust Company of Richmond, Virginia, one of Virginia's largest banks. He was responsible for the Broad Street Commercial Lending Center of the bank, to which Padgett's account was assigned because its small executive offices were on an upper floor of the same building in which the center was located. It was a significant account for the center and an important one to its profitability.

Padgett had borrowed small amounts off and on from Caslon since it had first established an account with the bank in 1947. Even the acquisition of several small companies (for less than $1 million each) in the 1980s did not require high levels of debt. The acquisition of a long-coveted competitor at an attractive price on short notice in early 1996 brought Padgett suddenly to the bank, asking for an additional $3.6 million loan. Combined with the $3.6 million already outstanding at that time, Caslon's total exposure could rise to $7.2 million, well in excess of the $5 million advised credit line that had been approved for the company. The request was granted nevertheless, under an internal guidance line of $8 million, and the rate was continued at prime. Libris had been working since then to structure the arrangements on a more orderly basis than 90-day notes with no protective covenants.

It was now January 1997. Libris hoped to have the new terms worked out so they could be reflected on the financial statements for the 1997 fiscal year that would end April 30. There was a chance that a negotiation completed before the auditors finished their fieldwork, roughly two months after the April ending of Padgett's fiscal year,

This case was prepared from material written by Paul H. Hunn, Visiting Lecturer, whose cooperation is acknowledged with appreciation. Copyright © 1996 by the University of Virginia Darden School Foundation, Charlottesville, VA, 22906. All rights reserved.

could be incorporated in the auditor's report. Libris preferred, however, to have the agreement signed before the end of the fiscal year to avoid this complication.

Libris wondered whether he should take a fresh look at the situation. He had originally tried to persuade Padgett's management to finance part of the company's requirements in the form of long-term debt from a life insurance company. When the financial vice president declined the private-placement proposal, Libris decided to see how the loan could be repaid to the bank within the period initially suggested by his superiors. As time had gone on, he began to think that these constraints might not be appropriate to the situation and that a more creative solution might prove acceptable both to departmental senior management and to Padgett's management. Because Libris knew he would have to get the approval of his superiors before he undertook a different initiative with Padgett's management, time was getting exceedingly short. He had to develop both the implications of the original decision and of any alternatives that appeared more attractive.

PADGETT PAPER PRODUCTS COMPANY

Padgett Paper Products Company, a closely held but publicly traded (over-the-counter) company, manufactured a variety of stationery products including notebooks, loose-leaf binders, forms, and filler paper for students and record-keeping purposes. The company was over 100 years old. Its ownership remained primarily with the descendants of the founders, now a large and widely spread group. Few family members were active in the company's management, and the major connection with most of the owners came in the form of the quarterly dividend check. A few members of the family depended on the dividends for most of their income. Most of the shareholders considered Padgett just another investment, and an illiquid one at that because the market for the company's stock was extremely thin. A significant payout was considered important by management.

Management, which was primarily professional, appeared competent, responsible, and reasonably effective. Its expertise was largely in operations, which were carried on at several plants in the Mid-South, and in marketing, which was controlled out of the executive office in Richmond. Management was not financially oriented, Libris had observed.

Padgett's customers were some 5,000 wholesalers and retailers in the United States and Canada. No single customer or small group of customers accounted for a substantial share of Padgett's sales. Terms were 2/10, net 30, but few customers took the discount. Many stretched payment for an additional 30 days. The business had a slight seasonal peak in the late summer when big back-to-school sales took place. Because the company tried to maintain level production to reduce unit cost in the highly competitive market, a seasonal variation of about $2 million occurred in its borrowing pattern. The peak occurred in the summer.

A consolidation had been taking place in the business since the late 1970s, initially caused by the high inflation rate of the period that made it difficult for small firms to finance their current assets. Financial difficulties and inventory problems resulting from the subsequent recession in the early 1980s further reduced the level of the competition. Changes in the tax rules periodically provided new impetus for the smaller companies to sell. The sharp drop in the stock market in October 1987 had frightened some owners into selling out. Most recently, a sudden increase in paper prices, which had risen over 50 percent from mid-1994 and exceeded the previous high prices of 1988–89, had again created financial strains for firms such as Tri-State Tablet. These pressures had become great enough, and the price-earnings multiples attractive enough because of the booming equity market, that many of the remaining owners (including Tri-State's) put their firms on the market. Tri-State had not been able to pass all the price increases through to its customers because of strong competition from large, integrated paper companies. In Padgett's case, a drop in its tax rate helped compensate for smaller margins.

Over the years, many of Padgett's competitors had been acquired by national corporations with strong marketing skills and good financial resources. The response of Padgett's management had been to acquire smaller companies that fit into its product or marketing needs. The acquisition of its competitor, Tri-State Tablet Company, in April 1996 was the culmination of these efforts.

Padgett's financial statements for fiscal year 1996 had been given an unqualified opinion by the national CPA firm that audited them. Straight-line depreciation was used for reporting purposes, with accelerated depreciation used for taxes. Inventory had been valued on a lower of cost (FIFO) or market basis despite the potential cash savings from the favorable tax effect if there were a change to LIFO. Padgett's management had always concluded that it was not worth the complexity to change inventory accounting methods. Financial statements for the 1993–96 fiscal years are presented in Exhibits 1 and 2. Exhibit 3 is a standard computerized spread used by Caslon's credit department to organize a company's financial statements for analysis.

PADGETT'S RELATIONSHIP WITH CASLON TRUST

Caslon Trust had historically been Padgett's only lending bank and was its only lending bank in early 1997. Among other benefits of this relationship, Padgett used Caslon Trust as the depository for its substantial Virginia and federal tax payments. So far during the 1997 fiscal year, Padgett's average collected balance with Caslon had been $524,000. Affiliated companies and subsidiaries had balances that had averaged $231,000. The loan balances outstanding had ranged from $3.3 to $7.2 million, with an average of $5.05 million. The loan had last been cleaned up for an extended period from March 31, 1993, to January 8, 1994.

Padgett maintained a small deposit relationship with the Phoenix Bank, a major North Carolina bank that had long been soliciting a more important role in the company's financial arrangements. In addition, several local banks were used to service the various plant locations.

The speed with which the Tri-State Tablet acquisition had been made had not allowed for careful planning of the financial arrangements. Libris's group management had been reluctant to double the loan to Padgett without a carefully structured financial program as well as appropriate protective covenants. With Libris's assurance that these questions could be quickly resolved, the group's senior vice president had authorized the loan and established a new temporary credit limit of $8 million. It had been expected, however, that the loan would be formally structured long before January 1997, which was a source of embarrassment to Libris. He knew he also would be embarrassed and his profit plan damaged if he should lose the account to Phoenix.

Once the dust created by the acquisition had settled down, Libris met with John Ruhl, Padgett's financial vice president, to discuss the company's plans. Based on these conversations, Libris and Caslon's credit department prepared a preliminary financial forecast for Padgett's 1997–2000 fiscal years. Summary figures from this forecast are presented in Exhibit 4.

Libris was distressed to note that, even under what he thought were assumptions that minimized the need for funds, Padgett would still have $4.4 million in short-term debt on the books at the end of the fiscal year 2000. Assuming the company could generate about $1 million in "undedicated" cash each subsequent year, a total of eight years would be required to retire the debt. This was considerably longer than the typical bank five-year term loan that a company of Padgett's size might expect. Caslon was willing to stretch to six years for important relationships, but a seven-year term loan would be considered a bit long for a company like Padgett, which did not enjoy the financial flexibility afforded firms having easy entry to the public capital markets.

Libris decided that a need of this duration appropriately called for insurance company financing. After he had met with officers of several companies, he wrote Ruhl to propose a 12- to 15-year loan and to quote terms an insurance company might offer. (Libris's letter is reproduced as Exhibit 5.) He also pointed out that Caslon might be able to structure an arrangement that would allow the bank to take the seasonal needs while the insurance company would take the long-term core requirements of $5 million.

Ruhl's response was emphatically negative. While he appreciated the information, he reported that management believed the current long-term fixed rates were too high. Although it was tempting to take advantage of the fact that long-term corporate rates had not yet returned to their early-1995 peak, his board was somewhat pessimistic about the future of the economy. "Politicians like low rates before elections," he said, "but they pay the piper afterwards. I think they're pumping up the economy now. We'll probably have high rates soon after the election, and then we'll have a recession. Maybe that will be the time to lock in really low rates." He admitted, however, that a repeat of the interest-rate runup of the 1970s would again have a serious effect on Padgett.

Furthermore, Padgett's management did not like the idea of an elaborate set of covenants. Ruhl said that he particularly disliked the type of covenant that could throw the company in default without management's explicit action. "Violation of a debt/capital ratio, for instance," explained Ruhl, "could occur as the result of an adverse year rather than anything we do. I don't mind agreeing not to borrow or pay dividends if certain conditions would result, but I just don't see agreeing to a lot of things that are out of my control. I can't see getting tied up in all these technicalities." Ruhl indicated that he did not see anything wrong with the present friendly, informal loan. "After all," he said, "if you don't like what we're doing—anything at all—you can call your entire loan at the end of any 90-day period. Isn't this better protection for you than fancy agreements?"

In the months that followed this disappointing outcome, Libris met frequently with Ruhl to get a thorough understanding of the business. He planned to prepare a forecast of future needs that would accurately reflect Padgett management's thinking and his own insights into the company. By late in 1996, preliminary estimates for the 1997 fiscal year were becoming available so Libris could incorporate them into his forecasts. The forecasts, which were prepared showing the effects of 5 percent, 10 percent, and 15 percent growth in sales over the 1998–2000 fiscal years, are included as Exhibit 6.

Ruhl thought that this effort was most helpful, although he noted that two last-minute changes should be incorporated in the planning. First, he had finally persuaded Padgett's directors that a shift to LIFO inventory valuation would save more cash than the cost of implementing the system. LIFO would be adopted for the 1997 fiscal year, which would result in a tax benefit of $500,000. Second, management had decided to dispose of a redundant warehouse that had been part of the Tri-State acquisition. Management expected to receive $700,000 from the cash sale and tax refunds on the book loss.

ALTERNATIVES

Libris still thought that splitting the loan—maybe with the bank's own real estate department—had promise. For instance, Padgett owned outright a large, general-purpose warehouse. Its appraisal value of $3 million was more than the amount at which it was carried on the books. Although Libris was not an experienced real-estate lending officer, he believed the property would be attractive collateral for a mortgage loan. Another alternative might be to wait until the loan had been partly retired and then invite another bank to share the remainder for the duration of the repayment. Part of the loan could be rotated between banks to allow each a cleanup period of several months. Finally, he had discovered that Padgett's small Canadian operation was self-contained with a negligible amount of intercompany transfers and charges. With net current assets of $1.8 to $2.0 million to offer as collateral and no direct debt, the Canadian subsidiary could probably raise $1.0 million from Canadian banks. The Canadian banks would require a "floating charge," a form of security agreement, against all current assets of the subsidiary.

Although U.S. banking law and practice was not identical to Canadian and British practice with respect to "floating liens," asset-based finance might offer useful alternatives. It would be expensive to take effective security against Padgett's receivables because the company had so many customers and the average account was small. A factoring arrangement might be suitable, in which Padgett could sell its accounts on a nonrecourse basis to a commercial finance company. Caslon Bank itself did not operate a factoring function, however. It would be necessary to find one that had experience in the paper distribution business or the costs of the factoring, which were usually about 2 percent of accounts purchased, would be too high. On the other hand, if Padgett factored its accounts, it could eliminate its credit department and would have no bad debts.

Caslon could always grant credit against the security of the accounts receivable even though the bank would not monitor the accounts as closely as a factor would. The loan would be limited to a percentage of receivables to provide some protection against losses. A security interest in the inventory also could be required, although the granting of this security could upset some major paper companies who were Padgett's sources of supply.

MONEY MARKET CONSIDERATION AND PRICING ASPECTS

Funds were readily available in the financial markets in January 1997. Although the prime rate had risen rapidly during 1994, it had then declined modestly during 1995 and 1996 to 8¼ percent. The prime's low in recent years had been 6 percent from mid-1992 to early 1994. Thirty-day commercial paper was currently yielding 5.38 percent. The Treasury yield curve was relatively flat: 90-day bills yielded 5.04 percent; 1-year notes, 5.6 percent; 5-year notes, 6.10 percent; 10-year bonds, 6.59 percent; and 30-year bonds, 6.73 percent. During the recent election campaign, however, there had been much debate about whether the economy was growing too slowly or too rapidly. Rates had therefore been very volatile. Whenever the market began to suspect that the Federal Reserve would raise rates to curb inflation, rates spiked up.

The interest-rate volatility was an issue that Libris would have to address in preparing a proposal for Ruhl. Should the loan (or loans) be priced at a fixed rate or at a floating rate? Fixed-rate loans were generally offered at a premium of 1/2 to 1 percent above the floating rate.

In adjusting the prime rate to the conditions of the borrower, Caslon bank officers often used what they termed a risk-premium system. This approach added or subtracted 25 basis points (1/4 percent) to the price for such factors as the size of the company's sales (add points for small size and lack of access to public markets), purpose, term, escalating versus level payments, debt profile, liquidity posture, and relationship benefits (for example, subtract points for balances, tax payments, and corporate trust). Of course, the final rate had to be checked against the market, which in Padgett's case was highly competitive as the result of Phoenix's interest.

Because of the complications that had already been experienced and that were likely to arise while completing the negotiations, Libris knew that he had no more time to collect information. He had to work quickly toward a satisfactory resolution of the loan structure with Padgett's management.

EXHIBIT 1   Income Statements for the Fiscal Years Ended April 30, 1993–96
(thousands of dollars except per share figures)

	1993	1994	1995	1996
Net sales	$26,331	$27,219	$36,897	$41,308
Cost of goods sold	15,728	16,077	21,937	24,555
Depreciation and amortization*	—	510	667	739
	$10,603	$10,632	$14,293	$16,014
General and administration expense	5,814	5,087	7,139	7,821
Selling expense†	—	1,878	2,603	3,147
Operating expenses	$ 5,814	$ 6,965	$ 9,742	$10,968
Operating profit	$ 4,789	$ 3,667	$ 4,551	$ 5,046
Interest expense	—	32	220	379
Other expenses (income)	83	(42)	(39)	(71)
Profit before taxes	$ 4,706	$ 3,677	$ 4,370	$ 4,738
Income taxes	2,702	1,893	2,216	2,132
Profit after taxes	$ 2,004	$ 1,784	$ 2,154	$ 2,606
Number of shares (000)	1,000	1,115	1,116	1,118
Earnings per share	$ 2.00	$ 1.60	$ 1.93	$ 2.33
Dividends per share	1.00	1.00	1.00	1.00

*Included in cost of goods sold in 1993.

†Included in general and administrative expenses in 1993.

EXHIBIT 2   Balance Sheets as of April 30, 1993–96 (thousands of dollars)

	1993	*1994*	*1995*	*1996*
Assets				
Current assets				
Cash and securities	$ 1,691	$ 266	$ 658	$ 834
Accounts receivable	4,734	5,542	6,350	7,754
Inventory	7,276	7,743	10,959	14,360
Prepayments and other	233	194	153	563
Total current assets	$13,934	$13,745	$18,120	$23,511
Property, plant, equipment	—	8,718	11,265	12,468
Less: Accumulated depreciation	—	3,384	4,912	5,209
Net property, plant, equipment	$ 4,797	$ 5,334	$ 6,353	$ 7,259
Other assets	59	257	386	224
Total assets	$18,790	$19,336	$24,859	$30,994
Liabilities and owners' equity				
Current liabilities				
Short-term notes	$ —	$ —	$ 3,118	$ 7,221
Accounts payable	1,127	1,619	2,158	1,958
Accruals	395	397	703	1,014
Other current liabilities	271	251	418	824
Current portion, long-term debt	615	117	51	52
Total current liabilities	$ 2,408	$ 2,384	$ 6,448	$11,069
Long-term debt	338	221	507	455
Deferred taxes	538	568	714	756
Other liabilities	136	126	116	151
Total liabilities	$ 3,420	$ 3,299	$ 7,785	$12,431
Owners' equity				
Common stock	5,587	5,587	5,587	5,587
Retained earnings	9,783	10,450	11,487	12,976
Total owners' equity	$15,370	$16,037	$17,074	$18,563
Total liabilities and net worth	$18,790	$19,336	$24,859	$30,994

EXHIBIT 3   Cash-Flow and Ratio Analysis, Fiscal Years Ended April 30, 1993–96 (dollar figures in thousands)

	1993	*1994*	*1995*	*1996*
Sources				
Profit after taxes plus depreciation and amortization*		$ 2,294	$ 2,821	$ 3,345
Deferred taxes		30	146	42
New long-term debt		—	337	—
New short-term debt		—	3,118	4,103
Accounts payable		492	539	(200)
Accruals		2	306	311
Other current liabilities		(20)	167	406
Other liabilities		(10)	(10)	35
Total sources		$ 2,788	$ 7,424	$ 8,042
Uses				
Dividends paid in cash		$ 1,117	$ 1,117	$ 1,117
Capital expenditure		979	1,575	1,530
Repayment of long-term debt		615	117	51
Accounts receivable		808	808	1,404
Inventory		467	3,216	3,401
Prepayments and other current assets		(39)	(41)	410
Other assets		198	129	(162)
Intangibles*		68	111	115
Total uses		$ 4,213	$ 7,032	$ 7,866
Change in cash and securities		$ (1,425)	$ 392	$ 176
Working capital	$11,526	$ 11,361	$11,672	$12,442
Profitability				
Sales growth	n.a.%	3.4%	35.6%	12.0%
Gross profit margin	40.3	39.1	38.7	38.8
Operating expenses ÷ Sales	22.1	25.6	26.4	26.5
Pretax margin	17.9	13.5	11.8	11.5
After-tax margin	7.6	6.6	5.8	6.3
Return on average owners' equity	n.a.	11.4	13.0	14.6
Return on total assets	10.7	9.2	8.7	8.4
EBIT ÷ Total assets	25.0	19.2	18.5	16.5
Dividend payout	50.2	62.6	51.9	42.9
Turnover on Sales				
Receivables	5.6×	4.9×	5.8×	5.3×
Inventory	3.6	3.5	3.4	2.9
Accounts payable	23.4	16.8	17.1	21.1
Working capital	2.3	2.4	3.2	3.3
Fixed asset	5.5	5.1	5.8	5.7
Net worth	1.7	1.7	2.2	2.2
Leverage				
Total debt ÷ Owners' equity	22.3%	20.6%	45.6%	67.0%
Long-term debt ÷ Owners' equity	2.2	1.4	2.9	2.4
Interest coverage	n.a.×	115.9×	20.9×	13.5×
Liquidity				
Quick ratio	2.7×	2.4×	1.1×	.8×
Current ratio	5.8	5.8	2.8	2.1

*Intangibles amortized as purchased.

EXHIBIT 4   Summary Figures from Preliminary Projection of Financial Position, Fiscal Years Ending
April 30, 1997–2000 (millions of dollars)

	1997	1998	1999	2000
Sources of funds				
Net sales	$55.2	$60.7	$66.8	$73.5
Profit after taxes	3.3	3.6	4.2	4.8
Noncash charges	.9	.9	1.0	1.1
Cash generated from operations	$ 4.2	$ 4.5	$ 5.2	$ 5.9
Disposition of assets	.2	—	—	—
Total sources	$ 4.4	$ 4.5	$ 5.2	$ 5.9
Uses of funds				
Dividends	$ 1.1	$ 1.1	$ 1.1	$ 1.1
Increase in working capital*	2.4	2.4	3.1	3.6
Capital expenditures	1.0	1.0	1.0	1.0
	$ 4.5	$ 4.5	$ 5.2	$ 5.7
Effect on short-term debt				
*Including retirement of short-term debt	.7	.2	.8	1.1
Leaving a balance in short-term debt of	$ 6.5	$ 6.3	$ 5.5	$ 4.4

Assumptions:
1. 10 percent sales growth.
2. 6.0 to 6.5 percent after-tax margin.
3. Accounts receivable turnover 5.7 (17.5 percent of sales).
4. Inventory turnover 3.6 (27.8 percent of sales).
5. Accounts payable turnover 21.3 (4.7 percent of sales).
Totals may not add because of rounding.

EXHIBIT 5 Libris's Letter Outlining Proposed Term-Loan Arrangement

---

Caslon Trust Company
Broad Street Commercial Lending Center
1111 Broad Street
Richmond, Virginia

May 15, 1996

Mr. John Ruhl
Vice President–Finance
Padgett Paper Products Company
Richmond, Virginia

Dear John:

Thank you for the opportunity last week to review the financial plans you have for Padgett. This letter sets forth our thoughts relating to the need for properly incorporating your bank loan into these plans.

Currently, Padgett has $6,853,000 outstanding in short-term 90-day notes, and we understand that an additional $1.0 to $1.5 million is likely to be borrowed to support new receivables of your new acquisition. This is in contrast with the circumstance of May 1994, when we financed your previous acquisition and our loan outstanding increased from $500,000 to $1,850,000. At that time, an anticipated restructuring of the loan was postponed until a clearer definition of longer-term corporate cash need could be ascertained.

In late 1995, we expressed an interest in discussing with you a restructuring of the then loan outstanding so that legitimately long-term funds could be sourced on a proper long-term basis. Our subsequent conversations and cash-flow study were complicated by the anticipated major acquisition and its impact.

Enclosed is a copy of our most recent Padgett forecast, the results of which we have jointly reviewed. On balance, our feeling is that the forecast may tend to understate the cash requirement in that it assumes moderate sales growth, the upholding of traditional margins, and tight control over capital expenditures and dividends. The forecast does seem to indicate a long-term need of at least $5 million, which cannot be properly funded through the bank on anything resembling a full-payout term-loan basis.

Given what appears to be the clear nature of the need, it seems appropriate that financing discussions with an insurance company be initiated. This suggestion is rooted in our firm feeling that it is strategically unwise from the

---

EXHIBIT 5   *(concluded)*

---

standpoint of the company, as well as that of the bank, to fulfill substantial long-term financial need through the continued use of 90-day notes.

On a confidential basis and without revealing your name, we have talked with three insurance companies within the last week. Discussions included the following generalized parameters for life insurance company lending:

Amount:	No problem.
Term:	12–15 years.
Rate:	Fixed, 9.5 percent minimum.
Payback:	Level payments desired, but flexibility offered (e.g., three years of grace).
Prepayment:	All want protection designed to discourage it; however, there are provisions for prepayment without penalty if they were to turn you down for a requested increase in amount and you were able to obtain a commitment from another source.
Availability of money:	Good.

Caslon would continue to provide for Padgett's seasonal working-capital financing on a floating-prime-rate basis. Our pricing, based on the structure of the long-term debt outlined, would probably be prime plus 0.5 percent.

We all recognize the fact that interest rates have started to rise again; however, our Economics Department does not feel that long-term interest rates will see reduced levels in the foreseeable future. Financing demands on the capital markets are expected to continue strong, inflation psychology seems to be rising, the deficits are not yet under control, and any advantage to be gained in avoiding the long-term market is, at best, marginal. It might, in fact, be dangerous.

For any needs consistent with prudent bank lending, Caslon Trust stands ready to finance your business. Our desire to assist in every way we can is complete and sincere.

> Sincerely,
>
> Frank
>
> Francis X. Libris
> Vice President

EXHIBIT 6 Projected Financial Statements for Fiscal Years Ending April 30, 1998–2000, Assuming 5, 10, and 15 Percent Sales Growth (dollar figures in millions except per share figures)

	1996 Actual	1997 Estimate	5% Growth			10% Growth			15% Growth		
			1998	1999	2000	1998	1999	2000	1998	1999	2000

A. Income Statements

	1996 Actual	1997 Estimate	1998	1999	2000	1998	1999	2000	1998	1999	2000
Sales, net	$41.32	$57.80	$60.69	$63.72	$66.91	$63.58	$69.94	$76.93	$66.47	$76.44	$87.91
Cost of sales	24.56	36.08	37.27	38.86	40.81	39.05	42.65	46.93	40.82	46.61	53.61
Depreciation and amortization	0.74	0.94	0.91	1.00	1.10	0.91	1.00	1.10	0.91	1.00	1.10
General and administrative	7.82	10.23	10.75	11.29	11.87	11.27	12.42	13.69	11.81	13.64	15.72
Selling expense	3.15	4.61	4.84	5.09	5.35	5.08	5.60	6.15	5.30	6.11	7.03
Operating profit	$ 5.05	$ 5.94	$ 6.92	$ 7.48	$ 7.78	$ 7.27	$ 8.27	$ 9.06	$ 7.63	$ 9.08	$10.45
Interest expenses*	0.38	0.95	0.80	0.72	0.61	0.89	0.84	0.77	.97	1.01	1.05
Other expenses (income)	(.07)	(.71)	0.07	0.07	0.07	0.07	0.07	0.07	0.07	0.07	0.07
Pretax earnings	$ 4.74	$ 5.70	$ 6.05	$ 6.69	$ 7.10	$ 6.31	$ 7.36	$ 8.22	$ 6.59	$ 8.00	$ 9.33
After-tax earnings	2.61	3.42	3.63	4.01	4.26	3.79	4.42	4.93	3.95	4.80	5.60
Earnings per share on 1,118,000 shares	$ 2.33	$ 3.06	$ 3.25	$ 3.59	$ 3.81	$ 3.39	$ 3.95	$ 4.41	$ 3.54	$ 4.29	$ 5.01
Dividends per share	1.00	1.03	1.08	1.19	1.27	1.13	1.31	1.47	1.18	1.43	1.66

EXHIBIT 6 (continued)

	1996	1997	5% Growth			10% Growth			15% Growth		
	Actual	Estimate	1998	1999	2000	1998	1999	2000	1998	1999	2000

B. Balance Sheets

	1996 Actual	1997 Estimate	1998	1999	2000	1998	1999	2000	1998	1999	2000
Assets											
Cash (minimum)	$ .83	$ 1.17	$ 1.23	$ 1.29	$ 1.36	$ 1.29	$ 1.42	$ 1.56	$ 1.35	$ 1.55	$ 1.78
Excess cash	—	—	.01	.73	1.24	—	—	—	—	—	—
Accounts receivable	7.75	10.12	10.62	11.15	11.71	11.13	12.24	13.46	11.63	13.38	15.38
Inventory	14.36	16.18	16.99	17.84	18.74	17.80	19.58	21.54	18.61	21.40	24.61
Prepayments, etc.	.56	.23	.24	.26	.27	.26	.28	.31	.27	.31	.36
Total current assets	$23.51	$27.71	$29.10	$31.27	$33.32	$30.48	$33.52	$36.87	$31.86	$36.64	$42.14
Plant and equipment	12.47	13.27	14.27	15.27	16.27	14.27	15.27	16.27	14.27	15.27	16.27
Less: accum. depreciation	5.21	6.04	6.95	7.95	9.05	6.95	7.95	9.05	6.95	7.95	9.05
Net plant and equipment	$ 7.26	$ 7.23	$ 7.32	$ 7.32	$ 7.22	$ 7.32	$ 7.32	$ 7.22	$ 7.32	$ 7.32	$ 7.22
Other	.22	.11	.11	.11	.11	.11	.11	.11	.11	.11	.11
Total assets	$30.99	$35.05	$36.54	$38.71	$40.65	$37.91	$40.95	$44.20	$39.29	$44.07	$49.47
Liabilities and owners' equity											
Short-term notes	$ 7.22	$ 7.45	$ 6.29	$ 5.50	$ 4.35	$ 6.29	$ 5.50	$ 4.35	$ 6.29	$ 5.50	$ 4.35
Accounts payable	1.96	2.72	2.85	3.00	3.14	2.99	3.29	3.62	3.12	3.59	4.13
Accruals	1.01	1.44	1.52	1.59	1.67	1.59	1.75	1.92	1.66	1.91	2.20
Other	.82	1.15	1.21	1.33	1.40	1.27	1.39	1.53	1.33	1.61	1.85
Current portion, LTD	.05	.05	.05	.05	.05	.05	.05	.05	.05	.05	.05
Total current liabilities	$11.06	$12.82	$11.93	$11.48	$10.61	$12.19	$11.98	$11.47	$12.46	$12.66	$12.58
Long-term debt	.46	.40	.35	.30	.25	.35	.30	.25	.35	.30	.25
Deferred taxes	.76	.80	.80	.80	.80	.80	.80	.80	.80	.80	.80
Other	.15	.20	.20	.20	.20	.20	.20	.20	.20	.20	.20
Cash deficit*	—	—	—	—	—	1.02	1.37	1.89	2.01	3.44	5.23
Total liabilities	$12.43	$14.22	$13.28	$12.78	$11.86	$14.56	$14.65	$14.61	$15.82	$17.40	$19.06
Common stock	5.59	5.59	5.59	5.59	5.59	5.59	5.59	5.59	5.59	5.59	5.59
Retained earnings	12.98	15.24	17.67	20.34	23.18	17.76	20.71	24.00	17.88	21.09	24.82
Total owners' equity	$18.56	$20.83	$23.25	$25.93	$28.77	$23.35	$26.30	$29.59	$23.47	$26.68	$30.41
Total liabilities and owners' equity	$30.99	$35.05	$36.53	$38.71	$40.63	$37.91	$40.95	$44.20	$39.29	$44.07	$49.47

EXHIBIT 6 (continued)

C. Cash Flow

	1997 Estimate	5% Growth			10% Growth			15% Growth		
		1998	1999	2000	1998	1999	2000	1998	1999	2000
Sources										
After-tax earnings	$3.42	$3.63	$4.01	$4.26	$3.79	$4.42	$4.93	$3.95	$4.80	$5.59
Noncash charges	.94	.91	1.00	1.10	.91	1.00	1.10	.91	1.00	1.10
Funds from operations	$4.36	$4.54	$5.01	$5.36	$4.70	$5.42	$6.03	$4.86	$5.80	$6.69
Deferred taxes	.04	—	—	—	—	—	—	—	—	—
Accounts payable	.76	.14	.14	.14	.27	.30	.33	.41	.47	.54
Accruals	.43	.07	.07	.08	.14	.16	.17	.22	.25	.29
Other and miscellaneous current liabilities	.33	.06	.12	.07	.12	.12	.14	.17	.27	.24
Other liabilities	.05	—	—	—	—	—	—	—	—	—
Other assets	.11	—	—	—	—	—	—	—	—	—
Total sources	$6.08	$4.81	$5.34	$5.65	$5.22	$6.00	$6.67	$5.66	$6.79	$7.76
Uses										
Dividends	$1.16	$1.21	$1.34	$1.42	$1.26	$1.47	$1.64	$1.31	$1.59	$1.86
Capital expenditures	.80	1.00	1.00	1.00	1.00	1.00	1.00	1.00	1.00	1.00
Short-term debt	(.23)	1.16	.79	1.15	1.16	.79	1.15	1.16	.79	1.15
Long-term debt	.05	.05	.05	.05	.05	.05	.05	.05	.05	.05
Minimum cash	.34	.06	.06	.06	.12	.13	.14	.18	.20	.23
Accounts receivable	2.36	.50	.53	.56	1.01	1.11	1.22	1.52	1.74	2.01
Inventory	1.82	.81	.85	.89	1.62	1.78	1.96	2.43	2.79	3.21
Prepay and deferred charge	(.33)	.01	.01	.01	.02	.02	.03	.04	.04	.05
Intangibles	.11	—	—	—	—	—	—	—	—	—
Total uses	$6.08	$4.80	$4.63	$5.14	$6.24	$6.35	$7.19	$7.69	$8.20	$9.56
Net cash flow	—	.02	.71	.51	(1.01)	(.35)	(.52)	(2.03)	(1.41)	(1.80)
Cumulative	—	.02	.73	1.24	(1.01)	(1.36)	(1.88)	(2.02)	(3.43)	(5.23)

EXHIBIT 6 (concluded)

	1996 Actual	1997 Estimate	5% Growth 1998	5% Growth 1999	5% Growth 2000	10% Growth 1998	10% Growth 1999	10% Growth 2000	15% Growth 1998	15% Growth 1999	15% Growth 2000
						D. Analytical Ratios					
Profitability											
Sales growth	12.0%	39.9%	5.0%	5.0%	5.0%	10.0%	10.0%	10.0%	15.0%	15.0%	15.0%
EPS growth	20.7	31.4	6.2	10.3	6.3	10.8	16.5	11.2	15.5	21.4	16.5
Gross profit margin	38.8	35.9	38.6	39.0	39.0	38.6	39.0	39.0	38.6	39.0	39.0
Operating exp. ÷ Sales	26.5	25.7	25.7	25.7	25.7	25.7	25.8	25.8	25.7	25.8	25.9
Pretax margin	11.5	10.3	10.0	10.5	10.6	9.9	10.5	10.7	9.9	10.5	10.6
After-tax margin	6.3	5.9	6.0	6.3	6.4	6.0	6.3	6.4	5.9	6.3	6.4
Return on average owners' equity	14.6	17.4	16.5	16.3	15.6	17.1	17.8	17.6	17.9	19.1	19.6
Return on total assets	8.4	9.8	9.9	10.4	10.5	10.0	10.8	11.2	10.1	10.9	11.3
EBIT ÷ Total assets	16.5	19.0	18.7	19.1	19.0	19.0	20.1	20.4	19.4	20.7	21.2
Dividend payout	42.9	33.8	33.3	33.3	33.3	33.3	33.3	33.3	33.2	33.2	33.2
Turnover											
Receivables	5.3×	5.7×	5.7×	5.7×	5.7×	5.7×	5.7×	5.7×	5.7×	5.7×	5.7×
Inventory	2.9	3.6	3.6	3.6	3.6	3.6	3.6	3.6	3.6	3.6	3.6
Accounts payable	21.1	21.3	21.3	21.3	21.3	21.3	21.3	21.3	21.3	21.3	21.3
Working capital	3.3	3.6	3.5	3.2	2.9	3.5	3.3	3.0	3.4	3.2	3.0
Fixed asset	5.7	8.0	8.3	8.7	9.3	8.7	9.6	10.6	9.1	10.4	12.2
Net worth	2.2	2.8	2.6	2.4	2.3	2.7	2.6	2.6	2.8	2.9	2.9
Leverage											
Total debt ÷ Owners' equity	67.0%	68.3%	57.1%	49.3%	41.3%	62.3%	55.7%	49.3%	67.4%	65.2%	62.7%
Long-term debt ÷ Owners' equity	2.4	1.9	1.5	1.1	0.9	1.5	1.1	0.8	1.5	1.1	0.8
Interest coverage	13.5	7.0	8.7	10.3	12.6	8.0	9.6	11.1	7.5	8.3	8.9
Liquidity											
Quick ratio	.8×	1.0×	1.0×	1.1×	1.3×	1.0×	1.1×	1.3×	1.1×	1.2×	1.4×
Current ratio	2.1	2.2	2.4	2.7	3.1	2.5	2.8	3.2	2.6	2.9	3.3
Working capital	$12.44	$14.89	$19.40	$29.98	$29.55	$18.29	$21.46	$25.23	$19.40	$23.98	$29.55

*Includes interest calculated on the cash deficit at 8 1/2%.

Note: Figures may not add because of rounding.

Sengupta Fibres, Ltd.

Mrs. Sharma, the managing director and principal owner of Sengupta Fibres, Ltd., discovered the problem when she arrived at the parking lot of the company's plant at 10:00 A.M. one morning in early January 1990. Trucks filled with rolls of fiber yarns were being unloaded, but they had been loaded just the night before and had been ready to depart that morning. The fiber was intended for customers who had been badgering Mrs. Sharma to fill their orders in a timely fashion. The government tax inspector, who was stationed at the company's warehouse, would not clear the trucks for departure because the excise tax had not been paid. The tax inspector required a cash payment, but in seeking to draw funds for the excise tax that morning, Mr. Ashoka, the bookkeeper, discovered that the company had overdrawn its bank account again—the third time in as many weeks. The truck drivers were independent contractors who refused to wait while the company and government settled their accounts. They cursed loudly as they unloaded the trucks.

Now this shipment would not leave for at least another two days, and angry customers would no doubt require an explanation. Moreover, before granting a loan with which to pay the excise tax, the branch manager of the All-India Bank & Trust Company had requested a meeting with Mrs. Sharma for the next day to discuss Sengupta's financial condition and plans for restoring the firm's liquidity.

Mrs. Sharma told Mr. Ashoka, "This cash problem is most vexing. I don't understand it. We're a very profitable enterprise, yet we seem to have to depend increasingly on the bank. Why do we need more loans just as our heavy selling season begins? We can't repeat this blunder."

This case was written by Thien T. Pham under the direction of Professor Robert F. Bruner as a basis for class discussion rather than to illustrate effective or ineffective handling of an administrative situation. Copyright © 1990 by the University of Virginia Darden School Foundation, Charlottesville, VA. All rights reserved. *No part of this publication may be reproduced, stored in a retrieval system, used in a spreadsheet, or transmitted in any form or by any means—electronic, mechanical, photocopying, recording, or otherwise—without the permission of the Darden School Foundation. For inquiries, please send an e-mail to dardencases@virginia.edu.* Rev. 1/98. Version 2.1.

COMPANY BACKGROUND

Sengupta Fibres, Ltd., was founded in 1962 to produce nylon fiber at its only plant, in Kota, India, about 100 kilometers south of New Delhi. By using new technology and domestic raw materials, the firm had developed a steady franchise among dozens of small local textile weavers. It supplied synthetic fiber yarns used in weaving colorful cloths for making saris, the traditional women's dress of India. On average, each sari required eight yards of cloth. An Indian woman typically would buy three saris per year. With a female population of over 500 million in India, the demand for saris would account for more than 12 billion yards of fabric. This demand was currently being supplied entirely from domestic textile mills that, in turn, filled their yarn requirements from suppliers such as Sengupta Fibres.

SYNTHETIC-TEXTILE MARKET

The demand for synthetic textiles was characterized by stable year-to-year growth and predictable seasonal fluctuations. Unit demand increased with both population and national income. In addition, India's population celebrated hundreds of festivals each year, in deference to a host of deities, at which saris were traditionally worn. The most important festival, the Diwali celebration in midautumn, caused a seasonal peak in the demand for new saris, which, in turn, caused a seasonal peak in demand for nylon textiles in late summer and early fall. Thus, the seasonal demand for nylon yarn would peak in midsummer. Unit growth in the industry was expected to be 15 percent per year.

Consumers purchased saris and textiles from cloth merchants located in villages around the country. A cloth merchant was an important local figure usually well known to area residents; the merchant generally granted credit to support consumer purchases. Merchants maintained relatively low levels of inventory and built stocks of goods only shortly in advance of and during the peak selling season.

Competition among suppliers (the many small textile-weaving mills) to these merchants was keen and was affected by price, service, and credit that the mills could grant to the merchants. The mills essentially produced to order, building their inventories of woven cloth shortly in advance of the peak selling season and keeping only maintenance stocks at other times of the year.

The yarn manufacturers competed for the business of the mills through responsive service and credit. The suppliers to the yarn manufacturers provided little or no trade credit. Being near the origin of the textile chain in India, the yarn manufacturers essentially banked the downstream activities of the industry.

PRODUCTION AND DISTRIBUTION SYSTEM

Thin profit margins had prompted Mrs. Sharma to adopt policies against overproduction and overstocking, which would require Sengupta to carry inventories through the slack selling season. She had adopted a plan of seasonal production, which meant that the yarn plant would operate at peak capacity for two months of the year and at modest levels the rest of the year. This policy imposed an annual ritual of hirings and layoffs.

To help ensure prompt service, Sengupta Fibres maintained two distribution warehouses, but getting the finished yarn quickly from the factory in Kota to the customers was a challenge. The roads were narrow and mostly in poor repair. A truck could take 10 to 15 days to negotiate the trip between Calcutta and Kota, a distance of about 1,100 kilometers. Except when they passed through cities, highways had only one lane. When two cars or trucks met, they had to slow down and squeeze past each other or else stop and wait for the traffic to pass. Journeys were slow and dangerous, and accidents frequent.

COMPANY PERFORMANCE

Sengupta Fibres had been consistently profitable. Moreover, sales had grown at an annual rate of 18 percent in 1989. Gross sales were projected to reach 78.2 million rupees (Rs) in the fiscal year ended December 31, 1990 (see Exhibit 1).[1] Net profits reached Rs2.6 million in 1989. Exhibits 2 and 3 present recent financial statements for the firm.

REASSESSMENT

After the episode in the parking lot, Mrs. Sharma and her bookkeeper went to her office to analyze the situation. She pushed aside the several items on her desk to which she had intended to devote the morning—a letter from a field sales manager requesting permission to grant favorable credit terms to a new customer (see Exhibit 4), a note from the transportation manager regarding a possible change in the inventory policy (Exhibit 5), a proposal from the purchasing agent regarding the delivery lead times of certain supplies (Exhibit 6), and a proposal from the operations manager for a scheme of level annual production (Exhibit 7).

To prepare a forecast on a business-as-usual basis, Mrs. Sharma and Mr. Ashoka agreed on various parameters. Cost of goods sold would run at 73.7 percent of gross sales—a figure that was up from recent years because of increasing price competition. Operating expenses would be about 6 percent of sales—also up from recent years to include the addition of a quality-control department, two new sales agents, and three young nephews in whom she hoped to build an allegiance to the Sharma family business. The company's income tax rate was 30 percent and, although accrued monthly, was actually paid quarterly in March, June, September, and December. The excise tax (at 15 percent of sales) was different from the income tax and was collected at the factory gate as trucks left to make deliveries to customers and the regional warehouses. Mrs. Sharma proposed to pay dividends of Rs450,000 per quarter to the 11 members of her extended family who held the entire equity of the firm. For years Sengupta had paid high dividends. The Sharma family believed that excess funds left in the firm were at greater risk than if the funds were returned to shareholders.

---

[1] At the time, the rupee was pegged to the U.S. dollar at the rate of 16 rupees per dollar.

Mr. Ashoka observed that sales collections in any given month had been running steadily at the rate of 40 percent of the last month's sales plus 60 percent of the sales from the month before last. The value of raw materials purchased in any month represented on average 55 percent of the value of sales expected to be made two months later. Wages and other expenses in a given month were equivalent to about 34 percent of purchases in the previous month. As a matter of policy, Mrs. Sharma wanted to see a cash balance of no less than Rs640,000.

Sengupta Fibres had a line of credit from All-India Bank & Trust Company, where it also maintained its cash balances. All-India's short-term interest rate was currently 16 percent, but Mr. Ashoka was worried that inflation and interest rates might rise in the coming year. The seasonal line of credit had to be cleaned up for at least 30 days each year. The usual cleanup month had been October,[2] but Sengupta Fibres had failed to make a full repayment at that time. Only after strong assurances by Mrs. Sharma that she would clean up the loan in November or December had the bank lending officer reluctantly agreed to waive the cleanup requirement in October. Unfortunately, Sengupta Fibres' credit needs did not abate as rapidly as expected in November and December, and although his protests increased each month, the lending officer agreed to meet Sengupta's cash requirements with loans. Now he was refusing to extend any more seasonal credit until Mrs. Sharma presented a reasonable financial plan for the company that demonstrated its ability to clean up the loan by the end of 1990.

FINANCIAL FORECAST

Mr. Ashoka hurriedly developed a monthly forecast of financial statements using the current operating assumptions (see Exhibit 8). As an alternative way of looking at the forecasted funds flows, Mr. Ashoka also prepared a forecast of cash receipts and disbursements (Exhibit 9). The monthly T-accounts underlying the forecasts are given in Exhibit 10, and a summary of the forecast assumptions is in Exhibit 11.

Mr. Ashoka handed over the forecast to Mrs. Sharma with a graph showing projected sales and month-end debt outstanding (Exhibit 12). After studying the forecasts for a few moments, Mrs. Sharma expostulated,

> This is worse than I expected. The numbers show that we can't repay All-India's loan by the end of December. The loan officer will not accept this forecast as a basis for more credit. We need a new plan, and fast. We need those loans in order to scale up for the most important part of our business season. Let's go over these assumptions in detail and look for any opportunities to improve our debt position.

Then, casting her gaze toward the stack of memos she had pushed aside earlier, she muttered, "Perhaps some of these proposals will help."

---

[2]The selection of October as the loan cleanup month was imposed by the bank on the grounds of tradition. Seasonal loans of any type made by the bank were to be cleaned up in October. Mrs. Sharma had seen no reason previously to challenge the bank's tradition.

EXHIBIT 1   Summary of Monthly Sales: Actual for 1989 and Forecast for 1990 (in rupees)

	1989	*1990*
January	1,341,600	1,744,080
February	2,005,692	2,507,115
March	2,964,936	3,854,417
April	6,104,280	7,630,350
May	10,464,480	12,034,152
June	13,255,008	15,243,259
July	12,295,764	14,140,129
August	6,191,484	7,429,781
September	3,488,160	4,360,200
October	2,964,936	3,854,417
November	2,354,508	3,060,860
December	1,918,488	2,398,110
Year	65,349,336	78,256,870

EXHIBIT 2   Historical and Forecasted Annual Income Statements (in rupees)

	1988 (Actual)	*1989* (Actual)	*1990* (Forecast)
Gross sales	55,546,936	65,349,336	78,256,870
Excise tax	8,332,040	9,802,400	11,738,530
Net sales	47,214,895	55,546,936	66,518,339
Cost of goods	38,327,385	46,398,029	57,675,313
Gross profits	8,887,510	9,148,907	8,843,026
Operating expenses	3,012,444	4,159,275	4,695,412
Depreciation	662,476	782,640	924,600
Interest expense	910,000	1,240,000	1,830,001
Pretax profit	4,965,066	3,749,632	1,400,013
Income tax	1,489,520	1,124,890	420,004
Net profit	3,475,546	2,624,742	980,009

EXHIBIT 3   Historical and Forecasted Balance Sheets (in rupees)

	1989 (Actual)	1990 (Forecast)
Cash	641,123	640,000
Accounts receivable	2,302,186	3,205,619
Inventories	1,076,000	1,806,344
Total current assets	4,019,309	5,651,964
Gross plant, property, and equipment	8,696,000	9,896,000
Accumulated depreciation	1,278,500	2,203,100
Net plant, property and equipment	7,417,500	7,692,900
Total assets	11,436,809	13,344,864
Accounts payable	654,234	998,962
Notes to bank	587,575	3,135,569
Accrued taxes	0	(164,677)
Total current liabilities	1,241,809	3,969,855
Owners' equity	10,195,000	9,375,009
Total liabilities and equity	11,436,809	13,344,864

EXHIBIT 4   Memo from Field Sales Manager

To: Mrs. G. Sharma
From: Mr. A. Bajpai

January 7, 1990

As you know, Pondicherry Textiles is considering us to be their prime yarn supplier for this year. Purchases would be in the neighborhood of Rs4,000,000 and are not reflected in our current sales forecast. Pondicherry would be one of our largest accounts. They have accepted our terms on price, but have asked for credit terms of 80 days, net. Unless we extend our credit terms, Pondicherry will not do business with us. We can expect that Pondicherry will purchase our yarn across the year in about the same pattern as our other customers.

If you approve this exception to our standard terms (45 days), the Pondicherry district sales office immediately will meet its quarterly sales quota. Please indicate your approval below.

Approved:

EXHIBIT 5   Memo from Transportation Manager

To: Mrs. G. Sharma
From: Mr. R. Sikh

January 2, 1990

I have been tracking our supply shipments in the last six months as you asked me to. The new road between Kota and New Delhi has improved reliability of the shipments significantly. Our supplier's new manufacturing equipment is now running consistently, and they have been meeting their shipment dates consistently. As a result, I would propose that we reduce our raw-material inventory requirement from 60 days to 30 days. This would reduce the amount of inventory we are carrying by one month, and should free up a lot of space in the warehouse. I am not sure if this will affect any other department since we will be buying the same amount of material, but it would make inventory tracking a lot easier for me. Please let me know so we can implement this in January.

EXHIBIT 6   Memo from Purchasing Agent

To: Mrs. G. Sharma
From: Mr. R. Mohan

January 5, 1990

Hibachi Chemicals of Yokohama has approached us with a proposal to supply us polyester pellets on a "just-in-time" basis from their plant in Majala (20 km away). These pellets account for 35 percent of our raw-material purchases. I am looking into the feasibility of this scheme—in particular, whether Hibachi can actually perform on this basis—and will report back in two weeks. If the proposal is feasible, it would reduce our inventory of pellets from 60 days outstanding to only 2 or 3 days.

EXHIBIT 7   Memo from Operations Manager

To: Mrs. G. Sharma
From: Mr. L. Gupta

January 7, 1990

   You asked me to estimate the production efficiencies arising from a scheme of level annual production. In essence, there are significant advantages to be gained:

- Gross profit margin would rise by 2 or 3 percent, reflecting labor savings and production efficiencies gained from a stable workforce and the absence of certain seasonal training and setup costs.
- Seasonal hirings and layoffs would no longer be necessary, permitting us to cultivate a stronger workforce and, perhaps, suppressing labor unrest. You will recall that the unions have indicated that reducing seasonal layoffs will be one of their major negotiating objectives this year.
- Level production entails lower manufacturing risk. With the load spread throughout the year, we suffer less from equipment breakdowns and can match the routine maintenance better with the demand on the plant and equipment.

EXHIBIT 8   Monthly Forecast of Income Statements and Balance Sheets for 1990 (in rupees)

	January	February	March	April	May
Income statement					
Gross sales	1,744,080	2,507,115	3,854,417	7,630,350	12,034,152
Excise taxes	261,612	376,067	578,163	1,144,553	1,805,123
Net sales	1,482,468	2,131,048	3,276,254	6,485,798	10,229,029
Cost of goods sold	1,285,387	1,847,744	2,840,705	5,623,568	8,869,170
Gross profit	197,081	283,304	435,549	862,230	1,359,859
Operating expenses	391,284	391,284	391,284	391,284	391,284
Depreciation	72,467	72,467	74,967	74,967	74,967
Interest expense (income)[a]	10,031	24,117	71,776	157,657	263,296
Profit before taxes	(276,701)	(204,564)	(102,478)	238,321	630,312
Income taxes	(83,010)	(61,369)	(30,743)	71,496	189,094
Net profit	(193,690)	(143,195)	(71,735)	166,825	441,219
Assets					
Cash[b]	640,000	640,000	640,000	640,000	640,000
Accounts receivable[c]	1,866,166	2,524,556	4,329,679	8,913,993	15,583,355
Inventories[d]	2,379,373	5,449,097	10,654,051	15,664,662	17,423,053
Total current assets	4,885,539	8,613,654	15,623,730	25,218,656	33,646,408
Net properties, plant and equipment[e]	7,345,033	7,272,567	7,497,600	7,422,633	7,347,667
Total assets	12,230,572	15,886,220	23,121,330	32,641,289	40,994,074
Liabilities and owners' equity					
Accounts payable[f]	1,395,250	3,472,013	5,894,104	7,659,113	7,052,391
Note payable—bank[g]	917,023	2,700,471	8,065,968	15,582,597	23,911,792
Accrued taxes[h]	(83,010)	(144,379)	(175,123)	(103,626)	85,467
Total current liabilities	2,229,263	6,028,105	13,784,950	23,138,084	31,049,651
Shareholders' equity[i]	10,001,310	9,858,115	9,336,380	9,503,205	9,944,424
Total liabilities and equity	12,230,572	15,886,220	23,121,330	32,641,289	40,994,074

[a]Interest expense 5 notes payable 3 16%/12months.
[b]See Exhibit 9.
[c]See panel 1, Exhibit 10.
[d]See panel 2, Exhibit 10.
[e]See panel 6, Exhibit 10.
[f]See panel 3, Exhibit 10.
[g]Plug figure.
[h]See panel 5, Exhibit 10.
[i]See panel 4, Exhibit 10.

June	July	August	September	October	November	December
15,243,259	14,140,129	7,429,781	4,360,200	3,854,417	3,060,860	2,398,110
2,286,489	2,121,019	1,114,467	654,030	578,163	459,129	359,717
12,956,770	12,019,109	6,315,314	3,706,170	3,276,254	2,601,731	2,038,394
11,234,282	10,421,275	5,475,748	3,213,467	2,840,705	2,255,854	1,767,407
1,722,488	1,597,835	839,565	492,703	435,549	345,877	270,986
391,284	391,284	391,284	391,284	391,284	391,284	391,284
77,467	77,467	77,467	79,967	79,967	79,967	82,467
353,264	354,537	255,856	147,386	85,153	55,982	43,948
900,473	774,547	114,959	(125,934)	(120,854)	(181,356)	(246,712)
270,142	232,364	34,488	(37,780)	(36,256)	(54,407)	(74,014)
630,331	542,183	80,471	(88,154)	(84,598)	(126,949)	(172,699)
640,000	640,000	640,000	640,000	640,000	640,000	640,000
21,434,744	22,257,077	14,884,851	7,789,062	5,441,530	4,344,504	3,205,619
12,919,354	6,285,558	3,745,096	2,935,878	1,986,514	1,426,124	1,806,344
34,994,098	29,182,636	19,269,948	11,364,940	8,068,044	6,410,628	5,651,964
7,570,200	7,492,733	7,415,267	7,635,300	7,555,333	7,475,367	7,692,900
42,564,298	36,675,369	26,685,214	19,000,240	15,623,378	13,885,994	13,344,864
3,361,700	1,673,431	1,395,250	958,794	594,281	522,338	998,962
29,077,842	24,102,636	14,275,704	7,832,191	4,940,696	3,456,612	3,135,569
0	232,364	266,852	0	(36,256)	(90,663)	(164,677)
32,439,543	26,008,431	15,937,805	8,790,985	5,498,721	3,888,287	3,969,855
10,124,755	10,666,938	10,747,409	10,209,255	10,124,657	9,997,708	9,375,009
42,564,298	36,675,369	26,685,214	19,000,240	15,623,378	13,885,994	13,344,864

EXHIBIT 9   Schedule of Cash Receipts and Disbursements for 1990 (in rupees)

	January	February	March	April	May
Assume:					
Sales	1,744,080	2,507,115	3,854,417	7,630,350	12,034,152
Purchases*	2,119,929	4,196,693	6,618,784	8,383,793	7,777,071
Debt outstanding	917,023	2,700,471	8,065,968	15,582,597	23,911,792
Receipts:					
Accounts receivable collected	2,180,100	1,848,725	2,049,294	3,046,036	5,364,790
New borrowings (repayments)	329,448	1,783,449	5,365,497	7,516,628	8,329,195
Disbursement:					
Accounts paid†	1,378,913	2,119,929	4,196,693	6,618,784	8,383,793
Capital expenditures	0	0	300,000	0	0
Interest payments	10,031	24,117	71,776	157,657	263,296
Excise tax paid	261,612	376,067	578,163	1,144,553	1,805,123
Operating expenses	391,284	391,284	391,284	391,284	391,284
Accrued income tax paid	0	0	0	0	0
Wages	468,831	720,776	1,426,875	2,250,386	2,850,489
Dividends	0	0	450,000	0	0
Subtotal: disbursements	2,510,671	3,632,173	7,414,791	10,562,664	13,693,985
Receipts − Disbursements	(1,123)	0	0	0	0
BOP cash balance	641,123	640,000	640,000	640,000	640,000
EOP cash balance	640,000	640,000	640,000	640,000	640,000

*Equal to 55 percent of sales in period $(T + 2)$.
†Equal to purchases in period $(T − 1)$.

June	July	August	September	October	November	December
15,243,259	14,140,129	7,429,781	4,360,200	3,854,417	3,060,860	2,398,110
4,086,379	2,398,110	2,119,929	1,683,473	1,318,961	1,247,017	1,723,642
29,077,842	24,102,636	14,275,704	7,832,191	4,940,696	3,456,612	3,135,569
9,391,871	13,317,795	14,802,007	11,455,989	6,201,948	4,157,887	3,536,994
5,166,051	(4,975,206)	(9,826,932)	(6,443,513)	(2,891,495)	(1,484,084)	(321,042)
7,777,071	4,086,379	2,398,110	2,119,929	1,683,473	1,318,961	1,247,017
300,000	0	0	300,000	0	0	300,000
353,264	354,537	255,856	147,386	85,153	55,982	43,948
2,286,489	2,121,019	1,114,467	654,030	578,163	459,129	359,717
391,284	391,284	391,284	391,284	391,284	391,284	391,284
355,609	0	0	229,071	0	0	0
2,644,204	1,389,369	815,357	720,776	572,381	448,447	423,986
450,000	0	0	450,000	0	0	450,000
14,557,922	8,342,589	4,975,074	5,012,477	3,310,454	2,673,803	3,215,952
0	0	0	0	0	0	0
640,000	640,000	640,000	640,000	640,000	640,000	640,000
640,000	640,000	640,000	640,000	640,000	640,000	640,000

EXHIBIT 10   Forecasted T-Accounts Supporting Financial Statements (in rupees)

	January	February	March	April	May
1. Schedule of accounts receivable					
Beginning of period	2,302,186	1,866,166	2,524,556	4,329,679	8,913,993
Plus sales	1,744,080	2,507,115	3,854,417	7,630,350	12,034,152
Less collections, last month[a]	767,395	697,632	1,002,846	1,541,767	3,052,140
Less collections, month before last[b]	1,412,705	1,151,093	1,046,448	1,504,269	2,312,650
End of period	1,866,166	2,524,556	4,329,679	8,913,993	15,583,355
2. Schedule of inventories					
Beginning of period	1,076,000	2,379,373	5,449,097	10,654,051	15,664,662
Plus purchases[c]	2,119,929	4,196,693	6,618,784	8,383,793	7,777,071
Plus labor	468,831	720,776	1,426,875	2,250,386	2,850,489
Less shipments (COGS)	1,285,387	1,847,744	2,840,705	5,623,568	8,869,170
End of period	2,379,373	5,449,097	10,654,051	15,664,662	17,423,053
3. Schedule of accounts payable					
Beginning of period	654,234	1,395,250	3,472,013	5,894,104	7,659,113
+ Purchases[c]	2,119,929	4,196,693	6,618,784	8,383,793	7,777,071
− Payments[d]	1,378,913	2,119,929	4,196,693	6,618,784	8,383,793
End of period	1,395,250	3,472,013	5,894,104	7,659,113	7,052,391
4. Schedule of shareholders' equity					
Beginning of period	10,195,000	10,001,310	9,858,115	9,336,380	9,503,205
Plus net profit	(193,690)	(143,195)	(71,735)	166,825	441,219
Less dividends	0	0	450,000	0	0
End of period	10,001,310	9,858,115	9,336,380	9,503,205	9,944,424
5. Schedule of accrued taxes					
Beginning of period	0	(83,010)	(144,379)	(175,123)	(103,626)
Plus monthly tax expense (@ 30%)	(83,010)	(61,369)	(30,743)	71,496	189,094
Less quarterly tax payments	0	0	0	0	0
End of period	(83,010)	(144,379)	(175,123)	(103,626)	85,467
6. Schedule of property, plant, and equipment					
Beginning gross PP&E	8,696,000	8,696,000	8,696,000	8,996,000	8,996,000
Plus capital expenditures	0	0	300,000	0	0
Ending gross PP&E	8,696,000	8,696,000	8,996,000	8,996,000	8,996,000
Monthly depreciation expense	72,467	72,467	74,967	74,967	74,967
Less cumulative depreciation	1,350,967	1,423,433	1,498,400	1,573,367	1,648,333
Ending net PP&E	7,345,033	7,272,567	7,497,600	7,422,633	7,347,667

[a]40 percent of sales in period $(T - 1)$.
[b]60 percent of sales in period $(T - 2)$.
[c]Equal to 55 percent of sales in period $(T + 2)$.
[d]Equal to purchases in period $(T - 1)$.

June	July	August	September	October	November	December
15,583,355	21,434,744	22,257,077	14,884,851	7,789,062	5,441,530	4,344,504
15,243,259	14,140,129	7,429,781	4,360,200	3,854,417	3,060,860	2,398,110
4,813,661	6,097,304	5,656,051	2,971,912	1,744,080	1,541,767	1,224,344
4,578,210	7,220,491	9,145,956	8,484,077	4,457,868	2,616,120	2,312,650
21,434,744	22,257,077	14,884,851	7,789,062	5,441,530	4,344,504	3,205,619
17,423,053	12,919,354	6,285,558	3,745,096	2,935,878	1,986,514	1,426,124
4,086,379	2,398,110	2,119,929	1,683,473	1,318,961	1,247,017	1,723,642
2,644,204	1,389,369	815,357	720,776	572,381	448,447	423,986
11,234,282	10,421,275	5,475,748	3,213,467	2,840,705	2,255,854	1,767,407
12,919,354	6,285,558	3,745,096	2,935,878	1,986,514	1,426,124	1,806,344
7,052,391	3,361,700	1,673,431	1,395,250	958,794	594,281	522,338
4,086,379	2,398,110	2,119,929	1,683,473	1,318,961	1,247,017	1,723,642
7,777,071	4,086,379	2,398,110	2,119,929	1,683,473	1,318,961	1,247,017
3,361,700	1,673,431	1,395,250	958,794	594,281	522,338	998,962
9,944,424	10,124,755	10,666,938	10,747,409	10,209,255	10,124,657	9,997,708
630,331	542,183	80,471	(88,154)	(84,598)	(126,949)	(172,699)
450,000	0	0	450,000	0	0	450,000
10,124,755	10,666,938	10,747,409	10,209,255	10,124,657	9,997,708	9,375,009
85,467	0	232,364	266,852	0	(36,256)	(90,663)
270,142	232,364	34,488	(37,780)	(36,256)	(54,407)	(74,014)
355,609	0	0	229,071	0	0	0
0	232,364	266,852	0	(36,256)	(90,663)	(164,677)
8,996,000	9,296,000	9,296,000	9,296,000	9,596,000	9,596,000	9,596,000
300,000	0	0	300,000	0	0	300,000
9,296,000	9,296,000	9,296,000	9,596,000	9,596,000	9,596,000	9,896,000
77,467	77,467	77,467	79,967	79,967	79,967	82,467
1,725,800	1,803,267	1,880,733	1,960,700	2,040,667	2,120,633	2,203,100
7,570,200	7,492,733	7,415,267	7,635,300	7,555,333	7,475,367	7,692,900

EXHIBIT 11 Forecast Assumptions

Ratio of:

Income tax/Profit before tax	30%
Excise tax/Sales	15%
This month's collections/Last month's sales	40%
This month's collections/Sales month before last	60%
Purchases/Sales two months later	55%
Wages/Purchases	34%
Annual operating expenses/Annual sales	6%
Capital expenditures (every third month)	Rs300,000
Interest rate on borrowings (and deposits)	16%
Minimum cash balance	Rs640,000
Depreciation/Gross PP&E (per year)	10%
(per month)	0.83%
Dividends paid (every third month)	Rs450,000

EXHIBIT 12 Trend of Certain Financial Accounts by Month (in millions of rupees)

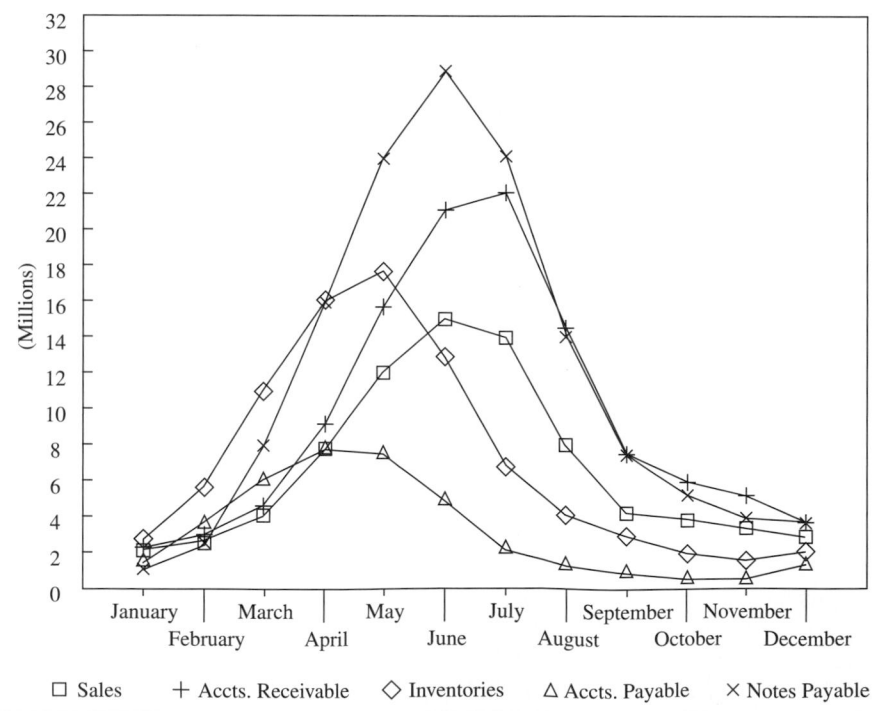

□ Sales + Accts. Receivable ◇ Inventories △ Accts. Payable × Notes Payable

Case 10

Bayern Brauerei

In early January 1993, Maria Ober arrived at Bayern Brauerei[1] to participate in her first meeting of the board of directors. She had recently joined the board at the behest of her uncle, the managing director of the company. August Ober had told her that the board could use her financial expertise in addressing some questions that would come up in the near future, but he would not be specific as to the nature of those questions. The company was owned entirely by 16 uncles, aunts, and cousins in the Ober family. Maria had received an MBA degree from a well-known business school and had worked for the past six years as a commercial loan officer for a leading bank in Frankfurt, Germany. With the permission of the bank, she agreed to join the Bayern Brauerei board.

The agenda for the January meeting of the directors consisted of three items of business: (1) approval of the 1993 financial budget, (2) declaration of the quarterly dividend, and (3) adoption of a compensation scheme for Max Leiter, the company's sales and marketing manager. Because she knew little about the company, Maria decided to visit it for a day before the first board meeting.

THE COMPANY

Bayern Brauerei produced two varieties of beer, dark and light, for which it had won quality awards consistently over the years. Its sales and profits in 1992 were DM102.3 million and DM2.6 million, respectively.[2] (See Exhibit 1 for historical and projected financial statements.) Founded in 1737, the Bayern Brauerei had been in the Ober family for 12 generations. An etching of Gustav Ober, the founder, graced the label of each bottle of beer.

---

[1]In English, Bayern Brauerei (BI-ern BROY-reye) means Bavarian Brewery.
[2]In January 1993, the deutsche mark could be exchanged for about U.S.$0.63.

This case was written by Professor Robert F. Bruner as a basis for class discussion rather than to illustrate effective or ineffective handling of an administrative situation. Bayern Brauerei is a fictional company reflecting the issues in actual organizations. Copyright © 1992 by the University of Virginia Darden School Foundation, Charlottesville, VA. All rights reserved. *No part of this publication may be reproduced, stored in a retrieval system, used in a spreadsheet, or transmitted in any form or by any means—electronic, mechanical, photocopying, recording, or otherwise—without the permission of the Darden School Foundation. For inquiries, please send an e-mail to dardencases@virginia.edu.* Rev. 5/98. Version 2.2.

The company was located in a village just outside Munich, Germany. Its modern equipment was capable of producing 700,000 hectoliters of beer per year. In 1992 the company sold 667,000 hectoliters. This equipment was acquired in 1987 following a fire that destroyed the old equipment.

Because of its efficiency improvements and slightly larger size, the new equipment increased the potential output of the brewery. This additional capacity remained unused, however, until late 1989. In that year, the Berlin Wall fell, and Germans were permitted to move freely between the eastern and western portions of Germany. August Ober envisioned a significant new market for high-quality beer in eastern Germany and resolved to penetrate that market. Accordingly, in 1990 he hired Max Leiter away from a major beer producer to rejuvenate the Bayern Brauerei sales staff and to move aggressively to position Bayern's beer in *die neuen Bundesländer* (the new federal states, *Länder*)[3] that joined with West Germany in the unification of 1990.

In early 1993, German consumers accounted for all of the company's sales, of which 81 percent were in western Germany (mainly the states of Baden and Bavaria) and 19 percent in the new federal states. Despite their relatively small portion of total sales, however, the eastern *Länder* had accounted for most of the unit growth in Bayern's sales over the past three years.

Bayern served its markets through a network of independent distributors. In western Germany, these distributors purchased Bayern's beer, stored it temporarily in their own refrigerated warehouses, and ultimately sold it to *their* customers at the retail end of the distribution chain (e.g., stores, restaurants, and hotels). Max Leiter had adopted a different distribution strategy with regard to the eastern *Länder.*

LUNCH WITH UNCLE AUGUST

After driving down from Frankfurt, Maria began her visit with a luncheon meeting with August Ober. Now age 57, August had worked at the brewery for his entire career. His experience had been largely on the production side of the brewery, where he had risen to the position of brewmaster before assuming general management of the company upon the retirement of his father. He said,

> Over the long history of this company, the Obers have had to be brewers, not marketers or finance people. As long as we made an excellent product, we always sold our output at the price we asked. Then, in 1989, I realized that we needed more than just production know-how. I wanted to enter

---

[3]Five new federal *Länder* emerged from the former German Democratic Republic, commonly known as East Germany. This region included an area of 106,000 square kilometers and a population of about 15.1 million. The region was dominated by Berlin, which added a population of about 3.4 million. Emigration from the eastern *Länder* was expected to reduce population slightly over the next few years. At the time of unification, manufacturing industry in this region was plagued by badly outdated premises, plant, and equipment. Shortly thereafter, industrial production and incomes fell dramatically as enterprises in the region closed their doors. In January 1993, the economic recovery of the eastern *Länder* was proving to be painfully slow.

the eastern *Länder* because it had traditionally been a good market for our beer before the partition in 1949. Returning to eastern Germany was, for me, reclaiming a lost market. Thus I hired Max Leiter to lead this initiative.

I'm quite pleased with what Max has been able to accomplish. He has organized five distributorships, taken us from 0 to 211 customer accounts, and set up warehousing arrangements—in 30 months, and on a small budget! He really produces results. I am afraid I will have to pay him a lot more money next year, if I am to keep him. As it is, I paid him DM122,860 in 1992, consisting of a base salary of DM80,000 and an incentive payment of DM42,860, which is calculated as 0.5 percent of the annual sales increase. As you know from my letter to the board of directors, I am proposing increases in both his base salary (to DM95,000) and incentive payment (to 0.8 percent of the annual sales increase).

Max was very helpful in pulling together the financial plan for 1993 [see Exhibit 1]. It shows handsomely rising sales and profits! Also, he prepared various analytical presentations, including a sources and uses of funds statement [Exhibit 2] and a detailed ratio analysis [Exhibit 3]. One very helpful analysis was the break-even chart[4] Max prepared [Exhibit 4]. It shows that, as we increase our volume above the break-even volume, our profits rise disproportionately faster.

If we keep on this growth course, we'll exhaust our existing unused productive capacity by late 1993. The budget for 1993 calls for investment of DM8.8 million in new plant and equipment. Max has proposed that in 1994 we invest DM8.6 million in a state-of-the-art warehouse and distribution center in Berlin. He argues that we won't be able to sustain our growth in the eastern *Länder* without these major investments. I haven't even begun thinking about how we will finance all this growth. In recent years, we have depended more on short-term bank loans than we used to. I don't know whether we should continue to rely on them to the extent we have. Right now, we can borrow from our long-standing Hausbank at an 11 percent rate of interest.[5] Our banker asked me to meet with him next week to discuss our expansion plans; I'm guessing that he can't wait to get more of our business!

With the improved profits, I am proposing an increase in dividends for this quarter to a total of DM650,000, one-fourth of the dividends projected to be paid in 1993. This should keep the Ober family happy. As you know, half of our family stockholders are retirees and rely on the dividend to help make ends meet. We have traditionally aimed for a 75 percent dividend payout from earnings each year, to serve our older relatives.

August Ober had been quite talkative during the meal, allowing Maria little opportunity to ask questions or offer her own opinions. She was disquieted by some of the statements she heard, however, and resolved to study the historical and forecasted financials in detail. Then, quite abruptly, Uncle August announced that lunch was done and he would take her to meet Max Leiter.

---

[4]This chart shows the relationship between revenues, costs, and volume of output. For instance, revenues are calculated as the volume of hectoliters of beer sold times the unit price of DM153.46 per hectoliter. Fixed costs (DM27.814 million) remain constant as unit output varies and are the sum of administration and selling expense plus depreciation. Variable costs are the sum of production costs, excise duties, and allowance for doubtful accounts, or DM102.29 per hectoliter. At any given level of output, total costs are the sum of variable and fixed costs. Profits or losses are illustrated as the difference between the revenue and total-cost lines, but note carefully that "profit" here is implicitly defined as earnings before interest and taxes (EBIT). This analysis identifies the break-even volume, where revenues just equal total costs. Bayern Brauerei's break-even volume was 543,607 hectoliters.

[5]In January 1993, the annual rate of return on short-term German government debt was 8.25 percent.

MEETING WITH MAX LEITER

After the introductory pleasantries, Maria asked Max to describe his marketing strategy and achievements in the eastern *Länder.* Max said,

Our beer almost sells itself; discount pricing and heavy advertising are unwarranted. The challenge is getting people to try it and getting it into a distribution pipeline, so that when the consumer wants to buy more, she can do so. But in 1990 and 1991, the beer distribution pipeline in eastern Germany was nonexistent. I had to go there and set up distributorships from nothing; there were willing entrepreneurs, but they had no capital. I provided the best financing I knew how, in the form of trade credit concessions. First, I extended credit to distributors in the East who could not bear the terms we customarily gave our distributors in western Germany. I relaxed the terms to these new distributors from 2 percent 10, net 40, to 2 percent 10, net 80.[6] Even on these terms, our distributors are asking for more time to pay; I plan to relax the payment deadline to 90 days. I am confident that we will collect on all of these receivables; my forecast assumes that bad debts as a percentage of accounts receivable will amount to only 2 percent.

These distributors are real entrepreneurs. They started with nothing but their brains. They have great ambitions and learn quickly. Some of them have gotten past due on their payments to us, but I suspect that they will catch up in due course. Virtually all the retailers and restaurateurs we supply are expanding and enhancing their shops, buying modern equipment, and restocking their own inventories—all without the support of big banks like yours in Frankfurt! Most of these retailers can't get bank credit; their "bootstrap" financing is ingenious and admirable. A little delay in payment is understandable. Where we see great opportunity in these distributors, the banks see no collateral, low profits, negative cash flow, and high risk. I know these distributors better than the banks know them. I think we'll make a profit on our investment there. My analysis [see Exhibit 5] suggests that we are earning a very high return on our investment in receivables in the eastern *Länder.* We borrow at 11 percent from our bank in the West, and use those funds to finance receivables in the East that give us a return of about 140 percent!

I should add that the other parts of my marketing strategy involve field warehousing, to permit rapid response to market demand, and quite a lot of missionary activity, to see that our beer received the proper placement in stores and restaurants. My policy on field inventories has been to support the fragile distributor network by carrying a substantial part of the inventory on behalf of the distributor. This resulted in a sizable increase in inventory for the company in 1991 and 1992.

These new marketing policies have paid off handsomely in terms of our unit growth in the new federal states. Sales in the eastern *Länder* grew 47 percent in 1992—a rate of increase that I aim to sustain for the foreseeable future. Without my changes in credit and inventory policy, we would have realized only a small fraction of our current level of sales there. In 1993 I hope to establish five more distributors and place our beer in 100 more stores and restaurants.

Maria inquired about the signs of economic recession in Germany and the deep recession in the eastern *Länder.* Max seemed relatively unconcerned and said confidently that unit sales in the new federal states would rise significantly in 1993. At the close of their meeting, Maria asked for information on Bayern's credit customers. Max supplied several files from which she extracted the summary information in Exhibit 6.

---

[6]"2 percent 10, net 40" means that Bayern's customer can take a 2 percent discount if payment is made within 10 days of invoice, and that otherwise the full payment is due within 40 days.

CONCLUSION

After a lengthy dinner that evening, at which she met the other directors, Maria returned to the information she had gathered that day. She would need to form an opinion on the three matters coming before the board the next day (the financial plan, the dividend declaration, and the compensation plan for Max). She also wanted to study the company's reliance on debt financing. The other directors would be interested to know why, if the company was operating so profitably above its break-even volume, it needed to borrow so aggressively. Maria also wondered about the wisdom of Bayern's aggressive penetration of the eastern *Länder:* Did rapid sales growth necessarily pay off in terms of more profits or dividends? All this would take more study. She yawned and then poured herself a cup of coffee before returning to scrutinize the numbers.

EXHIBIT 1   Historical and Projected Income Statements and Balance Sheets (fiscal year ended December 31; all figures in DM thousands)

| | Historical and Projected Income Statements | | | | | |
| | Actual | | | | Projected | |
	1989	*1990*	*1991*	*1992*	*1993*	*1994*
1. Sales: Western *Länder*	78,202	78,984	80,959	83,476	85,981	88,560
2. Sales: Eastern *Länder*	—	3,113	12,825	18,879	27,375	35,587
3. Net sales	78,202	82,097	93,784	102,355	113,355	124,147
Operating expenses						
4. Production costs and expenses	40,667	43,390	50,159	56,298	64,302	69,272
5. Administrative and selling expenses	15,734	15,967	18,663	20,164	21,000	24,000
6. Depreciation	4,550	5,439	7,367	7,650	7,650	8,530
7. Excise duties	11,526	11,174	11,734	11,949	12,469	13,656
8. Total operating expenses	(72,477)	(75,970)	(87,923)	(96,061)	(105,421)	(115,458)
9. Operating margin	5,725	6,127	5,861	6,294	7,935	8,689
10. Allowance for doubtful accounts	(9)	(6)	(28)	(19)	(188)	(46)
11. Interest expense	(841)	(778)	(2,260)	(2,085)	(2,406)	(2,679)
12. Earnings before taxes	4,875	5,343	3,573	4,190	5,341	5,964
13. Income taxes	(1,647)	(1,845)	(1,412)	(1,634)	(1,869)	(2,087)
14. Net earnings	3,228	3,498	2,161	2,556	3,471	3,877
15. Dividends to all common shares	2,428	2,628	1,622	1,917	2,604	2,908
16. Retention of earnings	800	870	539	639	868	969
Assets						
1. Cash	6,764	10,040	11,254	12,283	13,603	14,898
2. Accounts receivable						
Western *Länder*	8,740	9,004	9,104	9,477	9,658	9,948
Eastern *Länder*	0	310	2,987	4,505	6,750	8,775
Allowance for doubtful accounts	(87)	(93)	(121)	(140)	(328)	(374)
3. Inventories	7,732	7,853	8,965	14,330	15,870	17,381
4. Total current assets	23,149	27,114	32,189	40,455	45,552	50,627
5. Investments and other assets	3,911	3,913	3,918	3,914	3,000	3,000
6. Gross property, plant, and equipment	73,667	73,667	76,500	76,500	85,300	93,933
7. Accumulated depreciation	(29,505)	(34,944)	(42,311)	(49,961)	(57,611)	(66,141)
8. Net property, plant, and equipment	44,162	38,723	34,189	26,539	27,689	27,792
9. Total assets	71,222	69,750	70,296	70,908	76,242	81,419
Liabilities and stockholders' equity						
10. Bank borrowings (short term)	3,765	7,172	7,640	7,892	12,651	16,977
11. Accounts payable	4,511	4,607	4,705	5,328	5,668	6,207
12. Other current liabilities	9,325	9,031	10,316	11,259	12,469	13,656
13. Total current liabilities	17,601	20,810	22,661	24,479	30,788	36,841
14. Long-term debt, bank borrowings	20,306	14,755	12,911	11,066	9,222	7,378
15. Stockholders' equity	33,315	34,185	34,724	35,363	36,231	37,201
16. Total liabilities and stockholders' equity	71,222	69,750	70,296	70,908	76,242	81,419

Source: Casewriter analysis.

EXHIBIT 4 Break-even Chart for Bayern Brauerei, 1992

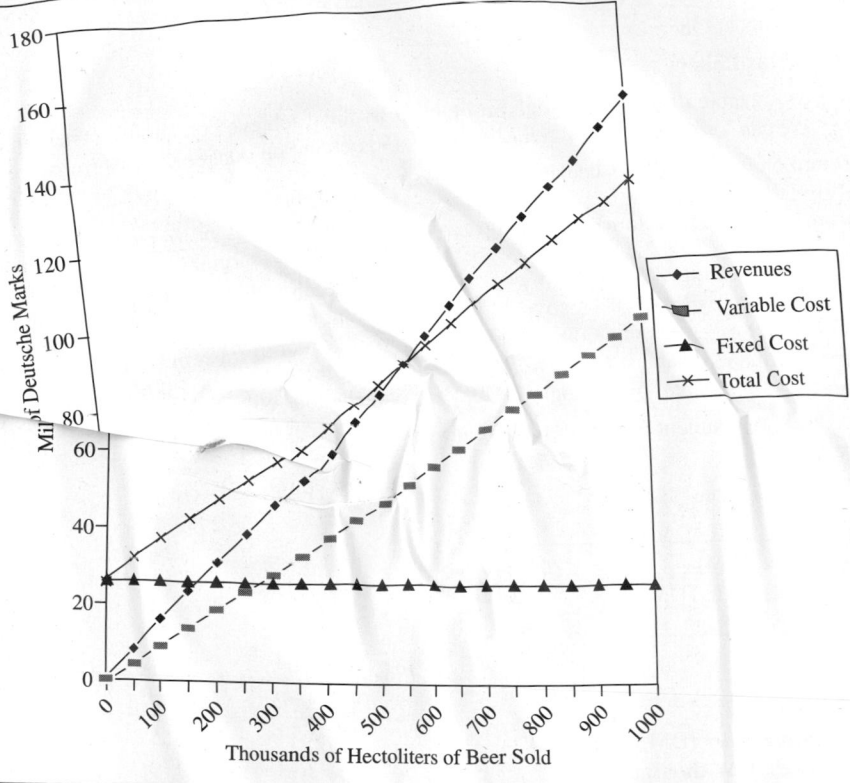

Source: Casewriter analysis.

EXHIBIT 5   Max Leiter's Analysis of the Return on Investment from Investment in Accounts Receivable in the Eastern *Länder*

To: August Ober

From: Max Leiter

The following table illustrates the high profitability we have achieved on our investment in receivables in the Eastern *Länder*. We can look forward to a return of about 140 percent on our receivables from the East.

The return on investment is calculated as follows:

$$\text{Return on investment} = \frac{\text{Marginal after-tax profit contribution}}{\text{Required marginal investment}}$$

The numerator is simply the profits we earn on new sales each year in the East. It excludes the fixed costs be—
we assume these costs have been covered already: we want to focus on the *marginal* events only. Al.... product
that, without the extension of credit, no sales growth would occur in Eastern Germany. The de——
investment in the receivables. This is *not* the face amount of the receivables; it is only t——
underlying the receivable. Accordingly, for 1993, the calculation is:

$$\text{Investment in accounts receivable } (AR) = (\text{Variable} \quad \text{....es}) \times \text{Change in AR}$$
$$= (102.29 \div 153.46) \times 2,245,000$$
$$= \text{DM}1,496,420$$

Assumptions

Revenue per HL (DM)	153.46
Variable Costs per HL (DM)	102.35
Contribution Percentage	33%
Tax Rate	35%

	1989 (Actual)	1990 (Actual)	1991 (Actual)	1992 (Actual)	1993 (Proj'd.)	1994 (Proj'd.)
Sales in Easter *Länder* (DM, thousands)	—	3,113	12,825	18,879	27,375	35,587
Change in sales (DM, thousands)	—	3,113	9,172	6,054	8,496	8,212
Variable costs on the marginal sales	—	(2,076)	(6,478)	(4,037)	(5,666)	(5,477)
Contribution on the marginal sales	—	1,037	3,235	2,016	2,829	2,735
Taxes on the marginal contribution	—	(363)	(1132)	(706)	(990)	(957)
Marginal after-tax profits (DM thousands)	—	674	2,103	1,311	1,839	1,778
Variable costs/Sales	—	67%	67%	67%	67%	67%
Change in accounts receivable, Eastern *Länder* (DM thousands)	—	310	2,677	1,518	2,245	2,025
Investment in accounts receivable (DM thousands)	—	207	1,785	1,012	1,497	1,351
Return on marginal investment in receivables	0%	326%	118%	129%	123%	132%

EXHIBIT 6   Selected Information on Bayern's Distributors in the Eastern *Länder*

Bayern Distributors by City

	Magdeburg	Chemnitz	Dresden	Gera	Berlin	Composite Ratios, German Beer-Distribution Industry
Income data						
Net sales, 1992	DM4,500,000	DM3,600,000	DM3,100,000	DM1,500,000	DM6,179,000	NA
Operating profit/Sales	1.8%	2.2%	3.0%	1.1%	3.5%	3.7%
Pretax profit/Sales	1.7%	1.9%	2.3%	0.7%	3.1%	3.5%
Assets (as % of total)						
Trade receivables	12.9%	13.5%	16.5%	19.5%	13.0%	12.0%
Inventory	15.1%	19.0%	30.0%	25.0%	22.0%	31.0%
Fixed assets	33.1%	29.1%	25.0%	21.0%	28.0%	24.0%
Total	100.0%	100.0%	100.0%	100.0%	100.0%	100.0%
Liabilities						
Short-term bank borrowings	0.1%	2.1%	1.5%	2.5%	4.0%	15.0%
Trade payables	29.2%	32.2%	28.7%	37.5%	19.0%	16.3%
Total current liabilities	35.0%	41.0%	33.2%	43.2%	27.0%	39.4%
Long-term debt	2.5%	0.0%	3.0%	0.0%	5.0%	16.0%
Net worth	32.5%	59.0%	63.8%	56.2%	68.0%	44.6%
Total	100.0%	100.0%	100.0%	100.0%	100.0%	100.0%
Ratios						
Current ratio	1.1	1.2	1.1	0.9	1.6	1.4
Days' sales outstanding	27.7	25.9	27.4	39.5	19.8	19.4
Sales/Assets	2.0	1.9	2.2	1.8	2.4	2.3
Pretax profit/Assets	2.9%	3.6%	5.1%	1.3%	7.4%	8.0%
Debt/Equity	8.0%	3.6%	7.1%	4.4%	13.2%	69.5%

Source: Casewriter analysis.

Merrill Electronics Corporation (A)

In early July 1991, Patricia Merrill, the president and largest shareholder of Merrill Electronics, was preparing to evaluate her company's operating results for the first half of 1991. She was particularly interested in these results for two reasons: first, she wished to determine the effectiveness of the policies and efforts of the company's new general manager, Charles Brown; and, second, she was to meet with Brown later in the day to discuss the company's cash position and the renegotiation of the lines of credit with its banks.

Since its founding in 1950 by Thomas Merrill, Merrill Electronics had been a distributor for GEC,[1] a large manufacturer of electrical and electronics products for consumer and institutional markets. Over the years, in addition to the GEC products, the company had added noncompeting lines of electrical appliances, records, compact discs, and cassettes. In 1980, it began to broaden its product lines by importing Japanese consumer electronics. Four years later, it entered into an exclusive import agreement with the Goldstone Corporation of Taiwan, a major producer of television and other electronic equipment. These products were distributed to retail firms and dealers throughout a broad geographical area.

By the mid-1980s, Merrill had entered into the personal computer (PC) market, distributing both hardware and software products. It became the national distributor for Fuji Electronics, a major Japanese manufacturer of PCs and related products, in March 1989. This had proven to be a fast-growing market, accounting for close to half of total sales and even more of the profits during the latest six-month period; but at the same time, it was becoming more and more competitive. By 1991, price-cutting had become rampant as mail-order and discount houses entered the business.

---

[1] Formerly, the Global Electrical Company. In 1982, the company's name and logo were changed to create a new image.

This case was prepared by Professor H. Lee Remmers at the European Institute of Business Administration (INSEAD), Fontainebleau, France.

Copyright H. L. Remmers, INSEAD, 1992.

Patricia Merrill had been working in the company for two years when her father, Thomas Merrill, died in January 1989. As the only family member with experience in the company, she succeeded him as president. Together with her mother, she controlled 75 percent of the share capital of the firm. The remaining shares were held by her father's brother and sister and their families. Although Patricia Merrill herself received a salary from the company, her mother and the other shareholders in the family relied on dividends from the company for a portion of their income.

Twenty-nine at the time of her father's death, Patricia Merrill had been working in the company as his personal assistant and heir apparent. During that period, he had delegated relatively little responsibility to her. Anxious to prove herself in her newly assumed capacity, she set ambitious growth targets for the company and then began to try to recruit a seasoned operating manager to help achieve those objectives. When she reviewed the operating statements for the first half of 1990, generally regarded as a good year in the industry, she was convinced she needed help. That October, she was able to attract Charles Brown into the company as general manager by offering him a share of the profits in addition to salary. Brown had been the general sales manager of a distributor handling the products of a major GEC competitor. It was agreed by them that, as general manager, Brown would have full authority to execute any changes he desired.

At the time of her father's death, Merrill had been troubled by the question of whether the family should retain its interest in the company or sell out. She had been aware of her father's concern over the steadily declining margins in the electrical distribution business in recent years, and, while the family enjoyed considerable wealth, she wondered whether they should not sell all or part of their shareholdings and invest the proceeds elsewhere. In fact, her uncle had been putting pressure on her to put the company up for sale ever since the death of her father.

At the end of 1990, her first year at the head of the company, Patricia Merrill had almost decided that they should sell out. In fact, she had told Brown at their first meeting that she might be interested in finding a buyer for the company because margins had fallen so drastically in recent years.

> My father worked on an average gross margin of about 20 percent not many years ago. Nowadays, aside from the computer line and records, we don't average 14 percent anymore. Television, which used to yield 15 percent, is now below 12 percent. The market for computers and software has become cutthroat and margins have fallen drastically during the past year and a half. So how can we make money? My feeling is that, if this keeps up, the distribution business will soon disappear. That's why I feel we should get out of this business now.

Brown replied that he was certainly familiar with the declining margins problem and that he had given it a great deal of thought. He was convinced, he said, that the answer lay in doing a high-volume business.

> I don't think we'll ever see average gross margins of 20 percent in the traditional lines of our business again, but I do think we can maintain the return on investment by building volume, adding new product lines and rationalizing or possibly dropping old ones, and controlling costs. It won't be easy, but I think it can be done.

Brown's confidence had been an important element in Merrill's decision to leave the family's money in the company, at least for the time being.

During his first few weeks with the company, Brown reviewed in detail the records of the operating and sales departments. He was particularly concerned with the market penetration achieved by the company's sales force in 1990 in relation to the estimated market potential as supplied by GEC, Fuji, and certain other suppliers. He was also interested in the gross margin trends and in the earnings shown by product lines.

As a result of his review, and with the aid of the operations manager, Julian McNeil, and the sales manager, Michael Teresi, Brown developed a forecast of sales, gross margins, operating expenses, and earnings for the first six months of 1991 (see Exhibit 1). The forecast was submitted to Merrill in late December of 1990, along with the following memorandum:

To: Patricia Merrill

From: Charles Brown

Summary of sales, gross margin and operating earnings objectives, January 1 to June 30, 1991.

1. The budgeted sales increase of $4,565,000 over the first six months of this past year is based primarily on the distribution of Fuji personal computers and accessories, and further growth in GEC's Vortex line of white goods,[2] which the company took on in late spring 1990. Sales of all other lines are also expected to increase. The primary emphasis in 1991 will be on adding volume to the PC Division while maintaining margins, and bringing white goods into a position where they will be a profitable addition to the company's existing lines of products.

2. The budgeted gross margins are in accordance with 1990 experience, except for televisions and VCRs, where a slight increase is predicted. PC margins have been under pressure, but we believe that our figures are realistic. The gross margin percentages on new products are based on factory representatives' estimates.

3. The budgeted operating earnings percentages are expected to be above 1990 figures since fixed costs will be spread over the greater volume that we expect to sell. In making these projections, we have included the cost of additional sales, office, service, and warehouse personnel to handle the planned increase in sales. We will continue to spend heavily on promotion and other investments to maintain a quality after-sales service.

4. Every effort will be made to speed up collection of accounts receivable and to obtain an overall inventory turnover of eight times in order to obtain the greatest use of the company's financial resources.

During the first six months of 1991, Brown began to put his plans into effect. Additional personnel were added to the staff and, as the monthly sales reports were received, Merrill observed a substantial overall increase in sales in comparison with the same period in 1990.

With the increased volume, however, the company began to have difficulty meeting payments to suppliers while holding borrowing within the credit lines agreed with its banks.

During the last three months of 1990, the company had found it necessary to increase the overall bank credit line limit to $2.5 million to finance larger inventories and receivables. It was planned that the credit line should be partially, if not wholly, paid

---

[2]Clothes washers and dryers, dishwashers, refrigerators, and freezers.

off during the first three months of 1991. However, sales in the first quarter of 1991 higher than had been anticipated, thus prolonging the company's need for borrow funds. The problem was compounded by the arrival in February and March of larg computer and software inventories; it worsened in May and June as white goods small appliances moved more slowly than expected.

Accordingly, Merrill and Brown approached the company's banks in March and arrang for an increase in their credit lines to $3 million and for them to be extended to Septem 30, 1991. During the next three months, sales continued to expand so that in late June made a further request to the banks for an extension of the $3 million limit to March 1992. The request was turned down. However, the bankers told Merrill and Brown would consider continuing the current line until December 31, 1991. But they would to be presented with a realistic operating plan including a cash-flow forecast to show the company could stay within the $3 million credit limit during the second half of the year, *and* reduce the amount of credit lines used to no more than $500,000 by December 31.

The chairman of the loan committee of the company's principal bank told Merrill and Brown that he believed part of the company's financial needs were long-term in nature and therefore should be supplied by an increase in equity or long-term capital. He insisted that without an increase of capital from the shareholders, his bank would find it very difficult to extend its present credit line of $1.5 million beyond the end of December if the conditions outlined above (preceding paragraph) were not met.

At the beginning of the second week in July, Merrill received from Julian McNeil, the operations manager, copies of the company's income statement and balance sheet for the six months ended June 30, 1991, together with his comments on sales, gross margins and earnings. (See Exhibits 1, 2, 3, and 4.) For comparative purposes, McNeil also gave Merrill a set of selected financial and operating statistics drawn from a sample of other companies in the consumer electronics distribution industry (see Exhibit 5). On receipt of these reports, Merrill began to analyze the effectiveness of Brown's plans and operations during the first half of 1991.

She next turned her attention to the company's financial position, giving consideration to a number of alternative ways of meeting its cash needs during the second half of 1991. In assessing these needs, she bore in mind that both Fuji and GEC recently had sent reminders that the credit terms *net 30 days* meant just that, that is, that they were going to be enforced. This could take a number of forms: interest could be charged on past-due payables, perhaps at considerably above market rates; much worse, the suppliers could stop shipping or ship only upon receipt of cash payment. Merrill also discussed with Brown, McNeil, and Teresi the expected sales targets for the company until the end of June 1991. Between them they agreed upon a sales forecast for the next 12 months (Exhibit 6).

Second, Merrill wondered to what extent the funds required for their ambitious sales program could be met internally—specifically, through a combination of reduced operating expenses, reduced inventory levels, improved collection of receivables, and, possibly, the dropping of one or more product lines.

Finally, she wondered whether—on the basis of Brown's performance to date and the long-term prospects of the business—the Merrill family might be justified in investing additional funds of their own in the company or, instead, begin to look for someone to buy them out sooner rather than later. Even if the family were to hold on to the company for now, investing additional capital if needed, she believed that within the next three to five years they should try to realize part of their investment by placing some of their shares on the over-the-counter market. To keep peace in the family, one way or another she would have to give the other shareholders a way to realize part of their investment. And she was well aware that to go public would require a solid track record—strong, stable growth of sales revenues and earnings, and a sound financial position.

EXHIBIT 1   Budgeted versus Actual Performance (January 1 to June 30, 1991)

	Budgeted $	% of Sales	Actual $	% of Sales	Variance in $	Actual as % of Budget	Difference in Percent
Net Sales							
PC products and services	6,500,000	100.0	7,261,500	100.0	+778,020	112	
Records, CDs, cassettes	736,125	100.0	986,730	100.0	+250,605	134	
Television and VCR	3,289,425	100.0	3,153,765	100.0	−135,660	96	
Hi-fi and electronics	1,311,840	100.0	1,397,160	100.0	+85,320	107	
Vortex	2,520,000	100.0	2,546,670	100.0	+26,670	101	
Small appliances	863,560	100.0	956,535	100.0	+92,970	111	
Total sales	15,220,950		16,302,360		1,097,925	107	
Gross Margin							
PC products and services	1,718,120	26.5	1,724,600	23.7	+6,480		−2.8
Records, CDs, cassettes	147,220	20.0	202,280	20.5	+55,060		+0.5
Television and VCR	332,240	10.1	352,365	11.1	+20,125		+1.0
Hi-fi and electronics	204,650	15.6	205,095	14.7	+445		−0.9
Vortex	348,090	13.8	312,225	12.3	−35,865		−1.5
Small appliances	99,730	11.5	107,130	11.2	+7,400		−0.3
Total gross margin	2,850,050	18.7	2,903,695	17.8	53,645		−0.9
Operating Expenses							
PC products and services	1,170,000	18.0	1,430,520	19.7	+260,520		+1.7
Records, CDs, cassettes	113,700	15.4	115,170	11.7	+1,470		−3.7
Television and VCR	250,000	7.6	253,380	8.0	+3,380		+0.4
Hi-fi and electronics	177,110	13.5	168,285	12.0	−8,825		−1.5
Vortex	317,850	12.6	285,290	11.2	−32,560		−1.4
Small appliances	91,550	10.6	105,720	11.1	+14,170		+0.5
Total expenses	2,120,210	13.9	2,358,365	14.5	238,155		
Earnings before Interest and Taxes (EBIT)							
PC products and services	548,120	8.5	294,080	4.1	−254,040		−4.4
Records, CDs, cassettes	33,520	4.0	87,110	8.8	+53,590		+4.2
Television and VCR	82,230	2.5	98,985	3.1	+16,755		+0.6
Hi-fi and electronics	27,540	2.1	36,810	2.6	+9,270		+0.5
Vortex	30,240	1.2	26,935	1.1	−3,305		−0.1
Small appliances	8,180	0.9	1,410	0.1	−6,770		−0.8
Total earnings before tax	729,830	4.8	545,330	3.4	−184,500		

EXHIBIT 2 Report of Operations (January 1 to June 30, 1991)

To: Patricia Merrill, President

From: Julian McNeil, Operations Manager

Re: Report of operations for six months ending June 30, 1991

1. Summary results are shown for the first half of 1991 on the previous page (Exhibit 1).

2. Division Analysis

PC Products Division

Sales volume during the past six months exceeded forecasts by over three-quarters of a million dollars. The new Fuji 2500XEC laptop has been especially popular and accounted for close to 20 percent of the total—in spite of some teething problems discussed below. However, gross margins have been under considerable pressure from discounters, especially for software products. We are concerned that this will continue and very likely become even more severe during the next few months. Margins overall may fall to as low as 20 percent before stabilizing. In addition, since well over half of this division's products are purchased from Japanese suppliers, margins may also be affected by currency fluctuations. Finally, we are beginning to explore the possibility of starting a mail-order operation with our own brand label—similar to Dell Computers.

Operating expenses are also running above those forecast. Part of this is due to problems with the color screens on the new F2500XEC laptop, but a number of other products have needed more service than planned. As our service and repair personnel become more experienced, expenses should be easier to control in this area. Inventories are still more than $500,000 over our target level, and competition will make it difficult to improve this situation much in the short term. There is some $200,000 in obsolete merchandise; we may be able to return some of this to our suppliers, but most will have to be sold off below cost.

Records Division

1991 should make history. Sales were especially strong in compact discs. Our most recent analysis of obsolete inventories indicates that we have approximately $30,000 to dispose of. We will probably have to sell this stock at below cost.

We are negotiating with another major producer and hope to add their label to our existing lines. This should have a favorable effect on revenues. On the other hand, margins continue to be under pressure from discounters.

Television and VCR Division

TV sales for the first six months are slightly below last year, although gross margin and operating earnings are ahead. On the negative side, ending June inventory is well above target and includes roughly $250,000 worth of older models. We will try to move these as fast as possible, but will probably mean discounting below cost.

According to GEC factory reports on television distributor sales to dealers, our market share in this area for the year to date is 14.7 percent. This compares to GEC's overall market share for 17.8 percent for this same period. In 1990, our market share was 15.2 percent, compared to the GEC national average of 16.9 percent. In 1989 we had 17.0 percent of the market in our area, compared to the GEC national average of 16.5 percent. Fortunately, our market share for Fuji TVs is up from the same period a year ago.

EXHIBIT 2   (*continued*)

VCR sales of the new Fuji and Goldstone lines as well as earnings are better than forecast, somewhat offsetting the currently weak TV market. We have had some servicing problems with the Goldstone VCRs, and although the factory has promised help, repair expenses may rise.

Hi-Fi and Electronics Division

Sales for the first half of 1991 have exceeded 1990 by $225,000. Although gross margins have decreased slightly in percentage terms, our operating earnings have increased. Factory reports of distributor sales of hi-fi equipment to dealers show our market share for the first months of 1991 to be 19.4 percent. This compares to the GEC national average of 12.0 percent for the same period. In 1990, our market share was 18.2 percent compared to the GEC national average of 11.8 percent. In 1989 the figures were 15.6 percent and 12.0 percent, respectively. Likewise, our market share for Fuji products is better than their overall national average.

Our order backlog amounts to more than $125,000. If business remains at or near the present level, this will be a banner year for this department. However, there are some orders in jeopardy because of slow delivery of merchandise from suppliers. Given this situation, our inventory target of 45 days may prove to be unrealistic.

Vortex Division

Because we took on the Vortex line in the middle of 1990, there are no comparable figures for the first half operation. We realize that this division has not done much more than break even for the first six months of 1991; however, in view of the promotional costs which we had (approximately $85,000) and some discounting, it may be considered satisfactory. Since most of these costs have been incurred, the balance of the year should be profitable.

Small-Appliance Division

Sales in this division include portable air conditioners, small kitchen appliances, and lamps. Sales and gross margins are running ahead of last year, but increased expenses from repairs on defective merchandise has virtually wiped out operating earnings.

The principal challenge we are facing is excessively high inventories. With interest rates at current levels, carrying costs exceed operating earnings.

We need to follow closely this division's performance during the next months. If results cannot be improved substantially, we might be advised to phase it out and focus our attention on the more promising lines.

3. Accounts Receivable

Our receivables are in good condition with 91.25 percent current. Bad-debt expense for the latest six months was $81,500, 0.5 percent of total sales. This amount is based on past experience, but may be conservative. Our bad-debt reserve is $191,410 of which about $120,000 will probably be written off when the final accounts for the year are prepared. The condition of our accounts receivable is shown by the following aging schedule:

	June 18, 1991	May 17, 1991
Current	91.25%	93.05%
Past due:		
1 to 30 days	4.15	3.85
31 to 60 days	1.85	1.55
61 to 90 days	1.10	0.81
91 days and over	1.65	0.74

EXHIBIT 2   (*concluded*)

4. Inventories

Our inventories as of June 30, 1991, amounted to $5,591,470. They are up considerably from a year ago, primarily as a result of the addition of the new line of personal computers, obsolete merchandise in the PC and TV divisions, problems with TVs that were mentioned earlier, and the need to carry a relatively broader range of Vortex washers and dryers than was previously the case. Our inventory position by product line is as follows:

Product Line	Actual Inventory Level		Target Inventory Level	
	Amount	In Days*	Amount	In Days†
PC products and services	$2,092,400	68	$1,526,000	50
Records, CDs, etc.	255,365	58	193,560	45
Televisions, VCRs	1,319,945	75	739,600	50
Hi-fi, electronics	450,300	65	285,750	45
Vortex	723,110	60	530,580	45
Small appliances	750,350	110	266,000	60
Total	$5,591,470	67	$3,541,490	49

*Based on anticipated sales volume (valued at cost) for July–October 1991.
†Based on our best estimates of optimum inventory levels, taking into account expected cost of product, delivery lead time from suppliers, diversity of products, sales-forecasting uncertainties.

EXHIBIT 3   Income Statements

	6 Months to 30 June 1990		6 Months to 31 December 1990		6 Months to 30 June 1991	
Net sales	$10,654,900	100.0	$18,096,400	100.0	$16,302,360	100.0
Cost of sales	8,939,610	83.9	15,020,010	83.0	13,398,665	82.2
Gross margin	1,715,290	16.1	3,076,390	17.0	2,903,695	17.8
Operating expenses:						
Direct selling	460,280	4.3	742,780	4.1	665,400	4.1
Advertising and promotion	119,680	1.1	231,300	1.3	205,200	1.3
After-sales service	253,250	2.4	522,650	2.9	566,800	3.5
Warehouse and shipping	178,150	1.7	262,400	1.5	236,400	1.5
General administration	542,550	5.1	575,005	3.1	608,115	3.7
Depreciation	44,175	0.4	54,590	0.3	76,450	0.5
Total expenses	1,598,085	15.0	2,388,725	13.2	2,358,365	14.5
Operating earnings (EBIT)	117,205	1.1	687,665	3.8	545,330	3.4
Interest expense	62,650	0.6	143,225	0.8	178,800	1.1
Earnings before taxes	54,555	0.5	544,440	3.0	366,530	2.3
Corporate taxes	22,900	0.2	206,890	1.2	146,850	0.9
Earnings after taxes	31,655	0.3	337,550	1.9	219,680	1.4
Dividends paid	20,000		50,000		50,000	

EXHIBIT 4   Balance Sheets (amounts in dollars)

	30 June 1990	*31 December 1990*	*30 June 1991*
Assets			
Current assets			
Cash and bank	58,900	38,850	35,220
Accounts receivable (net)	2,841,100	4,826,600	4,166,180
Inventories	2,895,200	3,534,120	5,591,470
Other current assets	29,700	41,450	65,980
Total current assets	5,824,900	8,441,020	9,858,850
Fixed assets			
Buildings and equipment (net)	632,900	718,200	789,750
Goodwill	100,000	100,000	100,000
Total	732,900	818,200	889,750
Total assets	6,557,800	9,259,220	10,748,600
Capital and liabilities			
Current liabilities			
Short-term bank loans	455,000	2,050,000	2,985,000
Long-term debt due in one year	80,000	80,000	80,000
Accounts payable (domestic)	1,155,700	1,819,130	1,705,110
Accounts payable (foreign)*	241,200	391,250	895,620
Accrued expenses	171,980	217,370	251,720
Total current liabilities	2,103,880	4,557,750	5,917,450
Long-term debt	560,000	520,000	480,000
Capital stock	1,000,000	1,000,000	1,000,000
Retained earnings	2,893,920	3,181,470	3,351,150
Owners' equity	3,893,920	4,181,470	4,351,150
Total capital and liabilities	6,557,800	9,259,220	10,748,600

*Primarily yen-denominated invoices.

EXHIBIT 5   Sales Forecasts, July 1991–June 1992 (in thousands of dollars)

Product Line	Jul.	Aug.	Sept.	Oct.	Nov.	Dec.	Jan.	Feb.	Mar.	Apr.	May	Jun.
PC products	1,200	1,200	1,350	1,450	1,600	1,500	1,300	1,450	1,750	1,900	1,850	1,800
Records, etc.	150	175	290	450	570	240	170	230	250	280	300	270
TV and VCRs	470	550	930	1,400	1,850	1,260	650	750	820	850	900	800
Hi-fi	210	250	400	630	800	640	225	325	345	360	350	320
Vortex	380	450	750	1,120	1,470	1,150	500	600	650	700	720	680
Appliances	135	170	275	420	550	450	180	240	250	270	280	250
Total	2,545	2,795	3,995	5,470	6,840	5,240	3,025	3,595	4,065	4,360	4,400	4,120

EXHIBIT 6   Selected Financial and Operating Data for Electronics Equipment Distributors[a]

	Average—Lower Quartile	Median	Average—Upper Quartile
Current ratio	1.5	2.0	2.7
Acid-test ratio	0.6	1.0	1.3
Debt ratio[b]	41.2%	48.6%	55.1%
Asset turnover[c]	3.0	3.5	3.9
Collection period[d]	28 days	33 days	39 days
Payment period[e]	29 days	31 days	35 days
Inventory turnover[f]	7.5 times	8.6 times	9.2 times
Gross margin	12.7%	15.4%	18.0%
Operating expenses/Sales	9.8%	12.2%	14.4%
Operating earnings (EBIT)/Sales	2.9%	3.2%	3.6%
Earnings after tax (EAT)/Sales	1.1%	1.3%	1.5%
Return on equity (ROE)[g]	4.7%	6.9%	9.5%

[a]Based on latest six-month results (January–June 1990).
[b]Total liabilities divided by total assets.
[c]Sales revenue for January–June 1991, divided by total assets for June 30, 1991 (annualized by multiplying by 2).
[d]Receivables on June 30, 1991, divided by sales revenue for January–June 1991 multiplied by 180 days.
[e]Payables on June 30, 1991, divided by purchases for January–June 1991 multiplied by 180 days.
[f]Inventories on June 30, 1991, divided by cost of sales for January–June 1991 (annualized by multiplying by 2).
[g]Earnings after tax for January–June 1991, divided by owners' equity for June 30, 1991 (annualized by multiplying by 2).

Part III

Estimating the Cost of Capital

"Best Practices" in Estimating the Cost of Capital: Survey and Synthesis

In recent decades, theoretical breakthroughs in such areas as portfolio diversification, market efficiency, and asset pricing have converged into compelling recommendations about the cost of capital to a corporation. By the early 1990s, a consensus had emerged prompting such descriptions as "traditional . . . textbook . . . appropriate," "theoretically correct" and "a useful rule of thumb and a good vehicle."[1] Beneath this general agreement about cost of capital theory lies considerable ambiguity and confusion over how the theory can best be applied. The issues at stake are sufficiently important that differing choices on a few key elements can lead to wide disparities in estimated capital cost. The cost of capital is central to modern finance touching on investment and divestment decisions, measures of economic profit, performance appraisal and incentive systems. Each year in the United States, corporations undertake more than $500 billion in capital spending. Since a difference of a few percent in capital costs can mean a swing in billions of expenditures, how firms estimate the cost is no trivial matter.

The purpose of this paper is to present evidence on how some of the most financially sophisticated companies and financial advisers estimate capital costs. This evidence is

[1]The three sets of quotes come, in order, from Ehrhardt (1994), Chapter 1; Copeland et al. (1990), p. 190; and Brealey and Myers (1993), p. 197.

This chapter was written by Robert F. Bruner, Kenneth M. Eades, Robert S. Harris, and Robert C. Higgins. Bruner, Eades, and Harris are professors at the Darden School, University of Virginia. Higgins is a professor at the University of Washington. The authors thank Todd Brotherson for excellent research assistance, and gratefully acknowledge the financial support of Coopers & Lybrand and the University of Virginia Darden School Foundation. The research would not have been possible without the cooperation of the 37 companies surveyed. These contributions notwithstanding, any errors remain the authors'. This chapter appeared in *Journal of Financial Practice and Education* (Spring 1998), and appears here with the permission of the Financial Management Association International, University of South Florida, College of Business Administration, Tampa, FL 33620-5500 (telephone: 813-974-2084).

valuable in several respects. First, it identifies the most important ambiguities in the application of cost-of-capital theory, setting the stage for productive debate and research on their resolution. Second, it helps interested companies benchmark their cost-of-capital estimation practices against best-practice peers. Third, the evidence sheds light on the accuracy with which capital costs can be reasonably estimated, enabling executives to use the estimates more wisely in their decision making. Fourth, it enables teachers to answer the inevitable question, "How do companies really estimate their cost of capital?"

The paper is part of a lengthy tradition of surveys of industry practice. Among the more relevant predecessors, Gitman and Forrester (1977) explored "the level of sophistication in capital budgeting techniques" among 103 large, rapidly growing businesses, finding that the internal rate of return and the payback period were in common use. Although the authors inquired about the level of the firm's discount rate, they did not ask how the rate was determined. Gitman and Mercurio (1982) surveyed 177 Fortune 1000 firms about "current practice in cost of capital measurement and utilization," concluding that "the respondents' actions do not reflect the application of current financial theory." Moore and Reichert (1983) surveyed 298 Fortune 500 firms on the use of a broad array of financial techniques, concluding among other things, that 86 percent of firms surveyed use time-adjusted capital budgeting techniques. Bierman (1993) surveyed 74 Fortune 100 companies reporting that all use some form of discounting in their capital budgeting and 93 percent use a weighted-average cost of capital. In a broad-ranging survey of 84 Fortune 500 large firms and Forbes 200 best small companies, Trahan and Gitman (1995) report that 30 percent of respondents use the capital asset pricing model.

This paper differs from its predecessors in several important respects. Existing published evidence is based on written, closed-end surveys sent to a large sample of firms, often covering a wide array of topics and commonly using multiple-choice or fill-in-the-blank questions. Such an approach often yields response rates as low as 20 percent and provides no opportunity to explore subtleties of the topic. Instead, we report the result of a telephone survey of a carefully chosen group of leading corporations and financial advisers. Another important difference is that the intent of existing papers is most often to learn how well accepted modern financial techniques are among practitioners, while we are interested in those areas of cost-of-capital estimation where finance theory is silent or ambiguous and practitioners are left to their own devices.

The following section gives a brief overview of the weighted-average cost of capital. The research approach and sample selection are discussed in Section II. Section III reports the general survey results. Key points of disparity are reviewed in Section IV. Section V discusses further survey results on risk adjustment to a baseline cost of capital, and Section VI offers conclusions and implications for the financial practitioner.

I. THE WEIGHTED-AVERAGE COST OF CAPITAL

A key insight from finance theory is that any use of capital imposes an opportunity cost on investors; namely, funds are diverted from earning a return on the next best equal-risk investment. Since investors have access to a host of financial market opportunities, corporate uses of capital must be benchmarked against these capital market alternatives. The cost of capital provides this benchmark. Unless a firm can earn in excess of its cost of capital, it will not create economic profit or value for investors.

A standard means of expressing a company's cost of capital is the weighted average of the cost of individual sources of capital employed. In symbols, a company's weighted-average cost of capital (or WACC) is

$$\text{WACC} = (W_{\text{debt}}(1 - t)K_{\text{debt}}) + (W_{\text{preferred}}K_{\text{preferred}}) + (W_{\text{equity}}K_{\text{equity}}) \qquad (1)$$

where:

K = Component cost of capital
W = Weight of each component as percent of total capital
t = Marginal corporate tax rate

For simplicity, this formula includes only three sources of capital; it can be easily expanded to include other sources as well.

Finance theory offers several important observations when estimating a company's WACC. First, the capital costs appearing in the equation should be current costs reflecting current financial market conditions, not historical, sunk costs. In essence, the costs should equal the investors' anticipated internal rate of return on future cash flows associated with each form of capital. Second, the weights appearing in the equation should be market weights, not historical weights based on often arbitrary, out-of-date book values. Third, the cost of debt should be after corporate tax, reflecting the benefits of the tax deductibility of interest.

Despite the guidance provided by finance theory, use of the weighted-average expression to estimate a company's cost of capital still confronts the practitioner with a number of difficult choices.[2] As our survey results demonstrate, the most nettlesome component of WACC estimation is the cost of equity capital; for unlike readily available yields in bond markets, no observable counterpart exists for equities. This forces practitioners to rely on more abstract and indirect methods to estimate the cost of equity capital.

II. SAMPLE SELECTION

This paper describes the results of a telephone survey of leading practitioners. Believing that the complexity of the subject does not lend itself to a written questionnaire, we wanted to solicit an explanation of each firm's approach told in the practitioner's own words. Though our interviews were guided by a series of questions, these were sufficiently open-ended to reveal many subtle differences in practice.

Since our focus is on the gaps between theory and application rather than on average or typical practice, we aimed to sample practitioners who were leaders in the field. We began by searching for a sample of corporations (rather than investors or financial advisers) in the belief that they had ample motivation to compute WACC carefully and to resolve many of the estimation issues themselves. Several publications offer lists of firms that are well-

---

[2]Even at the theoretical level, Dixit and Pindyck (1994) point out that the use of standard net present value (NPV) decision rules (with, for instance, WACC as a discount rate) does not capture the option value of being able to delay an irreversible investment expenditure. As a result, a firm may find it better to delay an investment even if the current NPV is positive. Our survey does not explore the ways firms deal with this issue; rather we focus on measuring capital costs.

regarded in finance;[3] of these, we chose a research report, *Creating World-Class Financial Management: Strategies of 50 Leading Companies* (1992), which identified firms,

> selected by their peers as being among those with the best financial management. Firms were chosen for excellence in strategic financial risk management, tax and accounting, performance evaluation and other areas of financial management . . . The companies included were those that were mentioned the greatest number of times by their peers.[4]

From the 50 companies identified in this report, we eliminated 18 headquartered outside North America.[5] Of those remaining, five declined to be interviewed, leaving a sample of 27 firms. The companies included in the sample are given in Exhibit 1. We approached the most senior financial officer first with a letter explaining our research, and then with a telephone call. Our request was to interview the individual in charge of estimating the firm's WACC. We promised our interviewees that, in preparing a report on our findings, we would not identify the practices of any particular company by name—we have respected this promise in the presentation that follows.

In the interest of assessing the practices of the broader community of finance practitioners, we surveyed two other samples:

- *Financial advisers.* Using a "league table" of merger and acquisition advisers presented in *Institutional Investor* issues of April 1995, 1994, and 1993, we drew a sample of 10 of the most active[6] advisers. We applied approximately[7] the same set of questions to representatives of these firms' merger and acquisition departments. We wondered whether the financial advisers' interest in promoting deals might lead them to lower WACC estimates than those estimated by operating companies. This proved not to be the case. If anything, the estimating techniques most often used by financial advisers yield higher, not lower, capital cost estimates.
- *Textbooks and trade books.* From a leading textbook publisher we obtained a list of the graduate-level textbooks in corporate finance having the greatest unit sales in 1994. From these, we selected the top four. In addition, we drew on three trade books that discuss the estimation of WACC in detail.

Names of advisers and books included in these two samples are shown in Exhibit 1.

---

[3]For instance, *Institutional Investor* and *Euromoney* publish lists of firms with the best CFOs, or with special competencies in certain areas. We elected not to use these lists because special competencies might not indicate a generally excellent finance department, nor might a stellar CFO.

[4]*Creating World-Class Financial Management: Strategies of 50 Leading Companies,* Research Report No. 1-110, Business International Corporation, New York, 1992 (238 pages), pages vii–viii. This survey was based upon a written questionnaire sent to CEOs, CFOs, controllers, and treasurers, followed up by a telephone survey.

[5]Our reasons for excluding these firms were the increased difficulty of obtaining interviews, and possible difficulties in obtaining capital market information (such as betas and equity market premiums) that might preclude using American practices. The enlargement of this survey to firms from other countries is a subject worthy of future study.

[6]*Activity* in this case was defined as four-year aggregate deal volume in mergers and acquisitions. The sample was drawn from the top 12 advisers, using their *average* deal volume over the 1993–95 period. Of these 12 firms, 2 chose not to participate in the survey.

[7]Specific questions differ, reflecting that financial advisers infrequently deal with capital budgeting matters and that corporate financial officers infrequently value companies.

III. SURVEY FINDINGS

The detailed survey results appear in Exhibit 2. The estimation approaches are broadly similar across the three samples in several dimensions:

- Discounted cash flow (DCF) is the dominant investment-evaluation technique.
- WACC is the dominant discount rate used in DCF analyses.
- Weights are based on *market,* not book, value mixes of debt and equity.[8]
- The after-tax cost of debt is predominantly based on *marginal* pretax costs, and *marginal or statutory* tax rates.
- The capital asset pricing model (CAPM) is the dominant model for estimating the cost of equity. Some firms mentioned other multifactor asset pricing models (e.g., arbitrage pricing theory), but these were in the small minority. No firms cited specific modifications of the CAPM to adjust for any empirical shortcomings of the model in explaining past returns.[9]

These practices differ sharply from those reported in earlier surveys.[10] First, the best-practice firms show much more alignment on most elements of practice. Second, they base their practice on financial economic models rather than on rules of thumb or arbitrary decision rules.

On the other hand, disagreements exist within and among groups on how to apply the CAPM to estimate cost of equity. The CAPM states that the required return (K) on any asset can be expressed as

$$K = R_f + \beta(R_m - R_f) \qquad (2)$$

where:

$$
\begin{aligned}
R_f &= \text{Interest rate available on a risk-free bond} \\
R_m &= \text{Return required to attract investors to hold the broad} \\
    &\quad \text{market portfolio of risky assets} \\
\beta &= \text{the relative risk of the particular asset}
\end{aligned}
$$

According to CAPM, then, the cost of equity, K_{equity}, for a company depends on three components: returns on risk-free bonds (R_f); the stock's equity beta, which measures risk of the company's stock relative to other risky assets ($\beta = 1.0$ is average risk); and the market risk premium ($R_m - R_f$) necessary to entice investors to hold risky assets generally versus risk-free bonds. In theory, each of these components must be a forward-looking estimate. Our survey results show substantial disagreements on all three components.

---

[8]The choice between target and actual proportions is not a simple one. Because debt and equity costs clearly depend on the proportions of each employed, it might appear that the actual proportions must be used. However, if the firm's target weights are publicly known and if investors expect the firm soon to move to these weights, then observed costs of debt and equity may anticipate the target capital structure.

[9]For instance, even research supporting the CAPM has found that empirical data are better explained by an intercept higher than a risk-free rate and a price of beta risk less than the market risk premium. Ibbotson (1994) offers such a modified CAPM, in addition to the standard CAPM and other models, in its cost of capital service. Jagannathan and McGrattan (1995) provide a useful review of empirical evidence on the CAPM.

[10]Gitman and Forrester (1977), and Gitman and Mercurio (1982).

Comments on Risk-Free Rates

Some of our best-practice companies noted that their choice of a bond market proxy for a risk-free rate depended specifically on how they were proposing to spend funds. We asked, "What do you use for a risk-free rate?" and heard the following:

- "Ten-year Treasury bond or other duration Treasury bond if needed to better match project horizon."
- "We use a three- to five-year Treasury note yield, which is the typical length of our company's investment. We match our average investment horizon with maturity of debt."

The Risk-Free Rate of Return. As originally derived, the CAPM is a single-period model, so the question of which interest rate best represents the risk-free rate never arises. But in a many-period world typically characterized by upward-sloping yield curves, the practitioner must choose. Our results show the choice is typically between the 90-day T-bill yield and a long-term Treasury bond yield. (Because the yield curve is ordinarily relatively flat beyond 10 years, the choice of which particular long-term yield to use is not a critical one.)[11] The difference between realized returns on the 90-day T-bill and the 10-year T-bond has averaged 150 basis points over the long run; so choice of a risk-free rate can have a material effect on the cost of equity and WACC.[12]

The 90-day T-bill yields are more consistent with the CAPM as originally derived and reflect truly risk-free returns in the sense that T-bill investors avoid material loss in value from interest rate movements. However, long-term bond yields more closely reflect the default-free holding period returns available on long-lived investments and thus more closely mirror the types of investments made by companies.

Our survey results reveal a strong preference on the part of practitioners for long-term bond yields. Of both corporations and financial advisers, 70 percent use Treasury-bond yield maturities of 10 years or greater. None of the financial advisers and only 4 percent of the corporations used the Treasury-bill yield. Many corporations said they matched the term of the risk-free rate to the tenor of the investment. In contrast, 43 percent of the books advocated the T-bill yield, while only 29 percent used long-term Treasury yields.

---

[11]In early January 1996, the differences between yields on the 10- and 30-year T-bonds was about 35 basis points. Some aficionados will argue that there *is* a difference between the 10- and 30-year yields. Ordinarily the yield curve declines just slightly as it reaches the 30-year maturity—this has been explained to us as the result of life insurance companies and other long-term buy-and-hold investors who are said to purchase the long bond in significant volume. It is said that these investors command a lower liquidity premium than the broader market, thus driving down yields. If this is true, then the yields at this point of the curve may be due not to some ordinary process of rational expectations, but rather to an anomalous supply–demand imbalance, which would render these yields less trustworthy. The counterargument is that life insurance companies could be presumed to be rational investors too. As buy-and-hold investors, they will surely suffer the consequences of any irrationality and therefore have good motive to invest for yields "at the market."

[12]This was estimated as the difference in arithmetic mean returns on long-term government bonds and U.S. Treasury bills over the years 1926 to 1994, given in Ibbotson Associates (1995).

Beta Estimates.   Finance theory calls for a forward-looking beta, one reflecting investors' uncertainty about the future cash flows to equity. Because forward-looking betas are unobservable, practitioners are forced to rely on proxies of various kinds. Most often this involves using beta estimates derived from historical data and published by such sources as Bloomberg, Value Line, and Standard & Poor's.

The usual methodology is to estimate beta as the slope coefficient of the market model of returns:

$$R_{it} = \alpha_i + \beta_i(R_{mt}) \qquad (3)$$

where:

R_{it} = Return on stock i in time period (e.g., day, week, month) t
R_{mt} = Return on the market portfolio in period t
α_i = Regression constant for stock i
β_i = Beta for stock i

In addition to relying on historical data, use of this equation to estimate beta requires a number of practical compromises, each of which can materially affect the results. For instance, increasing the number of time periods used in the estimation may improve the statistical reliability of the estimate, but risks the inclusion of stale, irrelevant information. Similarly, shortening the observation period from monthly to weekly, or even daily, increases the size of the sample but may yield observations that are not normally distributed and may introduce unwanted random noise. A third compromise involves choice of the market index. Theory dictates that R_m is the return on the market portfolio, an unobservable portfolio consisting of *all* risky assets, including human capital and other nontraded assets, in proportion to their importance in world wealth. Beta providers use a variety of stock market indices as proxies for the market portfolio on the argument that stock markets trade claims on a sufficiently wide array of assets to be adequate surrogates for the unobservable market portfolio.

The table below shows the compromises underlying the beta estimates of three prominent providers and their combined effect on the beta estimates of our sample companies. Note, for example, that the mean beta of our sample companies according to Bloomberg is 1.03, while the same number according to Value Line is 1.24. Exhibit 3 provides a complete list of sample betas by publisher.

Compromises Underlying Beta Estimates and Their Effect
on Estimated Betas of Sample Companies

	Bloomberg*	*Value Line*	*Standard & Poor's*
Number of observations	102	260	60
Time interval	Weekly over 2 years	Weekly over 5 years	Monthly over 5 years
Market index proxy	S&P 500	NYSE composite	S&P 500
Sample mean beta	1.03	1.24	1.18
Sample median beta	1.00	1.20	1.21

*With the Bloomberg service it is possible to estimate a beta over many differing time periods, market indices, and smoothed or unadjusted. The figures presented here represent the base-line or default-estimation approach used if one does not specify other approaches.

Over half of the corporations in our sample (item 10, Exhibit 2) rely on published sources for their beta estimates, although 30 percent calculate their own. Among financial advisers, 40 percent rely on published sources, 20 percent calculate their own, and another 40 percent use what might be called "fundamental" beta estimates. These are estimates which use multifactor statistical models drawing on fundamental indices of firm and industry risk to estimate company betas. The best-known provider of fundamental beta estimates is the consulting firm BARRA.

Within these broad categories, the following comments indicate that a number of survey participants use more pragmatic approaches, which combine published beta estimates or adjust published estimates in various heuristic ways.

We asked our sample companies, "What do you use as your volatility or beta factor?" A sampling of responses shows that the choice is not always a simple one:

- "[We use] adjusted betas reported by Bloomberg. At times, our stock has been extremely volatile. If at a particular time the factor is considered unreasonably high, we are apt to use a lower (more consistent) one."
- "We begin with the observed 60-month covariance between our stock and the market. We also consider Value Line, BARRA, S&P betas for comparison and may adjust the observed beta to match assessment of future risk."
- "We average Merrill Lynch and Value Line figures and use Bloomberg as a check."
- "We do not use betas estimated on our stock directly. Our company beta is built up as a weighted average of our business segment betas—the segment betas are estimated using pure-play firm betas of comparable companies."

Equity Market Risk Premium.   This topic prompted the greatest variety of responses among survey participants. Finance theory says the equity market risk premium should equal the excess return expected by investors on the market portfolio relative to riskless assets. How one measures expected future returns on the market portfolio and on riskless assets are problems left to practitioners. Because expected future returns are unobservable, all survey respondents extrapolated historical returns into the future on the presumption that past experience heavily conditions future expectations. Where respondents chiefly differed was in their use of *arithmetic* versus *geometric* average historical equity returns and in their choice of realized returns on T-bills versus T-bonds to proxy for the return on riskless assets.

The arithmetic mean return is the simple average of past returns. Assuming the distribution of returns is stable over time and that periodic returns are independent of one another, the arithmetic return is the best estimator of expected return.[13] The geometric mean return is the internal rate of return between a single outlay and one or more future receipts. It measures the compound rate of return investors earned over past periods. It accurately

---

[13]Several studies have documented significant negative autocorrelation in returns—this violates one of the essential tenets of the arithmetic calculation, since if returns are not serially independent, the simple arithmetic mean of a distribution will not be its expected value. The autocorrelation findings are reported by Fama and French (1986), Lo and MacKinlay (1988), and Poterba and Summers (1988).

portrays historical investment experience. Unless returns are the same each time period, the geometric average will always be less than the arithmetic average and the gap widens as returns become more volatile.[14]

Based on Ibbotson Associates' (1995) data from 1926 to 1995, the matrix below illustrates the possible range of equity market risk premiums depending on use of the geometric as opposed to the arithmetic mean equity return and on use of realized returns on T-bills as opposed to T-bonds.[15] Even wider variations in market risk premiums can arise when one changes the historical period for averaging. Extending U.S. stock experience back to 1802, Siegel (1992) shows that historical market premiums have changed over time and were typically lower in the pre-1926 period. Carleton and Lakonishok (1985) illustrate considerable variation in historical premiums using different time periods and methods of calculation even with data since 1926.

The Equity Market Risk Premium ($R_m - R_f$)

	T-Bill Returns	T-Bond Returns
Arithmetic mean return	8.5%	7.0%
Geometric mean return	6.5%	5.4%

Of the texts and trade books in our survey, 71 percent support use of the arithmetic mean return over T-bills as the best surrogate for the equity market risk premium. For long-term projects, Ehrhardt advocates forecasting the T-bill rate and using a different cost of equity for each future time period. Kaplan and Ruback (1995) studied the equity risk premium implied by the valuations in highly leveraged transactions and estimated a mean premium of 7.97 percent, which is most consistent with the arithmetic mean and T-bills. A minority view is that of Copeland, Koller, and Murrin (1990, pp. 193–94) writing on behalf of the Corporate Financial Practice at McKinsey & Company: "We believe that the geometric average represents a better estimate of investors' expected returns over long periods of time." Ehrhardt (1994) recommends use of the geometric mean return if one believes stockholders are "buy-and-hold" investors.

Half of the financial advisers queried use a premium consistent with the arithmetic mean and T-bill returns, and many specifically mentioned use of the arithmetic mean. Corporate respondents, on the other hand, evidenced more diversity of opinion and tend to favor a lower market premium: 37 percent use a premium of 5 to 6 percent, and another 11 percent use an even lower figure.

---

[14]For large samples of returns the geometric average can be approximated as the arithmetic average minus one-half the variance of realized returns. Ignoring sample size adjustments, the variance of returns in the current example is .09 yielding an estimate of $.10 - 1/2(.09) = .055 = 5.5\%$ versus the actual 5.8% figure. Kritzman (1994) provides an interesting comparison of the two types of averages.

[15]These figures are drawn from Table 2–1, Ibbotson (1995), where the R_m was drawn from the "Large Company Stocks" series, and R_f drawn from the "Long-Term Government Bonds" and "U.S. Treasury Bills" series.

Comments Regarding Market Risk Premium

"What do you use as your market risk premium?" A sampling of responses from our best-practice companies shows the choice can be a complicated one.

- "Our 400-basis-point market premium is based on the historical relationship of returns on an actualized basis and/or investment bankers' estimated cost of equity based on analysts' earnings projections."
- "We use an Ibbotson arithmetic average starting in 1960. We have talked to investment banks and consulting firms with advice from 3 to 7 percent."
- "A 60-year average of about 5.7 percent. This number has been used for a long time in the company and is currently the subject of some debate and is under review. We may consider using a time horizon of less than 60 years to estimate this premium."
- "We are currently using 6 percent. In 1993 we polled various investment banks and academic studies on the issue as to the appropriate rate and got anywhere between 2 and 8 percent, but most were between 6 and 7.4 percent."

Comments from financial advisers also were revealing. While some simply responded that they use a published historical average, others presented a more complex picture.

- "We employ a self-estimated 5 percent (arithmetic average). A variety of techniques are used in estimation. We look at Ibbotson data and focus on more recent periods, around 30 years (but it is not a straight 30-year average). We use smoothing techniques, Monte Carlo simulation, and a dividend discount model on the S&P 400 to estimate what the premium should be, given our risk-free rate of return."
- "We use a 7.4 percent arithmetic mean, after Ibbotson, Sinquefeld. We used to use the geometric mean following the then scholarly advice, but we changed to the arithmetic mean when we found later that our competitors were using the arithmetic mean and scholars' views were shifting."

Comments in our interviews (see box above) suggest the diversity among survey participants. While most of our 27 sample companies appear to use a 60-plus-year historical period to estimate returns, one cited a window of less than 10 years, two cited windows of about 10 years, one began averaging with 1960 and another with 1952 data.

This variety of practice should not come as a surprise, since theory calls for a forward-looking risk premium, one that reflects current market sentiment and may change with market conditions. What is clear is that there is substantial variation as practitioners try to operationalize the theoretical call for a market risk premium. A glaring result is that few respondents specifically cited use of any forward-looking method to supplement or replace reading the tea leaves of past returns.[16]

---

[16]Only two respondents (one advisor and one company) specifically cited forward-looking estimates although others cited use of data from outside sources (e.g., a company using an estimate from an investment bank) where we cannot identify whether forward-looking estimates were used. Some studies using financial analyst forecasts in dividend growth models suggest market risk premiums average in the 6 to 6.5 percent range and change over time with higher premiums when interest rates decline. See for instance, Harris and Marston (1992). Ibbotson (1994) provides industry-specific cost-of-equity estimates using analysts' forecasts in a growth model.

IV. THE IMPACT OF VARIOUS ASSUMPTIONS FOR USING CAPM

To illustrate the effect of these various practices, we estimated the hypothetical cost of equity and WACC for Black & Decker, which we identified as having a wide range in estimated betas, and for McDonald's, which has a relatively narrow range. Our estimates are "hypothetical" in that we do not adopt any information supplied to us by the companies but rather apply a range of approaches based on publicly available information as of late 1995. Exhibit 4 gives Black & Decker's estimated costs of equity and WACCs under various combinations of risk-free rate, beta, and market risk premiums. Three clusters of practice are illustrated, each in turn using three betas as provided by S&P, Value Line, and Bloomberg (unadjusted). The first approach, as suggested by some texts, marries a short-term risk-free rate (90-day T-bill yield) with Ibbotson's arithmetic mean (using T-bills) risk premium. The second, adopted by a number of financial advisers, uses a long-term risk-free rate (30-year T-bond yield) and a risk premium of 7.2 percent (the modal premium mentioned by financial advisers). The third approach also uses a long-term risk-free rate but adopts the modal premium mentioned by corporate respondents of 5.5 percent. We repeated these general procedures for McDonald's.

The resulting ranges of estimated WACCs for the two firms are as follows:

	Maximum WACC	*Minimum WACC*	*Difference in Basis Points*
Black & Decker	12.80%	8.50%	430
McDonald's	11.60%	9.30%	230

The range from minimum to maximum is large for both firms, and the economic impact is potentially stunning. To illustrate this, the present value of a level perpetual annual stream of $10 million would range between $78 million and $118 million for Black and Decker, and between $86 million and $108 million for McDonald's.

Given the positive but relatively flat slope of the yield curve in late 1995, most of the variation in our illustration is explained by beta and the equity market premium assumption. Variations can be even more dramatic, especially when the yield curve is inverted.

V. RISK ADJUSTMENTS TO WACC

Finance theory is clear that a single WACC is appropriate only for investments of broadly comparable risk: A firm's overall WACC is a suitable benchmark for a firm's average risk investments. Finance theory goes on to say that such a company-specific figure should be adjusted for departures from such an average risk profile. Attracting capital requires payment of a premium that depends on risk.

We probed whether firms use a discount rate appropriate to the risks of the flows being valued in questions on types of investment (strategic vs. operational), terminal values, synergies, and multidivisional companies. Responses to these questions displayed in Exhibit 3 do not display much apparent alignment of practice. When financial advisers were asked how they value parts of multidivision firms, all 10 firms surveyed reported that they use different discount rates for component parts (item 17). However, only 26 percent of companies always adjust the cost of capital to reflect the risk of individual investment opportunities (item 12). Earlier studies (summarized in Gitman and Mercurio (1982) reported that between a third and a half of firms surveyed did *not* adjust for risk differences among capital projects. These practices stand in stark contrast to the recommendations of textbooks and trade books: The books did not explicitly address all subjects, but when they did, they were uniform in their advocacy of risk-adjusted discount rates.

A closer look at specific responses reveals the tensions as theory based on traded financial assets is adapted to decisions on investments in real assets. Inevitably, a fine line is drawn between use of financial market data versus managerial judgments. Responses from financial advisers illustrate this. As shown in Exhibit 2, all advisers use different capital costs for valuing parts (e.g., divisions) of a firm (item 17); only half ever select different rates for synergies or strategic opportunities (item 18); only 1 in 10 state any inclination to use different discount rates for terminal values and interim cash flows (item 16). Two simplistic interpretations are that (1) advisers ignore important risk differences or (2) material risk differences are rare in assessing factors such as terminal values. Neither of these fits; our conversations with advisers reveal that they recognize important risk differences but deal with them in a multitude of ways. Consider comments from two prominent investment banks who use different capital costs for valuing parts of multidivision firms. When asked about risk adjustments for prospective merger synergies, these same firms responded as follows:

- "We make these adjustments in cash flows and multiples rather than in discount rates."
- "Risk factors may be different for realizations of synergies, but we make adjustments to cash flows rather than the discount rate."

While financial advisers typically value existing companies, corporations face further challenges. They routinely must evaluate investments in new products and technologies. Moreover, they deal in an administrative setting that melds centralized (e.g., calculating a WACC) and decentralized (e.g., specific project appraisal) processes. As the next box of comments illustrates, these complexities lead to a blend of approaches for dealing with risk. A number of respondents mentioned specific rate adjustments to distinguish between divisional capital costs, international versus domestic investments, and leasing versus nonleasing situations. In other instances, however, these same respondents favored cash-flow adjustments to deal with risks.

Why do practitioners risk-adjust discount rates in one case and work with cash-flow adjustments in another? Our interpretation is that risk-adjusted discount rates are more likely used when the analyst can establish relatively objective financial market benchmarks for what rate adjustments should be. At the business (division) level, data on comparable companies provide cost-of-capital estimates. Debt markets provide surrogates for the risks in leasing cash flows. International financial markets shed insights on cross-country differences. When no such market benchmarks are available, practitioners look to other methods for dealing with risks. Lacking a good market analog from which to glean investor opinion (in the form of differing capital costs), the analyst is forced to rely more on internal focus. Practical implementation of risk-adjusted discount rates thus appears to depend on the ability to find traded financial assets that are comparable in risk to the cash flows being valued and then to have financial data on these traded assets.

Comments Regarding Adjustments for Project Risk

When asked whether they adjusted discount rates for project risk, companies provided a wide range of responses:

- "No, it's difficult to draw lines between the various businesses we invest in, and we also try as best we can to make adjustments for risk in cash-flow projections rather than in cost of capital factors . . . We advocate minimizing adjustments to cost of capital calculations and maximizing understanding of all relevant issues (e.g., commodity costs and international/ political risks)." At another point the same firm noted that "for lease analysis only the cost of debt is used."

- "No [we don't risk adjust cost of capital]. We believe there are two basic components: (1) projected cash flows, which should incorporate investment risk, and (2) discount rate." The same firm noted, however, "For international investments, the discount rate is adjusted for country risk." and "For large acquisitions, the company takes significantly greater care to estimate an accurate cost of capital."

- "No, but use divisional costs of capital to calculate a weighted average company cost of capital . . . for comparison and possible adjustment."

- "Yes, we have calculated a cost of capital for divisions based on pure play betas and also suggest subjective adjustments based on each project. Our feeling is that use of divisional costs is the most frequent distinction in the company."

- "Rarely, but at least on one occasion we have, for a whole new line of business."

- "We do sensitivity analysis on every project."

- "For the most part we make risk adjustments qualitatively; i.e., we use the corporate WACC to evaluate a project, but then interpret the result according to the risk of the proposal being studied. This could mean that a risky project will be rejected even though it meets the corporate hurdle rate objectives."

- "No domestically; yes internationally—we assess a risk premium per country and adjust the cost of capital accordingly."

The pragmatic bent of application also comes to the fore when companies are asked how often they reestimate capital costs (item 13, Exhibit 2). Even for those firms that reestimate relatively frequently, the next box of comments shows that they draw an important distinction between estimating capital costs and policy changes about the capital cost figure used in the firm's decision making.

Firms consider administrative costs in structuring their policies on capital costs. For a very large venture (e.g., an acquisition), capital costs may be revisited each time. On the other hand, only large material changes in costs may be fed into more formal project evaluation systems. Firms also recognize a certain ambiguity in any cost number and are willing to live with approximations. While the bond market reacts to minute basis-point changes in investor return requirements, investments in real assets, where the decision process itself is time-consuming and often decentralized, involve much less precision. To paraphrase one of our sample companies, we use capital costs as a rough yardstick rather than the last word in project evaluation.

Our interpretation is that the mixed responses to questions about risk adjusting and reestimating discount rates reflect an often sophisticated set of practical trade-offs; these involve the size of risk differences, the quality of information from financial markets, and the reali-

---

Comments Regarding Reestimating WACC

How frequently do you reestimate your company's cost of capital? Here are responses from best-practice companies:

- "We usually review it quarterly but would review more frequently if market rates changed enough to warrant the review. We would only announce a change in the rate if the recomputed number was materially different than the one currently being used."
- "We reestimate it once or twice a year, but we rarely change the number that the business units use for decision and planning purposes. We expect the actual rate to vary over time, but we also expect that average to be fairly constant over the business cycle. Thus, we tend to maintain a steady discount rate within the company over time."
- "Usually every six months, except in case of very large investments, in which it is reestimated for each analysis."
- "Whenever we need to, such as for an acquisition or big investment proposal."
- "Reevaluate as needed (e.g., for major tax changes), but unless the cost of capital change is significant (a jump to 21 percent, for instance), our cutoff rate is not changed; it is used as a *yardstick* rather than the last word in project evaluation."
- "Probably need a 100-basis-point change to publish a change. We report only to the nearest percent."

---

ties of administrative costs and processes. In cases where there are material differences in perceived risk, a sufficient scale of investment to justify the effort, no large scale administrative complexities, and readily identifiable information from financial markets, practitioners employ risk adjustments to rates quite routinely. Acquisitions, valuing divisions of companies, analysis of foreign versus domestic investments, and leasing versus nonleasing decisions were frequently cited examples. In contrast, when one or more of these factors is not present, practitioners are more likely to employ other means to deal with risks.

VI. CONCLUSIONS

Our research sought to identify the "best practice" in cost-of-capital estimation through interviews of leading corporations and financial advisers. Given the huge annual expenditure on capital projects and corporate acquisitions each year, the wise selection of discount rates is of material importance to senior corporate managers.

The survey revealed broad acceptance of the WACC as the basis for setting discount rates. In addition, the survey revealed general alignment in many aspects of the estimation of WACC. The main area of notable disagreement was in the details of implementing the capital asset pricing model (CAPM) to estimate the cost of equity. This paper outlined the varieties of practice in CAPM use, the arguments in favor of different approaches, and the practical implications.

In summary, we believe that the following elements represent "best current practice" in the estimation of WACC:

- Weights should be based on *market-value* mixes of debt and equity.
- The after-tax cost of debt should be estimated from *marginal* pretax costs, combined with *marginal or statutory* tax rates.

- CAPM is currently the preferred model for estimating the cost of equity.
- Betas are drawn substantially from published sources, preferring those betas using a long interval of equity returns. Where a number of statistical publishers disagree, best practice often involves judgment to estimate a beta.
- Risk-free rate should match the tenor of the cash flows being valued. For most capital projects and corporate acquisitions, the yield on the U.S. government Treasury bond of 10 or more years in maturity would be appropriate.
- Choice of an equity market risk premium is the subject of considerable controversy both as to its value and method of estimation. Most of our best-practice companies use a premium of 6 percent or lower, while many texts and financial advisers use higher figures.
- Monitoring for changes in WACC should be keyed to major changes in financial market conditions, but should be done at least annually. Actually flowing a change through a corporate system of project valuation and compensation targets must be done gingerly and only when there are material changes.
- WACC should be risk adjusted to reflect substantive differences among different businesses in a corporation. For instance, financial advisers generally find the corporate WACC to be inappropriate for valuing different parts of a corporation. Given publicly traded companies in different businesses, such risk adjustment involves only modest revision in the WACC and CAPM approaches already used. Corporations also cite the need to adjust capital costs across national boundaries. In situations where market proxies for a particular type of risk class are not available, best practice involves finding other means to account for risk differences.

Best practice is largely consistent with finance theory. Despite broad agreement at the theoretical level, however, there remain several problems in application that can lead to wide divergence in estimated capital costs. Based on these remaining problems, we believe that further applied research on two principal topics is warranted. First, practitioners need additional tools for sharpening their assessment of relative risk. The variation in company-specific beta estimates from different published sources can create large differences in capital cost estimates. Moreover, use of risk-adjusted discount rates appears limited by lack of good market proxies for different risk profiles. We believe that appropriate use of averages across industry or other risk categories is an avenue worth exploration. Second, practitioners could benefit from further research on estimating equity market risk premiums. Current practice displays large variations and focuses primarily on averaging past data. Use of expectational data appears to be a fruitful approach. As the next generation of theories gradually sharpen our insights, we feel that research attention to implementation of existing theory can make for real improvements in practice.

Finally, our research is a reminder of the old saying that too often in business we measure with a micrometer, mark with a pencil, and cut with an ax. Despite the many advances in finance theory, the particular "ax" available for estimating company capital costs remains a blunt one. Best-practice companies can expect to estimate their weighted-average cost of capital with an accuracy of no more than plus or minus 100 to 150 basis points. This has important implications for how managers use the cost of capital in decision making. First, do not mistake capital budgeting for bond pricing. Despite the tools available, effective capital appraisal continues to require thorough knowledge of the business and wise business judgment. Second, be careful not to throw out the baby with the bath water. Do not reject the cost of capital and attendant advances in financial management because your finance people are not able to give you a precise number. When in need, even a blunt ax is better than nothing.

REFERENCES

Aggarwal, Raj. "Corporate Use of Sophisticated Capital Budgeting Techniques: A Strategic Perspective and a Critique of Survey Results." *Interfaces* 10, no. 2 (April 1980), pp. 31–34.

Bierman, Harold J. "Capital Budgeting in 1992: A Survey." *Financial Management* 22, no. 3 (Autumn 1993), p. 24.

Brealey, Richard, and Stewart Myers. *Principles of Corporate Finance.* 4th ed. New York: McGraw-Hill, 1991.

Brigham, Eugene, and Louis Gapenski. *Financial Management, Theory and Practice.* 6th ed. Chicago: Dryden Press, 1991.

Carleton, Willard T., and Josef Lakonishok. "Risk and Return on Equity: The Use and Misuse of Historical Estimates." *Financial Analysts Journal* 4, no. 1 (January–February 1985), pp. 38–48.

Copeland, Tom; Tim Koller; and Jack Murrin. *Valuation: Measuring and Managing the Value of Companies.* 2nd ed. New York: John Wiley & Sons, 1994.

Dixit, Avinash K., and Robert S. Pindyck. *Investment under Uncertainty.* Princeton, NJ: Princeton University Press, 1993.

_____. "The Options Approach to Capital Investment." *Harvard Business Review* 73, no. 3 (May–June 1995), pp. 105–15.

Ehrhardt, Michael. *The Search for Value: Measuring the Company's Cost of Capital.* Boston: HBS Press, 1994.

Fama, Eugene F., and Kenneth R. French. "Dividend Yields and Expected Stock Returns." *Journal of Financial Economics* 22, no. 1 (October 1986), pp. 3–25.

Gitman, Lawrence J. *Principles of Managerial Finance.* 6th ed. New York: Harper Collins, 1991.

Gitman, Lawrence J., and John R. Forrester, Jr. "A Survey of Capital Budgeting Techniques Used by Major U.S. Firms." *Financial Management* 6, no. 3 (Fall 1977), pp. 66–71.

Gitman, Lawrence J., and Vincent Mercurio. "Cost of Capital Techniques Used by Major U.S. Firms: Survey and Analysis of Fortune's 1000." *Financial Management* 11, no. 4 (Winter 1982), pp. 21–29.

Harris, Robert S., and Felicia C. Marston. "Estimating Shareholder Risk Premia Using Analysts' Growth Forecasts." *Financial Management* 21, no. 2 (Summer 1992), pp. 63–70.

Ibbotson Associates. *1995 Yearbook: Stocks, Bonds, Bills, and Inflation.* Chicago: Author, 1995.

_____. *1994 Yearbook: Cost of Capital Quarterly.* Chicago: Author, October 1994.

Jagannathan, Ravi, and Ellen R. McGrattan. "The CAPM Debate." *The Federal Reserve Bank of Minneapolis Quarterly Review* 19, no. 4 (Fall 1995), pp. 2–17.

Kaplan, Steven N., and Richard S. Ruback. "The Valuation of Cash Flow Forecasts: An Empirical Analysis." *Journal of Finance* 50, no. 4 (September 1995), pp. 1059–93.

Kritzman, Mark. "What Practitioners Need to Know . . . About Future Value." *Financial Analysts Journal* 50, no. 3 (May–June 1994), pp. 12–15.

Lo, Andrew W., and A. Craig MacKinlay. "Stock Market Prices Do Not Follow Random Walks: Evidence from a Simple Specification Test." *Review of Financial Studies* 1, no. 1 (Spring 1988), pp. 41–46.

Moore, James S., and Alan K. Reichert. "An Analysis of the Financial Management Techniques Currently Employed by Large U.S. Companies." *Journal of Business Finance and Accounting* 10, no. 4 (Winter 1983), pp. 623–45.

Poterba, James M., and Lawrence H. Summers. "A CEO Survey of U.S. Companies' Time Horizons and Hurdle Rates." *Sloan Management Review* 37, no. 1 (Fall 1995), pp. 43–53.

_____. "Mean Reversion in Stock Prices: Evidence and Implications." *Journal of Financial Economics* 22, no. 1 (October 1988), pp. 27–59.

Ross, Stephen; Randolph Westerfield; and Jeffrey Jaffe. *Corporate Finance* 4th ed. Chicago: Irwin, 1996.

Schall, Lawrence D.; Gary L. Sundem; and William R. Geijsbeek, Jr. "Survey and Analysis of Capital Budgeting Methods." *Journal of Finance* 33, no. 1 (March 1978), pp. 281–92.

Siegel, Jeremy J. "The Equity Premium: Stock and Bond Returns Since 1802." *Financial Analysts Journal* 48, no. 1 (January–February 1992), pp. 28–46.

Trahan, Emery A., and Lawrence J. Gitman. "Bridging the Theory-Practice Gap in Corporate Finance: A Survey of Chief Financial Officers." *Quarterly Review of Economics & Finance* 35, no. 1 (Spring 1995), pp. 73–87.

EXHIBIT 1   Three Survey Samples

Company Sample	Adviser Sample	Textbook/Trade Book Sample
Advanced Micro Devices	CS First Boston	Textbooks
Allergan	Dillon, Read	Brealey and Myers
Black & Decker	Donaldson, Lufkin, Jenrette	Brigham and Gapenski
Cellular One	J. P. Morgan	Gitman
Chevron	Lehman Brothers	Ross, Westerfield & Jaffe
Colgate-Palmolive	Merrill Lynch	
Comdisco	Morgan Stanley	Trade Books
Compaq	Salomon	Copeland, Koller & Murrin
Eastman Kodak	Smith Barney	Ehrhardt
Gillette	Wasserstein Perella	Ibbotson Associates
Guardian Industries		
Henkel		
Hewlett-Packard		
Kanthal		
Lawson Mardon		
McDonald's		
Merck		
Monsanto		
PepsiCo		
Quaker Oats		
Schering-Plough		
Tandem		
Union Carbide		
U.S. West		
Walt Disney		
Weyerhauser		
Whirlpool		

Note: For the full titles of textbooks and trade books, please see the list of references at the end of this paper.

EXHIBIT 2   General Survey Results

	Corporations	Financial Advisers	Textbooks/Trade Books
1. Do you use DCF techniques to evaluate investment opportunities?	89% Yes, as a primary tool 7% Yes, only as a secondary tool 4% No	100% rely on DCF, comparable companies multiples, comparable transactions multiples. Of these, 10% DCF is primary tool. 10% DCF is used mainly "as a check" 80% Weight the three approaches depending on purpose and type of analysis.	100% Yes
2. Do you use any form of a cost of capital as your discount rate in your DCF analysis?	89% Yes 7% Sometimes 4% N/A	100% Yes	100% Yes
3. For your cost of capital, do you form any combination of capital cost to determine a WACC?	85% Yes 4% Sometimes 4% No 7% N/A	100% Yes	100% Yes

4. What weighting factors do you use?
  a. target vs. current debt/equity?
  b. market vs. book weights?
	Target/Current
	    Market/Book
	52% Target 59% Market
	15% Current 15% Book
	26% Uncertain 19% Uncertain
	7% N/A 7% N/A
		Target/Current
		    Market/Book
		90% Target 90% Market
		10% Current 10% Book
			Target/Current
			   Market/Book
			86% Target
			100% Market
			14% Current/Target

5. How do you estimate your before tax cost of debt?	52% Marginal cost 37% Current average 4% Uncertain 7% N/A	60% Marginal cost 40% Current average	71% Marginal cost 29% No explicit recommendation
6. What tax rate do you use?	52% Marginal or statutory 37% Average historical 4% Uncertain 7% N/A	60% Marginal or statutory 30% Average historical 10% Uncertain	71% Marginal or statutory 29% No explicit recommendation

7. How do you estimate your cost of equity? (If you do not use CAPM, skip to question 12).	81% CAPM
	4% Modified CAPM
	15% N/A
		80% CAPM
		20% Other (including modified CAPM)
			100% Primarily CAPM
			Other methods mentioned:
			  dividend-growth model
			  arbitrage pricing model

EXHIBIT 2   (*continued*)

	Corporations	Financial Advisers	Textbooks/Trade Books
8. As usually written, the CAPM version of the cost of equity has three terms: a risk-free rate, a volatility or beta factor, and a market risk premium. Is this consistent with your company's approach?	85% Yes 0% No 15% N/A	90% Yes 10% N/A	100% Yes
9. What do you use for the risk-free rate?	4% 90-day T-bill 7% 3–7 year Treasuries 33% 10-year Treasuries 4% 20-year Treasuries 33% 10–30 year Treasuries 4% 10 yrs. or 90-day; depends 15% N/A (Many said they match the term of the risk-free rate to the tenor of the investment)	10% 90-day T-bill 10% 5–10-year Treasuries 30% 10–30-year Treasuries 40% 30-year Treasuries 10% N/A	43% T-bills 29% LT Treasuries 14% Match tenor of investment 14% Don't say
10. What do you use as your volatility or beta factor?	52% Published source 3% Financial adviser's estimate 30% Self-calculated 15% N/A	30% Fundamental beta (e.g., BARRA) 40% Published source 20% Self-calculated 10% N/A	100% mention availability of published sources
11. What do you use as your market risk premium?	11% use fixed rate of 4–4.5% 37% use fixed rate of 5–6% 4% Use geometric mean 4% Use arithmetic mean 4% Use average of historical and implied 15% Use financial adviser's estimate 7% Use premium over Treasuries 3% Use Value Line estimate 15% N/A	10% Use fixed rate of 5% 50% Use 7–7.4% (Similar to arithmetic) 10% LT arithmetic mean 10% Both LT arithmetic and geometric mean 10% spread above Treasuries 10% N/A	71% Arithmetic historical mean 15% Geometric historical mean 14% Don't say
12. Having estimated your company's cost of capital, do you make any further adjustments to reflect the risk of individual investment opportunities?	26% Yes 33% Sometimes 41% No	Not asked	86% Adjust beta for investment risk 14% Don't say

EXHIBIT 2   *(continued)*

	Corporations	*Financial Advisers*	*Textbooks/Trade Books*
13. How frequently do you reestimate your company's cost of capital?	4% Monthly 19% Quarterly 11% Semiannually 37% Annually 7% Continually/every investment 19% Infrequently 4% N/A (Generally, many said that in addition to scheduled reviews, they reestimate as needed for significant events such as acquisitions and high-impact economic events)	Not asked	100% No explicit recommendation
14. Is the cost of capital used for purposes other than project analysis in your company? (For example, to evaluate divisional performance?)	51% Yes 44% No 4% N/A	Not asked	100% No explicit discussion
15. Do you distinguish between strategic and operational investments? Is cost of capital used differently in these two categories?	48% Yes 48% No 4% N/A	Not asked	29% Yes 71% No explicit discussion
16. What methods do you use to estimate terminal value? Do you use the same discount rate for the terminal value as for the interim cash flows?	Not asked	30% Exit multiples only 70% Both multiples and perpetuity DCF model 70% Use same WACC for TV 20% No response 10% Rarely change	71% Perpetuity DCF model 29% No explicit discussion 100% No explicit discussion of separate WACC for terminal value

EXHIBIT 2 *(concluded)*

	Corporations	Financial Advisers	Textbooks/Trade Books
17. In valuing a multi-divisional company, do you aggregate the values of the individual divisions, or just value the firm as a whole? If you value each division separately, do you use a different cost of capital for each one?	Not asked	100% Value the parts 100% Use different WACCs for separate valuations	100%: Use distinct WACC for each division
18. In your valuations do you use any different methods to value synergies or strategic opportunities (e.g., higher or lower discount rates, options valuation)?	Not asked	30% Yes 50% No 20% Rarely	29%: Use distinct WACC for synergies 71% No explicit discussion
19. Do you make any adjustments to the risk premium for changes in market conditions?	Not asked	20% Yes 70% No 10% N/A	14% Yes 86% No explicit discussion
20. How long have you been with the company? What is your job title?	Mean: 10 years All senior, except one	Mean: 7.3 years 4 MDs, 2 VPs, 4 associates	N/A

EXHIBIT 3   Betas for Corporate Survey Respondents

	Bloomberg Betas		Value Line		Range
	Raw	Adjusted	Betas	S&P Betas	Maximum–Minimum
Advanced Micro	1.20	1.13	1.70	1.47	0.57
Allergan	0.94	0.96	1.30	1.36	0.42
Black & Decker	1.06	1.04	1.65	1.78	0.74
Cellular One			Not listed		
Chevron	0.70	0.80	0.70	0.68	0.12
Colgate-Palmolive	1.11	1.07	1.20	0.87	0.33
Comdisco	1.50	1.34	1.35	1.20	0.30
Compaq Computer	1.26	1.18	1.50	1.55	0.37
Eastman Kodak	0.54	0.69	NMF	0.37	0.32
Gillette	0.93	0.95	1.25	1.30	0.37
Guardian Industries			Not listed		
Henkel			Not listed		
Hewlett-Packard	1.34	1.22	1.40	1.96	0.74
Kanthal			Not listed		
Lawson Mardon			Not listed		
McDonald's	0.93	0.96	1.05	1.09	0.16
Merck	0.73	0.82	1.10	1.15	0.42
Monsanto	0.89	0.93	1.10	1.36	0.47
PepsiCo	1.12	1.08	1.10	1.19	0.11
Quaker Oats	1.38	1.26	0.90	0.67	0.71
Schering-Plough	0.51	0.67	1.00	0.82	0.49
Tandem Computers	1.35	1.23	1.75	1.59	0.52
Union Carbide	1.51	1.34	1.30	0.94	0.57
U.S. West	0.61	0.74	0.75	0.53	0.22
Walt Disney	1.42	1.28	1.15	1.22	0.27
Weyerhauser	0.78	0.85	1.20	1.21	0.43
Whirlpool	0.90	0.93	1.55	1.58	0.68
Mean	1.03	1.02	1.24	1.18	0.42
Median	1.00	1.00	1.20	1.21	0.42
Standard deviation	0.31	0.21	0.29	0.41	0.19

Note:
1. Bloomberg's adjusted beta is $\beta_{adj} = (.66)\beta_{raw} + (.33)1.00$

EXHIBIT 4 Variations in Cost-of-Capital (WACC) Estimates for Black & Decker Using Different Methods of Implementing the Capital Asset Pricing Model*

---

1. Short-term rate plus arithmetic average historical risk premium (recommended by some texts)
   R_f = 5.36%, 90-day T-bills
   $R_m - R_f$ = 8.50%, Ibbotson arithmetic average since 1926

Beta Service	Cost of Equity (K_e)	Cost of Capital (WACC)
Bloomberg, β = 1.06	14.40%	9.70%
Value Line, β = 1.65	19.40%	12.20%
S&P, β = 1.78	20.50%	12.80%

2. Long-term rate plus risk premium of 7.20% ("modal" practice of financial advisers surveyed)
   R_f = 6.26%, 30-year T-bonds
   $R_m - R_f$ = 7.20%, modal response of financial advisers

Beta Service	Cost of Equity (K_e)	Cost of Capital (WACC)
Bloomberg, β = 1.06	13.90%	9.40%
Value Line, β = 1.65	18.10%	11.60%
S&P, β = 1.78	19.10%	12.10%

3. Long-term rate plus risk premium of 5.50% ("modal" practice of corporations surveyed)
   R_f = 6.26%, 30-year T-bonds
   $R_m - R_f$ = 5.50%, modal response of corporations

Beta Service	Cost of Equity (K_e)	Cost of Capital (WACC)
Bloomberg, β = 1.06	12.10%	8.50%
Value Line, β = 1.65	15.30%	10.20%
S&P, β = 1.78	16.10%	10.50%

*In all cases the CAPM is used to estimate the cost of equity, the cost of debt is assumed to be 7.81 percent based on a Baa rating, the tax rate is assumed to be 38 percent, and debt is assumed to represent 49 percent of capital.

Grand Metropolitan PLC

*Grand Metropolitan PLC is the world's largest wine and spirits seller, and the only one ana-
lysts expect will show volume gains this year. Its Burger King hamburger chain, the world's
second biggest, has just completed a turnaround. So why is the price of GrandMet shares in
New York, compared with its earnings, 10% below the average price/earnings ratio of the
companies in the Standard & Poor's 500 index? And more important, why have rumors surfaced that GrandMet, valued at more than $14 billion in the stock market, may be a takeover
target?[1]*

*It is our goal to build on GrandMet's strengths and continue to create sustainable competi-
tive advantage in our businesses, which is the bedrock of shareholder value and wealth.[2]*

By April 1992, senior managers of Grand Metropolitan PLC could look back on a flurry
of financial activity. GrandMet had just acquired Cinzano, the Italian vermouth and wines
company, for £100 million. In the United States, GrandMet was negotiating a joint venture
in which it would receive £39.5 million in exchange for the U.S. flour-milling business it
had acquired when it bought Pillsbury in 1989. In 1991, the group sold off about £800 million in businesses in its effort to focus on core activities: food, drink, and retailing.

In spite of the world recession, Grand Metropolitan beat market forecasts in 1991 with
a 4.8 percent increase in pretax profits, which brought the group to a record £963 million.
This success was accomplished in what Chairman Sir Allen Sheppard believed was "one
of the toughest years in Grand Metropolitan's history." Sheppard emphasized that the positive results demonstrated the validity of GrandMet's strategic intent to focus on its core

---

[1]Peter Waldman, "Sir Allen Cools the Pace at Grand Met," *European Wall Street Journal,* October 8, 1991.
[2]"1990 Annual Report to Shareholders," Grand Metropolitan PLC.

This case was prepared by Philippe Demigne, Jean-Christophe Donck, Bertrand George, and Michael Levy
with Professor Robert F. Bruner. The financial support of the Citicorp Global Scholars Program is gratefully
acknowledged. This case was written as a basis for class discussion rather than to illustrate effective or ineffective handling of an administrative situation. Copyright © 1992 by the University of Virginia Darden School
Foundation, Charlottesville, VA, and INSEAD, Fontainebleau, France. All rights reserved. *No part of this publication may be reproduced, stored in a retrieval system, used in a spreadsheet, or transmitted in any form or by
any means—electronic, mechanical, photocopying, recording, or otherwise—without the permission of the
Darden Foundation. For inquiries, please send an e-mail to dardencases@ virginia.edu.* Rev. 3/98. Version 2.2.

businesses. While conceding that "1992 will be another tough year," he reiterated the company's goal "to constantly improve on rather than match previous achievements." The 1991 annual report carried the slogan ". . . adding value" imprinted under the company name. Achieving the goal, however, might mean selling off some of the group's poorly performing businesses, such as Pearle Vision. Furthermore, in the previous year, rumors had circulated that GrandMet might be a takeover target.

THE COMPANY

With a total 1991 turnover (sales) of £8.75 billion, Grand Metropolitan ranked among Britain's 10 largest companies. It currently acted as a pure holding company for a group of business units that were widely diversified both geographically and in terms of products. Exhibit 1 presents a summary and description of GrandMet's three major operating sectors: foods (30 percent of 1991 trading profit), drinks (46 percent), and retailing (24 percent). The brands it owned and managed ranked among the best known worldwide: Green Giant, Häagen-Dazs, Alpo, and Pillsbury in foods; Smirnoff, Bailey's, J&B, and Cinzano in drinks; Burger King and Pearle Vision in retailing. Geographically, 51 percent of GrandMet's 1991 turnover was generated in the United States, 34 percent came from the United Kingdom, and 10 percent from continental Europe. GrandMet's shares were listed on the London and New York[3] stock exchanges. The majority of GrandMet's shareholders were in the United Kingdom.

Exhibit 2 gives GrandMet's historical financial performance broken down by operating sector and by geographical region. Exhibit 3 summarizes the group's consolidated balance sheets and income statements for the past five years.

GrandMet was founded in the late 1940s as the Washington Group, a chain of hotels established by Sir Maxwell Joseph. With the acquisition of the Mount Royal Hotel in 1957, the company changed its name to Mount Royal Ltd. to reflect the fact that, with 712 rooms, this new acquisition was much larger than the group's existing hotels. In 1962, the group changed its name to Grand Metropolitan Hotels.

The 1960s saw the first in a series of acquisitions that would move GrandMet into non-hotel businesses. In 1966, the group bought Levy & Franks, owners of the Chef and Brewer pub and restaurant chain. By 1969, GrandMet had expanded into dairy products with the acquisition of Express Dairy (£32 million). During the 1970s, its most important purchases included the Mecca gaming establishments (bought for £33 million, sold in 1985 for £95 million) and Watney (£435 million), the owner of International Distillers and Vintners, which would form the core of GrandMet's drinks division.

GrandMet's pace of acquisition and divestiture accelerated during the 1980s. Its major acquisitions during this decade included the Liggett Group (owner of Alpo pet food, bought for $450 million); Intercontinental Hotels (bought for $500 million, sold in 1988

---

[3]In New York, GrandMet's actual shares were not traded. Rather, the trading was in the form of rights to shares held in trust. These rights were called American depositary receipts (ADRs). The prices of ADRs are denominated in dollars; dividends on ADRs are paid in dollars. The beta calculated on GrandMet's ADRs was estimated against the NYSE composite index.

for $2 billion); Pearle Optical ($385 million); Heublein (U.S. wines and spirits company and owner of Smirnoff vodka, bought for $1.2 billion); and, finally, Pillsbury (owner of Burger King and Häagen-Dazs, bought for £3.3 billion).

The 1990s started with a flurry of divestitures, as close to £800 million in businesses were sold off. By 1992, GrandMet had divested all of its hotels, breweries, gaming establishments, soft-drink bottling plants, fitness products, and all food brands that were judged not to have international branding potential. The result was a group focused on a "core competence": the management of international brands in food, drinks, and retailing. Exhibit 4 summarizes the transactions that GrandMet undertook from 1960 through 1992.

FINANCIAL STRATEGY

In an analysts' briefing given by GrandMet in December 1991, Ian Martin, group managing director and chief operating officer, stated that the group's positive financial results "demonstrate the effectiveness of our operational principles, which can be simplified down to just seven words: build brands, cut costs, develop products, all within the framework of total quality."[4] At this same briefing, David Nash, financial director, outlined the financial strategy that supported these operational principles: capitalize brand value, increase interest coverage, and dispose of products that do not provide an adequate return.

Brand Valuation.   In 1988, GrandMet was the first U.K. company to begin the practice of assessing the value of recently acquired brands and then capitalizing that value on the balance sheet. As shown in Exhibit 3, the value of the brands (principally, Smirnoff, Pillsbury, Green Giant, and Burger King), consolidated under the label *intangible assets,* constituted 40 percent of 1991 fixed assets and 27 percent of the company's 1991 total assets.

Interest Coverage and Debt Policy.   Senior management was committed to reducing GrandMet's financial gearing (leverage) and noted in announcing the results for 1991 that the ratio of debt/capital had fallen by 9 percentage points in the last year and that the firm's interest-coverage ratio had risen from 4.8 times to 6.6. Exhibit 5 shows the historical evolution of GrandMet's debt structure in terms of its maturity profile and currency profile.

Invest in Projects Meeting Growth Criteria.   At the December 1991 analysts' briefing, CEO Sheppard outlined GrandMet's investment policy as follows: "In addition to Brewing, we have continued to exit those businesses whose future potential earnings do not meet our growth criteria . . . All these decisions were driven by a thorough analysis of income growth prospects."[5] As Exhibits 2 and 3 indicate, during the 1987–91 fiscal years,

---

[4]GrandMet preliminary-results briefing, December 5, 1991.
[5]Ibid.

GrandMet had generated a compound growth rate in pretax profits of 20.5 percent per year. Implicit in Sheppard's statement was the assumption that only those investments that would not jeopardize this growth trend would be undertaken.

GROUP COST OF CAPITAL

Were GrandMet's financial objectives consistent with the creation of value? To approach this question, analysts often used the discounted cash flows of any project as a measure of value creation. This method required knowledge of the opportunity cost of capital for investments of similar risk. One commonly used discount rate was the weighted-average cost of capital (WACC), defined as follows:

$$\text{WACC} = (1 - T)I(D/V) + K_e(E/V)$$

where T is the corporate tax rate, I is the pretax cost of debt, D is the market value of debt, E is the market value of equity, K_e is the cost of equity, and V is the market value of the firm's assets ($V = D + E$).

In basic terms, the WACC blends the requirements of the different providers of capital—bondholders and shareholders. A separate WACC could be calculated for each of the three operating sectors as well as for the entire company.

Capital-Structure Weights

Exhibit 6 gives the book-value and market-value weightings for the company's capital structure.

Cost of Debt and Preferred Stock

Exhibit 7 estimates the weighted-average pretax cost of debt for GrandMet in both pounds sterling and U.S. dollars. The 1990 annual report stated,

> The group interest expense is arranged centrally and is not attributable to individual activities or geographical areas . . . The group has arranged interest rate swaps which have the effect of fixing the rate of interest at an average of 8.6 percent on US dollar and Deutsche mark borrowings totaling £616 million . . . In addition, the interest rate on borrowings of £1,070 million has been capped for one year by the purchase of interest rate caps at a rate of 9 percent. The interest rates shown . . . are those contracted on the underlying borrowings before taking into account any interest rate protection.

The firm noted that most of the commercial-paper borrowings were classified as *midterm* (i.e., longer in maturity than one year but shorter than long term), because the firm intended to roll over the maturing commercial paper indefinitely.

The statutory maximum corporate income tax rate prevailing in the United Kingdom in 1992 was 35 percent. In the United States, it was 34 percent.

Exhibit 7 also presents the cost of preferred stock (calculated as the annual dividend divided by the market value of the stock) and the cost of convertible debt. Convertible debt was recognized to be a hybrid, a mixture of "straight" debt and equity. Therefore, the cost of the convertible debt, 9.75 percent, was estimated[6] as an average of the cost of equity and after-tax cost of debt, weighted by proportions of debt and equity implicit in the convertible; that is, 9.75 percent was the blended after-tax required return on the convertible.

Cost of Equity

Several methods could be used for estimating the cost of equity. One approach was based on the theory that the current stock price was simply the discounted flow of future dividends. In this model, the after-tax cost of equity (K_e) could be approximated by the following equation:

$$K_e = DIV/P + g$$

where *DIV* is the current dividend per share, *P* is the current share price, and *g* is the expected growth rate of dividends to infinity.

Another approach was based on the capital asset pricing model (CAPM). This model explicitly sets required returns by considering the risk of the investment, where risk is defined with respect to a fully diversified portfolio. This model leads to the following expression for the expected after-tax cost of equity:

$$K_e = R_f + \beta(R_m - R_f)$$

where R_f is the risk-free rate (typically a government-bond rate), β is beta,[7] and $R_m - R_f$ is the stock market risk premium.

Exhibit 8 gives information for GrandMet relevant to measuring cost of equity, and Exhibit 9 presents the financial-market conditions in the United States and United Kingdom in April 1992. Which risk-free rate should one use—the U.S. rate (because half the company's revenues were dollar denominated) or the U.K. rate? How should the decision maker decide on which maturity to use (2 years, 10 years)? What did *risk free* really mean? The same questions arose in the case of the market risk premiums. Should the decision maker use the historical long-term geometric averages or short-term ones? With which market(s) should the decision maker be concerned?

---

[6]A convertible bond may be regarded as a hybrid of straight debt and straight equity. The mix of its debt and equity proportions depends on the degree to which the call option in the instrument is either in or out of the money. Convertibles that are deeply in the money are observed to trade like their share equivalents (i.e., move in value with their underlying share prices). Convertibles that are deeply out of the money are observed to trade like their debt equivalents (i.e., move in value with fluctuations in interest rates). Thus, determining the blended required return on a convertible begins with an observation of its "moneyness" from which a mix of debt and equity proportions is drawn. The weighted average of the after-tax debt and equity costs proceeds straightforwardly.

[7]In technical terms, beta is the normalized covariance of the asset's return with respect to the market return—basically, a measure of how the company's returns vary with respect to overall market fluctuations. A company with a beta of 1.0 experiences as much volatility as a broad portfolio of stocks, and it varies synchronously with the market. A company with a beta of less than 1.0 is less risky than the market portfolio. A beta greater than 1.0 indicates greater risk than the market portfolio.

The most recent Risk Measurement Services report from the London Business School reported that GrandMet had a beta of 1.14 with respect to the London stock market.[8] Value Line, the U.S. investment information service, had estimated GrandMet's beta at 0.8 with respect to the New York Stock Exchange.[9] Assuming no measurement differences or error in the estimation of these betas, one explanation for the deviation between these two numbers was the greater volatility of the London stock market with respect to the New York stock market.[10]

BUSINESS-SEGMENT CAPITAL-COST ESTIMATION

How should one estimate the cost of equity for each of GrandMet's individual sectors? Should each segment have a different risk-free rate based on different project lifetimes? How should one determine the beta for each sector? Finally, how should one determine the weights necessary to combine the business segments into an overall WACC for GrandMet? Should one base the weighting factor on revenues, profits, or some other measure?

The decision maker could examine the capital structures of comparable companies to facilitate the evaluation GrandMet's gearing in each of its segments. Exhibit 8 gives information on various companies that competed with GrandMet in each of its operating sectors.

COST OF CAPITAL AND CURRENCY

In evaluating GrandMet's performance, analysts wondered whether the cost of capital should be the same in London as in New York. If differences among local capital markets (such as those induced by country risk) existed, one might be able to diversify the differences away by holding a portfolio of international investments. Using this kind of assumption could free an analyst to work with local costs of capital.

The assumption of purchasing-power parity implied the following relationship between home and foreign local costs of capital:

$$\text{Local } K = (1 + \text{Home } K)\left(\frac{1 + \text{Local inflation rate}}{1 + \text{Home inflation rate}}\right) - 1$$

---

[8]Risk Measurement Services (RMS) estimated betas using five years of *monthly* returns. The returns included dividends and capital gains or losses. RMS noted, "Betas may change because the company changes. For example, if a company becomes more highly geared, the beta of its shares will increase. Similarly, if it acquires a less risky firm, the beta of the shares after the merger will be lower than before. You may find it helpful to bear this in mind when interpreting the estimates." (London Business School, "Your Questions Answered," *Risk Measurement Services,* October 1991, pp. 63–65.)

[9]Value Line estimated its betas by regressing *weekly* percentage changes in the price of a stock against the weekly percentage changes in the New York Stock Exchange Composite Index over a period of five years. Value Line noted, "There has been a tendency over the years for high Beta stocks to become lower and for low Beta stocks to become higher. This tendency can be measured by studying the Betas of stocks in consecutive five-year intervals. The Betas published in the *Value Line Investment Survey* are adjusted for this tendency and hence are likely to be a better predictor of future Betas than those based exclusively on the experience of the past five years." ("How to Use the Value Line Investment Survey: A Subscriber's Guide," *Value Line Investment Survey,* 1985, p. 57.)

[10]Analysts determined that the recent average equity market volatility (standard deviation of returns) in the United States was 10 percent, as opposed to about 14 percent in the United Kingdom. They believed the correlation in returns between the two markets was high, and assumed a correlation of 1.00.

This equation implies that real risk-free rates, equity risk premiums, and betas are constant across countries. Little evidence either to prove or refute such an assertion existed, although in competitive world capital markets, arbitrage activity would tend to drive the three elements into equilibrium. Using home capital costs to discount cash flows translated into home currencies would be a conservative response to these uncertainties.

CONCLUSION

Analysts noted with interest the circulation of rumors that the company might be the target of a takeover attempt. Had the company performed that badly? Were all segments of the group's business portfolio performing equally well? Might one or two of them be targeted for aggressive restructuring? The decision maker decided to compare the returns on net assets in Exhibit 2 against the segment WACCs.

EXHIBIT 1   Grand Metropolitan's Major Operating Sectors

Food *Trading Profit £300 m (30%)*	*Drinks* *Trading Profit £454 m (46%)*	*Retailing* *Trading Profit £ 236 m (24%)*
Pillsbury Brands (U.S.) Baked goods (biscuits, sweet foods, pizzas); fresh, frozen, and canned vegetables; milled flour and processed food. Brands included Pillsbury, Janos, Green Giant, Totino's. **Pillsbury Food Group (Europe)** Prepared meals; baked goods (cookies, cakes, gateaux, pies, savory pastries); savory products (meat pies, sausages, burgers, and buns). Brands included Erasco, Jokish, Peter's, Hofmann Menu, Fleur de Lys, Memory Lane, Kaysens, Brossard, Goldstein, Jus-rol, Bélin Surgelés, Vinchon Jeanette. **Häagen-Dazs (U.S., Europe, Far East)** Premium ice cream. **Alpo Pet Food (U.S.)** Cat and dog food. Brands included Alpo, Jim Dandy, Blue Mountain. **GrandMet Foodservice (U.S.)** Food goods for bakery and catering sectors.	**International Distillers and Vintners (worldwide)** Production and distribution of wines and spirits. Owned brands included Smirnoff vodka, J&B Rare Scotch whisky, Bailey's Irish Cream liqueur, Malibu liqueur, Croft Original sherry, La Plat d'Or wines, Metaxa Greek brandy, Popov vodka, Gilbey's gin, Bombay Dry gin, Cinzano vermouth, Ouzo 12, Inglenook, Almaden, and Beaulieu California wines. Agency brands included Grand Marnier liqueur, Cointreau, Jose Cuervo Tequila, Absolut vodka, Jack Daniel's bourbon. Note: This division also previously included Grand Metropolitan Brewing, with owned and licensed beer brands including Webster's, Watney, Foster's, Carlsberg, Budweiser, Holsten. This segment was sold to Courage in February 1991 as part of a pubs-for-breweries swap transaction (Inntrepreneur Estates).	**Grand Metropolitan Retailing (U.K.)** Management and operation of one small restaurant chain, Old Orleans, and around 1,540 managed pubs, both unbranded and under the Chef & Brewer, Clifton Inns, and Country Carvery brand names. **Pearle Inc. (U.S., Europe, Far East)** Retailing of eyecare products/services with over 1,100 stores. Brands included Pearle Vision. **Burger King (worldwide)** Chain of 6,400 franchised hamburger restaurants in 41 countries.

Property Interests
Grand Metropolitan Estates (U.K.) Property management and development. **Inntrepreneur Estates (U.K.)** 50% joint venture with Courage responsible for licensed estate of 7,350 tenanted pubs.

Source: Annual reports of Grand Metropolitan PLC.

EXHIBIT 2 Distribution of Turnover, Profits, and Assets by Segment and Region
(values except for percentages are £ millions)

	Absolute Performance					*As a Percentage of Totals*				
	1991	*1990*	*1989*	*1988*	*1987*	*1991*	*1990*	*1989*	*1988*	*1987*
Drinks										
Turnover	2,425	3,000	2,784	2,581	2,178	32	33	36	47	46
Operating profit	454	473	389	316	257	46	45	45	55	53
Net assets	1,536	1,623	1,626	1,479	1,504	26	26	26	40	49
Operating margin	18.7%	15.8%	14.0%	12.2%	11.8%					
RONA*	19.2%	18.9%	15.6%	13.9%	11.1%					
Food										
Turnover	3,026	3,506	2,872	1,253	1,047	40	39	37	23	22
Operating profit	300	309	245	84	69	30	29	28	15	14
Net assets	1,997	1,763	2,468	310	260	34	29	39	8	9
Operating margin	9.9%	8.8%	8.5%	6.7%	6.6%					
RONA	9.8%	11.4%	6.5%	17.6%	17.3%					
Retailing										
Turnover	2,051	2,531	2,040	1,671	1,467	27	28	27	30	31
Operating profit	236	278	230	179	160	24	26	27	31	33
Net assets	2,332	2,785	2,266	1,898	1,290	40	45	36	51	42
Operating margin	11.5%	11.0%	11.3%	10.7%	10.9%					
RONA	6.6%	6.5%	6.6%	6.1%	8.1%					
U.K. and Ireland										
Turnover	2,940	3,685	4,688	3,836	3,559	34	39	50	64	62
Operating profit	385	451	424	364	331	36	42	44	56	58
Net assets	1,816	2,500	2,626	2,700	1,945	30	40	41	64	62
Continental Europe										
Turnover	862	661	471	221	214	10	7	5	4	4
Operating profit	104	81	66	46	36	10	7	7	7	6
Net assets	557	427	330	384	335	9	7	5	9	11
United States										
Turnover	4,433	4,537	3,720	1,758	1,720	51	48	40	29	30
Operating profit	517	475	395	218	185	48	44	41	33	32
Net assets	3,466	3,149	3,314	1,034	759	57	50	51	25	24
Rest of America										
Turnover	216	216	174	54	58	2	2	2	1	1
Operating profit	20	21	20	14	13	2	2	2	2	2
Net assets	128	148	145	50	61	2	2	2	1	2
Rest of world										
Turnover	297	295	265	160	155	3	3	3	3	3
Operating profit	45	54	62	12	6	4	5	6	2	1
Net assets	86	91	68	22	24	1	1	1	1	1

*Return on net assets (RONA) is computed as earnings before interest and after taxes (EBIAT) divided by net assets (total assets less current liabilities). A benchmark against which to compare RONA is the weighted-average cost of capital.

Source: Annual reports of Grand Metropolitan PLC.

EXHIBIT 3 Historical Financial Statements (in £ millions)

	1991	1990	1989	1988	1987
	Balance Sheet				
Total assets	9,187	9,420	9,570	5,846	4,577
Fixed assets					
Intangible assets	2,464	2,317	2,652	588	0
Tangible assets	2,764	3,756	3,839	3,279	2,725
Investments	851	214	144	206	177
Total fixed assets	6,079	6,287	6,635	4,074	2,902
Current assets					
Stocks	1,286	1,349	1,269	761	734
Debtors	1,561	1,541	1,451	874	828
Cash at bank and in hand	261	243	215	138	113
Total current assets	3,108	3,133	2,935	1,772	1,675
Creditors (less than one year)					
Borrowings	(157)	(206)	(362)	(187)	(330)
Other creditors	(2,135)	(2,343)	(2,316)	(1,301)	(1,166)
Total current liabilities	(2,292)	(2,549)	(2,678)	(1,488)	(1,496)
Current assets − Current liabilities	816	584	257	284	179
Total assets − Current liabilities	6,895	6,871	6,892	4,358	3,081
Creditors (greater than one year)					
Borrowings	(2,703)	(2,925)	(3,494)	(702)	(1,142)
Other creditors	(169)	(191)	(231)	(163)	(103)
Total noncurrent liabilities	(2,872)	(3,116)	(3,725)	(865)	(1,245)
Provisions	(569)	(328)	(325)	(55)	(70)
Total assets − Total liabilities	3,454	3,427	2,842	3,438	1,765
Capital and reserves					
Capital	515	508	506	443	441
Reserves	2,907	2,893	2,304	2,964	1,296
Minority interests	32	26	32	31	28
Total equity	3,454	3,427	2,842	3,438	1,765
	Profit-and-Loss Account				
Turnover	8,748	9,394	9,298	6,029	5,706
Cost of sales	(7,473)	(8,119)	(8,159)	(5,262)	(5,016)
Depreciation	(204)	(216)	(190)	(125)	(126)
Trading profit	1,071	1,059	949	642	564
Income of related companies	10	23	18	12	8
Other income	18	79	80	39	14
Net interest	(171)	(239)	(280)	(93)	(120)
Exceptional items	35	(3)	(35)	(25)	(9)
Pretax profit	963	919	732	576	456
Taxation	(298)	(279)	(216)	(155)	(120)
Net income	665	640	516	421	336
Minority interests	(7)	(6)	(8)	(8)	(2)
Extraordinary items	(226)	435	560	290	128
Dividends payable	(218)	(198)	(167)	(129)	(104)
Retained earnings	214	871	901	574	358

Source: Annual reports of Grand Metropolitan PLC.

EXHIBIT 4 Acquisitions and Divestitures

	Acquisitions	Divestitures
1960s and 1970s	**1966** Levy & Franks: pub and restaurant chain **1967** Bateman & Midland Catering: contract catering **1969** Express Dairy: distribution of milk products **1970** Berni Inns: hotels in U.K.; Mecca: gaming, betting, and amusement centers **1971** Truman Hanbury Buxton: brewing, pubs, and hotels **1972** Watney (incl. IDV): brewing, distribution of wines and spirits	
1980s	**1980** Liggett Group (U.S.): cigarettes, wines and spirits, soft-drink bottling, fitness products, pet food (Alpo) **1981** Intercontinental Hotels: worldwide luxury hotel chain **1983** Childrens' World (U.S.): early education services **1985** Cinzano (25%): drinks; Quality Care (U.S.): home health care; Pearle Optical (U.S.): world's largest eye-care products retailing **1986** G. Ruddle & Co.: brewer **1987** Heublein (U.S.): wines and spirits; Almaden Vineyards (U.S.): wines; Saccone & Speed and Roberts & Cooper: wines and spirits; Dairy Produce Packers: dairy products; Martell (10%): cognac; two pet-food manufacturers (U.S.) **1988** Vision Express and Eye & Tech (U.S.): optical superstores; Kaysens: frozen desserts; Peter's Savoury Products: meat and pastry products; William Hill Org.: retail betting; Wienerwald/ Spaghetti Factory: German and Swiss restaurants **1989** The Pillsbury Company (U.S.): international food group: Burger King, Green Giant, Häagen-Dazs; Metaxa: Greek brandy; Ouzo-Kaloyannis (30%): Greek spirits; Brent Walker: pubs; UB Restaurants: Wimpy, Pizzaland, and Pizza Perfect fast-food chains	**1984** CC Soft Drinks: soft-drink manufacturer **1985** Express Dairy (northern area): milk/dairy products; Pinkerton Tobacco (U.S.): chewing tobacco (Liggett); L&M do Brasil: tobacco leaf (Liggett); Mecca Leisure: bingo halls/amusement centers **1986** Dryborough & Co. (U.K.), Stern Brauerei (D), Brouwerij Maes (B): brewing; Liggett Group (U.S.): cigarettes **1987** Compass Group: contract and other services; Children's World (U.S.): child care products; Quality Care (U.S.): home health-care products; Diversified Products (U.S.): fitness products (Liggett); McGuinness Distillers: Canadian spirits **1988** Hotel Meurice (F); Atlantic Soft Drink Co./Pepsi-Cola San Joaquin Bottling Co. (U.S.); Intercontinental Hotels **1989** Steak & Ale/Bennigans (U.S.): restaurant chain; London Clubs: London casino business; Van De Kamp's: branded frozen foods; Bumble Bee: branded seafood; William Hill: retail betting
1990s	**1990** Remy Martin-Cointreau (20%): joint-venture spirits/liqueurs; Anglo Espanola de Distribucion: Spanish wines and spirits distributor; Jus-rol: food manufacturer **1991** Belin Surgelés (France): frozen cakes and pastries; Inntrepreneur Estates (50%) joint venture with Courage: management company for all Courage and 3,570 GrandMet pubs under pubs-for-breweries swap **1992** Cinzano: remaining 75%	**1990** Berni Inns: family restaurant chain **1991** Pizzaland/Pastificio: pizza/pasta restaurant chains; Perfect Pizza: take-away/delivery pizza chain; Watney Truman, Ruddles Brewery, Samuel Webster and Wilsons: breweries; 4 Pillsbury flour mills (U.S.); 3,570 managed and tenanted pubs to Inntrepreneur Estates; The Dominic Group: off-license chain; Express Dairy: liquid milk products; Eden Vale: chilled products

Source: Annual reports of Grand Metropolitan PLC and IBCA report, "Grand Metropolitan" (October 1991).

EXHIBIT 5   Debt Profile

	1991	1990	1989	1988	1987
Debt maturity					
Current	5%	7%	9%	21%	22%
1 to 2 years	2	58	11	19	25
2 to 5 years	77	30	69	14	28
Over 5 years	16%	5%	11%	46%	25%
Debt currency					
U.S. dollar	77%	79%	11%	8%	11%
Pound sterling	18	15	9	47	33
Deutsche mark (DM)	2	1	1	0	0
Multicurrency	0	0	77	34	47
Various	3%	5%	3%	10%	8%

Market Value of Equity (as of April 15, 1992)	
Common share prices	£9.48 per share
Shares outstanding	1,005,896,041
Market value of equity	£9,535,894,468

Sources: Annual reports of Grand Metropolitan PLC and *The Wall Street Journal.*

EXHIBIT 6   Summary of Percentage Weights of the Various Classes of Capital

	£ Outstandings		£ Weights[a]		U.S.$ Outstandings		U.S.$ Weights	
	Book	*Market*	*Book*	*Market*	*Book*	*Market*	*Book*	*Market*
Column Number	*(1)*	*(2)*	*(3)*	*(4)*	*(5)*	*(6)*	*(7)*	*(8)*
Specified debts[b]	1,777.4	1,794.8	33.0%	15.6%	3,107	3,137	33.0%	15.6%
Unspecified debts[c]	87.0	87.0	1.6	0.8	152	152	1.6	0.8
Convertible debt	52.0	63.0	1.0	0.5	91	110	1.0	0.5
Preferred stock	12.2	6.3	0.2	0.1	21	11	0.2	0.1
Common stock	3,454.0	9,535.9	64.2	83.0	6,038	16,669	64.2	83.0
Total capital	5,382.6	11,487.1	100.0%	100.0%	9,409	20,079	100.0%	100.0%

[a]The £ weights are calculated by dividing the £ outstanding in each class of capital by the total amount of £ capital. The U.S.$ weights are estimated the same way.

[b]The balance sheet listed eight separate classes of debt capital to which costs could be attributed: bank loans, commercial paper, guaranteed notes, guaranteed debentures, debenture stock, and bonds.

[c]The balance sheet listed £87 million of debt outstanding without citing a specific cost. Presumably, this debt consisted of a number of small issues. One way to treat those issues in cost-of-capital estimation is to assume that their average cost is equal to a weighted-average cost of all the other specified debt securities.

EXHIBIT 7 Estimation of Average Costs of Debt and Preferred Stock

	Currency	Yield on Book Value	Yield on Market Value	£ Yields		U.S.$ Yields	
				Book Value	Market Value	Book Value	Market Value
Bank loans and overdrafts	£	9.54%	9.54%	9.54%	9.54%	7.86%	7.86%
Commercial paper	U.S.$	5.93	5.93	7.58	7.58	5.93	5.93
Guaranteed notes 1996	U.S.$	8.13	7.97	9.81	9.65	8.13	7.97
Guaranteed notes 2001	U.S.$	8.63	7.87	10.32	9.55	8.63	7.87
Guaranteed debentures 2011	U.S.$	9.00	8.02	10.70	9.70	9.00	8.02
Commercial paper	£	10.80	10.80	10.80	0.80	9.10	9.10
Debenture stock 2008	£	12.13	11.15	12.13	11.15	10.40	9.44
Bonds 1992	DM	6.63	8.57	6.93	8.88	5.29	7.21
Weighted-average cost of debt (pretax)		7.15	7.13	8.69	8.63	7.03	6.96
Subord. convert. bonds 2002 (after-tax)*	£	6.25	9.75	6.25	9.75	4.62	8.07
Preferred stock issues							
4.75%	£	4.75	10.05	4.75	10.05	3.14	8.36
6.25%	£	6.25	10.15	6.25	10.15	4.62	8.46
5.00%	£	5.00	10.35	5.00	10.35	3.39	8.66
Weighted-average cost of pfd.		5.31%	10.27%	5.31%	10.27%	3.76%	8.57%

Note: The weighted-average costs are based on the following estimated weightings given on page 193:

EXHIBIT 7 (concluded)

Securities	Book Value		Book % Weights		Market Value			Market % Weights	
Outstanding†	£	U.S.$	£	U.S.$	Outstanding	£	U.S.$	£	U.S.$
Bank loans and overdrafts £280	280	489	15.8	15.8	£280	280	489	15.6	15.6
Commercial paper $1,696	970	1,696	54.6	54.6	$1696	970	1,696	54.1	54.1
Guaranteed notes 1996 $170	97	170	5.5	5.5	$171	98	171	5.5	5.5
Guaranteed notes 2001 $170	97	170	5.5	5.5	$178	102	178	5.7	5.7
Guaranteed debentures 2011 $169	97	169	5.4	5.4	$185	106	185	5.9	5.9
Commercial paper £139	139	243	7.8	7.8	£139	139	243	7.7	7.7
Debenture stock 2008 £50	50	87	2.8	2.8	£54	54	94	3.0	3.0
Bonds 1992 DM137	47	82	2.6	2.6	DM136	46	80	2.6	2.6
Total specified debts	1,777	3,107	100.0	100.0		1,795	$3,137	100.0	100.0
Various unspecified debts £87	87	152							
Subord. convert. bonds 2002 £52	52	91			£63	63	110		
Preferred stock issues									
4.75% £1.2	1.2	2.1	9.8	9.8	£0.56	0.56	1.0	9.0	9.0
6.25% £3.3	3.3	5.8	27.0	27.0	2.03	2.03	3.5	32.1	32.1
5.00% £7.7	7.7	13.5	63.1	63.1	3.72	3.72	6.5	58.9	58.9
Total preferred stock £12.2	12.2	21.3	100.0	100.0	£6.31	6.31	11.0	100.0	100.0

*The cost of the convertible debt was estimated by the casewriters as a blend of the cost of equity and after-tax cost of debt.
†Currencies were translated to U.S. dollars or pounds sterling at the following rates of exchange prevailing in mid-April 1992: Dollar/Pound = 1.748; DM/Pound = 2.917; DM/Dollar = 1.669.

193

EXHIBIT 8   Information on Comparable Companies

	Sales (in U.S.$ mn)	*Dividend* Yield	*P/E* Ratio	*Interest* Coverage	*Senior* Debt Rating
Grand Metropolitan	15,222	3.4%	13.3	6.6	NR
Restaurant–Retailing					
Forte (U.K.)	4,600	5.7%	14.1	2.4	NR
McDonald's	6,695	0.8%	17.3	4.0	AA
Luby's	328	3.5%	14.2	nil	NR
National Pizza	305	0.0%	16.9	3.3	NR
TCBY Enterprises	129	3.9%	26.8	7.8	NR
Wendy's Int'l	1,060	2.0%	20.7	5.9	BBB
Average	**2,186**	**2.7%**	**18.3**	**3.9**	
Food Processing					
Argyll Group (U.K.)	7,830	4.3%	13.5	12.9	NR
Assoc. Brit. Foods (U.K.)	6,110	3.2%	9.6	8.3	NR
Borden	7,235	3.6%	14.1	3.9	A+
Cadbury-Schweppes (U.K.)	5,475	3.6%	17.4	3.8	NR
Campbell Soup	6,204	1.8%	21.1	5.9	AA
CPC International	6,189	2.7%	15.3	6.5	A
Dean Foods	2,158	1.9%	16.1	9.5	NR
Dreyer's Grd Ice Cream	355	0.7%	31.6	4.2	NR
Flowers Industries	825	4.1%	20.0	5.2	NR
General Mills	7,153	2.3%	23.3	8.6	A+
Heinz	6,800	2.8%	19.4	7.6	AA−
Michael Foods	455	1.3%	14.7	4.1	NR
Quaker Oats	5,491	2.8%	17.8	5.6	A+
Ralston Purina	7,375	2.2%	15.8	4.1	A−
Sara Lee	12,831	1.9%	22.0	6.6	AA−
Tate & Lyle (U.K.)	5,680	3.7%	10.1	3.1	NR
Tesco (U.K.)	11,050	3.3%	13.2	4.0	NR
Unilever (NL & U.K.)	42,250	3.2%	15.1	4.6	NR
United Biscuits (U.K.)	4,225	5.0%	13.7	8.5	NR
Universal Foods	834	2.6%	14.7	7.2	NR
Average	**7,326**	**2.9%**	**16.9**	**6.2**	
Drinks					
Allied Lyons (U.K.)	8,940	4.1%	23.4	2.3	NR
Anheuser-Busch	10,996	2.0%	15.7	8.2	AA−
Bass (U.K.)	7,630	4.8%	10.6	4.3	NR
Brown-Forman	1,250	2.8%	14.7	23.5	A+
Coors	1,917	2.3%	15.2	10.3	NR
Guinness (U.K.)	6,110	2.5%	15.9	4.7	NR
Labatt (Canada)	4,400	3.0%	14.3	2.9	NR
Molson (Canada)	2,500	2.1%	13.9	3.3	NR
Scottish & Newcastle (U.K.)	2,398	5.0%	13.5	5.8	NR
Seagram (Canada)	5,000	1.7%	17.2	3.1	NR
Whitbread (U.K.)	3,585	5.2%	10.7	5.6	NR
Average	**4,975**	**3.2%**	**15.0**	**6.7**	

Notes:
U.S. and Canadian companies: 1991 and expected annual growth rates until 1997.
U.K. companies: 1990 and average annual growth rates of the last five years.

Debt-to-Capital		Debt-to-Equity				Expected Growth Rate in:	
Book Value	Market Value	Book Value	Market Value	Average Tax Rate	Beta	Sales	Dividends
43%	21%	75%	27%	31%	UK: 1.14 US: 0.80	6.5%	12.0%
27%	30%	36%	42%	16%	1.18	12.3%	10.6%
42%	2%	72%	2%	34%	0.95	12.0%	13.5%
1%	0%	1%	0%	34%	0.90	10.0%	9.0%
49%	37%	96%	58%	36%	1.00	15.5%	0.0%
14%	3%	16%	3%	35%	1.25	9.0%	23.0%
33%	23%	49%	30%	34%	1.15	6.0%	0.0%
28%	**16%**	**45%**	**23%**	**31%**	**1.07**	**10.8%**	**9.4%**
32%	14%	47%	16%	28%	0.72	19.8%	18.3%
19%	19%	23%	23%	32%	0.47	2.3%	14.9%
43%	20%	75%	25%	36%	1.15	5.5%	9.5%
38%	17%	62%	21%	28%	0.83	10.9%	14.3%
30%	8%	43%	9%	40%	1.00	7.5%	15.5%
38%	12%	61%	14%	40%	1.10	8.5%	12.5%
26%	10%	35%	12%	42%	0.90	8.0%	7.0%
31%	22%	45%	28%	40%	1.05	16.5%	0.0%
35%	14%	54%	16%	40%	0.85	5.5%	6.5%
39%	6%	64%	6%	39%	1.00	11.0%	15.0%
10%	2%	11%	2%	38%	1.00	8.5%	11.0%
35%	26%	54%	36%	36%	1.15	9.5%	19.0%
40%	13%	67%	15%	43%	0.90	9.0%	11.5%
70%	18%	233%	23%	40%	0.90	9.5%	11.0%
29%	6%	41%	7%	36%	1.00	7.0%	13.5%
52%	32%	110%	47%	29%	1.10	14.7%	14.3%
19%	10%	23%	11%	32%	0.73	13.6%	22.8%
22%	31%	28%	44%	35%	0.86	8.5%	9.5%
32%	14%	48%	16%	33%	0.88	6.1%	12.2%
34%	13%	52%	15%	37%	0.90	9.0%	12.5%
34%	**15%**	**59%**	**19%**	**36%**	**0.92**	**9.5%**	**12.5%**
43%	30%	75%	44%	29%	0.97	9.2%	14.6%
38%	15%	61%	18%	38%	1.00	7.0%	12.0%
29%	38%	40%	62%	26%	0.77	10.1%	16.5%
14%	4%	16%	4%	35%	1.20	9.5%	11.5%
13%	10%	15%	11%	39%	0.85	5.0%	0.0%
31%	18%	44%	22%	28%	1.01	24.2%	21.1%
33%	28%	49%	38%	34%	0.75	2.0%	6.5%
45%	37%	82%	59%	34%	0.75	5.0%	13.0%
23%	20%	31%	25%	33%	0.59	19.3%	16.5%
29%	26%	41%	35%	22%	1.10	5.0%	12.0%
15%	15%	17%	17%	24%	0.70	6.1%	15.9%
28%	**22%**	**43%**	**30%**	**31%**	**0.88**	**9.3%**	**12.7%**

EXHIBIT 8   *(concluded)*

Restaurant

Forte (U.K.)	Active in contract catering and hotel- and motel-chain management.
Luby's Cafeteria (U.S.)	Operates a chain of cafeterias.
McDonald's (U.S.)	Licenses and operates a fast-food hamburger chain.
National Pizza (U.S.)	Largest franchisee of PepsiCo's Pizza Hut chain.
TCBY Enterprises (U.S.)	Largest franchisor of soft-frozen yogurt stores.
Wendy's Int'l (U.S.)	Licenses and operates a chain of quick-service hamburger restaurants.

Food Processing

Argyll Group (U.K.)	One of the leading food retailers in the United Kingdom.
Assoc. British Foods (U.K.)	Operator of grocery stores, retail bakeries, beauty shops.
Borden (U.S.)	Diversified producer of packaged food (dairy, snacks, pasta, popcorn, jams, potato chips) and adhesives (Elmer's Cement, Crazy Glue).
Cadbury-Schweppes (U.K.)	Manufacturer of bottled and canned soft drinks, candy and other confectionary products, food preparations.
Campbell Soup (U.S.)	A leading manufacturer of canned soups, spaghetti, fruit and vegetable juices, frozen foods, salads, bakery products, olives, pickles.
CPC International (U.S.)	A leading producer of grocery products (soups, mayonnaise, peanut butter, pasta, baked goods) and a large corn refiner (corn syrups, dextrose, starches).
Dean Foods (U.S.)	Manufactures, distributes dairy products (fluid milk, ice cream, cheeses) and processes canned and frozen vegetables, sauces, powdered drinks, and creamers.
Dreyer's Grand (U.S.)	Manufacturer and distributor of premium ice cream products.
Flowers Ind. (U.S.)	Producer of bakery and snack-food goods.
General Mills (U.S.)	Processes and markets consumer foods (cereals, flour, seafood, yogurt) and operates restaurants.
Heinz (U.S.)	Manufactures soups, ketchup, baby foods, cat food, frozen potatoes.
Michael Foods (U.S.)	Producer and distributor of egg and egg products, frozen potato products, ice cream products, refrigerator-case products.
Quaker Oats (U.S.)	Produces foods (cereals, breakfast products, beverages) and pet foods, owns Fisher-Price toys.
Ralston Purina (U.S.)	World's largest producer of dry dog and cat foods and dry-cell batteries.
Sara Lee (U.S.)	Diversified, international, packaged consumer goods (Hanes, Dim), with operations in coffee, specialty meats, frozen baked goods, and food-services distribution.
Tate & Lyle (U.K.)	Producer and distributor of sugar products, beverages, food products.
Tesco (U.K.)	One of the leading food retailers in the United Kingdom.
Unilever (NL and U.K.)	One of the world's largest producers and marketers of branded and packaged consumer goods.
United Biscuits (U.K.)	Maker of biscuits, cookies and crackers, snack foods, frozen foods and owner/operator of fast-food restaurant chain.
Universal Foods (U.S.)	International manufacturer and marketer of value-added food products and ingredients for food processing, baking, foodservice and retail markets.

Drinks

Allied Lyons (U.K.)	Active in beer and retailing, wines, spirits, eating and drinking places.
Anheuser-Busch (U.S.)	Largest U.S. brewer, also active in baked and snack goods, frozen foods, theme parks.
Bass (U.K.)	Active in malt beverages, amusement and recreation, hotels and motels, soft drinks.
Brown-Forman (U.S.)	A leading wine and spirits producer and importer, producer of fine china, crystal, and luggage.
Coors (U.S.)	U.S. brewer.
Guinness (U.K.)	Active in malt beverages, wines, brandy spirits, liquors.
Labatt (CN)	One of Canada's leading brewers, also active in foods, dairy products, fruit juices.
Molson (CN)	Engaged in brewing, cleaning and sanitizing, and retail merchandising.
Scottish & Newcastle (U.K.)	Active in malt beverages, wine and liquor stores, hotels and motels, soft drinks.
Seagram (CN)	One of the world's largest wine and spirits distillers/producers.
Whitbread (U.K.)	Maker of malt beverages, operator of hotels and motels, bottler of soft drinks, active in recreation.

Sources: *Value Line; Risk Measurement Services,* January–March 1992 (London Business School); Compact Disclosure (Digital Library System, Inc.); casewriters' estimates.

EXHIBIT 9 Capital-Market Conditions, April 1992

U.K. Gilt and U.S. Treasury Bond Yields (April 8, 1992)

Term	U.K. Gilts, Yield to Maturity	U.S. Treasuries, Yield to Maturity
1	10.50%	4.45%
2	10.40	5.29
3	10.30	5.95
5	10.00	6.82
10	9.80	7.45
15	9.60	7.59
20	9.60%	7.83%

Yields by Rating Category

Rating	Pound Yield	Dollar Yield
AAA	10.38%	8.69%
AA	10.56	8.86
A	11.08	9.38
BBB	11.16	9.45
BB	12.58	10.85
B	13.40%	11.66%

Foreign Exchange Rates

$/£ = 1.748
DM/£ = 2.917
DM/$ = 1.669

Long-Term Expected Rates of Inflation

United Kingdom   4.3% annually
United States   2.7% annually
Germany   4.0% annually

Equity Market Risk Premium

Market	Estimated Current Premium	Geometric Mean Historical Premium	Arithmetic Mean Historical Premium
London	3.9%	4.1%	6.9%
New York	2.7%	5.6%	8.4%

Sources: *Financial Times; The Wall Street Journal,* OECD *Economic Outlook,* June 1992; Banque Degroof, Belgium.

Case 14

The Boeing 777

The Boeing 777 will set a new standard for aircraft around the world. With the introduction of the 777, we will be able to offer our airline customers a complete family of Boeing airplanes that meets any seating requirement from approximately 100 to 500 passengers. We believe the 777 will allow us to offer the right product for the changing market requirements of the 1990s and beyond.[1]

Shrontz says his mission is raising Boeing's return on equity from the recent average of about 12 percent. Although Boeing makes money while its main competitors don't, Shrontz isn't satisfied. "We've got to enhance our earnings," he says.[2]

It takes a lot of courage to launch an industrial program in this uncertain economic environment.[3]

In October 1990, Frank Shrontz officially announced the launch of the latest addition to the Boeing family, the 777. This plane would fit in a market niche of medium-to-large passenger airframes and would carry 350 to 390 passengers up to 7,600 nautical miles (14,000 kilometers; for instance, from Sydney to Tokyo or Los Angeles to Frankfurt). The first planes were expected to be delivered in May 1995 to United Airlines, which had announced firm orders for the 777 on October 15, 1990. No other orders had as yet been received.

---

[1] Frank Shrontz, chief executive officer, The Boeing Company, October 29, 1990.

[2] Dorin Jones Yang, "To Frank Shrontz, the Blue Yonder Is Anything but Wild," *Business Week,* July 9, 1990, p. 49.

[3] A quotation of Howard A. Rubel, airline industry analyst with C. J. Lawrence, Morgan Grenfell, Inc., in "It's Fat and Snazzy—and Worth Billions to Boeing," *Business Week,* October 29, 1990, p. 32.

This case was written by Dena Gollish, Henrik Clausen, Niels Koggersvol, Peter Christey, and Professor Robert F. Bruner as a basis for class discussion rather than to illustrate effective or ineffective handling of an administrative situation. The financial support of the Citicorp Global Scholars Program is gratefully acknowledged. Copyright © 1992 by the University of Virginia Darden School Foundation, Charlottesville, VA, and INSEAD, Fontainebleau, France. All rights reserved. *No part of this publication may be reproduced, stored in a retrieval system, used in a spreadsheet, or transmitted in any form or by any means—electronic, mechanical, photocopying, recording, or otherwise—without the permission of the Darden Foundation. For inquiries, please send an e-mail to dardencases @virginia.edu.* Rev. 11/97. Version 1.5.

Industry analysts had mixed views on Boeing's decision to go ahead with the 777. Pessimists noted that Airbus Industrie and McDonnell Douglas both had already announced aircraft targeted for this niche and had sizable head starts on firm orders. This competition, they believed, would drive down prices for the aircraft. Furthermore, research-and-development expenditures on the 777—estimated at $4 billion to $5 billion—would be more than twice as high as for the 757 and 767 projects. If this new product failed, the financial loss would substantially deplete Boeing's book value of equity. Finally, Iraq's invasion of Kuwait and the ensuing international crisis had led to a sharp decline in airline travel. Political and economic conditions seemed to have turned against the project.

Optimists believed that the 777 would outperform its competitors and gain at least Boeing's historical 54 percent market share. Boeing believed that air travel would double by the year 2005, creating a large demand for new capacity. Moreover, the aging of large passenger aircraft would mean a replacement demand of 640 new units. Some analysts also pointed to the expected high growth rate on the routes targeted by the 777, resulting particularly from growth in the Asian market. In addition, many analysts believed that Boeing's R&D spending on the 777 could be used to develop other aircraft (for example, a new derivative of the 747) at a much reduced cost. Finally, the 777 offered airlines the most flexibility in designing the interior of the aircraft and the best cost efficiency of all its competitors.

In October 1990, perhaps the prime question was whether the Boeing 777 project remained a sensible investment for Boeing. Two and one-half years had elapsed since the start of the preliminary design effort. Political and economic conditions had worsened. Value Line noted:

> Boeing stock has been pummeled since Iraq's invasion of Kuwait [see graph of share prices], reflecting, we think, the surge in the cost of petroleum and jet fuel, which has sent airline fares rising and weakened global economies. As a result, passenger counts are under pressure and many investors are concerned that the boom in airliner demand will dissipate.[4]

Was the recent slump in Boeing's share price a result strictly of the Gulf Crisis, or was the stock market giving an advance signal of its evaluation of the Boeing 777? The advance orders for competitors' aircraft models to be launched in this segment had proved that demand existed for a new generation of aircraft, but would the new model be profitable at any level of demand? Finally, and most important, would the Boeing 777 project serve Frank Shrontz's ultimate mission of improving Boeing's return on equity?

COMMERCIAL AIRCRAFT INDUSTRY

Three companies dominated the large airframe market in 1990, with a combined 90 percent market share: Boeing (53 percent), Airbus Industrie (18 percent), and McDonnell Douglas (19 percent). Boeing was by far the largest player, not only in terms of current aircraft deliveries, but also in terms of revenues, earnings, and aircraft orders.

Airbus Industrie. Established 20 years earlier, Airbus had moved into second place in the world aircraft market, although it had yet to turn a profit. With the introduction of the A330 and A340 models in 1992–93, Airbus claimed it would have a full family of aircraft.

---

[4]Text quote from *Value Line Investment Survey,* October 12, 1990.

Share Prices, The Boeing Company, Compared to S&P 500

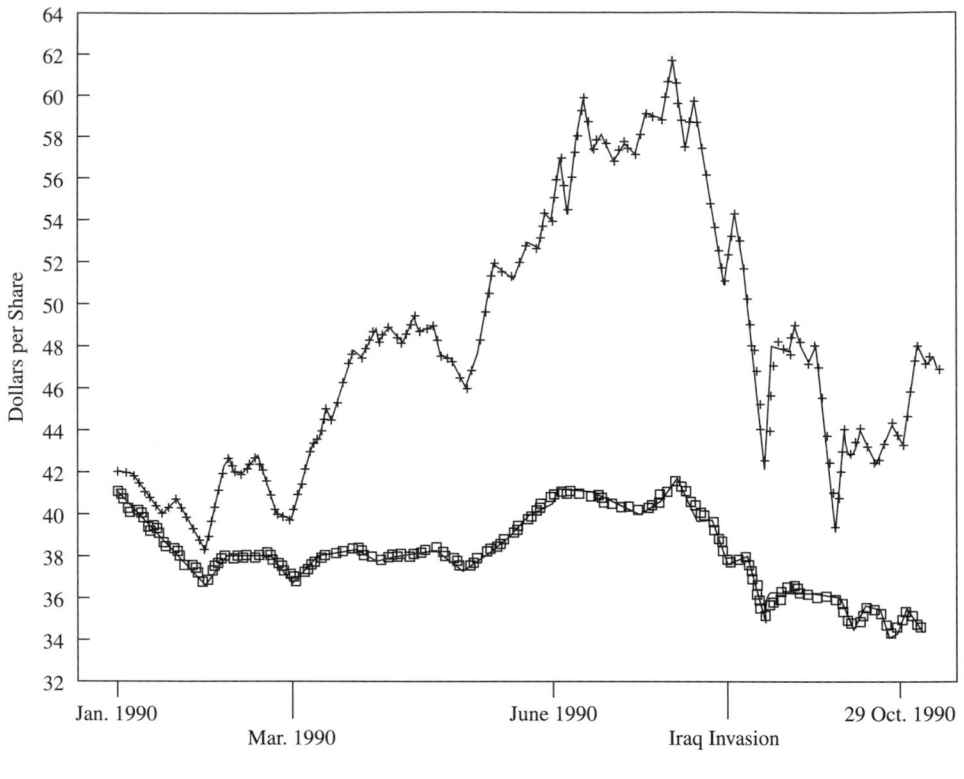

☐ S&P500 Index   + Boeing

Previously, Airbus competed mainly in the small-to-medium payload and distance segments. The A330/A340 would increase Airbus's offerings on both dimensions. These aircraft would compete directly with McDonnell Douglas's proposed MD-11 and the Boeing 777.

McDonnell Douglas.   Historically, McDonnell Douglas (MD) had been primarily a defense contractor, with commercial aircraft producing only one-third of revenues. Consequently, the company's commercial-jet product range was limited and had shown little development. The decline in U.S. defense spending and Airbus's entry into key market segments had severely weakened MD's financial position. Corporate debt stood at $4.9 billion (representing a ratio of book debt to equity of 1.5 times). MD's share of market had fallen over recent years to less than 13 percent of total orders in 1989. In 1989 the company had revenues of $14.6 billion, profits of $219 million, and outstanding orders for commercial aircraft worth $21 billion.

MD competed in the small-payload, short-haul end of the market with the MD-80 and the MD-90 and would compete in the medium segment with the MD-11. In response to the ending of the Cold War, the company planned to increase the commercial-aircraft portion of sales from current levels of 36 percent to 50 percent over the next few years. To meet these goals, it was developing another new aircraft, the MD-12X, to compete with Boeing's 747-400. This project would cost $4 billion to $5 billion.

The Boeing Company.   Boeing was the world's leading manufacturer of commercial-jet aircraft. Half of its aircraft sales were to airlines within the United States. Boeing's estimated sales for 1990 were $27 billion (compared with $20 billion in 1989), and profits were expected to be approximately $1.4 billion (up from $675 million in 1989). The company had a record-breaking order backlog of $97 billion, enough to keep its plants operating at full capacity over the next three years.

Boeing had two principal business segments: commercial aircraft and defense (the latter included space and missile products). Exhibit 1 gives a breakdown by segment for sales, assets, and profits for 1987–89. The commercial-aircraft segment produced and sold four main airframes (the 737, 747, 757, and 767) and numerous derivatives of them. Boeing's defense segment was the main contractor on numerous military transportation projects and major missile systems. While the defense division had recorded losses in the most recent years, it provided valuable support to the commercial-aircraft group through the manufacturing of parts and the design and manufacture of electronic systems. Analysts also believed there were significant technology transfers from defense R&D to the commercial-aircraft segment.

Boeing possessed a remarkably strong balance sheet, with book value of debt making up only 4 percent of total capital. Exhibit 2 presents Boeing's balance sheets, and Exhibit 3 presents income statements for 1988 and 1989. Analysts were predicting that Boeing would increase the debt ratio to 14 percent over the next year or so because of future financing needs. Nevertheless, the company had historically shown an aversion to debt financing. Therefore, analysts believed that, in the long run, Boeing's debt capitalization would remain quite low.

DEMAND FOR COMMERCIAL AIRCRAFT

In 1989 world commercial-aircraft revenues exceeded $25 billion; total jet aircraft delivered were 398; orders outstanding were valued at $165 billion. While overall airline traffic was expected to increase by 5.2 percent per year over the next 15 years, traffic in Asia was forecasted to grow at a rate of 10.6 percent a year. At the 5.2 percent overall rate of increase, new aircraft sales would aggregate $615 billion by 2005.

The growth in aircraft demand was a function of increases in passenger air traffic, which in turn was a function of economic growth. Air traffic was highly sensitive to variations in consumer and business confidence. In the brief time since Iraq had invaded Kuwait, fuel prices had risen, passenger air traffic had declined, the inflow of aircraft orders had stopped, and several airlines had canceled existing orders. While the long-term association between economic growth and aircraft orders tended to be quite stable, the health of the commercial airlines tended to be a major determinant of aircraft orders in the short term; airlines could postpone purchases for a year or two, creating havoc in the finances of the aircraft manufacturers.

The demand for aircraft could be segmented along two dimensions: seating capacity and range in nautical miles. As Exhibit 4 reveals, the three major producers of aircraft covered the entire range. Commercial aircraft varied in price from approximately $35 million for Boeing's 737 to $145 million for the 747-400. Boeing produced 21 737s per month, although many models of aircraft had production rates of 5 to 7 per year.

Despite the high up-front costs and the fact that most market segments could support only one model of aircraft, the major manufacturers tried to compete across all segments partly because of the gains expected from derivative aircraft that could be developed to serve selected subsegments or new major segments. Derivatives had design and many parts in common with the original aircraft and thus could be developed and manufactured relatively inexpensively. These derivatives expanded a model's market, extended its lifetime, and led to economies of scale and experience. Incremental development costs of stretching an aircraft design were believed to be usually less than 25 percent of the original cost. Other factors that led the manufacturers to develop a broad range of aircraft included image issues (being a major player), time-based competition (each company trying to preempt the others in a particular segment), and pressure from major customers to fill a market niche.

Boeing was particularly adept at exploiting the advantages of aircraft derivatives. Its 707, 727, 737, and 757 models had similar fuselage shapes, which reduced design costs and allowed them all to be built using common production facilities. These basic shapes were also stretched and shortened into several different models to fill numerous product niches. In addition to development work on the 777, Boeing was also expected to begin working on a super jumbo jet (600+ passengers).

AIRCRAFT DEVELOPMENT AND LIFE CYCLE

Any individual airframe was characterized by huge outlays (for research, development, and tooling) and a long life cycle. The average new airplane in the early 1990s would cost over $4 billion to bring to production and might require 12 to 20 years before breaking even. Substantial negative cash flows would accumulate before an airframe product line broke even. Because of the financial strains a new product line might create, each new airframe was a "bet the ranch" proposition for the aircraft manufacturers. Over time, survival in the industry depended on introducing successful products and having the financial "deep pockets" with which to survive the cash-flow trough. Most analysts concluded, in fact, that few airframes ever yielded positive cumulative cash flows—but the few financial successes were spectacular.

Boeing aircraft tended to follow predictable sales patterns across their lives. Deliveries tended to rise to a peak during the first few years of availability and then decline moderately until a new version of the aircraft (a derivative) was introduced. This pattern was followed by one or more additional cycles of decline and new introduction. Exhibit 5 illustrates these cycles for four of Boeing's aircraft over their first 20 years of delivery.

THE 777

Boeing had been working on a new, revolutionary aircraft since 1988. The aircraft would be the largest and longest haul twin-bodied jet and (according to Boeing) the most flexible and cost-efficient plane ever. The aircraft's most unique feature would be a folding wing tip, which would enable it to fit into the smaller slots in airport terminals. The 777 would also be the first jet to use fly-by-wire technology, an advanced flying system already used on Airbus turbo-prop planes.

Analysts estimated that R&D expense on the 777 had amounted to hundreds of millions of dollars in the 1980s and $200 million in 1990 alone. The new aircraft created a revolution in Boeing's design and manufacturing processes. In terms of the design process, two features were unique:

- *Up-front involvement of the airlines.* Boeing had asked six of its major customers to play active roles in designing the new aircraft in order to ensure that the aircraft would meet customer needs and, Boeing hoped, give it a competitive advantage over the A330/A340 and MD-11.
- *Use of "current engineering."* That is, having 400 or so project engineers work side by side with the aircraft's designers: Until this development, designers worked independently, sent the plans over to the engineers, and then continued to make improvements. Each subsequent change cost upward of $10,000, and hundreds of such changes were made. With the 777, Boeing intended to get the details right before production started. The change in the relationship between design and production was organizational (i.e., the two groups would talk to each other before production began) and technological. Through an advanced computer-aided design and manufacturing (CAD/CAM) system, Boeing engineers could fully simulate production of the aircraft. The bugs could be found and eliminated before the aircraft went into production. Boeing hoped this design/production approach would save as much as 20 percent of the 777's estimated $4 billion to $5 billion development cost.

Despite the many innovations, analysts believed that the R&D costs for the 777 would be higher than for any other plane to date. One analyst forecasted that the R&D expenditures would aggregate to $4.467 billion.[5] In addition to R&D, Boeing would incur major capital expenditures to double the size of the manufacturing facility in Renton, Washington, where the 747 and 767 aircraft were produced. A new facility would be built to produce the major wing components and advanced composite tailplanes. Analysts estimated that these facilities would cost nearly $1.5 billion. Boeing also planned to build a special laboratory for integrating and testing aircraft systems; the 777 and other aircraft would make use of this facility. The company would also increase its spending on employee training to focus on the CAD system used on the 777. Engineers would receive over 350,000 hours of training on this system. Some analysts predicted that all of these new facilities and training programs would increase Boeing expenditures by $2.5 billion over the next few years.

With these large initial outlays, Boeing would need significant revenues to make the 777 program a success. The company expected each aircraft to sell for $130 million on average. Several analysts, however, believed that the A330/A340 and MD-11 would put downward pressure on this price, forcing Boeing to price the 777 at $100 million.

The 777 was targeted to the fastest growing market segment in terms of passenger seats and distance. This segment serviced medium- and long-haul routes. Boeing estimated that over the next 15 years, two-thirds of aircraft sales by value would be in this market segment. If the company maintained its market share of approximately 50 percent, it would achieve unit sales of 1,000 aircraft in the 777's first 10 years of production. Production costs would begin at high levels and rapidly fall as the product moved down the learning curve. Boeing executives believed that the 777 would have a life span of 30 to 40 years.

---

[5]George Shapiro, Salomon Brothers.

FINANCIAL FORECAST AND ANALYSIS

Exhibit 6 contains a forecast of free cash flows from the Boeing 777 project based on the casewriters' analyses and drawing on numerous assumptions of securities analysts in their published commentaries on the 777 project. The appendix to this exhibit discusses these forecast assumptions in detail. The primary implication of the forecast is that the internal rate of return (IRR) in the base case would be 19 percent.

Numerous sensitivity analyses of the IRR could be made. One important question was the impact of variations in aircraft prices. Another key assumption was the size of demand in the first 10 years. If the recession in the early 1990s were particularly long or severe, planes sold could fall well short of the estimate of 1,000. On the other hand, a resumption of prolonged economic growth could trigger higher sales, not only to replace aging planes, but also to expand overall capacity. The IRRs associated with different unit prices and unit sales volumes in the first 10 years are given in Exhibit 7.

A key determinant of the attractiveness of the 777 project was Boeing's cost of capital. As Exhibit 8 reveals, relatively minor variations in discount rates produced rather large variations in project payback on a discounted-cash-flow (DCF) basis. If the cash flows were undiscounted, the payback would occur in the 10th year. At the other extreme, if cash flows were subject to a 20 percent discount rate, payback would never occur.

COST OF CAPITAL

Boeing's weighted-average cost of capital (WACC) could be estimated using the well-known formula:

$$\text{WACC} = [I \times (1 - t) \times W_d] + (K_e \times W_e)$$

where

I =   Pretax cost of debt capital
t =   Marginal tax rate
W_d =   Proportion of debt in a market-value capital structure
K_e =   Cost of equity capital
W_e =   Proportion of equity in a market-value capital structure

Exhibit 9 gives information about Boeing and comparable companies to use in the WACC equation. Exhibit 10 depicts five-year stock-price performance relative to the Standard & Poor's (S&P) 500 Index. Boeing had faced a relatively low effective tax rate in the past, but because of changes in tax and accounting regulations, its marginal effective tax rate was expected to rise to 34 percent in the future. In October 1990, the yield on long-term U.S. Treasury bonds was 8.82 percent, and the 64-year geometric average equity-market risk premium was 5.4 percent. At a recent stock price of $43.00 per share, Boeing's dividend yield was 2.5 percent. Value Line forecasted Boeing's dividends to grow at the rate of 17 percent over the next five years.

Analysts had pointed out that Boeing actually consisted of two separate businesses, the relatively more stable and (in the midst of the Gulf War crisis) thriving defense business and the more volatile commercial-aircraft business. Thus the question arose of whether one should estimate Boeing's cost of capital to serve as the benchmark required rate of return. Would a required return on a portfolio of these two businesses be appropriate for evaluating the 777 project? If necessary, how might it be possible to isolate a required return for commercial aircraft?

CONCLUSION

Within the aircraft-manufacturing industry, the magnitude of risk posed by the launching of a major new jet aircraft was accepted as a matter of course. One observer said,

> Sustained success demands a willingness to gamble regularly, even though the effects of guessing wrong may be fatal . . . The business of making and selling commercial airliners is not for the diffident or faint of heart. It is remarkably difficult and, by anyone's standard, intensely competitive. There are a few industries that consume as much or more capital; certain others rely as heavily on quantities of highly skilled personnel; probably no other is involved with as many advanced technologies.[6]

Other observers worried that the technical challenges might obscure the commercial considerations: "The mystery behind this business isn't building an airplane that flies and is safe. It's building an airplane that is salable and profitable."[7]

Frank Shrontz had indicated that his primary mission during his tenure as CEO of Boeing would be to raise the firm's return on equity. Given that the 777 would be the major new product introduction for Boeing in the 1990s, the prime question was whether it would help Shrontz pursue his objective.

EXHIBIT 1   Revenues, Operating Profits, and Identifiable Assets by Segment for the Boeing Company

	1987	*1988*	*1989*
Revenues			
Commercial aircraft	$9,827	$11,369	$14,305
Defense and other	5,986	5,971	6,318
Total	15,813	17,340	20,623
Operating Profit			
Commercial aircraft	352	585	1,165
Defense and other	306	235	(243)
Total	658	820	922
Identifiable Assets			
Commercial aircraft	5,170	4,558	6,675
Defense and other	7,396	8,050	6,603
Total	$12,566	$12,608	$13,278

Source: The Boeing Company annual reports.

---

[6]John Newhouse, *The Sporty Game* (New York: Knopf, 1982), p. 92.

[7]A quotation of Wolfgang Demisch of UBS Securities, Inc., in "How Boeing Does It," *Business Week,* July 9, 1990, p. 50.

EXHIBIT 2   Boeing Balance Sheets (dollars in millions)

	1988	*1989*
Assets		
Cash	$ 3,544	$ 1,863
Other current assets	5,017	6,797
Total current assets	8,561	8,660
Customer financing	1,039	822
Net property, plant, and equipment	2,703	3,481
Investments	305	315
Total assets	$12,608	$13,278
Liabilities and stockholders' equity		
Accounts payable	$ 4,697	$ 4,932
Current portion of long-term debt	7	5
Other current liabilities	697	291
Total current liabilities	6,705	6,673
Long-term debt*	251	275
Deferred taxes	205	174
Deferred investment credit	43	25
Stockholders' equity†		
Common shares	1,341	1,736
Retained earnings	4,137	4,452
Treasury stock	(74)	(57)
Total stockholders' equity	5,404	6,131
Total liabilities and stockholders' equity	$12,608	$13,278

*Boeing's long-term debt consisted entirely of two issues: $250 million of 8.375 percent notes due December 31, 1996, and $37 million of long-term notes payable believed to bear floating rates of interest and currently costing 9.31 percent. The market value of the first bond issue was $234.5 million, found by valuing the issue at a discount rate of 9.73 percent, the average yield to maturity of AA-rated debt with five years to maturity. Because the notes payable yielded a floating rate, their market value equaled book value. Thus, the total market value of the two debt issues was estimated to be $271.5 million.

†In October 1990, Boeing had 346,436,214 common shares outstanding. At a trading price of $43 per share, Boeing's market value of equity was $14,896.76 million.

Source: The Boeing Company annual report, 1989.

EXHIBIT 3   Boeing Income Statements (dollars in millions except per share data)

	1988	1989
Revenues	$16,962	$ 20,276
Costs and expenses	16,514	19,695
Earnings from operations	448	581
Other income (interest)	378	347
Interest expense	(6)	(6)
Profit before taxes	820	922
Taxes*	206	247
Effect of change in method of accounting for taxes		298
Net earnings	614	973
Earnings per share	2.68	4.23
Cash dividend per share	$1.0333	$1.11666

*Boeing's marginal tax rate was 34 percent

Source: The Boeing Company annual report, 1989.

EXHIBIT 4   Competitive Positioning of Major Jet Aircraft

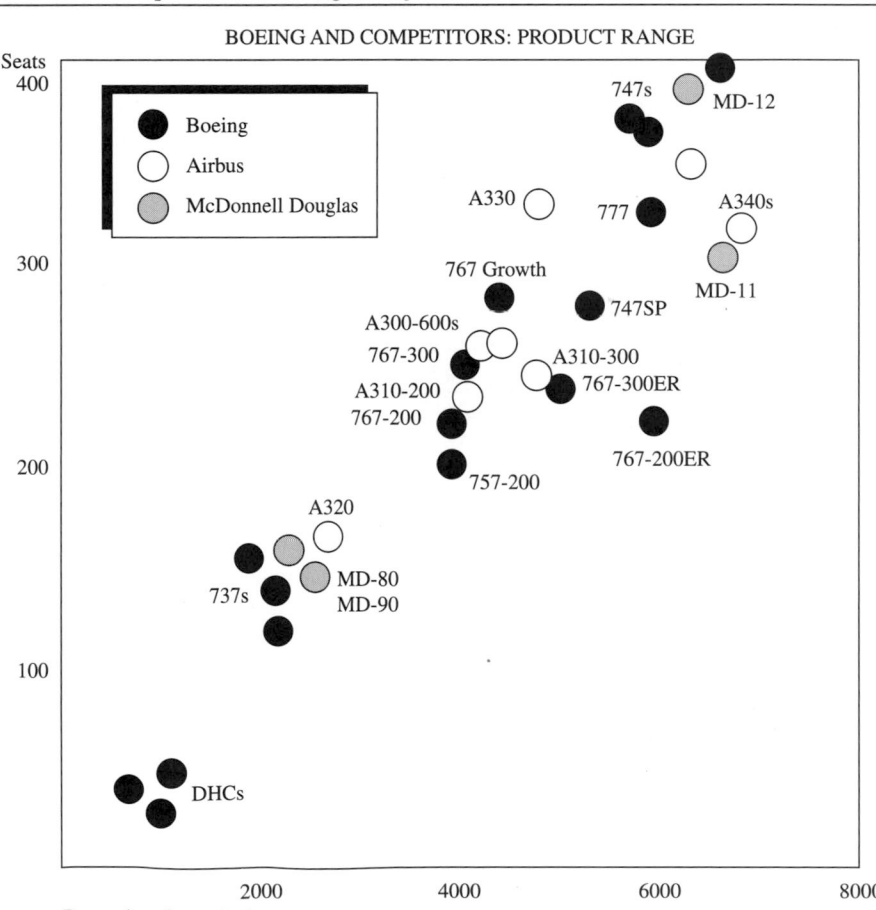

BOEING AND COMPETITORS: PRODUCT RANGE

EXHIBIT 5   Life Cycle of Unit Sales (averaged across the Boeing 707, 727, 737, and 747)

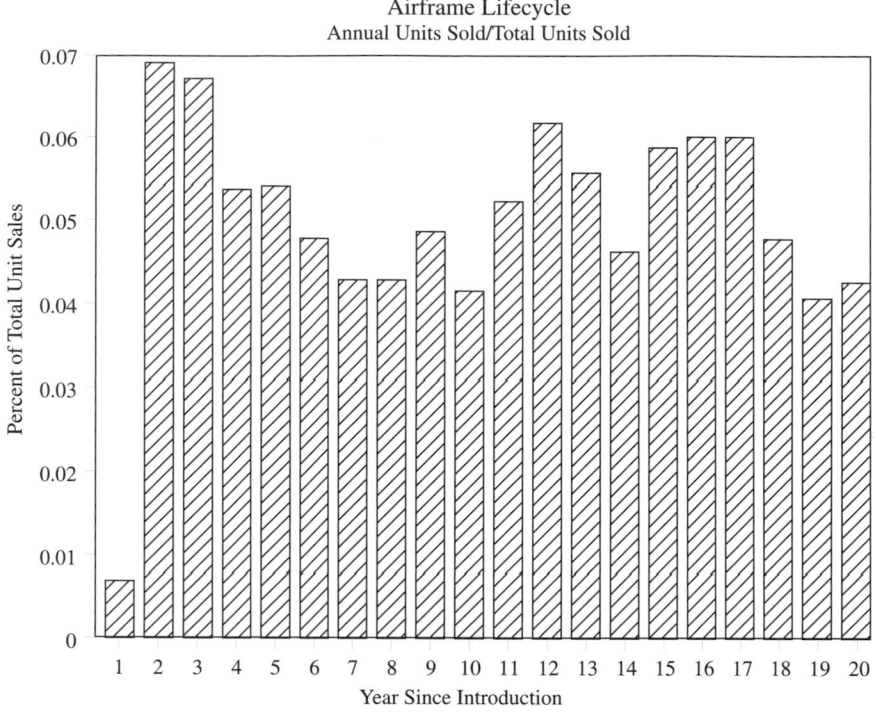

Source: The Boeing Company annual reports.

EXHIBIT 6   Forecast of Boeing 777 Free Cash Flows

Assumptions

Price per plane	130
Working-capital requirement (WCR) as % of sales	9.8%
General, selling, and administrative (GS&A) expense (% of sales)	4.0%
R&D expense (% of sales)	3.0% (excluding 1990–95)
Capital expenditure (% of sales)	0.1% (excluding 1990–94 and years before introduction of derivatives)
Depreciation	Double-digit accelerated method
Total number of planes yrs. 1–10	1,000
Total number of planes yrs. 11–20	1,000
Inflation	3.0%
Marginal effective tax rate	34.0%

EXHIBIT 6   (*continued*)

	1990	1991	1992	1993	1994	1995
Revenues						
Number of planes delivered						14
Price per plane						$ 130.00
Total revenues						1,847.55
Cost of goods sold						1,662.79
Gross profit						184.75
Depreciation	$ 0.00	$ 40.00	$ 96.00	$ 116.40	$ 124.76	112.28
GS&A expense						73.90
Operating profit						
(before R&D)	0.00	(40.00)	(96.00)	(116.40)	(124.76)	(1.43)
R&D expense	142.00	865.00	1,340.00	1,240.00	840.00	240.00
Pretax profit	(142.00)	(905.00)	(1,436.00)	(1,356.40)	(964.76)	(241.43)
Taxes (or tax credit)	(48.28)	(307.70)	(488.24)	(461.18)	(328.02)	(82.09)
After-tax profit	(93.72)	(597.30)	(947.76)	(895.22)	(636.74)	(159.34)
Capital expenditure	0.00	400.00	600.00	300.00	200.00	1.85
Depreciation add-back	0.00	40.00	96.00	116.40	124.76	112.28
Change in WCR						181.06
Annual free						
cash flow	$ (93.72)	$(957.30)	$(1,451.76)	$(1,078.82)	$(711.98)	$(229.97)

	1996	1997	1998	1999	2000	2001	2002
Revenues							
Planes delivered	145	140	111	111	102	92	92
Price per plane	$ 133.90	$ 137.92	$ 142.05	$ 146.32	$ 150.71	$ 155.23	$ 159.88
Total revenues	19,418.96	19,244.23	15,737.95	16,257.35	15,333.42	14,289.29	14,717.97
Cost of goods sold	16,506.12	15,202.94	12,275.60	12,518.16	11,653.40	10,859.86	11,038.48
Gross profit	2,912.84	4,041.29	3,462.35	3,739.19	3,680.02	3,429.43	3,679.49
Depreciation	101.06	90.95	82.72	77.75	75.63	75.00	75.00
GS&A expense	776.76	769.77	629.52	650.29	613.34	571.57	588.72
Operating profit							
(before R&D)	2,035.03	3,180.57	2,750.11	3,011.14	2,991.06	2,782.86	3,015.77
R&D expense	582.57	577.33	472.14	487.72	460.00	428.68	441.54
Pretax profit	1,452.46	2,603.24	2,277.97	2,523.42	2,531.05	2,354.18	2,574.23
Taxes (or tax credit)	493.84	885.10	774.51	857.96	860.56	800.42	875.24
After-tax profit	958.62	1,718.14	1,503.46	1,665.46	1,670.49	1,553.76	1,698.99
Capital expenditure	19.42	19.24	15.74	16.26	15.33	14.29	14.72
Depreciation add-back	101.06	90.95	82.72	77.75	75.63	75.00	75.00
Change in WCR	1,722.00	(17.12)	(343.62)	50.90	(90.54)	(102.33)	42.01
Annual free							
cash flow	$ (681.74)	$ 1,806.97	$ 1,914.06	$ 1,676.05	$ 1,821.34	$ 1,716.79	$ 1,717.27

EXHIBIT 6 (*continued*)

	2003	2004	2005	2006	2007	2008	2009
Revenues							
Planes delivered	105	89	111	130	118	94	123
Price per plane	$ 164.68	$ 169.62	$ 174.71	$ 179.95	$ 185.35	$ 190.91	$ 196.64
Total revenues	17,233.97	15,066.42	19,468.56	23,307.53	21,911.40	17,944.00	24,103.23
Cost of goods sold	12,925.47	11,299.82	16,548.27	18,879.10	17,310.01	13,996.32	20,487.75
Gross profit	4,308.49	3,766.61	2,920.28	4,428.43	4,601.39	3,947.68	3,615.49
Depreciation	99.46	121.48	116.83	112.65	100.20	129.20	96.99
GS&A expense	689.36	602.66	778.74	932.30	876.46	717.76	964.13
Operating profit	3,519.67	3,042.47	2,024.71	3,383.48	3,624.73	3,100.72	2,554.37
R&D expense	517.02	451.99	584.06	699.23	657.34	538.32	723.10
Pretax profit	3,002.65	2,590.47	1,440.65	2,684.25	2,967.39	2,562.40	1,831.27
Taxes (or tax credit)	1,020.90	880.76	489.82	912.65	1,008.91	871.22	622.63
After-tax profit	1,981.75	1,709.71	950.83	1,771.61	1,958.48	1,691.19	1,208.64
Capital expenditure	244.64	244.64	19.47	23.31	21.91	567.22	24.10
Depreciation add-back	99.46	121.48	116.83	112.65	100.20	129.20	96.99
Change in WCR	246.57	(212.42)	431.41	376.22	(136.82)	(388.81)	603.60
Annual free cash flow	$ 1,590.00	$ 1,798.97	$ 616.79	$ 1,484.73	$ 2,173.59	$ 1,641.97	$ 677.92

	2010	2011	2012	2013	2014	2015	2016
Revenues							
Planes delivered	125	125	98	84	89	89	89
Price per plane	$ 202.54	$ 208.61	$ 214.87	$ 221.32	$ 227.96	$ 234.79	$ 241.84
Total revenues	25,316.97	26,076.48	21,133.07	18,550.25	20,321.64	20,931.29	21,559.23
Cost of goods sold	20,506.75	20,600.42	16,483.79	14,283.69	15,444.45	15,907.78	16,385.01
Gross profit	4,810.22	5,476.06	4,649.27	4,266.56	4,877.19	5,023.51	5,174.21
Depreciation	76.84	65.81	61.68	57.96	54.61	52.83	52.83
GS&A expense	1,012.68	1,043.06	845.32	742.01	812.87	837.25	862.37
Operating profit	3,720.71	4,367.19	3,742.27	3,466.59	4,009.72	4,133.43	4,259.02
R&D expense	759.51	782.29	633.99	556.51	609.65	627.94	646.78
Pretax profit	2,961.20	3,584.89	3,108.28	2,910.08	3,400.07	3,505.49	3,612.24
Taxes (or tax credit)	1,006.81	1,218.86	1,056.82	989.43	1,156.02	1,191.87	1,228.16
After-tax profit	1,954.39	2,366.03	2,051.46	1,920.65	2,244.05	2,313.63	2,384.08
Capital expenditure	25.32	26.08	21.13	18.55	20.32	20.93	21.56
Depreciation add-back	76.84	65.81	61.68	57.96	54.61	52.83	52.83
Change in WCR	118.95	74.43	(484.45)	(253.12)	173.60	59.75	61.54
Annual free cash flow	$ 1,886.97	$ 2,331.34	$ 2,576.47	$ 2,213.18	$ 2,104.74	$ 2,285.77	$ 2,353.81

EXHIBIT 6   (*continued*)

	2017	2018	2019	2020	2021	2022	2023	2024
Revenues								
Planes delivered	89	89	89	89	89	89	89	89
Price per plane	$ 249.09	$ 256.57	$ 264.26	$ 272.19	$ 280.36	$ 288.77	$ 297.43	$ 306.35
Total revenues	22,206.00	22,872.18	23,558.35	24,265.10	24,993.05	25,742.85	26,515.13	27,310.58
Cost of goods sold	16,876.56	17,382.86	17,904.35	18,441.48	18,994.72	19,564.56	20,151.50	20,756.04
Gross profit	5,329.44	5,489.32	5,654.00	5,823.62	5,998.33	6,178.28	6,363.63	6,554.54
Depreciation	52.83	52.83	47.52	35.28	28.36	28.36	28.36	16.05
GS&A expense	888.24	914.89	942.33	970.60	999.72	1,029.71	1,060.61	1,092.42
Operating profit	4,388.38	4,521.61	4,664.15	4,817.74	4,970.25	5,120.21	5,274.67	5,446.07
R&D expense	666.18	686.17	706.75	727.95	749.79	772.29	795.45	819.32
Pretax profit	3,722.20	3,835.45	3,957.40	4,089.78	4,220.46	4,347.92	4,479.21	4,626.75
Taxes (or tax credit)	1,265.55	1,304.05	1,345.52	1,390.53	1,434.96	1,478.29	1,522.93	1,573.09
After-tax profit	2,456.65	2,531.39	2,611.89	2,699.26	2,785.50	2,869.63	2,956.28	3,053.65
Capital expenditure	22.21	22.87	23.56	24.27	24.99	25.74	26.52	27.31
Depreciation add-back	52.83	52.83	47.52	35.28	28.36	28.36	28.36	16.05
Change in WCR	63.38	65.29	67.24	69.26	71.34	73.48	75.68	77.95
Annual free cash flow	$ 2,423.88	$ 2,496.06	$ 2,568.60	$ 2,641.01	$ 2,717.53	$ 2,798.77	$ 2,882.44	$ 2,964.44

EXHIBIT 6   Appendix: Discussion of Assumptions Underlying the Estimation of Cash Flows

Revenue Estimation

In order to project revenues for the project, several assumptions were made about market size, market share, units per year, initial 777 price, the rate of price increases, and introduction of derivatives.

Market size: Boeing estimated that, from 1990 to 2005, the total aircraft market would be worth approximately $615 billion.[1] The company predicted that two-thirds of this market would be in the aircraft segment in which the 777 would compete.[2] Because the 777 would not be available until 1995, this forecast uses a total market base from 1995 to 2005, estimated as two-thirds of the 1990–2005 number (i.e., $410 billion). If the 777 segment had two-thirds of this market, it would have a market of $275 billion. The $130 million per aircraft (Boeing's estimate for the 777 price tag) would translate into a market size of over 2,000 planes during the 777's first 10 years of production. The replacement market alone was expected to demand 670 aircraft,[3] and this market was supposed to be the fastest growing in the aircraft industry.

Market share: If Boeing maintained its historical 50+ percent market share, its absolute share of the market between 1995 and 2005 would accumulate to $135 billion. With the 777s expected to sell for approximately $130 million each, the figures translate into a projection of 1,000 units during the 777's first 10 years of production.

Units per year: The number of units sold per year is based on historical trends for other Boeing aircraft for the first 10 years of their lives. The percentage distributions estimated from these other aircraft are then applied to the total 10-year figure (i.e., 1,000 aircraft) to yield annual unit sales. Units per year for years 21 to 30 are estimated to be the same as year 20 to reflect an average of two possibilities: (1) another derivative aircraft is introduced, resulting in higher unit sales, and (2) no new derivatives are introduced and the plane's sales decline.

Initial price: Boeing estimated that the 777 would sell for $130 million—the high end of the aircraft market; analysts' estimates ranged between $100 and $130 million. The forecast presented here assumes a price of $130 million.

EXHIBIT 6   *(concluded)*

Rate of price increases: Aircraft prices are assumed to increase at the rate of inflation. Inflation is assumed to be 3 percent annually for the next 35 years.

Introduction of derivatives: Based on historical trends from other Boeing aircraft, the forecast assumes that Boeing will introduce a derivative plane after 10 years and again after 15 years of 777 production. These moves would lead to temporary increases in sales in the following years.

Expense Estimation

Cost of goods sold: Based on gross-profit-margin experience from other Boeing aircraft models, the forecast assumes that gross profit begins at 10 percent of sales and reaches 25 percent when the company has produced 500 units. Gross profit margin remains at this level until a derivative model is introduced, when the profit margin falls to 15 percent and then recommences the improvement to 25 percent at a faster rate.

General, selling, and administrative expense: Boeing's ratio of GS&A to sales has run historically at about 4 percent. In certain years, the ratio has been as low as 2 percent, and in others, as high as 5 percent.

Depreciation: Boeing depreciated its assets on an accelerated basis. The forecast uses double-declining depreciation with a 20-year asset life and zero salvage value as the base.

Research and development: The forecast uses an analyst's[4] estimate of up-front R&D expenses of $4.467 billion. The cash flows exclude $200 million that Boeing spent on the project in early 1990, on the principle that the expenditures prior to October 1990 are sunk costs. After this period, annual R&D expense is estimated to be 3 percent of sales, a figure that draws on various analysts' assumptions and historical levels of R&D spending. The forecast assumes that this level of expenditure is sufficient to enable Boeing to introduce two 777 derivatives, in 2005 and 2009. This forecast does not assume Boeing's belief that its development-process innovations will reduce the cost of development by 20 percent.

Tax expense: Boeing has historically had a low marginal effective tax rate. Analysts believed this rate would increase in the future, however, to about 34 percent. The forecast reflects this expectation.

Other Adjustments to Cash Flow

Capital expenditures: The forecast assumes total capital expenditures of $1.5 billion for the original version of the 777 and future capital expenditures for the two derivatives at 25 percent of the original but increased at the rate of inflation. One might use a higher estimate, $2.5 billion, but it is believed to include facilities and systems not incremental to this project.

Working-capital requirement: The forecast assumes the past 5-year average of the Boeing Company ratio of working capital to sales—9.8 percent.

---

[1]McDonnell Douglas estimates are significantly higher, but Boeing estimates are used here to be consistent with the expectations of Boeing executives.

[2]"It's Fat and Snazzy," *Business Week,* October 29, 1990, p. 32.

[3]Lawrence Harris, "The Boeing Company, Attractive for Value-Oriented Accounts," Kemper Securities Group, Inc., December 26,1991.

[4]George Shapiro, Salomon Brothers.

EXHIBIT 7 Sensitivity Analysis of Project IRRs by Price, Volume, GS&A, and R&D Expenses

Unit Volume	*Unit Price (Millions)*			
(First 10 Years)	*$100*	*$110*	*$120*	*$130*
700	13.9%	14.8%	15.5%	16.3%
800	14.7	15.5	16.4	17.2
900	15.4	16.3	17.2	18.0
1,000	16.1	17.1	18.0	18.9
1,100	16.9	17.9	18.9	19.8
1,200	17.6%	18.6%	19.7%	20.6%

	R&D Expense/Sales				
GS&A Sales	*1.0%*	*2.0%*	*3.0%*	*4.0%*	*5.0%*
1.0%	23.5%	22.7%	21.8%	20.9%	19.9%
2.0	22.6	21.8	20.8	19.9	19.0
3.0	21.7	20.8	19.9	18.9	17.9
4.0	20.8	19.9	18.9	17.9	16.9
5.0	19.9	18.9	17.9	16.9	15.8
6.0	18.9	17.9	16.9	15.8	14.7
7.0%	17.9%	16.8%	15.8%	14.7%	13.5%

Source: Casewriters' analysis.

EXHIBIT 8 DCF Breakeven by Different WACCs

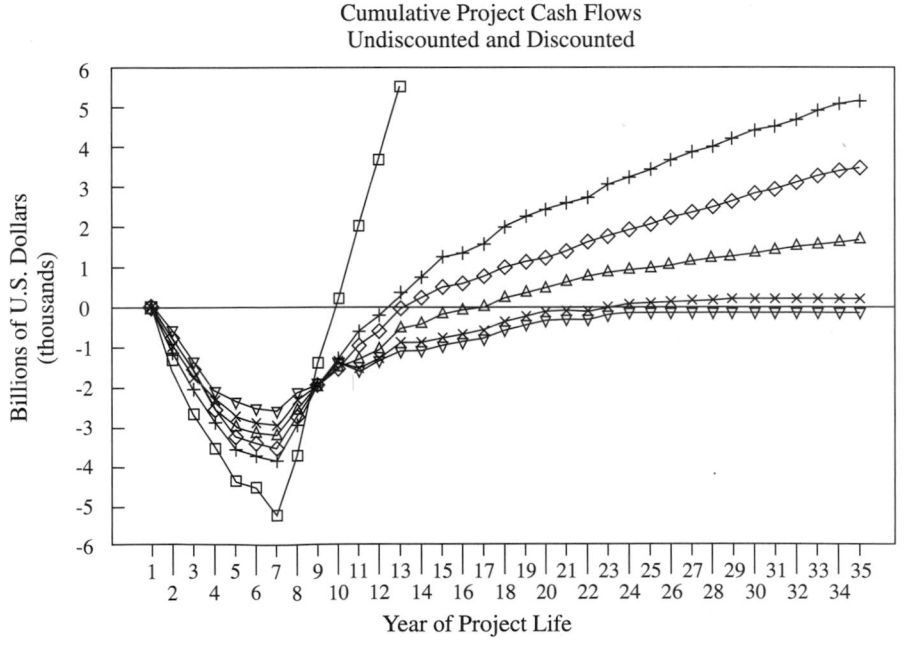

Cumulative Project Cash Flows
Undiscounted and Discounted

□ Undiscounted   + Discounted, K=10%   ◇ Discounted, K=12%   △ Discounted, K=15%

× Discounted, K=18%   ▽ Discounted, K=20%

EXHIBIT 9   Information on Comparable Companies (specially calculated betas estimated from *daily* stock returns and market returns over the periods indicated)

	Boeing	Grumman	Northrop	Lockheed	McDonnell Douglas
Percentage of revenues derived from defense and U.S. space program	26%	87%	89%	85%	66%
Estimated betas					
1. Statistical services:					
Value Line*	1.00	0.95	1.00	1.10	0.85
Datastream†	1.06	0.53	0.94	0.97	0.51
2. Calculated against the S&P 500 index:					
58 months	0.81	0.80	0.74	0.87	0.60
12 months	1.37	0.73	0.72	0.69	0.63
60 days	1.65	0.68	0.50	0.52	0.64
3. Calculated against the NYSE composite index:					
58 months	0.87	0.86	0.79	0.95	0.66
12 months	1.51	0.80	0.77	0.75	0.71
60 days	1.79	0.73	0.53	0.57	0.71
Market-value debt/equity ratio	0.018	1.756	1.288	1.182	2.714

*Value Line betas are calculated from a regression analysis between the weekly percentage changes in the price of a stock and the weekly percentage changes in the New York Stock Exchange Composite Index. The beta is calculated over the last five years of data.

†Datastream betas are calculated from a regression analysis between weekly adjusted prices of the stock and Datastream's own composite index. The betas are calculated over a four-year-period.

EXHIBIT 10   Daily Boeing Stock Prices Compared with the S&P 500 Index, January 1, 1986, to October 29, 1990

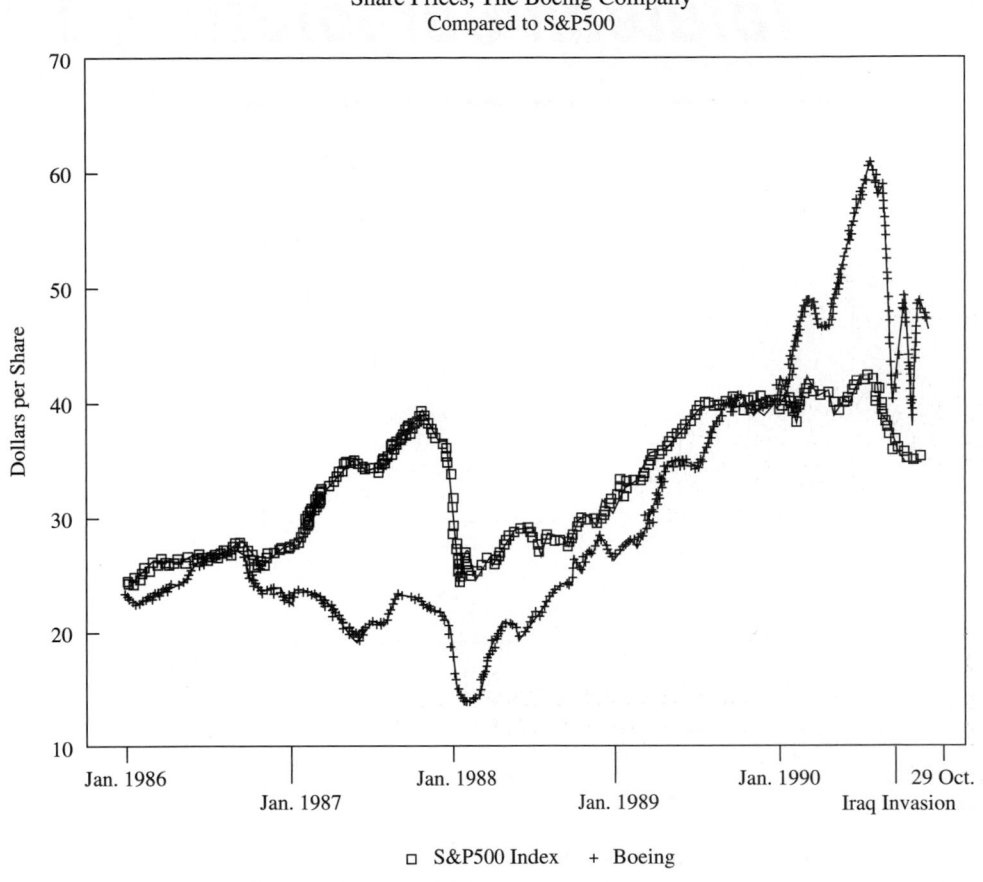

Share Prices, The Boeing Company
Compared to S&P500

Share Prices, The Boeing Company, DATASTREAM, 1990.

Teletech Corporation, 1996

Raider Dials Teletech

"Wake-Up Call Needed"
Says Investor

New York (AP)—The reclusive billionaire Victor Yossarian has acquired a 10 percent stake in Teletech Corporation and has demanded two seats on the firm's board of directors. The purchase was revealed yesterday in a filing with the Securities and Exchange Commission, and separately in a letter to Teletech's CEO, Maxwell Harper. "The firm is misusing its resources and not earning an adequate return," the letter said. "The company should abandon its misguided entry into computers, and sell the Products and Systems segment. Management must focus on creating value for shareholders." Teletech issued a brief statement emphasizing the virtues of a link between computer technology and telecommunications.

Source: *Wall Street Daily News,* January 9, 1996

Margaret Weston, Teletech's chief financial officer, learned of Victor Yossarian's letter late one evening in early January 1996. Quickly she organized a team of lawyers and finance staff to assess the threat. Maxwell Harper, the firm's CEO, scheduled a teleconference meeting of the firm's board of directors the next afternoon. Harper and Weston agreed that before the meeting they needed to fashion a response to Yossarian's assertions about the firm's returns.

This case was written by Robert F. Bruner and is dedicated to the memory of Professor Robert F. Vandell, a scholar in corporate finance and investment analysis, and the author of an antecedent case upon which the present case draws. Teletech Corporation is a fictional company, reflecting the issues facing actual firms and is used as a basis for class discussion rather than to illustrate effective or ineffective handling of an administrative situation. Copyright © 1997 by the University of Virginia Darden School Foundation, Charlottesville, VA. All rights reserved. *No part of this publication may be reproduced, stored in a retrieval system, used in a spreadsheet, or transmitted in any form or by any means—electronic, mechanical, photocopying, recording, or otherwise—without the permission of the Darden School Foundation. For inquiries, please send an e-mail to dardencases@virginia.edu.* Rev. 1/98. Version 2.0.

Ironically, returns had been the subject of debate within the firm's circle of senior managers in recent months. A number of issues had been raised about the hurdle rate used by the company in evaluating performance, and in setting the annual capital budget. Since the company was expected to invest nearly $2 billion in capital projects in 1996, gaining closure and consensus on these issues had become an important priority for Margaret Weston. Now, Yossarian's letter lent urgency to the discussion. In the short run, she needed to respond to Yossarian. In the long run she needed to assess the competing viewpoints and recommend new policies as necessary. What *should* be the hurdle rates for Teletech's two business segments? Was the Products and Systems segment really paying its way?

THE COMPANY

Teletech Corporation, headquartered in Dallas, Texas, defined itself as a "provider of integrated information movement and management." The firm had two main business segments: Telecommunications Services and the manufacture of computing and telecommunications equipment, a segment named Products and Systems. In 1995, Telecommunications Services had earned a return on capital (ROC)[1] of 9.8 percent; Products and Systems had earned 12.0 percent. The firm's current book value of net assets was $16 billion, consisting of $11.4 billion allocated to Telecommunications Services, and $4.6 billion allocated to Products and Systems. An internal analysis suggested that Telecommunications Services accounted for 75 percent of the market value of Teletech, while Products and Systems accounted for 25 percent. The current capital expenditures proposed by Telecommunications Services offered prospective internal rates of return averaging of 9.8 percent; the IRR for prospective Products and Systems projects averaged 12.0 percent. Overall, it appeared that the firm's prospective return on capital would be 10.35 percent. Top management applied a hurdle rate of 10.41 percent to all capital projects, and in evaluating the performance of business units.

Teletech Share Prices versus Market and Industry Indexes

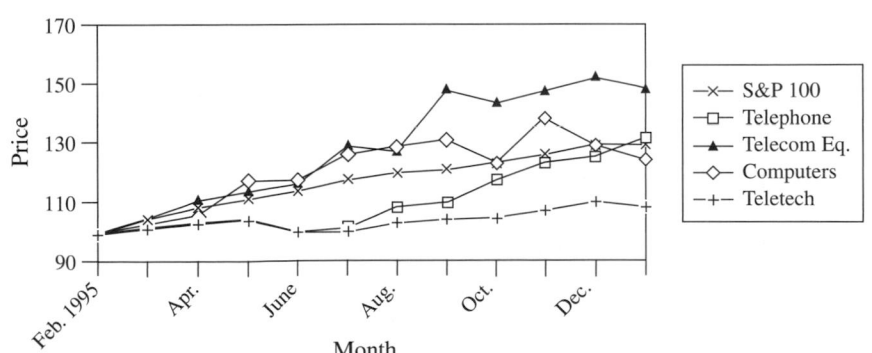

---

[1]Return on capital is calculated as the ratio of net operating profits after tax (NOPAT) to capital.

Over the past 12 months, the firm's shares had not kept pace with the overall stock market indices, or with industry indexes for telephone, equipment, or computer stocks. Securities analysts had remarked on the firm's lackluster earnings growth, pointing especially to increasing competition in telecommunications, as well as disappointing performance in the Products and Systems segment. A prominent commentator on television opined that "there was no precedent for a hostile takeover of a telephone company, but in the case of Teletech, there is every reason to try."

TELETECH'S TELECOMMUNICATIONS SERVICES SEGMENT

The Telecommunications Services segment provided long-distance, local, and cellular telephone service to more than 7 million customer lines throughout the Southwest and Midwest United States. Revenues in this segment grew at an average rate of 3 percent over the 1989–95 period. In 1995 segment revenues, net operating profit after taxes (NOPAT), and net assets were $11 billion, $1.18 billion, and $11.4 billion, respectively. Since the court-ordered breakup of the Bell System telephone monopoly in 1983, Teletech had coped with gradual deregulation of its industry through aggressive expansion into new services and geographic regions. Most recently, the firm had been a leading bidder for cellular telephone operations, and for licenses to offer personal communications services (PCS). In addition, the firm had purchased a number of telephone operating companies in privatization auctions in Latin America. Finally, the firm had invested aggressively in new technology, primarily digital switches and optical fiber cables in an effort to enhance its service quality. All of these strategic moves had been costly: The capital budget in this segment had varied between $1.5 and $2 billion in each of the previous 10 years.

Unfortunately, profit margins in the telecommunications segment had been under pressure for several years. Government regulators had been slow to provide rate relief to Teletech for its capital investments. Other leading telecommunications providers had expanded into Teletech's geographic markets and invested in new technology and quality enhancing assets. Teletech's management noted that large cable TV companies might enter the telecommunications market and continue the pressure on margins.

On the other hand, Teletech was the dominant service provider in its geographic markets and product segments. Customer surveys revealed that the company was the leader in product quality and customer satisfaction. Teletech's management was confident that the company could command premium prices, however the industry might evolve.

TELETECH'S PRODUCTS AND SYSTEMS SEGMENT

Prior to 1990, telecommunications had been the company's core business, supplemented by an equipment manufacturing division that produced telecommunications components. In 1990, the company acquired a leading computer workstation manufacturer with the goal of applying state-of-the-art computing technology to the design of telecommunications equipment. The explosive growth in the microcomputer market and the increased use of telephone lines to connect home- and office-based computers with mainframes convinced Teletech management of the potential value of marrying telecommunications equipment and computing technology. Using Teletech's capital base, borrowing ability, and distribution network to catapult growth, the Product and Systems segment increased its sales by nearly 40 percent in 1995. This segment's 1995 NOPAT and net assets were $480 million and $4.6 billion, respectively.

Products and Systems was acknowledged to be a technology leader in the industry. While this accounted for its rapid growth and pricing power, maintenance of that leadership position required sizable investments in R&D and fixed assets. The rate of technological change was increasing, as witnessed by sudden major write-offs by Teletech on products that until recently management had thought were still competitive. Major computer manufacturers were entering into the telecommunications equipment industry. Foreign manufacturers were proving to be stiff competitors in bidding on major supply contracts.

FOCUS ON VALUE AT TELETECH

Teletech's mission statement said in part,

> We will create value by pursuing business activities that earn premium rates of return.

Translating that statement into practice had been a challenge for Margaret Weston. First, it had been necessary to help managers of the segments and business units understand what "create value" meant for them. Since the segments and smaller business units did not issue securities into the capital market, the only objective measures of value were the securities prices of the whole corporation—but the activities of any particular manager might not be significant enough to drive Teletech's securities prices. Therefore, the company had adopted a measure of value creation for use at the segment and business unit level that would provide a proxy for the way investors would view each unit's performance. This measure, called economic profit, multiplied the excess rate of return of the business unit times the capital it used:

Economic profit = (ROC − Hurdle rate) × Capital employed

where:

$$\text{ROC} = \text{Return on capital} = \frac{\text{NOPAT}}{\text{Capital}}$$

NOPAT = Net operating profit after taxes

Each year, the segment and business unit executives were measured on the basis of economic profit. This measure was an important consideration in strategic decisions about capital allocation, manager promotion, and the awarding of incentive compensation.

A second way in which the value creation perspective influenced managers was in the assessment of capital investment proposals. For each investment, projected cash flows were discounted to the present using the firm's hurdle rate to give a measure of the net present value (NPV) of each project. A positive (negative) NPV indicated the amount by which the value of the firm would increase (decrease) if the project were undertaken. The following equation shows how the hurdle rate was used in the familiar NPV equation:

$$\text{Net present value} = \sum_{t=1}^{n} \left[\frac{\text{Free cash flow}_t}{(1 + \text{Hurdle rate})^t} \right] - \text{Initial investment}$$

HURDLE RATES

The hurdle rate used in the assessments of economic profit and NPV had been the focus of considerable debate in recent months. This rate was based on an estimate of Teletech's weighted average cost of capital (WACC). Management was completely satisfied with the intellectual relevance of a hurdle rate as an expression of the opportunity cost of money. The notion that the WACC represented this opportunity cost had been debated. Its measurement was never considered wholly scientific, but it had been accepted. For instance, Teletech was "split-rated" between AA− and A+. An investment banker recently suggested that, at these ratings, new debt funds might cost Teletech 7.03 percent (about 4.22 percent after a 40 percent tax rate.) With a beta of 1.041, the cost of equity might be about 11.77 percent. At market value weights of 18 percent for debt and 82 percent for equity, the resulting WACC would be 10.41 percent. Exhibit 1 summarizes the calculation. The hurdle rate of 10.41 percent was applied to all investment and performance measurement analyses in the firm.

ARGUMENTS FOR RISK-ADJUSTED HURDLE RATES

How the rate should be used within the company in evaluating projects was another point of debate. Given the different natures of the two businesses and the risks each one faced, differences of opinion arose at the segment level over the appropriateness of measuring all projects against the corporate hurdle rate of 10.41 percent. The chief advocate of multiple rates was Rick Phillips, executive vice president of Telecommunications Services, who presented his views as follows:

> Each phase of our business is different, must compete differently, and must draw on capital differently. Until recently, telecommunications was a regulated industry, and the return on our total capital highly certain, given the stable nature of the industry. Because of the recognized safety of the investment, many telecommunications companies can raise large quantities of capital from the debt markets. In operations comparable to Telecommunications Services, 75 percent of the necessary capital is raised in the debt markets at interest rates reflecting solid AA quality, on average— this is better than the corporate bond rating of AA−/A+. Moreover, I have to believe that the cost of equity of Telecommunications Services is lower than for Products and Systems. I contrast this with the Products and Systems segment where, although sales growth and profitability are strong, risks are high. Independent equipment manufacturers are financed by higher yield BBB-rated debt and more equity with higher expected total returns.
>
> In my book, the hurdle rate for Products and Systems should reflect these higher cost of funds. Without the risk-adjusted system of hurdle rates, Telecommunications Services will gradually starve for capital, while Products and Systems will be force-fed—that's because our returns are less than the corporate hurdle rate, and theirs are greater. Telecommunications Services lowers the risk of the whole corporation, and should not be penalized.
>
> Here's a rough graph of what I think is going on. Telecommunications Services, which can earn 9.8 percent on capital, is actually profitable on a risk-adjusted basis, even though it is not profitable compared to the corporate hurdle rate. The triangle shape on the drawing shows about where Telecommunications Services is located. My hunch is that the reverse is true for Products and Systems, which promises to earn 12.0 percent on capital. Products and Systems is located on the graph near the little circle.

Constant versus Risk-Adjusted Hurdle Rates

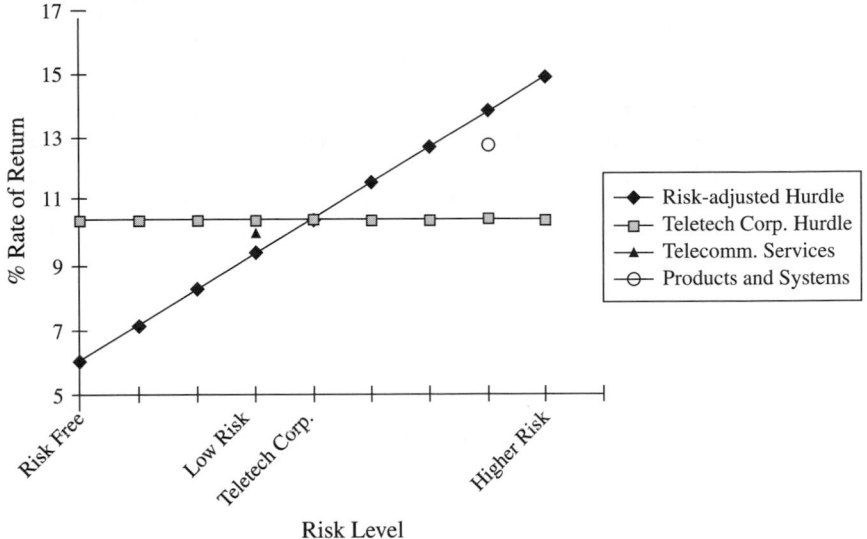

In deciding how much to loan us, lenders will consider the composition of risks. If money flows into safer investments, over time the cost of their loans to us will decrease.

Our stockholders are just as much concerned with risk. If they perceive our business as being more risky than other companies, they will not pay as high a price for our earnings. Perhaps this is why our price/earnings ratio is below the industry average most of the time. It is not a question of whether we adjust for risk—we already do informally. The only question in my mind is whether we make these adjustments systematically or not.

While multiple hurdle rates may not reflect capital-structure changes on a day-to-day basis, over time they will reflect prospects more realistically. At the moment, as I understand it, our real problem is an inadequate and very costly supply of equity funds. If we are really rationing equity capital, then we should be striving for the best returns on equity for the risk. Multiple hurdle rates achieve this objective.

Implicit in Phillips's argument, as Weston understood it, was the notion that if each segment in the company had a different hurdle rate, the costs of the various forms of capital would remain the same. However, the mix of capital used would change in the calculation. Low-risk operations would use leverage more extensively, while the high-risk divisions would have little or no debt funds. This lower-risk segment would have a lower hurdle rate.

OPPOSITION TO RISK-ADJUSTED HURDLE RATES

Phillips's views were supported by several others within Teletech; opposition was just as strong, however, particularly within the Products and Systems segment. Helen Buono, executive vice president for the segment, expressed her opinion as follows:

All money is green. Investors can't know as much about our operations as we do. To them the firm is an opaque box; they hire us to take care of what is inside the box, and judge us by the dividends coming out of the box. We can't say that one part of the box has a different hurdle rate than another part of the box, if our investors don't think that way. Like I say, all money is green: All investments at Teletech should be judged against one hurdle rate.

Multiple hurdle rates are illogical. Suppose that the hurdle rate for Telecommunications Services was much lower than the corporatewide hurdle rate. If we undertook investments that met the *segment* hurdle rate, we would be destroying shareholder value because we weren't meeting the *corporate* hurdle rate.

Our job as managers should be to put our money where the returns are best. A single hurdle rate may deprive an underprofitable division of investments in order to channel more funds into a more profitable division, but isn't that the aim of the process? Our challenge today is simple: We must earn the highest absolute rates of return we can get.

In reality, we don't finance each division separately. The corporation raises capital based on its overall prospects and record. The diversification of the company probably helps keep our capital costs down and enables us to borrow more in total than the sum of the capabilities of the divisions separately. As a result, developing separate hurdle rates is both unrealistic and misleading. All our stockholders want is for us to invest our funds wisely in order to increase the value of their stock. This happens when we pick the most promising projects, irrespective of their source.

MARGARET WESTON'S CONCERNS

As she listened to these arguments, presented over the course of several months, Weston became increasingly concerned with several related considerations. First, the corporate strategy directed the company toward integrating the two divisions. One effect of using multiple hurdle rates would be to make justifying high-technology research and application proposals more difficult, since the required rate of return would be increased. Perhaps, she thought, multiple hurdle rates were the right idea, but the notion that they should be based on capital costs rather than strategic considerations might be wrong. On the other hand, perhaps multiple rates based on capital costs should be used, but in allocating funds some qualitative adjustment should be made for unquantifiable strategic considerations. In Weston's mind, theory was certainly not clear on how to achieve strategic objectives when allocating capital.

Second, using a single measure of the cost of money (the hurdle rate or discount factor) made the net present value results consistent, at least in economic terms. If Teletech adopted multiple rates for discounting cash flows, Weston was afraid the NPV and economic profit calculations would lose their meaning and comparability across business segments. To her, a performance criterion had to be consistent and understandable, or it would not be useful.

In addition, Weston was concerned with the problem of attributing capital structures to divisions. In Telecommunications Services, a major new switching station might be financed by mortgage bonds. But in Products and Systems, it was not possible for the division to borrow directly; indeed, any financing was feasible only because the corporation guaranteed the debt. Such projects were considered highly risky—perhaps at best warranting only a minimal debt structure. Also, Ms. Weston considered the debt-capacity decision difficult enough to make for the corporation as a whole, let alone for each division. Judgments could only be very crude.

In further discussions with those in the organization about the use of multiple hurdle rates, Weston ran across two predominant trains of thought. One argument held that the investment decision should never be mixed with the financing decision. A firm should decide what its investments should be and then how to finance them most efficiently. Adding leverage to a present value calculation would distort the results. Use of multiple hurdle rates was simply a way of mixing financing with investment analysis. This argument also held that a single rate left the risk decision clear cut: Management could simply adjust its standard (NPV or economic profit) as risks increased.

The contrasting line of reasoning noted that the weighted-average cost of capital tended to represent an average market reaction to a mixture of risks. Lower-than-average-risk projects should probably be accepted even though they did not meet a weighted-average criterion. Higher-than-normal-risk projects should provide a return premium. While the multiple-hurdle-rate system was a crude way of achieving this end, it at least was a step in the right direction. Moreover, some argued that Teletech's objective should be to maximize return on equity funds, and because equity funds were and would remain a comparatively scarce resource, a multiple-rate system would tend to maximize returns to stockholders better than a single-rate system.

To help resolve these questions, Weston asked her assistant, Bernard Ingles, to summarize academic thinking about multiple hurdle rates. His memorandum is given in Exhibit 2. She also requested that he draw samples of comparable firms for Telecommunications Services and Products and Systems that might be used in deriving segment WACCs. The summary of data is given in Exhibit 3. Information on capital market conditions in January 1996 is given in Exhibit 4.

CONCLUSION

Weston could not realistically hope that all the issues before her would be resolved in time to influence Victor Yossarian's attack on management. But the attack did dictate the need for an objective assessment of the performance of Teletech's two segments—the choice of hurdle rates would be very important in this analysis. However, she did want to institute a pragmatic system of appropriate hurdle rates (or one rate) that would facilitate judgments in the changing circumstances Teletech faced. What were the appropriate hurdle rates for the two segments? Was Products and Systems underperforming as Yossarian suggested? How should Teletech respond to the raider?

EXHIBIT 1   Summary of WACC Calculation for Teletech Corporation, and Segment Worksheet

	Corporate	Telecommunications Services	Products and Systems
MV asset weights	100%	75%	25%
Bond rating	AA−/A+	AA	BBB−
Pretax cost of debt	7.03%	7.00%	7.78%
Tax rate	40%	40%	40%
After-tax cost of debt	4.22%	4.20%	4.67%
Equity beta	1.04		
R_f	6.04%		
$R_M - R_f$	5.50%		
Cost of equity	11.77%		
Weight of debt	18.0%		
Weight of equity	82.0%		
WACC	10.41%		

EXHIBIT 2   Theoretical Overview of Multiple Hurdle Rates

To: Margaret Weston

From: Bernard Ingles

Subject: Theory of Segment Cost of Capital

Date: January 1996

You requested an overview of theories about multiple hurdle rates. Without getting into minutiae, the theories boil down to the following points:

1. The central idea is that required returns should be driven by risk. This is the dominant view in the field of investment management, and is based on a mountain of theory and empirical research stretching over several decades. The extension of this idea from investment management to corporate decision making is straightforward, at least in theory.

2. An underlying assumption is that the firm is transparent (i.e., that investors can see through the corporate veil and evaluate the activities going on inside). No one believes firms are *completely* transparent, or that investors are perfectly informed. But financial accounting standards have evolved toward making the firm more transparent. And the investment community has grown tougher and sharper in its analysis: Teletech now has 36 analysts publishing reports and forecasts on the firm. The reality is that for big publicly held firms, transparency is not a bad assumption.

3. Another underlying assumption is that the value of the whole enterprise is simply the sum of its parts—this is the concept of Value Additivity. We can define "parts" as either the business segments (on the left-hand side of the balance sheet) or the layers of the capital structure (on the right-hand side of the balance sheet). Market values (MVs) have to balance.

$$MV_{\text{Teletech}} = (MV_{\text{Telecommunications Services}} + MV_{\text{Products + Systems}}) = (MV_{\text{debt}} + MV_{\text{equity}})$$

If these equalities did not hold, then a raider could come along and exploit the inequality by buying or selling the whole and the parts. This is "arbitrage." By buying and selling, the actions of the raider would drive the MVs back into balance.

4. Investment theory tells us that the only risk that matters is nondiversifiable risk, which is measured by "beta." Beta indicates the risk that an asset will add to a portfolio. Because the investor is assumed to be diversified, she is assumed to seek a return for only that risk that she cannot shed, the nondiversifiable risk. Now, the important point here is that the beta of a portfolio is equal to a weighted average of the betas of the portfolio components. Extending this to the corporate environment, the "asset beta" for the firm will equal a weighted average of the components of the firm—again, the components of the firm can be defined in terms of either the right-hand side, or the left-hand side of the balance sheet.

$$\beta_{\text{Teletech Assets}} = (w_{\text{Tel.Serv.}}\beta_{\text{Tel.Serv.}} + w_{P+S}\beta_{P+S}) = (w_{\text{debt}}\beta_{\text{debt}} + w_{\text{equity}}\beta_{\text{equity}})$$

where:

w = Percentage weights based on market values

$\beta_{\text{Tel. Serv.}}, \beta_{P+S}$ = Asset betas for business segments

β_{debt} = β for the firm's debt securities

β_{equity} = β of firm's common stock (given by Bloomberg, etc.)

This is a very handy way to model the risk of the firm, for it means that we can use the capital asset pricing model to estimate the cost of capital for a segment (i.e., using segment asset betas).

EXHIBIT 2   *(concluded)*

5. Given all the previous points, it follows that the weighted average of the various costs of capital (K) for the firm (WACC), which is the theoretically correct hurdle rate, is simply a weighted average of segment WACCs:

$$\text{WACC}_{\text{Teletech}} = (w_{\text{Tel. Serv.}} \text{WACC}_{\text{Tel. Serv.}}) + (w_{P+S} \text{WACC}_{P+S})$$

where:

$w_{\text{Tel. Serv.}}, w_{P+S}$ = Market value weights

$\text{WACC}_{\text{Tel. Serv.}} = (w_{\text{debt, Tel. Serv.}} K_{\text{debt, Tel. Serv.}}) + (w_{\text{equity, Tel. Serv.}} K_{\text{equity, Tel. Serv.}})$

$\text{WACC}_{P+S} = (w_{\text{debt, } P+S} K_{\text{debt, } P+S}) + (w_{\text{equity, } P+S} K_{\text{equity, } P+S})$

6. The notion in point 5 may not hold exactly in practice. First, most of the components in the WACC formula are estimated with some error. Second, because of taxes, information asymmetries, or other market imperfections, assets may not be priced strictly in line with the model—for a company like Teletech, it is reasonable to assume that any mispricings are just temporary. Third, the simple two-segment characterization ignores a hidden third segment: the corporate treasury department that hedges and aims to finance the whole corporation optimally—this acts as a "shock absorber" for the financial policies of the segments. Modeling the WACC of the corporate treasury department is quite difficult. Most companies assume that the impact of corporate treasury isn't very large, and simply assume it away. As a first cut, we could do this too, though it is an issue we should revisit.

Conclusions

- In theory, the corporate WACC for Teletech is appropriate *only* for evaluating an asset having the same risk as the whole company. It is not appropriate for assets having different risks than the whole company.
- Segment WACCs are computed similarly to corporate WACCs.
- In concept, the corporate WACC is a weighted average of the segment WACCs. In practice, the weighted-average concept may not hold, due to imperfections in the market and/or estimation errors.
- If we start computing segment WACCs, we must use the cost of debt, cost of equity and weights *appropriate to that segment*. We need a lot of information to do this correctly, or else we really need to stretch to make assumptions.

EXHIBIT 3   Samples of Comparable Firms

	1995 Revenues	Equity Beta	Asset Beta	Bond Rating	Book Value Debt/ Capitalization	Price/ Book	Market Value Debt/ Capitalization	Market Value Debt/ Equity	Price/ Earnings
Teletech Corporation	$16,000	1.041	0.92	AA−/A+	40%	3.01	18%	22%	12.9
Telecommunications Services Industry									
AT&T	$80,000	0.90	0.85	AA	39%	6.60	8.8%	9.7%	30.8
Alltel Corp.	3,160	0.75	0.63	A	49%	2.99	24.3%	32.2%	16.0
Ameritech	13,325	0.75	0.67	AA	47%	4.72	15.8%	18.8%	16.9
Bell Atlantic	13,500	0.80	0.68	AA	57%	4.53	22.6%	29.3%	17.5
Bell South	17,780	0.75	0.72	AAA	44%	11.90	6.2%	6.6%	19.0
Century Telecommunication Enterprises	625	1.00	0.84	BBB+	46%	2.63	24.5%	32.4%	15.8
Cincinnati Bell	1,350	0.80	0.69	AA	56%	4.72	21.2%	27.0%	18.8
Citizens Utilities Co.	1,070	0.70	0.56	AA	42%	1.68	30.1%	43.1%	15.8
Comsat	850	0.95	0.68	A	40%	1.03	39.2%	64.6%	16.8
Frontier Corp.	1,750	0.80	0.74	A	42%	5.50	11.6%	13.2%	28.3
GTE Corp.	20,250	0.80	0.66	BBB	69%	6.52	25.4%	34.1%	16.9
MCI Communications	15,100	1.25	1.14	A	24%	1.87	14.4%	16.9%	17.9
NYNEX Corp.	13,425	0.75	0.59	A−	62%	3.75	30.3%	43.6%	15.6
Pacific Telesis	9,070	0.85	0.68	AA−	74%	6.94	29.1%	41.0%	13.6
SBC Communications	12,560	0.90	0.80	A	54%	5.59	17.3%	21.0%	18.0
Southern New England	1,840	0.75	0.58	AA	57%	2.63	33.5%	50.4%	15.4
Sprint Corp.	13,550	1.05	0.87	BBB	52%	3.13	25.7%	34.7%	15.0
U.S. West	9,450	0.65	0.52	AA−	66%	4.67	29.4%	41.6%	14.3
Average		0.84	0.72		51%	4.52	22.8%	31.1%	17.9

EXHIBIT 3   *(concluded)*

	1995 Revenues	*Equity Beta*	*Asset Beta*	*Bond Rating*	*Book Value Debt/ Capitalization*	*Price/ Book*	*Market Value Debt/ Capitalization*	*Market Value Debt/ Equity*	*Price/ Earnings*
Telecommunications Equipment Industry									
ADC Telecomm. Inc.	$ 586	1.35	1.35	NR	0%	4.05	0.0%	0.0%	28.0
Acme-Cleveland	120	1.50	1.49	NR	1%	1.51	0.7%	0.7%	12.8
Allen Group	325	1.60	1.55	NR	13%	2.75	5.2%	5.4%	18.8
Andrew Corp.	626	1.25	1.23	NR	13%	4.40	3.3%	3.4%	19.7
DSC Communications	1,450	1.30	1.26	NR	18%	3.72	5.6%	5.9%	17.9
Newbridge Networks	675	1.55	1.55	NR	1%	5.48	0.1%	0.1%	23.9
Qualcomm Inc.	386	1.55	1.52	NR	9%	3.41	2.8%	2.9%	58.3
Tellabs Inc.	645	1.50	1.50	NR	1%	7.96	0.1%	0.1%	26.6
Average		1.45	1.43		7%	4.16	2.2%	2.3%	25.8
Computer and Network Equipment Industry									
Amdahl Corp.	$1,500	1.30	1.20	NR	12%	0.95	12.5%	14.3%	14.1
Bay Networks Inc.	1,342	1.75	1.74	NR	10%	9.03	1.2%	1.2%	26.0
Cabletron Systems	1,060	1.60	1.60	NR	0%	6.57	0.0%	0.0%	21.8
Cisco Systems	1,979	1.75	1.75	NR	0%	13.83	0.0%	0.0%	26.9
Digital Equipment	13,813	1.10	1.04	NR	22%	2.87	8.9%	9.8%	17.1
General Datacomm	221	1.85	1.79	NR	17%	3.96	4.9%	5.2%	NMF
Hewlett-Packard	31,519	1.25	1.24	NR	6%	3.33	1.9%	1.9%	14.6
SCI Systems	2,673	1.20	1.06	NR	32%	2.20	17.6%	21.4%	12.7
Sequent Computer	535	1.95	1.92	NR	3%	1.24	2.4%	2.5%	12.0
Standard Microsystems	345	1.60	1.52	NR	10%	1.31	7.8%	8.5%	29.8
Stratus Computer	580	1.60	1.59	NR	2%	1.36	1.5%	1.5%	13.3
Sun Microsystems	5,902	1.55	1.54	NR	3%	4.18	0.7%	0.7%	17.6
Tandem Computers	2,285	1.55	1.50	NR	6%	1.05	5.7%	6.1%	33.3
3Com Corp.	1,295	1.60	1.59	NR	12%	11.90	1.1%	1.1%	25.8
Average		1.55	1.51		10%	4.56	4.7%	5.3%	20.4

EXHIBIT 4   Debt Capital Market Conditions, January 1996

Corporate Bond Yields, by Rating		*U.S. Treasury Securities*	
Industrials			
AAA	6.50%	Short-term bills	5.20%
AA	7.00%	Intermediate-term notes	5.43%
A	7.64%	Long-term bonds	6.04%
BBB	7.78%		
BB	8.93%		
B	10.49%		
Utilities			
AA	6.53%		
A	7.94%		
BBB	8.06%		

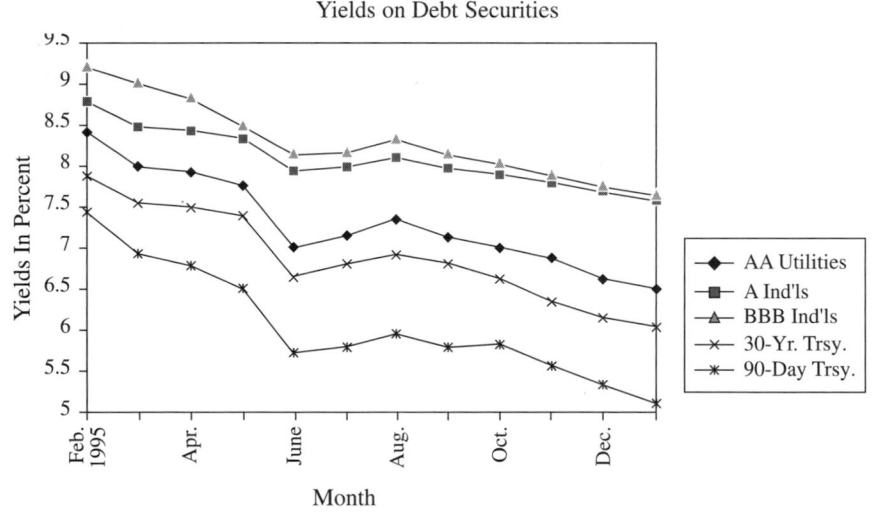

Yields on Debt Securities

Legend:
- ◆ AA Utilities
- ■ A Ind'ls
- ▲ BBB Ind'ls
- ✕ 30-Yr. Trsy.
- ✱ 90-Day Trsy.

Part IV

Capital Budgeting and Resource Allocation

Case 16

The Investment Detective

The essence of capital budgeting and resource allocation is a search for good investments in which to place the firm's capital. The process can be simple when viewed in purely mechanical terms, but a number of subtle issues can obscure the best investment choices. The capital-budgeting analyst is necessarily, therefore, a detective who must winnow good evidence from bad. Much of the challenge is knowing what quantitative analysis to generate in the first place.

Suppose you are a new capital-budgeting analyst for a company considering investments in the eight projects listed in Exhibit 1. The chief financial officer of your company has asked you to rank the projects and recommend the "four best" that the company should accept.

In this assignment, only the quantitative considerations are relevant. No other project characteristics are deciding factors in the selection, except that management has determined that projects 7 and 8 are mutually exclusive.

All the projects require the same initial investment, $2 million. Moreover, all are believed to be of the same risk class. The weighted-average cost of capital of the firm has never been estimated. In the past, analysts have simply assumed that 10 percent was an appropriate discount rate (although certain officers of the company have recently asserted that the discount rate should be much higher).

To stimulate your analysis, consider the following questions:

The case was written as a basis for class discussion rather than to illustrate effective or ineffective handling of an administrative situation. Robert Bruner prepared this with the permission of Gordon Donaldson, the author of an antecedent case. Copyright © 1988 by the University of Virginia Darden School Foundation, Charlottesville, VA. All rights reserved. *No part of this publication may be reproduced, stored in a retrieval system, used in a spreadsheet, or transmitted in any form or by any means—electronic, mechanical, photocopying, recording, or otherwise—without the permission of the Darden Foundation. For inquiries, please send an e-mail to darden-cases@virginia.edu.* Rev. 11/97. Version 2.0.

1. Can you rank the projects simply by inspecting the cash flows?
2. What criteria might you use to rank the projects? Which quantitative ranking methods are better? Why?
3. What is the ranking you found by using quantitative methods? Does this ranking differ from the ranking obtained by simple inspection of the cash flows?
4. What kinds of real investment projects have cash flows similar to those in the exhibit?

EXHIBIT 1   Project Free Cash Flows (dollars in thousands)

				Project Number				
	1	*2*	*3*	*4*	*5*	*6*	*7*	*8*
Initial investment	$(2,000)	$(2,000)	$(2,000)	$(2,000)	$(2,000)	$(2,000)	$(2,000)	$(2,000)
Year								
1	$ 330	$ 1,666		$ 160	$ 280	$ 2,200*	$ 1,200	$ (350)
2	330	334*		200	280		900*	(60)
3	330	165		350	280		300	60
4	330			395	280		90	350
5	330			432	280		70	700
6	330			440*	280			1,200
7	330*			442	280			$ 2,250*
8	$ 1,000			444	280*			
9				446	280			
10				448	280			
11				450	280			
12				451	280			
13				451	280			
14				452	280			
15			$10,000*	$(2,000)	$ 280			
Sum of cash-flow benefits	$ 3,310	$ 2,165	$10,000	$ 3,561	$ 4,200	$ 2,200	$ 2,560	$ 4,150
Excess of cash flow over initial investment	$ 1,310	$ 165	$ 8,000	$ 1,561	$ 2,200	$ 200	$ 560	$ 2,150

*Indicates year in which payback is accomplished.

Case 17

Vesuvio Fonderia S.p.A.

In November 1992, Angela Lombardi, managing director of Vesuvio Fonderia S.p.A.,[1] was considering the purchase of a "Bond-O-Matic" automated molding machine. This machine would prepare the sand molds into which molten iron was poured to obtain iron castings. The Bond-O-Matic would replace an older machine and would offer improvements in quality and some additional capacity for expansion. Similar molding-machine proposals had been rejected by the board of directors for economic reasons on three previous occasions, however, most recently in 1990. Therefore, and given the size of the proposed expenditure, about 1.5 billion lira,[2] Lombardi was seeking a careful estimate of the project's costs and benefits.

THE COMPANY

Vesuvio Fonderia specialized in the production of precision metal castings for use in automotive, aerospace, and construction equipment. The company had acquired a reputation for quality products, particularly for safety parts (i.e., parts where failure would result in loss of control for the operator). Products included crankshafts, transmissions, brake calipers, axles, wheels, and various steering-assembly parts. Customers were original-equipment manufacturers (OEMs), mainly in Europe. OEMs were growing especially demanding of product quality, and Vesuvio's response had reduced the reject rate of its castings by the OEMs to 70 parts per million.

---

[1]S.p.A. stands for "Societa per Azioni," literally, a business under share ownership, like a public corporation in the United States.

[2]In November 1992, the exchange rate of the Italian lira to the U.S. dollar was about 1,300:1.

This case was prepared by Robert F. Bruner from field research and public information and draws its structure and some data from an antecedent case written by Brandt Allen. Vesuvio is a fictional company representing the issues that faced actual firms. The author gratefully acknowledges the financial support of the Citicorp Global Scholars Program. Copyright © 1992 by the Darden Graduate Business School Foundation, Charlottesville, VA. *No part of this publication may be reproduced, stored in a retrieval system, used in a spreadsheet, or transmitted in any form or by any means—electronic, mechanical, photocopying, recording, or otherwise—without the permission of the Darden Foundation. For inquiries, please send an e-mail to dardencases@ virginia.edu.* Rev. 1/98. Version 1.6.

This record had won the company coveted quality awards from BMW, Ferrari, and Peugeot and had resulted in strategic alliances with those firms: Vesuvio and the OEMs exchanged technical personnel and design tasks; in addition, the OEMs shared confidential market-demand information with Vesuvio, which increased the precision of Vesuvio's production scheduling. In certain instances, the OEMs had provided cheap loans to Vesuvio to support capital expansion. Finally, Vesuvio received relatively long-term supply contracts from the OEMs and had a preferential position for bidding on new contracts.

Vesuvio, located in Naples, Italy, had been founded in 1912 by Angela Lombardi's great-grandfather, Benito Lombardi, a naval engineer, to produce castings for the armaments industry. In the 1920s and 1930s, the company expanded its customer base into the automotive industry. Although the company barely avoided financial collapse in the late 1940s, Benito Lombardi predicted a postwar demand for precision metal casting and positioned the company to meet it. From that time, Vesuvio Fonderia grew slowly but steadily; its sales for calendar-year 1992 were expected to be 230 billion lira. It was listed for trading on the Milan stock exchange in 1991, but the Lombardi family owned 55 percent of the common shares of stock outstanding. (The company's beta was 1.25.)[3]

The company's traditional hurdle rate of return on capital deployed was 12 percent. (This rate had not been reviewed since 1984.) In addition, company policy sought payback of an entire investment within five years. At the time of the case, the market value of the company's capital was 33 percent debt and 67 percent equity. The debt consisted entirely of loans from Banco Nazionale del Ercolano bearing an interest rate of 16 percent. The company's effective tax rate was about 46 percent, which reflected the combination of national and local corporate income tax rates.

Angela Lombardi, age 57, had assumed executive responsibility for the company 20 years earlier upon the death of her father. She held a doctorate in metallurgy and was the matriarch of an extended family. Only a son and a niece worked at Vesuvio Fonderia, however. Over the years, the Lombardi family had sought to earn a rate of return on its equity investment of about 18 percent—this goal had been established by Benito Lombardi and had never since been questioned by management.

THE BOND-O-MATIC MOLDING MACHINE

Sand molds used to make castings were prepared in a semiautomated process in 1992. Workers stamped impressions in a mixture of sand and adhesive under heat and high pressure. The process was relatively labor intensive, required training and retraining to obtain consistency in mold quality, and demanded some heavy lifting from workers. Indeed, medical claims for back injuries in the molding shop had doubled since 1982 as the mix of Vesuvio's casting products shifted toward heavy items. (Items averaged 20 kilograms in 1992.)

---

[3]The 10-year rate of return on Italian government bonds was 14.25 percent. Angela Lombardi assumed that the equity risk premium would be 5.6 percent. Also, she believed that current bond yields impounded an expected inflation rate of 10 percent for the foreseeable future.

The new molding machine would replace six semiautomated stamping machines that, together, had originally cost 700 million lira. Depreciation of 220 million had already been charged against this original cost; total depreciation on these machines had been averaging 80 million lira yearly. Vesuvio's management believed that these semiautomated machines would need to be replaced after six years. Lombardi had received an offer of 250 million lira for the six machines.

The current six machines required 12 workers per shift[4] (24 in total) at 13,000 lira per worker per hour, plus the equivalent of 3 maintenance workers, each of whom was paid 14,000 lira per hour, plus maintenance supplies of 5 million lira per year. Lombardi assumed that the semiautomated machines, if kept, would continue to consume electrical power at the rate of 21.6 million lira per year.

The Bond-O-Matic molding machine was produced by a company in Allentown, Pennsylvania. Vesuvio Fonderia had received a firm offering price of 1.25 billion lira from the Allentown firm. The estimate for modifications to the plant, including wiring for the machine's power supply, was 250 million lira. Allowing for shipping, installation, and testing, the total cost of the Bond-O-Matic machine was expected to be 1.502 billion lira, all of which would be capitalized and depreciated for tax purposes over eight years. (Lombardi assumed that, at a high and steady rate of machine utilization, the Bond-O-Matic would need to be replaced after the eighth year.)

The new machine would require two skilled operators (one per shift), each receiving 20 thousand lira per hour (including benefits), and contract maintenance of 90 million lira per year and would incur power costs of 40 million yearly. In addition, the automatic machine was expected to save at least 10 million lira yearly through improved labor efficiency in other areas of the foundry than the molding area.

With the current machines, over 30 percent of the foundry floor space was needed for the wide galleries the machines required; raw materials and in-process inventories had to be staged near each machine in order to smooth the work flow. With the automated machine, almost half of this space would be freed for other purposes (although at present there was no need for new space).

Certain aspects of the Bond-O-Matic purchase decision were difficult to quantify. First, Lombardi was not sure whether the tough collective-bargaining agreement her company had with the employees' union would allow her to lay off the 24 operators of the semiautomated machines. Reassigning the workers to other jobs might be easier, but the only positions needing to be filled were those of janitors, who were paid 6,000 lira per hour. The extent of any labor savings would depend on negotiations with the union. Second, Angela believed that the Bond-O-Matic would result in even higher levels of product quality and lower scrap rates than the company was now boasting. In light of the ever-increasing competition, this outcome might prove to be of enormous, but currently unquantifiable, competitive importance. Finally, the Bond-O-Matic had a theoretical maximum capacity that was 30 percent higher than the six semiautomated machines, but these machines were operating at only 90 percent of capacity, and Lombardi was not sure when added capacity would be needed. The latest economic news suggested that the economies of Europe were slipping into recession.

---

[4]The foundry was operating two shifts per day. The foundry did not operate on weekends or holidays. At maximum, the foundry would produce for 210 days per year.

Empirical Chemicals Ltd. (A): The Merseyside Project

Late one afternoon in January 1992, Jim Hawkins told Frances Trelawney, "No one seems satisfied with the analysis so far, but the suggested changes could kill the project. If solid projects like this can't swim past the corporate piranhas, the company will never modernize."

Trelawney was plant manager of Empirical Chemicals' Merseyside Works in Liverpool, England. Her controller, Jim Hawkins, was discussing a capital project she wanted to propose to senior management. The project consisted of a £7 million expenditure to renovate and rationalize the polypropylene production line at the Merseyside plant in order to make up for deferred maintenance and exploit opportunities to achieve increased production efficiency.

Empirical Chemicals was under pressure from investors to improve its financial performance as a result of both the worldwide recession in the chemicals industry and the accumulation of the firm's common shares by a well-known corporate raider, William Lord Bones. Earnings per share had fallen to £4.55 at the end of 1991 from £12.75 at the end of 1990. Trelawney thus believed that the time was ripe to obtain funding from corporate headquarters for a modernization program for the Merseyside Works—at least she had believed so until Hawkins presented her with several questions that had only recently surfaced.

This case was written by Professor F. Bruner as the basis for classroom discussion rather than to illustrate effective or ineffective handling of an administrative situation. Empirical Chemicals is a fictional company, reflecting the issues facing actual firms. The author wishes to acknowledge the helpful comments of Dr. Frank H. McTigue and the financial support of the Citicorp Global Scholars Program. Copyright © 1992 by the University of Virginia Darden School Foundation, Charlottesville, VA. All rights reserved. *No part of this publication may be reproduced, stored in a retrieval system, used in a spreadsheet, or transmitted in any form or by any means—electronic, mechanical, photocopying, recording, or otherwise—without the permission of the Darden Foundation. For inquiries, please send an e-mail to dardencases@virginia.edu.* Revised 1/98. Version 2.3.

EMPIRICAL CHEMICALS AND POLYPROPYLENE

Empirical Chemicals (EC), a major competitor in the worldwide chemicals industry, was a leading producer of polypropylene, a polymer used in an extremely wide variety of products (ranging from medical products to packaging film, carpet fibers, and automobile components) and known for its strength and malleability. Polypropylene was essentially priced as a commodity.

The production of polypropylene pellets at Merseyside began with propylene, a refined gas received in tank cars. Propylene was purchased from four refineries in England that produced it in the course of refining crude oil into gasoline. In the first stage of the production process, polymerization, the propylene gas was combined with a diluent (or solvent) in a large pressure vessel. In a catalytic reaction, polypropylene precipitated to the bottom of the tank and was then concentrated in a centrifuge.

The second stage of the production process compounded the basic polypropylene with stabilizers, modifiers, fillers, and pigments to achieve the desired attributes for a particular customer. The finished plastic was extruded into pellets for shipment to the customer.

The Merseyside production process was old, semicontinuous at best, and therefore higher in labor content than competitors' newer plants. The Merseyside plant was constructed in 1967.

EC produced polypropylene at Merseyside and in Rotterdam, Holland. The two plants were of identical scale, age, and design. The managers of both plants reported to Trevor Livesey, executive vice president and manager of the Intermediate Chemicals Group (ICG) of EC. The company positioned itself as a supplier to customers in Europe and the Middle East. The strategic-analysis staff estimated that, in addition to numerous small producers, seven major competitors manufactured polypropylene in EC's market region. Their plants operated at various cost levels. Exhibit 1 presents a comparison of plant output and indexed costs.

THE PROPOSED CAPITAL PROGRAM

Trelawney had assumed responsibility for the Merseyside Works only 12 months previously, following a rapid rise from an entry position of shift engineer eight years before. When she assumed responsibility, she undertook a detailed review of the operations and discovered significant opportunities for improvement in polypropylene production. Some of these opportunities stemmed from the deferral of maintenance over the preceding five years. In an effort to enhance the operating results of the Works, the previous manager had limited capital expenditures to only the most essential. Now, what had been routine and deferrable was becoming essential. Other opportunities stemmed from correcting the antiquated plant design in ways that would save energy and improve the process flow: (1) relocating and modernizing tank-car unloading areas, which would enable the process flow to be streamlined; (2) refurbishing the polymerization tank to achieve higher pressures and thus greater throughput; and (3) renovating the compounding plant to increase extrusion throughput and obtain energy savings.

Trelawney proposed the expenditure of £7 million on this program. The entire polymerization line would need to be shut down for 60 days, however, and because the Rotterdam plant was operating near capacity, Merseyside's customers would buy from competitors. Hawkins believed the lost customers would not be permanent. The benefits would be a lower energy requirement[1] as well as a 7 percent greater manufacturing throughput. In addition, the project was expected to improve gross margin (before depreciation and energy savings) from 11.5 percent to 12.9 percent. The engineering group at Merseyside were highly confident that the efficiencies would be realized.

Merseyside currently produced 135,000 metric tons of polypropylene pellets per year. Currently, the price of polypropylene averaged £611 per ton for EC's product mix. The tax rate required in capital-expenditure analyses was 35 percent. Hawkins discovered that any plant facilities to be replaced had been completely depreciated. New assets could be depreciated on an accelerated basis[2] over 15 years, the expected life of the assets. The increased throughput would necessitate a one-time increase of work-in-process inventory equal in value to 3.0 percent of cost of goods. Hawkins included in the first year of his forecast "preliminary engineering costs" of £500,000, which had been spent over the preceding nine months on efficiency and design studies of the renovation. Finally, the corporate manual stipulated that overhead costs be reflected in project analyses at the rate of 3.5 percent times the book value of assets acquired in the project, per year.[3]

Hawkins had produced the discounted-cash-flow (DCF) summary given in Exhibit 2. It suggested that the capital program would easily hurdle EC's required return of 13 percent for engineering projects.

---

[1]Hawkins characterized the energy savings as a percentage of sales and assumed that the savings would be equal to 1 percent of sales in the first 5 years and .5 percent in years 6–10. Thereafter, without added aggressive "green" spending, the energy efficiency of the plant would revert to its old level, and the savings would be 0. He believed that the decision to make further environmentally oriented investments was a separate choice (and one that should be made much later) and therefore that to include such benefits (of a presumably later investment decision) in the project being considered today would be inappropriate.

[2]The company's capital-expenditure manual suggested the use of double-declining-balance (DDB) depreciation, even though other more aggressive procedures might be permitted by the tax code. The reason for this policy was to discourage jockeying for corporate approvals based on tax provisions that could apply differently for different projects and divisions. Prior to senior-management approval, the controller's staff would present an independent analysis of special tax effects that might apply. Division managers, however, were discouraged from relying heavily on these effects. In applying the DDB approach to a 15-year project, the formula for accelerated depreciation was used for the first 10 years, after which depreciation was calculated on a straight-line basis. This conversion to straight-line was commonly done so that the asset would depreciate fully within its economic life.

[3]The corporate policy manual stated that

"new projects should be able to sustain a reasonable proportion of corporate overhead expense. Projects which are so marginal as to be unable to sustain these expenses and also meet the other criteria of investment attractiveness should not be undertaken. Thus, all new capital projects should reflect an annual pretax charge amounting to 3.5 percent of the value of the initial asset investment for the project."

CONCERNS OF THE TRANSPORT DIVISION

EC owned the tank cars with which Merseyside received propylene gas from four petroleum refineries in England. The Transport Division, a cost center, oversaw the movement of all raw, intermediate, and finished materials throughout the company and was responsible for managing the tank cars. Because of the project's increased throughput, Transport would have to increase its allocation of tank cars to Merseyside. Currently, the Transport Division could make this allocation out of excess capacity, although doing so would accelerate from 1996 to 1994 the need to purchase new rolling stock to support anticipated growth of the firm in other areas. The purchase would cost £2 million. The rolling stock would have a depreciable life of 10 years, but with proper maintenance, the cars could operate much longer. The rolling stock could not be used outside of Britain because of differences in track gauge.

A memorandum from the controller of the Transport Division suggested that the cost of these tank cars should be included in the initial outlay of Merseyside's capital program. But Hawkins disagreed. He told Trelawney,

> The Transport Division isn't paying one pence of actual cash because of what we're doing at Merseyside. In fact, we're doing the company a favor in using its excess capacity. Even *if* an allocation has to be made somewhere, it should go on the Transport Division's books. The way we've always evaluated projects in this company has been with the philosophy of "every tub on its own bottom"—every division has to fend for itself. The Transport Division isn't part of our own Intermediate Chemicals Group, so they should carry the allocation of rolling stock.

Accordingly, Hawkins had not reflected any charge for the use of excess rolling stock in his preliminary DCF analysis given in Exhibit 2.

The Transport Division and Intermediate Chemicals Group reported to separate executive vice presidents, who themselves reported to the chairman and chief executive officer of the company. The executive VPs received an annual incentive bonus pegged to the performance of their divisions.

CONCERNS OF THE ICG SALES AND MARKETING DEPARTMENT

Hawkins's analysis had led to questions from the director of sales. In a recent meeting, the director told Hawkins,

> Your analysis assumes that we can sell the added output and thus obtain the full efficiencies from the project, but, as you know, the market for polypropylene is extremely competitive. To move the added volume, we will have to shift capacity away from Rotterdam toward Merseyside. Is this really a gain for EC? Why spend money just so one plant can cannibalize another?

The vice president of marketing was less skeptical. He said that, with lower costs at Merseyside, EC might be able to take business from the plants of competitors such as Saone-Poulet or Vaysol. In the current severe recession, competitors would fight hard to keep customers, but sooner or later, the market would revive, and it would be reasonable to assume that any lost business volume would return at that time.

Hawkins had listened to both the director and vice president and chose to reflect no charge for a loss of business at Rotterdam in his preliminary analysis of the Merseyside project. He told Trelawney,

Cannibalization really isn't a cash flow; there is no check written in this instance. Anyway, if the company starts burdening its cost-reduction projects with fictitious charges like this, we'll never maintain our cost competitiveness. A cannibalization charge is rubbish!

CONCERNS OF THE ASSISTANT PLANT MANAGER

Harry Mulvaney, the assistant plant manager and direct subordinate of Trelawney, proposed an unusual modification to Hawkins's analysis during a late-afternoon meeting with Hawkins and Trelawney. Over the past few months, Mulvaney had been absorbed with the development of a proposal to modernize a separate and independent part of the Merseyside Works, the production line for ethylene-propylene-copolymer rubber (EPC). This product, a variety of synthetic rubber, had been pioneered by Empirical Chemicals in the early 1960s and was sold in bulk to European tire manufacturers. Despite hopes that this oxidation-resistant rubber would dominate the market in synthetics, in fact, EPC remained a relatively small product in the European chemical industry. Empirical, the largest supplier of EPC, produced the entire volume at Merseyside. EPC had been only marginally profitable to Empirical because of entry by competitors, the development of competing synthetic rubber compounds, and the slump in tire sales over the past five years.

Mulvaney had proposed a renovation of the EPC production line for a cost of £1 million. The renovation would give Empirical the lowest EPC cost base in the world and improve cash flows by £25,000 *ad infinitum.* Even so, at current prices and volumes, the net present value (NPV) of this project was −£750,000. Mulvaney and the EPC product manager had argued strenuously to the executive committee of the company that the negative NPV ignored strategic advantages from the project and increases in volume and prices when the recession ended. Nevertheless, the executive committee had rejected the project, mainly on economic grounds.

In a hushed voice, Mulvaney said to Trelawney and Hawkins,

Why don't you include the EPC project as part of the polypropylene line renovations? The positive NPV of the poly renovations can easily sustain the negative NPV of the EPC project. This is an extremely important project to the company, a point that senior management doesn't seem to get. If we invest now, we'll be ready to exploit the market when the recession ends. If we don't invest now, you can expect that we will have to exit the business altogether in three years. Do you look forward to more layoffs? Do you want to manage a shrinking plant? Recall that our annual bonuses are pegged to the size of this operation. Also remember that in the last 20 years no one from corporate has monitored renovation projects once the investment decision was made.

CONCERNS OF THE TREASURY STAFF

After a meeting on a different matter, Jim Hawkins described his dilemmas to Andrew Deakins, who worked as an analyst on EC's Treasury Staff. Deakins scanned Hawkins's analysis, and pointed out that:

Cash flows and discount rate need to be consistent in their assumptions about inflation. The 13 percent hurdle rate you're using is a nominal target rate of return. The Treasury staff think this impounds a long-term inflation expectation of 4 percent per year. Thus, EC's real (i.e., zero-inflation) target rate of return is 9 percent.

The conversation was interrupted before Hawkins could gain a full understanding of Deakins's comment. For the time being, Hawkins decided to continue to use a discount rate of 13 percent, because it was the figure promoted in the latest edition of EC's capital budgeting manual.

EVALUATING CAPITAL-EXPENDITURE PROPOSALS AT EMPIRICAL CHEMICALS

In submitting a project for senior-management approval, the proposers had to identify it as belonging to one of four possible categories: (1) new product or market, (2) product or market extension, (3) engineering efficiency, or (4) safety or environment. The first three categories of proposals were subject to a system of four performance "hurdles," of which at least three had to be met for the proposal to be considered. The Merseyside project would be in the engineering efficiency category.

1. *Impact on earnings per share.* For engineering-efficiency projects, the contribution to net income from contemplated projects had to be positive. This criterion was calculated as the average annual EPS contribution of the project over its entire economic life, using the number of outstanding shares at the most recent fiscal year-end as the basis for the calculation. (At fiscal year-end 1991, Empirical Chemicals had 92,891,240 shares outstanding.)
2. *Payback.* This criterion was defined as the number of years necessary for free cash flow of the project to amortize the initial project outlay completely. For engineering-efficiency projects, the maximum payback period was six years.
3. *Discounted cash flow.* DCF was defined as the present value of future cash flows of the project (at the hurdle rate of 13 percent for engineering-efficiency proposals), less the initial investment outlay. This net present value of free cash flows had to be positive.
4. *Internal rate of return.* IRR was defined as being that discount rate at which the present value of future free cash flows just equaled the initial outlay—in other words, the rate at which the NPV was 0. The IRR of engineering-efficiency projects had to be greater than 13 percent.

CONCLUSION

Trelawney wanted to review Hawkins's analysis in detail and settle the questions surrounding the tank cars and potential loss of business volume at Rotterdam. As Hawkins's analysis now stood, the Merseyside project met all four investment criteria:

1. Average annual addition to EPS: £0.0103.
2. Payback period: 5 years.

3. Net present value: £2.36 million.
4. Internal rate of return: 19.2 percent.

Trelawney was concerned that further tinkering might seriously weaken the attractiveness of the project.

EXHIBIT 1   Comparative Information on the Seven Largest Polypropylene Plants in Europe

	Plant Location	*Age*	*Plant Annual Output (Metric Tons)*	*Production Cost per Ton (Indexed to Low-cost Producer)*
CBTG A.G.	Saarbrün	1981	200,000	1.00
Empirical Chemicals	Liverpool	1967	135,000	1.09
Empirical Chemicals	Rotterdam	1967	135,000	1.09
Hosche A.G.	Hamburg	1977	200,000	1.02
Montecassino S.p.A.	Genoa	1961	90,000	1.11
Saone-Poulet S.A.	Marseilles	1972	145,000	1.07
Vaysol S.A.	Antwerp	1976	160,000	1.06
Next 10 largest plants			450,000	1.19

Source: Casewriter's analysis.

EXHIBIT 2   Jim Hawkins's DCF Analysis of Merseyside Project (financial values in millions of British pounds)

Assumptions

Annual output (metric tons)	135,000	Discount rate	13.0%
Output gain/Original output	7.0%	Depreciable life (years)	15
Price/ton (pounds sterling)	611	Overhead/Investment	3.5%
Inflation rate (prices and costs)	0.0%	Salvage value	0
Gross margin (ex. deprec.)	12.90%	WIP inventory/Cost of goods	3.0%
Old gross margin	11.5%	Months downtime, construction	2
Tax rate	35.0%	After-tax scrap proceeds	0
Investment outlay (mill.)	7.00	Preliminary engineering costs	0.5
Energy savings/Sales			
Yr. 1–5	1.0%		
Yr. 6–10	0.5%		
Yr. 11–15	0.0%		

	Now	Year 1: 1992	Year 2: 1993	Year 3: 1994	Year 4: 1995	Year 5: 1996
1. Estimate of incremental gross profit						
New output (tons)		144,450	144,450	144,450	144,450	144,450
Lost output—construction		(22,500)				
New sales (millions)		74.51	88.26	88.26	88.26	88.26
New gross margin		13.9%	13.9%	13.9%	13.9%	13.9%
New gross profit		10.36	12.27	12.27	12.27	12.27
Old output		135,000	135,000	135,000	135,000	135,000
Old sales		82.49	82.49	82.49	82.49	82.49
Old gross profit		9.49	9.49	9.49	9.49	9.49
Incremental gross profit		0.87	2.78	2.78	2.78	2.78
2. Estimate of incremental depreciation						
New depreciation		0.93	0.81	0.70	0.61	0.53
3. Overhead		0.25	0.25	0.25	0.25	0.25
4. Preliminary engineering costs		0.50				
5. Pretax incremental profit		−0.81	1.73	1.84	1.93	2.01
6. Tax expense		−0.28	0.60	0.64	0.68	0.70
7. After-tax profit		−0.52	1.12	1.19	1.25	1.31
8. Cash-flow adjustments						
Less capital expenditures	−7.00					
Add back depreciation		0.93	0.81	0.70	0.61	0.53
Less added WIP inventory		0.27	−0.36	0.00	0.00	0.00
After-tax scrap proceeds		0.00				
9. Free cash flow	−7.00	0.67	1.58	1.89	1.86	1.83
NPV	2.36					
IRR	19.2%					

Year 6: 1997	Year 7: 1998	Year 8: 1999	Year 9: 2000	Year 10: 2001	Year 11: 2002	Year 12: 2003	Year 13: 2004	Year 14: 2005	Year 15: 2006
144,450	144,450	144,450	144,450	144,450	144,450	144,450	144,450	144,450	144,450
88.26	88.26	88.26	88.26	88.26	88.26	88.26	88.26	88.26	88.26
13.4%	13.4%	13.4%	13.4%	13.4%	12.9%	12.9%	12.9%	12.9%	12.9%
11.83	11.83	11.83	11.83	11.83	11.39	11.39	11.39	11.39	11.39
135,000	135,000	135,000	135,000	135,000	135,000	135,000	135,000	135,000	135,000
82.49	82.49	82.49	82.49	82.49	82.49	82.49	82.49	82.49	82.49
9.49	9.49	9.49	9.49	9.49	9.49	9.49	9.49	9.49	9.49
2.34	2.34	2.34	2.34	2.34	1.90	1.90	1.90	1.90	1.90
0.46	0.40	0.34	0.32	0.32	0.32	0.32	0.32	0.32	0.32
0.25	0.25	0.25	0.25	0.25	0.25	0.25	0.25	0.25	0.25
1.64	1.70	1.75	1.78	1.78	1.33	1.33	1.33	1.33	1.33
0.57	0.60	0.61	0.62	0.62	0.47	0.47	0.47	0.47	0.47
1.07	1.11	1.14	1.15	1.15	0.87	0.87	0.87	0.87	0.87
0.46	0.40	0.34	0.32	0.32	0.32	0.32	0.32	0.32	0.32
0.00	0.00	0.00	0.00	0.00	0.00	0.00	0.00	0.00	0.00
1.52	1.50	1.48	1.47	1.47	1.19	1.19	1.19	1.19	1.19

Empirical Chemicals Ltd. (B): Merseyside and Rotterdam Projects

Trevor Livesey, executive vice president of the Intermediate Chemicals Group (ICG) of Empirical Chemicals (EC), met with his financial analyst, Karen Cooper, to review two mutually exclusive capital-expenditure proposals. The firm's capital budget would be submitted for approval to the board of directors early in February 1992, and any projects proposed by Livesey for the ICG had to be forwarded soon to the chief executive officer of EC for his review. Plant managers in Liverpool and Rotterdam had independently submitted expenditure proposals, each of which would expand the polypropylene output of their respective plants by 7 percent.[1] EC's strategic-analysis staff argued strenuously that a companywide increase in polypropylene output of 14 percent made no sense, but half that amount did. Thus, Livesey decided he could not accept *both* projects; he could sponsor only one for approval by the board.

Corporate policy was to evaluate projects based on four criteria: (1) net present value (NPV), computed at the appropriate cost of capital, (2) internal rate of return (IRR), (3) payback, and (4) growth in earnings per share. In addition, the board of directors was receptive to "strategic factors"—considerations that might be difficult to quantify. The manager of the Rotterdam plant, Johan Silver, argued vociferously that his project easily hurdled all the relevant quantitative standards and that it had important strategic benefits.

---

[1]Background information on Empirical Chemicals and the polypropylene business is given in "Empirical Chemicals (A): The Merseyside Project" (UVA-F-1020).

This case was written by Professor Robert F. Bruner as the basis for classroom discussion rather than to illustrate effective or ineffective handling of an administrative situation. Empirical Chemicals is a fictional company, reflecting the issues facing actual firms. The author wishes to acknowledge the helpful comments of Dr. Frank H. McTigue and the financial support of the Citicorp Global Scholars Program. Copyright © 1992 by the University of Virginia Darden School Foundation, Charlottesville, VA. All rights reserved. *No part of this publication may be reproduced, stored in a retrieval system, used in a spreadsheet, or transmitted in any form or by any means—electronic, mechanical, photocopying, recording, or otherwise—without the permission of the Darden Foundation. For inquiries, please send an e-mail to dardencases@virginia.edu.* Revised 1/98. Version 2.3.

Indeed, Silver had interjected these points in two recent meetings with senior management and at a cocktail reception for the board of directors. Livesey expected to review the proposal from Frances Trelawney, manager of the Liverpool plant, at this meeting with Cooper, but he suspected that neither proposal dominated the other on all four criteria. Livesey's choice would apparently not be straightforward.

THE PROPOSAL FROM MERSEYSIDE, LIVERPOOL

The project for the Merseyside plant entailed the enhancement of existing facilities and production process. Based on the type of project and the engineering studies, the potential benefits of the project were fairly certain. (See "Empirical Chemicals [A]" for a detailed discussion of this project.) To date, Trelawney, manager of the Merseyside Works, had limited her discussions about the project to conversations with Livesey and Cooper. Cooper had raised various exploratory questions about the project and had presented preliminary analyses of it to managers in Marketing and Transportation for their comments. The revised analysis emerging from these discussions would be the focus of discussion with Cooper in the forthcoming meeting.

Cooper had indicated that Trelawney's final memo on the project was short, only three pages and one exhibit. Trevor wondered whether this memo would satisfy his remaining questions.

THE ROTTERDAM PROJECT

Johan Silver's proposal consisted of a 90-page document replete with detailed schematics, engineering comments, strategic analyses, and financial projections. The basic discounted-cash-flow (DCF) analysis is presented in Exhibit 1 and shows that the project had an NPV of £12.28 million and an IRR of 17.2 percent. Accounting for a "worst-case" scenario, which assumed erosion of Merseyside's volume equal to the gain in Rotterdam's volume, the NPV was £10.85 million.

In essence, Silver's proposal called for the expenditure of £7.5 million spread over three years to convert the plant's polymerization line from batch to continuous-flow technology and to install sophisticated state-of-the-art process controls throughout the polymerization and compounding operations. The heart of the new system would be an analog computer driven by advanced software written by a team of engineering professors at an institute in Japan. The three-year-old process-control technology had been used on a smaller polypropylene production facility in Japan and had produced significant improvements in cost and output. Other major producers were known to be evaluating this system for use in their plants.

Silver explained that installing the sophisticated new system would not be feasible without also obtaining a continuous source of supply of propylene gas. He proposed to obtain this gas by pipeline from one refinery five kilometers away (rather than by railroad tank cars sourced from three refineries). EC had an option to purchase a pipeline and its right-of-way for £3 million; then, for relatively little cost, the pipeline could be extended to the Rotterdam plant and the refinery at the other end. The option had been purchased several years earlier. A consultant had informed Silver that to purchase a right-of-way at today's prices and to lay a comparable pipeline would cost approximately £6 million, a value at which the consultant believed the right-of-way could be sold today in an auction. The consultant also forecasted that in 15 years the value of the right-of-way would be £35 million.[2] This option was to expire in six months.

Some senior EC executives believed firmly that if the Rotterdam project were not undertaken, the option on the right-of-way should be allowed to expire unexercised. The reasoning was summarized by Henry Digbee, chairman of the executive committee:

> Our business is chemicals, not land speculation. Simply buying the right-of-way with an intention of reselling it for a profit takes us beyond our expertise. Who knows when we could sell it, and for how much? How distracting would this little side venture be for Johan Silver?

Younger members of senior management were more willing to consider a potential investment arbitrage on the right-of-way.

Silver expected to realize benefits (such as increased output and gross margin) of this investment gradually over time as the new technology was installed and shaken down and as learning-curve effects were realized. He advocated a phased investment program (as opposed to all at once) in order to minimize disruption to plant operations and to allow the new technology to be calibrated and fine-tuned.

Given the complexity of the technology and the extent to which it would permeate the plant, the system would be very expensive to dismantle. Practically, there would be no going back once the decision had been made to install the new controls. Silver's project would represent an irrevocable commitment to the analog technology at the Rotterdam plant.

Livesey recalled that the "strategic factors" to which Silver referred had to do with the obvious cost and output improvements expected from the new system, as well as from an advantage from being the first major European producer to implement the new technology. Being the first to implement the technology probably meant a head start in moving down the learning curve toward reducing costs as the organization became familiar with the technology. Silver argued,

> The Japanese, and now the Americans, exploit the learning-curve phenomenon aggressively. Fortunately, they aren't major players in European polypropylene, at least for now. This is a once-in-a-generation opportunity for EC to leapfrog its competition through the exploitation of new technology.

In an oblique reference to the Merseyside proposal, Silver went on to say,

> There are two alternatives to implementation of the analog process-control technology. One is a series of myopic enhancements to existing facilities, but this is nothing more than sticking one's head in the sand, for it leaves us at the mercy of our competitors who *are* making choices for the long term. The other alternative is to exit the polypropylene business, but this amounts to walk-

---

[2]The right-of-way had several alternate commercial uses. Most prominently, the Dutch government had expressed an interest in using the right-of-way for a new high-speed railroad line. However, the planning for this line had barely begun, which suggested that land-acquisition efforts were years away. Moreover, government budget deficits threatened the timely implementation of the rail project. Another potential user was Medusa Communications, an international telecommunications company that was looking for pathways along which to bury its new optical-fiber cables. Power companies and other chemical companies or refiners might also be interested in acquiring the right-of-way.

ing away from the considerable know-how we've accumulated in this business and from what is basically a valuable activity. Our commitment to analog controls makes the right choice at the right time.

The analog process-control system seemed to be the most advanced on the market. There were rumors, however, that an engineering design team at Glüsingen University in Germany was testing a radically different process-control technology—based on lasers, spectral chromatography, and digital computing—and that it was outperforming the Japanese system on cost reduction and output improvement by a factor of 1.1:1. If these rumors were true, such a system might become commercially available within five years. While it would be possible to switch to the German technology in five years, doing so would mean writing off entirely the investment in the Japanese system.

Livesey wondered how to take the potential new technology into account in making his decision. Even if he recommended the Merseyside project today, the new controls (either Japanese, or German if successfully commercialized) could later be installed at Merseyside. Frances Trelawney, the plant manager at Merseyside, told Trevor Livesey that she preferred to "wait and see" how the German technology evolved before entertaining a technology upgrade at her plant. Livesey believed that the flexibility to change technologies differed between the Rotterdam and Merseyside proposals, and this difference might affect the value of the respective projects.[3]

CONCLUSION

Trevor Livesey wanted to give this choice careful thought, because the plant managers at Merseyside and Rotterdam seemed to have so much invested in their own proposals. He wished that the capital-budgeting criteria would give a straightforward indication about the relative attractiveness of the two mutually exclusive projects. He wondered by what rational, analytical process he could extricate himself from the ambiguities of the present measures of investment attractiveness. Moreover, he wished he had a way to evaluate the primary technological difference between the two proposals: The Rotterdam project firmly committed EC to the new process technology; the Merseyside project did not, but it retained the flexibility to allow the technology in the future.

---

[3]Using Monte Carlo simulation, she had estimated that the cash returns from both the German and Japanese technologies had standard deviations of 8 percent and that the correlation of the two returns was predictably high: 80 percent. The nominal risk-free rate of return was about 9.5 percent. The view of Empirical's engineers was that the German digital-based process-control system would emerge in the next five years or not emerge at all and that the probability of successful commercialization of the German technology was 50 percent.

EXHIBIT 1   Analysis of Rotterdam Project (values in British pounds)

Assumptions

Annual output (metric tons)	135,000	Setup and labor savings/Sales (yr. 1)	0.0%
Output gain per year/Prior year	2.0%	Discount rate	9.0%
Maximum possible output	144,450	Depreciable life (years)	15
Price/ton (pounds sterling)	611	Overhead/Investment	3.5%
Inflation (prices and costs)	0.0%	Salvage value	0
Gross margin growth rate/Year	0.80%	WIP inventory/Cost of goods sold	3.0%
Maximum possible gross margin	16.5%	Terminal value of right-of-way	35
Old gross margin	11.5%	Months downtime, construction	
Tax rate	35.0%	1992	5
Investment outlay (millions)		1993	4
Now	3	1994	3
End, 1992	2	1995	0
1993	1.5		
1994	1		

	Now	Year 1: 1992	Year 2: 1993	Year 3: 1994	Year 4: 1995	Year 5: 1996
1. Estimate of incremental gross profit						
New output		137,700	140,454	143,263	144,450	144,450
Lost output—construction		(57,375)	(46,818)	(35,816)	0	
New sales (millions)		49.08	57.21	65.65	88.26	88.26
New gross margin		11.6%	11.8%	12.1%	12.5%	13.0%
New gross profit		5.69	6.74	7.92	10.99	11.44
Old output		135,000	135,000	135,000	135,000	135,000
Old sales		82.49	82.49	82.49	82.49	82.49
Old gross profit		9.49	9.49	9.49	9.49	9.49
Incremental gross profit		−3.80	−2.75	−1.57	1.51	1.95
2. Estimate of incremental depreciation						
Year 1 outlays		0.27	0.23	0.20	0.17	0.15
Year 2 outlays			0.21	0.18	0.16	0.13
Year 3 outlays				0.15	0.13	0.11
Total, new depreciation		0.27	0.45	0.54	0.46	0.40
3. Overhead		0	0	0	0	0
4. Pretax incremental profit		−4.06	−3.19	−2.10	1.04	1.56
5. Tax expense		−1.42	−1.12	−0.74	0.37	0.54
6. After-tax profit		−2.64	−2.08	−1.37	0.68	1.01
7. Cash-flow adjustments						
Add back depreciation		0.27	0.45	0.54	0.46	0.40
Less added WIP inventory		0.89	−0.21	−0.22	−0.59	0.01
Capital spending	3.00	2.00	1.50	1.00		
Terminal value, land						
8. Free cash flow	−3.00	−5.26	−2.92	−1.61	1.73	1.39
DCF, Rotterdam	12.28					
IRR, Rotterdam	17.2%					
9. Adjustment for erosion in Merseyside volume:						
Lost Merseyside output		—	—	—	9,450	9,450
Lost Merseyside revenue		—	—	—	5.77	5.77
Lost Merseyside gross profits		—	—	—	0.66	0.66
Lost gross profits after taxes		—	—	—	0.43	0.43
Change in Merseyside inventory		—	—	—	0.17	0.17
Total effect on free cash flow		—	—	—	−0.26	−0.26
DCF, erosion Merseyside	(1.43)					
DCF, Rotterdam adjusted for full						
erosion at Merseyside	10.85					

Year 6: 1997	Year 7: 1998	Year 8: 1999	Year 9: 2000	Year 10: 2001	Year 11: 2002	Year 12: 2003	Year 13: 2004	Year 14: 2005	Year 15: 2006
144,450	144,450	144,450	144,450	144,450	144,450	144,450	144,450	144,450	144,450
88.26	88.26	88.26	88.26	88.26	88.26	88.26	88.26	88.26	88.26
13.6%	14.4%	15.3%	16.5%	16.5%	16.5%	16.5%	16.5%	16.5%	16.5%
12.00	12.69	13.52	14.53	14.56	14.56	14.56	14.56	14.56	14.56
135,000	135,000	135,000	135,000	135,000	135,000	135,000	135,000	135,000	135,000
82.49	82.49	82.49	82.49	82.49	82.49	82.49	82.49	82.49	82.49
9.49	9.49	9.49	9.49	9.49	9.49	9.49	9.49	9.49	9.49
2.51	3.20	4.04	5.04	5.08	5.08	5.08	5.08	5.08	5.08
0.13	0.11	0.10	0.10	0.09	0.09	0.09	0.09	0.09	0.09
0.12	0.10	0.08	0.08	0.08	0.07	0.07	0.07	0.07	0.07
0.09	0.08	0.07	0.06	0.06	0.05	0.05	0.05	0.05	0.05
0.34	0.29	0.25	0.24	0.23	0.21	0.21	0.21	0.21	0.21
0	0	0	0	0	0	0	0	0	0
2.17	2.91	3.79	4.80	4.85	4.87	4.87	4.87	4.87	4.87
0.76	1.02	1.33	1.68	1.70	1.70	1.70	1.70	1.70	1.70
1.41	1.89	2.46	3.12	3.15	3.16	3.16	3.16	3.16	3.16
0.34	0.29	0.25	0.24	0.23	0.21	0.21	0.21	0.21	0.21
0.02	0.02	0.03	0.03	0.00	0.00	0.00	0.00	0.00	0.00
									35.00
1.74	2.16	2.69	3.33	3.38	3.37	3.37	3.37	3.37	38.37
9,450	9,450	9,450	9,450	9,450	9,450	9,450	9,450	9,450	9,450
5.77	5.77	5.77	5.77	5.77	5.77	5.77	5.77	5.77	5.77
0.66	0.66	0.66	0.66	0.66	0.66	0.66	0.66	0.66	0.66
0.43	0.43	0.43	0.43	0.43	0.43	0.43	0.43	0.43	0.43
0.17	0.17	0.17	0.17	0.17	0.17	0.17	0.17	0.17	0.17
−0.26	−0.26	−0.26	−0.26	−0.26	−0.26	−0.26	−0.26	−0.26	−0.26

Case 20

Glaxo Italia S.p.A.: The Zinnat Marketing Decision

The laws of the marketplace now apply as much to pharmaceuticals as to consumer electronics: once armed with a new product, a company must establish its market share as quickly as possible, before rival firms produce competitive brands . . . In the past, drugs brought in good profits for a decade or more.

Ernest Mario, *chief executive officer of Glaxo Holdings PLC[1]*

In September 1990, the laws of the pharmaceutical marketplace prompted Emilio Rottoli, financial controller of Glaxo Italia S.p.A.,[2] to evaluate competing strategies for the launch of a promising new product in Italy. Zinnat was a new formula of oral antibiotic. After a research-and-development cost of more than 200 billion Italian lira,[3] the product represented a significant innovation in its market segment. However, the huge quantity of competing antibiotics and antihistaminics made success of the product launch unpredictable.

---

[1]Quoted in *The Economist,* September 6, 1990.

[2]Societa per Azioni; literally, a business under share ownership, like a public corporation in the United States. Also, PLC means a public limited company.

[3]On September 14, 1990, one U.S. dollar could purchase 1,165 lira.

This case was prepared from field interviews and public information by Matteo Davoli, Giuseppe Geneletti, Marco Ghiotto, Diogo Rezende, and Professor Robert F. Bruner. Some financial information has been disguised. The cooperation of Emilio Rottoli and Glaxo Italia S.p.A. is gratefully acknowledged, as is the financial support of the Citicorp Global Scholars Program. Copyright © 1992 by the University of Virginia Darden School Foundation, Charlottesville, VA, and INSEAD, Fontainebleau, France. All rights reserved. *No part of this publication may be reproduced, stored in a retrieval system, used in a spreadsheet, or transmitted in any form or by any means—electronic, mechanical, photocopying, recording, or otherwise—without the permission of the Darden School Foundation. For inquiries, please send an e-mail to dardencases@virginia.edu.* Rev. 1/98. Version 2.1.

Glaxo's general approach to launching a new product called for rapid and massive distribution into the target market in order to capture a large market share quickly, but Rottoli had decided to evaluate two competing strategies for selling Zinnat:

- *Comarketing distribution,* under which Glaxo would permit another pharmaceutical company to make and market the same product but under a different brand name. Glaxo would receive a fee from the comarketer, plus profits on the sales of certain ingredients to that firm. This arrangement would sacrifice some market share for Glaxo's own brand, Zinnat. Glaxo had used comarketing arrangements to promote other products. The major market for Glaxo's best-selling product, Zantac, an antiulcer drug, was developed under a comarketing agreement with Hoffmann–La Roche, whose sales teams organized the introduction of the product among doctors in the United States. The tremendous success of this initiative had built up an appetite (and an expertise) within the company for such arrangements.
- *Direct sales,* under which Glaxo's own sales force would be the sole channel of distribution. This approach would permit the company to exploit the potential gains from its new product most fully. Under this approach, demands on Glaxo's sales organization would be greater than in comarketing, however, and market penetration for the product would take longer.

The choice between the two approaches would hinge not only on financial criteria (such as payback and internal rate of return) but also on qualitative factors such as the potential strength of the brand, uncertainties about the future regulation of a possible over-the-counter (OTC) product, the need to generate cash in the short term to sustain a large R&D budget, uncertainties about the rate of technological change in the pharmaceutical industry and the development of products competitive to Zinnat, potential price wars, and the peculiar aspects of the Italian market.

GLAXO HOLDINGS PLC

Glaxo Italia S.p.A. was a wholly owned operating company of Glaxo Holdings PLC, headquartered in London. Glaxo Holdings was the world's second largest pharmaceutical company in terms of sales, which totaled £2,894 million in the fiscal year ending June 30, 1990, and were expected to grow to £3.4 billion in 1991.[4] The company's growth had been phenomenal: £1 invested in the company in 1979 was worth £85 in 1990, approximately a 50 percent annual compound rate of growth in value (see Exhibit 1). Glaxo's shares were listed for trading in London, New York (as American depositary receipts), Tokyo, and Paris. With an equity market value of $23 billion, the company had the distinction of being the largest capitalization stock traded on the London stock market and the 26th largest traded in the United States.

Glaxo was a leader in products for the relief of peptic ulcers and of asthma and was a major supplier of antibiotics and of treatments for skin disorders. For several reasons, many of Glaxo's new drugs eventually achieved dominant market positions. First, Glaxo focused its

---

[4]On September 14, 1990, £1 = 2,212 Italian lira and U.S.$1.898.

research on unmet medical needs. Second, the company always coupled its R&D strategy with a fast track record in new-drug approval time. Third, Glaxo had built up one of the world's biggest sales forces for drugs, 9,500 representatives. Fourth, its marketing machine went into action early in a product's life. While the new drug was being developed, Glaxo held costly symposiums to which it invited opinion leaders who knew about the disease the drug was designed to treat. The idea was to build and gauge market potential. Once a drug was presented to regulators for approval, the marketers used public relations firms to work out ways to create demand. Doctors were flooded with medical literature and given guidelines on how to diagnose the disease. Medical authorities were persuaded of the economic savings from the product introduction. Almost immediately after a drug had been launched, Glaxo established small studies to monitor the performance of the drug in a normal population in order to spot any new adverse effect. Doctors were paid for their contributions to these studies.

GLAXO ITALIA S.p.A.

Glaxo Italia S.p.A. was the oldest Glaxo subsidiary. Exhibit 2 reveals that the subsidiary had the third largest market share in the highly fragmented Italian pharmaceutical market. Based in Verona (in the northeastern part of the country and the setting of Shakespeare's *Romeo and Juliet*), Glaxo Italia had manufacturing facilities producing most of Glaxo Holdings' products. The company workforce was about 2,000 people, 400 of whom were involved in research.

Glaxo Holdings granted unusual autonomy to its operating subsidiaries, including discretion over product positioning, the choice of promotional mix, the timing of line extensions, and resource allocation to various products. Glaxo Italia's objectives were to achieve a turnover[5] of 2 trillion lira, which would represent 9 percent of the market, with a 50 percent profit margin, by the turn of the century. In order to achieve these challenging goals, the company was rapidly expanding its sales force and had invested heavily in new research facilities (156 billion lira), which was one of the five most important R&D centers for Glaxo Holdings. Last but not least, Glaxo Holdings had selected Italy as the site for the Glaxo Management School.

As shown in Exhibit 3, this expansion strategy was expected to dampen profitability in the short term, but within five years, the heavy investment and debt-based financing were forecasted to pay off in a sevenfold growth of profits. Glaxo Italia sales in 1991 were expected to be 719 billion lira, which included 183 billion lira of sales by licensees and comarketers. The total would represent 6.2 percent of the pharmaceutical market (3.8 percent through direct sales only). Exhibit 4 reveals that a quarter of these sales would derive from licensees in comarketing agreements; Exhibit 5 indicates that continued sales growth depended significantly on new products and sales by licensees.

ZINNAT

The Zinnat oral antibiotic offered a new competitive remedy to current drugs for influenza-like feverish diseases. Zinnat's launch would be a major opportunity and challenge for the company to support and expand its presence in the antibiotic segment. The product would

---

[5]*Turnover* is equivalent to sales revenue.

be introduced in two formulations: (1) a package of 12 pills of 250 milligrams each, with a retail price of 34,400 Italian lira (ITL), and (2) a 2.5-gram syrup with a retail price of 29,880 ITL. The manufacturer's price was 61 percent of the retail price. Gross margin was 53 percent of the manufacturer's price. The cost of goods sold consisted mainly of costs of raw materials, local production, bottling, and fees. The raw material was sold to Glaxo Italia S.p.A. and any comarketers from Glaxo Holdings at a transfer price of 1,566 ITL/gram. Glaxo Italia would pay an additional 4 percent of this price for customs fees, transportation, and so on. The transfer price consisted of variable costs (20 percent) and the product's share of R&D expenses incurred (80 percent). Glaxo Italia and any comarketers had to anticipate a 20 percent cost for local production and bottling.

THE ETHICAL AND OTC PHARMACEUTICAL MARKETS

Glaxo planned to introduce Zinnat solely into the ethical-drug market, although at some point in the future, Zinnat might convert into an OTC drug. (When a drug was prescribed over a long period of time, it could develop a strong brand image.) These two main segments of the market were significantly different.

In the ethical-drug market, a doctor's prescription was necessary to obtain the product; therefore, the doctor was the "gatekeeper" to the end user and the target of marketing efforts by the manufacturers.

Italian doctors were renowned in Europe for their interest in new drugs. As a result, the average life cycle of ethical drugs tended to be shorter in Italy than elsewhere. Glaxo managers believed that aggressive use of sales-force marketing (both direct and co-marketed) would have a strong effect on Zinnat's market share.

OTCs, by definition, could be purchased directly from retailers (usually, but not necessarily, pharmacies). No patents applied in the case of OTCs, and all OTCs were branded. In most countries, OTCs could be directly advertised to the public, while ethical drugs were subjected to government regulations that allowed them to be advertised only in media targeted to the medical profession.

In general, manufacturers decided whether a drug they were developing fit the ethical or the OTC market, but a final decision was made by national drug-control authorities. OTC drugs were usually established remedies for minor illnesses such as coughs, colds, and flu or preventive preparations such as vitamins and tonics. For a new drug to be launched straight into the OTC market was extremely rare.

Ethical drugs might, however, be sold over the counter when their patents expired. This conversion could occur when an ethical drug, after a number of years on the market, was found not to have significant side effects and its potency for conditions other than those for which it was prescribed was limited. When government regulators were satisfied that a drug's side effects and potency were limited, they would permit the drug to be sold without a prescription.

Marketers at Glaxo believed that OTC marketing would increase for several reasons: (1) tighter control of national health-service budgets was leading to increasing incentives for self-medication; (2) patients were becoming more and more able to take on active roles as consumers; (3) liberalization in national drug-approval agencies had increased the number of products in this market (for instance, in Denmark, H2 antagonists[6] such as Zantac had been permitted to go OTC since 1989).

Antibiotics, because of their consumption patterns and intrinsic characteristics, were one product category that might experience movement into the OTC market early in their life cycles. Glaxo Holdings wanted to enter this segment first, however, because of its large share of revenues. But Glaxo Holdings considered itself an ethical-drug company and was structured accordingly (substantial R&D facilities and investments, marketing and distribution organizations centered on sales representatives rather than on advertising or brand management). One Glaxo Holdings executive was quoted as saying that "strong brand images were not our area. OTC was a different sort of business."[7] But the company was prepared to adapt.

THE POLICY OF RAPID PRODUCT LAUNCH: THE ROLE OF COMARKETING

Glaxo's strategy of rapid market penetration for new products sought to create several advantages: (1) the "snowball" effect of word-of-mouth advertising within the medical community; (2) economies of scale and scope (the introduction costs, such as presentations to doctors and hospitals, conferences, advertising, were relatively fixed) could be gained if the costs were spread across the largest possible volume; and (3) raised barriers to entry (preemption of market space). Rapid penetration also served the fundamental need to generate positive cash flows in the shortest possible time in order to finance investments in R&D for future products. Glaxo Holdings' new products that reached the launch phase were, in fact, extremely profitable, with internal rates of return generally greater than 200 percent. In the pharmaceutical industry, 1 R&D project in 10 became a commercialized new product; thus new-product development in a growing company such as Glaxo required significant investment.

Glaxo Italia possessed two direct sales-force teams (called "lines") currently employing 320 sales representatives each. In comarketing agreements, Glaxo would pursue rapid market penetration by adding the sales efforts of the comarketer as each marketed its own brands of the same product.[8] With comarketing, Glaxo anticipated various benefits: volumes would be higher and reached in shorter times than when marketing alone. In addition, establishing close ties with other firms could provide additional lobbying leverage in regulatory environments where the registration process for new products was particularly slow and bureaucratic. The comarketer could benefit in two ways. First, that firm's sales force could carry more products and thereby make each sales call more productive. Second, a broader product line might help keep the sales force productive during any trough in the firm's business cycle.

On the other hand, the presence of a distribution partner had several disadvantages. First, Glaxo had to increase its sales force and marketing efforts to compete against the comarketer's products. Second, the comarketer, which was also a pharmaceutical company in 90 percent of the cases, might be tempted to reformulate the product (and thus sidestep

---

[6]H2 antagonists (also called H2 blockers) block the histamine receptor (H2) in the body and thus reduce the production of gastric acids believed to cause stomach ulcers.

[7]In the *Financial Times,* November 8, 1989.

[8]Another classic joint marketing arrangement included co-detailing (same product, same brand name).

licensing fees) if it proved to be successful. Comarketing strategies were also vulnerable to price wars and litigation over allocation of resources and territories, and risked saturation of the doctors' attention.

PRODUCT LIFE AND PATENT LIFE

Product life and patent life were important influences on the Zinnat marketing decision. Product life consisted of the remaining years of effective patent life, plus any years thereafter when the product might continue to be sold without the benefit of patent protection. In theory, the product life of Zinnat could be infinite. Even after the patent expired, Zinnat might continue to be prescribed. The earliest antibiotic—penicillin—was still being prescribed by doctors, well after the expiration of patent protection. But the rate of innovation in the development of new antibiotics was increasing, raising the likelihood that Zinnat would be displaced by some new drug. Practically, Mr. Rottoli doubted there would be any appreciable sales of Zinnat after the 15th year.

Patent life was the number of years of protection for inventors from uncompensated direct imitation of their invention. The total patent life in the United States was 17 years, whereas in Europe it was 20 years. Patent life was taken up by (1) the time required to develop the specific application after the new compound had been developed, (2) the time necessary for registration, (3) the time required to introduce the product, and (4) the remaining "effective" patent life. Exhibit 6 shows that effective patent life fell from 13 to 5 years between 1965 and 1985. As Sir Peter Girolami, chairman of Glaxo, had recently said,

> Medicines which are now emerging from the development pipeline are more complex and more powerful than their predecessors; this inevitably complicates the necessary process of satisfying regulatory authorities.

A shortening of effective patent life could reduce the period of time during which protected profits on a drug could be made. Rottoli forecasted the Zinnat cash flows out to the sixth year in the belief that the product should prove that it could earn its return during that window of effective patent protection.

While patent life had shortened, R&D expenditures were constantly increasing. One widely accepted estimate of the average cost to discover and bring a major new drug to the market was U.S.$100 million. The implication of these high costs was that large revenues had to be generated to pay for them. According to one study of the Wellcome Foundation, to achieve an adequate return on an R&D expenditure of U.S.$100 million, a drug had to reach peak annual sales of over U.S.$200 million and total sales revenues of 11 times the R&D spent.[9] Rottoli estimated that a delay of just one week in development time represented a loss in terms of revenues of U.S.$1–U.S.$2 million. At the same time, the reduction in effective patent life led to a quicker significant drop in sales revenues when the price had to be reduced to face competition from the generic product. Comarketing could increase the risk of competition when a patent expired, because the comarketer might be prepared to manufacture the product in house. To manufacture Zinnat, for instance, the

---

[9]Trevor M. Jones, "Improving the Development Process," paper presented at the World Pharmaceutical Conference, London, March 1990.

comarketer would have to pay a licensing fee and would be required to purchase some ingredients from Glaxo Holdings. Without the protection of a patent, the fee and the supply arrangement would disappear.

FINANCIAL CRITERIA

Glaxo Italia used two main criteria as the basis for evaluating decisions about sales strategies: payback and internal rate of return (IRR).

- *Payback.* Any new product launched had to have a payback period of less than three years. This period reflected the company's strategic emphasis on rapid market penetration. The use of the payback criterion was justified on two grounds. First, given the extended industry practice of "cross-subsidization" among products, senior managers needed to know when a new product would start to generate cash surpluses that could be used to finance new R&D projects. Payback helped focus managers' attention on the cash-flow breakeven. Second, uncertainty about the time at which competitors could launch a similar product made it relevant to know how much time was necessary to recover the additional investment to market the product.
- *IRR.* The more desirable strategy would have the higher IRR. The minimum required IRR in Italy was a firm's cost of debt there (12.5 percent in September 1990).[10] Exhibit 7 contains information on current capital-market conditions.

When asked if an appropriate discount rate should take into account the cost of equity capital as well as the cost of debt, Rottoli answered:

> Investors expect to get higher returns? Well, if I produce good returns, they'll get them. If I don't, they won't! To begin with, let's start from zero cash and a new project on the way. At this point in time, the firm, hypothetically, can borrow money from a bank at, say, 12.5 percent; that represents the cost of debt. After this initial cost is entirely paid back from the project cash flows, what is left to the shareholders is the project net IRR (i.e., net of financial charges). Thus we do not fix any a priori target for shareholders' returns, be they based on market averages or historical trends or even future forecasts. It is sufficient for the net IRR to be greater than zero to justify the investment. It then falls to the investors to accept the expected rate of return on the project or to reject it. However, the net IRR is still clearly higher than what the shareholders will ultimately get from the business. I mean, we need yet to include and subtract all the fixed and structural costs necessary to run the business before getting to the investors' payoff. These are basically the reasons why I tend to consider discounted cash flow based on the project WACC (weighted-average cost of capital) premature at this stage.

Referring to the choice of costs and cash flows included in the forecast, Rottoli said,

> Only manufacturing and promotional cost are considered relevant. The remaining items—such as G&A (general and administrative), historical and future R&D (at local and group level), medical testing cost, real financial charges, taxes—are not taken into account.[11] Not at all! We are really

---

[10]The yield-to-maturity of Glaxo Holdings' long-term debt in the United Kingdom was 12.5 percent. Its book value of debt amounted to £420 million. Its market value of equity was £12,193 million.

[11]Glaxo Italia's marginal tax rate was 47 percent. Glaxo holdings' marginal tax rate in the United Kingdom was 29 percent.

interested in evaluating the marginal profitability between direct sales and comarketing. Therefore, all of those items being shared by the two alternatives end up complicating the measures while not dramatically improving the final decision.

FINANCIAL PROJECTIONS

To evaluate the strategic choice between direct sales and comarketing, Rottoli had prepared a financial model as presented in Exhibits 8, 9, and 10. Assumptions underlying the model are summarized in Exhibit 8. Aspects of the forecast that required some judgment were the following:

- *Product mix.* In the first year, the model assumed this mix: 85 percent pills and 15 percent syrup. From the second year on, the mix was assumed to be 80 percent pills and 20 percent syrup. The licensee was assumed to weight the product mix differently: 40 percent pills and 60 percent syrup. These assumptions were based on prior experience.
- *Marketing costs.* These costs included (1) the cost of drug samples given to doctors and clinics; (2) the cost of medical promotions (trials to hospitals, clinics, and local healthcare units); (3) the cost of seminars, congresses, and social promotions (one-hour short conferences plus dinners held by technical/scientific sales reps); (4) the cost of training the sales force; and (5) sales force compensation. Assumptions about these costs were based on prior experience. Sales-force compensation costs could be saved if Glaxo chose to market Zinnat directly rather than with a comarketer. Rottoli believed that the sales force would spend about 25 percent less time on Zinnat if the product were marketed directly instead of with a comarketer—this reflected the highly motivational effects of competition.
- *Market share.* The effect of competition from the comarketer would be reflected in higher market share for Zinnat in the antibiotic market, and earlier attainment of a notable position. Figure 1 compares the two market share forecasts projected by the Glaxo Italia staff. The lower market shares for Zinnat under the direct sales strategy were consistent with experience on other products, though Rottoli believed that the share forecast for direct sales was perhaps conservative. The market shares for the direct sales strategy could be as much as 1, 2, or 3 percent higher.
- *Sales force.* Zinnat was assigned principally to the sales force named "Line 1." In the first year only, sales force "Line 2" would support the launch. The cost of the direct sales force was calculated according to the estimated percentage time to be spent on the specific product. Historically, the cost per salesperson had increased by 12 percent each year on average; the forecast assumed this growth rate in salesperson costs over the forecast period.[12] The sales force in Line 1 was supposed to grow from 320 to 440 reps within three years, but Rottoli wrestled with the question of whether this increased sales-force promotional time was a marginal item or just a reallocation of corporate resources that would be needed anyway. He said,

---

[12]Beyond year six, one could assume that the cost per salesperson would grow at the rate of inflation in the lira, 4 percent.

FIGURE 1 Zinnat Market Share by Strategy

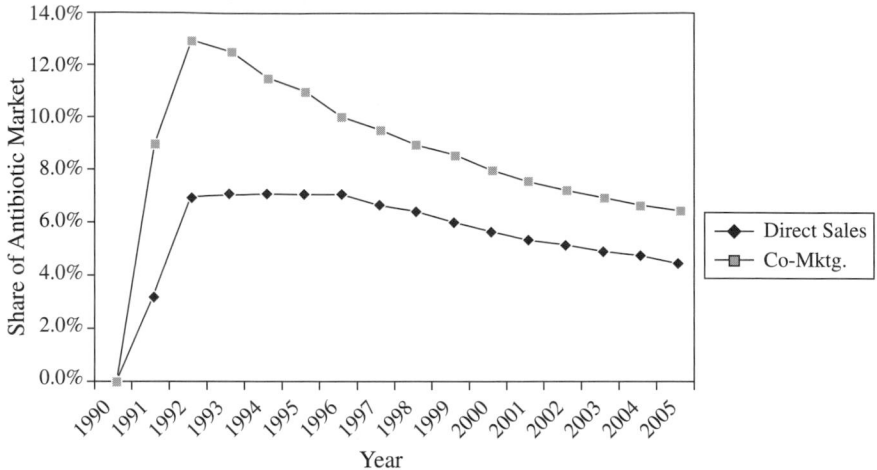

It was an eternal source of discussion between me and Mr. (Giuseppe) Ferrari, the Sales V.P. I told him that as long as new employees were hired for new-product promotional support, the sales structure was an incremental expense of this product launch. Mr. Ferrari argued that the sales force supported the company as a whole and that therefore the cost of new sales recruits should not be included in the forecast.

The financial forecast prepared by Rottoli charged Zinnat for the percent of actual sales-force time that the product was assumed to require.

- *Group profit on parent–subsidiary transfer of ingredients.* This figure was the profit that Glaxo Holdings PLC (the parent) made on the sales of the key chemical compounds to Glaxo Italia (the subsidiary). Glaxo explained that this profit was a means of reimbursing the parent for R&D expenses. The ingredients could be directly packaged by Glaxo Italia or possibly resold to the comarketer. The price per gram of the ingredients was 1,566 lira, which included a gross profit of 80 percent to Glaxo Holdings.

- *Capital generated and interest.* Glaxo Holdings viewed the product launch as having a cash flow (or flow of "capital generated") equal to the product margin less the working-capital requirement (equivalent to two months of sales.) The Zinnat product line in Italy would be charged interest for capital used, or credited interest for net capital supplied to Glaxo Holdings. The interest charge or credit was equal to the current yield on Glaxo Holdings' debt, multiplied by the cumulative capital used or generated at the end of the previous year. The initial phase of a project was somewhat similar to an entrepreneur venturing upon a new business. Initial exposure for a new-product launch was burdened by interest expenses at the stated rate until the early outlays were recovered. From then on, the business's profits would be "loaned" to new emerging projects at the same stated rate, according to the following logic: "One line generates cash, while another—internally—absorbs part of it," as Mr. Rottoli said. The capital employed then turned from a use (−) to a generation of cash (+). Investors expected higher returns from a project, however, than from purchasing securities on the market.

- *Time horizon.* Although the product life cycle of pharmaceutical products was typically between 10 and 20 years, the forecast was carried out to only 6 years. Product managers and marketing directors found extending a forecast beyond six years difficult. They believed that Zinnat in Italy would enjoy its strongest competitive standing in its first six years of life. From the seventh year on, the product's share of the antibiotic market would decline. Mr. Rottoli estimated that a reasonable rate of decline would be 5 percent per year.[13] He wondered, however, whether the rate of decline and/or the cash flows beyond the forecast horizon mattered.
- *Fees from the licensee.* Under the contemplated arrangement, the Italian co-marketer would pay Glaxo Holdings an annual fee equal to 4 percent of its revenues from Zinnat sales. However, the size of this fee would be the focus of tough negotiation. The ultimate arrangement could entail a fee lower or higher than 4 percent.

CONCLUSION

The data in the forecasts Rottoli was holding (Exhibits 8, 9, and 10) suggested he should undoubtedly recommend that the company go forward with comarketing instead of direct sales:

	Direct Sales	*Comarketing*
IRR	218%	1,013%
Payback	2.5 years	1 year

He wondered, however, whether these base-case results adequately captured the richness of the problem. For instance, how robust was the preference for comarketing to considerations such as these:

- What combinations of license fees, sales-force savings, and market share would leave Glaxo indifferent between the two marketing strategies?
- Taking Mr. Ferrari's argument, should the cost of the field sales force be considered to be incremental to the Zinnat launch?
- The combined action of two firms would allow reaching a high maximum market share in 24 months, whereas the effort of only one firm required 36 months in the forecast to achieve a lower market share. How significant was the benefit of the incremental speed and market penetration?
- After the product proved itself in the marketplace, a comarketer might defect to its own brand; thus, direct selling could have a distinctly different set of cash flows beyond year 6. In addition, the appearance or nonappearance of newer products could affect the more distant cash flows. What should be done about cash flows beyond the five-year forecast horizon?

On top of these concerns, Rottoli wondered if the forecasting system with which he was endowed captured the best insights. Glaxo had delivered abundant value to shareholders. Would the current financial evaluation of the Zinnat marketing decision promote that value? Were IRR and payback the best decision criteria? Was he missing any relevant cash flows?

---

[13]That is, share of market in year 2 would be 95 percent of the share of market in year 1.

EXHIBIT 1   Annual Value of £1 Invested in Glaxo Holdings Stock in 1979 (indexed so that the value for 1979 equals £1; uses yearly median stock prices; adjusted for 100% stock dividends in 1983 and 1985)

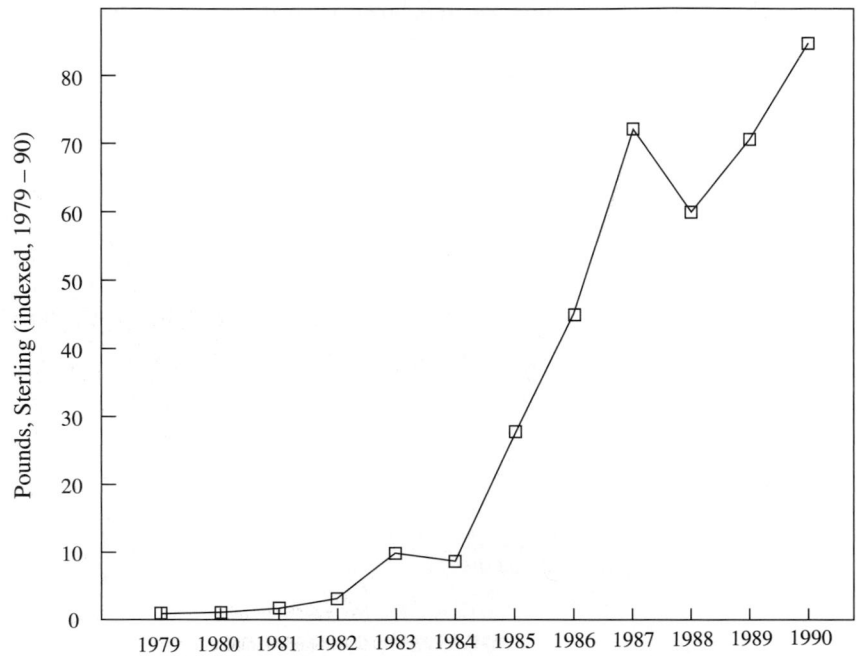

The Annual Market Value of Investment
In Glaxo Holdings

EXHIBIT 2   Shares of Pharmaceutical Market (Italy, 1990)

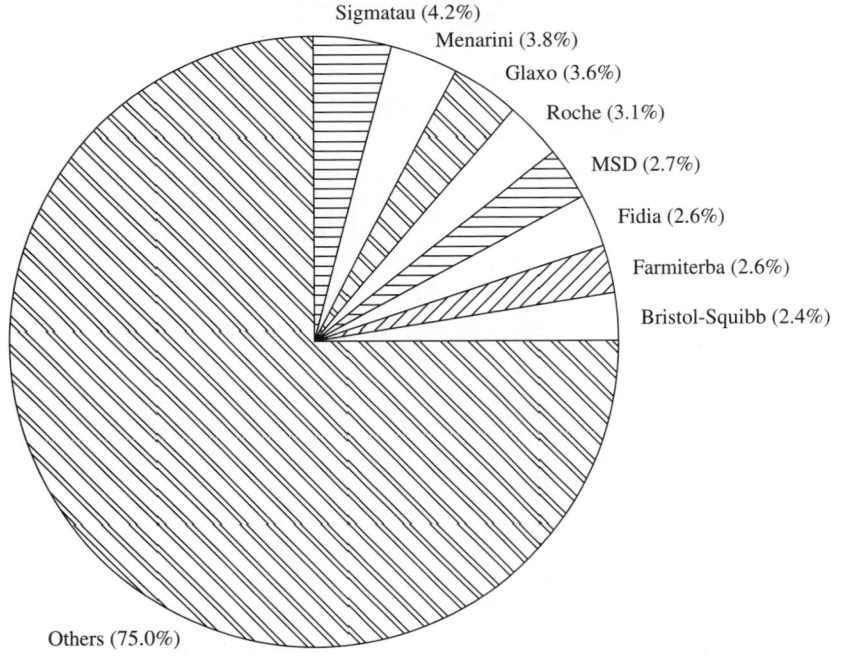

Sigmatau (4.2%)
Menarini (3.8%)
Glaxo (3.6%)
Roche (3.1%)
MSD (2.7%)
Fidia (2.6%)
Farmiterba (2.6%)
Bristol-Squibb (2.4%)

Others (75.0%)

Source: Glaxo Marketing Department.

EXHIBIT 3   Glaxo Italia Financial Performance, Historical and Projected, 1989–95

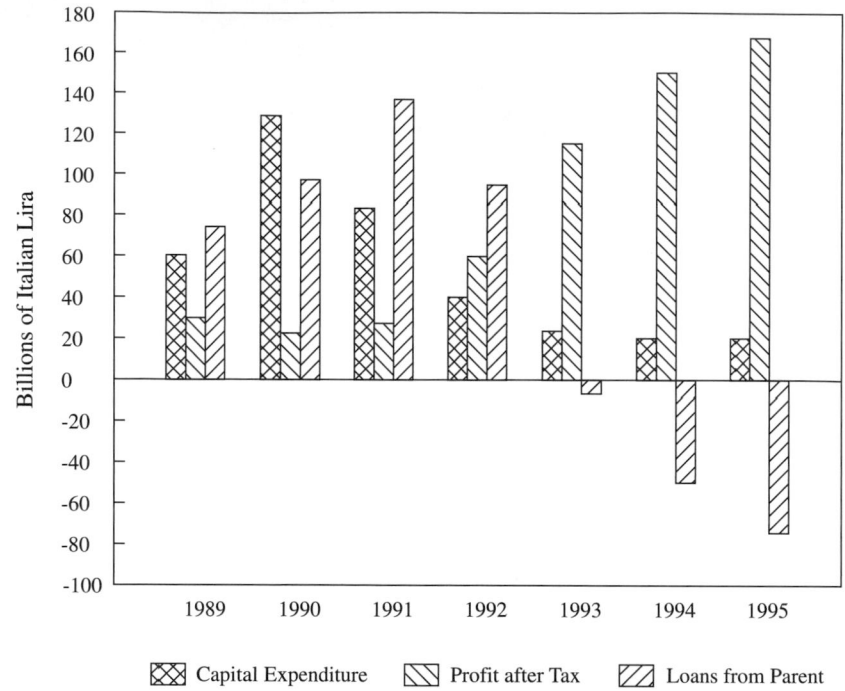

Source: Glaxo Italia S.p.A.

EXHIBIT 4   Glaxo Italia Product Portfolio, 1991 (projected revenues, 720 billion ITL)

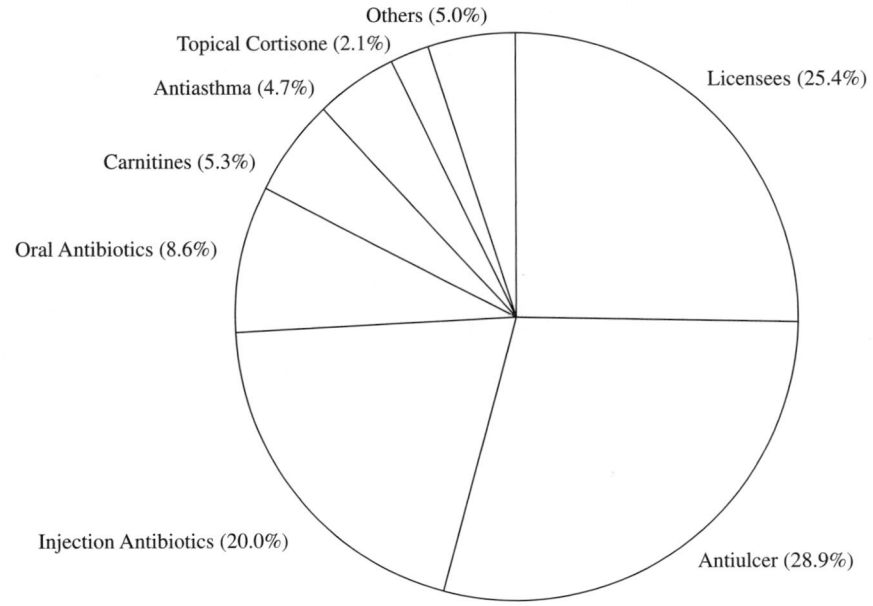

Glaxo Italia Product Portfolio, 1991
Projected Revenues, 720 bn ITL

Others (5.0%)
Topical Cortisone (2.1%)
Antiasthma (4.7%)
Carnitines (5.3%)
Oral Antibiotics (8.6%)
Licensees (25.4%)
Injection Antibiotics (20.0%)
Antiulcer (28.9%)

Source: Glaxo Italia S.p.A.

EXHIBIT 5   Glaxo Italia Sales Composition, Historical and Projected, 1980–95

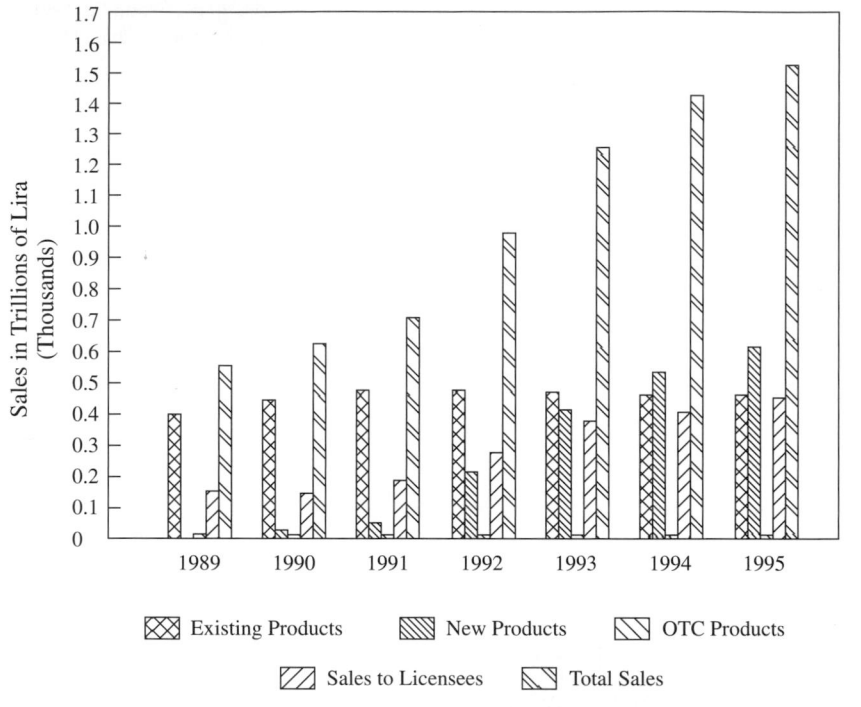

Source: Glaxo Italia S.p.A.

EXHIBIT 6   Effective Patent Life of Drugs in EC 1965 and 1985

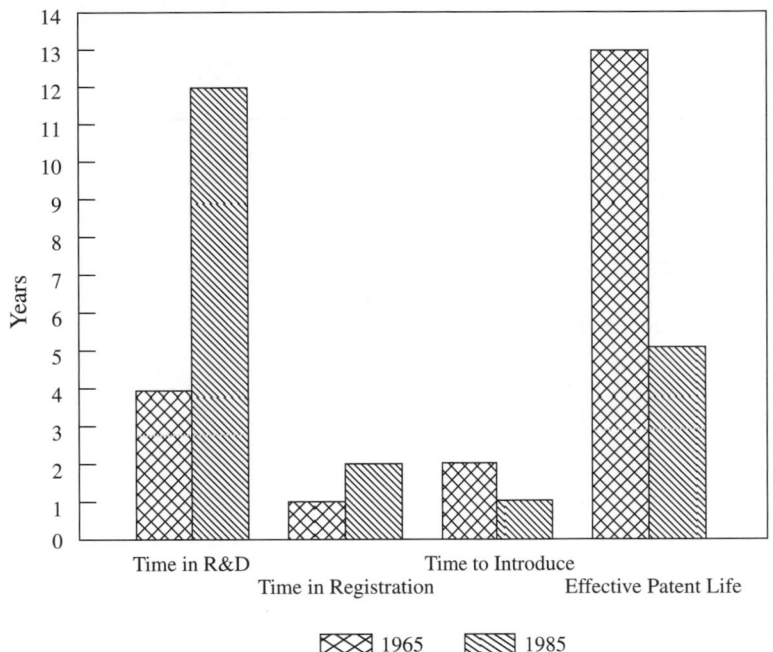

Source: Economist Intelligence Unit, 1989.

EXHIBIT 7   Capital-Market Conditions, September 1990

	United Kingdom	*Italy*
Yield on long-term government bonds		
June	11.01%	11.32%
September	11.32%	11.60%
Expected inflation rate	5%	4%

	Price/Earnings Ratio	*Share Price (U.S.$)*	*Beta*
Glaxo Holdings PLC	15.6	30	.90
Bristol Myers-Squibb	18.5	66	1.00
Eli Lilly	17.6	77	1.10
Pfizer	16.1	81	1.05
Rhône-Poulenc Rorer	7.5	9 3/8	1.05
Schering Plough Corp.	17.5	16	1.15
Equity market risk premium (64-year geometric mean)	5.6%		

Sources: *Financial Times, Risk Measurement Services, Value Line Investment Survey.*

EXHIBIT 8   Forecast Assumptions

	First-Year Product Mix
Pills sold by Glaxo	85%
Syrup sold by Glaxo	15%
Pills sold by licensee	40%
Syrup sold by licensee	60%
Marginal tax rate—Italy	47.0%
Marginal tax rate—UK	29.0%
Expected inflation rate—Italian lira	0.0%
Expected inflation rate—UK, pounds, sterling	5.0%
Yearly percentage increase in cost per sales rep.	12.0%
Yearly decline in market share after year 6	5.0%
Extra growth in direct sales	0.0%
Savings in promotional effort direct sales vs. comarketing	25.0%
Licensee fee (% of Zinnat revenues to licensee)	4.0%
Working capital required/Sales	16.7%
Glaxo Holdings, interest rate and internal charge for capital	12.5%

	1990	*1991*
Market forecast of antibiotic demand (millions of units)		52.3
Market share for Zinnat, direct sales strategy	0.0%	3.1%
Market share for Zinnat, comarketing strategy	0.0%	9.0%
% Zinnat volume sold by Glaxo, comarketing strategy		45.35%
Years from Sept. 1990	0.25	1.25
Transfer price of ingredients per gram (lira)	1,566.0	1,566.0
Glaxo price to customer—pills (lira)	20,984.0	20,984.0
Glaxo price to customer—syrup (lira)	18,226.8	18,226.8
Gross margin/Direct sales, Glaxo Italia		53%
Gross margin/Ingredient sales, Glaxo Holdings	80%	80%
Sales force 1—salespeople		320
% time on Zinnat (if direct marketing)		20%
% time on Zinnat (if comarketing)		26%
Sales force 2—salespeople		320
% time on Zinnat (if direct marketing)		13%
% time on Zinnat (if comarketing)		18%
Cost per sales rep (millions of lira)		105.0

Sources: Company analysis and casewriters' analysis.

Years 2+ Product Mix	1990 Price to Retail Cust. (Lira)	Content of Key Raw Materials (Grams)	1990 Manufacturer Price to Retailer	1990 Price of Ingredients (Lira/Grams)
80%	34,400.0	3.0	20,984.0	1,566.0
20%	29,880.0	2.5	18,226.8	1,566.0
40%				
60%				

1992	1993	1994	1995	1996
46.6	46.6	44.6	46.3	47.2
7.0%	7.1%	7.1%	7.1%	7.1%
13.0%	12.5%	11.5%	11.0%	10.0%
61.79%	63.78%	67.40%	71.38%	71.63%
2.25	3.25	4.25	5.25	6.25
1,566.0	1,566.0	1,566.0	1,566.0	1,566.0
20,984.0	20,984.0	20,984.0	20,984.0	20,984.0
18,226.8	18,226.8	18,226.8	18,226.8	18,226.8
53%	53%	53%	53%	53%
80%	80%	80%	80%	80%
350	400	400	400	440
25%	18%	16%	17%	17%
33%	24%	21%	23%	23%
117.6	131.7	147.5	165.2	185.0

EXHIBIT 9   Financial Forecast: Direct Sales (all figures in ITL billions)

	1990	1991	1992	1993	1994	1995	1996
Quantities of units (000)							
Volume sold direct		912	2560	2711	2764	2889	3003
Samples		710	700	600	400	400	350
Glaxo Italia: Profit							
Revenues	0.0	18.76	52.31	55.40	56.49	59.04	61.37
Gross margin		9.9	27.7	29.4	29.9	31.3	32.5
Marketing expense, direct sales							
Samples expense		3.3	3.2	2.7	1.8	1.8	1.6
Medical promotions (trials)	0.2	0.2	0.5	0.6	0.6	0.6	
Seminars, congresses, etc.	0.2	2.6	3.7	3.3	1.7	1.8	1.9
Sales force training	0.3	0.7	0.3	0.3	0.9	0.9	1.0
Compensation: sales force 1		6.6	10.2	9.5	9.3	11.4	14.0
Compensation: sales force 2		5.9					
Total marketing expense	0.7	19.2	17.9	16.4	14.3	16.6	18.5
Profit: Direct sales	−0.7	−9.2	9.8	12.9	15.7	14.7	14.0
Glaxo Holdings							
Profit on sales of ingredients to Glaxo Italia		5.9	11.8	12.0	11.5	12.0	12.2
Capital charge (−), income (+)	0.0	−0.1	−0.9	1.0	4.2	8.1	12.4
Profit: Zinnat product line	−0.7	−3.4	20.8	26.0	31.3	34.7	38.6
Investment in NWC	0.0	3.1	5.6	0.5	0.2	0.4	0.4
Capital generated	−0.7	−6.5	15.2	25.5	31.2	34.3	38.2
Cumulative capital used (−) or generated (+)	−0.7	−7.2	8.0	33.4	64.6	98.9	137.1
IRR on capital employed	218%						
Payback period	2.5 years						

Sources: Company analysis and casewriters' analysis.

EXHIBIT 10   Financial Forecast: Comarketing (all figures in ITL billions)

	1990	1991	1992	1993	1994	1995	1996
Quantities of units (000)							
Volume sold direct by Glaxo		1,813	3,308	3,336	3,185	3,352	3,132
Samples distributed free	50	710	700	600	400	400	350
Sold by licensees	200	2,895	2,746	2,494	1,941	1,744	1,591
Total	250	5,419	6,754	6,430	5,526	5,496	5,073
Glaxo Italia: Profit							
Direct sales by Glaxo Italia	0.0	37.3	67.6	68.2	65.1	68.5	64.0
Gross margin, direct sales	0.0	19.8	35.8	36.1	34.5	36.3	33.9
Marketing expense, direct sales							
Samples expense	0.2	3.3	3.2	2.7	1.8	1.8	1.6
Medical promotions (trials)	0.2	0.4	0.7	0.7	0.7	0.7	
Seminars, congresses, etc.	0.2	5.2	4.7	4.1	2.0	2.1	1.9
Sales force training	1.0	1.3	0.3	0.3	1.0	1.1	1.0
Compensation: sales force 1		8.7	13.6	12.6	12.4	15.2	18.7
Compensation: sales force 2		5.9					
Total marketing expense	1.6	24.8	22.5	20.5	17.9	20.9	23.2
Profit: Direct sales, Glaxo Italia	−1.6	−5.0	13.3	15.6	16.6	15.4	10.7
Glaxo Holdings: Profit and Fees							
Ingredient sales to Glaxo Italia and licensee	1.1	22.9	28.6	27.2	23.4	23.2	21.4
Profit: ingredient sales, Glaxo Holdings	0.8	18.3	22.8	21.7	18.7	18.6	17.2
Fee from licensee	0.2	2.2	2.1	1.9	1.5	1.3	1.2
Capital charge (−), income(+)	0.0	−0.1	0.6	4.7	10.2	16.3	22.6
Profit: Zinnat product line	−0.6	15.5	38.9	44.0	47.1	51.7	51.8
Change in working capital	0.2	9.9	6.0	−0.1	−1.2	0.5	−1.0
Capital generated	−0.8	5.6	32.9	44.2	48.2	51.1	52.8
Cumulative capital used (−) or generated (+)	−0.8	4.8	37.7	81.9	130.1	181.2	234.0
IRR on capital employed	1,013%						
Payback period	1 year						

Sources: Company analysis and casewriters' analysis.

Case 21

Pan-Europa Foods S.A.

In early January 1993, the senior-management committee of Pan-Europa Foods was to meet to draw up the firm's capital budget for the new year. Up for consideration were 11 major projects that totaled over (European currency unit) ECU208 million. Unfortunately, the board of directors had imposed a spending limit of only ECU80 million; even so, investment at that rate would represent a major increase in the firm's asset base of ECU656 million. Thus, the challenge for the senior managers of Pan-Europa was to allocate funds among a range of compelling projects: new-product introduction, acquisition, market expansion, efficiency improvements, preventive maintenance, safety, and pollution control.

THE COMPANY

Pan-Europa Foods, headquartered in Brussels, Belgium, was a multinational producer of high-quality ice cream, yogurt, bottled water, and fruit juices. Its products were sold throughout Scandinavia, Britain, Belgium, the Netherlands, Luxembourg, western Germany, and northern France. (See Exhibit 1 for a map of the company's marketing region.)

The company was founded in 1924 by Theo Verdin, a Belgian farmer, as an offshoot of his dairy business. Through keen attention to product development, and shrewd marketing, the business grew steadily over the years. The company went public in 1979 and by 1993 was listed for trading on the London, Frankfurt, and Brussels exchanges. In 1992, Pan-Europa had sales of almost ECU1.1 billion.

This case was prepared by Casey Opitz and Robert F. Bruner and draws certain elements from an antecedent case by them. Copyright © 1993 by the University of Virginia Darden School Foundation, Charlottesville, VA. All rights reserved. *No part of this publication may be reproduced, stored in a retrieval system, used in a spreadsheet, or transmitted in any form or by any means—electronic, mechanical, photocopying, recording, or otherwise—without the permission of the Darden Foundation. For inquiries, please send an e-mail to dardencases@ virginia.edu.* Rev. 1/98. Version 1.1.

Ice cream accounted for 60 percent of the company's revenues; yogurt, which was introduced in 1982, contributed about 20 percent. The remaining 20 percent of sales was divided equally between bottled water and fruit juices. Pan-Europa's flagship brand name was Rolly, which was represented by a fat, dancing bear in farmers' clothing. Ice cream, the company's leading product, had a loyal base of customers who sought out its high butterfat content, large chunks of chocolate, fruit, nuts, and wide range of original flavors.

Pan-Europa sales had been static since 1990 (see Exhibit 2), which management attributed to low population growth in northern Europe and market saturation in some areas. Outside observers, however, faulted recent failures in new-product introductions. Most members of management wanted to expand the company's market presence and introduce more new products to boost sales. These managers hoped that increased market presence and sales would improve the company's market value. Pan-Europa's stock was currently at eight times earnings, just below book value. This price/earnings ratio was below the trading multiples of comparable companies, but it gave little value to the company's brands.

RESOURCE ALLOCATION

The capital budget at Pan-Europa was prepared annually by a committee of senior managers who then presented it for approval by the board of directors. The committee consisted of five managing directors, the *président directeur-général* (PDG), and the finance director. Typically, the PDG solicited investment proposals from the managing directors. The proposals included a brief project description, a financial analysis, and a discussion of strategic or other qualitative considerations.

As a matter of policy, investment proposals at Pan-Europa were subjected to two financial tests, payback and internal rate of return (IRR). The tests, or hurdles, had been established in 1991 by the management committee and varied according to the type of project:

Type of Project	Minimum Acceptable IRR	Maximum Acceptable Payback Years
1. New product or new markets	12%	6 years
2. Product or market extension	10%	5 years
3. Efficiency improvements	8%	4 years
4. Safety or environmental	No test	No test

In January 1993, the estimated weighted-average cost of capital (WACC) for Pan-Europa was 10.5 percent.

In describing the capital-budgeting process, the finance director, Trudi Lauf, said,

We use the sliding scale of IRR tests as a way of recognizing differences in risk among the various types of projects. Where the company takes more risk, we should earn more return. The payback test signals that we are not prepared to wait for long to achieve that return.

OWNERSHIP AND THE SENTIMENT OF CREDITORS AND INVESTORS

Pan-Europa's 12-member board of directors included three members of the Verdin family, four members of management, and five outside directors who were prominent managers or public figures in northern Europe. Members of the Verdin family combined owned 20 percent of Pan-Europa's shares outstanding, and company executives combined owned 10 percent of the shares. Venus Asset Management, a mutual-fund management company in London, held 12 percent. Banque du Bruges et des Pays Bas held 9 percent and had one representative on the board of directors. The remaining 49 percent of the firm's shares were widely held. The firm's shares traded in London, Brussels, and Frankfurt.

At a debt-to-equity ratio of 125 percent, Pan-Europa was leveraged much more highly than its peers in the European consumer-foods industry. Management had relied on debt financing significantly in the past few years to sustain the firm's capital spending and dividends during a period of price wars initiated by Pan-Europa. Now, with the price wars finished, Pan-Europa's bankers (led by Banque du Bruges) strongly urged an aggressive program of debt reduction. In any event, they were not prepared to finance increases in leverage beyond the current level. The president of Banque du Bruges had remarked at a recent board meeting,

> Restoring some strength to the right-hand side of the balance sheet should now be a first priority. Any expansion of assets should be financed from the cash flow after debt amortization until the debt ratio returns to a more prudent level. If there are crucial investments that cannot be funded this way, then we should cut the dividend!

At a price-to-earnings ratio of eight times, shares of Pan-Europa common stock were priced below the average multiples of peer companies and the average multiples of all companies on the exchanges where Pan-Europa was traded. This was attributable to the recent price wars, which had suppressed the company's profitability, and to the well-known recent failure of the company to seize significant market share with a new product line of flavored mineral water. Since January 1992, all of the major securities houses had been issuing "sell" recommendations to investors in Pan-Europa shares. Venus Asset Management in London had quietly accumulated shares during this period, however, in the expectation of a turnaround in the firm's performance. At the most recent board meeting, the senior managing director of Venus gave a presentation in which he said,

> Cutting the dividend is unthinkable, as it would signal a lack of faith in your own future. Selling new shares of stock at this depressed price level is also unthinkable, as it would impose unacceptable dilution on your current shareholders. Your equity investors expect an improvement in performance. If that improvement is not forthcoming, or worse, if investors' hopes are dashed, your shares might fall into the hands of raiders like Carlo de Benedetti or the Flick brothers.[1]

At the conclusion of the most recent meeting of the directors, the board voted unanimously to limit capital spending in 1993 to ECU80 million.

---

[1]De Benedetti of Milan and the Flick brothers of Munich were leaders of prominent hostile-takeover attempts in recent years.

MEMBERS OF THE SENIOR MANAGEMENT COMMITTEE

The capital budget would be prepared by seven senior managers of Pan-Europa. For consideration, each project had to be sponsored by one of the managers present. Usually the decision process included a period of discussion followed by a vote on two to four alternative capital budgets. The various executives were well known to each other:

Wilhelmina Verdin (Belgian), PDG, age 57. Granddaughter of the founder and spokesperson on the board of directors for the Verdin family's interests. Worked for the company her entire career, with significant experience in brand management. Elected "European Marketer of the Year" in 1982 for successfully introducing low-fat yogurt and ice cream, the first major rollout of this type of product. Eager to position the company for long-term growth, but cautious in the wake of recent difficulties.

Trudi Lauf (Swiss), finance director, age 51. Hired from Nestlé in 1982 to modernize financial controls and systems. Had been a vocal proponent of reducing leverage on the balance sheet. Also had voiced the concerns and frustrations of stockholders.

Heinz Klink (German), managing director for distribution, age 49. Oversaw the transportation, warehousing, and order-fulfillment activities in the company. Spoilage, transport costs, stock-outs, and control systems were perennial challenges.

Maarten Leyden (Dutch), managing director for production and purchasing, age 59. Managed production operations at the company's 14 plants. Engineer by training. Tough negotiator, especially with unions and suppliers. A fanatic about production-cost control. Had voiced doubts about the sincerity of creditors' and investors' commitment to the firm.

Marco Ponti (Italian), managing director for sales, age 45. Oversaw the field sales force of 250 representatives and planned changes in geographical sales coverage. The most vocal proponent of rapid expansion on the senior-management committee. Saw several opportunities for ways to improve geographical positioning. Hired from Unilever in 1985 to revitalize the sales organization, which he successfully accomplished.

Fabienne Morin (French), managing director for marketing, age 41. Responsible for marketing research, new-product development, advertising, and, in general, brand management. The primary advocate of the recent price war, which, although financially difficult, realized solid gains in market share. Perceived a "window of opportunity" for product and market expansion and tended to support growth-oriented projects.

Nigel Humbolt (British), managing director for Strategic Planning, age 47. Hired two years previously from a well-known consulting firm to set up a strategic-planning staff for Pan-Europa. Known for asking difficult and challenging questions about Pan-Europa's core business, its maturity, and profitability. Supported initiatives aimed at growth and market share. Had presented the most aggressive proposals in 1992, none of which were accepted. Becoming frustrated with what he perceived to be his lack of influence in the organization.

THE EXPENDITURE PROPOSALS

The forthcoming meeting would entertain the following proposals:

Project	Expenditure (ECU millions)	Sponsoring Manager
1. Replacement and expansion of the truck fleet	22	Klink, Distribution
2. A new plant	30	Leyden, Production
3. Expansion of a plant	10	Leyden, Production
4. Development and introduction of new artificially sweetened yogurt and ice cream	15	Morin, Marketing
5. Plant automation and conveyer systems	14	Leyden, Production
6. Effluent water treatment at four plants	4	Leyden, Production
7. Market expansion eastward	20	Ponti, Sales
8. Market expansion southward	20	Ponti, Sales
9. Development and rollout of snack foods	18	Morin, Marketing
10. Networked, computer-based inventory-control system for warehouses and field representatives	15	Klink, Distribution
11. Acquisition of a leading schnapps brand and associated facilities	40	Humbolt, Strategic Planning

1. *Replacement and expansion of the truck fleet.* Heinz Klink proposed to purchase 100 new refrigerated tractor-trailer trucks, 50 each in 1993 and 1994. By doing so, the company could sell 60 old, fully depreciated trucks over the two years for a total of ECU1.2 million. The purchase would expand the fleet by 40 trucks within two years. Each of the new trailers would be larger than the old trailers and afford a 15 percent increase in cubic meters of goods hauled on each trip. The new tractors would also be more fuel and maintenance efficient. The increase in number of trucks would permit more flexible scheduling and more efficient routing and servicing of the fleet than at present and would cut delivery times and therefore possibly inventories. It would also allow more frequent deliveries to the company's major markets, which would reduce the loss of sales caused by stockouts. Finally, expanding the fleet would support geographical expansion over the long term.

As shown in Exhibit 3, the total net investment in trucks of ECU20 million and the increase in working capital to support added maintenance, fuel, payroll, and inventories of ECU2 million was expected to yield total cost savings and added sales potential of ECU7.7 million over the next seven years. The resulting IRR was estimated to be 7.8 percent, marginally below the minimum 8 percent required return on efficiency projects. Some of the managers wondered if this project would be more properly classified as "efficiency" than "expansion."

2. *A new plant.* Maarten Leyden noted that Pan-Europa's yogurt and ice-cream sales in the southeastern region of the company's market were about to exceed the capacity of its Melun, France, manufacturing and packaging plant. At present, some of the demand was being met by shipments from the company's newest, most efficient facility, located in Strasbourg, France. Shipping costs over that distance were high, however, and some sales were undoubtedly being lost when the marketing effort could not be supported by delivery. Leyden proposed that a new manufacturing and packaging plant be built in Dijon, France, just at the current southern edge of Pan-Europa's marketing region, to take the burden off the Melun and Strasbourg plants.

The cost of this plant would be ECU25 million and would entail ECU5 million for working capital. The ECU14 million worth of equipment would be amortized over 7 years, and the plant over 10 years. Through an increase in sales and depreciation, and the decrease in delivery costs, the plant was expected to yield after-tax cash flows totaling ECU23.75 million and an IRR of 11.3 percent over the next 10 years. This project would be classified as a market extension.

3. *Expansion of a plant.* In addition to the need for greater production capacity in Pan-Europa's southeastern region, its Nuremberg, Germany, plant had reached full capacity. This situation made the scheduling of routine equipment maintenance difficult, which in turn created production-scheduling and deadline problems. This plant was one of two highly automated facilities that produced Pan-Europa's entire line of bottled water, mineral water, and fruit juices. The Nuremberg plant supplied central and western Europe. (The other plant, near Copenhagen, Denmark, supplied Pan-Europa's northern European markets.)

The Nuremberg plant's capacity could be expanded by 20 percent for ECU10 million. The equipment (ECU7 million) would be depreciated over 7 years, and the plant over 10 years. The increased capacity was expected to result in additional production of up to ECU1.5 million per year, yielding an IRR of 11.2 percent. This project would be classified as a market extension.

4. *Development and introduction of new artificially sweetened yogurt and ice cream.* Fabienne Morin noted that recent developments in the synthesis of artificial sweeteners were showing promise of significant cost savings to food and beverage producers as well as stimulating growing demand for low-calorie products. The challenge was to create the right flavor to complement or enhance the other ingredients. For ice-cream manufacturers, the difficulty lay in creating a balance that would result in the same flavor as was obtained when using natural sweeteners; artificial sweeteners might, of course, create a superior taste.

ECU15 million would be needed to commercialize a yogurt line that had received promising results in laboratory tests. This cost included acquiring specialized production facilities, working capital, and the cost of the initial product introduction. The overall IRR was estimated to be 17.3 percent.

Morin stressed that the proposal, although highly uncertain in terms of actual results, could be viewed as a means of protecting present market share, because other high-quality ice-cream producers carrying out the same research might introduce these products; if the Rolly brand did not carry an artificially sweetened line and its competitors did, the Rolly brand might suffer. Morin also noted the parallels between innovating with artificial sweeteners and the company's past success in introducing low-fat products. This project would be classed in the new-product category of investments.

5. *Plant automation and conveyer systems.* Maarten Leyden also requested ECU14 million to increase automation of the production lines at six of the company's older plants. The result would be improved throughput speed and reduced accidents, spillage, and production tie-ups. The last two plants the company had built included conveyer systems that eliminated the need for any heavy lifting by employees. The systems reduced the chance of injury by employees; at the six older plants, the company had sustained an average of 75 missed worker-days per year per plant in the last two years because of muscle injuries sustained in heavy lifting. At an average hourly wage of ECU14.00 per hour, over ECU150,000 per year was thus lost, and the possibility always existed of more serious injuries and lawsuits. Overall cost savings and depreciation totaling ECU2.75 million per year for the project were expected to yield an IRR of 8.7 percent. This project would be classed in the efficiency category.

6. *Effluent water treatment at four plants.* Pan-Europa preprocessed a variety of fresh fruits at its Melun and Strasbourg plants. One of the first stages of processing involved cleaning the fruit to remove dirt and pesticides. The dirty water was simply sent down the drain and into the Seine or Rhine rivers. Recent European Community directives called for any waste water containing even slight traces of poisonous chemicals to be treated at the sources and gave companies four years to comply. As an environmentally oriented project, this proposal fell outside the normal financial tests of project attractiveness. Leyden noted, however, that the water-treatment equipment could be purchased today for ECU4 million; he speculated that the same equipment would cost ECU10 million in four years when immediate conversion became mandatory. In the intervening time, the company would run the risks that European Community regulators would shorten the compliance time or that the company's pollution record would become public and impair the image of the company in the eyes of the consumer. This project would be classed in the environmental category.

7 and **8.** *Market expansions eastward and southward.* Marco Ponti recommended that the company expand its market eastward to include eastern Germany, Poland, Czechoslovakia, and Austria and/or southward to include southern France, Switzerland, Italy, and Spain. He believed the time was right to expand sales of ice cream, and perhaps yogurt, geographically. In theory, the company could sustain expansions in both directions simultaneously, but practically Ponti doubted that the sales and distribution organizations could sustain both expansions at once.

Each alternative geographical expansion had its benefits and risks. If the company expanded eastward, it could reach a large population with a great appetite for frozen dairy products, but it would also face more competition from local and regional ice-cream manufacturers. Moreover, consumers in eastern Germany, Poland, and Czechoslovakia did not have the purchasing power that consumers did to the south. The eastward expansion would have to be supplied from plants in Nuremberg, Strasbourg, and Hamburg.

Looking southward, the tables were turned: more purchasing power and less competition but also a smaller consumer appetite for ice cream and yogurt. A southward expansion would require building consumer demand for premium-quality yogurt and ice cream. If neither of the plant proposals (i.e., proposals 2 and 3) were accepted, then the southward expansion would need to be supplied from plants in Melun, Strasbourg, and Rouen.

The initial cost of either proposal was ECU20 million of working capital. The bulk of this project's costs was expected to involve the financing of distributorships, but over the 10-year forecast period, the distributors would gradually take over the burden of carrying receivables and inventory. Both expansion proposals assumed the rental of suitable warehouse and distribution facilities. The after-tax cash flows were expected to total ECU37.5 million for eastward expansion and ECU32.5 million for southward expansion.

Marco Ponti pointed out that eastward expansion meant a higher possible IRR but that moving southward was a less risky proposition. The projected IRRs were 21.4 percent and 18.8 percent for eastern and southern expansion, respectively. These projects would be classed in the market-extension category.

9. *Development and rollout of snack foods.* Fabienne Morin suggested that the company use the excess capacity at its Antwerp spice- and nut-processing facility to produce a line of dried fruits to be test-marketed in Belgium, Britain, and the Netherlands. She noted the strength of the Rolly brand in those countries and the success of other food and beverage companies that had expanded into snack-food production. She argued that Pan-Europa's reputation for wholesome, quality products would be enhanced by a line of dried fruits and that name association with the new product would probably even lead to increased sales of the company's other products among health-conscious consumers.

Equipment and working-capital investments were expected to total ECU15 million and ECU3 million, respectively, for this project. The equipment would be depreciated over seven years. Assuming the test market was successful, cash flows from the project would be able to support further plant expansions in other strategic locations. The IRR was expected to be 20.5 percent, well above the required return of 12 percent for new-product projects.

10. *Networked, computer-based inventory-control system for warehouses and field representatives.* Heinz Klink had pressed for three years unsuccessfully for a state-of-the-art computer-based inventory-control system that would link field sales representatives, distributors, drivers, warehouses, and even possibly retailers. The benefits of such a system would be shortening delays in ordering and order processing, better control of inventory, reduction of spoilage, and faster recognition of changes in demand at the customer level. Klink was reluctant to quantify these benefits, because they could range between modest and quite large amounts. This year, for the first time, he presented a cash-flow forecast, however, that reflected an initial outlay of ECU12 million for the system, followed by ECU3 million in the next year for ancillary equipment. The inflows reflected depreciation tax shields, tax credits, cost reductions in warehousing, and reduced inventory. He forecasted these benefits to last for only three years. Even so, the project's IRR was estimated to be 16.2 percent. This project would be classed in the efficiency category of proposals.

11. *Acquisition of a leading schnapps brand and associated facilities.* Nigel Humbolt had advocated making diversifying acquisitions in an effort to move beyond the company's mature core business but doing so in a way that exploited the company's skills in brand management. He had explored six possible related industries, in the general field of consumer packaged goods, and determined that cordials and liqueurs offered unusual opportunities for real growth and, at the same time, market protection through branding. He had identified four small producers of well-established brands of liqueurs as acquisition candidates. Following exploratory talks with each, he had determined that only one company could be purchased in the near future, namely, the leading private European manufacturer of schnapps, located in Munich.

The proposal was expensive: ECU15 million to buy the company and ECU25 million to renovate the company's facilities completely while simultaneously expanding distribution to new geographical markets.[2] The expected returns were high: After-tax cash flows were projected to be ECU134 million, yielding an IRR of 28.7 percent. This project would be classed in the new-product category of proposals.

CONCLUSION

Each member of the management committee was expected to come to the meeting prepared to present and defend a proposal for the allocation of Pan-Europa's capital budget of ECU80 million. Exhibit 3 summarizes the various projects in terms of their free cash flows and the investment-performance criteria.

---

[2]Exhibit 3 shows negative cash flows amounting to only ECU35 million. The difference between this amount and the ECU40 million requested is a positive operating cash flow of ECU5 million in year 1 expected from the normal course of business.

EXHIBIT 1   Nations Where Pan-Europa Competed

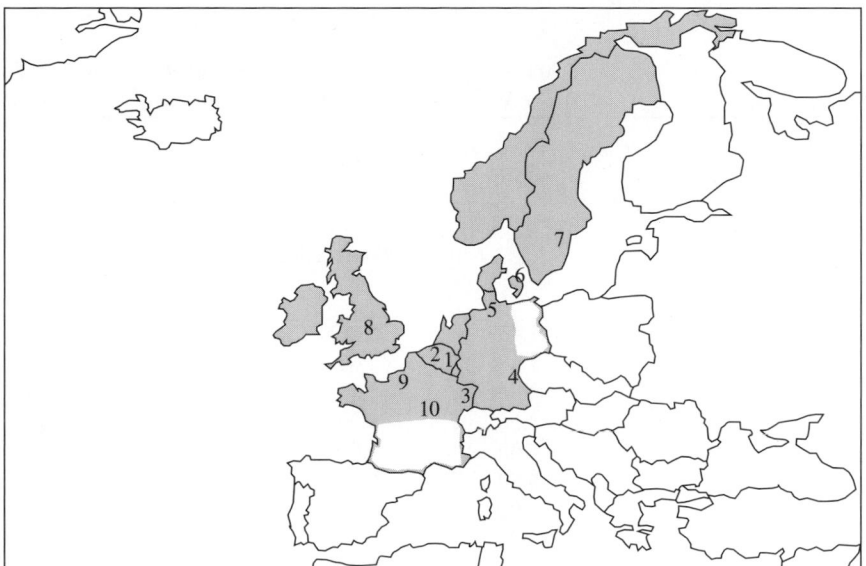

Note: The shaded area in this map reveals the principal distribution region of Pan-Europa's products.
Important facilities are indicated by the following figures:

1	Headquarters, Brussels, Belgium
2	Plant, Antwerp, Belgium
3	Plant, Strasbourg, France
4	Plant, Nuremberg, Germany
5	Plant, Hamburg, Germany
6	Plant, Copenhagen, Denmark
7	Plant, Svald, Sweden
8	Plant, Nelly-on-Mersey, England
9	Plant, Caen, France
10	Plant, Melun, France

EXHIBIT 2   Summary of Financial Results (all values in ECU millions except
per share amounts)

	Fiscal Year Ending December 31		
	1990	*1991*	*1992*
Gross sales	1,076	1,072	1,074
Net income	51	49	37
Earnings per share	0.75	0.72	0.54
Dividends	20	20	20
Total assets	477	580	656
Shareholders' equity (book value)	182	206	235
Shareholders' equity (market value)	453	400	229

EXHIBIT 3   Free Cash Flows and Analysis of Proposed Projects[a] (all values in ECU millions)

	1	*2*	*3*	*4*	*5*
					Automation
	Expand		*Expanded*	*Artificial*	*and Conveyer*
	Truck Fleet[c]	*New Plant*	*Plant*	*Sweetener*	*Systems*
Investment					
Property	20.00	25.00	10.00	15.00	14.00
Working capital	2.00	5.00			

Expected Free Cash Flows[d]

Year					
0	(11.40)	(30.00)	(10.00)	(5.00)	(14.00)
1	(7.90)	2.00	1.25	(5.00)	2.75
2	3.00	5.00	1.50	(5.00)	2.75
3	3.50	5.50	1.75	3.00	2.75
4	4.00	6.00	2.00	3.00	2.75
5	4.50	6.25	2.25	4.00	2.75
6	5.00	6.50	2.50	4.50	2.75
7	7.00	6.75	1.50	5.00	2.75
8		5.00	1.50	5.50	
9		5.25	1.50	6.00	
10		5.50	1.50	6.50	
Undiscounted sum	7.70	23.75	7.25	22.50	5.25
Payback (years)	6	6	6	7	6
Maximum payback accepted	4	5	5	6	4
Internal rate of return	7.8%	11.3%	11.2%	17.3%	8.7%
Minimum accepted rate of return	8.0%	10.0%	10.0%	12.0%	8.0%
Spread	−0.2%	1.3%	1.2%	5.3%	0.7%
NPV at corp. WACC (10.6%)	−1.92	0.99	0.28	5.21	−0.87
NPV at minimum rate of return	−0.13	1.87	0.55	3.88	0.32
Equivalent annuity[b]	−0.02	0.30	0.09	0.69	0.06

[a]The effluent treatment program is not included in this exhibit.
[b]The equivalent annuity of a project is that level annual payment over 10 years that yields a net present value equal to the NPV at the minimum required rate of return for that project. Annuity corrects for differences in duration among various projects. For instance, project 5 lasts only 7 years and has an NPV of 0.32 million; a 10-year stream of annual cash flows of 0.05 million, discounted at 8.0 percent (the required rate of return) also yields an NPV of 0.32 million. In ranking projects on the basis of equivalent annuity, bigger annuities create more investor wealth than smaller annuities.
[c]This reflects ECU11 million spent both initially and at the end of year 1.
[d]Free cash flow = Incremental profit or cost savings after taxes + Depreciation − Investment in fixed assets and working capital.
[e]Franchisees would gradually take over the burden of carrying receivables and inventory.
[f]ECU15 million would be spent in the first year, 20 million in the second, and 5 million in the third.

6	7	8	9	10
			Inventory-Control	*Strategic*
Eastward Expansion[e]	*Southward Expansion*[e]	*Snack Foods*	*System*	*Acquisition*[f]
		15.00	15.00	30.00
20.00	20.00	3.00		10.00

Expected Free Cash Flows

(20.00)	(20.00)	(18.00)	(12.00)	(15.00)
3.50	3.00	3.00	5.50	(20.00)
4.00	3.50	4.00	5.50	5.00
4.50	4.00	4.50	5.00	9.00
5.00	4.50	5.00		11.00
5.50	5.00	5.00		13.00
6.00	5.50	5.00		15.00
6.50	6.00	5.00		17.00
7.00	6.50	5.00		19.00
7.50	7.00	5.00		21.00
8.00	7.50	5.00		59.00
37.50	32.50	28.50	4.00	134.00
5	6	5	3	5
6	6	6	4	6
21.4%	18.8%	20.5%	16.2%	28.7%
12.0%	12.0%	12.0%	8.0%	12.0%
9.4%	6.8%	8.5%	8.2%	16.7%
11.99	9.00	8.95	1.16	47.97
9.90	7.08	7.31	1.78	41.43
1.75	1.25	1.29	0.69	7.33

Astral Records Ltd., North America: Some Financial Concerns

On August 24, 1993, her first day as chief executive officer (CEO) of Astral Records Ltd., North America (Astral NA), Sarah Conner confronted a host of management problems at the company. One week earlier, Astral NA's president and CEO had been killed in a tragic accident. Soon thereafter, Sarah was appointed to fill the position—starting immediately. Several issues in her in-box that first day were financial in nature, either requiring a financial decision, or with outcomes that would have major financial implications for the firm. That evening, Conner asked to meet with her assistant, Louis Tang, to begin addressing the most prominent issues.

ASTRAL RECORDS AND THE COMPACT-DISC MANUFACTURING INDUSTRY

Astral Records North America had been founded as a joint venture between Astral Records Ltd., U.K., and an American venture-capital firm, Bendini, Lambert and Locke (BLL). Astral NA's sole business mission was to manufacture compact discs mainly as a subcontractor to major recording companies. Astral NA was known for producing the highest-quality compact discs in the industry.

_____

This case was prepared by Robert Bruner, Robert Conroy, and Kenneth Eades. The firms and individuals in this case are fictional. This case was written as a basis for class discussion rather than to illustrate effective or ineffective handling of an administrative situation. Copyright © 1993 by the University of Virginia Darden School Foundation, Charlottesville, VA. All rights reserved. *No part of this publication may be reproduced, stored in a retrieval system, used in a spreadsheet, or transmitted in any form or by any means—electronic, mechanical, photocopying, recording, or otherwise—without the permission of the Darden Foundation. For inquiries, please send an e-mail to dardencases@virginia.edu.* Revised 2/98. Version 1.5.

Compact discs were first mass-produced in 1980. By 1993, the manufacturing technology was fairly mature. Accordingly, small manufacturers had proliferated in the industry, exploiting the low entry barriers: A new, small plant would cost between $8 million and $10 million. Easy entry had led to price competition in recent years among disc replicators. One analyst said,

> The gross margins on CDs have eroded tremendously over the past five years. I don't see there's any more maneuvering left on the price.

FINANCIAL QUESTIONS FACING SARAH CONNER

That evening, Conner met with Louis Tang, a promising new associate whom she had brought along from BLL. Sarah's brief discussion with Louis went as follows:

Sarah

Back at BLL we looked at Astral as one of our most promising venture-capital investments. Now it seems that such optimism may not be warranted—at least until we get a solid understanding of the firm's past performance and its forecasted performance. Did you have any success on this?

Louis

Yes, the bookkeeper gave me these: the historical-income statements [Exhibit 1] and balance sheets [Exhibit 2] for the last four years. The accounting system here is still pretty primitive. However, I checked a number of the accounts, and they look orderly. So I suspect that we can work with these figures. From these statements, I calculated a set of diagnostic ratios [Exhibit 3].

Sarah

I see you have been busy. Unfortunately, I can't study these right now. I need you to review the historical performance of Astral NA for me, and to give me any positive or negative insights that you think are significant.

Louis

When do you need this?

Sarah

At 7:00 A.M. tomorrow. I want to call on our banker tomorrow morning and get an extension on Astral's loan.

Louis

The banker, Mr. Farmington, said that Astral was "growing beyond its financial capabilities." What does that mean?

Sarah

It probably means that he doesn't think we can repay the loan within a reasonable period. I would like you to build a simple financial forecast of our performance for the next two years (ignore seasonal effects) and show me what our debt requirements will be at the fiscal years ended 1994 and 1995. I think it is reasonable to expect that Astral's sales will grow at 15 percent each year. Use whatever assumptions seem appropriate to you based on your historical analysis of results. For this forecast, you should assume that any external funding is in the form of debt.

Louis

But what if the forecasts show that Astral cannot repay the loan?

Sarah

Then we'll have to go back to Astral NA's owners, BLL and Astral Records U.K.,[1] for an injection of equity. Of course, BLL would rather not invest more funds unless we can show that the returns on such an investment would be very attractive, and/or that the survival of the company depends on it. Thus, my third request is for you to examine what returns on book assets and book equity Astral NA will offer in the next two years and to identify the "key driver" assumptions of those returns. Finally, let me have your recommendations about operating and financial changes I should make based on the historical analysis and the forecasts.

Louis

The plant manager revised his request for a new packaging machine and thinks these are the right numbers [see the plant manager's memorandum in Exhibit 4]. Essentially, the issue is whether to invest now or wait three years to buy the new packaging equipment. The new equipment can save significantly on labor cost but carries a price tag of $1 million. My hunch is that our preference between investing now versus waiting three years will hinge on the discount rate.

Sarah

[laughing] The joke in business school was that the discount rate was always 10 percent.

Louis

That's not what my business school taught me! BLL always uses a 40 percent discount rate to value equity investments in risky start-up companies. But Astral is reasonably well established now and shouldn't require such a high-risk premium. I managed to pull together some data [see Exhibit 5] on comparable companies with which to estimate the required rate of return on equity.

Sarah

Fine. Please estimate Astral's weighted-average cost of capital and assess the packaging-machine investment. I would like the results of your analysis tomorrow morning at 7:00 A.M.

---

[1]Benedini, Lambert and Locke owned a 60 percent interest in the equity of Astral NA. Astral Records Ltd., U.K., owned the remaining 40 percent interest.

EXHIBIT 1   Historical Income Statements (fiscal year ended August 23; all figures in thousands of dollars)

	1990 (Actual)	1991 (Actual)	1992 (Actual)	1993 (Actual)
1. Sales	$26,202	$28,822	$34,010	$39,792
Operating expenses:				
2. Production costs and expenses	11,950	13,380	17,847	22,335
3. Administrative and selling expenses	5,734	5,967	7,020	7,970
4. Depreciation	2,376	2,367	2,667	2,667
5. Total operating expenses	(20,060)	(21,714)	(27,534)	(32,972)
6. Operating margin	6,142	7,109	6,476	6,820
7. Interest expense	(2,427)	(2,535)	(3,265)	(3,222)
8. Earnings before taxes	3,715	4,574	3,212	3,598
9. Income taxes	(1,647)	(1,845)	(1,269)	(1,403)
10. Net earnings	2,068	2,729	1,943	2,195
11. Dividends to all common shares	1,000	1,000	1,000	1,000
12. Retentions of earnings	$ 1,068	$ 1,729	$ 943	$ 1,195

EXHIBIT 2   Historical Balance Sheets (fiscal year ended August 23; all figures in thousands of dollars)

	1990 (Actual)	1991 (Actual)	1992 (Actual)	1993 (Actual)
Assets:				
1. Cash	$ 1,764	$ 2,040	$ 2,905	$ 1,540
2. Accounts receivable	8,113	9,125	10,311	13,316
3. Inventories	15,861	17,147	25,643	34,717
4. Total current assets	25,738	28,312	38,859	49,573
5. Gross property, plant, and equipment	23,667	26,667	26,667	26,667
6. Accumulated depreciation	(2,505)	(4,872)	(7,538)	(10,205)
7. Net property, plant, and equipment	21,162	21,795	19,129	16,462
8. Total assets	46,900	50,107	57,988	66,035
Liabilities and stockholders' equity:				
9. Short-term borrowings (bank)*	12,060	13,042	19,680	25,802
10. Accounts payable	4,511	4,607	4,705	5,328
11. Other current liabilities	9,014	9,414	9,616	9,723
12. Total current liabilities	25,585	27,063	34,001	40,853
13. Long-term debt†	10,000	10,000	10,000	10,000
14. Shareholders' equity	11,315	13,044	13,987	15,182
15. Total liabilities and stockholders' equity	$46,900	$50,107	$57,988	$66,035

*Short-term debt was borrowed from Yurbank at an interest rate equal to LIBOR + 1 percent. LIBOR (London Interbank Offered Rate) was a common benchmark for expressing the floating rate of interest on bank loans.
†The company's long-term debt of $10 million had been issued privately in 1989 to Bendini, Lambert and Locke and to Astral Records Ltd., U.K. This debt was subordinate to any bank debt outstanding.

EXHIBIT 3 Ratio Analyses of Historical Financial Statements (fiscal year ended August 23)

	1990 (Actual)	1991 (Actual)	1992 (Actual)	1993 (Actual)
Profitability:				
1. Operating profit margin	23.4%	24.7%	19.0%	17.1%
2. Average tax rate	44.3%	40.3%	39.5%	39.0%
3. Return on sales	7.9%	9.5%	5.7%	5.5%
4. Return on equity	18.3%	20.9%	13.9%	14.5%
5. Return on assets	4.4%	5.4%	3.4%	3.3%
Leverage:				
6. Debt/Equity	1.95	1.77	2.12	2.36
7. Debt/Total assets	0.47	0.46	0.51	0.54
8. EBIT/Interest ($\times$)	2.53	2.80	1.98	2.12
Asset utilization:				
9. Sales/Assets	55.9%	57.5%	58.7%	60.3%
10. Sales growth rate	4.0%	10.0%	18.0%	17.0%
11. Assets growth rate	6.0%	6.8%	15.7%	13.9%
12. Days in receivables	113.0	115.6	110.7	122.1
13. Payables to COGS	17.2%	16.0%	13.8%	13.4%
14. Inventories to COGS	60.5%	59.5%	75.4%	87.2%
Liquidity:				
15. Current ratio	1.01	1.05	1.14	1.21
16. Quick ratio	0.39	0.41	0.39	0.36

EXHIBIT 4   O'Rourke's Memo Re: New Packaging Equipment

MEMORANDUM

TO:	Sarah Conner, President and CEO, Astral Records
FROM:	Harvey O'Rourke, Plant Manager
DATE:	August 24, 1993
SUBJECT:	New Packaging Equipment

Although our CD packaging equipment is adequate at current production levels, it is terribly inefficient. The new machinery on the market can give us significant labor savings as well as increased flexibility with respect to the type of packaging used. I recommend that we go with the new technology. The considerations relevant to the decision are included in this memo.

Our current packaging equipment was purchased five years ago as used equipment in a liquidation sale of a small company. Although the equipment was inexpensive, it is slow, requires constant monitoring, and is frequently shut down for repairs. Since the packaging equipment is significantly slower than the production equipment, we routinely have to use overtime labor to allow packaging to catch up with production. When the packager is down for repairs, the problem is exacerbated and we may spend several two-shift days catching up with production. I cannot say that we have missed any deadlines because of packaging problems, but it is a constant concern around here and things would run a lot smoother with more reliable equipment. In 1994 we will pay about $5,000 per year for maintenance costs. The operator is paid $30,000 per year for his regular time, but he has been averaging $40,000 per year because of the overtime he has been working. The equipment is on the tax and reporting books at $100,000 and will be fully depreciated in three years time (we are currently using the straight-line depreciation method for both tax and reporting purposes and will continue to do so). Because of changes in packaging technology, the equipment has no market value other than its worth as scrap metal. But its scrap value is about equal to the cost of having it removed. In short, we believe the equipment has no salvage value at all.

The new packager offers many advantages over the current equipment. It is faster, more reliable, more flexible with respect to the types of packaging it can perform, and will provide enough capacity to cover all our packaging needs in the foreseeable future. With suitable maintenance, we believe the packager will operate indefinitely. Thus, for the purposes of our analysis, we can assume that this will be the last packaging equipment we will ever have to purchase. Because of the anticipated growth at Astral, the current equipment will not be able to handle our packaging needs by the end of 1996. Thus, if we do not buy new packaging equipment by this year's end, we will have to buy it after three years time anyway. Since the speed, capacity, and reliability of the new equipment will eliminate the need for overtime labor, we feel strongly that we should buy now rather than wait another three years.

The new equipment currently costs $1 million, which we would depreciate over 10 years at $100,000 per year. It comes with a lifetime factory maintenance contract that covers all routine maintenance and repairs at a price of $2,000 for the initial year. The contract stipulates that the price after the first year will be increased by the same percentage as the rate of increase of the price of new equipment. Thus, if the manufacturer continues to increase the price of new packaging equipment at 5 percent per annum as it has in the past, our maintenance costs will rise by 5 percent also. We believe that this sort of regular maintenance should ensure that the new equipment will keep operating in the foreseeable future without the need for a major overhaul.

Astral's labor and maintenance costs will continue to rise due to inflation at approximately 5 percent per year over the long term. Because the manufacturer of the packaging equipment has been increasing its prices at about 5 percent per year, we can expect to save $157,625 in the purchase price by buying now rather than waiting three years. The marginal tax rate for this investment would be 40 percent.

EXHIBIT 5 Data on Comparable Companies and Capital-Market Conditions

Name	Percent of Sales from CD Production	Price/ Earnings Ratio	Beta	Book D/E	Book Value per Share	Market Price per Share	Number of Shares Outstanding (Millions)	Last Annual Dividend per Share	Analysts' (5)-Year Earnings Growth Forecast (%)	Bond Rating
Dickenson, Inc.	20%	9	1.50	.45	$ 5.50	$10.00	5.0	$0.95	4	A
Harris-Beshel	95%	8	1.30	.70	12.75	14.00	7.5	1.00	6	AA
Donaldson, Inc.	90%	12	1.20	1.40	5.25	18.00	10.0	.75	8	AA
IBBEX Corp.	40%	16	1.45	.10	16.80	20.00	15.0	0.00	10	Baa
ZEPORT	60%	10	1.60	1.30	25.00	40.00	10.0	2.20	7	B

Recently Issued Bonds (as of 8/24/93)

Name		Coupon	Maturity	Price	Rating
Dickenson, Inc.		7.2%	1998	102.95	A
Harris-Beshel		7.0%	2013	100.00	AA
Donaldson, Inc.		8.0%	2008	109.20	AA
IBBEX Corp.		8.0%	2003	100.00	Baa
ZEPORT		9.0%	2008	100.00	B

LIBOR		5.0%
U.S. Treasury Bills	3-month	2.8%
U.S. Treasury Bills	1-year	3.0%
U.S. Treasury Bills	3-year	4.6%
U.S. Treasury Bills	5-year	5.1%
U.S. Treasury Bonds	10-year	6.0%
U.S. Treasury Bonds	30-year	6.2%

EXHIBIT 5 (*concluded*)

Description of Companies

Dickenson, Inc.

This company was founded 50 years ago in Detroit. Its major business activities historically have been production of original artist recordings, management and production of rock-and-roll road tours, and personal management of artists. It only recently has entered the CD production market.

Harris-Beshel

This company was a spin-off from a large conglomerate in 1978. Although the company was a leader in the production of CDs, it has recently suffered a decline in sales. Infighting among the principal owners has fed concerns about the firm's prospects.

Donaldson, Inc.

This company, founded only two years ago, has emerged as a very aggressive competitor in the area of CD production. It is Astral's major competitor and its sales level is about the same.

IBBEX Corp.

This company has recently been an innovator in the production of CDs. Although CD manufacturing is not a majority of its business (film production is its main focus), the company is projected to be a major competitor within the next three years.

ZEPORT

This company was an early pioneer in the CD industry. Recently, however, it began to invest in new areas and has been moving away from CD production as its main focus of business.

Source: Casewriters' estimates.

Part V

Management of Shareholders' Equity

Northboro Machine Tools Corporation

Does it matter whether we pay a high or low dividend—or no dividend at all? To whom? And why? Our board is hearing some conflicting claims about dividend policy. I need to resolve this and recommend a dividend decision to the board for the third quarter of 1992.

With these words, Christine Olsen, the chief financial officer of Northboro Machine Tools Corporation, explained that she had become the judge in a debate over dividend policy within the company. After years of traditionally strong earnings and predictable dividend growth, the company had faltered in the late 1980s. In response, management implemented two extensive restructuring programs, both of which were accompanied by net losses. For three years in a row, dividends had exceeded earnings. Then, in 1990, dividends were decreased to a level below earnings. Despite extraordinary losses in 1991, the board of directors had declared a small dividend. For the first two quarters of 1992, the board had declared no dividend. But in a special letter to shareholders the board had committed itself to resuming the dividend as early as possible—ideally, in 1992. Now, in the summer of 1992, Olsen had to recommend to the board a dividend policy for implementation in the quarter ending September 30.

As a related matter, senior management was considering embarking on a campaign of corporate-image advertising along with changing the name of the corporation to Northboro Advanced Systems International, Inc. Management felt that this would help improve the perception of the company in the investment community. Olsen needed to recommend action to the board on this proposal.

This case is dedicated to Professors Robert F. Vandell and Pearson Hunt, the authors of an antecedent case, long out of print, that provided the model of the economic problem for this case. Northboro is a fictional firm, though it draws on facts of contemporary companies. Copyright © 1997 by the University of Virginia Darden School Foundation, Charlottesville, VA. All rights reserved. *No part of this publication may be reproduced, stored in a retrieval system, used in a spreadsheet, or transmitted in any form or by any means—electronic, mechanical, photocopying, recording, or otherwise—without the permission of the Darden Foundation. For inquiries, please send an e-mail to dardencases@ virginia.edu.* Rev. 12/97. Version 1.0.

Overall, management's view was that Northboro was a resurgent company that demonstrated great potential for growth and profitability. The restructurings had revitalized the company's operating divisions, and a new product promised to make its predecessors' and competitors' products obsolete. Many within the company viewed 1992 as the dawning of a new era that in spite of the company's recent performance would turn Northboro into a growth stock. The company had no Moody's or Standard & Poor's rating because it had no bonds outstanding, but Value Line rated it an "A" company.[1]

Out of this combination of a troubled past and a bright future arose Olsen's dilemma. Did the market view Northboro as a loser, as a blue-chip stock, or as a potential growth stock? How, if at all, could Northboro affect that perception? Would a change of name help frame investors' views of the firm? Did the company's investors expect capital growth or steady dividends? And, if those questions could be answered, what were the implications for Northboro's future dividend policy?

THE COMPANY

Northboro Corporation was founded in 1923 in Concord, New Hampshire, by two mechanical engineers, James North and David Peterboro. The two men had gone to school together and were disenchanted with their positions and prospects as mechanics at a farm-equipment manufacturer.

In its early years, Northboro had designed and manufactured a number of machinery parts, including metal presses, dies, and molds. In the 1940s, the company's large manufacturing plant produced tank and armored-vehicle parts and miscellaneous equipment for the war effort, including riveters and welders. After the war, the company concentrated on the production of industrial presses and molds, for plastics as well as metals. By 1975, the company had developed a reputation as an innovative producer of industrial machinery and machine tools.

In the late 1970s, Northboro entered the new field of computer-aided design and computer-aided manufacturing (CAD/CAM). Working with a small software company, it developed a line of presses that would manufacture metal parts by responding to computer commands. Northboro merged the software company into its operations and, over the next several years, perfected the CAM equipment. At the same time, it developed a superior line of CAD software and equipment that would allow an engineer to design a part to exacting specifications on a computer. The design could then be entered into the company's CAM equipment, and the parts would be manufactured without the use of blueprints or human interference. By year-end 1991, CAD/CAM equipment and software were responsible for about 45 percent of sales; presses, dies, and molds for 40 percent; and miscellaneous machine tools for 15 percent.

Most press and mold companies were small local or regional firms with limited clientele. For this reason, Northboro stood out as a true industry leader. Within the CAD/CAM

---

[1]Value Line's financial-strength ratings, from A++ to C, were a measure of a company's ability to withstand adverse business conditions and were based on leverage, liquidity, business risk, company size, and stock-price variability, as well as analysts' judgments.

industry, however, a number of larger firms, including General Electric, Hewlett-Packard, and Digital Equipment, competed for dominance of the growing market.

Throughout the 1980s Northboro helped set the standard for CAD/CAM, but the aggressive entry of large foreign firms into CAD/CAM and the rise of the dollar dampened sales. Moreover, Northboro fell behind some of its competition in the development of user-friendly software and the integration of design and manufacturing. As a result, revenues declined from a high of $607 million in 1985 to $504 million in 1991.

To combat the decline in revenues and improve weak profit margins, Northboro took a two-pronged approach. First, it devoted a greater share of its research and development budget to CAD/CAM in an effort to reestablish leadership in the field. Second, the company underwent two massive restructurings. In 1989, it sold two unprofitable lines of business with revenues of $31 million, sold two plants, eliminated five leased facilities, and reduced personnel. Restructuring costs totaled $44 million. Then, in 1991, the company began a second round of restructuring by altering its manufacturing strategy, refocusing its sales and marketing approach, and adopting administrative procedures that allowed for a further reduction in staff and facilities. The total cost of the operational restructuring in 1991 was $60 million.

The company's recent income statements and balance sheets are provided in Exhibits 1 and 2. Although the two restructurings produced losses totaling $135 million in 1989 and 1991, by 1992 the restructurings and the increased emphasis on CAD/CAM research appeared to have launched a turnaround. Not only was the company leaner, but also the CAD/CAM research led to the development of a system that Northboro management believed would redefine the industry. Known as the Artificial Workforce, the system was an array of advanced control hardware, software, and applications that could distribute information throughout a plant.

Essentially, the Artificial Workforce allowed an engineer to design a part on the CAD and input the data into a CAM that could control the mixing of chemicals or the molding of parts from any number of different materials on different machines. The system could also assemble and can, box, or shrink-wrap the finished product. Thus, no matter how intricate, a product could be designed, manufactured, and packaged solely by computer.

Northboro had developed applications of the product for the plastics, food-processing, and pulp-and-paper industries in 1991 and by the next year was developing applications for the oil- and gas-refining and chemicals industries.

By October 1991, when the first Artificial Workforce was shipped, Northboro had orders totaling $75 million; by year-end, the backlog totaled $100 million. The future for the product looked bright. Several securities analysts were optimistic about the product's impact on the company. The following comments paraphrase their thoughts:

> Artificial Workforce products have compelling advantages over competing entries and will enable Northboro to increase its share of a market that, ignoring periodic growth spurts, will expand at a real annual rate of about 5 percent over the next several years.

> The company is producing the Artificial Workforce in a new automated facility which, when in full swing, will help restore margins to levels not seen for years.

> The important question now is how quickly Northboro will be able to ship in volume. Manufacturing foul-ups and missing components have delayed production growth through May 1992, about six months beyond the original target date. And start-up costs, which were a signifi-

cant factor in last year's deficits, have continued to penalize earnings. Our estimates assume that production will proceed smoothly from now on and that it will approach the optimum level by year's end.

Northboro management expected domestic revenues from the Artificial Workforce series to total $90 million in 1992 and $150 million in 1993. Thereafter, growth in sales would depend on the development of more system applications and the creation of system improvements and add-on features. International sales through Northboro's existing offices in Frankfurt, London, Milan, and Paris, and new offices in Hong Kong, Seoul, Manila, and Tokyo were expected to provide additional revenues of $150 million as early as 1994. Currently, international sales accounted for about 15 percent of total corporate revenues.

Two factors that could affect sales were of some concern to Northboro. First, although the company had successfully patented several of the processes used by the Artificial Workforce system, management had received hints through industry observers that two strong competitors were developing comparable products and would probably introduce them within the next 12 months. Second, sales of molds, presses, machine tools, and CAD/CAM equipment and software were highly cyclical, and predictions about the strength of the U.S. economy were mixed. The economy had been weak for almost two years. As shown in Exhibit 3, the projected indicators were sending mixed messages. Domestic real GNP was expected to grow at 3.2 and 2.8 percent in the next two years. On the other hand, capital spending on industrial durable equipment was expected to increase dramatically over the next two years, at 7.5 and 8.7 percent.

CORPORATE GOALS

A number of corporate objectives had grown out of the restructurings and recent technological advances. First and foremost, management wanted and expected the firm to grow at an average annual compound rate of 15 percent. A great deal of corporate planning had been devoted to that goal over the past three years and, indeed, second-quarter financial data suggested that Northboro would achieve revenues of about $580 million in 1992, as shown in Exhibit 1. If Northboro achieved a 15 percent compound rate of growth through 1998, the company would reach $1.3 billion in sales and $107 million in net income.

In order to achieve this growth goal, Northboro management proposed a strategy relying on three key points. First, the mix of production would shift substantially. CAD/CAM and peripheral products on the cutting edge of industry technology would account for three-quarters of sales; the company's traditional presses and molds would account for the remainder. Second, the company would expand aggressively internationally, where it would hope to obtain half of its sales and profits by 1998. This expansion would be achieved through opening new field sales offices around the world. At present, Northboro was represented only in Europe. Third, the company would expand through joint ventures and acquisitions of small software companies, which would provide one-half of the new products through 1998; internal research would provide the other half.

From its beginning Northboro had an aversion to debt. Management believed that small amounts of debt, primarily to meet working-capital needs, had its place, but that anything beyond a 40 percent debt-to-equity ratio was, in the oft-quoted words of the founder David

Peterboro, "unthinkable, indicative of sloppy management, and flirting with trouble." Senior management was aware that equity was typically more costly than debt but took great satisfaction in the company "doing it on its own." Northboro's highest debt-to-capital ratio in the past 25 years—28 percent—occurred in 1991, and was still the subject of conversations among senior managers.

Although 11 members of the North and Peterboro families owned 30 percent of the company's stock and three were on the board of directors, management placed the interests of the public shareholders first. (Shareholder data are provided in Exhibit 4.) Stephen North, chairman of the board and grandson of the cofounder, sought to maximize the growth in the market value of the company's stock over time.

At the age of 61, Mr. North was actively involved in all aspects of the company's growth and future. He was conversant with a range of technical details of Northboro's products and was especially interested in finding ways to improve the company's domestic market share. His retirement was no more than four years into the future, and he wanted to leave a legacy of corporate financial strength and technological achievement. The Artificial Workforce, a project he had taken under his wing four years earlier, was beginning to bear fruit. He now wanted to ensure that the firm would also soon be able to pay a dividend.

Mr. North took particular pride in selecting and developing young managers with promise. Olsen had a bachelor's degree in electrical engineering and had been a systems analyst for Motorola before graduate school. She had been hired in 1982 out of a well-known MBA program. By 1991 she had risen to the position of chief financial officer.

DIVIDEND POLICY

Northboro's dividend and stock-price histories are presented in Exhibit 5. Prior to 1986, both earnings and dividends per share had grown at a relatively steady pace, but the recession in the early 1980s and the restructurings took their toll on earnings. As a consequence, dividends were pared back in 1990 to $0.25 per share—the lowest dividend since 1977. In 1991, the board of directors declared a payout of $0.25 per share despite reporting the largest per share earnings loss in the firm's history and, in effect, borrowing to pay the dividend. In the first two quarters of 1992, the directors had not declared a dividend. In a special letter to shareholders, however, the directors declared their intention to continue the annual payout later in 1992.

In August 1992, Olsen contemplated choosing among three possible dividend policies to recommend:

• *Zero dividend payout.* This option could be justified in light of the firm's strategic reposition to advanced technologies and CAD/CAM, and reflected the huge cash requirements of that move. The proponents of this policy argued that it would signal that the firm belonged in a class of high-growth and high-technology firms. Some securities analysts wondered whether the market still considered Northboro as a traditional electrical-equipment manufacturer or as a more technologically advanced CAD/CAM company. The latter category would imply that the market was expecting strong capital appreciation but, perhaps, little in the way of dividends. Others cited Northboro's recent performance problems. One "questioned the wisdom of ignoring the financial statements in favor of acting like a blue chip." Was a high dividend in the long-term interests of the company and its stockholders, or would the strategy backfire and make investors skittish?

- *40 percent dividend payout,* or a dividend of $0.20 per share. This would restore the firm to an implied annual dividend payment of $0.80 per share, the highest since 1988. Proponents of this policy argued that there was undoubtedly some anticipation of such an announcement in the current stock price of $32 per share, and that this was justified by expected increases in orders and sales. Northboro's investment banker suggested that the market might be expecting a strong dividend in order to bring the payout back in line with the 52 percent average within the electrical-industrial-equipment industry and with the 68 percent average in the machine-tool industry. Still others believed that it was important to send a strong signal to shareholders, and that a large dividend (on the order of a 40 percent payout) would suggest that the company had conquered its problems and that its directors were confident of future earnings. Supporters of this view argued that borrowing to pay dividends was not inconsistent with the behavior of most firms. Finally, some older members of management opined that a growth rate in the range of 10 to 20 percent should accompany a payout of 30 to 50 percent.

- *Residual dividend payout policy.* A small segment on the finance staff argued that Northboro should pay dividends only after funding all projects offering positive net present values (NPVs). Their view was that investors were paying managers to deploy their funds at returns better than they could achieve otherwise, and that by definition such investments would yield positive NPVs. By deploying funds into these projects, and otherwise returning unused funds to investors in the form of dividends, the firm would build trust with investors and be rewarded with higher valuation multiples. General Motors was the preeminent example of a firm that had followed such a policy, though few large publicly held firms followed GM's example.

    Another argument in support of this policy was that dividend policy was "irrelevant" in a growing firm: any dividend paid today would be offset by dilution at some future date by the issue of shares necessary to make up for the dividend. This argument reflected the theory of dividends in a perfect market advanced by two finance professors, Merton Miller and Franco Modigliani.[2] The main disadvantage of this policy to Christine Olsen was that dividend payments would be unpredictable. In some years, dividends could be cut—even to zero—possibly imposing negative pressure on the firm's share price. Olsen was all too aware of Northboro's own share price collapse following its dividend cut. She recalled a study by another finance professor, John Lintner,[3] which found that firms' dividend payments tended to be "sticky" upward—that is, dividends would rise over time and rarely fall, and that mature slower-growth firms paid higher dividends, while high-growth firms paid lower dividends.

In response to this internal debate, Olsen's staff pulled together Exhibits 6 and 7, which present comparative information on companies in three industries—CAD/CAM, machine tools, and electrical-industrial equipment—and on a general sample of high- and low-payout

---

[2]M. H. Miller and F. Modigliani, "Dividend Policy, Growth and the Valuation of Shares," *Journal of Business* 34 (October 1961), pp. 411–33.

[3]J. Lintner, "Distribution of Incomes of Corporations among Dividends, Retained Earnings, and Taxes," *American Economic Review* 46 (May 1956), pp. 97–113.

companies. To test the feasibility of a 40 percent dividend payout rate, Olsen developed the projected sources and uses of cash provided in Exhibit 8. She took the boldest approach by assuming that the company would grow at a 15 percent compound rate, that operating margins would improve over the next few years to historical levels, and that the firm would pay a dividend of 40 percent of earnings every year. In particular, the forecast assumed that the firm's net margin would hover between 5.6 and 6.0 percent over the next six years, and then increase to 7.95 percent in 1998. The firm's operating executives believed that this increase in profitability was consistent with economies of scale to be achieved upon the attainment of higher operating output of the Artificial Workforce.

IMAGE ADVERTISING AND NAME CHANGE

As part of a general review of the firm's standing in the financial markets, Northboro's director of Investor Relations, Alice Dent, had concluded that investors misperceived the firm's prospects and that the firm's current name was more consistent with the firm's historical product mix and markets than with those expected in the future. Dent commissioned surveys of readers of financial magazines which revealed a relatively low awareness of Northboro or its business. Surveys of stockbrokers revealed higher awareness of the firm, but a low or mediocre outlook on Northboro's likely returns to shareholders and growth prospects. Dent retained a consulting firm that recommended a program of corporate "image" advertising targeted toward opinion-leading institutional investors, and individual investors. The objective was to enhance the awareness and image of Northboro. Through focus groups, the consultants identified a name that appeared to suggest the firm's promising strategy, "Northboro Advanced Systems International, Inc." Alice Dent estimated that the image advertising campaign and name change would cost approximately $10 million.

Stephen North, the firm's board chair, was mildly skeptical. He said, "Do you mean to raise our stock price by 'marketing' our shares? This is a novel approach. Can you sell claims on a company the way Procter & Gamble markets soap?" The consultants could give no empirical evidence that stock prices responded favorably to corporate image campaigns or name changes, though they did offer some favorable anecdotes.

CONCLUSION

Christine Olsen was caught in a difficult position. Members of the board and management disagreed on the very nature of Northboro's future. Some managers saw the company as entering a new stage of rapid growth and thought that a large (or in the minds of some, any) dividend would be inappropriate. Others believed that it was important to make a firm gesture to the public that management believed Northboro had turned the corner and was about to return to the levels of growth and profitability seen in the 1970s. This action could only be accomplished through a dividend. As she wrestled with the different points of view, she wondered whether management might be representative of the company's shareholders. Did the majority of public shareholders own stock for the same reason, or were their reasons just as diverse as those of management?

EXHIBIT 1   Consolidated Income Statements (dollars in thousands, except per share data)

	For the Years Ended December 31			
	1989	*1990*	*1991*	*Projected 1992*
Net sales	$572,175	$543,986	$504,425	$580,000
Cost of sales	360,498	334,305	332,586	366,500
Gross profit	211,677	209,681	171,839	213,500
Research and development	51,785	47,030	50,278	51,500
Selling, general, and administrative	153,314	149,089	154,005	141,000
Restructuring costs	43,632	0	59,607	0
Operating profit (loss)	(37,054)	13,562	(92,051)	21,000
Other income (expense)	(3,000)	710	(2,305)	(2,800)
Income (loss) before taxes	(40,054)	14,272	(94,356)	18,200
Income taxes (benefit)	827	5,610	(500)	6,188
Net income (loss)	$ (40,881)	$ 8,662	$(93,856)	$ 12,012
Earnings (loss) per share	$ (3.31)	$ 0.70	$ (7.62)	$ 0.97
Dividends per share	$ 0.78	$ 0.25	$ 0.25	$ 0.40[*]

[*]Assuming a $0.20 dividend per share for the last two quarters of 1992.

EXHIBIT 2   Consolidated Balance Sheets (dollars in thousands)

	1990	*1991*	*Projected 1992*
		December 31	
Cash and equivalents	$ 9,278	$ 14,820	$ 17,110
Accounts receivable	139,027	124,824	145,000
Inventories	153,561	135,925	145,000
Prepaid expenses	9,506	8,677	10,000
Other	14,789	13,809	14,000
Total current assets	326,161	298,055	331,110
Property, plant, and equipment	218,402	239,227	274,000
Less depreciation	111,609	122,324	137,000
Net property, plant, and equipment	106,793	116,903	137,000
Intangible assets	6,286	1,399	1,000
Other assets	10,482	11,792	12,000
Total assets	$449,722	$428,149	$481,110
Bank loans	$ 22,797	$ 47,563	$ 50,000
Accounts payable	24,299	22,826	25,000
Current portion of long-term debt	200	100	1,000
Accruals and other	86,249	107,734	122,000
Total current liabilities	133,545	178,223	198,000
Deferred taxes	11,324	9,179	11,000
Long-term debt	6,000	5,850	20,000
Deferred pension costs	29,860	42,886	47,000
Other liabilities	1,545	3,629	5,000
Total liabilities and equity	182,274	239,767	281,000
Common stock, $1 par value	12,570	12,570	12,570
Capital in excess of par	71,916	71,938	71,938
Cumulative translation adjustment	(4,377)	13,472	18,000
Retained earnings	194,332	97,398	104,598
Less treasury stock at cost:			
1990—256,151; 1991—255,506	(6,993)	(6,996)	(6,996)
Total shareholders' equity	267,448	188,382	200,110
Total liabilities and equity	$449,722	$428,149	$481,110

EXHIBIT 3   Economic Indicators and Projections

	1989	1990	1991	June 1992	Projected 1993	1994
3-month Treasury bill rate (at auction)	8.12%	7.51%	5.37%	3.43%	3.51%	4.52%
30-year Treasury bond rate	8.45	8.61	8.14	7.67	7.68	8.00
AAA corporate bond rate	9.26	9.32	8.77	8.14	8.16	8.39
Change in:						
Real gross national product	2.5	0.8	−1.2	2.0	3.2	2.8
Producer price index	4.8	6.0	0.01	1.7	0.3	1.1
Industrial durable equipment purchases	7.8	−2.6	−9.1	−1.6	7.5	8.7
Price deflator	3.6	4.7	4.1	2.3	2.5	3.1
Consumer spending	6.9%	6.4%	3.7%	5.3%	6.2%	6.5%

Sources: *U.S. Economic Outlook,* WEFA Group, January 1993; *Federal Reserve Bulletin,* June 1992; *Value Line Investment Survey,* July 17, 1992.

EXHIBIT 4   Stockholder Comparative Data, 1981 and 1991 (thousands of shares)

	1981 Shares	1981 Percentage	1991 Shares	1991 Percentage
Founders' families	1,540	13	1,540	13
Employees and families	2,483	20	2,063	17
Institutional investors				
A. Growth-oriented	1,546	13	786	6
B. Value-oriented	987	8	1,590	13
Individual investors				
A. Long-term; retirement	4,598	38	3,324	27
B. Short-term; trading-oriented	587	5	1,586	13
C. Other; unknown	429	4	1,425	12
	12,170	100	12,314	100

The investor relations department identified these categories from company records. The type of institutional investor was identified from promotional materials stating the investment goals of the institutions. The type of individual investor was identified from a survey of subsamples of investors.

Note: Percentages do not foot exactly because of rounding.

EXHIBIT 5 Per Share Financial and Stock Data[*]

	Sales/ Share	EPS	Dividends per Share	Cash Flow/ Share	Stock Price			Average P/E	Payout Ratio	Average Yield	Shares Out (Millions)
					High	Low	Average				
1976	$14.62	$0.45	$0.18	$0.98	$20.50	$ 9.75	$14.58	32.4	40%	1.2%	10.25
1977	16.11	0.74	0.22	1.30	21.25	10.25	14.95	20.2	30	1.5	10.31
1978	22.40	0.90	0.27	1.44	21.38	8.25	13.59	15.1	30	2.0	10.62
1979	25.81	1.60	0.31	2.06	18.63	10.25	13.44	8.4	19	2.3	11.83
1980	27.37	2.31	0.40	2.85	22.63	12.25	18.48	8.0	17	2.2	11.97
1981	30.26	2.61	0.57	3.27	24.00	18.13	21.14	8.1	22	2.7	12.17
1982	31.87	2.63	0.72	3.36	26.88	18.38	22.88	8.7	27	3.2	12.42
1983	37.97	2.71	0.82	3.62	29.63	19.63	24.39	9.0	30	3.4	12.42
1984	40.97	2.58	0.87	3.64	40.00	20.25	29.67	11.5	34	2.9	12.43
1985	48.56	3.60	0.93	4.84	41.25	27.50	34.20	9.5	26	2.7	12.50
1986	43.88	2.81	1.04	4.28	39.00	21.50	32.03	11.4	37	3.2	12.35
1987	43.16	0.65	1.04	2.24	47.50	29.75	37.05	57.0	160	2.8	12.35
1988	41.76	0.35	1.04	2.01	40.50	27.00	31.47	89.9	297	3.3	12.35
1989	46.32	-3.31	0.78	2.88	30.75	22.13	26.45	NMF	NMF	2.9	12.35
1990	44.18	0.70	0.25	2.00	31.88	22.50	27.20	88.2	36%	1.0	12.31
1991	$40.96	-$7.62	$0.25	-$0.98	$39.88	$18.38	$29.15	NMF	NMF	0.9%	12.31

Note: NMF = Not a meaningful figure.
[*] Adjusted for 3-for-2 stock split in January 1982 and 50 percent stock dividend in June 1986.

EXHIBIT 6 Comparative Industry Data (as of December 31, 1991)

	Sales (Millions)	Annual Growth Rate of Cash Flow		Current Payout Ratio	Current Dividend Yield	Debt/ Equity	Insider Ownership	P/E Ratio
		Last 10 Years	Next 3–5 Years					
Northboro	$ 504	−1.5%	+15.0%	Nil	Nil	28%	30.0%	NMF
CAD/CAM companies (software and hardware)								
Autodesk	285	41.5*	10.0	20%	1.3%	0	10.0	22
GM-EDS	7,028	27.0	9.5	27	1.2	11	Nil	24
Digital Equipment	13,911	13.0	10.0	Nil	Nil	1	3.5	NMF
Intergraph	1,195	32.5	5.5	Nil	Nil	2	28.0	13
Mentor Graphics	400	16.0*	16.0	>100	1.2	20	27.0	NMF
SCI Systems	1,129	24.5	9.5	Nil	Nil	100	7.6	22
Sun Microsystems	3,221	57.9	29.5	Nil	Nil	25	3.7	12
Gerber Scientific	250	14.5	5.5	59	1.7	3	13.7	39
Hewlett-Packard	14,494	14.0	12.5	16	1.0	3	18.1	16
Electrical-industrial equipment manufacturers								
Emerson Electric	7,427	9.0	10.0	47	2.7	14	0.9	18
General Electric	43,089	10.0	10.0	41	3.0	15	0.7	14
General Signal	1,616	3.5	7.0	54	2.8	50	6.6	17
Honeywell	6,193	3.5	8.5	33	2.4	33	0.6	16
Measurex	254	11.5	12.5	86	1.9	1	4.0	16
Machine-tool manufacturers								
Acme-Cleveland	184	−10.5	8.0	91	5.3	14	3.4	30
Cincinnati Milacron	754	−5.5	15.5	>100	2.3	100	10.3	33
Giddings & Lewis	327	NMF	NA	13	1.3	50	1.2	21
Monarch	$ 106.6	−16.0%	14.0%	68%	2.0%	1%	2.1%	32

NMF = Not a meaningful figure because of recent reported losses.
*Last 5 years only.

Source: Comparative Industry Data, Northboro Machine Tools Corporation. *Value Line Investment Survey*, December 31, 1991.

EXHIBIT 7 Selected Healthy Companies with High- and Zero-Dividend Payouts (as of December 31, 1991)

	Industry	Expected Return on Total Capital (Next 3–5 Years)	Expected Growth Rate of Dividends (Next 3–5 Years)	Current Dividend Payout	Current Dividend Yield	Expected Growth Rate of Sales (Next 3–5 Years)	Current P/E Ratio
High-payout companies							
BRE Properties	Real estate investment	13.5%	3.0%	125%	7.7%	8.0%	12.1
Federal Realty	Real estate investment	10.0	9.0	500	7.2	7.0	52.5
Idaho Power	Electric power	8.5	1.5	118	7.2	+3.0	16.1
Sierra Pacific	Electric power	7.5	0	103	8.0	−0.5	13.7
Halliburton	Oilfield services	14.5	6.5	97	3.4	9.0	39.7
Consolidated	Natural gas	10.5	5.5	97	4.0	7.5	21.1
Sonat	Gas transmission	8.5	0	110	4.7	+4.0	20.0
Pacific Enterprises	Gas utility	8.0	0	125	15.2	−11.0	10.3
Zero-payout companies							
Oracle Systems	Software	20.0	0	0	0	15.0	37.2
Novell	Software	22.5	0	0	0	25.0	33.9
King World Productions	TV shows	19.0	0	0	0	9.5	10.4
Harley-Davidson	Motorcycles	15.5	0	0	0	10.5	24.1
Duty Free International	Retail	16.5	0	0	0	31.0	28.9
50-Off Stores	Retail	18.5	0	0	0	24.0	24.3
Lands' End	Retail	19.5	0	0	0	16.5	17.8
Cabletron	Network systems	21.0	0	0	0	32.5	22.2
Cisco Systems	Network systems	23.0%	0%	0%	0%	34.0%	30.3

Source: Selected Healthy Companies with High- and Zero-Dividend Payouts, Northboro Machine Tools Corporation, December 31, 1991.

EXHIBIT 8 Projected Sources and Uses Statement Assuming a 40 Percent Payout Ratio[*] (dollars in millions)

	1992	1993	1994	1995	1996	1997	1998	Total, 1992–98
Sales	$580	$667	$767	$882	$1,015	$1,167	$1,342	
Sources of cash:								
Net income	12	27	38	49	61	65	107	$358
Depreciation	15	17	20	23	27	31	35	168
	27	44	58	72	88	96	142	526
Uses of cash:								
Capital expenditure	35	40	45	50	55	60	65	350
Working capital	13	10	10	10	10	10	10	73
	48	50	55	60	65	70	75	423
Excess cash (borrowings needed)[*]	(21)	(6)	3	12	23	26	67	103
Dividend[†]	5	11	15	19	24	26	43	143
Excess cash (borrowings needed) after dividend[*]	$ (26)	$ (17)	$(12)	$ (8)	$ (1)	$ 0	$ 24	$ (40)

[*]This analysis ignores the effects of borrowing on interest and amortization. It includes all increases in long-term liabilities and equity items other than retained earnings.
[†]Dividend calculated as 40 percent of net income.

Case 24

Donaldson, Lufkin & Jenrette, 1995 (Abridged)

On the afternoon of October 24, 1995, John Chalsty, president and CEO of the investment bank, Donaldson, Lufkin & Jenrette (DLJ), met with several colleagues to price the initial public offering (IPO) of 9.2 million shares of DLJ's stock. Also present, either in person or over the phone, were most of the board members of the Equitable Companies Incorporated (Equitable), DLJ's parent and 100 percent owner. For nearly six months, Chalsty had worked to prepare for an offering of DLJ shares to the public.

Equitable's chairman, Richard Jenrette, would watch while the firm he founded, and which still bore his name, went public for the second time. The sale would mark another milestone of the successful restructuring of Equitable led by Jenrette. Investors could now see how much DLJ was worth on its own. Equitable had purchased DLJ in 1985 for $465 million. The filing range in the initial prospectus had been from $26.00 to $29.00 per share, placing a value on DLJ from $1.5 billion to $1.7 billion. Equitable would continue to own approximately 80 percent of DLJ after the offering.

The DLJ bankers who had worked with Chalsty and Equitable for six months, Pedro Galban, Bill Wheeler, Stephan Kiratsous, and Cameron Fleming, sat with the others. They had coordinated the offering and valued DLJ, primarily by comparing its results to those of other comparable publicly traded investment banks. However, DLJ proved to be a difficult comparison: Its strategy was unlike that of larger investment banks. It focused on competing in higher-margin business lines where it could be a leader. Traditionally, investors thought that the larger investment banks earned higher returns on capital, yet

This case was prepared by Douglas Fordyce, under the direction of Professor Robert F. Bruner, and is a condensed version of two other cases prepared by Fordyce and Bruner, "Donaldson, Lufkin & Jenrette (A) and (B)" (UVA-F-1145, F-1146). This case was written as a basis for class discussion rather than to illustrate effective or ineffective handling of an administrative situation. Copyright © 1996 by the Trustees of the University of Virginia Darden School Foundation, Charlottesville, VA. All rights reserved. *No part of this publication may be reproduced, stored in a retrieval system, used in a spreadsheet, or transmitted in any form or by any means—electronic, mechanical, photocopying, recording, or otherwise—without the permission of the Darden Foundation. For inquiries, please send an e-mail to dardencases@virginia.edu.* Rev. 1/98. Version 1.2.

DLJ was smaller, and earned higher returns than most of the six largest firms in recent years. Like other DLJ employees, the bankers were excited because DLJ would soon be able to raise debt and equity on its own and aggressively pursue its strategy. They, too, would be able to own a part of DLJ. In fact, many employees would be exchanging their interests in long-term compensation plans for shares and options in DLJ after the offering.

Joining the bankers from DLJ was Duff Anderson, managing director of Equity Capital Markets. As lead manager of the offering, DLJ was responsible for marketing the stock and coordinating the efforts of the other underwriters. Anderson bore responsibility for working with other securities firms in explaining the investment opportunity the stock represented to investors and in gauging demand for the issue. He had to represent the investors who purchased shares from the underwriters, making sure they got a fair return. Yet, he wanted to ensure that Equitable and DLJ received a good price for the stock they sold. And finally, he had to represent the underwriters, who could be stuck with any shares that went unsold.

While the DLJ offering was oversubscribed by investors, some had questioned how successful DLJ would be in the future. Critics wondered if DLJ had sufficiently diverse businesses and enough of an international presence to compete in the ever-competitive securities industry. Others questioned if DLJ could maintain its enviable, collegial atmosphere in the face of public scrutiny. Pointing to the high prices for other securities firms, a few investors said that, while DLJ possessed one of the finest franchises on Wall Street, they worried that Equitable might be selling at the peak of the market. The stocks of investment banks had traded down 7.5 percent on average over the last week. Perhaps, the indications of interest given by investors would prove less firm than expected.

Now, after the lengthy process of due diligence, SEC filings, road-show presentations, and meetings, all that remained for those present was setting the offering price of the stock.

THE SECURITIES INDUSTRY

Perhaps Wall Street had changed more in the last 20 years than it had since 1624 when Dutch traders erected what became the namesake wall on the southern tip of Manhattan. Before the mid-1970s, investment banks served as orderly financial intermediaries, underwriting "plain-vanilla" stocks and bonds, brokering securities for clients for a fixed fee and offering financial advice on mergers and acquisitions when asked. Investment banks maintained close relationships with a select group of corporations, acting as capital raiser and trusted advisor. The investment banks required little capital of their own, quickly moving securities from corporations to investors, rarely holding inventories of securities.

In this regulated environment, the function of investment banks was to bear capital market risks, in contrast to other firms. In an underwriting, investment banks purchased clients' securities at a fixed price, to resell later in the market at an uncertain price. Commercial banks accepted credit risk: the uncertainty of a borrower's ability to meet contractual interest and principal payments. Insurance companies underwrote event risk. Nonfinancial corporations accepted business risk, the operational risks inherent in their businesses.

Three regulatory changes threw this calm, profitable environment into turbulence. In 1974, the government enacted the Employee Retirement Income Security Act (ERISA), requiring pension managers to follow the "prudent man" rule when making investment decisions. Freed from investing just in bonds and blue-chip stocks, pension managers diversified their portfolios into new markets, both domestically and abroad. The managers were compensated according to how they performed relative to the market. With competition, managers grew hungry for financial products that could enhance their performance and manage unwanted risks. They also demanded that securities firms be ready to buy or sell nearly any security to them, requiring brokers to establish large securities inventories.

A year later, the government hit the brokerage industry with May Day, when fixed brokerage commissions were eliminated. The new regulations dissolved the fixed commission structure and allowed investors to negotiate commissions with their brokers. Large institutions cut their commissions by up to 80 percent instantly.[1] Smaller brokerages combined with each other to rationalize their businesses, meet capital requirements, and take advantage of economies of scale in the "back office," the processing and record-keeping side of the business. In the new environment, firms started to compete even more intensely with each other for clients.

Finally, in 1982 the SEC introduced Rule 415 which permitted "shelf registration" of securities. Under a shelf registration, a company filed one comprehensive registration statement to cover the issuance of a fixed amount of capital over a stated period, but left open the types of securities to be sold and when they would be brought to market. During that period, the company could quickly issue securities in two days, "pulling them off the shelf," to take advantage of favorable rates or conditions. Companies needed only to make quick updates to the initial registration statement. To win their underwriting business, issuers forced underwriters to bid more aggressively for their securities. This bidding cut the "gross spread," the percentage underwriters earned in the issuance process. Guy Moszkowski, the securities industry analyst at brokerage Sanford C. Bernstein, estimated that in 1982 underwriters earned 1.5 percent of the value of securities underwritten. By 1993 the gross spread had shrunk to just 0.67 percent.[2]

Technology, too, played a role in shaping the new financing arena. Computers supported the creation and pricing of more complex financial instruments, such as derivatives. In corporate finance, bankers could test multitudes of capital structures and their effects on a company through the use of spreadsheets. While margins eroded in the brokerage and underwriting businesses, blossoming fields like derivatives, junk bonds, and mergers and acquisition (M&A) services for leveraged buyouts (LBOs) kept overall margins healthy. Innovation proved profitable for those who could create the newest security or M&A tactic. Though temporarily lucrative for their inventors, these innovations tended to be quickly duplicated by competitors.

Contemporaneously, governments deregulated interest rates and foreign-exchange rates. Underwriters introduced products, like swaps and Yankee bonds, to take advantage of global capital markets. In most developed economies, deregulation and tighter monetary policies by reserve banks eventually led to a steady decline in interest rates from the early 1980s until 1994. This environment translated into an extended bull market, with a corresponding torrent of debt and equity issuances from companies. Investment banks received less for their services but were more than compensated with higher volumes of transactions and increased trading activity.

---

[1]"Other People's Money," *The Economist,* April 15, 1995.
[2]Ibid.

Power shifted from individual investors to institutional investors during this period. With the rise of pension and mutual funds, institutional investors came to dominate the market. In 1980, individuals owned 60.9 percent of all equities, and institutions owned 29.1 percent. In 1994, individuals owned just 48.2 percent, and institutions 51.8 percent.[3] Exhibit 1 details the growth of the financial markets. Exhibit 2 documents the expansion of the securities industry.

In search of higher margins, investment banks moved into new areas, accepting new risks. They blurred the historical lines between financial institutions. They even moved into nonfinancial businesses. To compete with commercial banks, investment banking firms accepted credit risk by developing bridge loan funds and syndication departments. Investment bankers lent money to firms on a short-term basis to facilitate pending M&A transactions. These loans, called bridge loans, assisted acquirors in acquisitions by "bridging" the gap in financing until the companies could replace the bridge loan with more permanent capital. Separately, loan-syndication departments in investment banks competed with commercial banks to take commercial loans, divide them into smaller loans, and sell off the loans to a syndicate of banks. If they properly executed the transaction, syndicate managers could earn fees for the work, while never taking the loan onto their balance sheet. Syndication constituted one of the commercial banks' most profitable areas. They resented Wall Street invasion of their profit centers, even though the commercial banks were quickly moving into securities trading, advisory services, and underwriting: Wall Street's businesses.

With the rise of derivatives, investment banks came to price and take on event risk. They insured against risks that corporations desired to shed. For example, an investment bank might offer to limit an airline's exposure to fluctuating jet fuel prices, allowing the airline to "lock in" a set price for its fuel needs for the year. To accomplish this hedge, the bank would sell a series of forward contracts on jet fuel prices to the airline. The bank then might sell offsetting positions to another party who wanted exposure to jet fuel prices, or might keep the contract on its books. The derivative market soared to become a multitrillion-dollar market. As the derivatives market expanded, investment banks tailored generic contracts to meet companies' specific needs. The specialized use of derivatives played a large part in the development of the collateralized-mortgage and asset-backed debt markets.

With their knowledge of the markets and constant flow of information, investment banks moved into principal trading. They used their own capital, often leveraged, to bet on the directions of the markets. To varying degrees, firms established proprietary trading operations, with firms like Salomon Brothers and Goldman Sachs leading the pack. Profits could be quite high if the traders were right, but losses could be severe if their insights proved wrong. In 1994, Salomon Brothers lost $831 million pre-tax, largely due to misguided bets on the bond market. Many critics charged Wall Street with a conflict of interest in its principal trading because many of its clients were making similar market bets. In effect, critics charged, the banks competed against their own clients.

Finally, many investment banks participated in merchant banking and venture-capital investments. They risked their own funds to buy all or part of other companies outside the securities industry. Merchant-banking deals often involved mature companies and took on

---

[3]"Equities, Corporate Bonds and Tax Exempt Securities," *Statistical Abstract of the United States 1995,* no. 825, p. 532.

large amounts of debt, while venture-capital investments tended to be in growth-stage companies. If the investment strategy proved correct, these investments could provide huge returns to the equity capital invested, garnering annual returns of 30 percent or greater. In the LBO field, investment banks competed for deals with LBO partnerships, like Kolberg, Kravis, Roberts & Co., Clayton Dubilier & Rice, and Saunders Karp & Co. In venture capital, they competed with other venture capitalists like Kleiner, Perkins, Caufield & Byers, and Welsh, Carson, Anderson & Stowe, as well as others.

Recently, many investment banks focused on trying to limit their exposure to U.S. interest rates. When rates increased almost 200 basis points from 1993 to 1994, firms were reminded of how much their businesses depended on low rates. Net profits for NYSE member firms declined from record-breaking heights in 1993 of $8.6 billion to $1.4 billion in 1994.[4] Underwritings dried up and bond portfolios plummeted. To dampen the effects of interest-rate swings, firms have tried to increase their presence overseas and to develop fee-based asset management businesses.

In the 1970s and 1980s, investment banks flocked to Europe and Japan as U.S. companies expanded abroad. The expansion required capital for equipment and for regulatory purposes. Many foreign regulatory bodies insisted that branch offices maintain regulatory capital on site. In the 1990s, investment banks built up trading and corporate finance operations in emerging markets, like Mexico, Brazil, Hong Kong, and India. These markets often offered lower levels of competition from local securities firms, excellent growth and higher profits. Morgan Stanley placed great emphasis on growing abroad, allocating roughly one-half of its capital overseas, generating 40 percent of its revenues.[5] Even with its strong presence abroad, Morgan made an attempt to merge with S. G. Warburg, one of the leading European investment banks, in 1995, though the merger fell through.

Many investment banks built or bought asset management businesses. Unlike other areas tied to interest rates, these businesses provided reliable revenue streams. They earned a fee based on a percentage of assets under management. Merrill Lynch created an asset management business that oversaw over $170 billion of assets. Annual management fees on the assets generated approximately $1.74 billion in revenues, roughly enough to cover the entire firm's fixed costs for a year. In 1995, Morgan Stanley paid $350 million for Miller Anderson & Sherrerd, an asset manager, to bulk up its business.

All of the changes in the industry necessitated capital—from holding more inventory for clients to building overseas operations to merchant banking investments. With so much capital at risk, earnings became more volatile. Profits could swing drastically with changes in underwriting volumes or interest rates.

Many analysts expected further consolidation within the securities industry in the future. They hypothesized that two factors would drive consolidation: globalization, and the long-expected repeal of the Glass-Steagall regulations. They argued that firms needed a strong international presence to successfully compete for large underwriting assignments and to mitigate oscillations in U.S. interest rates.

The Glass-Steagall Act of 1933 separated investment banks and commercial banks after the Crash of 1929. Regulators assigned a portion of the blame for the crash on the conflicts

---

[4]"Securities Industry—Revenues and Expenses: 1980–1994," *Statistical Abstract of the United States 1995,* no. 833, p. 535.

[5]"Other People's Money."

of interest in the two businesses. Commercial banks eventually earned the right to petition the Federal Reserve for underwriting powers. By 1995, J. P. Morgan, Chase Manhattan, and Bankers Trust had successfully requested these powers. They competed with investment banks in trading, debt underwriting, and advisory services. They had limited success in their efforts to underwrite stock offerings. The repeal of Glass-Steagall, which many predicted to occur by the end of the decade, would undoubtedly bring more participants to the securities industry. More competition would put further pressure on margins as newcomers competed for market share on price.

Many analysts expected that the European universal banks and U.S. money-center banks would be acquirors of U.S. investment banks once the act was repealed. Conventional wisdom stated that three firms—Goldman Sachs, Merrill Lynch, and Morgan Stanley—were sufficiently global and well capitalized as to remain immune from being acquired. Some speculated that Lehman Brothers, PaineWebber, and Salomon Brothers were prime merger or takeover targets.

COMPANY HISTORY

In 1959, William Donaldson, Dan Lufkin, and Richard Jenrette set out with $100,000 to create an equity-research firm that would serve institutional shareholders. Until that time, brokerage houses primarily catered to individual investors. The three Harvard Business School graduates saw that institutional investors were not adequately served.

The young firm prospered, offering sophisticated equity analysis to institutional investors in the hope of receiving their lucrative fixed-commission trading business. Gradually, the firm diversified in the face of competition and clients' demands for more services. As new businesses required more capital, the firm decided to go public in 1970. However, the New York Stock Exchange, of which DLJ was a member, prohibited members from having public shareholders. No NYSE member had ever offered shares to the public. *Business Week* reported on the controversial transactions, writing:

> Wall Street is, rather proudly, the home of the Big Risk and the Big Stake. Last week, three young men staked their 10-year-old, $24-million firm in one of the most remarkable wagers in recent financial history. If they lose, they forfeit their membership in the nation's wealthiest club, the New York Stock Exchange. If they win, they can increase the value of their firm tenfold, literally overnight. Win or lose, they have already set in motion forces that in the coming decade will wrench the sinews of power in every quarter of the U.S. securities industry.[6]

DLJ kept its NYSE membership, and in April of 1970, DLJ offered shares of itself to the public. At the time, DLJ had just over 400 employees with revenues of $21.9 million. The market valued the company at approximately $115 million.

DLJ continued its strategy of diversification during the seventies and early eighties. Faced with more capital requirements, DLJ chose to sell itself to Equitable in 1985 for $465 million. Equitable was then a mutual life insurance company, owned by policyholders. Richard Jenrette, head of DLJ, joined Equitable as chief investment officer shortly after the merger. He became chairman in 1990. Jenrette initiated a restructuring of Equitable in response to

---

[6]"Changing Wall Street's Rules," *Business Week,* May 31, 1969, pp. 70–74.

serious problems. In the restructuring, Jenrette cut $150 million in annual costs, and sold 49 percent of Equitable to AXA, a French holding company for a group of international insurance and financial services companies.[7] He also demutualized Equitable, raising $450 million in an initial public offering (IPO).[8] Equitable separated DLJ's original asset-management operations, Alliance Capital Management ("Alliance"), from DLJ. Later Equitable sold part of Alliance to the public. In June of 1995, Alliance's market capitalization stood at approximately $2 billion. By 1995, AXA owned approximately 60 percent of Equitable.

Under Equitable, DLJ built industry and product groups as opportunity presented itself. DLJ focused on building higher-margin businesses, like underwriting IPOs and high-yield ("junk") debt, creating specialized issues of mortgage-backed debt and merchant banking. It strove to be a leader in each market it selected. DLJ's strategy was one of patience, keeping lean in the good times and taking chances when others saw gloom. For example, while many securities firms fired employees following Black Monday—the October 17, 1987, crash—DLJ actively hired select professionals. Similarly, after the junk-bond market collapsed in 1990, DLJ sought out and hired a core group of junk-bond specialists from fallen market leader Drexel Burnham Lambert.

DLJ's careful strategy excelled, pushing DLJ up the industry league tables, as shown in Exhibit 3. By the mid-1990s, DLJ required more capital to continue its growth. Together, DLJ and Equitable sought a solution.

DLJ BUSINESS GROUPS

The company was a leading investment and merchant bank that served institutional, corporate, government, and individual clients. In terms of capital, DLJ ranked as the 11th largest securities firm. DLJ's businesses included securities underwriting, sales and trading, merchant banking, venture capital, financial advisory services, investment research, correspondent brokerage services, and asset management. It operated through three principal groups: the Banking Group, the Capital Markets Group, and the Financial Services Group.

DLJ Business Groups		
Banking Group	*Capital Markets Group*	*Financial Services Group*
Investment Banking	Institutional Equities	Pershing Division
Merchant Banking	Taxable-fixed Income	Investment Services Group
Emerging Markets	Equity Derivatives	Wood, Struthers & Winthrop
	Sprout Venture Capital	

In 1995, DLJ employed 4,676 people, including 431 professionals in the Banking Group, 821 professionals in the Capital Markets Group, and 998 professionals in the Financial Services Group. Exhibit 4 shows the revenue growth by group from 1990 until 1995.

---

[7]"Equitable Chairman to Step Down," *Bloomberg Business News,* February 13, 1996.

[8]A mutual insurance company is owned by policyholders. In a demutualization, ownership is converted to common stock and distributed to policyholders. Often times, new shares are sold to the public.

The Banking Group

The professionals in the Banking Group assisted clients in raising capital through the issuance of debt and equity securities in the public and private markets. The Investment Banking group also provided its clients with financial advice concerning mergers, acquisitions, restructurings, and other transactions. Since 1990, the Investment Banking group had assisted its clients in raising over $150 billion in capital and completed over 300 M&A transactions, worth approximately $65 billion. While DLJ worked with clients from all industries, it focused on 17 sectors where it believed it had a competitive advantage. The firm also maintained successful groups in private placements, private fund-raising (raising money for LBO funds, for example), structured finance, and restructurings.

The Merchant Banking group invested capital directly into companies, often in concert with the firm's clients. Institutional investors, DLJ itself, and DLJ employees provided the capital. DLJ utilized two investment funds with combined capital of $2.25 billion: DLJ Merchant Banking Partners L.P. and the DLJ Bridge Fund. These investments resulted in DLJ's owning a minority or majority position in a company's equity and debt. Since its inception in 1985, the group had invested in 46 companies with an aggregate purchase price of over $18 billion. Since 1992, DLJ had placed $580 million in 20 companies and realized $610 million from seven partial or whole realizations. DLJ earned one of the highest returns among principal investors, with annual returns thought to exceed 90 percent.[9] The bridge fund had completed 74 transactions totaling $12 billion of commitments to clients. The fund had $230 million of bridge loans outstanding as of June 30, 1995. The merchant banking activities earned money by charging a small fixed percentage for assets under management and keeping approximately 20 percent of the profits realized through the investments. The bridge operations earned money for committing to lend money and on the interest on money it lent out.

Due to its success in merchant banking, DLJ planned to form four new funds in the near future: DLJ Investment Partners, to seek out lower risk investments in debt and equity mezzanine securities and joint ventures; the DLJ Real Estate Fund, which would participate in the real-estate markets; the DLJ Senior Debt Fund, which would offer senior-debt financing to the firm's clients, replacing traditional senior bank loans; and Global Retail Partners L.P., to invest in early-stage retailers. The Merchant Banking group utilized DLJ's underwriting, M&A and research resources in exploring and executing merchant banking transactions.

In February 1995, the firm founded the Emerging Markets group to provide a broad array of investment banking, merchant banking, sales, and trading services to clients in Latin America and Asia. Additionally, the company agreed to invest $7 million in Pleiade Investments, a South African merchant bank.

The Banking Group produced high margins with lower levels of risk in favorable environments. Most of its costs were personnel related. These costs were tied to the group's performance through year-end bonuses; if performance fell, bonuses and costs fell. Merchant Banking offered more risk as DLJ put in its own capital with its limited partners

---

[9]Tom Pratt, "The Very Private World of Donaldson, Lufkin & Jenrette," *Investment Dealers Digest,* September 21, 1992.

in purchasing securities in companies. While Merchant Banking had performed spectacularly in the past, its investments were subject to being totally lost at any time if the companies in which it invested had difficulties.

Capital Markets Group

The Capital Markets Group offered trading, research, and sales services in fixed-income and equity securities. In these markets, DLJ focused on serving its clients and had not undertaken a large amount of proprietary trading.

The Taxable Fixed-Income division concentrated on serving institutional investors in high-yield corporate, investment-grade corporate, U.S.-government (as a primary dealer), and mortgage-backed securities. The division employed 450 professionals—including 72 traders, 137 institutional salespeople, and 52 fixed-income research analysts.

The Institutional Equities division covered major U.S. institutions with 100 traders and salespeople. For listed equities, the company acted as principal and agent, often taking long and short positions to help clients quickly gain liquidity. Most trades were made in blocks of 10,000 shares or more. DLJ also made markets in approximately 350 securities traded on the National Association of Securities Automated Quotation System (NASDAQ). The division primarily made markets for stocks of companies that had been underwritten by Investment Banking or covered by the research department.

DLJ earned the moniker *The House that Research Built,* referring to DLJ's founding as a research firm and continued strength in providing high-quality research. While the firm offered a broad array of services, it still maintained one of the highest rated research departments on Wall Street. Approximately 90 investment analysts analyzed and made recommendations on nearly 1,000 companies in 75 industries. The firm was only one of two companies that had ranked in the top 10 in each of the 23 years of *Institutional Investor's* annual All-America research survey.

The company provided a limited number of derivative products, mostly equity and index options through the Equity Derivatives division. Most of its products were tailored to meet a client's specific needs, in contrast to taking on trading risk or generating large volumes of generic derivatives. The Equity Derivatives division also participated in trading and distributing convertible securities.

Sprout, one of the oldest and largest venture-capital operations, resided in the Capital Markets group. Sprout managed over $1 billion in capital, focusing on investments in business services, computer graphics and peripherals, health care, leveraged transactions, office automation, retailing, and telecommunications. The professionals in Sprout worked closely with those in research and Investment Banking.

To serve clients, the Capital Markets Group held large inventories of stocks and bonds. While these positions were hedged to varying extents, their values changed with changes in the overall market. Under U.S. generally accepted accounting principles (GAAP), DLJ had to continuously mark its positions to market, creating losses and gains that appeared on the income statement. It financed much of its inventory through repurchase agreements with other financial institutions. These lenders would carefully watch DLJ and its financial condition in determining the rate they charged DLJ, which in turn would impact DLJ's overall profitability.

Financial Services Group

The Financial Services Group (FSG) provided a broad array of services targeted to individual investors and the financial intermediaries who represented them. Approximately 1,000 professionals worked in FSG. In FSG, Pershing offered correspondent brokerage services, clearing transactions for over 500 U.S. brokerage firms and lending clients money for margin trades. Pershing's clients collectively managed over 1 million accounts with assets of $100 billion. In clearing trades for others, Pershing accounted for approximately 10 percent of the daily volume on the New York Stock Exchange. It earned its revenues on a fee-for-service basis and on the interest made on money it lent for margin trades. Pershing's Financial Network™ was the largest on-line discount broker in the United States, providing trading through several on-line services, like America On-Line, PRODIGY, and Reuters Money Network. Between 1990 and 1994, the average daily volume traded through this service soared at an annual rate of 128 percent.

The Investment Services Group (ISG) served high-net-worth investors and smaller institutions. ISG gave its clients access to DLJ's research and sales and trading capabilities. DLJ purchased Wood, Struthers & Winthrop in 1977 to provide investment management and trust services to its clients. Wood, Struthers & Winthrop managed $2.5 billion, and operated three U.S. equity funds and two fixed-income funds.

FSG required a significant commitment of people and equipment to cover its clients and clear trades. While tied to the overall market, it made money more through market volatility than market direction. DLJ earned interest income by lending to customers to purchase securities and by holding higher-yielding inventory funded with lower-cost capital. In this capacity, DLJ made money much like a bank did, on the spread between the rate at which it lent or invested money and the rate at which it borrowed money. In 1994, DLJ made $288.1 million in net interest income.

Separate to the above three groups, DLJ owned Autranet, a distributor of independent research. Approximately 450 independent research firms, who had no affiliation with underwriters, supplied Autranet with research. Autranet distributed the research to over 400 institutions.

DLJ'S PERFORMANCE AND OUTLOOK

Overall, the firm's growth outpaced most of the industry over the last five years, steadily advancing DLJ up the industry league tables. Its strategy to compete in several higher margin businesses seemed to be succeeding. Revenues and profits grew at rates consistent with its increased market share: From 1990 to 1994 revenues increased at a compound average rate of 21.9 percent, while net income increased at 75.4 percent, generating an average annual pretax return on common equity of 33.6 percent. Each of the three operating groups expanded at roughly equal rates, though due to market conditions each experienced some fluctuation in year-to-year growth. Exhibits 5 and 6 present DLJ's financial statements and pro forma capitalization.

Investors would soon have the opportunity to share in DLJ's success. Many securities-industry analysts called DLJ one of the most desirable franchises on Wall Street. The analysts pointed to DLJ's focus on competing in select, high-margin businesses like initial public offerings, high-yield underwriting and trading, and merchant banking. Unlike some of its competitors, it did not commit large amounts of resources to the lower-margin businesses of underwriting and trading of investment-grade debt and municipal bonds. Investors who purchased DLJ's stock would be betting that DLJ could continue expanding its market share in its traditional areas and grow successfully in new areas with attractive profits. To continue gaining market share in many of its markets, however, DLJ would have to increasingly compete against much larger firms, like Goldman Sachs, Merrill Lynch, and Morgan Stanley.

While recognizing DLJ's strengths, critics worried that DLJ did not have sufficient operations overseas or large, recurring-fee operations. DLJ maintained seven offices in Europe and Asia, though it had not stated that it planned on committing the necessary capital to develop its operations around the world to compete in all aspects of the securities industry. DLJ seemed to choose foreign markets where it could obtain and maintain an advantage. And while DLJ's securities clearance division did generate significant recurring revenues, its profits were still tied to trading activity by its clients. It was not the steady, detached revenue stream that could come from extensive asset-management businesses. The critics were unsure that DLJ could find new business lines that would maintain its growth rates and profit margins.

Writer Anne Schwimmer brought out some questions in a cover story about DLJ and the offering in *Investment Dealers' Digest* (IDD). The article postulated that DLJ may have problems that could hinder post-IPO profits, such as an increasingly competitive high-yield market and a lack of diversified business lines. She questioned whether DLJ would maintain its culture with the increased scrutiny that public shareholders would bring.

In the high-yield market, she pointed to increasing competition where DLJ had enjoyed success and good margins. She speculated that the competition may have driven DLJ to underwrite some more speculative deals in high yield. She quoted a banker from a competing bank:

> Being a market leader, and in essence a firm that specializes in junk, they're not like a Goldman Sachs or Merrill Lynch or Morgan Stanley where you have a huge global business. Their mistake this year has been . . . (that) they saw so many competitors rushing into this market competing for mandates that they came down the credit quality spectrum, and started doing financings they wouldn't have done a year or two ago.

However, the banker continued, "To be honest with you, when we work with other firms, I like working with them the best.[10]

The article credited DLJ for building successful new businesses, like its institutional equities practice, but said that it needed further diversification. It also questioned whether or not DLJ's collegial atmosphere could survive in the face of public scrutiny. This atmosphere had been successful in nurturing professionals and keeping them at DLJ. Retaining key professionals was core to its mission. In the 1990s, DLJ had not suffered the talent drain and job-hopping that had plagued some firms. Employees strove to work hard, yet recognized the need to pursue interests outside of work. Indeed, DLJ's philosophy was that

---

[10]Anne Schwimmer, "Home Improvement" *Investment Dealers' Digest,* October 30, 1995.

the best employees managed to maintain balance in their lives. While the firm endeavored to serve its clients and earn a fair return for shareholders, it also included in the last line of its statement of principles: "Have fun!"

Others were not as sure that the stock would be a good investment at the offering. In a *Wall Street Journal* article, James Gipson, manager of a $340-million equity fund that invested heavily in investment banking stocks, said that he didn't plan on buying DLJ stock at the offering. He stated, "DLJ has been more consistently profitable than the typical Wall Street firm . . . but stock offerings take place when the owners think it's a good time to sell."[11]

VALUING DLJ

DLJ organized a "road show" to present the company to investors. On the road show, John Chalsty, president and CEO, and Anthony Daddino, CFO, traveled to 16 cities in four countries making over 30 presentations in just 19 days. DLJ expected to sell the stock to investors who wanted exposure to the securities industry. These investors would examine DLJ and its prospects relative to other publicly traded securities firms.

Earnings and cash flows at these firms were difficult to predict. Many external factors beyond the industry's control affected business dramatically, such as interest rates in the United States and abroad, merger-and-acquisition activity, domestic savings and investment rates, and the overall direction of the stock market. Additionally, analysts couldn't accurately predict how the firms would fare in their principal activities like trading, merchant banking, and venture capital. On the trading side, strategies that succeeded in the past might fall flat or key traders might leave. Realization of profits from principal investments depended upon the opportunity to exit the investment through a public offering or a sale, and results fluctuated from year to year.

DLJ posed extra valuation challenges due to its concentration in several key areas that were especially difficult to forecast, like high yield and IPO underwritings, and merchant banking. Picking comparable companies would be tenuous, as many of the other firms maintained large retail divisions, extensive principal trading activities, and broad investment-grade debt underwriting and trading operations.

The market tended to segregate the firms into four categories: bulge bracket, special bracket, regional and boutique firms, and discount brokers. The bulge brackets tended to compete for the business of large corporations, maintaining extensive staffs domestically and abroad in corporate finance and sales and trading. They were the largest firms, offering extensive services in almost every area of investment banking and brokerage. Special bracket firms often competed with the bulge brackets for business in selected industries and products, though keeping smaller operations and focusing primarily on U.S. clients. They generally possessed fewer people and less capital than the bulge-bracket firms. Regional investment banks and boutiques catered to companies and investors in their regions or industry specialties. Most concentrated on covering a few key industries.

---

[11]Michael Siconolfi, "DLJ Sets Sale of 20% Stake in Public Offering," *The Wall Street Journal,* August 30, 1995, Section A, 3:1.

Discount brokerages competed on price for retail investors' brokerage business, but generally didn't maintain underwriting or advisory departments. Exhibit 7 presents a segmentation of the industry. Exhibits 8, 9, and 10 present market and financial information on other securities firms.

Certainly, investors would count on receiving dividends from DLJ. During the past five years investors in other brokerage stocks had fared well, as dividends from these firms had grown considerably and stock prices had increased. Beginning in the first quarter of 1996, DLJ's board of directors planned on instituting a $0.125 quarterly dividend per share, or $0.50 at an annual rate.

Securities-industry analyst Guy Moszkowski of Sanford C. Bernstein & Company offered a separate valuation technique. He stated that he had observed a historical relationship between the current return on equity and the price-to-book ratio for capital markets firms like DLJ. Moszkowski noted that these firms often possessed a price-to-book ratio of 10 times the current return on equity in this part of the earnings cycle.[12]

In addition to its "fundamental" value, DLJ would have to contend with prevailing prices in the stock and bond markets and demand for IPOs in pricing the stock. If interest in IPOs dried up, DLJ might have to accept a lower price for its shares or postpone the offering. Generally, bankers priced IPOs 10 to 15 percent below their estimated value (the so-called IPO discount) in order to entice investors to purchase shares and to compensate them for buying stocks that lacked prior market prices. Exhibit 11 presents data on the IPO market and the overall equity and credit markets.

THE OFFERING

As an underwriter, DLJ planned to offer 9.2 million shares of stock to public investors. Of these, 5.9 million shares consisted of secondary shares sold by Equitable, and 3.3 million were primary shares offered by the company. The proceeds from secondary shares sold by Equitable would go to Equitable. Since these shares were already outstanding, they would not increase the number of shares outstanding. DLJ would receive the proceeds from the primary shares sold, which would increase the number of shares outstanding by 3.3 million. DLJ slated 7.36 million shares to be sold domestically and 1.84 million shares to be offered abroad.

Equitable also granted the underwriters a "green shoe." The green shoe was a 30-day option to purchase 1.38 million additional shares to cover any over-allotments made by the underwriters. DLJ anticipated that it would have 51.5 million shares outstanding after the offering. Equitable would own approximately 83 percent of DLJ's stock (80 percent if the green shoe were exercised). In connection with the stock offering, DLJ registered with the SEC to sell $300 million of senior subordinated notes for general uses and to repay existing bank borrowings.

---

[12]Guy Moszkowski, "Donaldson, Lufkin & Jenrette—Company Report," Sanford C. Bernstein & Co., Inc. December 1, 1995.

Technically, the shares offered by Equitable constituted an equity carve-out. In an equity carve-out, the parent company sold some of its interest in a subsidiary to the public. Many times, the parent sold less than 20 percent of its holdings in order to keep control of the subsidiary and to be able to consolidate the earnings and assets of the subsidiary on its own books. As long as the parent retained at least 80 percent of the equity of the subsidiary, it could consolidate its financial statements with those of its subsidiary under U.S. GAAP and thus be able to file a consolidated tax return.

Equity carve-outs and spin-offs (where a subsidiary's shares were distributed pro rata to existing investors) were very popular in the early 1990s as a way to increase shareholder value by unlocking hidden values, and creating "pure play" stocks that were easier for investors to value.

With the concurrent senior notes offering, DLJ obtained its own debt rating from Standard & Poor's of A − and Baa1 from Moody's. The credit markets could judge and lend to DLJ on its individual merits. If DLJ decided to increase its leverage, the ratings agencies would not penalize Equitable's debt ratings of A+ and A2. In return, Equitable still retained control of DLJ and received cash from the sale of its shares. It got a "fair market value" for part of its investment in DLJ and established a public price for its remaining interest.

EMPLOYEE OWNERSHIP

In conjunction with the offering, DLJ offered approximately 500 employees the opportunity to exchange $100 million of their interests in compensation plans for approximately 5.2 million shares of restricted stock. This stock was subject to vesting and forfeiture in certain circumstances. Additionally, these employees could exchange $55.7 million of future compensation under these plans for options to purchase approximately 9.2 million shares of DLJ stock at the offering price. Employees who opted to not exchange their interests would receive cash instead. The number of shares and options issued would depend on the final offering price.

Additionally, DLJ asked the underwriters to reserve approximately 550,000 shares for sale to directors and current and former employees of DLJ and Equitable. These groups would have the opportunity to purchase the reserved shares at a price equal to the initial public offering price less underwriting discounts and commissions. If these parties purchased these shares, they would be prohibited from selling them for five months. The underwriters would sell any shares they did not buy to the general public.

Since DLJ was not previously a public firm, it had to use various cash-compensation plans to give employees long-term incentives and rewards. After it went public, DLJ could use options as many of its peers did.[13] The employees of Merrill Lynch, for example, owned roughly 25 percent of the firm's stock, and employees of Morgan Stanley owned 39 percent. DLJ desired that its employees have their fortunes tied to those of the firm's other shareholders. If the employees gained control of the restricted stock and exercised the options gained under the exchange, they would own over 20 percent of DLJ's outstanding shares.

---

[13]While the cash incentives DLJ used in the past counted as compensation expense, options granted as compensation did not count as an expense under GAAP.

THE IPO PROCESS

Equitable and DLJ had selected the underwriters, choosing DLJ to serve as lead manager of the offering. They picked Goldman Sachs, Merrill Lynch, and Morgan Stanley to act as comanagers of the underwriting syndicate.[14] These four investment banks held responsibility for buying the shares from Equitable and DLJ and reselling them to investors. The four managers would receive the management fee, underwriting fee, and selling concession for their services.

In addition, the comanagers invited 26 securities firms to participate in the underwriting syndicate. These firms would be allocated a certain number of shares to sell, receiving the underwriting fee and selling concession for compensation. The managers asked 73 firms to be in the selling group. Members of this group received the selling commission if they sold their allotted shares, but could return any unsold shares to the underwriters. This option reduced the risks borne by the selling group.

On October 24, 1995, Equitable and DLJ stood at the end of the IPO process, ready to price DLJ's shares. The process had begun months before, when Equitable decided to offer shares to the public. Equitable and DLJ had chosen the other comanagers. The comanagers then investigated DLJ and its operations, performing due diligence, trying to ascertain the nature and status of the company. The underwriters risked their reputations with every IPO they underwrote and had to ensure that the issuer fairly and accurately represented itself. Investors counted on the investment banks' due diligence as a blessing or sign of trust on the quality of the issuer.

After completing the due diligence process, the comanagers, executives from DLJ, and their lawyers wrote the Form S-1 registration statement. Both DLJ and the underwriters had legal counsel assisting them through the entire process. In the S-1, DLJ offered extensive disclosures and descriptions of its business, history, risks, management, stock, and performance, as prescribed by the regulations surrounding the issuance of securities established in the Securities Act of 1933.

The issuer included a preliminary filing range for the expected price of the stock in the S-1. For DLJ, the filing range was $26.00 to $29.00 per share. The range implied an offering size of $239.2 million to $266.8 million (if the underwriters exercised their over-allotment option the range increased to $275.1 million to $306.8 million). Equitable and DLJ were not bound by this range, and could change the range with little effort. The S-1 also contained a copy of the preliminary prospectus to be used in the offering. On August 29, DLJ filed the S-1 with the SEC, establishing the registration date and starting the official registration process.[15]

From the registration date, the SEC had a period of at least 20 business days to review and comment on the S-1. This task fell to the SEC's division of corporation finance. The SEC did not comment on the quality or future prospects of the issuer, but instead focused on compliance with the regulations and the level of disclosure in the registration statement.

---

[14]As a member of the NASD, DLJ complied to Schedule E, which stipulated that in an offering of a member firm's parent company's stock, the price could be no higher than the price recommended by a "qualified independent underwriter." Goldman Sachs served in this capacity for the offering.

[15]For a more complete exploration of the offering process, see UVA-F-1129, "The Issue Process for Public Securities."

The SEC issued a letter of comment to the issuer, stating either that it found no problems with the registration or that the registration required further amendments. If the registration required refinements, the issuer made the changes and amended the registration. If the SEC found major problems in the statement, the issuer had to refile the registration with the SEC and issue a separate preliminary prospectus to potential investors.

While the SEC reviewed the registration statement, the issuer and managers were busy establishing the underwriting syndicate and marketing the security. The managers worked with the syndicate departments of other investment banks and brokerage firms to form the underwriting syndicate and selling group. These firms would ultimately sell the stock to investors.

The issuer and managers circulated the preliminary prospectus, known as a "red herring," and embarked upon a road show. During the road show, John Chalsty and Anthony Daddino made presentations to potential investors around the world. They met with investors in groups and in one-on-one sessions with large investors who requested these meetings. The first presentation was to the underwriters' sales forces to inform them of the particulars of the offering and issuing company. Salespeople from the underwriters spoke with potential investors about their interest in purchasing the securities. The investors often indicated how willing they would be to purchase the securities at a given price. For example, an institutional investor might have said that she would consider buying 100,000 shares at $27.00 per share, 75,000 at $28.00, and 60,000 at $29.00. Other investors, particularly in issues with heavy demand, might offer to buy as much as they could within the filing range. These indications were not obligations to buy the security; the investors could back out and refuse to purchase the shares.

Duff Anderson and the rest of DLJ's Capital Markets group oversaw this process. They coordinated the information-gathering process. The lead manager was known as the book manager or book runner because that firm gathered and controlled the information concerning the potential orders from all of the underwriters. The book manager consolidated this information into a "book" that was used to gauge demand at different prices and to price the issue. The professional book manager had to use his expertise in deciphering the firmness of the indications and the intent of the investors in owning the security. Many times, investors tried to game the process, especially for "hot" issues. For example, investors might place orders for more shares than they actually desired, knowing that all orders would be scaled down to the available supply. Certain short-term investors might want to buy the stock at issuance then quickly sell the stock for a profit (a technique known as flipping). Flipping added volatility to the after-market trading. Most issuers preferred to place their stock with longer-term investors. The book manager had to decide the depth and quality of the book.

When the underwriters and managers were satisfied with the level of indications and the conditions of the overall market, they negotiated the price of the security. After the issuer and underwriters agreed on the price, they filed an amendment to the registration statement that informed the SEC of the price of the security. The final prospectus then became effective. The issuer printed a final prospectus that included the price of the stock and circulated a copy of the prospectus to investors. After an issue went effective, the underwriters allocated and sold the shares to those who indicated their intent to purchase the securities.

The sale of the securities occurred on the public offering date, usually later on the day the issue went effective or the next morning. Underwriters tried to minimize the time between when the price was set—the price at which they committed to buy the securities—and the time when they sold the securities to the public. Three days after the offering date, the settlement occurred. Investors paid for and received their shares and the issuer received the net proceeds from the underwriters.

The pricing process before Equitable, DLJ, and the other underwriters was one of negotiation. The underwriters and issuer faced conflicting pressures in pricing the security. The underwriters had to consider the interests of both of their clients—issuer and investor—while mitigating their own risks. If the price were too low, the issuer would not be content with the performance of the underwriters. The issuer might believe that the underwriter left too much money "on the table." When selecting an underwriter, prospective issuers took into account an underwriter's prior performance. An underwriter who consistently underpriced securities would find that few companies wanted to use the firm. On the other hand, the investor would be happy to receive an underpriced security that would quickly appreciate in the aftermarket. However, underwriters received their remuneration as a percentage of the offering price, directly tying their pay to the price they obtained for the securities.

Conversely, if the security were overpriced, the investor would be unhappy as the stock fell in trading after the initial issuance. The investor might try to cut her losses and sell the security, further driving down the price of the stock. The investor would be left with a "bad taste" from the loss and might reconsider purchasing shares from the underwriter and the issuer in the future. Future issuances from the underwriter and issuer might receive less demand. The issuer may have received more money than expected from the issuance, but the preexisting shareholders (perhaps founders and managers) were now probably "long" a declining stock. They, too, might be upset. In this offering, Equitable would still own 80 percent of DLJ's stock that it might want to sell in the future.

The underwriters faced additional problems when a security was overpriced. They had purchased the stock from the issuer at a set price, but might not be able to sell all of it at this price. In this case, the underwriters might "break syndicate" and sell the stock at whatever price they could get. Additionally, the underwriters might try to support a falling issue in the aftermarket by buying it to keep it from dropping further. The underwriters had then taken the stock and its risks on to their balance sheets with their own capital. Losses generated by these activities could quickly offset underwriting profits.

In the end, many capital market professionals said that while there were many potential prices for any new issue, there was only one "right" price. The right price was a precarious balance of concerns for the issuer, for the investors, and for the investment banks themselves. Ideally, the price would satisfy all three constituents. The capital-markets bankers wanted to get the issuer the required money at a fair price without too much dilution. They strove to give each investor the stock he wanted, though many times the demand for shares was greater than the supply. They attempted to allocate the shares fairly, yet wanted an allocation that would move investors to purchase more shares in the aftermarket and in future offerings by the issuer. When investors didn't get all they wanted at the pricing, they would go out and buy more shares, driving the price up in the aftermarket. If the price went up, the underwriters would not have to support the stock, and the investors would be pleased. But if the stock went up too much, the issuer would feel that the underwriter left too much money on the table.

THE PRICING

Those sitting in the 49th-floor boardroom needed to make their decision. Although each party might have different objectives in setting a price, they had to reach a consensus. Richard Jenrette and Equitable would receive cash and a marketable security for their investment in DLJ. Investors would get the chance to invest in a very profitable, fast-growing firm that might be on its way to becoming one of the largest firms in the industry. Yet the firm would encounter many challenges in its drive to grow. Employees were eagerly awaiting the price to know how many shares and options they would obtain through the exchange. They were also anxious to see how the market would value what they had created under Equitable's ownership and guidance. The pricing decision would finish the IPO process and set DLJ off on its new course—as a separate public company.

EXHIBIT 1   The Expansion of the Financial Markets 1986–1995 (dollars in billions)[a]

	1986	1987	1988	1989	1990	1991	1992	1993	1994	09/95
Indices										
Fed Funds Rate (%)	9.2	6.8	8.9	8.0	5.5	4.1	2.7	2.9	4.9	6.2
Treasury bonds (%)	7.8	9.1	9.1	8.0	8.3	7.4	7.4	6.4	7.9	6.5
Dow Jones industrial average	1896	1939	2169	2753	2633	3168	2201	3754	3834	4789
NYSE average daily										
Shares traded (million)	141	189	162	165	157	179	202	265	291	338
Underwriting volumes										
Debt	$163	$131	$136	$149	$113	$195	$306	$452	$380	$568[b]
Common stock	43	42	30	23	19	56	71	102	62	91
IPOs	22	24	24	14	10	26	39	57	34	28
High-yield bonds	42	38	35	33	3	17	47	67	37	36
Mortgage and asset-backed	69	94	117	139	170	284	427	478	255	168
M&A and LBOs										
Value of transactions	$251	$221	$314	$314	$189	$124	$114	$179	$272	$406
Number of deals	2,619	2,723	3,171	3,846	3,615	3,354	3,697	4,822	5,704	6,572
LBOs as % of activity	18.3	18.1	17.0	22.8	1.8	4.4	5.5	5.2	2.7	1.5
Institutional activity										
Total long-term funds	424	454	472	554	569	853	1,100	1,510	1,551	1,908[c]
Stock funds % of total	38	40	41	45	43	48	48	50	56	60
Bond funds % of total	62	60	59	55	57	52	52	50	44	40

Note: January 1990 = 100
[a]Smith Barney "Broker and Asset Managers-Industry Report," October 9, 1995.
[b]Underwriting and M&A data for September 30, 1995, is annualized.
[c]Data are through August and annualized.

EXHIBIT 2 Securities Industry Revenues and Expenses 1980 to 1993* (in millions of dollars)

	1980	1985	1988	1989	1990	1991	1992	1993
Revenues								
Commissions	$ 6,777	$10,955	$11,932	$13,452	$12,032	$14,210	$16,249	$19,938
Trading and investment gains	5,091	14,549	16,667	16,247	15,746	22,641	21,838	25,526
Underwriting profits	1,571	4,987	5,607	4,537	3,728	6,593	8,300	11,251
Mutual fund sales	278	2,754	2,644	3,038	3,242	4,176	5,950	8,116
Other	2,960	13,854	26,096	35,731	33,428	34,498	35,557	41,343
Non-interest revenue	17,677	47,099	62,946	73,005	68,176	82,118	87,894	106,174
Margin interest income	2,151	2,746	3,155	3,860	3,179	2,771	2,690	3,242
Total revenues	19,829	49,844	66,100	78,864	71,356	84,890	90,584	109,416
Expenses								
Compensation	7,619	18,112	23,418	23,740	22,931	26,916	32,071	39,167
Exchange fees	1,055	2,314	2,804	3,057	2,959	3,200	3,722	5,364
Other expenses	4,119	11,446	16,899	17,422	16,583	18,605	21,908	24,766
Non-interest expenses	12,793	31,872	43,121	44,219	42,473	48,721	56,891	69,297
Interest expense	3,876	11,470	19,502	29,822	28,093	27,512	24,576	27,061
Total expenses	16,668	43,342	62,623	74,041	70,566	76,234	81,467	96,358
Pretax profits	$ 3,160	$ 6,502	$ 3,477	$ 2,823	$ 790	$ 8,656	$ 9,117	$13,058
Pretax margin	15.9%	13.0%	5.3%	3.6%	1.1%	10.2%	10.1%	11.9%
Margin excluding interest	27.6%	32.3%	31.5%	39.4%	37.7%	40.7%	35.3%	34.7%

*"Securities Industry—Revenues and Expenses: 1980–1994," *Statistical Abstract of the United States 1995,* no. 833, p. 535.

EXHIBIT 3   Selected Market Share Information for DLJ 1990–95[a]

	Years Ended December 31					*Six Months*	
	1990	*1991*	*1992*	*1993*	*1994*	*1994*	*1995*
U.S. M&A[b]							
Number of transactions	34	35	38	56	70	36	34
Rank based on value	12	12	9	11	11	7	7
Lead managed equity offerings[c]							
All common stock							
Number of issues	2	17	26	48	22	15	21
Rank based on value	25	8	6	7	10	8	7
IPOs							
Number of issues	1	8	14	24	15	9	13
Rank based on value	17	13	6	7	7	8	3
Lead managed high-yield issues[d]							
Number of issues	0	3	24	52	26	19	9
Rank based on value	—	4	3	1	2	2	1
Equity research rankings[e]							
"All-American" positions	35	37	43	45	44	NA	36
Overall rank	5	2	4	4	3	NA	2
"Completion percentage" rank[f]	1	1	1	1	2	NA	2
ISG statistics							
Number of account executives	127	137	170	190	233	NA	236
Assets in accounts (billions)	$2.5	$3.2	$4.5	$6.0	$8.0	NA	$9.9

[a]Source: DLJ.
[b]Source: DLJ, from *Investment Dealers' Digest,* includes completed domestic deals.
[c]Source: DLJ, from *Investment Dealers' Digest,* includes domestic transactions and excludes closed-end funds.
[d]Source: DLJ, from *Investment Dealers' Digest,* includes domestic transactions and excludes split-rated issues and private placements.
[e]Source: DLJ, from *Institutional Investor.*
[f]Completion percentage rank is based on the number of analysts divided by the number of All-American placements.

EXHIBIT 4   DLJ's Revenue Growth by Operating Group 1990–95

	Years Ended December 31 (dollars in millions)					*4-Year*	*Six Months*	
Operating Group	*1990*	*1991*	*1992*	*1993*	*1994*	*CAGR*	*1994*	*1995*
Banking	$152.4	$192.1	$ 428.4	$ 491.8	$ 390.0	26.5%	$178.2	$320.7
Capital markets	275.4	506.6	713.0	994.6	638.1	23.4%	345.4	344.5
Financial services	229.3	273.9	336.9	455.3	458.2	19.0%	233.6	284.9
Other	24.4	5.6	(26.5)	(38.1)	18.6	NM	2.9	1.7
Total	$681.8	$978.2	$1451.8	$1903.6	$1504.9	21.9%	$760.1	$974.8

Source: DLJ.

EXHIBIT 5 Summary DLJ Historical Statements (dollars in millions)

Income Statement Data	Years Ended December 31					Six Months Ended June 30		Last 12 Months Ended June 30
	1990	1991	1992	1993	1994	1994	1995	1995
Revenues:								
Commissions	$228.9	$257.9	$289.7	$358.8	$376.1	$194.2	$225.0	$406.9
Underwritings	150.3	170.9	350.3	574.6	261.1	139.5	171.2	292.8
Fees	88.9	166.2	158.1	211.3	281.3	112.9	173.5	341.9
Interest—Net[a]	362.3	323.0	381.7	657.3	791.9	391.4	423.6	824.1
Principal transactions—Net								
Trading	98.9	264.2	272.0	381.5	165.7	99.2	154.9	221.4
Investment	37.9	17.3	195.9	79.9	97.6	28.8	99.1	167.9
Other	16.9	15.1	16.4	21.9	35.0	15.2	26.4	46.2
Total revenues	984.1	1,214.6	1,664.1	2,285.3	2,008.7	981.2	1,273.7	2,301.2
Costs and expenses:								
Compensation and benefits	413.1	567.9	886.6	1,200.4	897.8	477.1	598.1	1,018.8
Interest	302.3	236.4	212.3	381.7	503.8	221.1	308.9	591.6
Other expenses	254.2	321.3	320.2	401.2	402.1	183.0	234.2	453.3
Total costs and expenses	969.6	1,125.6	1,419.1	1,983.3	1,803.7	881.2	1,141.2	2,063.7
Pretax income	14.5	89.0	245.0	302.0	205.0	100.0	132.5	237.5
Provision for income taxes	1.5	31.2	98.0	115.9	82.0	40.0	53.0	95.0
Net income before preferred dividends	$ 13.0	$ 57.8	$147.0	$186.1	$123.0	$ 60.0	$ 79.5	$142.5
Dividends on preferred stock	—	—	—	—	21.0	13.0	9.9	17.9
Net income applicable to common shares	$ 13.0	$ 57.8	$147.0	$186.1	$102.0	$ 47.0	$ 69.6	$124.6
Earnings per share					$ 1.98	$0.91[c]	$ 1.35	$ 2.42[c]
Dividends per share					$ 0.65	NA[c]	$ 0.33	NA[c]
Common shares outstanding[b]					51.5	51.5[c]	51.5	51.5[c]

[a]Interest is net of interest expense to finance U.S. government and agency instruments.
[b]Actual shares outstanding adjusted for the dilutive effect of the restricted stock units using the Treasury stock method.
[c]DLJ did not report earnings per share nor shares outstanding for these periods, and are estimated for illustrative purposes.

Source: DLJ Prospectus.

EXHIBIT 6 Summary Balance Sheets and Pro Forma Capitalization (dollars in millions)

	Years Ended December 31					Six Months Ended June 30	
	1990	1991	1992	1993	1994	1994	1995
Summary balance sheet data							
Securities purchased under agreements to resell and securities borrowed	$ 6,405.3	$ 10,942.5	$ 14,378.4	$ 21,575.2	$ 19,166.9	$ 22,886.1	$ 26,750.8
Total assets	$ 13,997.1	$ 18,721.7	$ 24,436.2	$ 38,766.7	$ 33,161.1	$ 41,628.8	$ 42,417.1
Liabilities and stockholders' equity							
Securities sold under agreements to repurchase and securities loaned	$ 7,619.0	$ 11,200.8	$ 19.7	$ 24,116.7	$ 20,385.4	$ 25,705.6	$ 27,895.9
Long-term borrowings	270.5	268.1	478.6	549.0	539.9	544.9	723.1
Preferred stock	—	—	—	225.0	225.0	225.0	225.0
Stockholders' equity	$ 294.1	$ 340.3	$ 454.6	$ 750.3	$ 820.3	$ 775.9	$ 873.6
Other financial data (at end of period)							
Ratio of net assets to stockholders' equity	25.81 x	22.86 x	22.12 x	22.91 x	17.01 x	24.16 x	17.93 x
Ratio of long-term borrowings to total cap	0.47	0.42	0.51	0.34	0.30	0.33	0.35
Pretax return on average equity	5.0%	28.1%	61.6%	50.1%	23.4%	23.3%	28.9%

EXHIBIT 6 (concluded)

Current Implied Dividend Yield	As of June 30, 1995		Percent of Total Capital	
	Actual	As Adjusted	Actual	As Adjusted
Pro forma capitalization (in thousands)*				
Short-term borrowings	$1,651,914	$1,523,881		
Notes	$ —	$ 300,000	0.0%	14.2%
Senior subordinated revolving credit	250,000	250,000	13.7%	11.9%
Term loan agreement	250,000	100,000	13.7%	4.7%
Swiss franc bonds	105,022	—	5.8%	0.0%
Medium-term notes	97,000	97,000	5.3%	4.6%
Other borrowings	21,067	21,067	1.2%	1.0%
Total long-term borrowings	723,089	768,067	39.7%	36.4%
Cumulative exchangeable preferred stock, at redemption value	225,000	225,000	12.4%	10.7%
Stockholders' equity				
Common stock ($0.10 par value) 150,000,000 shares authorized; 50,000,000 actual shares issued and outstanding; 53,300,000 as adjusted	1,000	5,330	0.1%	0.3%
Restricted stock units; number actual units issued and outstanding; 5,178,664 as adjusted units issued and outstanding	—	106,163	0.0%	5.0%
Paid-in capital	232,080	368,055	12.7%	17.4%
Retained earnings	640,855	637,157	35.2%	30.2%
Cumulative translation adjustment	(321)	(321)	0.0%	0.0%
Total stockholders' equity	873,614	1,116,384	48.0%	52.9%
Total capitalization (excl. short-term borrowings)	$1,821,703	$2,109,451	100.0%	100.0%

*Pro forma effects include offering at midpoint of filing range for illustrative purposes and $300,000 proposed debt issuance.

EXHIBIT 7 Groupings of Selected U.S. Investment Banks

Bulge Bracket	*Special Bracket*	*Regional Firms*
C.S. First Boston[a]	Alex. Brown & Sons	Advest Group
Goldman, Sachs (private)	Bankers Trust (commercial bank)	Bowles, Hollowell (private)
Lehman Brothers	Bear Stearns	Cowen & Co. (private)
Merrill Lynch & Co.	Dean Witter Discover	Inter-Regional Financial[b]
Morgan Stanley	Dillon, Read (private)	Interstate/Johnson Lane
Salomon Brothers	A. G. Edwards	Jefferies Group
	Hambrecht & Quist (private)	Legg Mason
	Lazard Freres & Co. (private)	Morgan Keegan
	Montgomery Sec. (private)	Piper Jaffray Cos.
	J. P. Morgan (commercial bank)	Raymond James Financial
	Paine Webber Group	Scott & Stringfellow
	Prudential Securities[c]	Stephens Inc. (private)
	Robertson, Stephens (private)	Tucker Anthony[d]
	Smith Barney[e]	Stephens Inc. (private)
		Wheat, First (private)

[a]C.S. First Boston was owned by Credit Suisse.
[b]Inter-Regional Financial Group owned Dain Bosworth and Rausher Pierce Resfnes.
[c]Prudential Securities was owned by The Prudential.
[d]Tucker, Anthony was owned by John Hancock.
[e]Smith Barney was owned by The Travelers.

EXHIBIT 8 Comparable Analysis of Selected Securities Firms (dollars in millions, except per share data)

	Alex. Brown	Bear Stearns	DLJ	A. G. Edwards	Lehman Brothers	Merrill Lynch	Morgan Stanley	Paine Webber	Salomon Brothers
Stock price as of October 23, 1995	$46.63	$20.00	NA	$25.13	$ 22.50	$ 56.98	$ 87.50	$21.50	$ 36.75
Shares outstanding (millions)	15.5	118.8	58.5	62.3	104.6	175.7	77.6	97.4	106.4
Market capitalization	$ 723	$2,376	NA	$1,565	$ 2,353	$10,011	$ 6,790	$2,095	$ 3,911
Long-term debt and preferred stock	173	4,792	993	0	13,605	16,775	9,929	2,710	14,353
Total market capitalization	$ 897	$7,168	NA	$1,565	$15,958	$26,787	$16,719	$4,805	$18,264
Last 12 months earnings per share	$ 5.29	$ 3.40	$2.42	$ 2.64	$ 1.59	$ 3.72	$ 4.06	$(0.26)	$ 0.58
Last 12 months book value per share	29.53	16.59	19.72	15.80	27.95	31.06	52.34	15.04	34.64
Cal. yr. 1995 est. earnings per share (Value Line)	6.16	1.70	NA	2.58	2.25	5.44	6.66	0.52	3.50
Cal. yr. 1996 est. earnings per share (Value Line)	6.10	2.80	NA	2.80	2.45	5.85	8.00	2.40	3.75
Current implied dividend	0.80	0.60	0.50	0.56	0.20	1.00	1.28	0.48	0.64
Stock price / LTM earnings per share	8.7 x	5.9 x	NA x	9.5 x	14.2 x	15.3 x	21.6 x	NMF x	63.4 x
Stock price / Book value per share	1.6	1.2	NA	1.6	0.8	1.8	1.7	1.4	1.1
Stock price / Cal. yr. 1995 est. earnings per share	7.6	11.8	NA	9.7	10.0	10.5	13.1	41.3	10.5
Stock price / Cal. yr. 1996 est. earnings per share	7.6	7.1	NA	9.0	9.2	9.7	10.9	9.0	9.8
Current implied dividend yield	1.7%	3.0%	NA	2.2%	0.9%	1.8%	1.5%	2.2%	1.7%
Value Line's Estimated 1996–2000									
Revenue growth	7.5%	12.0%	NA	9.5%	8.0%	13.0%	7.5%	9.0%	7.5%
Earnings	5.0%	10.0%	NA	9.5%	14.5%	8.0%	10.0%	10.5%	NMF
Dividends	10.5%	8.0%	NA	11.5%	19.0%	11.5%	9.0%	11.5%	2.0%
Book value	14.5%	14.0%	NA	13.0%	8.5%	14.5%	11.5%	9.0%	8.5%
Beta vs. S&P 500	1.27	1.64	NA	1.41	1.20	1.79	1.66	1.67	1.13
Employees	2,300	7,500	4,676	10,741	7,771	46,023	9,236	16,025	6,400

Sources: Bloomberg Financial Services, Value Line Investment Survey.

EXHIBIT 8   *(concluded)*

Descriptions of Selected Publicly Traded Securities Firms

Alex. Brown & Sons	Founded in 1800, Alex. Brown was a Baltimore-based investment bank with traditional strengths in underwriting IPOs and common stock. Alex. Brown had focused on diversifying revenues into M&A and sales and trading. It maintained a strong banking and research presence in a selected number of industries where it could be a leader. Alex. Brown was perennially rumored to be a takeover target for someone wanting to enter the securities industry.
Bear Stearns & Co.	Bear Stearns traced its roots to 1923 and went public in 1985. Bear Stearns was one of the largest dealers in fixed-income products, especially mortgage-backed securities. It operated a large clearance business for smaller brokerage firms. It had recently experienced strong gains in its corporate finance and M&A practices. While it covered all types of clients, its primary focus was on middle-market companies and selected products.
A. G. Edwards	St. Louis–based A. G. Edwards was founded in 1887 and went public in 1971. A. G. Edwards had 534 brokerage branches with 5,600 brokers, serving over 1 million clients. An estimated 95 percent of these were retail clients. A. G. Edwards maintained investment-banking operations, focusing on regional clients. A. G. Edwards also offered other products targeted to individual investors.
Lehman Brothers	Lehman was a major global investment bank specializing in investment-grade debt and equity underwriting, and sales and trading (approximately 40 percent of revenues came from abroad). Founded in 1850, Lehman was acquired by American Express in 1983, then spun-off to shareholders in 1994. It had undergone a major cost-reduction program in recent years to increase profitability.
Merrill Lynch & Co.	Merrill Lynch was the number one global underwriter for debt and equity in the 1990s. Its primary focus was on Fortune 500 clients in corporate finance. Recently, Merrill had strengthened its M&A and international businesses. It supplemented its investment-banking operations with a massive asset-management business. Merrill operated the largest retail brokerage network in the United States. Merrill had a large and excellent research staff. The firm actively participated in real estate, mortgage banking, cash management, and insurance, as well. Its recent problems with an Orange County derivatives suit seemed to be lessening.
Morgan Stanley	Morgan Stanley was a major international investment bank, with particular strengths in global offerings, M&A, merchant banking, and high-yield underwriting. Morgan Stanley had a reputation of being able to effectively handle the most complex transactions. It was building its asset management business. The firm was one of the first to expand overseas, and earned 40 percent of its revenues abroad. Its historical focus on Fortune 100 companies was expanding to cover emerging companies, especially in high technology.
Paine Webber	Paine Webber maintained the third largest brokerage force, with 6,025 brokers handling 2.5 million clients. Its corporate finance and research strengths were focused on covering middle-market companies. Paine Webber had embarked on a cost-cutting initiative to improve its profitability. It recently settled limited partnership claims against it for $200 million. In an effort to expand its trading and investment banking operations, Paine Webber purchased Kidder, Peabody in 1994.
Salomon Brothers	Salomon Inc. conducted business through Salomon Brothers and Phibro Energy. Phibro was a commodities trading and oil-refining company. Salomon was a traditional leader in fixed-income underwriting and trading. Recently, Salomon increased its emphasis on its corporate finance operations. It had a reputation as the premier proprietary trader. The firm was attempting to cut costs. The cost-cutting efforts led to a new salary plan that had caused many top professionals to leave. It had suffered through a trading scandal with the U.S. Treasury that had nearly caused the firm to collapse.

EXHIBIT 9   Inventory Holdings and Capital Structure Analysis of Selected Securities Firms (dollars in millions)

	Alex. Brown	Bear Stearns	DLJ	A. G. Edwards
Securities inventory analysis				
Government obligations	$ 3.3	$ 7,620.0	$ 7,336.4	$ 28.5
Municipals	44.1	136.1	0.0	96.8
Mortgage-backed	1.7	2,497.4	411.2	0.0
Corporate debt	19.6	2,501.4	3,450.3	0.0
Corporate stock	29.0	6,182.2	392.0	25.2
CDs and money market instruments	0.0	0.0	0.0	0.0
Commodities and other	0.0	1,841.2	0.0	0.0
Total	$ 97.7	$ 20,778.3	$ 11,589.9	$ 150.5
Percent of total inventory:				
Government obligations	3.4%	36.7%	63.3%	18.9%
Municipals	45.1%	0.7%	0.0%	64.3%
Mortgage-backed	1.7%	12.0%	3.5%	0.0%
Corporate debt	20.1%	12.0%	29.8%	0.0%
Corporate stock	29.7%	29.8%	3.4%	16.7%
CDs and money market instruments	0.0%	0.0%	0.0%	0.0%
Commodities and other	0.0%	8.9%	0.0%	0.0%
Total assets	$ 1,915	$ 79,517	$ 42,417	$ 2,617
Note: Resell agreements	$ 7	$ 24,741	$ 16,652	$ 114
Capitalization structure				
Short-term debt	$ 73	$ 9,230	$ 1,524	$ 0
Repurchase agreements	0	31,907	25,076	0
Long-term debt	173	4,205	768	0
Preferred stock	0	588	225	0
Total common equity	458	1,971	1,116	985
Total equity	458	2,558	1,341	985
Total capital excluding repos	$ 705	$ 15,993	$ 3,633	$ 985
Percent of total capital structure (excl. repos):				
Short-term debt	10.4%	57.7%	41.9%	0.0%
Long-term debt	24.6%	26.3%	21.1%	0.0%
Preferred stock	0.0%	3.7%	6.2%	0.0%
Total common equity	65.0%	12.3%	30.7%	100.0%
Total debt / Total equity	53.8%	525.2%	170.9%	0.0%
Long-term debt / Total equity	37.8%	164.4%	57.3%	0.0%
Total equity as % total assets	65.0%	16.0%	36.9%	100.0%
Senior debt rating (Moody's/S&P)	NR	A2/A	Baa l/A−	NR
Data as of	9/30/95	9/30/95	6/30/95	8/31/95

Source: D. P. Eberling, "Donaldson, Lufkin & Jenrette—Company Report," Prudential Securities, December 15, 1995, and company reports.

Lehman Brothers	Merrill Lynch	Morgan Stanley	Paine Webber	Salomon Brothers
$ 24,162.0	$ 17,938.6	$ 23,582.0	$ 6,539.6	$ 66,959.0
0.0	996.2	0.0	989.0	0.0
6,014.0	2,923.7	0.0	3,734.0	1,616.0
9,250.0	18,254.8	10,128.0	2,254.8	10,247.0
5,950.0	9,875.2	7,980.0	835.5	4,385.0
2,799.0	1,551.5	0.0	820.4	0.0
0.0	11,463.1	7,987.0	0.0	8,412.0
$ 48,175.0	$ 63,003.1	$ 49,677.0	$ 15,173.3	$ 91,619.0
50.2%	28.5%	47.5%	43.1%	73.1%
0.0%	1.6%	0.0%	6.5%	0.0%
12.5%	4.6%	0.0%	24.6%	1.8%
19.2%	29.0%	20.4%	14.9%	11.2%
12.4%	15.7%	16.1%	5.5%	4.8%
5.8%	2.5%	0.0%	5.4%	0.0%
0.0%	18.2%	16.1%	0.0%	9.2%
$ 117,518	$ 185,473	$ 132,264	$ 49,545	$ 162,586
$ 37,173	$ 45,502	$ 47,849	$ 27,622	$ 43,497
$ 9,167	$ 31,762	$ 6,707	$ 1,673	$ 6,420
57,887	54,274	62,322	29,540	77,817
12,897	16,156	9,111	2,423	13,341
708	619	818	287	1,012
2,923	5,459	4,062	1,466	3,687
3,631	6,077	4,880	1,752	4,699
$ 25,695	$ 53,996	$ 20,698	$ 5,848	$ 24,460
35.7%	58.8%	32.4%	28.6%	26.2%
50.2%	29.9%	44.0%	41.4%	54.5%
2.8%	1.1%	4.0%	4.9%	4.1%
11.4%	10.1%	19.6%	25.1%	15.1%
607.7%	788.5%	324.1%	233.8%	420.5%
355.2%	265.8%	186.7%	138.3%	283.9%
14.1%	11.3%	23.6%	30.0%	19.2%
Baa l/A	A1/A+	A1/A+	Baa l/BBB+	Baa l/BBB
8/31/95	9/30/95	8/31/95	9/30/95	9/30/95

EXHIBIT 10   Revenue and Income Analysis of Selected Securities Firms (dollars in millions)

	Alex. Brown	*Bear Stearns*	*DLJ*	*A. G. Edwards*
Income statement statistics				
1990–94 compound average growth rates				
Gross revenues	22.2%	8.6%	17.7%	17.0%
Net revenues	23.6%	14.8%	21.9%	17.1%
Commissions	19.8%	12.5%	13.1%	20.3%
Investment banking revenues	21.4%	17.0%	22.7%	15.2%
Principal transactions	40.3%	14.9%	17.8%	11.4%
Net income	74.2%	21.1%	75.4%	24.7%
Earnings per share	74.2%	37.0%	NA	23.9%
Dividends per share	26.3%	1.7%	NA	17.9%
Last 12 months' information				
Gross revenues	$ 716.5	$ 4,019.5	$ 3,818.6	$ 1,298.5
Net revenues	686.2	2,258.9	1,904.8	1,294.6
Commissions	163.3	581.9	437.3	621.9
Investment banking revenues	241.0	377.8	767.5	97.0
Principal transaction revenues	125.9	944.4	421.6	216.0
Net income	82.4	298.9	159.0	148.6
Last 12 months earnings per share	$ 5.39	$ 3.40	$ 2.42	$ 2.64
Current implied dividend per share	$ 0.80	$ 0.60	$ 0.50	$ 0.56
Dividend payout (Implied div./LTM EPS)	14.8%	17.6%	20.7%	21.2%
Net margin (gross revenues)	11.5%	7.4%	4.2%	11.4%
Net margin (net revenues)	15.3%	16.3%	10.6%	21.7%
Percent change in line items				
YTD 1994 – YTD 1995				
Gross revenues	24.6%	28.8%	6.6%	15.1%
Net revenues	23.6%	20.9%	36.5%	15.4%
Commissions	22.1%	24.3%	22.1%	−17.2%
Investment banking revenues	28.1%	18.3%	63.2%	−9.5%
Principal transaction revenues	8.0%	21.3%	79.3%	−1.7%
Net income	22.6%	40.9%	42.1%	26.6%
Earnings per share	24.2%	51.2%	48.1%	4.2%
Dividend per share	15.0%	0.0%	NA	10.5%
Business composition analysis				
Revenue source as a percent of net revenues				
Commissions	23.8%	25.8%	23.0%	48.0%
Investment banking revenues	35.1%	16.7%	40.3%	7.5%
Principal transactions	18.3%	41.8%	22.1%	16.7%
Other	22.7%	15.7%	14.6%	27.8%
Average ROE for previous three years	24.0%	24.4%	27.8%	20.3%

Source: D. P. Eberling, "Donaldson, Lufkin & Jenrette—Company Report," Prudential Securities, December 15, 1995, and company reports.

Lehman Brothers	Merrill Lynch	Morgan Stanley	Paine Webber	Salomon Brothers
NA	13.1%	12.4%	7.4%	−8.5%
NA	13.6%	12.9%	9.9%	−17.5%
NA	13.1%	13.0%	10.4%	12.9%
NA	11.7%	9.0%	4.9%	4.0%
NA	12.8%	5.2%	2.4%	NM
NA	51.7%	9.9%	−1.1%	NM
NA	56.1%	5.5%	NM	NM
NA	15.5%	12.9%	20.2%	0.0%
$ 11,040.0	$ 20,703.8	$ 10,391.0	$ 4,985.0	$ 8,086.0
2,781.0	9,744.8	3,862.0	3,077.1	2,421.0
452.0	2,917.6	479.0	1,156.0	331.0
652.0	1,165.2	1,076.0	295.3	413.0
1,227.0	2,406.3	1,366.0	814.5	493.0
202.0	1,061.5	532.0	2.7	132.0
$ 1.59	$ 3.72	$ 4.06	$ (0.26)	$ 0.58
$ 0.20	$ 1.00	$ 1.28	$ 0.48	$ 0.64
12.6%	26.9%	31.5%	NM	110.3%
1.8%	5.1%	5.1%	0.1%	1.6%
13.6%	13.9%	24.6%	0.1%	5.7%
37.7%	18.0%	22.3%	34.9%	38.1%
3.0%	1.6%	20.0%	28.2%	80.2%
3.0%	2.1%	13.0%	25.0%	−1.9%
24.8%	−7.3%	33.3%	4.9%	−19.4%
−16.4%	3.8%	44.3%	76.5%	NM
207.1%	5.5%	57.6%	−56.8%	NM
243.2%	−25.9%	−2.5%	−100.0%	NM
−40.0%	13.6%	8.0%	0.0%	0.0%
16.3%	29.9%	12.4%	37.6%	13.7%
23.4%	12.0%	27.9%	9.6%	17.1%
44.1%	24.7%	35.4%	26.5%	20.4%
16.2%	33.4%	24.4%	26.4%	48.9%
NA	23.8%	17.7%	17.5%	11.0%

EXHIBIT 11   IPO and General Capital Market Data: Number of IPO Transactions and Values

	1994		*1995*	
	Number	*Dollar Value*	*Number*	*Dollar Value*
January	40	$ 3,319.9	25	$ 1,422.6
February	77	5,101.1	46	1,541.3
March	75	5,822.9	36	1,741.8
April	54	3,154.9	47	2,951.0
May	78	2,359.8	42	1,908.7
June	66	4,089.7	69	3,379.8
July	47	3,521.6	60	2,729.5
August	54	2,540.4	55	2,861.0
September	41	2,400.1	38	2,362.0
October	65	4,556.6	—	—
November	49	3,235.8	—	—
December	38	2,014.1	—	—
Annual total	684	$42,116.9	—	—
January–September	532	$32,310.0	418	$20,897.7

General Credit and Equity Markets Data

	October 23, 1994	*October 23, 1995*
Fixed-income rates		
LIBOR (1 Month)	5.000%	5.875%
3-month Treasury	5.131%	5.426%
6-month Treasury	5.700%	5.575%
1-year Treasury	6.216%	5.645%
2-year Treasury	6.803%	5.757%
3-year Treasury	7.105%	5.816%
5-year Treasury	7.504%	5.921%
10-year Treasury	7.844%	6.073%
30-year Treasury	8.043%	6.392%
Equity Market Indices		
Dow Jones Industrial Avg.	3,891.30	4,755.48
S&P 500 Index	464.89	585.06
S&P Financials Index	42.92	59.69
S&P Investment Bank & Brokerage Index	120.80	172.09

Source: "IPO and General Capital Market Data," Bloomberg Business News, 1995.

British Aerospace PLC (A)

In the summer of 1991, Sir Roland Smith, chairman of the board of directors of British Aerospace (BAe), concluded that the company required £432 million in additional equity. This capital would be used to finance export sales, to continue the delivery of products already financed by customer advances, to fund ongoing restructuring and rationalization of the firm, and to rebuild the firm's equity base. In January 1991, Sir Roland had told securities analysts that he expected BAe's pretax profit for the year would total £300 million. In late August, however, there was troubling news that the recession in Britain was imposing a significantly greater strain on the company's performance and finances than had been expected. Results for the first six months ending in June 1991 showed a pretax profit of £86 million, off from £146 million in the first half of 1990. BAe's financial staff estimated that pretax profits for the year would drop to −£85 million.

In these circumstances, should BAe go to the market immediately, just as news of the first-half results were being absorbed by the financial community? Or should it wait a few months and risk a rights offering of shares under the darker cloud of the full-year results? The financial results and a sale of new shares would depress the share price from the 565-pence level prevailing in late August. If the company moved quickly, before it had to report first-half results in early September, it might exploit the high current price. Although capital market conditions were improving, BAe could not predict how soon it would be able to return to the market at August's 565-pence share price once it released first-half results. On the other hand, a rights offering of shares would require the firm to forecast near-term financial performance, which might also depress share prices. If the firm did proceed soon with a rights offering, what should its terms be? Specifically, where should BAe set the exercise price of each right, and how many rights should be issued per share of outstanding stock?

This case was prepared by Professor Robert F. Bruner. This case was written as a basis for class discussion rather than to illustrate effective handling of an administrative situation. Copyright © 1993 by the University of Virginia Darden School Foundation, Charlottesville, VA. All rights reserved. *No part of this publication may be reproduced, stored in a retrieval system, used in a spreadsheet, or transmitted in any form or by any means— electronic, mechanical, photocopying, recording, or otherwise—without the permission of the Darden Foundation. For inquiries, please send an e-mail to dardencases@virginia.edu.* Revised 11/97. Version 1.5.

THE COMPANY

British Aerospace was among the largest industrial firms in the United Kingdom, with 1990 sales and net income of £10.54 billion and £278 million, respectively. Its principal business sectors consisted of (1) defense systems, (2) commercial aircraft, (3) the Rover automobile group, and (4) property and construction. Exhibit 1 presents the contributions of each of these sectors to the firm's total annual sales and profits in recent years.

Defense Systems.   The company was a significant competitor in the defense-systems market: It led all Western European defense contractors, and it ranked third, after McDonnell Douglas and General Dynamics, among all defense contractors in the industrialized countries. BAe's products included military airframes, missiles, ammunition, explosives, and guns. The company declared that its objective was to "consolidate its position as one of the world's leading defense contractors as the industry restructures." Given the decline of the Soviet bloc from 1989 to 1991, it appeared that the defense-systems industry would enter a period of reduced demand and major rationalization. Although the demand for defense products was dropping in August 1991, BAe's management believed that demand would recover to previous levels by the year 2000. Outside analysts were especially interested in the "Al Yamamah" defense construction program for Saudi Arabia, for which BAe was the prime contractor. This program supplied defense systems, construction services, training, and support to the Saudi government. As of August 1991, BAe's gross revenues from this program exceeded £8.3 billion. BAe's management believed that sales from the contract would amount to £2 billion per year to the year 2000.

Commercial Aircraft.   BAe participated in Airbus Industrie and produced regional commercial aircraft and executive jets. Airbus was a consortium venture between BAe, Aerospatiale of France, Deutsche Airbus of Germany, and CASA of Spain. BAe designed and manufactured wings for the various Airbus models. Airbus was expected to grow and introduce new models over the next few years, which suggested that BAe would have to make significant commitments of working capital to the project.

Although demand for regional commercial aircraft was expected to grow, competition was expected to be particularly keen. Analysts believed that no manufacturers would earn a satisfactory return on capital employed in this sector; consequently, they expected the regional aircraft industry to undertake a substantial program of rationalization. BAe intended to participate in this rationalization and to introduce new models in conjunction with partners. The executive-jet segment was growing well and provided a satisfactory return on capital.

The Rover Automobile Group.   BAe produced and sold automobiles under the Rover, Land Rover, MG, and Sterling marques. BAe acquired Rover in August 1988, in what most observers agreed was a distress sale. Rover had been operating unprofitably for years prior to 1988. Since the acquisition, BAe had focused on improving profitability in the Rover group. This had entailed emphasizing export sales, repositioning Rover's car products toward the upper quartile of its respective market sectors, raising prices, changing the management process and working practices, and collaborating closely with Honda in product engineering and manufacturing. BAe expected that continued product enhancement and expansion would require capital expenditures greater than £350 per year over the next three years. Even with declining demand for automobiles in late 1990, management believed that the Rover group would be self-financing over the next three years.

Property and Construction. BAe entered this sector in 1987 when it acquired Ballast Nedham, an engineering and construction firm. In 1989, BAe also acquired Arlington, a developer of industrial parks. BAe offered three reasons for its entry into this sector: (1) the defense-systems sector required construction capability; (2) BAe's own restructuring would create surplus land and industrial facilities that BAe would want to sell or develop; and (3) complete infrastructure projects were generally viewed as an important industrial-growth segment. The recession in real estate that began in 1990 was gaining in severity, however, and depressing the financial performance of this sector of BAe's business.

PAST FINANCIAL PERFORMANCE AND ANALYSTS' EXPECTATIONS

In late 1990, securities analysts openly acknowledged the business and financial challenges facing BAe: one analyst cited BAe as "one of the last really inefficient U.K. manufacturing companies." Nevertheless, he also issued a "buy" recommendation at 526 pence per share, arguing:

> There is obviously a lot wrong with British Aerospace. The company is, however, aggressively coming to terms with its difficulties through a radical programme of restructuring that will improve trading margins. The buy case rests upon defense profits stabilizing on a much reduced cost base, upon which recovery in motors, aerospace, and property can build. With growth in telecommunications and asset sales reducing debt, these could double profits on a five-year view . . . 1991 will be a particularly strong year for BAe.[1]

Other analysts echoed this view. Their forecasts of financial performance for the year ending December 31, 1991, projected pretax profits at about £465 million, earnings per share at about 110 pence, and a dividend per share at 27.5 pence. These forecasts were, in part, an extrapolation of favorable historical trends in the company (see Exhibit 1). They were also founded on expectations of a robust market for automobiles, a strong recovery in property, and large exports under the Al Yamamah program.

RESULTS FOR FIRST-HALF 1991 AND FUTURE FINANCING REQUIREMENTS

Exhibit 1 presents the financial results for the first half of 1991, which Sir Roland would soon be obliged to report to investors. The figures showed that pretax income had fallen to £86 million as compared with £146 million for the same period a year earlier. Even worse, BAe analysts projected that, although the pretax income for the full year would be no greater than £150 million, it would be offset by £235 million in extraordinary restructuring

---

[1]P. Compton, "British Aerospace—Company Report," UBS Phillips & Drew Global Research Group, December 5, 1990.

charges. Thus, Sir Roland's staff projected that pretax earnings would be −£85 million *at best*. These results would be a stunning reversal of the historical trend and of the expectations of securities analysts.

The earnings decline was due to softening of business in the commercial aircraft and property sectors of the firm's activities. The defense sector remained robust, although growth in orders under the Al Yamamah program had not yet materialized. The Rover group had been saddled with £45 million in extraordinary expenses arising from its withdrawal from the North American automobile market.

Against this backdrop, management sought to raise £432 million in new common equity. The cash position of the firm had deteriorated sharply in the first half of 1991, because of heavy capital expenditures and seasonal buildup of working capital in the Rover group; reductions in customer advances as deliveries continued under the Al Yamamah program; and extraordinary rationalization expenses. The firm's net cash balance (cash less short-term debt) had declined from £711 million outstanding at the end of 1990 to −£120 million by the end of the first half of 1991. BAe's financial staff believed that net cash would return to a positive balance of £100 million by the end of 1991, although this would be well below prior years' balances (see Exhibit 1).

Exhibit 2 presents the prevailing price trends for BAe shares. BAe shares had enjoyed a surge in value in February 1991, along with the rest of the stock market, upon the conclusion of the Gulf War. Since then, the share value had subsided somewhat. At a level of 565 pence, shares were trading at a multiple of 5.8 times 1990 earnings per share (compared with a market-average multiple of 13.9 times 1990 earnings per share), and at a substantial discount from the 1990 book value per share of 845 pence. One analyst argued that the book value understated the true breakup value of the firm because it ignored future cash flows from the Al Yamamah program, the intangible values in the Rover group's brand names, and potential gains in more than 6,000 acres of developable land.[2]

RIGHTS-OFFERING METHOD OF ISSUING COMMON STOCK

In Britain, as in the rest of the European Community,[3] securities regulations required public companies to offer new shares of common stock to existing shareholders first. Shareholders retained the right (but not the obligation) to purchase shares offered to them; in other words, shareholders had "preemptive rights" over newly issued shares. The prevailing method of selling common stock was called a rights offering of shares. In a typical rights offering, existing shareholders were offered the opportunity to buy new shares

---

[2]Ibid.

[3]The rights offering, a preemptive offering of shares to existing shareholders, was the predominant method of share issuance outside the United States. The technique preferred in the United States was the "general cash offer," or "bought deal," where an underwriter would buy the shares from the issuing company and resell them to *any* interested investor. Some evidence suggested that rights offerings were less than or equally as costly as general cash offers to the issuer. Rights offerings differed from general cash offers mainly in that (1) in a rights offering, the price of the new shares was theoretically irrelevant and (2) rights offerings protected existing investors against involuntary dilution.

in proportion to their current holdings; the exercise price was fixed at some discount to prevailing market prices; and the option to buy lasted for a limited time, such as 30–50 days. The task for the shareholder was to decide whether to (1) exercise the rights, (2) sell the rights to someone else, or (3) do nothing and allow the rights to expire worthless. If the shareholder exercised the rights, his or her percentage interest in the company would remain unchanged; but if the rights were sold or allowed to expire, the shareholder's interest would be *diluted* to the extent of new shares issued.

The primary task for the issuing company was to design the rights issue to promote its success. Three elements needed to be decided:

- *Proportion of new shares to current holdings.* The right typically entitled the shareholder to purchase a specified number of new shares in proportion to the number of shares he or she currently held. For instance, a two-for-five rights issue meant that two new shares were offered for every five shares already owned.
- *The price discount.* Most rights offerings discounted the shares by 12 to 20 percent from prevailing prices. It was commonly believed that shares were discounted as an incentive to investors to buy the shares. Some analysts argued that the price at which shares were to be issued was irrelevant, because any discount affected the number of shares to be issued, which, in turn, affected the dilution of preexisting shares. Thus, discount and dilution might offset each other. Exhibit 3 illustrates the theoretical effect of a rights offering by BAe on its share price and market value of equity. The exhibit reveals that, if the shareholder failed to exercise or sell the rights, he or she would sustain a loss in value, and that loss would grow with increases in the rights ratio or the price discount, or both.
- *Underwriting.* In theory, companies had no need of an intermediary for the share issue because they would be selling shares to their own shareholders. An intermediary would, however, ensure that the company would receive the desired amount of proceeds in the issue: a firm underwriting commitment was essentially a put option that enabled the issuer to sell its shares to the underwriter in the event that its own shareholders did not exercise their rights. The typical fee for a standby commitment was 1.25 percent of the gross proceeds of the issue. Sir Roland wondered whether this would be a fair fee in BAe's case.[4]

CONCLUSION

The decisions about the timing and terms of the share rights offering seemed to depend on the financial information that the firm would soon release. How would the stock market respond to this information? Was there a way to frame the information to best advantage? Raising £432 million from existing shareholders meant a significant addition to the book value of the firm's equity and an even larger addition to its market value. Sir Roland Smith would, however, need to proceed cautiously in taking any action.

---

[4]The commitment would need to be outstanding for 30 to 50 days. BAe's sigma, or volatility, was .36; its beta was 1.08. Short-term British government Treasury bills were yielding 10.07 percent at the end of August 1991. BAe's dividend yield was about 5 percent. The stock price currently was 565 pence. The exercise price of the standby commitment would be the same as the exercise price of the shareholder right.

EXHIBIT 1   Historical, Projected, and Expected Financial Performance (values expressed in £ millions, except
per share amounts, which are in pence, and shares outstanding, which are in millions)

	1988	1989	1990 Actual	1991 Projected	1992 Projected	First Half 1990 Actual	First Half 1991 Actual
Revenues							
Defense	3,000	3,800	4,423	5,500	5,000	2,055	1,918
Aircraft	978	1,525	1,560	1,950	2,300	687	910
Rover	1,179	3,430	3,785	4,000	4,000	1,863	1,863
Property	409	547	577	570	800	269	315
Other	80	100	195	155	165	−88	−120
Total	5,646	9,402	10,540	12,175	12,265	4,786	4,886
Operating profit							
Defense	315	300	486	460	420	177	273
Aircraft	−9	19	35	20	20	12	−33
Rover	52	64	55	80	120	33	−45
Property	18	58	9	20	60	9	15
Intercompany	−34	0	NA	10	11	3	5
Total	342	441	585	590	631	234	213
Interest expense	−40	−103	−138	−90	−90	−45	−100
Exceptional items	−40	−5	−71	−35	−35	−43	−27
Pretax profit	236	333	376	465	506	146	86
Tax rate (%)	34	28	26	28	28	28	31
Minority interest	0	−26	−18	−42	−45	−3	15
EPS (p)	62	83	98.2	112	123	35.6	24.7
DPS (p)	20.6	22.7	28.7	27.5	31	10.5	13.8
Net cash	215	1,142	711	600	500	576	−120
Book value/Share (p)	860	826	845	1,000	1,050	821	1,678
Shares outstanding	—	—	299.89	—	—	294.94	238.8

Sources: Company annual reports and "British Aerospace—Company Report," UBS Phillips & Drew, December 5, 1990.

EXHIBIT 2   British Aerospace Prices per Share versus London Stock Market Index (FTSE100)*

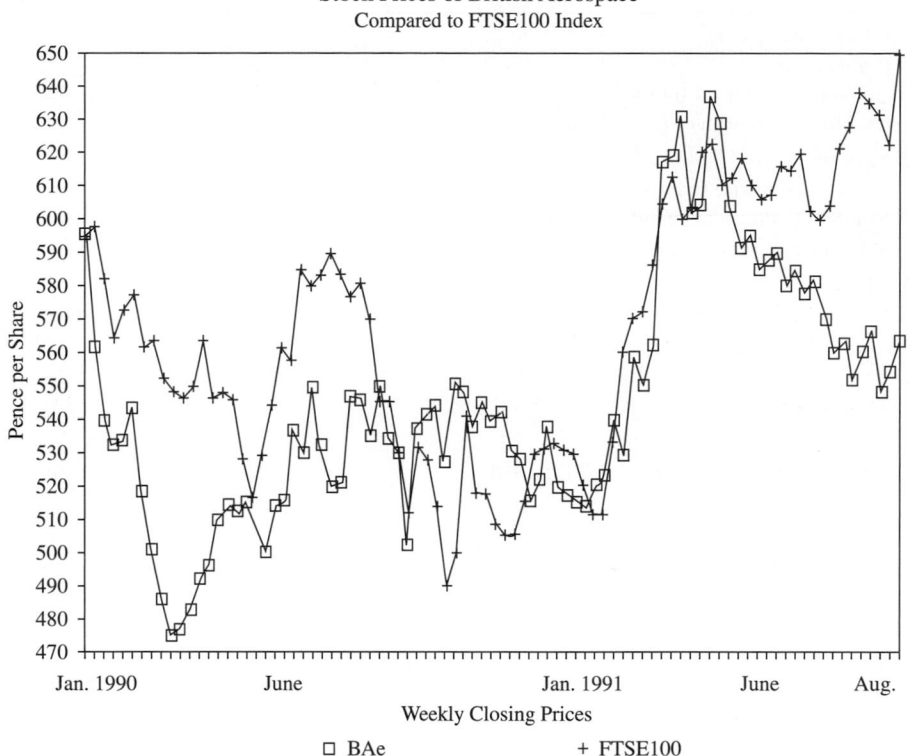

Stock Prices of British Aerospace
Compared to FTSE100 Index

*For the sake of comparison, the FTSE100 has been indexed to the British Aerospace share price at January 1, 1990.

Source of price data: Datastream, Inc.

EXHIBIT 3 Example of a Rights Offering Using Values for BAe, Summer 1991

	Scenario 1	Scenario 2	Scenario 3
Some key assumptions			
1. Rights ratio	2:5	3:5	4:5
2. Amount to be raised (£mm)	432	432	432
3. Exercise price (pence) [Line 2/Line 7]	452	302	226
Before issue			
4. Stock price before (pence)	565	565	565
5. Number of shares outstanding (mm)	238.8	238.8	238.8
6. Market value of shares (£mm)	1,349	1,349	1,349
After issue			
7. New shares added (mm) [Line 2 × Line 5]	95.52	143.28	191.04
8. Cost of new shares (£mm) [Line 2]	432	432	432
9. Total value of outst. sh. (£mm) [Line 8 + Line 6]	1,781	1,781	1,781
10. Total number of shares (mm) [Line 5 + Line 7]	334.32	382.08	429.84
Results			
11. New share price (pence) [Line 9/Line 10]	533	466	414
12. Value of a right (pence) [Line 4 − Line 11]	32	99	151
Impact of dilution if you exercise or sell the right:			
13. + Value of right (pence)	32	99	151
14. − Decline in stock price (pence)	(32)	(99)	(151)
15. = Dilution in value (pence)	0	0	0
Dilution in value if you do not exercise or sell the right:			
16. + Value of right (pence)	0	0	0
17. − Decline in stock price (pence)	(32)	(99)	(151)
18. = Dilution in value (pence)	(32)	(99)	(151)

Comment: The amount to be raised (Line 2) is assumed to remain constant across different rights offering deals. Thus, the rights ratio (Line 1) and the exercise price (Line 3) are interdependent. The *ex post* share price (Line 11) declines as more shares are issued. The value of the right (Line 12) rises as the exercise price (Line 3) declines, consistent with option pricing theory. Lines 13–15 reveal the hypothesized value neutrality of rights offerings. Lines 16–18 reveal the consequences for the unwitting.

Source: Casewriter's analysis.

Part VI

Management of the Corporate Capital Structure

Case 26

An Introduction to Debt Policy and Value

Many factors determine how much debt a firm takes on. Chief among them ought to be the effect of the debt on the value of the firm. Does borrowing create value? If so, for whom? If not, then why do so many executives concern themselves with leverage?

If leverage affects value, then it should cause changes in either the discount rate of the firm (i.e., its weighted-average cost of capital) or the cash flows of the firm.

1. Please fill in the following:

	0% Debt/ 100% Equity	25% Debt/ 75% Equity	50% Debt/ 50% Equity
Book value of debt	0	$2,500	$5,000
Book value of equity	$10,000	$7,500	$5,000
Market value of debt	0	$2,500	$5,000
Market value of equity	$10,000	$8,350	$6,700
Pretax cost of debt	.07	.07	.07
After-tax cost of debt	.0462	.0462	.0462
Market value weights of:			
Debt	0	_____	_____
Equity	1.0	_____	_____
Unlevered beta	.8	.8	.8
Risk-free rate	.07	.07	.07
Market premium	.086	.086	.086
Cost of equity	_____	_____	_____
Weighted-average cost of capital	_____	_____	_____
EBIT	$ 2,103	$2,103	$2,103
− Taxes (@ 34%)	_____	_____	_____
EBIAT	_____	_____	_____
+ Depreciation	$ 500	$ 500	$ 500
− Capital expenditures	($ 500)	($ 500)	($ 500)
Free cash flow	_____	_____	_____
Value of assets (FCF/WACC)	_____	_____	_____

Why does the value of assets change? Where, specifically, do the changes occur?

2. In finance, as in accounting, the two sides of the balance sheet must be equal. In the previous problem, we valued the asset side of the balance sheet. To value the other side, we must value the debt and the equity, and then add them together.

	0% Debt/ *100% Equity*	*25% Debt/* *75% Equity*	*50% Debt/* *50% Equity*
Cash flow to creditors:			
Interest	0	$ 175	$ 350
Pretax cost of debt	.07	.07	.07
Value of debt:			
(CF/r_d)	_____	_____	_____
Cash flow to shareholders:			
EBIT	$2,103	$2,103	$2,103
− Interest	_____	($ 175)	($ 350)
Pretax profit	_____	_____	_____
Taxes (@ 34%)	_____	_____	_____
Net income	_____	_____	_____
+ Depreciation	$ 500	$ 500	$ 500
− Capital expenditures	($ 500)	($ 500)	($ 500)
− Debt amortization	0	0	0
Residual cash flow	_____	_____	_____
Cost of equity	_____	_____	_____
Value of equity (CF/r_e)	_____	_____	_____
Value of equity plus value of debt	_____	_____	_____

As the firm levers up, how does the increase in value get apportioned between creditors and shareholders?

3. In the preceding problem, we divided the value of all the assets between two classes of investors—creditors and shareholders. This process tells us where the change in value is *going,* but it sheds little light on where the change is *coming from.* Let's divide the free cash flows of the firm into *pure business flows* and cash flows resulting from *financing effects.* Now, an axiom in finance is that you should discount cash flows at a rate consistent with the risk of those cash flows. Pure business flows should be discounted at the unlevered cost of equity (i.e., the cost of capital for the unlevered firm). Financing flows should be discounted at the rate of return required by the providers of debt.

This exercise was prepared by Professor Robert F. Bruner. This exercise was written as a basis for class discussion rather than to illustrate effective or ineffective handling of an administrative situation. Copyright © 1989 by the University of Virginia Darden School Foundation, Charlottesville, VA. All rights reserved. *No part of this publication may be reproduced, stored in a retrieval system, used in a spreadsheet, or transmitted in any form or by any means—electronic, mechanical, photocopying, recording, or otherwise—without the permission of the Darden Foundation. For inquiries, please send an e-mail to dardencases@virginia.edu.* Revised 11/97. Version 1.3.

	0% Debt/ 100% Equity	25% Debt/ 75% Equity	50% Debt/ 50% Equity
Pure business cash flows:			
EBIT	$2,103	$2,103	$2,103
Taxes (@ 34%)	($ 715)	($ 715)	($ 715)
EBIAT	$1,388	$1,388	$1,388
+Depreciation	$ 500	$ 500	$ 500
− Capital expenditures	($ 500)	($500)	($ 500)
Cash flow	$1,388	$1,388	$1,388
Unlevered beta	.8	.8	.8
Risk-free rate	.07	.07	.07
Market premium	.086	.086	.086
Unlevered WACC	_____	_____	_____
Value of pure business flows: (CF/Unlevered WACC)	_____	_____	_____
Financing cash flows			
Interest	_____	_____	_____
Tax reduction	_____	_____	_____
Pretax cost of debt	.07	.07	.07
Value of financing effect: (Tax reduction/pretax cost of debt)	_____	_____	_____
Total value (sum of values of Pure business flows and Financing effects)	_____	_____	_____

The first three problems illustrate one of the most important theories in finance. This theory, developed by two professors, Franco Modigliani and Merton Miller, revolutionized the way we think about capital-structure policies. The M&M theory says:

$$\underset{\text{Problem 1}}{\underset{\wedge}{\begin{array}{c}\text{Value of}\\\text{assets}\end{array}}} = \underset{\text{Problem 2}}{\underset{\wedge}{\begin{array}{c}\text{Value of}\\\text{debt}\end{array}}} + \begin{array}{c}\text{Value of}\\\text{equity}\end{array} = \begin{array}{c}\text{Value of}\\\text{unlevered firm}\end{array} + \underset{\text{Problem 3}}{\underset{\wedge}{\begin{array}{c}\text{Value of}\\\text{debt tax shields}^{1}\end{array}}}$$

4. What remains to be seen however, is whether shareholders are better or worse off with more leverage. Problem 2 does not tell us, because there we computed total value of equity, and shareholders care about value *per share*. Ordinarily, total value will be a good proxy for what is happening to the price per share, but in the case of a relevering firm, that may not be true. Implicitly we assumed that, as our firm in problems 1–3 levered up, it was repurchasing stock on the open market (you will note that EBIT did not change, so management was clearly not investing the proceeds from the loans in cash-generating assets).

---

[1]Debt tax shields can be valued by discounting the future annual tax savings at the pretax cost of debt. For debt that is assumed to be outstanding in perpetuity, the tax savings is the tax rate, t, times the interest payment, $r \times B$. The present value of this perpetual savings is $trB/r = tB$.

We held EBIT constant so that we could see clearly the effect of financial changes without getting them mixed up in the effects of investments. The point is that, as the firm borrows and repurchases shares, the total value of equity may decline, but the price per share may *rise*.

Now, solving for the price per share may seem impossible, because we are dealing with two unknowns—share price and change in the number of shares:

$$\text{Share price} = \frac{\text{Total market value of equity}}{(\text{Original shares} - \text{Repurchased shares})}$$

But by rewriting the equation, we can put it in a form that can be solved:

$$\text{Share price} = \frac{\text{Total market value of equity} + \text{Cash paid out}}{\text{Number of original shares}}$$

Referring to the results of problem 2, let's assume that all the new debt is equal to the cash paid to repurchase shares. Please complete the following table:

	0% Debt/ 100% Equity	25% Debt/ 75% Equity	50% Debt/ 50% Equity
Total market value of equity	_____	_____	_____
Cash paid out	_____	_____	_____
Number of original shares	1,000	1,000	1,000
Total value per share	_____	_____	_____

5. In this set of problems, is leverage good for shareholders? Why? Is levering/unlevering the firm something shareholders can do for themselves? In what sense should shareholders pay a premium for shares of levered companies?

6. From a macroeconomic point of view, is society better off if firms use more than zero debt (up to some prudent limit)?

7. As a way of illustrating the usefulness of the M&M theory and consolidating your grasp of the mechanics, consider the following case and complete the work sheet. On March 3, 1988, Beazer PLC, a British construction company, and Shearson Lehman Hutton, Inc. (an investment banking firm), commenced a hostile tender offer to purchase all the outstanding stock of Koppers Company, Inc., a producer of construction materials, chemicals, and building products. Originally the raiders offered $45 per share; subsequently the offer was raised to $56, and then finally $61 per share. The Koppers board generally asserted that the offers were inadequate and its management was reviewing the possibility of a major recapitalization.

To test the valuation effects of the recapitalization alternative, assume that Koppers could borrow a maximum of $1,738,095,000 at a pretax cost of debt of 10.5 percent and that the aggregate amount of debt will remain constant in perpetuity. Thus, Koppers will take on additional debt of $1,565,686,000 (i.e., $1,738,095,000 minus $172,409,000, the pre-existing long-term debt). Also assume that the proceeds of the loan would be paid as an extraordinary dividend to shareholders. Exhibit 1 presents Koppers's book- and market-value balance sheets assuming the capital structure before recapitalization. Please complete the worksheet for the recapitalization alternative.

EXHIBIT 1   Koppers Company, Inc. (values are in thousands)

	Before Recapitalization	*After Recapitalization*
Book-value balance sheets		
Net working capital	$ 212,453	_____
Fixed assets	601,446	_____
Total assets	813,899	_____
Long-term debt	172,409	_____
Deferred taxes, etc.	195,616	_____
Preferred stock	15,000	_____
Common equity	430,874	_____
Total capital	$ 813,899	_____
Market-value balance sheets		
Net working capital	$ 212,453	_____
Fixed assets	1,618,081	_____
PV debt tax shield	58,619	_____
Total assets	1,889,153	_____
Long-term debt	172,409	_____
Deferred taxes, etc.	0	_____
Preferred stock	15,000	_____
Common equity	1,701,744	_____
Total capital	$1,889,153	_____
Number of shares	28,128	_____
Price per share	$ 60.50	_____
Value to public shareholders		
Cash received	0	_____
Value of shares	$1,701,744	_____
Total	1,701,744	_____
Total per share	$ 60.50	_____

Case 27

MCI Communications Corp.: Capital Structure Theory

On a cold winter morning in February 1996, Katzu Mizuno stood admiring the panoramic view of New York Harbor from the 19th floor of the World Trade Center. In his first five months in New York as a first-year associate for Lynch Investments, Katzu had been pleasantly surprised to have some free time to explore the Big Apple. During this period, he had found an apartment, been to Madison Square Garden for a Knicks game, attended the symphony at Lincoln Center, and had made frequent trips to a sushi bar in his neighborhood. The tranquillity of the moment ended, however, with an urgent phone call from his boss, Anna Curti.

Earlier that morning, MCI Communications Corp., a longtime client of the firm, had called seeking advice about establishing a program to repurchase some of its outstanding common stock. As Exhibit 1 shows, throughout most of 1995 MCI's stock had been a sluggish performer in an otherwise buoyant market, and management sensed a growing restlessness on the part of shareholders. At a recent meeting of the board of directors, discussions had centered on repurchasing some of company's stock as a means to enhance shareholder value. One longtime director, Gavin Philips, pushed hard to finance the repurchase by increasing MCI's debt financing. He argued that this action would send a bold signal to the market about the future prospects of the firm. To be effective as a signal, Philips suggested that the company would need to increase its debt-equity ratio from its current level of around 36 percent to "at least twice that." He said, "Even at that debt level, MCI's debt-to-cap would be moderate relative to the industry." He estimated that such action would require MCI to issue approximately $2 billion in additional debt. Other direc-

This case was prepared by Susan Chaplinsky, Associate Professor of Business Administration and Robert S. Harris, Professor of Business Administration, University of Virginia. This case is drawn entirely from public data. All persons and events recounted are fictionalized to facilitate the teaching objectives of the day. Copyright © 1997 by the University of Virginia Darden School Foundation, Charlottesville, VA. All rights reserved. *No part of this publication may be reproduced, stored in a retrieval system, used in a spreadsheet, or transmitted in any form or by any means—electronic, mechanical, photocopying, recording, or otherwise—without the permission of the Darden Foundation. For inquiries, please send an e-mail to dardencases@ virginia.edu.*

tors, concerned that the increased debt burden might impede the company's current capital-expansion program, argued for a less extreme approach. They favored an open-market purchase program instead. Under this option, the company would announce its intentions to repurchase its stock from "time to time" but only as corporate funds allowed. This course of action, therefore, did not call for any increase in debt.

On hearing the directors' concerns, a senior vice president of MCI, William Duran, called Curti to seek advice on the repurchase and particularly whether debt financing would be advisable. Duran also indicated that since the board hoped to disclose the details of its plan to improve shareholder value by the end of next week, it would be necessary to get back to him as soon as possible. Curti responded quickly: She assigned a second-year associate, Lance Alton, to gauge the possible interest in any debt securities MCI might choose to issue, and she asked Mizuno to examine the consequences of substantially increasing the firm's use of debt. She instructed both of them to report their initial findings to her the following day.

Mizuno decided to compare MCI with its major competitors in long-distance telecommunications. However, he grew somewhat alarmed when his initial screen of peer companies produced approximately 40 firms in long-distance communications.[1] He knew that all of these firms could not be considered comparable to MCI based on their business risk, the markets they operated in, and their tax and regulatory environments. After comparing them to MCI on these dimensions, he narrowed his list to certain companies.

Exhibit 2 contains financial data for the peer companies. In assembling the data, Mizuno made several assumptions to help ensure consistency across the peer firms. First, although he was not certain of the tax status of each firm, he decided to initially assume that all companies faced a 40 percent tax rate. Second, it was the usual practice at Lynch to use a market-risk premium of 7.0 percent, the latest estimate of the arithmetic mean return of stocks over Treasury bonds.

Mizuno recalled from his finance classes that the maximum value of the firm corresponded to the lowest overall cost of capital. Thus, he intended to estimate what the cost of equity and the weighted-average cost of capital (WACC) might be if MCI pursued this capital-structure change. After discussions with other personnel at the bank, he concluded that the higher debt/equity ratio would increase MCI's borrowing costs from its current level of 6.10 percent. Exhibit 3 contains the latest capital market rates from which an estimate of the revised borrowing costs could be obtained. But what would the cost of equity (k_e) be? Mizuno decided that one approach was through "levering" and "unlevering" betas using the following equation:

$$\beta_{E,L} = \beta_U (1 + D(1 - T)/E)$$

where $\beta_{E,L}$ and β_U are the betas for levered and unlevered equity, respectively; D and E are the market values of debt and equity, respectively; and T is the corporate tax rate.

---

[1]The domestic companies competing with MCI in telecommunication services were Ameritech, Bell Atlantic, BellSouth, NYNEX, Pacific Telesis, SBC Communications, US West, AT&T, Sprint, Worldcom, Frontier Communication, GTE, Southern New England, IntelCom, and MFS Communications. In addition, there were 25 international telecommunication services companies.

Description of Industry Comparables

Company	*Description*
Ameritech	Ameritech is a holding company for Illinois, Indiana, Michigan, Ohio, and Washington State Bells and other subsidiaries, providing communications services directly to 75 percent of the population in these states. In October 1983, Ameritech became the first regional holding company to offer cellular phone service (21 million POPs, or persons served). 1994 revenue breakdown: local service, 42 percent; long-distance, 12 percent; network access, 23 percent; other, 23 percent. Purchased 49.9 percent stake in Telecom Corporation of New Zealand in September 1990 (now 25 percent after additional equity offerings). Ameritech will be among the first of the Baby Bells to offer long-distance telephone services. Bond rating AA2.
AT&T	AT&T Corporation is the world's largest long-distance telephone company. Formerly American Telephone and Telegraph, AT&T resulted from a court-ordered breakup of the Bell System in 1983, when it received about 23 percent of the former company's assets. AT&T operates in global information management, financial services, and leasing. 1994 revenue breakdown: telecommunication services, 59 percent; product and system sales, 28 percent; rentals and other, 10 percent; financial services and leases, 3 percent. Acquired McCaw Cellular in 1994, NCR in 1991; LIN Broadcasting in 1995. Bond rating AA3.
MCI Communications	MCI Communications Corporation, the second largest long-distance carrier, offers long-distance services domestically and internationally. Primary business is U.S. voice, using MCI's 3,556-million-circuit-mile microwave and fiber network. Offers 800 service, operator assistance, worldwide direct dialing, fax, and 900 service. British Telecom holds 100 percent of Class A common stock representing a 20 percent voting interest. Bond rating A2.
Sprint Corporation	Sprint Corporation operates the second largest independent-telephone system in the United States. Merged with Centel Corporation in a pooling-of-interests in March 1993. Provides long-distance services through U.S. Sprint and local telecommunication services to 6.65 million access lines. Cellular business serves a market of 20.2 million POPs. Also has directory publishing and supply distribution operations. 1994 revenue breakdown: long-distance, 53 percent; local phone, 34 percent; other, 13 percent. Bond rating BBB−.
Worldcom, Inc.	Worldcom, Inc. (formerly LDDS Communications, Inc.) is the fourth largest long-distance carrier in the nation. The company offers long-distance service through its 15,000-mile owned-and-leased network. Serves the entire United States and points to 230 countries. The company derives a predominant share of its total revenues from sales to commercial customers. Products include switched and dedicated lines for voice and data. Acquired IDB Communications, December 1994; WiTel Network Services, January 1995. Bond rating BBB−.

In addition to the information on peer firms, Exhibits 4 and 5 contain the latest income statement and balance sheet for MCI. This information could be used to estimate the expected changes in earnings per share and the tax benefits that would occur with a debt-financed stock repurchase. Mizuno knew that both issues would be of great interest to MCI's senior management.

As Mizuno prepared to tackle the analysis, he was concerned that his approach might not capture all the complexities of the decision. While shareholders' required returns typically increase as a firm uses more debt financing, he knew that the theoretical predictions of the cost of equity were only approximations. Mizuno had prepared a "to-do" list from his readings on capital costs (Exhibit 6) and thought these might help guide him through the analysis. To be sure no issues had been ignored, he would pursue a three-pronged approach: (1) examine the effects of debt on the firm's future coverage ratios under both expected and downside cash-flow projections, (2) check with Lance on the reactions gathered from potential creditors (i.e., would severe covenants be required?), and (3) review the company's need for future flexibility and consider how this financial strategy might affect business decisions.[2]

It would be a long night ahead. However, before he pursued these additional issues, Mizuno decided to start with the guidance theory offered.

---

[2]A useful framework for analysis is the FRICTO framework, in which the analyst looks at Flexibility, Risk, Income, Control, Timing, and Other factors.

EXHIBIT 1 Telecommunications Industry Stock Price Performance (value of $1,000 investment made January 22, 1993, as of December 29, 1995)

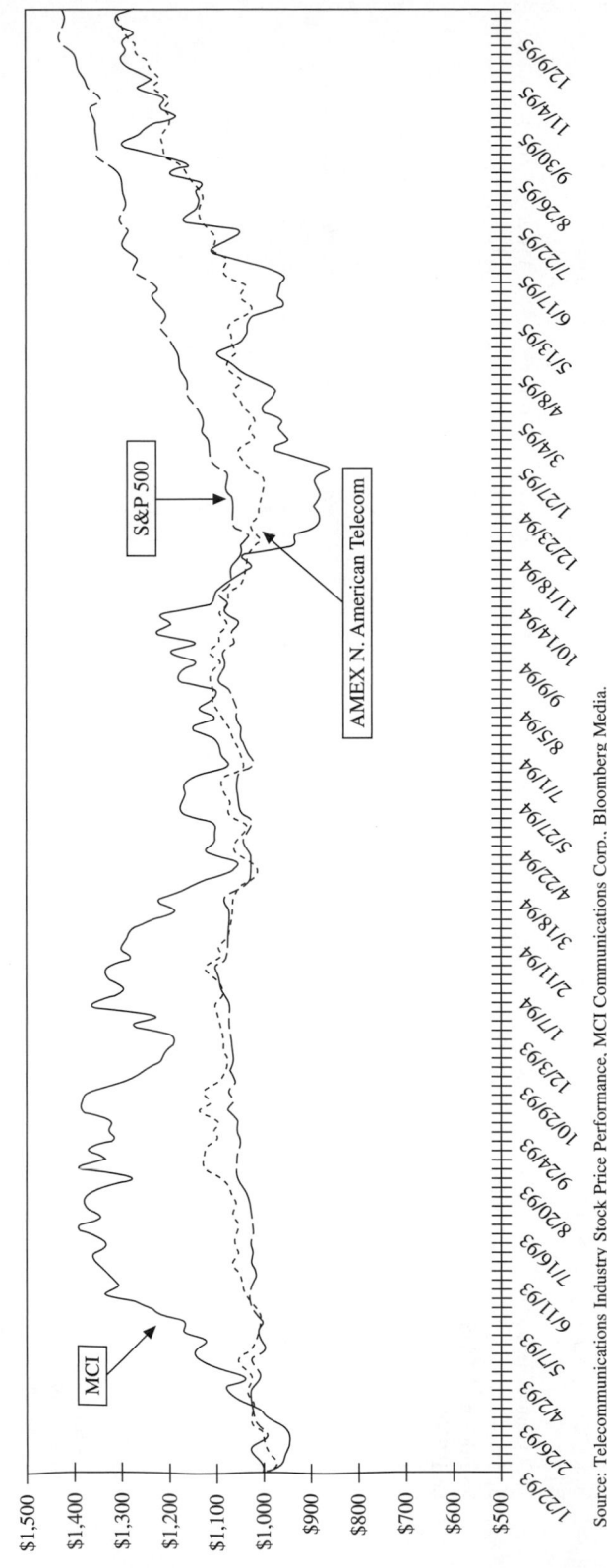

Source: Telecommunications Industry Stock Price Performance, MCI Communications Corp., Bloomberg Media.

Stock/Index	Total Return
MCI Communications	25.53%
S&P 500	41.23%
AMEX North American Telecom	30.25%

EXHIBIT 2 Financial Characteristics for Long-Distance Telecommunications Firms

Company	Recent Share Price	Number of Shares (Millions)	Market Capitalization (Millions)	Long-Term Debt, Incl. Capitalized Leases (LTD)	Total Interest Coverage (EBIT/ Interest)	LTD/(LTD + Book Value of Equity)	LTD/(LTD + Market Value of Equity)	LTD/Book Value of Equity	LTD/Market Value of Equity
Ameritech	$ 59.50	554	$ 32,963	$ 4,547	7.1	0.392	0.121	0.645	0.138
AT&T	66.88	1,592	106,473	13,073	9.6	0.392	0.109	0.645	0.123
MCI Communications	27.75	681	18,898	3,444	7.6	0.264	0.154	0.359	0.182
Sprint	40.00	351	14,040	5,474	4.7	0.573	0.281	1.342	0.390
WorldCom (LDDS)	35.25	193	6,803	3,392	2.9	0.632	0.333	1.717	0.499
S&P 500	608.24								

Company	Stock Beta[a]	Estimated Year-End EPS[b]	Price/ Earnings Ratio[c]	Annual Dividend	Dividend Payout (%)	Dividend Yield (%)	Historic 5-Year Growth EPS (%)[d]	Projected 5-Year Growth EPS (%)[e]	Firm Value[f] /1996 EBITDA
Ameritech	1.06	$ 3.75	15.9	$2.12	56.6	3.6	4.5	8.5	6.7
AT&T	1.11	4.00	16.7	1.32	33.0	2.0	7.0	11.5	8.9
MCI Communications	1.00	1.75	15.9	0.05	2.9	0.2	14.5	11.5	5.4
Sprint	1.05	2.90	15.8	1.88	64.9	4.7	17.5	13.5	6.1
WorldCom (LDDS)	1.77	1.75	20.1	0	0.0	0.0	35.0	NA	9.0
S&P 500	1.00	39.00	15.6	13.9	35.6	2.3	7.0		9.0

[a]Stock betas are from Bloomberg, Inc., and Value Line.
[b]Estimated 1996 year-end EPS.
[c]Based on 1996 estimated EPS.
[d]Growth rates in EPS are from Value Line.
[e]Firm value is the sum of long-term debt (LTD) and the market value of equity.

Source: February 1996 Salomon Brothers Global Equities Report and Value Line. Financial statement data are from year-end 1995.

EXHIBIT 3   Capital Market Conditions, February 15, 1996

U.S. Treasury obligations	*Yield*
3-month bills	4.898%
6-month bills	4.894
1-year notes	4.832
2-year notes	4.872
3-year notes	4.977
5-year notes	5.235
10-year notes	5.697
30-year notes	6.168
Corporate debt obligations (10-year)	
AAA	6.030
AA1	6.160
A1	6.190
BBB1	6.470
BB1	7.090
BB2	8.260
B1	9.420
AAA phones	6.090
AA1 phones	6.150
A1 phones	6.260
BBB1 phones	6.460
Other instruments	
Federal Reserve Bank discount rate	5.125
Certificates of deposit (6-month)	4.633
Commercial paper (6-month)	4.840

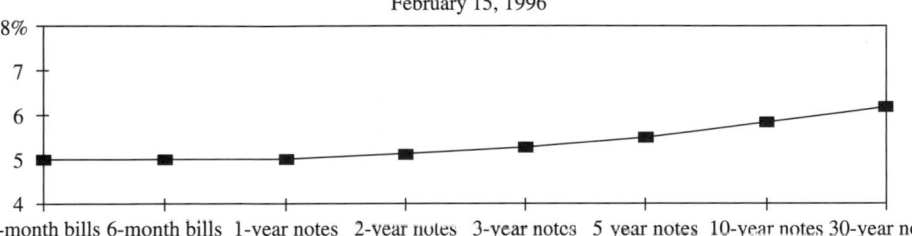

U.S. Treasury Yield Curves
February 15, 1996

Source: Capital Market Conditions, Bloomberg Media, 1995.

EXHIBIT 4   Income Statement, MCI (in millions, except per share amounts)

	Year Ended December 31, 1995
Revenue	$15,265
Operating expenses	
Telecommunications	7,813
Sales, operations, and general	4,506
Depreciation	1,308
Asset write-down	520
Total operating expenses	14,147
Income from operations	1,118
Interest expense	181
Income before taxes and extraordinary item	937
Income tax provision	364
Income before extraordinary item	573
Net income	$ 573
Earnings applicable to common stockholders	$ 573
Earnings per common and common equivalent shares	
Income before extraordinary item	$ 0.83
Total	$ 0.83
Weighted-average number of common shares	687

EXHIBIT 5   Balance Sheet, MCI (in millions)

	December 31, 1995
Assets	
Current assets	
Cash and cash equivalents	$ 471
Marketable securities	373
Receivables	2,954
Other current assets	749
Total current assets	4,547
Property and equipment	14,243
Accumulated depreciation	(5,238)
Construction in progress	1,304
Total property and equipment, net	10,309
Other assets	4,445
Total assets	$19,301
Liabilities and stockholders' equity	
Current liabilities	$ 706
Accrued telecommunications expense	1,936
Other accrued liabilities	1,728
Long-term debt due within one year	500
Total current liabilities	4,870
Long-term debt	3,444
Deferred taxes and other	1,385
Total noncurrent liabilities	4,829
Stockholders' equity	9,602
Total liabilities and stockholders' equity	$19,301

EXHIBIT 6   Analysts' Checklist for Cost-of-Capital Estimates

Principle	*Why*
Think like an investor and be forward looking.	You are estimating investor-required returns for the future.
Use financial market data.	Use market values and other financial market data because that's what investors deal with.
Find comparable companies with similar business risk.	Different levels of risks carry different required rates of return.
Be sensitive to trade-offs in looking for the best comparable versus using many companies.	If you focus on the one "best" comparable you have higher chances of large estimation errors in statistical estimates you may be using (e.g., betas). If you include a wide range of comparables, estimation errors may average out but you may not have as good a match on risk.
Cost of equity must reflect not only business risk but also financial risk.	Shareholder required returns (and betas) are based on both business risk and financial risk introduced by the use of debt.
Look to yields in debt markets for cost of debt.	In bond markets, yields to maturity and quotes on new issues (e.g., from banks or investment banks) provide forward-looking costs of debt.
Use a number of models and approaches to triangulate your estimate.	Theoretical models are useful but not perfect in their application. Assumptions and comparables are sometimes hard to specify exactly. See if your results are very sensitive to what appears to be reasonable alternatives.
Be wary of false precision.	Estimating costs of equity and weighted-average costs of capital involve many judgments and approximations. Your final estimate is subject to these approximations.
Match cash flows and discount rates in terms of currencies.	Increasingly, companies operate in many countries. If you are analyzing cash flows denominated in a currency (say DM), you must make sure that the cost of capital estimate reflects investor perceptions of investments in that specific currency.

Avoid using historical costs such as the historical interest rate.

Use market-value weights and forward-looking estimates of debt costs, equity costs, and tax rates.

Try to find companies that are comparable on important risk dimensions. These may include lines of business, international activity, competitive position, and strategic plans.

Look at both industry averages and specific comparables. If they differ, think about why.

The cost of equity (and cost of debt) used in a WACC calculation must be consistent with the weights used. If looking at comparable companies, check to see if they have similar capital structures. One technique is to compute WACCs for each company. Another approach tries to unlever costs of equity to adjust for financial risk. The first approach assures numbers are consistent but doesn't directly address differences in debt policy. The second requires use of theoretical approximations.

Know your banker and debt markets well.

Try different methods to estimate cost of equity. Look at how sensitive your results are to these and your choice of comparables.

Cost of capital estimates are approximate. Narrow your range but don't think you've got it exactly right.

There are two basic approaches. One is to estimate a cost of capital for each different currency, making sure to adjust for differential inflation among currencies. The second is to translate cash flows to a common currency using forecasted exchange rates and then use the common currency for cost of capital.

Polaroid Corporation, 1996

In late March 1996, Ralph Norwood, the recently appointed treasurer of Polaroid Corporation, reflected on several matters of concern about the firm's debt policy that would require his attention in the coming months. One immediate concern was Polaroid's outstanding $150-million, 7.25 percent notes, which were due to mature in January 1997. Investment bankers, keenly interested in garnering advisory and underwriting business from Polaroid, had sought to present proposals for refunding the issue. However, Norwood felt that any refunding decision should be part of a larger review of the firm's financial policies. Accordingly he undertook a review of the firm's overall debt policy, focusing primarily on the mix of debt and equity and on the maturity structure of the debt. He also sought to consider issues of control, the establishment of any special advisory relationships, and the use of new financial instruments.

In recent years Polaroid's share price had traded in a narrow range, reflecting small sales and earnings growth. However, a new plan to exploit aggressively the existing Polaroid brand, introduce product extensions, and enter new emerging markets (such as Russia) had been proposed to spur the firm's performance. The restructuring plan was spearheaded by Gary T. DiCamillo, the first outsider appointed chief executive officer (CEO) in the firm's history. DiCamillo had only recently joined the firm in November 1995. Norwood believed the plan would reinvigorate the company without materially increasing its operating risk. With important changes in the works, Norwood felt it essential that his financial policies afford Polaroid the necessary funding and flexibility to pursue the initiatives of the new CEO.

This case was written by Professors Robert Bruner and Susan Chaplinsky as a basis for class discussion rather than to illustrate effective or ineffective handling of an administrative situation. Copyright © 1997 by the University of Virginia Darden School Foundation, Charlottesville, VA. All rights reserved. *No part of this publication may be reproduced, stored in a retrieval system, used in a spreadsheet, or transmitted in any form or by any means—electronic, mechanical, photocopying, recording, or otherwise—without the permission of the Darden School Foundation. For inquiries, please send an e-mail to dardencases@virginia.edu.* Revised 6/98. Version 1.6.

THE EARLY YEARS

Polaroid Corporation was founded in 1937 by Edwin Land, who had dropped out of Harvard College to pursue ideas on the polarization of light. The early years of Polaroid reflected the characteristics of Land: inventive, determined, and single-minded. The first instant camera was produced in 1948, and from that moment 90 percent of the company's efforts were dedicated to the development of the field. Within four decades, sales of the firm grew from $142,000 to over $1 billion, largely on the basis of Land's interest and oversight of the research effort in instant photography. Significant breakthroughs included instant black-and-white film (1954), instant color film (1960), and the SX-70 camera and film (1972), which freed the user from having to coat the developing picture.

In 1977 the firm's sales exceeded $1 billion for the first time, though this achievement was offset by increasing pressures from the sales force for new sources of growth, in the form of cheaper products. Internally there had been major efforts to develop products beyond instant photography: document copiers, and an instant movie camera and film. The movie project debuted in 1977 as Polavision, an instant motion-picture technology. Unfortunately, sales languished largely because of the advent of video-camera technology. In 1979, the directors wrote off the inventory of Polavision products and effectively exited from the business. In 1980, Edwin Land stepped down as CEO of the firm; he retired from the board in 1982 and a year later sold his Polaroid stock in a public offering.

RECENT FINANCIAL PERFORMANCE

The two most notable events of the past decade were prompted by the actions of others. In 1976 Eastman Kodak Company introduced an instant camera and film product that threatened Polaroid's dominance of the instant-photography field. Polaroid sued Kodak for patent infringement, and 10 years later in 1986 was awarded the largest patent judgment in history, some $900 million. Meanwhile, few significant new products were developed during this time. In 1988, with no large shareholder like Edwin Land to protect the firm and expecting the proceeds from the Kodak patent judgment, Polaroid received an unsolicited tender offer from Shamrock Holdings. Shamrock proposed to pay the shareholders an extraordinary dividend from the Kodak proceeds, and to manage the company more tightly. Polaroid's management wanted to reinvest the proceeds in the business. To fend off the takeover threat, the firm conducted a leveraged recapitalization that involved the innovative use of an employee stock ownership plan (ESOP). The leveraged recap dramatically increased the firm's debt-to-capital ratio from 0 in 1988 to 56 percent in 1989. Shortly thereafter the firm began a program of steady share repurchases. Despite the repurchase program, long-term debt-to-capital fell to 42 percent by 1995. Exhibit 1 gives a 10-year summary of the financial characteristics of the firm.

Over the past 10 years, the firm's share price growth had lagged the growth in the broad market indexes. From 1986 to 1995, Polaroid's compound annual sales growth rate was 3.6 percent in nominal terms and, after adjusting for inflation, virtually 0. Earnings losses appeared in 1988, 1993, and 1995, and were associated with both declines in operating profit, and restructuring costs (consisting of both severance payments and write-offs). The sales and earnings results reflected the growing maturity of the instant photography market in the United States, and the absence of major new-product introductions. Consistent with the perceived maturity of their market segment, Polaroid's price/earnings (P/E) ratio of 12.1 fell well below the market's P/E of 15.2 in 1995.

The concerns over profitability and the lack of strong sales growth in cameras and film were also echoed in the comments of analysts following the firm. One analyst described Polaroid's challenge:

> Instant photography is a razor-blade business. Cameras are sold at low margins to encourage film sales. The company's instant film sales are its primary margin product. Expanding the "installed base" of cameras enhances the opportunities to sell film. The "burn rate" of film on newly purchased cameras, as might be expected, is highest and trails off in a reasonably predictable pattern thereafter. This correlation allows the company to make reasonable estimates of film unit sales volume. It also, obviously, means that there is a strong emphasis on selling cameras.[1]

The patents the company held protected it from any significant competition domestically in the field of instant photography. In international markets, Polaroid's only competitor was Fuji, which had a film and instant-camera product it marketed in Europe and Japan. However, even in Japan, Polaroid enjoyed a dominant market share. Thus, in the consumer market, Polaroid's strength for instant photography was unrivaled. In the commercial market, Polaroid's sales derived primarily from the use of instant photography for identification purposes (e.g., ID badges), and other applications in medicine and law enforcement. Increasingly the expansion of digital imaging threatened to erode the firm's base of users, as customers shifted from instant photography to digital solutions. In recent years, Polaroid's Commercial Group accounted for approximately half of its total sales and one-third of instant-film sales.[2] In the digital area, Polaroid faced stiff competition from many well-capitalized technology companies, such as Xerox, 3M, and Sony. To date, Polaroid's development efforts in digital imaging had entailed heavy start-up costs.

Norwood acknowledged many of the same concerns, but felt that the analyst community had taken a shortsighted view of Polaroid's potential. Echoing its past, the firm continued to be "engaged primarily in one line of business, the design, manufacture, and sale of instant photographic imaging products worldwide,"[3] with photographic products accounting for 90 percent of the firm's revenues in 1995. Norwood said, "The basic business is low growth; but it's an incredible annuity." Second, sales to interna-

---

[1] Duff & Phelps, Inc., *Duff & Phelps Credit Rating Report, Polaroid Corporation,* November 18, 1996, p. 2.
[2] Prudential Securities, *Polaroid—Company Report,* December 4, 1996, p. 4.
[3] Polaroid annual report, 1995, p. 44.

tional markets had strong growth potential. In many emerging-market countries, no infrastructure existed to develop 35-mm film. With rising standards of living worldwide, there was a large untapped market for instant photography, and Polaroid's cameras were in high demand. Exhibit 2 illuminates the growth in international revenues. The percentage mix of U.S. versus international sales had almost precisely reversed from 1993 to 1995. This reversal reflected steady growth in the international segment of between 3 and 8 percent per year. In contrast, sales in the United States had fallen 2 percent in 1994 and 12 percent in 1995. Sales to Russia alone accounted for 9 percent of total sales in 1995.

Exhibits 3 and 4 give the latest years' income statement and balance sheet for Polaroid.

CURRENT FINANCING AND FUTURE OUTLOOK

Against this backdrop, Norwood assessed the current and future financing requirements of the firm. One important issue for consideration was the extent to which the financing of the firm would be impacted by the plans of the new CEO. Gary DiCamillo was appointed Polaroid's chairman and CEO following a successful term as president of Black & Decker's PowerTools unit. At Black & Decker, DiCamillo was viewed as an energetic leader, whose efforts were instrumental in developing a line of new products that helped to revive Black & Decker's brand name. DiCamillo brought similar energy and plans to Polaroid. Shortly after his arrival, he announced a major restructuring of the firm, to reduce the workforce by some 2,500 positions (roughly 20 percent), and to reduce expenses by more than $150 million annually. In particular, he terminated the production of the Captiva camera and curtailed several major research and engineering programs, emphasizing instead projects having the greatest potential for commercialization. Finally, he sharply reduced corporate overhead costs. The effect of this restructuring was to trigger a special charge to earnings in 1995 of $247 million caused by the severance and early retirement programs, and by the write-down of equipment and inventory. As a result, Polaroid reported a net loss of $140.2 million, compared with 1994 earnings of $117.2 million.

In February 1996, DiCamillo announced a new management structure built around three core areas: Consumer, Commercial, and New Business. The purpose of the new structure was to focus the organization more effectively on customers' imaging needs, and to integrate product-development responsibilities within each group. DiCamillo wrote:

> Both the restructuring and reorganization reflect my conviction that we can grow our core photographic and emerging electronic imaging businesses. I believe we can leverage our considerable brand power, technological expertise, and global distribution reach to create new growth opportunities and revitalize our instant photography business.[4]

---

[4]Quoted from Letter to Shareholders, Polaroid annual report 1995, p. 3.

To meet its various financing needs, Polaroid maintained a five-year $150 million working capital line of credit to be used for general purposes. This line was to expire in 1999. In 1994 and 1995 there had been no borrowings under this line. The company maintained international lines of credit to support the firm's foreign currency balance sheet exposure. At the end of 1995, borrowings outside the United States were $160.4 million. Additional unused borrowings under these lines of credit were $160 million.

Polaroid's long-term debt outstanding consisted of three issues:

- *Notes.* $150 million, 7.25 percent notes due January 15, 1997, had been issued at a discount (to yield 7.42 percent). $200 million, 8 percent notes were due March 15, 1999, and had been issued with a discount to yield 8.18 percent. Both issues of notes were non-callable.
- *ESOP loan.* The loan had been drawn in 1988 to establish Polaroid's leveraged employee stock ownership plan (ESOP), as part of the leveraged recapitalization of the firm. Scheduled principal payments were made semiannually through 1997, when a final payment of $37.7 million was due. The weighted-average interest rate on the loan was 5.2 percent, 4.4 percent, and 3.6 percent during 1995, 1994, and 1993, respectively. Special tax benefits to providers of ESOP loans accounted for the unusually low interest rates.
- *Convertible subordinated debentures.* $140 million, 8 percent convertibles due in 2001. These carried an annual interest rate of 8 percent and were convertible to common stock at $32.50 per share. These were redeemable by the company after September 30, 1998, or sooner if the stock price exceeded $48.75 per share for 20 of 30 consecutive trading days. All of the debentures were held by Corporate Partners.[5]

Virtually all of the firm's debt was due within six years. As Ralph Norwood commented, "The weighted-average maturity structure of our debt was about four years. All our borrowings would need to be repaid or refinanced in a relatively short time." Exhibit 5 illustrates the estimation of Polaroid's weighted-average maturity of its debt.

In addition to the scheduled debt repayments, Ralph Norwood reviewed other possible demands on the firm's resources. He believed that capital expenditures would about equal depreciation for the next few years. Also, though sales might grow, working capital turns should decline, resulting in a reduction in net working capital in the first year, followed by increases later. Both of these effects reflected the tight asset management under the new CEO. While cash dividends would be held constant for the foreseeable future, the firm would continue with its program of opportunistic share repurchases, which had varied between $20 and $60 million per year. Exhibit 1 summarizes the firm's share repurchase activity in recent years.

---

[5]If the rights were fully exercised, the resulting stock would represent approximately a 9 percent stake in Polaroid. The company was currently attempting to negotiate the repurchase of the conversion rights from Corporate Partners. On March 29, 1996, Polaroid's share price closed at $44.00. The annualized volatility or "sigma" of returns on Polaroid's shares over the previous 100 days was 17.7 percent. The yield on six-year U.S. Treasury notes was 6.05 percent.

Exhibit 6 gives a five-year forecast of Polaroid's income statement, balance sheet, and free cash flow. The forecast was consistent with the lower end of analysts' projections for revenue growth and realization of the benefits of DiCamillo's restructuring program. It assumed that the existing debt will be refinanced with similar debt. Major share repurchases were not presumed in the forecast. The forecast would need to be revised to reflect the impact of any recommended changes in financial policy.

CONSIDERATIONS IN ASSESSING FINANCIAL POLICY

In addition to assessing the firm's internal financing requirements, Norwood also recognized that his policy recommendation would have an important role in shaping the perceptions of the firm by the bond-rating agencies and investors.

Bond Rating.   Polaroid currently had a "split" rating, where Standard & Poor's rated the firm's senior[6] long-term debt BBB and Moody's rated it Baa3 (roughly equivalent to a BBB− in the Standard & Poor's system). Exhibit 7 presents the bond-rating definitions for this and other rating categories. BBB/Baa3 was an "investment-grade" rating, whereas the next grade lower (BB/Ba) was "non-investment-grade" rating and often referred to as "high-yield or junk debt." Some large investors (such as pension funds and charitable trusts) were barred from investing in non-investment-grade debt. Many individual investors shunned it as well. For that reason, the yields on non-investment-grade debt over U.S. Treasury securities (i.e., spreads) were typically considerably higher than the spreads for investment-grade issues. Also, the ability to issue non-investment-grade debt depended to a much greater degree on the strength of the economy, and on favorable credit market conditions than did investment-grade debt. Norwood said:

> You don't pay much of a penalty in yield as you go from A to BBB. There's a range over which the risk you take for more leverage is *de minimus.* But you pay a big penalty as you go from BBB to BB. The penalty is not only in the form of higher costs, but also in the form of possible damage to the Polaroid brand. We don't want the brand to be sullied by the association with junk debt.

For these reasons, Ralph Norwood sought to preserve an investment-grade rating for Polaroid. But where in the investment-grade range should Polaroid be positioned? Exhibit 8 summarizes the bond ratings for a sample of Polaroid's peer firms, which Norwood described as "large global consumer technology products companies," and for a large sample of firms in general. Exhibit 9 gives financial ratios associated with the various rating categories. Although Norwood knew the ratings agencies also looked closely at the debt-to-capital ratio (debt capitalization), he believed that the

---

[6]The convention in finance is that the firm's bond rating refers to the rating on the firm's *senior* debt, with the understanding that any subordinated debt issued by the firm will ordinarily have a lower bond rating. For instance, Polaroid's senior debt had the split BBB/Baa3 rating, while its subordinated convertible bonds were rated BB/Ba.

EBIT coverage ratio was the single best measure of credit quality. Exhibit 10 gives Polaroid's EBIT coverage ratios for the past 10 years. Norwood's decision would require him to first choose a target bond rating. Thereafter, he would have to determine the minimum and maximum amounts of debt that Polaroid could carry to achieve the desired rating.

Flexibility.   Norwood was also aware that choosing a target debt level based on an analysis of industry peers might not fully capture the flexibility Polaroid would need to meet its own possible future adversities. Norwood said:

> Flexibility is how much debt you can issue before you lose the investment-grade bond rating. I want flexibility, and yet I want to take advantage of the fact that with more debt, you have lower cost capital. I am very comfortable with our strategy and internal financial forecasts for our business; if anything, I believe the forecasts probably underestimate, rather than overestimate, our cash flows. But let's suppose that a two-sigma adverse outcome would be an EBIT equal to $150 million—I can't imagine in the worst of times an EBIT less than that.

Accordingly, Norwood's final decision on the target bond rating would have to be one that maintained reasonable reserves against Polaroid's worst-case scenario.

Cost of Capital.   Consistent with management's emphasis on value creation, Norwood believed that choosing a financial policy that minimized the cost of capital was important. He understood that exploitation of debt tax shields could create value for shareholders—up to a reasonable limit—and that beyond the limit, costs of financial distress would become material and cause the cost of capital to rise. One investment bank, Hudson Guaranty, presented Norwood with estimates of the pretax cost of debt and cost of equity by rating category. These estimates are given in Exhibit 11. The cost of debt was estimated by averaging the current yield-to-maturity of bonds within each rating category. The cost of equity (k_e) was estimated by Hudson Guaranty using the capital asset pricing model. The cost of equity was computed for each firm using its beta and other capital market data. The individual estimates of k_e were then averaged within each bond-rating category. Norwood remarked on the relatively flat trend in the cost of equity within the investment-grade range. Hudson Guaranty replied that "changes in leverage within the investment-grade range are not regarded as material to investors." It remained for Norwood to determine which rating category provided the lowest costs of capital.

Current Capital Market Conditions.   Any policy recommendations would need to acknowledge the feasibility of implementing those policies today as well as in the future. Exhibit 12 presents information about current yields in the U.S. debt markets. The current situation in the debt markets was favorable as the U.S. economy continued in its fifth year of economic expansion. The equity markets seemed to be pausing after a phenomenal advance in prices in 1995. The outlook for interest rates was stable, though any sign of inflation might cause the Federal Reserve Board to lift interest rates. Major changes in taxes and regulations were in abeyance, at least until the outcome of the presidential elections to be held in November 1996.

CONCLUSION

Ralph Norwood leafed through the analyses and financial data he had gathered for his recommendations. He reflected on the competing goals of value creation, flexibility, and bond rating. His plan would have to afford Polaroid low costs and continued access to capital under a variety of operating scenarios. This would require him to test the possible effect of downside scenarios on Polaroid's coverage and capitalization ratios under alternative debt policies. He aimed to recommend a financial policy that would balance these goals and provide guidance to the directors and the financial staff regarding the target mix of capital and the maturity structure of the company's debt. With so many competing factors to weigh, Norwood felt it unlikely that his plan would be a perfect plan. But then he remembered one of Gary DiCamillo's favorite sayings: "If you wait until you have a 99 percent solution, you'll never act; go with an 80 percent solution."

EXHIBIT 1   Ten-Year Financial Summary (in U.S. millions except per share values and numbers of shares)

	At Fiscal Years Ended, December 31		
	1995	*1994*	*1993*
Selected income statement information			
Net sales			
U.S.	$1,019.0	$1,160.3	$1,178.8
International	1,217.9	1,152.2	1,066.1
Total	2,236.9	2,312.5	2,244.9
Operating expenses	2,147.7	2,112.2	2,059.5
Profit from opns. before restructuring exp.	89.2	200.3	185.4
Restructuring expense	247.0	0.0	44.0
Interest expense	52.1	46.6	47.9
Net earnings	−140.2	117.2	−51.3
Common shares, end of year (000s)	45,533	45,998	46,806
Common shares repurchased (000s)	1,218	941	0
Repurchase outlay ($ millions)	$40.2	$ 30.6	$ 0.0
Common shares issued (000s)	753	133	138
Earnings per share	−$ 3.09	$ 2.49	−$ 1.10
Dividend per share	$ 0.60	$ 0.60	$ 0.60
Selected balance sheet information			
Working capital	$ 738.5	$ 886.8	$ 833.6
Net property, plant, and equipment	691.0	747.3	718.2
Total assets	2,261.8	2,316.7	2,212.3
Long-term debt	526.7	566.0	602.3
Redeemable preferred stock	0.0	0.0	0.0
Common stockholders' equity	717.7	864.4	767.3
Additions to property, plant, and equipment	167.9	146.7	165.6
Depreciation	$ 132.7	$ 118.2	$ 100.3
Book value LT debt/Capital	42.3%	39.6%	44.0%
Market value LT debt/Capital	19.6%	27.5%	27.8%
Selected valuation information (at years' ends)			
Polaroid stock price	$ 47.38	$ 32.50	$ 33.50
S&P 500 index	615.93	459.27	466.25
Polaroid average P/E*	12.1	13.3	15.6
S&P industrials average P/E*	15.2	15.5	18.4
Polaroid market/book ratio	3.01	1.73	2.04
Polaroid beta	1.05	1.05	1.15
Yield on 30-year T-bonds	6.88%	7.37%	6.59%
Yield on 90-day T-bills	5.49%	4.25%	3.00%
Total annual return on large co. stocks	33.00%	1.30%	9.90%

*P/E ratios are computed on earnings before restructuring charges, litigation award, and other extraordinary items.

Sources: Polaroid annual report 1995; *Value Line Investment Survey; Federal Reserve Bulletin;* Standard & Poor's *Current Statistics;* Ibbotson Associates, *Stocks, Bonds, Bills, Inflation 1995.*

	At Fiscal Years Ended, December 31						
1992	*1991*	*1990*	*1989*	*1988*	*1987*	*1986*
$1,145.7	$1,113.6	$1,058.3	$1,091.8	$1,048.3	$1,009.3	$ 964.3
1,006.6	957.0	913.4	812.9	814.6	754.6	664.9
2,152.3	2,070.6	1,971.7	1,904.7	1,862.9	1,763.9	1,629.2
1,938.5	1,824.0	1,687.4	1,600.5	1,689.1	1,610.1	1,493.5
213.8	246.6	284.3	304.2	173.8	153.8	135.7
0.0	0.0	0.0	40.5	151.9	0.0	0.0
58.5	58.4	81.3	86.2	29.0	15.0	18.6
99.0	683.7	151.0	145.0	−22.6	125.2	108.2
46,668	48,919	50,070	52,110	71,635	61,918	61,918
2,258	1,151	2,040	19,525	0	0	0
$ 63.4	$ 30.6	$ 55.6	$ 950.6	$0.0	$ 0.0	$ 0.0
7	0	0	0	9,717	0	0
$ 2.06	$ 12.54	$ 2.20	$ 1.96	−$ 0.34	$ 2.02	$ 1.75
$ 0.60	$ 0.60	$ 0.60	$ 0.60	$ 0.60	$ 0.60	$ 0.50
$ 789.0	$ 695.3	$ 609.1	$ 642.0	$ 980.0	$ 652.6	$ 602.4
657.3	549.4	461.0	430.9	433.8	359.6	357.7
2,008.1	1,889.3	1,701.3	1,776.7	1,957.2	1,599.4	1,444.6
637.4	471.8	513.8	602.2	402.3	0.0	0.0
0.0	0.0	348.6	321.9	0.0	0.0	0.0
808.9	772.9	207.7	148.8	1,011.5	1,048.2	960.1
201.5	175.8	120.9	94.5	127.0	116.6	82.9
$ 89.1	$ 85.5	$ 87.2	$ 87.4	$ 81.9	$ 75.7	$ 71.2
44.1%	37.9%	48.0%	56.1%	28.5%	0.0%	0.0%
30.5%	26.6%	25.3%	28.5%	23.4%	0.0%	0.0%
$ 31.13	$ 26.63	$ 23.38	$ 22.88	$ 18.38	$ 11.88	$ 33.25
435.71	417.09	330.22	353.40	277.72	247.08	242.17
14.2	12.2	15.6	21.8	NMF	14.7	16.6
19.8	19	14.4	12.6	10.8	15.3	17.5
1.80	1.69	5.63	8.01	1.30	0.70	2.14
1.15	1.20	1.25	1.25	1.25	1.20	1.10
7.67%	8.14%	8.61%	8.45%	8.96%	8.59%	7.80%
3.43%	5.38%	7.50%	8.11%	6.67%	5.78%	5.97%
7.67%	30.55%	−3.17%	31.49%	18.81%	5.23%	18.47%

EXHIBIT 2   Information on International Revenues

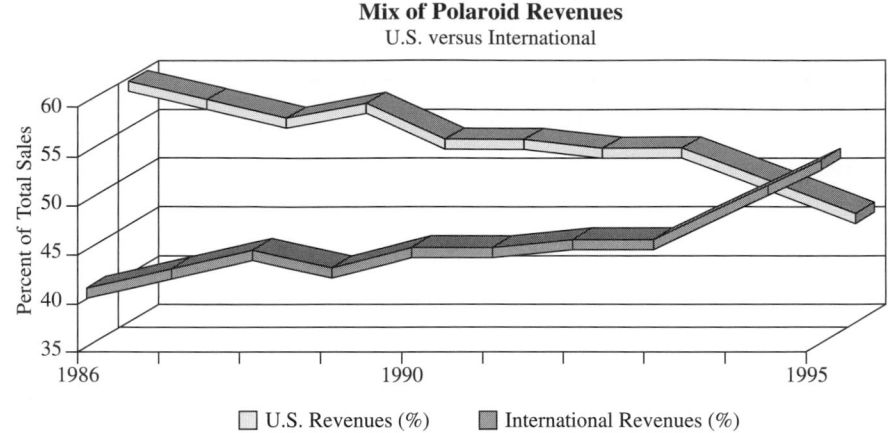

Mix of Polaroid Revenues
U.S. versus International

Source of graph data: *Polaroid Annual Report 1995,* pp. 48–49.

Estimated Quarterly Polaroid Sales to Russia ($ millions)

	1993	1994	1995
1st Quarter	$ 0	$ 22	$ 38
2nd Quarter	0	24	35
3rd Quarter	10	51	74
4th Quarter	10	57	49
Full Year	$20	$154	$196

Source: B. L. Landry, "Polaroid—Company Report," Morgan Stanley & Co., October 25, 1996.

Performance by Geographic Segment ($ millions, eliminations of interregional amounts not shown)

	1993	1994	1995
Sales			
United States	$1,609.6	$1,656.6	$1,498.4
Europe	945.2	1,051.7	1,106.9
Asia Pacific, Canada, Latin and South America	524.7	531.1	602.4
Profits/(loss)			
United States	$ 44.1	$ 100.8	$(179.4)
Europe	43.7	81.8	20.6
Asia Pacific, Canada, Latin and South America	56.8	45.2	24.4
Assets			
United States	$1,532.7	$1,480.5	$1,526.1
Europe	556.0	613.8	669.9
Asia Pacific, Canada, Latin and South America	216.9	248.1	258.4

Source: *Polaroid Annual Report 1995,* p. 45.

EXHIBIT 3   Consolidated Statement of Earnings (in $ millions)

	Years ended December 31	
	1995	*1994*
Net sales		
United States	$1,019.0	$1,160.3
International	1,217.9	1,152.2
Total net sales	2,236.9	2,312.5
Cost of goods sold	1,298.6	1,324.2
Marketing, research, and administration	849.1	788.0
Restructuring and other	247.0	0.0
Total costs	2,394.7	2,122.2
Profit (loss) from operations	−157.8	200.3
Interest income	8.7	9.7
Other income	−0.2	−2.7
Interest expense	52.1	46.6
Earnings (loss) before taxes	−201.4	160.7
Tax expense	−61.2	43.5
Net earnings (loss)	−140.2	117.2

Source: Polaroid annual report 1995.

EXHIBIT 4   Balance Sheet

	1995	*1994*
Assets		
Current assets		
Cash and cash equivalents	$ 73.3	$ 143.3
Short-term investments	9.8	85.6
Receivables, less allowances	550.4	541.0
Inventories	615.5	577.4
Prepaid expenses and other	208.5	141.4
Total current assets	1,457.5	1,488.7
Gross property, plant, and equipment	2,164.4	2,043.4
Less accumulated depreciation	1,473.4	1,296.1
Net property, plant, and equipment	691.0	747.3
Prepaid taxes—noncurrent	113.3	80.7
Total assets	$2,261.8	$2,316.7
Liabilities and stockholders' equity		
Current liabilities		
Short-term debt	$ 160.4	$ 117.1
Current portion of long-term debt	39.7	35.9
Payables and accruals	274.9	275.7
Compensation and benefits	197.4	121.4
Taxes payable	46.6	51.8
Total current liabilities	719.0	601.9
Long-term debt	526.7	566.0
Accrued postretirement benefits	257.2	247.2
Accrued postemployment benefits	41.2	37.2
Total liabilities	1,544.1	1,452.3
Preferred stock	0.0	0.0
Common stockholders' equity		
Common stock	75.4	75.4
Additional paid-in capital	401.9	387.2
Retained earnings	1,525.8	1,692.1
Less treasury stock, at cost	1,205.4	1.174.5
Less deferred compensation	80.0	115.8
Total common stockholders' equity	717.7	864.4
Total liabilities and stockholders' equity	$2,261.8	$2,316.7

Source: Polaroid Annual Report 1995.

EXHIBIT 5 Maturity Structure of Debt

	Debt Repayment ($ millions)	*Debt Repayment (% of total)*	*Maturity (years)*	*Weighted Maturity (years)*
1996	$ 39.7	8.0	1	.08
1997	187.8	36.0	2	.72
1998	0	0	3	0
1999	200.0	38.0	4	1.52
2000	0	0	5	0
2001	140.0	27.0	6	1.62
Total	$527.8	100.0		3.94

Note: For simplicity, this table assumes all debt payments are made on an annual basis. Any semiannual or quarterly principal payments would reduce slightly the estimated weighted maturity.

Source: Casewriters' analysis.

EXHIBIT 6   Financial Forecast (values in U.S. $millions)

	Actual	Projected				
	1995	1996	1997	1998	1999	2000
Annual increase in sales	−3.2%	2.0%	5.0%	6.0%	6.0%	7.0%
Operating profit/sales	4.0%	8.0%	9.5%	10.0%	10.0%	10.0%
Tax rate		40.0%				
Working capital/sales		37.0%				
Dividend payout ratio		25.0%				
Income statement						
Net sales	$2,236.9	$2,281.6	$2,395.7	$2,539.5	$2,691.8	$2,880.3
Operating profit	89.2	182.5	227.6	253.9	269.2	288.0
Interest income	8.5	5.0	5.0	5.0	5.0	5.0
Interest expense	(52.1)	(52.1)	(52.1)	(52.1)	(52.1)	(52.1)
Pretax income	45.6	135.4	180.5	206.8	222.1	240.9
Tax expense	(61.2)	(54.2)	(72.2)	(82.7)	(88.8)	(96.4)
Net income	(15.6)	81.3	108.3	124.1	133.2	144.6
Dividends	27.3	27.3	27.3	27.3	27.3	27.3
Retentions to earnings	$ (42.9)	$ 53.9	$ 81.0	$ 96.8	$ 105.9	$ 117.2
Balance sheet						
Cash	$ 83.1	$ 148.3	$ 187.1	$ 230.7	$ 280.3	$ 327.8
Working capital (without debt)	855.5	844.2	886.4	939.6	996.0	1,065.7
Prepaid tax	113.3	113.3	113.3	113.3	113.3	113.3
Net fixed assets	691.0	691.0	691.0	691.0	691.0	691.0
Total assets	$1,742.9	$1,796.8	$1,877.8	$1,974.6	$2,080.5	$2,197.8
Debt (long and short term)	$ 726.8	$ 726.8	$ 726.8	$ 726.8	$ 726.8	$ 726.8
Postretirement benefits	298.4	298.4	298.4	298.4	298.4	298.4
Equity	717.7	771.6	852.6	949.4	1,055.3	1,172.6
Total capital	$1,742.9	$1,796.8	$1,877.8	$1,974.6	$2,080.5	$2,197.8
Free cash flows						
EBIT		$ 182.5	$ 227.6	$ 253.9	$ 269.2	$ 288.0
Less taxes on EBIT		(73.0)	(91.0)	(101.6)	(107.7)	(115.2)
Plus depreciation		140.0	140.0	140.0	140.0	140.0
Less capital expenditures		(140.0)	(140.0)	(140.0)	(140.0)	(140.0)
− Additions (+ Reductions) working capital		11.3	(42.2)	(53.2)	(56.4)	(69.7)
Free cash flow		$ 120.8	$ 94.3	$ 99.2	$ 105.1	$ 103.1

Source: Casewriter analysis, consistent with forecast expectations of securities analysts.

EXHIBIT 7   Moody's Bond-Rating Definitions

Aaa   Bonds which are rated *Aaa* are judged to be of the best quality. They carry the smallest degree of investment risk and are generally referred to as "gilt edge." Interest payments are protected by a large or exceptionally stable margin, and principal is secure. While the various protective elements are likely to change, such changes as can be visualized are most unlikely to impair the fundamentally strong position of such issues.

Aa   Bonds which are rated *Aa* are judged to be of high quality by all standards. Together with the *Aaa* group they comprise what are generally known as high-grade bonds. They are rated lower than the best bonds because margins of protection may not be as large as in Aaa securities, or fluctuations of protective elements may be of greater amplitude, or there may be other elements present which make the long-term risks appear somewhat larger than in Aaa securities.

A   Bonds which are rated *A* possess many favorable investment attributes and are to be considered as upper-medium-grade obligations. Factors giving security to principal and interest are considered adequate, but elements may be present which suggest a susceptibility to impairment sometime in the future.

Baa   Bonds which are rated *Baa* are considered as medium-grade obligations; i.e., they are neither highly protected nor poorly secured. Interest payment and principal security appear adequate for the present but certain protective elements may be lacking or may be characteristically unreliable over any great length of time. Such bonds lack outstanding investment characteristics and in fact have speculative characteristics as well.

Ba   Bonds which are rated *Ba* are judged to have speculative elements; their future cannot be considered as well assured. Often the protection of interest and principal payments may be very moderate and thereby not well safeguarded during both good and bad times over the future. Uncertainty of position characterizes bonds in this class.

B   Bonds which are rated *B* generally lack characteristics of the desirable investment. Assurance of interest and principal payments or of maintenance of other terms of the contract over any long period of time may be small.

Caa   Bonds which are rated *Caa* are of poor standing. Such issues may be in default or there may be present elements of danger with respect to principal or interest.

Ca   Bonds which are rated *Ca* represent obligations which are speculative in a high degree. Such issues are often in default or have other marked shortcomings.

C   Bonds which are rated *C* are the lowest rated class of bonds, and issues so rated can be regarded as having extremely poor prospects of ever attaining any real investment standing.

Source: Moody's Bond Rating for Polaroid Corporation, *Moody's Industrial Manual* 1995, p. vi.

EXHIBIT 8   Distribution of Peer Firms' Bond Ratings

Peers	Moody's Rating	S&P's Rating
Minnesota Mining and Manufacturing (3M)	Aaa	AAA
Eastman Kodak	Aa	AA
Hewlett-Packard		
Fuji		
Xerox	A	A
Sony		
Black & Decker	Baa	BBB
Polaroid		
Tektronix		
Digital Equipment	Ba	BB

Source: Company document.

Distribution of Large Companies by Senior Debt Rating

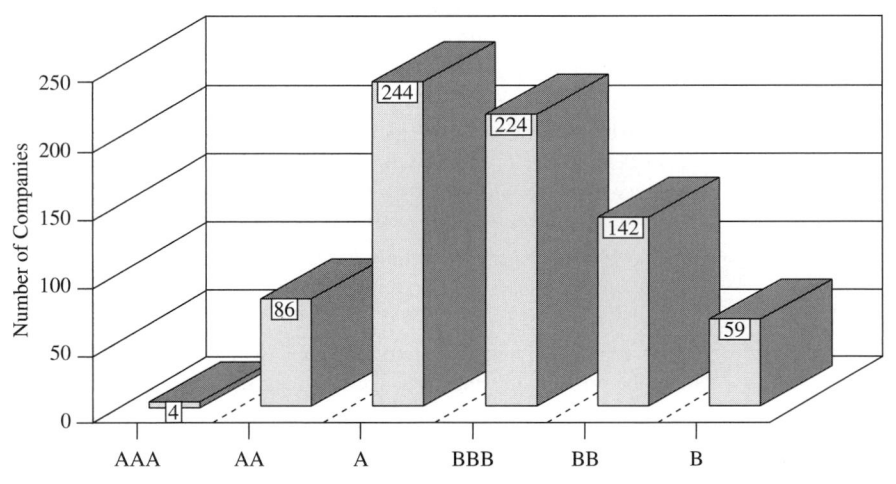

Source of graph: Company documents, and Hudson Guaranty analysis reflecting all rated firms with market value between $250 million and $10 billion at year-end 1995.

EXHIBIT 9   Key Industrial Financial Ratios by Rating Categories, Median Values for the Three Years, 1993–95

	AAA	*AA*	*A*	*BBB*	*BB*	*B*
Pretax interest coverage ($\times$)	13.50	9.67	5.76	3.94	2.14	1.17
EBITDA interest coverage ($\times$)	17.08	12.80	8.18	6.00	3.49	2.16
Funds from operations/Total debt (%)	98.20	69.10	45.50	33.30	17.70	12.80
Free operating cash flow/Total debt (%)	60.00	26.80	20.90	7.20	1.40	−0.90
Pretax return on permanent capital (%)	29.30	21.40	19.10	13.90	13.50	12.30
Operating income/Sales (%)	22.60	17.80	15.70	13.50	13.50	12.30
Long-term debt/Capital (%)	13.30	21.10	31.60	42.70	55.60	65.50
Total debt/Capitalization including short-term debt (%)	25.90	33.60	39.70	47.80	59.40	69.50

Note: Pretax interest coverage is EBIT/interest expense.

Source: Standard & Poor's *CreditWeek*, October 30, 1996, p. 26.

EXHIBIT 10   EBIT Coverage Ratios by Year, 1987 to 1995

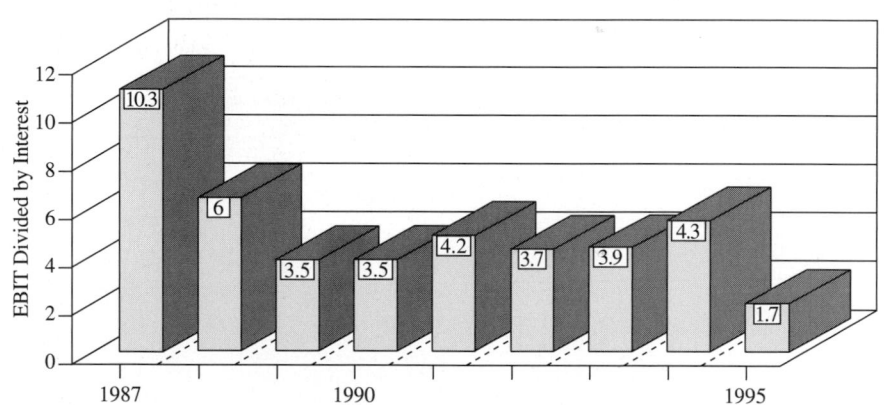

Note: The interest coverage ratio is calculated as EBIT before restructuring costs, divided by interest expense.

Source: Company document.

EXHIBIT 11   Capital Costs by Rating Category

	AAA	AA	A	BBB	BB	B
Cost of debt (Pretax)	6.70%	6.90%	7.00%	7.40%	9.00%	10.60%
Cost of equity	10.25%	10.3%	10.4%	10.5%	11.75%	13.00%

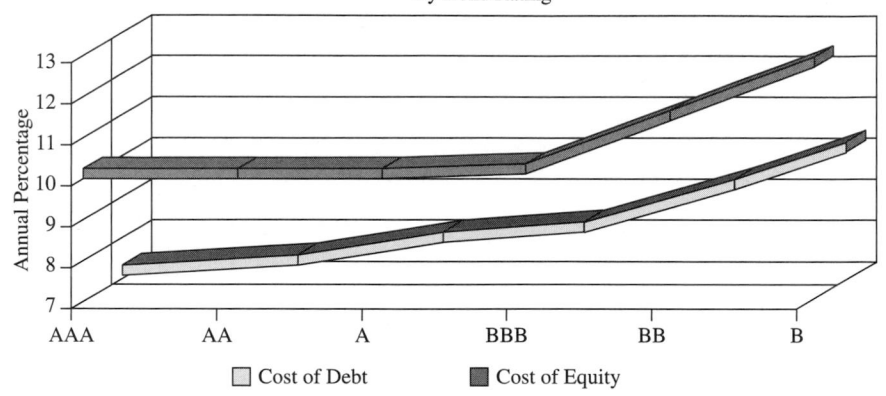

Cost of Debt and Equity
By Bond Rating

Source: Company documents and analysis by Hudson Guaranty using August 1995 data calculated for 314 publicly rated industrial firms, and adjusted to reflect capital market conditions in March 1996.

EXHIBIT 12   Capital Market Conditions, March 26, 1996

	Yield
U.S. Treasury obligations	
90-day bills	5.08%
1-year notes	5.37
5-year notes	6.00
10-year bonds	6.24
15-year bonds	6.42
20-year bonds	6.72
25-year bonds	6.77
Corporate debt obligations (10-year)	
AAA	6.73%
AA	6.87
A	7.04
BBB	7.40
BB+	7.85
BB/BB−	9.45
B (5-year)	10.52
Other instruments	
Prime rate loans	8.25%
Federal Reserve Bank	
Discount rate	5.00
Certificates of deposit (90-day)	5.29
Commercial paper (6 months)	5.26

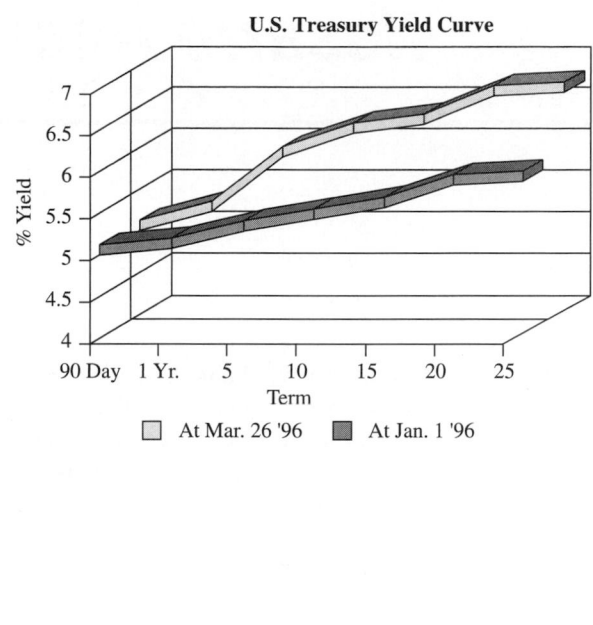

U.S. Treasury Yield Curve

Rosario Acero S.A.[1]

In March 1997, Pablo Este sat in a comfortable chair in the living room of his home in Buenos Aires, reflecting on the future of the small steel mill he owned. The initial years of Rosario Acero S.A., the former Rosario Works of Giganto Acero S.A., had been one challenge after another—the divestiture of Rosario from Giganto, downsizing the operations and workforce, searching for new customers during the six-month Giganto Acero strike at a time when sales to Giganto Acero accounted for nearly one-half the company's total sales, and arguing with local bankers over the value of receivables due from customers facing possible bankruptcy.

Now, after six profitable quarters, the company was preparing to issue its first long-term securities since its incorporation in 1993. The concern Pablo Este faced in March 1997 was the type of capital to acquire. The company's size—revenues were below $35 million (pesos)[2]—definitely limited options, but Sr. Este, as majority shareholder and chairman of Rosario Acero S.A.'s board of directors, wanted to consider all the options available at the time.

He had engaged Raul Martinez, an independent financial consultant, to investigate a private placement of eight-year senior notes with warrants. Sr. Martinez's initial report stated that Rosario Acero S.A. could raise its required $7.5 million at a coupon rate of 13 percent. Another option Sr. Este was interested in evaluating was an initial public offering of Rosario Acero S.A.'s stock through a local investment bank. And perhaps now was the time to sell the entire company to another firm.

---

[1]*Acero* is Spanish for "steel." *S.A.* stands for *sociedad anonimo,* the equivalent of a corporation.

[2]The Argentine peso was fixed at a 1:1 exchange rate with the U.S. dollar. Local convention was to indicate the currency with the dollar sign.

This case adapts an earlier study written by Renee Weaver and revised by Casey Opitz under the direction of Professor Robert F. Bruner. The case was written as a basis for class discussion rather than to illustrate effective or ineffective handling of an administrative situation. All names and financial data have been disguised. Copyright © 1998 by the University of Virginia Darden School Foundation, Charlottesville, VA. All rights reserved. *No part of this publication may be reproduced, stored in a retrieval system, used in a spreadsheet, or transmitted in any form or by any means—electronic, mechanical, photocopying, recording, or otherwise—without the permission of the Darden Foundation. For inquiries, please send an e-mail to dardencases@virginia.edu.* Revised 6/98. Version 1.1.

THE COMPANY

History.   Just two days after Christmas 1992, Giganto Acero announced the closing of 15 unprofitable business units, among which was the Rosario, Argentina, plant, operated by Giganto Acero since 1932. In April 1993, Pablo Este, a Rosario native, Harvard Business School graduate, and successful small-business entrepreneur, was introduced by Rosario civic leaders to members of the plant's top management. After reviewing the situation, Sr. Este agreed to commit the necessary capital, time, and managerial expertise to save the operation and make the mill a viable company in Rosario. Giganto Acero would remain an important customer. After brief negotiations, Sr. Este and a group investment partners purchased the assets of the plant for $14 million, the bulk of which was financed by seller notes from Giganto Acero—Este and his partners invested only $250,000 in the equity of the firm. The plant began operating as Rosario Acero S.A. in July 1993.

Product Lines and Sales.   Taking advantage of existing facilities and numerous opportunities to cut costs, Rosario management positioned the company as a niche player in the industry. Rosario Acero S.A. sold a variety of cast and fabricated steel products to over 35 steel and other heavy-industry customers. The percentage of sales in each major product category for the years 1994–96 is shown in Exhibit 1. Six product managers located in Rosario oversaw each of six product categories: rolling-mill rolls, steel castings, staves, mill liners, continuous caster rolls, and miscellaneous products. The company employed five outside salespersons on straight salary, located in Buenos Aires and Rosario, Argentina; Montevideo, Uruguay; Sao Paulo, Brazil; and Santiago, Chile.

The vast majority of the company's sales were to integrated steel producers (Giganto Acero and Brasilia Metal together accounted for 65 percent of sales in 1994; 49 percent in 1995; and 42 percent in 1996) and minimills. These buyers were very different types of customers. The integrated producers tended to multisource orders, which made them less price-sensitive consumers than minimills; they also tended to place more value on their long-standing supplier relationships. Minimills tended to be price sensitive, and though they relied on a single supplier, they were more likely to consider purchasing from suppliers outside of Mercosur.[3]

The company's chief product was rolling-mill rolls, which were like rolling pins found in a kitchen. These rolls were sold in pairs, and were used to squeeze moving slabs of hot or cold steel into a certain shape and thickness. Rolling-mill rolls accounted for nearly half of the firm's net sales in 1996. The company estimated its gross margins on this product at 32 percent. The company ranked itself second in the Mercosur market for rolling-mill rolls, with a 17 percent share.

Continuous caster rolls were used to channel molten steel as it was cooled during the casting process.[4] Repair and remachining of caster rolls was required on a regular basis. Rosario

---

[3]Mercosur was the South American free-trade association formed by treaty among Argentina, Brazil, and Uruguay.

[4]Molten steel would be poured into rectangular boxes where it would harden into steel ingots. This process was known as casting the steel. More generally, there were two ways to shape steel: (1) bend, stretch, cut, drill, or squeeze it under pressure, or (2) pour it into a preformed mold where it would harden into the desired shape—the latter was casting.

Acero S.A. provided this refurbishment, in addition to preparation of new rolls, to its customers who did not have the in-house capability to refurbish rolls. Company officials estimated gross margins on continuous caster rolls at 12 percent. The market for new rolls in Mercosur was approximately $25 million in 1996, so Rosario's sales gave it about a 13 percent share.

Rosario Acero S.A. produced both machined[5] (finished) and nonmachined (rough) steel castings in a variety of sizes from 1,500 to 45,000 kilograms for a diverse group of customers, including steel makers, cement producers, shipbuilders, automotive manufacturers, and extrusion-press operators, and rock and coal crushers. One example of steel castings was the slag pot, a steel vessel used to receive the impurities thrown off from blast furnaces and reheating furnaces. The company estimated the total potential slag pot market in Mercosur at $5 million, of which its share in the manufacture of small pots (those under 30,000 kilograms) was 80 percent. Overall, gross margins on rough castings were approximately 18 percent; gross margins on finished castings were just 2 percent.

A mill liner was a rolled steel liner plate and lift bar used in industrial grinding machines for grinding cement, pulverizing coal, and grinding high-silica sand for glass production. Rosario Acero S.A. produced mill liners from purchased parts at gross margins of 40 percent.

Facilities and Operations.   All of Rosario Acero S.A.'s production took place at the company's sole facility in Rosario, Argentina. The plant housed two electric furnaces used to melt scrap metal for production (for a total melting capacity of 61,000 kilograms). All melting and pouring was done from 17:00 to 9:00 on weekdays, or on weekends, to minimize energy costs. This practice saved an estimated $50,000 in monthly electricity costs. Factory overhead accounted for 63 percent of Rosario Acero S.A.'s cost of goods sold.

Plant equipment and facilities had been well maintained under Giganto Acero ownership, with capital spending totaling over $25 million from 1976 to 1989. Capital spending by Rosario Acero S.A. totaled $3 million from 1993 to March 1997, with additional spending planned from a portion of the long-term capital to be raised.

Rosario Acero S.A. relied on one primary source, located in Buenos Aires, for the scrap metal used in its production of rolls and castings. Exhibit 2 lists scrap prices during the most recent year. Within the structure of Rosario Acero S.A.'s costs, direct materials including scrap accounted for 26 percent of the cost of goods sold in 1996.

The company's plant operated seven days a week on three shifts as of the end of 1996, with an hourly workforce of 816. The unionized workforce (40 percent semiskilled, 60 percent skilled) earned an average hourly wage of $3.75 during 1996. Direct labor accounted for 11 percent of Rosario Acero S.A.'s cost of goods sold in 1996. All hourly employees were represented by the Union de Obreros Metalurgicos (Metalworkers' Union) under a contract that expired in June 1998. The hourly wage rate for comparable work was $4.25. Union leaders had told Pablo Este that the hourly employees would demand a better-than-competitive contract at the expiration of the current contract—this was to compensate the employees for staying with the firm through its difficulties.[6]

---

[5]Machining was a process of shaping the steel through cutting or drilling.
[6]The financial forecasts by Pablo Este assumed modest increases in wage rates, consistent with expectations for competitive market conditions.

The company also operated with 118 administrative employees, and a new CEO, Enrique Salazar, was appointed in May 1996 to assume operational responsibility under Pablo Este. Other members of senior management under Giganto Acero ownership held the same positions now, with the exception of the former company president, who had resigned in February 1997.

Six top managers other than Pablo Este held 25 percent of the stock outstanding at the end of 1996. Sr. Este held 58 percent. Este's investment partners held the balance of the shares outstanding.

THE STEEL INDUSTRY IN 1997

In 1996 the Argentine steel industry enjoyed a moderately profitable year. Several factors accounted for this turnaround in the industry. First, capacity cutbacks and modernization programs of the past half decade paid off; the industry reached 80 percent capacity in 1996, with utilization for high-demand items near 100 percent. In addition, the birth of the Mercosur trade group promoted more trade by Argentine firms with customers in Brazil and Uruguay.

Forecasts for 1997 and the next three to five years were favorable but contingent on producers continuing their recent efforts to remain competitive in the industry. Domestic steel shipments were estimated to be 70 million metric tons, slightly below 1996 because of cutbacks in inventories rather than lower consumption. Imports were expected to continue their decline from the 1996 level of 20 million metric tons to less than 19 million tons in 1997.

ROSARIO ACERO S.A.'S OUTLOOK

Rosario Acero S.A.'s revenues and earnings had grown since the company began operations in July 1993. The company's balance sheets and income statements for this period are provided in Exhibits 3 and 4. Management predicted continued growth into the new century, with different product lines growing at different rates. Annualized rates of growth from 1996 to 2002 were projected by product line as follows:

Product Line	1996 Sales (in millions)	1996–2002 Projected Growth Rate
Rolling-mill rolls	$16.0	13.9%
Castings	9.0	1.4
Slag pots	1.4	19.6
Mill liner	1.6	14.5
Continuous caster rolls	3.3	5.7
Fabricated and other	3.5	6.8
Total	$34.8	10.32% (Average)

In addition to continuing to serve present customers, Sr. Este wanted the company to pursue customers outside Mercosur. As yet, management had taken no action to investigate external markets, largely because of capital constraints on the firm.

ROSARIO ACERO S.A.'S FINANCING ALTERNATIVES

Management was seeking $7.5 million in long-term capital for three purposes in early 1997: (1) $4.8 million to pay down the company's present working-capital line of credit; (2) $975,000 to repay long-term debt that would mature in mid-1997; and (3) the remaining $1,725,000 for capital improvements and general purposes. The company would retain its recently negotiated $5 million working-capital line of credit with Banco de Sol of Buenos Aires. This line, at 2 percent above the local lending base rate, was not secured by any collateral,[7] though Pablo Este had given a personal guarantee backed by certain commercial real estate he owned. The banker had stated emphatically that an increase in the line of credit and release of Pablo Este from his guarantee would be out of the question without more long-term capital supporting the loan and a longer record of successful financial performance.

The private placement of eight-year notes recommended by Raul Martinez would have the terms set forth in Exhibit 5. The potential purchasers were two Spanish investment funds. The fee associated with issuing the placement through Sr. Martinez would be $52,000. The prospective investors demanded warrants with the debt, because of the firm's small size, relatively high leverage, and absence of a long history of operating profitability. Sr. Martinez explained that the warrants were a "kicker" that increased the effective return to the investors. The covenants associated with this placement were yet to be negotiated. The Spanish investors told Martinez that the minimum acceptable EBIT coverage ratio (i.e., EBIT divided by interest expense) would be 2.0. As a foundation for valuing the warrants, Sr. Martinez estimated the average volatility of peer steel companies' shares at 0.35. Martinez had also determined that in several recent comparable private placements of debt, the effective annual cost of the financing to the issuer had been between 14 and 16 percent, representing a huge premium over the Argentine base lending rate of 8.5 percent.

A second financing alternative that Pablo Este considered was an initial public offering (IPO) of the company's stock. While the 233,000 shares of stock currently outstanding were not presently traded, six senior managers had been offered (and had accepted) a chance to invest three times since the company's inception at prices as follows:[8]

December 1994: 15,480 shares at $3.00/share.

January 1995: 14,220 shares at $4.00/share.

December 1996: 28,550 shares at $9.00/share.

These purchases accounted for management's 25 percent equity interest in the firm.

---

[7]The custom of extending working-capital loans "clean" (i.e., unsecured by the firm's receivables and inventory) was due to the difficulties in Argentina of getting a perfected lien, and filing new paperwork to keep up the lien as the inventory and receivables rolled over.

[8]The number of shares currently outstanding, 233,000, includes these recent share sales.

Fees associated with an IPO were expected to be about 8 percent, but they could be reduced to 2 percent if a "best efforts" placement was selected rather than a guaranteed underwriting. Public trading of the stock would have implications for the shares held by top management and Sr. Este. For instance, Sr. Este wanted to see the issue open at a price higher than the $9.00 that managers had most recently paid for their shares of Rosario Acero S.A. For this reason, he had concluded that the size of the issue would have to be determined after a market value had been placed on the company.

The IPO market had recovered modestly since the Mexican peso crash of November 1994. By March 1997, the stock market had rebounded from the "tequila effect" of the peso crash. The Merval index had risen over the previous three years, suggesting a growing optimism among equity investors in Argentina. The market for IPOs was following this same recovery route, although the volume of IPOs was still relatively light.

The success of IPOs in recent months had depended a great deal on the quality of the offering; issues in more stable and mature industries that appealed to the knowledgeable investors were faring better than media and communications issues. A number of the recent IPOs involved privatizations of state-owned enterprises. Other IPOs were spin-offs from larger industrial groups seeking to rationalize their operations. One recent example was a spin-off of a subsidiary involved in a commodity fertilizer business that brought $22 a share on 11 million shares, surpassing expectations of $17 to $20 a share set for the issue prior to the November crash. In contrast was a retailer's first issue that had been planned for the end of November 1996. The company had expected to issue $9 million in equity, but it was forced to look elsewhere for funds when it could not locate another underwriter after its first banker withdrew.

Pablo Este had recently entertained the idea of selling Rosario Acero to another concern, although no specific price had been estimated for the company at that time. This option could be considered in more detail, this time as a means of obtaining funds or issuing stock to the public.

To value Rosario Acero S.A., Sr. Este had forecasted the financial performance of the firm under either financing option, the debt-and-warrants issue (see Exhibits 6, 7, and 8) or the equity issue (see Exhibits 9, 10, and 11). Also, he obtained average valuation multiples for minimills from a recent investment report; these indicated an average equity value of 1.5 times book value, 21 times 1996 earnings, and 18 times estimated 1997 earnings. Sr. Este had also gathered information on several publicly held steel producers in Mercosur that were somewhat similar to Rosario Acero S.A. This information is contained in Exhibit 12. He wondered whether to simply average the results of all the peers given in that exhibit or to exclude any; Picasso Acero, for instance, had experienced a turbulent year due to a strike and vandalism at its plant. Based on his own experience with leveraged buyouts, Sr. Este believed that a potential LBO purchaser might place a value on the company's equity by using a multiple of 4 times EBIT and then subtracting total debt.

Interest rates over the past few years are provided in Exhibits 13 and 14. Research by Raul Martinez revealed that economists and financial institutions were forecasting annual rates of inflation between 2.5 and 4.0 percent, and real GNP growth at 1.5 to 6.0 percent.

Pablo Este was 66 years old and the patriarch of a large extended family. While he had no intention of retiring from Rosario's board of directors soon, he was concerned about the liquidity of his valuable investment in the firm. It was important to him and the other equity investors to increase the marketability of Rosario's common stock. However, tempering any momentum to choose the IPO was the cautious sentiment among senior management regarding the impact of any securities issuance on their administrative control of the firm.

Sr. Este realized that, as chairman of the board, he could easily rely on someone else to explore the various options that might be available to Rosario Acero S.A. As the key framer of the company's success so far, however, he had an interest in seeing the board select the alternative that would best assure a continuation of that financial and employment success. With much information in front of him and all of his knowledge of Rosario Acero S.A. in his head, Pablo Este sat down to determine which long-term financing option he would support.

EXHIBIT 1   Percentage of Company Sales by Product Line*

	1994	1995	1996	Feb. 1997†	Recent Gross Profit Margins
Rolls	40%	46%	46%	68%	32%
Castings	29	27	29	20	18 (rough) 2 (finished)
Continuous caster rolls	4	6	9	6	12
Mill liners	8	5	5	2	40
Staves	0	3	1	1	
Other products	17	8	5	4	80 (small pots)
Services	2	4	4	0	
Total	100%	100%	100%	100%	

*Columns may not add to 100 because of rounding.
†1997 percentages based on bookings as of February 1997.

Source: Company records.

EXHIBIT 2   Scrap Prices of Dealer Bundles (price per metric ton delivered from Buenos Aires)

Date of Estimate	Price Range
December 1995	$ 96–$ 97
January 1996	99– 100
February 1996	104– 105
March 1996	98– 99
April 1996	93– 94
May 1996	103– 104
June 1996	114– 115
July 1996	115– 116
August 1996	119– 120
September 1996	131– 132
October 1996	159– 160
November 1996	159– 160
December 1996	144– 145
January 1997	139– 140

Source: Company records.

EXHIBIT 3   Balance Sheets (pesos in thousands)

	As of December 31		
	1994	1995	1996
Cash	$ 119	$ 0	$ 245
Accounts receivable	3,077	3,845	6,846
Inventories	5,186	4,786	4,682
Other current assets	865	168	381
Total current assets	9,247	8,799	12,154
Property, plant, and equipment	13,938	14,054	14,210
Other	193	187	116
Total assets	$23,378	$23,040	$26,480
Working capital notes payable	$ 4,650	$ 4,998	$ 4,821
Current portion long-term debt	1,706	1,171	1,335
Accounts payable	3,313	3,048	4,663
Other current liabilities	804	1,993	2,315
Total current liabilities	10,473	11,210	13,134
Long-term debt	11,804	8,847	8,467
Deferred taxes and leases	312	1,258	1,282
Total liabilities	22,589	21,315	22,883
Common stock (Par = $1/sh)	210	202	233
Additional paid-in capital	71	114	191
Retained earnings	508	1,409	3,173
Total owners' equity	789	1,725	3,597
Total liabilities and equity	$23,378	$23,040	$26,480

Source: Company financial statements.

EXHIBIT 4   Income Statements (in thousands of pesos, except per share data)

	As of December 31		
	1994	1995[a]	1996
Revenues	$25,084	$26,605	$34,836
Cost of goods sold (including depreciation)[b]	18,138	21,784	27,654
Selling, general, and administrative	3,598	3,767	3,959
Interest	1,586	1,461	1,098
Restructuring expenses	445	142	537
Profit before tax	1,317	(549)	1,588
Tax provision (benefit)	577	(285)	4
Income (loss) before extraordinary item	740	(264)	1,584
Extraordinary item[c]	265	1,165	179
Net income	$ 1,005	$ 901	$ 1,763
Earnings per share	$ 4.79	$ 4	$ 7.57

[a]Company loss in 1995 was attributed to sales lost as a result of a six-month strike against Giganto Acero, a major account for Rosario.
[b]COGS includes depreciation of $736,000 in 1994; $876,000 in 1995; and $935,000 in 1996.
[c]Extraordinary income resulted from refunding of debt, net of applicable income taxes in 1995 and 1996. Credits on income taxes due to net operating loss carryovers resulted in extraordinary income in 1994.

Source: Company financial statements.

EXHIBIT 5   Summary of Terms of Proposed Private Placement

Amount	$7,500,000
Issue	Senior notes with warrants
Maturity	Eight years due 2004
Takedown	Second quarter 1997
Interest rate	Thirteen percent per annum, payable semiannually
Amortization	Interest only for the first six years. Mandatory principal payments of $1,875,000 in the seventh year and $5,625,000 in the eighth year.

Optional redemption   None for the first six years. Callable thereafter at the following redemption prices as a whole or in part:

Year 7	105%
Year 8	100% (no premium)

Warrants   The notes will be accompanied by an eight-year nondetachable warrant entitling the holder to purchase 40,000 shares of common stock at an exercise price of $1 per share. The warrant shares will be subject to antidilution provisions and be adjusted for stock splits, stock dividends, recapitalizations, mergers, and the sale of stock, issuance of options, or securities or warrants convertible or issuable into common stock, all at a price in excess of $1 per share.

The number of warrant shares will be adjusted on a one-time basis based on the average of net operating income for the years 1997 and 1998. Such adjustment will occur in the first quarter of 1999.

Net Operating Income	Number of Shares	Percentage of Ownership
$6,000,000 or greater	40,000	15.0%
$5,999,999–$5,000,000	47,725	17.5
$4,999,999–$4,000,000	56,250	20.0
$3,999,999–$3,000,000	65,325	22.5
Less than $3,000,000	75,000	25.0

Net operating income will be defined as stated in the company's audited financials, before interest and provision for income taxes, and will conform with generally accepted definitions of operating income.

Optional put   The warrant shares can be put to the company, starting at the end of the fifth year by the holder of the warrant at a price per share equivalent to the then "appraised market value per share." Such value shall be calculated by taking operating income before taxes and interest for the latest four quarters and multiplying the sum by 6, adding cash and marketable securities, and deducting short-term and long-term debt. This sum will be divided by fully diluted shares outstanding to arrive at an "appraised market value per share." The warrant holder may not put in excess of 25 percent of his warrant shares to the company in any one year.

Provision for early redemption   Redemption of the senior notes before maturity would not be permitted.

Registration rights   The warrant shares will be subject to one free right of registration after the company's initial public offering and unlimited rights to piggyback other public offerings of the stock, subject to consent of underwriters.

Restrictive covenants on the notes   To be negotiated.

Source: Raul Martinez, second draft of private placement memorandum.

EXHIBIT 6   Forecast of Income Statement: Growth Financed with the Privately Placed Debt-and-Warrants Issue
(in millions of pesos except per share data)

Common Assumptions

Revenue growth rate	10.30%	Inventory/Revenues	13.00%
COGS/Revenues	78.00%	Other curr. assets/Revenues	1.00%
SG&A/Revenues	13.00%	Gross fixed assets/Revenues	48.00%
Tax rate	34.00%	Accts. payable/Revenues	14.00%
Depreciation/Gross fixed assets	5.60%	Other. curr. liabs./Revenues	7.00%
Cash/Revenues	1.00%	Interest rate	10.00%
Accts. receivable/Revenues	20.00%	Change in def'd tax/Taxes	25.00%
Base lending rate	8.50%	Primary shares	233,000
		Fully-diluted shares	273,000

	Actual	Projected					
	1996	1997	1998	1999	2000	2001	2002
Income statement							
Revenues	$34.80	$38.38	$42.34	$46.70	$51.51	$56.81	$62.67
Cost of goods sold	(27.65)	(29.94)	(33.02)	(36.43)	(40.18)	(44.32)	(48.88)
Selling, gen'l, and admin.	(3.96)	(4.99)	(5.50)	(6.07)	(6.70)	(7.39)	(8.15)
Earnings before interest and taxes	3.19	3.45	3.81	4.20	4.64	5.11	5.64
Interest (notes and old loans)*	(1.10)	(0.73)	(0.70)	(0.65)	(0.59)	(0.51)	(0.41)
Interest (new loan @ 13%)		(0.98)	(0.98)	(0.98)	(0.98)	(0.98)	(0.98)
Profit before taxes	2.09	1.75	2.13	2.57	3.07	3.63	4.26
Taxes	0.00	(0.59)	(0.72)	(0.88)	(1.04)	(1.23)	(1.45)
Profit after taxes	$ 2.09	$ 1.15	$ 1.41	$ 1.70	$ 2.03	$ 2.40	$ 2.81
Profit with extraord. item	1.76						
Earnings per share	$ 7.57	$ 4.96	$ 6.04	$ 7.29	$ 8.70	$10.28	$12.06

*The firm is assumed to borrow at base rate plus 2 percent, and lend at base rate less 2 percent.

EXHIBIT 7   Forecast of Balance Sheets: Growth Financed with the Private Placement of Debt-and-Warrants (pesos in millions except per share data)

	Actual	*Projected*					
	1996	*1997*	*1998*	*1999*	*2000*	*2001*	*2002*
Balance sheet							
Cash	$ 0.20	$ 0.38	$ 0.42	$ 0.47	$ 0.52	$ 0.57	$ 0.63
Accounts receivable	6.80	7.68	8.47	9.34	10.30	11.36	12.53
Inventory	4.70	4.99	5.50	6.07	6.70	7.39	8.15
Other current assets	0.40	0.38	0.42	0.47	0.52	0.57	0.63
Total current assets	12.10	13.43	14.82	16.34	18.03	19.88	21.93
Gross fixed assets	16.70	18.42	20.32	22.42	24.72	27.27	30.08
Accumulated depreciation	(2.50)	(3.53)	(4.67)	(5.93)	(7.31)	(8.84)	(10.52)
Net fixed assets	14.20	14.89	15.65	16.49	17.41	18.43	19.56
Other assets	0.10	0.10	0.10	0.10	0.10	0.10	0.10
Total assets	$26.40	$28.43	$30.57	$32.93	$35.54	$38.42	$41.59
Notes payable (or excess cash)	$ 4.80	$ (0.76)	$ (0.84)	$ (0.81)	$ (1.00)	$ (1.44)	$ (2.17)
Accounts payable	4.60	5.37	5.93	6.54	7.21	7.95	8.77
Other current liabilities	2.30	2.69	2.96	3.27	3.61	3.98	4.39
Total current liabilities	11.70	7.30	8.05	9.00	9.82	10.49	10.99
Old long-term debt	9.80	7.43	7.23	6.73	6.23	5.73	5.23
New long-term debt		7.50	7.50	7.50	7.50	7.50	7.50
Deferred taxes	1.30	1.45	1.63	1.85	2.11	2.42	2.78
Total liabilities	22.80	23.67	24.41	25.07	25.66	26.14	26.50
Common stock	0.20	0.20	0.20	0.20	0.20	0.20	0.20
Paid-in surplus	0.20	0.20	0.20	0.20	0.20	0.20	0.20
Retained earnings	3.20	4.35	5.76	7.46	9.49	11.88	14.69
Total liabilities and equity	$26.40	$28.43	$30.57	$32.93	$35.54	$38.42	$41.59
Comparative ratios							
EBIT/Interest	2.90	2.03	2.27	2.58	2.96	3.45	4.08
EBIT/(Interest + Amort.)	1.93	0.36	1.95	2.00	2.06	2.11	2.16
Liabilities/Equity	6.33	4.98	3.96	3.19	2.59	2.13	1.76
(Debt + Notes)/Equity	4.06	2.98	2.25	1.71	1.29	0.96	0.70
Profit/Revenues NPM	5.1%	3.0%	3.3%	3.6%	3.9%	4.2%	4.5%
Profit/Equity ROE	49.0%	24.3%	22.8%	21.6%	20.5%	19.5%	18.6%

EXHIBIT 8   Forecast of Free Cash Flow: Growth Financed with Debt and Warrants (pesos in millions)

	Projected					
	1997	*1998*	*1999*	*2000*	*2001*	*2002*
Earnings before interest and taxes	3.45	3.81	4.20	4.64	5.11	5.64
Taxes	(1.17)	(1.30)	(1.43)	(1.58)	(1.74)	(1.92)
Earnings before interest and after taxes	2.28	2.51	2.77	3.06	3.37	3.72
Plus depreciation	1.03	1.14	1.26	1.38	1.53	1.68
Less capital expenditures	(1.72)	(1.90)	(2.09)	(2.31)	(2.55)	(2.81)
Less additions to net working capital	(0.17)	(0.55)	(0.61)	(0.67)	(0.74)	(0.82)
Free cash flow	1.41	1.20	1.33	1.46	1.61	1.78

EXHIBIT 9   Forecast of Income Statements: Growth Financed with Equity, Shares Sold at $9.00 Each (pesos in millions except per share data)

Common Assumptions

Revenue growth rate	10.30%	Inventory/Revenues	13.00%
COGS/Revenues	78.00%	Other curr. assets/Revenues	1.00%
SG&A/Revenues	13.00%	Gross fixed assets/Revenues	48.00%
Tax rate	34.00%	Accts. payable/Revenues	14.00%
Depreciation/Gross fixed assets	5.60%	Other. curr. liabs./Revenues	7.00%
Cash/Revenues	1.00%	Interest rate	10.00%
Accts. receivable/Revenues	20.00%	Change in def'd tax/Taxes	25.00%
Base lending rate	8.50%	1996 primary shares	233,000
		1997 + primary shares	1,066,333

	Actual	Projected					
	1996	*1997*	*1998*	*1999*	*2000*	*2001*	*2002*
Income statement							
Revenues	$34.80	$38.38	$42.34	$46.70	$51.51	$56.81	$62.67
Cost of goods sold	(27.65)	(29.94)	(33.02)	(36.43)	(40.18)	(44.32)	(48.88)
Selling, gen'l, and admin.	(3.96)	(4.99)	(5.50)	(6.07)	(6.70)	(7.39)	(8.15)
Earnings before interest and taxes	3.19	3.45	3.81	4.20	4.64	5.11	5.64
Interest (notes and old loans)*	(1.10)	(0.68)	(0.60)	(0.50)	(0.37)	(0.23)	(0.07)
Interest (new loan @ 13%)		0.00	0.00	0.00	0.00	0.00	0.00
Profit before taxes	2.09	2.77	3.21	3.71	4.26	4.88	5.57
Taxes	0.00	(0.94)	(1.09)	(1.26)	(1.45)	(1.66)	(1.89)
Profit after taxes	$ 2.09	$ 1.83	$ 2.12	$ 2.45	$ 2.81	$ 3.22	$ 3.68
Profit with extraord. item	1.76						
Earnings per share	$ 7.57	$ 1.72	$ 1.99	$ 2.29	$ 2.64	$ 3.02	$ 3.45

*The firm is assumed to borrow at base rate plus 2 percent, and lend at base rate less 2 percent.

EXHIBIT 10 Forecast of Balance Sheets: Growth Financed with Equity, Shares Sold at $9.00 Each (in millions of pesos except per share data)

	Actual	*Projected*					
	1996	*1997*	*1998*	*1999*	*2000*	*2001*	*2002*
Balance sheet							
Cash	$ 0.20	$ 0.38	$ 0.42	$ 0.47	$ 0.52	$ 0.57	$ 0.63
Accounts receivable	6.80	7.68	8.47	9.34	10.30	11.36	12.53
Inventory	4.70	4.99	5.50	6.07	6.70	7.39	8.15
Other current assets	0.40	0.38	0.42	0.47	0.52	0.57	0.63
Total current assets	12.10	13.43	14.82	16.34	18.03	19.88	21.93
Gross fixed assets	16.70	18.42	20.32	22.42	24.72	27.27	30.08
Accumulated depreciation	(2.50)	(3.53)	(4.67)	(5.93)	(7.31)	(8.84)	(10.52)
Net fixed assets	14.20	14.89	15.65	16.49	17.41	18.43	19.56
Other assets	0.10	0.10	0.10	0.10	0.10	0.10	0.10
Total assets	$26.40	$28.43	$30.57	$32.93	$35.54	$38.42	$41.59
Notes payable (or excess cash)	4.80	(1.53)	(2.40)	(3.21)	(4.29)	(5.66)	(7.37)
Accounts payable	4.60	5.37	5.93	6.54	7.21	7.95	8.77
Other current liabilities	2.30	2.69	2.96	3.27	3.61	3.98	4.39
Total current liabilities	11.70	6.54	6.49	6.59	6.53	6.27	5.79
Old long-term debt	9.80	7.43	7.23	6.73	6.23	5.73	5.23
New long-term debt		0.00	0.00	0.00	0.00	0.00	0.00
Deferred taxes	1.30	1.54	1.81	2.12	2.49	2.90	3.37
Total liabilities	22.80	15.50	15.52	15.44	15.24	14.89	14.39
Common stock	0.20	1.20	1.20	1.20	1.20	1.20	1.20
Paid-in surplus	0.20	6.70	6.70	6.70	6.70	6.70	6.70
Retained earnings	3.20	5.03	7.15	9.59	12.41	15.63	19.30
Total liabilities and equity	$26.40	$28.43	$30.57	$32.93	$35.54	$38.42	$41.59
Comparative ratios							
EBIT/Interest	2.90	5.08	6.32	8.45	12.37	21.95	81.14
EBIT/(Interest + Amort.)	1.93	0.37	2.27	2.32	2.38	2.43	2.48
Liabilities/Equity	6.33	1.20	1.03	0.88	0.75	0.63	0.53
(Debt + Notes)/Equity	4.06	0.46	0.32	0.20	0.10	0.00	-0.08
Profit/Revenues	5.1%	4.8%	5.0%	5.2%	5.5%	5.7%	5.9%
Profit/Equity	49.0%	14.2%	14.1%	14.0%	13.8%	13.7%	13.5%

EXHIBIT 11 Forecast of Free Cash Flow: Growth Financed with Equity, Shares Sold at $9.00 Each (in millions of pesos)

			Projected			
	1997	*1998*	*1999*	*2000*	*2001*	*2002*
Earnings before interest and taxes	3.45	3.81	4.20	4.64	5.11	5.64
Taxes	(1.17)	(1.30)	(1.43)	(1.58)	(1.74)	(1.92)
Earnings before interest and after taxes	2.28	2.51	2.77	3.06	3.37	3.72
Plus depreciation	1.03	1.14	1.26	1.38	1.53	1.68
Less capital expenditures	(1.72)	(1.90)	(2.09)	(2.31)	(2.55)	(2.81)
Less additions to net working capital	(0.17)	(0.55)	(0.61)	(0.67)	(0.74)	(0.82)
Free cash flow	1.41	1.20	1.33	1.46	1.61	1.78

EXHIBIT 12 Selected 1996 Data on Publicly Listed Peer Firms

	Description of Business
Acero Dali S.A. (AD)	Production and fabrication of steel reinforcing and merchant bars. Principal customers: building, road, and bridge contractors; municipal, county, and state agencies; concrete manufacturers; railroad, utility, and industrial companies. Marketing areas: Argentina, Uruguay, Brazil, and the Caribbean. Directors own 3% of stock.
Colon S.A. (CSA)	Makes and distributes furnace lining materials (69% of sales), mainly to the steel industry. Produces filter media, filters, and oil control products. Mines a variety of ores and clays (14%). Insiders control about 55% of stock.
Greco Acero (GA)	Produces carbon steel products exclusively by the electric furnace method. Steel scrap is a major raw material. Makes 75% of sales in Argentina to steel service centers, fabricators, and hardware jobbers. Main markets: agriculture and construction. Escobar family owns about 45% of stock.
Velasguez S.A. (VAZ)	Manufactures steel and steel joists (holds 30% of regional market for joists). Major markets: construction, energy, rail, agriculture.
Picasso Acero S.A. (PI)	Leading processor of ferrous scrap (75% of sales) and nonferrous scrap (10%). Picasso family holds about 25% of stock; Tiger group about 15%. Sustained losses in the most recent year due to a strike, and strike-related vandalism at its plant.

EXHIBIT 12   *(concluded)*

Operating Information*	AD	CSA	GA	VAZ	PI
Sales	$381.0	$362.8	$397.4	$755.2	$117.1
Operating margin	55.6	11.7	26.0	144.9	(1.1)
Net income	16.9	7.5	10.3	46.4	(5.1)
Operating margin/Sales	14.6%	3.2%	6.5%	19.2%	(0.9%)
Net income/Sales	4.4	2.1	2.6	6.1	(4.4%)
Long-term debt/Capital (book)	40.0%	56%	22%	33%	42%
Total debt/Capital (book)	57.0%	66%	40%	37%	65%
Total debt/Equity (book)	1.33	1.94	0.67	0.59	1.86
Market equity/Book equity	1.85	1.25	1.50	2.10	0.90
Total debt/Equity (market)	0.72	1.55	0.44	0.28	2.06
Dividend payout ratio (3-year average)	27.0%	0%	15%[†]	12%	0%
Dividend yield	3.0%	0%	3.3%	1.0%	0%
P/E ratio	9.5	15.9	11.3	15.0	7.3
Beta	1.35	1.05	1.00	1.15	2.50
Stock price range	$ 44½- 18¼	$ 20¼- 13½	$ 24¼- 11⅛	$ 49½- 29½	$ 54- 18¾
Close March 1, 1997	$ 32¾	$ 18⅝	$ 19½	$ 42½	$ 33

Five-year Annualized per Share Growth Projections	AD	CSA	GA	VAZ	PI
Sales	10%		9%	10%	5%
Earnings	17%			12%	
Dividends	14%			12%	8%

*All operating information for most recent fiscal year as of March 1997 and in millions of pesos. Other information current as of March 1997 unless noted.
[†]Payout based on 1996 only. No dividends paid previously.
All data are disguised.

EXHIBIT 13   Debt Market Conditions

	March 1997
Average corporate bond yield	9.86%
Base lending rate	8.50
10-year Argentine T-bond	8.50
3-month Argentine T-bill	5.70

Interest Rate Trends

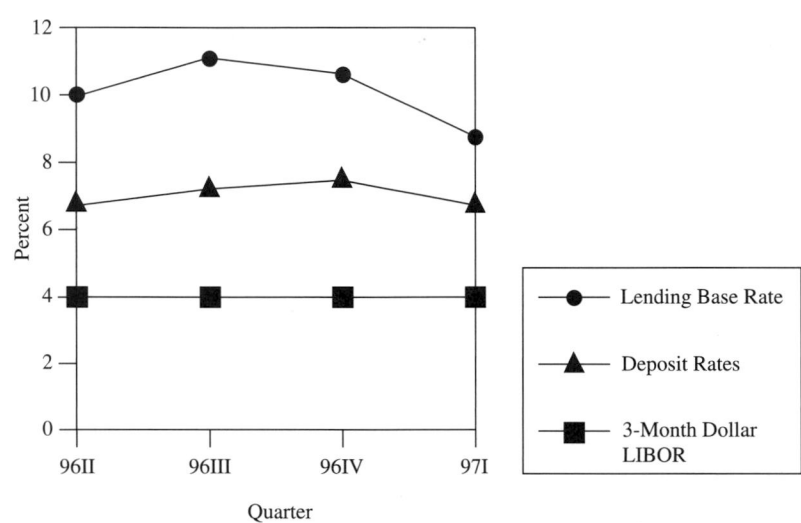

EXHIBIT 14   Current Yields on Selected Debt Issues in South America

Company	Rating*	Form of Debt	Coupon	Maturity Date	Current Yield	Yield to Maturity
Sola S.A.	BBB	Notes	8.625	2005	9.02	9.41
HABASA	BBB−	Subordinated notes	9.300	2003	10.35	10.49
Mercado S.A.	CCC+	Subordinated debenture	11.990	2005	16.89	13.05
Orientar S.A.	BBB−	Notes	10.500	2004	10.47	10.45
Serenidad S.A.	CCC−	Senior sinking-fund debenture	7.750	2004	12.86	17.42
Turismo S.A.	CCC+	Senior subordinated notes	13.250	2003	13.25	13.25
Util S.A.	CCC	Subordinated sinking-fund debenture	5.000	2003	15.25	16.10
Tulipan S.A.	CCC−	Sinking fund debenture	8.100	2005	15.88	19.08

Recent Private Placement Yields, BBB− Issues

	Company	Form of Debt	Maturity Date	Coupon
January	Grua S.A.	Fixed rate notes	2005	11.25%
	Globo S.A.	Senior notes	2001	11.35
	Disquete S.A.	Senior notes	2001	11.40
February	Energa S.A.	Senior notes	2006	11.20
	Energa S.A.	Senior notes	2002	11.60
	Vemco S.A.	Subordinated secured notes	2001	11.50
March	Luza Solaro S.A.	Secured nonrecourse notes	2001	10.90
	Dorar S.A.	Secured notes	1999	10.80
	Contrahacer S.A.	Senior secured notes	2002	10.85
	Coronar S.A.	Senior notes	2001	10.20

*According to a well-known international debt rating agency, "Debt rated BBB is believed to have a satisfactory capacity to pay interest and repay principal, though that capacity would decline readily if adverse economic conditions or changing circumstances should arise . . . Debt rated . . . CCC . . . is predominantly speculative."
Data have been disguised.

Planet Cópias & Imagem

In March 1996, the founders of Planet Cópias & Imagem reflected on their ambitious growth goals for the firm and began to plan the financing program that would help them achieve those goals. Planet, which was headquartered in Lisbon, Portugal, had successfully established five document centers with a unique, "high-tech, high-touch" store concept that included complete document preparation services, the newest reproduction technology, 24-hour service, food service, musical entertainment, and a pleasant atmosphere.

The founding entrepreneurs of Planet, Michael Melloy, Pascal Monteiro de Barros, and Luis Quartin Bastos—who called themselves "the three amigos"—sought to position the firm as a "breakout growth, category-killer" retail chain in Europe and worldwide. They aimed to become the dominant retail document center chain. Luis expressed Planet's growth plans when he told Portugal's leading newspaper, "Our goal is to have 100 megastores in 5 years."

The founders ideally wanted to take Planet public by 1999 (but no later than 2002) in an international initial public offering (IPO) on American and European exchanges. They hoped this would monetize and make liquid their "sweat equity" in the firm, and compensate them for the risks they had taken. Currently, most of the world's equity markets were receptive to IPOs (see Exhibit 1), though in the past the IPO "window of opportunity" for young firms had opened and closed. Thus, the timing of an IPO would be uncertain and would depend on market opportunities.

This case was prepared from field research by Kent Carstater under the direction of Professor Robert F. Bruner. Certain facts and all financial data have been disguised at the request of the company. This case was written as a basis for class discussion rather than to illustrate effective or ineffective handling of an administrative situation. Copyright © 1997 by the University of Virginia Darden School Foundation, Charlottesville, VA. All rights reserved. *No part of this publication may be reproduced, stored in a retrieval system, used in a spreadsheet, or transmitted in any form or by any means—electronic, mechanical, photocopying, recording, or otherwise—without the permission of the Darden Foundation. For inquiries, please send an e-mail to dardencases@virginia.edu.* Revised 6/98. Version 2.1.

The fundamental task of Luis, Michael, and Pascal was to craft a financial strategy that would accommodate Planet's cash needs in the near term while not sacrificing its long-term equity interest. The strategy would need to reflect expectations of Planet's capital requirements from now until the IPO. Also, the strategy needed to preserve the firm's financial flexibility, enhance the firm's value, expand its competitive position, and preserve the founders' control. Estimating the value of Planet would be an important element in deciding how much equity to surrender (i.e., sell) in order to raise capital. Finally, the strategy needed to indicate the types of capital to be issued, the amounts, timing, and bets implied in the sequencing of capital issues.

THE PLANET CONCEPT

Planet Cópias & Imagem focused on the creation, design, reproduction, and distribution of documents for students, businesses, and government agencies. The company owned five retail document services centers that integrated an extensive and technologically diverse design, copy, and finishing product mix. Exhibit 2 gives a complete listing of Planet's services.

Planet stores were intended to be places to work, create, learn, mingle, and relax. The Planet document services center offered modern and clean architecture. The entire store was kept cool to aid the performance of modern technology workstations. The space was light and uncluttered, with ambient music sounding throughout the store. The store staff was young, energetic, bright, well trained, and anxious to help. Someone working late on an urgent project could step over to the café for an espresso or pastry. Planet served food because Portuguese law prohibited any trade or business to remain open around the clock unless it served food. The stores combined pleasing design, bright signage, unobtrusive music, friendly and knowledgeable staff, food and drink, 24-hour by seven-day availability, and highly visible locations. Equipment offered the latest technology in each field and reflected strategic alliances with the main suppliers at the European headquarters level. Exhibit 3 summarizes Planet's client base in Portugal and illustrates that the firm's business drew on a blend of corporate and retail customers. Michael Melloy said,

> Most of our competitors have small copy centers in the basements of buildings. Shops are crowded, dirty, and dark. They are using small-capacity machines, many of which are three to five years old. They are not fun places to go. We want clients to make a favorable comparison of our stores with their former centers.

Planet currently operated in Lisbon only and employed a "cluster" strategy, combining a small store, two standard-size stores, a megastore, and a production center. This permitted Planet to exploit economies of scale in production and marketing, to provide service backups, and to be managed efficiently by a seasoned area manager. The Lisbon area model was the prototype for future Planet markets. This structure permitted a lower investment per market, as the area model could have a large product portfolio, without replicating the technological investment in every store.

Planet's core retail concept and its customer feedback mechanism permitted the product mix to evolve with the clients' changing needs. Likely additions to the Planet product line included Internet home-page and CD-ROM design; specialized product sales (computing, engineering, design, arts, presentation); software sales; computer training and demonstrations; presentation and conference areas; and paging and cellular sales. New services would contribute to internal sales growth and to more rapid amortization of existing space and equipment investments.

Marketing was primarily in the form of heavily promoted store openings and the corporate sales force. Effective word-of-mouth advertising was an important reason for Planet's success. To build the word of mouth, Planet focused its marketing efforts on existing clients, and augmented its marketing with press coverage in leading business publications, publication of its own magazine, press conferences, and presentations at trade shows where potential customers could try Planet's innovative services. Planet gained a great deal of attention in the press and was featured in 12 different leading Portuguese business and computing publications in its first year.

The founders intended to enter multiple new markets with Planet's specialty retail document centers. In order to take advantage of the unique window of opportunity presented by its highly fragmented competition, the founders planned to replicate its concept in new, larger, and richer markets. Luis, Michael, and Pascal believed that Planet's concept had worldwide potential.

The success of the Planet store concept seemed confirmed by the pilot store's first-year sales, which were 241 million escudos, much greater than the average mature store sales for America's leading quick printing and reprographic chain. Within three years, the firm had grown to four retail locations, one production center, and 230 employees. But the costs and investments necessary to support the start-up and expansion produced the firm's net losses for 1994 and 1995. The operating cash flow for 1995 was also negative. Exhibits 4, 5, 6, and 7 present historical and forecasted financial statements, and financial ratios—these are expressed in U.S. dollars,[1] as the three founders were preparing to present a proposal for financing to a group of international banks and investment firms.

COMPANY HISTORY

In the summer of 1992, Luis Quartin Bastos evaluated strategic investment opportunities for a Portuguese holding company. This firm had been offered the opportunity to buy the franchise for Portugal of a chain of copying centers. Luis was the likely candidate to manage this new venture. To help him better evaluate the proposal, Luis asked a business-school classmate, Michael Melloy, to prepare reviews of the industry, other possible franchisers, and the Portuguese market.

---

[1]Assumes 150 escudos per U.S. $1, the rate prevailing in March 1996.

Melloy's final report was submitted in late February 1993 and proved to be the genesis of Planet Cópias. Luis and the holding company disagreed with regard to the implementation of the report. Therefore, Luis quit his job and, with Michael, enlisted a third classmate, Pascal, to found Planet. The three entrepreneurs gained the support of a leading Portuguese investor. Altogether they invested 60 million escudos to open a pilot store in the center of Lisbon. The three founders owned 51 percent, and the silent partner retained the balance. After settling on the name, Planet Cópias & Imagem, they hired a design firm to create their corporate logo and image. For the initial site, they selected a 210-square-meter location, in a busy area near two arts universities, in the Chiado section of Lisbon. Key vendors were chosen, and construction began in November 1993. The pilot store (Planet Chiado) opened on January 4, 1994.

The first nine months were spent educating the market, training the workforce, and launching and testing the concept. The pilot store grew from one color copier to eight. Competitors quickly responded to Planet's initial success with similar product introductions and pricing. Planet's high-visibility entrance spawned four copycat firms in 1994. The three founders knew that they had a strong brand identity when unrelated businesses, such as a fast-food restaurant, began using their logo to attract customers.

Planet's board agreed to raise capital to open another four stores in Lisbon. The aim was to consolidate Lisbon rather than spread out to different Portuguese cities. Lisbon represented over 70 percent of Portugal's GNP and an even higher percentage of Planet's corporate target clients—service companies. By clustering the stores in a small geographic region and pricing for share, Planet's intention was to achieve brand dominance. Spreading the locations out further might have extended the reach of the brand, but the spacing of the stores would have precluded shared asset investment. The three concurred that there was a temporary window of opportunity to expand aggressively and prevent against possible new entrants and would-be imitators. Luis said,

> Each store needs to be viewed as a distribution point. Imagine having an amazing product and only one location. The likely competitive behavior is to bring in imitations, which is happening with increasing frequency. The likely consumer behavior is to demand that we open new locations or look for approximate substitutes, which we also saw happening.

Banco Mello was retained to sell 1.2 million new shares in Planet at 535 escudos per share, resulting in 1.6 million shares after the offering. The offering closed in May 1995, was oversubscribed, and raised a total of 643 million escudos. The new shares were placed among 35 individuals and institutions in Portugal and abroad. When the offering was completed, Planet bought back 10 percent of the stock to be used as treasury stock for an ESOP for management. After the capital increase, in which founding investors also invested at the offering price, the "three amigos" controlled about 48 percent of the equity.

On June 1, Planet opened its second store, Planet Liberdade, in the heart of Lisbon's premier business district. After some initial delays due to a shortage of optimal real estate locations, Planet opened a large production center outside Lisbon in September. The megastore on Avenida da Republica, Lisbon's main avenue, opened in December and was the largest of its kind in Europe. Also in December, Planet opened in Carnaxide, a growing office park location on the outskirts of Lisbon. The following chart lists Planet's locations as of January 1996:

Location	Type	Size (m²)	Opening
Planet Chiado	Store	200	January 1994
Planet Liberdade	Store	220	June 1995
Planet Meramar	Production center	450	September 1995
Planet Republica	Store	1,100	December 1995
Planet Carnaxide	Store	500	December 1995

Source: Company documents.

The four Planet stores and one production center met aggressive sales targets. There was no evidence of cannibalization. On the contrary, it appeared that each new store was reaching operating efficiency and higher sales levels increasingly earlier than expected due to growing brand identity.

PROFILE OF THE "BREAKOUT FIRM"

Conscious of having created a successful specialty retail concept, Luis, Michael, and Pascal identified and researched specialty retail firms which they called breakout firms. Breakout firms demonstrated sustainable per store growth and profitability with a rapid rate of expansion in number of stores. Kinko's (convenience documents), Barnes & Noble (books), Starbucks Coffee (specialty coffee), Blockbuster Video (video rental), and Boston Market (restaurants) were deemed illustrative breakout firms. The defining features of breakout growth specialty retailers were as follows:

- *Redefinition and professionalization of a fragmented sector.* Barnes & Noble and Planet competed against the smaller "mom-and-pop" stores in their respective markets.
- *Branding, and development of a store concept.* Blockbuster and Planet took their businesses out of inadequate retail space and provided large, well-lit, user-friendly environments.
- *Use of state-of-the-art information systems.* Blockbuster used its information technology to build a client profile to better manage content and build customer loyalty. Planet designed and was in the process of implementing a comprehensive management information system.
- *Infrastructure development and investment before growth.* Infrastructure consisted of headquarters, information technology, training, store design, and real estate functions. Though this led to operating losses in the early years of their histories, breakout firms were able to sustain much more rapid growth rates because of the infrastructure in place.
- *Use of joint ventures and/or licensing.* Boston Market and Planet both had well-defined partnering agreements.

Breakout firms aggressively expanded in target areas to gain large market share and name recognition. Expansion would begin with placement of a single store, followed by others in the region—the aim was market saturation. Such strategies were inherently *pre-*

emptive: the goal was to create a strong market share ahead of potential competitors. Through branding and careful location of stores, breakout firms would raise barriers to entry. As the dominant firms in their respective segments, these firms came to be called category killers (i.e., killers of competition within the retail category). Exhibit 8 presents financial and operating information on breakout growth firms.

The three founders believed that Planet's store economics compared favorably to these breakout firms. They pointed to a study by Hambrecht & Quist, an American investment bank, which suggested that in the current market environment, the highest valuation multiples were given to firms that offered both brand strength and distribution strength—Luis, Michael, and Pascal believed that Planet offered both.

EXPECTED TRENDS IN THE QUICK PRINTING AND REPROGRAPHICS INDUSTRY

Luis, Michael, and Pascal believed in several industry trends that would affect the outlook for their firm, and their plans. In an internal study, the three founders drew on their own knowledge and information of other sources to highlight these trends:[2]

- *Technological performance and customer convenience* will remain the two major critical success factors for firms in this industry.
- The significant *shift from printing to copying* will continue. Shorter product life cycles, price volatility, smaller target markets, and the need for speed contribute to the economic efficiency of copying. Technological innovation in copying equipment will continue to improve image quality, computer connectivity, and speed.
- *Improvements in technology.* Use of color copiers will grow dramatically during the next five years. Copy speed will continue to increase. The variety of copier papers will continue to broaden. The cost per copy will continue to drop. Each of these factors improves the advantage of copying versus printing.
- *Payback periods for investments will continue to shorten.* One study of color servers indicated a total economic life of 18 months, with its greatest performance/price advantage in the first 6 months.
- Within retail communication service stores, *peripheral services offered will continue to grow.* Users want convenience and "one-stop shopping." With accelerating innovation and obsolescence of technology, consumers will increasingly be reluctant to invest in equipment that they can access at any time of day and need not purchase to use.
- The combination of customers wanting minimal costs, immediate access, equipment with advanced power and ease of use will contribute to the *growth of self-service concepts.* People do not want to wait. Self-service allows people to do their own work, when they want it, without paying extra for it. The pressures for disintermediation of non- or low-value-added intermediaries within retail services will accelerate.

---

[2]The following points are quoted from a company document.

KINKO'S: INDUSTRY LEADER IN RETAIL CONVENIENCE DOCUMENT COPYING

The leading competitor in the retail convenience document copying industry was Kinko's Service Corporation, a California-based chain of about 800 stores and annual per store sales estimated to be in the neighborhood of $1 million.[3] Founded in September 1970 by Paul Orfalea, the company began with a 100-square-foot copy shop at a California college.

The three amigos attributed the growth and position of Kinko's to several factors:

- *Rapid adoption of substitute document technologies,* such as self-service computers linked to high-resolution printers.
- *Service speed and expansion of service.* By offering service 24 hours a day, seven days a week, Kinko's achieved a 200 percent operating capacity advantage over its competitors. As businesses increasingly focused on smaller market segments and produced products with shorter life cycles and more volatile prices, they needed documents faster. The 24-hour operational strategy increased the speed advantage of copying, which increased the economic run size for firms that valued time.
- *Unique management and ownership structure.* Instead of using the franchise basis of organization, stores were operated as Subchapter S corporations, with Kinko's holding a majority or total ownership position of a store. Minority positions were held by store manager/owners. Kinko's was a privately held company. All employees who had been with the firm for six months received benefits, including profit sharing. The incentive system promoted rapid growth with highly localized management focus.

By the late 1980s Kinko's had become a major resource for small and midsized firms who wanted the advantages of a well-equipped large firm. By offering modern computing and copying equipment, self-service work areas, fax machines, and Federal Express services, Kinko's invented the virtual office before it became the popular business buzzword. However, Kinko's growth was almost entirely in North America. As of 1994, Kinko's had 11 international stores—8 in Canada, 1 in the Netherlands, and 2 in Japan.

In comparing Kinko's and Planet, Michael Melloy said,

Kinko's does about 60 percent of what we do, the part (i.e., copying) that is low margin and requires a lot of volume. The other 40 percent (graphic design, Internet, etc.) is beyond Kinko's current operational and technological capabilities, and serves as the platform for tomorrow's value-added office services. Nobody has a service mix that matches Planet's.

GROWTH OPPORTUNITIES

In December 1995, it became evident that the Planet concept was viable, even in Europe's second-poorest national market, Portugal. The three founders decided that the Planet concept should be exported to other, richer markets in order to grow the firm.

---

[3]Kinko's is a privately held corporation. The estimate was developed by the three founders from interviews with shop managers, employees, clients, and industry experts.

In 1996, Planet aimed to sign agreements with partners to open Planet stores in Portugal, Spain, and the United States. From 1997 to 2000, Planet would seek to grow as a specialized retail chain worldwide through numerous local joint ventures.

Identified Target Store Locations Possible for 1996	
Market	*Stores*
Northern Portugal	3–5
Greater Lisbon	3–5
Spain	10–20
United States	3–5

Source: company document.

Historically, Planet had invested 125 million to 225 million escudos per store in Portugal. For the purposes of their own financial forecasting, the founders assumed a per store investment of 137.7 million escudos ($900,000)—this assumed economies in purchasing and store-opening expenses. Traditionally, 55 percent of the investment had been for equipment, 40 percent for leasehold improvements, and 5 percent for miscellaneous store-opening expenses (commissions, training, recruiting, etc.).

Planet had a geographically diverse existing shareholder base (distributed in the United States, Greece, Portugal, Brazil, Sweden, and the United Kingdom). The founders hoped to attract new investors looking for a successful concept with high growth through stock appreciation. After several years of aggressive geographic expansion into new markets, the company would seek a public listing, preferably in the United States.

ANALYSIS OF GROWTH AND FINANCING STRATEGY

Luis, Michael, and Pascal set forth an ambitious plan to grow the number of stores at the rate of 50 percent per year. They believed this target was the maximum rate their organization could handle at present. The three considered several possible sources of financing the growth of their firm:

- *Internal generation of cash.* The operating cash flow of the firm could be reinvested. This source of funds was the most attractive (of all sources) to the founders because it came without covenants and did not change the voting structure of the shareholders. The founders sought to interpret the forecast for the efficacy of a strategy focusing solely on internally generated cash.
- *Bank loans* were the next most preferred source of funds. Preliminary discussions with two institutions had indicated a willingness to consider a loan proposal that offered a minimum EBIT coverage ratio in the range of 3.0 times. And for both banks, that coverage ratio would be acceptable for only the first year. Thereafter, the minimum would rise higher than 3 times. The contemplated interest rate would be 14 percent. Finally, the banks required personal guarantees of all debt by the founders.

- *Equity investment by the three founders.* If the preceding sources of funds fell short of requirements, equity investment would be indicated. The founders sought to preserve their equity interest and voting control in the firm. But practically, they had already invested their entire net worth in the firm and provided guarantees for loans. Further acquisition of Planet shares by them would have to be earned (i.e., as sweat equity) rather than purchased with cash.

- *Equity investment by Planet's "angel" investors.* Wealthy individuals who provided seed capital for the start-up of new ventures were called angel investors. These investors were known and trusted by the founders. Planet's angels had invested in the expectation that an IPO or buyout by an institutional investor would give them a profitable exit from their investment in Planet. They would be surprised at the request for more equity. They might be induced to invest another $2 or $3 million, for another 20 percent of the shares. But they would probably not invest more than that. Investment by angels would dilute the interests of the three founders.

- *Equity investment by international private-equity groups.* One well-regarded group based in London had expressed an interest in the aggressive growth plans of Planet. This group had invested over £2 billion in private equity deals over the previous 20 years and had achieved a compound rate of return for their investors of 40 percent. They sought to invest in situations offering equity returns (IRRs) of no less than 35 percent. The investment vehicle would be common shares or convertible preferred stock. For most of the situations in which this group invested, the returns would come not from dividends, but rather from the capital gain received upon exit. The target investment horizon was five to seven years. This group typically applied a multiple of 6 times EBITDA[4] to estimate the terminal exit value of their investments. In unusually mature "cash cow" situations, the exit multiple might be increased to 12 times. Generally, the more that the IRR of the investment depended on terminal value, the higher would be the target rate of return used by the private equity group. Ordinarily, private equity groups sought voting control of the firms in which they invested, and tended to intervene actively in management if there were any adverse variances from plan. Financing by a private equity group might enhance Planet's reputation and ability to go public. But Luis, Michael, and Pascal ranked this source of funds least because of its high cost and effect on control.

Exhibits 4, 5, 6, and 7 present the forecasts of Planet's financial statements consistent with the three founders' growth plans. Exhibit 9 computes the discounted-cash-flow (DCF) value of the firm using a weighted-average cost of capital consistent with that DCF value.[5] Exhibit 10 estimates the dilution of the founders' equity interest and the EBIT coverage ratio consistent with assumptions about growth and equity financing. Exhibit 11 presents a sensitivity analysis of dilution, EBIT coverage, founders' future wealth, and market/book

---

[4]*EBITDA* stands for "earnings before interest, taxes, depreciation, and amortization," and is often used as one approximate measure of a firm's cash-operating income.

[5]The valuation in Exhibit 9 employs a circular reference so that the weights of debt and equity used in the valuation depend on the market value of equity that is estimated with the WACC.

ratio. These forecasts were expressed in U.S. dollars, to present the results in a currency most likely to appeal to a range of international investors and banks. Important assumptions of the forecast (see Exhibit 4) were as follows:

- *Annual growth rate in number of stores: 50 percent.* The founders believed that the organization could sustain a growth rate of, at most, 50 percent per year. The reason they chose not to model a lower rate of growth was their sense that they faced an extraordinary window of opportunity in the marketplace which they wanted to exploit rapidly before another competitor (such as Kinko's) stepped in. The resulting number of stores each year is given in Exhibit 7, line 18. In this line, fractional amounts could be explained by partial expansions of existing stores. As one of the founders, Pascal, said:

  The number of stores we open each year is the most important driver of the growth of our firm. Stores and sales per meter drive revenues. Stores drive capital spending. The number of stores drives EBITDA for determining exit values. Planet's creation of value derives from breakout growth.

- *Growth in sales per square meter: 4 percent.* For stores already in place, sales would increase each year due to inflation, currently 2.4 percent in Portugal (versus 2.7 percent in the United States), and due to an expansion of services. The founders believed that it was reasonable to assume that continual expansion of the product range would account for at least 1.6 percent real growth in sales per year. Pascal explained:

  This is a conservative assumption. We think we can do better than 4 percent. But the forecast ignores the fact that each store does not leap into full-blown operation from the opening day. Usually, a store operates at less than capacity for a year or so until it establishes its franchise. The net impact is that the forecast is a little more optimistic in the early years when we are investing heavily and operating young stores at less than capacity, and a little pessimistic in the later years when we have a large portfolio of "cash cows" growing their sales per square meter each year at a healthy rate. The impact of these life-cycle effects is something we can model later.

- *Sales per square meter in 1996: $2,000.* This compared to an estimate of $2,200 for Kinko's. Pascal believed $2,000 was a conservative assumption; since Planet had a broader product line than Kinko's, it should be possible to exceed the competitor's experience.
- *Capital investment per store in 1996: $900,000.* This compared to an estimate of $1 million per store for Kinko's. Pascal believed that with careful purchasing, supplier alliances, and special expertise in store development, it should be possible to lower the per store investment.
- *Gross margin: 75 percent.* This was consistent with the founders' estimate for Kinko's. But it was significantly lower than Planet's gross margin achieved in 1994 (81 percent) and 1995 (80 percent).
- *Percentage of financing need filled by equity: 0 percent.* As a starting point, the forecasts assumed that all external financial requirements would be funded by the issuance of debt securities. This assumption implied no dilution in the founders' interest in the firm, consistent with their strong desire to retain control.

The income statement projected in Exhibit 5 suggested that by 2002 the firm would grow to revenues of $97.3 million and earnings of $14.6 million. Also by that year, assets (see Exhibit 6) would grow to $149.6 million, for which debt would provide $98.6 million in financing. Shareholders' equity would amount to $31.2 million. Over the forecast period, the interest coverage ratio (see Exhibit 7, line 10) would fall to 1.2 times in 1996, and rise to 2.6 times by 2002. The three founders pondered the implications of this forecast for their growth and financing strategies.

An analyst had tested the sensitivity of the model results with a series of two-way tables. Exhibit 11 shows how variations in growth rate and equity mix affected EBIT coverage, market/book value, founders' wealth, and dilution. The "base case" model implicitly assumed that Planet would meet no significant competition to its breakout growth concept. Exhibit 12 relaxed this assumption by varying margin and same-store growth rates to test their effects on financial performance—unlike Exhibit 11, Exhibit 12 assumed all of the external financing need was fulfilled with debt financing.

THE FOUNDERS' GOALS

Pascal summed up the strategic aims of the three amigos in the following words:

> We are builders, not caretakers. We want to implement our growth plan in order to realize our breakout vision for Planet and win recognition in the industry and the capital markets. We have invested our capital and our sweat. We look forward to earning a sizable return on our investment, to be realized through an initial public offering. Throughout the financing process, we want to resist diluting our economic and voting interest in the company.

THE MARKET FOR INITIAL PUBLIC OFFERINGS

Analysts observed that both Europe and the United States were in the midst of an impressive wave of initial public offerings (IPOs). Exhibit 1 presents information on offerings in recent years. Over long periods, the equity markets' interest in the shares of new public companies waxed and waned. During periods of high interest, many firms went public; during periods of low interest, few firms did. Thus, the ability of a firm to go public might depend both on the firm's readiness for a public offering, as well as the receptiveness of the equity markets. Analysts cautioned entrepreneurs to prepare their firms to be ready to exploit a capital market window of opportunity.

In early 1996 the equity markets in Europe and the United States were near the highest levels in the past 10 years. Luis, Michael, and Pascal believed that if Planet were to sell equity to investors, the firm would realize higher prices in the current market environment than if they waited and had to issue equity later in a less buoyant market.

CONCLUSION

In March of 1996, Portugal's leading business periodical nominated Luis, Michael, and Pascal as "Entrepreneurs of the Year." But the feeling of honor was matched with a sense of urgency to set a strategy that would prepare the firm for a successful international IPO. How could the firm finance itself in ways that would best meet the founders' goals and vision? How could the founders grow the firm rapidly, achieve their wealth aspirations, and yet minimize dilution and meet the requirements of the potential providers of capital? Luis, Michael, and Pascal settled in for yet another long night of work.

EXHIBIT 1 Information on Recent Initial Public Offerings in Europe ($ billions)

	1991	*1992*	*1993*	*1994*	*1995*
France	$1.0	$0.7	$2.4	$ 3.7	$ 2.2
Denmark	0.2	0.0	0.0	2.9	0.3
Netherlands	0.6	0.0	0.4	2.8	0.5
Italy	0.1	0.5	0.4	2.1	2.5
Sweden	0.0	0.0	0.3	1.3	0.9
Germany	0.7	0.0	0.2	1.3	2.7
United Kingdom	1.9	0.0	3.7	1.0	1.4
Spain	0.1	0.2	1.4	0.8	0.6
Total	$4.6	$1.4	$8.8	$15.9	$11.1

Note: IPOs of equities in international offerings.

Source: OECD /DAF.

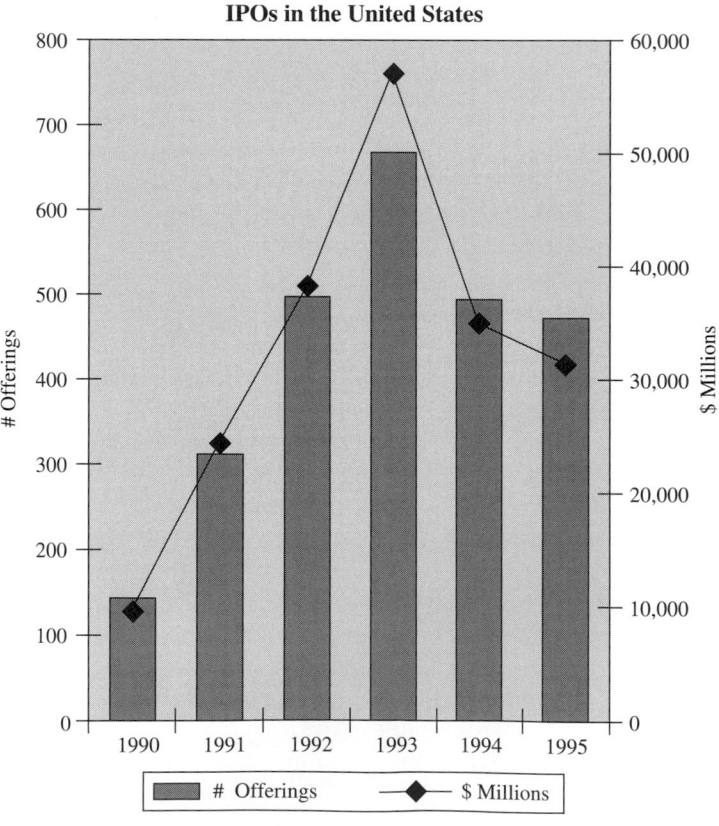

EXHIBIT 2   Services Provided by the Company

Copying
    Full service black/white, color laser copies
    Rapid offset printing
    Binding and finishing
    Specialty papers and materials
    Self-service black/white, color laser copies
    Oversize copies

Imaging
    Rapid photo development
    Slide development
    Promotional gift items, T-shirts, mouse pads,
       puzzles, etc.

Postal
    Mailbox rental
    DHL pickup and delivery
    Public fax

Self-service computing
    Self-service PCs and Macs
    Self-service white printing (different levels)
    Self-service scanning
    Internet access*
    Database access
    CD-ROM rental
    Video-aided training
    Silicon graphics training center

Design
    Operator-aided graphic design
    Desktop publishing
    Scanning
    Printing

Output
    Full-color poster printing, mounting, and laminating
    35-mm slide output
    Color plotting and CAD output

Planet Café
    Beverages
    Coffees
    Sandwiches, cookies, etc.
    Specialty newspaper and magazines sales

Supplies
    Impulse purchase stationery products
    Design products
    Computer consumables

*In its attempts to provide quality self-service Internet access to its customers, Planet accidentally came across a unique opportunity to play an essential role in Internet access in Portugal. This could fit in with two other key strategic objectives: (1) electronically link all customers to Planet in an Internet-based IT system and (2) explore other ways to maximize the value of Planet's thousands of loyal customers. The Internet opportunities for Planet were to be studied on a market-by-market basis.

Source: Company documents.

EXHIBIT 3 Planet's Client Base in Portugal

Walk-in retail clients

75% of total transactions

50% of total sales

Young (85% between 16 and 35 years old)

Computer literate, upwardly mobile

Mainly designers, artists, freelancers, students, and teachers

Corporate service

25% of total transactions

50% of total sales

Popular services included graphic design, color output, presentations, and copying.

Regular corporate clients include these firms:

ABN-Amro Bank	EMI Songs	Philip Morris, Portugal
Afga Gevaert, Lba	Entreposto Nissan	Portucel
Air France	Ernst & Young	Portugal Telecom
Alcatel-Comunicaçao	Esso	Price Waterhouse
Aliança-UAP	Euro RSCG—Melorosa,	Printemps
Amway	Lda	Procter & Gamble
Atlas Copco	Europ Assistance	Repsol
Banco Bilbao Vizcaya	Europcar	Richard Ellis
Banco Chemical	Rerrovial, S.A.	Roche Farma
Banco Comercial Português	Filmes Castelo Lopes	Royal Brands
Banco Espírito Santo	Filmes Lusomundo, SA	RTP
Banco ESSI	Glaxo Farmeutica, Lda	Sanofi Beauté
Banco Finantia	Grupo Argentaria	Securitas
Banco Fonsecas & Burnay	Hay Consulting/Hay Group	SIC
Banco Mello	Healey & Baker	SmithKline Beecham
Banco Santander	Hewlett Packard Portugal	Soci
Banco Totta & Açores	Honeywell	Tabaqueira
Barclays Bank	J. Walter Thompson	Telecel
Bates	Johnson & Johnson	Tetra Pak
British Airways	Kellogg's	Tranquilidade
Bull Portuguesa	Lintas	Unisys
Caiza Geral de Depósitos	Marconi	United Distillery
Carrier Portugal	Mattel	Valentim de Carvalho
Citibank	McDonald's	Vista Alegre
Colgate-Palmolive	McKinsey International	Walt Disney
Compaq Computer Portugal	Merck Sharp & Dohme	Warner Lambert Portugal
Crédit Lyonnais	Michelin	Willis Faber
Danone	Miele	WundermanCato Johnson
DDB Needham	Nestlé	Young & Rubicam
DHL	Novodesign	
Diário de Noticias	Ogilvy & Mather	
Dun & Bradstreet	Opel Portugal	
Eagle Star Vie	Pepsi-Cola International	
El Corte Inglés	Petrogal	

Source: Company documents.

EXHIBIT 4 Summary of Forecast Assumptions

Description

Growth in number of stores, 1997+	50%
Growth in sales per square meter	4%
Sales per square meter, 1996	$2,000
Average square meters per store	450
Capital investment per store in 1996	$900,000
Gross margin	75%
Dividend payout	0%
Equipment rentals per store	$220,000
Employee costs per store	$130,000
Tax rate	35%
Percent of financing need met by equity issuance	0%
Interest rate	14%

	Actual		Projected						
	1994	1995	1996	1997	1998	1999	2000	2001	2002
Cash and investments to sales	0.3%	0.4%	0.5%	0.5%	0.5%	0.5%	0.5%	0.5%	0.5%
Days in receivables	15.4	31.5	30.0	30.0	30.0	30.0	30.0	30.0	30.0
Days in payables	528.2	644.4	60.0	60.0	60.0	50.0	45.0	40.0	40.0
Days in inventory	21.5	161.6	90.0	60.0	60.0	50.0	40.0	30.0	30.0
Other current assets/Sales	44.8%	207.4%	75.0%	50.0%	25.0%	15.0%	10.0%	10.0%	10.0%
Other current liabilities/Sales	2.2%	59.4%	8.0%	6.0%	6.0%	6.0%	6.0%	6.0%	6.0%
Gross intangible assets/Sales	48%	77%	60%	50%	50%	40%	30%	30%	30%
Annual depreciation/Gross PP&E	N.A.	4.8%	3.2%	3.2%	3.2%	3.2%	3.2%	3.2%	3.2%

Source: Casewriter analysis.

417

EXHIBIT 5   Historical and Forecasted Income Statements (in U.S. dollars)

	Actual		
	1994	*1995*	*1996*
Years elapsed from present			1
1. Net sales	$1,577,390	$ 2,815,380	$6,750,000
2. Cost of goods sold	294,700	562,280	1,687,500
3. Gross profit	1,282,690	2,253,100	5,062,500
4. Operating expenses			
5. Equipment rentals	916,170	2,384,650	1,650,000
6. Miscellaneous taxes	5,460	4,030	13,500
7. Employee costs	357,130	1,160,680	1,014,000
8. Other operating costs	0	6,350	13,500
9. Depreciation	136,720	408,630	228,282
10. Extraordinary	10	29,720	1,000
11. Total operating expenses	1,415,490	3,994,060	2,920,282
12. Operating income	(132,800)	(1,740,960)	2,142,218
13. Interest expense	(143,940)	(212,630)	(1,775,613)
14. Earnings before taxes	(276,740)	(1,953,590)	366,605
15. Income taxes	0	1,640	128,312
16. Net earnings	($276,740)	($1,955,230)	$238,293
17. Common shares and equivalents	400,000	1,600,000	1,600,000
18. EPS (fully diluted)	($0.69)	($1.22)	$0.15
19. EPS(primary)	($0.69)	($1.22)	$0.15
20. Primary number/shares	400,000	1,600,000	1,600,000
21. Dividends per share	$0.00	$0.00	$0.00

Source: Casewriter analysis.

	Projected				
1997	*1998*	*1999*	*2000*	*2001*	*2002*
2	3	4	5	6	7
$10,530,000	$16,426,800	$25,625,808	$39,976,260	$62,362,966	$97,286,228
2,632,500	4,106,700	6,406,452	9,994,065	15,590,742	24,321,557
7,897,500	12,320,100	19,219,356	29,982,195	46,772,225	72,964,671
2,475,000	3,712,500	5,568,750	8,353,125	12,529,688	18,794,531
21,060	32,854	51,252	79,953	124,726	194,572
1,581,840	2,467,670	3,849,566	6,005,323	9,368,303	14,614,553
21,060	32,854	51,252	79,953	124,726	194,572
340,602	515,821	789,163	1,215,577	1,880,781	2,918,501
1,000	1,000	1,000	1,000	1,000	1,000
4,440,562	6,762,699	10,310,982	15,734,929	24,029,224	36,717,731
3,456,938	5,557,401	8,908,374	14,247,266	22,743,001	36,246,940
(2,352,048)	(3,528,278)	(4,559,809)	(5,703,070)	(8,900,245)	(13,810,153)
1,104,890	2,029,123	4,348,565	8,544,197	13,842,755	22,436,787
386,711	710,193	1,521,998	2,990,469	4,844,964	7,852,875
$718,178	$1,318,930	$2,826,567	$5,553,728	$8,997,791	$14,583,911
1,600,000	1,600,000	1,600,000	1,600,000	1,600,000	1,600,000
$0.45	$0.82	$1.77	$3.47	$5.62	$9.11
$0.45	$0.82	$1.77	$3.47	$5.62	$9.11
1,600,000	1,600,000	1,600,000	1,600,000	1,600,000	1,600,000
$0.00	$0.00	$0.00	$0.00	$1.00	$2.00

EXHIBIT 6 Historical and Forecasted Balance Sheets (in U.S. dollars)

	Actual		Projected	
	1994	*1995*	*1996*	*1997*
Assets				
1. Cash	$ 5,230	$ 10,980	$ 33,750	$ 52,650
2. Accounts receivable	66,620	243,330	554,795	865,479
3. Merchandise inventories	17,330	248,990	416,096	432,740
4. Other current assets	132,107	1,166,060	1,265,625	1,316,250
5. Total current assets	221,287	1,669,360	2,270,265	2,667,119
6. Security deposits	0	0	—	—
7. Gross property and equipment	1,061,040	4,883,810	7,133,810	10,643,810
8. Accumulated depreciation	74,710	310,820	539,102	879,704
9. Net property and equipment	986,330	4,572,990	6,594,708	9,764,106
10. Gross intangible assets	750,770	2,180,600	4,050,000	5,265,000
11. Amortization of intangible assets	62,020	234,860	545,150	1,012,500
12. Net intangible assets	688,750	1,945,740	3,504,850	4,252,500
13. Total assets	$1,896,367	$8,188,090	$16,419,823	$21,948,725
Liabilities and owners' equity				
14. Accounts payable	$ 426,440	$ 992,620	$ 277,397	$ 432,740
15. Notes payable	0	1,552,760	—	—
16. Sales and income taxes payable	34,350	77,240	135,000	210,600
17. Other shareholder payables	0	43,020	11,915	—
18. Other creditors	—	354,500	540,000	631,800
19. Accruals and deferrals	43,510	220,610	337,500	526,500
20. Total current liabilities	504,300	3,240,750	1,301,812	1,801,640
21. New debt issued (repur.) since 1995	—	—	12,682,948	16,800,344
22. Long-term debt	658,667	550,000	0	0
23. PV of leasing contracts	610,150	2,587,570	387,000	580,500
24. Total liabilities	1,773,117	6,378,320	14,371,760	19,182,483
25. Common stock	400,000	1,600,000	1,600,000	1,600,000
26. Paid-in capital	0	3,000,000	3,000,000	3,000,000
27. New equity issued (repur.) since 1995			0	0
28. Retained earnings	(276,750)	(2,231,980)	(1,993,687)	(1,275,508)
29. Less treasury stock	0	(558,250)	(558,250)	(558,250)
30. Total stockholders' equity	123,250	1,809,770	2,048,063	2,766,242
31. Total liabilities and stockholders' equity	$1,896,367	$8,188,090	$16,419,823	$21,948,725
Memo:				
32. Dividends		$ 0	$ 0	$ 0
33. Capital expenditures		3,822,770	2,250,000	3,510,000
34. Depreciation expense		236,110	228,282	340,602
35. Additions to net working capital		(1,288,377)	2,539,843	(102,974)
36. Incr. new external fing.		—	12,682,948	4,117,396
37. Total new financing required			$12,682,948	$16,800,344
38. New debt issued (repur.) since 1995			12,682,948	16,800,344
39. New equity issued (repur.) since 1995			—	—
40. Check: total capital issued since 1995			12,682,948	16,800,344
41. New debt issued by year			10,580,188	4,117,396
42. New equity issued by year			0	0

Source: Casewriter analysis.

		Projected		
1998	*1999*	*2000*	*2001*	*2002*
$ 82,134	$ 128,129	$ 199,881	$ 311,815	$ 486,431
1,350,148	2,106,231	3,285,720	5,125,723	7,996,128
675,074	877,596	1,095,240	1,281,431	1,999,032
1,026,675	960,968	999,407	1,559,074	2,432,156
3,134,031	4,072,924	5,580,248	8,278,043	12,913,747
—	—	—	—	—
16,119,410	24,661,346	37,986,766	58,774,422	91,203,164
1,395,525	2,184,688	3,400,265	5,281,046	8,199,547
14,723,885	22,476,658	34,586,502	53,493,376	83,003,617
8,213,400	10,250,323	11,992,878	18,708,890	29,185,868
1,316,250	2,053,350	2,562,581	2,998,220	4,677,222
6,897,150	8,196,973	9,430,297	15,710,670	24,508,646
$32,968,466	$44,996,878	$61,589,925	$96,190,979	$149,611,878
$ 675,074	$ 877,596	$ 1,232,145	$ 1,708,574	$ 2,665,376
—	—	—	—	—
328,536	512,516	799,525	1,247,259	1,945,725
—	—	—	—	—
985,608	1,537,548	2,398,576	3,741,778	5,837,174
821,340	1,281,290	1,998,813	3,118,148	4,864,311
2,810,558	4,208,951	6,429,059	9,815,760	15,312,586
25,201,986	32,570,063	40,736,211	63,573,179	98,643,951
0	0	0	0	0
870,750	1,306,125	1,959,188	2,938,781	4,408,172
28,883,294	38,085,139	49,124,458	76,327,721	118,364,708
1,600,000	1,600,000	1,600,000	1,600,000	1,600,000
3,000,000	3,000,000	3,000,000	3,000,000	3,000,000
0	0	0	0	0
43,422	2,869,989	8,423,717	15,821,508	27,205,420
(558,250)	(558,250)	(558,250)	(558,250)	(558,250)
4,085,172	6,911,739	12,465,467	19,863,258	31,247,170
$32,968,466	$44,996,878	$61,589,925	$96,190,979	$149,611,878
$ 0	$ 0	$ 0	$ 1,600,000	$ 3,200,000
5,475,600	8,541,936	13,325,420	20,787,655	32,428,743
515,821	789,163	1,215,577	1,880,781	2,918,501
(542,007)	(459,500)	(712,784)	(688,906)	(861,122)
8,401,642	7,368,077	8,166,149	22,836,968	35,070,771
$25,201,986	$32,570,063	$40,736,211	$63,573,179	$98,643,951
25,201,986	32,570,063	40,736,211	63,573,179	98,643,951
—	—	—	—	—
25,201,986	32,570,063	40,736,211	63,573,179	98,643,951
8,401,642	7,368,077	8,166,149	22,836,968	35,070,771
0	0	0	0	0

EXHIBIT 7   Financial Ratios

	Actual		Projected	
	1994	*1995*	*1996*	*1997*
Profitability				
1. Gross margin (%)	81.3%	80.0%	75.0%	75.0%
2. Operating expenses to sales (%)	89.7%	141.9%	43.3%	42.2%
3. Cost of goods sold	−8.4%	−61.8%	31.7%	32.8%
4. Gross profit	0.0%	−0.1%	35.0%	35.0%
5. Return on sales (%)	−17.5%	−69.4%	3.5%	6.8%
6. Equipment rentals	−224.5%	−108.0%	11.6%	26.0%
7. Miscellaneous taxes	−14.6%	−23.9%	1.5%	3.3%
Leverage				
8. Other operating costs	10.29	2.59	6.19	6.07
9. Depreciation	91.1%	72.2%	86.5%	86.3%
10. Extraordinary	0.9	8.2	1.2	1.5
Liquidity				
11. Operating income	0.14	0.08	0.45	0.51
12. Current ratio (×)	0.44	0.52	1.74	1.48
Growth and returns				
13. Primary earnings per share ($)	($0.69)	($1.22)	$0.15	$0.45
14. Change in EPS (%)	NMF*	−76.6%	NMF	201.4%
15. Dividends per share ($)	$0.00	$0.00	$0.00	$0.00
16. Dividends to net income (%)	0.0%	0.0%	0.0%	0.0%
17. Sales growth rate (%)	NMF	78.5%	139.8%	56.0%
Store numbers, size, and sales				
18. Ending number of stores	1.00	5.00	7.50	11.25
19. New stores added	1.00	4.00	2.50	3.75
20. Unit growth (%)	23.0%	23.0%	50.0%	50.0%
21. Ending square meters	200	2,270	3,375	5,063
22. Change in square meters (%)	NMF	1035.0%	48.7%	50.0%
23. Average square meters per store	200	350	450	450
24. Average sales per square meter ($)†	$ 7,887	$ 1,240	$ 2,000	$ 2,080
25. Average sales per store ($)	1,577,390	563,076	900,000	936,000
26. Same store sales increase (%)†	NMF	−64.3%	59.8%	4.0%
27. Capital investment per store ($)	$1,061,040	$976,762	$900,000	$936,000

*NMF stands for "not meaningful."
†Average sales per square meter (line 24) and same store sales increase (line 26) declined in 1995 because new stores were not in operation for full year.

Source: Casewriter analysis.

	Projected			
1998	*1999*	*2000*	*2001*	*2002*
75.0%	75.0%	75.0%	75.0%	75.0%
41.2%	40.2%	39.4%	38.5%	37.7%
33.8%	34.8%	35.6%	36.5%	37.3%
35.0%	35.0%	35.0%	35.0%	35.0%
8.0%	11.0%	13.9%	14.4%	15.0%
32.3%	40.9%	44.6%	45.3%	46.7%
4.0%	6.3%	9.0%	9.4%	9.7%
6.17	4.71	3.27	3.20	3.16
86.5%	83.1%	77.4%	77.0%	76.7%
1.6	2.0	2.5	2.6	2.6
0.51	0.53	0.54	0.55	0.55
1.12	0.97	0.87	0.84	0.84
$0.82	$1.77	$3.47	$5.62	$9.11
83.6%	114.3%	96.5%	62.0%	62.1%
$0.00	$0.00	$0.00	$1.00	$2.00
0.0%	0.0%	0.0%	17.8%	21.9%
56.0%	56.0%	56.0%	56.0%	56.0%
16.88	25.31	37.97	56.95	85.43
5.63	8.44	12.66	18.98	28.48
50.0%	50.0%	50.0%	50.0%	50.0%
7,594	11,391	17,086	25,629	38,443
50.0%	50.0%	50.0%	50.0%	50.0%
450	450	450	450	450
$ 2,163	$ 2,250	$ 2,340	$ 2,433	$ 2,531
973,440	1,012,378	1,052,873	1,094,988	1,138,787
4.0%	4.0%	4.0%	4.0%	4.0%
$973,440	$1,012,378	$1,052,873	$1,094,988	$1,138,787

EXHIBIT 8   Information on Breakout Firms as of January 1996 (all currency amounts are in $ millions)

Company Name	Business Description	Prior Year's Sales	EBIT	Net Income	Assets	Book Value of Equity
Autozone	Auto superstores	$ 1,808	$ 275	$139	$1,112	$ 685
Baby Superstores	Infant care products	175	14	7	92	58
Barnes & Noble	Book superstores	1,623	107	24	1,026	358
Bed, Bath & Beyond	Household goods stores	440	59	30	177	109
Benson Eyecare Corp.	Optical goods stores	169	22	8	262	109
Best Buy Co.	Consumer electronics	5,080	122	48	1,507	379
Boston Chicken	Fast-food stores	160	79	34	1,074	717
Circuit City Stores	Consumer electronics	5,583	279	179	2,004	893
Gymboree	Child amusement	188	38	22	127	93
Herlitz AG	Stationery/office supplies	940	72	24	1,205	950
Home Depot Inc.	Building materials	15,470	1,232	732	7,354	4,930
Just for Feet	Footwear	56	5	3	90	73
Office Depot Inc.	Office supplies	5,313	266	132	2,531	1,022
Petco	Pet food and supplies	189	12	5	77	41
PetsMart	Pet food and supplies	818	27	(10)	448	259
Rio Hotel & Casino Inc.	Coin-op amusement	193	37	19	309	166
Staples	Office supplies	2,000	110	40	1,009	385
Starbucks	Coffee and supplies	465	65	26	468	312
Sunglass Hut	Sunglasses	$ 290	$ 45	$ 17	$ 154	$ 72
Mean						

Sources of data: *Value Line Investment Survey* and Bloomberg Financial Services.

Market Value of Equity	Book Debt to Equity	Tax Rate	Beta	Five-Year Annual Revenue Growth	EBIT Multiple	Market to Book Value Multiple	Price/ Earnings Multiple
$ 5,047	0.00	39%	1.25	30%	18.4	7.4	29.5
874	0.03	38%	1.78	67%	64.3	15.1	68.9
1,154	0.73	47%	0.93	22%	18.7	3.2	38.9
1,806	0.20	41%	1.19	38%	36.7	16.6	46.3
261	0.60	34%	0.88	343%	19.0	2.4	32.6
758	0.60	39%	0.93	66%	9.9	2.0	15.8
2,203	0.46	39%	1.38	167%	40.7	3.1	51.6
3,305	0.20	37%	0.67	25%	14.2	3.7	18.5
642	0.07	43%	2.02	48%	18.1	6.9	24.8
629	0.26	34%	0.64	64%	11.0	0.7	30.1
22,185	0.10	39%	1.24	33%	19.8	4.5	30.3
497	0.06	46%	1.98	81%	105.4	6.8	72.6
3,578	0.38	40%	1.09	46%	18.5	3.5	27.1
232	0.17	29%	0.47	27%	22.6	5.7	47.1
1,782	0.30	11%	1.58	109%	85.8	6.9	NMF
366	0.70	37%	1.01	25%	16.8	2.2	19.3
2,465	0.71	33%	1.39	109%	38.3	6.4	45.0
1,656	0.27	45%	1.70	71%	32.4	5.3	53.0
$ 1,605	0.59	38%	1.68	43%	56.7	22.3	83.6
	0.34	37%	1.25	74%	34.1	6.6	40.8

EXHIBIT 9   Estimate of DCF Value, Free Cash Flows, and Weighted-Average Cost of Capital

Assumptions			
1. EBITDA multiple at exit	6		
2. Tax rate	35%		

	Jan. 1, 1996	1996	1997
Estimation of Free Cash Flows			
3. Operating income		$ 2,142,218	$ 3,456,938
4. Taxes		749,776	1,209,928
5. EBIAT		1,392,442	2,247,010
6. + Depreciation		228,282	340,602
7. Capital expenditures		(2,250,000)	(3,510,000)
8. − Additions (+ reductions) to wkg. cap.		987,083	(102,974)
9. Free cash flow		357,807	(819,414)
10. Terminal value			
11. Total free cash flow		$ 357,807	−$819,414
DCF value at end of year			
12. Annual discount rate	32.47%	29.53%	29.44%
13. Value of enterprise	$48,047,886	$61,878,330	$80,912,505
14. Value of debt	4,690,330	13,069,948	17,380,844
15. Value of equity	$43,357,556	$48,808,382	$63,531,661
16. Market/Book value of equity	23.96	23.83	22.97
Estimation of annual weighted-average cost of capital			
17. Book value of debt	$ 4,690,330	$13,069,948	$17,380,844
18. Book value of equity	1,809,770	2,048,063	2,766,242
19. Book value of capital	6,500,100	15,118,012	20,147,086
20. Book value debt/equity ratio	2.59	6.38	6.28
21. Market/Book value of equity	23.96	23.83	22.97
22. Market value debt/equity ratio	0.11	0.27	0.27
23. Cost of equity	35.00%	35.00%	35.00%
24. Cost of debt (pretax)	14%	14%	14%
25. Tax rate on income	0.35	0.35	0.35
26. After-tax cost of debt	9.10%	9.10%	9.10%
27. Weight of debt	9.8%	21.1%	21.5%
28. Weight of equity	90.2%	78.9%	78.5%
29. WACC	32.47%	29.53%	29.44%

Notes: This discounted-cash-flow valuation of the firm employs the following features:

1. Terminal value (line 10, year 2002) is calculated as the multiple (line 1) times EBITDA (lines 3 plus 6) in the final year.
2. The weighted average cost of capital (line 29) is reestimated every year, to reflect changes in the financial leverage of the firm (lines 27 and 28).
3. The calculation intentionally models a circular reference so that the weights of capital (lines 27 and 28) are consistent with the DCF value of equity in each year (line 15).
4. The value of equity each year equals the value of the enterprise (line 13), less the value of debt outstanding (line 14).
5. The value of the enterprise each year equals the following year's value of the enterprise (line 13) plus free cash flow (line 11) discounted at the WACC for that year. For instance, to obtain the enterprise value at year-end 2001, the model "looks ahead" to the free cash flow for 2002 and the value of the enterprise at year-end 2002, and discounts the sum of those values back to year-end 2001 at 23.64 percent, the WACC for 2002.
6. The cost of equity of 35 percent (line 23) uses the private equity investors' required rate of return.

Source: Casewriter analysis.

1998	1999	2000	2001	2002
$ 5,557,401	$ 8,908,374	$ 14,247,266	$ 22,743,001	$ 36,246,940
1,945,090	3,117,931	4,986,543	7,960,050	12,686,429
3,612,311	5,790,443	9,260,723	14,782,950	23,560,511
515,821	789,163	1,215,577	1,880,781	2,918,501
(5,475,600)	(8,541,936)	(13,325,420)	(20,787,655)	(32,428,743)
(542,007)	(459,500)	(712,784)	(688,906)	(861,122)
(805,462)	(1,502,830)	(2,136,337)	(3,435,018)	(5,088,609)
				234,992,647
$ 805,462	$ 1,502,830	$ 2,136,337	$ 3,435,018	$229,904,038
28.56%	28.56%	28.77%	27.51%	—
$104,824,947	$136,267,064	$177,612,942	$229,904,038	$234,992,647
26,072,736	33,876,188	42,695,399	66,511,961	103,052,123
$ 78,752,212	$102,390,876	$134,917,543	$163,392,078	$131,940,524
19.28	14.81	10.82	8.23	4.22
$ 26,072,736	$ 33,876,188	$ 42,695,399	$ 66,511,961	$103,052,123
4,085,172	6,911,739	12,465,467	19,863,258	31,247,170
30,157,908	40,787,927	55,160,866	86,375,219	134,299,292
6.38	4.90	3.43	3.35	3.30
19.28	14.81	10.82	8.23	4.22
0.33	0.33	0.32	0.41	0.78
35.00%	35.00%	35.00%	35.00%	35.00
14%	14%	14%	14%	14%
0.35	0.35	0.35	0.35	0.35
9.10%	9.10%	9.10%	9.10%	9.10%
24.9%	24.9%	24.0%	28.9%	43.9%
75.1%	75.1%	76.0%	71.1%	56.1%
28.56%	28.56%	28.77%	27.51%	23.64%

EXHIBIT 10 Analysis of Founders' Dilution and Wealth (values in U.S. dollars)

Assumptions

1. Percent of equity used to meet need			0%
2. Annual growth rate in number of stores			50%
		Jan. 1, 1996	*1996*
3. Incremental external financing need (from Exhibit 6, line 35)			$12,682,948
4. Total value of equity raised (repurchased) (from Exhibit 6, line 42)			—
5. Total market value of equity (Exhibit 9, line 15)		$43,357,556	$48,808,382
6. Shares outstanding at beginning of year			1,600,000
7. Sale price of new shares*			$30.51
8. New shares sold (shares repurchased)			—
9. Ending shares outstanding			1,600,000
10. % voting control of founders (if no further outlays)			48.0%
11. Loss of voting % from present base of 48%†			0.0%
12. EBIT coverage ratio (Exhibit 7, line 10)			1.21
13. Market/Book ratio (Exhibit 9, line 16)		23.96	23.83
14. Wealth of founders (line 10 times line 5)		$20,811,627	$23,428,023
15. Cumulative external financing need (Exhibit 6, line 21)		—	$12,682,948

*The sale price of new shares is estimated as the current market value of equity less the cash to be raised through share issuance, divided by the shares outstanding at the beginning of the year.
†Line 11 is a measure of the founders' voting dilution, and is calculated as the percentage of shares held by the founders, less 48 percent, their initial interest.

1997	*1998*	*1999*	*2000*	*2001*	*2002*
$ 4,117,396	$ 8,401,642	$ 7,368,077	$ 8,166,149	$ 22,836,968	$ 35,070,771
—	—	—	—	—	—
$63,531,661	$78,752,212	$102,390,876	$134,917,543	$163,392,078	$131,940,524
1,600,000	1,600,000	1,600,000	1,600,000	1,600,000	1,600,000
$39.71	$49.22	$63.99	$84.32	$102.12	$82.46
—	—	—	—	—	—
1,600,000	1,600,000	1,600,000	1,600,000	1,600,000	1,600,000
48.0%	48.0%	48.0%	48.0%	48.0%	48.0%
0.0%	0.0%	0.0%	0.0%	0.0%	0.0%
1.47	1.58	1.95	2.50	2.56	2.62
22.97	19.28	14.81	10.82	8.23	4.22
$30,495,197	$37,801,062	$49,147,621	$64,760,421	$78,428,197	$63,331,452
$16,800,344	$25,201,986	$32,570,063	$40,736,211	$63,573,179	$98,643,951

EXHIBIT 11 Sensitivity Analysis of Outcomes by Growth Rate of Stores, and Equity Issuance

	% Equity Financing				
Growth Rate in Stores	50%	60%	70%	80%	90%

1996 EBIT Coverage

Growth Rate in Stores	50%	60%	70%	80%	90%
0%	2.81	3.55	4.78	7.24	14.63
5%	2.77	3.50	4.71	7.13	14.41
10%	2.73	3.45	4.65	7.04	14.21
15%	2.70	3.41	4.59	6.95	14.04
20%	2.67	3.37	4.54	6.87	13.88
25%	2.64	3.34	4.49	6.81	13.74
30%	2.62	3.31	4.45	6.74	13.62
35%	2.60	3.28	4.41	6.69	13.50
40%	2.58	3.25	4.38	6.63	13.40
45%	2.56	3.23	4.35	6.59	13.30
50%	2.54	3.21	4.32	6.54	13.21

1996 Market Value/Book Value Ratio

Growth Rate in Stores	50%	60%	70%	80%	90%
0%	0.6	0.6	0.6	0.7	0.7
5%	0.8	0.8	0.8	0.8	0.8
10%	1.0	1.0	0.9	0.9	0.9
15%	1.3	1.2	1.1	1.1	1.0
20%	1.6	1.5	1.4	1.3	1.2
25%	2.0	1.8	1.7	1.6	1.5
30%	2.5	2.2	2.0	1.9	1.8
35%	3.0	2.7	2.5	2.3	2.1
40%	3.7	3.3	3.0	2.7	2.5
45%	4.6	4.0	3.6	3.2	3.0
50%	5.5	4.8	4.3	3.9	3.6

Founders' Wealth in 2002 ($ millions)

Growth Rate in Stores	50%	60%	70%	80%	90%
0%	$ 0.2	$ 0.0	$ 0.0	$ 0.0	$ 0.0
5%	$ 2.3	$ 1.9	$ 1.5	$ 1.2	$ 0.9
10%	$ 4.8	$ 4.3	$ 3.8	$ 3.4	$ 3.0
15%	$ 7.9	$ 7.3	$ 6.7	$ 6.2	$ 5.8
20%	$11.6	$11.0	$10.4	$ 9.8	$ 9.3
25%	$16.3	$15.6	$14.9	$14.3	$13.7
30%	$22.0	$21.3	$20.6	$19.9	$19.3
35%	$29.1	$28.4	$27.7	$27.0	$26.3
40%	$37.9	$37.2	$36.5	$35.7	$35.0
45%	$48.7	$48.0	$47.2	$46.5	$45.7
50%	$61.9	$61.2	$60.5	$59.7	$58.9

Founders' Loss of Voting % from Present Base of 48%

Growth Rate in Stores	50%	60%	70%	80%	90%
0%	−46.4%	−47.7%	−47.8%	−47.8%	−47.8%
5%	−34.6%	−37.5%	−39.8%	−41.7%	−43.1%
10%	−27.5%	−30.3%	−32.7%	−34.7%	−36.3%
15%	−23.1%	−25.8%	−28.0%	−30.0%	−31.6%
20%	−20.4%	−22.8%	−24.9%	−26.8%	−28.4%
25%	−18.6%	−20.9%	−22.9%	−24.6%	−26.2%
30%	−17.4%	−19.6%	−21.5%	−23.1%	−24.6%
35%	−16.6%	−18.6%	−20.4%	−22.1%	−23.5%
40%	−16.0%	−18.0%	−19.7%	−21.3%	−22.7%
45%	−15.5%	−17.5%	−19.2%	−20.7%	−22.1%
50%	−15.2%	−17.1%	−18.8%	−20.3%	−21.6%

Source: Casewriter analysis.

EXHIBIT 12   Sensitivity Analysis of Outcomes by Gross Margin and Growth in Sales per Square Meter

	% Gross Margin				
Growth in Sales/Meter	*70%*	*72%*	*75%*	*77%*	*80%*

1996 EBIT Coverage

0%	1.00	1.09	1.23	1.33	1.49
1%	0.99	1.08	1.23	1.32	1.48
2%	0.98	1.08	1.22	1.32	1.47
3%	0.98	1.07	1.21	1.31	1.47
4%	0.97	1.06	1.21	1.31	1.46
5%	0.97	1.06	1.20	1.30	1.46
6%	0.96	1.05	1.19	1.29	1.45
7%	0.96	1.05	1.19	1.29	1.44
8%	0.95	1.04	1.18	1.28	1.44

1996 Market Value/Book Value Ratio

0%	14.0	14.6	15.3	15.8	16.4
1%	16.0	16.6	17.3	17.7	18.3
2%	18.1	18.7	19.4	19.8	20.3
3%	20.4	20.9	21.5	21.9	22.4
4%	22.8	23.2	23.8	24.2	24.6
5%	25.3	25.7	26.2	26.6	27.0
6%	27.9	28.3	28.8	29.0	29.4
7%	30.7	31.0	31.4	31.7	32.0
8%	33.6	33.8	34.2	34.4	34.7

Founders' Wealth in 2002 ($ millions)

0%	$19.5	$25.7	$35.1	$ 41.4	$ 50.8
1%	$25.2	$31.8	$41.7	$ 48.4	$ 58.3
2%	$31.1	$38.1	$48.6	$ 55.6	$ 66.1
3%	$37.4	$44.7	$55.8	$ 63.2	$ 74.3
4%	$43.9	$51.7	$63.3	$ 71.1	$ 82.8
5%	$50.7	$58.9	$71.2	$ 79.4	$ 91.7
6%	$57.8	$66.4	$79.4	$ 88.0	$101.0
7%	$65.2	$74.3	$88.0	$ 97.1	$110.7
8%	$72.9	$82.5	$96.9	$106.5	$120.9

Cumulative External Financing Needed by 2002 ($ millions)

0%	$ 96.7	$ 92.9	$ 87.1	$ 83.3	$77.5
1%	$ 99.8	$ 95.8	$ 89.8	$ 85.8	$79.7
2%	$103.0	$ 98.8	$ 92.6	$ 88.4	$82.1
3%	$106.4	$102.1	$ 95.5	$ 91.2	$84.6
4%	$110.0	$105.5	$ 98.6	$ 94.1	$87.3
5%	$113.8	$109.0	$101.9	$ 97.2	$90.1
6%	$117.7	$112.8	$105.4	$100.5	$93.1
7%	$121.9	$116.7	$109.0	$103.9	$96.2
8%	$126.2	$120.9	$112.9	$107.5	$99.5

Source: Casewriter analysis.

Part VII

Analysis of Financing Tactics: Leases, Options, and Foreign Currency

Merton Electronics Corporation

Patricia Merton, president and majority shareholder of Merton Electronics, was dissatisfied with her company's results over the past year (see Exhibits 1 and 2). Sales had risen by over 12 percent compared to the previous year, very close to budget, but at a considerably slower pace than what had been enjoyed during the previous three years. At the same time, 1997 earnings fell by more than 40 percent, reflecting increasingly difficult market conditions. Margins had been flat or falling for the past three years, but 1997 was the worst. Operational improvements had been maintained, keeping working capital and cash needs under control. Also, Merton had secured additional long-term financing and an increase in the company's credit line. Although continued growth would require additional investment in new computer and office equipment and other fixed assets, she expected this could be largely financed out of cash flow—if margins did not deteriorate further and working capital could be kept in line with sales.

Since its founding in 1950 by Thomas Merton, Merton Electronics had been a distributor for GEC, a large manufacturer of electrical and electronics products for consumer and institutional markets. Over the years, in addition to the GEC products, the company had added noncompeting lines of electrical appliances, records, compact discs, and cassettes. In 1980, it began to broaden its product lines by importing Japanese consumer electronics. Four years later, it entered into an exclusive import agreement with the Goldstone Corporation of Taiwan, a major producer of television and other electronic equipment. These products were distributed to retail firms and dealers throughout a broad geographical area.

By the beginning of the 1990s, the company had entered into the personal computer (PC) market, distributing both hardware and software products. It became the national distributor for Fuji Electronics, a major Japanese manufacturer of PCs and related products, in September 1993. This market had proven to be fast growing, accounting for more than

---

This case was written by Professor Lee Remmers. Copyright © 1998 by Lee Remmers.

half of total sales, although only about a third of profits, in 1997; this part of the business was becoming more and more competitive, as price-cutting had become rampant from mail-order and computer-discount houses.

Patricia Merton had been working in the company for two years when her father, Thomas Merton, died in the spring of 1991. As the only family member with experience in the company, she succeeded him as president. Together with her mother, she controlled 65 percent of the share capital of the firm. The remaining shares were held by her father's brother and sister, their families, and a few long-service employees.

During the first weeks of 1998, Merton had been taking advantage of the relative calm that usually marked that time of the year. This was when they took the semiannual inventory, tended to various small problems that had been pushed aside during the past few months, and thought about the future.

One of the things that continued to disturb her was the volatility of the yen, and more recently, the Taiwanese dollar (see Exhibit 3). Over half of the equipment sold in the PC, TV and VCR, and hi-fi product lines was imported from Japanese suppliers. From a volume of about $20 million two years earlier, yen-denominated purchases had approached $27 million during the past 12 months. Annual purchases totaling another $4 million were from Taiwanese suppliers. With the volume expected in the consumer electronics and PC product lines, Patricia Merton foresaw purchases from Fuji Electronics, the company's principal supplier, and other Asian manufacturers to increase in the future.

Typical of Merton's Japanese suppliers, Fuji Electronics had always insisted on invoicing in yen. In contrast, at the beginning of their agreement, Goldstone Corporation had invoiced in U.S. dollars. This changed in 1989, when the company was informed that from then on, the Taiwanese dollar would be used for billing.

Once an order was placed, the Asian suppliers shipped by airfreight, normally within 60 days. Payment terms were 30 days from the end of the delivery month; hence the ¥284 million value of goods delivered in January 1998 would be paid at the end of February (Exhibit 4). With few exceptions, the spot price on the last day of the month in which the order was placed was used for the invoice. This meant that Merton had on average a 90-day currency exposure for each order.

Two years earlier, toward the end of January 1996, concerned that the falling margins were at least partially due to the impact of a rising exchange rate, Patricia Merton had asked her general manager, Charles Brown, to gather some data on the monthly volume of purchases from Japanese suppliers as well as the yen–dollar exchange rates. The data gathered by Brown at the time astonished her. The effect of the yen's more or less continual appreciation against the dollar until the summer of 1995 meant that purchases during that period appeared to have cost the company significantly more—in dollar terms—than if the exchange rate had been stable. Fortunately, thanks to the popularity of the Fuji products, they had been able until 1995 to increase prices to partially offset their higher dollar costs. Also, the Japanese suppliers had absorbed some of the yen's rise by cutting prices significantly. But as the dollar fell through the ¥100 "barrier," it became more and more difficult to maintain margins. During the first four months of 1995, the rising yen translated into an almost $1.1 million higher cost of purchases. Although Brown did not prepare a detailed analysis of purchases before 1995, he estimated that "losses" were, if anything, considerably larger. On the other hand, his data had shown that between July and December 1995, a strengthening dollar produced "gains" of over $1.4 million. As a result of this analysis, they had sought the advice of their banker in January 1996.

Listening to his clients' story, the banker agreed that Merton did face significant currency risk. Further, he reminded them that since Merton Electronics imported a higher portion of its products from Japan than some of its principal competitors, its profit margins were much more sensitive to the value of the yen than theirs were. In view of this, he advised them to hedge their yen purchases. The bank would arrange hedges to cover the orders placed during the month. They agreed that this would be on a monthly basis to obtain the better rates relatively large transactions would provide. The hedges would, he explained, fix in advance the dollar cost of each month's orders. This would effectively remove the currency problem from their everyday concerns and allow them to concentrate on running the business. As for purchases from the Taiwanese suppliers, the banker told them the Taiwanese authorities managed their currency so that it stayed more or less fixed to the U.S. dollar, that even if it were to move it was likely to depreciate and, for these reasons, hedging would not be worthwhile. This advice was taken. Since 1996, Merton had systematically hedged each yen purchase order; purchases from Taiwanese suppliers were not hedged.

Now, after two years, Patricia Merton thought it was time to review this policy. Once again she asked Brown to look at their experience over the past year, going back to January 1997. What this showed was completely different from the previous analysis. Although the yen was still volatile, it had mainly weakened against the dollar during this period. By hedging, the dollar cost of yen purchases had been about $25.5 million during 1997. If the purchases had not been hedged, but the yen bought on the spot market when the invoices came due, the dollar cost would have been about $24.6 million—an almost $900,000 difference! This was almost exactly the pretax earnings for 1997. Extremely disturbed by what Brown told her, Patricia Merton immediately contacted the firm's banker and arranged to see him later in the day.

Merton's meeting with her banker was strained at the beginning. Somewhat defensive, he maintained that since neither he nor anyone else could have accurately predicted how the yen–dollar exchange rate would have moved during the past two years, hedging the exposures was the most prudent policy for Merton. Furthermore, with so much economic and political uncertainty in Japan and the rest of Asia at the present time, he could not recommend in good conscience a better solution to managing the yen risk. When Patricia Merton asked him why he had not encouraged them earlier to hedge the Taiwanese dollar payments, he recalled his advice at the time was that it had been basically pegged to the U.S. dollar for several years and anyway was difficult to hedge satisfactorily because of exchange controls imposed by the Taiwan authorities. He reckoned that by following his recommendation not to hedge the Taiwanese dollar purchases, the U.S. dollar costs had been lower in 1997 by some $125,000 compared to what they would have been if hedged. Not entirely satisfied by his explanation, Merton asked him what he thought they should do now.

The issue boiled down to whether the company should take on currency risk or not, and, if so, how much. With over 60 percent of its purchases subject to currency fluctuations, the banker stuck to his earlier view that the firm could not afford to ignore this risk. He admitted that, with hindsight, not hedging would have been the best policy over the past one to two years. This meant that Merton would have bought the foreign currency on the spot market each time payments to the Asian suppliers were made. This, he said, was essentially a bet on a stronger dollar, which turned out to be the case. Quickly checking the numbers, he noted that if the ¥880 million worth of goods on order or already invoiced at the end of January were to be settled at the current spot rate of ¥127, this would cost Merton about $6.93 million. As it stood, the company was already committed to pay $7.04 million since these purchases had been hedged when the goods were ordered. In other words, hedging appeared to have cost them some $110,000 at the present time. This lost opportunity would be larger or smaller depending on what the yen would do between now and when the invoices were settled. Nevertheless, he still would not advise the company to "do nothing" and expose itself to large possible currency losses in the future. Patricia Merton, as president and major shareholder of the company, would have to decide.

Accepting his arguments that it would be unwise to "do nothing," she thought it would be useful to review the alternative courses that the company might follow. Although the company had been using forward contracts for some 18 months to hedge the yen purchases, Merton felt she needed to have her memory refreshed and asked the banker to outline once again how the different hedges worked.

According to the banker, there were two basic choices when hedging. It could "lock in" today an exchange rate that would be close to the current spot rate; the forward contracts they had been using provided this type of hedge. Or they could enter into an option contract that would set an upper bound on the cost of yen but allow them to take advantage of cheaper yen if that should happen by the time the invoices had to be paid. The option would provide some of the advantages of not hedging and limit the disadvantages—but at a cost.

To lock in an exchange rate, the banker went on, meant that the future price of a foreign currency—the *future spot rate*—would in effect be set today; in other words, the hedge was a bet on a stronger yen. This type of hedge ensured that whatever the future spot rate might turn out to be, the *effective* price paid for yen would still be that which was agreed today. There were three ways to lock in an exchange rate: a forward contract, a money-market transaction, and a currency futures contract. Each of these carried precisely defined terms with regard to price, maturity, and certain other performance measures. Any modifications in the terms of the contract, such as changing its maturity, would have to be negotiated and agreed with the party providing the hedge, possibly resulting in additional cost.

The *forward contract hedge,* which the company had used for the past 18 months, was an arrangement by which it bought from the bank a specified quantity of yen to be delivered at a specified date in the future—normally when the invoice had to be settled. The exchange rate was fixed at the outset. At ¥125.50, the 90-day forward rate was at present nearly 1.5 percent more "expensive" than the spot rate. With this hedge, Merton would receive yen from the bank on the agreed maturity date, pay the bank the amount of dollars at the forward exchange rate set earlier (¥125.50), and then use the yen to pay the Japanese suppliers.

The *money market hedge* was also an arrangement with the bank. Merton would buy yen today on the spot market and place it in a yen time deposit or some other yen asset until needed to pay the suppliers. The purchase of yen would be financed in dollars by a short-term loan or by using cash reserves if they were available. The cost of this hedge would be the difference between the interest paid on the dollar loan and that received from the yen deposit. The banker reminded them that Merton could borrow dollars at 25 *basis points*[1] over the current *prime* rate (8.50 percent); but they would only earn at present ⅜ percent on a three-month Euroyen time deposit, Japanese rates being at an all-time low (see Exhibit 6 for rates).

The *yen futures hedge* was provided by an instrument traded on the Chicago Mercantile Exchange (CME).[2] Quotations for yen futures on January 22 appear on Exhibit 5. As protection against loss from currency fluctuations, this hedge was very similar to the forward contract provided by the bank. Merton would *buy* a sufficient number of futures to create the hedge. It could then wait until the futures contracts came to maturity and take delivery of the yen. Alternatively, if Merton decided the hedge was no longer needed *before* the futures contracts reached maturity, they could be sold. If a rise in the value of the yen meant it cost more dollars to settle the purchase account with the Japanese suppliers, it also meant that the futures would be sold at a profit, thereby providing an offset. However, the mechanics of futures contracts differ considerably from forwards. The contracts are made through a member of the futures exchange, usually a broker. Currency futures come in standard contract sizes (for the yen ¥12.5 million) and standard maturity dates (the third Wednesday of March, June, September, December). They are revalued daily (marked-to-market) with any profit or loss immediately settled between broker and client. To trade on the futures market, the client must open and maintain collateral (a margin account) with the broker. This changes from time to time but at present is a minimum of $1,500 per contract. In addition, the broker will charge a small commission.

The *currency option contract* was available from either banks or exchanges. Option contracts give the *right but not the obligation* to buy (a *call*) or to sell (a *put*) currency or some other asset within a specified period and at a predetermined price known as the *strike* or *exercise price.*

Bank or OTC[3] options can be tailored to meet the client's precise needs for maturity, amount, or currency. They are usually European-type options; that is, they may only be exercised at expiration. Most bank options are on spot currency. Merton's banker pointed out that besides dealing in "plain vanilla" (standard) call and put options, he could also offer them *synthetic* or *exotic* instruments. Synthetics were combinations of calls, puts, and sometimes forward contracts that were designed to meet particular risk/return objectives of a client. A so-called *zero-cost option* is one of the more widely used of these. Exotics were options that had some particular feature that gave the buyer a lower premium at the price of a more risky payoff.[4]

Like futures, *exchange traded* options have standardized maturities and amounts. The expiration dates are similar to those for futures: March, June, September, and December. In addition, the American exchanges offer some "nearby" expiration dates (see Exhibit 5). For example, at the end of January, contracts were offered for February and April expiration as well as for the March and June standard months. Only a few major currencies are available. Most are priced in U.S. dollars, even those traded on European or Asian

---

[1] A basis point is ¹⁄₁₀₀ of a percent, i.e., 0.0001. Basis points are generally used in pricing loans and certain other financial instruments. Rates are usually quoted on an annual basis.

[2] Currency futures are also traded on exchanges in London (LIFFE), Singapore (SIMEX), Sidney, and elsewhere in the world.

[3] OTC: over the counter.

[4] Among the most popular were average rate and barrier or knockout options.

exchanges. They are usually so-called American-type options; in other words, they may be exercised at any time before expiration. Recently, European-style options have been introduced on some exchanges—they can only be exercised at maturity. Those traded on the Philadelphia exchange are on spot currency. Chicago's CME and London's LIFFE contracts are on currency futures. To buy an option on an exchange, the full premium[5] must be paid in advance. To sell (or write) an option requires a specified margin to be maintained with the broker.

Besides going over the hedging instruments, the banker raised a number of other issues for Merton to consider. The company imported goods from its Japanese suppliers on a continuous basis throughout the year. If they did decide to continue hedging these purchases, should it be when the orders were placed as they have been doing up to now? Or should they wait until the time when the purchase invoice was actually received? What about hedging periodically for a longer period of 6 to 12 months once operating plans and budgets were agreed? Finally, if they do continue to hedge, should it be for the entire amount at risk—however it was measured—or only some portion of it?

Merton's banker concluded by stressing that there was no "correct" hedging approach. It depended on the particular needs and financial position of the company, and the attitudes of its management and shareholders towards risk. Whether or not the hedge was profitable would only be known ex post, when the supplier was paid. In the case of Merton Electronics, hedging yen during the past months turned out to be the wrong decision; in contrast, it was the correct decision for the Taiwanese dollar. If instead yen had strengthened against the dollar, locking in the rate would have been the correct decision. Further, he cautioned that under some competitive situations, hedging could actually increase risk rather than decrease it.

The discussion left Merton nearly as baffled as when she arrived at the bank. On leaving, she told the banker that she needed a few days to decide what to do. Back at the office, Merton told Brown that she was pretty much convinced that they should begin to devote a bit more time and thought to managing their currency position. Although they had "lost" some $900,000 on yen purchases during the past few months from a rather simplistic "hedge everything" policy, there was clearly too much uncertainty for a "do nothing" policy to be justified. The problem was to decide quickly what to do.

Anxious to resolve this matter quickly, Patricia Merton asked Brown to prepare a brief report on how their company's currency risk should be managed. In particular, she asked him to set out the relative advantages in terms of cost and risk for each of the alternatives that had been described to them by the banker. To provide a practical example, he could use the ¥300 million exposure arising from the goods that were ordered in January and which would be due for payment in April, 90 days from then. She suggested that Brown use the January 22 market rates which they had picked up at the bank (Exhibit 6) and, for the purpose of the analysis, assume that the suppliers would be paid and the hedges lifted on April 22. She also asked him to check out whether they would have been better off hedging with options over the past months than with forwards. She herself intended to give some thought to broader policy issues, including whether they should hedge at all and, if so, how much, when, and under what circumstances?

---

[5]The LIFFE exchange uses a margin system similar to that for futures trading. Hence, a specified minimum margin is maintained with the broker rather than paying a cash premium up front.

EXHIBIT 1   Comparative Income Statements (dollars in thousands)

	Year Ending December 31, 1996	*Year Ending December 31, 1997*
Sales revenue	53,682	60,392
Cost of goods sold	44,336	51,228
Gross margin	9,346	9,164
Variable expenses	3,277	3,687
Fixed expenses	3,652	4,009
Depreciation	171	207
Operating earnings (EBIT)	2,246	1,261
Interest expense	565	348
Earnings before taxes	1,681	913
Corporate taxes	581	301
Earnings after taxes	1,100	612

EXHIBIT 2   Comparative Balance Sheets (dollars in thousands)

	December 31, 1996	*December 31, 1997*
Assets		
Current assets		
Cash and deposits	95	115
Prepaid expenses	96	70
Accounts receivable	7,816	8,794
Inventories	8,880	9,350
	16,887	18,329
Fixed assets (net)	1,290	1,585
Goodwill	150	150
Total assets	18,327	20,064
Capital and liabilities		
Current liabilities		
Bank credit	4,257	2,237
Mortgage—current	150	150
Accrued expenses	392	359
Accounts payable		
Domestic	2,215	2,497
Foreign (yen)	3,312	3,670*
	10,826	8,913
Mortgage loan	750	600
Subordinated loan	—	500
Capital stock	1,500	1,500
Retained earnings	5,751	6,313
Owners' equity	7,251	7,813
Total capital and liabilities	18,327	20,064

*Dollar value of foreign currency accounts payable (¥375.2 million at spot rate of ¥130.5/U.S.$; Taiwan $25.9 million at spot rate of TWD 32.6/U.S.$).

EXHIBIT 3   Foreign Exhange Data

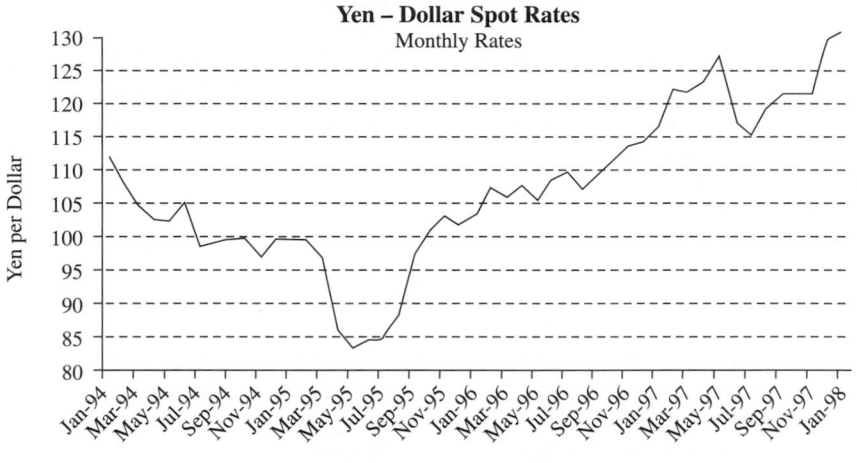

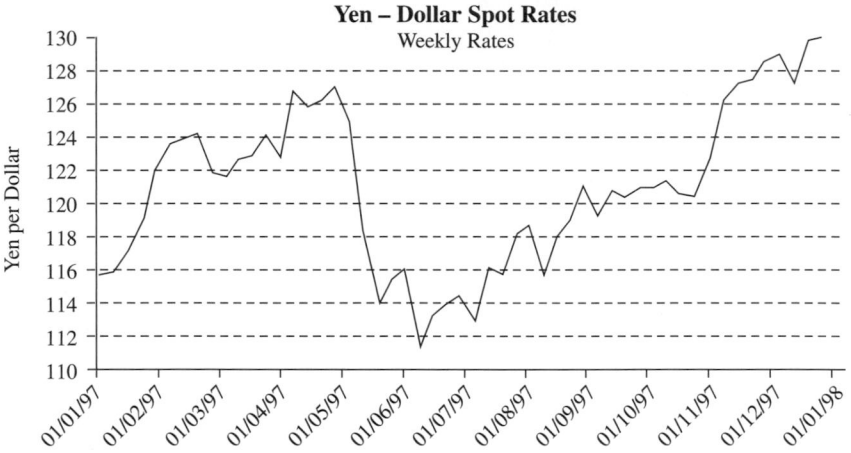

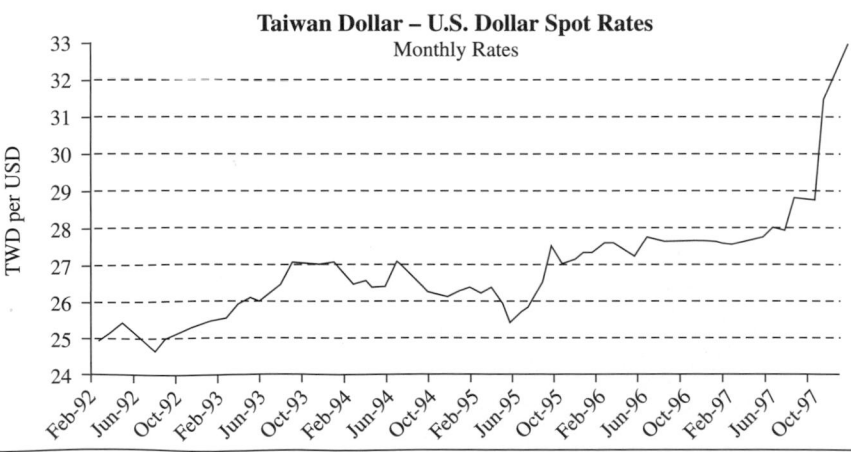

EXHIBIT 4   Actual and Forecasted Purchases from Japanese Suppliers, January 1997–April 1998

Purchase Amount ¥ Million	Order Date	Average ¥ /$ Spot	Delivery and Invoice Date	Payment Date	Average ¥ /$ Spot	Change in Order Value in $ 000
224.7	January 97	116	March 97	April 97	123	+110.2
261.1	February 97	122	April 97	May 97	127	+84.3
276.6	March 97	121	May 97	June 97	117	−78.2
271.1	April 97	123	June 97	July 97	115	−153.3
237.6	May 97	127	July 97	August 97	118	−142.7
192.2	June 97	117	August 97	September 97	121	+54.3
253.5	July 97	115	September 97	October 97	121	+109.3
294.5	August 97	118	October 97	November 97	121	+61.9
395.3	September 97	121	November 97	December 97	129	+202.6
330.8	October 97	121	December 97	January 98	130	+189.3
284.6	November 97	121	January 98	February 98	?	?
295.5	December 97	129	February 98	March 98	?	?
300.0	January 98	130	March 98	April 98	?	?
325.0	February 98	?	April 98	May 98	?	?
375.0	March 98	?	May 98	June 98	?	?
340.0	April 98	?	June 98	July 98	?	?

EXHIBIT 5   Interest Rates

Short Term Interest Rates

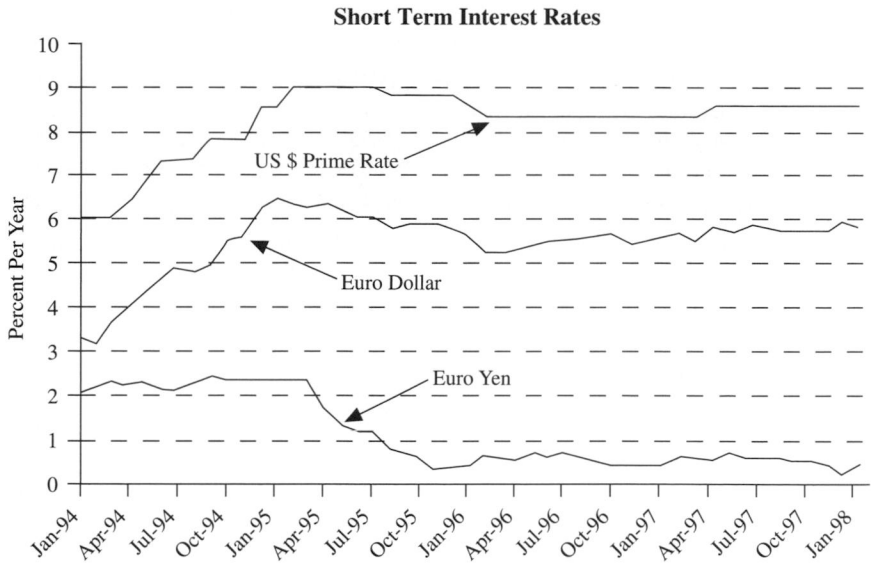

Futures Prices

Japan Yen (CME)—12.5 million yen; $ per yen (.00)

	Open	High	Low	Settle	Change	Lifetime High	Lifetime Low	Open Interest
Mar	.7928	.7970	.7890	.7917	−.0024	.9375	.7512	88,937
Jun	.8046	.8046	.7950	.8017	−.0024	.9090	.7637	2,293
Sept	—	—	—	.8117	−.0024	.8695	.7735	413

Est. vol. 20,416; vol Th 36,578; open int. 91,647, +608.

The Wall Street Journal, January 23–24, 1998.

Futures Option Prices

Japanese Yen (CME)—12.5 million yen; cents per 100 yen

Strike Price	Calls—Settle February	Calls—Settle March	Calls—Settle April	Puts—Settle February	Puts—Settle March	Puts—Settle April
7,800	1.66	2.21		0.49	1.05	1.12
7,850	1.32	1.92		0.65	1.25	1.30
7,900	1.03	1.65		0.86	1.48	
7,950	0.80	1.42		1.12	—	—
8,000	0.62	1.21	2.08	1.45	2.02	
8,050	0.48	1.03	1.84	1.81	—	—

Est. vol. 4,445; Wed. 6,552 calls 4,970 puts
Op. int. Wed. 49,854 calls 65,330 puts

Source: *The Wall Street Journal,* January 23–24, 1998.

EXHIBIT 6 Currency and Other Financial Market Data, January 22, 1998

Spot yen: 127.35–127.40 per $; $0.7849–$0.7852 per ¥100
90-day forward yen: 125.50–125.75 per $; $0.7952–$0.7968 per ¥100

90-day Euroyen interest rates: 3/8%–1/2% per annum
Japanese 10-year government bond yield: 1 3/4%
90-day Eurodollar interest rates: 5 1/2%–5 5/8% per annum
Merton short-term borrowing rate: Prime (8 1/2%) + 25 basis points

March 1998 yen futures (CME): $0.7928; June 1998 yen futures (CME): $0.8031

90-day yen call options [OTC]: $0.7852 strike—$0.0249 per 100 yen
                                   $0.7968 strike—$0.0188 per 100 yen

Burlington Northern Railroad Company: Equipment Leasing

On July 9, 1990, Paul Weyandt, director of equipment finance at Burlington Northern Railroad Company (BNRR), was leafing through the bids he had received for the lease-financing deal being proposed by his office. Included in the $150 million of equipment to be leased were new and remanufactured diesel electric locomotives, bilevel and trilevel auto racks, box cars, coal gondola cars, and covered hopper cars (see Exhibit 1 for equipment descriptions). Weyandt had decided that the bid submitted by Phyllis Grossman, vice president of Norwest Equipment Finance, had the most attractive attributes for the auto racks. In addition to a reasonable annual lease payment, Grossman's proposal also granted BNRR an option to purchase the auto racks at the end of the 15-year period.

Because of BNRR's good working relationship with Norwest over the years, Weyandt was confident that Rob McKenney, vice president and treasurer of BNRR, would support the choice of Norwest. Before accepting the bid, however, Weyandt needed to demonstrate to McKenney that leasing through Norwest would be better for BNRR than borrowing $22 million to purchase the auto racks directly. Weyandt had already demonstrated to McKenney that the equipment was a good investment by showing that the discounted expected cash flows exceeded BNRR's 20 percent investment hurdle rate; now he had to determine the best way to finance the investment.

This case was written by Kenneth Eades for the purposes of classroom discussion with the support of the Foundation for Leasing Education, the education foundation of the Equipment Leasing Association of America. Some figures have been altered at the request of the participating companies. Copyright © 1991 by the University of Virginia Darden School Foundation, Charlottesville, VA. All rights reserved. *No part of this publication may be reproduced, stored in a retrieval system, used in a spreadsheet, or transmitted in any form or by any means— electronic, mechanical, photocopying, recording, or otherwise—without the permission of the Darden School Foundation. For inquiries, please send an e-mail to dardencases@virginia.edu.*

BURLINGTON NORTHERN RAILROAD COMPANY

In 1990, Burlington Northern Railroad Company was the primary subsidiary of Burlington Northern, Inc. (BNI), a holding company. With over 25,000 miles of track in the system, BNRR operated one of the largest railroads in the United States. When the railroad industry was essentially deregulated in 1980, BNRR's revenues became subject to the competition of the market place. Revenues were generated by transporting bulk freight across the country. Coal, the most important, accounted for approximately one-third of the company's total revenues. Other major products transported included those from the agricultural, forest, and automotive industries.

In May 1988, Burlington Resources, another subsidiary of BNI, was spun off as an independent corporation, and certain aspects of this spin-off were still having an effect on BNRR's financing decisions in 1990. Burlington Resources had contained the natural-resource operations of BNI, including the exploration, development, and production of oil, gas, coal, and other minerals. It also included the transportation and sale of natural gas, the sale of timber and logs, the manufacture and sale of forest products, and the management and development of real estate.

In the Burlington Resources spin-off, BNI stockholders were distributed shares of Burlington Resources, Inc., proportionate to their ownership of BNI.[1] After the spin-off, BNI stockholders held both their old BNI shares plus new Burlington Resources shares. Because the BNI shares no longer represented a claim on the assets of Burlington Resources, the price of BNI shares dropped in value as soon as the Burlington Resources shares were distributed. The total wealth of BNI shareholders increased, however, because the loss in value of the BNI shares was more than offset by the market value of the new Burlington Resources shares distributed.

The spin-off had a significant effect on BNI's capital structure, because virtually no long-term debt was transferred along with Burlington Resources' assets. The act of removing Burlington Resources' assets and yet retaining the debt associated with those assets left BNI in the position of being a highly levered company with long-term debt representing 76 percent of its total capital in 1988. The company had publicly stated its intent of reducing the debt by $1 billion during 1989–94 to keep its financial leverage within manageable limits. The combination of heavy capital needs and a recent fall in BNRR's revenue (see Exhibits 2 and 3 for financial data on BNI) made the reduction of debt an ambitious undertaking.

Capital expenditures were projected at $550 million in 1990 and had been $465 million in 1989. For 1990, $325 million was being invested in roadwork (railway track, track bedding, and track equipment), and the remaining $225 million was being spent on equipment (locomotives, rail cars, auto racks, etc.). Despite these heavy investments, BNRR had managed to fund most of its needs internally. The choices of external financing, however, were limited by the philosophy of BNI management that the interest of BNI shareholders should be the overriding consideration with every decision. Issuing new equity, for exam-

---

[1]A spin-off is a form of corporate divestiture in which a holding company distributes shares of one of its subsidiaries to the holding company's shareholders. Thus, a spin-off creates a new company by slicing off part of the holding company.

ple, had been ruled out because railroads rarely went to the equity markets and doing so might be interpreted negatively by the marketplace. Rather than risk a fall in the stock price, management had decided that if new investments could not be funded internally, they would either have to be funded with debt or be in the form of leases.

NORWEST EQUIPMENT FINANCE

On December 31, 1989, Norwest Corporation, with $24.3 billion in assets, was one of the largest regional bank holding companies in the United States. Despite the difficult times facing many members of the banking industry, Norwest maintained a strong return on common equity of 19.6 percent and, on December 1, 1990, had increased its quarterly dividend to $0.205 from $0.185, the second increase for the year. The strong return on equity and increased dividends resulted in a record-high stock price of $24.13 on a book value of $13.67/share. The premium over book value reflected Norwest's relatively low number of highly levered transactions and the depressing effect that real estate loans were having on the market values of many other banks. The proportion of nonperforming assets in Norwest was less than half that of the average regional bank holding company.

Norwest Equipment Finance, which specialized in leasing to corporations, was a wholly owned subsidiary of Norwest Corporation. For over 20 years, Norwest Equipment Finance had leased equipment ranging from trucks to machine tools, computers, and railroad equipment to some of the largest companies in the United States. BNRR had been leasing equipment through Norwest for over 15 years.

LEASING AT BNRR

Leasing played an important role at BNRR because of the company's tax status in 1990. The 1986 Tax Reform Act required that corporations not only compute their taxes as they had in the past but also compute an alternative minimum tax (AMT). The AMT amount had to be paid if it exceeded the tax liability computed by the regular method. The 20 percent tax rate for AMT was much lower than the normal rate of 34 percent, but taxable income for AMT was computed much differently and could be much higher than the regular taxable income.[2]

A likely candidate for AMT was a company that reported large amounts of "tax-preference items," which included depletion allowances, intangible drilling costs, and accelerated depreciation of assets placed in service after 1986. Tax-preference items were deductible under the regular tax method but were not allowable deductions when taxable income was computed for AMT. The heavy demands for capital equipment in a railroad meant that BNRR carried a great deal of equipment on its books, and as a result, the company incurred large accelerated-depreciation expenses. The accelerated-depreciation expenses combined with other tax-preference items had been sufficient to make BNI subject to the AMT in the past and into the foreseeable future.

---

[2]For a more complete discussion of the AMT for corporations, see Richard Contino, *Handbook of Equipment Leasing* (New York: AMACOM, 1989).

As long as BNI was subject to the AMT, the value of owning an asset would be reduced, because assets would have to be depreciated on a straight-line basis rather than on an accelerated basis. As a lessee, however, the lease payments made by BNRR were deductible regardless of whether the company was subject to AMT or not. Regarding BNRR's use of leases, Weyandt had recently stated:

> For the most part, leasing is either credit motivated or tax motivated. Sometimes a company will lease because it's a relatively weak credit and wants to use the lessor's ability to borrow money at a lower rate. Burlington, however, is a good credit. Our equipment-backed securities are rated Aa3 by Moody's and A+ by Standard & Poor's, so even a AAA-rated lessor could not realize enough advantage in the markets to make it worthwhile for us to lease through them. Because of our current tax situation, on the other hand, we are in a position of benefiting by leasing from a company that is not subject to AMT like we are. If a company is paying the 34 percent tax rate, it can fully utilize the depreciation expenses of an asset and then pass the depreciation benefits along to Burlington by leasing us the asset. So right now, leasing is basically a tax play for Burlington Northern.[3]

The leasing terms proposed by Norwest for the auto racks had the added advantage for BNRR of being an off-balance-sheet item. According to accounting principles, a lease had to be classified as either an operating or a capital lease (see Exhibit 4). If a lease were capitalized, the lessee had to report the value of the leased equipment as an asset and the value of the lease as a liability. Assuming that the asset value and lease value were identical, capitalizing a lease was equivalent to adding a 100 percent debt-financed asset to the books, which would increase BNRR's debt-to-equity ratio. Operating leases, on the other hand, were reported in the footnotes of the company's annual reports but were not required to be reported on the company's balance sheets. To achieve the objective of decreasing its financial leverage, therefore, BNRR was careful to make sure that all its new leases were classified as operating leases.

Two of the four criteria necessary to qualify as an operating lease were critical—the economic-life test and the value test. The estimated life of the auto racks was approximately 22 years; thus, the 15-year lease was shorter than required by the economic-life test—75 percent of the asset's life. For purposes of the value test, Weyandt had computed the present value of the lease payments by discounting them at BNRR's cost of equipment-secured debt. His preliminary calculations indicated that the value test was also satisfied, as the present value of the lease payments was less than 90 percent of the auto racks' current value.

LEASING THE AUTO RACKS

Exhibit 5 illustrates the various methods of structuring a lease. In a *direct lease,* the manufacturer either leased directly to the lessee or sold the asset to an intermediary who acted as the lessor. In a *sale-and-lease-back* arrangement, the owner of an asset sold the asset to a lessor and then leased it back. Like most large leasing deals, however, BNRR's equipment lease would be structured as a *leveraged lease.*

Typical of most leveraged leases, the auto-rack deal involved three parties: a lessee, an equity-participant lessor, and a debt participant. The auto racks would be purchased from the manufacturer by Norwest, who would act as the lessor and realize all the tax benefits

---

[3]Casewriter interview, March 25, 1991.

of ownership. The leverage aspect of the lease arose because Norwest would contribute only 20 percent of the purchase price, with the remaining 80 percent being borrowed with either a public or private debt offering. Because of the large amount of debt required and the relatively attractive rates in the public market, it had been decided to issue public debt. To limit Norwest's exposure in the deal, however, the debt would be structured as a nonrecourse loan. Under such a loan, the debtholders had a first lien on the auto racks and, in the event of default, could repossess the auto racks directly from BNRR. The debtholders would not, however, have recourse to any other assets held by either BNRR or Norwest. The debt would therefore provide leverage for Norwest, without being a general liability to the firm. From the debtholders' perspective, the nonrecourse debt would be virtually identical to an equipment-secured loan issued directly by BNRR.

The bankruptcy laws treated default on equipment-secured loans for railroads and airlines differently from the way they treated default on identical loans in other industries. If a railroad was forced into bankruptcy, the equipment-secured creditors had the right to repossess the pledged asset directly without waiting more than 60 days for a judgment from the bankruptcy court. In the case of a company in another industry, bankruptcy meant that the secured creditors would receive the proceeds of the sale of their collateral, but only if the courts deemed liquidation to be the appropriate action and only after protracted and costly legal proceedings. Thus, the special treatment by the bankruptcy laws made equipment-secured loans less risky for railroads than for other companies and allowed railroads to pay much lower interest rates for secured borrowing than for general credit. The nonrecourse loan arranged by BNRR for the auto racks gave the lenders virtually the same rights they would have had if the bonds had been issued by BNRR as a loan secured directly by the auto racks.

Morgan Stanley, an investment-banking firm retained by BNRR for the deal, had advised that the $17.6 million, 15-year bond issue would be rated by the rating agencies as Aa3/A+ and carry a rate of 9.81 percent with annual coupon payments and principal due at maturity. The notes would be serviced by BNRR's lease payments made to a trustee who would be obligated to make the interest and principal payments on the debt before any excess rent, renewal, or purchase option payments could be distributed to Norwest. In the event that BNRR missed a lease payment, Norwest could take one of several actions: keep the lease alive by making the missed payment for BNRR, pay off the debtholders and keep the auto racks, or cut its losses by allowing the debtholders to repossess the racks.

As part of the bidding process, Weyandt had informed the bidders what the terms of each lease should be for each class of equipment. For example, the new locomotives were to be bid as a 23-year lease and the auto racks were to be bid as a 15-year lease. The leases were to have annual payments and allow BNRR to purchase the assets at a predefined price at the end of each lease. According to FASB 13, an operating lease could not give the lessee the right to purchase the asset at a bargain price (i.e., at substantially below its residual value, the fair market value of the asset at the end of the lease [see the alternative-ownership test in Exhibit 4]). Typically, industry practice was for the lessor to hire an independent appraiser and offer a purchase price to the lessee of no less than the inflation-adjusted appraised residual value. Currently, the industry was using a rate of 3.5 percent per annum to inflate the purchase price to future dollars. Thus, if an asset worth $1 million were to be leased for 15 years and the appraised residual value equaled 25 percent of its current value, the lowest purchase price Norwest would offer was $0.42 million [$0.25 \times \$1$ million $\times (1 + .035)^{15}$].

The estimate of the auto racks' residual value played a significant role in how Norwest and BNRR valued the lease. The lease gave BNRR the right to buy the auto racks at a predefined purchase price, but neither Grossman nor Weyandt knew with any certainty what the market for used auto racks would be in 15 years. The major determinants of the residual value would be inflation and supply-and-demand forces. If inflation turned out to be higher than anticipated during the term of the lease, the value of the auto racks would also be high (and vice versa). If another railroad happened to go out of business close to the termination of the lease, a glut of used auto racks on the market would keep the market price of auto racks low. New auto racks being produced at significantly reduced prices or significantly higher quality would also exert downward pressure on the price of used auto racks.

Grossman realized that the purchase price was a critical part of the lease. If the purchase price ended up being higher than the market value of the auto racks at the end of the lease, BNRR would simply decline to buy from Norwest unless the auto racks were offered at the prevailing market price. On the other hand, if Grossman offered BNRR a purchase-option price that was too low, BNRR would almost certainly end up buying the racks and Norwest's yield on the lease would suffer. The trick was to offer Weyandt an attractive purchase price that satisfied the IRS's interpretation of the alternative-ownership test and also kept enough of the upside value of the asset to give Norwest a reasonable return on the lease.

For the auto racks, Norwest had bid a two-tier lease payment of $2.3 million for the first seven years and $2.8 million for the last eight years. The 15 lease payments were to be made annually beginning at the end of the first year. At the end of the lease, BNRR had the right to purchase the auto racks for $9.2 million, 25 percent of $22.1 million inflated at 3.5 percent per year for 15 years.

ANALYZING THE LEASE

The lease-versus-buy analysis required several assumptions. In particular, BNRR's tax status was critical to how it assessed the value of the lease. BNRR's tax department had told Weyandt that the company would, assuming that the tax laws were not changed in the interim, be subject to AMT for at least the next 15 years. The auto racks would be depreciated on a straight-line basis over 14 years (to a $0 salvage value) rather than an accelerated basis (modified accelerated cost recovery system [MACRS] for seven-year property). See Exhibit 6 for MACRS depreciation schedule. Leasing meant, of course, that BNRR would forfeit the right to depreciate the asset altogether.

Another assumption critical to the analysis was the residual value of the auto racks. Because of the fixed purchase price, a high residual value in 2005 increased the value of the lease significantly. A low residual value in 2005 meant that the fixed purchase price would have no value to BNRR. Because of the uncertainty associated with its estimation and its potential impact on the overall decision, Weyandt had decided to compute the present value of the residual value separately. If the overall value of the lease depended too much on his estimate of residual value, he would have to reconsider whether he should recommend that BNRR lease the auto racks.

EXHIBIT 1   Equipment Descriptions

Equipment Type	Market Value	Description
New locomotives	$ 19,600,000	Built by Electro-Motive Division, General Motors Corporation, 3,800 horsepower diesel electric locomotive.
Remanufactured locomotives	47,740,000	Remanufactured by Morrison-Knudsen Company, Inc., Electro-Motive Division, General Motors Corporation, and VMV Enterprises, Inc. Remanufactured locomotives met or exceeded the performance standards and requirements for new locomotives.
Auto racks	22,067,600	Bilevel and trilevel auto racks built by Trinity Industries, Inc., and Thrall Car Manufacturing Company. Completely enclosed structures used to haul automobiles.
Box cars	7,680,000	Built by Gunderson Inc. 50.5-foot hi-cube box cars with 8-foot double plug doors.
Gondolas	12,288,000	Built by Bethlehem Steel Corp. Aluminum-bodied rotary coal gondolas, 4,400-cubic-foot capacity with a maximum load of 120 tons of coal.
Covered hoppers	43,500,000	Built by Trinity Industries, Inc. Trough hatch-covered hoppers designed for 4,750 cubic feet of grain up to a maximum of 110 tons.
Total	$152,875,600	

EXHIBIT 2   BNI Income Statements, Bond, and Equity Data (in thousands of dollars)

Consolidated Income Statements

	As of December 31	
	1989	*1988*
Revenue	$4,606,286	$4,699,517
Costs and expenses	3,949,750	4,020,617
Operating income	656,536	678,900
Interest expense on long-term debt	(270,272)	(292,050)
Other income (expense), net	4,397	(207,655)*
Income from continuing operations before taxes	390,661	179,195
Provision for income taxes	147,670	80,493
Income from continuing operations	242,991	98,702
Income from discontinued operations net of income taxes	—	57,048
Net income	$ 242,991	$ 155,750

Bond Data as of July 9, 1990

	Annual	Maturity	52-Week		
Rating	*Coupon*	*Date*	*High*	*Low*	*Current*
Baa1	9⅜	1996	102	97¾	100½
Baa1	9	2016	95	88	90¼
Baa1	8½	1996	98⅞	95¾	97½

Equity Data as of July 9, 1990

Shares common stock outstanding: 75,678,974 (March 31, 1990)
Share price: $37
Beta: Not a meaningful figure because of recent spin-off; 0.9 prior to spin-off.

*Includes litigation settlement of $175,000.

EXHIBIT 3 Consolidated Balance Sheets, as of December 31 (in thousands of dollars)

	1988	1989
Assets		
Cash and equivalents	$ 82,627	$ 83,620
Accounts receivable, net	430,355	685,018
Materials and supplies	133,286	157,954
Current portion of deferred income taxes	119,589	98,339
Other current assets	31,137	39,740
Total current assets	$ 796,994	$ 1,064,671
Property and equipment		
Road, roadway, and real estate	$ 6,566,015	$ 6,362,153
Equipment	1,777,927	1,766,458
Total PP&E	8,343,942	8,128,611
Accumulated depreciation and amortization	3,189,410	3,050,349
Property and equipment, net	5,154,532	5,078,262
Other assets	196,254	187,401
Total assets	$ 6,147,780	$ 6,330,334
Liabilities		
Accounts payable	$ 645,077	$ 628,008
Compensation and benefits payable	222,218	178,957
Accrued interest on long-term debt	77,375	96,972
Taxes payable	135,564	117,684
Other current liabilities	94,242	85,053
Current portion of long-term debt	113,490	112,083
Total current liabilities	$ 1,287,966	$ 1,218,757
Long-term debt	$ 2,219,619	$ 2,722,625
Other liabilities	268,721	270,702
Deferred income taxes	1,277,715	1,186,124
Total liabilities	$ 5,054,021	$ 5,398,208
Preferred stock	$ 13,512	$ 14,101
Common stock	967,528	992,405
Retained earnings (deficit)	131,544	(20,624)
Cost of treasury stock	(18,825)	(53,756)
Net worth	$ 1,093,759	$ 932,126
Total liabilities and net worth	$6,147,780	$6,330,334

EXHIBIT 4 Rules for Determining Operating versus Capital Lease

According to the Financial Accounting Standards Board in Financial Accounting Standard No. 13, a lease must be capitalized if it meets any one of the following criteria:

1. *Ownership test*
   The lessee automatically is transferred ownership of the asset by the end of the lease.
2. *Alternative-ownership test*
   The lessee has the right to buy the asset at a price substantially below the fair market price.
3. *Economic-life test*
   The lease term is greater than or equal to 75 percent of the estimated economic life of the asset.
4. *Value test*
   The present value of the minimum lease payments is greater than or equal to 90 percent of the fair market value of the asset at the time of the lease.

EXHIBIT 5   Burlington Northern Railroad Company: Equipment Leasing

Lease Structures

1. Direct Lease

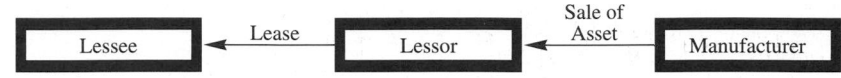

2. Sale and Lease Back

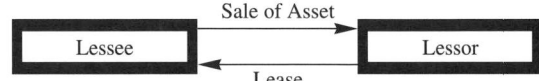

3. Leveraged Lease

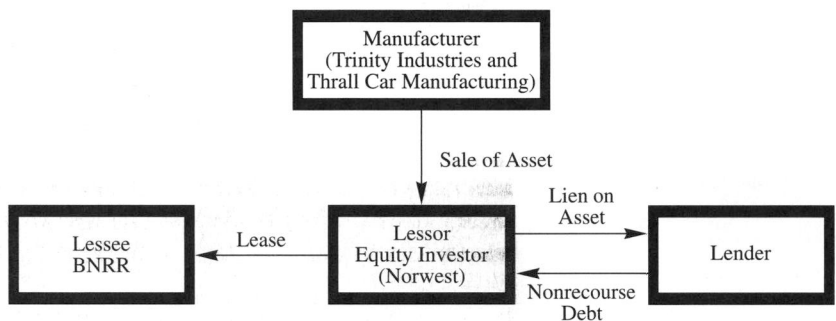

EXHIBIT 6   MACRS Seven-Year Property-Depreciation Schedule*

Tax Year	MACRS Schedule	Beginning Tax Basis
1	0.1429	1.0000
2	0.2449	0.8571
3	0.1749	0.6122
4	0.1249	0.4373
5	0.0893	0.3124
6	0.0892	0.2231
7	0.0893	0.1339
8	0.0446	0.0446

*Because of the half-year convention, seven-year MACRS involves eight years of depreciation expenses.

Boston Chicken, Inc.: 4½% Convertible Subordinated Debentures Due 2004

On January 25, 1994, Boston Chicken announced that it would issue $130 million in convertible subordinated debentures yielding 4 1/2 percent, and would be priced at par. A summary of terms is given in Exhibit 1. The issue surprised analysts, who noted that the company had never reported an annual profit. It had gone public less than two months earlier, making it the fastest bond financing after an IPO on record. And its business concept and growth prospects were uncertain. The shares were initially offered on November 16, 1993, at $20.00 and closed in the first day's trading at $48.50, for a whopping 143 percent one-day gain. One source reported,

> Not surprisingly, in view of the millions that the company left on the table, some capital markets pros criticized Merrill's [Lynch's] performance in pricing the offering. But Boston Chicken officials insisted at the time that they were satisfied with Merrill's performance, noting that the pricing already was quite aggressive at 40 times estimated 1994 earnings. "We thought it was kind of pushing the edge of the envelope."[1]

Analysts wondered if investors in the forthcoming issue of convertible bonds would enjoy the same short-term gain. On January 25, 1994, the closing share price for Boston Chicken was $44.75 per share. The company stated that it did not anticipate paying any cash dividends in the foreseeable future.

---

[1]Tom Pratt, "Boston Chicken Sets Converts with Merrill in the Lead," *Investment Dealer's Digest,* January 17, 1994, p. 12.

This case was written by Professor Robert Bruner as a basis for class discussion rather than to illustrate effective or ineffective handling of an administrative situation. Copyright © 1996 by the University of Virginia Darden School Foundation, Charlottesville, VA. All rights reserved. *No part of this publication may be reproduced, stored in a retrieval system, used in a spreadsheet, or transmitted in any form or by any means—electronic, mechanical, photocopying, recording, or otherwise—without the permission of the Darden Foundation. For inquiries, please send an e-mail to dardencases@virginia.edu.* Revised 11/97. Version 1.3.

The issue of Boston Chicken convertibles came to the attention of Martha Lovejoy, senior vice president and portfolio manager of the Growth and Income Fund, one of the Allegiance Group of mutual funds. Allegiance Group offered 36 different funds and held over $100 billion under management. The objective of the Growth and Income Fund was to seek "long-term growth, current income, and growth of income, consistent with reasonable investment risk." About 5 percent of the fund's $8 billion under management was devoted to convertible bonds.

Lovejoy wanted to assess the new issue of Boston Chicken convertibles. She needed to decide that day whether to purchase some of these bonds for the Growth and Income Fund. To assist her in the analysis was C. K. Pao, a new associate with Allegiance Group. The day before, Lovejoy had asked Pao to gather information on the company and the issue, and to meet with her at 7:30 the next morning.

THE COMPANY

Boston Chicken operated and franchised food-service stores that specialized in complete meals featuring rotisserie-roasted chicken.[2] The strategy of the company was to combine the fresh, flavorful, and appealing meals associated with traditional home cooking with the convenience and value associated with fast-food restaurants. Elements of the strategy included providing convertible debt financing to its franchise area developers; hiring veteran multiunit food-service operators; emphasizing complete, reasonably priced meals; using visible and high-traffic store locations; and employing advanced point-of-sale information technology. The company's goal was to become the leader in the emerging food-service category of fresh, convenient meals associated with traditional home cooking. Management believed that the company competed with other take-out food-service companies, fast-food restaurants, casual full-service dining restaurants, delicatessens, cafeteria-style buffets, and convenience stores. One other company, Kenny Rodgers' Roasters, offered direct competition in the rotisserie-roasted chicken concept.

The first Boston Chicken store was opened in Newton, Massachusetts, in 1985. In early 1992, a team of managers who had built the Blockbuster Video store chain purchased control of Boston Chicken. Seeking to apply to Boston Chicken the strategy of explosive growth that they had perfected at Blockbuster, the management team moved rapidly to transform the company. As of January 14, 1993, the company had 228 stores, of which 40 were operated directly by the company and 188 were operated by franchisees. The company had entered into agreements to open more than 765 additional stores in the next three years and estimated that there would be about 450 stores in the system by the end of 1994.

The initial phase of store expansion had been financed with loans from banks and equity investments of $38 million by the management team. On November 16, 1993, Boston Chicken sold 2,960,000 shares in an initial public offering, realizing $60 million in proceeds. The proceeds were applied mainly to store expansion.

---

[2]On March 2, 1995, Boston Chicken changed the name of its restaurants to Boston Market, and introduced turkey, ham, and meatloaf dishes. The corporate name remained Boston Chicken, Inc.

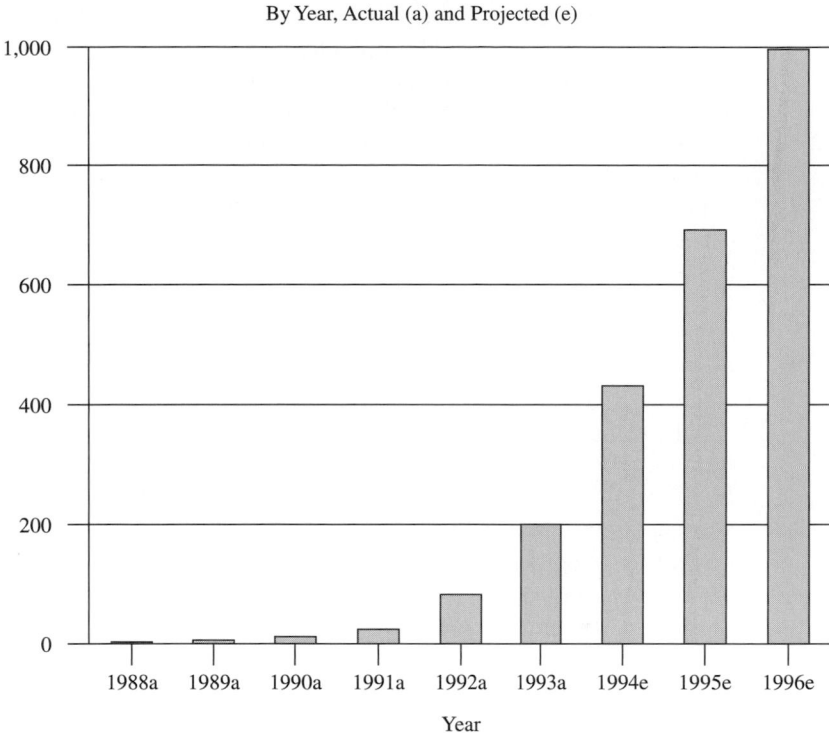

Number of Boston Chicken Stores
By Year, Actual (a) and Projected (e)

The proceeds of the convertible bond offering would be applied to the development of new stores, including financing certain of its area developers. Area developers were, in effect, "superfranchisees" who committed to developing rapidly a geographical region, such as Southern California. Boston Chicken financed developers and franchisees with convertible loans which, when exercised, would deliver majority control in the stores to Boston Chicken. One securities analyst argued that this scheme insulated the company's financial statements from the initial operating losses and negative cash flows associated with opening stores, and presented a more optimistic picture of growth and profitability than actually existed. While the company viewed royalties and fees as revenues, critics believed that these were actually intercompany fund transfers (i.e., assuming that Boston Chicken effectively controlled its franchisees). Exhibit 2 presents a summary of financial performance in recent years.

LOVEJOY'S ANALYTICAL APPROACH

In briefing Pao on the information required, Lovejoy explained that a convertible bond (or "convert") would require more analysis than a nonconvertible (or "straight") bond. Straight bonds were usually evaluated on the adequacy of their yield to maturity relative to the risk and maturity of the bond. The standard approach was to find a sample of bonds similar in risk rating and term to maturity and estimate the average yield of that sample—this average was the investor's "opportunity cost" for the bond being evaluated.

Converts were more complicated to compare to one another because of their widely differing terms. Nevertheless, convertible-bond traders traditionally used a number of ratios as a basis of comparison. Lovejoy requested that Pao estimate these ratios for the Boston Chicken 4⅛s and for a sample of issues comparable in rating and maturity. Exhibit 3 gives the definitions of these ratios, and Pao's results.

> **Pao's first task:**
> Interpret the results in Exhibit 3.

Rather than rely only on the traditional ratios, Lovejoy advocated *valuing* the converts directly as a test of the appropriateness of the offering price. Converts were actually hybrid securities that combined elements of a simple bond, plus various embedded options. The value (V) of a convertible bond was just the sum of the simple (or "straight") bond value, and the values of various embedded options:

$$V_{\text{CV bond}} = V_{\text{Straight bond}} + V_{\text{Option 1}} + V_{\text{Option 2}} + \ldots + V_{\text{Option } n}$$

She said that valuing the bond element was relatively easy, while identifying and valuing the embedded options was challenging. But, she said, this analysis often exposed arbitrage opportunities in the pricing of securities. For instance, if the Boston Chicken 4⅛s were *over*priced, she might try to short-sell those bonds, and with the proceeds, buy an offsetting portfolio of straight bonds and options. If they were *under*priced, she could do the reverse: buy the 4⅛s and sell a portfolio of bonds and options. To begin with, she needed to answer the basic question of whether the bonds were worth their offering price of par.[3]

VALUING THE STRAIGHT-BOND PORTION

Lovejoy began the analysis by asking Pao for his valuation of the straight-bond portion. He explained that he had valued the straight bond on a handheld calculator.[4] An important assumption was the yield assumption used to price the straight bond. He drew a sample of intermediate-term CCC-rated straight bonds (see Exhibit 4) and used the average yield to maturity of this sample, 13.4 percent. The resulting value was $517.40 per $1,000 bond.

Lovejoy said,

Pao, in light of what you have just told me, isn't this bond a rip-off? Why would you ever buy a security whose present value of cash flows was less than the price of the security? Stated alternatively, why would you buy a bond whose yield was less than yields on comparable securities? Here's a statement by an analyst about the Boston Chicken 4⅛s that

> **Pao's second task:** Explain why yields and PV's are lower for converts than for straights.

---

[3]To say that a bond is offered at par is to indicate that the offering price is identical to the principal amount (or par value) of the bond. For instance, to offer at par a bond that promises to repay $1,000 at maturity is to price that bond today at $1,000. Note that the convention is to quote bond prices on a base of $100, rather than $1,000—thus, a bond quoted at par would have a price of 100.

[4]Settlement date was February 1, 1994. Maturity date was February 1, 2004. Coupon rate was 4.5 percent.

showed up on my Bloomberg screen a couple of weeks ago: "___ The company [Boston Chicken] most likely chose to raise more money using convertible debt rather than a secondary offering because it is less expensive and won't dilute shares outstanding."[5]

Pao's third task: Determine what is wrong with the quotation from Bloomberg.

I can't believe he said that.

Lovejoy's attention was drawn to the risk ratings of the Boston Chicken 4⅛s: Standard & Poor's rated it CCC+,[6] while Moody's rated it B3.[7] She noted that these were both "high-yield bond" ratings and indicated a material risk of default.[8] "Why do you suppose," she asked Pao,

Pao's fourth task: Suggest why the company or the bond issue would merit a junk-bond rating.

"that the 4⅛s carry such a low risk rating?" She said that if their preliminary analysis suggested that the Boston Chicken 4⅛s might be an attractive investment, she would ask Pao to complete a deeper credit analysis of the issue, to check the assessment of the rating agencies.

Lovejoy pointed out that an alternate way to value the straight-bond component was to view it as composed of a default-risk-free bond, and a default-risk discount:

$$V_{\text{Risky straight bond}} = V_{\text{Default-risk-free straight bond}} - V_{\text{Default-risk discount}}$$

Pao asked what was the value of a default-risk discount. Lovejoy said that the default-risk discount was the value of an insurance policy (or loan guarantee) that was just sufficient to turn a risky bond into a risk-free bond. The insurance policy was nothing other than owning a put option that would permit the lender to exchange a defaulted loan for the par value of that loan. In theory, the value of the default-risk discount and the put option would be equal.

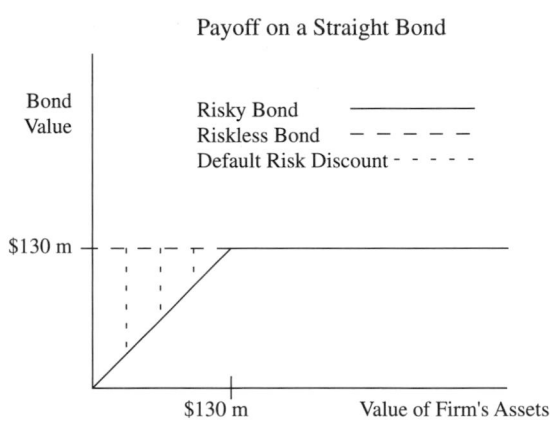

---

[5]"Update: Boston Chicken to Raise $100 Million through Debt Sale," *Bloomberg Business News,* January 7, 1994.

[6]Standard & Poor's defined debt rated CCC as having a currently identifiable vulnerability to default. It is dependent upon favorable conditions. The company is not likely to have the capacity to pay interest and repay principal.

[7]Moody's defined the debt rated B as generally lacking characteristics of the desirable investment. Assurance of interest and principal payments may be small. Within the B category, ratings varied from B1 (at the highest) to B3 (at the lowest).

[8]The universe of bonds could be segmented into "investment-grade" bonds, which carried ratings from AAA/Aaa at the high end, to BBB/Baa at the low end. Non-investment-grade, or "high-yield" or "junk," bonds carried ratings below BBB/Baa. Many institutional investors were prohibited from investing in junk bonds, or limited in their capacity to invest in them. Junk bonds had higher rates of default, and offered higher yields.

Lovejoy drew a graph on a chalkboard and said, "The payoff on a default-risk-free $130 million bond issue would be $130 million across all asset values of the firm. But for a risky loan, as the asset value of the firm declined below the par value of the bond, the payoff on the bond would decline dollar for dollar. This accounts for the 'kink' in the payoff diagram of the risky loan. The only way to 'iron out the kink' is to buy an insurance policy (or loan guarantee) that would promise to pay the lender any shortfall in the firm's ability to repay."

VALUING THE CONVERSION OPTION

Next Lovejoy turned to the conversion option embedded in the security.

Lovejoy   The right to convert is a call option on Boston Chicken's shares. For this we can use the standard-option pricing model. This is an option lasting the life of the bond, 10 years. The risk-free rate of return is 5.74 percent, the yield on contemporaneous U.S. Treasuries (i.e., 10-year maturities). Today's stock price of Boston Chicken is $44.75. The exercise price of the option is the conversion price indicated in the terms of the bond (see Exhibit 1), $55.938 per share. We can assume that there will be no dividend paid on the shares for the life of the bond. The main assumption we need to estimate is the volatility of returns on Boston Chicken stock. What is your estimate of volatility?

Pao   My analysis shows that over the 66 trading days since the IPO, Boston Chicken's volatility has been .666.[9] This is not a very long observation period. It might not reflect the average volatility of the firm's shares over the next 10 years. So I drew a sample of peer companies' volatilities. These are given in Exhibit

> **Pao's fifth task:**
> Recommend a volatility assumption.

5. The average volatility of the firms in this sample is .323. In comparison, the volatilities of intermediate-term U.S. Treasuries are 5 to 10 percent. The volatilities of 10-year junk bonds are 15 to 20 percent.

Before Pao offered an estimate of the value of the conversion option, Lovejoy pointed out that conversion of the bond into shares would *dilute* the per share value of the common stock. On the current base of 16,723,546 shares outstanding, 2,324,400 new shares would be issued by the company to meet the conversion.[10] This would mean that the value of the conversion option would be reduced by the extent of dilution. Lovejoy explained that the dilution was simply the ratio of new shares issued under the conversion to the sum of new and old shares. Thus, the value of the option after accounting for dilution would be:

$$V_{\text{Option after dilution}} = \left[1 - \left(\frac{\text{Number of new shares}}{\text{Number of new shares} + \text{Existing shares}} \right) \right] V_{\text{Option before dilution}}$$

---

[9]To derive this estimate, Pao calculated the standard deviation of the 66 lognormalized daily price relatives (i.e., today's price divided by yesterday's price) and then annualized the result.

[10]Note that adjusting for dilution is *not* necessary when calculating the value of an exchange-traded option. In that case, exercising the option results in no new shares being issued by the company. But in the cases of convertible bonds and warrants, where the counterparty to the investor is the company itself, new shares ordinarily will be issued and dilution must be reflected in the valuation of the option.

Lovejoy asked Pao to make the dilution adjustment in this case, but noted that as a practical matter it was not always necessary to adjust for dilution. Exercise of the option dilutes the share price but also increases the value of the equity—these two effects tend to offset each other when the dilution is relatively small. But then Pao raised a concern that dilution might be greater than first appeared:

Pao   Come to think of it, the management team owns long-lived options that would almost certainly be exercised by then. The company has employee options outstanding for 3.469 million shares, exercisable between $2.92 and $11.00 per share. The converts have the highest exercise price of any options outstanding on Boston Chicken shares. It seems reasonable to assume that the employee options will be exercised before the converts. Therefore, our dilution adjustment ought to take into account these other options too.

Lovejoy   You have the correct intuition: We need to consider other options maturing during the life of the 4½s. But the options you mentioned are already deep in the money. In an efficient market, the effect of their exercise should *already* be impounded in the price of Boston Chicken common. One other thing: We're trying to estimate the market value of the 4½s. Each bond will convert into 17.88 shares.[11] Therefore, the total value of the conversion option embedded in the 4½s will equal the option value per share times 17.88. What is the total value of the conversion option per bond?

> **Pao's sixth task:** Estimate the value of the conversion option in the bond. Estimate the value of the call option per share, adjust for dilution, and multiply by 17.88.

While Pao was estimating the value of the embedded conversion option, Lovejoy considered how valuable the firm would need to be in order to put the conversion option "in the money." She observed that the value of the assets would need to be greater than $1.26 billion[12] in order for the bond to be worth more as equity. Moving to the

Payoff on a Convertible Bond

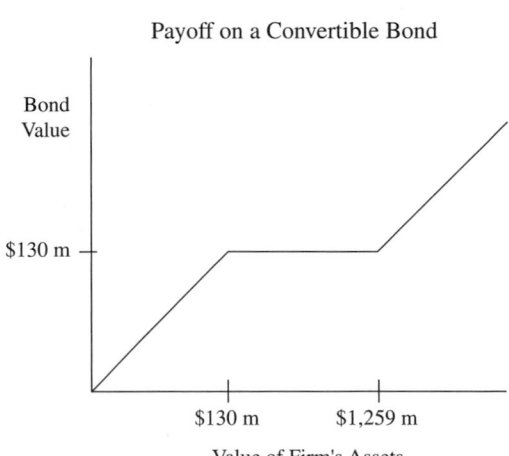

Value of Firm's Assets

---

[11]The number of shares per bond is determined by dividing the par value of the bond, $1,000, by the conversion price, $55.938 per share.

[12]Lovejoy's calculation assumed that the convertible-bond issue was completed and that the fully diluted number of shares was 22,516,946—this assumes that all options on the company's shares were exercised and that the 4½s had converted. Using the exercise price of the 4½s ($55.938 per share) as the break-even price and multiplying by the total number of shares gives a value of the firm at $1.259 billion. If there were any other debt outstanding (e.g., senior debt), it would need to be added to the base of capital used in this break-even calculation. In comparison, on January 24, 1994, the market value of the firm was about $776 million.

chalkboard, she modified her diagram of the payoff on a risky straight bond to reflect the conversion to equity when the asset value of the firm rose above $1.26 billion. Referring to this, she told Pao,

> Just as I said we have to be credit analysts to assess the "kink" on the lower end of the payoff diagram, this shows that we need to be *equity analysts* to assess the "kink" on the higher end of the diagram. In theory, the volatility estimate we use in the option-pricing model should be all the equity analysis we need. But in reality, we need to arrive at our own assessment of the desirability and timing of converting the bond to shares.
>
> For instance, given the rate of growth of Boston Chicken, the probability could be high that the bonds are converted to shares rather soon. As a practical matter, this may not be a 10-year bond. To illustrate, consider that Boston Chicken forecasts growing from 288 stores today to 993 stores in three years—roughly a factor of four times. Merrill Lynch has forecasted the firm's annual growth rate in EPS at 40 percent,[13] Alex Brown & Sons has forecasted a 50 percent annual growth rate.[14] Some analysts believe that Boston Chicken will earn $0.40 per share in 1994. What do you think the Boston Chicken shares will be worth at the end of 1996? If this forecast is realized, is early conversion likely?

> **Pao's seventh task:** Decide how likely will be voluntary conversion by 1996. Hint: Using an appropriate multiple, assess the value of shares in 1996.

VALUING THE COMPANY'S EARLY REDEMPTION OPTION

Lovejoy observed that the terms of the bond allowed the company to "call," or redeem, the bond issue before maturity. To redeem a bond was to repay it.

Lovejoy   If this were a straight bond, the redemption provision would give the issuer flexibility to repay the bond early, from cash or possibly by refunding the bond by issuing another bond and using the cash proceeds to repay this bond. The *company* owns this option, not the bondholder. The company is "long" a call; the bondholder is "short" a call.

This means that from our standpoint as investors, this particular embedded option reduces the value of the bond to us. To see this, just focus on the value of the bond as interest rates vary. Suppose that interest rates decline, in which case the issuer could truly expropriate investor's value by buying in the bonds at prices well below their market value. Graphically, the value of a

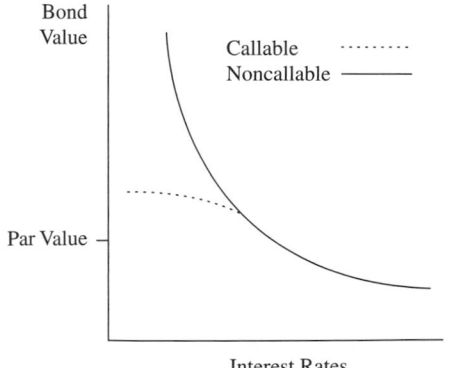

Value of Callable and Noncallable Bonds

---

[13]P. H. Oakes, "Boston Chicken, Inc.—Company Report," Merrill Lynch Capital Markets, December 21, 1993.

[14]S. Rockwell, "Boston Chicken—Company Report," Alex Brown & Sons, Inc., December 16, 1993.

callable bond as interest rates vary looks like this. With a noncallable bond, as yields decline, the bond value rises. But with callable bonds, the increase in price "tops out" because of the expectation that the issuer will exercise the option to refund the bond with cheaper debt. The difference between the dashed and solid lines is a gain for the stockholders of the firm at the expense of the bondholders. The value of the option to redeem accounts for the probability of this wealth transfer.

Lovejoy explained that in the case of convertible bonds, *redemption provision* was a confusing misnomer, for it suggested that the issuer would use this provision to repay the bonds early *with cash.* She noted that with the low coupons of most convertible bonds, cash redemption almost never made sense.[15] Instead, redemption provisions had a different purpose: to permit the issuer to *force the conversion* of the bonds into common stock.[16] Of course, this only occurred when the conversion option was "in the money."[17]

Lovejoy   Without being forced to convert to stock by some threat of redemption, I *might* continue to hold the convertible bond even if the option is in the money. As long as the annual cash flow I receive is higher on the bond than the dividends on the underlying stock, it will make sense for me to hold the bond. Since Boston Chicken pays no dividend, I would continue to hold the bond until just before maturity. The company wants to induce me to make the conversion, so it threatens to redeem the bond at par, which at that point would be less than its market value. From my standpoint, being forced to do anything is a negative. Therefore, the value of this redemption provision has to reduce the value of the bond.

Pao   The redemption terms look pretty complicated. For the first two years, early redemption is not possible. Then, for the next year, redemption is possible only if the stock price exceeds 140 percent of the exercise price, or $78.31. Then, for years 4 through 10, the company may redeem the issue between 103 and 100 percent of par value. I don't know how to begin valuing that option.

Lovejoy   Indeed, valuing redemption provisions is usually so complicated that we have to model it precisely to get an estimate. The careful approaches are to model the exact terms of redemption using a custom-designed binomial option pricing model or to use a numerical approach like Monte Carlo simulation. The main reason for this complexity

---

[15]With a low coupon rate, interest rates would have to fall dramatically in order for it to be economically attractive to refund the bond with another, even lower, coupon issue, or to use interest-generating cash to repay the bond.

[16]Rapidly growing companies often force conversion in order to expand their base of equity capital as a foundation for greater debt financing. Creditors usually make lending decisions on the basis of conventional definitions of debt and equity. The conventional definitions may ignore economic reality. An in-the-money convertible bond trades like, and is economically similar to, common equity. From this standpoint, forced conversion to expand the borrowing capacity of the firm is unnecessary window dressing. Nevertheless, very few issuers of convertible bonds permit them to run their full term as debt.

[17]The fact that bond investors usually need to be "forced" to convert in-the-money convertible bonds is one of the interesting paradoxes in finance. This paradox is not explained by the difference between coupon rates and dividend rates—even after the dividend-equivalent cash flow on a bond rises higher than the coupon cash flow, bondholders will still tend not to convert voluntarily. The only explanation is that convertible bondholders are not particularly alert to investment strategies in these instruments.

is that the likelihood that the firm will call the bond early depends on *two* key drivers: interest rates and stock prices.[18] No off-the-rack option pricing model exists to model an option with two sources of variability, and with a complex exercise.

Pao   Uh . . . so what do we do now?

Lovejoy   Well, at this stage, I'm mainly interested in solving for the implied value of the redemption provision. Once we know the values of the other pieces of this bond, we can determine what is the implied value of the redemption provision.

PUTTING IT ALL TOGETHER

Lovejoy   So, Pao have we found all the embedded options in the bond?

Pao   What about the "overallotment option" mentioned in the terms? Shouldn't we reflect that in the valuation too?

Lovejoy   No. It's an option agreement between Boston Chicken and the underwriters, not between the issuer and investors. It *would* affect the number of shares outstanding, which would affect the dilution calculations in the conversion option. You could rerun your numbers using the larger number of shares with the overallotment option, but for now, let's just stick with the base-case assumption of a $130 million bond issue.

Pao   What about this "change in control" provision? It says that the investors have the right to repurchase the bonds at par if control changes.

Lovejoy   Very good! You've found another option. This is what is called a "poison put." It protects the bondholder against someone buying the company and loading it up with debt, in which case the value of the convertible bonds would decline. Like the redemption provision, this option is also difficult to value. But let's assume that because the managers are growth-oriented and own a large percentage of equity in this company, a change of control is pretty unlikely. Therefore, I'll assume that the value of this option is very small.

Pao   Is the issue really $130 million? It says in the terms that the *net* proceeds will be $126 million—shouldn't that be the figure we use in all our calculations?

Lovejoy   No. From our standpoint as investors, we paid $130 million for securities, and that's the benchmark against which we should value this issue.

Pao   These bits and pieces of value sure get confusing. Where do we go with all of this?

Lovejoy   Well, let's put them all in the framework that we started with. Here, let me modify my initial model, and you write in the values you found underneath. How big are the various components? What drives the value of each? Also, summarize for me where you think are the biggest guesses or leaps of assumption.

> **Pao's eighth task:** Sum the parts and estimate the implied value of the redemption option.

---

[18]It is rational for the issuer to call the bond if the redemption price of the bond is less than either its "bond equivalent value" (i.e., present value of principal and interest) or its "equity equivalent value" (current stock price times conversion ratio of the bond). Interest rates determine bond equivalent value. Stock prices determine equity equivalent value. To complicate matters, interest rates and stock prices are correlated. This correlation should be modeled in a careful estimate of the redemption option.

$$V_{\text{Boston Chicken } 4\frac{1}{2}s} = V_{\text{Straight bond}} + V_{\text{Conversion option}} - V_{\text{Redemption option}}$$

$$\underline{\hspace{2cm}} = \underline{\hspace{2cm}} + \underline{\hspace{2cm}} - \underline{\hspace{1cm}?\hspace{1cm}}$$

Lovejoy   Oh. One last question. An options trader once told me that investing in options was actually "trading on risk." That is, traders don't think in terms of prices so much as they think in terms of the volatilities implied by the prices. If the volatility is greater than they think it should be, the trader

> **Pao's ninth task:** Develop an attitude on Boston Chicken volatilities, and make a recommendation.

shorts the option. If smaller, the trader goes long. Why do they think this way? What relevance does it have for our decision about investing in the Boston Chicken 4⅛s? And what is your rough-cut recommendation—should we invest?

EXHIBIT 1   Summary of Terms of the Offering

Debentures offered	$130 million principal amount of 4 1/2% convertible subordinated debentures due February 1, 2004.
Pricing	The debentures will be offered for sale at par value.
Interest payment dates	February 1 and August 1, commencing August 1, 1994.
Conversion rights	The debentures are convertible into shares of common stock at any time prior to maturity or redemption at a conversion price of $55.938 per share, or 17.88 shares per $1,000 bond. If all bonds were converted, this issue would create 2,324,400 new shares.
Optional redemption by company	The debentures are not redeemable prior to February 1, 1996. Thereafter, the debentures are redeemable at any time and from time to time at the option of the company, at redemption prices plus accrued interest. Between February 1, 1996, and February 1, 1997, the debentures cannot be redeemed unless the closing price of the common stock equals or exceeds 140% of the conversion price for 20 trading days. In 1996, the redemption price will be 103.6 percent of the principal amount of the bonds. From 1997 to 2004, the redemption price will decline ratably to 100 percent.
Change in control	Upon a change in control, holders of the debentures have the right to require the company to purchase all or any part of their debentures at the principal amount plus accrued interest.
Subordination	The debentures are subordinated to all existing and future senior indebtedness of the company. As of December 26, 1993, the company had no senior debt.
Use of proceeds	The company intends to use the net proceeds from this offering primarily for store development, including purchasing real estate in the Philadelphia area.
Underwriters	Merrill Lynch & Co., Alex. Brown & Sons. These two firms were the underwriters for the company's IPO in November 1993.
Underwriting discount	The company will receive the gross proceeds of the offering less an underwriting discount of 2.75%. Under the terms of this discount, the gross proceeds, underwriting discount, and net proceeds to the company will be $130,000,000, $3,575,000, and $126,425,000.
Overallotment option	The company has granted the underwriters an option to purchase up to an additional $19,500,000 in principal amount of debentures on the same terms per debenture solely to cover overallotments, if any. If such option is exercised in full, the gross proceeds, underwriting discount, and net proceeds to the company will be $149,500,000, $4,111,250, and $143,388,750, respectively.

Source: Prospectus, Boston Chicken, Inc., January 25, 1994.

EXHIBIT 2   Summary Information, Historical Financial Performance of Boston Chicken (in millions of dollars, except per share amounts)

| | Fiscal Years Ended December 31 | | | | | October 3, |
	1988	*1989*	*1990*	*1991*	*1992*	*1993 (40 weeks)*
Revenue						
Company-owned stores	$ —	$ 981	$2,939	$ 3,865	$ 5,656	$ 20,241
Royalties and franchise fees	—	87	476	1,375	2,627	7,990
Total	—	1,068	3,415	5,240	8,283	28,231
Costs						
Cost of products sold	—	392	1,286	1,429	2,242	7,671
Salaries and benefits	44	646	1,813	2,872	7,111	10,651
General and administrative	68	983	1,666	2,696	4,818	8,657
Provision for loss on store closings	—	—	—	834	423	833
Income						
Income (loss) from operations	(112)	(953)	(1,350)	(2,591)	(6,311)	419
Net income (loss)	(98)	(929)	(1,304)	(2,568)	(5,851)	263
Earnings per share	$(0.01)	$(0.12)	$ (0.15)	$ (0.27)	$ (0.41)	$ 0.04
Store data						
Systemwide revenue	$—	$2,825	$8,162	$20,752	$42,654	$101,128
Number of company-operated stores	—	2	4	5	19	25
Number of franchise-operated stores	—	2	10	29	64	142
Total number of stores	—	4	14	34	83	167
Balance sheet data						*
Working capital	$ 956	$ 478	$ 68	$ 1,134	$ 7,816	$ 3,399
Total assets	1,003	1,638	2,852	5,607	22,670	68,155
Long-term debt	—	—	—	—	—	28,769
Stockholders' equity	993	1,259	1,191	3,006	17,037	29,289

*Balance sheet data as of October 3, 1993, do not reflect the effect of initial public offering and conversion of convertible debt that occurred November 16, 1993.

Source: Offering prospectus, Boston Chicken, Inc., January 25, 1994.

EXHIBIT 3 Analytical Ratios on Comparable Convertible Bonds

Ratio	Indication	Boston Chicken 4½s 2004 Rated CCC/B3	Adv. Medical 7¼s, 2002 Rated CCC−	Cellular Comm. 8⅜s, 2000 Rated CCC+	Datapoint 8⅞s, 2006 Rated CCC	Orbital Sciences, 6¾s, 2003 Rated CCC+
Yield to maturity	Return from principal and interest only	4.5%	24.81%	2.0%	12.15%	1.71%
Bond price (for $1,000 par value)	Current quote	$1,000 (par)	$400	$1,562.50	$795	$1,426.50
Conversion ratio = $1,000/Conversion Price	Number of shares to be received in exchange for $1,000 par value of bond	17.88	55.13	69.44	55.231	69.656
Market conversion price, also called **conversion parity** = (Market price of bond)/(Conversion ratio)	The price at which the stock must sell to equal the current bond price. Also, the price that an investor *effectively* pays for the common stock. This is based on market, not par, value.	$55.938	$7.375	$22.625	$14.375	$20.625
Current share price		$44.75	$1.44	$22.50	$5.875	20.50
Market conversion premium ratio = Market conversion price*/Current market price	The "mark-up" of exercise price over current stock price	25%	412%	1%	145%	1%
Premium payback period or **break-even time** = Market conversion premium per share divided by Favorable income differential/Share*	Time it takes to recover the premium per share	4.45 years	4.51 years	0.11 year	5.29 years	0.13 year
Premium over straight value = Market price of the CV bond*/ Straight value of bond	Extent of "downside risk" between the current price, and the bond-only "floor"	93%	nil	100%	9%	118%

*The dollar conversion premium per share is the exercise price per share minus the current market price per share of stock. The favorable income differential per share is equal to [Coupon interest from bond − (Conversion ratio × Dividend per share)]/Conversion ratio.

Source: Standard & Poor's *S&P Bond Guide,* January 1994, and casewriter analysis. Reprinted by permission of Standard & Poor's, a division of The McGraw-Hill Companies.

EXHIBIT 4 Sample of Comparable "Straight" Bonds

Issuer	Rating	Matures	Yield to Maturity
Baltimore Bancorp	CCC+	1999	11.11%
Burlington Motor	CCC+	2003	11.67
Calmar Spraying Sys.	CCC+	1999	14.48
Collins & Aikman	CCC+	2001	11.49
Cullum Companies	CCC+	1998	12.50
Horsehead Invs. Inc.	CCC−	1999	16.88
Nortek, Inc.	CCC	1997	13.22
NWA, Inc.	CCC	1996	12.57
PCPI Funding	CCC+	1998	13.88
Pilgrim's Pride Corp.	CCC+	2003	10.74
Trans World Airlines	CCC+	1998	18.43
World Corp.	CCC−	1997	13.86
Mean			13.40%
Median			12.90%
Standard deviation			2.33%

Source: Standard & Poor's *Bond Guide,* January 1994.

EXHIBIT 5 Financial Information on Peer Companies

Name	Number of Units	1993 Revs. ($ mil.)	Opng. Margin (%)	Net Margin (%)	Expected EPS Growth (%)	Price/ Earnings	Market/ Book	Debt/ Capital (%)	Beta	Volatility
Applebee's Second largest casual dining chain in the United States	475	117.1	16.1	8.3	31.0	36.5	6.4	3	1.45	.47
Au Bon Pain Bakery cafés	200	123	15.0	5.2	18.0	42.4	3.6	50	1.66	.47
Bertucci's Gourmet pizza restaurants	50	74.6	16.0	8.0	12.0	41.0	16.4	15	1.31	.60
Bob Evans Farms Runs family-style restaurants and makes pork products	292	700	14.0	7.1	13.5	19.2	2.9	0	.95	.23
Brinker International Operates a portfolio of theme restaurant chains for casual dining	366	653	16.7	7.5	23.5	33.7	6.6	1	1.35	.31
Luby's Cafeterias Chain of cafeterias	168	368	19.1	9.7	12.5	16.6	2.7	0	.85	.26
McDonald's Corp.	12,418	7,408	33.0	14.6	13.5	18.7	3.7	37	1.05	.21
Morrison Restaurants Runs chains of cafeterias and casual restaurants	426	1,099	8.8	3.5	15.0	19.2	3.9	3	1.00	.32
Perkins Family Restaurants Targets budget-conscious family market	422	218	14.5	7.8	10.5	10.6	2.8	34	.70	.17
Ryan's Family Steak Houses Family-style steakhouse restaurants	221	397	17.3	7.2	18.0	13.6	1.8	0	1.30	.31
Wendy's International Third largest chain of fast-food hamburger restaurants	3,962	1,320	14.5	6.0	20.0	20.7	3.0	29	1.10	.20

Sources: *Value Line Investment Survey*, March 25, 1994 (all information except volatilities). Volatilities are from *Bloomberg Business News*.

EXHIBIT 6 Capital Market Conditions, on or about January 24, 1994

Yields on U.S. Treasuries	
3-month	2.96%
1-year	3.51
3-year	4.44
5-year	5.05
7-year	5.38
10-year	5.74
20-year	6.35
30-year	6.29

Yields on Corporates, by Rating	
Aaa	6.80%
Aa	7.06
A	7.27
Baa	7.63

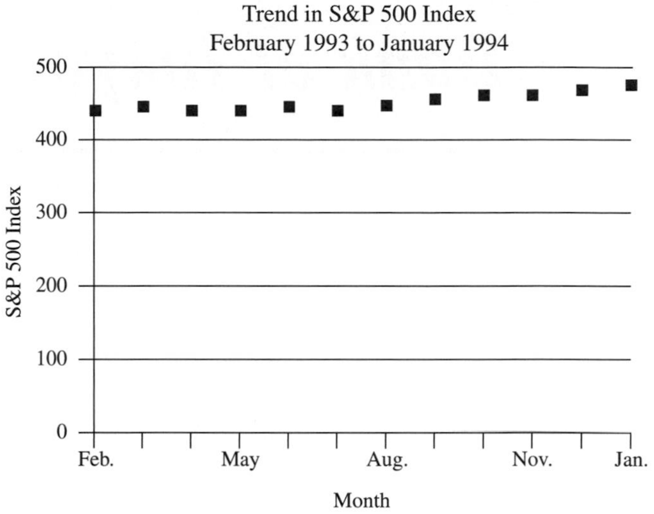
Trend in S&P 500 Index
February 1993 to January 1994
500
400
300
200
100
0
S&P 500 Index
Feb.
May
Aug.
Nov.
Jan.
Month

Sources: *Federal Reserve Bulletin, The Wall Street Journal,* and *Moody's Bond Record.*

Bank of Tokyo

In October 1990, Tasuku Takagaki, recently appointed president of the Bank of Tokyo (BOT), wrestled with the first major challenge of his presidency: achieving a capital structure for the bank that would meet the capital-adequacy standards set by the Bank for International Settlements (BIS). BIS required that all banks engaged in international banking maintain a 7.25 percent capital/asset ratio by the end of the fiscal year 1991. The standards were imposed on all banks by governmental agreement in 1988 and would be in effect at the end of BOT's current fiscal year, March 1991. Failure to meet the standards would trigger restrictions in BOT's ability to engage in international banking activities. The massive paper losses incurred by the Bank of Tokyo, however, primarily a result of the downturn in the stock market, had dropped its ratio from a solid 8.0 percent in March 1990 to 6.8 percent by the semiannual book closing in September 1990.

To conform to the BIS standards, Mr. Takagaki could respond in one or more of the following ways:

Limit asset growth, the denominator of the capital/assets ratio, by restraining lending activity. Mr. Takagaki preferred increasing BOT's capital, the numerator, through a new issue so as not to restrain growth.

Issue ¥60 billion of common stock. Common stock was the purest form of capital from the BIS's standpoint and would contribute significantly to the perception of solidity. However, Mr. Takagaki questioned whether the time was right to sell shares. The year 1990 had been characterized as the year of the "bursting of the bubble economy" in the Japanese financial industry. By October 1990, the Nikkei 225 index (leading shares on the Tokyo stock exchange) had plunged 48 percent from its all-time high

---

This case was written by Michael J. Schill under the direction of Professor Robert F. Bruner as a basis for class discussion rather than to illustrate effective or ineffective handling of an administrative situation. Copyright © 1992 by the University of Virginia Darden School Foundation, Charlottesville, VA, and INSEAD, Fontainebleau, France. All rights reserved. *No part of this publication may be reproduced, stored in a retrieval system, used in a spreadsheet, or transmitted in any form or by any means—electronic, mechanical, photocopying, recording, or otherwise—without the permission of the Darden Foundation. For inquiries, please send an e-mail to dardencases@virginia.edu.* Version 1.3.

reached on the last day of 1989. At its current share price of ¥1,050, BOT would need to sell 57.142 million shares. With 1,993,933,000 shares outstanding, the old shareholders' interest in BOT would be diluted 2.8 percent.

Issue ¥60 billion of convertible subordinated bonds. Equity-linked bonds had been a favorite form of financing for Japanese firms since the mid-1980s. The conventional view was that they permitted shares to be sold at a higher price than prevailed at present, and carried a lower coupon rate. Some observers were skeptical of these benefits and pointed to difficulties issuers had encountered when their bonds did not convert. Because of the equity-market downturn, Mr. Takagaki was worried that the demand for such issues was limited. He speculated, however, that being the first bank to float securities in the current capital markets might help maximize the value of the issue. The financial staff of the bank was studying a possible issue of five-year notes convertible at 2.5 percent over the current stock price of ¥1,050. The coupon rate and bond price had yet to be determined.

Mr. Takagaki wondered what the cost of the funds obtained from this convertible would be and how it would compare with the cost of common stock, which even at the current depressed prices had a low dividend yield. Should he consider other possible terms? How did the convertible bond compare with an issue of warrant bonds, an extremely popular form of financing for Japanese companies? What were the strengths and weaknesses of convertibles versus bonds with warrants? Were any other advantages and disadvantages associated with a convertible-bond issue that he should take into account?

Whatever he decided, Mr. Takagaki wished to move quickly. The capital markets were still unsettled—the Nikkei fell 40 percent in September. On October 1, 1990, the Nikkei index briefly fell below the psychological barrier of 20,000 and then recovered. The apparent stability of the Nikkei in the few weeks that followed gave financial planners some breathing room, but the underlying weaknesses in the market had not subsided.

JAPANESE BANKING INDUSTRY

The Japanese banks steadily built their global presence throughout the post–World War II era. By 1970, 4 Japanese banks ranked in the world's top 20 banks based on total assets in dollars. By 1980, the Japanese banks boasted 6 in the world's top 20. Over the course of the 1980s, Japanese banks suddenly emerged as the world's dominant financial leaders in terms of global mass and resources. By the end of the decade, Japan's largest banks had achieved a spectacular compound growth rate of over 17 percent and represented 8 of the largest 10 banks in the world, as shown in Exhibit 1. Observers attributed much of this record to six factors:

1. *Growth in the manufacturing sector.* A major share of the banking-sector growth could be linked to the dramatic global success of the Japanese manufacturing sector. Japanese banks followed their clients around the world as Americans and Europeans did more business with Japanese firms.

2. *Appreciation of the yen.* A portion of the shift in size resulted from decisions made in New York City's Plaza Hotel in 1985. A meeting of the Group of Seven (G-7)[1] finance ministers made an accord collectively to reduce the value of the U.S. dollar in foreign-exchange markets. The results of the actions vaulted the yen from an average dollar exchange rate of ¥239 in 1985 to ¥128 in 1988. This appreciation of the yen was an important factor in the ability of Japanese banks to make large dollar-denominated investments in real estate and company acquisitions.

3. *Advantageous cost of capital.* From 1980 to February 1987, the Bank of Japan, Japan's central bank, consistently lowered Japan's discount rate, from 9.0 percent to 2.5 percent. The banks were able to use these comparatively low interest rates to raise inexpensive capital. Moreover, interest-rate regulation allowed banks to pay very low interest on bank deposits.

4. *Bullish stock market.* Two structural factors linked Japanese lending capacity directly to changes in the stock market. First, because of the significant cross-ownership within Japanese *keiretsu* relationships, banks maintained large investments in equity securities. The second factor was the BIS agreement to Japanese demands that a bank be allowed to recognize a portion of unrealized gains on stock holdings in the banks' capital calculation. Consequently, when large securities holdings increased in value, Japanese banks were able to generate loans backed by the unrealized gains applied to their capital base. Exhibit 2 shows the rise of the Nikkei versus the other major world markets over the late 1980s. This bull market generated vast capital gains, which could then be leveraged to create loans at the ratio of over 12 to 1.

5. *Appreciating real estate values.* The Japanese philosophy was that the price of real estate would never decrease. This traditional belief had long convinced most Japanese that land ownership provided a riskless asset. Moreover, in step with the cash generated during the prosperous 1980s, land prices soared. Banks loaned against land values; lenders then used the cash to invest further in the rising stock market and real estate market; the increase in the land value provided more backing for further lending; and the speculative cycle continued. Although the U.S. land area was 25 times larger than that of Japan in 1990, the Japanese total land value of ¥20 trillion was 4 times the total U.S. land value. By March 31, 1990, Japanese property-backed loans had increased to 23 percent of the city banks' (Tokyo financial-center banks') total loans.[2]

6. *Deregulation of the Japanese financial system.* Even though the banking and securities businesses were separated by law in Japan (as in the United States), Japanese banks had gained experience in universal banking in foreign markets beyond the Ministry of Finance's control. The Ministry of Finance was studying reforms to abolish the barriers between commercial banks, trust banks, and securities houses, moreover, and the proposed reforms were expected by 1993.

---

[1]The Group of Seven nations were the United States, Canada, Japan, France, Britain, Germany, and Italy.

[2]David Lake, *Japanese Capital—How Corporations Tap the World's Largest Liquidity Pool,* Special Report No. P333 (London: The Economist Intelligence Unit, Business International Limited, February 1992).

CRASH OF THE JAPANESE STOCK MARKET

While the Nikkei average was approaching 40,000 during the latter part of 1989, underlying macroeconomic factors were undermining the buoyancy of the market. The Bank of Japan had already demonstrated its concern over rising inflation through back-to-back discount-rate hikes, from 2.50 percent to 3.75 percent, in May and October 1989. The increases in interest rates were particularly damaging to the banks because of the deregulation of interest rates previously mentioned. Even though banks were increasingly required to pay higher market rates on deposits, the banks maintained their low lending rates in order to hold or gain market share, even at near 0 percent spreads.[3]

In early December 1989, Yasushi Mieno was asked to assume the position of governor of the Bank of Japan, and he communicated his determination to shrink the speculative bubble in the stock market. Within one week of his appointment, he announced the third increase of the discount rate, to 4.25 percent. The repeated, unexpected discount-rate increases stunned short-term lenders, who reacted immediately with higher yields. The bond-market yields remained unchanged.

The interest-rate instability was accompanied by political instability created by worry that the long-ruling Liberal Democratic Party would lose its majority in the February 1990 elections. In the early months of 1990, the market remained jittery in anticipation of the election and further expected hikes in the discount rate; bond yields finally increased to meet the short-term rates.

When the election votes were counted on February 18, the Liberal Democratic Party had achieved a landslide victory in the House of Representatives and managed better than expected in the lower house. Analysts expected the results to send the yen and the Nikkei up. The appreciation of the yen never materialized, however, and when the Tokyo stock market closed February 19, the Nikkei was down. Within one week, the Nikkei dropped 5,000 points—a 14 percent drop from its peak level. A month later, Governor Mieno upped the discount rate another full 100 basis points; the market continued in a downward spiral through April. A rebound in the early summer brought the Nikkei back to a steady 32,000.

Hopes that the market would make a quick recovery were dashed in August with the invasion of Kuwait by Iraq. The resulting global bear market had a doubling impact in Tokyo as the Bank of Japan raised the discount rate again on August 30 to 6.0 percent. To make matters worse, Daiwa Securities was found guilty of compensating losses incurred by preferred clients. The Sumitomo Bank chairman, Ichiro Isoda, accepted responsibility for illegal speculative lending activities by both a local branch and through direct support of a speculative real estate client, and announced his resignation. On October 1, 1990, the Nikkei dropped below 20,000, 48 percent below its peak eight months previously. This drop represented a paper-value loss of ¥300 trillion,[4] or 70 percent of Japan's 1990 gross domestic product.

---

[3]A lending "spread" was the difference between the interest rate charged by the bank to its customer and the bank's own cost of funds.

[4]Christopher Wood, "A Survey of Japanese Finance," *The Economist,* December 8, 1990.

CAPITAL ADEQUACY: BIS CAPITAL RATIOS

In July 1988, the Banking Regulations and Supervisory Practices committee of the Bank for International Settlements in Basel, Switzerland, adopted a set of capital-adequacy guidelines to reduce the sources of competitive inequality in the international banking industry. The original framework was devised jointly by the banking authorities in the United Kingdom and United States in January 1987. Banking regulators from each of the Group of Ten (G-10), as well as Luxembourg and Switzerland, having reviewed and approved the proposal, had the measure ratified within their home countries.

The regulation required all banks involved in international transactions to exceed a minimum capital-to-asset ratio based on two different estimates of capital and a risk-adjusted asset calculation.[5] Exhibit 3 displays the comparative BIS ratios for the major Japanese banks.

Although the BIS could not enforce restrictions on the international banking activities of banks that were unable to meet the requirement, banks were compelled to clear the hurdles in order to maintain goodwill within the banking community. In 1987, as the proposal was first being considered, Japanese banks awoke to the important impact the BIS regulations would have on their financing. Based on prior-year financial statements, the average capital ratio of Japanese banks, 2.7 percent, was far below the 7.25 percent required rate. The Japanese banks pleaded that they were as stable as banks that met the requirement because of their operations, Japanese interbank support, and the Bank of Japan's protection. The Ministry of Finance (MOF) refused the Japanese bank arguments and demanded full adherence to the BIS guideline. By December 1988, the MOF had set a new capital-ratio requirement in line with BIS regulation.

The BIS believed that its regulation created much more equitable competition in the international banking industry than in the past. The existence of an international standard promoted better regulatory and commercial monitoring of banks' soundness. The emphasis on Tier 1 capital required banking operations to focus on profitability rather than volume. The risk-adjustment calculation discouraged excessive high-risk lending and off-balance-sheet exposure.

Faced with grossly deficient capital ratios in the late 1980s, the Japanese banks had two alternatives to prepare for the 1991 deadline. First, they could reduce their asset bases by

---

[5]The BIS required capital to back assets only in proportion to their relative risk. Tests of capital adequacy required calculating three quantities. *Tier 1 ("core") capital* was defined as retained earnings, common stock, qualifying noncumulative perpetual preferred stock, and minority interests, *less* goodwill. *Tier 2 ("supplementary") capital* included preferred stock, hybrid capital instruments, subordinated debt, and 45 percent of unrealized gains on marketable securities. Tier 2 capital was restricted to a maximum of 100 percent of Tier 1 capital. *Risk-adjusted assets:* all bank assets were assigned to one of four risk categories. Then the sum of each category was assigned a risk rating. For example, cash was assigned to the least risky category and received a risk weighting of 0 percent, meaning that none of the cash balance was required to be backed by capital. Loans to private corporations were assigned to the most risky category; their full value had to be backed by capital. Moreover, off-balance-sheet items that also increased claims on the bank's capital were added to the BIS asset calculation.

The BIS regulation required banks to meet two standards, to be phased in over two years. By March 1991, the minimum acceptable capital ratios would be 3.25 percent Tier 1 capital to risk-adjusted assets and 7.25 percent Tiers 1 and 2 capital to risk-adjusted assets. In March 1993, the respective minimum ratios would rise to 4 and 8 percent.

slowing lending activities or by selling their large investments in the ownership of client companies (through *keiretsu* cross-ownership patterns). Second, the banks could raise Tier 1 capital through common equity issues or Tier 2 capital through issues of common stock, preferred stock, or subordinated debt.

The near trebling of the Nikkei 225 from 13,083 (end of 1985) to 38,916 (end of 1989) provided Japanese banks with the opportunity to raise all the required capital. Over the course of these three years, the 13 city banks issued ¥6 trillion in equity and equity-related financing.[6] In addition, Tier 2 capital was automatically increased through the ballooning of unrealized capital gains on the banks' security holdings. By March 1990, one year ahead of schedule, almost all of the banks were well above the 7.25 percent requirement.

The collapse of the Tokyo stock market reversed both effects; unrealized gains shrank, and investor demand for new securities issues ebbed. In April 1990, the Ministry of Finance froze all new issues of both equity and debt in order to avoid further depression of the equity market. (The MOF was particularly worried that large life-insurance companies would dump their equity holdings in search of the new subordinated-debt issues.)

In June the ban on subordinated issues was eased. Over the summer, Japanese banks issued ¥2 trillion of subordinated debt at an uncomfortable 8.4 percent. Contrary to the spirit of the BIS regulations, however, many of these new issues were completed by subtle agreements between the banks and buyers. The banks loaned the necessary funds to their clients in order to allow them to purchase the banks' debt issue.

Nevertheless, by September 1990, all of the city banks except Kyowa Bank were still below the 7.25 percent ratio. The deficiency came primarily from the requirement that 50 percent of the total capital come from Tier 1 capital. Additional subordinated debt was effective only at increasing Tier 2 capital. After further decline of the Nikkei in September, the Ministry of Finance, believing that the market had reached bottom at 24,000, lifted the restriction on equity issues. Exhibit 3 shows the September 1990 status of city banks' capital ratios.

BANK OF TOKYO

Founded in 1946 as the successor to the Yokahama Specie Bank, the Bank of Tokyo was granted the exclusive right to specialize in international finance. The bank used this opportunity to build Japan's most extensive international network, with over 250 overseas offices. Although the Ministry of Finance had later granted foreign-exchange licenses to the other city banks, the BOT continued to maintain Japan's largest share of foreign-exchange volume. The BOT also acted as the agent for all government or government-guaranteed bonds.

The BOT considered itself a "global service banker." It made a concerted effort to meet international-client needs through the most extensive network and internationally seasoned staff of any Japanese bank. The success of this strategy was seen in its profits, 70 percent of which were generated beyond Japanese shores. The BOT was also the largest lender among Japanese banks to debtor nations. Exhibit 4 provides peer comparisons for the BOT.

The company's president, Tasuku Takagaki, had joined the BOT at age 25 after receiving a degree at Tokyo University. By 1963, he was assistant manager at the New York agency and later became general manager of the International Investment Division and

---

[6]Wood, "A Survey of Japanese Finance."

resident director for Europe. After six years as director of the head office, Mr. Takagaki was asked to assume the bank's presidency in June 1990.[7]

The BOT was different from the other 12 city banks in five key areas: (1) the majority of the firm's profits were generated abroad; (2) the BOT did not maintain a strong retail banking effort in Japan; in fact, the bank had three times the number of offices in California as it had in Japan; (3) because of its unique access to the debenture-issue market, the BOT maintained a much smaller portion of its assets in loans than the other banks; (4) the bank derived its income mostly from fees and commissions and bond and foreign-exchange trading rather than from interest income; and (5) the bank belonged to no *keiretsu* group and was thus free to do business with any of them.

Some believed that the BOT would not be competitive in the long run. Critics cited the BOT's inability to penetrate the large, lucrative Japanese retail banking market. In effect, while the BOT's competitors were beginning to squeeze it in the international market, the BOT had not successfully established itself in Japan. Furthermore, the BOT's high exposure to LDC debt[8] was almost twice the amount of any other bank. Nevertheless, even though Moody's had twice lowered the BOT's debt rating (from AAA to Aa2), the BOT still had a rating higher than almost any large American bank.

Rumors of a possible merger of the BOT with a bank with a stronger domestic business had spread throughout the financial community. The Industrial Bank of Japan and Mitsubishi Bank were most often cited as potential merger candidates.

Exhibit 5 summarizes the BOT's issues of financial securities over the recent years. It reveals a strong appetite for Euromarket financings and a shift toward issuing hybrid bonds in the 1987–89 period.

MARKET DIRECTION

Mr. Takagaki was particularly concerned over the future direction of the stock market. A quick recovery would heal most of the bank's current wounds. Continued decline at the pace endured in 1990 would spell disaster.

Japanese equity had long been trading at extraordinary multiples of earnings relative to other world markets. In the late 1980s, price/earnings (P/E) ratios had averaged over 60 times. By late 1990, the ratio had fallen to nearly 30 times but was still well above the U.S. average of 14 times. Although the shares of over 50 U.S. companies were listed for trading in Tokyo, they continued to be priced at American P/E levels,[9] and observers wondered whether the pricing disparity did not presage further declines in Japanese share prices.

One analyst at Nikko Securities countered that the causes of the P/E discrepancies were embedded in the accounting and economic structure of Japanese industry. By adjusting for such factors as depreciation rates, interlocking ownerships, and consolidations, he demon-

---

[7]*International Who's Who 1991–92,* 55th ed. (Europa Publications, Ltd.).

[8]LDC debt, loans to less-developed countries, was viewed as being riskier than sovereign or commercial loans to the industrially developed countries. In 1990, BOT's LDC loans outstanding amounted to ¥574 billion.

[9]Ted Fikre, "Equity Carve-Outs in Tokyo," *Federal Reserve Board of New York Quarterly Review,* Winter 1991, p. 60.

strated a decrease in Japanese P/E ratios to match the levels observed in other markets.[10] Furthermore, this analyst studied all the other Japanese stock-market declines of over 30 percent and concluded that a stock-market upturn would only begin when Japanese fiscal and monetary policy eased.[11]

THE USE OF EQUITY-LINKED SECURITIES

In the late 1980s, Japanese companies issued large volumes of Eurodollar convertible bonds or bonds with attached warrants in London. Given the already low interest rates on the bonds and the spectacular returns expected from the convertible portions of the issues arising from the increase in stock prices, investors were willing to accept very low coupon rates on the bonds. The payment exposure could then be swapped from a fixed-rate liability to a floating rate and from dollars into yen, which resulted in zero-to-negative cost of funds.

If the BOT were to issue convertible bonds now, the issue would be the first such issue in several months, well after the tail end of what had been a surge in convertibles and warrant bonds. The use of convertible-bond financing had dramatically dominated the volumes of straight corporate bonds issued, as the graph in Exhibit 6 indicates. Similarly, the new-issue volume in warrant bonds had grown from insignificant in 1985 to U.S. $70 billion in 1989. The bull market in warrant bonds peaked in March 1989 when three companies issued equity warrant packages of $1.5 billion each.

Both convertible bonds and warrant bonds would result in the release of new shares by the issuer. Although nominally both consisted of a call option and a straight bond, there were significant differences between the two:

Convertible bonds offered the option of exchanging the bond for shares at some conversion ratio, or conversion price. The option component and bond component were inseparable in these securities.

Warrant bonds offered the option of buying shares at a certain exercise price either by paying in cash or, in certain instances, by exchanging bonds. In these cases, the warrants were *detachable* and could be traded (and held) separately from the bonds. The theory behind these bonds was that they permitted the investor to enjoy fixed bond income and a capital gain simultaneously; the two returns were not mutually exclusive. Even though the bulk of these Japanese bonds[12] was issued in the Euromarkets, 70 to 80 percent of the warrants found their way into the hands of

---

[10]H. Takahashi, "The Sense of Overpricing on the Japanese Stock Market Gradually Subsides," *Nikko Monthly Report,* The Nikko Research Center, Ltd., October 25, 1990.

[11]H. Takahashi, "The Point at Which Stock Prices Will Bottom Out in the Correctional Phase," *Nikko Monthly Report,* The Nikko Research Center, Ltd., February 25, 1991.

[12]The issuance of convertibles and warrant bonds in the Euromarkets never gained great favor among corporations domiciled in other countries. In America and Britain, issuers had to account for dilution resulting from exercise of the warrants and therefore were discouraged from relying on hybrids; Japanese companies were not subject to such rules. In efficient markets, the presence or absence of reporting requirements regarding warrant dilution should be immaterial, but some observers believed that these rules have a material effect in the unregulated Euromarkets. (See, for instance, "Japan's Warrant Hangover," *The Economist,* September 8, 1990, p. 95.)

Japanese institutions and individuals.[13] Typically, the warrants were issued with an exercise price very close to the prevailing share price (usually only 2.5 percent higher) at the time of issue.

The allure these hybrid securities had for issuers lay in the belief that they represented a cheaper source of financing than either subordinated bonds or common stocks. If the issuer performed poorly, the option would not be exercised and the issuer would enjoy a lower-than-normal coupon rate. If the issuer performed well, the options would be exercised and the shares sold—at a higher price than prevailing when the bonds were issued.

Some observers believed that these hybrid securities offered remarkably low costs of funds, especially those issued near the peak of the stock-market cycle. In April 1989, Nomura Securities revealed that, taking into account currency-swap factors, the average current cost of funds issued would be 0.3 percent (which compared with 1.8 percent for an issue denominated in yen terms).[14] The lowest recorded coupon for a Japanese warrant bond was 0.875 percent in a June 1987 five-year issue by Tokyu Corporation. After swapping the proceeds, Tokyu realized a negative cost of funds (i.e., Tokyu was paid to issue the package). Coupon rates on convertible bonds could be even lower: In 1989, the Bank of Tokyo issued Swiss franc convertible notes with a coupon rate of 25 basis points. One journal commented, "At coupon levels up to 3 percent, Japanese issuers [of hybrid securities] are able to swap into yen funds at effectively no cost."[15]

Other analysts were not sure about this logic and questioned whether the advocates were making fair comparisons. Moreover, the advocates usually ignored the potential implications of a stock-market slump; one market-maker estimated that 80 percent of the warrants issued in warrant-bond deals were out of the money in early September 1990.[16] The implications were that investors would not exercise the warrants and thus not provide the cash with which the issuer could repay the bonds.

Similarly, regarding convertible bonds, one journal commented:

> Japan's banks were forbidden from issuing warrants by the Ministry of Finance. Instead they resorted to the next best thing: convertible bonds, which give investors the right to convert their loans into shares. The party may have been slightly different to the warrant issuers' one; the morning after looks almost as painful. Japan's 12 commercial city banks have issued some ¥2 trillion ($14 billion) of convertible bonds since 1987. Most of the bonds are denominated in Swiss francs and most will mature during the financial year beginning April 1991. The share prices of the banks have fallen so far below their conversion prices that it looks as if the banks will probably have to pay most of the money back. Finding ¥2 trillion will not be easy.[17]

---

[13]Richard Downes and Chris Elven, *Japanese Equity Warrants: A Clear and Comprehensive Guide* (London: Eurostudy Publishing, 1990), p. 23.

[14]The examples of Nomura Securities and Tokyu Corporation ignore the implicit cost of the option and focus wholly on the cost of the bond component.

[15]Quoted by Downes and Elven, *Japanese Equity Warrants,* p. 27, from *International Insider,* August 3, 1987.

[16]The market value of these warrants outstanding in September 1990 was $140 billion. Figures are taken from "Japan's Warrant Hangover," *The Economist,* September 8, 1990, p. 95.

[17]"More Trouble," *The Economist,* September 8, 1990, p. 96. © 1990 The Economist Newspaper Group, Inc. Reprinted with permission. Further reproduction prohibited.

One approach to valuing hybrid securities such as convertibles and warrant bonds was to estimate the value of the components (bond and option) separately and then sum the component values. Exhibit 7 presents estimates of volatility on BOT common stock. Exhibit 8 gives information on current yields to maturity of "straight" and convertible bonds issued by Japanese corporations. Exhibit 9 presents a summary of equity-investment information for the Bank of Tokyo and a forecast of performance. The BOT was currently paying dividends at the rate of ¥8 per year, to give a dividend yield of about 0.8 percent.

CONCLUSION

The BOT needed to raise roughly ¥60 billion by March to conform to the BIS regulations. Typically, the par value of each Japanese yen bond was ¥100,000. Reflecting on the success of the convertible-bond issues of the BOT and other firms, Mr. Takagaki wondered whether the current low level of the stock market might be an ideal time for a new five-year convertible-bond issue.

EXHIBIT 1 World's 20 Largest Banks in 1990 (dollars in millions)

Bank	Assets	Capital	Capital/ Assets	Pretax Profits	Profits/ Assets
1. Dai-Ichi Kangyo Bank	455,069	14,350	3.2%	2,136	0.5%
2. Mitsui Taiyo Kobe Bank	420,539	11,402	2.7	1,478	0.4
3. Sumitomo Bank	415,384	14,476	3.5	2,611	0.6
4. Fuji Bank	408,954	12,782	3.1	2,201	0.5
5. Sanwa Bank	398,674	12,407	3.1	2,276	0.6
6. Mitsubishi Bank	395,765	11,571	2.9	1,916	0.5
7. Industrial Bank of Japan	289,759	9,177	3.2	1,130	0.4
8. Crédit Agricole	273,204	11,784	4.3	1,428	0.5
9. Banque Nationale de Paris	261,269	7,065	2.7	1,036	0.4
10. Tokai Bank	256,951	7,313	2.8	750	0.3
11. Barclays Bank	246,025	11,051	4.5	1,334	0.5
12. Crédit Lyonnais	237,897	6,339	2.7	1,060	0.4
13. Deutsche Bank	229,787	9,615	4.2	2,364	1.0
14. Citicorp	227,084	7,317	3.2	1,538	0.7
15. Bank of Tokyo	**226,119**	**6,608**	**2.9**	**1,150**	**0.5**
16. National Westminster Bank	224,058	10,732	4.8	779	0.3
17. ABN-Amro Bank	208,882	8,011	3.8	1,147	0.5
18. Long-Term Credit Bank of Japan	196,527	7,266	3.7	825	0.4
19. Groupe des Caisses d'Epargne	172,307	5,843	3.4	707	0.4
20. Union Bank of Switzerland	167,079	12,495	7.5	1,072	0.6

Source: *The Banker.* Data on Japanese institutions are as of March 1990; other data are as of December 1989.

EXHIBIT 2   Changes in the Stock-Market Indexes of Major Countries

	1985	*1989*	*October 31, 1990*	*1985–89 Compound Annual Growth Rate*	*1989–90 Compound Annual Growth Rate*
Japan (Nikkei 225)	13,083	38,916	25,194	31%	−41%
United States (Dow Jones 30)	1,541	2,732	2,422	15	−13
United Kingdom (FT 100)	1,414	2,399	2,050	14	−17
Germany (FAZ)	626	741	622	4	−19

EXHIBIT 3   BIS Total Capital Ratios for Selected Japanese Banks

Bank	*March 1990*	*Sept. 1990*
Kyowa	8.8	7.5
Sanwa	8.5	7.2
Daiwa	8.4	7.1
Sumitomo	8.4	7.1
Mitsubishi	8.4	7.1
Saitama	8.3	7.1
Fuji	8.3	7.1
Hokkaido Takushoku	8.3	7.1
Dai-Ichi Kangyo	8.3	7.1
Long-Term Credit Bank	8.2	7.0
Bank of Tokyo	**8.0**	**6.8**
Industrial Bank of Japan	7.8	6.6
Tokai	7.8	6.6
Nippon Credit	7.3	6.2
Mitsui Taiyo Kobe	7.1	6.0

Source: James Capel, Inc., quoted in Christopher Wood, "A Survey of Japanese Finance," *The Economist,* December 8, 1990.

EXHIBIT 4 Information on Comparable Companies, 1990

Bank	Market Value/ Book Value	International Profits/ Total Profits	International Profit Margin	Operating Return on Assets	Costs as Percentage of Operating Revenues	Costs as Percentage of Assets
Dai-Ichi Kangyo	2.0	20.0%	0.4%	—	—	—
Mitsui Taiyo Kobe	1.6	14.8	0.5	—	—	—
Sumitomo	2.0	32.6	0.8	—	—	—
Fuji	2.0	23.3	0.6	—	—	—
Mitsubishi	1.8	27.2	0.6	—	—	—
Sanwa	1.8	27.4	0.7	—	—	—
Bank of Tokyo	**2.3**	**56.0%**	**1.0%**	**0.39%**	**58.9**	**0.39**
Composite average of other city banks	—	—	—	0.24%	64.7	0.60

Source: "Japanese Equity Research—City Banks," Salomon Brothers, March 5, 1992. Data in the three right-hand columns are as of March 1990; the rest of the data are as of September 1990.

EXHIBIT 5   History of Security Issuance

Year	Currency,* Amount	Rate and Type of Security
1985	C$ 75m	10 7/8s Eurobonds, 7-year
	U.S.$ 100m	11 1/4s Eurobonds, 10-year
	C$ 75m	10 7/8s Eurobonds, 10-year
	U.S.$ 100m	10 3/8s Eurobonds, 10-year
	C$ 60m	11s Eurobonds, 10-year
	U.S.$ 100m	Guaranteed floating-rate Euronotes, 12-year
1986	C$ 70m	10 1/2s Eurobonds, 10-year
	U.S.$ 100m	8 3/8s guaranteed Eurobonds, 10-year
	U.S.$ 100m	Zero-coupon guaranteed Eurobonds, 5-year
	Yen 15bn	6 1/8s Eurobonds, 7-year
	U.S.$ 50m	8 1/4s guaranteed deferred-coupon Eurobond, 5-year
	U.S.$ 100m	7 5/8s guaranteed Eurobonds, 7-year
	Yen 20bn	8 1/2s Eurobonds, 7-year
	U.S.$ 120m	8s Eurobonds, 7-year
1987	ItL 50bn	10 1/4s guaranteed Euronotes, 5-year
	DM 100m	5 3/4s guaranteed Eurobonds, 6-year
	U.S.$ 100m	1 3/4s convertible Eurobonds, 15-year
	SFr 100m	8 3/4s convertible Swiss notes, 5-year
	FFr 400m	Floating-rate Euronotes, 5-year
	ECU 70m	8 1/8s guaranteed Eurobonds, 5-year
1988	C$ 120m	8 1/2s guaranteed Eurobonds, 6-year
1989	U.S.$ 100m	3 3/8s convertible Eurobonds, 15-year
	SFr 200m	0 1/4s convertible Swiss notes, 5-year
	SFr 300m	0 1/4s convertible Swiss notes, 5-year
1990 (to Oct.)	U.S.$ 225m	9s guaranteed Luxembourg bonds, 10-year
	DM 150m	0 1/4s floating/fixed-rate dual-coupon Eurobond, 6-year
	U.S.$ 800m	Guaranteed subordinated floating-rate Euronotes, 10-year

*C$ = Canadian dollar; ItL = Italian lira; SFr = Swiss franc; FFr = French franc; ECU = European currency unit; DM = German mark.

Source: *Moody's Global Ratings,* Moody's Investor Services, April 1991.

Exhibit 6   Issuance of Japanese Corporate Bonds, by Year

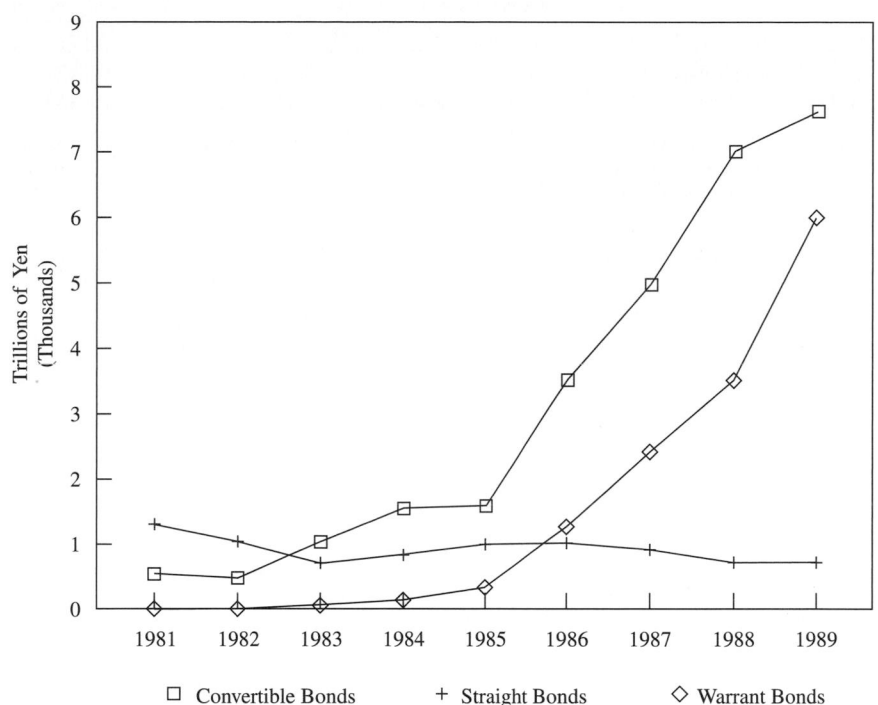

Issuance of Japanese Corporate Bonds
By Year

Sources: Data obtained from Bond Underwriters Association of Japan, and Richard Downes and Chris Elven, *Japanese Equity Warrants,* London: Eurostudy Publishing, 1990.

EXHIBIT 7   Estimated Standard Deviation of Equity Returns and Selected Prevailing Interest Rates

	Annualized Standard Deviations Based on Monthly Observations	*Annualized Standard Deviations Based on Weekly Observations*
May–October 1990	0.1272	0.1717
November 1989–October 1990	0.1824	0.1427
January 1987–October 1990	0.2234	0.1345

Note: The stock prices underlying these volatility estimates were adjusted for splits and dividends. The estimates were derived from log-normalized price relatives of stock prices. For a discussion of the estimation procedure, see J. Cox and M. Rubinstein, *Options Markets* (Englewood Cliffs, NJ: Prentice-Hall, 1985), pp. 255–58.

Issuer and Term to Maturity	*Yields to Maturity (%)*
Japanese government	
3 years	7.40
5 years	7.55
15 years	7.38
Industrial corporations (AAA)	
Average "long-term"	7.44
Financial institutions	
Average "long-term"	7.14

Source of stock-price data: Datastream, Inc. (weekly data) and Global Disclosure, Investext (monthly data).
Source of interest-rate data: Tokyo Stock Exchange Factbook (Tokyo, 1991).
Source of estimated volatilities: Casewriters' analysis.

EXHIBIT 8   Comparable Bond Issues

Bond Issuer	*Matures*	*Coupon (%)*	*Conversion Price*	*Current Bond Price*	*Yield to Maturity (%)*
U.S. dollar convertible bonds					
Fuji Bank	31 Mar 95	1.2	2,971	79.3	6.9
Fuji Bank	30 Sep 92	1.0	2,971	89.3	7.2
Dai-Ichi Kangyo Bank	30 Sep 92	1.0	2,966	89.0	7.4
Dai-Ichi Kangyo Bank	29 Sep 92	1.1	2,966	78.0	6.5
Mitsubishi Bank	30 Sep 92	1.1	2,867	89.2	7.4
Mitsubishi Bank	29 Sep 95	1.2	2,867	78.0	6.6
Sumitomo Bank	30 Sep 92	1.0	3,261	89.0	7.4
Sumitomo Bank	30 Sep 92	1.1	3,261	80.3	7.1
U.S. dollar "straight" bonds					
Bank of Tokyo	1995	10.4	(Not	103.3	9.53
Bank of Tokyo	1999	10.8	applicable)	101.5	9.28
Bank of Tokyo	1995	11.3		106.3	9.50
Bank of Tokyo	1993	7.6		96.3	9.14
Bank of Tokyo	1993	8.0		97.1	9.10
Bank of Tokyo	1996	8.4		95.5	9.45
Bank of Tokyo	2000	9.0		91.8	10.32
Industrial Bank of Japan	1995	11.5		107.8	9.30
Industrial Bank of Japan	1995	10.9		105.3	9.29
Industrial Bank of Japan	1995	10.5		104.3	9.30
Industrial Bank of Japan	1993	9.5		101.0	9.10
Industrial Bank of Japan	1997	7.9		91.9	9.60
Industrial Bank of Japan	2004	9.4		96.0	9.91
Sumitomo Bank	1993	9.4		100.8	9.07

Sources: *International Herald Tribune* and *Financial Times*.

EXHIBIT 9   Summary Financial Report on Bank of Tokyo

BANK OF TOKYO

8313
東京銀行

Only foreign exchange specialized bank with worldwide network. Formerly Yokohama Shokin Bank. Issues bank debentures in Japan, and racks up 70% of gross profit from international operations. Issued high-coupon bonds, first ever issued by Japanese bank. Lending to debtor nations largest among Japanese banks.

Outlook: Domestic fund management profit reaching projected mark, although profit margin sagging in 2nd half. Covering loss from credits to Mexico with gains on securities sold. Net operating profit outlook may be revised slightly downward due to extra appropriation for bad-debt reserves. In Mar '91 term, suspended payment of interest on credits by debtor nations hurting, but domestic profit margin picking up. Small-lot discount bonds with currency option winning consumer's favor.

Income (¥mil)	Current Revenues	Net Oper. Profit	Current Profit	Net Profit	Earnings per sh	Dividend per sh	Equity per sh
Mar '86	1,133,517	–	71,919	39,126	¥22.0	¥6.5	¥203.3
Mar '87	1,020,690	–	81,969	47,125	26.6	7	222.8
Mar '88	1,116,006	–	88,068	51,061	28.5	7	255.9
Mar '89	1,443,715	–	102,294	59,237	30.9	7.5	318.5
Mar '90∗	1,900,000	76,000	98,000	54,000	27.1	8	
•Sep '89	954,997	42,443	49,432	32,684	16.5	4	374.7
•Sep '90∗	1,100,000	40,000	47,000	31,000	15.6	4	
□Mar '88	1,344,812	–	92,361	47,321	26.4		273.1
□Mar '89	1,734,095	–	121,825	60,691	31.7		334.5
□Mar '90∗	2,250,000	–	119,500	56,000	28.1		

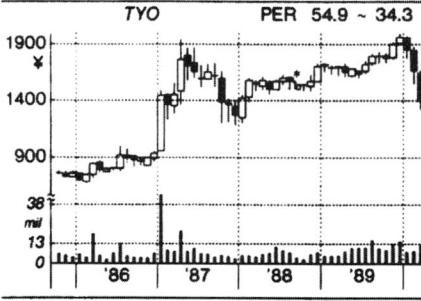

TYO   PER 54.9 ~ 34.3

Funds Breakdown   (Sep '89, %)

Time Deposits	56
Deposits at Notice	4
Bonds	21
Other Deposits	19

Prices

	High	Low	G/L(%)
~'86	999 ('86)	37 ('50)	
'87	1940 (Apr)	954 (Jan)	33.1
'88	1730 (Dec)	1200 (Jan)	36.0
'89	1990 (Dec)	1600 (Jun)	14.6
#'90	1970 (Jan)	1320 (Mar)	(-)29.1

Finance   (000shs)

Apr '88 CB ¥20bil (¥1640.8)	
May '88 Pub 60 (¥1554)	1,852,415
Nov '88 100:3 Gratis	1,913,110
Mar '89 CB $100mil (¥1772.9)	
Mar '89 CB SFr200mil (¥1772.9)	
Mar '89 CB SFr300mil (¥1772.9)	
May '89 Pub 60 (¥1622)	1,975,519

Loans Breakdown   (Sep '89, %)

To Small Firms, etc.	33
To Consumers	1

Stocks   (¥50 par value, 1000 per unit)

Shares Out. (Feb 28 '90 000shs) 1,993,933
No. of Shareholders (Sep 30 '89) 25,823

Major Holders(%)		Foreign Owners	1.3
Meiji Life Ins.	5.7	Mitsubishi Trust	1.6
Nippon Life Ins.	5.4	Tokio M.& F.Ins.	1.5
Dai-ichi Life Ins.	5.2	Nippon Steel	1.5
Taiyo Life Ins.	2.7	Norinchukin Bank	1.4
Mitsubishi Corp.	2.0	Mitsui Trust	1.3

Financial Data (¥mil)

	•Sep '89	□Mar '89
Total Assets	29,610,697	29,525,748
Cash & Due	7,140,844	6,519,506
Investment Securities	3,042,260	2,895,421
Loans & Bills Disc.	11,874,245	12,998,303
Deposit Certificates	1,571,014	1,850,344
Call & Borrowed	4,041,522	3,958,590
Capital Stock	225,140	171,380
Capital Surplus	143,520	89,767
Shareholders' Equity	742,169	640,370
Equity Ratio(%)	2.5	2.2
Funds Available	20,088,360	20,019,209

Highest in Current Profit (¥mil)
Mar '89   102,294

No.of Branch Offices: 82
Exchanges: TYO, OSA
Underwriters: Yamaichi, Nomura, Daiwa, Nikko, Sanyo, Kokusai, Dainana
Est: Dec 1946   **Listed:** May 1949
Employees (Age) 8,019(36)
Chairman: Yusuke Kashiwagi
President: Minoru Inoue
Overseas Offices   ⇒ See P. 1321
U.S.A., U.K., Hong Kong

Principal Office   **Tel:** 03-245-1111
1-3-2, Nihonbashi-Hongokucho, Chuo-ku, Tokyo 103   **Telex:** 22220 **Fax:** 03-279-3926

Source: *Japan Company Handbook,* First Section (Tokyo: Tokyo Keizai, Summer 1990.)

General Motors: 1991 Equity Financing

The past year had been extremely challenging for General Motors (GM) and its director of corporate finance, Follin Smith. The crisis in the Middle East coincided with the first recession in eight years, and GM's profits had dropped precipitously (see Exhibits 1–3). As the end of the second quarter 1991 approached, Smith was coming to grips with the fact that for the last two quarters of 1990 and the first two of 1991, General Motors had lost an astounding $4.5 billion. Prospects for improvement in the near term were not bright: The industry continued to be plagued by overcapacity and weak consumer demand, putting severe pressure on margins. As the high-cost producer among the "Big 3," General Motors had suffered the most from the adverse economic conditions. Despite extraordinary efforts to conserve cash internally, GM would have to tap the capital markets to meet its financial needs, and it was up to Follin Smith to develop a financing strategy that specified which of the many alternatives available to the company should be used to raise the first $500–$750 million of those funds.

GENERAL MOTORS AND THE AUTO INDUSTRY

GM senior management had recognized a softening in the economy during the first half of 1990. Although sales figures were roughly comparable to the year before, profits were down almost 50 percent as General Motors sought to draw down inventory levels by reducing

This case was adapted from a Supervised Business Study written by Alex McCormick (Darden '93) under the direction of Associate Professor Kenneth Eades. The authors acknowledge the helpful assistance of Follin Smith (Darden '85) and Darren Berry (Darden '94). This case was written as a basis for class discussion rather than to illustrate effective or ineffective handling of an administrative situation. Copyright © 1995 by the University of Virginia Darden School Foundation, Charlottesville, VA. All rights reserved. *No part of this publication may be reproduced, stored in a retrieval system, used in a spreadsheet, or transmitted in any form or by any means—electronic, mechanical, photocopying, recording, or otherwise—without the permission of the Darden Foundation. For inquiries, please send an e-mail to dardencases@virginia.edu.* Revised 3/98.

production and offering dealers and customers higher sales incentives. While GM's balance sheet was strong, a deep or protracted recession could easily drain its cash reserves. The Saturn division was about to launch a new line of small cars, and the company was in the midst of redesigning virtually all its other car lines. If these projects were delayed as the result of insufficient resources, the strategic position of the company would be jeopardized.

Consequently, Smith and her staff began to closely analyze all expenditures in an attempt to identify any that were either unnecessary or outsized. Their first action was to temporarily suspend the stock repurchase program. In 1989, General Motors had spent $1.65 billion to retire its outstanding stock. While the board of directors had viewed the repurchase program as helpful in supporting the price of the stock and demonstrating management's positive outlook about the future, it was not deemed critical to the daily operations of the business.

GM had also just finished some very difficult labor contract negotiations with the United Auto Workers. After a marathon bargaining session on September 17, 1990, the two parties came to an agreement which was both a blessing and a curse for GM. Management granted wage and benefit increases averaging 6.7 percent over the next three years. Additionally, the company agreed to unprecedented job security provisions. Workers with more than two years' seniority could not be laid off for more than 36 weeks during the length of the contract. During the 36-week layoff, GM had to pay supplementary unemployment benefits to ensure that employees were guaranteed approximately 95 percent of their normal take-home pay. Beyond 36 weeks, the company agreed to pay employees a full 100 percent of their regular paycheck. This arrangement effectively made labor part of GM's fixed costs by making it uneconomical to lay off workers. In exchange for these concessions, GM was allowed more flexibility in work rules, the ability to increase worker buyout programs, and the right to consolidate or close plants.

GM wasted little time in exercising its new power. On November 1, 1990, GM announced, along with third-quarter results, a special $2.1 billion restructuring charge covering the closure of four assembly plants and the consolidation of five distribution centers. The total quarterly loss of $1.98 billion was the largest in the history of the automobile industry. GM's action aimed to reduce costs and bring capacity more in line with demand. Excluding the charge, net income was $109 million, as General Motors sold 10.3 percent fewer vehicles in the United States than the previous year and sales incentives averaged over $1,000 for each unit sold.

As 1990 drew to a close, with sales languishing and losses mounting, it became apparent that more aggressive measures would have to be taken. On February 4, 1991, General Motors outlined a sweeping plan to reduce costs. Specific measures included reducing the dividend from $3.00 to $1.60. The dividend cut, which was the first decrease in 11 years, represented a cash-flow reduction to shareholders of almost $850 million annually. Given the fundamental weakness in the industry, the dividend change had been expected by analysts, and the stock price was not adversely affected (see Exhibit 4 for a graph of GM's stock price). One action that did raise questions in the market was the announcement that capital spending would be reduced by $500 million annually, which would be achieved primarily by delaying certain development projects. Furthermore, General Motors would seek to squeeze $2 billion in annual savings from its suppliers by demanding material cost reductions as a condition for continued relationships.

In an unprecedented action two days after the cost-reduction plan announcement, Standard & Poor's downgraded the debt of all three U.S. automakers. Citing "continuing aggressive moves by foreign players to gain North American market share and persisting production overcapacity," the agency said, "the resulting heightened price competition is being magnified by a cyclical downturn and further exacerbated by the situation in the Mideast."[1] GM's rating was reduced to A from AA minus.

As expected, on February 14, General Motors reported a fourth-quarter loss of $1.62 billion, bringing the total loss for 1990 to $1.99 billion. Much of the loss was attributed to the restructuring charge, which, if excluded from 1990 expenses, would have resulted in the company's earning $100 million for the year. Regardless of how 1990 results were reported, however, the company was clearly suffering because of declining demand, vigorous competition, increased sales incentives, and an unfavorable shift in the product mix toward lower-priced vehicles.

Despite a $403-million gain on the sale of its New York office tower, GM's results in the first half of 1991 looked no better than the year before. Unless the company resorted to selling additional assets or further reduced the dividend, it would have to go to the external markets to raise $500–$750 million. Moreover, if the recession continued, it was quite likely that the company would have to return to the markets in a relatively short time to raise additional funds. Because of GM's ongoing financing needs, the choice of which financial instrument to issue for the first $500–$750 million was particularly important because of the message it would convey to the market about how GM was going to react to the challenge it was currently facing.

FINANCING ALTERNATIVES

Smith felt that GM's current financial condition left few financing alternatives that were feasible. The recent downgrading of GM's debt made it unlikely that a new debt issue would be well received by the markets. Not only would the cost of the new debt be higher, but there was a good chance that GM's debt would be downgraded again if any more leverage were added to the balance sheet during a time when the company was losing money. Because a second downgrading would almost certainly result in a significant fall of the stock price, Smith felt it was an unacceptable risk to take. With debt being infeasible and GM's capital structure having deteriorated significantly due to recent operating losses, Smith felt that it was imperative to inject equity into the company. The added equity would serve to increase the company's borrowing capacity, which would in turn give GM more flexibility about its choices for the company's future financing needs.

Several equity or "near equity" alternatives had been proposed. Based on current market conditions, GM's investment banking advisers had estimated that any of the instruments could be used to raise $500–$750 million.

Convertible Debt

A strategy often employed by companies having trouble accessing the straight debt market was to issue convertible bonds. The coupon for a convertible debt issue was usually set about 200 basis points lower than the rate for a comparable straight debt issue. The market

---

[1] *Bond Buyer,* February 7, 1991.

was willing to receive a lower interest rate in consideration of the upside potential afforded by the conversion option. Because a convertible bond had both debt and equity characteristics, some analysts viewed convertible debt as "quasi equity." The rating agencies, however, had made it clear to GM that they would consider a convertible bond as full-fledged debt in their debt-ratio calculations. Thus, even though a new issue of convertible debt would be subordinate to the existing debt outstanding, it would not meet the company's primary objective of strengthening its debt-equity position.

Common Equity

After eliminating both straight and convertible debt, Smith turned her attention to the equity alternatives. As a result of its innovative equity financing over the years, GM had three classes of common stock outstanding in 1991: class H, class E, and $1⅔ shares. The $1⅔ shares were the regular GM common shares with par value equal to $1⅔ per share. The H-class shares were issued in 1985 in connection with the acquisition of Hughes Aircraft Company (now called Hughes Electronics). The E-class shares were issued in connection with the purchase of EDS Corporation in 1984. The H- and E-class shares differed from the $1⅔ shares with respect to voting rights and dividends. H shares carried one-half vote per share, and E shares carried one-quarter vote per share. In addition to having different voting rights, the stocks had independent dividend policies linked directly to the performance of their respective businesses.[2] The table below summarizes the characteristics of the E, H, and $1⅔ shares as of June 25, 1991:

Common Class	Shares Outstanding (Millions)	Average Daily Trading Volume	Closing Price ($)	Voting Rights per Share	Dividend per Share ($)
$1⅔	615	1,395	41⅜	1	1.60
E	98	334	46½	¼	0.64
H	70	10	17	½	0.72

Of the three classes of common stock, the $1 2/3 shares were the most recognizable and would be the easiest to place in the market. As shown in Exhibit 4, the market price of the stock had recently rebounded to $41 3/8 per share, a significant improvement from a low of $30 3/8 per share in January. Assuming fees and price discounting of 2 percent, an issue of approximately 12 million $1 2/3 shares would be required to raise $500 million. With 615 million shares outstanding, an extra 12 million would represent only a 2 percent increase. The relatively low amount of dilution, however, was not enough to make issuing new shares attractive. The last time GM had raised funds by issuing its $1 2/3 shares was 1955, and during the past few years the company had been actively involved in repurchasing its shares on the open market. For GM to now announce a large share issuance

---

[2]For example, an investor holding an E share received a dividend that was dependent on the earnings performance of EDS, not GM.

might be interpreted by the market as a signal that either the company was truly in desperate financial trouble and could not issue any other type of security or that GM management was trying to take advantage of an overpriced common by issuing shares before the market corrected its error. In either case Smith wanted to avoid issuing the $1 2/3 shares unless she felt there was no other viable alternative.

GM could also issue the E-class or H-class shares to raise the funds. Of the two issues, the E-shares were more actively traded and had experienced much stronger price appreciation over recent years (see Exhibit 5). As a result of the price appreciation, the E-class stock had a much lower yield than the H stock (1.4 versus 4.2 percent). GM's investment bankers had advised the company that the low trading volume and low number of shares outstanding would mean that an H-share issuance would have to be treated as if it were an initial public offering (IPO). IPOs required much more time to prepare because the market had to be educated about the stock. Moreover, there was always the risk that an IPO could fail and the issue would have to be either postponed or canceled.

Preferred Stock

As an alternative to issuing straight common equity, GM's investment bankers had suggested several different plans for raising the money with preferred stock. Preferred stock would be viewed by analysts and the rating agencies as primarily equity (i.e., adding preferred to the capital structure would increase GM's borrowing capacity, although not as much as if straight equity had been added). On the other hand, because a preferred would not be linked directly to the performance of GM's stock, its issuance was not likely to send a negative signal to the market. Preferred stock carried some risk for the issuing company because no common dividends could be distributed until all preferred dividends had been fully paid. For example, if a company had missed its preferred dividends for several quarters, it would have to pay all preferred dividends in arrears before the common dividend could be reinstated. Missing a dividend payment on a preferred did not, however, constitute a default, as would be true if an interest payment were missed on a bond. Thus, the risk for an issuer was lower for preferreds than for bonds.

GM had issued preferred stock in the past and currently had two straight perpetual preferreds outstanding with coupons of $3.75 and $5.00. If GM were to issue another straight perpetual preferred with standard features, current market conditions would demand a coupon rate of 8.75 percent. Standard features would include a seven-year call protection period, cumulative dividends, and no voting rights unless dividends were missed for more than six quarters. At 8.75 percent the yield on the preferred would be approximately 90 basis points lower than the yield to maturity on GM's outstanding senior debt and 55 basis points higher than the yield on the company's outstanding preferred issues (see Exhibit 6). Existing preferreds commanded lower yields because of very stringent covenants which made the issues less risky than the proposed new issue. The 90-basis-point spread below the yield of GM's outstanding bonds was due to a couple of factors. First, yields on some preferreds were bid down by corporate investors who could take advantage of a provision in the tax law which treated 70 percent of dividend income received by corporations as nontaxable. And second, the 8.75 percent yield was close enough to the bond yield to attract a segment of the individual investor market who wanted to hold preferred stocks from blue-chip companies like GM.

An alternative to issuing straight preferreds would be to issue a convertible preferred. A convertible would carry a lower coupon than a straight preferred as compensation for the upside potential associated with the conversion option. Current market conditions would demand a coupon rate of 7.50 percent and a conversion ratio of 2 shares of $1⅔ common per $100 preferred share. Like a convertible bond issue, a convertible preferred could carry a somewhat negative signal to the market because of GM's willingness to sell the conversion option. Selling a conversion option was equivalent to selling a call option, and a company would be motivated to sell a call option when it believed its stock was overpriced or felt the upside potential of the stock had become limited. In either case, the market was likely to react negatively to the announcement that GM was issuing a convertible.

PERCS

A new preferred derivative known as a preferred equity redemption cumulative stock (PERCS) had also been suggested by GM's investment bankers. A PERCS was a convertible preferred with a built-in ceiling on the stock price appreciation. In exchange for the limited upside, investors were given a higher dividend yield than the common stock. The dividend, conversion ratio, and appreciation cap were designed such that the PERCS would be issued at the same price per share as the underlying common stock. Thus, a PERCS was similar to perpetual straight preferred in that it paid a dividend that was substantially higher than the common stock. The unusual feature of the PERCS was that it automatically converted into common stock at the end of three years subject to a predefined cap between 30 to 45 percent above the price of the PERCS at issuance.

To illustrate how the conversion provision in a PERCS works, assume that the current price of a company's stock is $50 per share and that a PERCS is brought to the market with a 40 percent appreciation cap. At the end of three years, if the price of the common is below the $70 cap ($50 + 40 percent), each PERCS would be exchanged for one full share of common stock. If the common stock is selling above $70 after three years, however, say at $100, each PERCS would receive a fraction of one share of common that was equivalent to $70. The exchange ratio would be determined as follows:

$$\text{Shares of common received} = \text{Cap price/Common stock price}$$

Thus, for this example where the common stock had risen to $100, each PERCS would be exchanged for 0.7 shares of common ($70/$100), resulting in lower dilution.

In the event that the common stock rose above the cap price prior to the PERCS's maturity, the issuing company had the option to force early conversion by calling the issue. An early conversion meant that investors would forfeit whatever dividend yield advantage the PERCS might have over the common. To offset the investor's potential loss of income, the call price was set above the cap price initially and declined daily until it reached the cap price at maturity. Thus, the initial call price was computed as the cap price plus the sum of the dividend premium of the PERCS over the common. To illustrate how a call price would be determined, suppose that the common stock from the above example paid no dividend, while the PERCS paid $3.65 annually (a 7.3 percent yield), and the cap price remained at $70. At issuance the call price would be set at $80.95, a $10.95 premium over the cap price of $70. The premium equals the expected sum of the dividend differential between the PERCS and the common dividend over the life of the PERCS. Because the common pays no dividend, the excess dividend of the PERCS equals the annual dividend multiplied by three years ($3.65 × 3 = $10.95). Thus, the call price would decline by exactly one cent every day during the three years prior to maturity, at which time it would have fallen to exactly the cap price of $70.

Exhibit 6 summarizes the PERCS proposal and the market conditions for June 25, 1991. Exhibit 7 lists the closing prices for put and call options traded on GM stock on the Chicago Board Options Exchange on June 25, 1991.

THE DECISION

As Follin Smith considered the financing choices, she was torn between taking the safer route of issuing a straight common or straight preferred versus using a derivative security like the convertible preferred or the PERCS. Only one PERCS issue had been done in the markets to date, and that was an exchange offer by Avon Products. Avon offered one PERCS share in exchange for one common share on which the company had recently cut the dividend. Thus, the PERCS was to serve as a means of allowing investors to trade their lower-yielding common for a higher-yielding and somewhat safer preferred stock, which also had some potential upside gain associated with it. If GM were to issue PERCS, however, it would be the first company to use PERCS to raise new money, and it was not clear how the market would react. Smith was also uncomfortable about how to judge the terms of the PERCS. Was the proposed $3.31 annual dividend on the PERCS too much of a yield premium over the $1.60 dividend on the common to compensate for the appreciation rights the investors were giving up? What type of investor would be interested in buying a PERCS? What kind of signal would issuing a PERCS send to the market, compared with issuing a convertible preferred or straight equity?

EXHIBIT 1   Income Statement with GMAC on an Equity Basis (in millions of dollars)

	Years Ended December 31		
	1990	*1989*	*1988*
Net sales and revenues			
Manufactured products	107,748	109,894	108,076
Computer systems and services	3,049	2,639	2,153
Total net sales and revenues	110,797	112,533	110,229
Costs and expenses			
Cost of goods sold	96,366	94,049	92,751
SG&A	8,667	8,105	7,391
Depreciation and amortization of property	5,487	5,088	4,951
Amortization of intangible assets	373	506	545
Special provision for restructurings	3,314	—	—
Total costs and expenses	114,207	107,747	105,638
Operating income (loss)	(3,410)	4,786	4,591
Other income	1,814	2,331	1,847
Interest expense	(2,049)	(2,228)	(1,537)
Income (loss) before income taxes	(3,645)	4,889	4,901
Income taxes (credit)	(890)	1,733	1,493
Income (loss) after taxes	(2,755)	3,156	3,408
Earnings of nonconsolidated affiliates	769	1,069	1,224
Income (loss) before cumulative effect of accounting changes	(1,986)	4,224	4,632
Cumulative effect of accounting changes	—	—	224
Net income (loss)	(1,986)	4,224	4,856

Source: General Motors annual reports.

EXHIBIT 2   Balance Sheet Statements with GMAC on an Equity Basis (in millions of dollars)

	Years Ended December 31		
	1990	*1989*	*1988*
Current assets			
Cash and marketable securities	4,607	7,071	6,837
Accounts and notes receivable			
Trade	16,691	18,037	17,337
Nonconsolidated affiliates	3,098	3,759	3,743
Inventories	9,331	7,992	7,984
Contracts in process	2,349	2,073	2,035
Prepaid expenses and deferred income taxes	3,968	2,374	2,476
Total current assets	40,044	41,306	40,412
Equity in net assets of nonconsolidated affiliates	9,752	9,000	8,332
Other investments and miscellaneous assets	6,693	5,762	5,636
Property	36,035	33,895	31,832
Intangible assets	10,356	6,802	5,013
Total assets	102,879	96,765	91,225
Current liabilities			
Accounts payable	8,189	7,659	7,750
Loans payable	3,118	2,302	1,931
Accrued liabilities and deferred income taxes	17,822	14,116	13,022
Total current liabilities	29,129	24,077	22,683
Long-term debt	4,615	4,255	4,243
Payable to GMAC*	13,018	14,461	14,840
Other liabilities, deferred income taxes, and credits	24,447	17,030	13,495
Stocks subject to repurchase	1,284	1,650	—
Stockholders' equity	30,047	34,983	35,672
Total liabilities and stockholders' equity	102,879	96,765	91,225

*For marketing and financial reasons, GM assumed part of the dealer inventory financing previously provided by GMAC. Primarily to support these receivables, General Motors entered into a financing agreement with GMAC through 1996 which provides that GMAC will extend loans to GM up to a maximum of $17 billion, which bear interest at floating market rates. GMAC services these receivables for a fee. This financing agreement ensures that GMAC's ongoing funding activities continue, and returns to GMAC the approximate amount of interest and fees it would have earned had it retained the dealer-inventory financing business.

Source: General Motors annual reports.

EXHIBIT 3   Cash-Flow Statements with GMAC on an Equity Basis (in millions of dollars)

	Years Ended December 31		
	1990	*1989*	*1988*
Cash flows from operating activities			
Income before cumulative effects of accounting change	(1,986)	4,224	4,632
Adjustments to reconcile income to net cash provided by operating activities:			
Depreciation and amortization of property	5,487	5,088	4,951
Amortization of intangible assets	373	506	545
Special provision for plant closings and other restructurings	2,848	(83)	
Deferred income taxes and undistributed earnings of Nonconsolidated affiliates	(2,010)	(111)	312
Change in operating assets and liabilities:			
Accounts receivable	32	(95)	2,194
Inventories	(1,340)	(7)	312
Contracts in process	(276)	(38)	(48)
Prepaid expenses	988	558	(698)
Accounts payable	530	(91)	662
Other liabilities	1,515	1,602	(1,768)
Net cash provided by operating activities	6,161	11,553	11,093
Cash flows from investing activities			
Investment in companies, net of cash acquired	(907)	(198)	(675)
Expenditures for real estate, plants, and equipment	(3,990)	(4,079)	(2,992)
Expenditures for special tools	(3,156)	(2,928)	(2,194)
Change in marketable securities, notes, and accounts receivable	2,575	(1,435)	(978)
Net cash used in investing activities	(5,478)	(8,639)	(6,841)
Cash flows from financing activities			
Net increase (decrease) in loans payable	816	371	(948)
Net increase in long-term debt	360	12	294
Net increase (decrease) in payable to GMAC	(1,543)	(380)	859
Repurchases of common stocks/Redemption of preference stocks	(569)	(1,655)	(787)
Proceeds from issuing common and preference stocks	376	173	253
Cash dividends paid to stockholders	(1,957)	(1,964)	(1,658)
Net cash used in financing activities	(2,517)	(3,443)	(1,986)
Effect of exchange rate changes on cash and cash equivalents	(131)	(50)	(36)
Net increase (decrease) in cash and cash equivalents	(1,964)	(123)	2,231
Cash and cash equivalents at beginning of the year	5,456	5,579	3,348
Cash and cash equivalents at the end of the year	3,491	5,456	5,579

Source: General Motors annual reports.

EXHIBIT 4 GM Stock Price History

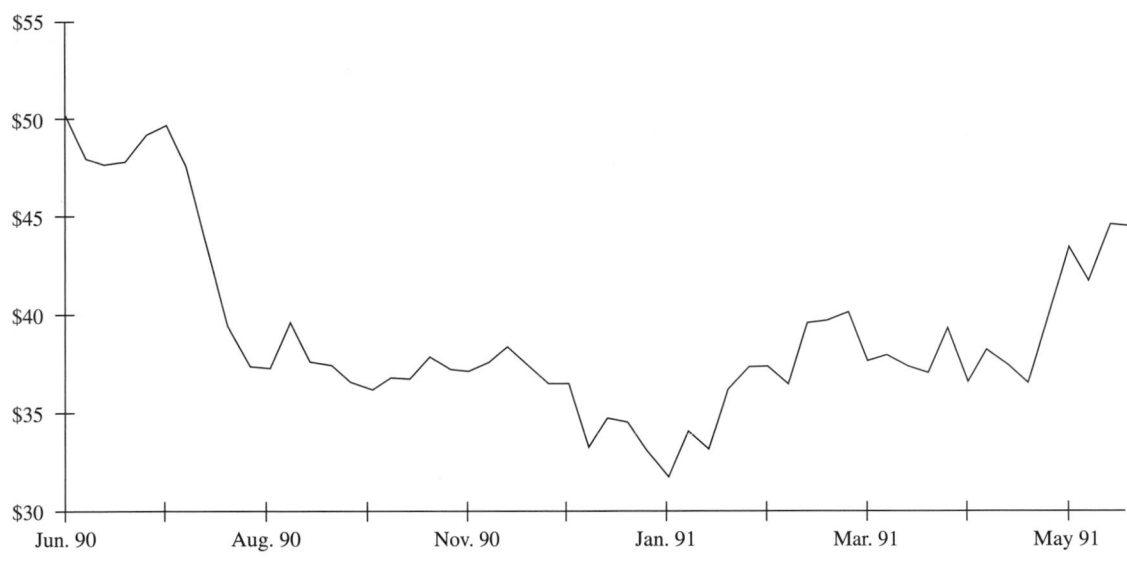

EXHIBIT 5 GM-E and GM-H Stock Price History

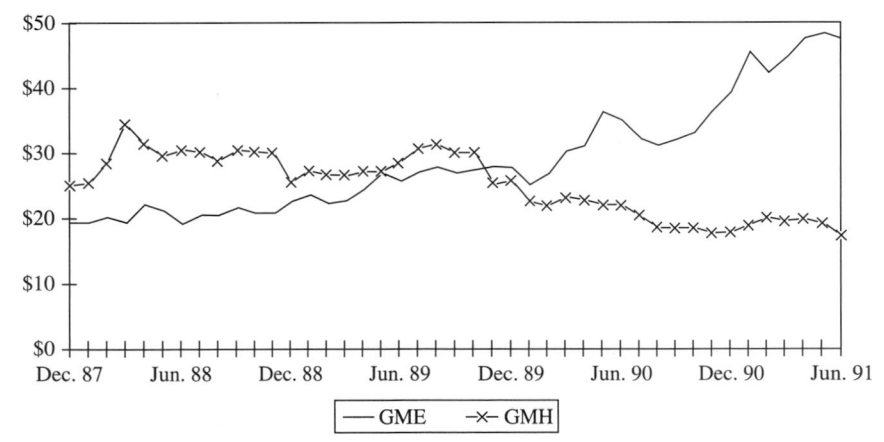

EXHIBIT 6 PERCS Proposal and Market Conditions

PERCS Proposal

Size of offering	$500–$750 million
Issue date	June 25, 1991
Expiration date	July 2, 1994
Issue price	$41 3/8
Strike price	$53.79
Dividend	$3.31

GM Common

Price	$41 3/8
Dividend	$1.60

Yields

Preferreds	
GM pf $3.75	8.13%
GM pf $5.00	8.26%
Bonds	
GM 8 5/8	9.65%
Government	
1-year	6.24%
3-year	7.35%
5-year	7.93%
10-year	8.25%
30-year	8.47%

EXHIBIT 7   Premiums for GM Options, Chicago Board Options Exchange Closing Prices for June 25, 1991

Option and NY Close	Strike Price	Calls				
		July	*August*	*September*	*September 1, 1992*	*March 1, 1993*
41⅜	30	s*	s	s	14	14¼
41⅜	35	r*	s	7⅜	s	s
41⅜	40	2⅜	3⅛	3½	r	8
41⅜	45	⅜	⅞	1⅜	5	6

Option and NY Close	Strike Price	Puts				
		July	*August*	*September*	*September 1, 1992*	*March 1, 1993*
41⅜	35	r	s	½	s	s
41⅜	40	¹¹⁄₁₆	1½	1¾	s	s
41⅜	45	3¾	r	4½	s	s
Days to maturity		24	52	87	451	627
Treasury rate (%)		5.08	5.44	5.71	6.73	6.99

*s = no option; r = not traded.

Source: *The Wall Street Journal.*

Part VIII

Valuing the Enterprise: Acquisitions, Buyouts, Restructurings, and Projects

Rocky Mountain Advanced Genome Inc.

In January 1996, negotiations neared conclusion for a private equity investment by Big Sur Capital Management Company in Rocky Mountain Advanced Genome (RMAG). The owners of RMAG, who were also its senior managers, proposed to sell a 90 percent equity interest to Big Sur for $46 million. The proceeds of the equity sale would be used to finance the growth of the firm. Big Sur's due-diligence study of RMAG had revealed a highly promising high-risk investment opportunity. It remained for Kate McGraw, a managing director with Big Sur, to negotiate the specific price and terms of investment. McGraw aimed to base her negotiating strategy on an assessment of RMAG's economic value, and to structure the interests of Big Sur and the managers of RMAG to create the best incentives for value creation.

McGraw's analysis so far had focused on financial forecasting of equity cash flows. The final steps would be to estimate a terminal value for the company (also called continuing value) and to discount the cash flows and terminal value to the present. She also sought an assessment of forecast assumptions. In this regard, she requested help from Janice Kelley, a new associate with Big Sur.

BIG SUR CAPITAL MANAGEMENT COMPANY

Big Sur, located in San Francisco, California, had been organized in 1968 as a hedge fund, though over the years it proved more successful in a variety of "private equity" investments and had gradually shifted its activities to this area. The firm had $2 billion under management. The firm's portfolio consisted of 64 investments, about evenly split between venture capital investments and participations in leveraged buyouts.

This case was prepared by Professor Robert F. Bruner as a basis for class discussion rather than to illustrate effective or ineffective handling of an administrative situation. Rocky Mountain Advanced Genome and the individuals in this case are fictitious, and reflect the issues facing actual firms and managers. Copyright © 1996 by the University of Virginia Darden School Foundation, Charlottesville, VA. All rights reserved. *No part of this publication may be reproduced, stored in a retrieval system, used in a spreadsheet, or transmitted in any form or by any means—electronic, mechanical, photocopying, recording, or otherwise—without the permission of the Darden Foundation. For inquiries, please send an e-mail to dardencases@virginia.edu.* Revised 1/98. Version 1.2.

ROCKY MOUNTAIN ADVANCED GENOME

RMAG, headquartered in Colorado Springs, Colorado, had been founded 15 months earlier by seven research scientists who had taken leaves of absence from major universities and pharmaceutical companies to establish the firm. The company used gene sequencing techniques with a computer-driven search algorithm to identify genes in human DNA. In the firm's short life span, it had uncoded about 60 percent of all human genes and was using that information to design treatments for diseases. RMAG and its pharmaceutical partners had identified 97 possible drug therapies. But given that it typically took 15 years and $350 million to take a drug from the lab bench to the drugstore, it would be years before the company determined whether any of these therapies would be effective.

The company's business consisted of three segments:

- *Diagnostic test kits* would afford low-cost and virtually error-free detection of a wide range of medical conditions. Development of the kit technologies was finished; the products were moving rapidly through the Food and Drug Administration (FDA) approval process and, because of their noninvasive and nontherapeutic nature, might be available for sale within 12 months. After the conclusion of the genome mapping process, more test kit applications were expected to emerge.
- *Agricultural biogenetic engineering.* Management believed that applying the same gene-mapping technology to corn and other commodity plants would permit the realization of truly disease-resistant, high-growth varieties. RMAG worked with two hybrid seed producers in a joint venture. RMAG's development costs were underwritten by the producers, and RMAG would receive a royalty on sales of new varieties produced by the joint venture. Management believed that revenues in this segment could begin within 24 to 36 months.
- *Human therapeutics.* The search for vaccines and antibiotics with which to fight incurable diseases was potentially the most economically attractive segment. Most of the activity in this segment was funded by major pharmaceutical companies under joint venture/royalty arrangements similar to the agricultural segment. RMAG also conducted proprietary research in this area. Management's long-term strategy was to use external funding (through joint venture arrangements) to the fullest extent possible, as a means of carrying the firm until its first major proprietary breakthrough. But despite external funding, RMAG still faced significant capital requirements stemming from investment in infrastructure, staffing, and its own proprietary research program.

RMAG's management believed that the genome mapping activity would pay off dramatically and quickly: By the year 2003, they believed, the revenues of the firm (consisting of underwritten research, royalties, and sales of proprietary products) would top $1 billion. Kate McGraw was less optimistic, believing that the FDA approval process would slow down the commercialization of RMAG's new products. The cash-flow forecasts of management, and of Kate McGraw, are given in Exhibits 1 and 2. Kate assumed that the firm would not finance itself with debt; thus, the forecasted free cash flows were identical with equity cash flows.

In assessing RMAG, Kate McGraw could look toward two small publicly held companies in this general field:

- *Human Genome Sciences, Inc.,* of Rockville, Maryland. This firm was the leader in the field and had uncoded 90 percent of the human genome. The firm claimed to have developed over 150 new therapies. On January 18, 1996, the firm announced that it had cracked the genetic code to the *staphylococcus aureus* bacterium, the most common cause of infections in hospitals, and the major cause of toxic shock syndrome and wound infection. At the announcement, Human Genome's stock price rose 21 percent. Over the previous 12 months, the firm's stock price had risen 220 percent. CEO William Haseltine said that the stock price was "based on people's perception of how many product opportunities there are going to be. It's a projection of what the future value is going to be, based on what the present value is."[1] The firm's beta was 0.82; the price/expected earnings ratio was 87.77; the price/book ratio was 11.71; price/sales was 15.61; and price/free cash flow was 88.67. The firm had no debt outstanding. The firm's sales had grown from zero in 1992, to $22 million in 1993, $41 million in 1994, and an expected $76.5 million in 1995. The company paid no dividend.

• *Myriad Genetics Inc.* of Salt Lake City, Utah, used the well-documented family trees of Utah families as a tool to help identify genetic defects and possible remedies—this was a much more targeted research strategy than Human Genome's approach of mechanistically sequencing thousands of unknown genes. Myriad concentrated on cancers and cardiovascular diseases. In December 1995, the firm filed a patent for the full gene sequence of a tumor suppressor gene that produced susceptibility to breast cancer—this would permit the company to commercialize tests and therapeutics exploiting the gene sequence. The firm went public on October 6, 1995, at $18 per share; in January 1996 the firm's shares traded around $31. With negative historical and expected earnings, the firm's price/earnings ratio was meaningless. However, the firm traded at 4.55 times book value. Revenues were $600,000 in 1994, and were expected to be $1.3 million in 1995.

Securities analysts were cautious about the fledgling gene-sequencing industry. The widespread belief was that gene sequencing would deliver *some* breakthrough. One analyst said, "Nearly everyone is into genomics. Everyone is a believer."[2] Yet there was almost no consensus on how soon the breakthroughs would occur, or how significant they would be. Filing for patents on gene sequences was at the edge of the legal envelope. The field was being flooded with entrepreneurial research scientists. The FDA approval process was, at best, uncertain in this area. And established firms witnessed internal clashes over direction.

THE IDEA OF TERMINAL VALUE

To assist her in the final stages of preparing for the negotiations, Kate McGraw called in Janice Kelley, who had just joined the firm after completing an undergraduate degree. To lay the groundwork for the assignment, Kate began by describing the concept of terminal value:

---

[1]"Bloomberg Forum: Human Genome Has 150 Potential Drugs, CEO Says," *Bloomberg Financial News Service,* February 13, 1996.

[2]David T. Molowa, analyst with Bear, Stearns & Co., quoted in "The Gene Kings," *Business Week,* May 8, 1995, p. 78.

Kate	Terminal value is the lump-sum of cash flow at the *end* of a stream of cash flows; that's why we call it *terminal.* The lump-sum represents either (*a*) the proceeds to us from exiting the investment or (*b*) the present value (at that future date) of all cash flows beyond the forecast horizon.

Jan	Since they are way off in the future, terminal values really can't be worth worrying about, can they? I don't believe most investors even think about them.

Kate	Terminal values are worth worrying about for two reasons. First, they are present in the valuation of just about every asset. For instance, in valuing a U.S. Treasury bond, the terminal value is the return of your principal at the maturity of the bond.

Jan	Some investors might hold to maturity, but the traders who really set the prices in the bond markets almost never hold to maturity.

Kate	For traders, terminal value equals the proceeds from selling the bonds when you exit from each position. You can say the same thing about stocks, currencies, and all sorts of hard assets. Now, the second main reason we worry about terminal value is that in the valuation of stocks and whole companies terminal value is *usually a very big value driver.*

Jan	I don't believe it. Terminal value is a distant future value. The only thing traders care about is dividends.

Kate	I'll bet you that if you took a random sample of stocks—I'll let you throw darts at the financial pages to choose them—and looked at the percentage of today's share price *not* explained by the present value of dividends for the next five years, you would find that the unexplained part would dominate today's value. I believe that the unexplained part is largely due to terminal value.[3]

> **Jan's first task:**
> Present and explain the data in Exhibit 3.

Jan	I'll throw the darts, but I still don't believe it—I'll show you what I find.

VARIETIES OF TERMINAL VALUES

Kate	We can't really foresee terminal value, we can only *estimate* it. For that reason, I like to draw on a wide range of estimators as a way of trying to home in on a best guess of terminal value. The estimators include (*a*) accounting book value, (*b*) liquidation value, (*c*) multiples of income, and (*d*) constant growth perpetuity value. Each of these has advantages and disadvantages, as my chart here shows [see Exhibit 4]. I like the constant growth model best and the book value least, but they all give information, so I look at them all.

Jan	Do they all agree?

Kate	They rarely agree. Remember that these are imperfect estimates. It's like picking the point of central tendency out of a scatter diagram or triangulating in on the height of a tree, using many different points of observation from the ground. It takes a lot of careful judgment

---

[3]The unexplained part could also be due to option values that are not readily captured in a discounted-cash-flow valuation.

because some of the varieties of terminal value are inherently more trustworthy than others. And from one situation to the next, the different estimators have varying degrees of appropriateness. In fact, even though I usually disregard book value, there are a few situations in which it might be a fair estimate of terminal value.

Jan Like when?

Kate Give it some thought; you can probably figure it out. Give me some examples of where the various estimators would be very appropriate and rather inappropriate. But remember that no single estimator will give us the truth. Wherever possible, we want to use a variety of approaches.

> **Jan's second task:**
> Draw on Exhibit 4.

TAXES

Jan What about taxes in terminal values? Shouldn't I impose a tax on the gain inherent in any terminal value?

Kate Sure, if you are a taxpaying investor and if it is actually your intent to exit the investment at the forecast horizon. But lots of big investors in the capital markets (such as pension funds and university endowments) do not pay taxes. And other investors really do not have much tax exposure because of careful tax planning. Finally, in M&A analysis and most kinds of capital budgeting analysis, the most reasonable assumption is *buy and hold,* in perpetuity. Overall, the usual assumption is *not* to tax terminal values. But we all need to ask the basic question at the start of our analysis, is the investor likely to pay taxes?

LIQUIDATION VERSUS GOING-CONCERN VALUES

Jan Now I'm starting to get confused. I thought *terminal* meant the end . . . and now you're talking about value in perpetuity. If terminal value is really the ending value, shouldn't we be talking about a *liquidation value?* Liquidation values are easy to estimate: we simply take the face value of net working capital, add the proceeds of selling any fixed assets, and subtract the long-term debt of the company.

Kate *Easy* isn't the point. We have to do what's economically sensible. For instance, you wouldn't want to assume that you would liquidate Microsoft in three years just because that's as far into the future as you can forecast. Microsoft's key assets are software, people, and ideas. The value of those will never get captured in a liquidator's auction. The real value of Microsoft is in a stream of future cash flows. When we come to a case like Microsoft, we see the subtlety of "terminal value"—in the case of *most* companies it means "continuing value" derived from the going concern of the business. Indeed, many assets live well beyond the forecast horizon. Terminal value is just a summary (or present value) of the cash flows beyond the horizon.

Jan So when would you use liquidation value?

Kate I've seen it a lot in corporate capital budgeting, cases like machines, plants, natural resources projects, etc. The assets in those cases have definite lives. But companies and *businesses* are potentially very long-lived and should be valued on a going-concern basis. But I still look at liquidation value because I might find some interesting situations where liquidation value is higher than going-concern value. Examples would be companies subject to oppressive regulation or taxation and firms experiencing weird market conditions—in the late 1970s and early 1980s, most oil companies had a market value *less* than the value of their oil reserves. You don't see those situations very often, but still it's worth a look.

MARKET MULTIPLES AND CONSTANT GROWTH VALUATION

Jan Aren't multiples the best terminal value estimators? They are certainly the easiest approach.

Kate I use them, but they've got disadvantages, as my chart [Exhibit 4] shows. They're easy to use, but too abstract for my analytical work. I want to get real close to the assumptions about value, and for that reason, I use this version of the constant growth valuation model to value a firm's assets:

$$TV_{Firm} = \frac{FCF \times (1 + g^{\infty}_{FCF})}{WACC - g^{\infty}_{FCF}}$$

FCF is free cash flow. *WACC* is weighted-average cost of capital. And $g\infty$ is the constant growth rate of free cash flows to infinity. This model was derived from an infinitely long DCF valuation formula:

$$PV_{Firm} = \frac{FCF_0 \times (1 + g^{\infty}_{FCF})}{(1 + WACC)} + \frac{FCF_0 \times (1 + g^{\infty}_{FCF})^2}{(1 + WACC)^2} +$$

$$\frac{FCF_0 \times (1 + g^{\infty}_{FCF})^3}{(1 + WACC)^3} + \ldots + \frac{FCF_0 \times (1 + g^{\infty}_{FCF})^{\infty}}{(1 + WACC)^{\infty}}$$

If the growth rate is constant over time, this infinitely long model can be condensed into the easy-to-use constant growth model.

When I'm valuing equity instead of assets, I use the constant-growth valuation formula, but with equity-oriented inputs:

$$TV_{Equity} = \frac{\text{Residual cash flow} \times (1 + g^{\infty}_{RCF})}{\text{Cost of equity} - g^{\infty}_{RCF}}$$

Residual cash flow (RCF) is the cash flow which equityholders can look forward to receiving—a common name for RCF is *dividends*. A key point here is that the growth rate used in this model should be the growth rate appropriate for the type of cash flow being valued; and the capital cost should be appropriate for that cash flow as well.

You may have seen the simplest version of the constant growth model—the one that assumes zero growth—which reduces to dividing the annual cash flow by a discount rate.

Jan Sure, I have used a model like that to price perpetual preferred stocks. In the numerator, I inserted the annual dividend; in the denominator I inserted whatever we thought the going required rate of return will be for that stream.

Kate If you insert some positive growth rate into the model, the resulting value gets bigger. In a growing economy, the assumption of growing free cash flows is quite reasonable. Sellers of companies always want to persuade you of their great growth prospects. If you buy the optimistic growth assumptions, you'll have to pay a higher price for the company. But the assumption of growth can get unreasonable if pushed too far. Many of the abuses of this model have to do with the little infinity symbol, ∞: the model assumes *constant growth at the rate,* g, *to infinity.*

"PETER PAN" GROWTH: *WACC* < *g*

Jan   Indeed, if you assume a growth rate greater than WACC, you'll get a *negative* terminal value.

Kate   That's one instance in which you cannot use the constant growth model. But think about it: WACC less than *g can't* happen; a company cannot grow to infinity at a rate greater than its cost of capital. To illustrate why, let's rearrange the constant growth formula to solve for WACC:

$$\text{WACC} = \frac{\text{FCF}_{\text{Next period}}}{\text{Value of firm}_{\text{Current period}}} + g^{\infty}_{FCF}$$

If WACC is less than *g,* then the ratio of FCF divided by value of the firm would have to be *negative.* Since the value of the healthy firm to the investors cannot be less than zero,[4] the source of negativity must be FCF—that means the firm is absorbing rather than throwing off cash. Recall that in the familiar constant growth terminal value formula, FCF is the flow that compounds to infinity at the rate *g.* Thus, if FCF is negative, then the entire stream of FCFs must be negative—the company is like Peter Pan: *it never grows up;* it never matures to the point where it throws off positive cash flow. This is a crazy implication, for investors would not buy securities in a firm that never paid a cash return. In short, you cannot use the constant growth model where WACC is less than *g,* nor would you want to because of the unbelievable implications of that assumption.

USING HISTORICAL GROWTH RATES; SETTING FORECAST HORIZONS

Kate   A more common form of abuse of this model is to assume a very high growth rate, simply by extrapolating the past rate of growth of the company.

Jan   Why isn't the past growth rate a good one?

Kate   Companies typically go through life cycles. A period of explosive growth is usually followed by a period of maturity and/or decline. Take a look at the three deals in this chart [see Exhibit 5]: a start-up of an animation movie studio in Burbank, a bottling plant in Mexico City, and a high-speed private toll road in Los Angeles.

• *Movie studio.* The studio has a TV production unit with small but steadily growing revenues and a full feature-length film production unit with big but uncertain cash flows. The studio does not reach stability until the 27th year. The stability is largely due to the

---

[4]This is a sensible assumption for healthy firms, under the axiom of the limited liability of investors: Investors cannot be held liable for claims against the firm, beyond the amount of their investment in the firm. However, in the cases of punitive government regulations or an active torts system, investors may be compelled to "invest" further in a losing business. Examples would include liabilities for cleanup of toxic waste, remediation of defective breast implants, and assumption of medical costs of nicotine addiction. In these instances, the value of the firm to investors could be negative.

firm's film library, which should be sizable by then. After year 27, exploiting the library through videos and re-releases will act as a shock absorber, dampening swings in cash flow due to the production side of the business. Also, at about that time, one can assume that the studio reaches production capacity.

- *Bottling plant.* The bottler must establish a plant and an American soda brand in Mexico, which accounts for the initial negative cash flows and slow growth. Then, as the brand takes hold, the cash flows increase steeply. Finally, in year 12, the plant reaches capacity. After that, cash flows grow mainly at the rate of inflation.
- *Toll road.* This will take 18 months to build, and will operate at capacity almost immediately. The toll rates are government regulated, but the company will be allowed to raise prices at the rate of inflation. The cash flows reach stability in year 3.

A key point of judgment in valuation analysis is to *set the forecast horizon at that point in the future where stability or stable growth begins.* You can't use past rates of growth of cash flows in each of these three projects because the explosive growth of the past will not be repeated. Frankly, over long periods of time, it is difficult to sustain cash-flow growth much in excess of the economy. If you did, you would wind up owning everything!

Jan   So at what year in the future will you set the horizon and estimate a terminal value for these three projects? And what growth rate will you use in your constant growth formula for them? Uh-oh. I know, "Figure it out for yourself . . ."

> **Jan's third task:**
> Set the forecast horizon for the three projects. See Exhibit 5.

GROWTH RATE ASSUMPTION

Kate   There are two classic approaches for estimating a growth rate to use in the constant-growth formula. The first is to use the self-sustainable growth rate formula:

$$g^\infty = \text{ROE} \times (1 - \text{DPO})$$

This assumes that the firm can only grow as fast as it adds to its equity capital base (through the return on equity, or ROE, less any dividends paid out, indicated through the dividend payout ratio, or DPO). I'm not a big fan of this approach, because most naive analysts simply extrapolate *past* ROE and DPO without really thinking about the future. Also it relies on accounting ROE and can give some pretty crazy results.[5]

The second approach assumes that nominal growth of a business is the sum of *real growth* and *inflation.* In more proper mathematical notation the formula is

$$g^\infty_{\text{Nominal}} = [\,(1 + g^\infty_{\text{Units}}) \times (1 + g^\infty_{\text{Inflation}})\,] - 1$$

This formula uses the economist's[6] notion that the nominal rate of growth is the product of the rate of inflation and the "real" rate of growth. We commonly think of real growth as a percentage increase in units shipped. But in rare instances, real growth could come from price increases due, for instance, to a monopolist's power over the market. For simplicity, I just use a short version of the model (less precise, though the difference in precision is not material):

---

[5]For a full discussion of the self-sustainable growth rate model, see "A Critical Look at the Self-Sustainable Growth Rate Concept," a technical note published by Darden Educational Materials Services (UVA-F-951).

[6]The economist Irving Fisher derived this model of economic growth. Its common name is the Fisher formula.

$$g^{\infty}_{Nominal} = g^{\infty}_{Unit} + g^{\infty}_{Inflation}$$

Now, this formula focuses you on two really interesting issues: the real growth rate in the business, and the ability of the business to pass along the effects of inflation. The consensus inflation outlook in the United States today calls for about a 3 percent inflation rate indefinitely. We probably have not got the political consensus to drive inflation to zero, and the Fed has shown strong resistance to letting inflation rise much higher. Well, if inflation is given, then the analyst can really focus her thinking on the more interesting issue of the real growth rate of the business.

The real growth rate is bound to vary by industry. Growth in unit demand of consumer staple products (like Band-Aids) is probably determined by growth rate of the population—less than 1 percent in the United States. Growth in demand for luxury goods is probably driven by growth of real disposable income—maybe 2 percent today. Growth in demand for industrial commodities like steel is probably about equal to the real rate of growth of GNP—about 2.5 percent on average through time. In any event, all of these are small numbers.

When you add these real growth rates to the expected inflation rate today, you get a small number—this is intuitively appealing since, over the very long run, the increasing maturity of a company will tend to drive its growth rate downward.

TERMINAL VALUE FOR ROCKY MOUNTAIN ADVANCED GENOME

Kate   We're negotiating to structure an equity investment in RMAG. We and management disagree on the size of the cash flows to be realized over the next 10 years [see Exhibits 1 and 2]. I'm willing to invest cash on the basis of *my* expectations, but I'm also willing to agree to give RMAG's management a contingent payment if they achieve *their* forecast. To begin the structuring process, I needed valuations of RMAG under their and our forecasts. We have the cash-flow forecasts, and we both agree that the weighted-average cost of capital (WACC) should be 20 percent—that's low for a typical venture capital investment, but given that RMAG's R&D partners are bearing so much of the technical risk in this venture, I think it's justified. All I needed to finish the valuation was a sensible terminal value assumption—I've already run a sensitivity analysis using growth rates to infinity ranging from 2 to 7 percent [see Exhibit 6]. The rate at which the firm grows will place different demands on the need for physical capital and net working capital—the higher the growth rate, the greater the capital requirements. So, in computing the terminal value using the constant growth model, I adjusted the free cash flow for these different capital requirements. Here are the scenarios I ran:

> **Jan's fourth task:**
> Interpret Exhibit 6.

Nominal Growth Rate to Infinity	Capital Expenditures in Terminal Year, Net of Depreciation	Net Working Capital Investment in Terminal Year
2%	$0 million	$0 million
3	−$5	−$3
4	−$12	−$5
5	−$15	−$7
6	−$20	−$8
7	−$28	−$9

RMAG's management believes that they can grow at 7 percent to infinity, assuming a strong patent position on breakthrough therapeutics. I believe that a lower growth rate is justified, though I would like to have your rec-

Jan's fifth task:
What drives g^{∞}?

ommendation on what that rate should be. Should we be looking at the population growth rate in the United States (about 0.5 percent per year), or the real growth rate in the economy (about 2.5 percent per year), or the historical real growth rate in pharmaceutical industry revenues (5 percent per year)? Are there other growth rates we should be considering?

We ought to test the reasonableness of the DCF valuations against estimates afforded by other approaches. Estimates of book and liquidation values of the company are not very helpful in this case, but multiples estimates would help. Price/earnings multiples for RMAG are expected to be 15 to 20 times at the forecast horizon—this is considerably below the P/Es for comparable companies today, but around

Jan's sixth task:
Estimate terminal values using multiples and prepare present value estimates using them.

the P/Es for established pharmaceutical companies today. Price-to-book ratios for comparable companies today are between 4 and 12 times—RMAG's book value of equity is $3.5 million. Please draw on any other multiples you might know about. We do not foresee RMAG paying a dividend for a long time.

Jan   This makes me skeptical about the whole concept. Terminal value for a high-tech company will be an awfully mushy estimate. How do you estimate growth? How sensitive is terminal value to variations in assumed growth rates? And with several terminal value estimates, how do you pick a "best guess" figure necessary to complete the DCF analysis? And once you've done all that, how far apart are the two valuations?

Kate   You need to help me find intelligent answers to those questions. Please let me have your recommendations about terminal values, their assumptions, and, ultimately, about what you believe is a sensible value range today for RMAG, from our standpoint and management's. By *value range*, I mean high and low estimates of value for the equity of RMAG that represent the bounds within which we will start negotiating (the low value), and above which we will abandon the negotiations.

Jan's seventh task:
Triangulate in on value ranges and recommend a deal structure.

CONCLUSION

Later, Kate McGraw reflected on the investment opportunity in RMAG. It looked as if management's asking price was highly optimistic; $46 million would barely cover the projected cash deficit for 1996. This implied that further rounds of financing would be needed for 1997 and beyond. But buying into RMAG now was like buying an option on future opportunities to invest—the price of this option was high, but the potential payoff could be immense if the examples of Human Genome Sciences and Myriad Genetics were accurate reflections of the potential value creation in this field. Indeed, it was reasonable to assume that RMAG could go public in an initial public offering (IPO) shortly after the first major breakthrough was announced. An IPO would accelerate the exit from this investment. If an IPO occurred, Big Sur would not sell its shares in RMAG, but instead would distribute the RMAG shares tax-free to clients for whom Big Sur was managing investments. Kate wondered how large the exit value might be, and what impact an early exit would have on the investment decision.

Kate's task:
Assess early exit values, and impact on decision.

EXHIBIT 1   Rocky Mountain Advanced Genome Cash Flow Forecast, by RMAG Management (values in millions of dollars)

	Actual				
	1995	1996	1997	1998	1999
Income statement					
Sales					
Cancer diagnostics	$0	$1	$15	$56	$107
Other diagnostics	2	12	28	45	75
Agriculture	0	0	2	13	52
Human therapeutics	0	0	0	0	8
Total sales	2	13	45	114	242
Cost of sales	7	10	21	41	84
Gross profits	−5	3	24	73	158
Contract revenue	16	21	23	15	12
Operating expenses					
R&D	14	20	24	18	21
SG&A	12	15	24	45	93
Total expenses	26	35	48	63	114
Other income	3	2	2	0	−3
Income before taxes	−12	−9	1	25	53
Taxes	0	0	5	9	19
Net income	−12	−9	−4	16	35
Free cash flow					
Net income	−12	−9	−4	16	35
Noncash items	0	1	2	2	6
Working capital	−4	−8	−12	−22	−63
Capital expenditures	−15	−6	−5	−23	−53
Free cash flow	−$31	−$22	−$19	−$27	−$76

Source: Casewriter analysis.

2000	2001	2002	2003	2004	2005
$181	$249	$274	$282	$285	$289
110	135	165	190	210	225
106	146	166	174	186	189
57	171	250	330	352	362
454	701	855	976	1,033	1,065
159	246	322	335	350	361
295	455	533	641	683	704
4	3	3	3	3	3
21	32	43	51	52	50
176	259	323	369	372	349
197	291	366	420	424	399
−10	−25	−38	−43	−37	−20
92	142	132	181	225	288
32	57	76	89	90	85
60	85	56	92	135	203
60	85	56	92	135	203
10	18	19	15	8	−1
−101	−118	−100	−61	1	39
−93	−111	−98	−66	−10	−10
−$124	−$126	−$123	−$20	$134	$231

EXHIBIT 2   Rocky Mountain Advanced Genome Cash Flow Forecast, by Big Sur Analysis (values in millions of dollars)

	Actual 1995	1996	1997	1998	1999
Income statement					
Sales					
Cancer diagnostics	$0	$0	$2	$11	$22
Other diagnostics	2	4	11	22	40
Agriculture	0	1	4	7	12
Human therapeutics	0	0	0	0	0
Total sales	2	5	17	40	74
Cost of sales	7	17	20	25	39
Gross profits	−5	−12	−3	15	35
Contract revenue	16	22	22	15	12
Operating expenses					
R&D	14	23	25	27	29
SG&A	12	21	25	32	44
Total expenses	26	44	50	59	73
Other income	3	0	0	1	−1
Income before taxes	−12	−34	−31	−29	−27
Taxes	0	0	0	1	4
Net income	−12	−34	−31	−30	−31
Free cash flow					
Net income	−12	−34	−31	−30	−31
Noncash items	2	3	3	3	4
Working capital	−6	−6	−6	−7	−14
Capital expenditures	−15	−9	−9	−9	−10
Free cash flow	−$31	−$46	−$43	−$43	−$51

Source: Casewriter analysis.

2000	2001	2002	2003	2004	2005	2006
$36	$56	$71	$85	$95	$106	$114
59	89	135	145	160	185	199
15	25	50	60	75	91	105
0	0	14	56	80	110	140
110	170	270	346	410	492	558
54	72	96	124	142	154	160
56	98	174	222	268	338	398
4	4	4	4	4	4	4
33	37	44	52	53	54	58
64	87	104	127	138	136	136
96	124	147	179	191	191	194
−2	−2	−3	−2	0	0	3
−38	−24	28	45	80	152	210
−13	4	11	15	27	39	48
−25	−28	17	30	53	112	162
−25	-28	17	30	53	112	162
6	8	10	14	18	20	23
−17	−19	−20	−28	−16	−6	–6
−11	−15	−18	−24	−27	−28	−30
−$47	−$54	−$11	−$8	$28	$98	$149

EXHIBIT 3   Jan Kelley's Dart-Selected Sample of Firms with Analysis of Five-Year Dividends as a Percent
of Stock Price

	Recent Price	Annual Dividend	Five-Year Dividend Growth %
Allied Signal	$42.00	$0.78	14.5%
Burlington Northern	78.00	1.20	0.0
Caterpillar	57.00	1.20	30.0
Cooper Inds.	34.00	1.32	2.5
Cummins Engine	35.00	1.00	26.0
Delux Corp.	28.00	1.48	1.5
Donnelley R. R.	39.00	0.68	16.0
Dun & Bradstreet	62.00	2.63	4.0
Eaton Corp.	51.00	1.50	6.5
Emerson Electric	71.00	1.75	9.5
Equifax	20.00	0.32	6.5
Federal Express	82.00	0.00	0.0
Fluor Corp.	58.00	0.60	11.5
Honeywell	44.00	1.01	11.5
Illinois Tool Works	59.00	0.62	10.5
Kelly Services	28.00	0.78	11.0
Owens-Corning	44.00	0.00	0.0
Raychem	57.00	0.32	4.5
ServiceMaster	30.00	0.95	2.5
Sherwin-Williams	40.00	0.64	6.5
Stone Container	18.00	0.15	7.0
Tenneco	47.00	1.60	6.0
WMX Technologies	30.00	0.60	5.5
Westinghouse	$16.00	$0.20	0.0%

Note: To illustrate the estimate of 90% for Allied Signal, the annual dividend of $0.78 was projected to grow at 14.5% per year
to $0.89 in 1997, $1.02 in 1998, $1.17 in 1999, $1.34 in 2000, and $1.54 in 2001. The present value of these dividends discounted
at 12.3% is $4.14. This equals about 10% of Allied Signal's stock price, $42.00. The complement, 90%, is the portion of market
price not attributable to dividends.

Source of data: *Value Line Investment Survey* for prices, dividends, growth rates, and betas. Other items calculated by casewriter.

Beta	Equity Cost	Present Value of Five Years' Dividends	Percent of Market Price Not Attributable to Dividends
1.15	12.3%	$ 4.14	90%
1.15	12.3	4.30	94
1.25	12.8	9.37	84
1.15	12.3	5.06	85
1.10	12.0	7.22	79
0.90	10.9	5.71	80
1.05	11.7	3.81	90
1.00	11.5	10.73	83
1.05	11.7	6.51	87
1.05	11.7	8.24	88
1.25	12.8	1.35	93
1.35	13.4	0.00	100
1.25	12.8	2.90	95
1.10	12.0	4.98	89
1.10	12.0	2.98	95
1.10	12.0	3.80	86
1.50	14.2	0.00	100
1.30	13.1	1.27	98
0.80	10.4	3.82	87
1.10	12.0	2.76	93
2.25	18.2	0.56	97
1.15	12.3	6.75	86
1.20	12.6	2.48	92
1.15	12.3%	0.72	96%
		Average	90%

EXHIBIT 4   Key Terminal Value Estimators

Approach	Advantages	Disadvantages
Book value	Simple "Authoritative"	Ignores some assets and liabilities Historical costs: backward-looking Subject to accounting manipulation
Liquidation value	Conservative	Ignores "going-concern" value (Dis)orderly sale?
Replacement value	"Current"	Replace *what?* Subjective estimates

Multiples, earnings
  capitalization
Price/Earnings
Value/EBIT
Price/Book
	Simple
	  Widely used
		"Earnings" subject to accounting
		  manipulation
		"Snapshot" estimate: may ignore cyclical,
		  secular changes
		Depends on comparable firms: ultimately
		  just a measure of relative, not absolute
		  value

Discounted cash flow	Theoretically based Rigorous Affords many analytical insights Cash focus Multiperiod Reflects time value of money	Time-consuming Risks "analysis paralysis" Easy to abuse, misuse Tough to explain to novices

Source: Casewriter.

EXHIBIT 5   Cash Flows of Three Deals with Differing Rates of Development (values in millions of dollars)

Year	Movie Studio	Bottling Plant	Toll Road
1	($20)	($20)	($20)
2	(40)	(60)	90
3	(60)	(100)	169
4	(20)	5	172
5	0	10	176
6	20	20	179
7	30	40	183
8	50	65	187
9	75	115	190
10	100	150	194
11	90	180	198
12	80	190	202
13	60	200	206
14	55	204	210
15	70	208	214
16	85	212	219
17	95	216	223
18	105	221	227
19	130	225	232
20	150	230	237
21	140	234	241
22	160	239	246
23	190	244	251
24	225	249	256
25	240	254	261
26	230	259	266
27	255	264	272
28	260	269	277
29	265	275	283
30	270	280	288
31	+Steady growth to infinity		

Projected Cash Flows by Investment

- Toll Road
- Bottling Plant
- Movie Studio

Source: Casewriter analysis

EXHIBIT 6   Sensitivity Analysis of RMAG Terminal Value and Present Value by Variations in Terminal Value Scenarios (values in millions of dollars)

RMAG's View

Annual growth rate to infinity	2%	3%	4%	5%	6%	7%
WACC	20%	20%	20%	20%	20%	20%
Annual cap. ex. (net of depr'n.) 2006	$0	($5)	($12)	($15)	($20)	($28)
Annual addition to NWC 2006	—	(3)	(5)	(7)	(8)	(9)
Adjusted free cash flow 2006	202	194	185	180	174	165
Terminal value 2005	1,142	1,173	1,200	1,257	1,314	$1,355
Present value of terminal value 2005	185	189	194	203	212	219
Present value free cash flows 1996–2005	($151)	($151)	($151)	($151)	($151)	($151)
Total present value	$33	$38	$43	$52	$61	$68

Big Sur's View

Annual growth rate to infinity	2%	3%	4%	5%	6%	7%
WACC	20%	20%	20%	20%	20%	20%
Annual cap. ex. (net of depr'n.) 2007	$0	($5)	($12)	($15)	($20)	($28)
Annual addition to NWC 2007	—	(3)	(5)	(7)	(8)	(9)
Adjusted free cash flow 2007	185	177	168	163	157	148
Terminal value 2006	1,049	1,073	1,093	1,142	1,189	1,219
Present value of terminal value 2006	141	144	147	154	160	164
Present value free cash flows 1996–2006	($118)	($118)	($118)	($118)	($118)	($118)
Total present value	$23	$26	$29	$35	$42	$46

Source: Casewriter analysis

McCaw Cellular Communications: The AT&T/McCaw Merger Negotiation

In September of 1992, Craig O. McCaw, the founder and CEO of McCaw Cellular Communications, mused about the recent discussions he had engaged in with Robert Allen, chairman and CEO of AT&T. Allen had approached Craig McCaw regarding a possible partnership. Such a deal would enable AT&T to enter the wireless industry and at the same time provide McCaw Cellular Communications, Inc., with sorely needed capital to exploit its cellular operating licenses. McCaw had sacrificed much of its financial flexibility in its hostile takeover of LIN Broadcasting in 1990 and now was saddled with over $5 billion in debt, which had depleted cash reserves and reduced net income. A potential offer from AT&T, the global telecommunications powerhouse, intrigued McCaw as he reflected on the difficult road he and his family had traveled in growing the family-run cable operation into the nation's leading cellular service provider.

McCaw considered the possible reasons AT&T was pursuing McCaw Cellular. One reason might have been that AT&T sold cellular phones but offered no cellular service, while McCaw offered cellular service but sold no equipment. Or perhaps it was future access to Personal Communications System (PCS), the next generation in wireless technology. Or maybe it was McCaw Cellular's existing seamless wireless national network for voice and data transmissions,

This case was prepared from public information by Michael J. Innes and William J. Passer under the direction of Professor Robert F. Bruner. The comments and assistance of John B. Muleta are gratefully acknowledged. Copyright © 1996 by the University of Virginia Darden School Foundation, Charlottesville, VA. All rights reserved. *No part of this publication may be reproduced, stored in a retrieval system, used in a spreadsheet, or transmitted in any form or by any means—electronic, mechanical, photocopying, recording, or otherwise—without the permission of the Darden School Foundation. For inquiries, please send an e-mail to dardencases@virginia.edu.* Revised 6/98. Version 2.2.

a network behind which AT&T could throw its brand name, data banks, marketing clout, and technical expertise. A deal between these two firms would offer to McCaw AT&T's undisputed expertise in the industry and its global marketing and sales-force power to expand its overseas presence. McCaw would be AT&T's cellular arm and could help it expand into Europe, where laws prohibited wired services but did not restrict cellular service.

Craig McCaw believed synergies might exist between AT&T and his company. Collaboration, or even outright purchase, would enable McCaw Cellular to take the next step in both market and technical dominance. Selling to AT&T would be cleaner than a joint venture, since a combined cellular/wired network would be created without the players fussing over which part of the business belonged to which entity. One major issue concerned Craig about selling out: control. In every prior deal, Craig and his family had been in control, and yet a deal with AT&T might require him to relinquish control of the empire he had built over nine years. Currently, Craig maintained control of more than 60 percent of McCaw's voting stock and thus had the final say on any strategic action undertaken by the company. Giving up this control would require *substantial* compensation.

Negotiations had not yet progressed into detailed terms of an acquisition, but McCaw liked Allen and hoped discussions would continue into the fall. The key points to negotiate in the coming weeks would be establishing the price and terms for control of McCaw. Given a lull in mergers and acquisitions activity in the capital markets, a merger of this magnitude, if signed by year's end, would likely surprise many Wall Street types and enable McCaw to earn an above-average premium.

THE BEGINNINGS OF MCCAW CELLULAR

McCaw Cellular was a Kirkland, Washington–based wireless provider operating in the largest urban areas under the name *Cellular One.* McCaw had been one of the first to recognize that cellular, or wireless, communication technology offered consumers incredible conveniences never before dreamed possible in a largely wired nation. In the early 1980s, McCaw realized that communications could occur between people instead of only between locations. He commented that "if you can communicate from wherever you are, then you don't need to be at the office to do your job." While the technology existed for this, it was only a matter of time until the buying public became comfortable enough to embrace it. McCaw continued, "Wireless takes away any place limitations—people are an intellectual asset, not a physical one."[1]

When Craig was 16 years old, he received his first taste of business ownership. His father, John McCaw, sold Craig and his three brothers a small, 2,000-subscriber cable system in Centralia, Washington (two hours south of Seattle), which he had purchased in 1937.[2] The boys paid no cash for the station, and instead gave only preferred stock to their parents as compensation. John McCaw died in 1969, while Craig was a sophomore at Stanford University. Craig's entrepreneurial spirit was stronger than his brothers', and he decided to manage the cable system out of his college dormitory, in addition to managing a small aircraft leasing firm he had started.

---

[1]"The Future for McCaw Is Only a Vision Away," *Sacramento Bee,* January 17, 1994, p. C1. AT&T Corp., *Hoover's Company Information,* HOOVER'S INC., Austin, TX, 1998.

[2]"Would You Believe It? Craig McCaw Says He Is Risk-Averse," *Forbes,* March 1, 1993, p. 78. AT&T Corp., *Hoover's Company Information,* HOOVER'S INC., Austin, TX, 1998.

Craig drew from the experience of operating his family's cable system to expand his cable holdings by pledging existing assets to secure new loans. With a keen eye to the bottom line, Craig slashed costs, raised rates, and improved station programming. In 1981, Craig formed a partnership with Affiliated Publications, then the owner of the *Boston Globe,* to purchase more cable stations. As McCaw's leverage increased, Affiliated's initial $12-million stake grew steadily and by the mid-1980s had reached $85 million, or 43 percent of McCaw's cable company, McCaw Communications. Cellular technology attracted Craig McCaw, and he was among the first to purchase several FCC-awarded franchises with the money he raised from the sale of his cable stations in the mid-1980s. At the time McCaw commented, "We were never going to have a major influence on the cable business . . . Cellular was the place where we thought we could make a difference."[3] Wireless communication, noted McCaw, represented the future because it was more functional for both the businessperson *and* the consumer.

With Affiliated's approval, McCaw aggressively acquired any cellular licenses he could find, including the Florida licenses held by the *Washington Post,* financing the purchases using junk debt. Nobody else at that time seemed to realize the potential of cellular, enabling Craig to buy licenses at very cheap prices, around $5.00/POP.[4] POPs were the total number of potential subscribers for a cellular operator. By 1987, McCaw Communications' debt level had risen too high, forcing Craig to deleverage the company by selling his cable operations to Jack Kent Cooke for $755 million.[5] Craig took his company public in August of that year, selling 13 million shares at $21.75 per share, or 12 percent of McCaw Cellular Communications, Inc. (NASDAQ: MCAWA). Craig used $2.3 billion of fresh capital resulting from both the initial public offering and subsequent debt financing to acquire additional cellular licenses over the next 18 months.

By 1989, the company's debt burden had risen to 87 percent of capital. More equity was needed to keep the company afloat. In that year, McCaw sold its southeastern cellular system for $1.3 billion to Contel Cellular, a large regional operator. In addition, the company sold shares to British Telecom PLC (BT) bearing 22 percent of the votes outstanding.[6] This transaction surprised analysts both for the global alliance it created, and for the price: The price of $41.50 per share dramatically exceeded the preannouncement closing price of $29.00 and valued McCaw's equity at $5.5 billion. One analyst said, "These numbers are off our charts. It values McCaw shares 40 percent more than previous takeover values. A controlling interest for a cellular company could require even more of a premium."[7] Shares of other cellular companies rose at the announcement of the BT purchase.

By September 1992, McCaw Cellular employed 4,400 people and was the market leader, with 1.2 million subscribers and 58 million POPs in 21 states.[8] Its licenses gave it a strong competitive advantage in 5 of the 10 most populated metropolitan areas in the nation.

---

[3]Ibid. AT&T Corp., *Hoover's Company Information,* HOOVER'S INC., Austin, TX, 1998.

[4]Ibid. POPs are defined in the Industry Perspective section of this case; see p. 531.

[5]"The Forbes Four Hundred," *Forbes,* October 18, 1993, p. 160.

[6]At the time, U.S. law limited the ownership or voting of McCaw stock to no more than 25 percent. Because of share issues by McCaw between 1989 and 1992, BT's interest had declined to 20.3 percent.

[7]Quotation of Drexel Burnham Lambert analyst John Reidy in "British Telecom Buys into U.S. Cellular Leader McCaw," Reuters, January 19, 1989.

[8]POPs, mentioned earlier, are defined below in the Industry Perspective section of this case; see p. 531.

Approximately 80 percent of McCaw's licenses were located in the 30 most populated U.S. areas. In nine years, the company had become not only the largest domestic player in cellular, with 83 percent of 1991 revenues contributed by cellular service operations, but also a national communications powerhouse. At this subscriber level, penetration totaled only 2 percent, but enormous growth potential existed since penetration was projected to increase between 16 percent and 24 percent annually over the next decade.

McCaw provided cellular service under the brand name of Cellular One in Florida, the Midwest, California/Nevada, the Northeast, the Pacific Northwest, Texas/Louisiana, the Rocky Mountain region, and the Upper Midwest. In addition, the company provided voice messaging, two-way mobile phone service, one-way radio messaging, and telephone answering services. McCaw had also partnered with ClairCom to provide air-to-ground communications for commercial air travel and owned 12.5 percent of American Mobile Satellite, which used satellite technology to provide cellular service to rural America.[9] Exhibits 1 and 2 detail McCaw's historical operating statements and balance sheets, while Exhibit 3 displays relevant information relating to the company's stock price.

CRAIG MCCAW—A VISIONARY

Craig McCaw, 42, was the second oldest of four brothers raised by an entrepreneurial father and mother who bought and sold dozens of radio, TV, and cable stations as Craig was growing up. Marion McCaw, his mother, was one of the first women to earn an accounting degree at the University of Washington and had shared her interest in financial order with her sons. Craig, however, was the son who took to this most strongly.

The tiny station in Centralia, Washington, proved to be the first step in Craig's entrepreneurial career. Owning and running the station revealed to Craig the importance of controlling businesses one invests in, an attribute that characterized his investment philosophy in September 1992. Of his brothers, Bruce (age 46), John Jr. (age 42), and Keith (age 39), only Keith was not actively involved in the business.

Over the years, Craig had become a shrewd businessman and had surrounded himself with equally strong financial and business talent. Exhibit 4 identifies McCaw's board of directors, who, along with Craig, had determined that "the coming revolution in personal communications was too big for one company. McCaw needed a partner so it could occupy that emerging marketplace."[10]

As far as any deal went, Craig was willing to take cash but preferred AT&T stock because of the tax deferral a stock-for-stock deal gave McCaw and his family. A simple exchange ratio could be derived by dividing the per share market value of McCaw by the per share market value of AT&T, but that ignored any premium for McCaw's seamless network or its operating potential. McCaw, of course, expected to have a say in the direction of the joint company's future, but confided to James Barksdale, McCaw Cellular president, that he would "walk away if it frustrates me, as neither of us feel any obligation to have my participation."[11]

---

[9]"McCaw Cellular Communications," *Hoovers Handbook Database,* The Reference Press, Inc., Austin, 1994.
[10]"Going Public," *Seattle Times,* April 7, 1993, p. F1.
[11]"The Future to McCaw Is Only a Vision Away," *Sacramento Bee,* January 17, 1994, p. C1.

THE APPEAL OF AMERICAN TELEPHONE & TELEGRAPH (AT&T)

The history of telecommunications can be traced back to Alexander Graham Bell's 1876 invention of the telephone. Bell's original backers, fathers of deaf students he tutored, founded Bell Telephone in 1877.[12] In what would foreshadow the competitive nature of the telecommunications industry, rival Western Union tried to market a competing patent filed by Elisha Gray just a few hours after Bell's.[13] In 1879, after several years of litigation, Bell successfully had Western Union barred from the telephone business. And in 1882, Bell wrested control of Western Electric, the nation's premier electrical-equipment manufacturer, from Western Union.

Bell's patents expired in the 1890s, and independent phone contractors quickly entered the market. Bell battled the larger competitors, bought up smaller players, and blocked independents from access to Bell System phone lines.[14] The company changed its name to American Telephone & Telegraph and relocated from Boston to New York City in 1899. J. P. Morgan and his allies gained control of AT&T and appointed Theodore Vail president of the company in 1907. AT&T won control of Western Union in 1909 but was threatened with antitrust action by the Wilson administration. The company's renowned research facility, Bell Labs, was founded in 1925.

Regulation has played a significant role in the development of the telecommunications industry. Prior to 1982, the government had allowed AT&T to develop, through its control of the Bell System of local telephone companies and Western Electric, a near monopoly over long-distance services, local-exchange services, and telephone-equipment manufacturing. AT&T's dominance of the telecommunications industry had always been a cause for concern with the Department of Justice (DOJ) investigations of AT&T and the Bell System for antitrust violations starting in the 1950s and lasting through the early 1980s. In 1982, the U.S. District Court in Washington, D.C., entered a consent decree settling the DOJ's antitrust case against AT&T and its affiliates. This decree, more commonly known as the Modified Final Judgment (MFJ), required AT&T to divest the 22 local telephone companies that comprised the Bell System. In return, AT&T was allowed to keep Western Electric and Bell Labs and, most important, its long-distance and international businesses. As part of the settlement the divested companies were organized into seven regional companies, known as the Regional Bell Operating Companies (RBOCs), which served close to 75 percent of the local telephone exchange lines in the country. The MFJ, which was administered by Judge Henry Greene starting January 1, 1984, restricted AT&T from entering the local-exchange business and required it to deal with its former affiliates in a nondiscriminatory manner. In addition, the MFJ restricted the RBOCs from entering three lines of business without prior approval from Judge Greene: (1) long-distance telephone service, (2) manufacturing, and (3) information services.[15]

---

[12]"AT&T Corp.," *Hoover's Handbook Database* (Austin, TX: The Reference Press, Inc. 1996).

[13]Ibid.

[14]Ibid.

[15]*United States* v. *AT&T Co.,* 552 F. Supp. 131 (D.C. Cir. 1982), aff'd sub nom., *Maryland* v. *United States,* 460 U.S. 1001 (1983).

One consequence of deregulation was that AT&T now had to pay each RBOC an access fee for use of the local network at the end of a long-distance connection. AT&T set out to look beyond local telephone service for alternative sources of revenue. Robert Allen was appointed CEO in April 1988, and he brought a vision for an intelligent long-distance network that allowed people to move information in new ways. The increasingly global nature of the telecommunications business enabled Allen and his management team to view AT&T not as the largest long-distance provider in the nation, but rather as a communications concern.

AT&T had faced almost unprecedented business challenges going forward since the divestiture of its local telephone companies in 1984. Smith Barney research analyst C. W. Schelke believed AT&T "had to fight a business war on two fronts: It had to minimize the loss of its historic business despite structural changes that dramatically increased the degree of competition in those businesses; and it had to seek to capitalize on changes in information processing and transmission that were occurring worldwide."[16]

Since 1988, Allen had engineered a string of acquisitions aimed at realizing his vision. He assembled a number of computer, software, multimedia, and other key technology interests. Each acquisition was a deliberate attempt to supplement AT&T's existing network with the tools to achieve communications anywhere and at any time. Exhibits 5 and 6 detail historical operating statements and balance sheets of AT&T since 1989. Exhibit 7 displays AT&T's share price information.

Transforming AT&T into a global communications giant presented Allen with challenges; however, the advances that the company had made toward that goal were unmistakable. Particular steps had been taken in the company's equipment manufacturing businesses, and Smith Barney's Schelke believed that the company was now positioned to show much better results from those businesses than in recent years.[17] In fact, other signs of progress were already evident. Despite a decline in the market share of its core long-distance business from 97 percent to 65 percent,[18] AT&T had been more profitable as of late than it was in the early 1980s. Operating income as a percentage of revenue had grown from approximately 5 percent in 1984 to nearly 9 percent in 1990.[19] Earnings per common share before extraordinary items and cumulative effects of accounting changes rose from $1.14 to $2.38 over the same period.[20] While there was some concern in the analyst community over the $26 billion in charges and write-offs the company had taken over the past eight years, to the company's credit it had delivered total shareholder returns superior to the S&P 500 since divestiture.[21]

---

[16]C. W. Schelke, "AT&T Company Report," Smith Barney, Harris Upham & Co., September 25, 1992, p. 1.

[17]Ibid., p. 2.

[18]*Cellular Investor* (Carmel, CA: Paul Kagan & Associates, Inc., May 14, 1993), p. 7.

[19]AT&T 1991 annual report, p. 21.

[20]Operating income as a percentage of revenue (2.2 percent) and earnings per common share before extraordinary items ($.40) fell off in 1991 in conjunction with the merger with NCR. Excluding charges associated with the merger and gains associated with the sale of investments in Sun Microsystems and UNIX System Laboratories, earnings per common share in 1991 was $2.51. AT&T 1991 annual report, p. 19.

[21]S. L. Mintz, "Can AT&T Stay on Top?" *CFO: The Magazine for Senior Financial Executive* 10 (April 1994), p. 4.

	AT&T's Recent Activities under CEO Robert E. Allen
Date	*Event*
July 1988	$112 million investment in joint venture with GTE to develop digital switching equipment
March 1989	Buys Paradyne, a data communications equipment company, and Eaton Financial, an equipment financing company
June 1989	Exchanges $135 million and a 20 percent stake in AT&T Network Systems International for 20 percent of Italtel, an Italian communications equipment maker
July 1989	Gives up on 1983 Olivetti investment, exchanging it for a 17.3 percent stake of Olivetti parent Compagnie Industriali Riunite
December 1989	Spends $285 million to acquire ISTEL Group, a British high-tech company
December 1989	Buys Western Union's Business Services Group for $180 million; renamed AT&T EasyLink Services
June 1991	The Sun Microsystems deal unravels; sells 19 percent interest in workstation maker, acquired in 1988
September 1991	NCR joins AT&T portfolio for $7.5 billion in stock

WIRELESS NETWORK TECHNOLOGY

Wired and Wireless Communication

The terms *wireline* and *wireless* referred to network facilities owned by a company providing communication services. Wireline, also referred to as *wired*, meant that the communications path between the company's switch and the customer is a wire (copper, coaxial, or fiber-optic cable), commonly called the local loop.[22] Traditional phone and data networks such as the Internet were examples of wireline networks. Wireless meant that an additional over-the-air component existed in the pathway. Mobile radio and cellular phone networks, which rely on signals transmitted over the air, were examples of wireless networks. In certain instances, these two types of networks worked together, when wireline networks provided the means for linking independent wireless networks to one another. Thus, when a customer placed a cellular call to someone located beyond the limits of that customer's cellular network, a switching interface in a wireline network made the connection.

Exhibit 8 shows the distinguishing features of typical wireless network architecture. A defined service region, typically a metropolitan service area (MSA) or a rural service area (RSA), was subdivided into hexagonal sectors or "cells." Each cell represented the area that was covered by a single transmitter (sending and receiving communications signals over the air) that was located at a "cell site" placed somewhere within the cell. The equipment at the

---

[22]C. Weinhaus, C. Lagerwerff, R. Lock, et al., *Cellular to PCS: A Wireless Primer, Telecommunications Industries Analysis Project,* University of Florida, December 1995, p. 5.

cell site functioned like an air-traffic controller, communicating with traffic in the tower's range to ensure that no "collisions" between various calls occurred.[23] Each call was on a different channel or each channel was subdivided to prevent interference.

The intelligent-electronic-switching-system technology for wireline networks was used in cellular networks as well, particularly when a customer's call crossed cell boundaries and it was necessary to hand off the call from one transmitter to the next. This handoff, done electronically, allowed the customer to move beyond the limits of one calling area into an adjacent calling area without a service interruption. When a customer moved outside his or her home system's service area (the aggregation of a number of cells), that individual became "roaming." "Blocked" calls, which resulted in lost potential revenue, occurred when the channels of a particular cell were full. Therefore, it was critical to develop ways to increase the capacity of a given network as use increased. The concept of "frequency reuse" was developed for that purpose. What resulted was the creation of different channels among adjacent cells allowing the advanced switching technology to hand off a call from a channel in one cell to a different channel in an adjacent cell.

Analog and Digital Technologies

Most mobile communication systems were analog (i.e., carried voice waves in their original wave form), where the voice signal varied in a consistent manner. For example, in an analog watch, the hands continuously sweep around the numbers on the dial without interruption. The information is a continuously varying representation of time—the position of the moving hands in relation to the stationary dial.[24] New wireless applications such as data transmission and imaging favored digital technology, a more expensive yet higher quality alternative. Digital systems transformed the voice wave into digital form—short bursts of information that represented the height of the voice wave by a number. Digital transmissions therefore used complex mathematical manipulations to drastically reduce the amount of information necessary for speech recognition at the other end of the call. Thus, additional space was made available, which in turn could be used to augment a network's capacity.

INDUSTRY PERSPECTIVE

Beginning around 1982, the FCC began awarding licenses for a new class of communications services known as cellular mobile radio, which used the airwaves to provide simultaneous two-way voice communications and was the functional equivalent of the service provided by the traditional wired phone network. In order to provide incentives for developing this new service, the FCC devised a license grant scheme that limited the number of licensees to two in each predefined market area. To stimulate competition, the commission decreed that each local telephone company, which included the RBOCs, within a defined

---

[23]Ibid. p. 9.
[24]Weinhaus, Lagerwerff, Lock, et al., *Cellular to PCS,* p. 11.

geographic market would automatically be awarded one of the licenses (known as A licenses), while the other ones would be issued through the use of lotteries (known as B licenses). Because most of the license lottery winners were permitted to transfer their licenses to another party (albeit for a fee and not to the competing local exchange telephone company), most licenses eventually ended up with entrepreneurs like Craig McCaw who wanted to take advantage of the duopoly the FCC had created.

Starting in the mid-80s, McCaw Cellular began systematically to acquire and operate a number of licenses. By 1992, it had become the market leader with 1.2 subscribers, 60 million POPs, and a national penetration rate of 2 percent.[25]

Between 1984 and 1991 the cellular market grew rapidly at a compounded annual growth rate of 86.9 percent in subscribers and 64.1 percent in revenues (see Exhibit 9). In 1992 the industry had approximately 11 million subscribers and was projected to sign up, on average, almost 10,000 new subscribers per day in 1993.[26] The total subscriber base was estimated at nearly 14.5 million by December 1993. As technology continued to improve quality and availability of cellular service, it became attractive not only to the traditional businessperson but also to the individual user.[27] Customers' usage was predicated on service quality rather than cost. As a result, cellular operators had begun experimenting with flexible pricing plans designed to cater to different segments of the cellular markets and thus grow their overall subscriber base.[28] And as the number of cellular users inevitably increased in the near term, those companies that effectively combined service and value pricing emerged as market leaders.

Local and Long-Distance

The 1984 divestiture paved the way for new competition in the long-distance market. Since then, many new companies had entered the market, driving the prices of long-distance service down for the consumer and increasing call volume. By 1992, approximately 90 percent of revenues in the long-distance market were attributable to three independent carriers: AT&T, MCI, and Sprint. In that year, the long-distance market was projected at $65–$70 billion; AT&T captured a 62 percent share.

On the local side, the market was dominated by the Baby Bells. These seven operating companies provided service to over 75 percent of the estimated 145 million access lines in 1992, with the remainder served by smaller, independent firms.[29] In 1984 these local-exchange companies generated operating revenues of approximately $74 billion, but by 1992 revenues had grown to $93 billion. Growth for plain old telephone service (POTS) in the United States was projected to be moderate. Thus, market expansion would be

---

[25]POP stands for point of presence. POPs represented potential subscribers for a cellular operator, and were calculated as the population of a particular geographic area multiplied by a firm's fractional ownership in the cellular system serving that area. For example, in a metropolitan area with 1 million POPs and two licensed cellular operators, each of which held half of the market, each operator would have 500,000 POPs. *Penetration* was a term that described the percentage of potential subscribers that had already subscribed.

[26]"Survey of Mobile Communications," *The Financial Times,* September 8, 1993, p. XIV.

[27]"Centel Corporation," University of Virginia Darden School Foundation, UVA-F-1078, 1995.

[28]"Cellular Phones Plug in Flexible Pricing Plans," *Crain's New York Business,* July 19, 1993, p. 25.

[29]"Centel Corporation," p. 5.

driven by demand for and availability of technologically advanced products and services such as cellular, data transmission, and imaging, as long as they could be provided at reasonable prices.

It was no secret that the nation's long-distance providers wanted somehow to get back into the local telephone business. While the traditional way had been blocked by Judge Greene's order, cellular technology enabled companies such as AT&T to circumvent this ruling legally and offer its customers both long-distance and local cellular service, bypassing the traditional RBOC wirelines. Thus, as cellular service became increasingly affordable, RBOCs would lose a much needed and relied-upon source of revenues—the local access charges that long-distance companies currently paid the regionals to complete each call.[30] This was sure to evoke a strong legislative response, although it was unsure when that might occur.

Strategic Opportunities and PCS

Communications companies wanted to create broader strategic alliances to capture market growth anticipated by the technological advances and convergence between the computer and telecommunications industries. Thus, the overall goal of cellular firms was slowly being transformed from just offering simple phone service to having a seamless communications network for its subscribers being a one-stop shop for all communications activity. With new competition looming on the horizon, the successful execution of these strategic moves was critical if market share was to be maintained. Given the high fixed-cost structure of the industry, high barriers to entry could be erected if these alliances created synergies such as cost savings, market access, and/or cross-promotion.

Technology was advancing very rapidly by 1992, as voice communications, data, and images were being developed to fit together in one portable device. Personal Communications Systems (PCS) technology was based on person-to-person rather than point-to-point communication. However, nobody was certain when it would become available to the public. Some industry professionals believed it would be as early as 1997. In fact, some analysts anticipated that as digital and data services expanded beyond cellular, the market for these services would grow at 25–30 percent annually throughout the 1990s, with spending approaching $10 billion by the year 2000.[31] By late 1993, it was anticipated that the FCC would issue auction guidelines for the portion of the radio spectrum that would be used by PCS.

Whereas current cellular technology used cells spaced 30 miles apart to hand off a call from one location to the next, PCS digital technology employed smaller, more densely packed microcells spaced a quarter mile apart, making PCS ideal for densely populated metropolitan areas. However, the cost for building a large PCS network was certain to be prohibitive, notwithstanding the large learning curve that would be required to successfully manage this type of network. It was estimated that a rival trying to enter the PCS mar-

---

[30]"Survey of Mobile Communications."
[31]"The Financial Report," Reuters, August 16, 1993.

ket would pay between $7 billion and $10 billion to obtain the necessary licenses, and then spend additional billions to build the network.[32] Indeed, many were skeptical that PCS, when finally developed, would be substantially better than cellular, arguing that cellular could already do everything PCS could. And given the fact that cellular operators like McCaw would be switching to digital service by 2000, the advantages PCS offered became even less compelling.[33] Regardless of one's view, it was important to consider the implementation of PCS in any 10-year projections of the industry.

Potential Obstacles for Cellular

While the consumer appeal of cellular was evident, the financial success could not be assured. This was due to the fact that the U.S. telecommunications industry in 1992 had yet to turn its technology from a high-priced business tool into a lower-priced mass-market product. In addition, companies offering cellular service continued to be unprofitable because of the huge up-front capital expenditures required to acquire licenses and expand their customer bases. In total, $11 billion was spent in 1992. The cost of acquiring new subscribers in the early 1990s ran between $500 and $1,300 per person at a time when revenues per subscriber had begun to flatten as the more price-sensitive consumer market was being tapped. Indeed, the average monthly bill dropped from over $100 in the late 1980s to about $70 in 1992.

Another risk of cellular arose in recent weeks and focused on whether handheld phones posed a health hazard. At issue was whether the radiation levels from portable cellular signals had the strength to permeate healthy human tissues and cause cancer. Medical professionals said that it did not, citing the absence of conclusive evidence to link handheld phones with the disease. The debate, however, continued and frightened some consumers.[34] In response, the Cellular Telecommunications Industry Association (CTIA) took the lead in the research effort. Industry leaders such as McCaw Cellular reassured the buying public that cellular phones were safe by offering their customers the chance to exchange their current phones for new ones. The health hazard allegations, if true, would seriously jeopardize the growth potential of the industry. The CTIA, it was expected, would publish its findings in early 1993.

Cellular Industry Outlook

A general industry outlook is given in Exhibit 10—this incorporates the optimistic expectations of Craig McCaw. Recent domestic economic data can be found in Exhibit 11. Industry analysts largely agreed on the number of POPs because the FCC had awarded all its cellular licenses and the U.S. population growth rate was steady at approximately 1 percent annually. Analysts differed on how quickly penetration growth would occur. McCaw

---

[32]"PCS Advantages Still Up in the Air," *Seattle Times,* September 24, 1993, p. E1.
[33]Ibid.
[34]"Cellular Firms Grapple with Cancer Scare," *USA Today,* February 1, 1993, p. 1B.

believed that the number of subscribers would grow at about 25 percent annually from 1993 to 2003. This was in excess of what some analysts estimated. However, McCaw believed the mass-market appeal of cellular would be realized more rapidly as monthly service costs continued to fall. Customers had already demonstrated that the convenience of cellular was highly valued. Also, he believed that PCS would complement cellular communications and that demand would expand as wireless communication became more popular and less costly.

Consolidation among industry leaders would likely occur in an effort to preserve market dominance and fend off new competition in cellular communications. Exhibit 12 presents recent economic data and financial information relating to comparable cellular firms. Given the recent lull in mergers and acquisitions activity, though, as shown by Exhibit 13, it was uncertain when consolidation might commence. To be profitable, cellular companies had to have one eye on costs in order to maximize margins and the other eye on subscriber growth. Technology and service upgrades would likely necessitate large capital expenditures in the future if firms are to maintain low churn rates (the annual percentage of existing customers who changed or disconnected service).

McCaw's optimism about industry growth and penetration was echoed by a 1991 study by Arthur D. Little that suggested that 10 years after PCS became universally available, it might serve as many as 60 million subscribers. It remained unclear, however, what impact PCS would have on current cellular customers. While PCS might initially convince some cellular customers to switch, industry specialists largely agreed that PCS would complement, not compete with, cellular, and would thus expand the market. PCS might be used more by pedestrians, but cellular technology was anticipated to be used more by vehicular callers.[35]

Regulatory Environment

The U.S. telecommunications industry was heavily regulated, with the FCC, the DOJ, the various states, and more recently Judge Harold Greene all having a say in the industry's regulatory oversight. The risks associated with the high level of regulation were normally allocated by business activities and could range from having changes in a company's stock price due to delays in obtaining regulatory approval for certain transactions to having to put in place new and costly operating procedures as a result of a regulatory edict. Most companies in this industry were adept at keeping close contact with the regulatory and legislative bodies in order to mitigate or minimize the potentially negative impact of regulations.

Others argued that the recent rate of technological change in telecommunications had made past regulatory policy obsolete, no longer indicative of the state of the industry. Judge Green, who oversaw the breakup of AT&T's monopoly, was clear in what he hoped divestiture would accomplish: independent competition in long-distance, local-exchange service, and equipment manufacture. The impact of current cellular technology, which could not have been known in 1982, might allow certain companies to cross the lines between these three separate business categories. In fact, it became possible for long-distance companies such as AT&T to offer local service via cellular networks. If Judge

---

[35]"Survey of Mobile Communications."

Green's intent could be circumvented, perhaps the entire regulatory establishment needed to be reevaluated. The prospect of regulatory change would add another element of uncertainty to the futures of McCaw and AT&T.

The U.S. Radio Spectrum

The U.S. government, through the FCC, assigned various locations in the airwaves for public services, such as police and emergency preparedness systems, and for private services, such as broadcast TV, CB radio, and paging systems. What spectrum was available, and who could use it, had an impact that cut across local, state, national and international boundaries.

Exhibit 14 shows the location of the most common commercial communications services on the radio spectrum and their assigned transmission frequencies. A frequency was energy in the form of an electromagnetic wave commonly measured in hertz (cycles per second), and a band of frequencies was a range between two defined limits. Earlier technologies (AM and FM radio, broadcast TV) tended to lie at the low end of the spectrum (0 to 108 megahertz [MHz]), while newer technologies tended to lie at the higher end of the spectrum (824 to 1990 MHz).

Cellular versus PCS

Currently, cellular was the only significant commercial, mobile, wireless communication product. While the FCC recently completed its allocation of the cellular spectrum via license auctions, strong demand for additional cellular licenses remained. The FCC, equipment manufacturers, and service providers were therefore looking at new ways to grow the number of players in the rapidly expanding mobile communications industry.

One such possibility was PCS, the digital-based technology. The development of PCS was driven by two major factors: the demand for more mobile licenses and the potential for worldwide mobile services. As noted, when the cellular spectrum was originally allocated by the FCC in the early 1980s, duopolies were created in each cellular market. McCaw was the early winner, having successfully bid for many of these licenses throughout the United States with the intention of creating a nationwide cellular network. This methodology guaranteed customers a choice, albeit limited, in the selection of a cellular service provider. As the demand for cellular service rose, firms anxious to provide cellular services could not gain access because firms like McCaw held the exclusive licenses.

The FCC defined PCS "as a family of mobile or portable radio communications services which could provide services to individuals and business, and be integrated with a variety of competing networks."[36] No one knew what mobile services, including PCS, would look like in the future, although some believed PCS would supplement current mobile services (cellular, paging, and mobile radio), combining individual customer mobility with various communication services. While PCS was seen by some as a cellular competitor, others argued that the development of PCS would likely expand, not contract, the total mobile communications market. Although it demonstrated considerable economic potential on paper, PCS remained an unproven technology.

---

[36]Ibid., p. 3.

It was hoped that PCS ultimately would create new services and lower the price of existing cellular services to the customer. Further, foreign nations had developed their own cellular services, with different spectrum bands than are the standard in the United States. As a result, global equipment manufacturers have pressured domestic firms to customize their products and services for use abroad. The successful development of PCS would therefore represent a unique market opportunity, as it would respond to these pressures by creating a new class of mobile communications that fit an international standard, without affecting the domestic cellular spectrum.

PREPARING TO NEGOTIATE THE DEAL

On September 30, 1992, Alex Mandl, lead negotiator for AT&T, and Craig McCaw were discussing the possibility of embarking on some sort of collaborative effort in cellular communications. McCaw was reluctant to sell but would probably do so at the right price because he recognized the strong synergies that would exist if AT&T were to throw its muscle behind McCaw's billion-dollar cellular operation. Craig anticipated that AT&T might make a proposal, and he believed the company must be prepared to respond immediately. James Barksdale joined McCaw in 1992 as president after nine years as CFO at Federal Express and assumed a primary role in the negotiations. His concern for the customer impressed McCaw and helped Craig understand why an AT&T/McCaw deal might work—AT&T was great at signing up customers, and that was currently one of McCaw's most important strategic objectives.[37]

The potential synergies between McCaw and AT&T were extraordinary—for McCaw, cost savings through SG&A consolidation, access to new technology from Bell Labs, vertical integration with AT&T and its switching equipment, increased advertising power, use of the well-recognized AT&T name, and the ability to refinance company debt at AT&T's more favorable AA credit rating.[38] AT&T would receive local-access fee reductions and instant access to state-of-the-art technology without directly confronting the RBOCs or having to infuse capital to build an independent cellular network. Allen noted that he was certain a merger would work to "extend AT&T's presence around the globe."[39]

In order for these synergies to be realized, two potential issues would have to be addressed. First, would British Telecom (BT) agree to go along with a merger that would concede the dominant cellular network in the lucrative U.S. market to AT&T, its archrival, and allow it to become a global communications services provider? And second, how would Craig McCaw fit into the new management picture?

British Telecom had invested $1.5 billion in McCaw in 1989 as a way to participate in the growth of the North American telecommunications market. BT had attempted through acquisition to expand its reach into North America and, in addition to cellular, wanted a piece of the emerging market for movies on demand at home, interactive games, home

---

[37]"Craig McCaw's Cautious Gambles," *Forbes,* March 1, 1993, p. 10.
[38]"McCaw Megamerger Won't Slow Its Growth Here," *Puget Sound Business Journal* 14, no. 14, Sec. 1, p. 1.
[39]Ibid.

shopping, and vast information databases.[40] It had been rumored that BT was looking for acquisition candidates that would help capture some of this anticipated market. While McCaw provided access to the cellular market and positioned BT to take advantage of PCS when it materialized, some speculated that the home-data highway could be more lucrative than mobile communications. Further, if BT were going to maximize its access to North America through McCaw, BT wanted management control of McCaw, a goal that was almost impossible since U.S. laws in 1992 limited foreign ownership in radio licensees to less than 20 percent.[41]

British Telecom stood to realize a loss on its investment if it were to sell its 20 percent interest at the current market price of about $24 per share. While there was no guarantee BT would go along with a McCaw/AT&T deal, Craig was on favorable terms with the BT directors on his board and believed they would be amenable to a transaction if it arose for two reasons. First, BT had been experiencing poor earnings recently and might welcome a chance to end its alliance with loss-ridden McCaw. Second, a sale of shares through an acquisition by AT&T would probably deliver a premium price above the current market price and reduce (if not eliminate) any loss on the investment. (BT's investment basis was $41.50 per share.) Third, BT would welcome any opportunity to redeploy any cash proceeds of the sale into the home-data highway.

THE ACQUISITION OF LIN BROADCASTING

LIN Broadcasting, a large New York–based communications firm, owned television properties (seven stations, five in top-10 markets) and cellular licenses in the lucrative markets of New York, Los Angeles, Philadelphia, Houston, and Dallas. Since 1969, LIN had been headed by Donald Pels, a respected media executive who left a lucrative position at Capital Cities to take the helm there. Under his leadership, LIN had become a media powerhouse having broad access to the nation's largest markets. By June 1989, LIN's market price had grown to $116 per share, up from $0.17 per share in the early 1970s. In September 1992, LIN's stock price was $67.60 per share, giving it a market capitalization of roughly $3.5 billion. Analysts guessed that the noncellular segment of LIN represented at most $1 billion of LIN's equity value.

Craig McCaw was particularly interested in LIN for two reasons: (1) its New York and Los Angeles penetration, two markets McCaw had been unable to break into, and (2) its below-average service in the markets in which it competed. Therefore, McCaw moved to acquire LIN in 1989. A recent equity infusion by BT in exchange for 20 percent of McCaw Cellular and McCaw's 40 percent common equity ownership in LIN had given him the financial flexibility he needed to pursue this acquisition. In early 1989, though, BellSouth emerged as a "white knight" for LIN and McCaw found himself in the middle of an auction. To improve his bargaining position, McCaw showed his tactical brilliance by secretly arranging to purchase John Kluge's 45 percent interest in LIN's New York cellular franchise

---

[40]Paul Andrews and Casey Corr, "Deal Takes Data Highway Global," *Seattle Times,* June 2, 1993.
[41]47 U.S.C. 310 (1992).

for $1.9 billion. If BellSouth eventually acquired LIN, the company would be forced to either buy Kluge out at a premium or allow McCaw to come in as a full partner, per the terms of McCaw's side deal with Kluge.

Finally, in November 1989, after months of bidding against BellSouth, McCaw, in a hostile takeover, successfully bid $3.4 billion, or $154.11 per share, for 52 percent of LIN Broadcasting and control. He owned about 27 million common shares. The $3 billion financing package had been arranged previously through a consortium of 43 lenders. As shown in Exhibit 15, the new debt added substantially to the firm's leverage and severely limited the company's financial flexibility.

The terms of the deal treated Pels extraordinarily well, allowing him to sell his 1.3 million stock options to McCaw for about $200 million, giving him the equivalent of a $25 per share premium over what common shareholders were to receive. Common shareholders could sell 47 percent of their LIN holdings to McCaw for $154.11 per share and would also receive $17 of McCaw stock for each remaining share of LIN they held. A final condition of the deal was that McCaw Cellular had to purchase the remaining 48 percent of LIN by October 1995 or divest itself of its current 52 percent ownership.

If McCaw bought LIN in its entirety, it would get the benefit of 100 percent of LIN's POPs but would spend billions for that privilege.[42] If McCaw chose to sell LIN, however, the company would lose the revenues it currently derived from its 52 percent ownership of LIN but would likely receive several billion dollars from the sale.[43] AT&T, as a potential buyer, would therefore be betting on LIN's volatility over the next five years. The deciding component in valuing LIN would therefore be establishing a reasonable market price, five years in the future. Some analysts estimated an asset value by applying a multiple of 11 to 13 to LIN's projected 1995 operating cash flow—this was a standard valuation approach in September 1992. Several industry sources noted that LIN's market value under these assumptions might be as low as $95 per share or as high as $125 per share. LIN's stock price information is shown in Exhibit 3.

Valuing McCaw Cellular

Many questions remained in Craig McCaw's mind as he thought about a potential deal with AT&T. Determining a fair value for his company, given the projected growth in the cellular/PCS market, was certain to be a difficult task. At issue was how much the company was actually worth at current and projected subscriber rates, revenue per subscriber, and anticipated penetration. Exhibit 16 provides information regarding interest rates and current capital market conditions. Exhibit 17 presents information on recent cellular industry mergers and acquisitions transactions.

Substantial savings in marketing and SG&A would probably result from a deal with AT&T—how large an impact would those have on McCaw's profitability? And what impact would the future capital expenditures required to add PCS and convert to digital

---

[42]Exhibit 18 models the purchase result, though it does not include a payment for the remaining shares of LIN.

[43]Exhibit 18 can be adjusted to reflect the sale of McCaw's shares in LIN. The proceeds of a share sale are not automatically included in the forecasted free cash flows.

have on his firm's value? Industry experts expected that the average value for cellular firms in 1993 would grow to over \$200/POP, but that, of course, was the average.[44] Some of these concerns are dealt with in Exhibit 18, which details McCaw's 10-year cash-flow forecast, assuming it would purchase LIN in 1995.

McCaw anticipated growth in POPs to be relatively stable at 1 percent per year, but expected the gains in annual penetration to be high—as shown in Exhibit 10, the penetration would be nearly 46 percent by year-end 2003. This reflected his belief that subscriber volume would increase rapidly. Even though monthly revenue per subscriber would drop, the increased volume would make up for the smaller incremental revenue. PCS would emerge as a complementary technology, and expand demand for all wireless services, including cellular. Marketing expenses were going to drop and McCaw expected them to decline to slightly more than the industry average of 7 percent. Capital expenditure and net working capital requirements per subscriber would also drop as the industry matured, technology improved, and subscribers increased. Exhibit 18 incorporates McCaw's assumptions about these items.

Exhibit 18 assumes that McCaw would purchase LIN's remaining 48 percent of equity outstanding in 1995. Revenues, expenses, depreciation, capital expenditures, and changes in net working capital are adjusted for the expansion of McCaw's interest in LIN. The "yes/no" switch in the upper left-hand corner of the model adjusts the cash-flow forecasts for whether or not LIN would be acquired in 1995. However, the forecast *does not* reflect the outlay associated with McCaw buying the remaining 48 percent, or the proceeds from selling its 52 percent interest.

An informal McCaw survey of its subscribers revealed that the cellular service brand with the most national recognition was Cellular One (the McCaw brand name), and the second most recognized name was AT&T—even though AT&T did not sell cellular service.[45] Perhaps a merger with AT&T was a good match after all, thought McCaw. The critical issue was to structure a deal that maximized shareholder value and minimized the tax burden to the McCaw family, given their very low basis. McCaw would also have to answer to the FCC. The FCC could be a skeptical audience for a transaction that would enable two industry powerhouses to outpace their rivals, thereby reducing the benefits to customers brought about by industry competition.

Exhibit 4 lists members of McCaw's board of directors, who were experienced business executives and sophisticated investors. They would be willing to entertain offers for the company in cash, common stock of the acquirer, and even somewhat "exotic" forms of consideration such as preferred stock and convertible debentures. Perhaps Craig would even consider sharing in the upside potential of the cellular business going forward through a preferred dividend. What might be the appropriate debt/equity mix and form of structure that would be necessary to ensure the long-term survival and fiscal health of McCaw Cellular? Craig knew that any deal would require a vote by all company shareholders. And while Exhibit 19 (which presents a breakdown of the company's stock ownership) suggests such approval was a formality, it was important that Craig show his investors the ways in which value would be created for them, so as to avoid any litigation.

---

[44]*Reuters,* August 13, 1993.
[45]"Craig McCaw's Cautious Gambles," p. 12.

McCaw had two classes of stock: Class A and Class B. Each Class B share was convertible into one Class A share, but each Class B share had 10 votes while a Class A share had a single vote. Craig McCaw and his family were the principal holders of the Class B shares, thus furthering his voting control over the other shareholders.

Craig had the sense that AT&T was eager to jump into the cellular industry, having ignored the market opportunity that had previously arisen in the mid-1980s, namely, purchasing cellular licenses at bargain prices and waiting for demand to catch on. Perhaps Craig could even convince Allen to assume McCaw's $5 billion in debt, thus improving the company's cash-flow situation. How much did Craig think he needed—depending upon how desperate AT&T was, could Craig and his family be cashed out at a very favorable multiple? In addition to the benefits derived from the stock options and shares held by Craig and his family (see Exhibit 19), Craig received $155,385 in cash compensation in 1991.

Craig knew that a deal with AT&T was an incredible opportunity. However, if the deal were not lucrative enough, Craig was happy to sit tight with his seamless network of cellular communication, sign up cellular customers, position himself to exploit PCS and convert his network over to digital, and wait for another bidder to come along. After all, as the undisputed market leader, he could afford to.

EXHIBIT 1 Historical Income Statements McCaw Cellular Communications, Inc. (in millions, except where noted)

	1989	1990	1991	Year-to-Date September 30, 1992
Revenues:				
Cellular	$ 446,503	$ 830,497	$ 1,135,240	$ —
Broadcast	—	116,820	129,481	—
RCC and other	57,635	90,136	100,850	—
Net revenues	$ 504,138	$ 1,037,453	$ 1,365,571	$ 1,249,102
Expenses:				
Operating	437,745	715,288	888,419	767,679
Corporate	14,254	20,860	16,514	15,522
Depreciation	65,059	103,288	143,231	129,928
Amortization of intangibles	127,312	149,637	201,376	154,767
Subtotal	644,370	989,073	1,249,540	1,067,896
Operating income (loss)	$ (140,232)	$ 48,380	$ 116,031	$ 181,206
Other income:				
Interest expense	(245,523)	(496,602)	(577,992)	(377,955)
Interest income	54,097	45,612	30,072	13,979
Net gain on assets sold	28,204	1,172,896	249,479	2,589
Equity in income of unconsolidated investees	6,885	16,752	22,874	38,258
Nonrecurring benefit (charge)	—	(16,621)	6,241	—
Subtotal	722,037	(269,326)	(323,129)	(156,337)
Profit before tax	$ (296,569)	$ 770,417	$ (153,295)	$ (141,923)
Taxes	760	314,505	49,486	(23,062)
Profit after tax	$ (297,329)	$455,912	$ (202,781)	$ (164,985)
Minority interest				
(Income) loss of consolidated subsidiaries	8,790	(32,165)	(14,000)	(16,439)
Provision of pref. stock dividend to subsidiary	—	(52,348)	(134,300)	(100,725)
Income tax benefit of prior year's losses	—	190,919	—	—
Net income	$ (288,539)	$ 562,318	$ (351,081)	$ (282,149)
Weighted avg. number of shares outstanding	148,157,863	182,414,174	181,487,060	182,499,000
Proportionate subscribers[a]	434,000	687,000	985,000	1,252,000
Proportionate POPs[b]	52,066,000	55,900,000	57,400,000	58,500,000

[a]In thousands; includes McCaw's 52 percent ownership of LIN's subscribers.
[b]Figure is as-is; includes McCaw's 52 percent ownership of LIN's POPs.

Sources: McCaw Cellular Communications 1991 annual report; 1992 SEC 10-Q Filings.

EXHIBIT 2   Historical Balance Sheet Information McCaw Cellular Communications, Inc. (in thousands)

	FYE 12/31/89	*FYE 12/31/90*	*FYE 12/31/91*	*3Q Ended 9/30/92*
Current assets				
Cash and cash equivalents	$ 461,806	$ 345,309	$ 138,184	$ 161,982
Marketable securities	435,847	65,691	258,243	153,276
Accounts receivable, net[a]	63,835	155,250	202,196	241,268
Federal tax benefit receivable	—	47,825	—	—
Other	34,185	36,855	39,103	50,651
Total current assets	$ 995,673	$ 650,930	$ 637,726	$ 607,177
PPE, net[b]	630,264	874,725	1,196,482	1,328,240
Licensing costs, net[c]	789,211	4,403,825	3,996,628	4,783,390
Other intangibles, net[d]	139,392	687,237	823,441	—
Investments	358,326	1,855,407	1,861,016	1,876,336
Other	128,478	242,041	201,403	186,405
Subtotal	2,045,671	8,063,235	8,078,970	8,174,371
Total assets	$3,041,344	$8,714,165	$8,716,696	$8,781,548
Current liabilities				
Current portion of long-term debt	$ 13,422	$ 37,452	$ 48,117	$ 68,199
Accounts payable	194,197	82,312	107,859	69,459
Accrued expenses[e]	—	210,083	290,669	294,824
Unearned revenues/Customer deposits	14,637	32,113	44,324	54,800
Total current liabilities	$ 222,256	$ 361,960	$ 490,969	$ 487,282
Long-term debt	1,738,896	5,224,777	5,198,838	5,526,499
Minority interests	29,743	—	—	—
Mandatory repurchase obligation	46,480	—	—	—
Other	—	180,369	245,580	168,286
Subtotal	1,815,119	5,405,146	5,444,418	5,694,785
Total liabilities	$2,037,375	$5,767,106	$5,935,387	$6,182,067
Redeemable preferred stock of subsidiary	—	902,348	1,036,648	1,137,373
Preferred stock outstanding, $0.01 par 10 million shares authorized	—	—	—	—
Common stock outstanding, $0.01 par				
Class A: 400 million shares authorized[f]	935	1,128	1,212	1,225
Class B: 200 million shares authorized[g]	705	666	611	601
Additional paid-in-capital	1,646,247	2,156,722	2,226,167	2,232,780
Less Class B stock held in Treasury, at cost[h]	(10,958)	—	—	—
Cumulative accretion of mandatory repurchase obligation	(42,725)	—	—	—
Deficit	(590,235)	(113,805)	(483,329)	(772,498)
Total stockholders' investment	$1,003,969	$2,947,059	$2,781,309	$2,599,481
Total liabilities and stockholders' investment	$3,041,344	$8,714,165	$8,716,696	$8,781,548

[a]Allowance for doubtful accounts: 1989—$10,860; 1990—$22,331; 1991—$25,334.
[b]Accumulated depreciation and amortization: 1989—$139,630; 1990—$212,401; 1991—$336,409. Total capital expenditures for 1991 were $305,078,000.
[c]Accumulated amortization: 1989—$166,868; 1990—$206,425; 1991—$302,050.
[d]Accumulated amortization: 1989—129,020; 1990—$170,043; 1991—$269,514; Included in Licensing Costs for September 30, 1992.
[e]Included with accounts payable in 1989.
[f]1989–93—538,454 shares outstanding; 1990—112,810,611 shares outstanding; 1991—121,205,785 shares outstanding.
[g]1989—70,126,906 shares outstanding; 1990—66,389,937 shares outstanding; 1991—61,072,994 shares outstanding.
[h]385,000 shares of Class B stock.

Sources: McCaw Cellular Communications 1991, 1992 annual reports.

EXHIBIT 3   Monthly Closing Stock Price McCaw Cellular Communications and LIN Broadcasting

McCaw Cellular		LIN Broadcasting	
Month	*Stock Price*	*Month*	*Stock Price*
October 1990	$12.00	October 1990	$39.70
November 1990	$15.13	November 1990	$53.02
December 1990	$17.50	December 1990	$56.45
January 1991	$17.50	January 1991	$59.89
February 1991	$23.38	February 1991	$61.05
March 1991	$25.13	March 1991	$57.83
April 1991	$26.00	April 1991	$62.66
May 1991	$23.75	May 1991	$62.19
June 1991	$23.88	June 1991	$53.70
July 1991	$24.00	July 1991	$62.19
August 1991	$27.38	August 1991	$67.02
September 1991	$30.13	September 1991	$67.70
October 1991	$28.13	October 1991	$65.64
November 1991	$26.63	November 1991	$57.38
December 1991	$29.63	December 1991	$65.64
January 1992	$33.25	January 1992	$68.39
February 1992	$34.88	February 1992	$72.06
March 1992	$30.13	March 1992	$68.39
April 1992	$28.00	April 1892	$67.02
May 1992	$27.75	May 1992	$61.50
June 1992	$24.25	June 1992	$58.75
July 1992	$27.25	July 1992	$63.69
August 1992	$24.25	August 1992	$61.27
September 1992	$24.38	September 1992	$67.70
High	$34.88	High	$72.06
Low	$12.00	Low	$39.70
Average	$24.78	Average	$61.70
Beta*	3.16	Beta*	2.07
Volatility†	39.81%	Volatility†	31.84%

*Beta was calculated against the S&P 500 index from weekly data over the period October 1, 1990, to September 30, 1992.
†Volatility was calculated from daily data for the 260 most recent trading days ending September 30, 1992.

Sources: Bloomberg Financial Service, *Value Line Investment Survey.*

EXHIBIT 4   McCaw Cellular Communications, Inc., Board of Directors

Member	Age	Details
Craig O. McCaw	42	Chairman of the board and chief executive officer, McCaw Cellular Communications, Inc.
Wayne M. Perry	42	Vice chairman of the board and former president, McCaw Cellular Communications, Inc.
James L. Barksdale	49	President and chief operating officer (COO), McCaw Cellular Communications, Inc., and former EVP and COO Federal Express Corp. Mr. Barksdale serves as a director of 3Com Corporation, Envoy Corporation, and Promus Companies Incorporated.
Harold S. Eastman	53	Former president and vice chairman of the board, McCaw Cellular Communications, Inc.
John W. Stanton	36	Chairman, Stanton Communications, chairman of the board, General Cellular Corporation, and former vice chairman of the board, McCaw Cellular Communications, Inc.
John E. McCaw, Jr.	41	Director and former EVP Acquisitions, McCaw Cellular Communications, Inc.
Bruce R. McCaw	45	Director. Mr. McCaw serves as a director of Forbes Westar, Inc.
John P. Giuggio	61	President and chief operating officer, Affiliated Publications.
Harold W. Anderson	68	Contributing editor and former publisher, Omaha World-Herald; former chairman, president and CEO Omaha World-Herald Company. Mr. Anderson serves as a director of Raleigh (North Carolina) News and Observer Publishing Co.; The Williams Companies; Great Lakes Forest Products, Ltd.; and Morrison Knudsen Corporation.
John C. Malone	51	President and chief executive officer Tele-Communications, Inc. Dr. Malone serves as a director of various companies including United Artists Entertainment, Inc., Turner Broadcasting Systems, Inc., and the Bank of New York.
Daniel J. Evans	66	U.S. senator and former governor, State of Washington. Senator Evans serves as a director of various companies including Puget Sound Power and Light, Tera Computer Company, and Burlington Northern Inc.
Malcolm Argent	56	Secretary and director, British Telecommunication PLC (BT).
Barry D. Romeril	48	Group finance director, BT.
Bruce R. Bond	45	Group Products and Services Director, BT. Mr. Bond is a former vice president of US West and Mountain Bell Telephone Company.
R. C. M. Baker	45	President and chief executive officer, BT North America.

Source: McCaw Cellular Communications, Inc., 1991 annual report.

EXHIBIT 5   Historical Income Statements American Telephone & Telegraph (all figures in millions)

	FYE 12/31/89	*FYE 12/31/90*	*FYE 12/31/91**	*YTD 9/30/92*
Revenues				
Telecommunications services	$38,475	$38,263	$38,805	$29,856
Sales of products and systems	15,241	16,124	15,941	11,167
Rentals and other services	6,956	6,993	6,959	5,060
Financial services and leasing	428	811	1,384	1,317
Net revenues	$61,100	$62,191	$63,089	$47,400
Costs				
Telecommuncations services	26,045	25,633	25,276	19,050
Products and systems	8,849	9,228	9,134	6,665
Rentals and other services	3,596	3,377	3,344	2,379
Financial services and leasing	244	645	1,071	940
Subtotal	38,734	38,883	38,825	29,034
Gross margin	$22,366	$23,308	$24,264	$18,366
Operating expenses				
SG&A	14,244	14,782	16,220	11,574
R&D	3,098	2,935	3,114	2,204
Provision for business restructuring	—	95	3,572	39
Subtotal	17,342	17,812	22,906	13,817
Operating income (loss)	5,024	5,496	1,358	4,549
Other income, net	427	257	251	344
Interest expense	(720)	(874)	(726)	(500)
Profit before tax	$ 4,731	$ 4,879	$ 883	$ 4,393
Taxes	(1,622)	(1,775)	(361)	(1,586)
Profit after tax	$ 3,109	$ 3,104	$ 522	$ 2,807
Income tax benefit of prior year's losses	—	—	—	—
Net income	$ 3,109	$ 3,104	$ 522	$ 2,807
Weighted-average number of shares outstanding	1,294	1,282	1,293	1,329
Capital expenditures	$ 3,959	$ 4,120	$ 4,086	1,057
Earnings per share	$2.40	$2.42	$0.40	$2.11
Dividends per common share	$1.20	$1.32	$1.32	$0.99

*Considers $4,500 of business restructuring, which reduced net income by $2,863, or $2.21 per common share.

Sources: AT&T 1991, 1992 annual reports and SEC 10-Q filings.

EXHIBIT 6   Historical Balance Sheets American Telephone & Telegraph (in millions)

	FYE 12/31/89	FYE 12/31/90	FYE 12/31/91	3Q end. 9/30/92
Current assets				
Cash and temporary cash investments	$ 1,183	$ 1,875	$ 2,148	$ 905
Receivables less allowances	9,555	—	—	—
Accounts receivable, net[a]	—	10,226	11,050	11,312
Finance receivables	—	3,187	5,476	7,601
Inventories	3,206	3,125	3,125	3,256
Deferred income taxes	942	1,315	2,311	2,158
Other	405	618	503	561
Total current assets	$15,291	$20,346	$24,613	$25,793
PPE, net	15,919	18,661	18,689	18,823
Investments	1,187	1,471	976	978
Finance receivables	—	2,658	3,180	3,668
Prepaid pension costs	—	3,094	3,084	3,615
Other[b]	5,290	2,092	2,813	3,388
Subtotal	22,396	27,976	28,742	30,472
Total assets	$37,687	$48,322	$53,355	$56,265
Current liabilities				
Current portion of long-term debt	$ 2,426	$ 5,090	$ 7,053	$ 6,721
Benefit and payroll related	2,571	2,896	3,259	3,446
Accounts payable	4,763	4,846	4,989	5,105
Dividends payable	323	383	432	441
Other	2,154	3,817	5,258	5,247
Total current liabilities	$12,237	$17,032	$20,991	$20,960
Long-term debt including capital leases	8,144	9,354	8,484	8,851
Other	1,390	1,599	2,902	2,714
Deferred income taxes	2,070	3,153	3,426	4,450
Other deferred credits	819	250	339	281
Unamortized investment tax credits	289	736	568	414
Subtotal	12,712	15,092	15,719	16,710
Total liabilities	$24,949	$32,124	$36,710	$37,670
Minority interests	—	315	417	395
Common stock outstanding, $1.00 par				
1.5 billion shares authorized[c]	1,076	1,275	1,309	1,333
Additional paid-in-capital	8,700	9,497	10,624	11,163
Guaranteed ESOP obligation	—	(519)	(462)	(407)
Foreign currency translation	—	50	158	191
Retained earnings	2,962	5,580	4,599	5,921
Total shareholders' equity	$12,738	$15,883	$16,228	$18,201
Total liabilities and shareholders' equity	$37,687	$48,322	$53,355	$56,266

[a]Includes capital and operating lease receivables.
[b]Includes amortization of goodwill: 1990—$50; 1991—$52.
[c]Year ending 12/89—1,290,075,798 shares outstanding; 12/90—1,275,202,000 shares; 12/91—1,309,352,000 shares; 9/92—1,332,861,000 shares.

Sources: AT&T Corporation 1991 annual report, third-quarter 1992 10-Q filing with SEC.

EXHIBIT 7   Historical Stock Prices American Telephone & Telegraph

Month	Stock Price
January 1991	$32.75
February 1991	$33.38
March 1991	$34.38
April 1991	$37.50
May 1991	$37.13
June 1991	$38.25
July 1991	$39.88
August 1991	$39.00
September 1991	$37.50
October 1991	$38.75
November 1991	$36.25
December 1991	$39.13
January 1992	$37.25
February 1992	$37.13
March 1992	$40.75
April 1992	$43.25
May 1992	$42.50
June 1992	$43.00
July 1992	$44.00
August 1992	$42.25
September 1992	$43.63
High	$44.00
Low	$32.75
Average	$38.94
Beta:*	0.97
Volatility:†	18.19%

*Beta was calculated with respect to the S&P 500 index from weekly data over the period January 1, 1991, to September 30, 1992.
†Volatility was calculated from daily data for the 260 most recent trading days ending September 30, 1992.

Source: Bloomberg Financial Services.

EXHIBIT 8   Cellular Architecture

Cellular Architecture

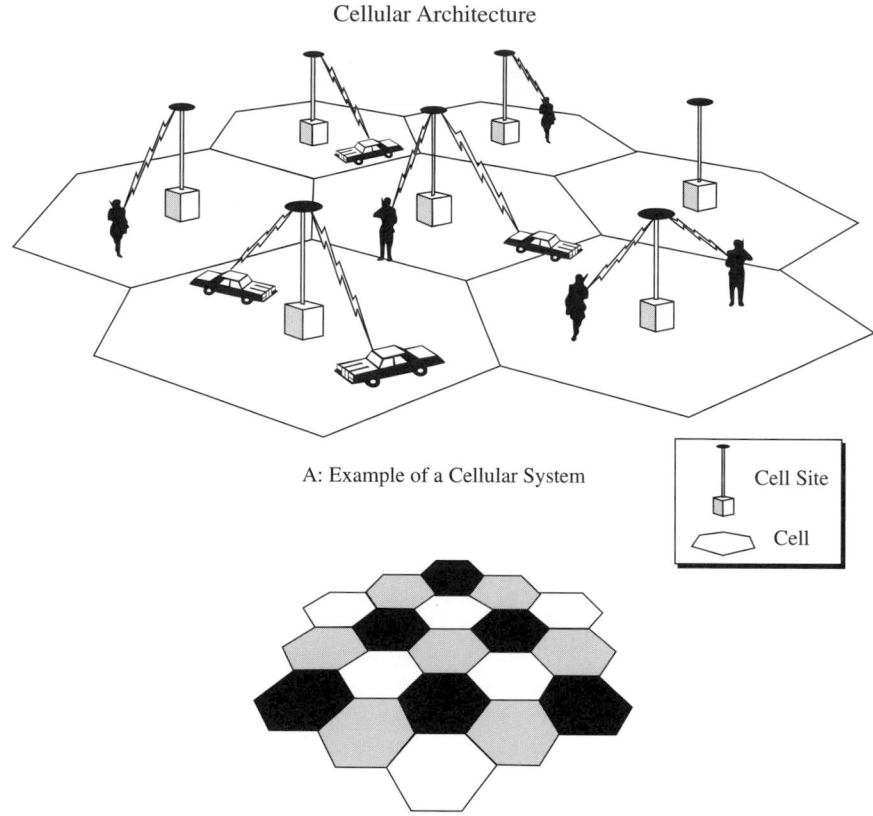

A: Example of a Cellular System

Cell Site

Cell

B: Frequency Re-Use Cellular Architecture

Source: Figure 5B: U.S. Congress, Office of Technology Assessment (OTA), *Wireless Technologies and the National Information Infrastructure,* OTA-ITC-622 (Washington, D.C.: U.S. Government Printing Office, July 1995), p. 83.

Copyright © 1995 Carol Weinhaus and the Telecommunications Industries Analysis Project Work Group, Boston, Massachusetts.

EXHIBIT 9 Historical Domestic Cellular Industry Growth: The AT&T/McCaw Cellular Merger Negotiation

Year	Subscribers (000s)	Revenues (MMs)	Capital Expenditures (MMs)	Revenues/ Subscriber	Capital Expenditures to Revenues	Capital Expenditures per Subscriber
1984	91.6	$ 178	$ 355	$1,943.23	199%	$3,873
1985	340.2	306	911	900.06	298	2,678
1986	681.8	463	1,437	678.35	311	2,107
1987	1,230.9	672	2,235	545.94	333	1,815
1988	2,069.4	1,074	3,274	518.75	305	1,582
1989	3,508.9	1,934	4,480	551.20	232	1,277
1990	5,188.0	4,569	6,219	880.65	136	1,199
1991	7,290.0	5,709	8,672	783.06	152	1,190
Compound annual growth rate 1984–91:		86.87%	64.12%	57.87%		
Compound annual growth rate 1989–91:		44.14%	71.80%	39.12%		
Annual growth rate 1990–91:		40.52%	24.94%	39.45%		

Original Source: Cellular Telephone Industry Association.

EXHIBIT 10   McCaw's 10-Year Cellular Industry Projections

	1991	*1992*	*1993*	*1994*	*1995*
Population (millions)*		256.10	258.60	261.10	263.60
% coverage	96%	96%	97%	97%	97%
Net POPs covered (millions)	—	245.86	250.84	253.27	255.69
% penetration year-end† (McCaw view)	8.89	4.5%	5.5%	6.8%	8.5%
Annual penetration gain (McCaw view)		1.3%	1.1%	1.3%	1.6%
Subscriber market size (mm) (McCaw view)		11.04	13.91	17.34	21.63
Annual growth (McCaw view)		46.0%	26.0%	24.7%	24.7%
Average subscribers (mm) (McCaw view)		9.30	12.47	15.63	19.48
Churn rate		2.2%	2.1%	2.0%	1.9%
High-use % of local subscribers		32.9%	29.6%	26.6%	23.9%
Mid-range % of local subscribers		38.1%	37.4%	36.4%	35.1%
Low-use/PCS % local subscribers		29.0%	33.0%	37.0%	41.0%
High-use local revenue/Subscribers		$107.64	$106.86	$104.56	$102.32
Mid-range local revenue/Subscribers		$ 64.41	$ 64.26	$ 63.92	$ 63.58
Low-use/PCS local revenue/Subscribers		$ 25.25	$ 25.50	$ 26.01	$ 26.79
Combined local revenue/Subscribers per month		$ 67.28	$ 64.08	$ 60.70	$ 57.75
Combined local annual revenue/Subscribers		$807.32	$768.95	$728.44	$693.06
Total local revenue (millions)		$ 7,508	$ 9,592	$11,383	$13,504
Roaming revenue/Subscribers per month		$ 9.61	$ 8.70	$ 8.00	$ 7.43
Combined roaming annual revenue/Subscribers		$115.32	$104.40	$ 96.00	$ 89.16
Total roaming revenue (millions)		$ 1,072	$ 1,302	$ 1,500	$ 1,737
Total revenue/Average subscribers per month		$ 76.89	$ 72.78	$ 68.70	$ 65.18
Total annual revenue (millions)		$ 8,581	$10,894	$12,884	$15,241

*Population growth assumed at 1 percent.
†Assumes two carriers per market.

Source for items other than "McCaw Outlook": *Cellular Investor,* Paul Kagan & Associates, Inc.
Source for "McCaw Outlook": Casewriter analysis.
"Wireless Cellular Architecture," from *Cellular to PCS: A Wireless Primer*, Copyright © 1995 by Carol Weinhaus and the Telecommunications Industries Analysis Project Work Group, Boston, MA, 1995.

1996	1997	1998	1999	2000	2001	2002	2003
266.20	268.80	271.40	274.00	276.60	279.30	282.00	284.80
97%	97%	97%	97%	97%	97%	97%	97%
258.21	260.74	263.26	265.78	268.30	270.92	273.54	276.26
10.4%	12.9%	15.9%	19.7%	24.3%	30.0%	37.1%	45.8%
2.0%	2.5%	3.0%	3.7%	4.6%	5.7%	7.1%	8.7%
26.97	33.63	41.94	52.29	65.19	81.30	101.38	126.44
24.7%	24.7%	24.7%	24.7%	24.7%	24.7%	24.7%	24.7%
24.30	30.30	37.79	47.12	58.74	73.25	91.34	113.91
1.8%	1.8%	1.7%	1.6%	1.6%	1.6%	1.6%	1.6%
21.6%	19.4%	17.5%	15.7%	14.1%	12.7%	11.6%	10.7%
33.4%	32.5%	31.0%	29.4%	27.4%	25.3%	23.4%	22.0%
45.0%	48.1%	51.5%	54.9%	58.5%	62.0%	65.0%	67.3%
$100.15	98.05	$ 96.00	$ 94.02	$ 92.10	$ 90.24	$ 86.43	$ 86.68
$ 63.24	$ 62.91	$ 62.58	$ 62.26	$ 61.93	$ 60.98	$ 60.05	$ 59.15
$ 27.60	$ 28.70	$ 29.85	$ 31.04	$ 31.35	$ 31.67	$ 31.98	$ 32.30
$ 55.17	$ 53.27	$ 51.57	$ 50.11	$ 48.29	$ 46.52	$ 44.86	$ 44.03
$662.09	$639.27	618.87	$601.28	$579.54	$558.29	$538.37	$528.31
$16,088	$19,371	$23,385	$28,330	$34,044	$40,893	$49,174	$60,179
$ 6.89	$ 6.43	$ 5.96	$ 5.51	$ 5.04	$ 4.58	$ 4.35	$ 4.07
$ 82.68	$ 77.16	$ 71.52	$ 66.12	$ 60.48	$ 54.96	$ 52.20	$ 48.84
$ 2,009	$ 2,338	$ 2,703	$ 3,115	$ 3,553	$ 4,026	$ 4,768	$ 5,563
$ 62.06	$ 59.70	$ 57.53	$ 55.62	$ 53.33	$ 51.10	$ 49.21	$ 48.10
$18,097	$21,710	$26,088	$31,445	$37,596	$44,918	$53,942	$65,743

EXHIBIT 11 Recent Economic Data United States of America

Unemployment		Inflation			Quarterly GDP Growth	
			CPI	PPI	1Q90	1.70%
1991	6.70%				2Q90	1.40%
January 1992	7.30	1988	4.10%	2.50%	3Q90	1.00%
February 1992	7.30	1989	4.80	5.20	4Q90	−0.50%
March 1992	7.20	1990	5.40	4.90		
April 1992	7.50	1991	4.20	2.10	1Q91	−2.00%
May 1992	7.80	1992	3.10	1.20	2Q91	−1.75%
June 1992	7.70	1993	3.70	2.60*	3Q91	−1.00%
July 1992	7.60				4Q91	0.00%
August 1992	7.50				1Q92	1.75%
September 1992	7.50				2Q92	1.75%
					3Q92	2.00%

Note: Constant 1987 dollars.

*First quarter projection

Source: *Federal Reserve Bulletin*, December 1992.

Source: *Industry Week.*

Source: William O'Neil & Co., Inc. Los Angeles, CA.

"U.S. Radio Spectrum Location of Commercial Services," from *Cellular to PCS: A Wireless Primer*, Copyright © 1995 by Carol Weinhaus and the Telecommunications Industries Analysis Project Work Group, Boston, MA, 1995.

EXHIBIT 12 Comparative Telecommunications Firms (in millions, except per share data)

	1991 Revenues	1991 Profits	Long-Term Debt	Average Share Price 1991	Shares Outstanding	Capital Expenditure per Share	Beta*	D/E Ratio	Value Line Financial Strength Rating†
Cellular									
McCaw Cellular	$ 1,366	$ (351)	$ 5,199	$30.00	182	$1.26	1.75	0.95	C+
AirTouch Cellular	782	17	257	N/A	424	0.55	1.45	N/A	A
British Telecom	23,206	3,268	6,563	62.60	616	6.91	0.85	0.17	A++
LIN Broadcasting	468	(838)	1,770	72.00	51	N/A	1.60	0.48	C++
US Cellular	99	24	193	19.75	48	1.19	1.70	0.20	B
Vanguard Cellular	89	(33)	184	27.00	25	N/A	2.20	0.27	NA
Contel Cellular	235	(119)	1,777	23.00	100	N/A	2.40	0.77	NA
Long-distance									
ATT Corp.	63,089	522	8,484	39.00	1,309	3.16	0.85	0.17	A+
MCI Communications	8,433	551	3,104	12.40	519	2.65	1.15	0.48	B+
Sprint	8,780	368	3,696	26.40	218	5.70	1.05	0.64	B+
Local									
Centel	1,181	160	1,331	33.00	85	N/A	1.05	0.47	B++
Bell Atlantic	12,280	1,332	7,960	48.60	396	6.21	0.80	0.41	A+
BellSouth	14,445	1,507	7,735	25.10	970	3.20	0.90	0.32	A+
SouthWestern Bell	9,332	1,076	5,675	32.00	600	N/A	0.90	0.30	N/A
GTE	19,621	1,733	16,037	31.25	889	4.46	0.95	0.58	A
Ameritech	10,818	1,233	4,963	31.40	533	4.04	1.75	0.30	A+
NYNEX	13,229	1,151	6,828	36.90	408	6.13	0.85	0.45	A+
PacTel	9,895	1,109	5,505	42.00	401	4.66	0.90	0.33	A+
US West	10,577	553	7,629	38.00	410	N/A	0.90	0.49	A+
AllTel Corporation	1,748	186	992	18.75	158	2.03	0.75	0.33	B++

*Information calculated using monthly stock prices over the past five years.
†Financial strength measures the likely capacity to obtain new debt financing, and ranges from strongest (A) to weakest (C).

Source: *Value Line Investment Survey;* and University of Virginia Darden Graduate School of Business Administration: Case "Centel Corporation," UVA-F-1078.

EXHIBIT 13 General Trends in Recent Mergers and Acquisitions Activity (values in billions, except where noted)

	4th Quarter 1991		1st Quarter 1992		2nd Quarter 1992		3rd Quarter 1992	
	Number of Deals	*Value*	*Number of Deals*	*Value*	*Number of Deals*	*Value*	*Number of Deals*	*Value*
All activity								
U.S. acquisitions	438	$24.31	414	$16.74	423	$18.66	427	$12.70
Non-U.S. acquisitions	41	3.02	31	0.98	31	2.06	21	0.80
U.S. acquisition, non-U.S.	41	3.13	50	0.24	60	0.69	53	2.41
Total	520	30.47	495	17.95	514	21.42	501	15.91
Number reporting price	160		119		137		168	
Divestitures only*	262	7.48	248	4.97	215	4.82	258	7.86
Number reporting price	77		54		55		81	
LBOs only*	32	1.69	20	0.66	19	1.18	22	2.19
Number reporting price	12		4		4		8	

*Included in all activity.

12-Month Moving-Average Stock Premiums

One Month before Announcement		Two Months before Announcement	
4Q91	54.68%	4Q91	53.78%
1Q92	54.20	1Q92	64.06
2Q92	53.10	2Q92	53.25
3Q92	50.00	3Q92	49.85

Mode of Payment

	Combined*	Cash	Stock
4Q91	65%	51%	28%
1Q92	50	51	43
2Q92	71	46	35
3Q92	69	88	40

Sales Volumes of Target Companies, October 1, 1991–September 30, 1992

Sales†	Number of Firms
$1–$5	88
$5.1–$10	52
$10.1–$15	27
$15.1–$25	50
$25.1–$35	35
$35.1–50	49
$50.1–$75	31
$75.1–$100	22
$100.1–$500	106
$500–	133

*"Combined" includes mixture of cash and stock.
†Sales are in millions.

Source: *Mergers & Acquisitions,* January/February 1993.

EXHIBIT 14 U.S. Radio Spectrum Location of Commercial Services

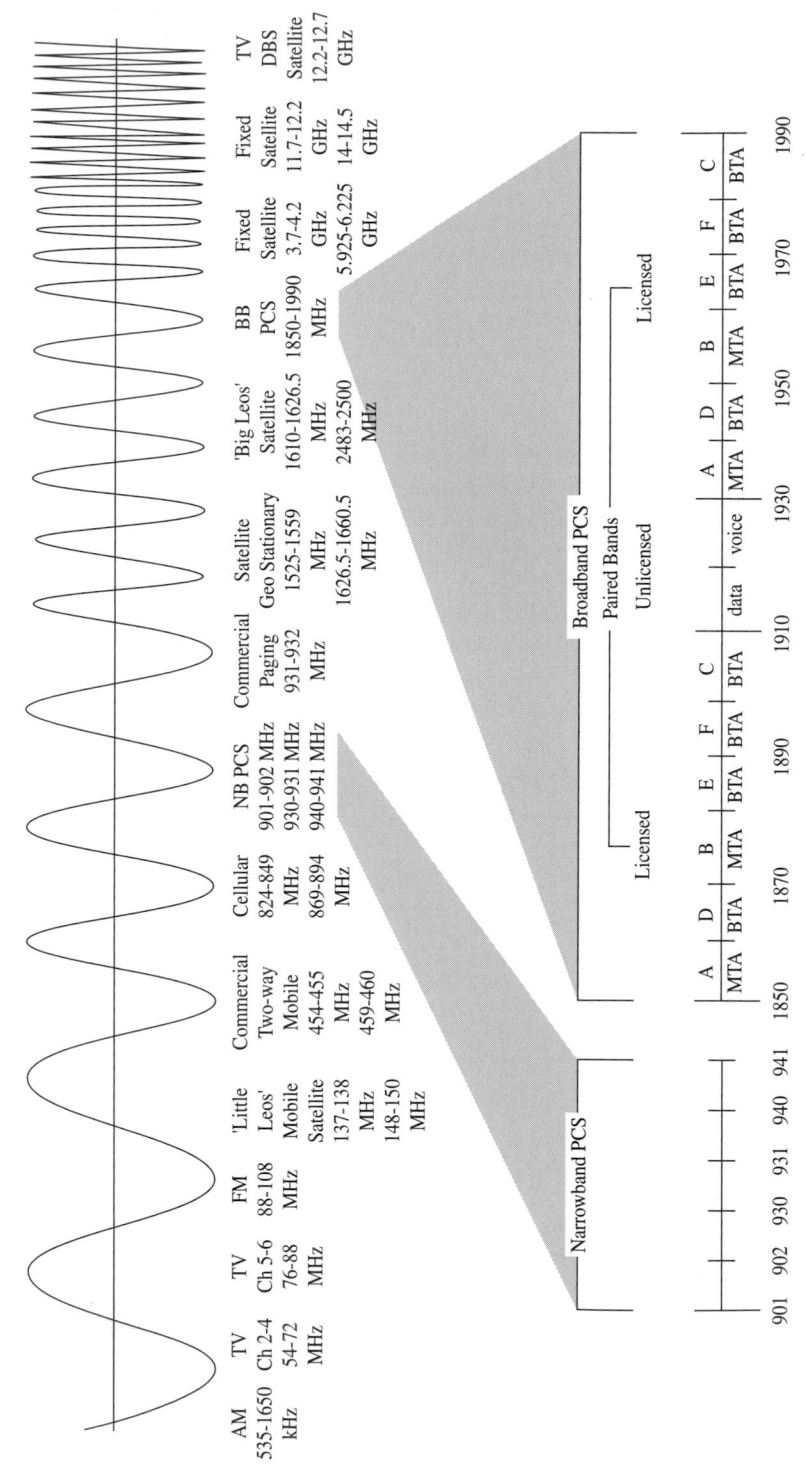

U.S. Radio Spectrum Location of Commercial Services

Source: Personal communications with the Federal Communications Commission (FCC), National Telecommunications and Information Administration (NTIA), and Nortel.
Copyright © 1995 Carol Weinhaus and the Telecommunications Industries Analysis Project Work Group, Boston, Massachusetts.

554

EXHIBIT 15 McCaw Long-Term Debt Structure as of 12/31/91 (in $ millions)

	1991	1990	LTD Repayment Schedule (in Millions)	
Revolving credit/loan agreement[a]	$1,790.0	$1,820.0	1992	$ 48.1
LIN Broadcasting facilities[b]	1,801.5	1,740.0	1993	90.8
12.75% senior notes of McCaw, due 1994	123.4	122.7	1994	435.5
13% senior subordinated notes, due 1996	146.4	145.8	1995	598.3
12.95% senior subordinated debentures, due 1999[c]	528.1	596.1	1996	797.3
14% senior subordinated debentures, due 1998[c]	396.1	395.5	Thereafter	3,302.3
8% convertible senior subordinated debentures, due 2008[c,d]	114.2	114.2		$5,272.4
Other convertible senior subordinated debentures, due 2008[c,e]	272.4	243.5	Less unamortized discounts	(25.4)
Other	74.9	82.2		$5,247.0
	5,247.0	5,260.2		
Less current portion	48.1	37.5		
Total long-term debt	$5,198.9	$5,222.8		

[a]$3,000 available; weighted-average rate of 7.76%; quarterly amortization payments amortizing the debt are due through March 2000.
[b]$2,100 available; weighted-average rate of 7.11%; quarterly amortization payments amortizing the debt are due through August 2000. This represents 100% of LIN Broadcasting's outstanding debt.
[c]Unsecured.
[d]Conversion price of $29.75 per share of Class A common stock.
[e]Conversion at 23.25 shares of Class A common stock per $1,000 of principal; effective rate of 11.5%; semiannual payments of interest begin December 15, 1992.

Source: McCaw Cellular Communications, Inc. 1991 annual report.

EXHIBIT 16 Current Capital Market Conditions

Historical Prime Rates

1988	9.32%
1989	10.87
1990	10.11
1991	8.46
1992	6.25
1993*	6.00

*Projected

Recent Money Rates

	June 1992	July 1992	August 1992	Average September 1992	Close September 25, 1992
Federal funds	3.76%	3.25%	3.30%	3.22%	3.07%
3-mo. commercial paper	3.92	3.44	3.38	3.24	3.25
6-mo. commercial paper	3.99	3.53	3.44	3.26	3.27
1-yr. Treasury bill	4.17	3.60	3.47	3.18	3.16
3-yr. Treasury bond	5.60	4.91	4.72	4.42	4.44
5-yr. Treasury note	6.48	5.84	5.60	5.38	5.46
10-yr. Treasury bond	7.26	6.84	6.59	6.42	6.47
30-yr. Treasury bond	7.84	7.60	7.39	7.34	7.41

*Corporate Bond Ratings & Yields**

	Aaa	Aa	A	Baa
June 1992	8.22%	8.56%	8.70%	9.05%
July 1992	8.07	8.37	8.49	8.84
August 1992	7.95	8.21	8.34	8.65
September 1992	7.92	8.17	8.31	8.62
Week Ending September 25, 1992	7.96	8.22	8.37	8.69

*Based on yields to maturity on selected long-term corporate bonds.

S&P 500 Index Performance

	Index*	P/E*
1989	323.05	15.45
1990	335.01	15.47
1991	376.20	26.22
January 1992	416.08	25.69
February 1992	412.56	25.94
March 1992	407.36	24.92
April 1992	407.41	25.61
May 1992	414.81	25.64
June 1992	408.27	24.88
July 1992	415.05	24.28
August 1992	417.93	23.16
September 1992	418.48	23.21

*Data at ends of respective periods.

S&P Bond

AT&T	AA
McCaw Cellular	CCC+

Yield to Maturities of Selected Issues as of September 1992

	AT&T	McCaw Cellular	
0–5 years	5.43%	14.0%/98	12.03%
5–10 years	6.80	12.95%/99	11.69%
10+ years	8.13		

Sources: *Federal Reserve Bulletin;* Compustat; *S&P Bond Guide.* Projected prime rate is casewriter's estimate.

EXHIBIT 17   Recent Cellular Mergers and Acquisitions Transactions (in millions, except where otherwise noted)

Purchaser	Target	Date	Value	POPs	Value/ POP
Bell Atlantic Corp.	Metro Mobils CTS	September 1991	$2,450	11.50	$213.04
McCaw Cellular	Crowley Cellular	June 1991	105	0.61	172.91
Comcast Corp.	Metromedia (AWACS)	May 1991	675	4.90	137.76
BellSouth Corp.	McCaw Cellular (Southern)	April 1991	360	2.70	133.33
GTE Corp.	Providence Journal (cellular unit)	October 1990	710	3.50	202.86
McCaw Cellular	Metromedia (NY)	August 1990	1,900	6.80	279.41
Time Warner, Inc.	Pricellular Corp.	March 1990	13	0.43	30.93
Price Communications	Utica/Rome MSA Wireless	March 1990	35	0.22	159.82
Contel Corp.	McCaw Cellular (Southeast)	January 1990	1,300	6.10	213.11
Vanguard Cellular	Palmer Communications (ME)	October 1989	NA	N/A	148.00
Vanguard Cellular	Palmer Communications (NH)	October 1989	NA	N/A	145.00

Sources: Paul Kagan & Associates, Inc.; and University of Virginia Darden Graduate School of Business Administration case "Centel Corporation," UVA-F-1078.

EXHIBIT 18 Financial Forecast of McCaw Cellular Prepared by McCaw, Assuming Remaining Portion of LIN Broadcasting Is Purchased

Modeling Assumptions				
Annual population growth rate	1.00%			
Annual penetration growth	23.50%			
Purchase remainder of LIN in 1995*	y			
	12/31/91	*Three Months*		
Direct costs and exp. (except mktg) (% service rev.)	33.19%	33.0%	32.5%	31.9%
Direct cost increment (%)	−1.70%			
Marketing expenses (% service rev.)	26.43%	25.9%	23.8%	21.9%
Marketing expense increment (%)	−8.00%			
Depreciation plus amortization (% service rev.)†	35.24%	34.8%	33.1%	31.4%
D&A increment (%)	−5.00%			
Capital expenditures per net subscriber additions ($)	1,147	1,000	850	750
Net working capital (NWC) per subscriber	198	150	60	24
Tax rate	36%			
	9/30/92	*12/31/92*	*12/31/93*	*12/31/94*
McCaw Pops (millions)	45.00	45.11	45.56	46.02
Penetration (from penetration growth factor)	2.12%	2.24%	2.76%	3.41%
McCaw subscribers	0.94	1.01	1.26	1.57
LIN Pops (millions)	26.40	26.47	26.73	27.00
LIN penetration	2.38%	2.51%	3.10%	3.83%
LIN subscribers	0.60	0.66	0.83	1.03
McCaw share of LIN subscribers	0.31	0.35	0.43	0.54
McCaw share of LIN POPs	13.73	13.76	13.90	14.04
Proportionate McCaw POPs	58.50	58.88	59.46	60.06
Proportionate McCaw subscribers				
Beginning subscribers (millions)	—	1.25	1.35	1.69
Subscribers added	—	0.10	0.33	0.42
Ending subscribers	1.25	1.35	1.69	2.11
Period average subscribers	—	1.30	1.52	1.90
Avg. net rev./Sub per month ($)		$76.00	$72.00	$68.20
Total net service revenue (millions)		297	1,314	1,553
% Growth net service revenue				18%
Direct costs and expenses (except marketing)		(98)	(427)	(496)
Marketing		(77)	(313)	(340)
Operating cash flow		122	574	717
Depreciation and amortization (millions)		(103)	(434)	(487)
Cellular operating income (millions)		19	140	229
After-tax cellular operating income (millions)		12	89	147
(+) Depreciation and amortization		103	434	487
(−) CapEx		(105)	(284)	(314)
(−) ΔNWC		—	104	46
Free cash flow		10	344	366

*McCaw must act on its option to purchase the remaining 47.5% of LIN Broadcasting prior to October 1995. If LIN is purchased, approximately 13 million additional POPs will be allocated to the purchaser. If remainder of LIN is not purchased, McCaw will lose approximately 14 million POPs. Assume either transaction is effective January 1, 1996.

†Amortization represents annual expense of intangible assets.

			Full Year				
31.4%	30.9%	30.3%	29.8%	29.3%	28.8%	28.3%	27.9%
20.2%	18.5%	17.1%	15.7%	14.4%	13.3%	12.2%	11.2%
29.8%	28.3%	26.9%	25.6%	24.3%	23.1%	21.9%	20.8%
650	575	550	520	500	500	450	450
10	4	2	2	2	2	2	2

12/31/95	*12/31/96*	*12/31/97*	*12/31/98*	*12/31/99*	*12/31/00*	*12/31/01*	*12/31/02*
46.48	46.95	47.42	47.89	48.37	48.84	49.34	49.84
4.21%	5.20%	6.43%	7.94%	9.80%	12.06%	14.96%	18.48%
1.96	2.44	3.05	3.80	4.74	5.89	7.38	9.21
27.27	27.54	27.82	28.10	28.38	28.65	28.95	29.24
4.73%	5.84%	7.22%	8.91%	11.01%	13.53%	16.80%	20.74%
1.29	1.61	2.01	2.50	3.12	3.88	4.86	6.06
0.67	1.61	2.01	2.50	3.12	3.88	4.86	6.06
14.18	27.54	27.82	28.10	28.38	28.65	28.95	29.24
60.66	74.49	75.23	75.98	76.74	77.50	78.29	79.07
2.11	2.63	4.05	5.05	6.30	7.86	9.77	12.24
0.52	1.42	1.00	1.25	1.56	1.90	2.48	3.03
2.63	4.05	5.05	6.30	7.86	9.77	12.24	15.27
2.37	3.34	4.55	5.68	7.08	8.82	11.01	13.76
$62.35	$58.10	$50.71	$48.47	$47.08	$46.36	$45.69	$45.06
1,771	2,329	2,771	3,304	4,003	4,904	6,034	7,439
14%	31%	19%	19%	21%	23%	23%	23%
(556)	(719)	(841)	(985)	(1,174)	(1,414)	(1,710)	(2,072)
(357)	(432)	(473)	(518)	(578)	(652)	(737)	(836)
858	1,178	1,458	1,800	2,251	2,838	3,587	4,531
(528)	(660)	(746)	(845)	(972)	(1,133)	(1,323)	(1,549)
330	519	712	955	1,279	1,705	2,265	2,982
211	332	456	611	819	1,091	1,450	1,909
528	660	746	845	972	1,133	1,323	1,549
(339)	(463)	(551)	(650)	(780)	(951)	(1,115)	(1,363)
22	10	4	(2)	(3)	(3)	(4)	(6)
423	539	654	804	1,008	1,269	1,653	2,089

EXHIBIT 19 McCaw Cellular Communications: Security Ownership of Certain Beneficial Owners and Management

	Class A Common[a]		
	Shares	*Options[e]*	*Total*
Management and directors			
Craig O. McCaw[c]	400,000	50,000	450,000
BT USA	22,140,136	4,000	22,144,136
John E. McCaw	4,500	24,250	28,750
Keith W. McCaw	251,050	—	251,050
Bruce R. McCaw	104	1,000	1,104
Other Directors	273,495	53,436	326,931
Subtotal[d]	23,069,285	132,686	23,201,971
Other equity investors			
Jordan Voting Trust	9,254,233		9,254,233
Equitable Insurance	13,500,000		13,500,000
74 Mutual Funds	19,636,654		19,636,654
113 Investment Advisors	49,427,531		49,427,531
46 Banks	8,101,287		8,101,287
Individuals and Other	2,763,320		2,763,320
Subtotal	102,683,025		102,683,025
Total outstanding A and B shares (primary)		185,485,712	
Total outstanding A and B shares (fully diluted)		191,578,181	

[a]400 million shares authorized.
[b]200 million shares authorized.
[c]Craig McCaw may vote all shares of Class B common except for BT's holdings and the vested options held by John McCaw and those owned by the other directors. He may vote only his Class A common shares and options.
[d]B shares carry 10 votes each; A shares carry 1 vote each.
[e]At December 31, 1991, options on shares were exercisable at prices ranging from $0.41 per share to $39 per share.

Sources: McCaw Cellular Communications, Inc., Annual meeting of stockholders, May 14, 1992; William O'Neil & Co., Inc. Los Angeles, CA.

Class B Common[b]			Votes, Primary Shares	Votes, Fully Diluted Shares[e]	% of Total Fully Diluted Votes
Shares	*Options[e]*	*Total*			
13,717,506	3,310,289	17,027,795	137,575,060	170,727,950	63.08%
13,709,063	—	13,709,063	159,230,766	159,234,766	20.34%
9,044,500	562,186	9,606,686	90,449,500	96,095,610	0.72%
10,815,361	—	10,815,361	108,404,660	108,404,660	0.03%
11,357,273	—	11,357,273	113,572,834	113,573,834	0.00%
1,089,699	2,087,308	3,177,007	11,170,485	32,097,001	2.71%
59,733,402	5,959,783	65,693,185	620,403,305	680,133,821	
			9,254,233	9,254,233	1.18%
			13,500,000	13,500,000	1.72%
			19,636,654	19,636,654	2.51%
			49,427,531	49,427,531	6.31%
			8,101,287	8,101,287	1.03%
			2,763,320	2,763,320	0.35%
			102,683,025	102,683,025	13.12%
			723,086,330	782,816,846	100.0%

Case 38

Euro Disneyland S.C.A.: The Project Financing

> *Anyone who has had builders in knows that the first law of building is that the estimate is a figure approximating to half the eventual cost of a project. The second law of building is that the customer always pays. The third law of building is not to assume that just because the figures have a row of naughts on the end that the costing is any more accurate than that which is employed to build your conservatory. Time will tell. Meanwhile we ought also perhaps to take a sanguine look at the projections for the number of people who are going to visit the site ... What I find difficult to square, if this is such a cast iron certainty, is why [Disney] has not kept the whole project for itself, and why it is so keen to use other people's money. Disney may have made Cinderella, but the rest of us should not believe in good fairies.[1]*

In the spring of 1989, The Walt Disney Company (Disney, or WDC) set in motion a complex series of transactions that would have several effects on its Euro Disneyland project, the largest metropolitan development project in western Europe. These effects would include the following:

- The reduction of The Walt Disney Company's equity interest from 100 to 49 percent.
- The repayment to Disney of (French francs) FF2.8 billion in project-development costs.
- A massive increase in leverage; FF12.3 billion in debts and lease obligations.
- One of the largest European initial public offerings of common stock, by a company that had no revenues or earnings.
- The creation of a bewildering ownership and governance structure for the project.
- The generation of a cascade of French government subsidies, investments, and tax breaks.

---

[1]"Fact and Fantasy in Disneyland," *Evening Standard,* October 10, 1989.

This case was prepared from public information by Professors Robert F. Bruner of the Darden Graduate Business School and Herwig Langohr of INSEAD, with the assistance of Anne Campbell, research associate. The authors thank S. G. Warburg Securities for its cooperation with the research. Neither the Walt Disney Company nor Euro Disneyland S.C.A. has been involved in the preparation of this case, and neither company takes any responsibility for its contents. Copyright © 1992 jointly by INSEAD, Fontainebleau, France, and the University of Virginia Darden School Foundation, Charlottesville, VA. *No part of this publication may be reproduced, stored in a retrieval system, used in a spreadsheet, or transmitted in any form or by any means—electronic, mechanical, photocopying, recording, or otherwise—without the permission of the Darden School Foundation. For inquiries, please send an e-mail to dardencases@virginia.edu.* Revised 4/98. Version 1.6.

Some analysts viewed these developments with alarm, voicing suspicions about Disney's partial removal from the project. Others welcomed the opportunity to invest alongside the world's most successful theme park operator. Virtually everyone struggled to understand the implications for Disney and other stakeholders in Euro Disneyland.

THE EURO DISNEYLAND PROJECT

Disney planned to build the park on approximately 1,945 hectares[2] (4,800 acres) 32 kilometers due east of Paris. Disney chose this site on the basis of availability, communications, and proximity to a potential audience after considering 200 possible sites in France and Spain. About half of the developable land, 857 hectares, would be devoted to entertainment and resort facilities: another 808 hectares would be set aside for retail, commercial, industrial, and residential purposes. Regional and primary infrastructure such as roads and railway tracks would constitute the balance of 280 hectares.

The heart of the entertainment area would feature two separate theme parks: (1) the Magic Kingdom, modeled after similar parks operating in the United States and Japan, and (2) a park based on Disney's MGM Studio theme park in Florida. The Magic Kingdom's five themed "lands," Main Street, Frontierland, Adventureland, Fantasyland, and Discoveryland, would occupy 160 hectares and were expected to cost FF8.6 billion. The Disney MGM Studio theme park, which would offer visits to studio film sets and presentations on Hollywood filmmaking, was expected to cost FF5.9 billion.

Disney planned to make hotels the linchpin of a comprehensive resort facility. Six hotels (with 5,200 rooms) were to be ready by 1992: By 2011, these facilities would increase to more than 20 hotels with 18,200 rooms. Future entertainment facilities would include two golf courses, a water-recreation area, campgrounds providing 2,100 sites, and a 60,000-square-meter retail/entertainment complex.

Euro Disneyland's commercial development would lie just beyond the ring road that would surround the entertainment core on the southern part of the site. Facilities would consist of single and multifamily residences, time-share apartments, 700,000 square meters of office space, 750,000 square meters of industrial space, and 95,000 square meters of retail space.

Visitors would access Euro Disneyland using an interchange from a high-speed, multi-lane highway, an extension of the suburban railroad system serving Paris, or the high-speed *train à grande vitesse* (TGV) railroad train system serving travelers from more distant regions of France and neighboring countries.

Disney planned to open the Magic Kingdom theme park in April 1992. A total cost of FF14 billion was budgeted for "Phase IA," the initial capital investment in the Magic Kingdom; the Magic Kingdom Hotel; and peripheral development, organization, interest, and preopening expenses. About FF4.9 billion of this amount would be spent by the end of September 1989.

---

[2]A hectare is a measure of area equal to 10,000 square meters, or 2.471acres.

PROJECT OWNERSHIP AND GOVERNANCE

Euro Disneyland would be organized as a *société en commandité par actions* (S.C.A.), a type of French company that had certain features similar to those of a limited partnership. Exhibit 1 summarizes the ownership structure and percentages of investment in the Euro Disneyland project. There were four primary participants in this structure:

- Euro Disney S.A., a *gérant* or management company and a wholly owned subsidiary of the Walt Disney Company, would manage and direct the project. The *gérant*'s responsibility would be to manage Euro Disneyland S.C.A. in the company's best interests. The *gérant*'s compensation would consist of a base fee and a management incentive fee.[3]
- The shareholders, or *associés commanditaires,* could elect the supervisory board and approve the annual accounts and dividend payments. Shareholders would have no liability for the debts of the company. By agreement with the French government, The Walt Disney Company would use its best efforts to ensure that, until opening day, investors living in the European Community would hold the shares that Disney did not own. Shares would be listed for public trading in Paris, London, and Brussels. EDL Holding Company S.A., a French *société anonyme* and a wholly owned subsidiary of The Walt Disney Company, would hold the other 49 percent of the shares.
- The role of the supervisory board, or *conseil de surveillance,* would be to monitor the general affairs and management of Euro Disneyland S.C.A., to report on the performance of the *gérant,* to approve contracts between the *gérant* or its affiliates and Euro Disneyland S.C.A., and to prepare an annual report. This board could not, however, remove the *gérant* or require the *gérant* to take any action.
- The *associé commandité,* or general partner, had unlimited liability for all debts and liabilities of the company. The general partner would be EDL Participations S.A., which was wholly owned by Disney through EDL Holding Company S.A. It would receive a distribution each year of 0.5 percent of Euro Disneyland S.C.A.'s net after-tax profits. EDL Participations could not be removed as general partner without its consent. On the other hand, it could not dispose of its interest as general partner without a majority vote of the shareholders of Euro Disneyland S.C.A.

As part of the general financing plan for the project, one other entity would be established:

- Euro Disneyland S.N.C., *société en nom collectif,* or "financing company," would serve as a vehicle to finance the construction of the Magic Kingdom through the use of a tax-leveraged

---

[3]The base fee in any year would equal 3 percent of Euro Disneyland S.C.A.'s total revenues in that year, less 0.5 percent of the S.C.A.'s net after-tax profits, until the later of (1) the expiration of five financial years of Magic Kingdom operations or (2) the end of the financial year in which the company satisfied certain financial tests under the bank-loan agreement. Thereafter, the base fee would be 6 percent per year less 0.5 percent of the S.C.A.'s net after-tax profits. The base fee was reflected in the operating expenses of the theme parks. The incentive fee would be equal to 35 percent of any pretax gains on sales of hotels, plus a percentage of the S.C.A.'s pretax cash flow. This percentage would range from zero if the cash flow was below 10 percent of the actual cost of Phase IA; 30 percent if the cash flow was between 10 and 15 percent of the cost of Phase IA; 40 percent if the cash flow was between 15 and 20 percent of the cost of Phase IA; and 50 percent if the cash flow was above 20 percent of the cost of Phase IA. These thresholds would increase proportionately if inflation were more than 5 percent per year, or decrease proportionately if inflation were less than 4 percent per year.

financing lease. Euro Disneyland S.C.A. would build the Magic Kingdom and sell it to the financing company for the cost of the land and construction.[4] The financing company would lease the Magic Kingdom back to Euro Disneyland S.C.A. for 20 years, with lease payments essentially matching the debt service and incidental costs of the financing company. Upon complete amortization of its liabilities, the financing company would sell the Magic Kingdom back to Euro Disneyland S.C.A. for a nominal value, whereupon the S.N.C. would be dissolved. Euro Disneyland Participations S.A., a wholly owned subsidiary of The Walt Disney Company, would provide 17 percent of the partners' equity capital in Euro Disneyland S.N.C. During the construction and early years following completion of the Magic Kingdom, interest expenses and depreciation of assets over a 10-year period were expected to produce tax losses for the S.N.C. The structure of the financing company would permit the partners to take these losses directly into their accounts for tax purposes.[5]

In addition to its 49 percent interest in S.C.A., and its 17 percent interest in S.N.C., The Walt Disney Company would receive royalties[6] in return for granting a 30-year intellectual and industrial-property-rights license to Euro Disneyland S.C.A.

THE MASTER AGREEMENT WITH THE FRENCH GOVERNMENT

Although it did not appear in a listing of investors, the French government would be an influential participant in Euro Disneyland's development. The Walt Disney Company and the French government signed a master agreement in February 1988 that committed each party to certain obligations. France agreed to:

1. Provide 1,665 hectares for theme-park resort, commercial, and residential development at a fixed price; the price was set at the 1971 cost of raw agricultural land, or approximately FF140,000[7] per hectare. By comparison, raw land zoned for commercial uses in

---

[4]Of the total Phase IA budgeted cost of FF14 billion, S.N.C. would effectively finance FF10.3 billion, leaving S.C.A. to finance the balance, FF3.7 billion. These investments would be financed as follows:

	S.N.C.	S.C.A.	Total
Market debt	4,300	200	4,500
Government loans	3,000	1,800	4,800
S.N.C. equity	2,000	—	2,000
S.C.A. equity	1,000*	1,700	2,700
Total	10,300	3,700	14,000

* This amount is invested by the S.C.A. in the S.N.C.

[5]Although the partners were legally liable for the financing company's debt, Euro Disneyland S.C.A. waived any right of recourse against the partners in the event of the financing company's default. Moreover, Euro Disneyland S.C.A., Euro Disneyland Participations S.A., and The Walt Disney Company agreed to indemnify the partners for any liabilities they might incur.

[6]The royalties would be equal to 10 percent of the gross revenues at theme parks, plus 5 percent of gross revenues from merchandise, food and beverage sales, plus 10 percent of fees due from participants who invested money toward the construction of specific rides, plus 5 percent of gross revenues of theme hotels.

[7]This is the casewriters' estimate. The master agreement actually cited a land cost of FF111,000 per hectare, but added to this cost would be direct and indirect infrastructure costs (not including roads and railroads), and certain overhead and financing expenses.

the Île-de-France region was listed for prices ranging from FF170,000 to FF210,000 per hectare. Euro Disneyland S.C.A. would have 20 years to complete the land purchases at the same price. The government explained that it wished to "damp down" property speculation in the area.[8]

2. Finance, construct, and operate a 20-kilometer extension of the Paris suburban railroad to provide direct access from central Paris to the gates of the Magic Kingdom. This would entail building two railroad stations, a car park, and a bus station.

3. Finance and construct two junctions to link the A4 motorway with the Euro Disneyland site.

4. Contribute FF200 million toward the construction of secondary roads.

5. Provide up to FF4.8 billion in loans at an annual fixed rate of 7.85 percent—a rate less than the French government's own borrowing rate.[9] The loans would mature in 20 years and would amortize from years 6 through 20.

6. Apply the lowest VAT rate of 5.5 percent on all Euro Disneyland's consumer products (compared with 18.6 percent for consumer durables and cars and 33 percent for luxury goods).

In addition to the master agreement, the French government agreed to provide TGV train service to Euro Disneyland starting in June 1994. France also confirmed that the Magic Kingdom could depreciate assets over a 10-year period, rather than the usual 20-year period. One journalist estimated that the entire package of concessions would cost the French taxpayer $54,000 (about FF297,000) for each new job the park would create.[10] Other analysts estimated the value of the government concessions at up to FF6 billion.[11]

The master agreement required Euro Disneyland S.C.A. and Euro Disneyland S.N.C. to open the Magic Kingdom by April 1992 and complete Phase IA. In addition, Euro Disneyland had to guarantee a minimum amount of suburban rail system traffic,[12] pay FF45 million for utility and electrical networks, guarantee a minimum level of tax revenues to the Department of Seine-et-Marne,[13] encourage share ownership by EC nationals, use French and other EC contractors and suppliers (subject to their availability on a competitive basis), and include at least one attraction in the Magic Kingdom depicting French and European civilization.

---

[8]George Sivell, "Mickey Mouse Weaves a Magic Deal," *Times of London,* May 29, 1989.

[9]The 20-year French government bond was currently priced to yield 9.1 percent in the market.

[10]The journalist Gilles Smadja was quoted in "Presto! Let the Magic Begin," *Newsweek,* April 13, 1992, p. 14. Euro Disneyland was projected to employ over 11,000 people, implying that the estimated value of the concessions was FF3.267 billion ($594 million).

[11]"Disney President Pelted with Eggs at Stock Announcement," Associated Press article, October 5, 1989.

[12]Euro Disneyland guaranteed a minimum of 9.13 million one-way journeys each year for a five-year period after opening day. Failing that, Euro Disneyland would make payments varying from four to seven French francs (measured in 1986 francs) per journey to the extent that actual traffic would fall below 75 percent of the minimum agreed level.

[13]This aimed to reimburse the Department of Seine-et-Marne for the FF 200 million in expenditures for primary and secondary infrastructure. The aggregate taxes would have to reach FF200 million by 1999 (measured in 1986 francs). Any shortfall would be filled jointly by Euro Disneyland and the Republic of France.

The Walt Disney Company agreed to refrain from opening or licensing another theme park within 800 km of Euro Disneyland for five years after opening the Magic Kingdom. Disney agreed to hold at least 17 percent of the shares of Euro Disneyland S.C.A. and Euro Disneyland S.N.C. until the fifth anniversary of opening day.

THE WALT DISNEY COMPANY

The Walt Disney Company, headquartered in Burbank, California, was the parent, or sponsor, of the Euro Disneyland project. Disney derived 60 percent of its revenues from the development and operation of theme parks. Observers generally acknowledged that The Walt Disney Company dominated the theme-park industry by virtue of its size, customer franchise, and product leadership. Fifty million visitors attended Disney's four theme parks annually, an average of more than 12 million a park. The next largest competing park attracted 4.6 million. Disney achieved dominance in the theme-park industry through the nature and quality of its facilities,[14] its crowd-handling techniques, its use of entertainment culture, and its operational and marketing[15] skills.

FINANCIAL FORECAST AND VALUATION

In a departure from usual practice, Disney intended to publish a detailed financial forecast for the project in advance of the initial public offering of shares. Exhibit 2 presents a forecast of the operating statement and dividends by year from 1992 to 1996 and for each fifth year thereafter to 2016. This exhibit concludes with the total annual return to shareholders. Exhibit 3 presents the sources and applications of funds for the forecast period, evincing a substantial reliance on debt financing in the first few years followed by steady debt amortization. Exhibit 4 gives the debt/equity ratio by year for Euro Disneyland S.C.A.

---

[14]Disney designed all of its own rides and attractions, using an in-house "imagineering" department. This approach guaranteed uniqueness, consistency, and high product quality. Rides could be tailored to the unique needs of the theme area and of the entire park and designed especially for Disney's high-volume attendance. Finally, the in-house approach guaranteed Disney exclusive ownership of the numerous design innovations (many of which were patented).

[15]Disney aimed to maximize attendance at the parks and to achieve high occupancy at the Disney resort hotels. The company's main marketing tools were public relations, media promotions, participant campaigns, national advertising campaigns, and special events. Some attractions and services were comarketed with "participants," such as Renault, Banque Nationale de Paris, and France Telecom, that had committed to sponsoring an attraction at Euro Disneyland. Special pricing and travel packages played a key role in maintaining demand throughout the year.

Disney made the unusual assumption that certain revenue items would grow at a greater rate than inflation. Magic Kingdom ticket prices, hotel rates, campsite rates, and lease rates in the retail/entertainment center were projected to grow at 6.5 percent, versus 5 percent for inflation. Analysts wondered what might account for a 1.5 percent *real growth rate* over Disney's forecast period. By comparison, ticket prices at Disney theme parks in the United States had grown at a real rate of 2.6 percent per annum since 1972.

On the basis of a discounted cash flow analysis of this forecast, S. G. Warburg, the prospective lead underwriter for the initial public offering (IPO), concluded that shares in Euro Disneyland S.C.A. would be worth approximately FF70 each. Warburg's analysis used a 12 percent discount rate.[16] Warburg also conducted an extensive sensitivity analysis of the share values, the results of which are given in Exhibit 5.

FINANCIAL TRANSFORMATION

The Euro Disneyland project would be transformed in a two-stage process from an all-equity, wholly owned unit of The Walt Disney Company into a leveraged public firm, minority-owned by Disney. Exhibit 6 presents the balance sheet of Euro Disneyland S.C.A. and adjustments that resulted from the two-stage process.

Step 1: Sale of ORAs, March 1989. To set in motion the complex project financing, the Caisse des Depôts et Consignations (the large pension-fund-management company operated by the French government) required that Euro Disneyland prove its ability to sell shares of stock in the project. Accordingly, in March 1989, Euro Disneyland arranged for four investor banks to purchase 510,000 shares of stock at FF15 per share. These banks were Banque Indosuez, Banque Nationale de Paris, S. G. Warburg

---

[16]In estimating a discount rate for the project, S. G. Warburg acknowledged that "there are currently no quoted investment opportunities which are directly comparable to Euro Disneyland in the sense that they offer a direct and undiluted play on the theme park industry." The Walt Disney Company in the United States offered one comparison. Warburg identified two comparable companies in the French business community. The first was Club Mediteranée, the world leader in holiday villages which, like Euro Disneyland, provided the concept of a "total" destination resort. Club Med and Euro Disneyland differed in that Club Med offered a globally diversified portfolio of destination resorts, whereas Euro Disneyland offered only one. The countries where the Club Med resorts were located, however, experienced greater weather and political risks than Europe. Warburg also compared Euro Disneyland with Accor, the leading French hotel operator. Accor's assets were located primarily in France, and the properties were, on average, quite young. They therefore held the prospect of long lives and capital gains similar to Euro Disneyland. Warburg forecasted dividends and estimated an internal rate of return (IRR) for Disney, Accor, and Club Med. Against an estimated IRR of 9 percent for The Walt Disney Company, 11.3 percent for Accor, and 11.9 percent for Club Med, Warburg reasoned that the market would fix on a discount rate of 12 percent for Euro Disneyland's return to share investors after April 1993. Warburg suggested that during the development period (October 1989 to April 1992) investors would look for an implicit return of 20 percent on their investments. This higher rate would reflect the development risks prior to opening and the fact that Euro Disneyland was not a going concern at the initial public offering.

& Co., and Caisse Nationale de Crédit Agricole. At the same time, EDL Holding Company purchased 465,000 shares at FF10 per share.[17] The investor banks and EDL Holding Company also purchased debt securities of Euro Disneyland, called *obligations remboursables en actions* (ORAs), which were to be repaid substantially from the proceeds of the forthcoming initial public offering.[18]

Step 2: Initial public offering of common stock, Fall 1989. The sale of shares was expected to raise net proceeds of FF5.73 billion. The proceeds would be used to repay the ORAs that were issued by the company in March 1989, and to support the funding of Phase IA and subsequent phases. Following the IPO, The Walt Disney Company would own 49 percent of the shares, the investor banks would own about 0.5 percent, and the public would own about 50.5 percent. Immediately following the IPO, the issued share capital of S.C.A. would be FF1.7 billion, divided into 170 million shares of FF10 each.

Analysts noted that The Walt Disney Company would receive a substantial gain through this initial public offering. Disney's shares, carried at the purchase price of FF10 each, would be revalued at FF72 each. Disney responded that the resulting total value of its shares (FF5.997 billion) would be fair recognition of an already substantial investment of know-how, personnel resources, and cash expenditure, and an acknowledgment of Disney's role as the risk-bearing sponsor of the project. As of September 30, 1989, the total assets of Euro Disneyland S.C.A. amounted to FF4.833 billion. Disney's projected net cash invested in the equity of Euro Disneyland S.C.A. would be approximately FF833 million.[19]

Analysts puzzled over various cash flows that composed the return to The Walt Disney Company from the Euro Disneyland project: (1) royalties, (2) incentive fees (see footnote 3),

---

[17]In March 1989, shareholders approved an increase in capital: 510,000 shares were issued at FF15 per share to the investor banks (i.e., Banque Indosuez, Banque Nationale de Paris, S. G. Warburg & Co., and Caisse Nationale de Crédit Agricole). In addition, 465,000 shares were issued at par (FF10) to EDL Holding Company. Prior to the IPO, shares were held as follows: EDL Holding Company (490,000), Banque Indosuez (204,000), Banque Nationale de Paris (153,000), S. G. Warburg & Co. (102,000), and Caisse Nationale de Crédit Agricole (51,000); for a total of 1,000,000 shares. On June 30, 1989, the share capital would amount to FF10 million, comprising 1 million fully paid FF10 ordinary voting shares. Shareholders' equity would increase by FF5.73 billion from the net IPO proceeds, plus FF828.1 million from the conversion of Disney ORAs. In September 1989, 85,880,000 new shares would be issued in order to be subscribed in cash as part of the IPO. This would increase S.C.A.'s share capital by FF858 million to a total of FF868 million.

[18]In March 1989, S.C.A. completed a private placement of ORAs and stock purchase warrants which raised FF2,129,950,000. EDL Holding Company subscribed for 828,100 non-interest-bearing ORAs at par with a nominal unit value of FF1,000. Upon completion of the public equity offering, these ORAs would convert into 82,810,000 shares of S.C.A. The investor banks subscribed pro rata for a total of 861,900 ORAs at par with a nominal unit value of FF1,500. These ORAs bear interest at 12.5 percent per year. Upon completion of the IPO, the ORAs held by the investor banks would be redeemed in cash at their par value plus accrued interest. On June 30 this amounted to FF13,469,000. The investor banks also received warrants to purchase between 310,000 and 3,260,000 additional shares, depending on the redemption date of their ORAs.

[19]Disney's cash investment in equity consisted of outlays for the initial 25,000 shares at FF10 in 1985, another 465,000 shares at FF10 in March 1989, and FF828.1 million for the ORAs, also in March 1989.

(3) dividends from the S.C.A., (4) depreciation tax shields from the S.N.C.,[20] (5) Disney's participation in net profits, and (6) the reimbursement of FF2.762 billion of development costs previously incurred by WDC. Exhibit 7 presents a forecast of these various cash flows to The Walt Disney Company based on the pro forma for the project financing. Because the extent of WDC's future tax burden was unclear, this exhibit presents the total cash flows to WDC under two scenarios: (1) WDC pays no taxes on its returns from Euro Disneyland and (2) WDC pays taxes at the maximum 35 percent rate on *all* returns from Euro Disneyland. To provide a basis of comparison for the project-financing results, Exhibit 8 gives a forecast assuming no project financing but holding the capital structure constant.

CONCLUSION

The transactions of 1989 would transform the Euro Disneyland project dramatically: from a private to a publicly owned project; from a simple governance and ownership structure to a complex one; from one stakeholder to many; from internal financing to external financing; from an unlevered to a levered project. Analysts pondered the implications of this transformation. Most important, they asked why WDC brought many players into the project. Why should banks, equity investors, and the French government participate so massively? Who stood to gain what?

---

[20]As stated earlier, because the lease payments received by the S.N.C. from the S.C.A. would just equal the S.N.C.'s financing expenses, the only source of income to the investors in the S.N.C. would come from the tax losses generated from depreciation of the Magic Kingdom theme park. This annual return would be a tax savings to the investors equal to the tax rate times annual depreciation.

EXHIBIT 1   Management and Control Structure of the Euro Disneyland Project

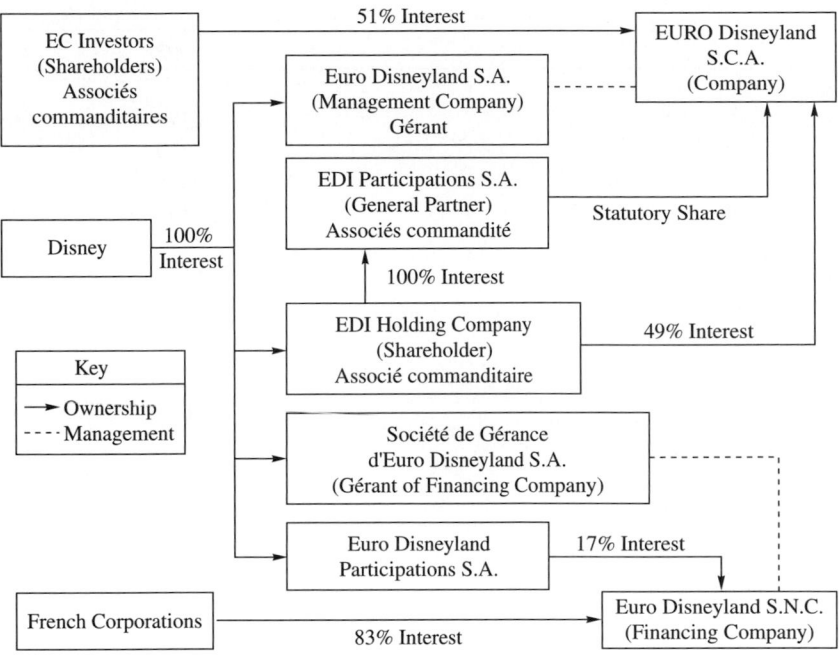

EXHIBIT 2 Profit Projections (in millions of French francs)

	Years Beginning April 1		
	1992	*1993*	*1994*
Revenues			
Magic Kingdom*	4,246	4,657	5,384
Second theme park	0	0	0
Resort and property development	1,236	2,144	3,520
Total revenues	5,482	6,801	8,904
Operating expenses			
Magic Kingdom*	2,643	2,836	3,161
Second theme park	0	0	0
Resort and property development	796	1,501	2,431
Total operating expenses	3,439	4,337	5,592
Operating income	2,043	2,464	3,312
Other expenses (income)			
Royalties	302	333	387
Preopening amortization	341	341	341
Depreciation	255	263	290
Interest expense	567	575	757
Interest and other income	(786)	(788)	(768)
Lease expense	958	950	958
Management incentive fees	55	171	477
Total other expenses (income)	1,692	1,845	2,492
Profit before taxation	351	620	870
Taxation	147	260	366
Net profit	204	360	504
Dividends payable†	275	425	625
Tax credit or payment (*avoir fiscal*)	0	138	213
Total return	275	563	838

*Includes Magic Kingdom Hotel.
†After transfers to legal reserve and deduction of a distributive share of 0.5 percent of net profits after tax payable to the *associé commandité*. In later years, dividends payable reflect the availability of cash. Dividends from 1992 through 1996 include distribution of profits carried forward from earlier years arising from interest income.

Source: Initial public offering circular, Euro Disneyland S.C.A., September 1989, p. 36.

		Years Beginning April 1			
1995	*1996*	*2001*	*2006*	*2011*	*2016*
5,853	6,415	9,730	13,055	18,181	24,118
0	3,128	4,565	6,656	9,313	12,954
5,077	6,386	8,133	9,498	8,979	5,923
10,930	15,929	22,428	29,209	36,473	42,995
3,370	3,641	5,504	7,384	10,175	13,097
0	1,794	2,644	3,695	5,020	6,830
2,970	3,694	5,210	6,369	5,753	2,211
6,340	9,129	13,358	17,448	20,948	22,138
4,590	6,800	9,070	11,761	15,525	20,857
422	717	1,085	1,509	2,120	2,802
341	341	0	0	0	0
296	625	658	723	842	228
708	1,166	920	623	352	0
(778)	(790)	(615)	(266)	0	0
962	975	1,242	882	83	0
963	1,820	2,747	3,916	5,590	7,876
2,914	4,854	6,037	7,387	8,987	10,906
1,676	1,945	3,034	4,375	6,539	9,951
704	818	1,274	1,837	2,746	4,180
972	1,127	1,760	2,538	3,793	5,771
900	1,100	1,750	2,524	3,379	5,719
313	450	536	865	1,908	2,373
1,213	1,550	2,286	3,389	5,287	8,092

EXHIBIT 3   Cash-Flow Projections (in millions of French francs)

	Years Beginning April 1		
	1992	*1993*	*1994*
Source of funds			
Profit before taxation	351	620	870
Depreciation and amortization	597	604	631
Issuance of long-term debt	990	693	2,950
	1,938	1,917	4,451
Application of funds			
Capital expenditures			
Magic Kingdom	310	326	293
Second theme park	0	0	2,950
Resort and property development	31	139	62
Acquisition of land	51	145	103
Repayment of long-term debt	0	24	540
Loan to financing company	0	(24)	(47)
Taxes paid	139	414	519
Dividends payable	275	425	625
	806	1,449	5,045
Movement in working capital*	(779)	(668)	516
Movement in net liquid funds	353	(200)	(78)

*The yearly movement in working capital may be analyzed as follows:

	1992	*1993*	*1994*
(Increase) decrease in resort and property-development inventories due to funding of projects and sales	(979)	(678)	507
Increase in current liabilities	200	10	9
	(779)	(668)	516

Source: Initial public offering circular, Euro Disneyland S.C.A., September 1989, p. 37.

		Years Beginning April 1			
1995	*1996*	*2001*	*2006*	*2011*	*2016*
1,676	1,945	3,034	4,375	6,539	9,951
638	967	658	723	842	228
2,950	0	779	1,146	0	0
5,264	2,912	4,471	6,244	7,381	10,179
313	334	335	471	658	114
2,950	102	101	134	178	196
0	0	0	0	5	0
198	450	205	339	0	0
781	1,600	1,872	1,584	440	0
(71)	(94)	(259)	0	0	0
858	971	1,280	1,843	2,746	4,180
900	1,100	1,750	2,524	3,379	5,719
5,927	4,463	5,284	6,895	7,406	10,209
997	1,548	683	100	45	57
334	(3)	(130)	(551)	20	27
1995	*1996*	*2001*	*2006*	*2011*	*2016*
785	1,527	656	65	0	0
212	21	27	35	45	57
997	1,548	683	100	45	57

EXHIBIT 4   Forecasted Debt/Equity Ratio

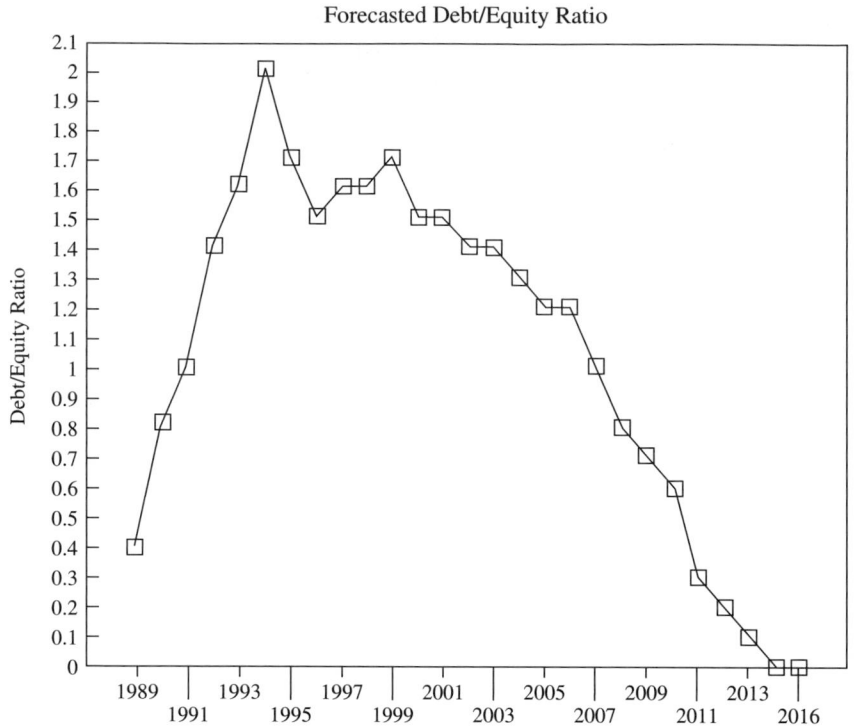

Source: "Euro Disneyland S.C.A.: The Project Financing," *Research Report,* S. G. Warburg, p. 106.

EXHIBIT 5 Returns to Investors and Sensitivity Analysis (in French francs)

The table below illustrates the projected returns to the investor based on the assumptions previously described and demonstrates the effect on these returns of variations in certain of the key assumptions. At the end of the period, the company is assumed to be capitalized at 12.5 times net profit available for distribution in the year ending March 31, 2017.

		Net Dividend per Share Years Beginning April 1					Net Value in April 1993*	Internal Rate of Return over Period to 2017 Issue Price (FF72)
	1992	1995	2001	2006	2011	2016		
Company's Projections	1.6	5.3	10.3	14.8	19.9	33.6	131	13.3%
Reduced attendance (*assuming 10 million visits in the first year of operations of the Magic Kingdom*)	1.6	5.3	9.4	13.8	18.4	31.7	119	12.7
Increased attendance (*assuming 12 million visits in the first year of operations of the Magic Kingdom*)	1.6	5.3	11.1	15.9	21.3	35.6	141	13.8
Reduced per capita spending (*assuming per capita spending at both theme parks is lower by 10 percent*)	1.6	4.8	8.9	12.9	17.4	30.3	112	12.3
Increased per capita spending (*assuming per capita spending at both theme parks is higher by 10 percent*)	1.6	5.3	11.6	16.6	22.3	37.0	147	14.1
Delay (*assuming a six-month delay in the opening of the Magic Kingdom*)	1.6	4.5	9.7	12.6	21.8	33.6	122	12.8
Increased construction costs (*assuming costs of construction of Phase IA are higher by 10 percent*)	1.6	5.3	10.2	15.1	20.4	34.0	129	13.2
Reduced resort and property-development income (*assuming that income from all resort and property development is lower by 10 percent*)	1.6	5.3	9.8	14.3	19.3	33.0	126	13.0
Increased resort and property development income (*assuming that income from all resort and property development is higher by 10 percent*)	1.6	5.3	10.8	15.4	20.4	34.3	135	13.5%

*Net value in April 1993 reflects gross dividends per share and assumed residual value in 2017 discounted at an illustrative rate of 12 percent.

Source: Initial public offering circular, Euro Disneyland S.C.A., September 1989, pp. 38–39.

EXHIBIT 6 Pro Forma Balance Sheet of Euro Disneyland S.C.A. (in thousands of French francs)

	Actual (Dec. 31, 1988)	Project Devel. Activities	Sale of ORAs and Shares
Fixed assets			
Intangible assets	0	8,644	
Tangible assets	0	475,630	
Deposits	0	4,232	
Total fixed assets	0		
Construction in progress	0	1,748,653	
Current assets			
Accounts receivable	0	761,994	
Cash and investments	251	(1,010,518)	2,133,250
Total current assets	251		
Deferred charges	0	710,460	
Total assets	251	2,699,095	2,133,250
Shareholders' equity			
Share capital	250		9,750
Share premium	25		2,550
Accumulated losses	(24)		
Current period net income	0	7,333	
Subtotal	251		
ORAs and warrants	0		2,120,950
Deferred taxes	0	4,688	
Current liabilities			
Payable to Euro Disneyland S.A.	0	1,908,567	
Other accounts payable	0	537,124	
Total current liabilities	0		
Deferred revenues	0	241,383	
Total equity and liabilities	251	2,699,095	2,133,250

Expected (Sept. 30, 1989)	Repay. and Conversion of ORAs	Exercise of Warrants	IPO	Pro Forma (Sept. 30, 1989)
8,644				8,644
475,630				475,630
4,232				4,232
488,506				488,506
1,748,653				1,748,653
761,994				761,994
1,122,983	(1,292,850)		5,730,000	5,560,133
1,884,977				6,322,127
710,460				710,460
4,832,596	(1,292,850)	0	5,730,000	9,269,746
10,000	828,100	3,100	858,800	1,700,000
2,575		1,550	4,866,550	4,870,675
(24)				(24)
7,333				7,333
19,884				6,577,984
2,120,950	(2,120,950)			0
4,688				4,688
1,908,567				1,908,567
537,124				537,124
2,445,691				2,445,691
241,383				241,383
4,832,596	(1,292,850)	4,650	5,725,350	9,269,746

EXHIBIT 7 Projected Cash Flows to The Walt Disney Company Assuming Euro Disneyland Is Financed as Proposed (in millions of French francs)

	Base Fees	Incentive Fees	Royalties	Profit Particip.	Dividends
1989					
1990					
1991					
1992	197.4	55.0	302.0	1.0	137.0
1993	244.8	171.0	333.0	1.9	281.0
1994	320.5	477.0	387.0	2.5	419.0
1995	393.5	963.0	422.0	4.8	606.0
1996	573.4	1,820.0	717.0	5.6	775.0
1997	614.1	1,976.2	778.9	6.1	850.1
1998	657.6	2,145.8	846.2	6.7	932.6
1999	704.1	2,329.9	919.3	7.3	1,023.0
2000	754.0	2,529.9	998.7	8.0	1,122.2
2001	807.4	2,747.0	1,085.0	8.8	1,231.0
2002	851.2	2,948.9	1,159.0	9.6	1,306.9
2003	897.4	3,165.6	1,238.0	10.4	1,387.4
2004	946.1	3,398.2	1,322.5	11.4	1,472.9
2005	997.4	3,647.9	1,412.7	12.4	1,563.6
2006	1,051.5	3,916.0	1,509.0	13.5	1,660.0
2007	1,099.3	4,204.9	1,615.2	14.5	1,843.6
2008	1,149.2	4,515.1	1,728.8	15.5	2,047.6
2009	1,201.4	4,848.2	1,850.4	16.6	2,274.1
2010	1,256.0	5,205.9	1,980.6	17.7	2,525.6
2011	1,313.0	5,590.0	2,120.0	19.0	2,805.0
2012	1,356.9	5,986.7	2,241.6	20.7	2,989.8
2013	1,402.3	6,411.6	2,370.2	22.5	3,186.8
2014	1,449.2	6,866.7	2,506.2	24.5	3,396.7
2015	1,497.7	7,354.1	2,650.0	26.6	3,620.5
2016	1,547.8	7,876.0	2,802.0	29.0	3,859.0

*This takes into account the fullest possible tax burden, imposed on *all* cash inflows at the rate of 35 percent per year.
†The terminal value was estimated by capitalizing the sum of base fees, incentive fees, royalties, profit participation, and dividends at a rate of 12 percent, S. G. Warburg's estimate of a discount rate appropriate for this project. Estimated this way, the terminal value assumes no growth after the investment horizon.

Source: Offering circular, Euro Disneyland S.C.A., September 1989, and casewriters' analysis.

S.N.C. Return	Reimb. Payments	Invest. Outlay	Cash Flow to The Walt Disney Company	
			(Untaxed)	*(Maximum Tax*)*
		(833.0)	(833.0)	(833.0)
(340.0)	1,909.0		1,569.0	900.9
	360.0		360.0	234.0
61.3	493.0		1,246.6	810.3
61.3			1,093.0	710.5
61.3			1,667.3	1,083.8
61.3			2,450.6	1,592.9
61.3			3,952.3	2,569.0
61.3			4,286.7	2,786.4
61.3			4,650.1	3,022.6
61.3			5,045.0	3,279.3
61.3			5,474.1	3,558.2
61.3			5,940.5	3,861.3
			6,275.5	4,079.1
			6,698.8	4,354.2
			7,151.0	4,648.2
			7,634.0	4,962.1
			8,150.0	5,297.5
			8,777.4	5,705.3
			9,456.2	6,146.5
			10,190.7	6,624.0
			10,985.9	7,140.8
			11,847.0	7,700.6
			12,595.8	8,187.3
			13,393.5	8,705.8
			14,243.3	9,258.2
			15,148.9	9,846.8
		134,281.7[†]	150,395.5	97,957.1

EXHIBIT 8 Projected Cash Flows to The Walt Disney Company Assuming Euro Disneyland Is a Fully Integrated Internal Project (in millions of French francs)

	Operational Income	Amort. and Deprec.	Net Interest Expense	Taxes	Capital Expend.	+/- Debt	Terminal Value	Residual Cash Flow to WDC
1989					3,800.0	2,767.5		(1,032.5)
1990					5,100.0	2,767.5		(2,332.5)
1991					5,100.0	2,767.5		(2,332.5)
1992	2,043.0	700.0	(219.0)	546.7	392.0	990.0		2,313.3
1993	2,464.0	684.6	(213.0)	697.3	610.0	669.0		2,038.7
1994	3,312.0	680.9	(11.0)	924.7	3,408.0	2,410.0		1,400.3
1995	4,590.0	817.2	(70.0)	1,345.0	3,461.0	2,169.0		2,023.0
1996	6,800.0	949.4	376.0	1,916.1	886.0	(1,600.0)		2,021.9
1997	7,203.3	946.2	360.6	2,063.7	830.5	(1,498.6)		2,449.9
1998	7,630.4	940.5	345.8	2,220.5	778.4	(1,397.2)		2,888.6
1999	8,082.9	932.4	331.6	2,386.6	729.6	(1,295.8)		3,339.3
2000	8,562.2	922.2	318.0	2,562.7	683.9	(1,194.4)		3,803.2
2001	9,070.0	910.3	305.0	2,749.1	641.0	(1,093.0)		4,281.9
2002	9,553.8	896.8	314.8	2,919.8	692.6	(962.0)		4,664.7
2003	10,063.3	886.6	324.8	3,098.2	748.3	(831.0)		5,061.0
2004	10,600.1	879.7	335.2	3,284.8	808.6	(700.0)		5,471.5
2005	11,165.5	876.2	345.9	3,480.2	873.7	(569.0)		5,896.7
2006	11,761.0	876.0	357.0	3,684.8	944.0	(438.0)		6,337.2
2007	12,432.6	879.4	356.0	3,919.0	922.4	(438.4)		6,796.8
2008	13,142.5	881.6	355.0	4,167.1	901.4	(438.8)		7,280.3
2009	13,893.0	882.6	354.0	4,429.8	880.8	(439.2)		7,789.3
2010	14,686.4	882.5	353.0	4,707.8	860.7	(439.6)		8,325.3
2011	15,525.0	881.4	352.0	5,002.1	841.0	(440.0)		8,889.9
2012	16,469.3	879.4	43.4	5,441.3	688.8	(352.0)		9,943.8
2013	17,471.1	869.8	5.3	5,808.6	564.2	(264.0)		10,829.0
2014	18,533.8	854.6	0.7	6,187.5	462.1	(176.0)		11,707.5
2015	19,661.1	834.9	0.1	6,589.1	378.5	(88.0)		12,605.4
2016	20,857.0	812.1	0.0	7,015.7	310.0	0.0	112,760.8[†]	126,292.1

*Pretax income is taxed at 35 percent per year.
[†]The terminal value was estimated by capitalizing the residual cash flow of the project at 12 percent, S. G. Warburg's estimate of a discount rate appropriate for this project. Estimated this way, the terminal value assumes no growth after the investment horizon.

Source: Pro forma adjustment of projections contained in the offering circular, Euro Disneyland S.C.A., September 1989.

Calaveras Vineyards

In March 1994, Anne Clemens, a senior vice president at Goldengate Capital, received a loan proposal from Tom Howell, a managing director with NationsBank's investment banking group. The brochure described the prospective management acquisition of Calaveras Vineyards and solicited Goldengate's participation in the $4.5 million senior financing facility. The facility would consist of a $2 million term loan and a revolving credit of up to $2.5 million. Clemens would need to decide quickly whether the proposed terms were attractive, where to position Goldengate in this credit, and whether to offer a counterproposal on terms.

Goldengate Capital was a large West Coast financial institution with main activities in commercial lending, asset-based financing, leasing, mezzanine lending, and equity investing. Clemens had worked with Howell on a previous deal and had participated in two other business deals structured by him. These had proved to be very profitable deals for Goldengate, so Clemens planned to give this new proposal careful study. NationsBank N.A. was the third largest financial institution in the United States.

CALAVERAS VINEYARDS

Calaveras Vineyards was situated on 220 acres in Alameda Valley, California. The vineyards occupied 175 acres. The remaining acres consisted of various equipment sheds (to house the farming equipment); the winery building (containing storage tanks, aging barrels,

---

This case was prepared by Robert F. Bruner as a basis for discussion of an administrative situation, rather than to illustrate effective or ineffective decision making. Information about the company has been disguised. Some information on peer firms is fictional and has been added for the sake of deepening student analysis. The cooperation of NationsBank is gratefully acknowledged. Copyright © 1995 by the University of Virginia Darden School Foundation, Charlottesville, VA. All rights reserved. *No part of this publication may be reproduced, stored in a retrieval system, used in a spreadsheet, or transmitted in any form or by any means—electronic, mechanical, photocopying, recording, or otherwise—without the permission of the Darden School Foundation. For inquiries, please send an e-mail to dardencases@virginia.edu.* Revised 6/98. Version 2.1.

and a small bottling operation); and a small farmhouse with guestrooms, offices, and the requisite tasting and sales room. Exhibit 1 summarizes the major assets of the vineyard.[1]

Calaveras Vineyards was founded by Esteban Calaveras in 1883 to make wine for the Catholic Church. By the 1950s, the winery and vineyard had expanded into the production of table wines for sale to retailers and restaurants. Through the 1960s and 1970s, the Calaveras family, which continued to own the vineyards, made few changes despite dramatic growth in demand for California wines and the entry of large corporations in the production of California wines. Ownership of the vineyard changed hands in 1986, 1990, and 1992, as the vineyard was caught up in a frenzy of deal-doing among large corporate wine producers. With each change, the vineyard changed marketing organizations (i.e., independent firms that managed the sales and marketing of the vineyard's products). Thus, over the preceding nine years, there had been no fewer than three changes in ownership and three changes in the marketing organization.

Most recently, Stout PLC, a British conglomerate with interests in alcoholic beverages and branded consumer products, had acquired Calaveras Vineyards in a purchase of a portfolio of vineyards from another conglomerate. Stout had decided to sell Calaveras as part of a drive to focus on large, well-known wine and spirits brands.

PRODUCTS, MARKETING, AND COMPETITION

Despite the many changes in ownership and marketing, Calaveras managed to improve its brand image and market position through a strategy of careful quality control, market segmentation, and capital improvements (such as converting from redwood to oak cooperage, upgrading the winery with a bladder press, and installing a sprinkler system). As a result of these improvements, Calaveras was able to increase its average wholesale prices from $29.52 in 1989 to $44.26 in 1993.

Calaveras's products could be broken down into five main categories:

1. *Estate wines* were made and bottled at the winery from a few selected varieties. The Sauvignon Blanc and Cabernet Sauvignon had been highly praised by numerous influential wine writers, while the Petite Sirah was one of Calaveras's oldest and best-known varieties. All of Calaveras's estate wines were sold in the super-premium category.

2. *Selected-vineyards* wines were made from grapes purchased from selected vineyards (under long-term contracts) and aged and bottled separately to preserve their special characteristics. The Chardonnay was highly praised by numerous influential wine writers and had brought prestige to the Calaveras brand. All selected-vineyards wines were sold in the super-premium category.

3. *California wines* were made from medium-quality Calaveras produce. This category was declining in importance as Calaveras was able to elevate its wines to a higher status and pricing category under either the estate or selected-vineyards programs.

---

[1]Clemens had heard that choice vineyard land might sell for between $5,000 and $10,000 an acre, but that acreage was usually sold in units sufficient in size to constitute a winery business. She suspected that, in a forced liquidation, receivables could be sold for 85 percent of face value and inventory (virtually all of which was finished goods) could be sold for 75 percent of book value, while plant and equipment would fetch 40 percent of book value.

4. *Generic wines* were made from lesser-quality produce of the estates, selected-vine-yards, and California categories.
5. *Special-accounts* wines were made from surplus, lesser-quality wine, and from nonvarietal grapes. This wine was sold under special programs to airlines, hotels, and church parishes.

Exhibit 2 summarizes the breakdown of 1993 revenues among these categories.

In recent years, Calaveras's corporate owners had aimed to lift it out of the bulk-wine category and into the premium-brand segment of the market. Dr. Lynna Martinez was hired in 1987 to develop and implement a strategy to reach this goal. Martinez's strategy called for developing estate wines that would put the Calaveras brand in the premium category and focusing the product line on a few premium varieties of grapes. Accordingly, Calaveras introduced the Sauvignon Blanc, Cabernet Sauvignon, and Petite Sirah wines and reduced the number of varietal grapes grown at the vineyard from 22 in 1987 to 7 in 1994. In 1990, Dr. Martinez introduced the Chardonnay to broaden Calaveras's position in the premium category. Having attained the goal of moving Calaveras to the premium segment of the wine market, management's strategy now called for cautious price increases and the development of the special-accounts segment in order to use more fully Calaveras's wines of lesser quality.

Calaveras management planned to adopt a new marketing company upon consummation of the acquisition. The new company, Winston-Fendall, was well established as a wine marketer on the West Coast, where Calaveras had its strongest sales. Also, Winston-Fendall had just lost its flagship account and promised to position Calaveras in that capacity. The contract with the marketing company called for Winston-Fendall to collect all receivables on behalf of Calaveras and remit them to Calaveras. In addition, Winston-Fendall would pay Calaveras on a nonrecourse basis any receivables that were left unpaid after 90 days. Management believed these requirements would relieve Calaveras of credit risk.

About two-thirds of Calaveras's case sales were made through its wholesale-distribution network, with most of the remaining cases sold directly to special commercial accounts, including airlines and hotels. Roughly 60 percent of Calaveras's wholesale-case sales were made by its distributors to restaurants. The other 40 percent were made primarily to high-end retail outlets. Calaveras management planned to make no significant changes in its current wholesale-distribution network. All major distributorships had expressed keen interest in a continuing or increasing relationship with Calaveras. Nine distributors handled 80 percent of total volume, with two distributors in California handling 50 percent of total volume.

Calaveras had developed special commercial accounts with airline and hotel companies, which represented sales volume of approximately 15,000 to 25,000 cases a year. These accounts permitted Calaveras to sell wine that would ordinarily be sold in bulk. Because these were direct sales, margins to Calaveras were higher than if the cases had been sold through intermediaries. Gigantic Airlines, a major national air-transportation company, purchased 4,000 cases of this wine in 1987 and had raised the volume to 12,715 cases in 1993. At the same time, free-on-board (FOB) prices increased from $21 per case in 1987 to $39.70 per case in 1993. Gigantic had committed to a minimum of 16,500 cases in 1994 and had told management that future purchases should be no less than 16,500 cases per year.

A common practice in the industry was to segment demand by price, ranging from "low-price" (under $2.75 per 750-milliliter equivalent bottle at retail); "economy" ($2.76–$4.25); "popular" ($4.26–$5.75); "premium" ($5.76–$7.50); "super-premium" ($7.51–$10.00); and "ultra-premium" ($10.01 and over). Competition in the super-premium and premium wine segments was fragmented. Nevertheless, management identified several brands with characteristics similar to Calaveras, namely, high visibility, a reputation based on a well-respected brand and/or personality of the owners/winemakers, and a competitive position in the super-premium/premium segment. These competitors included Clos du Val, Cakebread, Acacia, Sonoma-Cutrer, and Jordan, all of which were privately owned and typically secretive about their finances and operations.

Nationwide, demand for alcoholic beverages was stagnating. Unit sales of spirits were declining. Dollar sales of beer had grown only 2.2 percent in 1992, less than the rate of inflation. Wine sales in supermarkets, however, had grown 7.4 percent, in part because "supermarket operators are becoming increasingly sophisticated in their selections of quality wines with higher price points, and because they are doing a better job of merchandising."[2] Another source noted:

> Domestic table wine, in particular, outshone the overall wine market . . . In recent years, this category has been fueled by premium California varietals. American consumers have increasingly been moving away from the generic wines popular in the 1970s to the more upscale, higher quality varietal wines. Several commercial wine manufacturers, most notably Gallo, Heublein, and The Wine Group have moved into the premium varietal market to reap its profits. And that is what they did in 1991. Both Gallo's Reserve Cellars and Heublein's Blossom Hill posted double-digit gains in 1991.[3]

Offering one unusual explanation for these sales improvements, Standard & Poor's noted:

> Much of the gains can be traced to the continued effects of the publicity surrounding the so-called "French Paradox"—scientific studies indicating that while the French consume 30 percent more fat per year than do Americans, they have a 40 percent lower incidence of coronary disease. The report gained widespread attention following a program on the subject that first aired on CBS's *60 Minutes* in November 1991. The show aired again in the summer of 1992. In the report, both American and French doctors suggested that the "paradox" could be related to the fact that the French drink more wine than Americans. The researchers concluded that moderate consumption of alcoholic beverages—particularly red wine—could reduce the risk of heart disease by as much as half. There has been a significant upturn in wine sales, especially red wine, since the *60 Minutes* report aired.[4]

OPERATIONS

The vineyard supplied about half the grape requirements of the Calaveras winery. Exhibit 3 details the acreage under production and the yield by variety of grape. To fulfill its grape requirements, the new company would assume two long-term supply contracts from Stout

---

[2]*Progressive Grocer* (July 1993), p. 74.

[3]*Jobson's Wine Marketing Handbook 1992* (Jobson Publishing Corporation, 1992), p. 6.

[4]From *Standard & Poor's Industry Surveys,* 26 August 1993, pg. F31. Reprinted by permission of Standard & Poor's, a division of The McGraw-Hill Companies.

PLC. Exhibit 4 outlines the purchase terms under these contracts for 1993. Clemens learned that the price under these long-term contracts was variable with the market; she assumed that this year's price per ton would be a fair predictor of next year's price, although the uncertainty about the cost of goods meant that gross margins for each of the product lines could vary by as much as 4 percent up or down from target. She assumed that gross margins had a standard deviation of 2 percent.

The production of wine from grapes entailed four main steps: crushing, fermenting, aging, and bottling. The winery was located on the vineyard property, with total capacity of approximately 65,000 cases per year for estate and selected-vineyards production. Although the winery had adequate production capacity in most areas, a moderate amount of fermentation, storage, and aging capacity was leased from Seraphim Winery, a neighbor. Also, all finished bottled goods were warehoused at Seraphim.

MANAGEMENT

Management of the new company would be headed by Dr. Lynna Martinez, who was vice president and general manager of the property for Stout PLC. The operations manager, Peter Newsome, would remain in that capacity. Martinez would purchase 85 percent of the equity of the new company; Newsome would purchase the remaining 15 percent. Exhibit 5 presents abbreviated résumés for these individuals.

HISTORICAL FINANCIAL PERFORMANCE

Stout PLC had provided pro forma historical profit-and-loss statements and balance sheets for Calaveras's fiscal years ended March 1990, 1991, 1992, and 1993. These statements are presented in Exhibit 6. Management believed that sales and operating profit were approximately as follows (all values in thousands):

	1991	1992	1993
Sales	$2,848	$2,836	$2,534
Operating profit	$ (54)	$ 13	$ 260

Sales increased from $2.4 million in 1990 to $2.8 million in 1991 and 1992 as Calaveras's strategy of introducing premium wines began to show tangible results with increasing average prices. Sales dropped to $2.5 million in 1993 as Stout's dismantling of its vineyard operations began to have an impact on Calaveras's volumes; in particular, Calaveras had no effective sales organization representing it. Operating cash flow improved dramatically because of increased average prices for Calaveras wines.

FINANCIAL PROJECTIONS

Management had developed a financial forecast with the assistance of the prominent accounting firm, Ernst and Anderson. Forecasted balance sheets, income statement, and assumptions are given in Exhibits 7, 8, and 9, respectively. Because many factors varied predictably with the planned production level, the primary variable was case revenues. Management had developed what it believed was a conservative projection of case sales, which took into account three main factors: case sales trends and demand, inflation, and real price increases reflecting Calaveras's strengthening brand recognition.

Historical and projected case sales are given in Exhibits 10 and 11. Sales in Calaveras Vineyards' first year were expected to rebound to the levels of 1992, as the company's marketing effort was revitalized. Case-sales forecasts for the second year and beyond represented a continuation of the increasing demand for Calaveras's estate Sauvignon Blanc, Cabernet Sauvignon, and selected-vineyard's Chardonnay, while recognizing the constraints of vineyard and production capacity for these and other varieties—overall, this displayed a shift in product mix toward white wines. Clemens learned that the theoretical maximum capacity of the winery was 110,000 cases per year. Without further information, she assumed that, to sustain unit growth shown in the forecasts, it would be necessary to invest $350,000 per year starting in 1996, rather than the $250,000 per year shown in the loan-proposal forecast. The forecast also showed an ambitious real growth rate in unit prices of 2 percent. Anne Clemens wondered how long real price growth could continue and generally believed that it was an especially uncertain number.[5] In defense of this assumption, the proposal document pointed to the strong past success of Lynna Martinez in elevating the winery's brand recognition and shifting the product mix into the higher-price categories.

For the sake of comparison, Anne Clemens's assistant had gathered information on manufacturers of wine and brandy (Exhibit 12). Unfortunately, there were very few publicly listed "pure-play" firms comparable to Calaveras. Clemens's assistant had identified three possible comparables, all traded over the counter:

- Canandaigua Wine Company was the second largest producer of wines in the United States, with sales in 1993 of $471 million. Once derisively called "Chateau Screwcap" and "a wino's winemaker"[6] for its focus on low-price product segments, the firm was building a record of solid growth and profit improvement through the acquisition and consolidation of small wineries. The firm was located in upstate New York.
- Finn & Sawyer Wine Company had sales of $25 million and was headquartered in Mendocino, California. It operated four California vineyards and produced only ultra-premium and super-premium wines.
- Frogg's Jump Winery, Inc., had sales of $67 million and was located in Livermore Valley, California. This firm specialized in the production of private-label wines for hotels, resorts, and airlines, and in servicing the higher-volume wine needs of wine-cooler manufacturers and of large religious organizations.

---

[5]Indeed, Clemens believed that real price growth could vary between +3 percent and −1 percent with equal probability.

[6]Jay Palmer, "Sampling Chateau Screwcap," *Barron's* (July 20, 1992), p. 36.

Valuation information about these firms included the following:

	Canandaigua	Finn & Sawyer	Frogg's Jump
Beta (levered)*	0.59	1.35	0.95
Beta (unlevered)	0.54	1.312	0.867
Book-value debt/equity ratio	0.86	0.12	0.35
Market-value debt/equity ratio	0.277	0.048	0.156
Market/book ratio	3.11	2.50	2.25
Price/earnings ratio (on expected EPS)	14	13	15
Tax rate	38%	40%	39%
Expected EPS growth rate, next five years	25%	11%	14%

*These betas are taken from Value Line and casewriter analysis. Such betas are estimated by regressing the difference between return on the company and the risk-free rates of return against the equity market premium (calculated as the return on a large portfolio of stocks including both large and small capitalization companies less the risk-free rate of return).

Clemens was conscious of the fact that Calaveras was a considerably smaller company than any of these comparables and that, with the performance turnaround and change in management, some conservative equity investors might demand a venture-capital type of return from Calaveras. Target venture-capital equity returns were at least 30 percent. As for future financing, Clemens believed that Calaveras would gravitate toward the industry-average capital structure.

In the first quarter of 1994, long-term corporate interest rates had risen 150 basis points on fears of rising inflation. Similarly, the stock-market indexes had receded 4 percent. Exhibit 13 gives a summary of historical rates of inflation in recent years. Clemens learned that between 1926 and 1992 inflation averaged 3.1 percent per year and had a standard deviation of 4.7 percent. Exhibit 14 presents information on current capital market conditions.

CONCLUSION

The specific terms of financing would need to be determined through negotiations between the buyers and their creditors. The NationsBank proposal, however, contemplated the following structure at closing:

Uses of Funds		Sources of Funds	
(in Millions of Dollars)		*(in Millions of Dollars)*	
Net working capital*	$2,116	Revolving loan	$1,122
Land	1,124	Term loan	2,000
Plant and equipment	582	Equity investment	1,000
Organization expenses	300	Total sources	$4,122
Total uses	$4,122		

*Net working capital at closing was projected to be the sum of cash ($50,000) and inventory ($2,196,000), less payables and accruals ($130,000).

NationsBank had proposed that the revolving loan be secured by accounts receivable and inventory. The maximum commitment under the revolver would be $2.5 million, though the borrowing base (the amount actually permitted to be outstanding under the loan) would be equal to 85 percent of receivables and 75 percent of inventories.[7] The interest rate on the revolving loan would be prime plus 2.0 percent. The term loan would amortize equally over five years, and would be secured by land, plant, and equipment. The interest rate on the term loan would be prime plus 3.0 percent. The prime rate was currently 6.75 percent.[8] As a rough initial assumption, Anne Clemens decided to assume a total interest rate of 9.5 percent on both the revolver and term loan. Also, Clemens assumed that, over the long term, Martinez would lever Calaveras's balance sheet at levels typical for other wine-producing companies, and proposed to use a discount rate consistent with this assumption.

The proposal from Tom Howell noted that Calaveras was currently carried on Stout's books for approximately $7 million and that the fair market value of the assets of Calaveras was estimated to be $5–$7 million. Therefore, the purchase price for the assets of the firm of $4.122 million represented a significant discount.

Anne Clemens had to decide quickly whether to participate in this deal, and how. Could the new company service the debt? What was the value of the assets on both an asset and a cash-flow basis? What were the "key drivers" of these values, and how sensitive were the values to variations in those assumptions? How attractive was this deal from the standpoint of the equity investors? Should she propose alternative terms, and, if so, what should they be?

As the sun set over the Pacific Ocean, Clemens decided to tackle these questions with the help of her assistant. After telephoning for supper from a nearby deli, she booted up her computer and accessed the spreadsheet model of the financial forecast that her assistant had prepared.

---

[7]Privately, Anne Clemens estimated that in liquidation, a sale of the plant and equipment would fetch a value equal to only 40 percent of their gross book value.

[8]Anne Clemens believed that *changes* in the prime rate of interest were normally distributed with a mean of zero and a standard deviation of about 1.75 percent.

EXHIBIT 1   Summary of Major Assets

Acreage	220 gross acres 175 planted acres
Buildings	8 structures (2 of wood frame and batten siding; 6 of metal sides and roof, and concrete floor)
Grape-crushing equipment	
Bottling equipment	(@ 70 bottles per minute)
Cooperage	40 stainless-steel tanks; 254,774 gallons capacity 33 wooden tanks; 61,298 gallons capacity 1,161 French oak barrels; 69,760 gallons capacity 1,197 barrels used for generic wines; 63,667 gallons capacity

Source: NationsBank offering document.

EXHIBIT 2   Breakdown of 1993 Revenues by Product Category

Products	*Percentage of 1993 Revenues*
Estates	
Sauvignon Blanc (w)	13.8%
Cabernet Sauvignon (r)	8.6
Petite Sirah (r)	4.5
Selected vineyards	
Chardonnay (w)	30.0
Sauvignon/Fume Blanc (w)	4.9
White Zinfandel (w)	2.5
California	
Petite Sirah (r)	8.1
Chenin Blanc (w)	1.6
Other (r)	0.4
Generic	
White table wine	6.9
Red table wine	2.1
Special accounts (r,w)	16.6
Total	100.0%

Note: *r* indicates a red wine; *w* indicates a white wine.

Source: NationsBank proposal document.

EXHIBIT 3   Summary of Acres under Production and Tons per Acre by Variety of Grape

Variety and Acres Growing in 1993	*1991 Tons/Acre*	*1992 Tons/Acre*	*1993 Tons/Acre*
Sauvignon Blanc			
(71 acres)	3.4	3.1	2.9
Semillon			
(20.1 acres)	4.4	4.7	3.4
Chenin Blanc			
(5.7 acres)	7.5	11.9	7.3
White Riesling			
(7.8 acres)	3.0	2.4	1.4
Muscat Blanc			
(0 acres)	2.7	0.8	0
White total			
(107.15 acres)	3.7	3.7	3.0
Cabernet Sauvignon			
(40.5 acres)	2.8	2.9	2.8
Petite Sirah			
(26.7 acres)	2.9	2.7	2.2
Red total			
(67.2 acres)	2.8	2.8	2.5
Grand total			
(174.35 acres)	3.4	3.4	2.8

Notes:
1. Tonnage figures have been rounded from the actual. In 1989, 50 acres of the 175 were replanted. This acreage has not yet reached full production.
2. The grand total tons/acre is a weighted average (by acres) of the yield for red and white wine grapes.

Source: NationsBank proposal document.

EXHIBIT 4   Summary of Purchases in 1993 of Grapes under Long-Term Contract

	Acres	*Price/Ton*	*Tons*	*Years Remaining*	*Pricing Changes*
Contract with Helsingor Vineyards				9 years	Variable at market
Chardonnay	96.0	$750.76	320		
Sauvignon Blanc	35.0	469.90	140		
Pinot Blanc	27.0	$583.58	100		
Contract with Cleaver Winery				3 years	Variable at market
Zinfandel	15.0	$412.90	50		

Source: NationsBank proposal document.

EXHIBIT 5   Résumés for Martinez and Newsome

Lynna Martinez

Position	Vice president/general manager and winemaker, Calaveras Vineyard, Alameda, California (1987– present).
Education	University of Burgundy, Dijon, France. Degrees, Diplôme des Hautes Honneurs, Microbiology.
	University of California at Davis. Degrees: M.S. Food Science, Ph.D. Microbiology.

Experience:

1980–81	Technical director—Casa Blanca Winery, Trujillo, Mexico.
1981–84	Technical director/winemaker—Domaine Millar, Fresno, California.
1984–87	Winemaker—Bullion Vineyards, La Plata, California.
Other	Training in family-owned winery and distillery. Teaching and research assistant at Department of Viticulture and Enology, University of California at Davis. Numerous training trips to Europe to gain experience in champagne and white-wine technology at the Moet et Chandon installation in Epernay.

Peter Newsome

Position	Operations manager.
Education	Macquarrie University, Australia. Degree in business administration.

Experience:

1984–86	Tasting-room manager.
1986–93	Manager of purchasing and warehousing.
1993 to present	Operations manager.

Source: NationsBank proposal document.

EXHIBIT 6 Pro Forma Historical Financial Statements

	1990	1991	1992	1993
Profit and loss statement				
Net sales	$2,378,041	$2,847,763	$2,836,062	$2,534,255
Cost of sales	1,992,461	1,782,811	2,197,367	1,779,809
Winery (under)/over absorbed costs	0	(612,000)	(96,998)	(53,303)
Gross profit	385,580	482,952	541,697	701,143
Marketing and advertising	62,354	109,647	103,047	61,333
Selling and administration	356,706	427,164	425,409	380,138
Total expenses	419,060	536,811	528,456	441,471
Operating profit	(33,480)	(53,859)	13,241	259,672
Balance sheets				
Cash	331,856	52,385	7,379	24,769
Receivables	337,492	397,864	354,508	316,782
Inventories	2,570,861	2,461,174	1,806,339	2,332,241
Prepaid expenses	1,083	1,179	8,191	0
Total current assets	3,241,292	2,912,602	2,176,417	2,673,792
Fixed assets				
Cost	3,984,287	4,303,372	4,429,552	4,487,193
Accumulated depreciation	178,484	377,253	771,765	1,067,086
Net fixed assets	3,805,803	3,926,119	3,657,787	3,420,107
Intangibles	486,822	340,421	493,656	62,233
Total assets	7,533,917	7,197,142	6,327,860	6,156,132
Trade liabilities	166,254	217,290	95,410	78,853
Parent equity and advances	7,367,663	6,961,852	6,232,450	6,077,279
Total liabilities and equity	$7,533,917	$7,179,142	$6,327,860	$6,156,132

Source: NationsBank proposal document. Figures have been disguised.

EXHIBIT 7   Forecasted Income Statement (all values in thousands)

	1994	1995	1996	1997	1998
Sales revenue	$3,704	$4,193	$4,681	$4,967	$5,348
Cost of goods sold					
Estates	422	560	638	664	781
Selected	259	310	365	380	395
Chardonnay	412	509	613	696	724
California	177	120	124	129	135
Generic	215	224	233	242	252
Special accounts	625	650	677	704	732
Winery	85	88	92	96	100
Total	(2,196)	(2,461)	(2,742)	(2,911)	(3,119)
Gross profit	1,508	1,731	1,939	2,056	2,229
Selling, general, and administration	(519)	(587)	(655)	(695)	(749)
Amortization of organizational costs	(60)	(60)	(60)	(60)	(60)
EBIT	930	1,085	1,224	1,301	1,420
Interest expense (average balance)	(306)	(308)	(280)	(235)	(173)
Profit before taxes	624	777	944	1,066	1,247
Tax expense	231	287	349	394	461
Net income	$ 393	$ 489	$ 594	$ 671	$ 786
Dividends to common shareholders	0	0	0	0	0
Retentions to equity	$ 393	$ 489	$ 594	$ 671	$ 786

Source: Casewriter's analysis, drawing on NationsBank proposal document. Figures have been disguised.

EXHIBIT 8 Forecasted Balance Sheets (all values in thousands)

	(At Closing)	1994	1995	1996	1997	1998
Cash	$ 50	$ 50	$ 50	$ 50	$ 50	$ 50
Accounts receivable	0	370	419	468	497	535
Inventory	2,196	2,461	2,742	2,911	3,119	3,245
Organization costs, current	60	60	60	60	60	0
Total current assets	2,306	2,942	3,272	3,489	3,726	3,830
Land	1,124	1,124	1,124	1,124	1,124	1,124
Plant and equipment	582	832	1,082	1,332	1,582	1,832
Gross PP&E	1,706	1,956	2,206	2,456	2,706	2,956
Accumulated depreciation	0	116	283	499	766	1,082
Net PP&E	1,706	1,840	1,923	1,957	1,940	1,874
Organization costs, noncurrent	240	180	120	60	0	0
Total assets	$4,252	$4,961	$5,315	$5,506	$5,666	$5,704
Payables and accruals	$130	$246	$274	$291	$312	$324
Debt, current portion LTD	400	400	400	400	400	0
Revolving line of credit	1,122	1,722	1,958	1,938	1,806	1,446
Total current liabilities	1,652	2,368	2,633	2,630	2,518	1,770
Debt, noncurrent	1,600	1,200	800	400	0	0
Total liabilities	3,252	3,568	3,433	3,030	2,518	1,770
Common stock	1,000	1,000	1,000	1,000	1,000	1,000
Retained earnings	0	393	882	1,477	2,148	2,934
Total equity	1,000	1,393	1,882	2,477	3,148	3,934
Total liabilities and equity	$4,252	$4,961	$5,315	$5,506	$5,666	$5,704
Memorandum:						
Borrowing base (85% AR, 75% Inv.)	$1,647	$2,161	$2,413	$2,581	$2,761	$2,888
Revolver	$1,122	$1,722	$1,958	$1,938	$1,806	$1,446

Source: Casewriter's analysis, drawing on NationsBank proposal document. Figures have been disguised.

EXHIBIT 9 Forecast Assumptions

Summary of Key Assumptions

Case sales	Exh. 11	Cash minimum (m)	$50
$/Case	Exh. 11	AR/sales	0.10
Gross margins		INV(*T*)/COGS(*T*+1)	1.00
Estates	0.50	CL(*T*)/COGS(*T*+1)	0.10
Select, other	0.38	SGA/sales	0.14
Chardonnay	0.40	Depreciation	5-yr, S-L
California	0.36	Capital expenditure	250
Generic	0.29	Interest rate	9.50%
Special accounts	0.38	Tax rate	37.00%
Winery	0.49	Inflation rate	2.00%
Dividend payout:		Real price growth	2.00%
Now—1996	0%	Amortization of organization costs	5 years
1997 and after	0%		

Discussion of Certain Assumptions

1. Production and inventory. Grapes are processed into wine in the year of harvest and all wine processed is sold approximately one year after processing, with the exception of estate reds (about 10 percent of production), which are sold two years after processing. The forecast assumes overall average processing time of one year. Thus, cost of sales and current liabilities are based on costs capitalized the previous year.

2. Beyond the forecast period, prices are expected to increase 2 percent per year, *before* inflation. This is consistent with management's strategy of lifting the brand recognition of Calaveras Vineyards wines, and of improving the quality of all wines.

3. Depreciation is based on a five-year average life of allocated asset (purchased) values. Assets are depreciated using the straight-line method.

4. The tax rate is a blended Federal and California State blended rate of 37 percent. There are no significant differences between book and tax income.

5. Organization costs of $300,000 will be amortized over five years. These cash costs were to be paid at closing and would consist mainly of legal, accounting, and financial advisory fees incurred to consummate the transaction.

6. The vineyard yield per acre and production rate per ton of grapes are expected to remain constant.

7. The term loan is assumed to be amortized over five years. The interest rate of the term loan and revolver is assumed constant at 9.5 percent, 25 basis points lower than currently, to reflect the expected moderation of inflation, over the longer term.

EXHIBIT 10   Historical Case Sales and Prices

	1991 Cases	1991 $/Case	1992 Cases	1992 $/Case	1993 Cases	1993 $/Case
Estates						
Sauvignon Blanc (w)	4,436	$46.85	2,924	$48.25	6,133	$49.70
Cabernet Sauvignon (r)	3,258	45.56	2,887	46.92	2,993	48.33
Petite Sirah (r)	2,547	46.42	1,574	47.82	1,599	49.25
Select vineyards						
Chardonnay (w)	8,633	38.88	16,537	40.05	11,569	41.25
Sauvignon/Fume Blanc (w)	11,794	37.85	9,750	38.98	3,444	40.15
White/Rose Zinfandel (w)	5,835	38.03	4,482	39.17	2,112	40.35
California						
Petite Sirah (r)	9,472	32.52	7,666	33.50	5,864	34.50
Chenin Blanc (w)	5,393	33.13	5,210	34.13	1,353	35.15
Other (r)	7,299	30.73	1,350	31.65	322	32.60
Generic						
White table wine	17,685	22.42	13,301	23.10	7,716	23.79
Red table wine	4,657	20.09	2,976	20.69	2,337	21.31
Total wholesale	81,009		68,657		45,442	
Special accounts						
Hotels (w, r)	0	37.61	0	38.74	2,090	39.90
Gigantic Airlines (w, r)	11,320	37.42	23,465	38.54	12,715	39.70
Altar wines (w, r)	2,388	41.59	2,157	42.83	3,155	44.12
Winery (w, r)	3,633	$54.15	2,957	$55.78	2,188	$57.45
Total nonwholesale	17,341		28,579		20,148	
Total case sales	98,350		97,236		65,590	

Note: *r* indicates a red wine; *w* indicates a white wine.

Source: NationsBank proposal document and casewriter's analysis.

EXHIBIT 11 Forecasted Case Sales and Prices

	1994 Cases	1994 $/Case	1995 Cases	1995 $/Case	1996 Cases	1996 $/Case	1997 Cases	1997 $/Case	1998 Cases	1998 $/Case
Estates										
Sauvignon Blanc	9,000	$51.71	12,000	$53.80	14,000	$55.97	14,000	$58.23	16,000	$60.58
Cabernet Sauvignon	5,000	50.28	6,000	52.31	6,000	54.43	6,000	56.63	7,000	58.91
Petite Sirah	2,500	51.24	3,000	53.31	3,000	55.46	3,000	57.70	3,000	60.04
Select vineyards										
Chardonnay	16,000	42.92	19,000	44.65	22,000	46.45	24,000	48.33	24,000	50.28
Savignon/Fume Blanc	8,000	41.77	8,000	43.46	8,000	45.22	8,000	47.04	8,000	48.94
White/Rosé Zinfandel	2,000	41.98	3,500	43.68	5,000	45.44	5,000	47.28	5,000	49.19
California										
Petite Sirah	5,000	35.89	5,000	37.34	5,000	38.85	5,000	40.42	5,000	42.06
Chenin Blanc	1,728	36.57	0	38.05	0	39.58	0	41.18	0	42.85
Other	1,000	33.92	0	35.29	0	36.71	0	38.20	0	39.74
Generic										
White table wine	10,000	24.75	10,000	25.75	10,000	26.79	10,000	27.87	10,000	29.00
Red table wine	2,500	22.17	2,500	23.07	2,500	24.00	2,500	24.97	2,500	25.98
Total wholesale	62,728		69,000		75,500		77,500		80,500	
Special accounts										
Hotels	4,000	41.51	4,000	43.19	4,000	44.93	4,000	46.75	4,000	48.64
Gigantic Airlines	16,500	41.30	16,500	42.97	16,500	44.71	16,500	46.51	16,500	48.39
Altar wines	3,500	45.90	3,500	47.76	3,500	49.69	3,500	51.69	3,500	53.78
Winery	2,790	59.77	2,790	62.19	2,790	64.70	2,790	67.31	2,790	70.03
Total nonwholesale	26,790		26,790		26,790		26,790		26,790	
Total case sales	89,518		95,790		102,290		104,290		107,290	

EXHIBIT 12   Comparative Information on Manufacturers of Wine and Brandy (81 establishments for 1993)

Financial Statement	Average Dollar Amount	Percentage of Assets or Sales
Cash	$59,256	4.6%
Accounts receivable	99,189	7.7
Notes receivable	6,441	0.5
Inventory	560,356	43.5
Other current	25,763	2.0
Total current	751,005	58.3
Fixed assets	376,147	29.2
Other noncurrent	161,022	12.5
Total assets	1,288,174	100.0
Accounts payable	95,325	7.4
Bank loans	0	0.0
Notes payable	76,002	5.9
Other current	204,820	15.9
Total current	376,147	29.2
Other long-term liabilities	235,736	18.3
Deferred credits	2,576	0.2
Net worth	673,715	52.3
Total liabilities and net worth	1,288,174	100.0
Net sales	752,554	100.0
Gross profit	298,011	39.6
Net profit	$14,299	1.9%

Ratios	Upper Quartile	Median	Lower Quartile
Solvency			
Quick ratio (×)	1.2×	0.4×	0.2×
Current ratio (×)	5.5	2.5	1.5
Curr. liab. to net worth (%)	8.0	44.0	102.7
Total liab. to net worth (%)	28.8	103.4	186.4
Efficiency			
Collection period (days)	29.2	51.3	69.2
Sales to inventory (×)	2.6	1.4	0.8
Assets to sales (%)	95.8	136.7	287.9
Acct. payable to sales (%)	4.9	11.3	17.7
Profitability			
Return on sales (%)	7.3	2.8	(0.2)
Return on assets (%)	8.1	2.3	(0.1)
Return on net worth (%)	16.6	7.7	1.1

Source: Dun & Bradstreet Business Services, *Industry Norms and Key Business Ratios* (1994). Copyright 1994, Dun & Bradstreet, a company of The Dun & Bradstreet Corporation.

EXHIBIT 13   A Summary of Industry Rates of Inflation in 1991

	Percentage Change in 1991
Producer price index	
Wine, brandy, and brandy spirits	3.4%
Grape table wine	4.2
White wine	3.3
Red wine	4.4
Rosé wine	6.6
All farm products	−6.3%
Consumer price index	
Wine	13.6%
Total beverage alcohol	10.5
Food	2.9
All items	4.26%

Source: *Jobson's Wine Marketing Handbook 1992* (Jobson Publishing Corporation, 1992).

EXHIBIT 14   Current Capital Market Conditions (February 28, 1994)

Interest Rates

Federal funds	3.75%
Prime rate	6.75
90-day T-bills	3.25
30-year T-bonds	5.85
Corporate bonds (10+ years)	
High-quality	7.0
Medium-quality	7.3
High-yield	9.35

Stock Market

P/E multiples	
Dow	14.5×
S&P 500	15.5×
NASDAQ	16.8×

Average Equity Market Premiums (1926–92)

	Geometric Mean Premium	Arithmetic Mean Premium
Returns on all common stock less returns on:		
Long-term government bonds	5.5%	7.2%
U.S. Treasury bills	6.6	8.6
Returns on small-company stocks less returns on:		
Long-term government bonds	7.4	12.4
U.S. Treasury bills	8.5	13.8

Sources: *Federal Reserve Board Bulletin;* and Ibbotson Associates, *1993 Yearbook, Stocks, Bonds, Bills, and Inflation.*

Mirth Press, Inc.

In November of 1994, Alexandra Pointer sat in her office at Quincyshire Management, Inc., and pondered a possible acquisition. Pointer was a principal at Quincyshire, a "private equity" investment firm engaged in the acquisition, ownership, and supervision of business enterprises for the account of the $100 million Quincyshire Equity Fund. Quincyshire had identified a humor-book and audio publisher, Mirth Press, Inc., as a possible acquisition. In partnership with another private equity firm, Quincyshire had structured a winning bid for the company. The equity group had signed a letter of intent granting it the exclusive right to negotiate the purchase of Mirth. Since the due-diligence research had been completed, the closing of the transaction was approaching. Pointer and her partners had to decide on the appropriateness of the proposed deal structure and whether to commit to the acquisition terms as finally negotiated.

Pointer was impressed with the firm's recent growth and its prospects for growth in the future. Mirth's sales grew from $4,716,000 in 1992 to $21,595,000 in 1994. (See Exhibits 1 and 2 for historical financial statements.) This rapid growth was attributable to the introduction of a line of audio products. These products included recordings of readings of classic humor literature, famous comedy acts, excerpts from films and TV shows, and compilations of the work of promising new comedians.

The Quincyshire group could buy the company for a price, including fees, of $48.4 million. The transaction would be structured as a management buyout. The current management, the company's founders, would buy into the new company. Management believed that the market for its audio products was largely untapped and that their innovative, interactive marketing program would continue to produce strong sales growth. Quincyshire, its partner, and current stockholders would contribute $13.4 million in equity (common and preferred). The remainder of the purchase price would be funded by a $23 million senior-

This case was prepared from field research by Thomas Halverson under the direction of Professor Robert F. Bruner. Names, locations, and products have been disguised at the request of the company. The case was written as a basis for class discussion rather than to illustrate effective or ineffective handling of an administration situation. Copyright © 1997 by the University of Virginia Darden School Foundation. All rights reserved. *No part of this publication may be reproduced, stored in a retrieval system, used in a spreadsheet, or transmitted in any form or by any means—electronic, mechanical, photocopying, recording, or otherwise—without the permission of the Darden School Foundation. For inquiries, please send an e-mail to dardencases@virginia.edu.* Revised 1/98. Version 1.3.

term loan secured by Mirth's intellectual properties and a $12 million subordinated term note with warrants. The new company also planned to negotiate a $4 million revolving credit facility to fund any working capital shortfalls.

QUINCYSHIRE MANAGEMENT, INC.

Quincyshire was founded in 1986 as a vehicle for investing in management buyouts (MBOs). These were typically leveraged acquisitions and recapitalizations where Quincyshire partnered with a management team and provided the majority equity capital. Quincyshire evaluated its investments against a target annual hurdle rate of 40 percent over a five-year holding horizon. At the end of 1993, Quincyshire raised $100 million for its Quincyshire Equity Fund. Prior to this, Quincyshire had raised capital for each transaction. The fund allowed Quincyshire more flexibility and facilitated the firm's ability to act quickly. At the time of the Mirth acquisition, Quincyshire principals had made over 40 investments in a wide range of industries. The firm boasted a total internal rate of return of over 55 percent on all of its investments before the new fund had been organized. While some investments performed better than others, Quincyshire had experienced several "home runs." For example, the firm bought an industrial fasteners business from a major industrial company in 1992 and sold the business less than two years later, realizing an internal rate of return of well over 100 percent.

THE PRIVATE EQUITY INDUSTRY

The private equity industry gained prominence in the early 1980s as firms like Kohlberg Kravis Roberts & Co. (KKR) and Forstmann Little & Co. started closing big, public leveraged buyouts (LBOs). Institutional money poured into leveraged buyout funds as buyout firms consistently posted returns well above that of the stock market. LBO funds were able to pay large premiums for undervalued assets in the public markets and leverage these transactions as much as 10 to 1. Fund-raising and deal flow continued to be strong until the late 1980s. At that time, the junk-bond market collapsed and all credit tightened; corporations downsized, restructured, and increased operating efficiency; and the public markets reflected higher asset valuations.

In 1992, money started to flow back into private-equity deals (see Exhibit 3 for a history of deal volume). By 1994 private-equity deal volume had eclipsed the record set in 1987. Pension funds and other institutional investors were allocating more of their portfolios to this sector. The money under institutional management was growing as well. Private equity firms were getting a bigger piece of a bigger pie. But banks were not allowing 1980s-type leverage: ratios of 4 to 1 and 3 to 1 were the norm. Strategic buyers were dominating the acquisition world. In 1988 financial buyers represented 34 percent of all acquisitions, while in 1994 financial buyers accounted for only 6.9 percent of all acquisitions.[1] In addition, the quality of seller representation in the middle market had improved substantially. Companies were increasingly being auctioned, and prices as measured by multiples of cash flow or EBITDA were climbing.

---

[1]Marcia Berss, "How Long Can You Twiddle Your Thumbs?" *Forbes,* September 11, 1995, p. 47.

The competition for deals made it difficult for private equity firms to put their money to work. There was a constant conflict for firms between the desire to empty their full coffers and the need to maintain price discipline. Most firms had a five-year horizon to invest their funds. Traditionally, firms charged a management fee for funds committed over that horizon. Investors were becoming more demanding, though. Private-equity firms had to cut management fees or change the fee structure such that fees were charged only on funds invested rather than committed. These factors pressured fund managers to do deals.

Investors were aware of the changed deal environment. A study by Pathway Capital Management found the median gross return of 447 LBOs completed between 1970 and 1993 to be 35 percent. In 1994, however, Blackstone Capital Partners had marketed its latest fund with a 25 percent gross return target, down from 35 percent for its previous fund. Morgan Stanley Capital Partners III was marketed with a target of 30 percent pretax gross rate of return. Institutional investors' expectations for returns had decreased significantly since the 1980s. Investors were funding at expected rates of return in the 20s.[2]

The downward pressure on returns spurred private equity firms to seek new strategies. Some firms sought deals that were not being auctioned by an intermediary. Others entered traditionally difficult industries like retail. Still others were employing "platform" strategies where they would acquire a leading firm in an industry and then use that firm (or "platform") as a vehicle to consolidate the industry. Platform strategies in effect converted private-equity firms from financial buyers into strategic buyers. Still others had started taking minority positions through which they could exert significant control.

Quincyshire had raised a new fund in this environment. Its target rate of return was high compared to the trends in the industry. Even so, since late 1993, Quincyshire completed or was in the process of completing five deals representing approximately 35 percent of its capital under management. This ranked Quincyshire among the leaders of all private-equity firms in terms of number of transactions.

HISTORY OF MIRTH PRESS

Tom and Pat Nikle were lifelong enthusiasts of humor literature. Prior to venturing into the publishing business, Tom was professor of English at University of California at Napa. Pat was a freelance writer who had led script development on three major comedy films. Together, they owned one of the largest private collections of first-edition humor literature in the United States. In the early 1980s the couple pooled their interest in humor literature and conceptualized a collection of compilations of regional humor, which would group stories, poems, and cartoons. This resulted in a five-volume collection of books, representing New England, the South, New York, the Upper Midwest, the Mountain Region, and California. To publish their collection, they incorporated Mirth in the summer of 1984. In January of 1985 the Nikles sold additional shares in Mirth to two individual investors and by the spring of 1985 their collection of regional humor, *Hinterland Humor,* was ready for the press.

Hinterland Humor sold out and additional issues were printed. Mirth acquired the domestic rights to a Canadian company's regional humor books to increase its offerings. Mirth con-

---

[2]"Industry Returns May Fall, but Funds Say 'Not Ours,' " *Buyouts* 7, sec. 15 (July 25, 1994).

tinued to add titles over the next few years by acquiring small publishers and internally generating titles. The growth was financed by two separate venture capital infusions.

In 1990 Mirth developed a proprietary line of audio products marketed under the Mirthful brand. Mirth had sold audiotapes of readings and comedians' skits produced by another company since 1986. The audiotapes sold impressively, and management realized that there was a large potential market for humor audio products. To maximize profitability in this potential market, Mirth decided that it had to control its own audio products. In July of 1990, the Mirthful brand was launched. These records, tapes, and compact discs were manufactured on contract by outside firms. The audio line was an immediate success. Mirth as a humor audio publisher was born.

By 1994 Mirth's audio line encompassed several product categories such as Holiday Titles (humorous readings with a holiday theme); Downeast Folklore (New England folklore readings); Kids' Humor (tall tales, jokes, and puns); Inspired Broadcast Skits (classic segments from Groucho Marx, *The Honeymooners,* Lucille Ball, and Jack Benny); and Komedy Tonight! (nightclub skits of new comedians). Sales of audio products had grown from $676,000 in fiscal year 1990 to over $15 million in fiscal year 1994. While Mirth's catalog sales and direct marketing efforts remained strong, the bulk of the Mirth's growth could be attributed to its innovative retail approach.

In late 1991 the company began developing an interactive retail display for its audio products—the Komedy Kiosk. This was a stand-alone kiosk that allowed the customer to sample Mirth products. Occupying only five square feet of floor space, Komedy Kiosk was a six-foot-tall wooden structure that displayed Mirth audio products. Using a motion sensor, it greeted passing customers and encouraged them to sample Mirth titles. Komedy Kiosk was capable of playing 60-second samples of 34 different titles. In August of 1992, Mirth placed its first 10 Komedy Kiosk units in retail locations. By 1994, more than 3,000 units were in stores. These units generated 68 percent of Mirth's sales. Management realized that future growth would be dominated by the audio area. The Komedy Kiosk retail program was the key to this growth. Before the implementation of this program, Mirth was unable to reach customers directly through its original channels. Komedy Kiosk not only reached new customers, but actually sold to them interactively.

By 1994 Mirth had become the leader in the humor audio niche. It had 140 titles and a library of 300 hours of original recordings. The company expected audio sales to grow from $15.1 million in 1994 to $66.1 million in 1998 and to dominate its product niche. While Mirth anticipated strong growth in its sales of books, sales of audio products were expected to generate the bulk of the firm's growth.

THE HUMOR AUDIO BUSINESS

The audio business offered high profit margins. Mirth typically maintained a trade gross profit margin of 83 percent on compact discs and 80 percent on cassettes. The company was able to maintain these margins because it paid little in royalties. (Exhibit 4 presents expense ratios for a typical audio publisher as compared to Mirth.) Most of the properties were either in the public domain (such as the stories of Pecos Bill) or were purchased with lump-sum initial payments.

The humor audio industry was a small but growing niche market. Unfortunately, there was little public information about the size of the market or consumer buying habits. Mirth had begun to assess its category by means of primary research. The initial evidence suggested that the customer sought a humorous experience rather than a particular artist. Customers were looking to find happiness or relieve stress. Because of these buying traits, customers bought into the concept rather than the individual brand, writer, or comedian. These factors presented obstacles to maintaining a strong brand.

Mirth's competition consisted of several small publishers. None of the large music companies had entered the market in a serious way. Theoretically, barriers to entry were low in the industry. The key assets were humor properties, which could be acquired relatively cheaply. Channels of distribution were very different for Mirth than for typical music products. While music publishers sold their titles primarily through record stores, Mirth did not. Humor audio seemed to get lost in typical record stores; the category's turns were too low. Record stores changed displayed product weekly or even daily, while Mirth products changed only three to four times a year. Record stores would not dedicate sections to humor audio.

Mirth sold its titles in specialty stores, in discount stores, by mail order, and in record clubs. This was typical for the humor audio industry. The company did not experience its explosive growth until it introduced its Komedy Kiosk marketing program. The kiosks gave Mirth visibility. Potential customers were drawn to the display and could sample the titles. The program worked. It seemed that if people were exposed to these products, they would buy them. Exhibit 5 compares Mirth's channels of distribution to those of a typical music publisher.

Mirth would continue to create and market its full line of products, including calendars, books, audio books, posters, and T-shirts. As humor audio sales increased, nonaudio products would represent a decreasing percentage of revenue. From 1990 to 1994, audio sales increased from 17 percent of the total, to 68 percent.

COMPETITION

Tom and Pat Nikle believed that competition in this category was highly fragmented. Competitors were mostly relatively small, private companies. Mirth's main competitors included these:

> *Gib Hobson Productions* was a private company producing the Parody label in Vancouver. Hobson had 13 humor-only titles and 12 humor-and-music titles. Mirth acted as Hobson's U.S. distributor from 1986 until 1993. Its distribution system was underdeveloped, and management estimated that total sales were in the $5 to $8 million area. Hobson did have a 12-title interactive listening system similar to Komedy Kiosk.

> *Global Disk Productions, Inc.,* had competed in the industry for eight years. It had 4 humor-and-music titles, 60 music-only titles, and an interactive-music listening system. Global Disk was located in Washington and had solid distribution in the Northwest. Global Disk estimated that its total 1994 sales would be about $5 million.

> *The Comedy Company* of Roslyn, New York, had 50 titles, all of which were related to nightclub comedy skits. The Comedy Company's products could be found most often in airports and gift shops.

Belly Laugh Partners was an eight-title organization in Tucson. It had no national distribution program.

The Wall-to-Ceiling Records Company had 15 humor titles sold exclusively in its retail stores. Management estimated Wall-to-Ceiling Records Company sales between $4 and $5 million for these products.

Downeast Humor Company of Maine was very strong in the Northeast. It offered 12 humor-and-music titles in a rack display with headphones. It did not distribute much outside of the Northeast. Management estimated sales to be around $5 million.

Harebrained Audio was a division of Uitland Inc. of Memphis. Its humor-and-music products were marketed in mass-merchant stores with no interactive display. Tom Nikle believed that sales for its compact discs were in the $4 to $5 million range.

Sigma Music marketed 25 "New Age" humor titles under the *Climbing the Wall* label. These humor-and-music recordings were of very low quality.

MARKETING STRATEGY

Mirth planned to grow aggressively by capitalizing on its key corporate assets. The company maintained strong in-house creative prowess. This creative force drove the introduction of new recordings, new packaging, and new lines of product. The creative focus was not only a development asset, but because creative development was in-house, Mirth enjoyed cost advantages over its competitors. The company led the industry in kiosk technology and coverage. The kiosk marketing program had been the backbone of the sales growth at Mirth. The company pioneered this selling technique and continued to experiment with new kiosk locations and formats. Mirth led the industry in audio expertise. It possessed a large library of humor in the public domain. Management felt that Mirth produced the highest quality recordings in the industry. It had the artistic resources and production know-how to continue to be a leader in quantity and quality of titles.

The company planned to build on this strong base and increase brand awareness and distribution. The goal was to maintain and build upon its reputation as the category leader in quality of sound and product presentation. While management felt that its trial rate was high, they planned to promote and enhance the Mirth brand in order to protect its premium price and encourage more repeat purchases. Mirth planned to enhance its distribution by increasing the number of kiosks in both specialty stores and mass merchandisers domestically and internationally. Management was also exploring the possibility of placing kiosks in other high-traffic areas such as airports. An increase in kiosk coverage would act as a barrier to competition. A large retail network was an asset not easily obtained due to the "mom-and-pop" nature of many Mirth carriers. The company had success as a private-label manufacturer for a mass retailer. Mirth would continue to explore such opportunities and was considering launching a lower quality line for mass retailers. A less expensive, slightly lower quality line would enable the company to compete on price in the mass retail market without cannibalizing higher quality product sold in specialty and higher end stores. Perhaps the company's greatest asset was its ability to innovate and adapt. Only a few years ago, Mirth was a small book publisher. Since then it had increased its offerings, pioneered a new distribution method, and expanded a growing category.

THE TRANSACTION

The $48.4 million purchase price would be financed from a number of sources, as indicated in Table 1.

A single commercial bank (Institution A) proposed to fund a revolver, a senior-term loan, and a subordinated loan. Although not necessary to finance the transaction, a revolving credit facility of $4 million would be negotiated. Quincyshire anticipated interest rates of 10.5 percent on the senior-term loan and the revolver (based on a formula of prime plus 2 percent) and 12.5 percent on the subordinated note. The subordinated note had been structured so that the principal did not amortize in the first five years. The senior note followed a regular amortization schedule (Exhibit 6).

About $5.68 million in preferred stock would be issued with a face value of $9 million, and an original issue discount (OID) of $3.32 million. This issue would carry an 8 percent accumulating dividend payable upon sale of the company. Quincyshire and Institution A would purchase this preferred issue, along with Institution B, another private equity fund that had participated in many of Quincyshire's deals. Exhibit 6 gives a schedule of dividends and accreted value for the preferred issue.

Common stock would be purchased by cash contributions from Quincyshire and Co-investor B, as well as the private equity subsidiary of Institution A (called Co-Investor A). In addition, management and its two historical venture capital investors would roll over some of their shares in the company (i.e., swap "OldCo" shares for "NewCo" shares).

As part of this transaction, Institution A was to receive 10-year warrants attached to the preferred stock to purchase 2,250 shares of preferred stock, exercisable at $1,000 per share. The price of the preferred stock implied in the transaction was $1,000 per share.

TABLE 1   Sources and Uses of Funds

Uses		Sources	
Seller consideration	$45,000,000	Revolver	
Repay existing debt	900,000	Senior term	$23,000,000
Fees and expenses	2,000,000	Subordinated debt	12,000,000
Cash to new company	500,000	Institution A preferred stock	2,250,000
	$48,400,000	Co-investor B preferred stock	325,800
		Quincyshire preferred stock	3,105,000
		Common stock acquired by cash contribution	
		Co-investor A common stock	1,000,000
		Co-investor B common stock	144,615
		Quincyshire common stock	1,380,000
		Common stock acquired by rollover of shares	
		Management common stock	4,365,001
		Venture capital A common	433,538
		Venture capital B common	396,046
			$48,400,000

Institution A's private equity investment affiliate, Co-investor A, was to receive 1,165 10-year warrants to purchase common exercisable at $615 per share. The sellers were to be issued earn-out warrants as well, to be paid if certain EBITDA targets were reached. (See Exhibit 7 for a complete summary of security purchases and contributions.)

CONCLUSION

As part of her final review of the deal, Pointer wished to check the expected returns and value creation to all of the participants, and their sensitivity to changes in assumptions. Her assistant had prepared a forecast of cash flows for Mirth Press (see Exhibit 8), as well as projected balance sheets (see Exhibit 9). Exhibit 10 contains selected financial information on potential comparable companies. Current capital market conditions are summarized in Exhibit 11.

Mirth had grown explosively over the last year. Pointer wondered if this were just a fad. Could the company maintain its momentum? Would the existing competitors roll out their own kiosks and steal Mirth's market share? Could Mirth maintain its margins in a more competitive environment? As Mirth grew in sales and gained recognition, would a giant music publisher like Sony recognize the opportunity and enter the market? Should Mirth move to acquire its competitors and consolidate the industry? What was the proper exit strategy for Quincyshire? All of these questions had to be addressed by Pointer and her partners before the papers were signed.

EXHIBIT 1   Historical Income Statements (fiscal year ending June 30, in thousands)

	1992	Actual 1993	1994	Five Months Ending Nov. 1994
Net sales	$4,716	$7,166	$21,595	$18,147
Sales growth	N/A	51.95%	201.36%	N/A
Cost of sales	($2,472)	($3,372)	($7,133)	($5,994)
(as % of sales)	52.42%	47.06%	33.03%	33.03%
Depreciation and amortization	($36)	($65)	($161)	($98)
Gross profit	$2,208	$3,729	$14,301	$12,055
Gross margin	46.82%	52.04%	66.22%	66.43%
SG&A Expense	($1,836)	($2,926)	($9,179)	($7,229)
(as % of sales)	38.93%	40.83%	42.50%	39.84%
Operating profit	$372	$803	$5,122	$4,826
Operating margin	7.89%	11.21%	23.72%	26.59%
Interest expense	($117)	($93)	($112)	NA
Interest income	$0	$0	$2	NA
Pretax earnings	$255	$710	$5,013	NA

Source: Company reports.

EXHIBIT 2   Historical Balance Sheets (fiscal year ending June 30, in thousands)

	1992	1993	1994
Current assets			
Cash	$ 11,216	$ 21,092	$ 56,076
Accounts receivable (net)	749,686	1,610,210	6,916,365
Inventory	1,353,393	1,591,072	2,649,532
Prepaid expenses:			
Royalty advances	146,123	223,774	278,248
Other	64,815	74,502	347,566
Total current assets	2,325,233	3,520,650	10,747,787
Long-term assets			
Gross PPE	523,942	809,544	1,324,200
Accumulated depreciation	−144,277	−209,325	−316,299
Net fixed assets	379,665	600,219	1,007,901
Deferred income taxes	6,000	33,500	142,000
Noncompete	0	96,160	60,100
Intangibles (net)	17,794	13,834	9,874
Debt and equity issuance costs (net)	39,277	27,337	15,397
Loan origination fees (net)	3,502	2,722	1,942
Goodwill	5,932	4,612	3,292
Total long-term assets	452,170	778,384	1,240,506
Total assets	$2,777,403	$4,299,034	$11,988,293
Current liabilities			
Current maturities:			
Notes payable	$ 113,000	$ 151,893	$ 66,425
Capital lease obligations	17,292	49,636	49,709
Notes payable—banks	545,000	667,346	—
Accounts payable	466,074	939,723	1,548,596
Accruals	221,297	509,024	3,813,507
Accrued income taxes	107,450	184,137	1,395,851
Noncompete		36,413	36,060
Total current liabilities	1,470,113	2,538,172	6,910,148
Long-term liabilities			
Notes payable	318,057	213,463	473,559
Capital lease obligations	27,064	104,439	104,069
Noncompete		60,100	24,040
Total long-term liabilities	345,121	378,002	601,668
Total liabilities	1,815,234	2,916,174	7,511,816
Equity			
Common stock, Class A	4,500	4,540	4,540
Common stock, Class B	3,250	3,500	3,500
Preferred stock	2,350	2,350	2,350
Additional paid-in capital	909,258	921,218	929,618
Retained earnings	42,811	451,252	3,536,469
Total equity	962,169	1,382,860	4,476,477
Total liabilities and equity	$2,777,403	$4,299,034	$11,988,293

Source: Company reports.

EXHIBIT 3   Volume of Funds Committed in Private Equity Deals by Year

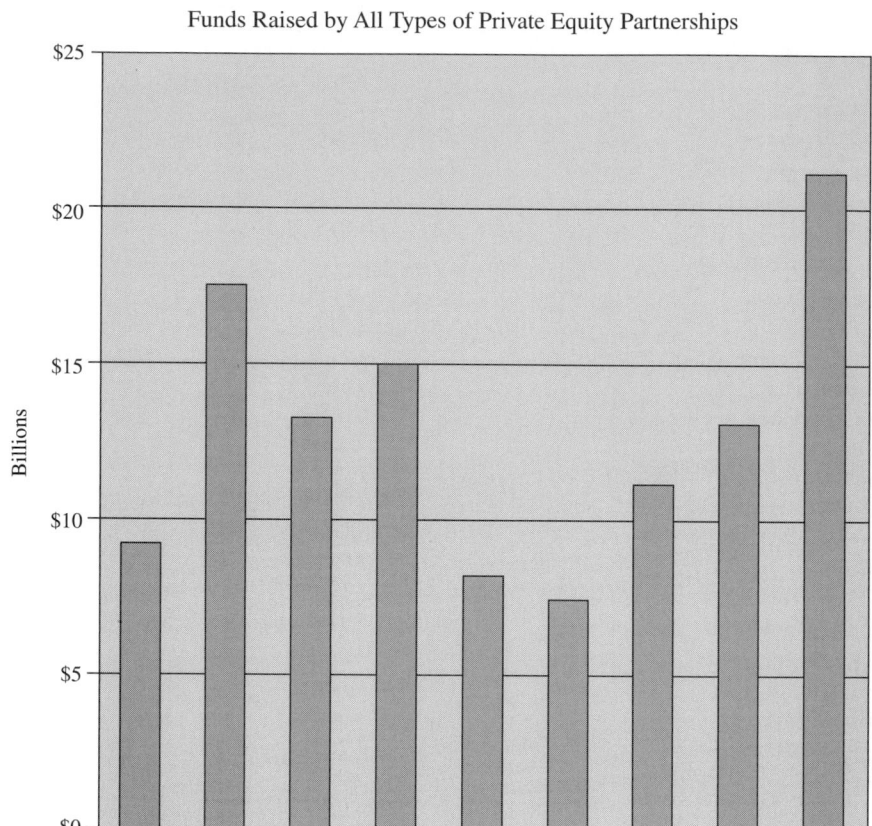

Funds Raised by All Types of Private Equity Partnerships

Source: *The Private Equity Analyst,* January 1996.

EXHIBIT 4   Expense Percentages Compared

Mirth Press versus Prerecorded Music/Entertainment Industry

Typical Audio Publisher		*Mirth Press*	
Royalties	29%	Manufacturing	32%
G&A expense	25	Marketing	21
Manufacturing	20	Operating profit	20
Depreciation	10	G&A expense	10
Marketing	6	Royalties	8
Distribution	5	Fulfillment	6
Operating profit	5	Editorial	2
		Depreciation	1

Source: Quincyshire Management memorandum.

EXHIBIT 5 Channels of Distribution, Mirth versus Typical Prerecorded
Music/Entertainment Publisher

	Music Publisher			Mirth
Record stores	61%	Specialty stores		53%
Discount stores	24%	Discount stores		35%
Record clubs	11%	Mail order		10%
Mail order	4%	Record clubs		2%

Source: Quincyshire Management memorandum.

EXHIBIT 6 Schedule of Debt Capitalization and Payments, and Preferred Dividend Accruals

		Projected						
		Jun-95	*Jun-96*	*Jun-97*	*Jun-98*	*Jun-99*	*Jun-00*	*Jun-01*
Senior debt								
$23,000	Principal BOY*	23,000	22,000	19,500	15,500	11,000	6,000	1,000
10.50%	Amortization	($1,000)	($2,500)	($4,000)	($4,500)	($5,000)	($5,000)	($1,000)
	% amortized	4.35%	10.87%	17.39%	19.57%	21.74%	21.74%	4.35%
	Cumulative % amortized	4.35%	15.22%	32.61%	52.17%	73.91%	95.65%	100.00%
	Principal EOY*	22,000	19,500	15,500	11,000	6,000	1,000	—
	Average balance	22,500	20,750	17,500	13,250	8,500	3,500	500
	Interest rate	10.50%	10.50%	10.50%	10.50%	10.50%	10.50%	10.50%
	Interest	$1,378	$2,179	$1,838	$1,391	$893	$368	$53
	Debt service	$2,378	$4,679	$5,838	$5,891	$5,893	$5,368	$1,053
Subordinated debt								
$12,000	Principal BOY	$12,000	$12,000	$12,000	$12,000	$12,000	$12,000	$12,000
12.50%	Amortization	$0	$0	$0	$0	$0	$0	$0
	% amortized	0.00%	0.00%	0.00%	0.00%	0.00%	0.00%	0.00%
	Cumulative % amortized	0.00%	0.00%	0.00%	0.00%	0.00%	0.00%	0.00%
	Principal EOY	12,000	12,000	12,000	12,000	12,000	12,000	12,000
	Average balance	12,000	12,000	12,000	12,000	12,000	12,000	12,000
	Interest rate	12.50%	12.50%	12.50%	12.50%	12.50%	12.50%	12.50%
	Interest	$875	$1,500	$1,500	$1,500	$1,500	$1,500	$1,500
	Debt service	$875	$1,500	$1,500	$1,500	$1,500	$1,500	$1,500
Preferred								
$9,000	Amount outstanding BOY	9,000	9,420	10,174	10,987	11,866	12,816	13,841
8.00%	Accrued dividend	$420	$754	$814	$879	$949	$1,025	$1,107
	Accreted value	9,420	10,174	10,987	11,866	12,816	13,841	14,948
	Dividends paid	$0.00	$0.00	$0.00	$0.00	$0.00	$0.00	$0.00
	Amount outstanding EOY	9,420	10,174	10,987	11,866	12,816	13,841	14,948

Total Debt Service Calculation

	Senior interest	$1,378	$2,179	$1,838	$1,391	$ 893	$ 368	$ 53
	Senior debt service	$2,378	$4,679	$5,838	$5,891	$5,893	$5,368	$1,053
	Total interest	$2,253	$3,679	$3,338	$2,891	$2,393	$1,868	$1,553
	Total debt service	$3,253	$6,179	$7,338	$7,391	$7,393	$6,868	$2,553

*BOY and EOY stand for *beginning of year* and *end of year,* respectively.

Source: Quincyshire Management memorandum.

EXHIBIT 7   Schedule of Equity Investments

Schedule of Investors Who Acquire Equity with Cash

Rate of preferred	8.0%	(Accrues)
Purchase price of preferred share	$1,000	
Purchase price of common share:	$615.31	
Exercise price of preferred warrant:	$1.00	
Exercise price of common warrant:	$1.00	

	No. of Shares Preferred	Purchase Price Preferred	No. of Preferred Warrants	Exercise of Preferred Warrants
Quincyshire	3,105	$3,105,000		
Co-investor A				
Institution A	2,250	2,250,000	2,250	$2,250,000
Co-investor B	325.8	325,800		
	5,680.8	$5,680,800	2,250	$2,250,000

Schedule of Investors Who Acquire Equity with Shares*

	No. of Shares Preferred	No. of Shares Common	Value Contributed
Management	2,745	2,632	$4,365,001
Venture capital A	300	217	433,538
Venture capital B	274.2	198	396,046
	3,319.2	3,047	$5,194,585

Sellers issued earn-out warrants for 5% of preferred and 5% of common:

On June 30, 1996,
If EBITDA = $14.5 M–$15 M, then ⅓ of warrants earned.
If EBITDA = $15 M–$15.5 M, then ⅔ of warrants earned.
If EBITDA > $15.5 M, then all warrants earned.
Exercise price:

Preferred	$500.00
Common	$307.69

*Shares purchased via tax-free rollover.

Source: Quincyshire Management, Inc.

No. of Shares Common	Purchase Price Common	No. of Common Warrants	Exercise of Common Warrants	Contribution Total If All Warrants Are Exercised
2,243	$1,380,000			$ 4,485,000
1,625	1,000,000	1,625	$1,000,000	2,000,000
				4,500,000
235	144,615			470,415
4,103	$2,524,615	1,625	$1,000,000	$11,455,415

Summary of Number of Common and Preferred Shares

Preferred Shares	Primary	Fully Diluted	Common Shares	Primary	Fully Diluted
Institution A	2,250.0	4,500.0	Co-investor A	1,625.0	3,250.0
Co-investor B	325.8	325.8	Co-investor B	235.0	235.0
Quincyshire	3,105.0	3,105.0	Quincyshire	2,243.0	2,243.0
Management	2,745.0	3,195.0	Management	2,632.0	2,989.5
Venture capital A	300.0	750.0	Venture capital A	217.0	574.5
Venture capital B	274.2	724.2	Venture capital B	198.0	555.5
Total	9,000.0	12,600.0	Total	7,150.0	9,847.5

EXHIBIT 8   Forecast of EBIT and Cash Flow

	Actual	*Projected*	
	5 Months Ending November-94	*12 Months Ending June-95*	*7 Months Ending June-95*
Net sales	$18,147	$40,900	$22,753
Sales growth			
Cost of sales	($5,994)	($14,275)	($8,281)
Depreciation	($98)	($275)	($177)
Gross profit	$12,055	$26,350	$14,295
Gross margin	66.43%	64.43%	62.83%
SG&A expense	($7,229)	($15,600)	($8,371)
(as % of sales)	39.84%	38.14%	36.79%
Other (expense) income			
Total operating expenses	($7,229)	($15,600)	($8,371)
Operating income	$4,826	$10,750	$5,924
Operating margin	26.59%	26.28%	26.04%
Other income	$0	$0	$0
EBIT	$4,826	$10,750	$5,924
EBIT (after tax @ 34%)	$3,185	$7,095	$3,910
Add depreciation	$98	$275	$177
Less capital expenditures			($617)
Less additions to working capital			$60
Free cash flow			$3,530

		Projected		
June-96	*June-97*	*June-98*	*June-99*	*June-00*
$54,450	$70,900	$89,200	$102,580	$117,967
33.13%	30.21%	25.81%	15.00%	15.00%
($21,900)	($29,385)	($38,125)	($44,622)	($51,316)
($480)	($315)	($375)	($450)	($550)
$32,070	$41,200	$50,700	$57,508	$66,101
58.90%	58.11%	56.84%	56.06%	56.03%
($19,170)	($25,500)	($31,300)	($36,929)	($42,468)
35.21%	35.97%	35.09%	36.00%	36.00%
($19,170)	($25,500)	($31,300)	($36,929)	($42,468)
$12,900	$15,700	$19,400	$20,579	$23,633
23.69%	22.14%	21.75%	20.06%	20.03%
$0	$0	$0	$0	$0
$12,900	$15,700	$19,400	$20,579	$23,633
$8,514	$10,362	$12,804	$13,582	$15,598
$480	$315	$375	$450	$550
($1,100)	($300)	($500)	($500)	($500)
($2,375)	($2,654)	($1,929)	($2,277)	($2,615)
$5,519	$7,723	$10,750	$11,255	$13,033

EXHIBIT 9   Forecast of Balance Sheets

			Projected		
	Pro Forma	Jun-95	Jun-96	Jun-97	Jun-98	Jun-99
Assets						
Cash	$ 450	$ 0	$ 0	$ 0	$ 0	$ 0
Cash surplus	0	1,410	1,723	2,723	6,320	10,236
Accounts receivable, net	13,900	9,800	12,800	16,104	18,519	21,297
Inventory	3,200	3,750	5,400	7,006	8,200	9,430
Prepayments	615	500	600	600	600	600
Other	0	0	0	0	0	0
Total current assets	$18,165	$15,460	$20,523	$26,433	$33,639	$41,563
Gross PPE	$ 1,659	$ 2,276	$ 3,376	$ 3,676	$ 4,176	$ 4,676
Accumulated depreciation	0	(177)	(657)	(972)	(1,347)	(1,797)
Net fixed assets	1,659	2,099	2,719	2,704	2,829	2,879
Other assets and intangibles	210	178	124	124	124	124
Closing costs	2,000	1,767	1,367	967	567	167
Goodwill (fixed asset write-down)	37,751	37,200	36,257	35,313	34,369	33,425
Total LT assets	$41,620	$41,244	$40,466	$39,108	$37,889	$36,595
Total assets	$59,785	$56,704	$60,990	$65,541	$71,528	$78,158
Liabilities						
Revolving credit borrowings	$ 0	$ 0	$ 0	$ 0	$ 0	$ 0
Accounts payable	5,470	2,600	4,300	5,579	6,530	7,509
Accruals	3,200	2,600	3,300	4,282	5,011	5,763
Accrued income taxes	1,465	1,330	1,305	1,300	1,300	1,300
Current portion long-term debt	0	0	0	0	0	0
Other current liabilities	800	800	800	800	800	800
Total current liabilities	$10,935	$ 7,330	$ 9,705	$11,961	$13,641	$15,372
Senior debt	$23,000	$22,000	$19,500	$15,500	$11,000	$6,000
Subordinated debt	12,000	12,000	12,000	12,000	12,000	12,000
Original issue discount	(3,000)	(2,708)	(2,208)	(1,708)	(1,208)	(708)
Mortgages	320	320	320	320	320	320
Financing notes	130	130	138	138	138	138
Other LT liabilities	0	0	0	0	0	0
Total LT liabilities	$32,450	$31,742	$29,750	$26,250	$22,250	$17,750
Total liabilities	$43,385	$39,072	$39,455	$38,211	$35,891	$33,122
Common stock	$ 4,400	$ 4,400	$ 4,400	$ 4,400	$ 4,400	$ 4,400
Preferred stock	9,000	9,420	10,174	10,987	11,866	12,816
Warrants	3,000	3,000	3,000	3,000	3,000	3,000
Retained earnings	0	812	3,961	8,942	16,370	24,821
Total equity	$16,400	$17,632	$21,535	$27,330	$35,637	$45,036
Liabilities and equity	$59,785	$56,704	$60,990	$65,541	$71,528	$78,158

Source: Quincyshire Management memorandum.

EXHIBIT 10 Information on Potential Comparable Companies

Company	Description
1. Educational Development Corp.	Distributes, develops, produces, and sells books and educational materials.
2. Thomas Nelson, Inc.	Publishes, distributes, and produces primarily Christian books, music, and programming content.
3. Western Publishing Group, Inc.	Creates, publishes, prints, and markets children's books, videos, and audiotapes; makes paper tableware, gift products, and stationery; provides printing and publishing services to others.
4. Houghton Mifflin Co.	Publishes textbooks and other educational materials (80 percent of net sales) and general works of fiction, nonfiction, children's books, and reference materials.
5. K-Tel International, Inc.	Sells recorded-music products. Products are licensed from other record companies or are from K-Tel's master library.
6. All-American Communications	Produces and distributes television programming and recorded music.
7. Quality Dino Entertainment Ltd.	Acquires, produces, markets, and distributes recorded music in Europe, North America, and Australia. Headquarters is in Canada.
8. Integrity Music, Inc.	Produces, distributes, and publishes Christian music recordings and related products. 13.6 percent of sales are international.

Source of descriptions: Standard & Poor's *Stock Reports,* 1994.

EXHIBIT 10 (concluded)

	Educational Development Corp.	Thomas Nelson, Inc.	Western Publishing Group, Inc.	Houghton Mifflin Co.	K-Tel International, Inc.	All-American Communications, Inc.	Quality Dino Entertainment Ltd.	Integrity Music, Inc.
3-year average								
ROE	22.07%	14.36%	−5.22%	12.76%	91.10%	0.53%	NA	141% (2-yr.)
ROA	8.61%	5.92%	−0.14%	8.31%	7.86%	1.75%	NA	NA
Sales growth	18.77%	46.61%	8.08%	1.19%	16.58%	54%	18% (2-yr.)	21% (2-yr.)
EBIT growth	122.40%	37.63%	−50.41%	34.99%	8.98%	229%	−118% (2-yr.)	28% (2-yr.)
1994								
Sales (millions)	$8.02	$227.67	$613.46	$483.08	$54.27	$114.90	$75.09	$34.80
EBITDA (millions)	$1.03	$27.00	$(5.09)	$104.39	$1.47	$40.44	$1.53	$5.86
ROE	25.40%	15.37%	−30.31%	21.85%	8.65%	2.54%	3.93%	36.17%
Gross margin	53.01%	49.04%	29.50%	52.25%	50.54%	25.20%	1.27%	63.69%
Market cap. (millions)	$14.51	NA	$408.68	$654.76	$17.61	$49.66	NA	$33.08
ST + LT debt (millions)	$0.05	$105.08	$229.81	$99.44	$1.00	$115.34	$1.55	$2.26
Beta	1.00	0.75	0.85	1.11	0.56	1.21	2.06	0.65
Volatility*	57.70%	NA	36.06%	23.90%	102.95%	74.81%	68.17%	45.54%

*Annualized standard deviation of daily returns.

Source: Bloomberg; Standard & Poor's; Prophet Information Services, Inc.

EXHIBIT 11   Current Capital Market Conditions, November 1994

Corporate Bond Yield Average

Average corporate	7.30%
Aaa	7.02
Aa	7.18
A	7.32
Baa	7.68
High-yield corporates	11.00%
3-month	5.21%
6-month	5.75
1-year	6.22
2-year	6.91
3-year	7.15
5-year	7.58
10-year	7.90
30-year	8.06%

Other Interest Rates

Prime rate	7.34%
1-year CD	5.67
1-year LIBOR	6.50%

Index Price-to-Earnings Ratios

S&P 500	17.36
DJIA	18.99
MIDCAP	18.86
AMEX	17.40
NASDAQ	23.84

Source: Bloomberg's *Business News,* Moody's, and *The Wall Street Journal.*

MediMedia International, Ltd.

We had a clear vision that we could do much better on our own than as part of a bureaucracy. The demotivating factors of a big operation paralyze activity. We saw opportunities for revenue growth, cost savings, and asset management—all things that required people to take extra initiative at the local level. Across 25 countries this is quite a challenge: We wanted to be able to act locally under a common global understanding. Accordingly, we recreated the sense of partnership, the feeling that "it is our company" by inviting all the key managers in as equity investors. Raising the equity completely internally was not the hard part; indeed, the equity offering was oversubscribed by $2 million.

Dr. Martin Steinmeyer, chairman and chief executive officer of MediMedia

As Martin Steinmeyer later recounted, the major challenges in the buyout had to do with negotiating the transaction and arranging the debt financing. Buyout negotiations had been ongoing since February 1990. Now, in February 1991, the leveraged buyout (LBO) department of Kleinwort Benson, Ltd. (KB), in London, in collaboration with Berliner Handels und Frankfurter (BHF) Bank in Frankfurt, was circulating a confidential memorandum soliciting senior-debt financing for a management buyout. The total funds required, $70.13 million, would be raised in part with debt denominated in European currency units

This case was prepared by Robert F. Bruner and draws on field interviews and company documents. The cooperation of MediMedia International, Ltd., and Kleinwort Benson is gratefully acknowledged. This case was written as a basis for class discussion rather than to illustrate effective or ineffective handling of an administrative situation. Copyright © 1992 by the University of Virginia Darden School Foundation, Charlottesville, VA. All rights reserved. *No part of this publication may be reproduced, stored in a retrieval system, used in a spreadsheet or transmitted in any form or by any means—electronic, mechanical, photocopying, recording or otherwise—without the permission of the Darden Foundation. For inquiries, please send an e-mail to dardencases @virginia.edu.* Revised 6/98. Version 2.1.

(ECUs), the first time a buyout would be so financed. Was this structure appropriate? Could the debt financing be arranged? Was the purchase price sensible? What were the risks and potential returns to the various players in the deal: the senior creditors, Dun & Bradstreet (the seller and source of a vendor note), KB and BHF (mezzanine investors and financial advisers to management), and management (who were to provide the entire source of equity capital)?

THE COMPANY

The target of the buyout bid, MediMedia International, Ltd., had a corporate office in London and published medical journals and distributed promotional supplies primarily for prescribing doctors. MediMedia's business included 30 largely autonomous operations in 25 countries, producing more than 70 products. Table 1 presents a breakdown of revenues by global region and reveals that over two-thirds of MediMedia's business was in Europe. Most of the firm's products afforded pharmaceutical companies the opportunity to promote their prescription drugs to prescribers.

MediMedia occupied a leading position in almost all of the local markets in which it operated. No other pharmaceutical promotional companies operated on as wide a scale as MediMedia. Almost all of the company's products were exclusive to a specific geographical market; even where products were produced in one country and sold in another, they were tailored to local conditions and regulations.

MediMedia had four principal medical product groups: medical journals, drug directories, office media (such as prescription pads and other medical stationery), and custom media (such as single-sponsored publications, educational videos, and training services). Directories and office media represented the most stable products in terms of both revenue and margins, whereas several journal markets had recently experienced not only reduced growth in display advertising expenditures but also structural changes favoring certain types of journals over others. Competition, modest in office media and directories, was quite intense in journals.

The principal source of revenue from journals was the sale of display advertising to pharmaceutical companies. On the other hand, directories, office media, and custom media generated a substantial portion of their income from line fees, sponsorship and sale of

---

TABLE 1   MediMedia International Revenue by Region, 1990 (in U.S.$ millions)

Europe	$ 77.5
U.S.A.	17.5
Asia/Oceania	11.8
Other	5.0
Interco	(0.9)
Total	$110.9

products, and subscriptions from doctors, pharmacists, and veterinarians. Pharmaceutical companies used directories and office media to advertise and promote brand awareness of essential products in daily use. Journals and custom media tended to benefit from new-product launches.

MediMedia maintained its own editorial staff, many of whom had medical or pharmaceutical training. The staff was responsible for writing or commissioning journal articles and maintaining the databases for the various directories. On some products, the production process extended to photocomposition or even typesetting, but MediMedia was not a printing company. Virtually all physical production and distribution were performed by external suppliers or contractors.

Given the importance of government regulation in the drug industry (especially on promotional activities), MediMedia's national markets tended to behave independently. Few global trends existed, other than the expectation that the world pharmaceutical industry would continue to grow and to spend a fairly constant proportion of sales on marketing and promotional activities. However, MediMedia management identified five trends that warranted careful attention:

- Pharmaceutical advertisers were fine-tuning the targeting of advertising promotion to maximize the value of advertising spending. This strategy would tend to favor customized media, special editions of drug directories, and prescription pads.
- Pharmaceutical companies were concentrating advertising expenditures in the early stage of a product's life cycle. This focus would favor targeted and customized or educational media.
- European Community (EC) members as well as countries in other regions were considering proposals to extend patent lives for ethical drugs.
- Some markets were tending to favor high-frequency journals, often in tabloid format.
- The globalization of product sales was an ongoing trend.

Advertising-based journals were clearly less favored by the above factors, and the journal market in some countries already had been adversely affected. Where expenditures on journals had been reduced, however, the resulting detriment tended to be to the marginal players rather than across the board. MediMedia management had responded to these threats with higher publication frequency and increased circulation, coupled with some switches to tabloid formats.

HISTORICAL PERFORMANCE

The businesses that were to form the MediMedia International group hitherto had been structured, for management purposes, as a distinct subgroup of companies within Dun & Bradstreet. Accordingly, historical financial information existed on a pro forma, stand-alone basis only down to the operating-profit level, below which the business accounts were distorted by such items as goodwill amortization. Operating performance for the four years ended 1990 is summarized in Exhibit 1.

During the fiscal year ended November 30, 1990, the group's total revenue amounted to $110.9 million and its operating profit to $8.9 million. During the period 1987–90, the group's revenue grew at a compound annual rate of 7.8 percent and gross profit at 5.2 percent. Revenue from drug directories, journals, and office media together accounted for

83.4 percent of total revenue and had grown each year from 1987 to 1990. Sales in Europe accounted for 73 percent of the group's revenue, with France being the largest single contributor (37 percent of revenue and 30 percent of operating profit). No single product in any country accounted for a material portion of the group's total revenue or gross profit.

Printing and production, which accounted for half of the group's direct costs, were largely variable in nature and consisted principally of paper and third-party printing. The other half, while not completely variable, could be controlled by skillful management of the editing and production processes. Editorial costs accounted for about 17 percent of direct costs and were largely fixed, although some freelancers were used. Sales costs had a significant variable element, because a proportion of the sales staff's remuneration was in the form of commissions and bonuses. Distribution costs were substantially variable, because the group had no in-house distribution capabilities.

The slight decline of gross-margin percentages over the past three years generally was due to product reformatting and enhancement efforts in the journal segment. These efforts reflected the highly competitive nature of the journal sector, the significant costs incurred by the group to reposition and relaunch several major titles in response to market trends, and internal restructuring. Gross margins on office media were constant throughout the period.

The group's principal tangible assets were two French freehold properties in central Paris with a net book value of U.S.$3.5 million. Management estimated the current market value of the properties to be U.S.$10.8 million; the buildings were expected to be the only tangible security available to lenders. Intangibles consisted of deferred software costs and, following the acquisition, goodwill in the form of intellectual-property rights. Trade debt consisted of high-quality receivables from international pharmaceutical companies. Work-in-progress inventory was generally small. Current liabilities consisted mainly of amounts due suppliers and deferred income liabilities with respect to subscription amounts received in advance of delivery.

ORIGINS OF THE BUYOUT PROPOSAL

MediMedia was to be carved out of the IMS International unit of Dun & Bradstreet (D&B), which had acquired IMS International in May 1988. At the time, IMS consisted of two businesses, market research and communications. D&B, interested in only the market research segment of IMS, would have quickly sold the communications business; but because the acquisition had been completed by means of a tax-free exchange of stock and had been accounted for as a "pooling of interests," D&B was prohibited for two years from making any significant disposals from IMS under U.S. Securities and Exchange Commission regulations. Martin Steinmeyer commented:

> We expressed a desire to buy these businesses at the time when D&B bought IMS. D&B demurred because of the two-year waiting period. Toward the end of the period, D&B hired S. G. Warburg & Company to advise them on the sale of the medical publishing businesses. Five other bidders emerged—three others willing to pay much more than we. Among the potentially interested buyers was Elsevier (in Holland), who were themselves publishers of specialized journals and magazines. D&B called our offer ridiculous and told us to give up hope of

buying the business. But we insisted that our offer remain on the table. Ultimately, the other bidders withdrew. Maybe they did not want to bid against the people on whom they would have to rely to make the acquisition succeed.

To raise the debt financing, management approached BHF (which had known Dr. Steinmeyer for many years) and KB to comanage the deal. Exhibit 2 summarizes the principal hurdles faced by KB and BHF in structuring the financing for the acquisition.

TABLE 2   Sources and Uses of Funds (ECU securities translated at ECU 1 = U.S.$1.388)

	U.S.$ Millions
Sources	
Existing liabilities	1.13
Senior debt	32.00
Mezzanine debt	15.00
Vendor note	11.00
Equity	11.00
Total sources	70.13
Uses	
Purchase price	65.80
Decrease in net working capital	(4.47)
Interest on purchase price	1.30
Cost and expenses	7.50
Total uses	70.13

The sources and uses of funds are given in Table 2. Exhibits 3, 4, and 5 give the detailed terms for the senior debt, mezzanine debt, and vendor note, respectively. Almost half of the debt financing, or $29 million, would be denominated in ECU.[1] Following the freeing up of capital movements within the European Community, many observers believed the ECU would play a larger role in financial services. Indeed, by February 1991, a robust secondary market in ECU-denominated corporate bonds had formed. Until this time, however, no leveraged buyout had been funded in whole or part with the ECU.

The development of the buyout proposal for MediMedia occurred in a declining market for buyouts. The peak in buyouts had occurred in 1989 (see Exhibit 6); since then, the volume and average size of buyouts had dropped dramatically, as had the degree of financial

---

[1]The European currency unit (ECU) was created in 1979 as part of the founding of the European Monetary System. In value the ECU equaled a "basket" of 12 European national currencies, weighted as follows: Belgian franc, 7.6 percent; Luxembourg franc, 0.3 percent; Danish kroner, 2.45 percent; German mark, 30.1 percent; Spanish peseta, 5.3 percent; French franc, 19.0 percent; Irish pound, 1.1 percent; Italian lira, 10.15 percent; Dutch florin, 9.4 percent; U.K. pound, 13 percent; Greek drachma, 0.8 percent; and Portuguese escudo, 0.8 percent. The ECU could be valued in U.S.$ terms by translating each constituent currency into dollars at the prevailing exchange rate, multiplying by the weights, and summing. The easier approach would be to consult the published exchange rates given in financial newspapers. Although not used as legal tender, ECUs were recognized as foreign currency in all EC countries and were used in bond issues, bank deposits, and checks. In 1988, ECU-denominated bond issues accounted for 5.5 percent of all international bond issues and ranked sixth among all global currencies.

leverage, or gearing, in such deals. To a large extent, this trend was coincident with a softening in capital-market conditions over the 1988–91 period. The European leveraged buyout market was dominated by U.K. deals in terms of both transaction volume and value.

MANAGEMENT

MediMedia was expected to employ 537 persons at closing. Of these, 52 managers proposed to contribute the $11 million in equity necessary to consummate the buyout. Several managers were keen to participate in the auction themselves, because they had significant net worth from the profits they realized when they sold their publications to the group. After closing, 11 million shares would be outstanding; on a fully diluted basis, the total would rise to 12.94 million shares.

The board was to consist of four managers, plus two nonexecutive directors. Dr. Steinmeyer (German, age 55) would be the president and chairman of the board of MediMedia. He was president of IMS International's Communications Division and had personally founded some of the business units subsequently acquired by IMS International and then by D&B. Dr. Steinmeyer, who would be based in Germany, also would be responsible for group operations in Germany, Austria, Switzerland, and the United States.

Mr. Gerard Lashermes (French, age 47), to be based in Brussels, would be the chief operating officer and the director responsible for group operations in France, Belgium, Italy, Spain, and Portugal. He had joined the staff of Les Ordonnances Médicales de France (OMF) in 1968 and become its managing director and co-owner in 1972. OMF was acquired by the MediMedia group in 1976.

Mr. David Bromilow (British, age 48) would be manager of MediMedia's operations in the Australasia/Asia region and would be based in Bangkok. Qualified as a chartered accountant, he had joined IMS International in 1972 and served in the finance department until 1987, when he assumed his present operational responsibility in Bangkok.

Mr. Paul Keane (British, age 46) would be the chief financial officer, based in London. He had served as financial controller of the IMS International Communications Division since 1987 and was a chartered accountant. Prior to IMS, he had worked for various firms in auditing, merchant banking, and corporate planning.

DUN & BRADSTREET

D&B, the seller of the businesses that would form MediMedia, was a major purveyor of business information. It sold credit reports on more than 9 million businesses, published the Yellow Pages telephone directories, published bond ratings through its Moody's Investors Services subsidiary, and measured television audiences through its A. C. Nielsen subsidiary. D&B had been thrown on the defensive in late 1990 by charges that its Credit Services unit (which sold credit reports on companies) had engaged in systematic sales churning. In addition, its A. C. Nielsen subsidiary was being squeezed by price competition and rising costs. Value Line expected D&B's earnings to decline by 10 percent but believed the company was in "rock-solid" financial shape.

THE FINANCIAL ADVISERS

Kleinwort Benson, Ltd., was one of the major international merchant banks in the city of London and had acted as senior lender, mezzanine lender, equity investor, and corporate adviser to investors in over 100 buyouts. Its European Mezzanine Fund (formed in a partnership among KB and other major institutional investors) had committed resources available to it in excess of ECU million.[2] The fund aimed to place amounts between £3 million and £20 million with Western European borrowers that had cash flow, strong market share, high barriers to entry, strong management, the absence of cyclicality, and low capital intensity.

BHF was headquartered in Frankfurt and provided a full range of corporate-banking and investment-banking services. At the end of 1990, its total assets were (deutsche marks) DM38.8 billion. BHF's shares were listed for trading on all regional stock exchanges in Germany as well as on exchanges in Basel and Zurich.

MEDIMEDIA'S BUSINESS PLAN AND FINANCIAL FORECAST

The financial forecast for the period 1991–98 (see Exhibits 7, 8, and 9) suggested that the outstanding debt under the senior-term loan facility could be repaid in full within six years. The figures for 1991 were extracted from management's annual budget for D&B and reflected a consolidation of local operating units' own projections. The figures for 1992 also were based on local operating-unit estimates (the projections for 1993 a beyond had no detailed recourse to local operating units). An important feature of the projections

---

[2]A promotional brochure published by Kleinwort Benson, Limited, explained mezzanine debt as follows:

[It] is a form of capital that comes between equity and debt. In essence, it fills the gap between the amount of senior debt which can be advanced against the security of a company's assets and its cash flow, and the limited amount of equity normally available. Mezzanine finance is generally subordinated to senior debt. It will typically have a junior pledge of security or be unsecured. Therefore, mezzanine providers look almost exclusively towards the cash flow generated by the business (although sometimes they also consider asset sales) in order to assess the likelihood of repayment. To compensate for the lack of security and the greater risk of non-payment should the investee company encounter difficulty, mezzanine debt typically receives a higher rate of interest than a traditional bank loan. Specifically, the interest rate is often in the range of standard money market rates (LIBOR in the U.K.) plus 3 to 5%. There is also usually a further payment to the mezzanine provider after 3 or 5 years related to the increase in the value of the company over that period. This final payment can be made by issuing warrants which are convertible into ordinary shares in the company. Typically, the Fund would expect the mezzanine finance that it provides to have a 6 to 9 year nominal maturity but realistic prospects for refinancing or repayment from other sources within 3 to 5 years, if the business is as successful as planned . . . An institutional investor would usually expect an internal rate of return (IRR) of over 40% for providing equity capital in an MBO, whereas a mezzanine lender would aim for an IRR of between 20% and 30%, depending on interest rates and the risks inherent in the transaction. The use of mezzanine finance reduces the amounts required of senior debt and equity. This results in a safer senior loan in terms of better asset coverage and a larger capital base. It is, therefore, easier to raise senior debt and, since mezzanine can improve the return on investment, it becomes easier to raise equity capital.

was that they assumed no asset sales, acquisitions, capital expenditure cutbacks, or cost-reduction programs.

Revenue in 1991 was expected to grow at 21 percent; this forecast was significantly influenced by the weakening of the U.S. dollar against those European currencies that accounted for over two-thirds of the group's revenues. At constant rates, revenue growth would be 11 percent. Growth in 1991 was expected to be achieved through a combination of price increases (to keep pace with inflation), new products, increased publication frequency, and the publication of certain biannual products.

The modest improvement in gross margins projected for 1991 was believed to be conservative, because of the absence of substantial one-time costs for restructuring, relaunches, and redundancies taken to direct costs during 1990. Management forecasted no other significant margin improvements, although it expected improved performance from several products.

Management assumed no improvement in working-capital control in 1991 and only a modest improvement in 1992. Historically, there had been little incentive to speed cash collection, although management believed there was considerable room for improvement.

The projections assumed an effective tax rate rising from 25 percent to 30 percent, even though the marginal corporate tax rate throughout most of the European Community and the United States was about 35 percent. This lower rate reflected efforts to create a tax-efficient corporate structure by channeling earnings away from high-tax jurisdictions and debt toward those low-tax jurisdictions.

Exhibit 10 presents information on publishing and information services companies. Given MediMedia's peculiar market niche, no single company could be a perfect comparison; but the multiples and aggregate information could give a financial analyst a sense of comparative financial performance.

Exhibits 11, 12, and 13 summarize information on capital market conditions in dollars, pounds, and ECUs. KB analysts assumed, for the sake of their financial analyses (see projections in Exhibits 7, 8, and 9), that the ECU London Interbank Offering Rate (LIBOR) would be 10 percent and the dollar LIBOR would be 6.75 percent for the duration of the forecast period.

CONCLUSION

This proposed transaction was structured around the classic model for the leveraged buyout: the financing structure involved the aggressive use of debt, arrayed across several tiers of the capital structure; management also expected to service the debt from the strong cash flow of the business, its growth, and hoped-for operating economies; finally, the layer of mezzanine debt included warrants, giving those investors a play on MediMedia's equity. Observers wondered how large the gains from improved operating performance and debt financing would be in this instance, and how the new wealth thus created would be parlayed among the various participants in the transaction.

More important, were the prospective returns sufficient to attract lenders and investors? Kleinwort Benson had noted that mezzanine investors looked for internal rates of return of between 20 and 30 percent, and that institutional equity investors looked for internal rates of return of over 40 percent. To generalize about target rates of return for bank lenders was difficult, although most banks had difficulty producing returns of more than one percent on their entire loan portfolios. For highly leveraged transactions, some banks looked for internal rates of return of more than 2 percent on loans.[3]

The transaction also offered some unusual twists: (1) a significant part of the debt was denominated in ECUs, (2) the managers of the new company would be the sole providers of the equity capital—no outside equity investors would help consummate the deal, and (3) the structure included a vendor note that appeared to carry an extraordinarily low coupon. Observers wondered what motivated these unusual features and how, if at all, they might contribute to the success of the transaction.

---

[3]The 1 and 2 percent benchmarks assumed that the internal rate of return was calculated as *net* of funding costs and of the bank's taxes on profits from the loan. Observers estimated that 35 percent would be an appropriate marginal tax rate for a bank lender. Also, a bank's cost of funds was typically 200 basis points (two percentage points) *below* LIBOR.

EXHIBIT 1   Historical Operating Performance, 1987–90

	1987	1988 (11 Months Only)	1989	1990
Revenue	$89,387	$87,819	$97,772	$110,897
Costs	(76,874)	(77,666)	(85,201)	(98,466)
Local operating profit	12,513	10,153	2,521	12,431
Central costs	(3,953)	(2,523)	(2,984)	(3,525)
Operating profit	8,560	7,630	9,537	8,906
Local operating profit margin (%)	14.0	11.6	12.8	11.2
Operating profit margin (%)	9.6	8.7	9.8	8.0

Source: Offering memorandum.

EXHIBIT 2   Prominent Issues in Approaching the Buyout

---

1. *Price.* It is crucial to determine the appropriate purchase consideration for the target company. This is done using several different methods, the most common of which are (1) comparable transactions in the industry and (2) discounted cash flow. In a more general sense financiers seek to answer the question, "How much debt can the company prudently service given its industry, competitive position, growth potential, and other factors?"

2. *Capital structure.* Once the purchase price is determined, the question becomes how the buyout should be financed. That is, what proportion of the total capital should be equity, mezzanine (if applicable), or bank loans (senior debt). This decision is made on the basis of a variety of factors but must accommodate both the need for a decent return on the equity and mezzanine layers and the need for an amount of senior debt that banks are likely to provide.

3. *Identity of the financiers.* As the issues of capital structure are resolved, the lead debt arranger for the transaction must have a firm idea on which specific financial institution can be counted upon to finance the deal. The "target list" of senior and mezzanine lenders and equity providers (the latter is not applicable in this case) is drawn up by a combination of people from the LBO unit and the financing desk (bank syndications group) based on knowledge of the deal and the market.

4. *Deal timetable.* The various parties involved in an LBO often are driven by external constraints. These constraints need to be known and a realistic timetable designed, within those limits.

5. *Due diligence.* This term traditionally refers to the process of researching and investigating the target company, its competitive position, and the industry. With regard to the company, the emphasis is on the accounting and a legal examination of all relevant ledgers, books, contracts, and documents. The purpose of this examination is to determine the *historical* status and performance of the company: This forms the basis of a view on the *likely projected* performance of the business. The most time-consuming part of this process is undoubtedly the accountants' investigative report, usually called a "Long Form Report."

6. *Legal and tax structure.* Apart from the capital structure, parties in an LBO must decide how the new company will be organized, because organizational decisions will have a decisive impact on whether the financing can be arranged in a satisfactory form and whether an inappropriately high level of tax can be avoided. The advice of legal and tax counsel is necessary.

Source: Internal memorandum, Kleinwort Benson.

EXHIBIT 3   Proposed Terms, Senior Revolving and Term Debt, Kleinwort Benson, Ltd.

Borrowers: New holding companies in the Netherlands, Hong Kong, Switzerland, Germany, and France, as well as Les Editions du Médecin Généraliste S.A.

Guarantors: MediMedia (the ultimate parent), the regional holding companies, and Les Editions du Médecin Généraliste S.A., jointly and severally.

Purpose: To finance the acquisition, and pay the fees, costs, and expenses relating thereto.

Currency: The senior term loan facility will be divided into two tranches, A and B. Tranche A drawings will be denominated in ECUs, and tranche B drawings will be denominated in U.S. dollars. Advances under the revolving loan facility may be in U.S. dollars and other freely convertible foreign currencies.

Amounts: The senior term loan facility aggregate drawings under tranche A: ECU 10,090,000. Aggregate drawings under tranche B: U.S.$18,000,000. Revolving loan facility amount is U.S.$4,000,000, or the equivalent in other currencies.

Agent: BHF Bank, Frankfurt.

Lead managers: Kleinwort Benson, Ltd., and BHF Bank.

Repayment: Revolving loan facility must be repaid in full no later than the seventh anniversary of the senior facilities agreement.

Senior term loan installments:

	Tranche A	*Tranche B*
November 30, 1991	0	U.S.$2,000,000
November 30, 1992	0	U.S.$4,000,000
November 30, 1993	ECU1,550,000	U.S.$1,850,000
November 30, 1994	ECU1,800,000	U.S.$2,000,000
November 30, 1995	ECU2,150,000	U.S.$2,500,000
November 30, 1996	ECU2,525,000	U.S.$3,000,000
November 30, 1997	The balance	The balance

EXHIBIT 3   *(concluded)*

The facilities will be automatically repayable in full upon the occurrence of (1) a flotation or listing of MediMedia's share capital, (2) any material change in control, or (3) any event that would give rise to mandatory prepayment of the subordinated vendor note.

Prepayment: All prepayments shall be applied against scheduled repayment installments in inverse order of maturity. Drawings prepaid may not be reborrowed.

Voluntary prepayment: Permissible, subject to a prepayment fee equal to 2.5 percent of any amounts repaid in year 1 and 1.5 percent of any amounts prepaid in year 2.

Mandatory prepayment: Excess cash flow shall be applied in prepayment of outstanding principal. Excess cash flow shall mean (1) amounts received by way of rebate of the purchase consideration, (2) amounts received from asset disposals, (3) proceeds of any money-raising activities, and (4) cash generated for financing, less net interest accrued and scheduled principal payments.

Interest rate: For both the revolving loan facility and the senior term loan facility, 2.25 percent over LIBOR for the relevant currency and period.

Commitment fee: For the revolving loan facility, 0.5 percent per year on the unused portion of the facility.

Financial covenants included:

EBIT/Total interest expense	Minimum 2×
EBIT/Senior debt interest expense	Minimum 3×
Cash generated for financing/Total interest expense	Minimum 1.2×

General covenants:

Negative pledge by MediMedia and all companies in the group.
No payment of dividends or other distributions to investors.
No share repurchase or redemption of shares.
No change in the fiscal-year end.
No acquisitions or formations of subsidiaries.
No asset disposals.
No additional borrowings.

Security: A first charge over all the assets, including goodwill and other intangible assets, group revenue, and equity in subsidiaries.

Governing law: English law.

Source: Kleinwort Benson memorandum.

EXHIBIT 4   Proposed Terms, Mezzanine Debt (mezzanine debt: ECU 10,810,000, subordinated secured term loan)

Borrowers: New regional holding companies in the Netherlands, Hong Kong, and Switzerland.

Guarantors: MediMedia International (the ultimate parent company) and the regional holding companies, jointly and severally.

Repayment: One installment, due November 30, 1998. Repayment and prepayment provisions similar to senior debt facilities. Prepayment is not permitted while senior debt is outstanding.

Interest: 3.25 percent per annum over LIBOR.

Warrants: To subscribe for ordinary shares in MediMedia equivalent to 15 percent of its fully diluted ordinary share capital (or 1.94 million shares). Exercisable at any time for a nominal consideration (i.e., $0.01 per share) either in whole or in part at the option of the warrantholders. After the seventh anniversary of the financing, the warrantholders may put shares acquired through exercise of the warrants to MediMedia at a price per share equal to 7 times earnings per fully diluted share. There will be 12.94 million shares on a fully diluted basis.

Financial and general covenants: Similar to the senior debt facility.

Participants: Agent: Kleinwort Benson, Ltd. Lead managers: Kleinwort Benson, Ltd., and BHF. Investors: Kleinwort Benson European Mezzanine Fund L.P. and BHF.

Source: Offering memorandum.

EXHIBIT 5   Proposed Terms, Subordinated Vendor Note (subordinated vendor note: U.S.$11 million junior subordinated debt)

Issuer: Regional holding companies of MediMedia in the Netherlands, Hong Kong, and Switzerland.

Guarantors: MediMedia and its regional holding companies, jointly and severally.

Holder: Dun & Bradstreet Group.

Final maturity: 10 years from the issuance date.

Interest: Years 1 and 2: fixed rate equal to 0.52 percent per year over the average yield of 9- and 10-year U.S. Treasury bonds. During the first two years, interest will be paid by means of non-interest-bearing deferred notes, payable at final maturity of the subordinated vendor note.

Years 3–10: cash interest of 0.52 percent over the interpolated yield on the two U.S. Treasury bonds whose final maturities are, at the subordinated note's interest reset date, nearest to the final maturity of the subordinated vendor notes. Interest that cannot be paid in cash after year 2 will be satisfied by another issue of notes carrying same terms.

Mandatory prepayment: After satisfaction of the senior and mezzanine loans, prepayment must occur upon: (1) sale or disposal of all the assets; (2) sale of share capital; (3) listing of share capital; (4) merger or consolidation of MediMedia.

Security: Ranking junior to senior and mezzanine loans. Otherwise, security interest is similar to those facilities.

Subordination: Repayments of principal on these notes may not be made unless the senior and mezzanine loans have been fully discharged.

Profit participation: The noteholder will be entitled to share in gains arising from disposals made by, or flotation of, the MediMedia group while the notes are outstanding. The noteholder's share will be equal to 25 percent of the gain if sold in the first year, 20 percent if in the second, 15 percent in the third, and 10 percent each year thereafter until maturity of the loan. No amounts may be paid in cash until the senior and mezzanine loans have been fully discharged.

Source: Offering memorandum.

EXHIBIT 6   Volume of Deals, and Total Value Paid in U.K. Leveraged Buyouts, by Year

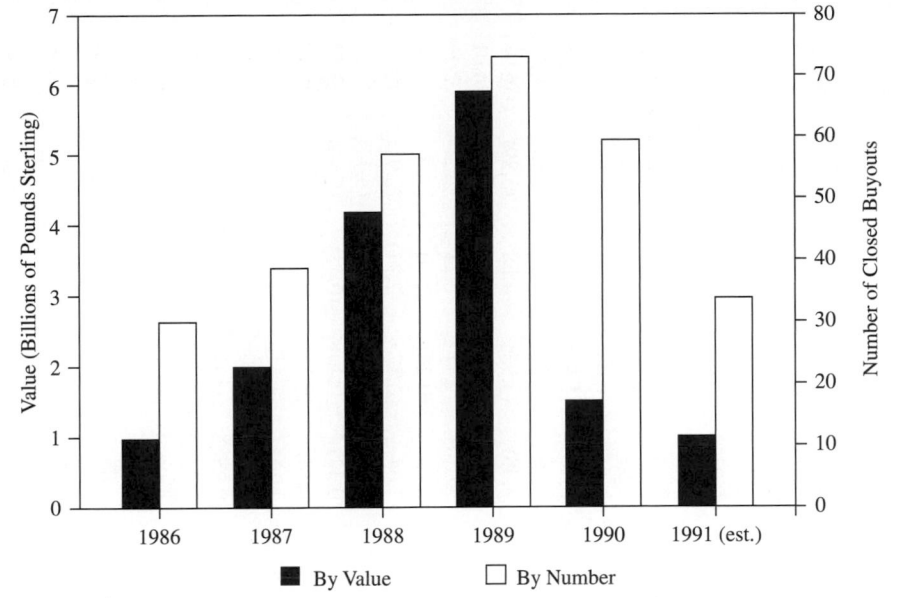

Source: Kleinwort Benson and KMPG Corporate Finance.

EXHIBIT 7 Forecasted Profits and Cash Flows, 1991–98, Fiscal Years Ending November 30 (U.S.$ millions)

	Historical			Projected							
	1988	1989	1990	1991	1992	1993	1994	1995	1996	1997	1998
EBIT	7.60	9.50	8.90	11.42	14.60	16.89	18.25	19.71	21.29	23.00	24.85
Less interest on:											
Existing debt	N.Av.	N.Av.	N.Av.	1.00	0.03	0.03	0.03	0.03	0.03	0.03	0.04
Working cap. revolver	N.Av.	N.Av.	N.Av.	0.17	0.17	0.17	0.17	0.17	0.17	0.17	0.17
Senior term loan	N.Av.	N.Av.	N.Av.	1.69	3.20	2.83	2.83	1.87	1.25	0.52	0.00
Mezzanine loan	N.Av.	N.Av.	N.Av.	0.99	1.99	1.99	1.99	1.99	1.99	1.99	1.99
Junior sub. debt	N.Av.	N.Av.	N.Av.	0.47	0.94	0.94	0.94	0.94	0.94	0.94	0.94
Total interest expense	N.Av.	N.Av.	N.Av.	(4.32)	(6.33)	(5.96)	(5.51)	(5.00)	(4.38)	(3.65)	(3.14)
Interest income	N.Av.	N.Av.	N.Av.	0.32	0	0.13	0.25	0.38	0.55	0.74	1.06
Tax expense	N.Av.	N.Av.	N.Av.	(1.82)	(2.53)	(3.38)	(3.95)	(4.58)	(5.29)	(6.08)	(6.89)
Net income	N.Av.	N.Av.	N.Av.	5.60	5.74	7.68	9.04	10.51	12.17	14.01	15.88
Depreciation	0	1.30	2.00	1.90	1.98	2.01	2.11	2.22	2.22	2.22	2.22
Incrs. deferred taxes	(0.10)	0	0.70	(0.25)	(0.19)	(0.20)	(0.20)	0	0	0	0
Capital expenditures	0	0	0	(2.69)	(1.40)	(2.64)	(2.77)	(2.91)	(2.91)	(2.91)	(2.91)
Decrs. accts. recvbl.	1.80	0.70	(6.40)	(0.02)	(2.24)	(2.73)	(2.95)	(3.19)	(3.44)	(3.72)	(4.02)
Decrs. inventories	0.30	0	(1.20)	0.17	(0.23)	(0.32)	(0.40)	(0.43)	(0.46)	(0.50)	(0.54)
Decrs. prepaid expense	0	(1.20)	(0.80)	0.40	(0.12)	(0.14)	(0.15)	(0.16)	(0.18)	(0.19)	(0.21)
Incrs. accts. payable	0.50	0.80	(10.80)	0.18	0.80	1.15	1.41	1.52	1.64	1.77	1.91
Incrs. taxes payable	0	0	1.30	0.45	0.57	0	0	0	0	0	0
Incrs. accrued liabs.	0	0	11.30	(1.33)	0.70	0.85	0.92	0.99	1.07	1.16	1.25
Noncash interest exp.	0	0	0	0.47	0.94	0.47	0	0	0	0	0
Cash avail. for debt repayment	N.Av.	N.Av.	N.Av.	4.88	6.55	6.13	7.01	8.55	10.11	11.84	13.58
Scheduled debt repayments											
Senior term	N.Av.	N.Av.	N.Av.	2.00	4.00	4.00	4.50	5.50	6.50	5.50	0
Mezzanine	N.Av.	N.Av.	N.Av.	0	0	0	0	0	0	0	15.00
Junior sub.	N.Av.	N.Av.	N.Av.	0	0	0	0	0	0	0	0
Total	N.Av.	N.Av.	N.Av.	2.00	4.00	4.00	4.50	5.50	6.50	5.50	15.00
Revolver repayment	N.Av.	N.Av.	N.Av.	(1.70)	0	0	0	0	0	0	0
Residual cash flow (Addition to cash balance)	10.10	11.10	5.00	4.58	2.55	2.13	2.51	3.05	3.61	6.34	(1.42)

Source: Offering memorandum.

EXHIBIT 8 Historical and Forecasted Net Assets and Capital Structure, 1991–98 (U.S.$ millions)

	Pre-Closing Nov. 1990	Changes	Pro Forma Nov. 1990	1991	1992	1993	1994	1995	1996	1997	1998
Net assets											
Net working capital	$11.04	$(4.47)	$ 6.57	$11.30	$14.37	$17.69	$21.37	$25.69	$30.67	$ 38.49	$ 38.68
Gross PPE	7.71		7.71	10.40	11.80	14.44	17.21	20.12	23.03	25.94	28.85
Accumulated depreciation	0		0	1.90	3.88	5.89	8.00	10.22	12.44	14.66	16.88
Net PP&E	7.71		7.71	8.50	7.92	8.55	9.21	9.90	10.59	11.28	11.97
Other LTA	2.42		2.42	2.42	2.42	2.42	2.42	2.42	2.42	2.42	2.42
Goodwill	0	45.93	45.93	45.93	45.93	45.93	45.93	45.93	45.93	45.93	45.93
Transaction costs	0	7.50	7.50	7.50	7.50	7.50	7.50	7.50	7.50	7.50	7.50
Total net assets	21.17	48.96	70.13	75.65	78.14	82.09	86.43	91.44	97.11	105.62	106.50
Capital structure:											
Existing debt	0.29		0.29	0.29	0.29	0.29	0.29	0.29	0.29	0.29	0.29
Revolver	0	0	0	1.70	1.70	1.70	1.70	1.70	1.70	1.70	1.70
Senior term debt	0	32.00	32.00	30.00	26.00	22.00	17.50	12.00	5.50	0	0
Mezzanine debt	0	15.00	15.00	15.00	15.00	15.00	15.00	15.00	15.00	15.00	0
Junior subordinated debt	0	11.00	11.00	11.47	12.41	12.88	12.88	12.88	12.88	12.88	12.88
Total debt	0.29	58.00	58.29	58.46	55.40	51.87	47.37	41.87	35.37	29.87	14.87
Deferred tax	0.84		0.84	0.59	0.40	0.20	0	0	0	0	0
Equity	32.33	(21.33)	11.00	16.60	22.34	30.02	39.06	49.57	61.74	75.75	91.63
Total capital	33.46	48.96	70.13	75.65	78.14	82.09	86.43	91.44	97.11	105.62	106.50
Ending debt/equity (×)	0.01	36.67	4.92	3.40	2.44	1.72	1.21	0.84	0.57	0.39	0.16
Avg. debt/equity (×)				4.16	2.92	2.08	1.46	1.03	0.71	0.48	0.28
EBIT/ interest (×)				2.6	2.3	2.8	3.3	3.9	4.9	6.3	7.9
EBIT/interest and principal (×)				2.5	1.4	1.7	1.8	1.9	2.0	2.5	1.4

Source: Offering memorandum.

EXHIBIT 9   Forecast of Free Cash Flows and Tax Savings from Debt (U.S.$ in millions)

	1991	*1992*	*1993*	*1994*	*1995*	*1996*	*1997*	*1998*
Free cash flow forecast								
EBIT	$11.42	$14.60	$16.89	$18.25	$19.71	$21.29	$23.00	$24.85
Taxes	−2.86	−4.53	−5.24	−5.48	−5.91	−6.39	−6.90	−7.46
EBIAT	8.57	10.07	11.65	12.78	13.80	14.90	16.10	17.40
Cash flow adjustments:								
+Depreciation	1.90	1.98	2.01	2.11	2.22	2.22	2.22	2.22
+Increase in deferred taxes	−0.25	−0.19	−0.20	−0.20	0	0	0	0
− Capital expenditures	−2.69	−1.40	−2.64	−2.77	−2.91	−2.91	−2.91	−2.91
+Decrease in accounts receivable	−0.02	−2.24	−2.73	−2.95	−3.19	−3.44	−3.72	−4.02
+Decrease in inventories	0.17	−0.23	−0.32	−0.40	−0.43	−0.46	−0.50	−0.54
+Decrease in prepaid expenses	0.40	−0.12	−0.14	−0.15	−0.16	−0.18	−0.19	−0.21
+Increase in accounts payable	0.18	0.80	1.15	1.41	1.52	1.64	1.77	1.91
+Increase in taxes payable	0.45	0.57	0	0	0	0	0	0
+Increase in accrued liabilities	−1.33	0.70	0.85	0.92	0.99	1.07	1.16	1.25
− Investment								
Free cash flow	7.38	9.94	9.63	10.75	11.84	12.84	13.93	15.10
	1991	*1992*	*1993*	*1994*	*1995*	*1996*	*1997*	*1998*
Forecast of annual debt tax shields								
Interest expense	4.32	6.33	5.96	5.51	5.00	4.38	3.65	3.14
− Interest income	(0.32)	0	(0.13)	(0.25)	(0.38)	(0.55)	(0.74)	(1.06)
− Interest not paid in cash	(0.47)	(0.94)	(0.47)	0	0	0	0	0
Net deductible interest expenses	3.53	5.39	5.36	5.26	4.62	3.83	2.91	2.08
Annual tax reduction	0.88	1.67	1.66	1.58	1.39	1.15	0.87	0.62

Source: Casewriter analysis, drawing on offering memorandum.

EXHIBIT 10 Information on Comparable Companies

| | Beta | Volatility or Sigma | Book Value Debt/Equity Ratio | Market Value Debt/Equity Ratio | Last Year Operating Margin | P/E | Expected Dividend | | Expected Five-Year Growth Rate of | |
							Ratio	Yield	Revenues	Divs.
Axel Springer Verlag AG (Germany) Publishes newspapers, specialty magazines, books, and market research data reports.	N.Av.	N.Av.	0.362	N.Av.	2.7%	N.Av.	N.Av.	N.Av.	N.Av.	N.Av.
Commerce Clearing House (U.S.) Publishes loose-leaf reports, periodicals, and books on current developments in tax and business law. Foreign operations account for 13 percent of revenues.	0.70	0.35	0.075	0.028	13.5	21.3		2.3%	7.5%	4.0%
Dun & Bradstreet (U.S.) Sells credit information, Yellow Pages, and financial ratings.	1.10	0.20	0.120	0.030	22.0	16.5		3.1	8.5	8.0
Elsevier N.V. (Netherlands) Publishes newspapers, consumer magazines, trade books, scholarly journals, and scientific and medical journals.	1.05	0.30	0.030	0.005	18.9	19.0		4.0	N.Av.	N.Av.
EMAP PLC (U.K.) Publishes consumer magazines, business magazines, and newspapers, and holds trade shows. Owns 13 radio stations.	1.03	0.32	0.061	0.021	12.3	11.1		N.Av.	N.Av.	N.Av.
Euromoney Publications PLC (U.K.) Publishes international financial news, information and analyses through magazines, surveys, books, directories, databases, conferences, and seminars.	1.05	0.23	0.037	0.010	19.0	15.5		4.5	N.Av.	N.Av.
Havas S.A. (France) Sells local media, directories, international multimedia, tour services, advertising, and consulting.	1.10	N.Av.	0.283	0.059	3.7	23.6		1.0	N.Av.	N.Av.

(continued)

EXHIBIT 10 *(concluded)*

	Beta	*Volatility or Sigma*	*Book Value Debt/Equity Ratio*	*Market Value Debt/Equity Ratio*	*Last Year Operating P/E Margin*	*Expected Dividend Ratio*	*Expected Dividend Yield*	*Expected Five-Year Growth Rate of Revenues*	*Expected Five-Year Growth Rate of Divs.*
Houghton Mifflin Co. (U.S.) Publishes textbooks and materials for colleges and schools.	1.20	0.20	0.250	0.176	17.0	18.3	2.1	9.5	9.5
International Thomson Organization Specialized publisher for professional groups (39% of revenues), publisher of regional newspapers in U.K. (21%), and operator of leisure travel business (40%).	1.20	0.65	0.294	0.200	3.0	27.0	1.9%	7.0%	6.5%
McGraw-Hill Inc. (U.S.) Publishes textbooks, technical, and popular books, business and industrial periodicals (e.g., *Business Week, Aviation Week,* etc.). Owns four TV stations.	1.20	0.20	0.500	0.249	19.5	15.3	2.7	6.5	6.5
Meredith Corp. (U.S.) Publishes *Better Homes and Gardens, Ladies Home Journal, Country Home, Metropolitan Home, Successful Farming,* plus books on cooking and hobbies. Owns seven TV stations. Insiders control 59 percent of shareholder votes.	1.20	0.65	0.294	0.200	3.0	27.0	1.9%	7.0%	6.5%
Pearson PLC (U.K.) Publishes newspapers and magazines (*Economist*) holds interests in entertainment, oil services, and investment banking.	1.00	0.30	0.570	0.250	16.0	14.0	N.Av.	N.Av.	N.Av.
Reed International PLC (U.K.) Principal activities are publishing and business information.	1.33	0.37	0.618	0.400	15.7%	11.3	N.Av.	N.Av.	N.Av.

Source: *Value Line Investment Survey,* March 8, 1991; *Moody's International Corporate Manual,* 1991; Risk Measurement Services, January 1991; and casewriter estimates.

EXHIBIT 11   Current Debt Capital Market Conditions as of Late February, 1991

Yields on U.S. Treasury Debt Securities

1-month	6.37%	4-years	7.41%
3-months	6.18	5-years	7.58
6-months	6.27	7-years	7.82
1-year	6.37	8-years	7.87
2-years	7.00	10-years	7.92
3-years	7.22%	30-years	8.08%

Yields on 10-Year Debt of Other Governments

United Kingdom	9.97%
Japan	8.06
Germany	8.29
France	8.97
Netherlands	8.56%

Yields on High-Grade U.S. Corporate Bonds

1–3 years	8.13%
5–10 years	8.66
15+ years	9.20%

Bank Lending Rates

U.S. prime rate	9.00%
U.K. base lending rate	13.50
LIBOR (U.S.$)	6.75%

Interest Rate Trends

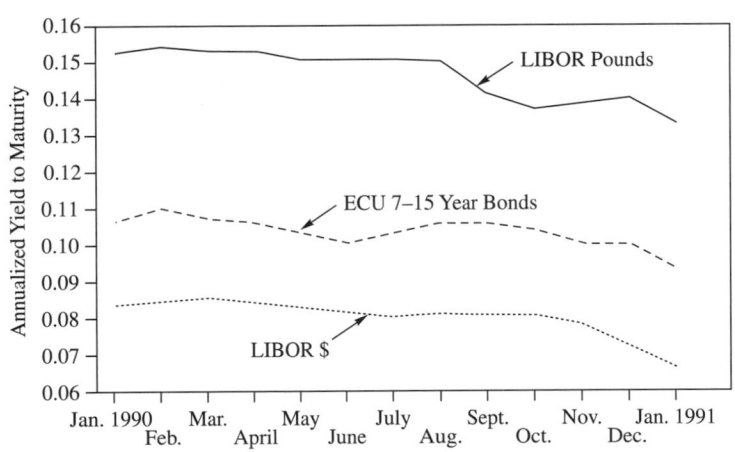

Source: *Financial Times,* February 26, 1991; and OECD *Financial Indicators,* March 1991 and June 1990.

EXHIBIT 12   Current Equity Capital Market Conditions as of Late February 1991

	Dividend Yield	*P/E Ratio*
FTSE 500 (London)	4.91%	11.49×
S&P 500 (New York)	2.19	17.77
Dow Jones Industrials	3.44	N.Av.

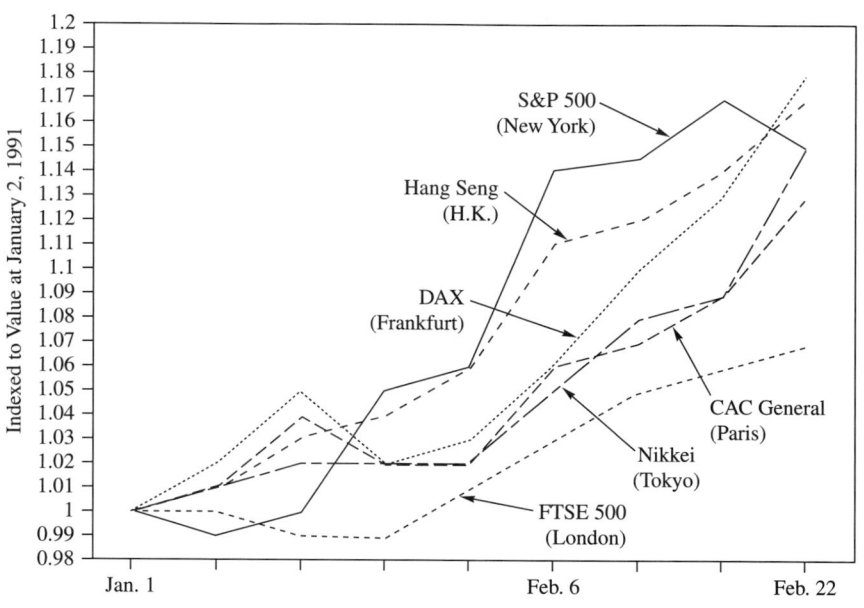

Equity Market Trends
Major World Equity Markets

Source: *Financial Times of London,* daily issues at seven-day intervals, January 1 to February 22, 1991.

EXHIBIT 13   Current Foreign Exchange Market Conditions as of Late February 1991

	Spot	*1-Month Forward*	*3-Month Forward*
U.S.$/ECU	1.3535	+0.31	+0.91
U.S.$/£	1.92225	+0.98	+2.76

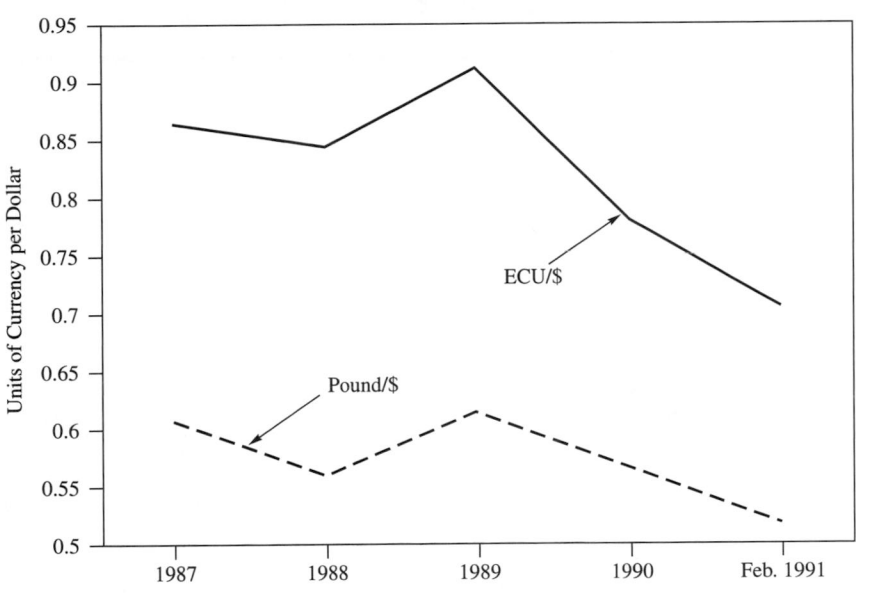

Trends in Foreign Exchange Rates
(Last Four Years)

Source: *Financial Times,* February 26, 1991; OECD *Financial Indicators,* March 1991 and June 1990.

Caledonian Newspapers Ltd. (Abridged)

The buyout was difficult from the word "go." First, our due diligence was a massive hurry-up, because the seller was anxious to close. The deal closed on June 30, 1989, three weeks after a venture capitalist brought it to us. We had to close the financing on a demand basis, because the lawyers couldn't get the documentation done in time. The documentation took longer because, just before the closing, we all discovered that, in its haste, the venture capitalist had negotiated one deal with us and another deal with management. It took three more months of negotiation to align everybody's participation.

Second, a month after closing, a difficulty in understanding the operations of the company led to a warranty claim against the seller involving a dispute on some of the terms of sale. The negotiations with the seller delayed the entire program of layoffs, which were crucial to meeting the financial projections. The old financial forecasts were irrelevant. We had to approach it as if the deal were starting over.

Third, a year after closing [the summer of 1990] advertising revenue in the entire regional newspaper industry went into free fall.

With these words, Ian Stirling recounted the unexpected difficulties with his debtor, Caledonian Newspapers Ltd., which had been taken private in June 1989. Stirling was a vice president at the London branch of Eagle American Bank (EAB), which had originally financed the acquisition with the expectation of realizing high returns on the loan, both

This case was prepared by Robert F. Bruner while he was professor at INSEAD, in Fontainebleau, France. The case draws extensively on interviews with and memoranda of a financial institution that chooses to remain unidentified. Names and numerous facts have been disguised. This case was written as a basis for class discussion rather than to illustrate effective or ineffective handling of an administrative situation. Copyright © 1992 by the University of Virginia Darden School Foundation, Charlottesville, VA. *All rights reserved. No part of this publication may be reproduced, stored in a retrieval system, used in a spreadsheet, or transmitted in any form or by any means—electronic, mechanical, photocopying, recording, or otherwise—without the permission of the Darden Foundation. For inquiries, please send an e-mail to dardencases@virginia.edu.* Revised 1/98. Version 1.5.

from high interest rates and from exercising a warrant for 9 percent of the shares of the company. Over the 18 months following the buyout, the company had fallen far short of its plan and its covenants, and two cash infusions were required to keep it solvent. Now, in December 1990, the company was nearly insolvent again: Just a few days previously, Stirling had recommended that his bank write off one-half the value of the loan, £1.25 million. He wanted to devise a plan of action that would put Caledonian on a sound financial basis permanently (permitting repayment of the loan) or at least terminate the bank's losses on the credit. He was contemplating two alternative courses of action:

- Restructure the company's capital in a way that would make available enough cash for the company to survive through some combination of new equity investment and debt rescheduling or forgiveness. Two separate proposals had recently been put forward.
- Liquidate the company. Because Caledonian was in default of its loan agreement, EAB could force an immediate sale of the business by demanding repayment of its £2.5 million loan in full.

To pursue the best course would require careful analysis of Caledonian, not only from a creditor's point of view, but also from an equityholder's. In addition, any analysis would have to take place fast: Stirling estimated that Caledonian's cash would run out completely in less than two months.

CALEDONIAN NEWSPAPERS

Caledonian published two newspapers, the *Glasgow News Clarion* (a morning daily except Sunday) and the *Sunday Leader* (circulation, 27,000). The *Glasgow News Clarion,* with a record of over 250 years of uninterrupted publication, was the English-speaking world's oldest daily newspaper. Published in Glasgow, its circulation, covering the whole of Scotland, had been declining gradually, since it peaked at 49,000 in 1963 to its current 39,000. In recent years, circulation had been relatively stable, because existing readers were extremely loyal.

The newspaper market in Glasgow was dominated by three local daily publications: Caledonian's *News Clarion* and two competitors, the *Glasgow Telegraph* and *Scots News*. The *Glasgow Telegraph* held 34 percent of circulation in Glasgow and Scotland at large. The *Scots News* held 10 percent, and the *News Clarion's* market share was 8 percent. Various "national" daily newspapers published in Edinburgh and England accounted for 48 percent of circulation. Like the *News Clarion,* the *Scots News* was a morning paper; the *Glasgow Telegraph* was published in the evening.

Caledonian's head office and plant were leased. Production equipment was up-to-date. Text was keyed directly by journalists; production employees set advertisements and made up the pages. Caledonian operated a rotary press that, although nearly 40 years old, provided a reasonable level of printing quality but a level below the quality provided by the web offset press in use at the *Glasgow Telegraph* and other national newspapers from England. Caledonian handled its own distribution through a fleet of 69 vehicles. The retailer margin on sales of Caledonian newspapers was in line with U.K. standards, 30 percent of cover price.

THE MANAGEMENT BUY-IN[1]

Caledonian Newspapers had been owned by the Rutherglen family since 1796 and was currently run by Captain William Rutherglen (age 64), who wanted to retire. With no "heir apparent" in the family, Rutherglen, as noted previously, had sought to sell the company to a large U.K. publisher. The price had been set at £3.8 million. Rutherglen was somewhat dismayed by the sudden failure of this deal and had quickly set out to close a deal with another purchaser. The management buy-in team negotiated a price of £3.25 million; subsequently, other offers had been made to Rutherglen in excess of £4 million, but he had agreed to honor his deal with the original buy-in team so long as the agreed time schedule was met.

John Dumbarton, an executive with years of experience in turning around regional daily newspapers, led the management buy-in team. Dumbarton had decided that reducing payroll costs was the key to improved profit margins at Caledonian. He targeted a workforce reduction of 67 employees which yielded annual savings of £767,000. The total one-time cost of these redundancies, £400,000, would be paid back in 9 to 18 months. New typesetting technology permitted the staff to be reduced without affecting the quality of the newspaper.

In addition to the program of cost reductions, Dumbarton developed an unusual proposal for increasing advertising revenue by issuing a free newspaper in Glasgow, essentially a clone of the *News Clarion* but under a different title, while continuing to sell the *News Clarion* outside Glasgow. This move would permit Caledonian to climb to circulation parity with the *Glasgow Telegraph* and compete more effectively for advertisers. More than 45 percent of advertising revenue in Scotland originated in Glasgow.

The acquisition was to involve £300,000 of equity financing to be provided by the new management team and £1.2 million by Emergent Ventures (EV), a large U.S. venture-capital company with which Eagle American Bank had participated in many profitable deals. The acquisition was an asset purchase with sources and uses of funds as follows:

	Sources (£000s)		Uses (£000s)
Bank debt (EAB)	2,500		
Convertible preferred stock (EV)	900		
Common stock: EV	300	Acquisition price	3,250
Common stock: management	300	Redundancies and working capital	750
Total	4,000	Total	4,000

Emergent Ventures' preferred stock would be convertible into common shares.

---

[1]*Buy-in* was a term used by Ian Stirling synonymously with *buyout*.

On a fully diluted basis, management and EV would control, respectively, 18.2 and 72.8 percent of the common shares.[2] The preferred stock would receive a 9 percent dividend if cash were available. EAB would provide a £2.5 million, six-year, revolving/term loan to finance £1.75 million of the purchase price and £750,000 toward restructuring costs and working-capital requirements for the first 12 months. Exhibit 1 details the terms of the loan agreement.

The sale transaction was structured so that Caledonian could occupy the leasehold premises rent free for two years and would pay £60,000 annually thereafter. Caledonian also had an option to buy the property at any time during the next three years exercisable at £900,000. Stirling learned from an outsider familiar with the property that the land had considerable potential and could be worth £2 million within two years. He did not include this possibility in his projections but believed that the potential property values provided some credit support in the event of liquidation.

Stirling's analysis of the deal, which suggested a "base-case" after-tax return on assets to the bank of 3 to 4.5 percent, reflected the benefits of fees, expected warrant conversion, high and rising interest rates, and the bank's ability to fund the loan through an interest-rate swap at an all-in cost of 11 percent. Over the previous four years, Eagle American Bank had realized after-tax returns on its entire loan portfolio of about 1 percent. On its portfolio of loans in highly leveraged transactions, EAB had realized returns of just over 2 percent. In addition, Stirling expected that participation in the deal would encourage Emergent Ventures to present other business opportunities to the bank.

THE SECOND- AND THIRD-ROUND FINANCINGS

Although the buyout nominally occurred in June 1989, the new management team was not free to begin its restructuring until January 1990, when the warranty settlement with Rutherglen, the seller, was agreed. Accordingly, a new business plan dated January 1990 was formulated.

Stirling continued:

In the first three months of 1990, the company started to underperform. Indeed, the company missed an interest payment, and management asked us to forgive interest. We were unhappy with that and told them that, if they needed more money, to raise it themselves. In March 1990, management and Emergent Ventures agreed to invest another £390,000. EAB also invested £14,000 to avoid dilution of its warrant equity interest. At the time, we were still fairly bullish on the company's prospects. By the spring, Dumbarton, in fact, was back on schedule with the program of redundancies: 40 had been completed. There were 27 more redundancies under the

---

[2]EV's £900,000 investment in convertible preferred stock would be exercisable into 54.6 percent of the fully diluted shares outstanding. EV's £300,000 investment in common equity would, like management's £300,000 investment, claim 18.2 percent of the shares on a fully diluted basis. EAB's warrants would be exercisable into the remaining 9 percent of shares on a fully diluted basis.

original program to go (at a cost of £160,000). Dumbarton had identified opportunities for 12 more redundancies beyond that to be incurred over 12 months, at a total cost of £257,000 and an annual saving of £15,000 per position.

By May 1990, it was apparent that the company would need more money. At that time, the U.K. recession was really beginning to bite. Advertising spending had dropped dramatically. Regional newspapers were hit badly. Even though the company was making the promised cost savings, these savings were chased by the declining revenue. EAB decided not to put any more money up. Emergent Ventures told management that they would put more money up, but if so, it was "good-bye management." Emergent Ventures invited management to put more money in.

John Dumbarton went to Sir Max Ealing,[3] a personal acquaintance of John's and a senior figure in the U.K. publishing industry. Dumbarton persuaded Ealing to invest £350,000 for 20 percent of the common stock of the company. All the former equity investors got diluted; EAB's interest upon exercise of the warrants would be 7.2 percent. The deal was closed in June 1990. Everyone thought this round had done it.

August 1990 was Armageddon for regional newspapers. Advertising revenues fell through the floor. There were several big business failures in the industry. By November 1990, the company was broke again. The money Ealing had invested was gone. There were no buyers for the company. We thought it was going to fail any day. This was a novel experience for Ealing. In November, Emergent Ventures went to Ealing with a new plan for restructuring [presented later] and said, "Put in another £250,000 in support of our plan, or you'll get diluted." He thought Emergent Ventures was taking the wrong approach and told them to go away; shortly thereafter, he put forward his own restructuring proposal [presented later].

At that point, a few things were clear to us. First, management couldn't seem to run the business for cash. Second, the outside equity investors were plainly not in accord, a situation that might grow into a stalemate with disastrous consequences for all. Unless we [EAB] took a more proactive role, the company seemed doomed. So, in late November, we managed to persuade everyone that the firm was to be managed for cash generation rather than for earnings growth, and found Henry Hounslow, who agreed to step in as finance director and run the business solidly for cash. In addition, we began spending our time with potential receivers in Scotland, to prepare for possible liquidation. We hired Hogarth Hobbes Partners [specialists in media investments] to place a value on the company. They opined that, in a breakup asset sale, Caledonian Newspapers was worth between £1 and £1.5 million. They said the company's receivables were worth 70 percent of book value, or about £700,000, and they believed that the titles were worth £800,000. The total value placed our loan underwater by £1 to £1.5 million.

In November 1990, EAB downgraded the loan to Caledonian to a risk rating indicating serious doubt of complete repayment and wrote off £1.25 million of the loan.

---

[3]Sir Max Ealing, age 67, was a leading figure in newspaper publishing in the United Kingdom. Starting from his origins as an orphan foundling in Battersea, he accumulated a personal net worth in excess of £20 million through the purchase and management of local and regional newspaper-publishing companies. Following a near failure of one of his publishing companies in the 1950s, he disavowed the use of debt financing as the basis for building his business interests; his personal and corporate balance sheets were thus virtually debt free. He was known to be an extremely shrewd negotiator and a tough controller of costs. In the present recession, none of his newspaper titles had folded, nor had any of his companies gone bankrupt. Also a leading figure in the Conservative Party, he was a personal friend of prime ministers and numerous cabinet ministers.

THE PUBLISHING INDUSTRY

Advertising revenue growth in the regional newspaper industry in real terms was 15 percent in 1988, 4 percent in 1989, and −2 percent in 1990. Many industry analysts expected that the real growth rate for 1991 would be −2 percent again but that the monthly rate of change would turn positive by the end of the year. One financial commentator had this to say for the industry:

> Publishing shares have had a rough time in 1990, with the more sluggish economy causing advertising cutbacks in many areas . . . It is difficult to see, too, when the upturn will come; magazine publisher EMAP has suggested that it won't be before next spring. A pick-up in the housing market would obviously help, with estate agents' advertising important for regional weeklies . . . publishing should be among the first businesses to benefit when upturn comes. Even if that isn't going to happen soon, the big share price falls seen in 1990—taking the sector index to its lowest level since 1986—are making a lot of allowance for dull results. This, then, is a sector with some good recovery situations.[4]

A financial analyst for Emergent Ventures characterized the market's attitude toward the publishing industry as "short-term paranoia." He also noted that the general recession had slowed the pace of acquisitions in newspaper publishing. Exhibit 2 summarizes four recent newspaper acquisitions, and Exhibit 3 gives valuation information on comparable companies. This analyst also called three large publishing firms that were potential buyers for a company such as Caledonian. The following is a sampling of the comments he received:

Firm A

Few deals are currently being done, and we perceive that prices have dropped dramatically in recent months. Many local papers are struggling; even we have had to close down some of our own titles. Caledonian's strategy of the free newspaper may be flawed; we've had, at best, mixed success with it. A more sensible strategy may be to tighten costs down as much as possible, play hard on the strengths of the core ("paid for") business, and market aggressively the overall readership size of the two daily titles. All things being equal, we wouldn't be looking to buy or sell a business at this point in time. You can't expect to receive more than seven to eight times earnings for a business like Caledonian.

Firm B

The advertising market is suffering and was particularly bad in July and August. Values have declined since then; there are several properties on the market at this time. A number of previously aggressive groups are not buying, and some publicly quoted companies like Adscene and Goodhead are in a mess. The current environment for a seller is not attractive.

Firm C

I should say that I am not looking to buy anything and haven't for a year or so. I would not buy anything on a multiple of earnings now, particularly historic ones. Frankly, I would look at asset values at this moment. The industry is struggling. A strategic buy (that is, if it was a newspaper located in the middle of our area) would be different. Then I would look at potential profits and beyond the present economic cycle. Market leaders are very much stronger than those in second or third position. I wouldn't pay much for goodwill unless it was a strategic buy.

---

[4]"Coping with Tougher Times," *Investors Chronicle,* November 9, 1990, p. 23.

LIQUIDATION ALTERNATIVES

Stirling weighed the possibility of simply liquidating the business in order to recover as much of the bank's principal as possible. Two liquidation scenarios were possible. First, the assets of Caledonian could be sold piecemeal, fetching between £1 and £1.5 million. Second, Caledonian might be sold as a single entity, on a going-concern basis. Hogarth Hobbes Partners opined that, on this basis, the firm would fetch about £2 million (see Exhibit 4) or more, if the economy turned up. Unfortunately, virtually no buyers for newspaper companies could be found in the current market climate. To obtain a going-concern price for the company would require waiting.

EMERGENT VENTURES' RESTRUCTURING PROPOSAL

In mid-November, Emergent Ventures had proposed to EAB a choice between two possible loan-restructuring alternatives. The first was that EAB sell its entire £2.5 million debt (including any accrued interest) for a total fixed consideration of £0.75 million, to be received within the next three-month period.

The second alternative called for Eagle American to remain as a debt lender, and Emergent Ventures and Ealing would invest £325,000 in total in non-interest-bearing junior secured convertible debt. Emergent Ventures believed this amount would restore the company to financial health and see it through even an extended downturn in its business. EAB's existing debt would be restructured as follows:

- £1.25 million would remain as senior secured debt. Interest would be paid at the London Interbank Offering Rate (LIBOR) plus 2 percentage points, with the first payment due on June 30, 1991, and quarterly payments thereafter. The rate of principal repayment on the senior debt would need to be negotiated.
- £1.25 million would become junior secured convertible debt, ranking equally with the new Emergent Ventures money. Interest would accrue at LIBOR plus 3 percent until December 31, 1992 (and be payable quarterly in arrears thereafter). Repayment of all junior secured convertible debt, plus accrued interest, would be scheduled in 10 equal annual installments commencing December 31, 1992. On the sale of the company, senior secured debt would become immediately repayable, and junior secured debt would automatically convert into ordinary shares.

EAB's junior debt would convert at the rate of £1 per share into a 25 percent interest on a fully diluted basis. Meanwhile, Ealing and Emergent Ventures would be able to exchange their junior debt for shares at the rate of £0.25 per share. Exhibit 5 describes the capitalization of the company, pro forma the Emergent Ventures proposal.

MAX EALING'S RESTRUCTURING PROPOSAL

At first tentatively and then over the course of several long conversations with Stirling, Ealing sketched out a competing restructuring plan for Caledonian that would call for the current equity investors to subscribe for new common shares in the following proportions:

	Cash Investment	Percentage of Shares	
		Primary Basis	*Fully Diluted*
Eagle American Bank	0	0	32.0%
Max Ealing	£360,000	50.7%	34.5
Emergent Ventures	250,000	35.2	23.9
Management	100,000	14.1	9.6
Total new equity	£710,000	100.0%	100.0%

EAB's warrant would increase to 32 percent of the shares (fully diluted), to be exercised at a price equal to the subscription price of the other equity investors, which implied a total exercise price of £334,000. In essence, the former equity claims on the company would cease to exist; any former equity investor who did not subscribe would be wiped out.

Ealing initially proposed that EAB forgive half of its loan to the company. Then later he suggested instead that the loan outstanding remain at £2.5 million, but if the company successfully met all of its interest payments and made the first principal payment in June 1992, EAB would formally forgive half the debt. At the date of forgiveness, the option on 32 percent of the common stock would become active. Until June 1992, Caledonian would have to make interest payments on only half of the loan (£1.25 million) at an interest rate of 12 percent. (EAB's cost of funding was 11 percent.) In effect, Ealing's proposal would decompose the Caledonian credit into a "bad" loan and a "good" loan. The "good" loan would be currently serviced; the "bad" loan would not be serviced, but if things went well would be converted into common stock.

Ealing was concerned that, if EAB exercised its large option on Caledonian's stock, he could lose majority control of the company. Therefore, he requested the right of first refusal on the sale of any shares by EAB. If Ealing refused to buy EAB's shares, the bank would have the right to find another buyer, and all other shareholders would be bound to sell their shares at the buyer's offering price or else pay that price to acquire Caledonian themselves.

STIRLING'S FINANCIAL FORECASTS IN DECEMBER 1990

Exhibit 6 presents Stirling's forecast of Caledonian's financial performance for the next 2.5 years, until Caledonian's fiscal year end in June 1993. He believed that the fortunes of the company would either have turned sharply better by then or it would be in liquidation. If things turned out well, Emergent Ventures would probably seek to cash out quickly by a partial or complete sale of the company. In either case a longer forecast horizon was not warranted.

Based on extensive conversations with Dumbarton and Ealing, Stirling came to believe that earnings before interest and taxes (EBIT) would turn positive and thereafter hover in the low £400,000 range. This outcome reflected modest increases in advertising and circulation revenues, roughly in line with inflation. Also, the new controller was proving to be quite capable in managing the cash costs of the business. More important, Stirling believed the now completed program of redundancies would finally show a significant effect in reducing production and editorial costs. In short, his EBIT forecast assumed no radical transformation of the business.

Exhibit 6 also shows the earnings and cash flow before debt amortization under three different financing scenarios: (1) the original loan remained outstanding (i.e., £2.5 million at rates of 17, 18, and 19 percent); (2) Ealing's "good loan/bad loan" proposal went into effect (i.e., £1.25 million at 12 percent); or (3) Emergent Ventures' senior/convertible sub-ordinated loan proposal was accepted. Stirling noted that, under the current loan structure, both EBIT and cash-flow coverage of interest payments were less than 1.0 for the three-year forecast period, which confirmed his view that the current loan structure was untenable. The two restructuring proposals produced EBIT coverage ratios of greater than 1.0.

Unknown to the other providers of capital to Caledonian Newspapers, Eagle American Bank had funded its loan to Caledonian with an interest-rate swap that effectively locked in a cost of funding at 11 percent. Half of this swap had been unwound when EAB wrote off half the loan in November 1990. However, Stirling viewed the balance of his loan exposure as being funded at 11 percent for the duration of the forecast period in Exhibit 6.

CONCLUSION

Stirling's response to the restructuring proposals was guarded. First, he wondered whether an asset liquidation might not be the highest valued strategy. Every other course of action ran large risks. At the rate at which Caledonian was expected to consume cash, simply waiting for things to get better might be simply waiting for the asset values to deteriorate. (Exhibit 7 presents a summary of current capital market conditions. The marginal corporate tax rate was 35 percent.) Emergent Ventures' proposal would partially impair EAB's seniority claim on Caledonian's assets. Ealing's proposal injected the unpalatable concept of loan forgiveness in EAB's dealings with Caledonian.

At present, Eagle American Bank was under pressure from U.S. government bank regulators to create reserves against nonperforming loans. The remainder of the loan to Caledonian, £1.25 million, was currently on nonaccrual status; if it stayed there, the bank would be expected to set aside up to 80 percent of that amount as a provision against loan loss in its income statement. Stirling noted,

> The bank wants to restructure troubled loans like this, to be proactive rather than just passively let the mud hit the fan,[5] but our attitude is that any restructuring has to have a strong commercial rationale and not just be driven by accounting rules and banking regulations.

---

[5]In late 1988, Sokol and Metla Garabedian, two well-known raiders, had bought 12 percent of Eagle American Bank's outstanding common shares at prices ranging between $14 and $19 per share. Now, in December 1990, EAB's shares were trading at around $5.00 per share, a reflection of depressed earnings in the U.S. banking industry stemming from the surprisingly high wave of loan losses being announced. EAB had had its share of these losses. The Garabedians were known to be extremely unhappy with the paper losses on their investment position.

Stirling believed that quick action was important because of Caledonian's weak cash position. Moreover, he was worried that the longer the restructuring negotiations continued, the more fractious and acrimonious they would become. Even though EAB had substantial power through its priority claim on the assets, using that claim would be a clumsy weapon. The highest valued solution from EAB's standpoint might require continued strong cooperation among the bank and equity investors.

EXHIBIT 1   Original Loan Terms

Facility amount:	£2.5 million revolver/term loan.
Purpose:	To finance acquisition of Caledonian and £750,000 of redundancy costs/working capital.
Maturity:	June 30, 1995 (Prepayment allowed without penalty.)
Amortization:	Revolving during year 1, then amortizing in line with the following repayment schedule (reduction to be scheduled half-yearly): year 2, £200,000; year 3, £400,000; year 4, £500,000; year 5, £500,000; year 6, £900,000; total, £2.5 million.
Pricing:	Year 1 fixed @ 16%
	Year 2 fixed @ 17%
	Year 3 fixed @ 18%
	Year 4 fixed @ 19%
	Year 5 fixed @ 20%
	Interest is payable quarterly in arrears. (Currently, EAB's cost of funding was 12.5%. However, the swap reduced the cost of funding *this loan* to only 11%.)
Facility fee:	1% payable at closing.
Security:	Fixed and floating charge over all assets of Caledonian.
Covenants:	A full range of covenants will be applied including, *inter alia:*

1. Quantitative tests:

		Minimum EBIT	Minimum EBIT/Interest
Months	1–6	£ 35,000	No minimum
Months	7–8	£ 15,000	No minimum
Months	9–12	£100,000	1.00
Months	13–18	No minimum	2.00
Months	19–24	No minimum	2.50
Year	3+	No minimum	3.00

2. Limitations on indebtedness, liens, guarantees, disposal of assets, investments, distributions, change of management.
3. Key-man insurance of £1 million on Dumbarton.
4. Assignment of property insurance.

Equity participation:	EAB to have a five-year option (exercisable at par value per share, aggregating to £22,000) to acquire 9% of Caledonian common stock.
Fully diluted ownership:	

Management	18.2%
Emergent Ventures	72.8%
EAB (via warrants)	9.0%
	100.0%

Policy issues:	This credit will initially qualify as a highly leveraged transaction, with debt/equity of 1.6:1.

Source: EAB memorandum, June 18, 1989.

EXHIBIT 2   Recent Newspaper Acquisitions (excerpted from an Emergent
Ventures memorandum)

Trinity/Pennysaver

Date: February 1990

Target country: USA

Trinity acquired Pennysaver Publications, a Pennsylvania group that published a weekly
advertisement-only publication, for £8.02 million. Profit before tax for the year to December 31,
1988, was £250,000, and the group had net assets at completion of £760,000. The valuation
represents a price of 32 times profit before tax.

Trinity/Richmond

Date: May 1990

Target country: Canada

Trinity acquired the Richmond Review, a triweekly paper with a Friday paid-for circulation of
17,000 and a free midweek and weekend edition (home delivered) of 40,000 circulation.
Turnover was (Canadian) C$4 million and the purchase price was C$6.9 million. Whether the
business was profitable was not disclosed. The price represents a multiple of 1.7 times revenue.

Guiton/Guernsey Press

Date: November 1989

Target country: Channel Islands

Guiton launched a hostile bid for its Channel Islands competitor, which failed. The bid value was
£17 million. Guernsey Press made pretax profits of £0.73 million on undisclosed turnover. This
represents a multiple of 23 times profit before tax.

Southnews/Fulham Times

Date: September 1989

Target country: England

Southnews acquired Fulham Times, which published three free weekly papers, for an up-front
consideration of £240,000 plus a maximum earnout (to March 31, 1991) of £200,000. The
Fulham Times group made a loss of about £100,000 on sales of about £500,000 in the year to
March 31, 1989. Thus the up-front consideration represents 50% of sales and the maximum
price might be 90% of sales.

EXHIBIT 3   Information on Comparable Companies

Company	Market Value of Equity	Annual Revenues
Adscene Group PLC	£9 million	£21 million
Published a portfolio of weekly newspapers (70% of revenues) and provided contract printing services (30%). Historical multiple less than half the sector average because of a 50% decline in profits and a reported 33% decline in turnover for the first 6 months of the year.		
Bristol Evening Post PLC	£41.8 million	£58 million
Published a number of regional newspapers and also operated a chain of regional newsagents and convenience stores. Publishing accounted for 60% of turnover. The group had been the subject of an offer from David Sullivan, proprietor of the *Sunday Sport.* The Monopolies and Mergers Commission recently blocked the offer; even so, the P/E was at a 10% premium to the market.		
Home Counties Newspapers PLC	£15.8 million	£16.9 million
Published a range of weekly newspapers in England. Since January, the company's share price had declined from 250p (pence) to its present level of 158p (a 2-year low). Recent statements from the company said that "it is well placed to withstand the effects of the current difficult economic climate."		
Independent Newspapers PLC	£143.0 million	£138 million
Printed and published a range of national and provincial newspapers in Ireland and the United Kingdom and owned a number of outdoor-advertising businesses around the world. Publishing represented 75% of turnover. The group had recently made a number of small acquisitions.		
Johnston Press PLC	£40.6 million	£41.7 million
Printed and published a portfolio of weekly newspapers, both paid-for and free. Chairman said he remained "cautiously optimistic" for the current year. Publishing was 75% of turnover.		
Portsmouth & Sunderland Newspapers PLC	£32.4 million	£71.7 million
Published daily and weekly paid-for and free titles in England. Also had a retailing division (newsagents) and small film and video interests. Chairman in his latest statement said that the outlook for the publishing business was uncertain and remarked on the slowdown in advertising revenue as "significant" and that vigorous action was being taken to control costs. The company was trading at its 12-month low. Publishing was 70% of turnover.		
Southnews PLC	£13.2 million	£19 million
Published a portfolio of paid-for and free local newspapers in England. Made a number of small acquisitions over the last 18 months. In his most recent statement, the chairman said that, despite the severity of the decline in advertising revenues suffered in England, the board remained confident of the company's future potential.		
Trinity International Holdings PLC	£100.8 million	£119 million
Published newspapers in the United Kingdom, United States, and Canada and was also engaged in the manufacture of papermaking and packaging products in the United Kingdom. Had recently been consolidating its overseas portfolio through acquisition and stated that it was considering a number of further acquisitions at home and abroad. Publishing was 63% of turnover.		

*Sigma is volatility of returns to shareholders and is a measure of risk commonly used in the valuation of options.

Source: Internal EAB memorandum, Risk Measurement Services, December 1990, and casewriter's estimates.

Historical Earnings (P/E)	Expected Earnings (P/E)	Equity Value to Revenues	Beta	Market-Value Debt-to-Equity Ratio	Sigma*
4.8×	9.5×	0.43×	1.06	.242	.42
12.3×	12.0×	0.72×	.67	.052	.26
5.7×	NAv	0.94×	.79	.133	.41
14.2×	NAv	1.04×	.89	.178	.28
10.8×	NAv	.097×	.73	.255	.21
8.7×	8.9×	0.45×	.58	.088	.26
10.7×	NAv	0.70×	.99	.089	.37
8.8×	NAv	0.85×	.96	.333	.36

EXHIBIT 4   Report of Hogarth Hobbes Partners

November 30, 1990

Dear Ian:

Re: Caledonian Newspapers

You asked for an immediate opinion on the strategy to pursue with your debtor; in addition you asked us to consider the price that Caledonian Newspapers might achieve in the event of an orderly sale of the company as a "going concern" during the course of the next six months. Our responses are as follows:

(1) It is crucial in this assessment exercise to maintain a clear analysis of trends. On acquisition, Caledonian appeared to be breaking even, including its frees, with a turnover of £6.9 million. In fact, it was losing about £250,000 on a turnover of £6.5 million in 1989. Profit was therefore disappearing because the Sunday paper was being hit extremely hard by recently increased competition. It is not difficult to see these facts, covered up during the sale, as good reasons for the long-standing owners seeking to sell. Alas, the launch of the free has in itself generated a loss of some £400,000 in its first year of operation. Consequently the Group in the first year post acquisition made a loss of around £500,000, against an anticipated profit of towards £900,000. In summary, therefore, we apportion this £1.4 million shortfall approximately evenly between the deterioration of the Sunday paper and the slower take-off in the new free paper.

(2) We would advise you to proceed most cautiously. There is a distinct downturn in newspaper advertising revenue creeping northwest from the Southeast. It has not yet hit Liverpool or Yorkshire or Scotland; we expect it is yet to reach Glasgow.

(3) The market for newspaper companies is very quiet at present. Almost all deals announced over the last six months are consolidation deals—outposts being relinquished to stronger local players. The Monopolies and Mergers Commission is not keen on giving you that option! The number of capable and willing purchasers and the price they might offer are reduced by: (*a*) low market ratings; (*b*) diminished profits; (*c*) lack of confidence; (*d*) high interest rates; (*e*) a feeling "cash is king"; (*f*) that the bottom has not yet been hit; (*g*) that it is a buyer's market . . .

(5) The investors' buy-in plans were, frankly, astonishingly bold. The price was not unreasonable, but it was later in the cycle . . . The plan was to destroy hard-won circulation revenue and high advertising yields by the launch of a daily free in the hope of a much bigger share of the market . . . It is a fundamental of publishing that paid-for circulation can achieve higher advertising yields than free; mixing them, as here, dilutes the strength . . .

(6) The first year, financially, has gone exceptionally badly . . .

(7) Assume you carry on. Even if budget is met, a further £1 million cash is needed for 1990–91 before, in the following year, interest payments can be resumed. In 24 months, the paper is projecting £600k and £7.2m. Its likely value would be 0.5 to £5m assuming lower interest rates and a moderate upturn in buyer's interest. The upside is not greater—and that assumes the budget will be met. We instinctively feel it is likely the budget would be missed by up to £500k.

(8) At some point, some of the other interested parties . . . could well lose confidence in their investment. While you are covered first, if they throw in the towel, you lose also . . .

EXHIBIT 4   *(concluded)*

(9) How saleable is Caledonian anyway? . . . It is a fundamentally unattractive place . . . The paper is far from dominant in its market . . . in a spatially isolated market [with] relatively little natural expansion possible . . . Why did no other established group come forward in 1989 when the market, while cooling, was more active than today?

(10) In summary, a sale in two to three years at £10 or even £5m—the odds, for all these reasons, seem very much against it. We therefore see very little light at the end of that tunnel.

(11) The standard guideline for the valuation of publishing businesses at the present time is 5 times actual operating profits for the period shortly about to end (i.e., calendar year 1990). By and large, publishers are assuming that 1991 will be around the same as 1990, and that 1990 in most cases will be about the same as 1989. Add backs and other development costs which used to be treated benevolently by purchasers in assessing value are now treated with much greater scepticism. Higher promotional expenditure, stated as exceptional, is being considered unexceptional. On this very simple basis, there is not significant rushing in to buy papers at breakeven or loss.

Based on our analysis, we feel it may be possible to construct an orderly sale for the company built around the profitability of the *News Clarion* at up to £2 million . . . In our opinion the value attaching to the *News Clarion* masthead is a relatively enduring value . . . As far as the rest of the group is concerned, we feel the case for the continued publication of the Sunday and the daily free remains unproven. The daily free may simply not be a viable publishing product . . . The battle ahead for the Sunday paper appears to be exceptionally tough . . . If the recession bites hard, and lingers, the sale value will fall sharply . . . However, it will rise if turnover moves towards £5 million and margins improve towards and beyond 10%. A value then of around £5 million could not be ruled out. If we owned the papers, we would not accept an offer of less than £2 million for the newsletter goodwill.

(12) Our advice has to be to protect your downside vigorously and immediately . . .

In conclusion, we strongly recommend against going further in . . . You need to bang the drum for immediate profit, even if it reverses management strategy, because that is the best chance of recovering your £2.5m.

We await your further instructions.

Yours faithfully,

(signed)

Michael Blimpson, Partner

EXHIBIT 5 Pro Forma Capitalization: Restructuring Proposal by Emergent Ventures

	Par Value Currently[a] (£ 000s)	Changes (£ 000s)	Par Value Pro Forma the Restructuring (£ 000s)	Par Value after Exercise of Debt And Options (£ 000s)	Number of Shares (000s)
Senior debt	2,500	(1,250)	1,250	1,250	
Convertible debt (mgt.)	100	(100)	0	0	
Junior convertible debt					
Eagle American	0	1,250	1,250	0	
Emergent Ventures (EV)		200	200	0	
Ealing		125	125	0	
Management		100	100	0	
Cv. pfd. stock (EV and Mgt.)	1,200	0	1,200	0	
Common stock					
Eagle American	14	0	14	1,264	1,264 (25.1%)
Emergent Ventures	305	0	305	1,665[b]	2,265 (44.9%)
Ealing	188[c]	0	188	313[d]	688 (13.6%)
Management	385	0	385	525	825 (16.4%)
Total capital	£4,692	£325	£5,017	£5,017	5,042 (100.0%)

[a]The capitalization and ownership of shares outstanding at the end of November 1990 could be broken down as follows:

	Number of Ordinary Shares	Number of Convertible Preference Shares	Par Value Originally Invested
Emergent Ventures	305,000	1,160,250	£1,465,250
Management	385,000	39,750	424,750
Eagle American	14,000	0	14,000
Ealing	188,375	0	350,000
Totals	892,375	1,200,000	£2,254,000

In addition to its share ownership, the management group had contributed £100,000 of loans in May 1990; these loans were still outstanding. Finally, completing the long-term capitalization of the company were Eagle American's loans totaling £2.5 million. Note that EV's investment in convertible preference shares rose from 900,000 shares to 1,160,250 in the third-round financing.

[b]The conversion price on Emergent Ventures' junior debt investment was £0.25 per share. Therefore, £200,000 par value of convertible debt amounted to 800,000 shares. In combination with the 305,000 initial shares, plus convertible preference stock with an exercise price of £1.00 per share, the total resulting shares for Emergent were 2,265,250.

[c]Max Ealing bought shares in the summer of 1990 at a premium. Of the total invested amount of £350,000, par value was £188,375 and premium or surplus was £161,625. The losses of the company through November 1990 had completely depleted the amount of the paid-in surplus.

[d]Ealing's junior debt investment converted to shares at the rate of £0.25 per share. The £125,000 converted to 500,000 shares. When combined with the initial 188,000 shares, Ealing's new total was 688,000.

EXHIBIT 6   Financial Forecast (fiscal years ending June 30)

	Estimate 1990–91	*Forecast 1991–92*	*Forecast 1992–93*
Revenues			
Advertising	£3,600,490	£3,823,322	£4,041,920
Circulation	2,294,462	2,428,102	2,523,284
Sundry	121,212	119,615	126,000
Total	6,016,164	6,371,039	6,691,204
Costs			
Production	2,007,719	1,730,230	1,804,536
Editorial	1,413,762	1,250,174	1,287,000
Advertising	691,822	721,558	760,185
Vehicles	80,877	136,527	145,600
Plant	355,491	338,603	496,961
Distribution	647,406	648,320	667,731
Publicity	54,453	39,987	45,500
Administration	1,014,388	871,441	857,624
Depreciation	147,916	200,889	200,888
Total	6,413,834	5,937,729	6,266,025
EBIT (earnings before interest and taxes)	£ (397,670)	£ 433,310	£ 425,179

Earnings and Cash Flow: Assuming the Original Loan Remained Outstanding

Interest expense	£ (425,000)	£ (450,000)	£ (475,000)
Other expenses			
Goodwill amortization	(122,668)	(116,079)	(116,077)
Redundancy	(304,955)	0	0
Pension-fund reversion	0	100,000	0
Profit before tax	(1,250,293)	(32,769)	(165,898)
Tax	0	0	0
Net earnings	(1,250,293)	(32,769)	(165,898)
Cash-flow adjustments:			
+ Depreciation	147,916	200,889	200,888
+ Goodwill amortization	122,668	116,079	116,077
− Capital expenditures	(10,000)	(25,000)	(25,000)
− Additions to net working capital	0	0	0
Cash flow before debt amortization	£ (989,709)	£ 259,199	£ 126,067
Ratios:			
EBIT/sales	−6.6%	6.8%	6.4%
EBIT/interest	NMF	0.96×	0.90×
Free cash flow/interest	NMF	1.58×	1.27×

EXHIBIT 6 *(concluded)*

	Estimate 1990–91	Forecast 1991–92	Forecast 1992–93
Earnings and Cash Flow Assuming Ealing's Proposal			
Interest expense	£ (287,500)	£(150,000)	£ (150,000)
Net earnings	(1,112,793)	267,231	159,102
Cash flow before debt amortization	£ (852,209)	£ 559,199	£ 451,067
Ratios:			
EBIT/interest	NMF	2.89×	2.83×
Free cash flow/interest	NMF	4.73×	4.01×
Earnings and Cash Flow Assuming Emergent Ventures' Proposal			
Interest expense	£ (250,000)	£(181,250)	£(316,875)*
Net earnings	(1,075,293)	235,981	7,773
Cash flow before debt amortization	£ (814,709)	£ 527,949	£ 284,192
Ratios:			
EBIT/interest	NMF	2.39×	1.34×
Cash flow/interest	NMF	3.91×	1.90×

*Interest expense in 1992–93 under the Emergent Ventures Proposal was calculated as follows:

Interest on the senior debt	£181,250
Current interest on the junior debt	96,875 (half year only)
One-tenth of accrued interest on junior debt	38,750
	£316,875

Source: Ian Stirling's notes.

EXHIBIT 7   Information on Current Capital-Market Conditions, December 7, 1990

London Money Rates

LIBOR (£) (offer rates)
   1 month   14.188%
   6 months   13.000
   1 year   12.500
Bank base rate   14.000
U.K. gilts (treasury securities)
   6 months   11.875
   1 year   11.582
   5 years   11.082
   10 years   10.655
   20 years   10.255
   25-year company bonds   12.030%

Equity Market

	June 1989	December 1991
Average P/E ratio, equity market	11.2×	10.46×
Average dividend yield	4.13%	5.43%
Share price index (1985 = 100)	180	161

Financial Outlook

	1991	1992	1993	1994	1995	1996
Inflation rate (consumer prices)	5.8%	4.4%	4.6%	4.5%	4.2%	4.0%
Bank prime rate (yearly average)	12.8%	11.7%	13.2%	12.0%	10.0%	9.8%

Source: *Financial Times,* December 7, 1990; OECD, *Economic Outlook,* January 1991; Economist Intelligence Unit, *Global Forecasting Service.*

Case 43

AB Volvo/Régie Nationale Des Usines Renault S.A.

If you want to win, you must go faster. The advantage of a complete merger is simplicity and speed. Agreement between the two companies does not go as fast as managing a single group. Speed is of the essence. We must go beyond the limits of cooperation to date.

Louis Schweitzer, *Chairman and CEO, Renault*[1]

On September 6, 1993, the chairmen of Volvo and Renault announced the terms by which their auto manufacturing businesses would merge. This announcement crowned a strategic alliance between the two firms, in effect since 1990. Renault was a French state-owned enterprise and had gained the approval for this merger from the French government. Volvo, however, was owned by 164,000 institutions and private investors. The proposed merger required approval by a majority of Volvo's shareholders. For this reason Volvo's chairman, Pehr G. Gyllenhammar,[2] called a special meeting of the shareholders for November 6, 1993, to obtain their approval. He was confident that the economic rationale for the merger would persuade the shareholders.

It remained for Volvo's shareholders to assess the merger proposal. Was this proposal in their own best interests? Would it create value? For whom? Was this the only strategic alternative for Volvo? Was it the best? Was the structure of this transaction appropriate? How would the newly merged auto business be managed?

---

[1]Quoted in "Hard Slog to Make the Marriage Work" by Kevin Done, *Financial Times,* September 7, 1993, p. 19.

[2]*Gyllenhammar* is pronounced YIL-en-hammar.

This case was prepared by Robert F. Bruner from field research to serve as a basis for classroom discussion and is not intended to indicate effective or ineffective handling of an administrative situation. The cooperation of numerous interviewees and the financial support of a Citicorp Global Scholarship are gratefully acknowledged. Copyright © 1994 by the University of Virginia Darden School Foundation, Charlottesville, VA. All rights reserved. *No part of this publication may be reproduced, stored in a retrieval system, used in a spreadsheet or transmitted in any form or by any means—electronic, mechanical, photocopying, recording or otherwise—without the permission of the Darden Foundation. For inquiries, please send an e-mail to dardencases @virginia.edu.* Revised 6/98. Version 2.1.

TRENDS IN THE WORLDWIDE AUTOMOTIVE INDUSTRY

After four decades of cyclical growth, the worldwide automotive industry was in the midst of a painful rationalization. As Exhibit 1 reveals, the number of European car and truck manufacturers fell dramatically over the past 40 years. Excess capacity was estimated to exceed 30 percent, prompting manufacturers to close plants.[3] This industry rationalization was due in part to the wave of economic recession which began in North America in 1991 and spread to Europe in 1992. But it was also due to several important structural trends in the industry:

- "Lean" manufacturing techniques were exploited by volume producers to achieve cost and quality advantages over other producers.[4]
- Rising new product development costs. Between 1979 and 1989, Volvo's annual expenditure on truck R&D rose from (Swedish kronor) SEK300 million[5] to SEK1,250 million. Similarly for cars, the annual R&D expenditure rose from SEK600 million to SEK4,300. This was attributable to tightening environmental regulations and to increasing competition, which made product enhancement an important competitive tool.
- Lower returns to commercial operators of automotive equipment (particularly trucks and buses) arising from the process of European integration and creation of a deregulated transport market. This reduced demand and sharpened price competition. Profitability in the automotive industry fell sharply between 1989 and 1992. (Exhibit 2 presents average operating margins and returns for leading producers.)

RÉGIE DES USINES NATIONALE RENAULT S.A.

Renault had produced automobiles since 1898 and was by 1993 the largest business enterprise in France, based on the number of employees (147,000 worldwide and 61,000 in France) and total revenues ([French francs] FF170 billion for the group). The company had been nationalized in 1945 by General Charles de Gaulle on charges that it collaborated with the enemy during the German occupation of France in the Second World War. The firm's "régie" status indicated that it was not simply a company, but a "state body" wholly owned by the government of France.

Renault's financial performance had varied considerably in the postwar period—it nearly entered bankruptcy in the early 1980s. Renault recovered in 1987[6] (see Exhibit 3) and in 1992

---

[3]Volvo, for instance, had recently made the decision to close the assembly plant at Kalmar, Sweden, the showcase for the firm's team-based manufacturing approach.

[4]Lean manufacturing techniques developed by Toyota and other major auto producers emphasized the reduction of unnecessary assets and time in the production process, along with continuous improvement in product quality. Successful application of these techniques gave the lean manufacturers cost advantages which they exploited to deliver higher returns to shareholders or price reductions to customers. For various reasons, smaller manufacturers (e.g., Jaguar and Porsche) had been slow to adopt these techniques, or resisted adopting them altogether; this contributed to the declining market position of smaller producers.

[5]Around the time of announcement of this merger, the French franc (FF) could purchase 1.369 Swedish kronor (SEK). Also, the U.S. dollar could purchase 7.83 Swedish kronor.

[6]Renault had entered the U.S. market in 1980 with acquisition of a 46 percent interest in American Motors Corporation. Renault-AMC produced the *Motor Trend* "car of the year" in 1983 (the "Alliance"). In 1987, Renault sold its interest in AMC and exited from the U.S. market.

was among the most profitable manufacturers. The corporate turnaround stemmed largely from the accession to power of a cadre of business-oriented enterprise managers, and by the introduction of a new line of products, including Clio (an inexpensive subcompact), Safrane (an expensive executive luxury car), and Espace (a van-style family car). Also, the new team had successfully implemented a comprehensive total quality management program.

In March 1993, the legislative elections brought to power a center-right coalition whose goals included the privatization of the large state-owned enterprises, most of which had been nationalized under the first Socialist government in the postwar period (1982–88). The government had indicated a strong desire to privatize these enterprises rapidly and targeted Renault for early privatization. However, the exact timing of privatization was uncertain. The government's minister of finance, Gérard Longuet, indicated that the sale of the government's shares would depend both on the suitability of capital market conditions and on the financial condition of the company. Observers believed that Renault could be privatized in late 1994 or early 1995. However, a shift in political fortunes back to the Socialist Party could halt Renault's privatization. Analysts were reluctant to estimate the offering price of Renault. But they offered the trading experience of Renault's French rival, PSA (Peugeot), as a benchmark for suggesting that Renault's expected market/book value ratio would be about 0.75.

Following a precedent set by Prime Minister Thatcher in the United Kingdom, the French government retained an unusual right in the enterprises it privatized. This right, called an *action specifique* (popularly called a golden share) reserved for the government, among other things, the ability to prevent an investor from acquiring (or voting) more than 20 percent of the shares in the newly privatized firm. This right would last indefinitely. The effect of such rights was to reserve for the government some power in determining the structure of competition in key industries. Observers also suspected that golden shares would be a way of preserving the independence of national champions such as Renault.

AB VOLVO

In mid-1993, Volvo was Scandinavia's largest industrial group, with headquarters in Gothenburg, Sweden. Total sales in 1993 were SEK83 billion, on which the firm lost SEK3.3 billion in earnings. Volvo's assets amounted to SEK117 billion. Exhibit 4 presents a graph of the Volvo price per share since 1971. Exhibit 5 gives selected financial data for AB Volvo over recent years. Volvo had two classes of common stock listed for trading, totaling 77,605,009 shares.[7]

Volvo's business portfolio in 1993 could be broken down into four main segments:

Automobiles. Car production accounted for 54 percent of total revenues in 1992. The company held 1.1 percent share of the world auto market, producing 311,000 cars in 1993. Over 90 percent of Volvo's auto sales were outside Sweden, principally to North America and the United Kingdom. Volvo also owned 20 percent of Renault, as part of the strategic alliance formed in 1990.

---

[7]Volvo A shares each carried one voting right. The B shares carried 1/10th of a voting right. Typically the A shares traded at a 5–10 percent premium in price to the B shares. The betas and sigmas (volatilities) of the two shares were not materially different.

Trucks and buses. Volvo was the second in world sales of heavy trucks and buses, with 51,300 units commanding a 10 percent share of market. Production of trucks and buses accounted for 37 percent of Volvo's total revenues in 1992. Over 95 percent of truck and bus sales were outside Sweden. As part of the Renault alliance, Volvo owned 45 percent of Renault Industrial Vehicles, the truck manufacturing operation.

Engines and aerospace. Through wholly owned subsidiaries, Volvo produced marine engines and aerospace components. This sector accounted for 7 percent of Volvo's revenues in 1992.

Other. Volvo also held a large investment portfolio of equity interests in other companies which accounted for 2.4 percent of revenues in 1992. The most significant of these investments was the holding of 39.5 percent[8] of the shares in Procordia, a state-controlled company, with operations mainly in branded consumer products (BCP) and pharmaceuticals. Separately from the merger of the Volvo and Renault automotive operations, AB Volvo had announced an offer to acquire the rest of BCP for Volvo shares and divest its interest in Procordia Pharmaceuticals.

Volvo (Latin for "I roll") began operations in 1927 as a manufacturer of cars. Diversifying gradually into trucks, buses, and marine engines, the company grew steadily. Plants were established in Belgium, Peru, and Canada. In 1966, Volvo introduced its model 144, which was acclaimed as the "car of the year"; thereafter, sales grew rapidly, especially in North America.

In 1971, Volvo's CEO, Gunnar Engellau, designated Pehr G. Gyllenhammar (his 36-year-old son-in-law) as the new CEO, and Volvo entered a new phase of its history. Gyllenhammar's rise to power coincided with a shift in strategy toward reducing the firm's dependence on cars. Sweden itself offered little room for sales growth; so any car-based strategy would need to be export oriented. But to compete in the export market meant regular style changes, which raised significant challenges from the high cost of product development. Accordingly, Gyllenhammar undertook a series of investments and merger attempts aimed at diversifying Volvo's business base, and/or attaining greater economies of scale and scope for Volvo cars. These included eight major transactions.[9]

---

[8]Volvo and the Swedish government were the principal owners of Procordia, each with 42.7 percent of the voting rights.
[9]The transactions included the following:

- Attempted merger with Saab-Scania, Sweden's other major car manufacturer. Plans for merger were announced in May 1977, but abandoned in August when opposition to the merger developed.
- Attempted investment in the Norwegian oil industry. In August 1977 Gyllenhammar initiated discussions with Norway's prime minister to exchange Volvo shares for a 40 percent interest in Norway's North Sea oil fields. The proposal was abandoned after a majority of Volvo shareholders opposed the plan.
- Attempted acquisition of Beijerinvest Group in late 1977 (broken off in January 1978). Gyllenhammar was attracted by Beijerinvest's oil trading firm, though the firm also operated food, engineering, and other businesses.
- 1980, sale of a 9.9 percent share interest in Volvo to Renault. This took place in combination with a public share offering. Other issues of stock took place in 1981 and 1982.
- In early 1980s, Volvo acquired a number of minority interests in consumer foods manufacturers.
- In 1986, Gyllenhammar negotiated the sale of Volvo's pharmaceutical businesses to Fermenta AB, and the acquisition of 20 percent of Fermenta's shares. This deal broke down when it appeared that Fermenta's CEO had engaged in fraud.
- In 1986, Volvo acquired a 25 percent interest in a pharmaceutical company, Pharmacia.
- In 1991, Volvo organized NedCar B.V. as a joint venture between Volvo, Mitsubishi, and the Dutch government. The objective of this joint venture was to manufacture car models in the medium-size segment for sale under the Volvo and Mitsubishi names.

STRATEGIC ALLIANCE BETWEEN VOLVO AND RENAULT

In 1990, Volvo and Renault agreed to establish a strategic alliance through a complicated scheme of cross-shareholdings, joint production and R&D agreements, and supervisory boards. While Renault had owned Volvo shares since 1980, Gyllenhammar and Raymond Lévy (CEO of Renault at the time) believed that closer cooperation was necessary to exploit opportunities that faced both companies. The structure of this alliance is shown in Exhibit 6. Volvo estimated that the undiscounted value of economies available through the alliance would amount to FF30 billion between the years 1994 and 2000.[10] One might assume that these alliance synergies had a present value in 1993 of FF18 billion[11] and that they would accrue 60 percent to Renault and 40 percent to Volvo.

Analysts speculated whether the alliance would survive a rejection of the merger proposal. If the merger were rejected and the alliance terminated, analysts believed that the alliance synergies would disappear. Also, unwinding the alliance would trigger cash penalties against the party seeking to exit.

At the end of 1992, Renault was the larger partner in the alliance. Exhibit 7 indicates the relative sizes of the two firms based on sales and income (denominated in U.S.$), employees, and units sold.

PEHR G. GYLLENHAMMAR

After 22 years at the helm of Volvo, Pehr Gyllenhammar was one of the most prominent businessmen in Scandinavia. Born in 1935, he had studied law in Sweden and other countries, after which he practiced briefly with a specialty in admiralty law. He joined Skandia Insurance Company (Sweden's largest insurer) in 1965 as an assistant manager, and by 1970 had risen to president and CEO. In late 1970, he joined AB Volvo and was appointed managing director and CEO in 1971. He was prominently associated with the series of investment and merger transactions proposed by Volvo over the next 22 years, having played a personal role in the design and proposal of them. From 1983 to 1990, he served as chairman of the board and CEO; and after 1990, his title was executive chairman of the board. He served on numerous boards of directors[12] and had received a number of honors.[13]

Gyllenhammar found time to cast his management ideas into numerous articles and five books: *Towards the Turn of the Century at Random* (1970), *I Believe in Sweden* (1973), *People at Work* (1977), *Industrial Policy for Human Beings* (1979), and *Also with Feeling* (1991). This body of writing conveyed a humanistic orientation toward factory work,

---

[10]These economies are reflected in the financial forecasts given in Exhibits 12–15. The SEK17 billion of merger synergies are *over and above* these alliance synergies.

[11]This is an estimate by the casewriter, and is mainly for illustrative purposes. The figure could vary substantially depending on the time pattern of the alliance synergy cash flows and on the discount rate used.

[12]Gyllenhammar's board memberships included Skandinaviska Enskilda Banken (Sweden's largest bank), United Technologies Corporation, Kissinger Associates, Pearson PLC, Reuters Holdings PLC, NV Philips Gloeilampenfabrieken, and Renault.

[13]His honors included four honorary doctorates and the Legion d'Honneur (France), King's Medal (Sweden), Lion of Finland (Finland), and Order of Merit (Italy).

emphasizing a concern for worker safety, dignity, and fulfillment. Two prominent innovations associated with his early years as CEO were the construction of a revolutionary car assembly plant at Kalmar, Sweden, in which Volvo developed the team-based manufacturing techniques for which it became famous, and the invention of individual industrial carriers to move cars through the plant, rather than using an assembly line—this technological innovation permitted the firm to experiment with team-based manufacturing techniques.

In 1993, the business press described Gyllenhammar with such words as "outspoken," "visionary," "ambitious," "industrial statesman," and "strong advocate of Sweden's need to move closer to the rest of Europe." He had been perceived as a charismatic and popular leader. But just recently, the tone of his press treatment changed when Aktiespararna (the association of individual shareholders) petitioned the board of directors to reveal his salary. At the April 1993 annual meeting, Gyllenhammar announced that his salary was SEK9.5 million, the highest individual pay package in Scandinavia. Aktiespararna charged that Gyllenhammar had taken advantage of a board which had no compensation committee to pay himself an "excessive" salary at a time when the company was closing plants, cutting the dividend, and losing money.

THE PROPOSED TERMS OF MERGER

The terms of merger were announced on September 6, 1993. The proposed merger would create Renault-Volvo RVA, to be owned 65 percent directly or indirectly by the French government, and 35 percent by AB Volvo. The pro forma 1992 sales of this group would have been FF241 billion, ranking the firm sixth in size in the worldwide auto industry. The firm would employ 200,000 persons. The memorandum of understanding contained the following items:

Brand names. The integrity of the brand names of the two organizations would be preserved through the maintenance of separate product lines and the operation of specific dealer networks. Renault-Volvo RVA would wholly own Renault Automobile Division, Volvo Car Corporation, Volvo Truck Corporation, Renault Industrial Vehicles, the other Renault industrial companies, and the financial subsidiaries of Renault and Volvo. Volvo's interests in engines, aerospace, food, and pharmaceuticals would not become part of RVA.

Internal governance, management, and supervisory boards. RVA would be directed by a management board under the supervision of a supervisory board. The supervisory board would have extended powers and would be called upon to decide on major financial issues. To be nominated chairman of the supervisory board would be Pehr Gyllenhammar. The supervisory board would have 14 members.[14] The management board would have overall management responsibility for the running of the Renault-Volvo RVA. The French government would nominate the chairman

---

[14]Of the 14 board members, 2 would represent French employees; 1, Swedish employees; 1, employees outside Sweden and France; 3, the French government (and later the public investors); and 3, AB Volvo. Four at-large members would generally represent the shareholders.

of the management board and CEO of RVA—the likely nominee was Louis Schweitzer, CEO of Renault. The management board would have five members, three to be proposed by France, and two by AB Volvo.

Share ownership. Renault-Volvo RVA would be owned by a shareholding structure indicated in Exhibit 8. AB Volvo would directly own 17.85 percent of RVA's shares. The French government would directly own 47.15 percent of the shares.[15] Finally, 35 percent would be owned by a holding company, RVC, owned 51 percent by Renault S.A. (a holding company organized by the French government) and 49 percent by AB Volvo. RVC would not have an operational role: Its purpose was to "secure the fundamental interests of its shareholders and ensure the stability of their investment in Renault-Volvo. It will be called upon to decide on major issues . . . such as capital increases."[16] The shareholders' agreement which would govern RVC would be valid for 25 years, though each side would have the right to terminate the agreement after the eighth year. The government and AB Volvo agreed not to sell or pledge their respective holdings in RVC until the listing of shares (privatization) of Renault-Volvo. Also, each agreed to give the other a right of first refusal on the sale of shares, and not to sell shares to a competitor. The net result of this ownership structure was that AB Volvo would control 35 percent of Renault-Volvo.[17] The changes in shareholdings necessary to effect this ownership structure are summarized in Exhibit 9.

The government announced that it intended to privatize Renault in 1994, and that it would sell its shares principally to a *noyau dur* (or "hard core") of investors. Observers believed that leading candidates for this hard core included Matra (a French industrial and automotive manufacturer) and French financial groups with ties to the French government, such as Société Générale, Groupe Suez, and Crédit Agricole.

In a November 17 letter to the Swedish prime minister, the French prime minister stated that the "golden share" would not be used against Volvo as long as Volvo's participation in Renault-Volvo RVA did not exceed a total of 35 percent. This letter appeared to relax the typical French golden share limitation of 20 percent. However, this limitation would still preclude any chance that Volvo's shareholders could gain absolute control of RVA.

The merger would substantially transform AB Volvo from principally an automotive manufacturer to an industrial conglomerate. A summary of AB Volvo's resulting asset portfolio is given in Exhibit 10. Pro forma financial statements for AB Volvo are given in Exhibit 11.

RATIONALE FOR THE MERGER

The Volvo merger prospectus pointed to three main reasons for the merger:

- *Competitive advantage.* The combined firm would rank second in world production of trucks after Daimler-Benz, and sixth in world production of passenger cars. In 1992,

---

[15]The 47.15 percent includes the 0.79 percent share attributable to Renault employees who had been issued nonvoting share certificates by Renault.

[16]"Information to Volvo Shareholders," AB Volvo, September 9, 1993, p. 3.

[17]The 35 percent figure is the sum of the direct holding, 17.85 percent, plus the indirect holding through RVC (49 percent times 35 percent).

Volvo and Renault combined sold 2.3 million passenger cars and 106,300 trucks and buses. Volvo and Renault were viewed as having complementary product lines both geographically and in product segments.

- *Exploit operating efficiencies* in procurement, research and development, and production. Volvo explained that these merger economies would amount to SEK16.43 billion (FF12 billion)[18] on an undiscounted basis between 1994 and 2000. About 60 percent of the savings would occur in car operations, and the remaining 40 percent would occur in trucks and buses. These economies might be used to reduce prices and increase the firm's share of market, or to raise earnings and increase the firm's capital base. These merger operating efficiencies would be on top of SEK41.07 billion (FF30 billion) of efficiencies to be realized through the existing strategic alliance between 1994 and 2000.

- *Achieve substantial financial strength* and the proper orientation to meet capital requirements estimated in Volvo's case to amount to between SEK5 and 8 billion. The Renault truck operation would require substantial additional capital as well. Sören Gyll, Volvo's president and CEO, wrote, "Without the merger with Renault, securing the long-term survival of Volvo would have required major infusions of capital. Combined with Renault, a large, sound and financially sustainable automotive operation is created, which becomes an important cornerstone in the new Volvo."[19] Volvo's car operations, which reported substantial profits in the 1980s, lost money since 1990 mainly due to lower sales volume. This resulted in increasing debt.

FINANCIAL OUTLOOK

Exhibits 12 to 15 present forecasts of free cash flows for the car and truck units of Volvo, for Renault, and for the expected SEK16.43 billion of synergies the merger would generate. These synergies are over and above the SEK41.07 billion in alliance synergies; the forecasts assume that synergy use is applied to expand profit margins rather than reduce prices. These exhibits were based on casewriter analysis but are consistent with the analyses and assumptions of securities analysts following AB Volvo at the time of the announcement. Generally, analysts believed that the new Renault-Volvo would have a debt/equity ratio of 35 percent,[20] that the new company could borrow SEK at 9.3 percent (or French francs at 8.1 percent), and that the company's marginal tax rate would be 38 percent[21] in Sweden. They expected that Renault's marginal tax rate would be 35 percent in France.

---

[18]The synergies were quoted by Volvo in French francs. For simplicity of presentation, these values were converted to Swedish kronor (SEK) at 1.369 SEK/FF, the rate prevailing on September 6, 1993, the date the merger proposal was announced.

[19]AB Volvo, "Information Prior to Extraordinary General Meeting of Shareholders in AB Volvo, November 9, 1993," p. 6.

[20]Capital-structure, interest-rate, and tax-rate figures are casewriter estimates consistent with forecasts of financial analysts. In particular, the debt/equity ratio is an average across the business cycle. Analysts believed that the debt/equity ratio would vary across the business cycle between 22 percent (at the cyclical high) and 45 percent (at the cyclical low).

[21]The analysts' expectations were different from the typical marginal tax rate faced by corporations in Sweden, 47 percent.

Exhibit 16 gives comparative financial data on automotive manufacturers. Exhibit 17 presents information on capital market conditions in early September 1993. Exhibit 18 shows the breakdown of share ownership of AB Volvo as of August 1993, and pro forma the merger with Renault and acquisition of BCP.

CONCLUSION

In promoting the merger of Renault and Volvo's automotive businesses, Pehr Gyllenhammar wrote to the shareholders:

> The risk that Volvo—and Sweden—run is that our country will not be competitive. Then there is no protection in a stand-alone alternative, whereas the new company with its strength and staying power may cushion any short-term harmful effects. Also, the French party is making the biggest ever foreign investment in Sweden—this in times of crisis. It demonstrates high confidence in Volvo and in our country. There is hardly any risk that one would erode the capital so invested by destroying the base. Mergers on this scale are delicate processes. We must maintain momentum and pace in the company while building a new and common organization . . . If we mean anything by participating from our small national base, in building Europe, we have to realize that such work requires both giving and taking.[22]

---

[22]AB Volvo, "Information Prior to Extraordinary General Meeting of Shareholders in AB Volvo, November 9, 1993," pp. 36–37.

EXHIBIT 1   Changing Competitive Structure of Industry

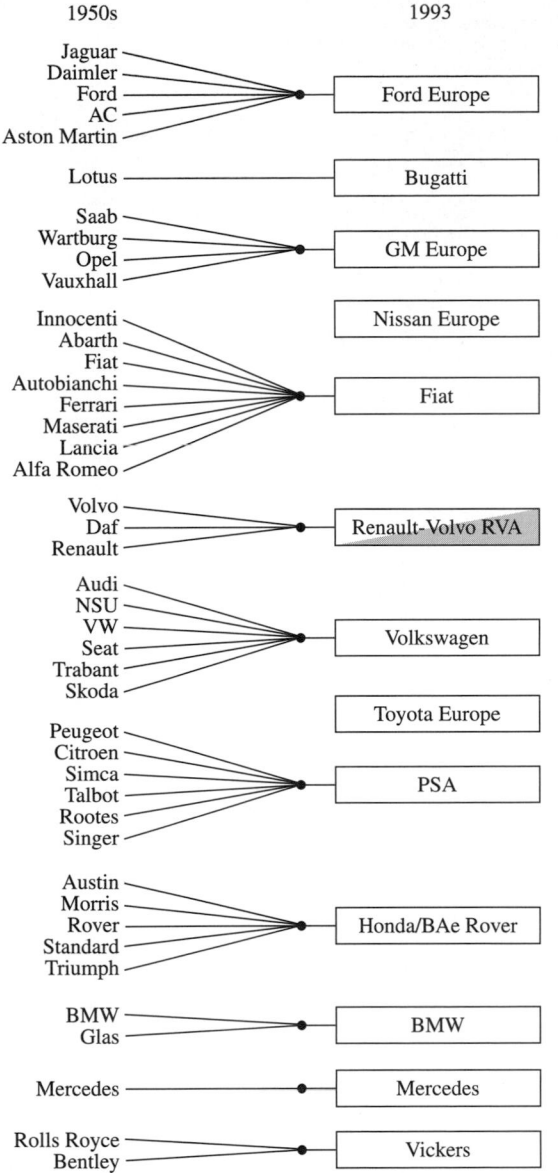

1950s	1993
Jaguar, Daimler, Ford, AC, Aston Martin	Ford Europe
Lotus	Bugatti
Saab, Wartburg, Opel, Vauxhall	GM Europe
	Nissan Europe
Innocenti, Abarth, Fiat, Autobianchi, Ferrari, Maserati, Lancia, Alfa Romeo	Fiat
Volvo, Daf, Renault	Renault-Volvo RVA
Audi, NSU, VW, Seat, Trabant, Skoda	Volkswagen
	Toyota Europe
Peugeot, Citroen, Simca, Talbot, Rootes, Singer	PSA
Austin, Morris, Rover, Standard, Triumph	Honda/BAe Rover
BMW, Glas	BMW
Mercedes	Mercedes
Rolls Royce, Bentley	Vickers

The number of independent European manufacturers of heavy trucks has fallen dramatically in the past decade, from 40 in 1965 to 20 in 1980, and to only 10 in 1992.

Joint ventures, with or without ownership interests, have become increasingly common in the automotive industry.

Objective is to achieve advantages of scale — and thereby greater profitability — while retaining and strengthening the identity and integrity of the various companies' trademarks.

Source: AB Volvo, "Information Prior to Extraordinary General Meeting of Shareholders in AB Volvo, November 9, 1993," p. 39.

EXHIBIT 2 Operating Margin as a Percentage of Sales for Leading Automotive Producers

	1979	1980	1981	1982	1983	1984	1985	1986	1987	1988	1989	1990	1991	1992
GM	7.0	-2.1	0.6	1.6	7.4	5.6	4.4	2.6	2.7	4.4	4.4	-0.1	-3.3	-2.5
Ford	2.0	-6.1	-3.3	-1.3	4.1	6.5	7.1	6.6	8.7	8.0	5.8	0.4	5.2	-2.1
Chrysler	-5.2	-12.9	0.1	1.0	6.9	11.5	9.4	8.5	7.6	5.1	2.3	-0.5	-2.4	2.7
VW	8.0	3.8	3.0	1.2	1.9	3.8	4.9	1.6	1.7	2.6	3.0	1.8	0.7	-0.2
Fiat			8.2	5.9	5.9	7.8	8.4	8.4	8.1	8.6	9.3	4.3	1.4	0.0
PSA	6.6	1.9	2.5	0.2	2.8	3.7	4.7	7.2	9.7	12.7	12.1	9.8	6.3	3.8
Renault		4.6	1.7	2.5	-0.1	-5.4	-3.9	2.9	6.2	8.9	7.4	3.9	2.8	4.4
Daimler-Benz	8.9	6.8	8.3	8.4	7.5	6.8	9.4	7.4	6.0	4.8	3.4	3.0	2.4	1.9
BMW	8.4	6.4	5.1	5.9	7.4	6.9	6.1	6.0	4.6	4.4	3.7	2.9	2.5	1.4
Volvo	5.5	4.4	6.3	7.5	9.4	11.4	10.1	9.1	8.7	8.5	5.3	0.7	-1.5	-2.7
Saab-Scania	7.9	7.9	7.5	8.3	10.0	9.5	7.9	7.9	6.9	6.0	1.8	7.2	6.2	4.6
Toyota	4.9	6.2	4.0	6.0	6.9	8.4	10.4	7.5	5.5	6.5	5.8	7.0	5.1	2.1
Nissan	7.8	5.4	7.1	6.0	3.6	5.6	1.9	-0.4	1.5	3.9	6.7	2.4	2.4	-0.1
Honda	6.6	10.5	8.3	8.6	9.9	11.3	10.5	5.9	5.0	5.1	5.2	3.4	3.5	2.6
Mazda				3.6	3.6	4.0	5.1	1.4	0.6	1.6	2.3	2.9	1.6	1.1
Mitsubishi				2.2	1.0	2.2	1.8	2.4	2.7	2.8	2.7	3.2	2.8	2.4
Isuzu				2.1	1.0	0.9	2.4	0.2	-1.7	1.1	1.3	0.8	-3.7	-1.5
Suzuki				1.3	2.6	3.8	3.3	3.3	4.1	1.6	3.2	5.1	3.9	4.1
Daihatsu				1.5	2.2	2.0	1.4	1.8	2.2	2.0	0.9	1.7	0.5	0.1
Fuji				5.7	4.0	3.7	3.0	1.6	1.0	0.5	-5.9	-9.6	-1.8	-1.6
Average of five best	8.0	7.1	7.6	7.8	8.8	10.4	10.0	8.3	8.6	9.3	8.3	6.0	4.3	3.9
RVA (pro forma)		4.6	3.0	4.0	3.1	0.8	1.3	5.1	7.1	8.8	6.7	2.8	1.5	2.3

Source: AB Volvo document.

EXHIBIT 3 Renault Financial Performance (all figures in millions of French francs)

	1985	1986	1987	1988	1989	1990	1991
Turnover (revenues)	111,382	134,935	147,510	161,438	174,480	163,620	165,794
Operating profit (loss)	(4,398)	3,549	9,204	14,385	12,940	6,299	4,663
Pretax profit (loss)	(12,255)	(5,210)	3,562	8,975	9,730	1,380	4,109
Tax expense (tax credit)	(1,330)	648	(127)	62	910	516	963
Minority interests	28	176	433	79	48	(346)	68
Net profit (loss)	(10,953)	(6,034)	3,256	8,834	9,300	1,210	3,078
Total assets	42,003	45,988	43,489	46,648	49,780	119,451	127,098
Net debt	61,962	55,627	46,377	23,786	17,590	81,854	72,733
Capital expenditures	8,269	5,551	7,021	7,295	10,360	10,669	9,434
Total equity	(9,450)	(11,433)	(7,811)	14,012	16,770	20,513	38,425

Source: Renault annual reports.

EXHIBIT 4 Price of Volvo Shares, 1971–93

Share Price Performance
Volvo versus Market Index

□ Volvo Stock Price   + Swedish Mkt. Index

Source of data used in this figure: PG Sitter Kvar," *Affarsvärlden,* December 8, 1993 (in Swedish).

EXHIBIT 5 Volvo Group Financial Performance (amounts in SEK millions unless otherwise stated)

	1988	1989	1990	1991	1992
Condensed consolidated statements of income					
Sales	96,639	90,972	83,185	77,223	83,002
Operating income (loss)	7,028	4,817	567	(1,168)	(2,249)
Restructuring costs	—	—	(2,450)	—	(1,450)
Income from equity method investments	—	1,015	1,322	1,218	96
Financial income (expense)	1,039	822	234	1,478	(1,146)
Income (loss) after financial income (expense)	8,067	6,654	(327)	1,528	(4,749)
Extraordinary income (expense)	176	313	—	(725)	—
Minority interests in (income) loss	—	(56)	40	310	1,437
Taxes	(3,200)	(2,124)	(733)	(431)	(8)
Minority interests in (income) loss	(103)	—	—	—	—
Net income (loss)	4,940	4,787	(1,020)	682	(3,320)
Income (loss) per share, SEK	63.70	61.70	(13.10)	8.80	(42.80)
Condensed consolidated balance sheets					
Liquid funds	15,632	18,470	17,585	18,779	21,760
Receivables and inventories	33,346	35,248	35,604	35,087	39,979
Investments in bonds	3,956	3,455	2,854	928	—
Restricted deposits in Bank of Sweden	4,034	5,293	2,072	41	2
Other assets	29,963	35,677	43,982	51,913	55,266
Total assets	29,983	35,677	43,982	51,913	55,266
Current liabilities	34,500	42,846	48,712	47,778	59,386
Long-term liabilities	18,727	17,244	17,794	20,120	23,981
Minority interests	484	414	300	4,986	3,919
Shareholders' equity	33,240	37,639	35,291	33,864	29,721
Total liabilities and shareholders' equity	86,951	98,143	102,097	106,748	117,007
Capital expenditures	3,948	6,281	4,598	2,874	2,915
Research and development costs	5,139	6,176	7,061	6,414	6,178
Number of employees, year-end	78,614	78,690	68,797	63,582	60,115
Wages, salaries and social costs	15,434	16,875	17,865	17,654	16,857
Share capital	1,940	1,940	1,940	1,940	1,940
Dividends to shareholders	1,086	1,203	1,203	1,203	601
Dividend per share, SEK	14.00	15.50	15.50	15.50	7.75
Return on capital employed, percent	17.2	13.8	4.4	6.8	0.7
Return on shareholders' equity, percent	15.8	13.3	Neg.	2.0	Neg.
Shareholders' equity and minority interests to total assets, percent	38.8	38.8	34.9	36.4	28.8

Source: AB Volvo, annual report 1992.

EXHIBIT 6   Structure of Strategic Alliance and Cross-Shareholdings (September 1993)

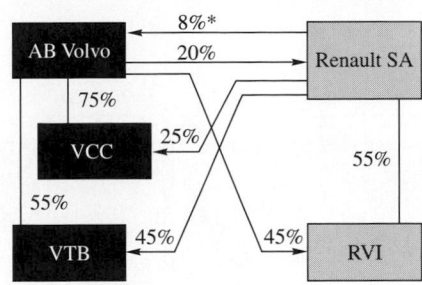

Abbreviations	Reference
VCC	Volvo's restructured car operations
VTB	Volvo's restructured truck and bus operations
Renault SA	Parent company of the Renault Group, following conversion to a capital stock company
RVI	Renault Véhicules Industriels SA

*Renault has acquired 8.24% of Volvo shares, and 10% of the votes.

Source of Information: AB Volvo, "Information Prior to Extraordinary General Meeting of Shareholders in AB Volvo, November 9, 1993," p. 40.

EXHIBIT 7   Composition of RVA Based on Pro Forma Financial Information

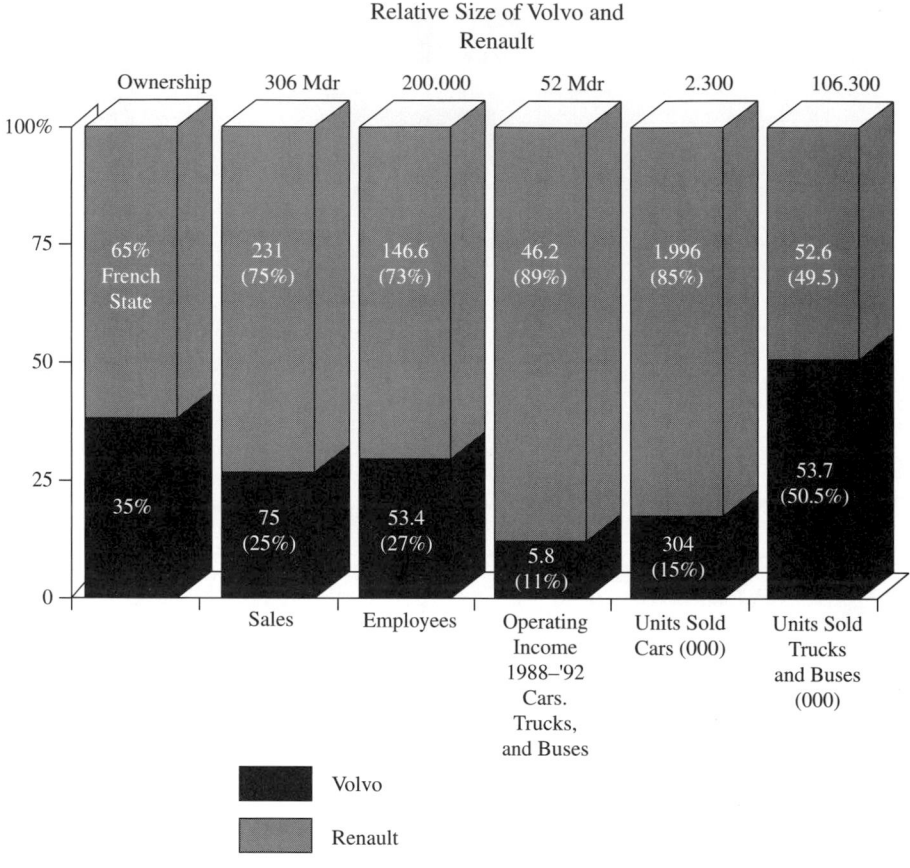

Source: AB Volvo document.

EXHIBIT 8 Proposed Ownership Structure of RVA

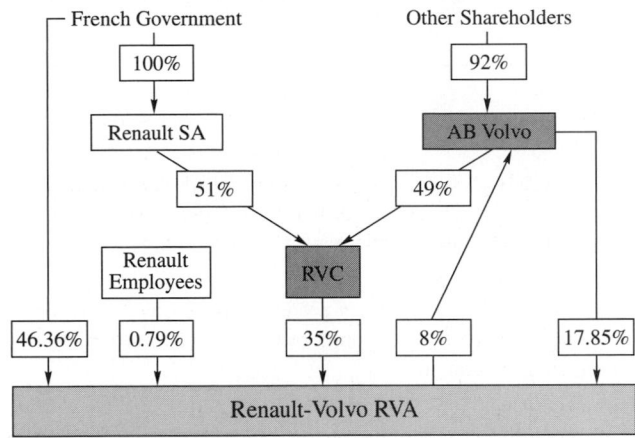

Source: AB Volvo, "Information Prior to Extraordinary General Meeting of Shareholders in AB Volvo, November 9, 1993," p. 43.

EXHIBIT 9 Changes in Ownership Position to Effect the Merger

	Before Merger	*Change*	*After Merger*
Changes in French Government Holdings			
Shareholding in AB Volvo	+8.24%	−8.24%	0.0%
Shareholding in Volvo Cars	+25.0%	−25.0%	0.0%
Shareholding in Volvo Trucks	+45.0%	−45.0%	0.0%
Shareholding in Renault Cars	+80.0%	−80.0%	0.0%
Shareholding in Renault Trucks	+55.0%	−55.0%	0.0%
Shareholding in RVC	0.0%	+51.0%	+51.0%
Shareholding in RVA	0.0%	+46.0%	+46.0%
Changes in AB Volvo Holdings			
Shareholding in Renault S.A.	+20.0%	−20.0%	0.0%
Shareholding in Renault Trucks	+45.0%	−45.0%	0.0%
Shareholding in Volvo Cars	+75.0%	−75.0%	0.0%
Shareholding in Volvo Trucks	+55.0%	−55.0%	0.0%
Shareholding in RVC	0.0%	+49.0%	+49.0%
Shareholding in RVA	0.0%	+17.5%	+17.5%
Changes in RVA Holdings			
Shareholding in AB Volvo	0.0%	+8.24%	+8.24%

Source: Casewriter analysis.

EXHIBIT 10 AB Volvo Asset Portfolio—after Merger with Renault and Acquisition of Branded Consumer Products (book value of assets by business segment)

	Percentage
Automotive	41
This consists of Volvo's investment in RVC and RVA.	
Engineering	4
This consists of Volvo's investment in two wholly owned companies: Volvo Penta (engines and transmissions for marine and industrial use), and Volvo Flygmotor (engines and components for aerospace).	
Branded consumer products	21
This consists of the consumer products operations obtained by Volvo in the breakup of Procordia, the conglomerate owned jointly by Volvo and the Swedish government.	
Pharmaceuticals	17
This consists entirely of the pharmaceutical portion of Procordia, spun off into a separate company called Pharmacia. This new company consists of two subsidiaries, Kabi Pharmacia and Biotech.	
Other	17
These other holdings consist of a portfolio of shares in listed and unlisted companies, with activities as diverse as real estate, car rental, automotive dealerships, pumps, medical technology, and miscellaneous shareholdings.	
Total	100

Source: AB Volvo, "Information Prior to Extraordinary General Meeting of Shareholders in AB Volvo, November 9, 1993," p. 27.

EXHIBIT 11   Financial Statements Pro Forma the Merger, AB Volvo (SEK billion)

	January–June 1993	
	After Formation of RVA	*After Formation of RVA and Acquisition of BCP*
Income statements		
Sales	0.09	0.09
Cost of operations	(0.36)	(0.36)
Operating loss	(0.27)	(0.27)
Dividends received	2.42*	2.20†
Net interest expense	(0.76)	(0.76)
Other financial income and expense	(0.43)	(0.43)
Income before allocations and taxes	0.96	0.74
Allocations	(0.24)	(0.24)
Income before taxes	0.72	0.50
Taxes	(0.02)	(0.02)
Net income	0.70	0.48

*Dividend from Renault-Volvo RVA is included pro forma in the amount of SEK446 million. The dividend revenue is assumed to be tax-exempt.
†In the pro forma calculation, the dividend from Procordia, SEK355 million, has been replaced with a dividend of SEK140 million from Pharmacia. Dividend from BCP is not included in the calculation.

	After Formation of RVA	*After Formation of RVA and Acquisition of BCP*
Balance sheets (June 30, 1993)		
Liquid funds	—	—
Other current assets	1.1	1.1
Shares in subsidiaries*	2.0	12.1
Shareholding in Renault-Volvo RVA*	16.6	16.6
Other shares and participations*	16.1	10.7
Other noncurrent assets	3.8	3.8
Total assets	39.6	44.3
Short-term loans	5.9	5.9
Other current liabilities	1.7	1.7
Long-term loans	9.1	9.1
Other long-term liabilities†	0.8	0.8
Untaxed reserves	1.5	1.5
Shareholders' equity	20.6	25.3
Total liabilities and shareholders' equity	39.6	44.3

*In the pro forma calculations for the parent company, it is assumed that all transactions related to the formation of Renault-Volvo RVA and the acquisition of BCP are carried out without any earnings effects, that is, as a pure exchange transaction. Depending on the final selection of accounting methods, deviations can arise with regard to both values of shares and participations as well as shareholders' equity.
†Non-interest-bearing.

Source: AB Volvo, "Information Prior to Extraordinary General Meeting of Shareholders in AB Volvo, November 9, 1993," pp. 29–30.

EXHIBIT 12 Free-Cash-Flow Forecasts: Renault Car and Truck Business, Premerger Basis, Including Alliance Synergies but Not Merger Synergies (values in billions of French francs, except as noted)

	1992pf	1993e	1994f	1995f	1996f	1997f	1998f	1999f	2000f
Forecast assumptions									
Sales growth	1.08	0.91	1.06	1.08	1.09	1.06	1.06	1.06	1.05
% operating margin	4.41	0.49	1.58%	3.59%	5.00%	5.00%	5.50%	5.50%	5.50%
Tax rate	35.00%	35.00%	35.00%	35.00%	35.00%	35.00%	35.00%	35.00%	35.00%
Depreciation/Sales	0.033	0.033	0.033	0.033	0.033	0.033	0.033	0.033	0.033
Cap. expend./Sales	0.038	0.038	0.038	0.038	0.038	0.038	0.038	0.038	0.038
Net wc/Sales	0.285	0.285	0.285	0.285	0.285	0.285	0.285	0.285	0.285
Inflation: France	0.023	0.023	0.019	0.016	0.02	0.02	0.02	0.02	0.02
Inflation: Sweden	0.016	0.023	0.02	0.025	0.02	0.02	0.02	0.02	0.02
SEK/FF exchange rate	1.100	1.369	1.383	1.395	1.395	1.395	1.395	1.395	1.395
Sales	179.4	163.5	172.5	186.5	203.3	215.5	228.4	242.1	254.2
Operating profit	7.9	0.8	2.7	6.7	10.2	10.8	12.6	13.3	14.0
Finance and real estate	1.7	1.7	1.7	1.7	1.7	1.7	1.7	1.7	1.7
Profit before tax	9.6	2.5	4.4	8.4	11.9	12.5	14.3	15.0	15.7
Tax expense	−3.4	(0.9)	(1.5)	(2.9)	(4.2)	(4.4)	(5.0)	(5.3)	(5.5)
Profit after tax	6.3	1.6	2.9	5.5	7.7	8.1	9.3	9.8	10.2
+Depreciation	5.8	5.3	5.6	6.1	6.6	7.0	7.4	7.9	8.3
−Capital expenditures	−6.8	(6.2)	(6.5)	(7.1)	(7.7)	(8.2)	(8.7)	(9.2)	(9.6)
−Addns. to net working cap.	−5.0	4.5	(2.6)	(4.0)	(4.8)	(3.5)	(3.7)	(3.9)	(3.4)
Free cash flow, FF	0.3	5.3	(0.6)	0.5	1.8	3.5	4.4	4.5	5.4
Free cash flow, SEK	0.3	7.2	(0.9)	0.6	2.6	4.8	6.1	6.3	7.5

pf = Actual results, pro forma the merger.
e = Expected, based on partial year data, pro forma the merger.
f = Forecasted.

Source: Casewriter estimates, consistent with forecast assumptions of securities analysts.

EXHIBIT 13 Free-Cash-Flow Forecasts: Volvo Cars, Premerger Basis, Including Alliance Synergies but Not Merger Synergies (amounts in billions of SEK)

	1992pf	1993e	1994f	1995f	1996f	1997f	1998f	1999f	2000f
Forecast assumptions									
Sales growth	1.20	1.19	1.08	1.10	1.1	1.09	1.08	1.05	1.05
% operating margin	−0.041	0.014	3.50%	5.00%	6.00%	6.00%	6.00%	6.50%	6.50%
Tax rate			38.00%	38.00%	38.00%	38.00%	38.00%	38.00%	38.00%
Depreciation/Sales	0.038	0.034	0.034	0.034	0.034	0.034	0.034	0.034	0.034
Cap. expend./Sales	0.051	0.046	0.046	0.046	0.046	0.046	0.046	0.046	0.046
Net working cap./Sales			0.0001	0.0001	0.0001	0.0001	0.0001	0.0001	0.0001
Sales	44.6	53.0	57.5	63.0	69.3	75.5	81.6	85.7	89.9
Operating profit	−1.8	0.7	2.0	3.2	4.2	4.5	4.9	5.6	5.8
Share of associates	−0.7	(0.7)	(0.4)	(0.1)	(0.1)	(0.1)	(0.1)	(0.1)	(0.1)
Restructuring charge		(0.8)							
Profit before tax			1.6	3.1	4.1	4.5	4.8	5.5	5.8
Tax expense			(0.6)	(1.2)	(1.6)	(1.7)	(1.8)	(2.1)	(2.2)
Profit after tax			1.0	1.9	2.5	2.8	3.0	3.4	3.6
+Depreciation			2.0	2.1	2.4	2.6	2.8	2.9	3.1
−Capital expenditures			(2.6)	(2.9)	(3.2)	(3.5)	(3.8)	(3.9)	(4.1)
−Addns. to net working capital			(0.0)	(0.0)	(0.0)	(0.0)	(0.0)	(0.0)	(0.0)
Free cash flow (SEK)			0.3	1.1	1.7	1.9	2.0	2.4	2.5

pf = Actual results, pro forma the merger.
e = Expected, based on partial year data, pro forma the merger.
f = Forecasted.

Source: Casewriter estimates, consistent with forecast assumptions of securities analysts.

EXHIBIT 14 Free-Cash-Flow Forecasts: Volvo Trucks, Premerger Basis, Including Alliance Synergies but Not Merger Synergies (amounts in billions of SEK)

	1992pf	1993e	1994f	1995f	1996f	1997f	1998f	1999f	2000f
Forecast assumptions									
Sales growth	1.25	1.3	1.03	1.025	1.1	1.1	1.08	1.08	1.08
% operating margin	−2.11%	1.94%	2.20%	3.40%	5.00%	6.80%	6.00%	6.00%	6.00%
Tax rate	38.00%		38.00%	38.00%	38.00%	38.00%	38.00%	38.00%	38.00%
Depreciation/Sales	0.038	0.034	0.034	0.034	0.034	0.034	0.034	0.034	0.034
Cap. expend./Sales	0.051	0.046	0.046	0.046	0.046	0.046	0.046	0.046	0.046
Net working cap./Sales	0.15	0.140	0.140	0.140	0.140	0.140	0.140	0.140	0.140
Sales	30.4	39.0	40.0	41.0	45.1	49.6	53.6	57.9	62.5
Operating profit	−0.6	0.3	0.7	1.3	2.3	3.4	3.2	3.5	3.7
Share of associates	−0.1	(0.1)							
Restructuring charge	−0.3								
Profit before tax			0.7	1.3	2.3	3.4	3.2	3.5	3.7
Tax expense			(0.3)	(0.5)	(0.9)	(1.3)	(1.2)	(1.3)	(1.4)
Profit after tax			0.4	0.8	1.4	2.1	2.0	2.2	2.3
+Depreciation			1.4	1.4	1.5	1.7	1.8	2.0	2.1
−Capital expenditures			(1.8)	(1.9)	(2.1)	(2.3)	(2.5)	(2.7)	(2.9)
−Addns. to net working capital			(0.1)	(0.1)	(0.6)	(0.6)	(0.6)	(0.6)	(0.6)
Free cash flow (SEK)			(0.2)	0.2	0.3	0.9	0.8	0.9	0.9

pf = Actual results, pro forma the merger.
e = Expected, based on partial year data, pro forma the merger.
f = Forecasted.

Source: Casewriter estimates, consistent with forecast assumptions of securities analysts.

EXHIBIT 15 Forecasts of Merger Synergies, over and above Alliance Savings (amounts in billions of SEK)

	1992pf	1993e	1994f	1995f	1996f	1997f	1998f	1999f	2000f
Forecast assumptions									
Savings (pretax)/Sales			0.0	0.004	0.005	0.0073	0.009	0.01	0.01
Renault car and truck sales			172.5	186.5	203.3	215.5	228.4	242.1	254.2
Volvo car sales			57.5	63.0	69.3	75.5	81.6	85.7	89.9
Volvo truck sales			40.0	41.0	45.1	49.6	53.6	57.9	62.5
Pretax savings			0.0	1.2	1.6	2.5	3.3	3.9	4.1
Taxes (at 35%)			0.0	0.4	0.6	0.9	1.1	1.3	1.4
After-tax savings			0.0	0.8	1.0	1.6	2.1	2.5	2.6

pf = Actual results, pro forma the merger.
e = Expected, based on partial year data, pro forma the merger.
f = Forecasted.

Source: Casewriter estimates, consistent with analysts' expectations. The time profile of pretax savings is drawn from AB Volvo, "Merger of Volvo's Automotive Operations with Renault," p. 4.

EXHIBIT 16   Comparative Financial Information, Major Automotive Manufacturers

	Beta (and exchange where estimated)	Market-Value Debt/Equity Ratio
Chrysler Corporation (cars and trucks)	1.30 (U.S., NYSE)	1.464
Ford Motors (cars and trucks)	1.20 (U.S., NYSE)	3.64
General Motors (cars and trucks)	1.10 (U.S., NYSE)	2.37
Navistar (trucks)	1.20 (U.S., NYSE)	0.436
Paccar (trucks)	1.10 (U.S., OTC)	0.257
Honda (cars)	0.75 (U.S., NYSE)	0.44
Nissan (cars)	0.70 (U.S., OTC)	1.283
Toyota (cars)	0.65 (U.S., OTC)	0.311
Volkswagen (cars)	0.35 (FTSE, London)	2.60
Volvo (cars and trucks)	1.40 (Stockholm)	0.64
	0.88 (CAC, Paris)	
	1.20 (S&P 500, U.S.)	
	1.11 (FTSE, London)	
	0.68 (Topix, Tokyo)	
PSA (Peugeot) (cars)	1.10 (Frankfurt)	0.47
Daimler-Benz (cars and trucks)	1.10 (Frankfurt)	1.15
Fiat (cars and trucks)	1.20 (U.S., NYSE)	2.85

NMF = Not a meaningful number, usually because of negative earnings.

Sources: *Value Line Investment Survey,* Bloomberg, Morgan Stanley Capital International *Perspective,* and casewriter estimates.

Tax Rate	Market/Book Value	Price/Earnings Ratio	Forecast Five-Year Growth Rate in Sales	Forecast Five-Year Growth Rate in Dividends
0.34	2.09	10.5	1.0%	10.5%
0.34	2.14	NMF	4.0	6.0
0.34	6.48	NMF	3.5	6.5
0.34	1.18	NMF	0.0	0.0
0.34	1.84	16.8	8.0	10.0
0.57	1.43	42.6	7.5	7.0
0.47	1.05	NMF	6.5	3.0
0.49	1.39	30.7	6.5	6.0
0.55	1.08	NMF	4.0	2.5
0.38	1.49	NMF	−2.5	−4.0
0.35	0.75	NMF	3.5	4.5
0.48	2.20	NMF	4.5	4.0
0.48	1.03	NMF	2.5	2.5

EXHIBIT 17 Capital Market Information (September 6, 1993)

Exchange Rates

Swedish krona/French franc	1.369
Swedish krona/U.S. dollar	7.83
Swedish krona/Deutsche mark	4.824
Swedish krona/Japanese yen	0.075

Interest Rates

Sweden

Central Bank discount rate (overnight funds)	11.5%
Long-term government bonds	7.79
Long-term corporate bonds (intermediate grade)	9.3

France

Central Bank discount rate (overnight funds)	10.0
Long-term government bonds	6.45
Long-term corporate bonds (intermediate grade)	8.1

Japan

Central Bank discount rate	2.50
Long-term government bonds	4.1

Germany

Bank discount rate	6.75
Long-term government bonds	6.2

United States

Central Bank discount rate	3.00
Long-term government bonds	5.6

Inflation Rates

Current annual rate (mid-1993)	Sweden	3.6%
	France	1.4
Expected inflation in 1994	Sweden	1.9
	France	2.0
Expected inflation in 1995	Sweden	2.5
	France	1.6
Beyond 1995		2.0% both countries

Equity Market Premium (Geometric)

Sweden	6.0%
France	4.5
United States	5.4
Japan	4.0
Germany	4.0

Sources: *OECD Economic Outlook,* June 1993; *Financial Times,* September 6, 1993; and casewriter estimates.

EXHIBIT 18   Share Capital and Ownership Structure

Share capital

Prior to the acquisition of BCP, AB Volvo's share capital was SEK 1,940 M, distributed among 25,282,716 Series A shares and 52,322,293 Series B shares, each with a par value of SEK 25. Series A shares carried 1 vote each and Series B shares ¹⁄₁₀ of a vote each. Series A and B shares carried equal rights to participation in the company's assets and profits.

In conjunction with the acquisition of BCP, a maximum of 11,131,749 new shares would be issued, each with a par value of SEK 25, of which a maximum of 3,441,358 Series A shares, assuming that all BCP shareholders chose to accept the new issue of Volvo shares as consideration. It was assumed that no conversion of Procordia's convertible debentures had occurred after October 20, 1993.

Convertible debenture loans

AB Volvo had convertible debenture loans outstanding in the amount of SEK 1,679 M. At full conversion, share capital increased by SEK 102 M and the number of shares by 4,076,784 B shares.

Ownership structure after the acquisition

The largest shareholders in Volvo, prior to and after the acquisition of BCP, were shown in the table here. The holdings were based on ownership of Volvo at September 30, 1993, and of Procordia at September 13, 1993, and assuming that all BCP shareholders accepted newly issued Volvo shares in the public offer, whereby holders of A shares were assumed to choose Series A Volvo shares.

Change in Share Capital

	No. of Shares	Share Capital (SEK M)
January 1, 1993	77,605,009	1,940
New issue in 1993	11,131,749	278

(continued)

EXHIBIT 18   (*concluded*)

	Volvo Before the New Issue			Volvo After the New Issue		
AB Volvo Shareholders	No. of Shares	% of Votes	% of Capital	No. of Shares	% of Votes	% of Capital
Régie Nationale des Usines Renault SA	6,424,195	10.0	8.3	6,424,195	8.8	7.2
The National Pension Insurance Fund, Fourth Fund managing board	3,066,501	7.5	4.0	4,391,799	7.8	4.9
S-E Bankers fonder AB (savings funds)	2,111,685	5.8	2.7	2,929,455	7.3	3.3
Svenska Handelsbanken pension fund	1,519,640	5.0	2.0	1,641,307	4.7	1.8
Investment AB Cardo (investment company)	1,470,000	4.8	1.9	1,470,000	4.2	1.7
Försäkringsbolaget SPP (pension fund)	3,780,000	4.5	4.9	4,709,098	4.8	5.3
Protorp Förvaltnings AB (investment company)	1,320,100	4.3	1.7	1,320,100	3.8	1.5
Skandia-Gruppen (insurance group)	2,067,516	3.7	2.7	2,518,237	3.9	2.8
Folksam Sak-och livförsäkring, including AMF sjuk (insurance group)	1,888,000	3.6	2.4	2,253,000	3.2	2.5
Parcitas investments SA	995,000	3.3	1.3	995,000	2.9	1.1
Skandinaviska Banken pension fund	800,000	2.6	1.0	806,333	2.3	0.9
Fond 92–94 (wage-earner fund)*	2,150,000	2.5	2.8	2,430,833	2.8	2.7
AMF Pensionsförsäkringar AB (pension fund)	2,269,224	2.5	2.9	2,844,394	2.6	3.2
Nordbanken savings funds†	2,381,970	1.9	3.1	3,024,378	2.0	3.4
Trygg-Hansa Sak-och livförsäkring (insurance group)	3,384,000	1.4	4.4	4,142,341	2.0	4.7
Other shareholders	41,977,178	36.6	53.9	46,836,288	36.9	53.0
Total	77,605,009	100.0	100.0	88,736,758	100.0	100.0

*As per August 31, 1993.
†As per August 25, 1993.

Source: AB Volvo, "Information Prior to Extraordinary General Meeting of Shareholders in AB Volvo, November 9, 1993," p. 31.

Rhône-Poulenc Rorer, Inc.

The interest with which industry analysts, the financial community, and our shareholders have responded to RPR has been encouraging. As evidenced in the strong performance of our stock during 1990 and the attendant decline in the CVR since issuance of the security by Rhône-Poulenc S.A. in August, many among our key audiences have moved from curiosity to confidence in RPR's ability to fulfill its ambitious sales and earnings goals for the future.

Company, 1990 annual report

Leadership requires, first, critical mass in order to compete effectively in research and marketing; second, a global presence to leverage these investments; and third, advantageous partnerships.

Company, 1989 annual report

Désormais, le succès dépend de notre talent et non plus de nos moyens.[1]

In August 1991, a year had elapsed since the $3.2 billion merger that created a major multinational pharmaceutical company, Rhône-Poulenc Rorer (RPR). The merger, noted for its size, novel terms, and ambitiousness, provoked considerable comment and some skepticism about the projected synergies. Now, a year later, the company had shown rapid post-merger integration and initial synergy gains. The skeptics were not completely muzzled, however; some doubted that the growth and cost savings could be sustained.

---

[1]"Henceforth, success depends more on our talents than on financing," a quotation of Igor Landau, president of the Health Sector at Rhône-Poulenc S.A. in Isabelle Chaperon, "Affairs a Suivre," *La Vie Francaise,* June 7, 1991.

This case was prepared by Robert F. Bruner, as a basis for classroom discussion, while he was a Citicorp Global Scholar and visiting professor at INSEAD in Fontainebleau, France. Copyright © 1992 by the University of Virginia Darden School Foundation, Charlottesville, VA. All rights reserved. *No part of this publication may be reproduced, stored in a retrieval system, used in a spreadsheet, or transmitted in any form or by any means— electronic, mechanical, photocopying, recording, or otherwise—without the permission of the Darden School Foundation. For inquiries, please send an e-mail to dardencases@virginia.edu.* Revised 6/98. Version 1.1.

The expected performance of RPR was of crucial importance to at least one shareholder of the company—Rhône-Poulenc S.A., the seventh largest chemical manufacturer in the world, which owned 68 percent of RPR's shares. In the merger, Rhône-Poulenc gave the minority shareholders a "contingent value right" (CVR) that, in effect, promised to pay them on July 31, 1993, any shortfall between $49.13 and the then prevailing stock price. At year-end 1990, Rhône-Poulenc carried this contingent liability on its balance sheet at (French francs) FF 4.96 billion (about U.S.$ 827 million). On August 1, RPR's shares closed at $45.75 and the CVRs closed at $2.50.

THE COMPANY

Rhône-Poulenc Rorer, Inc. (RPR), was created on July 31, 1990, in a merger between Rorer Group, Inc., and the Human Pharmaceutical Business (HPB) of Rhône-Poulenc S.A. As Exhibit 1 indicates, RPR reported sales of $2.9 billion for 1990, but if sales were annualized to include a full year of HPB's operations, RPR's sales would rise to $3.6 billion, ranking it as the 13th largest pharmaceutical firm in the world. (See Exhibits 2 and 3 for comparisons of RPR with its key competitors.) Contenders in the field were numerous, and even the largest firms did not account for more than a 5 percent share of the market.

Worldwide pharmaceutical sales were estimated to be $145 billion, having risen at a rate of 13 percent a year in recent years. The growth rate in worldwide pharmaceutical sales was expected to slow, however, to 9 percent per year.[2] The largest markets were in the United States and Japan, which represented, respectively, sales of $44.5 and $31.3 billion in 1989.

RPR's mission statement dedicated the company to becoming the best pharmaceutical company in the world. This statement had been revised somewhat from a version published in the 1988 annual report (see Exhibit 4 for the comparison). The company defined its products according to three categories. *Strategic products* involved those that already enjoyed a broad international market or were expected to do so. The merger positioned RPR as the leading seller in Europe of over-the-counter (OTC) drugs, with sales of $280 million (see Exhibit 5). These products were earmarked for heavy investment in marketing and were expected to grow at 19.2 percent per year through 1994. (One analyst assumed only 17.2 percent growth because of the maturity of the Maalox brand.)[3] *Specialty items* were defined as products with clearly defined regional markets, or limited sales potential, because of either maturity or the narrowness of the market. These products were expected to grow at about 8.5 percent per year. Finally, RPR estimated that *new products* to be rolled out in the near future would produce sales of $715 million in 1994. Given the uncertainties associated with introducing these products, however, one outside analyst expected only $422 million.[4]

---

[2]P. Chandarana, "Company Report—Rhône-Poulenc Rorer," Elysées Bourse, October 2, 1990.

[3]Chandarana, "Company Report," noted that *Informations Médicales et Statistiques* predicted demand for antacids sold OTC to rise 6.3 percent per year by the year 2000, compared with a 1.3 percent annual fall in sales for prescription antacids. Also, competitors were known to be increasing their marketing efforts to sell OTC antacids.

[4]Chandarana, "Company Report."

In its 1988 annual report, Rorer's chief executive officer, Robert Cawthorn, had celebrated this firm's sales level clearing $1 billion for the first time and reaffirmed the goal of producing growth in earnings of 15 percent or better. An important component of this growth strategy had been a program of acquisitions, because sales growth in the company's existing product lines was characterized as "mature." One observer described the Rorer strategy as "playing offense in an effort to remain independent."[5]

Rhône-Poulenc S.A. (RP), the diversified chemicals manufacturer, owned 68 percent of RPR shares. In turn, the French government owned 100 percent of RP's voting common stock. RP had been nationalized in 1982 and had since struggled to modernize and attain its goal of a ranking among the five largest chemicals producers worldwide. With the French government under its own budgetary pressures, RP's growth had been financed internally and through an increasingly sophisticated series of financings in the corporate capital markets. As yet, RP had not met its stated goals. Analysts expected that RP would be privatized in 1993 after the next general assembly elections in France, when the conservatives were expected to be returned to power.

Following the merger, Rorer's Robert Cawthorn continued as RPR's CEO, although the firm did assign a new chief financial officer and executive in charge of European operations and marketing. (These individuals are profiled in Exhibit 6.) The new senior executives came from Rhône-Poulenc. Outside observers believed that RP would slowly take over the company. Cawthorn, however, considered RPR to be a freestanding pharmaceutical operation with its own mission statement and Rhône-Poulenc S.A. to be merely an important shareholder.[6]

Some observers questioned RPR's claim to cultural integration and independence. The skeptics pointed to the predominantly American management team, an American-style mission statement, and a waning effort on the part of the American executives to learn French.

THE MERGER

Takeover rumors concerning Rorer had first appeared in the late 1980s, as the firm's relatively low cash balance and rising level of debt seemed to be handicapping its strategy of growth by acquisition. The final confirmation of this constraint surfaced in 1989, when Rorer bid for and lost the opportunity to take over the pharmaceutical business of A. H. Robins. Rorer thus surprised analysts with its announcement of a merger with the Human Pharmaceutical Business of Rhône-Poulenc. Later, the news emerged that several companies had expressed an interest in acquiring Rorer, including Hoffman–La Roche, Ciba-Geigy, Sandoz, Yamanouchi, Monsanto, and Du Pont.

The $3.2 billion combination with Rhône-Poulenc coincided with a wave of mergers in the pharmaceutical industry, including Merrill-Dow buying Marion Laboratories, the $2.1 billion acquisition of Genentech by Hoffman–La Roche, SmithKline and Beecham, Bristol-Myers and Squibb, and major joint ventures between Sanofi and Sterling Drug and

---

[5]Janet Novak, "Please Pass the Maalox," *Forbes*, August 7, 1988.
[6]Mike Ward, "RPR Takes the Global Stage," *Financial Times*, July 23, 1991.

between Du Pont and Merck. One observer commented, "Early evidence shows that the few mega-mergers that have been completed have been a stunning success, and we anticipate further duplication."[7]

Prior to the RPR combination, Rhône-Poulenc's Human Pharmaceutical Business had virtually no position in the United States and Japan, although it was strong in some European Community markets. Moreover, its channels of distribution were not fully utilized. Rorer, on the other hand, lacked a position in Europe and the channels with which to access the market. After the combination, the company ranked among the top three in Europe and had improved its position in the United States. One goal of the company was to rank in the top 10 pharmaceutical companies worldwide.

The merger was consummated in a three-stage transaction, by which Rhône-Poulenc obtained 68 percent of Rorer's common stock (91.6 million shares), which was enough to permit Rhône-Poulenc to consolidate Rorer's results for financial reporting.[8] First, Rhône-Poulenc would tender for 50.1 percent (43.2 million shares) of Rorer's common stock for $36.50 cash per share. (Rhône-Poulenc, by borrowing the funds to finance the tender offer, increased its debt/capital ratio to 45 percent, well above competitors' capitalizations of 20–30 percent.)

Second, Rorer assumed $265 million of RP debt (guaranteed by RP), made a $20 million cash payment to RP, and issued 48.4 million new common shares to RP in exchange for RP's HPB division.[9] Observers believed that Rorer's bylaws would require at least 85 percent of all shares be voted in favor of the issuance of new shares and, more generally, of this entire transaction.

Third, Rhône-Poulenc issued the 41.8 million CVRs to the remaining minority shareholders in Rorer. A CVR entitled the holder to the right at the end of three years, July 31, 1993 (or four years, at RP's option), to a cash payment of U.S.$49.13 (or $53.06 if the payment were made at the end of four years) reduced by the higher of the value of the RPR share at that date or $26.00. Thus, if the value of the RPR share exceeded $49.13 (or $53.06), there would be no payment. The maximum amount of RP's liability on December 31, 1990, was FF4,960 million (FF5,165 million at the date of the issuance of the rights).[10]

The total market value of the rights on December 31, 1990, was FF844 million (FF1,306 million at the date of their issuance). The maximum amount of RP's liability at the date of issuance was hedged. Any changes in the value of the CVRs resulting from fluctuations in exchange rates, as well as the amortization of the cost of the hedge, were recorded directly into the consolidated equity of RP. The CVRs were quoted on the American Stock Exchange and traded independently of the shares of RPR, which were listed on the New York Stock Exchange (NYSE).

---

[7]Alan Archer, "Alliances Offer a Model," *Financial Times,* July 23, 1991.

[8]RPR split its common shares 2:1 on May 17, 1991. To avoid unnecessary confusion, all share numbers and prices reported in this case are given on a post-split basis. Actually, the acquisition terms involved half the number of shares and twice the share price reported here.

[9]The transfer of RP's health sector excluded RP's business units in veterinary products, serums, and vaccines and the firm's minority interest in a French pharmaceutical concern, Roussel-Uclaf.

[10]In general, the disclosure of contingent liabilities by a firm depended on whether the likelihood of realizing the liability was probable, possible, or remote. If the probability of realization was less than 50 percent, accounting conventions required that the liability be disclosed in the footnotes to the financial statements. The accounting rules contained no prescribed way, however, to estimate the magnitude of contingent liabilities.

Rorer and Rhône-Poulenc jointly announced that they believed that the package of CVR and minority share in RPR was worth $36.50 and thus equal to the price at which RP was tendering for shares of RPR. Rorer investors responded favorably to the announcement of an agreement in principle to merge. During the week of the announcement (January 12–19, 1990), Rorer shares increased by $7.313 over the ex ante share price of $24.625, or 28 percent (net of the changes in the Standard & Poor's 500 index over the week). This gain equaled about $632 million in new value. Meanwhile, RP's nonvoting common shares, traded on the Paris Bourse and the NYSE, lost 4.4 percent net of market during the announcement week, or about $175 million.

On April 7, 1990, Warren Buffett, an American investor with an unusually successful money-management record, announced that he had acquired 8 million shares of Rorer (5.8 percent of the total) at an average price of $32.85. As of March 31, 1991, RPR's 8,175 minority common stockholders were dominated by large institutional investors, including 30 mutual funds (2.1 million shares), 61 investment advisors (22.1 million shares), 36 banks (2.77 million shares), and 8 insurance companies (4.4 million shares). The institutions accounted for 23 percent of the 137.4 million shares outstanding and 71 percent of the 44 million shares not held by RP.

CVRS AND CONTINGENT PAYMENTS IN ACQUISITIONS

Contingent payments tended to appear in acquisitions involving a large potential difference between the target transaction prices of buyers and sellers or when the sellers were seeking some protection for the remaining minority shareholders against unfair treatment by the acquirer. Acquisitions in the pharmaceutical industry featured some of the most innovative forms of these contingent-payment schemes; Exhibit 7 summarizes the terms of three other contingent deals and compares them with the RPR terms.

CVRs had been used as merger vehicles since 1985, although they did not gain widespread recognition until used in 1989 in the takeover of Marion Laboratories by Merrill-Dow, the pharmaceutical subsidiary of Dow Chemical. The creation of Rhône-Poulenc Rorer was modeled on the Marion/Merrill-Dow deal.

On September 13, 1991, Dow Chemical stunned the markets by announcing that it would redeem for cash the contingent value rights on Marion Merrill shares that were soon to mature. Analysts estimated that the payment per CVR would be about $10.00. Marion Merrill's share price plunged $8.125 to $29.50 on the announcement; the CVRs rose $4.875 to trade at $11.00. The announcement deflated investor expectations that Dow Chemical would extend the life of the CVRs for another year and make a bid for the 32 percent of Marion Merrill that it did not already own. Analysts pointed out that Marion Merrill's growth appeared to be slowing because of its failure to find new "blockbuster" drug products in the face of several imminent patent expirations. Indeed, analysts expected that Marion Merrill would not be able to market any new products for several years. Thus, they speculated that for Dow to redeem the rights now would be cheaper than to delay and redeem them in a year and cheaper than buying the remaining shares. Analysts also pointed out that Dow's earnings were under pressure. Dow's share price closed up $0.25 on September 13.

THE OUTLOOK

CEO Cawthorn implemented an aggressive postmerger integration process at RPR that rationalized the merging manufacturing operations, reorganized the R&D function to heighten collaboration and foster the exchange of ideas, and sold nonstrategic assets.[11] The successful postmerger integration permitted RPR to report that synergies and asset sales projected for 1990 were achieved. In its merger prospectus, the company had projected sales and earnings through 1994 (see Exhibit 8), and the results for 1990 and the first two quarters of 1991 were indeed consistent with these projections. Earnings and dividends per share for RPR showed the following trends:

	1988	1989	1990	1991 Quarter 1	1991 Quarter 2
Earnings per share (EPS)	$0.965	$1.215	$0.01	$0.39	$0.50
EPS (before restructuring charges)			1.26		
Dividends per share	$0.40	$0.41	$0.42	$0.105	$0.11
Return on equity	13.8%	14.7%	20.8%	—	—

Observers worried, however, about the sustainability of RPR's record. First, the cost of new-product development in the industry was rising—from an average $125 million per product in 1987 to $230 million in 1990. Industry R&D expenditures had been rising 15 percent per year since 1985, yet the number of new drug applications worldwide had fallen at the rate of 10 percent per year (also since 1985). Second, analysts predicted that governments would get tougher on the cost of drugs in an effort to slow down rapidly rising health costs. As a result, demand for drugs might shift from prescription remedies to OTC products. Other strategic risks included patent expiration and competition from low-priced generic drug manufacturers and decreasing product life cycles. On the positive side, analysts noted that computers and biotechnology were aiding new-product development, that the world population was aging, and that RPR was marketing harder than it had, which would boost the payback from its more aggressive R&D spending.

The following table summarizes comments by securities analysts about RPR in early 1991.

RPR's estimated beta was 1.1. The sigma (standard deviation of returns) on RPR shares was about .18 (see Exhibit 9) and compared with an average of .27 for 12 pharmaceutical companies.[12]

---

[11]RPR retained First Boston and Shearson Lehman to assist in the sale of certain assets. Asset sales were managed according to two key objectives: (1) to sell only if the net present value of future cash flows from retaining the assets would be less than the NPV of selling the assets and (2) to achieve earnings neutrality in the future.

[12]Exhibit 9 estimates sigma over the prior 31 weekly closing prices. If sigma were estimated over the prior 52 weeks, its value would be .1875. Estimated over the 79 weeks since RPR shares began trading, the sigma was .266.

Analyst and Date	Expectations for RPR	Comments
J. P. Riccardo, Bear, Stearns, & Co. May 10, 1991 Stock price = $41.00	EPS 1991e $2.33 1992e $3.08 Gross margins will improve from 62.8% to 68% of sales.	The company may struggle to achieve its sales target of $4,050 million in 1991 . . . While we remain concerned over the outlook for 1992, we believe that the Cawthorn-led team will pull off the right strategic moves to insure RPR's stated goals through 1994. On that basis, we would rate the stock a long-term buy.
R. C. Carryl, Value Line August 9, 1991 Stock price = $46.00	1991e $2.25 1992e $2.40	Rhône-Poulenc Rorer appears to be entering a period of sustainable double-digit earnings growth . . . reflecting the shuttering of redundant facilities, a reduction in the employee head-count, and the cross-selling of each other's products . . . Despite the positive long-term earnings outlook, investors looking for a drug stock would do well to consider other opportunities . . . RPR's margin remains well below that of its industry counterparts, primarily reflecting a higher cost of goods sold/sales ratio. Furthermore, with overseas operations accounting for a whopping 75–80% of its total business, the drug maker's income stream is far more sensitive to foreign currency exchange swings than any of its peers. Investors skeptical of RPR's growth prospects might want to consider the contingent value rights (CVRs) which guarantee a cash payment.
Jami Rubin, Smith Barney February 12, 1991 Stock price = $37.50	1991e $2.15 1992e $3.15	We rate Rhône-Poulenc Rorer a *buy*. Because of its dramatic profit margin expansion potential, [it] is expected to be the fastest-growing company in our universe—30% per year compared with 16% per year for our eight-company drug composite . . . Few major Wall Street brokers actively follow the company; therefore, these strong fundamentals are not efficiently reflected in the stock price, in our opinion . . . RPR's explosive EPS growth reflects dramatic margin expansion . . . RPR could trade around $46 per share in 12–18 months.
S. Weisbrod, Merrill Lynch February 26, 1991 Stock price = $40.50	1991e $1.95 1992e $2.90	We recommend purchase . . . by long-term investors. We think the stock is fully valued near term . . . The dramatic margin expansion gives us more confidence in our 1992 and 1993 projections.
P. Chandarana, Elysées Bourse October 2, 1990 Stock price = $30.50	1991e $2.25	A possible long-term buy, but risks on earnings growth and dollar . . . Our own more conservative projections call for sales to advance 12% a year and net 32% . . . Trading at $30.50, the stock has little upward potential . . . Investors could take an interest with an eye on the long term.
Zack's Earnings Estimates March 30, 1991	Average over Eight Analysts 1991e $2.75 1992e $3.63 EPS growth rate next 5 years 21.1% Industry EPS growth 14.2%	

On August 28, 1990, an analyst for Bear Stearns had recommended that investors buy CVRs and RPR common shares at a ratio of 1.4 to 1. At the time, the CVRs were trading at $6.56 and RPR common at $31.50. In March 1991, he recommended that the ratio be adjusted to 1.8 CVRs per 1 share of RPR common; by then the stock price had risen to $40.625. He said,

> You will not lose money (from today's prices) unless RPR EPS falls below $2.50 per share at the CVR expiration in 1993; if RPR does not fall lower than $15 per share, your return will be greater than 10 percent to the CVR expiration.[13]

Exhibit 10 graphs the price movements of RPR's common shares and CVRs after the merger, and Exhibit 11 gives information regarding current capital market conditions. Over the previous 18 months, the price/earnings ratio of the S&P 500 index had varied between 18.07 and 14.21; the P/E ratio at the last market peak (August 25, 1987) was 16.3 times and at the last market trough (August 12, 1982) was 7.6 times.

---

[13]B. Cohen, Bear Stearns & Co., "Rhône-Poulenc Rorer, Research Highlights," March 15, 1991.

EXHIBIT 1   RPR Selected Financial Data (dollars in thousands)

	1988	1989	1990
Net sales	$1,041,612	$1,182,152	$2,917,364
Cost of products sold	377,750	428,626	1,075,992
R&D expenses	103,952	121,806	350,178
Net interest	39,608	41,608	137,801
Restructuring costs	0	9,981	289,256
(Gain) loss on asset sales	7,065	(30,870)	(78,835)
Gain on contract termination fee		(19,949)	
Other expense	11,890	28,828	35,474
Income taxes	33,299	38,848	9,542
Minority interest			6,343
Net income	61,841	86,467	989
Capital expenditures			
New headquarters	10,835	29,308	92,073
Other	59,942	82,107	124,785
Depreciation	56,494	63,817	144,693
Working capital	312,403	436,922	391,391
Property, plant, and equipment	395,651	488,167	1,930,702
Total assets	1,388,012	1,791,716	4,084,982
Long-term debt	564,599	882,525	1,634,352
Shareholders' equity	$ 414,171	$ 439,944	$ 693,454
Employees	8,394	8,527	23,454
Sales per employee	132	140	150

Source: Company 1990 annual report.

EXHIBIT 2   Data on Leading Pharmaceutical Companies

	Home Country	1990 Sales ($m)	1990/91 Growth (%)
Merck	United States	6,425	9.4
Bristol-Myers Squibb	United States	5,980	8.0
Glaxo	United Kingdom	5,286	9.2
SmithKline Beecham	United Kingdom	5,001	0.0
Hoechst	Germany	4,628	18.2
Ciba-Geigy	Switzerland	4,592	11.7
Johnson & Johnson	United States	4,200	12.4
American Home Products	United States	4,022	−3.0
Sandoz	Switzerland	4,005	8.7
Eli Lilly & Co.	United States	3,720	16.8
Bayer	Germany	3,720	8.3
Pfizer	United States	3,684	10.7
Rhône-Poulenc Rorer	**United States/France**	**3,613**	**7.4**
Hoffman–La Roche	Switzerland	3,471	19.6
Takeda	Japan	2,670	−23.9
Schering-Plough	United States	2,652	6.4
ICI	United Kingdom	2,474	8.6
Marion/Merrill-Dow	United States	2,438	3.0
Upjohn	United States	2,420	3.8
Wellcome	United Kingdom	2,260	15.5

Source: Alan Archer, "Alliances Offer a Model," *Financial Times,* July 23, 1991. Sales reported in the article were given in pounds sterling and have been converted here to dollars at the rate of 1.78 to the pound.

EXHIBIT 3   Information on Comparable Firms in the Pharmaceutical Industry

	P/E Ratio	Beta	Long-Term Sigma	Expected Growth of Sales	Expected Growth of Profits	Debt/Equity	Expected Dividend-Payout Ratio
American Home Products	15.0	1.00	.25	7%	10.5%	.124	55%
Bristol-Myers Squibb	21.0	1.00	.29	11	15.0	.042	56
Eli Lilly & Co.	16.3	1.10	.23	16	19.5	.053	41
Marion/Merrill-Dow	17.6	n.a.	n.a.	13	16.0	.111	43
Merck	23.5	1.00	.23	14	17.5	.031	42
Pfizer	22.5	1.05	.28	13	14.0	.031	47
Rhône-Poulenc Rorer	**20.4**	**1.00**	**.176**	**15**	**27.5**	**2.00**	**20***
Schering-Plough	18.0	1.10	n.a.	11	17.5	.087	41
Upjohn	15.8	1.05	.25	9	12.5	.299	41
Warner-Lambert	16.9	1.10	.31	12%	17.0%	.220	42%

*RPR's quarterly dividend had been raised to $.11 per share at the June 30 payment date, up from $.105 per share.

Source: *Value Line Investment Survey,* August 9, 1991. The sigma for RPR was obtained from Exhibit 8 of this case. Sigmas on other firms were obtained from J. Cox and M. Rubinstein, *Options Markets* (Englewood Cliffs, NJ: Prentice-Hall, 1985), pp. 346–58.

EXHIBIT 4   Mission Statement

Mission Statement, 1990 Annual Report	*Mission Statement, 1988 Annual Report*

<table>
<tr>
<td>

Our Mission is to become the BEST pharmaceutical company in the world by dedicating our resources, our talents, and our energies to help improve human health and the quality of life of people throughout the world.

Being the best means:

- Being the BEST at satisfying the needs of everyone we serve, patients, health-care professionals, employees, communities, governments and shareholders;

- Being BETTER AND FASTER than our competitors at discovering and bringing to market important new medicines in selected therapeutic areas;

- Operating with the HIGHEST professional and ethical standards in all our activities, building on the Rhône-Poulenc and Rorer heritage of integrity;

- Being seen as the BEST place to work, attracting and retaining talented people at all levels by creating an environment that encourages them to develop their potential to the full;

- Generating consistently BETTER results than our competitors, through innovation and a total commitment to quality in everything we do.

</td>
<td>

The Rorer Mission

To improve human health while maximizing shareholder value by becoming a world-class pharmaceutical company, able to compete effectively with any other company in selected therapeutic areas in the major developed markets of the world.

The Rorer Credo

We believe:

- That customer satisfaction is our first responsibility. To provide value for the people who benefit from our products and services, we must emphasize quality and integrity in everything we do.

- That we must treat each other fairly, with trust and respect, in an environment that fosters involvement, open communication, and teamwork.

- That we must continually adapt and renew our business. We must encourage and reward innovation, experimentation, and change.

- That we are responsible to the communities in which we work and live. We will actively support civic improvement, better health, and education.

</td>
</tr>
</table>

Source: Company annual reports. Reprinted by permission of Standard & Poor's, a division of The McGraw Hill Companies.

EXHIBIT 5 Data on OTC Drug Sales

A. World Drug Sales (in $ billions)

	Prescription	*OTC*	*Total*
1990	120	25	145
1986	90	20	110

B. OTC Drug Sales in Europe by Company (in $ millions)

	Country of Headquarters	*1990 Sales*
Rhône-Poulenc Rorer	**United States/France**	**280**
Bayer	Germany	210
Sanofi	France	180
SmithKline Beecham	United Kingdom	170
Procter & Gamble	United States	170
Boeringer Ingelheim	Germany	150
Boots	United Kingdom	150
American Home Products	United States	140
Nicholas Laboratories	United States	120
Warner-Lambert	United States	110
Sterling Drug	United States	100
Hoffman–La Roche	Switzerland	100

Source: Clive Cookson, "Roche Deal Puts Fizz in Drugs Race," *Financial Times,* June 4, 1991.

EXHIBIT 6 Profiles of Senior RPR Executives

Robert E. Cawthorn (age 55)
Chairman, president, and CEO. Joined Rorer in 1982 as executive vice president (EVP) and president of its international pharmaceutical subsidiary. President from February 1984; CEO from May 1985. Chairman from May 1986.

Jean-Jacques Bertrand (age 51)
EVP and group president [specifically in charge of Europe, Africa, the Middle East, South America, and Asia (excluding Japan and Korea)]. Served as president, Worldwide Pharmaceutical Operations, of Rhône-Poulenc Santé from 1987 to 1990. From 1985 to 1987, served as president of various RP pharmaceutical operations.

Ralph H. Thurman (age 41)
EVP and group president, North America, Japan/Korea, Australia/New Zealand, and Worldwide Industrial Operations. Vice president, Personnel, from 1985 to 1987. Senior vice president (SVP), Organization and Administration, in 1988. EVP and president of U.S. subsidiary in 1989.

Gilles D. Brisson (age 39)
SVP, Corporate Development. 1989–90 area vice president of Northern Europe for Rhône-Poulenc. 1987–89 deputy SVP of Worldwide Pharmaceutical Operations of Rhône-Poulenc Santé. 1983–87 general manager of Theraplix.

Patrick Langlois (age 45)
SVP and chief financial officer. 1988–90 SVP, Corporate Finance and Acquisitions, of Rhône-Poulenc. 1975–86 director of International Financings of Rhône-Poulenc and finance director.

Source: Company merger proxy statement, 1990.

EXHIBIT 7   Landmark Acquisition Payment Structures in the Pharmaceutical/Biotechnology Industries

Deal	Eli Lilly and Company buys 100% of equity in Hybritech, Inc.	Rhône-Poulenc acquires 68% of equity in Rorer Group, Inc.	Dow Chemical acquires 67% of equity in Marion Laboratories	Roche Holding Ltd. acquires 60% of equity in Genentech
Date of closing	February 1986	July 1990	July 1989	February 1990
Total estimated payment (U.S.$)	$412.8 million	$1,600 million	$5,700 million	$1,295 million
General structure	One-stage exchange per each Hybritech share: (1) $22.00 cash or par value of 10-yr. conv. notes paying 6.75%. Conversion price $66.31 per share. (2) 1.4 warrants to buy Lilly common stock at $75.98 per share. (3) One contingent-payment unit (CPU) paying up to $22.00 in dividends over 10 years.	Three-stage transaction: (1) Cash tender offer for 50.1% of stock in Rorer. At $36.50 for 43.2 million shares, the initial cash outlay is $1,577 million. (2) RP transfers its worldwide HPB to Rorer. Rorer pays RP $20 million and assumes $265 million of RP debt. Rorer issues 48.4 million new common shares to RP. (3) RP issues 41.8 million CVRs (for terms of payment, see text of case).	Two-step transaction: (1) Dow acquires 38.9% of Marion through a cash tender offer at $38 per share. (2) Dow contributes its pharmaceutical subsidiary, Merrill-Dow, and 92 million CVRs in exchange for new Marion shares.	Two-step transaction: (1) Roche purchases a 20% interest in Genentech through the purchase of newly issued shares at $22 per share. (2) All non-Roche common shares are exchanged for $18 cash and ½ share of redeemable common stock. Following the transaction, public shareholders will own 40% of voting stock; Roche will own 60%.
Contingent terms	Annual dividend of CPU equal to: [6% of sales + 20% of gross profits − ($11 million * (1.35^t)] divided by number of Hybritech shares. t = years since 1986. Sales and gross profits are for Hybritech.	CVR entitles holders to receive from RP the amount by which $98.26 a share exceeds either a $52.00 floor price or the average market value of Rorer's share price 60 days before the rights' maturity date of July 31, 1993. Maximum payout $46.26 per share. RP has the right to extend maturity of CVRs for an additional year to July 31, 1994. In that event, the ceiling rises from $98.26 to $106.12. Maximum payout increased to $54.12.	Similar to RP CVR: a "put" spread guarantees shareholder returns within a predetermined range of stock prices through 1992.	Redeemable common stock entitles Roche to redeem the shares at predetermined prices until June 1995. Thereafter, these shares will automatically convert into an equal number of regular common shares. Redemption price starts at $38.00 at closing and rises $1.25 per quarter to the maximum of $60 per share in April–June 1995.

Source: Value Line Investment Survey, 1991. Rhône-Poulenc S.A., Forecasted Financial Performance for Selected Industries.

EXHIBIT 8 Five-Year Projected Financial Performance Forecasted by RPR* (in millions of dollars except per share data)

	1990	1991	1992	1993	1994
Revenues	$2,533	$4,053	$4,657	$5,276	$5,906
Interest expense, net	100	176	168	137	107
Depreciation	131	165	173	186	197
Restructuring costs	218	—	—	—	—
Income before tax	37	497	599	906	1,125
Net income	7	328	462	600	743
Earnings per share	0.065	2.43	3.42	4.45	5.50
Cash	184	135	95	95	95
Total assets	3,371	3,855	3,968	4,141	4,341
Debt (including current portion)	2,021	1,812	1,505	1,158	774
Stockholders' equity	640	902	1,225	1,615	2,061
Capital expenditures	$173	$208	$150	$157	$176
Ratio of debt to debt plus equity	76%	67%	55%	42%	27%
Pretax interest-expense coverage, excluding restructuring costs	3.4×	3.7×	5.0×	7.3×	10.8×

*The financial projections . . . were developed by the managements of Rhône-Poulenc and Rorer Group, Inc., over a period of several months. The projections . . . represent the "base" case in the view of senior management of both Rhône-Poulenc and Rorer Group, Inc. There are numerous assumptions and attendant uncertainties with respect to these projections which are set forth in more detail below.

The 1990 data assume that the transactions are completed on June 30, 1990, and that the combined accounts include 12 months of results for Rorer Group, Inc., and 6 months of results for the Human Pharmaceutical Business as well as interest on the debt incurred in the restructuring from June 30, 1990. The projections also assume provisions of $218 million (before taxes) in 1990 for one-time costs related to the transactions.

The financial projections reflect substantial benefits anticipated from the combination and assume, among other factors: (1) increases in sales of existing products and introduction of new products, receipt of regulatory approvals required for new products within the planned time frames and achievement of marketing plans for both new and existing products; (2) reduction of sales in certain markets from overlapping products; (3) some disruption in sales from the business combination together with declines over time on products which will be less actively marketed by the combined company than previously; (4) exclusion of sales increases which may result from increased marketing emphasis on certain core products by the combined sales force; (5) price increases on existing products of both companies throughout the period on a basis generally consistent with historical experience; (6) improvement in operating margins, particularly in the first three years after the transactions, which improvement is expected to result from the consolidation of manufacturing operations, sales forces, marketing, distribution and administrative functions, and research and development activities.

Source: Rorer Group, Inc., merger proxy statement, 1990.

EXHIBIT 9 Estimation of RPR Stock-Price Volatility across 31 Weeks, January 1991 to August 1991

	Weekly Closing Stock Prices*	Price Relative	Log of Price Relative	Squared Error of Log of Price Relative
Jan. 11	$34.69			
	33.75	0.973	−0.027	0.0012
	34.00	1.007	0.007	0.0000
	34.56	1.016	0.016	0.0001
	35.00	1.013	0.013	0.0000
	36.13	1.032	0.032	0.0006
	38.79	1.074	0.071	0.0041
	39.56	1.022	0.022	0.0002
	40.75	1.030	0.030	0.0005
	40.69	0.999	−0.001	0.0001
	41.44	1.018	0.018	0.0001
	40.44	0.976	−0.024	0.0010
	40.50	1.001	0.001	0.0000
	39.31	0.971	−0.030	0.0014
	39.75	1.011	0.011	0.0000
	39.44	0.992	−0.008	0.0002
	39.56	1.003	−0.003	0.0000
	39.38	0.995	−0.005	0.0001
	41.99	1.066	0.064	0.0033
	41.25	0.985	−0.015	0.0005
	41.19	0.999	−0.001	0.0001
	41.13	0.999	−0.001	0.0001
	41.88	1.018	0.018	0.0001
	42.00	1.003	−.003	0.0000
	42.50	1.012	0.012	0.0000
	41.50	0.976	−0.024	0.0010
	41.63	1.003	0.003	0.0000
	41.75	1.003	0.003	0.0000
	42.38	1.015	0.015	0.0001
	41.50	0.979	−0.021	0.0008
	43.38	1.045	0.044	0.0014
Aug. 2	$45.75	1.055	0.053	0.0021
Sum			0.304	0.017998
Average			0.010	0.000599

Number of price relatives	30
Number of stock prices	31
Adjusted weekly variance	0.000620
Annual variance	0.032
Annual standard deviation	0.180 = Sigma or volatility

Comment: In this table, stock prices are converted into price relatives (which are simply the ratio of today's price to yesterday's price). Then the price relatives are transformed into logarithmic values (in order to normalize the distribution). In the right-hand column, the squared deviations of the logarithmic values are computed from their mean value (0.010). The weekly variance is computed by dividing the sum of the right-hand column (.018) by the number of price relatives (30) and then multiplying by a correction factor (30/29) to adjust for sampling bias. The annual variance is obtained by multiplying the weekly variance by 52. The standard deviation is the square root of annual variance. For a more detailed discussion of this estimation procedure, see J. Cox and M. Rubinstein, *Options Markets* (Englewood Cliffs, NJ: Prentice-Hall, 1985), pp. 255–58.
*These stock prices include dividend payments as of ex dividend dates.

Source of stock prices: Datastream, Inc.

EXHIBIT 10   Graph of Prices of RPR Common Stock and CVRs, July 1990 to July 1991 (all values indexed to 1.00 from first day of trading)

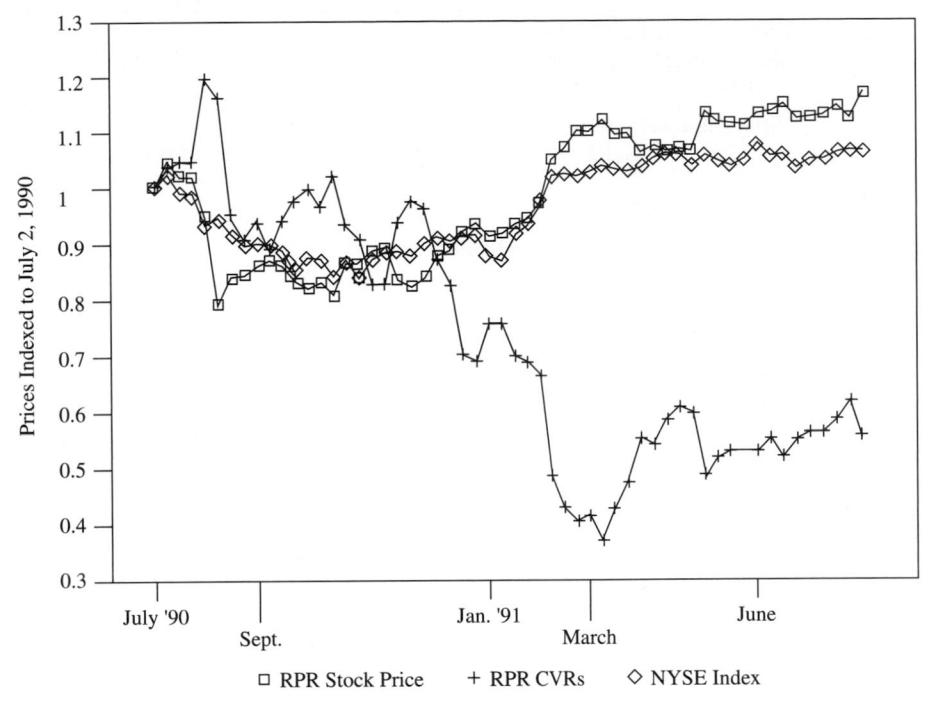

		Security Prices	
	July 2, 1990		*August 1, 1991*
RPR common stock	$36.88		$45.75
RPR CVRs	5.56		2.50
Standard & Poor's index	$196.23		$210.99

Source: Datastream, Inc.

EXHIBIT 11   Current Capital-Market Conditions, Early August 1991

	August 9, 1991	*July 26, 1990*
Equity-market multiples		
Median price/earnings ratio	15.2×	13.3×
Median dividend yield	3.0%	3.7%
Equity-market indexes		
Dow-Jones industrial average	3,017.67	2,920.79
S&P 500 index	380.96	365.91
NASDAQ*/OTC composite index	504.15	455.43
Change in equity-market indexes over past 12 months (%)		
Dow-Jones industrial average	+5.3	+10.8
S&P 500 index	+10.1	+4.1
NASDAQ/OTC composite index	+17.6	−1.6
U.S. Treasury yield curve (yields by maturity, %)		
3-month bills	5.69	7.83
6-month bills	5.89	7.85
1-year notes	6.17	7.90
2-year notes	6.85	8.09
3-year notes	7.09	8.20
5-year notes	7.74	8.26
10-year bonds	8.16	8.47
30-year bonds	8.35	8.53
Benchmark corporate costs of funds (%)		
Prime rate	8.5	10.0
Aaa corporate bond rate	8.9	9.3
Other bond rates:		
A-rated corporates (25 yrs.)	9.6	9.67
A-rated financials (10 yrs.)	9.15	N.Av.
Preferred stocks, dividend yield:		
A-rated utilities	8.99	N.Av.
A-rated financials	9.37	N.Av.

*National Association of Securities Dealers.

Source: *Value Line Investment Survey,* August 9, 1991, and August 3, 1990.

Part IX

Cross-Border Investments into Emerging Markets

The Procter & Gamble Company: Mexico 1991

Dick Druffel, associate director of Procter & Gamble's International Treasury Division, looked over the proposal from Procter & Gamble (P&G) (Mexico) to borrow an average of $55 million over the next three years. The funds would be used to expand and modernize P&G (Mexico)'s manufacturing capacity and to make strategic prepayments of advertising expenses. As part of P&G's globalization strategy, the finance needs of all P&G subsidiaries were coordinated through the head office in Cincinnati, Ohio, in order to "finance the Company's global business at the lowest cost of capital consistent with taking acceptable risk."[1]

The proposal had been presented as a "talk piece" to senior financial management two weeks earlier, on October 6, 1991, and had received preliminary approval. Erik Nelson, vice president of financial operations, had asked for a complete written analysis of the proposal for the board's consideration in November. Despite the soundness of the plan, Druffel knew that convincing the board to agree to the financing package would be an uphill battle, depending as it did on the stability of the Mexican economy for at least the next five years.

PROCTER & GAMBLE

In October 1837, James Gamble and William Procter each contributed $3,596 to start the Procter & Gamble Company as a soap and candle manufacturer in Cincinnati, Ohio. The

---

[1]E. G. Nelson, vice president of financial operations, to E. L. Artzt, chairman and chief executive officer, memorandum of October 14, 1991.

This case was prepared by Peter Williams, MBA 1994, under the supervision of Mark Eaker and Kenneth Eades, professors of business administration. The case was written as a basis for class discussion rather than to illustrate effective or ineffective handling of an administrative situation. Copyright © 1993 by the University of Virginia Darden School Foundation, Charlottesville, VA. All rights reserved. *No part of this publication may be reproduced, stored in a retrieval system, used in a spreadsheet, or transmitted in any form or by any means—electronic, mechanical, photocopying, recording, or otherwise—without the permission of the Darden Foundation. For inquiries, please send an e-mail to dardencases©virginia.edu.* Revised 1/95.

two partners had an eye on the future and, before their partnership was signed, bought land near the Miami-Erie Canal, close to the Cincinnati city limits, as a possible site for a soap and candle factory. Cincinnati's location—linked by rail with Cleveland, Ohio, and the major East Coast cities and by river to the Mississippi and thus the port of New Orleans, Louisiana—contributed to its rapid growth as a manufacturing and distribution center. P&G grew with the city and, by 1848, the company was showing an annual profit of $26,000.

Through careful stockpiling of raw materials and continual experimentation to improve its products, P&G prospered during the Civil War. In 1878, Ivory soap was introduced and proved an immediate success, which catapulted P&G from 40 years of trading in candles, soaps, lard oils, and glycerin into the development of brands that were recognized and requested by consumers. In 1913, P&G started selling directly to retailers in the New York area and, following World War I, expanded its direct selling to retailers nationally. P&G's ability to offer consistent deliveries to retailers paid off in increased profits and a steady flow of business.

Procter & Gamble celebrated its centennial in 1937 with sales of $230 million, 11 manufacturing plants in the United States, 5 in foreign countries (Canada, England, Cuba, and the Philippines), 12 cottonseed mills, and a cellulose-processing plant in Memphis, Tennessee, that was described as "the largest in the world."[2] At the same time, P&G was developing the brand-management system that was to become a fundamental part of its operations. The company continued to broaden its product range, and by 1955, with sales of $966 million and net earnings of $57 million, P&G was reorganized into three separate operating divisions representing the main areas of operations—foods, drugs, and soaps. By the late 1970s, the company had 10 operating divisions worldwide for consumer products and 5 for industrial products. P&G consistently chose products that moved through grocery stores and drugstores, primarily for use in the home. Its products were typically small-unit, low-priced, packaged goods that were purchased frequently.

As the company's product markets matured in the United States, P&G's strategy of expansion through broadening product ranges gave way to a strategy of aggressive geographical expansion in the 1980s. The company was competing in 26 product categories by 1981, 41 by 1990. By 1970, P&G had operations in 20 countries; by 1980, 22 countries; and by 1990, 46 countries. Net sales and earnings grew accordingly, as Exhibit 1 shows, driven by the growth in unit sales. By 1990, P&G's total sales had grown to $24.1 billion, with international sales exceeding $9.6 billion. Net earnings were $1,602 million, up 33 percent from 1989. The company's return on shareholders' equity exceeded 20 percent for the first time since 1950. Exhibit 2 shows net sales, net earnings, and asset distribution by geographical areas of operation for 1979–90.

P&G's chairman of the board and chief executive officer, Edwin Artzt, stated: "Virtually every business in the United States today is touched in some way by global competition. P&G is very well positioned to pursue a strategy of globalization. If we do it right, it will be our principal engine of growth."[3] In his report to the shareholders for the 1990 fiscal year, Artzt further expanded on P&G's global strategies:

> In the 1990s our major focus will be on global planning. We will plan the growth of our investments on a worldwide basis to achieve maximum competitive advantage. We will take advantage

---

[2]Oscar Schisgall, "Eyes on Tomorrow," *Advertising Age* (August 20, 1987).
[3]The Procter & Gamble Company, 1990 annual report.

of our strongest technologies and ideas by reapplying and tailoring them to meet consumer needs everywhere. We will market world brands that share global technology and common positioning, but with appropriate regional testing of product aesthetics and form, packaging materials, and market execution to best satisfy local customer demands for quality and value. Product innovation will flow not only from U.S. research facilities, but increasingly from our major technical centers around the world.

GLOBAL FINANCING AT P&G

In response to the global thrust of P&G's operations, global-financing strategies were needed to minimize overall costs of financing and to maximize overall returns from investments. In considering the financing requirements of its international operations, P&G broadly examined the costs, and risks, of sourcing funds by

- Having a subsidiary independently borrow the necessary capital in its country of operation and in local currency.
- Having a subsidiary independently borrow in the United States, in U.S. dollars.
- Having the parent company guarantee the borrowings of the subsidiary in the United States.
- Directly investing equity from the parent company into the subsidiary.

Each of the four approaches involved a different combination of interest-rate, currency, and sovereign risk. By comparing the anticipated net cost P&G was able to estimate the risk and reward advantages related to those basic options. With funds sourced in local currency, the most significant risk was typically that of fluctuating interest rates. In cases where funds were sourced from the United States, the risk of devaluation of the local currency and sovereign risk were greater. Sovereign risk represented the possibility that restrictions could be placed on the operations of foreign-owned enterprises by the government of the country of operation; such restrictions could range from capital-investment requirements to complete nationalization.

The broad outlines of P&G's global-financing strategy were expressed by Erik Nelson:

> When you look at the regions in which we are now operating around the world, they fall into three broad categories. First, there are the developed, "low-risk" regions, which primarily include North America, Western Europe, and Japan. In these areas, our policy is to borrow in local currency without a parent company guarantee . . . We might also guarantee debt in situations where doing so would provide an attractive interest rate discount versus non-guaranteed borrowing. We wouldn't expect to see this very often, since real interest rates (nominal rates less inflation) tend to be very comparable to the United States over time.
>
> Second, there are a number of countries which we classify as "medium risk." Mexico is one such country. They are characterized by high local-currency interest rates (because the governments are trying to keep inflation in check) but significantly lower rates of inflation and devaluation.
>
> Often, the devaluation risk is low enough that the interest-rate savings far outweigh the potential devaluation loss. In such cases . . . guaranteeing a dollar loan can often produce substantial savings to the Company . . .

Another option for financing in medium-risk countries would be a capital infusion, with dollars borrowed from the parent company. This is little different from a loan guarantee for borrowing by a subsidiary. The negative to an infusion is that the capital may be blocked by local regulations or involve a substantial dividend-withholding tax. This is usually not the case when repaying borrowed money since the withholding tax usually applies to interest but not principal.

Finally, there are the "high-risk" countries, with Brazil being the classic example. Here we typically have no choice but to infuse capital. Local interest rates are exorbitant. The devaluation risk and market volatility are so great that guaranteed dollar borrowing is imprudent.[4]

MEXICO

Mexico was a tightly controlled colony of Spain for more than 300 years. Independence in 1821 was followed by decades of political struggle, and economic development was slow until the 30 years of internal peace achieved at the end of the 19th century. This period was disrupted by the Mexican Revolution of 1910, which almost completely destroyed the country's economy. Accordingly, although Mexican culture, society, and politics reflected the cumulative development of over 450 years since the Spanish conquest and of the earlier civilizations, the economy of modern Mexico dated from only the 1920s.

Since the 1920s, Mexico's politics were dominated by the Partido Revolucionario Institucional (PRI). The PRI presided over 40 years of strong economic growth with accompanying peace and stability, during which "it became widely accepted that political office allowed exploitation of opportunities of personal enrichment while in office."[5] Real economic growth between 1958 and 1970 averaged 6.8 percent per year, which, with population growth averaging 3.5 percent per year, meant about 3.2 percent real economic growth per capita. Inflation was only 2.9 percent per year, and real interest rates were positive and stable.

The discovery of the massive Chiapas oil field in the late 1970s rapidly increased Mexico's economic growth and prosperity, financed by the massive influx of foreign loans during the presidency of Jose Lopez Portillo (1976–82). An unhealthy side effect of growth during this period was the rapid increase in inflation. With oil priced at the time at $32 per barrel and predicted to rise, to lose by investing in Mexico seemed impossible, but in 1982 the oil-price bubble burst and the economy collapsed. Mexico's external debt was driven to unmanageable levels, resulting in the debt crisis of 1982. To restrain capital flight, the government froze all hard-currency payments. All debts owed to foreign creditors—such as that owed by P&G (Mexico) to U.S. banks—were taken over by the government and converted to pesos. The government deferred all principal repayment on these debts for five years, and when it became apparent that this period would be extended, many foreign loans were discounted by creditors in return for early repayment. President Portillo's successor, Miguel de la Madrid, embarked on an austerity program of fiscal restraint and structural economic reform that caused high levels of political unrest and internal friction.

---

[4]E. G. Nelson, vice president of Financial Operations, to E. L. Artzt, chairman of the board and chief executive officer, memorandum of October 14, 1991.

[5]*Economist Intelligence Unit Country Profile 1992–93: Mexico*, p. 4.

Since 1987, Mexican economic policy had featured a series of government/labor/private-sector economic pacts that combined traditional austerity measures (tight fiscal and monetary policies) with wage, price, and exchange-rate controls. The policies had been successful in restoring economic confidence and reducing inflation, while avoiding a sharp recession. External debt as a ratio of gross domestic product (GDP) fell from 47 percent in 1989 to 36 percent in 1991 and was expected to decrease further in 1992. The government maintained tight fiscal control and the public-sector deficit had fallen accordingly, from 4.0 percent of GDP in 1990 to 1.5 percent of GDP in 1991. A federal-budget surplus of 0.8 percent of GDP was predicted for 1992, excluding revenue from sales of state-owned enterprises, many of which were privatized, with a reduction from 1,155 directly owned by the government in 1982, to 280 by 1990. Of these, nearly 150 were expected to be sold by the end of 1992. The changes in Mexican economic policy are reflected in the exchange- and interest-rate data for Mexico for the period 1970–89, shown in Exhibit 3. Overall economic data for Mexico for 1987–93 (estimated) are shown in Exhibit 4.

In 1991, Mexico had a mixed economy, with the government dominant in the areas of public utilities, petroleum, banking, and some manufacturing industries. The economy was becoming broad-based, and dependence on petroleum exports was reduced: Petroleum accounted for only 29 percent of exports in 1991, down from 77 percent in 1982. Agriculture was dominated by the government's support through crop purchases and financing of cooperatives. Private enterprise dominated in manufacturing, mining, commerce, entertainment, and service industries. Key economic indicators for 1990–91 are shown in Exhibit 5.

The major economic goals of the government of Mexico in 1991 were to lower inflation, modernize the economy, and improve living standards for the poorest segments of society. The policies adopted by the government to control inflation included (1) reducing the fiscal deficit and the public-sector internal debt, (2) controlling aggregate demand, (3) trying to temper real-wage increases, (4) limiting price increases through rapid growth in imports that forced price competition and through restraints on price increases, and (5) sterilizing a large proportion of capital inflows.

These policies were combined with measures designed to encourage foreign direct investment in Mexico: (1) control of the rate of devaluation of the peso to achieve a target of 5.5 percent devaluation per year; (2) lowered tax rates, with the maximum corporate tax rate declining from 39.2 percent in 1988 to 35 percent in 1991; and (3) relaxed restrictions on the movement of foreign capital. (Exhibit 6 shows money and credit data for Mexico for 1986–91. Comparisons of income-tax rates in the United States, Canada, and Mexico are shown in Exhibit 7.) The government planned to continue the current economic policies and hoped to see increased investment and economic growth from the North American Free Trade Agreement.

Mexico's political reform lagged behind its economic reform. *The Economist* reported:

President Salinas, who took office on December 1, 1988, promised a new era of pluralism and consultation as well as more transparency in political life. And, indeed, when the PRI conceded that gubernatorial elections held in Baja California Norte in July 1989 had been won by the PAN [an opposition party] candidate, he seemed to be sticking to his promises. Never before had the PRI lost a state governorship. However, since then, progress towards political modernization has been erratic . . . The numerous elections held since President Salinas came to office have demonstrated that a part of the ruling PRI is strongly opposed to relinquishing power and hence the practice of electoral alchemy has continued.[6]

The PRI won the July 1988 elections by its narrowest margin ever, with presidential candidate Carlos Salinas de Gortari receiving 50.4 percent of the official votes. In prior elections, the PRI had normally captured more than 90 percent of the official votes. The next elections were scheduled for December 1994.

PROCTER & GAMBLE (MEXICO)

Organized in 1948 under the laws of the United Mexican States as a limited liability company *(sociedad anonima de capital variable),* Procter & Gamble (Mexico) was a wholly owned subsidiary of Procter & Gamble. Within Mexico, P&G (Mexico) competed in 18 product categories, whose aggregate market size was approximately $2.5 billion. As P&G's largest operating subsidiary in Latin America, P&G (Mexico) was ranked first in 1991 in unit shipments and seventh in revenues among P&G's international subsidiaries. Headquartered in Mexico City, P&G (Mexico) owned two manufacturing facilities and operated another three, including the largest synthetic-detergent plant in the world. P&G (Mexico) had 18 product categories, as against 41 in the United States, and manufactured in Mexico all the established brands that were sold there.

During the 1980s, P&G (Mexico), like most international companies, suffered from the severely restrictive legislative environment in Mexico. Foreign corporations were allowed to expand in Mexico only with proportionately increasing Mexican partnerships. In addition, the debt crisis of 1982 and subsequent freezing of foreign-debt repayments locked P&G into repaying dollar loans with rapidly devaluing local peso income. P&G had been negatively affected by the rule changes that occurred during the period.

In 1990, as Dick Druffel later reported, "we sensed a change in the investment climate in Mexico and regained confidence in our opportunities. We began to lay plans to develop our business in Mexico in line with the dramatically improved business environment."[7] In an August 1991 report on Mexico (Exhibit 8), Treasury analyst E. Romero predicted a much-improved outlook for business and prepared a proposal for financing capital investment by P&G (Mexico).

Druffel reported that the proposal was

to grow the business we needed to increase and modernize our manufacturing capacity and [we] were looking to make capital investments of at least $150 million over the three-year period. On top of that, we would need to finance a significant increase in working capital and start-up costs from new-product introductions. At this point, our business plans were far from firm, but were well enough defined that we could begin planning on how to finance them.[8]

---

[6]Ibid.
[7]Dick Druffel, speech at Financial Executive Institute, Mexican conference.
[8]Ibid.

Approximately 20 percent of the capital needs would be in dollars, with the remaining 80 percent in pesos.

The investment program would be financed by cash surpluses generated by P&G (Mexico) and by borrowing. The average indebtedness over the three years was expected to be $55 million but could vary by as much as 20 percent more or less, depending on the needs of the capital-investment program as well as the cash surpluses generated by P&G (Mexico). In August 1991, Romero had prepared comparisons of financing costs based on borrowing in Mexico and in the United States. Equity investment was ruled out because of the relatively short time frame of the financing needed. Two basic options were considered:

- *Borrowing in Mexico, in pesos.* P&G (Mexico) could borrow directly from banks in Mexico on an "as-needed" basis. The P&G parent company would approve the borrowings but would play no active part in securing the loans. Only variable-interest loans for short- and medium-term financing were obtainable. Interest rates to P&G (Mexico) would start at about 29 percent but were expected to come down over the three years so that the average interest rate paid would be 22 percent per year. The dollar financing needed would be purchased when needed by P&G (Mexico), using pesos. The main risk in borrowing in pesos was that interest rates might remain high, or even increase. There would, however, be no devaluation risk and no increase in sovereign risk. Another advantage of borrowing in pesos was the closeness of contact and communication between P&G (Mexico) and the issuing banks in Mexico, which would result in greater flexibility in matching drawdowns of funds with investment needs.
- *Borrowing in the United States, in dollars.* There were two ways that P&G could effect borrowing in the United States to provide the financing needed by P&G (Mexico). First, P&G (Mexico) could borrow directly from U.S. banks, with the approval, but not active participation, of P&G. Indications were that the interest rate for such a loan would average 12 percent per year over the next three years. Second, P&G (Mexico) could borrow directly from U.S. banks, with the loans guaranteed by P&G. Citibank had quoted an average interest rate of 7 percent per year for the guaranteed loan. If the loan were not guaranteed by P&G, the risks would be borne largely by the lender, whereas the guarantee would bind P&G to repaying the funds should P&G (Mexico) default. Whether guaranteed or not, the funds would be drawn down by P&G (Mexico) as needed every quarter from the banks in the United States and converted to pesos or used as dollars, depending on investment needs. Both the guaranteed and unguaranteed loans would carry fixed interest rates, removing the risk of floating interest rates. However, sovereign risk and the risk of devaluation of the peso remained.

In preparing the financing-cost comparisons (Exhibit 9), Romero projected inflation in Mexico of 14 percent for 1991–92, declining to 9.3 percent by 1993–94. The expected devaluations of the peso against the dollar were projected to be 4.7 percent in 1991–92, declining to 4.3 percent by 1993–94. Income tax was expected to remain at 35 percent, with the social contribution tax of 10 percent of income bringing the overall tax rate payable by P&G (Mexico) on income to 45 percent per year.

In addition, the effect of the inflationary component tax had to be considered. The inflationary component tax provided monthly tax benefits to corporations equivalent to the book value of monetary assets at month-end, multiplied by the government's official estimate of inflation during the month, multiplied by 45 percent. Similarly, liabilities were penalized by the government by a tax equivalent to the book value of liabilities at month-end, multiplied by the government's official estimate of inflation during the month, multiplied by 45 percent.

As an example, a loan taken out in Mexico for $100,000 for a year in which the official estimate of inflation was 14 percent would result in a tax expense of 14% × $100,000 × 45% = $6,300. The $100,000 invested in the same year would result in a tax credit of the same amount. Thus, the effect of the inflationary component tax was to reward equity investments and discourage speculative investments in assets that would not be shown on a balance sheet in Mexico (such as foreign currency) using borrowed funds.

As an additional financing option, Citibank suggested that if P&G (Mexico) were to increase its borrowings, they would be able to issue medium-term maturity debt notes (MTNs), guaranteed by P&G, directly to the U.S. financial markets. The MTNs would carry fixed interest rates and terms. Citibank estimated that the interest rate payable could then be reduced to an average of 6 percent per year. If the average borrowings over three years were increased to $80 million, the issue would be large enough to warrant a public placement. Citibank's fees for structuring such a public placement would amount to $440,000.

Dick Druffel knew that the estimates of P&G (Mexico)'s borrowing needs could easily be understated. By issuing the MTNs, however, P&G would obtain the full amount of borrowing up front, resulting in cash surpluses initially and, possibly, for all three years. The placement of those surpluses could partially offset the costs of borrowing, depending on what returns could be obtained and at what risk levels. Investment returns in Mexico looked attractive, and establishing an investment portfolio would create an asset that would earn inflationary component tax benefits. The question was, Were the high yields on investment an expression by the market of the risks of investment, or were they being maintained artificially high by the government's economic policies? In either case, borrowing in the United States was exposing P&G to devaluation and sovereign risk. Increasing the borrowing and investing the cash surpluses in Mexico seemed to be doubling that exposure.

There was no doubt in Druffel's mind that conditions in Mexico had changed for the better, but how much and for how long?

EXHIBIT 1   Financial Review, 1981–90 (years ended June 30; dollars in millions except per share amounts)

	1981[a]	1982	1983[b]	1984
Net sales	$11,416	$11,994	$12,452	$12,946
Net earnings	$ 668	$ 777	$ 866	$ 890
Net earnings per common share	$ 2.02	$ 2.35	$ 2.61	$ 2.67
Net earnings as percentage of net sales	5.85%	6.48%	6.95%	6.87%
Dividends per common share	$ 0.95	$ 1.03	$ 1.13	$ 1.20

[a]Excludes in 1981 an extraordinary charge of $75 million ($.23 per common share) associated with the suspension of sale of Rely tampons.
[b]Net earnings and dividends per common share have been adjusted for the stock splits in 1983 and 1989.
[c]Includes in June 1987 a charge of $459 million ($1.36 per common share) associated with a provision for restructuring.

Source: The Procter & Gamble Company, 1990 annual report.

1985	1986	1987[c]	1988	1989[b]	1990
$13,552	$15,439	$17,000	$19,336	$21,398	$24,081
$ 635	$ 709	$ 327	$ 1,020	$ 1,206	$ 1,602
$ 1.90	$ 2.10	$ 0.94	$ 2.98	$ 3.56	$ 4.49
4.69%	4.59%	1.92%	5.28%	5.64%	6.65%
$ 1.30	$ 1.31	$ 1.35	$ 1.38	$ 1.50	$ 1.75

EXHIBIT 2   Net Sales, Net Earnings, and Asset Distribution by Geographical Area, 1979–90 (dollars in millions)

	United States	*International*	*Corporate*	*Total*
		Net Sales		
1979	$ 6,722	$2,871	$(264)	$ 9,329
1980	7,637	3,493	(358)	10,772
1981	8,044	3,750	(378)	11,416
1982	8,610	3,737	(353)	11,994
1983	9,074	3,685	(307)	12,452
1984	9,554	3,737	(345)	12,946
1985	10,243	3,625	(310)	13,552
1986	11,210	4,490	(261)	15,439
1987	11,805	5,524	(329)	17,000
1988	12,423	7,294	(381)	19,336
1989	13,312	8,529	(443)	21,398
1990	**$14,962**	**$9,618**	**$(499)**	**$24,081**
		Net Earnings		
1979	$ 467	$ 115	$ (7)	$ 575
1980	519	148	(27)	640
1981	556	130	(18)	668
1982	685	88	4	777
1983	758	105	3	866
1984	707	125	58	890
1985	521	96	18	635
1986	612	165	(68)	709
1987	329	120	(122)	327
1988	864	305	(149)	1,020
1989	927	417	(138)	1,206
1990	**$ 1,304**	**$467**	**$(169)**	**$ 1,602**
		Assets		
1979	$ 3,575	$1,360	$ 745	$ 5,680
1980	4,219	1,750	603	6,572
1981	4,397	1,769	795	6,961
1982	5,054	1,700	756	7,510
1983	5,344	1,614	1,177	8,135
1984	6,072	1,740	1,086	8,898
1985	6,829	1,946	908	9,683
1986	8,394	3,461	1,200	13,055
1987	8,483	3,849	1,383	13,715
1988	8,346	4,751	1,723	14,820
1989	8,669	5,260	2,422	16,351
1990	**$ 9,742**	**$6,516**	**$2,229**	**$18,487**

Source: The Procter & Gamble Company, annual reports.

EXHIBIT 3   Mexican Exchange Rates, Interest Rates, and Inflation, 1970–89

Year	Exchange Rate (Pesos per U.S.$)	Treasury Bill Rate	Time-Deposit Rate	Commercial-Bank Lending Rate	Consumer Price Index*
1970	12.50				21.68%
1971	12.50				22.82
1972	12.50				23.96
1973	12.50				26.62
1974	12.50				33.09
1975	12.50				38.03
1976	20.00				44.11
1977	22.70		11.00%		57.04
1978	22.70	12.75%	12.00	18.20%	66.93
1979	22.80	17.89	16.75	19.90	79.10
1980	23.30	27.73	26.15	28.10	100.00
1981	26.20	33.23	31.82	36.60	127.90
1982	96.50	57.44	52.54	46.02	203.30
1983	143.90	53.78	54.70	63.03	410.20
1984	192.60	49.18	47.78	54.73%	679.00
1985	371.70	63.20	59.48		1,070.98
1986	923.50	88.57	84.68		1,994.16
1987	2,209.70	103.07	97.24		4,623.41
1988	2,281.00	69.15	63.65		9,902.26
1989	2,641.00	45.01%	36.25%		11,883.57%

*Base year for inflation: 1980 = 100%.

Source: International Monetary Fund, *International Financial Statistics Yearbooks 1980, 1985, 1990, 1992.*

EXHIBIT 4   Mexican Economic Data, 1987–93

	1987	1988	1989	1990	1991*	1992*	1993*
Real GDP % change	1.70	1.40	3.10	3.90	3.80	4.60	5.30
CPI % change	132.00	114.00	20.00	27.00	16.00	12.00	10.00
Devaluation %	125.00	65.00	8.30	14.20	5.00	4.80	4.50
Central Bank reserves ($bn)	13.70	6.60	6.90	10.00	16.90	15.30	15.00
Govt. exp. as % of GDP	15.40	10.80	6.80	4.20	1.60	2.10	3.80
Oil as % of total exports	41.80	32.60	34.60	33.30	29.00	25.00	22.00

*Forecast.

Source: The Procter & Gamble Company, Treasury Division.

EXHIBIT 5   Key Mexican Economic Indicators, 1990–91

	1990	*1991*
Domestic economy		
Population (year-end, in millions)	82.40	$84.00
Population growth (% change, p.a.)	2.00%	2.00%
GDP, current U.S.$ (billion)	$241.90	$283.60
GDP per capita, current U.S.$	$2,935.70	$3,376.20
Real GDP growth (% change, p.a.)	4.40%	3.60%
Real GDP per capita growth (% change, p.a.)	2.40%	1.60%
Consumer price index (% change, p.a.)	29.90%	18.80%
Money supply (M1) (% change, p.a.)	62.60%	122.20%
Production and employment		
Labor force (year-end, in millions)	26.20	26.80
Open unemployment (% of workforce)	4.00%	3.20%
Real industrial production (% change, p.a.)	5.50%	3.10%
Gross fixed investment (% GDP)	18.80%	19.70%
Govt. financial deficit (% GDP)	4.00%	1.50%
Balance of payments (U.S.$bn)		
Exports (F.O.B.)	$26.80	$27.10
Imports (F.O.B.)	$31.20	$38.20
Trade balance	$(4.40)	$(11.10)
Current account balance	$(7.10)	$(13.30)
Foreign direct investment	$2.60	$4.80
Foreign portfolio investment	$2.00	$7.50
Capital account	$8.20	$20.20
E & OE	$2.20	$1.20
Foreign-exchange reserves (year-end)	$10.20	$17.50
Foreign debt (year-end)	$40.60	$35.60
Foreign debt/GDP (%)	40.60%	35.60%
Average exchange rate (pesos per dollar)	2,807.30	3,006.80
Foreign direct investment (U.S.$bn)		
Total (cumulative)	$30.30	$33.90
U.S. (cumulative)	$19.10	$21.50
U.S. share (%)	63.00%	63.40%
U.S.–Mexico trade (U.S.$bn)		
U.S. exports to Mexico (FAS)	$28.40	$33.30
U.S. imports from Mexico (CUS)	$30.20	$31.20
Trade balance	$(1.80)	$2.10
U.S. share of Mexican exports (%)	69.80%	70.00%
U.S. share of Mexican imports (%)	64.60%	67.00%

Source: Market reports, 1992 National Trade Data Bank.

EXHIBIT 6   Money and Credit Data for Mexico, 1986–91 (in billions of pesos unless otherwise indicated; year-end)

	1986	*1987*	*1988*	*1989*	*1990*	*1991*
Currency in circulation	3,067	7,339	13,201	18,030	24,689	32,513
Demand deposits	2,468	4,928	7,130	10,279	21,847	72,772
Money (M1), incl. others	5,790	12,627	21,191	29,087	47,439	106,227
M1 growth (%)	67.2	118.0	67.8	37.3	63.1	123.9
Quasi money	15,500	40,029	22,257	64,731	117,513	140,108
Money (M2)[*]	21,290	52,656	43,448	93,818	164,952	246,335
M2 growth (%)[*]	78.4	147.3	(19.0)	115.7	75.8	49.3
Domestic credit	33,815	69,118	115,328	167,930	237,896	322,575
Claims on central government	21,060	37,585	63,915	72,515	85,372	83,276
Claims on local government	92	251	322	1,506	2,695	3,902
Claims on public sector	2,838	5,789	6,737	9,484	6,835	3,321
Claims on private sector	8,758	22,608	41,346	81,693	141,733	228,924
Claims on other financial institutions	1,067	2,885	3,008	2,732	1,261	3,152
Net foreign assets	3,854	23,388	6,493	7,388	9,868	23,958
Memorandum item Average cost of funds (CPP, % annual rate)	80.9	94.6	67.6	44.6	37.1	22.6

[*]M2 does not include money-market instruments, an important component of bank funding in 1988–89. The figures for M2 growth in those years are thus somewhat misleading.

Source: IMF, *International Financial Statistics,* as reported in *Economist Intelligence Unit Country Profile 1992–93: Mexico.*

EXHIBIT 7   Comparative Tax Rates: Mexico, United States, Canada

	Combined Corporate Income Tax			
	Minimum	*Intermediate*	*Maximum*	*Average*
Mexico				35.00%[*]
United States	34.00%	38.60%	43.10%	38.30%
Canada	38.80%	43.80%	45.80%	43.30%

*Excludes social contribution tax of 10%.

Source: American Chamber of Commerce of Mexico, *Business Mexico,* 1992.

EXHIBIT 8

FILE MEMORANDUM   August 22, 1991
                                                                   R.L.: 9/92

MEXICO OUTLOOK

The ruling government has been able to achieve economic/political stability in a relatively short period of time by making fundamental changes to economic and fiscal policy. Included among these changes have been a lowering of tax rates, removing restrictions on foreign capital, and tight monetary control. As a result, Mexico is in the fourth year of economic growth, social spending is up, and inflation has dropped to midteens. The current government is in control and has strong support as evidenced by its 60% approval rating.

Satisfactory progress has been made on inflation. In May the CPI rose 1%, bringing accumulated inflation YTD to 8%. With no official price increases scheduled for the year, the government objective of 15% for 1991 appears feasible. More skeptical sources are forecasting a 21% inflation rate, which is still well below recent levels.

It is widely assumed that the managed devaluation of .04 pesos per day will continue until year-end, leading to a 5.5% annual devaluation. To date, Mexico has been able to devalue the peso at rates lower than inflation primarily because the demand for dollars has been easily satisfied by significant dollar inflows to capitalize on purposely high peso interest rates. Further, the current predictable daily devaluation policy has made the market comfortable that the peso is under control.

	1988	*1989*	*1990*	*1991(e)*
Inflation	52%	20%	30%	15%
Devaluation	40%	9.5%	11.5%	5.5%

Approval of the Free Trade Agreement is considered to be beneficial for Mexico's exports and growth prospects over the long-term. Further, it is felt this will provide additional momentum to keep the free market/economic rationalization programs moving ahead.

On the external side, the improvement on the trade and current accounts last year was almost entirely due to the windfall of temporarily higher oil prices. Recently, there is evidence of deterioration. Some factors contributing to an increasing deficit are rising imports, a fall in oil prices, and modest growth in non-oil exports. For perspective, the value of exports was 16% higher in the first five months of 1991 compared to a year ago, but imports were 42% higher.

The erosion of the current account will be more than offset by strong private capital inflows (repatriation of capital). In the year to May, approved foreign investment was estimated at U.S.$3.6 billion. Official reserves at the end of March were estimated at U.S.$13 billion, a U.S.$2 billion increase from year-end 1990.

Overall, Mexico currently has the strongest growth in North and Central America. It is estimated that GDP will expand by 4–5% in 1991 and this despite the U.S. recession. Further, the government continues to maintain an attractive investment environment. Moreover, the current administration will be in office through 1994, making a negative policy shift unlikely.

                                                                   E. Romero

Distribution: C. P. Slater, R. C. Stewart, R. T. Druffel, J. Martinez
0753J

EXHIBIT 9   Financing Options: Three-Year Summary

	Assumptions		
	1991–92	*1992–93*	*1993–94*
Debt at start of year ($mn)	0.00	$40.00	$70.00
Borrowings for cash needs ($mn)	$40.00	$30.00	$40.00
Inflation	14.00%	11.00%	9.30%
Devaluation (40 centavo/day by			
government fiat)	4.70%	4.50%	4.30%
Interest rates			
MTN	6.00%	6.00%	6.00%
U.S.$-guaranteed	7.00%	7.00%	7.00%
U.S.$-unguaranteed	12.00%	12.00%	12.00%
Peso	22.00%	22.00%	22.00%
MTN structuring fee ($mn)	$0.44	0.00	0.00
Tax			
Income tax	35.00%	35.00%	35.00%
Social contribution tax	10.00%	10.00%	10.00%
Inflationary component tax			
Penalty on liabilities	45.00%	45.00%	45.00%
Benefit on monetary assets	45.00%	45.00%	45.00%
Average investment return			
Peso	18.50%	14.40%	12.80%
Dollar	9.70%	8.70%	8.00%

Cost Comparisons	*Financing Method*		
	Guaranteed $	*Unguaranteed $*	*Peso*
3-year average debt ($mn)	$55.0	$55.0	$55.0
Interest rate	7.0%	12.0%	22.0%
Interest expense ($mn)	$(11.6)	$(19.8)	$(36.3)
Structuring fee	0.0	0.0	0.0
Devaluation effect	$(7.4)	$(7.4)	0.0
Total pretax cost	$(19.0)	$(27.2)	$(36.3)
Tax relief on debt	$8.5	$12.2	$16.3
Inflationary component tax	$(8.5)	$(8.5)	$(8.5)
Total after-tax cost	$(18.95)	$(23.5)	$(28.5)
Difference vs. minimum cost	0.0	$(4.54)	$(9.53)

Case 46

Paginas Amarelas

In July 1996, Brasil Investimentos retained J. P. Morgan & Company to advise it regarding a sale or restructuring of its subsidiary in the telephone-directory business, Paginas Amarelas. Juan Lopez, a new associate at J. P. Morgan's Latin America M&A group, was given the task of valuing the business. After several days of work and interaction with the client's management, Lopez was able to gain a better understanding of the business and the markets where they operated. He put together a forecast of the future cash flows (in U.S. dollars as requested by the client) for Paginas Amarelas' operations in the three countries in which it competed: Argentina, Brazil, and Chile. Exhibit 1 presents the cash-flow forecasts in local currencies and U.S. dollars. Exhibits 2, 3, and 4 give the discounted-cash-flow (DCF) estimates using various discount rates and growth rates.

The next logical step was to estimate the weighted-average cost of capital (WACC) to serve as a target rate of return for each country operation. This WACC would permit him to determine from the estimates in Exhibits 2, 3, and 4 the DCF value of the three country operations. As he started to work on the task of estimating appropriate discount rates, Lopez realized that this would be much more challenging than calculating the cost of capital for companies operating in the United States.

BRASIL INVESTIMENTOS

The client was a Brazilian industrial conglomerate with 1996 sales forecasted at $1.5 billion. Paginas Amarelas had net annual turnover close to $140 million. Company executives were concerned about major changes taking place in the markets where Paginas Amarelas competed. The recent trend of substantial increases in the number of telephone

This case was prepared from field research by Mario Wanderley under the direction of Professor Robert F. Bruner. The cooperation of P. B. Weymouth of J. P. Morgan & Co. is gratefully acknowledged. The name, industry, and financial data of the client have been disguised. Copyright © 1998 by the Trustees of the University of Virginia Darden School Foundation. *No part of this publication may be reproduced, stored in a retrieval system, used in a spreadsheet, or transmitted in any form or by any means—electronic, mechanical, photocopying, recording, or otherwise—without the permission of the Darden Foundation. For inquiries, please send an e-mail to dardencases@virginia.edu.* Revised 3/98. Version 1.5.

lines in the region was anticipated to continue, and the Brazilian state-owned telephone companies were expected to be privatized throughout 1997 and 1998. New players were expected to enter the telephone-directory business in the region, since many of the local telephone companies to be privatized would be bought by players that owned their own telephone-directory companies. These developments could soon result in a more competitive market place and in reduced margins. In light of this possible future scenario, management felt the need to evaluate quickly the prospective attractiveness of this business.

J. P. MORGAN & COMPANY

J. P. Morgan & Company was a global financial services provider, ranking among the top four U.S. commercial banks and considered a major global player in the investment-banking industry. The new mandate from Brasil Investimentos to advise it regarding strategic alternatives for its telephone-directory business was important to J. P. Morgan. The mandate would help strengthen the relationship with Paginas Amarelas' parent company and strengthen Morgan's leadership position in Latin America. Among the alternatives contemplated by the J. P. Morgan team working on this mandate were the sale or spin-off of Paginas Amarelas.

In estimating the value of a company, J. P. Morgan generally made use of three methods—the (DCF) discounted-cash-flow method, trading multiples, and transaction multiples. The DCF method consisted basically of projecting a company's free cash flows and discounting them by the weighted-average cost of capital (WACC).[1] The cost of capital needed to reflect the operational and financial risks presented by the business, given an estimated long-term capital structure. The trading multiples valuation "provides an estimate of value based on a public peer group"[2] while the transaction multiples valuation "provides a benchmark of value based on prices paid by strategic acquirers."[3]

THE TELEPHONE-DIRECTORY INDUSTRY IN LATIN AMERICA

Telephone-directory companies provided users with a listing of addresses and telephone numbers of essentially all local residential and commercial subscribers. Revenues were derived from advertising space on the listings, sold to businesses and professionals.

A telephone-directory enterprise shared characteristics with several other types of businesses. Similar to any publishing or printing company, it was affected by fluctuations in the cost of paper, printing, and distribution.[4] It provided information for its users, the telephone subscribers, just like information-service providers. It rendered its clients a channel to send

---

[1] WACC = [(After tax cost of debt × Percent of debt) + (Cost of equity × Percent of equity)]

After-tax cost of debt = Cost of debt × (1 − Tax rate)

Cost of equity = Risk-free rate + (Beta × Equity market premium)

[2] J. P. Morgan & Co., client presentation.

[3] Ibid.

[4] In general, telephone-directory companies that owned their own press facilities were not able to utilize 100 percent of their press lines capacity just with their in-house jobs, and were forced to seek contracts to produce other printed matter. Even those telephone-directory companies that outsourced printing and distribution of books were still affected by these price fluctuations.

messages to households, comparable to a direct-marketing company. The telephone-directory business also had a resemblance to newspapers and radio stations since it derived the vast majority of its revenues from advertising. Furthermore, the clientele of telephone-directory companies, newspapers, and radio stations was very similar—small and midsized local businesses and professionals.

In Latin America each municipality typically had only one phone directory. Directory companies were bound by contracts between them and local telephone operators or local authorities to provide a given municipality with the telephone directory. These contracts were awarded through a competitive bid. The highest bidder won on a mix of technical and economic factors. Normally, the economic aspect carried a much higher weight than the technical aspect. Economics usually corresponded to what percentage of advertising revenues (generated through the sale of advertising space on the listings) the directory company was willing to share with the local telephone company or authority. The percentage of revenues shared generally ranged from 40 to 45 percent. The technical part pertained to previous experience in the business and proven publishing and distribution expertise.

These contracts had durations ranging from one to seven years. There were no guarantees that the current provider would be awarded the next contract, since all firms had to go through the same competitive process once the contract expired. In projecting the future cash flows, Lopez estimated the probability of renewal for each local contract, and built that into the model.

The telephone-directory business in Latin America had a cyclical nature, with its level of activities following economic cycles. In recessions, companies typically cut their promotional budgets, spending less money on telephone-directory advertising. A depressed economic environment led clients either to place smaller ads or to forgo advertising. In a booming economy companies increased their advertising expenditures. This cyclicality was not common in developed countries, where advertisers typically viewed telephone directories as a relatively cheap promotional channel and maintained advertising levels even in economic downturns.

The expenses associated with printing the telephone books represented a major portion of a telephone-directory company's costs (see Exhibit 5). As a result, an increase in the number of telephone lines and subscribers raised the company's costs since more books had to be printed and distributed. In developed countries, this additional expense was more than offset by increased advertising revenues, as the expanded audience would give telephone-directory companies the opportunity to command a higher price per square inch of advertising space sold.

In Latin America telephone-directory companies faced a different reality. Local advertisers were very price sensitive and typically had not adopted concepts such as *cost per thousand readers* in allocating their promotional budgets. Therefore, local clients were not willing to pay higher prices for advertising space. Increases in costs could not be passed on to clients. In general, advertisers would only recognize the benefits of a higher audience long after this surge had taken place.

PAGINAS AMARELAS COUNTRY OPERATIONS

Paginas Amarelas had operations in Argentina, Brazil, and Chile. In 1995, the Argentine subsidiary contributed with 33 percent of Paginas Amarelas' total net revenues, while the Brazilian and Chilean units were responsible for 52 and 15 percent of total net revenues, respectively. In Argentina, Paginas Amarelas shared the market with two other telephone-

TABLE 1 Telephone Density under Selected Regional Carriers (as of September 1996 for Latin America)

Carrier	Telefonica Argentina	Telecom Argentina	Telebras (Brazil)	CTC (Chile)	Average of G-7 Countries*
Lines/100 people	20.5	17.2	9.3	14.7	50.4

*The Economist Intelligence Unit, Country Report, Argentina, December 16, 1996.

Source: J. P. Morgan & Co., Equity Research, Weekly Industry Update, January 14, 1997.

directory companies. It had around 32 percent of the total market[5] and had enjoyed a healthy profit margin of around 17 percent. See Exhibit 6 for a representative breakout of revenues and margins. The telephone-directory business in Brazil had four major players. Paginas Amarelas had around 15 percent of the market and had enjoyed net margins of around 18 percent. In Chile, Paginas Amarelas was one of three telephone-directory companies and earned margins similar to those of the Brazilian unit.

The telephone market in the three countries where Paginas Amarelas operated had undergone significant development. Previously, telephone companies in the three countries were state-owned and enjoyed a monopoly (in 1996, this situation still existed in Brazil). The combination of these two factors—government control and no competition—contributed to the low level of services offered, the high prices charged, and the low telephone density in each of these countries.[6]

In Argentina and Chile the privatization of state-owned carriers and the end of the monopoly resulted in superior service and lower service charges, which was followed by a significant increase in the number of lines. The privatization of the Brazilian telephone companies, anticipated to start in late 1997, was expected to yield similar results. Despite recent progress, the telephone density in these countries was still considerably lower than in developed countries (see Table 1), leaving a lot of room for growth.

The foreseen increase in the number of telephone lines in the three countries could lead to lower margins for Paginas Amarelas in the near term. The reduced margins would result from the incremental cost of printing more directories, combined with the inability to pass along the increased expenses to advertisers.

Another aspect often associated with privatization and elimination of monopolies was the entrance of international players into the local market. With the American and European markets maturing, leading telecommunications companies (many of which had a telephone-directory subsidiary) and telephone-directory companies were looking toward high-growth markets abroad. This international expansion had been observed recently in several countries throughout Latin America, including Chile, and was expected to affect the Argentine and Brazilian market.

---

[5]Keep in mind that there was usually only one phone directory per municipality. Therefore, the directory company serving that market enjoyed a 100 percent market share in that city. The 32 percent market share referred to the percent of telephone lines in the country served by Paginas Amarelas.

[6]In Brazil this situation was even more acute, as subscribers had to "buy" their telephone lines. In July 1996, a telephone line in Sao Paulo, Brazil, cost between $2,000 and $4,000 depending on the neighborhood, and would take up to 10 months to be connected after being purchased.

New players would bring increased competition and reduced margins. Municipalities that typically had only one telephone directory could have two or three in the near future. This would probably drive down the price of advertising in this medium.

MAJOR CHANGES IN LATIN AMERICA

Argentina, Brazil, and Chile had each, in the recent past, been under a military dictatorship. In the mid- and late 1980s, democratic systems had replaced these military regimes. The current political situations in all three nations were stable, with the respective democratic systems well established.

The economies of Argentina, Brazil, and Chile had experienced major changes in the past 5 to 10 years. High inflationary environments, especially in Argentina and Brazil, gave way to more stable economies with recent annual inflation rates below 15 percent (see Exhibit 6). Closed markets, protected by high import tariffs, were rapidly being replaced by market economies. International trade had increased significantly since the process of deregulation started to take place and since the creation of Mercosur.[7]

The current governments of each nation had a firm commitment to free markets, privatization, trade liberalization, and low inflation. Such policies had prompted a sharp increase in foreign direct investment and moderate economic growth (see Exhibit 6).

At the end of 1994, the Mexican peso crisis[8] depressed investors' confidence in the region and spread fears that similar problems would occur throughout Latin America. Foreign capital left the region, returning temporarily to the safe havens of developed countries' capital markets. As a result, the local equity markets and currencies from Latin American countries plummeted (see Exhibit 7).

RECENT DEVELOPMENTS IN EACH COUNTRY

Argentina.   With 34 million people, Argentina was the second largest country and economy in South America. It had the largest GDP per capita of the region. In 1983, the democratic regime was reestablished in the country. The Argentine economy reached stability in 1990 when Economy Minister Domingo Cavallo adopted the "Convertibility Plan," introducing a fixed 1:1 exchange rate between the peso and the U.S. dollar. The country enjoyed economic growth (and the president enjoyed great popularity) for almost four years until the Mexican crisis. The Argentine economy was the hardest hit by the peso crisis after the Mexican economy. The country went into deep recession with an economic contraction of 4.6 percent in 1995. Only recently did the Argentine economy show signs of recovery (see Exhibit 5).

---

[7]Mercosur was a free-table bloc comprised of Argentina, Brazil, Paraguay, and Uruguay. It represented a market with over 200 million people and a GDP close to $1 trillion.

[8]The Mexican peso crisis was the result of currency mismanagement. The Mexican government kept the currency at an artificially high value. Subsequently, massive capital flight forced the government to accept a major devaluation.

Notwithstanding recent improvements, unemployment remained at 17 percent. Unemployment rates and political scandals had reduced the popularity and power of President Carlos Menem. Concerns over a currency overvaluation also existed. The Economist Intelligence Unit projected a real GDP growth in Argentina of 3 percent in 1996 and 4.2 percent in 1997.

Brazil.   With a population in excess of 160 million people, Brazil was the largest country and economy in Latin America. It was also the most industrialized country in the region and its biggest market. Its democratic regime was reestablished in 1986. In 1994, after several unsuccessful plans aimed at reducing inflation, a new economic plan introduced by the current president and then finance minister, Mr. Fernando Henrique Cardoso, achieved the desired goal of price stabilization. The plan instituted a new currency, the real (the fifth new currency in a period of eight years). The value of the real was pegged to the dollar, being adjusted gradually within bands. Questions about the sustainability of the currency peg rose after the higher-than-expected fiscal deficit in 1996,[9] and deterioration of the country's balance of foreign trade.

Chile.   In 1996, this small country (with a population of close to 14 million people) was seen as an economic model for many Latin American nations. Under the dictatorship of General Augusto Pinochet, who ruled the nation for 18 years since 1973, the country started the change from a closed economy to a market economy. With the help of a group of Chilean economists, educated at the University of Chicago under Professor Milton Friedman, Pinochet cut government spending, reduced civil service, and privatized several state-owned companies. The government also reduced import tariffs and started an effort to diminish the country's reliance on copper exports. By 1996 the national government had become a constitutional democracy.

The results of such drastic changes were reductions in unemployment, inflation, and interest rates. National savings rates increased to levels comparable to Asian markets, and the Chilean economy had been growing at a pace similar to the economies of the "Asian tigers." Foreign investment was at its highest levels. In the mid-1990s Chilean companies were actually exporting capital and investing overseas.

For the past decade Chile had a much more stable economy than that of any other Latin American nation. The country's short-term outlook was also rosier, with the Economist Intelligence Unit projecting GDP growth of 6.7 percent in 1996 and an average GDP growth of 5.5 percent in 1997–98.

INVESTMENTS IN LATIN AMERICAN SECURITIES

Fixed-income securities of issuers from Argentina, Brazil, and Chile had gained considerable attention from foreign investors. With the growth in investors' appetites for emerging markets' instruments came an increase in the liquidity of some securities, particularly of sovereign debt[10] and local blue-chip companies.

---

[9]Government officials had set a target for 1996 fiscal deficit of 2.5 percent of GDP. It turned out to be 4.2 percent of GDP.

[10]Sovereign debt are debt instruments issued by a foreign nation's government or state-owned institutions that are fully backed by the foreign nation's government.

Foreign investors kept close track of social, economic, and political developments in emerging markets. Some observers believed that their expectations of the future economic and political conditions were reflected in exchange rates (see Exhibits 8, 9, and 10) and in the spread over U.S. Treasury bonds (of similar maturity) of local government bonds and high-quality corporate instruments (see Exhibits 11, 12, and 13). According to this view, yield spreads reflected investors' forward-looking assessment of the country's risk.[11]

VALUATION ANALYSIS

In preparing the cash-flow forecasts in Exhibit 1, Lopez tried to factor in the future impact of the changes occurring in the telephone-directory business in the region. He also sought to take into account any type of synergies that could be enjoyed by a potential buyer. Lopez assumed that all three units would be sold to a single acquirer. Thus, Paginas Amarelas would continue to enjoy some of the synergies that it currently enjoyed, including increased bargaining power when buying paper, printing efficiencies,[12] and the network of contacts that management had throughout the region. One potential source of synergy that Lopez purposely left out was the ability that the single buyer would have to issue international debt on behalf of the three combined units. This added financial flexibility was not taken into account, given the fact that Paginas Amarelas' parent company had not taken advantage of it.

First, he discovered that the telephone-directory industry in Latin America had no local "pure play" competitors,[13] making the determination of a beta for each country operation precarious at best. In addition, the efficiency of the local capital markets was questionable and so would be any estimate of the local market's equity premium. Finally, Lopez was not convinced he would be able to find a security from Argentina, Brazil, and Chile that offered no risk of default.

DETERMINING THE COST OF DEBT

Lopez needed to estimate the cost of capital (WACC) with which to discount free cash flows from Argentina, Brazil, and Chile. He decided to start with the easiest part, estimating the cost of debt.

Brasil Investimentos' executives had stated that the country operations had neither borrowed money at the corporate level, nor as one entity (i.e., the three country operations together as the telephone-directory subsidiary), but only at the country level. Lopez's assessment was that all three local operations were relatively small to issue debt independently in the international markets. They would have to rely on the local markets for their

---

[11]The spread over U.S. Treasury that a given security trades at reflects not only the country risk (risk of expropriation, devaluation/inflation, inconvertibility of currency, political instability, etc.), but also the risk of default that the issuer presents (credit risk).

[12]The Brazilian unit owned its own printing facility, which also served the Argentine and Chilean markets.

[13]Most of the players were subsidiaries of large diversified companies.

borrowing needs. With that in mind, Lopez called J. P. Morgan bankers working at the credit department in offices located in the three countries. He was able to get from them an estimate of the U.S. dollar rates at which each country unit could expect to borrow (see Exhibit 14 for estimated borrowing rates, tax rates, and long-term capital structure).

DETERMINING THE COST OF EQUITY

In pursuing the next step, calculating the cost of equity, Lopez could choose between two different approaches under the capital asset pricing model (CAPM). One approach would be to use local markets' parameters (local risk-free rate, local-market premium and beta). The other approach would be to use U.S. market parameters to come up with a cost of equity, which would then be adjusted to reflect the country risk.

The first path offered several difficulties. Lopez had problems in determining a risk-free rate for each country. He questioned whether there was such a thing as a risk-free rate for countries like Argentina, Brazil, or Chile. He knew that even sovereign bonds, like Brady bonds,[14] offered risk of default, since the governments of these countries had defaulted on debt and interest payments in the recent past.

Another challenge was estimating equity risk premiums for each market. Lopez knew that there was little historical information on equity markets for most Latin American countries. He also realized that when the data were available they usually covered short periods of time. Furthermore, most companies in Argentina, Brazil, and Chile were family owned, and many of them were not listed on stock exchanges. Of those companies listed, only very few were heavily traded and had enough liquidity. Lopez realized that any equity risk premium derived from the data available would not be a good estimate of the premium that investors required when undertaking equity investments in the respective countries.

In addition, he could not find any relevant pure play competitor in the telephone-directory industry. Substantially all the companies operating in this industry owned other types of businesses. Those that did not were too small to provide a realistic comparison. Lopez then wondered how he could come up with a beta for Paginas Amarelas.

Given the difficulties and potential flaws posed by the first alternative, Lopez considered using the second approach—a cost of equity using U.S. parameters but adjusted for country risks stemming from the local political and capital-market environments. This second approach posed the challenge of estimating the "adjusting factors" that would correctly reflect the higher risk offered by equity investments in Argentina, Brazil, and Chile (while still leaving unanswered the question of which beta to use). Lopez sat back and started to think about the appropriate "adjusting factors."

Risk ratings by institutions like the Economist Intelligence Unit (EIU) and DRI/McGraw-Hill furnished some indication of country risk. Risk ratings (for instance, see Table 2) were estimated using several economic data and economic ratios—like the ratio of debt service to exports or foreign reserves, and tried to take into account the

---

[14]Brady bonds were U.S.-dollar-denominated bonds issued by governments of developing countries that were used as exchange for existing bank loans in default. The principal payments of these securities were collateralized (partly or in total) by U.S.-government zero-coupon bonds.

TABLE 2   Economist Intelligence Unit Risk Ratings by Country

	Argentina	Brazil	Chile
EIU risk rating	65	60	25

Source: J. P. Morgan & Co. document.

political situation in the country. Lopez debated whether these ratings were relevant to the valuation that he was conducting. Looking at the EIU risk ratings above, he questioned whether they implied that making an investment in Brazil would be more than two times riskier than making the same investment in Chile.

The idea of calculating a WACC in U.S. dollars and adjusting it with an estimate of country risks brought additional questions to mind: Was this methodology theoretically sound? Should he use one "adjusting factor" for all Latin American countries or one for each country? Should the estimate of country risk used be the same, regardless of one being a foreign or a local investor? Should the discount rate be estimated using U.S. market parameters even when one is dealing with a local prospective buyer?

CONCLUSION

Lopez returned to consider the DCF values in Exhibits 2, 3, and 4. Given an estimate of the investors' required rates of return on investments in Argentina, Brazil, and Chile, he could determine the value of each segment in U.S. dollar terms. The key issue, then, was to find the appropriate dollar required rate of return for the telephone-directory business in each country.

EXHIBIT 1 Cash-Flow Forecasts in Local Currencies and U.S. Dollars

Free Cash Flows in Local Currency

	1997	1998	1999	2000	2001	2002	2003	2004
Argentina (pesos)	6,843	6,993	7,273	7,667	8,238	8,936	9,536	10,159
Brazil (reals)	11,469	12,122	12,850	13,740	14,833	16,167	17,335	18,553
Chile (pesos)	1,337,764	1,415,233	1,497,317	1,593,512	1,704,109	1,839,768	1,954,070	2,071,694

Inflation Forecast*

	1997	1998	1999	2000	2001	2002	2003	2004
Argentina	1.7%	2.5%	4.0%	4.5%	5.5%	5.5%	5.5%	5.5%
Brazil	6.9	6.0	6.0	6.0	6.0	6.0	6.0	6.0
Chile	6.5	6.1	5.8	5.5	5.0	5.0	5.0	5.0
United States	3.0	3.0	3.0	3.0	3.0	3.0	3.0	3.0

Spot Exchange Rates and Forward Exchange Rates (Local Currency: U.S. Dollar)

	July 1996	1997	1998	1999	2000	2001	2002	2003	2004
Argentine peso	1.000	0.987	0.983	0.992	1.007	1.031	1.056	1.082	1.108
Brazilian real	1.012	1.050	1.081	1.112	1.145	1.178	1.212	1.248	1.284
Chilean peso	410.73	424.69	437.47	449.36	460.27	469.21	478.32	487.60	497.07

Free Cash Flows in U.S. Dollars

	1997	1998	1999	2000	2001	2002	2003	2004
Argentina	$6,930	$7,117	$7,331	$7,617	$7,990	$8,462	$8,816	$9,169
Brazil	$10,920	$11,215	$11,551	$12,002	$12,591	$13,334	$13,893	$14,448
Chile	$3,150	$3,235	$3,332	$3,462	$3,632	$3,846	$4,007	$4,168

Note on the estimation of U.S.-dollar cash flows:

Cash flows were translated from local currency to U.S. dollars in the following manner:

1. Cash flows were projected in nominal local currency, taking inflation into account.

2. A forecast of the exchange rate (the forward rate) between the dollar and local currency was based on interest rate parity, which assumes that the exchange rate reflects differences in the inflation rate between the two countries.

3. Cash flows were then converted to U.S. dollars using the estimated exchange rate for each period.

*Casewriter's estimate.

EXHIBIT 2   Argentina: Analysis of Sensitivity of DCF to Variations in WACC and Growth Rate in Perpetuity

The two-way tables below give the DCF values of free cash flow and terminal value, where the terminal value is estimated using the constant growth valuation model with the indicated growth rates in perpetuity.

Argentine Unit—Free Cash Flows and Sensitivity Analysis (in 000s U.S.$)

	1997	1998	1999	2000	2001	2002	2003	2004
FCF	$6,930	$7,117	$7,331	$7,617	$7,990	$8,462	$8,816	$9,169

Discounted-Cash-Flow Values by Growth and WACC

Nominal Growth Rate in Perpetuity

WACC	1%	3%	5%	6%	7%	9%
10.0%	$89,434	$104,371	$131,258	$154,785	$193,995	$507,677
11.0	80,074	91,115	109,516	124,238	146,320	256,730
12.0	72,435	80,814	93,981	103,856	117,682	172,984
13.0	66,086	72,582	82,325	89,285	98,565	131,043
14.0	60,729	65,854	73,256	78,346	84,889	105,828
15.0	56,149	60,253	65,998	69,828	74,616	88,978
16.0	52,192	55,520	60,057	63,006	66,611	76,911
17.0	48,739	51,467	55,104	57,419	60,196	67,834
18.0	45,701	47,959	50,911	52,756	54,937	60,752
19.0	43,009	44,893	47,316	48,806	50,546	55,068
20.0	40,606	42,191	44,198	45,417	46,823	50,401
21.0	38,451	39,792	41,469	42,475	43,625	46,499
22.0	36,506	37,648	39,060	39,898	40,847	43,185
23.0	34,742	35,721	36,917	37,620	38,412	40,334
24.0	33,137	33,979	34,999	35,594	36,259	37,854
25.0	31,670	32,398	33,272	33,778	34,340	35,676

Casewriter's note:
A terminal value for each business unit was calculated using the perpetuity growth formula:

$$\text{Terminal value} = \frac{\text{Last year's cash flow} \times (1 + \text{Growth rate in perpetuity})}{\text{WACC} - \text{Growth rate in perpetuity}}$$

EXHIBIT 3 Brazil: Analysis of Sensitivity of DCF to Variations in WACC and Growth Rate in Perpetuity

The two-way tables below give the DCF values of free cash flow and terminal value, where the terminal value is estimated using the constant growth valuation model with the indicated growth rates in perpetuity.

Brazilian Unit—Free Cash Flows and Sensitivity Analysis (in 000s U.S.$)

	1997	1998	1999	2000	2001	2002	2003	2004
FCF	$10,920	$11,215	$11,551	$12,002	$12,591	$13,334	$13,893	$14,448

Discounted-Cash-Flow Values by Growth and WACC

Nominal Growth Rate in Perpetuity

WACC	1%	3%	5%	6%	7%	9%
10.0%	$140,927	$164,464	$206,831	$243,903	$305,689	$799,975
11.0	126,176	143,574	172,571	195,768	230,564	404,544
12.0	114,139	127,343	148,091	163,652	185,438	272,581
13.0	104,135	114,371	129,725	140,692	155,314	206,493
14.0	95,694	103,769	115,434	123,454	133,765	166,759
15.0	88,478	94,944	103,997	110,032	117,576	140,208
16.0	82,242	87,485	94,635	99,283	104,963	121,193
17.0	76,801	81,100	86,831	90,478	94,854	106,890
18.0	72,014	75,572	80,224	83,131	86,567	95,730
19.0	67,771	70,740	74,558	76,907	79,648	86,774
20.0	63,986	66,483	69,645	71,565	73,781	79,421
21.0	60,589	62,703	65,345	66,930	68,742	73,271
22.0	57,524	59,324	61,548	62,869	64,365	68,049
23.0	54,746	56,288	58,172	59,281	60,528	63,557
24.0	52,216	53,543	55,150	56,087	57,135	59,649
25.0	49,904	51,051	52,429	53,226	54,112	56,216

Casewriter's note:
A terminal value for each business unit was calculated using the perpetuity growth formula:

$$\text{Terminal value} = \frac{\text{Last year's cash flow} \times (1 + \text{Growth rate in perpetuity})}{\text{WACC} - \text{Growth rate in perpetuity}}$$

EXHIBIT 4   Chile: Analysis of Sensitivity of DCF to Variations in WACC and Growth Rate
                 in Perpetuity

The two-way tables below give the DCF values of free cash flow and terminal value, where the
  terminal value is estimated using the constant growth valuation model with the indicated growth
  rates in perpetuity.

Chilean Unit—Free Cash Flows and Sensitivity Analysis (in 000s U.S.$)

	1997	1998	1999	2000	2001	2002	2003	2004
FCF	$3,150	$3,235	$3,332	$3,462	$3,632	$3,846	$4,007	$4,168

Discounted-Cash-Flow Values by Growth and WACC

Nominal Growth Rate in Perpetuity

WACC	1%	3%	5%	6%	7%	9%
10.0%	$40,652	$47,442	$59,663	$70,357	$88,179	$230,762
11.0	36,397	41,416	49,780	56,472	66,509	116,695
12.0	32,925	36,734	42,719	47,207	53,492	78,629
13.0	30,039	32,992	37,421	40,584	44,802	59,565
14.0	27,604	29,933	33,298	35,612	38,586	48,104
15.0	25,522	27,388	29,999	31,740	33,916	40,445
16.0	23,724	25,236	27,299	28,639	30,278	34,959
17.0	22,154	23,394	25,047	26,099	27,362	30,834
18.0	20,773	21,800	23,141	23,980	24,971	27,615
19.0	19,549	20,406	21,507	22,185	22,975	25,031
20.0	18,457	19,178	20,090	20,644	21,283	22,910
21.0	17,478	18,087	18,849	19,307	19,829	21,136
22.0	16,593	17,113	17,754	18,135	18,567	19,630
23.0	15,792	16,237	16,780	17,100	17,460	18,334
24.0	15,062	15,445	15,909	16,179	16,481	17,206
25.0	14,395	14,726	15,124	15,354	15,609	16,216

Casewriter's note:
A terminal value for each business unit was calculated using the perpetuity growth formula.

$$\text{Terminal value} = \frac{\text{Last year's cash flow} \times (1 + \text{Growth rate in perpetuity})}{\text{WACC} - \text{Growth rate in perpetuity}}$$

EXHIBIT 5 1995 Operating Ratios of Paginas Amarelas

	% of Gross Revenues	*% of Net Revenues*
Revenues from ads and insertions		
− Refunds/provisions for bad debt	1.6%	3.0%
Total revenues		
− % to local telephone co.	45.0%	83.3%
Net revenues	54.0%	100.0%
Costs:		
Total printing costs	20.6%	38.2%
Layout costs	1.9%	3.5%
Distribution costs	0.4%	0.8%
Costs from information services	2.0%	3.7%
Variable costs	6.70%	12.4%
Fixed costs	5.08%	9.4%
Gross profit	17.2%	31.9%
Depreciation	0.16%	0.3%
SG&A	3.94%	7.3%
Operating income	13.2%	24.4%
Income taxes	4.6%	8.5%
Net income	8.5%	15.8%

EXHIBIT 6   Historical and Forecast Economic Data for Argentina, Brazil, and Chile

Nominal GDP in US$ Billion

	1992	1993	1994	1995	1996e	1997f	1998f
Argentina	$228.89	$257.85	$281.91	$275.43	$287.35	$305.87	$331.98
Brazil	$364.28	$423.53	$564.82	$717.42	$748.61	$772.43	$798.04
Chile	$ 42.75	$ 5.64	$ 52.18	$ 67.30	$ 75.27	$ 79.46	$ 85.79

Source: J. P. Morgan. *Emerging Markets: Economic Indicators,* January 10, 1997, p. 20.

Real GDP Growth

	1992	1993	1994	1995	1996e	1997f	1998f
Argentina	8.70%	6.00	7.40	−4.40	3.00	4.20	3.10
Brazil	−0.90%	4.70	5.80	4.20	3.20	3.40	3.40
Chile	11.00%	6.30	4.20	8.50	6.70	4.80	6.20

Source: The Economist Intelligence Unit. Country Report from the three countries.

Consumer Prices—% Change from Previous Year

	Dec 93	Dec 94	Dec 95	Jul 96	Nov 96	1997f	1998f
Argentina	7.4%	3.9	1.6	0.0	0.4	1.7	2.5
Brazil	2489.1%	929.3	22.0	14.9	10.6	6.9	6.0
Chile	12.2%	9.0	8.2	7.7	6.6	6.5	6.1

Source: J. P. Morgan. *Emerging Markets: Economic Indicators,* January 10, 1997, p. 7.

Total External Debt in U.S.$ Billion

	1992	1993	1994	1995	1996e	1997f	1998f
Argentina	$ 71.90	$ 76.65	$ 90.71	$ 97.21	$ 99.91	$103.56	$107.91
Brazil	$133.61	$147.35	$157.06	$173.14	$187.10	$194.40	$208.23
Chile	$ 18.96	$ 19.67	$ 21.77	$ 21.83	$ 21.48	$ 23.28	$ 25.98

Source: J. P. Morgan. *Emerging Markets: Economic Indicators,* January 10, 1997, p. 18.

EXHIBIT 6 *(concluded)*

Net Foreign Direct Investment (in U.S.$ Millions)

	1989	1990	1991	1992	1993	1994	1995
Argentina	$1,028	$1,836	$2,439	$2,562	$3,482	$ 477	$1,164
Brazil	$ 608	$ 324	$ 89	$1,924	$ 801	$2,035	$3,475
Chile	$1,279	$ 582	$ 400	$ 321	$ 375	$ 848	$1,008

Source: International Financial Statistics, January 1997, pp. 100, 150, 188.

International Reserves (Excluding Gold, $ Billions)

	1994	1995	Jul 96	Sep 96e	Nov 96e
Argentina	$14.3	$14.3	$14.4	$15.2	$14.9
Brazil	$38.8	$51.8	$59.5	$58.8	$60.5
Chile	$13.1	$14.1	$14.6	$14.6	$15.0

Source: J. P. Morgan. *Emerging Markets: Economic Indicators,* January 10, 1997, p. 15.

Foreign Currency Debt Ratings, July 1996

	Argentina	Brazil	Chile
Moody's	B1	B1	Baa1
S&P	BB−	B+	A−
S&P Outlook	Stable	Positive	Stable

Source: J. P. Morgan. *Latin American Credit Ratings,* January 1997, pp. 1–2.

Equity Markets

Country / Index	Dec 95	Aug 96	Sep 96	Oct 96	Nov 96e	Dec 96e
Argentina / Merval	100	96.8	104.4	103.1	107.5	113.9
Brazil / Ibovespa	100	145.6	150.0	152.0	155.1	163.8
Chile / IGPA	100	92.4	94.3	93.8	88.3	85.4

Source: J. P. Morgan. *Emerging Markets: Economic Indicators,* January 10, 1997, p. 4.

Dec 95 = 100
e = Estimate
f = Forecast

Source: *Emerging Markets: Economic Indicators,* January 10, 1997, p. 4.

EXHIBIT 7   Stock Market Performance

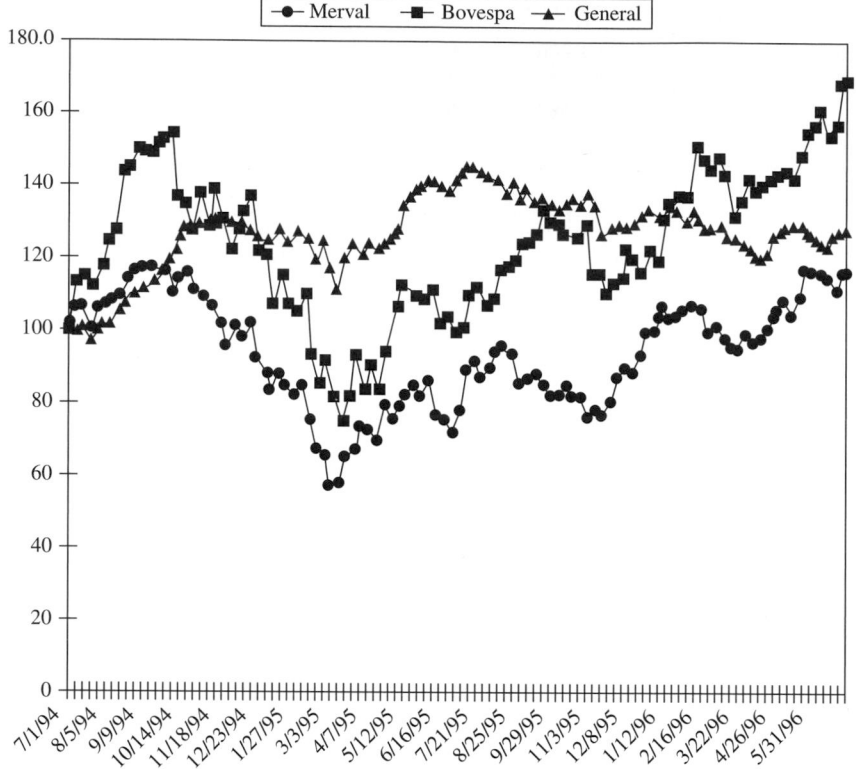

Stock Market Indexes – Comparative Performance
(Argentina - Merval, Brazil - Bovespa, Chile - General)

Figure by casewriter. Source of data: J. P. Morgan & Company.

EXHIBIT 8   Spot Foreign Exchange Rate: Argentine Peso to the U.S. Dollar

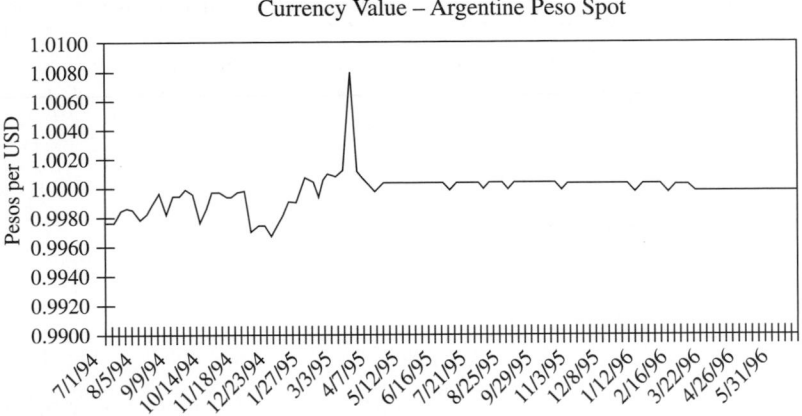

Currency Value – Argentine Peso Spot

Figure by casewriter. Source of data: J. P. Morgan & Company.

EXHIBIT 9   Spot Foreign Exhange Rate: Brazilian Real to the U.S. Dollar

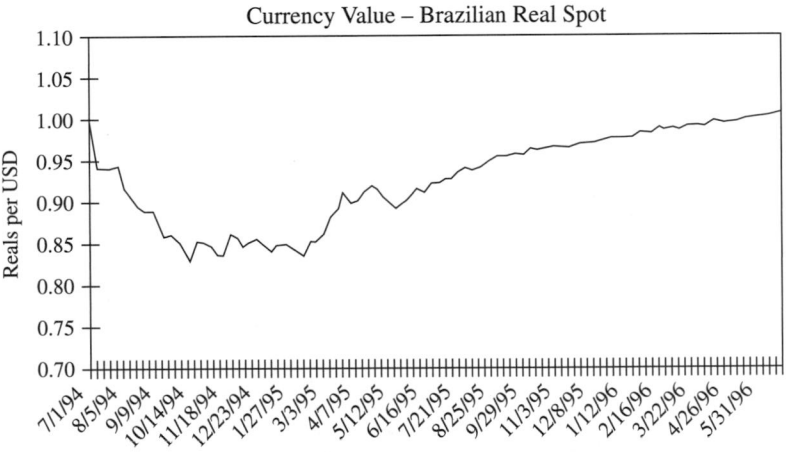

Currency Value – Brazilian Real Spot

Figure by casewriter. Source of data: J. P. Morgan & Company.

EXHIBIT 10   Spot Foreign Exchange Rate: Chilean Peso to the U.S. Dollar

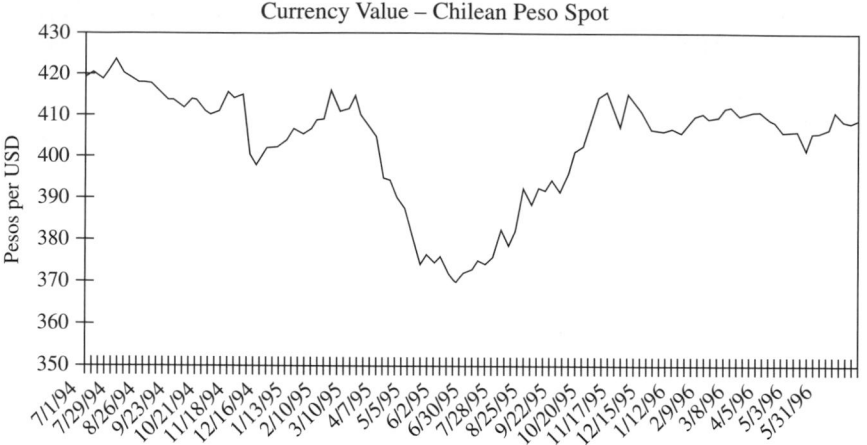

Figure by casewriter. Source of data: J. P. Morgan & Company.

EXHIBIT 11   Spread over U.S. Treasuries: Argentine Government Bonds

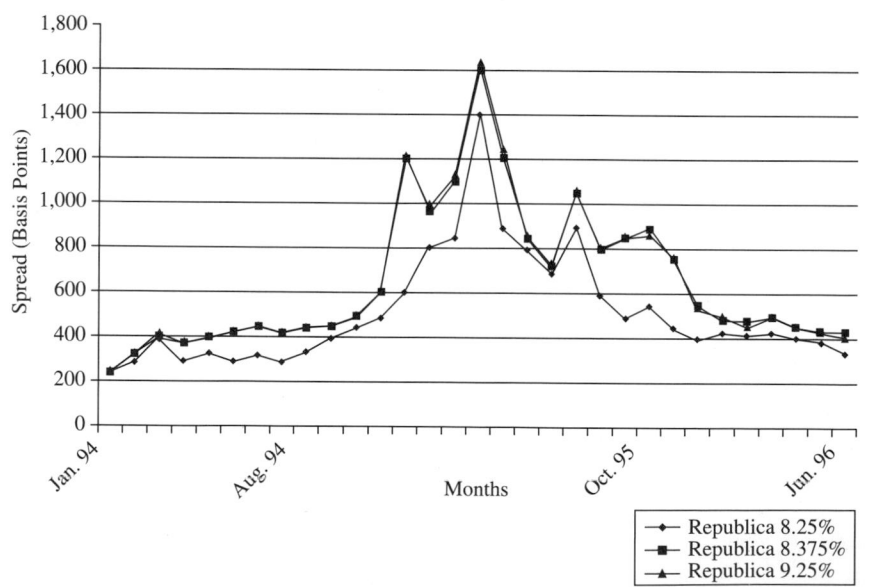

Figure by casewriter. Source of data: J. P. Morgan & Company.

EXHIBIT 12   Spread over U.S. Treasuries: Brazilian Government Bonds

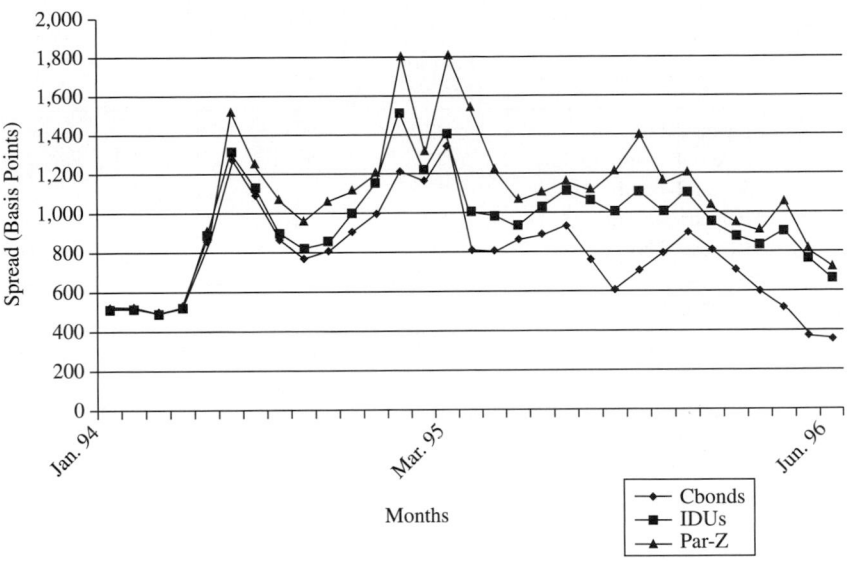

Figure by casewriter. Source of data: J. P. Morgan & Company.

EXHIBIT 13   Spread over U.S. Treasuries: Chilean High-Grade Corporate Bonds

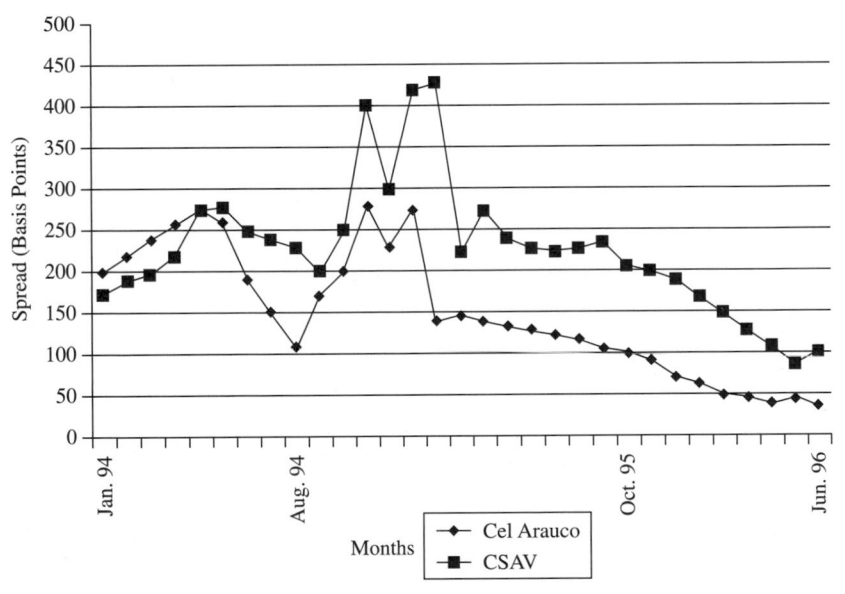

Figure by casewriter. Source of data: J. P. Morgan & Company.

EXHIBIT 14   Capital-Market Conditions, July 1996

U.S. Treasury Yields

	Yield to Maturity
1-year T-bill	5.92%
2-year T-bond	6.21
5-year T-bond	6.57
10-year T-bond	6.80
30-year T-bond	7.00

Source: Bloomberg.

Estimated Local Borrowing Rates, Income Taxes, Capital Structure, and Country Betas

	Argentina	Brazil	Chile
Local borrowing rate	8.0%	12.0%	8.0%
Income tax rate	35%	35%	15%
Country beta (vs. U.S. S&P 500 index)	1.96	2.42	0.65
Target market value debt-to-capital ratio for telephone-directory business	20%	20%	20%

Source: J. P. Morgan & Co. and International Finance Corporation, Emerging Stock Markets Factbook, 1996.

Median Beta and Capital Structure Information for Certain U.S. Industries, J. P. Morgan

	Direct Marketing	Information Services	Newspapers	Publishing / Printing	Radio Stations
Unlevered Median Beta	0.86	0.79	0.74	0.76	0.77
Mean Market Value Debt/Capital Ratio	20%	18%	17%	19%	21%

Source: J. P. Morgan & Co.

Continental Cablevision, Inc./Fintelco Joint Venture

On February 1, 1994, the senior management team at Continental Cablevision met to evaluate the terms of the proposed final agreement to establish a joint venture in Argentina. The venture partner was Fintelco, a leading television-cable operator in Buenos Aires owned by Samuel Liberman. The team at Continental consisted of CEO Amos Hostetter, Senior Vice President for Corporate and Legal Affairs Robert Sachs, CFO Nancy Hawthorne, and Senior Vice President for Programming Robert Stengel. After six months of start-and-stop negotiations, communication difficulties, and numerous trips between Argentina and the United States, the two cable companies fashioned terms for a joint venture structure that gave Continental a 50 percent equity stake in Fintelco for $80 million. The team believed that Continental would be the first U.S. cable company to initiate talks with one of the four main Argentine cable companies. Despite Continental's apparent jump on the competition, the senior management team wanted to reassess the returns and potential risks associated with conducting business in Argentina. The team wanted to move quickly to consummate the arrangement and needed to conclude the assessment within a few days. Was this an appropriate arrangement for Continental in terms of price, terms, risks, and returns? Was the joint venture structure the best option for Continental? How attractive was the Argentine market, and did the market fit with Continental's strategy? And finally, was Samuel Liberman the right partner for Continental?

This case was prepared by Katarina Paddack, research assistant, under the direction of Professor Robert F. Bruner. The development of this case was made possible with the financial support of the Darden Partnership Program. All financial data concerning Fintelco and some operating data have been disguised. Copyright © 1997 by the University of Virginia Darden School Foundation, Charlottesville, VA. All rights reserved. *No part of this publication may be reproduced, stored in a retrieval system, used in a spreadsheet, or transmitted in any form or by any means—electronic, mechanical, photocopying, recording, or otherwise—without the permission of the Darden School Foundation. For inquiries, please send an e-mail to dardencases@virginia.edu.* Revised 11/97. Version 1.1.

CONTINENTAL CABLEVISION

Continental Cablevision, Inc., was founded in 1963 by two young Harvard Business School graduates, Amos B. Hostetter, Jr., and H. Irving Grousbeck, who viewed the lack of cable service in small cities of the Midwest as a business opportunity. Installing a 520-foot antenna in a cornfield in Tiffin, Ohio, the two entrepreneurs began Continental Cablevision, which served an area of less than five square miles. Ten television channels were offered over coaxial cable to subscribers (see Exhibit 1 for definitions of cable terms). Continental grew to become the third largest cable multiple-system operator (MSO) in the United States by 1994, with revenues of $1.2 billion (see Exhibits 2 and 3 for Continental's income statement and balance sheet). Though Continental's balance sheet showed negative equity, creditors remained confident of the firm's ability to service its debt, in light of its very strong cash flow. High depreciation expense shielded the firm's income from taxes. As of December 1993, the company's S&P bond rating was BB. Remaining a privately held company, Continental served over 3 million subscribers in 16 states.[1]

During the 1980s, Grousbeck retired to pursue a teaching career. Under Hostetter's leadership, Continental grew to employ more than 7,000 people in 1994. Hostetter's decentralized management philosophy delegated broad operating authority to the regional vice presidents, who managed each of the company's five management regions. Approximately 90 employees worked at the corporate offices in a renovated pilot house on the edge of Boston Harbor.

Continental's success was based on a growth strategy that clustered cable systems in certain areas of the country in order to more effectively distribute operating costs over a large number of subscribers. Until the mid-1980s, Continental's core business concentrated on the construction and operation of new cable-television systems in the United States. By 1987, however, the U.S. cable market began to show signs of maturation, when growth in the number of homes passed dropped to 5 percent from a high of approximately 20 percent in 1980. Growth in basic cable subscriptions had also dropped from 20 percent in 1981 to 7 percent in 1987.

In 1987, government deregulation of the cable industry led to industry consolidation and a flurry of strategic partnerships as cable operators tried to position themselves competitively for the coming decade. The 1984 Cable Act (effective in 1987) allowed operators to raise basic rates and to reinvest a portion of the subsequent revenue into license fees paid to basic networks for original programming and program acquisition. As a result, cable operators began a fierce drive toward "content" investments in programming and created a powerful generation of basic networks. Annual network gross advertising-revenue growth rates doubled from 14.2 percent in 1986 to 28.5 percent in 1989. During the early 1990s, these networks grew to include the Discovery Channel, Turner Broadcasting, QVC Network, the Cartoon Channel, Comedy Central, and E! Entertainment. In 1994, U.S. cable programming, measured in terms of net advertising sales and affiliate fees, was estimated to have become a $5 billion business; projections called for a doubling of basic cable network revenues to $11 billion by 2004, a compound annual growth rate of 9.1 percent.[2]

---

[1]Continental serviced Massachusetts, New Hampshire, Maine, Connecticut, New York, Virginia, Georgia, Florida, Ohio, Michigan, Illinois, Minnesota, Iowa, Missouri, Nevada, and California.

[2]*The Economics of Basic Cable Networks 1994* (Carmel, CA: Paul Kagan Associates, Inc.).

Like its competitors, Continental looked for new ways to diversify its traditional revenue and asset base. Entering the programming market, Continental bought interests in Turner Broadcasting, QVC, and E! Entertainment. In collaboration with the Hearst Corporation, Continental also created its own programming—New England Cable News, an award-winning 24-hour regional news network viewed by more than 2 million New England residents.

The company also began to position itself for expansion into nontraditional cable markets. Upgrading its cable systems with an advanced fiber-optic coaxial-cable architecture, Continental positioned itself to enter nontraditional cable services, including interactive services as well as residential and commercial voice, video, and data communications.

Continental also began to form partnerships with industry competitors; by 1994, Continental had acquired a 10 percent interest in PrimeStar, a cable-industry-backed effort to provide the nation's first direct-broadcast satellite service, and a 20 percent interest in Teleport Communications, an alternate-access telecommunications company. In March 1994, Continental and Performance Systems International began testing cable Internet access at certain sites in Cambridge, Massachusetts. This link offered subscribers Internet connections that were 50 to 300 times faster than phone-line access.

International Expansion

Over the years, Continental had been approached by a number of international companies seeking capital investments. However, capital constraints and domestic priorities, including the need to upgrade and rebuild existing systems as well as build new systems, precluded international expansion. Two main motives later prompted Continental to seek overseas growth. First, the U.S. Congress passed the 1992 Cable Act, which limited the cable industry's ability to raise cable rates in the United States. Second, the domestic cable industry had matured, with average cable-television household penetration at approximately 62 percent in 1994.[3] Robert Sachs explained,

> The economics of building new systems was more attractive than acquiring existing systems, whose costs at market prices could reach $2,000/subscriber. Overseas we could build and purchase systems for one-third to one-half the cost of buying them in the United States. We were looking for investment opportunities in countries that were politically and economically stable. We were also looking for virgin markets that were comparable to what we had encountered in the United States during the 1970s and 1980s and for cable companies that had already achieved some operating success.[4]

Sachs also pointed out that Continental was not interested in either outright acquisition of cable companies overseas or de novo strategies:

> Knowledge of the local market is extremely important in this industry. This includes knowing customs and culture, programming tastes, and the political and regulatory environment. For this reason, it is essential to have the right local partner or partners. We believed that simply hiring someone was insufficient to align the local operations with the local market.

In 1993, Continental began to explore cable joint venture opportunities in Singapore and Australia. Continental did not have a formal division for international development, and

---

[3]Company estimate.

[4]All quotes from company personnel were obtained through company interviews by the casewriters in March 1996.

managers who were involved in initiating the joint ventures took on the development responsibilities. As a result, development responsibilities were split between President Bill Schleyer (Australia), Senior Vice President Robert Sachs (Argentina and Singapore), and Senior Vice President Robert Stengel (Argentina). Hostetter, a hands-on executive, worked closely with all three, allowing the company to make quick decisions on a number of issues surrounding international investment opportunities.

In the summer of 1993, Stengel received a call from an associate of Texas businessman Jack Crosby concerning an investment opportunity with Fintelco, an Argentine multiple-system operator (MSO). Sachs explained,

> Jack was a cable TV pioneer and an old friend of Amos Hostetter's. They had known each other for more than 25 years. Jack had a five-year relationship with Sam Liberman, an Argentine entrepreneur who was looking for a U.S. partner for his cable company, Fintelco. Jack knew this was a good investment opportunity but didn't have the ability to make this size of an investment himself. Jack said that Samuel was a successful businessman who had built a good cable business but recognized the need for a strong MSO partner in order to take the business to the next level.

Not knowing very much about Argentina's economic or political situation, Sachs commissioned Dr. Riordan Roett, professor and director of the Latin American Studies Program at the Johns Hopkins Nitze School of Advanced International Studies, to prepare an analysis of Argentina's political and economic situation. Sachs and CFO Nancy Hawthorne obtained information from the Bank of Boston, which had worked in Argentina for years and was familiar with the risks associated with doing business in Argentina. Stengel and Crosby made a series of visits to Argentina to get to know Liberman and his key employees, as well as the market itself.

ARGENTINA'S POLITICS AND ECONOMY

Argentina, the second largest country in South America after Brazil, had a population of approximately 33 million in 1991, with more than 11 million people in the greater Buenos Aires area. The country's largest demographic group was of European heritage (Spanish, Italian, and German), and Spanish was the country's official language. Ninety-three percent of the Argentine population was literate. The country had a large, cosmopolitan middle class.

In 1983, after seven years of military rule, Argentina returned to civilian government under a tripartite system of government (president, chamber of deputies, senate). The military's 1982 defeat by Great Britain in the Malvinas War and a deteriorating economy led to popular unrest and the election of Raul Alfonsín of the middle-class-oriented Radical Party. From 1983 to 1989, Alfonsín succeeded in restoring civilian government. However, Alfonsín's inability to institute economic reform led to the 1989 election of Carlos Menem of the Peronist Party, the oldest Argentine party, formed by Juan D. Peron in the 1940s.

During the next four years, Menem launched an unprecedented economic and financial reform program, defending political stability as the "bedrock of Argentina's new economic order."[5] Working with Argentina's third largest political party, the conservative Union

---

[5]Riordan Roett, "Argentina—Political and Economic Overview," Johns Hopkins University SAIS Latin American Studies Program, Washington, DC.

of the Democratic Center, and other smaller provincial parties, Menem put together a coalition in the Chamber of Deputies to support his experimental economic program.

In an attempt to restructure the Argentine economy in the midst of a two-year recession, Menem embarked on one of the most extensive privatization programs of state-owned companies in the world. The privatization program included industries such as telecommunications, airlines, petroleum, railway, roads, electricity, gas, steel mills, ports, maritime transport, reinsurance, and defense. Many public-sector operations were reformed to reduce the public-sector deficit from 17.2 percent of GDP in 1989 to 2.5 percent of GDP in 1990. Menem also liberalized foreign trade and investment, removing all but one (automobile) of the country's quantitative restrictions and simplified and reduced tariffs. Finally, Menem phased out many price controls and made significant changes to the country's tax system and financial sector. By December 1990, monthly inflation dropped to 4.7 percent from 95.5 percent in March 1990.

These improvements proved to be temporary. Despite Central Bank intervention, a steady depreciation of the overvalued currency, the austral (As), from As5,500/U.S.$1 to As9,500/U.S.$1 by the end of January 1991 led to the resignation of virtually every member of Menem's cabinet. During the first week of February, consumer prices rose 21.3 percent amid turmoil in the domestic financial markets.

In mid-1991, Argentina's economy made a profound transformation under the direction of Economy Minister Domingo Cavallo, who focused efforts on stabilizing the economy and deregulating the private sector. On April 1, 1991, Cavallo announced a comprehensive adjustment program including a convertibility plan, which promised the full convertibility of the austral at As10,000/U.S.$1 to stabilize the exchange rate. In January 1992, the austral was replaced by the peso (As10,000/1 peso) as the national currency of Argentina, setting the exchange rate at 1 peso/U.S.$1.

Following the restructuring plan, Argentina's economy boomed, with GDP growth at 8.9 percent in 1991 and 8.6 percent in 1992.

GDP Growth in Argentina, 1989–94						
GDP Growth	*1989*	*1990*	*1991*	*1992*	*1993*	*1994e*
Argentina	−6.3%	0.2%	8.9%	8.6%	6.0%	4.0%

Source: *World Tables 1995,* World Bank, Economist Intelligence Unit.

In 1993, following an impressive rise in the Argentine stock market, the Merval index plunged (see Exhibit 4). The Merval index is a capitalization-weighted index whose 22 equities are selected according to participation (number of transactions and trading volume). Following the crash, which severely damaged investor confidence, the market underwent significant changes including increased initial public offering (IPO) activity (especially of formerly government-owned enterprises), qualitative changes in trading volume, increased foreign investment, increased professionalism, and sector-based price differentiation. In the early 1990s, the Merval index was much more volatile than the U.S. equity markets, though it was also not well correlated with U.S. equity returns. The beta of Argentine equities with respect to U.S. equities was 1.96.

By 1994, Argentina's economy had rebounded. Argentina had the highest GDP/capita ($8,258) and the third largest GDP ($280 billion) in Latin America. Inflation rates were expected to reach a record low of 7 percent in 1994, one of the lowest in Latin America. Domestic lending interest rates had decreased from 1,000 percent in 1989 to 10.11 percent in January 1994; interest rates for fixed-term deposits averaged 8.3 percent by January 1994 (see Exhibits 5 and 6). Exhibit 7 displays the yield for an 8¼ Argentine government Brady bond, an 8¾ U.S. Treasury bond, and the difference in yield between the two bonds.[6] By the first half of 1994, there was no public-sector deficit and the bond-risk premium had dropped to 3.1 percent, as compared with approximately 4 percent in 1993 (see Exhibit 7).

In addition, economists began to question the sustainability of the government's use of a pegged exchange rate to fight inflation. Exhibit 8 presents historical and forecasted rates of inflation for Argentina and the United States up to 1998. Beyond 1998, some observers expected Argentina's inflation rate to converge to inflation in the dollar, about 2.5 percent. Many economists believed that the peso was overvalued; sharp increases in imports without an offsetting rise in exports had undermined the trade and current-account balances and had increased the country's dependence on capital inflows from 1993 to 1994 (see Exhibit 9). The Economist Intelligence Unit reported in December 1993 that "the weakness of the external accounts makes Argentina particularly vulnerable to external shocks, such as a rise in world interest rates or a strong revaluation of the dollar."[7]

Argentine presidential elections were scheduled for 1995. In late 1993, Menem championed a constitutional amendment allowing the president to run for a second term of office. To gain support for the amendment, Menem negotiated an agreement with Raul Alfonsín, opposition leader of the Radical Party and former president, whereby Alfonsín pledged Radical support of Menem's reelection in 1995 in return for greater opposition participation in government. In early 1994, Menem and his economic reforms remained popular with the Argentine population.

Argentina's Cable Market

By 1994, the Argentine cable market had become the most developed in Latin America, with approximately 4 million subscribers and a 50 percent cable-penetration rate (see Exhibit 10). Unlike many other Latin American countries, Argentina was the front-runner in government deregulation of the cable industry, resulting in a competitive but strong

---

[6]Brady bonds are obligations of a developing-country government, issued after lengthy negotiations between the sovereign, major commercial-bank lenders and international agencies, that are used to help restructure defaulted commercial-bank loans. Typically, a Brady bond's principal is collateralized by zero-coupon U.S. Treasuries and two or three semi-annual coupon payments backed by at least double-A-rated securities. The remaining coupons reflect the sovereign's country and credit risk. The blended yield of the Brady bond is a weighted average of U.S. government rates and the pure sovereign rate, or stripped yield. The principal on the bonds, denominated in U.S. dollars, is guaranteed by the U.S. government; while interest payments are not guaranteed, principal at maturity would be guaranteed in the case of default. Because interest is paid in dollars, there is virtually no currency risk in Brady bonds.

[7]*Economist Intelligence Unit,* "Financing Foreign Operations," Business International Corp., December 1, 1993.

FIGURE 1

Argentina

cable and programming market, especially in the areas in and around Buenos Aires, which had 32 percent of the country's population. The number of homes passed by wireline cable had an estimated 65 percent growth rate by the year 2004, with an estimated 67 percent increase in total subscribers. Subscribers' rates mirrored those found in the U.S. cable market, at approximately $28 per month (see Exhibit 11).

During the early 1990s, Argentina's cable industry began to consolidate around four of the largest MSOs, which served an estimated 46 percent of the total cable market:

- Multicanal: 689,000 subscribers.
- Cablevision: 523,900 subscribers.
- Fintelco: 390,000 subscribers.
- Fincable: 364,000 subscribers.[8]

Approximately 1,000 small operators (typically with less than 50,000 subscribers each) served the remaining 54 percent of the country's cable subscribers.

While most of Cablevision's and Fincable's subscribers were located in and around Buenos Aires, only 50 percent of Multicanal's subscribers were located in that area.

---

[8]Company estimates as of 1993.

Although the four MSOs had overbuilt the most lucrative areas of Buenos Aires, in the less-dense areas of the city competition diminished. Benjamin Gomez, Continental's assistant treasurer, described his impression of Buenos Aires:

> The cable market in Buenos Aires was extremely competitive. Customers had at least one, and in some cases two or three other operators to choose from in a given area. In addition to the major MSOs, there were several smaller entrepreneurial companies seeking subscribers as well. Competition outside of Buenos Aires, however, was much less.

In Córdoba, Argentina's second largest city, Fintelco held approximately 81 percent of the market share because of the acquisition of CCTV Video Vision in 1989 and Telecable Color in 1993. The remaining market share was controlled by Multicanal. In the other major cities in Córdoba Province, Fintelco's market share was even higher because of the acquisition of local cable operators.

Table 2 shows estimated market share of the four MSOs.

TABLE 2   MSOs' Estimated Market Shares

Operator	Buenos Aires Market Share	Argentina Market Share
Fintelco	23%	20%
Multicanal	28	35
Cablevision	32	27
Fincable	17	18

Source: Company estimates.

Generally, cable systems were valued on a per subscriber basis in Argentina. Estimated average prices per subscriber increased from $300–$400 in 1993 to $500–$1,200 in 1994.[9]

As part of the government's deregulation plan, the Reciprocal Protection and Encouraging of Investments Treaty was scheduled to be signed in October 1994 by the United States and Argentina. Similar to U.S. foreign-ownership rules, this treaty would allow U.S. investors to own up to 100 percent of Argentine cable systems and 25 percent of broadcast-television stations. Foreign investors would be subject to the same national and local laws as domestic cable operators, including approval applications to Argentina's regulatory body, the Comité Federal de Radiodifusion (COMFER). Application approval could take up to one year. COMFER granted cable operating licenses (15-year licenses with the possibility of a 10-year extension based on performance) and regulated cable programming content. COMFER also levied an 8 percent tariff in Buenos Aires and a 6 percent tariff in the rest of the country. Local municipalities levied additional annual fees based on how many meters of plant were installed.

---

[9]Company estimate.

Telephone and Satellite Markets

In addition to the cable market, Argentina's underdeveloped telecommunications market had untapped future growth potential. As described by one analyst,

> Global investment in cable, as in Latin American media and telecommunications, is changing the traditional communications paradigm. Cable is now an integral aspect of a regionwide broadband revolution aimed at delivering multiple services via coaxial and fiber-optic networks.[10]

Two local telephone companies, Telecom Argentina (north) and Telefónica de Argentina, S.A. (south), provided telephone services to Argentina's population under a 1989 contract that banned the two companies from providing video programming to customers until they relinquished their telephone monopoly in 1997. At that time, the government could extend the contract an additional three years. Analysts expected the government to open telephone service to additional competition and to allow telephone companies to enter the cable television market at that time. As in the U.S. market, Continental saw telephony as a major growth market in Argentina. Gomez noted that "when we looked at the Argentine market, one important issue for Continental was the future of telephony. We saw this market as a potential future driver of value for the cable industry in Argentina."

In 1994, the wireless-cable market was not fully developed in Argentina. The Argentine government awarded MMDS, or wireless-cable licenses, for channels throughout the country, allowing cable operators to own MMDS licenses in markets where they operated cable systems. Fintelco owned licenses in many of its cable operating areas. In addition, two international direct-to-home satellite services (Panamsat's Galavision and Hughes' Galaxy) were to be offered as early as 1996, and domestic satellite licenses would be awarded by the government in 1997.

FINTELCO

Fintelco was formed in 1980 by Samuel Liberman, an Argentine entrepreneur with diversified business interests. Pioneering one of the first cable companies in Buenos Aires, Liberman built and operated new cable systems using a growth strategy similar to that used by Hostetter at Continental, which emphasized creating large system clusters in order to maximize operating, technical, and marketing efficiencies. Liberman allowed the company to grow slowly, knowing that Buenos Aires would drive the cable market for the rest of the country. In the late 1980s, Fintelco bought VideoVision, the largest cable-television-system operator in Córdoba. By 1990, Fintelco's largest subsidiary, VCC, had grown to become one of the three largest MSOs in Buenos Aires. As one of the three largest cable operators in Argentina, Fintelco provided services for approximately 390,000 subscribers in 1993 and had experienced non-acquisition-related growth rates of 116 percent from 1992 to 1993 (see Exhibit 12).

Owing to his experience as an international entrepreneur, Liberman had a hands-on approach to running his businesses. Gomez observed,

---

[10]*The 1995 Latin American Cable/Pay TV Databook.* (Carmel, CA: Kagan World Media, Inc.), p. 1.

> Samuel Liberman has a coterie of people around him which includes longtime trusted business associates, his son, and one of his daughters. He likes to hear everyone's opinion and then makes decisions based on the best information available and his own instincts.

Until 1990, Fintelco's growth was primarily due to network expansion. However, deregulation of cable-industry segments by the Argentine government spurred acquisition activity and consolidation between the four largest MSOs. Liberman began to look to the acquisition of smaller MSOs outside of the Buenos Aires vicinity as an opportunity to leapfrog local competition and the arrival of foreign competition in order to become the dominant MSO in several of the smaller key markets. Liberman sought potential acquisition targets that had strong cash flow, were located in close proximity to existing systems for economies of scale, and were not overvalued.

In 1994, Liberman began to look for acquisition opportunities in Argentina's third largest city, Rosario, which was served by four different cable operators. He envisioned acquiring three of the four cable operators to give Fintelco control of approximately 85 percent of the Rosario market. One obstacle to continued growth was the lack of a well-developed local capital market. As a result, Fintelco had a difficult time obtaining long-term financing on reasonable terms. Gomez said that "Argentina's capital markets did not understand the cable market. Media lending, which is largely cash-flow based, was relatively new to Argentine banks."

Included in Liberman's strategic vision was growth in programming capabilities. In 1985, Liberman formed a programming subsidiary, Enequis S.A., which operated 14 program services, 4 of which showed locally produced programming. Liberman also felt that channel capacity would be a future success driver in Buenos Aires and sought funding for advanced plant capacity in several key competitive markets.

In 1993, Fintelco's revenues reached approximately $137 million. Fintelco's balance sheet as of February 1, 1994, can be found in Exhibit 13. A forecast of Fintelco's free cash flows is given in Exhibit 14. Information on comparable U.S. companies can be found in Exhibit 15.

THE JOINT VENTURE

The joint venture structure developed over a six-month period, during which Hostetter and Liberman got to know each other and each other's companies. Robert Sachs described the development of the relationship:

> The relationship clicked from the beginning. Like Amos, Samuel Liberman was a self-made man and shared many of the same personality characteristics. They were both private people. They both cherished their independence. From Sam's standpoint, he felt comfortable with Amos on more than just a business level. He was personally comfortable with him.
>
> Sam shared the same vision for the company as did Amos, who believed the value of cable operations would increase steadily over time. Like Continental, Fintelco had grown using a clustering strategy and believed the only way to generate operating efficiencies would be to concentrate subscribers geographically to spread operating, distribution, and advertising costs. Other companies had a more "scattershot" mentality. Fintelco was more focused and had a clear strategic vision of what type of expansion it was interested in.
>
> Throughout the negotiation period, both sides felt that if the deal would go through, it would be based on mutual trust and respect between Amos Hostetter and Samuel Liberman, not just between corporate entities.

Draft Joint Venture Structure

In February 1994, after six months of negotiations, a joint venture structure had been drafted by both Continental and Fintelco.

- *50-50 partnership.* The 50-50 partnership structure addressed concerns of both companies. Sachs commented, "Continental was not interested in becoming a company system operator in Argentina. We were looking to form a partnership whereby the local entity would continue to run the company. To make this work, we needed local market expertise." Not wanting to give up control of the company, Liberman's concerns centered around the current and future management structure of the company. Sachs continued,

> Sam went back and forth on what percentage of the company he wanted to sell. Amos felt that Sam would not be comfortable selling 75 percent of the business and cede control of the company's direction. So, after much discussion about Sam's long-term interests, Amos offered to buy 25 percent. Appreciating that Amos was not trying to wrest control from him, Sam said that he would be comfortable having Continental as a 50 percent partner. The two men ended up agreeing upon a 50-50 deal. This negotiation process brought the two companies closer and reinforced the personal trust upon which this joint venture was built.

This was the first time that Continental had entered into a 50-50 international deal. The existing management would remain in place, with Liberman as Fintelco's chairman. A management committee would consist of Hostetter, Liberman, Jeffrey DeLorme (Continental executive vice president), and Guillermo Liberman (Samuel's son and Fintelco's manager of administration and internal audit).

- *$80-million price tag.* Continental agreed to invest $80 million to acquire 50 percent of Liberman's ownership interest in Fintelco. Both companies agreed to provide additional capital to fund acquisitions as well as to deploy advanced technology as part of Fintelco's upgrading and rebuilding process. Over time, an additional $70 million would be invested by each partner.[11] Gomez said,

> One central financing issue that we needed to work into the deal was an assurance that the inflow of capital, from both Continental and Liberman, would stop at some ceiling amount. We didn't want to have to keep pumping capital into this venture years down the road, detracting from other company projects in both the short and long term.

Sachs commented, "We saw this deal as a win–win for both Continental and Fintelco. They needed capital, and we were interested in gaining a foothold in the Argentine market." Following Continental's equity investment, Continental and Fintelco planned to secure a line of credit from a consortium of U.S. and Argentine banks to help finance the company's expansion activities as well as to rebuild and upgrade capital expenditure programs. The joint venture would continue to bear the short- and long-term debt of Fintelco that predated the joint venture. However, one element of risk that could not be addressed was the significant currency risk that would result from the fact that Fintelco's revenues would be denominated in pesos while a significant portion of its liabilities, including interest expense and a portion of programming costs, would be denominated in U.S. dollars.

---

[11]This additional investment is already reflected in the free cash flows estimated in Exhibit 14.

- *Technical assistance.* To further emphasize Continental's commitment to the joint venture, Continental offered to provide Fintelco with technical assistance in the operating, programming, and financial areas of the business. Fintelco would only be charged for the costs associated with this assistance. Gomez commented, "The technical-assistance structure would allow us to develop a flexible relationship, which we believed would be important for the success of the joint venture."
- *Right of acquisition/divestiture.* Finally, the deal contained an exit agreement whereby after four years the partners, if they so chose, could either sell to one another or cause the outright sale of the company to a third party. Also, in the case that Hostetter would cease to run Continental, Liberman would have the option of buying back Continental's shares or selling his own shares to Continental.

JOINT VENTURE DECISION

Nancy Hawthorne, Robert Sachs, Robert Stengel, and Amos Hostetter considered the business opportunities of their own forecasts of operation and whether the joint venture terms could be improved to enhance the success of the new venture. They were especially eager to reply to Samuel Liberman promptly and to launch the venture before other U.S. cable companies entered the market. Hostetter had built Continental not only by decisive and aggressive entry into new markets, but also by careful business dealings that would ensure the success of Continental's investments. Would the entry into Argentina be consistent with Continental's expansion approach?

EXHIBIT 1   Definitions

Broadband refers to any system capable of delivering wideband channels and services and is often used as a synonym for cable television. Bandwidth refers to the frequency spectrum used to transmit pictures, sounds, or both. For example, the average television station uses bandwidth of 6 million cycles per second (6 megahertz).

Coaxial cable is a line of transmission for carrying television signals. Its principal conductor is either a pure copper or copper-coated wire, surrounded by insulation, and then encased in aluminum. Coaxial cable—20,000 times larger than telephone twisted-pair wires—can carry more than 100,000 times as much information as conventional telephone lines.

Fiber-optic cable, thin and pliable tubes of glass or plastic, are used to carry wide bands of frequencies. Telephone and data-communications companies have also installed fiber-optic lines, which could offer data-transfer speeds fast enough to handle video signals.

MMDS (multichannel/multipoint distribution system) or *wireless cable,* is a service using a very high frequency (2 gigahertz) to transmit multiple television signals via microwave.

Multiple-system operator (MSO) describes a company that owns and operates more than one cable-television system. Tele-Communications and Time Warner were the first and second largest U.S. cable MSOs; other competitors included Comcast, Viacom, Cox, Jones Intercable, and Newhouse/Advance.

Source: Company Web site.

EXHIBIT 2   Continental Cablevision Consolidated Operations, 1992–93 (in U.S.$ thousands)

	1992	*1993*
Revenues	1,113,475	1,177,163
Costs and expenses		
Operating	365,513	382,195
Selling, general and administrative	259,632	267,376
Depreciation and amortization	272,851	279,009
Restricted stock purchase program	9,683	11,004
Total	907,679	939,584
Operating income	205,796	237,579
Other (income) expense:		
Interest	296,031	282,252
Equity in net loss of affiliates	9,402	12,827
Gain on sale of marketable equity securities	0	−4,322
Gain on sale of investments	−10,253	−17,067
Partnership litigation	10,280	−2,325
Minority interest in net income (loss) of subsidiaries	136	184
Dividend income	−330	−650
Other	1,836	375
Total	307,102	271,274
Loss from operations before income taxes, Extraordinary item and cumulative effect of change in accounting for income taxes	−101,306	−33,695
Income tax expense (benefit)	1,654	−7,921
Loss before extraordinary item and cumulative effect of change in accounting for income taxes	−102,960	−25,774
Extraordinary item, net of income taxes	0	0
Loss before cumulative effect of change in accounting for income taxes	−102,960	−25,774
Cumulative effect of change in accounting for income taxes	0	−184,996
Net loss	−102,960	−210,770
Preferred stock preferences	−16,861	−34,115
Loss applicable to common stockholders	−119,821	−244,885
Loss per common share:		
Loss before extraordinary item and cumulative effect of change in accounting for income taxes	(1)	(0.53)
Extraordinary item	0	0.00
Loss before cumulative effect of change in accounting for income taxes	(1.00)	(0.53)
Cumulative effect of change in accounting for income taxes	0	(1.62)
Net loss	(1.00)	(2.15)

Source: Company data.

EXHIBIT 3   Continental Cablevision Consolidated Balance Sheet 1992–93 (in U.S.$ thousands)

	1992	*1993*
Assets		
Cash and cash equivalents	27,352	122,640
Accounts receivable—net	36,085	44,530
Prepaid expenses and other	5,172	4,800
Supplies	26,598	31,638
Marketable equity securities	35,517	58,676
Investments	35,275	136,186
Property, plant, and equipment—net	1,213,848	1,211,507
Intangible assets—net	623,349	387,719
Other assets—net	0	94,157
Total	2,003,196	2,091,853
Liabilities and stockholders' equity		
Accounts payable	40,851	43,342
Accrued interest	39,803	72,424
Accrued and other liabilities	168,149	145,191
Debt	3,011,669	3,177,178
Deferred income taxes	626	105,041
Minority interest in subsidiaries	4,613	2,217
Redeemable common stock ($.01 par value; 16,767,050 shares outstanding)	223,716	213,548
Stockholders' equity		
Preferred stock, $.01 par value; 1992: 1,557,142 shares authorized; none outstanding. 1993: 198,857,142 shares authorized; none outstanding	0	0
Series A convertible preferred stock, $.01 par value; 1992: 1,142,858 shares authorized and outstanding; 1993: 1,142,858 shares authorized and outstanding; liquidation preference $450,976,000	11	11
Class A common stock, $.01 par value; 1992: 7,500,000 shares authorized; 137,373 shares outstanding; 1993: 425,000,000 shares authorized; 6,201,500 shares outstanding	1	62
Class B common stock, $.01 par value; 1992: 7,500,000 shares authorized; 3,665,820 shares outstanding 200,000,000 shares authorized; 91,310,500 shares outstanding	37	913
Additional paid-in capital	558,679	577,076
Unearned compensation	−34,919	−23,577
Net unrealized holding gain on marketable equity securities	0	0
Deficit	−2,010,040	−2,221,573
Stockholders' equity	−1,486,231	−1,667,088
Total	2,003,196	−2,091,853

Source: Company data.

EXHIBIT 4   Argentine and U.S. Stock Markets (August 30, 1991, to January 31, 1994)

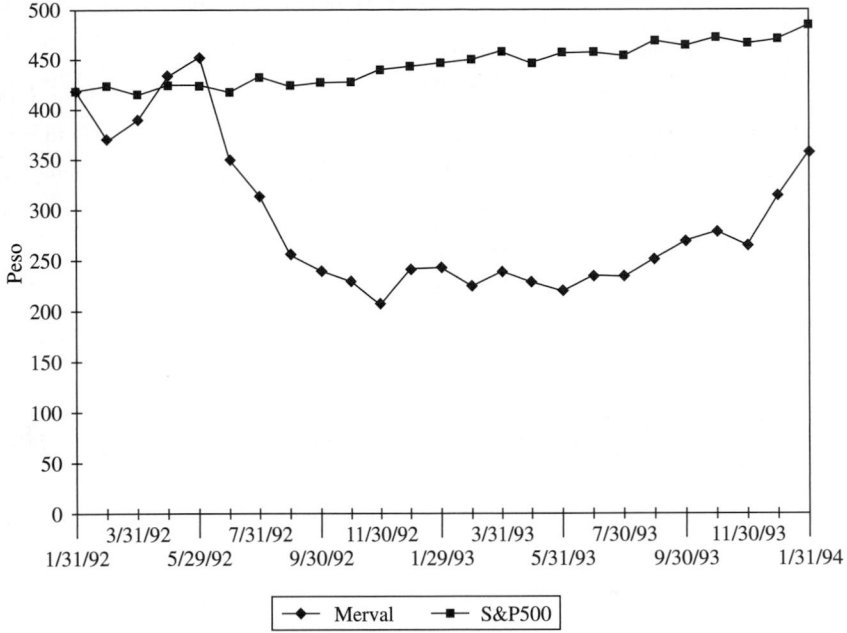

Note: The Argentine Merval index is the market value of a stock portfolio, selected according to participation in the Buenos Aires Stock Exchange, number of transactions, and trading volume. The index has a base value of $0.01 and is revised every three months.

Source: Bloomberg News Media.

EXHIBIT 5   Current Capital Market Rates and Yields (February 1, 1994)

U.S. Treasury Securities (Jan. 1994 average) (%)

3 months	2.98
6 months	3.15
1 year	3.54
2 years	4.14
3 years	4.48
5 years	5.09
10 years	5.75
20 years	6.39
30 years	6.29

Source: *S&P Bond Guide.*

Corporate Bond Yields (Jan. 1994 average)

Rating Category	Public Utilities (%)	Industrial (%)
AAA	n.a.	6.80
AA	7.36	7.26
A	8.35	7.84
BBB	8.31	8.28
BB	n.a.	9.01
B	n.a.	10.38

Source: *S&P Bond Guide.*

Other Interest Rates

Commercial Paper (%)		LIBOR (%)		Prime Rates (%)	
30 days	3.1	1 month	$3\frac{1}{8}$	United States	6
60 days	3.13	3 months	$3\frac{1}{4}$	Canada	5.5
90 days	3.15	6 months	$3\frac{3}{8}$	Germany	5.9
		1 year	$3\frac{11}{16}$	Japan	3
				Switzerland	7.5
				Great Britain	5.5

Sources: *The Wall Street Journal,* February 1, 1994; *Federal Reserve Bulletin,* 1994.

EXHIBIT 6   Argentina's Interest Rates (January 1994)

	Pesos	*U.S.$*
Deposits		
30 day	8.47%	5.75%
90 day	8.99	7.10
Average	8.29	6.43
Loans		
30 day	10.11	8.0
90 day	—	8.88

Source: Datastream.

EXHIBIT 7   Annualized Yield on Argentine Government Brady Bond 8¼ Maturity August 2, 2000, U.S. Treasury Bond 8¾ Maturity August 15, 2000, and Yield Difference

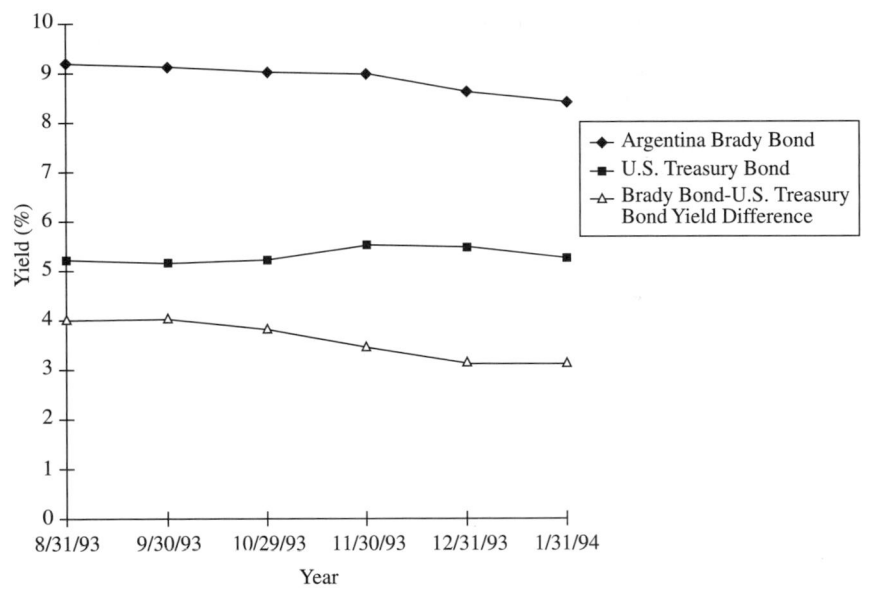

Source: Bloomberg.

EXHIBIT 8   Inflation and Foreign Exchange Market Data

Year	U.S. Inflation (%)	Argentine Inflation (%)	Foreign Exchange Rate Peso/$
1989 actual	4.8	3,079.8	.001577
1990 actual	5.4	2,314.7	.135024
1991 actual	4.2	171.7	.513900
1992 actual	3.0	24.9	.999000
1993 actual	3.0	11	

			Official Exchange Rate	Parity-implied Exchange Rate*
			.999000	1.077
1994 forecast	2.5	7	.999000	1.124
1995 forecast	2.5	8	.999000	1.184
1996 forecast	2.5	12	.999000	1.294
1997 forecast	2.5	10	.999000	1.389
1998 forecast	2.5	6	.999000	1.436

*The parity-implied forward-exchange rate was calculated based on the following purchasing-power-parity model:

$$\text{Peso/\$ (expected rate)} = \text{Peso/\$ (current rate)} \times (1 + \text{Argentine inflation rate})/(1 + \text{U.S. inflation rate})$$

Source: International Monetary Fund, *World Economic Outlook, October 1996.* Forecast: "Inflation," *Economist Intelligence Unit,* Business International Corp. (December 20, 1993).

EXHIBIT 9   Argentina's Balance of Payments (in millions of dollars)

	1993	*1992*	*1991*	*1990*
Current account				
Exports	13,117	12,235	11,978	12,354
Imports	(16,783)	(14,872)	(8,275)	(4,079)
Trade balance	(3,666)	(2,637)	3,703	8,275
Nonfinancial services	(1,146)	(1,128)	(908)	(321)
Interest and dividends	(2,922)	(3,661)	(4,260)	(4,400)
Transfers	446	749	793	998
Current account	(7,288)	(6,677)	(672)	4,552
Capital account				
Public sector	3,624	5,757	972	(271)
Private sector	13,908	9,559	(6,363)	(3,821)
Direct investments	587	518	465	305
Privatizations	5,718	3,661	1,974	1,531
Commercial/financial	4,968	3,195	1,913	451
Loans	(11)	(20)	(27)	(30)
Others	2,646	2,205	(10,678)	(6,078)
Capital account	17,532	3,802	(5,391)	(4,092)
Errors and omissions	55	(57	(125)	219
Net international reserves	10,099	(2,932)	(6,188)	679

Source: Banco Central de la Republica Argentina (BCRA).

EXHIBIT 10   Latin American Cable-Television Market, *International Cable,* 1994. (in thousands)

Country	*Population*	*Homes*	*TV Homes*	*Subscribers*	*Penetration (%)*
Argentina	33,800	8,700	8,000	4,000	50.0
Mexico	94,000	18,430	12,500	1,575	12.6
Brazil	146,200	35,650	32,000	250	.8
Venezuela	21,170	3,995	3,700	160	4.3
Chile	13,670	3,040	1,750	100	5.7
Paraguay	5,080	980	400	100	25.0
Panama	2,582	527	370	75	20.3
Colombia	35,210	6,520	4,310	62	1.4
Peru	23,265	4,475	2,000	31	1.6
Ecuador	11,252	2,205	1,200	25	2.1
Uruguay	3,145	952	500	20	4.0
Bolivia	7,505	1,700	936	16	1.7

Source: *International Cable,* 1994.

EXHIBIT 11 South American and Mexican Overview of Cable Markets

	1994	1999	2004
Basic Homes Passed by Wireline Cable (millions)			
Argentina	5.40	7.00	8.90
Mexico	3.50	6.90	14.00
Brazil	0.75	3.68	8.04
Chile	0.50	1.44	3.28
Paraguay	0.06	0.25	0.40
Uruguay	0.06	0.43	0.71
Colombia	0.06	0.86	3.30
Venezuela	0.06	0.46	1.70
Peru	0.04	0.36	0.97
Ecuador	0.04	0.11	0.24
Bolivia	0.01	0.13	0.44
Total	10.48	21.62	41.98
Total Multichannel Subscribers (millions)*			
Argentina	4.490	6.170	7.530
Mexico	2.150	6.390	9.850
Brazil	0.430	3.110	6.910
Chile	0.260	0.980	1.850
Venezuela	0.130	0.640	1.250
Colombia	0.081	0.637	2.002
Paraguay	0.053	0.097	0.130
Ecuador	0.029	0.076	0.120
Peru	0.029	0.197	0.400
Uruguay	0.029	0.249	0.370
Bolivia	0.009	0.093	0.155
Total	7.690	18.639	30.567
TV Households (millions)			
Brazil	33.10	38.80	42.60
Mexico	12.70	15.30	17.50
Argentina	8.60	10.10	11.10
Colombia	7.00	7.90	8.90
Chile	3.40	3.70	4.10
Venezuela	3.20	3.90	4.70
Peru	2.17	2.77	3.62
Uruguay	0.65	0.80	0.94
Ecuador	0.54	0.65	0.77
Bolivia	0.50	0.60	0.72
Paraguay	0.31	0.42	0.54
Total	72.17	84.94	95.49

*Includes wireline and wireless cable.

Source: Kagan World Media, Inc., *The 1995 Latin American Cable/Pay TV Databook.* Reprinted by permission of Paul Kagan Associates, Inc.

EXHIBIT 11   *(concluded)*

	1994	*1999*	*2004*
*Total Annual Multichannel Revenue ($ mil.)**			
Argentina	1,437.0	2,305.0	3,139.0
Mexico	374.0	1,315.0	2,353.0
Brazil	120.8	967.1	2,284.4
Chile	50.0	207.0	437.0
Venezuela	34.0	171.0	362.0
Colombia	13.2	171.9	593.4
Paraguay	10.9	24.9	38.3
Peru	10.0	86.0	184.0
Ecuador	5.1	17.0	30.3
Uruguay	3.9	51.1	88.9
Bolivia	0.8	19.1	37.2
Total	2059.7	5335.1	9547.5
Annual Monthly Fee for Basic Wireline Subscribers (U.S.$)			
Peru	40	41	40
Brazil	32	30	29
Argentina	28	32	35
Colombia	23	26	27
Paraguay	20	22	25
Venezuela	20	21	22
Chile	18	19	21
Ecuador	17	20	22
Uruguay	17	19	21
Mexico	16	17	19
Bolivia	10	24	25
Average basic fee	22	25	26

*Includes wireline and wireless cable.

EXHIBIT 12   Fintelco Growth Trends

	1992	*1993*
Homes passed (internal)	588,647	692,523
Homes passed (acquisitions)	0	73,320
Total	588,647	765,843
Growth per annum		
Without acquisitions	N/A	17.6%
Total	N/A	30.1%
Subscribers (internal)	164,559	355,456
Subscribers (acquisitions)	0	26,096
Total	164,559	381,552
Growth per annum		
Without acquisitions	40.5%	116.0%
Total	40.5%	131.9%
Penetration		
Without acquisitions	28%	51.3%
Total	28%	49.8%

Source: Company data.

EXHIBIT 13   Fintelco's Consolidated Balance Sheet, February 1, 1994 (in pesos)

Assets
Current assets

Cash	27,129,668
Investments	4,017
Accounts receivable	20,608,602
Other receivables	9,689,295
Inventories	19,792,676
Total current assets	77,224,258

Long-term assets

Other receivables	2,340,133
Inventories	12,197,656
Investments	6,499,054
Fixed assets	103,651,305
Intangible assets	209,144,150
Total long-term assets	333,832,296
Total assets	411,056,554

Liabilities
Current liabilities

Accounts payable	101,998,411
Loans	121,089,355
Payroll and related taxes	7,019,015
Taxes	11,849,551
Other liabilities	7,547,852
Other allowances	1,866,830
Total current liabilities	251,371,013

Long-term liabilities

Accounts payable	448,544
Loans	12,174,262
Taxes	4,493,561
Payroll and related taxes	3,120
Other allowances	10,003,401
Other liabilities	4,607,337
Total long-term liabilities	31,730,225
Total liabilities	283,101,238
Minority interest	1,552,057
Net worth	126,403,259
Total	411,056,554

Source: Company data.

EXHIBIT 14 Forecast of Fintelco Cash Flow (in thousands of pesos)

	Actual		Forecast Assumptions							
	1993	1994	1995	1996	1997	1998	1999	2000	2001	2002
Subscriber assumptions										
Annual growth, total homes passed				1.50%	1.50%	1.50%	1.50%	1.50%	1.50%	1.50%
Fintelco penetration of market, homes passed			32.04%	32.56%	33.54%	34.71%	36.56%	38.80%	41.20%	44.20%
Fintelco penetration of market, subscribers/homes	49.82%	49.94%	48.98%	49.09%	49.01%	48.80%	47.86%	46.75%	45.67%	44.49%
Tax rate	29.95%	62.05%	30.30%	17.95%	18.08%	18.76%	19.90%	26.04%	25.08%	27.61%
Operating expense/Revenues	8.00%	9.22%	9.74%	9.11%	8.80%	8.42%	8.14%	7.89%	7.65%	7.47%
Local origination expense/Revenues	3.56%	3.69%	3.66%	3.12%	2.93%	2.77%	2.70%	2.65%	2.62%	2.59%
Programming expense/Revenues	30.87%	38.72%	30.48%	28.67%	28.00%	27.34%	27.00%	26.75%	26.63%	26.61%
G&A/Revenues	14.55%	18.53%	26.15%	22.41%	20.83%	19.55%	18.75%	18.38%	18.08%	17.88%
Marketing/Revenues	18.32%	16.62%	8.99%	8.64%	8.38%	8.15%	8.07%	7.99%	7.93%	7.89%
Net working capital/Revenues	0.00%	0.00%	4.93%	0.54%	0.44%	0.31%	0.29%	0.36%	0.31%	0.34%
Basic revenues/Subscribers per month (in pesos)	36.00	23.84	29.48	31.44	32.43	33.40	34.19	34.78	35.35	35.88
Advertising/Subscribers per month	1.45	0.96	1.59	2.08	2.27	2.47	2.68	2.84	2.95	2.99
Other/Subscribers per month	4.24	2.26	3.08	2.72	2.51	2.39	2.06	1.93	1.81	1.68
Total revenues/Subscribers per month	41.69	27.06	34.15	36.24	37.21	38.26	38.93	39.55	40.11	40.55
Total homes passed by cable operators in Argentina			5,200,000	5,278,000	5,357,170	5,437,528	5,519,090	5,601,877	5,685,905	5,771,194
Homes passed (by Fintelco)	765,843	1,585,796	1,666,080	1,718,517	1,796,795	1,887,366	2,017,779	2,173,528	2,342,593	2,550,868
Fintelco growth		107.07%	5.06%	3.15%	4.55%	5.04%	6.91%	7.72%	7.78%	8.89%
Ending basic subscribers	381,553	791,947	816,046	843,620	880,609	921,035	965,709	1,016,124	1,069,862	1,134,881
Growth		107.56%	3.04%	3.38%	4.38%	4.59%	4.85%	5.22%	5.29%	6.08%
Average basic subscribers	273,056	586,750	803,996	829,833	862,115	900,822	943,372	990,917	1,042,993	1,102,372
Growth		114.88%	37.03%	3.21%	3.89%	4.49%	4.72%	5.04%	5.26%	5.69%

Revenue assumptions (thousands of pesos)

	Actual			Forecast						
	1993	1994	1995	1996	1997	1998	1999	2000	2001	2002
Revenues										
Basic	117,960	167,857	284,422	313,079	335,500	361,049	387,047	413,569	442,438	474,637
Advertising	4,751	6,759	15,340	20,713	23,484	26,700	30,339	33,770	36,922	39,553
Other	13,893	15,913	29,716	27,086	25,967	25,836	23,320	22,950	22,654	22,224
Total revenues	136,604	190,529	329,478	360,878	384,951	413,585	440,706	470,289	502,014	536,414
Growth		39.48%	72.93%	9.53%	6.67%	7.44%	6.56%	6.71%	6.75%	6.85%

Forecast of Free Cash Flows

	Actual			Forecast						
	1993	1994	1995	1996	1997	1998	1999	2000	2001	2002
Revenues (peso 000)	136,604	190,529	329,478	360,878	384,951	413,585	440,706	470,289	502,014	536,414
Expenses										
Operating	10,923	17,567	32,091	32,876	33,876	34,824	35,873	37,106	38,404	40,070
Local origination	4,858	7,031	12,059	11,259	11,279	11,456	11,899	12,463	13,153	13,893
Programming	42,163	73,773	100,425	103,464	107,786	113,074	118,991	125,802	133,686	142,740
G&A	19,878	35,305	86,158	80,873	80,185	80,856	82,632	86,439	90,764	95,911
Marketing	25,022	31,666	29,620	31,180	32,259	33,707	35,565	37,576	39,810	42,323
Total expenses	102,844	165,341	260,353	259,652	265,385	273,918	284,960	299,386	315,817	334,937
Operating income	33,760	25,188	69,124	101,226	119,566	139,668	155,745	170,903	186,197	201,477
Less depreciation	5,101	9,004	17,317	20,259	24,642	28,193	30,770	33,305	35,270	37,359
Less amortization	—	—	16,195	17,280	17,243	17,243	17,243	17,243	17,243	17,243
Less financial and other expenses	4,498	2,296	—	—	—	—	—	—	—	—
EBIT	24,161	13,888	35,612	63,687	77,681	94,232	107,732	120,355	133,684	146,875
Less taxes	7,236	8,617	10,791	11,432	14,045	17,678	21,439	31,340	33,528	40,552
EBIAT	16,925	5,270	24,822	52,255	63,636	76,554	86,294	89,015	100,156	106,323
Plus amortization	—	—	16,195	17,280	17,243	17,243	17,243	17,243	17,243	17,243
Plus depreciation	5,101	9,004	17,317	20,259	24,642	28,193	30,770	33,305	35,270	37,359
Less capital expenditures	13,320	22,762	84,500	71,500	58,500	45,500	32,500	32,500	26,000	26,000
Less additions to net working capital	—	—	16,243	1,949	1,694	1,282	1,278	1,693	1,556	1,824
Free cash flow	8,706	(8,488)	(42,409)	16,346	45,327	75,208	100,529	105,370	125,113	133,101

Source: Company data.

EXHIBIT 15   Information on Comparable U.S. Companies

	1993 Annual Revenues ($ mil.)	Subscribers (mil.)	Book Value of Debt ($ mil.)	Book Value of Equity ($ mil.)
Viacom	2,035	1.2	2,532	936.2
A wholly owned subsidiary of Viacom International with four units: cable-television systems (29% of 1992 operating profits); broadcasting (NBC and CBS) and radio (8%); cable-television channels (Showtime, Movie Channel, Nickelodeon) (49%); and television programs (*The Cosby Show, A Different World*) (14%).				
Cable and Wireless	6,800	—	1,750	5,023.2
A global communications company owning interests in local telephone companies. Operates digital and fiber-optic submarine cables. Major subsidiaries include Hong Kong Telecom (58% owned) and Mercury Communications (80%).				
Tele-Communications, Inc.	4,140	10.2	10,256	1680.9
The largest operator of cable-television systems in the United States. Also operates Encore. Divested in movie theaters in 1992 and publishes *Cabletime* television guide.				
CBS, Inc.	3,750	—	492	1061
Operates a radio and television network including 7 affiliate stations in New York City, Los Angeles, Chicago, Miami, Philadelphia, Minneapolis–St. Paul, and Green Bay and 21 radio stations. Sold its music and publishing operations in 1987.				
AT&T	67,030	—	16,376	15,096
Formed from court-ordered breakup of the Bell Telephone System, receiving 23% of the former company's assets. Operates interstate and international toll networks and portions of intrastate networks. Owns Western Electric and Bell Laboratories.				
A. H. Belo Corp.	555	—	282.2	315
Publishes the *Dallas Morning News* and 7 community newspapers in the Dallas–Ft. Worth area. Owns assets of the Times Herald Printing Co. and television stations in Dallas, Houston, Sacramento, Norfolk, and Tulsa. Owns a 40% interest in Falcon Video Communications.				

Sources: Value Line, Bloomberg, and *S&P Bond Rating Guide*.

Market Value of Equity ($ mil.)	Market Value/ Book Value of Equity	Price/ Earnings	Forecast Avg. Annual Price Earnings 1996–98	S & P Bond Rating	Beta	Volatility
5,798.4	6.19	36.6	24	BB+	1.2	.342
16,016	3.19	31.4	24	—	.95	.316
10,775	6.41	46.3	16	BBB−	1.65	.133
4,092	3.86	15.5	18	A	.95	.273
78,880	5.23	18.1	18	AA	.95	.147
920	2.92	19.3	22	BBB	.80	.294

Case 48

Westmoreland Energy, Inc.: Power Project at Zhangze, China

In November 1994, Dorothy Hampton reviewed with frustration the slow progress toward closing on the $540 million electric power generating project at Zhangze,[1] China. She was the project development manager at Westmoreland Energy, Inc. (WEI), a subsidiary of Westmoreland Coal. WEI specialized in the development of power projects in emerging economies. Hampton's responsibility was to seek out and consummate new project agreements in China. Negotiations with the Chinese government had begun more than a year ago. A joint venture agreement had been signed in March 1994—but this was merely a statement of intent of various parties that they would seek to complete a formal contract. Since March, a key potential investor had backed away from the deal. Decision making on the part of the Chinese was agonizingly slow. James Matthews, Hampton's boss and president of WEI, would be attending the parent company's board meeting in two days and needed to know when Hampton expected to close the Zhangze deal. Matthews mentioned that it was likely to be "now or never" on this deal because the company would not continue indefinitely to reserve the capital for this investment.

Hampton considered the alternatives. Should WEI push forward on its own? If so, on what terms? She knew that more than ample funds existed, given the recently announced sale of the parent company's largest eastern coal operation. WEI already had the essential development expertise in-house or under retainer through consulting agreements. Should

---

[1]See the pronunciation glossary in Exhibit 1 for phonetic pronunciation of this and other Chinese words.

This case was prepared by Reed Menefee and Andrew Meiman from field research under the direction of Professor Robert F. Bruner. Names of individuals and certain facts have been disguised. Copyright © 1996 by the University of Virginia Darden School Foundation, Charlottesville, VA. *No part of this publication may be reproduced, stored in a retrieval system, used in a spreadsheet, or transmitted in any form or by any means—electronic, mechanical, photocopying, recording, or otherwise—without the permission of the Darden School Foundation. For inquiries, please send an e-mail to dardencases@virginia.edu.* Revised 3/98. Version 2.1.

WEI drop out after a year of due diligence, fact finding, and negotiating? Hampton had to give Matthews her answer tomorrow morning.

WESTMORELAND ENERGY, INC.

Westmoreland Energy, Inc., based in Charlottesville, Virginia, was a subsidiary of Westmoreland Coal Company. WEI was formed in 1986 to compete in the independent power and cogeneration market. The company sought to achieve long-term growth through the development of energy projects in the domestic and international markets. Its project portfolio consisted of eight domestic projects with a gross capacity of 850 megawatts (MW) of electricity. The company's typical equity ownership in each of these projects was 30–50 percent.

Westmoreland Coal Company (WCX), WEI's parent, was established in 1854. WCX held substantial coal reserves and mining operations in the eastern United States and in Montana. In recent years, WCX had to contend with the oversupply and low price of Central Appalachian coal. These pressures resulted in a steady consolidation and downturn throughout the industry. Consequently, WCX was looking to reposition itself in new, higher growth markets. At fiscal year-end 1993, the company reported an operating loss of $97.6 million on revenues of $470 million. The loss was primarily attributable to the closing and write-off of several eastern mining operations. For the nine months ending September 30, 1994, the company reported a loss of $8.4 million on revenues of $305 million. The loss excluded a gain of $41.1 million on the sale of certain mining assets.

WEI's organization comprised three operating groups:

- The Development Group, which identified, created, and managed business opportunities.
- The Finance and Accounting Group, which obtained all necessary funding for projects and supported the overall financial needs of the company.
- The Venture and Asset Management Group, which oversaw the construction and operation of projects.

Over the past few years, the scope of the power industry had expanded from a predominantly domestic business to one dealing with diverse international projects. Projected annual growth in electricity demand in the United States through the year 2000 was less than 2 percent, with returns on investment in the range of 8–12 percent per annum.[2] In contrast, international markets were conservatively expected to grow between 5 percent and 10 percent annually during the same period, with potential returns in excess of 20 percent. WEI decided to focus on potential investments in China, Italy, and Mexico. Many of the international projects pursued by WEI were coal-fired electric-power generating plants, which complemented the firm's expertise in coal in independent power generation and mining.

WEI approached each of its international markets differently. In Mexico, WEI proposed an innovative energy supply partnership for an industrial complex and was exploring the acquisition of existing private cogeneration facilities. In Italy, WEI set out to work on a greenfield development.

---

[2]The investment returns noted here are returns on assets, not equity.

RATIONALE FOR PURSUING OPPORTUNITIES IN CHINA

In general, Hampton and others viewed China as a means not only to move WEI into an attractive power market, but to capitalize on WCX's historic strength in coal mining in a potentially high-growth coal-production market. In addition to the shortage of power in the Chinese countryside, there was also a shortage of rail and other transportation infrastructure. One objective of the Ministry of Electric Power was to encourage the development of power projects located near the coal mines. These projects would then export electricity via high-voltage transmission lines. This, in turn, would lessen the burden on the railroads by reducing the need to transport coal. Consequently, an attractive alternative to development of power plants in the rapidly growing coastal provinces was the development of projects in the interior provinces, such as Shanxi, near the fuel reserves. The interior mineral-rich province of Shanxi was at the heart of China's coal reserves.

Hampton believed that this strategy would appeal to WCX's board members who wanted to see "Coal" (the nickname for the coal company) revitalized. WCX had actively marketed the concept of mine-mouth power projects in the United States, but with minimal success due to the abundance of natural gas.[3] However, natural gas was not an alternative fuel in China. Coal was the fuel of choice, and it was estimated that its production would quadruple over the next decade in China.

With respect to China, Hampton had argued that project financing was the only feasible way for WEI to become involved with Zhangze given the scope and time horizon of the deal. She had considered putting together an all-equity financed plan to expedite government approvals and the building process. Equipment vendors, such as General Electric and Westinghouse, had been cited in the press for their eagerness to invest in China and open up new markets. Additionally, six investment funds (public and private), with a focus solely on Asian infrastructure, had recently raised more than $3.1 billion. Hampton, however, reminded herself of the principal reasons to rely on the project-financing structure that she had used so many times before. These reasons included the following:

- Elimination of, or limitation on, the recourse nature of the financing of a project.
- Off-balance-sheet treatment of debt financing.
- Leverage of debt to avoid dilution of existing equity.
- Avoidance of restrictive covenants in other debt or equity arrangements that may preclude project development.
- Arrangement of attractive debt financing and credit enhancement, available to the project itself but unavailable to the project sponsor as a direct loan.[4]

Admittedly, the advantages and disadvantages would be determined by the unique circumstances underlying the Zhangze Project. Hampton knew that there would be a constant tension among the various parties involved with respect to risk allocation, risk assumption, and risk avoidance.

---

[3]The "mine-mouth" concept provided for a power plant to be built at the mouth of a coal mine that supplied the fuel to the plant. This way, the coal transportation issues were minimized.

[4]"A Practical Guide to Transactional Project Finance: Basic Concepts, Risk Identification, and Contractual Considerations," *The Business Lawyer* 45, no. 1 (November 1989), pp. 181–85.

CHINA'S BUSINESS ENVIRONMENT

Hampton reflected on the general business environment in China, especially three broad subject areas: the political, the legal and regulatory, and the economic. Each area had positive and negative factors to consider.

Political Environment

In the political arena, a host of issues made Hampton wary. Unpredictable changes in China's top political leadership could dramatically change the attitude toward foreign investment. Moreover, China's communist ideology often left diplomatic relations with other nations under a cloud of uncertainty. If for any reason one or several leading nations cooled their relations with the PRC, foreign investment might be threatened. The United States' annual consideration of China's most-favored-nation status illustrated China's shaky position as a world-class trading partner. There was always the chance that a future radical change in government might have unfavorable results. As in many other countries around the world, there could be no strong guarantee that in the future the Chinese government would not nationalize or expropriate foreign-investment-backed projects.

Hampton felt that there were several positive aspects to China's political environment that balanced the apparent risks. In general, China's central leadership recognized the need to reform their central planning mentality and foster a more market-based approach. In 1992, senior leader Deng Xiaoping called for the establishment of a "socialist market economy." China also recognized the need for foreign-capital investment to meet their goals. To that end it was developing mechanisms such as open economic zones to encourage foreign capital and technology investment. Finally, local governments had become more autonomous and been given more authority to act on their own behalf. Officials in the Shanxi Province reflected this growing independence and were anxious to close deals to help them grow and improve the lives of their people. On a practical level, this meant developing the infrastructure, such as electricity-generation capacity, to support growth.

Legal and Regulatory Environment

Legal and regulatory concerns were closely related to the political environment through the laws and mandates from China's leadership. The PRC's legal system was a civil law system based on written statutes. Decided legal cases had little precedent value. No well-developed body of laws governing foreign investment enterprises existed. As a result, the administration of laws and regulations by government agencies was subject to considerable discretion. New laws, changes to existing laws, and inconsistent interpretation of laws might adversely affect foreign investment.[5] For example, laws that limited the controlling interests and returns on investment had widely varying interpretation and application

---

[5]AES China Generating Co. Ltd. prospectus, 1994, p. 10.

throughout China. Overall, the legal system might impede the development of competitive markets and the development of roles and responsibilities of the players in these markets.

Although it was under reform, much of the existing legal and institutional framework was based on government-owned enterprises and a command-and-control structure. Specifically, many aspects of the power sector operated without contractual arrangements, instead relying on the mechanisms of central planning.[6] The entire context of contractual obligation was vastly different in China than in further developed countries. For example, Chinese government agencies had signed hundreds of "letters of intent" to enter into joint venture arrangements with dozens of companies. In some cases, "exclusive" letters had been signed with several parties for the same project.

Hampton knew that the Chinese government had initiated a series of dramatic reforms targeted at the power industry. The proposed "electricity law" and the promotion of contractual arrangements through the Ministry of Electric Power would make a positive impact in the legal and regulatory environment of the industry.

Economic Environment

The final, and perhaps the most critical area, was China's economic environment. In the past, the PRC government had implemented policies to restrain economic growth rates, control inflation, and otherwise regulate economic expansion. See Exhibit 2 for a table of macroeconomic indicators. The recent market-based reforms had made a significant positive impact. However, the reforms were carried out on an incremental, piecemeal basis. There was no assurance that the reforms would continue, or continue to be successful. Furthermore, the reforms and economic expansion had been more effective in some provinces than in others.

Probably the most important economic issue, and one of the most difficult for Hampton to come to grips with, was the foreign-exchange aspect of the project. Although in the past China had used heavy-handed policies to prevent sustained high inflation rates, Hampton was still concerned with the potential for depreciation of the Chinese currency, the renminbi (RMB).

The Chinese government had implemented major changes in the country's foreign-exchange system. The new system emphasized external liberalization and a transparent system based on rules and prodevelopment macroeconomic policies.

> The new unified exchange arrangement is a managed float. At the start of each day, the PBC [People's Bank of China] announces a reference rate based on the average of the buying and selling rates against the U.S. dollar at the close of the previous day's trading. Movement of the renminbi against the U.S. dollar is limited to 0.3 percent on either side of the reference rate, with the PBC intervening in the interbank market through purchases and sales of foreign exchange to keep the exchange rate within this limit. During the first six months of 1994, the exchange rate remained stable at about Y [RMB] 8.7 per U.S. dollar . . . and the foreign exchange holdings of the PBC rose.[7]

---

[6]*China Power Sector Reform,* World Bank report, September 1994, p. 30.
[7]International Monetary Fund, "Exchange and Trade System Reforms," *Economic Reform in China: A New Phase,* November 1994.

Hampton knew that Matthews and the board had encountered similar dilemmas with regard to their dealings in Italy and Mexico. Had Zhangze been structured appropriately to account for these concerns? Was it adequately reflected in the terms and potential returns of the deal?

Turning toward the power industry, Hampton contemplated what she thought was a huge market opportunity. With approximately 1.1 billion people, China was the most populous country on earth. Compared to other developing countries, China's power sector was vastly underdeveloped. In 1993, China had 183,000 MW of installed capacity. This represented a rate of about 8 percent annual growth over the installed base of 66,000 MW in 1980. China's 10-year development program for the 1990s had recently been revised to target 8 to 9 percent gross domestic product (GDP) growth through the 1990s. Electricity demand and GDP growth occur at essentially the same rate. Chinese authorities estimated adding yearly capacity at a rate of 15,000–16,000 MW per year through 1997 and 17,000–20,000 MW per year from 1998 through 2000. This growth in capacity matched GDP growth, but still only reduced the existing power shortages from 10 percent to 5 percent of the total demand.[8]

By the year 2000, China's installed base was expected to be nearly 300,000 MW. During this period, private companies and non-Chinese parties could be involved in more than 70,000 MW worth of projects.[9] With the trend toward larger generation units and larger projects, in the range from 300 to 1,200 MW on average, this potential need represented 100 to 200 major projects for non-Chinese parties before the year 2000, with many more to follow. The Zhangze project could be the foot in the door that WEI needed to capitalize on this potentially huge market opportunity.

THE ZHANGZE POWER PLANT

The Zhangze Power Plant was located in the suburb of Changzhi City, which was in the southeastern part of Shanxi Province, which was in the north-central region of the country of China. Changzhi was one of the energy/chemical/heavy-industry bases of Shanxi province. Since the sixth five-year plan (1981–1985), the state had invested in a series of key projects, including the Shanxi Chemical Fertilizer Plant, the Changcun Coal Colliery, and the Zhangze Power Plant.[10]

In order to meet the demand of industrial and agricultural development in the southeastern district of Shanxi, and to maximize the advantage of rich coal resources in this area, the state arranged the construction of Zhangze Power Plant. Phase I (two 100-MW units) was finished and put into operation in 1986. Phase II (four 210-MW Soviet-made units) was operational by 1991. Recently, the Ministry of Energy and the Shanxi government had given instructions to prepare for the Phase III expansion of the plant. The scope of the Phase III expansion was 600 MW (two 300-MW units).

The Zhangze Power Plant was the only large regional plant project in the southeast of Shanxi. At the completion of Phase III, the plant would function as a mine-mouth power

---

[8]*China Power Sector Reform,* World Bank report, September 1994, p. 6.

[9]W. Meade and E. Roseman, "Entering China's Power Market," *Independent Energy,* October 1993.

[10]Shanxi Electric Design Institute, Feasibility Study for Zhangze Power Plant.

plant promoting industrial and agricultural development in the southeastern district of Shanxi. It would reduce the power shortfall in Shanxi, provide additional power to the Beijing-Tianjin district, and create conditions that would allow electricity to be sent to eastern and southern provinces.

Hampton and her colleagues selected the Zhangze Project as the best China opportunity available to WEI based primarily on the following considerations:

- *Extension project.* The project was an extension of an existing plant, which meant that the site was currently available and some of the necessary infrastructure for the next phase had already been planned, designed, or constructed as part of earlier phases. Ideally this would translate into a shorter development period and lower development costs.
- *Local and provincial support.* A high degree of government support would assist the project in gaining necessary approvals and funding.
- *Electricity sales.* All of the power generated by the project would be purchased by the Shanxi Provincial Electric Power Company rather than being sold directly to distant provinces. This would allow for a simpler development process since involvement with other provinces would not be required.
- *Project size and type.* Although the final size of the plant would be determined by the final selection of equipment (chosen to optimize plant economics), this was a well-established, conventional-size plant, and it would use proven technology.
- *Project schedule.* The Shanxi Power Bureau had indicated a desire for the project to be operational in 1998. This aggressive schedule would provide high visibility and an early foothold for WEI in China.

WEI'S INVOLVEMENT WITH ZHANGZE

In early July 1993, representatives from WEI and its U.S. law firm traveled to China to review project opportunities. Hampton arranged meetings with provincial leaders, representatives from the Shanxi Power Bureau, Taiyuan City officials, and Zhangze Power Plant officials. At the conclusion of the two-week trip, WEI signed a letter of intent[11] with the Zhangze Power Plant and Changzhi city government for the development of the Phase III Zhangze Project.

WEI arranged for a site trip and further discussions during December 1993. At the conclusion of these discussions, a preliminary joint venture agreement[12] was signed with the Shanxi Power Bureau. The agreement promised WEI the exclusive right to develop the project.

---

[11]The letter of intent was a one-page document that stated the Shanxi Provincial Electric Power Company's intention to build a coal-fired electric generating facility in Changzhi, Shanxi. The document was signed by WEI, WEI's law firm, and the Changzhi city government. The document closed by saying that "the parties to this agreement are prepared to enter into negotiations of final details for a memorandum of understanding for an equity joint venture, contract, and articles of association." (Source: company records.)

[12]The preliminary joint venture agreement incorporated the major points from negotiations subsequent to the letter of intent. Although 15 pages in length, the document was still tentative in detail and very far from a final agreement by U.S. standards. (Source: company records.)

The State Planning Commission issued an approval letter[13] for the project in early February 1994. WEI subsequently arranged for a site study to be performed by a U.S. engineering and construction firm. With the assistance of a number of consultants and an investment bank, a joint venture agreement[14] was signed on March 9, 1994. Key points in the agreement included the following:

Parties	1. Shanxi Provincial Electric Power Company
	2. WEI
	3. State Energy Investment Company (to be a party to the joint venture contract, but did not sign the agreement)
	4. Shanxi Provincial Planning Committee (signed agreement to demonstrate support, but will not be a party to the joint venture contract)
Type	Equity joint venture, whereby the venture will be capitalized at 75/25 (debt/equity).[15] In the base case, this meant that WEI would put in 40 percent of the equity capital and the Chinese would put in 60 percent.
Ownership interest	49 percent WEI; 51 percent to be divided among the Chinese parties
Size	600 MW; 2-unit coal-fired power plant
Term	Twenty years from start of construction. Build-operate-transfer (BOT), whereby WEI will build the plant, operate it during the contract period, and at the end of the term transfer the asset to the local partner at no additional cost.
Operation	1998

Thinking about the joint venture agreement brought Hampton back to the hard reality of the numbers and the task that lay before her. She turned her attention back to the model and focused on the critical assumptions that went into the project's valuation.

THE DETAILS OF THE DEAL AND THE MODEL

With the assistance of Rob Kost, an experienced financial analyst, Hampton built a detailed model of the project that allowed her to run sensitivities on a handful of key assumptions. She focused her efforts on the project's principal pressure points. Many uncertainties had already been put to rest with sound contractual agreements. The Chinese had shown flexibility on some items[16] and inflexibility on others.[17] Nonetheless, a handful of critical inputs

---

[13]The approval letter from the State Planning Commission was a formality that had to be received prior to embarking on the due diligence necessary for the joint venture agreement. (Source: company records.)

[14]Defined as a business undertaking by two or more parties in which profits, losses, and control are shared. A legally binding agreement subject to various conditions and requirements.

[15]The 75/25 debt/equity mix was approved by the Chinese authorities (through the State Planning Commission). WEI's investment banker had negotiated this point based on its view of the market and other deal precedents.

[16]Points of flexibility had been capital-cost escalations, term and rate on debt financing, and WEI's equity investment percentage. However, there was no guarantee that these items would be negotiable in the future.

[17]Points of inflexibility had been plant scale, and the 75 percent/25 percent mix of debt and equity financing.

had not been easy to pinpoint. See Exhibit 3 for a summary of the project's sources and uses of funds. Exhibits 4 through 10 give various financial exhibits from the project's forecasting model.

Operating Assumptions

Within the operating assumptions, Hampton knew that production hours per year had a major effect on the project's returns. The Chinese had set a very conservative goal of 6,000 hours per annum based on historical statistics from existing Chinese plants. WEI's power plants in the United States, however, typically operated at 90 percent utilization or better (7,884 hours per annum). Hampton believed that WEI could do substantially better than the Chinese had estimated. Of course, there was the likelihood that the labor and operating practices of the Chinese would depress production and capacity utilization levels. Hampton and Kost were comfortable with an operating hours per year range of 5,500 to 6,500. The upper end of the range (74 percent utilization) was within reach if everything went as planned.

The forecast assumed no increase in the scale of the plant through the year 2014. While there would be periodic overhauls of the equipment, all of the capital spending would be for maintenance. The accounting for this project assumed that all maintenance spending and expenditures would be an ordinary deduction for tax purposes.

Business Context Assumptions

Many of the core business contracts were set at this point. Hampton had received firm bids and indications as detailed in the model. The big unknown here was what would happen to the U.S. dollar and RMB inflation, and in turn how this would affect the capital costs and foreign exchange rate over the next 20 years. Most "authorities" viewed the U.S. dollar as likely to inflate at a rate between 2.5 and 4.0 percent over the next five years. Inflation in China, on the other hand, was anybody's guess. Optimistic investment banks opined that 10 percent RMB inflation was reasonable in the near term. China's inflation rate had fluctuated between 5 percent and 26 percent from 1992 through 1994 (see Exhibit 11). However, recent statistics showed enormous real growth in China, which could eventually offset the inflationary trends. Moreover, the Chinese government had publicly shown its resolve and ability to keep inflation under control. The capital-cost escalation figures (in the model) were used solely during the three-year construction period and then capitalized with the total construction cost.

Hampton believed that the inflation risk could be managed through properly structured pricing formulas and linkages between supply contracts and take-or-pay contracts. She questioned sensitivity analyses that compounded an assumed inflation rate over the entire term of the debt and sought to determine the project's level of vulnerability to rising inflation. She took some comfort in WEI's use of fixed-rate loans (or bonds) which would mitigate interest rate risk. She also took comfort in the strength of the project's cash flows and contractual mechanisms for annual upward adjustment of electricity prices.

Hampton believed that the electricity prices should be indexed to inflation. The Chinese would not permit a 1:1 match, but an escalation clause was permitted. There would not be a reduction if deflation occurred. Given the generous pricing at the plant's commencement and other tax incentives, Hampton assumed that the price escalation would be low for political reasons. It was currently set at 4 percent per annum for the duration of the contract.

Financing Assumptions

Hampton considered the proposed terms of the financing. WEI's investment banker had assured Hampton that the deal would be well received in the market. Due to the increasingly competitive international bond and bank markets, the proposed 10 percent rate (on the U.S.$ debt) was within reach if the deal could be closed within the next three months. It was possible that the all-in cost might push the coupon up another 50 basis points. The U.S. and Hong Kong markets were firm about the 10-year tenor, but several European banks had talked about going out to 12 years at 10.5 percent per annum. The Chinese had essentially agreed to the terms as detailed in the model (10-year RMB debt at 11 percent per annum). The RMB-debt interest rate might be pushed up another 100 basis points if the Chinese economy overheated with growth and inflation rose. Interest rates are contained in Exhibit 12.

Although WEI would receive a 49 percent ownership interest, meaning that it was entitled to 49 percent of the cash flows to equity, its actual equity investment would be somewhat less than 49 percent of the total project equity. The Chinese had negotiated that several transmission lines be included in the project costs. However, these transmission lines would not belong to the project. Consequently, the Chinese agreed to put in a higher proportion of the cash invested than they would receive in equity interest. It was also interesting to note that the Chinese equity contribution included some of the "soft" costs primarily associated with the initial feasibility studies. Hampton was confident that WEI would receive its 49 percent for something in the range of 37 percent to 45 percent of the total equity committed to the deal.

WEI and its advisers negotiated that the overall project would be funded with at least 25 percent equity, thereby leaving 75 percent for debt. This meant that the combination of local and foreign equity had to account for 25 percent of the total project investment. The model allowed Hampton to vary the debt and equity breakdown of WEI's investment and thereby vary the debt and equity breakdown of the U.S. and Chinese shares, but keep the overall project capital mix at 75 percent debt and 25 percent equity.

Hampton had prepared a financial forecast that went out through the year 2014, the termination date of the BOT contract. The entire model was driven by the "assumptions" section and resulted in a residual cash-flow analysis (cash flows to equity).

In considering which discount rate to use, Hampton leaned toward using the capital asset pricing model (CAPM). Matthews, however, was not convinced of CAPM's relevance. He felt that the board's desired 20 percent IRR was the best benchmark. But Hampton was not comfortable with the board's mandated 20 percent IRR. The capital asset pricing model showed that the expected risk premium on an investment was proportional to its beta. She identified several publicly traded comparables to Zhangze, and considered using their costs of equity to determine the relevant hurdle. The asset betas and market value debt/equity ratios of these companies are given in Exhibit 13. Matthews had doubted that CAPM would have much relevance in an emerging economy with spurious market data and with the comparability of Hampton's peer sample. Therefore, Hampton determined to take a closer look at each entity to make sure. Three of the comparable companies were listed on stock exchanges in the United States. The other two were listed on the Hong Kong exchange. She noted that the Hong Kong dollar was pegged to the U.S. dollar. Exhibit 14 gives information regarding yield premiums on Chinese "Yankee bonds"[18] and country betas of Asian equity markets relative to the U.S. equity market.

CONCLUSION

Hampton had to give Matthews her recommendation about Zhangze tomorrow morning. No matter which way the decision went, Matthews would want a detailed explanation, including a valuation analysis and a summary of risks. She would have to focus on the key value drivers and terms of the deal. Did the structure ensure the necessary coverage ratios,[19] debt/equity mix, and return requirements? Hampton was concerned that Matthews and the board were not consistently applying the appropriate cost of equity to prospective deals, and consequently their expectations were out of sync with the market. This issue needed to be thoroughly aired, as it would have a profound impact on her ability to do this or any deal. Hampton thought about the appropriate risk analysis for the board, which would entail exercising the model, carefully reviewing the deal design and examining its affect on the terms of the financing (such as coverage ratios, debt amortization, and the project's capitalization). Before proceeding with the analysis for the board, she had to resolve the issue of an appropriate discount rate. Regardless of whether she used the board's 20 percent hurdle, or determined a cost of equity using comparables, Hampton knew that determining the appropriate return would be fundamental to her analysis and decision.

---

[18]A "Yankee bond" is a security issued by a foreign government or corporation in the U.S. capital markets. The issue is denominated in U.S. dollars.

[19]WEI's investment banker had advised Hampton that the capital markets would expect a debt coverage ratio of no less than 1.1 in each of the two years of operation and then gradually approaching 1.5 for the remainder of the debt term. Similarly, the interest coverage ratio was expected to be generally twice that of the debt coverage ratio with some leeway allowed in the first few years.

EXHIBIT 1   Pronunciation Glossary

Changcun	′chawng-qun
Changzhi	′chawng-juh
Huabei	wah-′bay
Huaneng	wah-′nung
Shandong	shawn-′dong
Shanxi	shawn-′C
Taiyuan	′tie-you-in
Tianjin	tea-′en-ean
Zhangze	′thZong-zuh

Note: The (′) mark denotes the syllable for emphasis.

EXHIBIT 2   Macroeconomic Indicators (annual percentage change unless otherwise specified)

	1980	1981	1982	1983	1984	1985	1986
Real GNP	7.9	4.4	8.8	10.4	14.7	12.8	8.1
Real gross industrial output	9.3	4.3	7.8	11.2	16.3	21.4	11.7
Real gross fixed investment	2.9	−12.5	28.0	14.7	22.7	27.3	13.3
Consumer retail prices							
Period average	6.0	2.4	1.9	1.5	2.8	8.8	6.0
End of period	22.2	2.6	0.1	3.7	4.8	10.7	6.2
Merchandise exports							
(% change in U.S.$ terms)	33.7	20.5	−4.0	−2.0	15.4	5.0	2.6
Merchandise imports							
(% change in U.S.$ terms)	24.8	12.6	−16.4	−10.9	27.6	60.0	−8.7
Trade balance							
(billions of U.S.$)	1.9	—	3.0	0.8	−1.3	−14.8	−12.0
(In Percent of GNP)							
Current account balance	0.3	0.9	2.1	1.5	0.8	−4.0	2.6
Overall budgetary balance	−3.3	−1.3	−1.4	−1.7	−1.5	−0.5	−2.0
Revenue	29.4	29.0	27.2	27.4	26.4	26.6	25.1
Expenditure	32.7	30.3	28.6	29.1	27.9	27.1	27.1
(RMB per U.S.$)							
Official exchange rate							
(period average)	—	—	—	—	—	—	—

Source: International Monetary Fund, *Economic Reform in China,* November 1994; and *International Financial Statistics* magazine.

1987	1988	1989	1990	1991	1992	1993		Avg.		
10.9	11.3	4.4	4.1	7.7	13.0	13.4		9.4		
17.7	20.8	8.5	7.8	14.5	22.0	21.1		13.9		
14.7	10.4	−15.5	1.2	18.8	28.2	22.0		12.6		
7.3	18.6	17.8	2.1	2.9	5.3	13.0		6.9		
9.1	26.7	6.4	2.2	4.0	6.7	17.6		8.8		
34.9	18.2	5.3	19.2	17.8	18.6	8.0				
4.3	27.4	5.3	−13.3	22.3	26.2	29.0				
−3.8	−7.7	−6.6	8.7	8.1	4.4	−12.2				
			(In Percent of GNP)							
0.1	−1.0	−1.7	3.9	3.8	1.8	−2.5				
−2.2	−2.4	−2.3	−2.1	−2.5	−2.5	−2.1				
22.8	20.0	20.4	20.1	18.1	16.3	15.4				
25.0	22.4	22.7	22.1	20.5	18.9	17.5				
			(RMB per U.S.$)							

									1994	
								I	*II*	*III*
—	3.722	3.765	4.783	5.323	5.515	5.762		8.702	8.673	8.590

EXHIBIT 3 Sources & Uses (in millions)

	In RMB	*In U.S.$*
Sources		
Local currency loan	1,005.82	$114.30
Nonrecourse U.S.$ loan	2,647.74	300.88
WEI equity (40%)	402.83	45.78
Chinese equity (60%)	733.51	83.35
Total	4,789.90	$544.31
Uses		
Construction cost	3,664.00	$416.36
Cost escalation	646.56	73.47
Interest during construction	479.34	54.47
Total	4,789.90	$544.31

Notes:
Base-case values.
Investment bankers were confident that they could place all debt.
Assumed exchange rate (RMB/U.S.$) = 8.8

Source: Company documents and casewriter analysis.

EXHIBIT 4   Model Assumptions

Operating Assumptions

Installed plant capacity, megawatts	600	Major overhaul (% of total cost)	1%
Start of construction date	1995	Operation and maintenance (base year)	
Construction period, months	36	(water, material—RMB millions)	59.17
Date of operation	1998	Number of staff	400
Generation efficiency	92.2%	Staff salaries, RMB/year/staff member	10,000
Coal consumption, tons/hour	273.9	Management salaries, RMB/year	1,900,000
Coal cost, RMB/ton	100	*Operating hours/year*	6,000

Business Context Assumptions

Sales tax rate	5.0%	Coal price escalation, %	6.0%
Income tax rate		Operation and maintenance cost escalation, %	8.0%
Years 1–2	0.0%	*Electricity sale price escalation, %*	4.0%
Years 3–5	15.0%	*U.S.$ capital cost escalation, %*	3.2%
Years 6–end	30.0%	*RMB capital cost escalation, %*	10%
		U.S.$ official FX rate (RMB/U.S.$)	8.8

Financing Assumptions

Contract term, years	20	*U.S.$ debt repayment period, years*	10
		U.S.$ debt interest rate	10.0%
		RMB debt repayment period, years	10
		RMB debt interest rate	11.0%

Notes:
Base-case values.
Capital cost escalation applies only to the three-year construction period.
Italicized lines are adjustable inputs.

Source: Company documents and casewriter analysis.

EXHIBIT 5   Investment Summary and Investment Breakdown

Project Investment (Base Assumptions, Millions)

	Local Invest (RMB) *Base*	*U.S.$ Invest* *Base*	*U.S.$ to RMB* *Base*	*Total (RMB)* *Base*	*%*
Power Plant	1,200	280	2,464	3,664.0	100%
Debt	650.4	238.4	2,097.6	2,748.0	75%*
Equity	549.6	41.6	366.4	916.0	25%

Investment Breakdown as a % of Total Project

Equity			*Debt*	
WEI equity†	40.00%		U.S.$ debt	76.33%
Local equity	60.00%		Local debt	23.67%
Totals	100.0%			100.0%

Investment Breakdown of Individual Allocations

Chinese Portion			*WEI Portion*	
Local debt	54.20%		U.S.$ debt	85.13%
Local equity	45.80%		WEI equity	14.87%
Totals	100.00%			100.00%

Base-case values.
Italicized lines are adjustable inputs.
*75/25 debt/equity split dictated by Chinese authorities.
†In the model, changing WEI's % of equity allows different debt/equity mixes to be examined. Change only this cell and the model will calculate the remainder of the mix percentages. Dorothy felt confident that WEI would receive its 49% ownership interest for something in the range of 37% to 45% of the total equity contributed to the deal.

Source: Company documents and casewriter analysis.

EXHIBIT 6   Project Cost and Financing Summary

Project Cost Summary (millions)

	U.S.$ Invest	U.S.$ Convt'd. to RMB	Local RMB Invest	Total (RMB)
Construction cost	280.00	2,464.00	1,200.00	3,664.00
Cost escalation	27.84	245.00	401.56	646.56
Subtotal	307.84	2,709.00	1,601.56	4,310.56
Interest during construction	38.81	341.57	137.77	479.34
Total	346.66	3,050.57	1,739.33	4,789.90

Financing Summary (millions)

	U.S.$ Invest	U.S.$ Conv'td. to RMB	Local RMB Invest	Total (RMB)
Local currency loan			1,005.82	1,005.82
Nonrecourse U.S.$ loan	300.88	2,647.74		2,647.74
Total debt				3,653.55
WEI equity	45.78	402.83		402.83
Chinese equity			733.51	733.51
Total equity				1,136.34
Total debt + equity				4,789.90

Base-case values.

Source: Company documents and casewriter analysis.

EXHIBIT 7 Expenditure Schedule and Interest during Construction (IDC) (millions)

Construction year	0	1	2	3	
		1995	*1996*	*1997*	*Totals*
RMB (% of total spent/year)		30%	40%	30%	100%
Base debt schedule		195.12	260.16	195.12	650.40
Escalated debt schedule		236.10	346.27	285.68	868.04
Interest during construction		12.99	45.02	79.77	137.77
Subtotal		249.08	391.29	365.45	1,005.82
Equity schedule		199.50	292.61	241.40	733.51
Total		448.59	683.90	606.85	1,739.33
U.S.$ (% of total spent/year)		30%	40%	30%	100%
Base debt schedule		71.51	95.35	71.51	238.36
Escalated debt schedule		76.16	104.79	81.11	262.06
Interest during construction		3.81	12.86	22.15	38.81
Subtotal		79.97	117.65	103.26	300.88
Equity schedule		13.30	18.31	14.17	45.78
Total		93.27	135.96	117.43	346.66
Total in RMB (% of total spent/year)		30%	40%	30%	100%
Base debt schedule		824.40	1,099.20	824.40	2,748.00
Escalated debt schedule		906.29	1,268.47	999.45	3,174.21
Interest during construction		46.50	158.14	274.70	479.34
Subtotal		952.79	1,426.61	1,274.15	3,653.55
Equity schedule		316.57	453.69	366.08	1,136.34
Total		1,269.36	1,880.30	1,640.23	4,789.90

Base-case values.

Source: Company documents and casewriter analysis.

EXHIBIT 8   Debt Repayment Schedule (millions)

Year number	1	2	3	4	5	6	7
	1998	*1999*	*2000*	*2001*	*2002*	*2003*	*2004*
U.S.$ debt							
Beginning balance	300.88	282.00	261.23	238.39	213.26	185.62	155.22
Principal payment	18.88	20.77	22.84	25.13	27.64	30.40	33.44
Interest payment	30.09	28.20	26.12	23.84	21.33	18.56	15.52
Ending balance	282.00	261.23	238.39	213.26	185.62	155.22	121.77
Total debt service	48.97	48.97	48.97	48.97	48.97	48.97	48.97
RMB debt							
Beginning balance	1,005.82	945.67	878.90	804.79	722.53	631.22	529.86
Principal payment	60.15	66.77	74.11	82.26	91.31	101.36	112.50
Interest payment	110.64	104.02	96.68	88.53	79.48	69.43	58.29
Ending balance	945.67	878.90	804.79	722.53	631.22	529.86	417.36
Total debt service	170.79	170.79	170.79	170.79	170.79	170.79	170.79
U.S.$ and RMB debt in RMB							
Beginning balance	3,653.55	3,427.27	3,177.76	2,902.63	2,599.24	2,264.69	1,895.78
Principal payment	226.28	249.51	275.13	303.39	334.55	368.91	406.82
Interest payment	375.41	352.18	326.56	298.31	267.15	232.78	194.88
Ending balance	3,427.27	3,177.76	2,902.63	2,599.24	2,264.69	1,895.78	1,488.96
Debt service	601.70	601.70	601.70	601.70	601.70	601.70	601.70

Base-case values.

Source: Company documents and casewriter analysis.

8	9	10	11	12	13	14	15	16	17	
2005	*2006*	*2007*	*2008*	*2009*	*2010*	*2011*	*2012*	*2013*	*2014*	*TOTAL*
121.77	84.98	44.52	0.00	0.00	0.00	0.00	0.00	0.00	0.00	
36.79	40.47	44.52	0.00	0.00	0.00	0.00	0.00	0.00	0.00	300.88
12.18	8.50	4.45	0.00	0.00	0.00	0.00	0.00	0.00	0.00	188.79
84.98	44.52	0.00	0.00	0.00	0.00	0.00	0.00	0.00	0.00	
48.97	48.97	48.97	0.00	0.00	0.00	0.00	0.00	0.00	0.00	489.67
417.36	292.48	153.86	0.00	0.00	0.00	0.00	0.00	0.00	0.00	
124.88	138.62	153.86	0.00	0.00	0.00	0.00	0.00	0.00	0.00	1,005.82
45.91	32.17	16.93	0.00	0.00	0.00	0.00	0.00	0.00	0.00	702.07
292.48	153.86	0.00	0.00	0.00	0.00	0.00	0.00	0.00	0.00	
170.79	170.79	170.79	0.00	0.00	0.00	0.00	0.00	0.00	0.00	1,707.89
1,488.96	1,040.34	545.60	0.00	0.00	0.00	0.00	0.00	0.00	0.00	
448.63	494.74	545.60	0.00	0.00	0.00	0.00	0.00	0.00	0.00	3,653.55
153.07	106.96	56.10	0.00	0.00	0.00	0.00	0.00	0.00	0.00	2,363.41
1,040.34	545.60	0.00	0.00	0.00	0.00	0.00	0.00	0.00	0.00	
601.70	601.70	601.70	0.00	0.00	0.00	0.00	0.00	0.00	0.00	6,016.96

EXHIBIT 9   Operating Statement (millions)

Year number	1	2	3	4	5	6
	1998	*1999*	*2000*	*2001*	*2002*	*2003*
Gross output, MW	600	600	600	600	600	600
Net output, MW	553.2	553.2	553.2	553.2	553.2	553.2
Operating hours/Year	5500	6000	6000	6000	6000	6000
Net GWh/ Year	3,042.60	3,319.20	3,319.20	3,319.20	3,319.20	3,319.20
Sales price, RMB/kWh	0.328	0.341	0.355	0.369	0.384	0.399
Gross revenue, RMB	997.97	1,132.25	1,177.54	1,224.64	1,273.62	1,324.57
Sales tax	49.90	56.61	58.88	61.23	63.68	66.23
Net revenue	948.07	1,075.63	1,118.66	1,163.40	1,209.94	1,258.34
Variable costs						
Coal	150.65	174.20	184.65	195.73	207.48	219.92
Other						
Total variable costs	150.65	174.20	184.65	195.73	207.48	219.92
Fixed costs						
Operation and maintenance	54.3	59.17	63.9	69.0	74.5	80.5
Staff	5.9	6.4	6.9	7.4	8.0	8.7
Major overhaul	47.9	47.9	47.9	47.9	47.9	47.9
Total fixed costs	108.1	113.4	118.7	124.3	130.5	137.1
Operating profit	689.3	788.0	815.3	843.3	872.0	901.3
Debt interest paid	375.4	352.2	326.6	298.3	267.1	232.8
Depreciation	278.9	278.9	278.9	278.9	278.9	278.9
Profit before tax	35.0	156.9	209.9	266.1	326.0	389.7
Income tax	0.0	0.0	31.5	39.9	48.9	116.9
Profit after tax (net profit)	35.0	156.9	178.4	226.2	277.1	272.8
Debt principal repaid	226.3	249.5	275.1	303.4	334.5	368.9
Debt coverage ratio	1.15	1.31	1.36	1.40	1.45	1.50
= Operating profit/(Interest + Principal repaid)						
Interest coverage ratio	1.84	2.24	2.50	2.83	3.26	3.87
= Operating profit/Interest						

Notes:
Base-case values.
MW—megawatt; kWh—kilowatt hour; GWh—gigawatt hour.

Source: Company documents and casewriter analysis.

7	8	9	10	11	12	13	14	15
2004	*2005*	*2006*	*2007*	*2008*	*2009*	*2010*	*2011*	*2012*
600	600	600	600	600	600	600	600	600
553.2	553.2	553.2	553.2	553.2	553.2	553.2	553.2	553.2
6000	6000	6000	6000	6000	6000	6000	6000	6000
3,319.20	3,319.20	3,319.20	3,319.20	3,319.20	3,319.20	3,319.20	3,319.20	3,319.20
0.415	0.432	0.449	0.467	0.486	0.505	0.525	0.546	0.568
1,377.55	1,432.65	1,489.96	1,549.56	1,611.54	1,676.00	1,743.04	1,812.76	1,885.27
68.88	71.63	74.50	77.48	80.58	83.80	87.15	90.64	94.26
1,308.67	1,361.02	1,415.46	1,472.08	1,530.96	1,592.20	1,655.89	1,722.12	1,791.01
233.12	247.11	261.93	277.65	294.31	311.97	330.68	350.53	371.56
233.12	247.11	261.93	277.65	294.31	311.97	330.68	350.53	371.56
86.9	93.9	101.4	109.5	118.3	127.7	138.0	149.0	160.9
9.4	10.1	10.9	11.8	12.7	13.8	14.9	16.0	17.3
47.9	47.9	47.9	47.9	47.9	47.9	47.9	47.9	47.9
144.2	151.9	160.2	169.2	178.9	189.4	200.7	212.9	226.1
931.4	962.0	993.3	1,025.2	1,057.7	1,090.8	1,124.5	1,158.7	1,193.3
194.9	153.1	107.0	56.1	0.0	0.0	0.0	0.0	0.0
278.9	278.9	278.9	278.9	278.9	278.9	278.9	278.9	278.9
457.6	530.0	607.4	690.2	778.8	811.9	845.6	879.8	914.4
137.3	159.0	182.2	207.1	233.7	243.6	253.7	263.9	274.3
320.3	371.0	425.2	483.2	545.2	568.4	591.9	615.8	640.1
406.8	448.6	494.7	545.6	0.0	0.0	0.0	0.0	0.0
1.55	1.60	1.65	1.70	NA	NA	NA	NA	NA
4.78	6.28	9.29	18.28	NA	NA	NA	NA	NA

EXHIBIT 10   Equity Cash Flows (millions)

	1995	1996	1997	1998	1999	2000	2001	2002
Profit after tax				35	157	178	226	277
(+) Depreciation				279	279	279	279	279
(−) Debt amortization				(226)	(250)	(275)	(303)	(335)
(−) Equity investment	(317)	(454)	(366)					
Residual cash flow (total proj)	(317)	(454)	(366)	88	186	182	202	221
IRR (on equity total project)	18.79%							
WEI ownership interest	49.00%							
WEI equity investment %	40.00%							
RCF, WEI portion only	(117)	(161)	(125)	43	91	89	99	108
IRR (WEI equity in project)	23%							
Cost of equity	20.0%							
NPV	70.8 RMB							

EXHIBIT 11   China's Inflation Rate

Year	Change in Cost of Living Index (%)			
	1st Quarter	2nd Quarter	3rd Quarter	4th Quarter
1992	5.40	5.50	6.10	8.30
1993	11.10	13.90	16.10	17.10
1994	23.40	21.90	25.80	

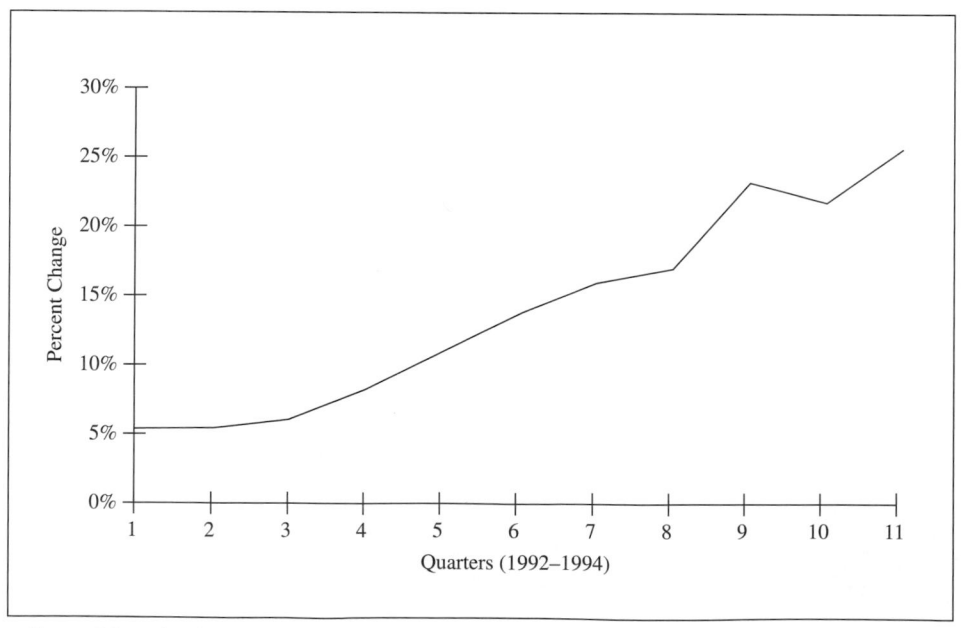

Source of data: *The China Business Review.*

2003	2004	2005	2006	2007	2008	2009	2010	2011	2012	2013	2014
273	320	371	425	483	545	568	592	616	640	664	688
279	279	279	279	279	279	279	279	279	279	280	281
(369)	(407)	(449)	(495)	(546)	—	—	—	—	—	—	—
183	192	201	209	216	824	847	871	895	919	944	969
90	94	99	103	106	404	415	427	438	450	462	475

EXHIBIT 12 U.S. Interest Rates

				Treasuries			
Date	*1-year*	*2-year*	*3-year*	*5-year*	*10-year*	*20-year*	*30-year*
12/1/93	3.62	4.20	4.54	5.14	5.82	6.44	6.28
1/1/94	3.67	4.30	4.66	5.29	5.92	6.54	6.41
2/1/94	3.60	4.20	4.53	5.10	5.77	6.37	6.31
3/1/94	4.16	4.81	5.19	5.74	6.28	6.86	6.79
4/1/94	4.50	5.21	5.66	6.23	6.77	7.23	7.11
5/1/94	5.12	5.81	6.20	6.69	7.09	7.45	7.33
6/1/94	5.36	5.98	6.33	6.74	7.12	7.52	7.39
7/1/94	5.50	6.19	6.53	6.95	7.34	7.74	7.62
8/1/94	5.40	6.03	6.35	6.75	7.13	7.47	7.41
9/1/94	5.56	6.15	6.44	6.81	7.19	7.60	7.46
10/1/94	6.06	6.69	7.01	7.35	7.66	8.02	7.86
11/1/94	6.25	6.93	7.21	7.58	7.91	8.20	8.06
11/14/94	6.59	7.15	7.45	7.73	7.97	8.22	8.09

Date	*Discount Rate*	*Federal Funds*	*Commercial Paper Rate*	*Corp. Rate BAA*	*Bond Yield Corporate*	*Prime Rate*
12/14/93	3.00	2.94	3.39	7.71	7.11	6.00
1/14/94	3.00	2.94	3.29	7.67	7.01	6.00
2/14/94	3.00	3.25	3.65	7.71	7.20	6.00
3/14/94	3.00	3.31	4.06	8.15	7.55	6.00
4/14/94	3.00	3.50	4.27	8.53	7.95	6.25
5/14/94	3.00	4.00	5.06	8.70	8.21	6.75
6/14/94	3.50	4.19	4.80	8.56	8.02	7.25
7/14/94	3.50	4.25	5.18	8.76	8.37	7.25
8/14/94	3.50	4.25	5.24	8.78	8.24	7.25
9/14/94	4.00	4.81	5.23	8.93	8.25	7.75
10/14/94	4.00	4.69	5.66	9.10	8.57	7.75
11/14/94	4.00	5.50	5.96	9.33	8.81	7.75

Source: *Federal Reserve Bulletin.*

EXHIBIT 13 Asset Betas for Comparable Firms

Company	Stock Exchange	Equity Beta	Market-Value Debt/Equity	Asset Beta
Power Companies with Capacity in China*				
AES Chigen	NASDAQ	1.56	1.65	0.78
Shandong Huaneng Power—ADR	NYSE	0.74	0.68	0.53
Consolidated Elec. Power	Hong Kong	0.72	0.60	0.53
China Overseas Land & Invest.	Hong Kong	0.91	0.80	0.61
Huaneng Power Intl.—ADR	NYSE	0.73	0.70	0.51
Average				0.59
U.S. Power Companies Using Mainly Coal-Fired Technology				
American Electric Power	NYSE	0.75	0.76	0.52
Centerior Energy	NYSE	0.55	1.72	0.27
Detroit Edison	NYSE	0.70	0.99	0.44
Empire District	NYSE	0.50	0.04	0.49
Interstate Power	NYSE	0.55	0.75	0.38
Ipalco Enterprises	NYSE	0.65	0.51	0.50
KU Energy Corp.	NYSE	0.65	0.42	0.52
LG&E Energy Corp.	NYSE	0.60	0.52	0.46
MDU Resources	NYSE	0.50	0.41	0.40
NIPSCO Industries	NYSE	0.70	0.64	0.51
Northwestern Public Service	NYSE	0.55	0.61	0.40
Potomac Electric Power	NYSE	0.65	0.64	0.47
PSI Resources Inc.	NYSE	0.70	0.64	0.51
Average				0.45

* Debt/equity ratios for the Chinese firms are approximations by the casewriter.

Sources: *Bloomberg's Business News* and *Value Line Investment Survey.*

EXHIBIT 14   Information Related to Political Risk and Country Risk

Yields on Selected Yankee Bonds

Issuer	Term	Yield Spread
China International Trust and Investment	9-year	+ 105 basis points vs. 10-year U.S. Treasury
People's Republic of China	10-year	+ 100 basis points vs. 10-year U.S. Treasury
Bank of China	5-year	+ 90 basis points vs. 5-year U.S. Treasury
Bank of China	20-year	+ 155 basis points vs. 20-year U.S. Treasury

Country Betas

Country	Volatility	Volatility Relative to U.S.	Correlation with U.S.	Country Beta Relative to U.S.
China	40.50	4.02	0.27	1.08
Indonesia	30.55	3.03	0.26	0.79
Japan	26.36	2.62	0.22	0.58
Korea	25.22	2.50	−0.03	−0.08
Taiwan	38.76	3.83	0.09	0.35
United States	10.80	1.00	1.00	1.00

Source of Yankee bond yields: Salomon Brothers, "The Executive's Guide to International Capital Budgeting: 1994 Update," August 1994, p. 13.
Source of country beta information: Donald Lessard, "Incorporating Country Risk in the Valuation of Offshore Projects," *Journal of Applied Corporate Finance* 9, no. 5 (Fall 1996), p. 60.

Case 49

Joint Venture Negotiating Committee: Slavagrad Government of Euroslavia: The GM-Euroslavia Joint Venture Investment Simulation

General Motors Corporation and the Government of Euroslavia commit themselves to work toward a final agreement on a joint venture to produce automobiles in Euroslavia, as contemplated in the terms outlined above. This agreement, however, does not preclude changes in the scale, form, or timing of investment since any ultimate agreement depends on specific terms yet to be negotiated between the two parties, and on revised assessments of market prospects.

Signed April 9, 1992

Leczak Stepanski, Minister of Industry, Euroslavia Jacques Schmidt, Vice President, General Motors

Conclusion of the Memorandum of Understanding

The "GM-Euroslavia Joint Venture Investment Simulation" cases were prepared by Professor Robert F. Bruner with the assistance of Jane Sommers-Kelly from field interviews and public information. The cooperation of General Motors–Europe is gratefully acknowledged, as is the financial support of the Citicorp Global Scholars Program. All financial data and some market data have been disguised. Protagonists are disguised or fictional. Some license had been taken in describing the business situation in order to heighten the differences in points of view. Copyright © 1993 by the University of Virginia Darden School Foundation, Charlottesville, VA. All rights reserved. *No part of this publication may be reproduced, stored in a retrieval system, used in a spreadsheet, or transmitted in any form or by any means—electronic, mechanical, photocopying, recording, or otherwise—without the permission of the Darden School Foundation. For inquiries, please send an e-mail to dardencases @virginia.edu.* Revised 6/98. Version 4.2.

Late one afternoon in April 1992, Anna Krzykowiak (kri-KO-vi-ak), special assistant to the finance minister of Euroslavia, called together a special committee to prepare for negotiations with the large American automobile producer, General Motors. Earlier that month, General Motors had concluded a memorandum of understanding with the Euroslav government committing both parties to work toward a final agreement under which GM would form a joint venture with the Euroslav state automobile manufacturer, AUTA,[1] to produce and sell Opel automobiles in Euroslavia. (See Exhibit 1 for a journalist's account of this agreement.) The memorandum of understanding nominally required GM to make an initial $113 million investment in interim assembly capacity, to be followed by a $400 million investment in a major, integrated (i.e., greenfield) auto assembly plant. The contemplated allocation of ownership interests in the joint venture was 70 percent to GM, 30 percent to Euroslavia. A final round of negotiations was needed to hammer out a detailed series of commitments for both parties. To conduct the negotiations with GM, the minister of finance had appointed Krzykowiak the new chief negotiator, aided by a committee of assistants and consulting advisers.

The memorandum of understanding had created the expectation that General Motors would make a major and long-term investment in Euroslavia. However, Euroslavia had experienced yet another change in government (the fourth in 18 months), which might create fears about political stability. The tightening of Euroslavia's anti-inflation policy had prolonged its current recession. Disturbing news was coming to light about the depth and severity of Euroslavia's recession that might discourage foreign investors. Finally, GM itself had experienced what some newspapers had called a management coup. For these reasons, Krzykowiak believed the scope of the forthcoming negotiations was wide open and might result in one of these three outcomes:

- GM would first invest $113 million in a temporary plant and then $400 million in a greenfield plant and joint venture with AUTA. This alternative was embedded in the memorandum of understanding.
- GM would invest in a complete "knock-down" plant and joint venture with AUTA. For a $113 million outlay, GM would construct a movable plant that would assemble automobiles from kits manufactured by Adam Opel, Inc., in Germany.
- GM would supply the Euroslav auto market with imports from its Adam Opel subsidiary, thus maintaining the status quo.

An assessment of GM's possible proposals and negotiations was urgently needed, because the talks were about to begin. To delay the timetable of the talks would not be possible. The potential stakes were huge: Euroslavia desperately needed inflows of hard (i.e., Western) currencies with which to finance the growth of its economy. GM's investment represented a huge potential source of new capital, know-how, technology, and credibility for Euroslavia's market reforms.

---

[1] AUTA stood for Autofabryka Azzotiazion and was the name of Euroslavia's second largest automobile manufacturer.

GENERAL MOTORS CORPORATION

General Motors was the world's largest industrial company in terms of sales (U.S.$125 billion in 1990). It employed over 761,000 people worldwide and held 19 percent of the world market (7.5 million GM vehicles sold in 1990). To maintain this share, the firm had to sell about 30,000 vehicles every day. General Motors' investment of over U.S.$25 billion worldwide between 1986 and 1989 reflected the firm's significant market positions in Europe, Asia and the Pacific region, and Latin America.

Once identified not only as a mainstay of American prosperity but also one of the nation's prime beneficiaries, GM was now reeling from a series of competitive setbacks and financial losses. In 1991, the company lost more money (U.S.$6 billion) than both of its two U.S. rivals *combined*. GM's U.S. market share dropped from 47 percent in the early 1980s to 35 percent by 1992. Falling consumer demand for new cars caused low use of capacity; high fixed costs resulted in a high break-even level and losses. By December 1991, GM's stock price was at a four-year low point. Moody's downgraded GM's senior debt rating from A1 to A2 in January 1992 because of poor financial performance in 1991. Newspapers speculated that General Motors' debt rating might be reduced below investment grade; this action would dramatically raise GM's cost of funds.

Robert Stempel became chairman and chief executive officer of General Motors upon the regular retirement of Roger Smith in early 1990. In a crisis atmosphere 20 months later, the board of directors became frustrated with management's slow response to the deteriorating performance of the firm. The board took action in an unprecedented coup in April 1992: Stempel's board position was restricted and his handpicked chief operating officer and chief financial officer were replaced. A major cash conservation program was initiated to stem losses. GM successfully sold $2.5 billion in new common shares to reduce its debt-to-capital ratio, which was at an unprecedented 70 percent (almost twice the historic 40 percent). Most important, the board appointed Jack Smith, the highly successful president of GM-Europe, as president and COO. Value Line, perhaps reflecting the optimism in the investment community, was cautiously bullish about GM's investment outlook (see Exhibit 2).

GENERAL MOTORS–EUROPE

GM's long-standing corporate policy was to establish local production and employment in its major markets whenever economic conditions permitted. In 1923, GM opened its first assembly operation outside North America in Copenhagen, Denmark. A second manufacturing plant was established in Antwerp, Belgium, in 1924. The firm acquired Vauxhall Motors in England in 1925; four years later it acquired Adam Opel A.G. in Germany. More recent acquisitions included Group Lotus, the U.K.-based performance-car-manufacturing firm, in 1986, and 50 percent of Saab Automobile AB, based in Sweden, in 1989.

General Motors' most extensive activities outside North America were in Europe and included facilities and sales companies in 20 European countries. The main car-related manufacturing operations were located in Germany (Rüsselsheim, Bochum, Kaiserslautern,

Eisenach); the United Kingdom (Ellesmere Port, Luton); Belgium (Antwerp); Spain (Zaragoza); Austria (Vienna-Aspern); and Portugal (Azambuja). GM's more than 30 automotive-component plants employed about 124,000 people.

GM-Europe's Opel and Vauxhall brands had the highest growth rates among all volume-car manufacturers in Europe. With an all-time high 1.545 million passenger cars sold, 1990 marked the sixth consecutive year of new-car sales records. Opel/Vauxhall's market penetration rose from 9.0 percent in 1986 to 11.6 percent in 1990, placing the company fourth among all car makers in Europe. In 12 European countries GM ranked among the top three sellers, and some industry observers had recently characterized Adam Opel A.G. as "the most profitable car company in the world" and "the engine of profitability for GM."

GM IN EASTERN EUROPE

As early as 1979, GM had established a joint venture, Industrial Delova Automobilia, in Belgrade, Yugoslavia. Since the political thaw that began in 1988, GM had successfully penetrated other Eastern European countries:

Former East Germany. In early 1990, Adam Opel A.G. established a joint-venture company with the state-owned Automobile Werke Eisenach (the former producer of Ladas and Trabants) to produce parts and assemble vehicles. The assembly of mid-size Vectras at an initial rate of 10,000 units per annum started on October 5, 1990, just two days after German reunification. A (deutsche mark) DM1 billion ($625 million) greenfield assembly plant, slated to open at Eisenach in July 1992, would produce 150,000 units annually.

Hungary. In 1988, GM signed a joint venture agreement with RABA, the state-owned automobile company, to produce up to 200,000 1.6-liter engines at a greenfield plant to be opened in 1992. Over 90 percent of the engines would be exported to Germany for Kadett/Astra production. In addition, a smaller plant would assemble 15,000 Astras annually. The GM engine-and-transmission plant in Aspern, Austria, would serve as a "sister plant" to facilitate training and technology transfer. GM's total investment in Hungary was DM320 million ($200 million), of which Opel was the conduit for DM200 million ($125 million).

Other initiatives in Eastern Europe included the following:

Former Soviet Union. GM was negotiating to set up a joint venture to manufacture catalytic converters.

Czechoslovakia. GM had begun negotiations in February 1990 to invest in a joint venture with BAZ, the state-owned automobile manufacturer. GM needed production capacity for automobile transmissions and wanted this capacity on-stream by March 1992, when it would complement other new productive capacity elsewhere in Europe. Disagreements between the Czech and Slovak negotiators had led to 12 months of delays. GM concluded that it would not be feasible to start up a transmission facility in Czechoslovakia within the time required and shifted the new capacity to Austria. No further discussions with the Czech government had occurred since then.

GM Europe continued to encourage GM's divisions to investigate East European investment opportunities. Several divisions were investigating possible future involvements.

COMPETITORS IN EASTERN EUROPE

GM's efforts to penetrate East European markets occurred against the background of a general thrust by European, American, and Asian automobile manufacturers into these markets. As one automobile executive noted:

> We could just about hold an industry conference at any of the international-class hotels in Warsaw, Budapest, or Prague right now. One day I saw my counterparts from Ford and Volkswagen at the Metropole in Budapest. The next day I saw my counterparts from Fiat and Peugeot at the Marriott in Warsaw. These people weren't just sightseeing. It's a frenzy of deal-doing. You have to understand: North America and Western Europe are mature markets, and the Japanese dominate Asia. Eastern Europe represents the only major remaining growth opportunity. No executive wants to be the one who missed the train . . . and the train is starting to leave the station.

The pattern of investment in Eastern Europe suggested that Western firms were more willing to invest in Eastern Europe if a competitor had already done so. In recent years several automobile companies had moved into Eastern Europe:

Volkswagen. In 1991, Volkswagen acquired a majority interest in the Skoda automobile company in Czechoslovakia for an initial DM1.4 billion ($875 million) and was committed to investing an additional DM9 billion ($5.6 billion) by 1998. In addition, VW had committed DM4.8 billion ($3 billion) for the conversion of the East German Trabant assembly plant by 1992. In June 1992, VW announced its intention to pursue a business venture with Euroslavia's smallest automobile manufacturer. This venture might entail an investment of DM130 million ($81 million), although no specific agreement had been struck.

Eurauto. In May 1992, Eurauto expanded its investment in a joint venture with BIS, the largest Euroslav automobile manufacturer, into a majority ownership for a total of DM3.2 billion ($2 billion).[2]

Ford. In 1991, Ford announced its intention to build a components factory in Hungary for DM132 million ($83 million).

Suzuki. In 1991, Suzuki committed DM425 million ($265 million) to assemble automobiles in a joint venture with Hungary's Autokoncern. The joint venture would construct a new assembly plant.

Mercedes-Benz. In 1991, Mercedes-Benz invested DM1.3 billion ($840 million) in the Liaz-Avia bus-manufacturing plant in Czechoslovakia.

Renault. Renault had been actively pursuing an East European partner and location but had failed to win a bid or close a transaction. The company complained that East European governments unfairly taxed imports and chose their partners on subjective, not economic, grounds. Nonetheless, Renault's bid for Skoda was only half of Volkswagen's successful bid of DM1.4 billion ($875 million).

---

[2]By July 1992, BIS workers were striking for higher wages and job guarantees in advance of Eurauto's assumption of control.

Notably absent from the list of major investors in Eastern Europe were Japanese automobile manufacturers. Some analysts believed the Japanese were taking a wait-and-see attitude about the future of East European automobile markets. Others suspected a policy of exclusion by the East European governments in an attempt to hasten integration of their countries with Western Europe.

THE EUROSLAV AUTOMOBILE MARKET

With a population of 40 million people, Euroslavia constituted one of the largest national markets in Eastern Europe—about the same population and area as Spain. It was also one of the youngest in terms of the demographic distribution of its population. Analysts believed that Euroslavia would have the largest number of new-car sales by the end of the decade, and even then would have the lowest vehicle density in terms of cars per 1,000 people. In Eastern Europe there were only 11 cars per 100 persons, compared with 35 in Western Europe and 60 in the United States. On average, Czech cars were 9.1 years old; East German cars were 12 years old. Although Euroslavia's purchasing power was below that of East Germany and Hungary, it was expected to improve. All in all, Euroslavia was extremely attractive in terms of size, geographical position, and potential growth in demand. By the year 2000, Euroslavia was expected to have the largest annual unit demand of any country in Eastern Europe.

No major automobile manufacturer could stay in the Euroslav market without a joint venture with the government. The import duties to be paid would either price cars out of the market or force the manufacturer to sell cars at a loss just to stay in the market. Under joint-venture agreements, the government promised joint venturers with AUTA, BIS, and BUZ[3] duty-free imports of 30,000 cars per year and granted each partner one-third of this quota.[4]

Demand for GM's products would be determined significantly by per capita income, and demand for *new* Western cars. With real wages at 75 percent of their prior levels, household budgets were increasingly strained. On average, individuals had a purchasing power equivalent to U.S.$3,900 per year, a standard of living 75 percent lower than the United States'. Demand would also be limited by steeply rising import prices and weakening exchange rates. One positive factor was that growth in private-sector activity would support increased spending on cars. Another important positive factor was cash payments from family members in Western Europe and the United States to their families in Euroslavia—these transfer payments represented a significant source of funds in the Euroslav private sector.

The composition of Euroslav automobile demand could be broken down into low-priced vehicles costing U.S.$5,000–$7,000 (DM8,000–11,000) and high-priced, new Western cars costing U.S.$12,000–$16,000 (DM19,000–25,000). The following table compares sales in Euroslavia of Opel cars and Euroslav new and used cars:

---

[3]BUZ was the third largest of the three Euroslav automobile companies.

[4]The proposed allocation of the duty-free import quota was contentious. Several manufacturers who had no plant capacity in Euroslavia complained to the government and to the European Community. This situation might prove to be an embarrassment and could force the government to share the quotas more broadly.

Segment	Marque	Price (DM)	1991 Unit Sales
Small cars	Opel Corsa	14,000	2,150
	BIS-Eurauto Pina	7,500	(new)
	AUTA Slavi	10,000	40,000
Used cars*	0–3 years	11–13,000	37,000
	3+–6 years	7–9,000	40,000
	6+ years	3–5,000	78,000
Compact	Opel Astra	21,000	600
Midsize	Opel Vectra	25,300	1,300
Upper-medium	Opel Omega	33,000	200
Luxury	Opel Senator	52,900	30
Sports coupe	Opel Calibra	41,000	75

*The used-car totals include compact cars as well as small cars.

The low-priced segment made up 90 percent of the market, largely because the average Euroslav worker could not afford a new car: it took a worker 7.5 years to earn the price of a new GM Astra. Although new Western cars had only captured 11 percent[5] of the total market, they were expected to make up 25 percent of the total market within five years. Some industry forecasts expected this market share to remain relatively constant through 1995, when incomes were expected to rise.

Total car demand was the key figure. Projections ranged from 200,000 to 230,000 units in 1993 to between 300,000 and 350,000 in the year 2000. This scenario gave all Western new-car manufacturers and their joint ventures roughly 22,000–25,000 potential annual sales in the short term and 75,000–87,500 by 2000.

The car-supply picture was changing rapidly. All local manufacturers would most likely have Western joint-venture backing and engineering capability by 2000. Cars of purely East European design had already fallen from half to a third of all new-car registrations, with Western imports and joint ventures making up the other two-thirds. The flood of used Western cars competing with the cheap Eastern models created tough price competition.

GM executives perceived that Euroslav automobile-manufacturing techniques were not competitive with those of Western European manufacturers. Jacques Schmidt, the leader of the GM negotiating team, told Anna Krzykowiak,

> We used statistics on manufacturing hours per car to indicate to the Euroslavs where Skoda in Czechoslovakia and AUTA are relative to the other manufacturers in Europe. We said, "If you are intent on keeping these car companies alive, the hours per car must go way down. If the hours per car go way down, please reset your expectations about employment at these plants. You take 3,000 people to produce 64,000 cars per year. We build 250,000 cars with the same number of people."

Krzykowiak believed that the Euroslav negotiating team would need to reconsider its objectives for large, guaranteed employment.

---

[5]Anna Krzykowiak noted that all estimates of the size of the Euroslav car market included the sales of used Western cars, which at the time were flooding into Euroslavia. When one focused only on *new* cars, and on cars in the GM price range, the resulting Western new-car market share of the total car market was relatively small.

ECONOMIC AND POLITICAL CONDITIONS IN EUROSLAVIA

Although the roots of many of Euroslavia's economic problems went back decades, any recent discussion of economic and political conditions in Euroslavia usually started with the watershed year, 1989, when the non-Communist trade union, Democracy, gained participation in the government. Shortly thereafter, the Communist Party leader, Bulban Militar, declared the first free elections in Euroslavia since World War II. Jan Svoboda, the charismatic leader of Democracy, was elected president of Euroslavia in 1990.

1. *The Euroslav economy receded seriously from 1989 to 1992.* Euroslavia's gross domestic product (GDP) fell 9 percent in 1991 following a 1990 decline of 11 percent. Industrial production was down 24 percent in 1990, 12 percent in 1991, and a further 14 percent decline was expected for 1992. Certain sectors were particularly hard hit, with transportation-equipment output falling a numbing 36 percent. Unemployment stood at 19 percent in 1992. Some analysts expected real wages to fall 5 percent in 1992 on top of a 22 percent decline in 1991. This economic deterioration was due to the combination of the collapse of Euroslavia's East European export markets and a sharp fall in domestic wages. On the positive side, the recession was considered a necessary transitional stage. The manufacturing sector needed to "clean house," eliminate unnecessary production facilities, and begin producing on demand instead of via central planning. The government was trying to reequilibrate the economy away from the unprofitable heavy-industry sector and toward the service sector.

2. *The economic outlook for 1993–95 was cautiously positive.* GDP was expected to grow 1 percent in 1993 and 2 percent in 1994. The austerity program had brought consumer-price increases down from 685 percent in 1990 to under 45 percent in 1992. Government public bonds were beginning to be sold, but only in 26-week maturities; they offered nominal interest rates of 53 percent.

The foreign-exchange rates for the bunt[6] were believed to reflect the underlying inflation differentials between Euroslavia and other countries. A 17 percent increase in exports had eliminated the trade deficit and brought in Western "hard currencies." The State Bank's reserves totaled DM5.8 billion ($3.6 billion), three times more than in the pre-1989 years.

Liberalization of ownership of state enterprises had been a key focus of economic reform. As a result, a million new jobs were created by private businesses alone in 1990–91. Newly privatized companies were listing themselves on the stock market, although less than 15 were quoted in June 1992. The regulatory environment for foreign direct investment (FDI) had been liberalized; the Ministry of Finance hoped FDIs would average DM1.9 billion (U.S.$1.2 billion) per year from 1992 to 1995. The government's restructuring programs—the most radical undertaken by any East European government— were considered successful by Western observers.

3. *Political and economic risks remained for foreign investors in Euroslavia.* The political uncertainty in Euroslavia had a strong bearing on economic performance. Unable to forge a coalition, four prime ministers had come and gone in three years. The most important economic tenet, fiscal discipline, required a government strong enough to withstand

---

[6]The Euroslav currency was the bunt, which traded at 13.760 to the U.S. dollar in April of 1992.

the resulting social unrest. In 1992, the lower house of Parliament temporarily turned from its anti-inflation policies to an antirecession spending program. Observers worried that this stop-and-go macroeconomic policy making could undermine the gains made to date.

JOINT VENTURE INVESTMENT ALTERNATIVES IN EUROSLAVIA

The Euroslav negotiating team had considered a range of potential joint venture strategies with GM and, by a process of elimination, had boiled them down to three main alternatives:

1. *Complete knock-down (CKD) plant operated in a joint venture between GM and AUTA.* A CKD plant would consist of the tools and equipment necessary to assemble up to 30,000 Opel Astras and Vectras a year from kits imported from Adam Opel A.G. in Germany. AUTA workers would assemble the cars and possibly add a few components of local origin. The output of the CKD plant would be sold in Euroslavia, although in theory the cars could be exported to other markets in Europe. The greatest value added would already be in the Opel kits; only marginal local value would be added by AUTA. In GM's experience—given the extra shipping and handling and the absence of economies of scale—cars produced in CKD plants were 20 percent more expensive than cars produced in high-volume, integrated facilities. The cost of this plant was estimated at DM180 million ($113 million). As a quid pro quo for investing in Euroslavia, GM might receive a one-third allocation of the quota of 30,000 duty-free cars, which would permit it to bring in other cars in the Opel product line.

2. *Greenfield assembly plant operated in a joint venture with AUTA.* Funds would be allocated now; construction would begin in six months. The Greenfield plant would be fully operational in 1996 and yield 100,000 Opel Astras and Vectras per year. In the meantime, a CKD plant would be constructed rapidly in order to begin production before year-end 1992 and would yield up to 30,000 Opel Astras and Vectras per year. The cost of the Greenfield plant would be DM640 million ($400 million). The CKD plant would employ 560 of AUTA's 3,000 workers at least through 1996, and the Greenfield plant would employ 1,600 workers after that.

3. *Status quo.* At the time, GM manufactured units in Germany and exported them to the Euroslav market. Despite the memorandum of understanding, GM might consider developing its dealer networks, building its distribution chain, and postponing an investment decision, with its attendant risk. GM would have to continue paying duties on its cars shipped to Euroslavia, but the forgone import concessions would be balanced by the saved investment capital. Krzykowiak's team concluded that this strategy would sacrifice any hope of a joint venture with AUTA, because the Euroslav government would not wait to marry its major automobile manufacturer to a Western car company—indeed, it would deliver AUTA to one of GM's European competitors.

Krzykowiak's staff prepared a financial analysis of the three alternatives (the summary memorandum and quantitative tables are contained in Exhibit 3).

EUROSLAV NEGOTIATING TEAM

The negotiating team owed its allegiance to at least four interest groups within the Euroslav government.

Ministry of Finance.   Jerzy Katowicz, the minister of finance, was closest to the prime minister and was bearing the brunt of pressures on the government to do something about the country's economic crisis. His first priority was balancing the government's budget (several International Monetary Fund loans depended on that); fighting inflation was number two; and spurring economic growth was third. He believed that the people and government of Euroslavia would accept a period of austerity necessary to achieve these goals. He genuinely believed that the austerity program would work, but that any retreat from the austerity program, while granting short-term relief, would have disastrous consequences in the long run. Unfortunately, austerity, the rate of inflation, and the recession had snowballed, and a political backlash was forming in the lower house of Parliament. Minister Katowicz had to show tangible progress, *fast.*

The announcement of the memorandum of understanding with GM had been a ray of sunshine for the government. Katowicz wanted no retreat from the major investment program outlined in the memorandum, because major hard-currency investments were crucially important to Euroslavia's economic growth, as were the export businesses those investments would create. Moreover, the government's budget could not afford any bunt contribution to the joint venture. Katowicz wanted a detailed agreement soon. In pursuit of these goals, he personally intervened with the prime minister to have his own special assistant, Anna Krzykowiak,[7] appointed president of the committee that would negotiate with GM. She had proved to have outstanding qualities in recent crisis negotiations and was an effective advocate of the free-market principles to which Minister Katowicz was committed.

Ministry of Industry and Trade.   Leczak Stepanski, the minister of industry and trade, viewed the negotiations with GM as one more opportunity to fashion the structure of Euroslavia's automotive industry for the long term. A fervent believer in the benefits of a national industrial policy, he wanted the negotiations to reinvigorate AUTA with modern plant and equipment, worker training, and new-product designs. AUTA's survival as an entity was important to Stepanski for symbolic and political reasons. In return, he was prepared to accept reductions in employees, offer high import tariffs as a protection against GM's competitors, and allow GM 10,000 duty-free car imports per

---

[7]Krzykowiak had been leader of the Euroslav team that had successfully concluded debt-rescheduling negotiations with the International Monetary Fund. In reporting on those negotiations, the *Financial Times* described her as "brilliant, tough, shrewd, and articulate." *Paris Match* profiled her as one of the 10 most promising European professional women for the 1990s:

> After fleeing Euroslavia with her parents in 1976, she studied physics at the Max Planck Institute in Munich, and then earned a doctorate in economics from the London School of Economics. Abandoning a brilliant academic career at Stanford University, she returned to Euroslavia in 1988 to serve as an economic adviser to the Democracy movement and Jan Svoboda, its leader. She proved her negotiating skills in 1991 when she persuaded a group of striking machinists to end their occupation of a nuclear power plant. Friends say she is an idealist with no personal political ambitions. However, political observers suggest that she will be prime minister or president before the decade is over. (Biographical blurb on Anna Krzykowiak, from "Ten Most Promising European Professional Women for the 1990s," *Paris Match,* (date not given).

In addition to the IMF negotiations, she had also led the negotiations with Eurauto over its $2.3 billion investment in BIS, the other major Euroslav automobile manufacturer.

year. He would worry later about problems such an agreement might create for Euroslavia's association with the European Community.[8]

Ministry of Ownership Transformation (formerly, Ministry of Privatization).

Bogdan Lobachoff[9] would represent the Ministry of Ownership Transformation, which was responsible for selling or arranging joint ventures with state-owned enterprises. AUTA was a particularly important focus of Lobachoff's attention: because of its size and market position, any action (or inaction) on the disposition of AUTA would affect his personal standing in the government. He was a realist who knew that AUTA's operations were essentially worthless when compared with those of Western manufacturers. Thus, a deal that attributed *any* value to AUTA's assets and its Slavi brand would be a victory. However, political opponents in the Parliament had charged that the ministry was giving Euroslavia's industrial "crown jewels" to greedy foreign investors for "next to nothing." Lobachoff's goal, therefore, was to achieve a deal attributing as much value as possible to AUTA. He believed AUTA provided both a distribution network and an organized pool of automotive workers that were worth *something*. Ultimately, he had one goal in mind: to eliminate further state support for AUTA, which he viewed as an ailing behemoth.

Autofabryka Azzotiazion.

Janucz Lewandewski,[10] the general director of AUTA itself, would participate on the negotiating committee. The signing of the memorandum of understanding had been an important victory, for it seemed to guarantee the survival of AUTA and provide the opportunity for his management team to participate in the new joint venture. The memorandum's statement that GM would own 70 percent of the venture held implications for daily control of the operation that would need to be hammered out: What role would Lewandewski and his management team have in this new venture? How much operational flexibility would they have to run the plant? What budget oversight? What salaries?[11]

Lewandewski's managers openly expressed concern about interference from "the Germans" at Opel. Euroslavs widely admired the quality and workmanship of German products. However, as Lewandewski noted,

---

[8]Euroslavia was at the time negotiating the agreement by which it would become an "associate" of the European Community (EC). Ordinarily, countries assumed associate status for a few years before becoming full members. The statutes of the EC prohibited import tariffs of the kind designed to protect domestic manufacturers. The European Commission gave special scrutiny to the automotive industry, which had become something of a lightning rod for EC investigators. The EC had requested the phasing out of the protective tariffs and had demanded equal apportionment of the duty-free import quotas across all companies selling cars in Euroslavia, whether manufacturing in Euroslavia or not. The Euroslav committee had promised a 30 percent share of the quota to GM, but to ignore the EC requests might jeopardize the progress of the association talks.

[9]Lobachoff (LOB-a-choff) was a career civil servant.

[10]Janucz Lewandewski (YAN-ush lev-an-DEV-ski) had worked for AUTA his entire career. Raised in Slavagrad as the son of the local Communist Party chairman, he joined the party at the age of 15. Trained as a mechanical engineer at the Moscow Institute for Heavy Machinery, his first job was as a production planner for AUTA. By 1992, he had been general director of AUTA for seven years.

[11]Shortly after the announcement of Eurauto's joint venture with BIS, the workers and *managers* went on strike for employment guarantees and higher pay. The standard aspiration of workers in a privatized company was for a 50 percent increase in hourly wages. For managers, the aspiration was for *a tenfold* increase (the typical take-home pay of an industrial manager of a state-owned enterprise in Euroslavia was on the order of U.S.$200 per month).

There is an ancient difference between Slavs and Germanics that is deeper than can be explained by World War II. Euroslavs resent German methods and culture: too rigid, exacting, serious, domineering. But you have these kinds of differences between neighbors all over the world: Mexicans feel this way toward the Americans, Egyptians toward the Israelis, Vietnamese toward the Chinese, etc. And so it is in Europe. I hope I won't have to take orders from a German.

In addition to these representatives on the negotiating committee, the Ministry of Ownership Transformation had retained various consultants to advise the committee:

- Credit Suisse First Boston would prepare financial and valuation analyses.
- Arthur Andersen would prepare a final audit of AUTA and advise on financial accounting questions that might arise.
- Skadden, Arps, Slate, Meagher & Flom, a prominent New York–based law firm specializing in mergers and acquisitions, would draft the agreement on the Euroslav side and advise on the design of terms.

Reflecting on the makeup of the committee representing the Euroslav government in negotiations with GM, Anna Krzykowiak commented,

To outsiders, we look monolithic. But the truth is that this committee has some potentially serious political divisions. In cutting the final deal with GM, we will have to make internal trade-offs. We must be careful that this doesn't trigger infighting between the various ministries and AUTA. To satisfy everyone on the committee, we must extract more of everything from GM: more invested deutsche marks, more guaranteed employment, and a faster timetable—while giving up less ourselves in the way of income-tax revenues, import duties, and control. Unfortunately, our bargaining strength is weakening as the economy stalls and as we spin through prime ministers. If I can simply hold GM to the broad outline of the memorandum of understanding (i.e., with an initial DM180 million [$113 million] investment in a temporary plant, followed by a DM640 million [$400 million] investment in a greenfield plant), the negotiations will be a success. The big question is, what will we have to give up to hold to the agreement? I am prepared to make deep concessions on

- Number of jobs guaranteed in the joint venture.
- Wages and salaries.
- Import duties (larger duty-free quota for GM and higher tariff on non-duty-free cars).

If forced to, I will give some ground on

- Transfer price of the kit in a CKD plant.
- Percentage ownership of the Euroslav government in the joint venture.
- Local content of cars.

I will be very reluctant to give ground on terms that affect overall hard-currency investment in Euroslavia, and that affect the government deficit:

- Total investment by GM in Euroslavia.
- Export allowances.
- Corporate tax rate.
- The amount distributed from the JV.

Under no circumstances will I agree to terms that require my government to contribute cash to the joint venture. We are under tremendous pressure from the IMF to curb government spending. We have no means to make a hard investment. I am prepared to give up some opportunity inflows in return.

I have communicated these priorities to my colleagues on the negotiating committee, but they have not as yet expressed agreement with my views. My committee members disagree with me vehemently on some of these items. I have to fight with my adversaries and my own "friends" at the same time.

GM NEGOTIATING TEAM

GM was scheduled to send a negotiating team consisting of representatives from the manufacturing, marketing, and finance functions of the firm.

1. *The planning and marketing views: Jacques Schmidt, vice president of Planning, GM-Europe, Zürich.* Schmidt had been the chief architect of the trailblazing 1988 joint venture agreement with the government of Hungary, which industry observers had termed a bold stroke into a receptive market and an illustration of ingenious integration of manufacturing resources between Eastern and Western Europe. Schmidt had negotiated the memorandum of understanding with the Euroslav government and was unquestionably the "champion" for significant investment in Euroslavia.

2. *The treasury view: James Sterling, manager of corporate finance, GM-Europe Regional Treasury Center, Brussels.* Sterling brought to the GM negotiating committee the financial point of view. In general, the Treasury Group, somewhat removed from the dominant car culture inside General Motors, was known for a tradition of independence and skepticism. The group thought of itself as a rigorous analytical shop and routinely scrutinized management's project proposals to make sure that risk-adjusted returns were sufficient. The Treasury staff believed that 15 percent was an appropriate discount rate for deutsche-mark cash flows associated with the automobile joint venture in Euroslavia. One of his major concerns was GM's global environmental policy. If they were to start a joint venture in Euroslavia, they might end up with the liability for all environmental problems caused by AUTA.

3. *The manufacturing view: Helmut Kunst, vice president of Manufacturing, Adam Opel A.G., Rüsselsheim, Germany.* An engineer by training and a lifelong manufacturing manager, Kunst would bring to the GM team an assessment of the operational feasibility of any joint-venture proposals. He would also represent the interests of Adam Opel, A.G. Based on preliminary discussions with him, the Euroslav negotiating team had concluded that Kunst was especially worried about workforce training and quality, potential logistical problems, condition of the facilities, and lack of management depth at AUTA.

CONCLUSION

Anna Krzykowiak anticipated hard work ahead for her negotiating team. Only that morning an analysis from the Ministry of Finance had described depressing developments in the Euroslav automobile market (see Exhibit 4). A second report had also just arrived that described AUTA's uncertain—possibly unhealthy—financial condition and a potentially worrisome environmental liability (see Exhibit 5).

Any final deal would have to be approved by the GM-Europe strategy board. Then the proposal would be presented to GM President Jack Smith and, ultimately, the board of directors. The Euroslavs also had an approval process that would culminate in review by the council of ministers and Parliament.

EXHIBIT 1   "GM and AUTA Jump-Start Stalled Talks"*

U.S. motor manufacturer General Motors Corp. (GM) has signed a memorandum of understanding to invest $113 million in a joint venture with Autofabryka Azzotiazion (AUTA), Euroslavia's largest car maker. For almost a decade, the country has been seeking a western partner for AUTA. This agreement brings an end to many months of ebbing negotiations and wild speculations.

The memorandum was signed by Euroslav industry minister Leczak Stepanski as well as directors of GM Europe and AUTA. It creates a new company, as yet unnamed, in which GM will hold a 70 percent stake.

The two sides have announced plans to build a new factory on the present AUTA site to assemble GM's Opel cars. This alone will cost $113 million.

Sources say GM has pledged to invest a further $400 million by 1996 in a separate joint venture to make an Opel-designed car for which Euroslavia will have exclusive production rights. Rollo Meyer, a spokesman for GM Europe in Zürich, concedes that "the $113 million is only an initial investment figure."

The new venture should be ready to assemble as many as 30,000 Astra and Vectra models by mid-1993. Meanwhile, it will oversee the replacement of AUTA's outdated Slavi car with a new model. GM will also sign a separate agreement with AUTA to modernize its Eurauto-derived Slavi.

GM's desire to establish a strong east European network is firmly underscored by plans for an extensive supplier development programme that will bring together AUTA and its Euroslav component manufacturers with leading western suppliers to the GM group. In support of this programme, GM's own European components arm has

signed a memorandum with FA Krosno to pursue a joint suspension manufacturing project.

Negotiations are still taking place, but a conclusion satisfactory to both sides will help offset the obstacles and delays of the past year. "Talks broke down twice officially and a few more times unofficially. Virtually every time, the Euroslav side refused to grant the incentives sought by the western side. These included the right to import cars into Euroslavia free of duty, which would save a considerable sum, and guidelines on government incentives," says Peter Hennessy, head of the Credit Suisse First Boston team, representing the Euroslav ministry of privatisation.

For this deal, Euroslavia was advised by a consortium coordinated by CSFB, which also included U.S. law firm Skadden, Arps, Slate Meagher & Flom and accountants Arthur Andersen. GM brought no external financial advisers to the table.

A number of western car manufacturers have been linked with AUTA, and talks with various parties ran aground many times. There was a major deadlock in October 1991, when AUTA and the Euroslav government rejected offers to form a venture from both GM and Citroën of France, and asked both to amend certain financial aspects of their proposals before returning to the table. Neither GM nor Citroën had accepted previous Euroslav government invitations to buy a stake in AUTA.

Another source close to the GM deal process comments: "One main problem was that the Euroslav side wasn't really unified in knowing what it wanted from this—which is understandable for a country that is still learning."

But Meyer at GM is more neutral about the reasons why it turned into one of eastern Europe's most

protracted set of talks: "At first, the Euroslavs concluded from their calculations that our terms were not good. That is a matter of interpretation. It is difficult to pinpoint the problems along the way, but the constant arrival and departure of Euroslav officials did not help. We were almost at the point of signing this in December. Then, the next day, the government changed."

He insists that the deal in its present form is attractive enough without sweeteners to lure GM into Euroslavia and there are no unorthodox investment terms attached to the agreement, because western motor companies are "all treated the same way in Euroslavia." But he admits that there is rough terrain ahead: "It is impossible to judge how long it will take to work. At the moment, we are not selling that many cars in Euroslavia. The market there is big but not very active."

This long-awaited deal is a setback for Citroën, a unit of French car maker Peugeot, which bid against GM until the very end. However, French newspapers report that AUTA and Citroën are still in talks over another, smaller deal. French car manufacturers have had some bad luck in eastern Europe, losing out on a number of major deals.

Renault lost a battle against Volkswagen to partner Czech plant Skoda in 1991, then lost out to Mercedes in a bid to link up with Czech truck makers Avia and Liaz, leaving it to pair off finally with bus maker Karosa Vysoke.

The other major deal to have been struck between the Euroslav car industry and a Western investor will see Euroauto take a majority stake in a joint venture with BIS (no connection with AUTA). The two signed a memorandum in October after a smooth but intense set of negotiations.

*Euromoney Publications, *Central European,* April 1992, p. 6. Some persons and companies have been disguised. The article incorrectly states that AUTA was Euroslavia's largest car maker. Actually, AUTA was approximately half the size of BIS, the largest Euroslav car maker.

EXHIBIT 2   Summary of General Motors' Financial Report, June 19, 1992.

GENERAL MOTORS NYSE-GM	RECENT PRICE	44	P/E RATIO	NMF	Trailing:NMF Median: 7.5	RELATIVE P/E RATIO	NMF	DIV'D YLD	3.6%	VALUE LINE	105

	High	29.0	32.3	40.0	41.4	42.5	44.3	47.1	44.1	50.5	50.5	44.4	44.3		Target Price Range
TIMELINESS 3 Average	Low	16.9	17.0	28.0	30.5	32.1	32.9	23.4	30.0	39.1	33.1	26.8	28.8		1995 1996 1997

SAFETY 2 Above Average (Scale: 1 Highest to 5 Lowest)

BETA 1.05 (1.00 = Market)

1995-97 PROJECTIONS

	Price	Gain	Ann'l Total Return
High	85	(+95%)	22%
Low	60	(+35%)	13%

Insider Decisions

	S	O	N	D	J	F	M	A	M
to Buy	0	0	0	0	0	2	0	0	0
Options	1	0	0	5	2	4	9	4	0
to Sell	7	1	0	2	0	0	9	1	1

Institutional Decisions

	1Q'91	4Q'91	1Q'92
to Buy	158	128	138
to Sell	234	253	230
Hld's(000)	212952	210319	216902

Percent shares traded: 9.0 / 6.0 / 3.0

Relative Price Strength

Shaded areas indicate recessions

Options: CBOE

1976	1977	1978	1979	1980	1981	1982	1983	1984	1985	1986	1987	1988	1989	1990	1991	1992	1993	© VALUE LINE PUB., INC.	95-97
82.42	96.23	110.80	114.58	97.51	103.25	98.27	118.43	132.97	152.40	162.43	162.77	196.42	203.43	201.49	194.83	203.00	210.55	Revenues per sh D	240.60
6.69	7.53	8.19	7.11	1.15	3.55	5.38	9.98	11.36	10.70	10.16	11.13	19.07	18.71	8.81	4.52	11.45	15.75	"Cash Flow" per sh	20.50
5.04	5.81	6.12	5.02	d1.33	.54	1.55	5.92	7.11	6.14	4.11	5.03	6.82	6.33	d4.09	d8.85	Nil	4.00	Earnings per sh A	8.00
2.78	3.40	3.00	2.65	1.48	1.20	1.20	1.40	2.38	2.50	2.50	2.50	3.00	3.00	3.00	1.60	1.60	1.60	Div'ds Decl'd per sh B ■	4.00
1.75	3.28	4.80	5.83	8.72	10.81	5.79	3.05	5.70	9.65	12.78	7.53	9.18	12.39	12.53	11.56	10.55	10.55	Cap'l Spending per sh	12.05
24.46	26.85	29.98	32.32	29.40	28.60	28.82	32.44	37.75	45.99	47.80	52.76	57.81	57.37	49.23	42.89	39.05	41.30	Book Value per sh F	54.00
572.43	571.14	570.56	578.73	592.03	607.25	623.54	629.77	630.90	632.37	632.37	625.31	612.91	605.68	605.59	631.59	665.00	665.00	Common Shs Outst'g C	665.00
6.9	5.9	4.9	5.7	--	NMF	14.9	5.8	5.0	5.9	9.1	7.7	5.5	6.9	--	--	Bold figures are		Avg Ann'l P/E Ratio	9.0
.88	.77	.67	.82	--	NMF	1.64	.49	.47	.48	.62	.51	.46	.52	--	--	Value Line estimates		Relative P/E Ratio	.70
8.0%	9.9%	9.9%	9.3%	6.0%	5.1%	5.2%	4.1%	6.7%	6.9%	6.7%	6.5%	6.6%	6.9%	7.0%	4.4%			Avg Ann'l Div'd Yield	5.6%

CAPITAL STRUCTURE as of 12/31/91

Total Debt $96.1 bill.   Due in 5 Yrs $78.3 bill.
LT Debt $42.8 bill.   LT Interest $10.1 bill.
(Interest not earned)

(61% of Cap'l)

Pension Liability $5.1 bill. in '91 vs. $4.9 bill. in '90.

Pfd Stock $238.3 mill.   Pfd Div'd $38.2 mill.
1,530,194 shs. $5.00 cum. ($100 par); 814,100
shs. $3.75 cum. ($100 par) (Less than 1% of Cap'l)
Common Stock 631,593,841 shs. (39% of Cap'l)
Excl. 103,833,719 Class E shs.; 75,382,054 Class H shs.

	60026	74582	83890	96372	102814	101782	120388	123212	122021	123056	135000	140000	Revenues ($mill) D	160000
	44.0%	44.0%	44.4%	42.8%	41.5%	36.7%	36.0%	35.3%	35.3%	34.6%	35.0%	35.0%	Market Share	35.0%
	5.6%	10.8%	8.8%	7.3%	4.8%	5.9%	16.0%	16.2%	13.0%	11.9%	9.0%	9.5%	Operating Margin E	10.0%
	962.7	3730.2	4516.5	3999.0	2944.7	3550.9	4632.1	4224.3	d1986	d4992	285	2960	Net Profit ($mill)	5620
	--	44.7%	32.8%	35.3%	--	--	31.2%	34.0%	NMF	NMF	34.0%	34.0%	Income Tax Rate	34.0%
	1.6%	5.0%	5.4%	4.1%	2.9%	3.5%	3.8%	3.4%	NMF	NMF	.2%	2.1%	Net Profit Margin	3.5%
	1658.1	5890.8	6276.7	1957.5	3920.3	14243	42581	47984	45441	42522	44510	44155	Working Cap'l ($mill) D	62050
	4745.1	3521.8	2772.9	2867.2	9825.3	18294	31614	36708	41627	42800	44685	42030	Long-Term Debt ($mill) D	50750
	18252	20710	24070	29335	30488	33225	35672	34983	30047	27328	26190	27685	Net Worth ($mill) D	36155
	5.4%	16.3%	17.5%	12.9%	8.3%	8.1%	9.8%	9.9%	.6%	NMF	.5%	8.5%	% Earned Total Cap'l	9.5%
	5.3%	18.0%	18.8%	13.6%	9.7%	10.7%	13.0%	12.1%	NMF	NMF	1.0%	10.5%	% Earned Net Worth	15.5%
	1.2%	13.9%	12.6%	8.2%	4.2%	5.7%	8.4%	6.5%	NMF	NMF	NMF	6.0%	% Retained to Comm Eq	7.5%
	78%	24%	34%	40%	58%	47%	36%	46%	NMF	NMF	NMF	46%	% All Div'ds to Net Prof	53%

CURRENT POSITION 1989 D / 1990 / 12/31/91 ($MILL.)

	1989 D	1990	12/31/91
Cash Assets	10213.3	7821.4	10192.4
Receivables	97802.0	95847.5	87872.3
Inventory (LIFO)	7991.7	9331.3	10066.0
Other	2073.3	2348.8	2283.1
Current Assets	118080.3	115349.0	110413.8
Accts Payable	7707.8	8824.4	10061.3
Debt Due	56717.1	57123.9	53339.6
Other	5671.4	3959.6	4491.2
Current Liab.	70096.3	69907.9	67892.1

ANNUAL RATES of change (per sh)

	Past 10 Yrs.	Past 5 Yrs.	Est'd '89-'91 to '95-'97
Revenues	6.5%	6.0%	3.0%
"Cash Flow"	10.5%	--	11.5%
Earnings	--	--	NMF
Dividends	3.5%	0.5%	8.0%
Book Value	5.0%	2.5%	1.5%

Cal-endar	QUARTERLY SALES ($ mill) E				Full Year
	Mar.31	Jun.30	Sep.30	Dec.31	
1989	26968	27438	22771	25070	102247
1990	23942	27911	24413	23391	99657
1991	22259	25180	22792	21400	91631
1992	25595	26000	22405	27000	101000
1993	26000	27000	24500	27000	104500

Cal-endar	EARNINGS PER SHARE A				Full Year
	Mar.31	Jun.30	Sep.30	Dec.31	
1989	2.37	2.23	.72	1.01	6.33
1990	1.02	1.32	d3.54	d2.89	d4.09
1991	d1.28	d1.44	d1.88	d4.25	d8.85
1992	.02	.03	d.25	.20	Nil
1993	.75	1.25	.75	1.25	4.00

Cal-endar	QUARTERLY DIVIDENDS PAID B				Full Year
	Mar.31	Jun.30	Sep.30	Dec.31	
1988	.625	.625	.625	.625	2.50
1989	.75	.75	.75	.75	3.00
1990	.75	.75	.75	.75	3.00
1991	.40	.40	.40	.40	1.60
1992	.40	.40			

BUSINESS: General Motors is the world's largest auto manufacturer. 1991 sales were 16.8% of worldwide total. Automotive products account for 85% of sales. Makes Chevrolet and GMC trucks, GM diesel locomotives, and engines. Operates plants in 17 foreign countries, principally in Western Europe, which make Vauxhall, Opel, and Holden cars and trucks. Acquired EDS in '84, Hughes Aircraft in '86. Foreign business accounts for 16%, labor costs, 24% of sales. '91 depreciation rate: 10.3%. Estimated plant age: 10 years. The company has 756,300 employees, 2 mill. stockholders. Insiders own 1% of stock. Chairman: Robert C. Stempel. Incorporated.: Delaware. Address: 3044 West Grand Boulevard, Detroit, Michigan 48202-3091. Telephone: 313-556-5000.

General Motors managed to earn a small profit in the March period. The news gave the share price a boost, and helped the company get a sympathetic hearing from investors when it recently offered $2.2 billion in new common stock intended to shore up its balance sheet and its underfunded pension plans. Still, GM's difficulties are hardly past. Such a major makeover of the company as is now under way will almost certainly take longer and cost more than anticipated, and labor peace (see below) cannot be assumed. Accordingly, we expect GM's return to profitability to be slower than that of its crosstown rivals. Assuming roughly 10% dilution from the new share issue, we now look for GM to earn its preferred dividend requirement in 1992; pent-up demand should drive a partial profit recovery in 1993, thus helping to keep the reduced common payout intact.

The changes being made at GM are real, and not everyone is going to like them. A recent example: In an effort to make its North American plants function more like its highly lucrative European operations, GM's new purchasing head has decreed that virtually all contracts with suppliers would be opened to new bids, and that the company's internal parts-making divisions would be given no preference in the coming competitions to supply GM world wide. This attempt to overhaul the way the company spends $50 billion annually on parts and raw materials is sure to cause bitter battles among suppliers and to alarm the United Auto Workers, 80,000 of whose members work in GM's sprawling parts operations fabricating 70% of the components that go into GM vehicles. Investors should note that several times in the past two years, the UAW has called strikes at key GM parts factories to protest similar decisions to "outsource" materials.

There's no urgent reason to commit to GM stock at this juncture, particularly after the recent share-price runup. For the 3- to 5-year term, we think that GM's resources (human and material) are larger than its problems by a wide margin. Still, dilution from the recent share issue has reduced the stock's attractiveness as a longer-term holding.

Mark Leach   *June 19, 1992*

(A) Primary earnings. Excludes nonrecurring gain: '91, $1.16; '92, 88¢. Next earnings report due early Aug. (B) Next dividend meeting about Aug. 4. Goes ex about Aug. 14. Approximate dividend payment dates: 10th of March, June, Sept., Dec. ■ Dividend reinvestment plan available. In '84, plus .05 shs. "E" stock. (C) In millions, adjusted for stock split. (D) Includes GMAC from 1988. (E) Excludes GMAC from 1988. (F) Includes intangibles. In '91: $10.2 billion, $16.12/sh.

Company's Financial Strength	A
Stock's Price Stability	80
Price Growth Persistence	25
Earnings Predictability	10

Source: *Value Line Investment Survey.*

EXHIBIT 3   Financial Analysis of Euroslav Market-Entry Strategies: Memorandum and Spreadsheet Model

To: Anna Krzykowiak
         President, Negotiating Team

From: Alexandre Chopin
Re: Financial Analysis of Euroslav Market-Entry Strategies

We have completed the financial modeling of the three market-entry strategies for Euroslavia and can report the following results for the base case of macroeconomic and operating assumptions:

	Status Quo	*CKD Plant*	*CKD/Greenfield Plant*
Base case			
Net present value	DM (64) million	DM 352 million	DM 1,526 million
IRR	8%	33%	36%
Profitability index*	Infinite	2.51×	3.75×
Payback	0 years	4 years	6 years
Hard-currency flow 1993–95	DM (382) million	DM 92 million	DM 638 million
Jobs created by 1996	0	560	1,600
Revenues			
Income taxes	DM 0 million	DM 79 million	DM 178 million
Import/export duties	DM 326 million	DM 31 million	DM 54 million
Dividend distributions	DM 0 million	DM 0 million	DM 54 million
Pessimistic case			
Net present value			
IRR			
Profitability index			
Payback			
Net hard-currency flow			
Jobs created by 1996			
Revenues			
Income taxes			
Import/export duties			
Dividend distributions			
Optimistic case			
Net present value			
IRR			
Profitability index			
Payback			
Net hard-currency flow			
Jobs created by 1996			
Revenues			
Income taxes			
Import/export duties			
Dividend distributions			

*The profitability index is computed as the ratio of the present value of future cash flows to the value of the initial-year investment outlay.

EXHIBIT 3   *(continued)*

Of course, these are just the basic results. When you think it is appropriate, we will exercise the model to complete the grid in this table, and to identify key value drivers or break-even assumptions for critical variables.

Also, we have undertaken no work yet to test the sensitivity of these results to variations in points to be negotiated with General Motors:

- Percentage ownership by GM in the joint venture.
- DM total investment by GM into Euroslavia.
- Duties on imported cars.
- Depreciation rate on facilities.
- Number of workers for whom we guarantee employment.
- Local-content percentage of each car.
- Income-tax rate for the joint venture.
- Dividend distributions.
- Transfer prices for the kit and complete cars.

Appendix
Description of Financial Model
of Entry Strategies for Euroslavia

The Excel spreadsheet model permits rapid sensitivity analysis of financial results and is intended to support the preparation of the Euroslavia government for the negotiations with the GM negotiating team.

The entire spreadsheet is summarized in the northwest corner, where a single screen of data lists 20 key assumptions and nine results for the three alternative strategies. One can conduct sensitivity analyses by varying assumptions and pressing "F9," the recalculation button on the computer. (Alternatively, one could construct data tables of results in an unused region of the spreadsheet.) Immediately below the summary screen on the spreadsheet is a summary of key macroeconomic assumptions underlying the financial forecasts. Farther down are the free-cash-flow (FCF) forecasts for the three strategies, each of which consists of two pages of calculations working from units produced and sold toward FCF. Projections extend for eight years (1993–2000) and are denominated in deutsche marks (DM). For simplicity, the spreadsheet uses one price for cars (revenue per car and variable cost), which represents the expected product mix.

The input variables located in the "Key Value Drivers" portion of the model are broken down into three sections: Market Assumptions, Joint Venture Assumptions, and Plant Assumptions.

Key Value Drivers
Market Assumptions
1. Percentage of total market held by new, Western-made cars.
2. Opel's percentage share of the new, Western-made-car demand.
3. Growth of export demand for Vectras (the anticipated growth in the markets for the Astra and Vectra models that would be filled from the Euroslav plant if a decision to export was made).
4. Vectra units demanded in Euroslavia.
5. Percent growth rate of car prices.
6. Import duties levied on cars into Euroslavia.
7. Export duties levied on cars out of Euroslavia.
8. DM inflation rate.
9. Real growth rate of demand after year 2000 (to be used in the terminal-value calculation).
10. Terminal value growth rate.

EXHIBIT 3   *(continued)*

Joint Venture Assumptions
1. The number of cars that GM will be permitted to import duty-free into Euroslavia.
2. Production strategy, where the value *1* indicates the plant is run at full capacity with the surplus production available for export to other countries, or *0,* which indicates that the plant produces only for Euroslav demand.
3. Depreciation rate on plant and equipment.
4. Percentage ownership of joint venture by GM and Euroslavia.
5. The amount above which cash flow would be paid out in the form of dividends. The Euroslav government had control over this through currency control, because GM currently did not have other investment opportunities in Euroslavia.
6. The transfer price of the kits. The transfer price would affect both which entity showed a profit and the flow of currency from Euroslavia.
7. Transfer price for completed cars.

Plant Assumptions
1. Local content of cars.
2. Employment for a CKD plant.
3. Employment for greenfield plant.

    The "Key Results" section of the model includes the following calculations on the performance of the investment in the joint venture:

- Net present value (PV) of the joint venture.
- Internal rate of return of the joint venture.
- Profitability index (ratio of PV inflows to PV outflows).
- Payback.
- Effect on Opel net income (JV results consolidated).
- GM share of Euroslav market.
- Number of jobs.
- Effect on Euroslav balance of payments.
- PV of tax revenues to Euroslavia (duties and income taxes).

The following exhibits present representative results for the base-case assumptions:
    Analysis of Joint-Venture Cash Flows, CKD Strategy.
    Analysis of Joint-Venture Cash Flows, CKD-Greenfield Strategy.
    Analysis of Joint-Venture Cash Flows, Status Quo Strategy.

EXHIBIT 3 (*continued*) Summary Screen of Excel Model

Key Value Drivers

	1993–1995	1996–1999	2000
Market assumptions			
New "Western" car mkt. share	13%	20%	49%
Opel mkt. share/new Western mkt.	36%	25%	18%
Growth for export demand of Vectra	31%		
Vectra units demanded in Euroslavia	60%		
Price real growth rate (%)	1%	2%	3%
Import duties	35%	35%	20%
Export duties	2%	2%	2%
DM inflation from year 2000	4.0%		
Real growth in unit sales from year 2000	2.0%		
Terminal value growth rate	6.0%		
Joint-venture assumptions			
Duty-free quota for GM	10,000		
Production strategy	1		
Straight-line depreciation years	8		
Euroslav government's % Own. of JV	30%		
Amount above CF distributed (DM millions)	500		
Transfer price: kit (DM)	11,500		
Transfer price: complete car (DM)	15,500		

	CKD	Greenfield	Status Quo
Plant assumptions			
Local content %	19%	100%	0%
Number of people employed, CKD	560		
Number of people employed, Greenfield	1,600		

Key Results

	CKD Euroslav JV Only	Greenfield Euroslav JV Only	Status Quo Euroslav Only
1. NPV of free cash flows (DM millions)	352	1,526	(64)
2. Internal rate of return (FCFs)	33%	36%	8%
3. Profitability index	2.51	3.75	Infinite
4. Payback (years)	4	6	0
5. Hard currency inflow (PV) (DM millions) 1993–95	92	638	(382)
Hard currency inflow (PV) (DM millions) 1996–2000	(182)	1,599	(625)
6. Jobs created by 1996	560	1,600	0
7. PV revenues to Euroslav government (DM millions)			
Import/export duties	31	54	326
Income taxes	79	178	0
Cash-flow distributions	0	54	0

EXHIBIT 3 *(continued)* Macroeconomic Assumptions Underlying Government Staff Analysis

Macroeconomic Assumptions		1993	1994	1995	1996	1997	1998	1999	2000
1. Euroslav car registrations (000)		200	210	220	230	240	250	265	280
2. Outside demand		12,000	15,720	20,593	26,977	35,340	46,295	60,647	79,448
3. Euroslav inflation		30%	30%	30%	20%	10%	10%	10%	10%
Compounded Bunt		130%	169%	220%	264%	290%	319%	351%	386%
DM inflation		6%	5%	4%	4%	4%	4%	4%	4%
Compounded DM		106%	111%	115%	120%	125%	130%	135%	140%
U.S. inflation		4%	4%	4%	4%	4%	4%	4%	4%
Compounded U.S.		104%	108%	112%	117%	122%	127%	132%	137%
4. Forward exchange rates:									
Bunt/DM	8,600	10,597	13,120	16,400	18,923	20,015	21,170	22,391	23,683
DM/$	1.6	1.62	1.64	1.64	1.64	1.64	1.64	1.64	1.64
Bunt/U.S.$	13,760	17,200	21,500	26,875	31,010	32,799	34,691	36,692	38,809
5. Euroslav corporate tax rate		40%							
6. German corporate tax rate		55%							
7. DM discount rate		15%							
8. Retail price new Opels in Euroslavia, 1993		19,000							
9. Opel costs:									
Opel var. cost/completed car		13,500							
Opel var. cost/kit		11,000							
Price to dealer completed car in West		17,000							
Opel incremental fixed costs/CKD 1993–95		10,000,000							
Opel incremental fixed costs/Greenfield 1996–98		50,000,000							
Opel incremental fixed costs/status quo		0							

	CKD	Greenfield	Status Quo
10. Cost of each alternative (DM millions)	180	640	0
($ millions @ 1.6 DM/$)	113	400	0
11. Value of AUTA investment (DM millions)	54	54	

EXHIBIT 3 *(continued)* Analysis of Joint Venture Cash Flows, CKD Strategy

This section calculates the JV's cash flow with a CKD plant.
Layout = Market demand, units assembled, imported, and/or exported from/to Opel. Unit prices, total revenue, unit costs, total costs, and operating
income. Cash flow in and out, NPV, and payback. GM-Opel pays for 100% of plant investment; JV realizes the depreciation.

		1993	1994	1995	1996	1997	1998	1999	2000
Production inputs									
Total Euroslav market purchases		200,000	210,000	220,000	230,000	240,000	250,000	265,000	280,000
New Western car market share, %		13%	13%	13%	20%	20%	20%	20%	49%
New Western car demand–units		26,000	27,300	28,600	46,000	48,000	50,000	53,000	137,200
Opel % of new Western demand		36%	36%	36%	25%	25%	25%	25%	18%
Opel units demanded		9,360	9,828	10,296	11,500	12,000	12,500	13,250	24,696
Vectra units demanded	60%	5,616	5,897	6,178	6,900	7,200	7,500	7,950	14,818
Opel unit actual demand for export		12,000	15,720	20,593	26,977	35,340	46,295	60,647	79,448
Production results									
Units assembled in Euroslavia		17,616	21,617	26,771	30,000	30,000	30,000	30,000	30,000
Units necessary to import from Opel		3,744	3,931	4,118	4,600	4,800	5,000	5,300	9,878
Surplus units for export		12,000	15,720	20,593	23,100	22,800	22,500	22,050	15,182
Revenue inputs	DM/unit								
1. /Unit sold to Euroslavia dealers	14,961	15,933	16,889	17,734	18,798	19,925	21,121	22,388	23,955
plus dealer margin and VAT tax	27%	4,302	4,560	4,788	5,075	5,380	5,703	6,045	6,468
= Retail price paid by consumer	19,000	20,235	21,449	22,522	23,873	25,305	26,824	28,433	30,423
2. /Surplus unit exported to Opel	15,500	16,353	17,170	17,857	18,571	19,314	20,087	20,890	21,726
Revenue results									
Revenue from Euroslav sales (DM 000)		149,134	165,986	182,584	216,171	239,104	264,011	296,643	591,600
Revenue from Export sales (DM 000) 1993–95		196,230	269,914	367,731	0	0	0	0	0
Revenue from Export sales (DM 000) 1996–2000		0	0	0	428,995	440,360	451,949	460,626	329,848
Total revenue		345,364	435,900	550,316	645,166	679,465	715,960	757,269	921,449

(continued)

EXHIBIT 3 *(continued)*

		1993	1994	1995	1996	1997	1998	1999
Costs	DM/unit							
1. Opel transfer price/unit								
Completed car transfer price	15,500	16,353	17,170	17,857	18,571	19,314	20,087	20,890
Kit cost/unit (− local input)	11,500	9,888	10,382	10,798	11,230	11,679	12,146	12,632
2. Material local content for assembly								
% of local content		19%	19%	19%	19%	19%	19%	19%
Material cost/unit for assembly		2,258	2,444	2,606	2,741	2,850	2,965	3,083
3. Wages per month								
Salary per month (bunts 000)	3,859	5,017	6,522	8,478	10,174	11,191	12,310	13,541
Social Sec./Unemployment fund	4,200	5,460	7,098	9,227	11,073	12,180	13,398	14,738
Monthly cost/employee	8,059	10,477	13,620	17,706	21,247	23,371	25,709	28,279
Number of Euroslav employees	560	560	560	560	560	560	560	560
Wage cost/month (bunts MM)	4,513	5,867	7,627	9,915	11,898	13,088	14,397	15,836
Wage cost/month (DM 000)	426	554	581	605	629	654	680	707
Total annual wage costs (DM 000)	5,110	6,644	6,976	7,255	7,545	7,847	8,161	8,487
Variable costs								
1. Paid to Opel								
Paid to Opel for completed car imports		64,591	74,772	84,725	102,354	115,520	130,152	149,219
Paid to Opel for kits		174,187	224,434	289,063	336,888	350,363	364,378	378,953
Total paid to Opel 1993–95		238,778	299,206	373,787	0	0	0	0
Total paid to Opel 1996–2000		0	0	0	439,242	465,883	494,530	528,172
2. Material local content		39,772	52,829	69,772	82,226	85,515	88,935	92,493
3. Annual wage costs		6,644	6,976	7,255	7,545	7,847	8,161	8,487
4. Export duties to Euroslav govt.		3,925	5,398	7,355	8,580	8,807	9,039	9,213
5. Import duties to Euroslav govt.		0	0	0	0	0	0	0
Total variable costs		289,118	364,410	458,169	537,593	568,052	600,665	638,364
Fixed costs								
Sales, gen., & admin.	2%	6,907	8,718	11,006	12,903	13,589	14,319	15,145
P&E maintenance	860	907	953	991	1,030	1,072	1,114	1,159
Depreciation, straight-line		29,250	29,481	29,723	29,975	29,736	30,510	30,793
(less tech. transfer/training)		10,550	11,078	11,521	0	0	0	0
Total fixed costs		47,615	50,229	53,241	43,909	44,397	45,943	47,098
Total costs		336,733	414,639	511,410	581,502	612,449	646,609	685,462

Operating income (DM000)

Operating income (DM000)		8,631	21,261	38,906	63,665	67,016	69,351	71,807	64,182
Less Euroslav taxes	40%	3,452	8,505	15,562	25,466	26,807	27,741	28,723	25,673
Loss carry forward		0	0	0	0	0	0	0	0
Taxes paid		3,452	8,505	15,562	25,466	26,807	27,741	28,723	25,673
After-tax (Euroslav) net income (DM 000)		5,178	12,757	23,344	38,199	40,210	41,611	43,084	38,509
Free-cash-flow calculations									
Plus depreciation	1,750	29,250	29,481	29,723	29,975	29,736	30,510	30,793	31,088
Less capital expenditures		(1,846)	(1,939)	(2,016)	(2,097)	(2,181)	(2,268)	(2,359)	(2,453)
Less NWC requirement	3%	(10,361)	(2,716)	(3,432)	(2,846)	(1,029)	(1,095)	(1,239)	(4,925)
Less GM CKD plant investment	(180,000)	0	0	0	0	0	0	0	0
Less AUTA asset valuation	(54,000)	0	0	0	0	0	0	0	0
Plus terminal value									1,105,738
Free cash flows	(234,000)	22,221	37,583	47,618	63,232	66,736	68,758	70,280	1,167,957
Beginning cash flow		22,221	59,804	107,422	170,654	237,390	306,148	376,428	1,544,385
Amount distributed 1993–95		0	0	0	0	0	0	0	0
Amount distributed 1996–2000		0	0	0	0	0	0	0	0
Remaining cumulative cash flow		22,221	59,804	107,422	170,654	237,390	306,148	376,428	1,544,385
PV free cash flows	352,337								
IRR free cash flows	33.2%								
Payback (years)	4								
Profitability index	2.5								

EXHIBIT 3 *(continued)* Analysis of Joint Venture Cash Flows, CKD-Greenfield Strategy

This section calculates the JV's cash flow with a CKD built immediately and followed by a Greenfield assembly plant built by 1996.

Layout = Market demand, units assembled, imported, and/or exported from/to Opel. Unit prices, total revenue, unit costs, total costs, and operating income. Cash flow in and out, NPV, and payback.

GM-Opel pays for 100% of plant investment; JV realizes the depreciation.

		1993	1994	1995	1996	1997	1998	1999	2000
Production inputs									
Total Euroslav market purchases		200,000	210,000	220,000	230,000	240,000	250,000	265,000	280,000
New Western car mkt. share %		13%	13%	13%	20%	20%	20%	20%	49%
New Western car demand-units		26,000	27,300	28,600	46,000	48,000	50,000	53,000	137,200
Opel expected % of new Western		36%	36%	36%	25%	25%	25%	25%	18%
Opel unit actual demand Euroslavia		9,360	9,828	10,296	11,500	12,000	12,500	13,250	24,696
Vectra units demanded	60%	5,616	5,897	6,178	6,900	7,200	7,500	7,950	14,818
Opel unit actual demand for export		12,000	15,720	20,593	26,977	35,340	46,295	60,647	79,448
Production results									
Units assembled in Euroslavia		17,616	21,617	26,771	0	0	0	0	0
Units manufactured in Euroslavia		0	0	0	33,877	42,540	53,795	68,597	94,265
Surplus units for export		12,000	15,720	20,593	26,977	35,340	46,295	60,647	79,448
Units imported from Opel		3,744	3,931	4,118	4,600	4,800	5,000	5,300	9,878
Revenue inputs	DM/unit								
1. /Unit sold to Euroslav dealers	14,961	15,933	16,889	17,734	18,798	19,925	21,121	22,388	23,955
plus dealer margin and VAT tax	27%	4,302	4,560	4,788	5,075	5,380	5,703	6,045	6,468
= Retail price paid by consumer	19,000	20,235	21,449	22,522	23,873	25,305	26,824	28,433	30,423
2. /Surplus cars' transfer price to Opel	15,500	16,353	17,170	17,857	18,571	19,314	20,087	20,890	21,726
Revenue results									
On Euroslav sales		149,134	165,986	182,584	216,171	239,104	264,011	296,643	591,600
On export sales 1993–95		196,230	269,914	367,731	0	0	0	0	0
On export sales 1996–2000		0	0	0	500,997	682,559	929,918	1,266,920	1,726,052
Total revenue		345,364	435,900	550,316	717,169	921,663	1,193,929	1,563,563	2,317,652

Costs

	DM/unit								
1. Opel transfer price/unit									
Completed car cost/unit	15,500	16,353	17,170	17,857	18,571	19,314	20,087	20,890	21,726
Kit cost/unit (− local input)	11,500	9,888	10,382	10,798	0	0	0	0	0
2. Local value added									
% for assembly	19%	19%	19%	19%	100%	100%	100%	100%	100%
Material cost/unit for assembly	11,500	2,258	2,444	2,606					
Material cost/unit for manufacturing	9,775				11,712	12,180	12,668	13,174	13,701
3. Annual wage costs									
Wage/employee/m (bunts)	3,859	5,017	6,522	8,478	10,174	11,191	12,310	13,541	14,896
Social Sec./Unemployment fund/m (bunts)	4,200	5,460	7,098	9,227	11,073	12,180	13,398	14,738	16,212
Monthly cost/employee (bunts)	8,059	10,477	13,620	17,706	21,247	23,371	25,709	28,279	31,107
Number of Euroslav employees	560	560	560	560	1,600	1,600	1,600	1,600	1,600
Wage cost/month (bunts millions)	4,513	5,867	7,627	9,915	33,995	37,394	41,134	45,247	49,772
Wage costs (DM 000)	426	554	581	605	1,796	1,868	1,943	2,021	2,102
Total annual wage costs (DM 000)	5,110	6,644	6,976	7,255	21,557	22,419	23,316	24,249	25,219

Variable costs

1. Paid to Opel for kits		174,187	224,434	289,063	0	0	0	0	0
Paid to Opel for completed car imports		61,224	67,499	73,542	85,428	92,707	100,433	110,717	214,615
Total paid Opel 1993–95		235,411	291,933	362,605	0	0	0	0	0
Total paid Opel 1996–2000		0	0	0	85,428	92,707	100,433	110,717	214,615
2. Material costs		39,772	52,829	69,772	396,763	518,151	681,455	903,712	1,291,545
3. Wage costs		6,644	6,976	7,255	21,557	22,419	23,316	24,249	25,219
4. Export Duties Paid		3,925	5,398	7,355	10,020	13,651	18,598	25,338	34,521
5. Import Duties paid		0	0	0	0	0	0	0	0
Total variable costs		285,751	357,137	446,986	513,768	646,929	823,802	1,064,017	1,565,900

Fixed costs

SG&A costs	3%	10,361	13,077	16,129	16,774	17,445	18,143	18,868	19,623
P&E maintenance		500	900	900	1,800	1,800	2,300	2,300	2,300
Depreciation		69,250	69,481	69,723	109,975	110,237.2	110,509.8	110,793.3	111,088.1
Technology transfer fees 1993–95		10,550	11,078	11,521	0	0	0	0	0
Technology transfer fees 1996–2000		0	0	0	59,907	62,303	64,796	0	0
Total fixed costs		90,661	94,535	98,273	188,456	191,786	195,748	131,962	133,011
Total costs		376,412	451,672	545,259	702,224	838,714	1,019,550	1,195,979	1,698,911

(continued)

EXHIBIT 3 *(continued)*

		1993	1994	1995	1996	1997	1998	1999	2000
Operating income (DM 000)		(31,048)	(15,772)	5,057	14,945	82,949	174,379	367,584	618,741
Less Euroslav taxes	40%	(12,419)	(6,309)	2,023	5,978	33,180	69,751	147,034	247,496
Less Carry forward		(12,419)	(18,728)	(16,705)	(10,727)	0	0	0	0
Taxes paid		0	0	0	0	22,452	69,751	147,034	247,496
After-tax (Euroslav) net income (DM 000)		(31,048)	(15,772)	5,057	14,945	60,497	104,627	220,551	371,245
Free-cash-flow calculations									
Plus depreciation		69,250	69,481	69,723	109,975	110,237	110,510	110,793	111,088
Less capital expenditures	1,750	(1,846)	(1,939)	(2,016)	(2,097)	(2,181)	(2,268)	(2,359)	(2,453)
Less NWC requirement	5%	(17,268)	(4,527)	(5,721)	(8,343)	(10,225)	(13,613)	(18,482)	(37,704)
Less GM plant investment	(500,000)	0	0	(320,000)	0	0	0	0	0
Less AUTA asset valuation	(54,000)	0	0	0	0	0	0	0	0
Plus terminal value									5,207,842
Free cash flows	(554,000)	19,087	47,243	(252,957)	114,480	158,329	199,256	310,504	5,650,017
Beginning cash flow		19,087	66,331	(186,626)	(72,146)	86,183	285,439	595,942	6,150,017
Amount distributed 1993–95		0	0	0				0	0
Amount distributed 1996–2000					0	0	0	95,942	442,175
Remaining cumulative cash flow		19,087	66,331	(186,626)	(72,146)	86,183	285,439	500,000	5,707,842
PV free cash flows	1,526,043								
Internal rate of return	36.1%								
Payback (years)	6								
Profitability index	3.8								

EXHIBIT 3 (*continued*) Analysis of Joint Venture Cash Flows, Status Quo Strategy

This section calculates cash flows in Euroslavia with no plant.
Layout = Market demand, units imported from Opel AG, unit prices to dealers, total revenue, unit costs, total costs, and operating income. Cash flow in and out, PV. JV pays duties.

	DM/unit	1993	1994	1995	1996	1997	1998	1999	2000
Production inputs									
Total Euroslavia market purchases		200,000	210,000	220,000	230,000	240,000	250,000	265,000	280,000
New Western car market share, %		13%	13%	13%	20%	20%	20%	20%	49%
New Western car demand-units		26,000	27,300	28,600	46,000	48,000	50,000	53,000	137,200
Opel % of new Western		36%	36%	36%	25%	25%	25%	25%	18%
Opel units demanded		9,360	9,828	10,296	11,500	12,000	12,500	13,250	24,696
Sales via dealers (capped)		9,360	9,828	10,296	11,500	12,000	12,500	13,250	24,696
Unsatisfied demand		0	0	0	0	0	0	0	0
Production results									
Production in Euroslavia		0	0	0	0	0	0	0	0
Imports from Opel AG		9,360	9,828	10,296	11,500	12,000	12,500	13,250	24,696
Revenue inputs									
1. /Unit sold to Euroslavia dealer	14,961	15,933	16,889	17,734	18,798	19,925	21,121	22,388	23,955
plus dealer margin and VAT tax	27%	4,302	4,560	4,788	5,075	5,380	5,703	6,045	6,468
= Retail price paid by consumer	19,000	20,235	21,449	22,522	23,873	25,305	26,824	28,433	30,423
Revenue results									
On Euroslav sales		149,134	165,986	182,584	216,171	239,104	264,011	296,643	591,600
On export sales		0	0	0	0	0	0	0	0
Total revenue		149,134	165,986	182,584	216,171	239,104	264,011	296,643	591,600

(*continued*)

EXHIBIT 3 *(concluded)*

	DM/unit	1993	1994	1995	1996	1997	1998	1999	2000
Costs									
1. Opel transfer price/unit									
Completed car transfer price	15,500	16,353	17,170	17,857	18,571	19,314	20,087	20,890	21,726
2. Local value added									
Material %	0%	0%	0%	0%	0%	0%	0%	0%	0%
a. Material DM		0	0	0	0	0	0	0	0
b. Wages									
Salary per month (bunts 000)		0	0	0	0	0	0	0	0
Social Sec./Unemployment fund		0	0	0	0	0	0	0	0
Monthly cost/employee		0	0	0	0	0	0	0	0
Number of Euroslav employees		0	0	0	0	0	0	0	0
Wage cost/month (bunts millions)		0	0	0	0	0	0	0	0
Wage costs/month (DM 000)		0	0	0	0	0	0	0	0
Total annual wage costs (DM 000)		0	0	0	0	0	0	0	0
Variable costs									
1. Paid to Opel for completed car imports 1993–95		153,059	168,748	183,855	0	0	0	0	0
Paid to Opel for completed car imports 1996–2000					213,569	231,769	251,083	276,794	536,538
2. Material local content		0	0	0	0	0	0	0	0
3. Annual wage costs		0	0	0	0	0	0	0	0
4. Export duty		0	0	0	0	0	0	0	0
5. Import duty to gov't on comp. cars	35%	53,571	59,062	64,349	74,749	81,119	87,879	96,878	107,308
Total variable costs		206,630	227,810	248,204	288,318	312,888	338,962	373,671	643,845
Fixed costs									
Sales, gen., and admin.		0	0	0	0	0	0	0	0
P&E maintenance		0	0	0	0	0	0	0	0
Depreciation		0	0	0	0	0	0	0	0
Total fixed costs		0	0	0	0	0	0	0	0
Total costs		206,630	227,810	248,204	288,318	312,888	338,962	373,671	643,845

Operating income (DM 000)									
Less Euroslav taxes	40%	(57,497)	(61,824)	(65,620)	(72,147)	(73,783)	(74,951)	(77,028)	(52,245)
Loss carry forward		(22,999)	(24,730)	(26,248)	(28,859)	(29,513)	(29,980)	(30,811)	(20,898)
Taxes paid		(22,999)	(47,728)	(73,976)	(102,835)	(132,348)	(162,328)	(193,140)	(214,038)
After-tax (Euroslav) net income (DM 000)		0	0	0	0	0	0	0	0
		(57,497)	(61,824)	(65,620)	(72,147)	(73,783)	(74,951)	(77,028)	(52,245)
Free-cash-flow calculations									
Plus depreciation		0	0	0	0	0	0	0	0
Less capital expenditures		0	0	0	0	0	0	0	0
Less NWC requirement		0	0	0	0	0	0	0	0
Plus terminal value									709,921
Free cash flow		(57,497)	(61,824)	(65,620)	(72,147)	(73,783)	(74,951)	(77,028)	657,676
Beginning cash flow	500	(57,497)	(119,321)	(184,941)	(257,087)	(330,871)	(405,821)	(482,850)	174,826
Amount distributed 1993–95		0	0	0	0	0	0	0	
Amount distributed 1996–2000								0	0
Remaining cumulative cash flow		(57,497)	(119,321)	(184,941)	(257,087)	(330,871)	(405,821)	(482,850)	174,826
Present value, FCF	(64,190)								
Internal rate of return	8.1%								
Payback	0								
Profitability index	Infinite								

EXHIBIT 4   Update on Euroslav Car Market

To: Anna Krzykowiak
           President, Negotiating Team

From: Jerzy Lobotonski
           Economics Research Staff
           Ministry of Finance

Re: Developments in Euroslav Car Market

The Economics Research Staff of the Ministry of Finance has just finished a lengthy analysis of the Euroslav car market. Their new conclusions can be summarized as follows:

1. Automobile demand is forecast to be 350,000 units in Euroslavia by the year 2000. It may take longer than expected to recover from the current deep recession. The standard of living is lower in Euroslavia than previously believed, and the long-term GDP growth rate we had previously used (3.5 percent) may be optimistic.
2. The trade accord with the European Community is projected to reduce tariffs on cars gradually over the next 10 years. A reduction of the tariff on new cars imported from the EC to 25 percent by 1996 effectively eliminates the advantage of a CKD plant and leaves a relative short window in which to make the project fully profitable.
3. Two distinct automobile markets exist in Euroslavia: low-priced vehicles (either newly made in Eastern Europe or used vehicles from Western Europe) and high-priced, new, Western-made cars. In Euroslavia, 25,000 new Western cars were sold last year (including 8,000 fairly low-priced cars from Hyundai), which corresponds to 11 percent of the total market for new and used cars (or 15 percent of the smaller market for new cars alone). The key question is: *How will the split in this dual market change and consequently affect the size of the Euroslav car market available to Opel?* The shift toward new Western cars will depend on how fast Euroslav incomes rise, which depends on how fast Euroslav products find acceptance in the West. The shift also will depend on import tariffs:
   • The trade accord with the European Economic Community is projected to reduce tariffs on cars gradually over the next 10 years. A reduction of the tariff on new cars imported from the EEC to 25 percent by 1996 effectively eliminates the advantage of a CKD plant and leaves a relatively short window in which to make the project fully profitable.
   • We (Euroslavia) offered manufacturers a duty-free quota of 30,000 cars starting in mid-1992 and rising gradually over the decade. If the market for new Western cars remains relatively small, this quota will be enough to supply most of the existing demand. On this basis a CKD operation could sustain 20 percent higher costs than duty-free imports from the West.
4. Of the 61,000 imports sold in Euroslavia in 1991, about two-thirds were either small or low-priced cars. The mix will shift toward larger cars by the end of the decade.

To summarize:

• Previous forecasts of demand for cars in Euroslavia could be optimistic.
• The dual market could persist, depressing growth in demand for new Western cars and resulting in a severe cost penalty for CKD units.
• Unit growth, if it comes, could be concentrated in the small rather than compact and larger-car segments, further jeopardizing the viability of a joint venture.

EXHIBIT 5   Assessment of AUTA Facilities, Operations, and Financial Condition

---

To: AUTA Negotiating Team

From: Ministry of Ownership Transformation

Subject: Summary of Audit and Physical Inspection of AUTA Facilities, Performed by General Motors

Date: December 11, 1991

Following is a summary of audit and inspection findings from a visit to AUTA by a General Motors team on
   December 9, 1991:

- The poor condition of AUTA's financial accounting systems prevented detailed audits of AUTA's financial condition. A moderate portion of the accounting system is computerized.
- Cash on hand and in various bank accounts on November 30, 1991, was 72,369,421.15 bunts (about U.S.\$5,169,244).
- Accounts receivable seem to be minimal (AUTA built only to order) although there have been irregularities in accounting for certain bad debts. The GM team was unable to make a final judgment on the magnitude of receivables.
- Raw material and work-in-process inventories appear to have been significantly understated in some vital commodities (e.g., glass and sheet steel) by as much as 25 percent. Exact quantities in stock are currently difficult to determine. However, on the basis of limited sampling, we estimate that market values of all inventories are 495,894,229 bunts (U.S.\$35,421,016), or approximately 18 percent *more* than reported in the financial statements (i.e., 89,260,961.22 bunts).
- Of the seven buildings at the AUTA complex, three were built in 1951, two in 1963, and two in 1969. All appear to be in fair repair. They have been completely depreciated. The environmental auditors, Enviro-audit of Fairfax, Virginia, report significant traces of gasoline, benzene, naphtha, lead, and other heavy metals at depths to 8 meters in more than 15 locations on the property.
- The machinery and tools have been fully depreciated but are in excellent repair. Approximately 80 percent of the machines are of Czech and Euroslav origin and were acquired in the 1960s and 1970s. Five percent are of unknown age and origin. Fifteen percent are of Western origin and appear to have been acquired between 1980 and 1986. The vast majority of these machines would require special fittings and retooling to permit integration into a GM assembly operation. Given the age of the machinery and the cost of refitting, the production audit team from Opel doubt that the investment return on refitting would be satisfactory.
- AUTA currently has an order backlog of 14,289 cars, of which only 1,321 would be for vehicles similar to the Opel Astra.
- The AUTA dealer network consists of 39 local "agents," most of whom operate private garages. All primary, secondary, and tertiary communities are covered by these agents.

Part X

Setting Corporate Financial Policy

Structuring Corporate Financial Policy: Diagnosis of Problems and Evaluation of Strategies

You can observe a lot just by watching.

Yogi Berra

This note outlines a diagnostic and prescriptive way of thinking about corporate financial policy. Successful diagnosis and prescription depend heavily on thoughtful creativity and careful judgment, so the note presents no "cookbook" solutions. Rather, it discusses the elements of good *process* and offers three basic stages in that process:

1. *Description.* The ability to describe a firm's financial policies (which have been chosen either explicitly or by default) is an essential foundation of diagnosis and prescription. Part I defines *financial structure* and discusses the design elements by which a senior financial officer must make choices. This section illustrates the complexity of a firm's financial policies.

2. *Diagnosis.* One derives a "good" financial structure by triangulating from benchmark perspectives. Then one compares the idealized and actual financial structures, looking for opportunities for improvement. Part II presents an overview of three benchmarks by

This note was prepared by Professor Robert F. Bruner and draws on collaborative work with Katherine L. Updike. Copyright © 1993 by the University of Virginia Darden School Foundation, Charlottesville, VA. All rights reserved. *No part of this publication may be reproduced, stored in a retrieval system, used in a spreadsheet, or transmitted in any form or by any means—electronic, mechanical, photocopying, recording, or otherwise—without the permission of the Darden School Foundation. For inquiries, please send an e-mail to dardencases@virginia.edu.* Revised 6/98. Version 1.5.

which the analyst can diagnose problems and opportunities: (1) the expectations of investors; (2) the policies and behavior of competitors; and (3) the internal goals and motivations of corporate management itself. Other perspectives may also exist. Parts III, IV, and V discuss in detail the estimation and application of the three benchmarks. These sections emphasize artful homework and economy of effort by focusing on key considerations, questions, and information. The goal is to derive insights unique to each benchmark rather than to churn data endlessly.

3. *Prescription.* Action recommendations should spring from the insights gained in description and diagnosis. Rarely, however, do unique solutions or ideas exist; rather, the typical chief financial officer (CFO) must have a *view* about competing suggestions. Part VI addresses the task of comparing competing proposals. Part VII presents the conclusion.

PART I: IDENTIFYING CORPORATE FINANCIAL POLICY: THE ELEMENTS OF ITS DESIGN

The first task for financial advisers and decision makers is to understand the firm's *current* financial policy. Doing so is a necessary foundation for diagnosing problems and prescribing remedies. This section presents an approach for identifying the firm's financial policy, based on careful analysis of the *tactics* by which that policy is implemented.

The Concept of Corporate Financial Policy

The notion that firms *have* a distinct financial policy is startling to some analysts and executives. Occasionally, a chief financial officer will say, "All I do is get the best deal I can whenever we need funds." Almost no CFO would admit otherwise. In all probability, however, the firm has a more substantive policy than the CFO admits to. Even a style of myopia or opportunism is, after all, a policy.

Some executives will argue that calling financing a policy is too fancy. They say that financing is reactive: It happens after all investment and operational decisions have been made. How can reaction be a policy? At other times, one hears an executive say, "Our financial policy is simple." Attempts to characterize a financial structure as reactive or simplistic overlook the considerable richness of choice that confronts the financial manager.

Finally, some analysts make the mistake of thinking one size fits all; that is, they assume that financial policy is mainly driven by the economics of a certain industry and they overlook the firm-specific nature of financial policy. Firms in the same, well-defined industry can have very different financial policies. The reason is that financial policy is a matter of *managerial choice.*

"Corporate financial policy" is a set of broad *guidelines* or a preferred *style* to guide the raising of capital and distribution of value. Policies should be set to support the mission and strategy of the firm. As the environment changes, policies should adapt.

The analyst of financial policy must come to terms with its ambiguity. Policies are guidelines; they are imprecise. Policies are products of managerial choice rather than dictates of an economic model. Policies change over time. Nevertheless, the framework in this note can help the analyst define a firm's corporate financial policy with enough focus to identify potential problems, prescribe remedies, and make decisions.

The Elements of Financial Policy

Every financial structure reveals underlying financial policies through the following seven elements of financial-structure design:[1]

1. *Mix* of classes of capital (such as debt versus equity): *How heavily does the firm rely on different classes of capital? Is the reliance on debt reasonable in light of the risks the firm faces and the nature of its industry and technology?* Mix may be analyzed through capitalization ratios, debt-service coverage ratios, and the firm's sources-and-uses-of-funds statement (where the analyst should look for the origins of the new additions to capital in the recent past). Many firms exhibit a pecking order of financing: They seek to fill their funds needs, through retentions of profits, then through debt, and, finally, through the issuance of new shares. *Does the firm observe a particular pecking order in its acquisition of new capital?*

2. *Maturity structure of the firm's capital.* To describe the choices made about the maturity of outstanding securities is to be able to infer the judgments the firm made about its priorities—for example, future financing requirements and opportunities or relative preference for refinancing[2] risk versus reinvestment[3] risk. A risk-neutral position with respect to maturity would be where the life of the firm's assets equals the life of the firm's liabilities. Most firms accept an inequality in one direction or the other. This might be due to ignorance or to sophistication: Managers might have a strong internal "view" about their ability to reinvest or refinance. Ultimately, we want managers to maximize value, not minimize risk. The absence of a perfect maturity hedge might reflect managers' better-informed bets about the future of the firm and markets. Measuring the maturity structure of the firm's capital can yield insights into the bets that managers are apparently making. The standard measures of maturity are term to maturity, average life, and duration. *Are the lives of the firm's assets and liabilities roughly matched? If not, what gamble is the firm taking (i.e., is it showing an appetite for refinancing risk or reinvestment risk)?*

3. *Basis of the firm's coupon and dividend payments.* In simplest terms, basis addresses the firm's preference for fixed or floating rates of payment and is a useful tool in fath-

---

[1]For parsimony, this note will restrict its scope to these seven items. One can, however, imagine other dimensions than those listed here.

[2]Refinancing risk exists where the life of the firm's assets is *more* than the life of the firm's liabilities. In other words, the firm will need to replace (or "roll over") the capital originally obtained to buy the asset. The risk of refinancing is the chance that the firm will not be able to obtain funds on advantageous terms (or at all) at the rollover date.

[3]Reinvestment risk exists where the life of the firm's assets is *less* than the life of the firm's liabilities. In other words, the firm will need to replace (or "roll over") the investment which the capital originally financed. The risk of reinvestment is the chance that the firm will not be able to reinvest the capital on advantageous terms at the rollover date.

oming management's judgment regarding the future course of interest rates. Interest-rate derivatives provide the financial officer with choices conditioned by caps, floors, and other structured options. Understanding the basis choices of management can reveal some of the fundamental "bets" management is placing, even when it has decided to "do nothing." *What is the firm's relative preference for fixed or floating interest rates? Are the firm's operating returns fixed or floating?*

4. *Currency* addresses the global aspect of a firm's financial opportunities. These opportunities are expressed in two ways: (*a*) management of the firm's exposure to foreign exchange rate fluctuations, and (*b*) exploitation of unusual financing possibilities in global capital markets. Exchange rate exposure arises when a firm earns income (or pays expenses) in a range of currencies. Whether and how a firm hedges this exposure can reveal "bets" that management is making about the future movement of exchange rates and the future currency mix of the firm's cash flows. The financial policy analyst should look for foreign-denominated securities in the firm's capital and for swap, option, futures, and forward contracts—all of these can be used to manage the firm's foreign exchange exposure. The other way that currency matters to the financial policy analyst is as an indication of the willingness of management to source its capital "offshore." This is an indication of sophistication and of "having a view" about the parity of exchange rates with security returns around the world. In a perfectly integrated global capital market, the theory of interest rate parity would posit the futility of finding "bargain financing" offshore. But global capital markets are not perfectly integrated, and interest rate parity rarely holds everywhere. Experience suggests that financing bargains may exist temporarily. Offshore financing may suggest an interest in finding and exploiting such bargains. *Is the currency denomination of the firm's capital consistent with the currency denomination of the firm's operating cash flows? Do the balance sheet footnotes show evidence of foreign exchange hedging? Also, is the company in effect sourcing capital on a global basis, or is it focusing narrowly on domestic capital markets?*

5. *Exotica.* Every firm faces a spectrum of financing alternatives, ranging from "plain vanilla" bonds and stocks to hybrids and one-of-a-kind, highly tailored securities.[4] This element considers management's relative preference for financial innovation. Where a firm positions itself on this spectrum can shed light on management's openness to new ideas, intellectual originality, and, possibly, opportunistic tendencies. As a general matter, option-linked securities often appear in corporate finance where there is some disagreement between issuers and investors about a firm's prospects. For instance, managers of high-growth firms will foresee rapid expansion and vaulting stock prices; bond investors, not having the benefit of inside information, might only see high risk—issuing a convertible bond might be a way to allow the bond investors to capitalize the risk[5] and enjoy

---

[4]Examples of highly tailored securities include exchangeable and convertible bonds (such as those issued by Chub Company), hybrid classes of common stock (such as General Motors' class E and H shares), and contingent securities (such as Eli Lilly's contingent payment unit, a dividend-paying equity issued in connection with an acquisition).

[5]In general, the call options embedded in a convertible bond will be more valuable the greater the volatility of the underlying asset.

the creation of value through growth, in return for accepting a lower current yield. Also, the circumstances under which exotic securities were issued are often fascinating episodes in a company's history. *Based on past financings, what is the firm's appetite for issuing exotic securities? Why have the firm's exotic securities been tailored as they are?*

6. *External control.* Any management team probably prefers little outside control. One must recognize that, in any financial structure, management has made choices about subtle control trade-offs, including *who* might exercise control (e.g., creditors, existing shareholders, new shareholders, or a raider) and the control *trigger* (e.g., default on a loan covenant, passing a preferred stock dividend, a shareholder vote). How management structures control triggers (e.g., the tightness of loan covenants) or forestalls discipline (e.g., through the adoption of poison pills and other takeover defenses) can reveal insights about management's fears and expectations. Clues about external-control choices may be found in credit covenants, collateral pledges, the terms of preferred shares, the profile of the firm's equity holders, the voting rights of common stock, corporate bylaws, and antitakeover defenses. *In what ways has management defended against or yielded to external control?*

7. *Distribution* seeks to determine any patterns in (*a*) the way the firm markets its securities (i.e., acquires capital) and (*b*) the way the firm delivers value to its investors (i.e., returns capital). Regarding marketing, insights emerge from knowing where a firm's securities are listed for trading, how often shares are sold, and who advises the sale of securities (the adviser a firm attracts is one indication of its sophistication). Regarding delivery of value, the two generic strategies involve dividends or capital gains. Some companies will pay low or no dividends and force their shareholders to take returns in the form of capital gains. Other companies will pay material dividends, even borrowing to do so. Still others will repurchase shares, split shares, and declare extraordinary dividends. Managers' choices about delivering value yield clues about management's beliefs about investors and about the company's ability to satisfy investor needs. *How have managers chosen to deliver value to shareholders, and with whose assistance have they issued securities?*

A Comparative Illustration

The value of looking at a firm's financial structure through these seven design elements is that the insights they provide can become a basis for developing a broad, detailed picture of the firm's financial policies. Also, the seven elements become an organizational framework for the wealth of financial information that is typically available on publicly owned companies.

Consider the examples of Reebok International Ltd., which manufactures high-quality footwear, and The Limited, Inc., a women's clothing retailer. Sources such as *Moody's Industrial Manual* distill information from annual reports and regulatory filings and permit the analyst to draw conclusions about the seven elements of each firm's financial policy. Drawing on the financial results for 1990, analysts may glean the following insights about the policies of Reebok and The Limited:

Elements of Financial Policy	*Reebok International Ltd.*	*The Limited, Inc.*
Mix	**Equity orientation** Debt/assets = 0.096 Sold equity 1986, 1987 Huge cash balance Debt rating A3 Acquisitions financed by stock swap or cash from stock sale	**Moderate debt** Debt/assets = 0.18 Debt rating A1 No equity sold since initial public offering in 1971 Finances acquisitions with stock swaps Unused bank lines equal $800 million
Maturity	**Medium to long** Avg. life = 7.5 years	**Barbell**[a] Avg. life = 3.7 years 78% @ 1 year 22% @ 9 years Long-term debt funds finance subsidiary
Basis	**Fixed rates** 7% of debt is floating rate Replaces floating-rate bank debt with equity and fixed-rate debt	**Mixed** 44% of debt is floating rate
Currency	**Exclusively U.S.$**	**Exclusively U.S.$**
Exotica	**No exotics** Modest use of leases	**No exotics, but . . .** Uses commercial paper as source of long-term capital Bonds sold in book-entry form to reduce administrative costs[b] A retailer with no large lease obligations! Apparently prefers to borrow and buy
Control	**Favors large stockholders** Noncumulative voting for directors Debt unsecured and callable	**Debt is unsecured but noncallable** **Significant investors** Two Wexner family members on board (Wexner is CEO) Cumulative voting[c] for directors

Distribution	**Steady dividends**
	Raised dividends when earnings
	   fell in 1988
	Payout 13–24%
	Some international
	Sold shares abroad in 1987
	   See name
	Loyal to adviser
	Kidder underwrote all equity and debt
	Agents: Citibank and Bank of Boston
		Capital gains
		Rapid growth
		Many stock splits
		Declining dividend-payout trend: 19%, 17.5%, 16.6%
		Some international
		Listed for trading in New York, London, Tokyo
		
		Various advisers
		Bear Stearns, Salomon, Morgan Stanley
		Agents: BONY, First Chicago

[a]A "barbell" maturity structure is bimodal, with debt coming due mainly in both the near term and the far term. Some experts believe that such a maturity structure hedges against future interest-rate movements: If rates fall, the short-term debt will exploit the trend; if rates rise, the long-term debt mitigates the impact.

[b]The Moody's citation reveals that the bonds will be represented by a single "global security" deposited with the Depository Trust Co., a subsidiary of the New York Stock Exchange that settles "paperless" securities transactions. Under "book-entry" registration, investors receive no securities, only an acknowledgment that securities are held for them on account at intermediaries such as Depository Trust. Book-entry registration may lower administrative costs for the issuer.

[c]Cumulative voting is a scheme of shareholder elections of directors whereby stockholders may cast their votes, cumulatively, for one person. Thus, if four directors' seats are to be filled, the shareholder may cast as many as four votes for one candidate. Cumulative voting is viewed as a means of protecting the representation of minority or dissident blocs of shareholders.

As the table shows, standard information available on public companies such as these yields important contrasts in the financial policies of the two firms. Note that the insights are *informed guesses:* Neither of these firms explicitly describes its financial policies. Nonetheless, with practice and good information, the validity of the guesses can be high.

Reebok and The Limited present distinctly different policy profiles. Reebok's is a conservative policy in almost every dimension. The Limited's is sophisticated and slightly more aggressive. Two such firms would warrant very different sets of questions by a director or outside financial adviser.

The key idea is that financial policies can be characterized by the tracks they leave. Good strategic assessment begins with good "tracking" of current or past policy.

PART II: GENERAL FRAMEWORK FOR DIAGNOSING FINANCIAL POLICY OPPORTUNITIES AND PROBLEMS

Having parsed the choices embedded in the firm's financial structure, one must ask, "Were these the *right* choices?" What is "right" is a matter of the context and the clienteles to which management must respond. A firm has many potential claimants.[6] The discussion that follows will focus on the perspectives of competitors, investors, and senior corporate managers.

1. *Does the financial policy create value?* From the standpoint of investors, the best financial structure will (*a*) maximize shareholder wealth, (*b*) maximize the value of the entire firm (i.e., the market value of assets), and (*c*) minimize the firm's weighted-average cost of capital. When these conditions occur, the firm makes the best trade-offs among choices on each of the seven dimensions of financial policy. This analysis is all within the context of the *market* conditions.

2. *Does the financial policy create competitive advantage?* Competitors should matter in the design of corporate financial policy. Financial structure can enhance or constrain competitive advantage mainly by opening or foreclosing avenues of competitive response over time. Thus, a manager should critically assess the strategic options created or destroyed by a particular financial structure. Also, assuming that they are reasonably well managed, competitors' financial structures are probably an indicator of good financial policy in a particular industry. Thus, a manager should want to know how his or her firm's financial structure compares to the peer group. In short, this line of thinking seeks to evaluate the relative position of the firm in its competitive environment on the basis of financial structure.

---

[6]With a moment's reflection, the analyst will call up a number of claimants, or "stakeholders," or clienteles, whose interests the company might serve. Managers, customers, and investors are often the first to come to mind. Creditors (e.g., bankers) often have interests that are different from equity investors. Workers (and unions) often make tangible claims on the firm. Governments, through their taxing and regulatory powers, do so as well. One might extend the list to environmentalists and other social activists. The possibilities are almost limitless. For parsimony, this discussion treats only the three perspectives that yield the most insight about financial policy.

3. *Does the financial policy sustain the vision of senior management?* The internal perspective tests the appropriateness of a capital structure from the standpoint of the expectations and capacities of the corporate organization itself. The analyst begins with an assessment of corporate strategy and the resulting stream of cash requirements and resources anticipated in the future. The realism of the plan should be tested against expected macroeconomic variations, as well as against possible but unexpected financial strains. A good financial structure meets the classic maxim of corporate finance, "Don't run out of cash." In other words, the ideal financial structure adequately funds the growth goals and dividend payouts of the firm without severely diluting the firm's current equity owners. The concept of self-sustainable growth provides a straightforward test of this ideal.

The next three sections will discuss these perspectives in more detail.

All three perspectives are not likely to offer a completely congruent assessment of financial structure. The investor's view looks at the *economic* consequences of a financial structure; the competitor's view considers *strategic* consequences; the internal view addresses the *survival and ambitions* of the firm. The three views ask entirely different questions; an analyst should not be surprised when the answers diverge.

Rather like estimating the height of a distant mountain through the haze, the analyst develops a concept of the best financial structure by a process of *triangulation*. Triangulation involves weighing the importance of each of the perspectives as *complements* rather than as substitutes, identifying points of consistency, and making artful judgments where the perspectives diverge.

The goal of this analysis should be to articulate concretely the design of the firm's financial structure, preferably in terms of the seven elements discussed in Section I. This exercise entails developing notes, comments, and calculations for every one of the cells of this analytical grid:

Elements of Financial Structure	Current Structure	Investor View	Competitor View	Internal View	Evaluation/ Comments
1. Mix					
2. Maturity					
3. Basis					
4. Currency					
5. Exotica					
6. External control					
7. Distribution					

No chart can completely anticipate the difficulties, quirks, and exceptions that the analyst will undoubtedly encounter. What matters most, however, is a way of thinking about the financial-structure design problem that encourages both critical thinking and organized, efficient digestion of information.

FIGURE 1   Overview of Financial-Structure Analysis

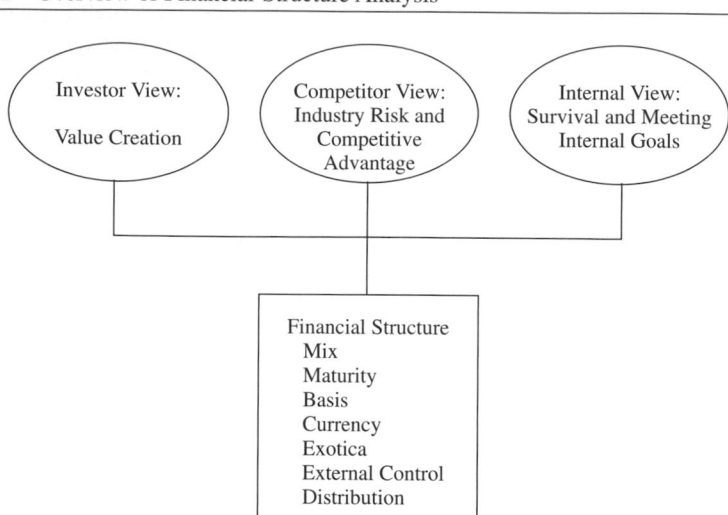

Figure 1 summarizes the approach presented in this section. Good financial-structure analysis develops three complementary perspectives on financial structure, then blends those perspectives into prescription.

PART III: ANALYZING FINANCIAL POLICY FROM THE INVESTORS' VIEWPOINT[7]

In finance theory, the investors' expectations should influence all managerial decisions. This theory follows the legal doctrine that firms should be managed in the interests of their owners. It also recognizes the economic idea that, if investors' needs are satisfied after all other claims on the firm are settled, then the firm must be "healthy." The investors' view also confronts the reality of capital market discipline: The best defense against a hostile takeover (or other type of intrusion) is a high stock price. The threat of capital market discipline has done more in the 1980s and 1990s to rivet the attention of management on *value creation* than any academic theories have done.

This perspective is extremely useful in identifying value-creating strategies. Economic value is held to be the present value of expected future cash flows discounted at a rate consistent with the risk of those cash flows. Considerable care must be given to the estimation of cash flows and discount rates (a review of discounted-cash-flow [DCF] valuation is

---

[7]Excellent summaries of the investors' orientation are found in Tom Copeland, Tim Koller, and Jack Murrin, *Valuation: Measuring and Managing the Value of Companies,* 2nd ed. (New York: Wiley, 1994); and Alfred Rappaport, *Creating Shareholder Value,* 2nd ed. (New York: Free Press, 1997).

beyond the scope of this note). Theory suggests that leverage can create value through the *benefits of debt-tax shields* and can destroy value through the *costs of financial distress.* The balance of these costs and benefits depends on specific capital market conditions, which are conveyed by the debt and equity costs that capital providers impose on the firm. Academic theory's bottom line is this:

> An efficient (i.e., value-optimizing) financial structure is one that simultaneously minimizes the weighted-average cost of capital and maximizes the share price and value of the enterprise.

The investors' perspective is a rigorous approach to evaluating financial structures: valuation analysis of the firm and its common stock under existing and alternative financial structures. The "best" structure will be one that creates the most value.

The phrase "alternative financial structures" is necessarily ambiguous but should be interpreted to include a wide range of alternatives, including leveraged buyout, leveraged recapitalization, spin-offs, carve-outs, and even liquidation. However radical the latter alternatives may seem, the analyst must understand that investment bankers and corporate raiders routinely consider these alternatives. To anticipate the thinking of these agents of change, the analyst must replicate their homework.

Careful analysis does not rest with a final number, but rather considers a range of elements:

Cost of debt	The analysis focuses on yields to maturity and the spreads of those yields over the Treasury yield curve. Floating rates are always effective rates of interest.
Cost of equity	The assessment uses as many approaches as possible, including the capital asset pricing model, the dividend-discount model, the financial-leverage equation, the earnings/price model, and any other avenues that seem appropriate. Though it is fallible, the capital asset pricing model has the most rigor.
Debt/Equity mix	The relative proportions of types of capital in the capital structure are important factors in computing the weighted-average cost of capital. All capital should be estimated on a *market-value* basis.
Price/Earnings ratio, Market/Book ratio, EBIT multiple	Comparing these values to average levels of the entire capital market or an industry group can provide an alternative check on the valuation of the firm.
Bond rating	The creditors' view of the firm is important. S&P and Moody's publish average financial ratios for bond-rating groups. Even for a firm with no publicly rated debt outstanding, simple ratio analysis can reveal a firm's likely rating category and its current cost of debt.
Ownership	The relative mix of individual and institutional owners and the presence of block holders with potentially hostile intentions can help shed light on the current pricing of a firm's securities.
Short position	A large, short-sale position on the firm's stock can indicate that some traders believe a decline in share price is imminent.

To conclude, the first rule of financial policy analysis is, *Think like an investor.* The investors' view assesses the value of a firm's shares under alternative financial structures and the existence of any strongly positive or negative perceptions in the capital markets about the firm's securities.

PART IV: ANALYZING FINANCIAL POLICY FROM A COMPETITIVE PERSPECTIVE

The competitive perspective matters to senior executives for two important reasons. First, it gives an indication about (1) "standard practice" in the industry and (2) the strategic position of the firm relative to the competition. Second, it implies rightly that finance can be a strategic competitive instrument.[8]

The competitive perspective may be the hardest of the three benchmarks to assess: there are few clear signposts in industry dynamics, and, as most industries become increasingly global, the comparisons become even more difficult to make. Despite the difficulty of this analysis, however, senior executives give inordinate attention to it. The well-versed analyst must therefore be able to assess the ability of current policy (and its alternatives) to maintain or improve its competitive position.

This analysis does not proceed scientifically but rather evolves iteratively toward an accurate assessment of the situation.[9] The steps might be defined as follows:

1. Define the universe of competitors.
2. "Spread" the data and financial ratios on the firm and its competitors in comparative fashion.
3. Identify similarities and, more important, differences. Probe into anomalies. Question the data and the peer sample.
4. Add information needed, such as a foreign competitor, another ratio, historical normalization, and so on.
5. Discuss or clarify the information with the CFO or industry expert.

As the information grows, the questions will become more probing. What is the historical growth pattern? Why did the XYZ company suddenly increase leverage or keep a large cash balance? Did the acquisition of a new line actually provide access to new markets? Are changes in dividend policy or debt mix and maturity related to new products and markets?

Economy of effort demands that the analyst begin with a few ratios and data that can be easily obtained (from Value Line, 10Ks, etc.). If a company is in several industries and does not have pure competitors, choose group-divisional competitors and, to the extent possible, use segment information to devise ratios that will be valid (i.e., operating income to sales rather than an after-tax equivalent). Do not forget information that may be outside the financial statements and may be critical to competitive survival, such as geographic diversification, research and development expenditures, and union activity. For some industries, other key ratios are available through trade groups, such as same-store sales and capacity analyses. Whatever the inadequacy of the data, the comparisons will provide direction for subsequent analysis.

---

[8]For a discussion of finance as a competitive instrument, see William E. Fruhan Jr.'s classic work, *Financial Strategy: Studies in the Creation, Transfer, and Destruction of Shareholder Value* (Homewood, IL: Irwin, 1979).

[9]A good overview of industry and competitor analysis may be found in Michael Porter, *Competitive Analysis* (New York: Free Press, 1979). An excellent survey of possible information sources on firms is in Leonard M. Fuld, *Competitor Intelligence* (New York: Wiley, 1985).

The ratios and data to be used will depend on the course of analysis. An analyst could start with the following general types of measures with which to compare a competitor group:

1. Size: sales, market value, number of employees or countries, market share.
2. Asset productivity: return on assets (ROA), return on invested capital, market to book value.
3. Shareholder wealth: price/earnings (P/E), return on market value.
4. Predictability: beta, historical trends.
5. Growth: 1–10 year compound growth of sales, profits, assets, and market value of equity.
6. Financial flexibility: debt-to-capital, debt ratings, cash-flow coverage, estimates of cost of capital.
7. Other significant industry issues: unfunded pension liabilities, postretirement medical-benefit obligations, environmental liabilities, capacity, research and development expense to sales, percentage of insider control, and so on.

One of the key issues to resolve in analyzing the comparative data is whether all the peer-group members display the same results and trends. Inevitably, they will not—which begs the question, Why not? Trends in asset productivity and globalization are affecting competitors differently and eliciting a range of strategic responses. This phenomenon should stimulate further research.

The analyst should augment personal research efforts with the work of industry analysts. Securities analysts, consultants, academicians, and journalists, both through their written work and via telephone conversations, can provide valuable insights based on extensive personal contacts in the industry.[10]

Analyzing competitors develops insights into the range of financial structures in the industry and the appropriateness of your firm's structure in comparison. Developing these insights is more a matter of qualitative judgment than of letting numbers speak for themselves. For instance:

1. Suppose your firm is a highly leveraged computer manufacturer with an uneven record of financial performance. Should it unlever? You discover that the peer group of computer manufacturers is substantially equity financed, owing largely to the rapid rate of technological innovation and the predation of a few large players in the industry. The *strategic rationale* for low leverage is to survive the business and short product life cycles. Yes, it might be good to unlever.
2. Suppose your firm is an airline and finances its equipment purchases with flotations of commercial paper. The average life of the firm's liabilities is four years, while the average life of the firm's assets is 15 years. Should the airline refinance its debt using securities with longer maturity? You discover that the peer group of airlines finances its assets with leases, equipment-trust certificates, and project-finance deals that almost exactly match the economic lives of assets and liabilities. The *strategic rationale* for lengthening the maturity structure of liabilities is to hedge against yield-curve changes

---

[10]See, for instance, *Nelson's Guide to Securities Research* for a directory of securities analysts. The indexes to *The Wall Street Journal* and the Frost & Sullivan *Predicast* can give quick overviews of industry trends.

that might adversely affect your firm's ability to refinance yet leave its peer competitors relatively unaffected.

3. Here's a trickier example: Your firm is the last nationwide supermarket chain that is publicly held; all other major supermarket chains have gone private in LBOs. Should your firm lever up through a leveraged-share repurchase? Competitor analysis reveals that other firms are struggling to meet debt-service payments on already thin margins and that a major shift in customer patronage may be under way. You conclude that price competition in selected markets would trigger a realignment in market shares in your firm's favor because the competitors have little pricing flexibility. In this case, adjusting to the industry-average leverage would not be appropriate.

PART V: DIAGNOSING FINANCIAL POLICY FROM AN INTERNAL PERSPECTIVE[11]

Internal analysis is the third major screen of a firm's financial structure. It accounts for the expected cash requirements and resources of a firm, and tests the consistency of the firm's financial structure with the profitability, growth, and dividend goals of the firm. The classic tools of internal analysis are the forecast cash flow, financial statements, and sources-and-uses-of-funds statements. The standard banker's credit analysis is consistent with this approach.

The essence of this approach is a concern for (*a*) the preservation of the firm's *financial flexibility,* (*b*) the *sustainability* of the firm's financial policies, and (*c*) the *feasibility* of the firm's strategic goals. For instance, the long-term goals may call for a doubling of sales in five years. The business plan for achieving this goal may call for the construction of a greenfield plant in year one, then regional-distribution systems in years two and three. Substantial working-capital investments will be necessary in years two through five. How this growth is to be financed has huge implications for your firm's financial structure *today.* Typically, an analyst addresses this problem by forecasting the financial performance of the firm, experimenting with different financing sequences and choosing the best one, then determining the structure that makes the best foundation for that financing sequence. This analysis implies the need to maintain future financial flexibility.

Financial flexibility

Financial flexibility is easily measured as the excess cash and unused debt capacity on which the firm might call. In addition, there may be other reserves such as unused land or excess stocks of raw materials which could be liquidated. All reserves that could be mobilized should be reflected in an analysis of financial flexibility. Illustrating with the narrower definition (cash and unused debt capacity), one can measure financial flexibility as follows:

---

[11]An excellent overview of the "internal" view of a firm's financial policies may be found in Gordon Donaldson, *Managing Corporate Wealth: The Operation of a Comprehensive Financial Goals System* (New York: Praeger, 1984).

1. Select a target minimum debt rating acceptable to the firm. Many CFOs will have in mind a target minimum, such as a BBB/Baa rating.
2. Determine the book value[12] debt/equity mix consistent with the minimum rating. Standard & Poor's, for instance, publishes average financial ratios (including debt/equity) that are associated with each debt-rating category.[13]
3. Determine the book value of debt consistent with the debt/equity ratio from step 2. This gives the amount of debt that would be outstanding if the firm moved to the minimum acceptable bond rating.
4. Estimate financial flexibility using the following formula:

$$\text{Financial flexibility} = \text{Excess cash} + (\text{Debt at minimum rating} - \text{Current debt outstanding})$$

The amount estimated by this formula indicates the financial reserves on which the firm can call to exploit unusual surprising opportunities (such as the chance to acquire a competitor) or to defend against unusual threats (such as a price war, sudden product obsolescence, or a labor strike).

Self-Sustainable Growth

A shorthand test for sustainability and internal consistency is the self-sustainable growth model. This model is based on one key assumption: Over the forecast period, the firm sells no new shares of stock (this assumption is entirely consistent with the actual behavior of firms over the long run).[14] As long as the firm does not change its mix of debt and equity, the self-sustainable model implies that assets can grow only as fast as equity grows. Thus the issue of sustainability is significantly determined by the firm's return on equity (ROE) and dividend payout ratio (DPO):

$$\text{Self-sustainable growth rate of assets} = \text{ROE} \times (1 - \text{DPO})$$

The test of feasibility of any long-term plan involves comparing the growth rate implied by this formula and the *targeted* growth rate dictated by a management plan. If the targeted growth rate equals the implied rate, then the firm's financial policies are just in balance. If the implied rate exceeds the targeted rate, the firm will gradually become more liquid, creating an asset-deployment opportunity. If the targeted rate exceeds the implied rate, the firm must raise more capital, either by selling stock, levering up, or reducing the dividend payout.

Management policies can be modeled finely by recognizing that ROE can be decomposed into various factors using two classic formulas:

---

[12]Ideally one would work with market values rather than book values. But the rating agencies compute their financial ratios only on a book-value basis. Since this analysis in effect mimics the perspective of the rating agencies, the analyst must work with book values.

[13]See *CreditWeek,* published by Standard & Poor's.

[14]From 1950 to 1989, only 5 percent of the growth of the U.S. economy's business sector was financed by the sale of new common stock. The most significant sources were short-term liabilities, long-term liabilities, and retained earnings, in that order.

1. Du Pont system of ratios:

   ROE = $P/S \times S/A \times A/E$
   P/S = Net margin, a measure of profitability
   S/A = Sales divided by assets, a measure of asset productivity
   A/E = Assets divided by equity, a measure of financial leverage

2. Financial-leverage equation:[15]

   ROE = $[\text{ROTC} + ((\text{ROTC} - K_d) \times (D/E))]$
   ROTC = Return on total capital
   K_d = Cost of debt
   D/E = Debt divided by equity, a measure of leverage

Inserting either of these formulas into the self-sustainable growth rate equation gives a richer model of the drivers of self-sustainability—one sees, in particular, the importance of internal operations. The self-sustainable growth model can be expanded to reflect explicitly measures of a firm's operating and financial policies.

The self-sustainable growth rate model tests the internal consistency of a firm's operating and financial policies. *This model, however, provides no guarantee that a strategy will maximize value.* Value creation does not begin with growth targets; growth per se does not necessarily lead to value creation, as the growth-by-acquisition strategies of the 1960s and 1970s abundantly illustrate. Also, the adoption of growth targets may foreclose other, more profitable strategies—these targets may invite managers to undertake investments yielding less than the cost of capital. Meeting sales or assets-growth targets can destroy value. Thus, any sustainable-growth analysis must be augmented by questions about the value-creation potential of a given set of corporate policies. These questions include (1) What are the magnitude and duration of investment returns as compared to the firm's cost of capital? and (2) With what alternative set of policies is the firm's share price maximized? With questions such as these, the investor orientation discussed in Section III is turned inward to double-check the appropriateness of any inferences derived from financial forecasts of sources-and-uses of funds statement and from the analysis of the self-sustainable growth model.

PART VI: WHAT IS BEST?

Any financial structure evaluated against the perspectives of investors, competitors, and the internal goals will probably show opportunities for improvement. Most often, CFOs choose to make changes at the margin rather than tinker radically with a financial structure. For changes large and small, however, the analyst must develop a framework for judgment and prescription.

The following framework is a way of identifying the trade-offs among "goods" and "bads" rather than finding the right answer. Having identified the trade-offs implicit in any alternative structure, it remains for the CFO and adviser to choose the structure with the most attractive trade-offs.

---

[15]This is the classic expression for the cost of equity, as originally presented in the work of Nobel Prize winners Franco Modigliani and Merton Miller.

The key elements of evaluation are the following:

Flexibility—the ability to meet unforeseen financing requirements as they arise. These requirements may be favorable (e.g., a sudden acquisition opportunity) or unfavorable (e.g., Source Perrier and the benzene scare). Flexibility may involve liquidating assets or tapping the capital markets in adverse market environments or both. Flexibility can be measured by bond ratings, coverage ratios, capitalization ratios, liquidity ratios, and the identification of salable assets.

Risk—the predictable variability in the firm's business. Such variability may be due to both macroeconomic factors (e.g., consumer demand) and industry- or firm-specific factors (e.g., product lifecycles, biannual strikes in advance of wage negotiations). To some extent, past experience may indicate the future range of variability in earnings before interest and taxes (EBIT) and cash flow. High leverage tends to amplify these predictable business swings. The risk associated with any given financial structure can be assessed by EBIT-EPS (earnings per share) analysis, break-even analysis, the standard deviation of EBIT, and beta. In theory, beta should vary directly with leverage.[16]

Income—this compares financial structures on the basis of value creation. Measures such as DCF value, projected ROE, EPS, and cost of capital indicate the comparative value effects of alternative financial structures.

Control—alternative financial structures may imply changes in control or different control constraints on the firm as indicated by the percentage distribution of share ownership and by the structure of debt covenants.

Timing—asks question of whether the current capital market environment is the right moment to implement any alternative financial structure, and what the implications for future financings will be if the proposed structure is adopted. The current market environment can be assessed by examining the Treasury yield curve, the trend in the movement of interest rates, the existence of any "windows" in the market for new issues of securities, P/E multiple trends, and so on. Sequencing considerations are implicitly captured in the assumptions underlying alternative DCF value estimates and can be explicitly examined by looking at annual EPS and ROE streams under alternative financing sequences.

This flexibility, risk, income, control, and timing (FRICT) framework can be used to indicate the relative strengths and weaknesses of alternative financing plans. To use a simple example, suppose that your firm is considering two financial structures: (1) 60 percent debt and 40 percent equity (i.e., debt will be issued); and (2) 40 percent debt and 60 percent equity (i.e., equity will be issued). Also, suppose that your analysis of the two structures under the investor, competitor, and internal-analysis screens leads you to make this basic comparison:

---

[16]This relationship is illustrated by the formula for estimating a firm's levered beta:

$B_1 = B_u \times [1 + (1 - t) \times D/E]$
B_1 = Levered beta
B_u = Unlevered beta
t = Firm's marginal tax rate
D/E = The firm's market-value, debt-to-equity ratio

	60 Percent Debt	*40 Percent Debt*
Flexibility	"Lowish," not bad BBB debt rating $50 million reserves	High AA debt rating $300 million reserves
Risk	High EBIT coverage = 1.5	Medium EBIT coverage = 3.0
Income	Good-to-high DCF value = $20/share	Mediocre DCF value = $12 per share (dilutive)
Control	Covenants tight No voting dilution	Covenants not restrictive 10% voting dilution
Timing	Interest rates low today Risky sequence	Equity multiples are low today Low risk sequence for future

The 60 percent debt structure is favored on the grounds of income, control, and today's market conditions. The 40 percent debt structure is favored on the grounds of flexibility, risk, and the long-term financial sequencing. This example boils down to a decision between "eat well" and "sleep well." It remains up to senior management to make the difficult choice between the two alternatives, giving careful attention to the views of the investor, competitors, and managers.

PART VII: CONCLUSION

Description, diagnosis, and prescription in financial structuring form an iterative process. It is quite likely that the CFO in the eat well/sleep well example would send the analyst back for more research and testing of alternative structures. Figure 2 presents an expanded view of the basic cycle of analysis and suggests more about the complexity of the financial structuring problem. With time and experience, the analyst develops an intuition for efficient information sources and modes of analysis. In the long run, this intuition makes the cycle of analysis manageable.

FIGURE 2   Expanded Illustration of Process of Developing a Financial Policy

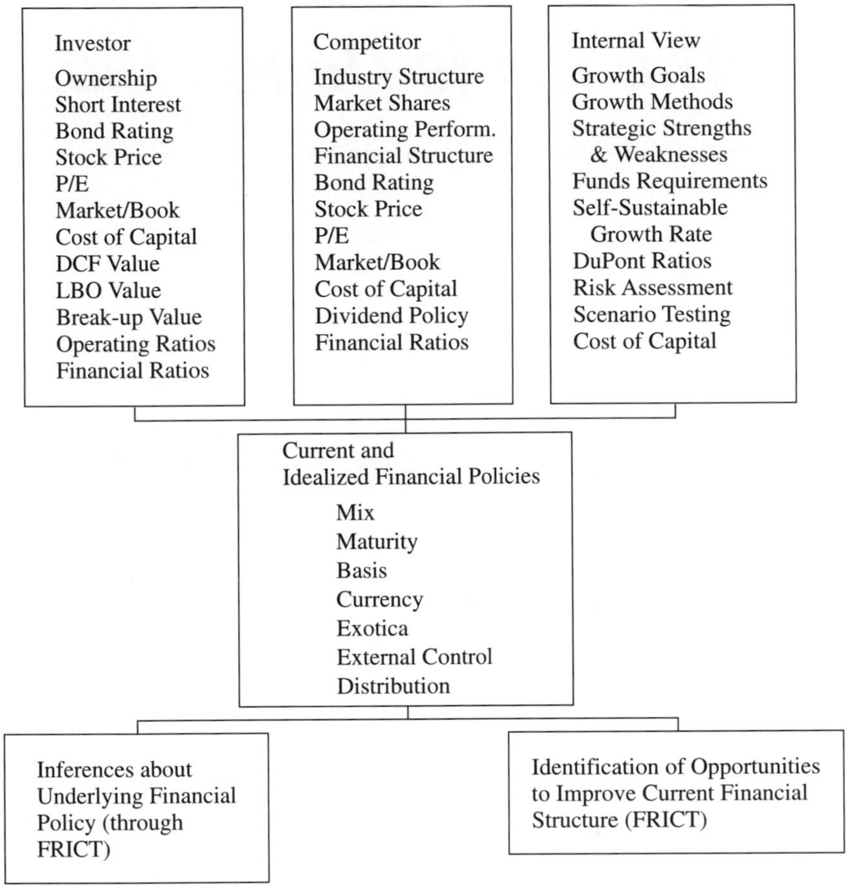

Investor	Competitor	Internal View
Ownership	Industry Structure	Growth Goals
Short Interest	Market Shares	Growth Methods
Bond Rating	Operating Perform.	Strategic Strengths
Stock Price	Financial Structure	& Weaknesses
P/E	Bond Rating	Funds Requirements
Market/Book	Stock Price	Self-Sustainable
Cost of Capital	P/E	Growth Rate
DCF Value	Market/Book	DuPont Ratios
LBO Value	Cost of Capital	Risk Assessment
Break-up Value	Dividend Policy	Scenario Testing
Operating Ratios	Financial Ratios	Cost of Capital
Financial Ratios		

Current and
Idealized Financial Policies

Mix
Maturity
Basis
Currency
Exotica
External Control
Distribution

Inferences about
Underlying Financial
Policy (through
FRICT)

Identification of Opportunities
to Improve Current Financial
Structure (FRICT)

The Home Depot, Inc.

The fastest-growing major area of retailing today is that of do-it-yourself/home improvement. The most dynamic company in the business is Home Depot.

M. Gilliam, securities analyst, First Boston[1]

Trying to wed two conflicting strategies—low-cost structure with broad assortment and a high level of customer service—is arguably one of the most difficult retail concepts to pull off. Home Depot is further along the learning curve than anyone else.

David Bolotsky, securities analyst, Goldman Sachs[2]

Right now, when Home Depot goes into an area, they just cut up and spit out the independents.

Walter Stoeppelwerth, consultant[3]

We love a fight, a fair fight.

Bernard Marcus, chief executive officer, The Home Depot[4]

---

[1]M. Gilliam, "The Customer Is Always Right," First Boston Corporation, May 19, 1989, p. 6.

[2]M. J. McCarthy, "Home Depot's Do-It-Yourself Powerhouse," *The Wall Street Journal,* July 17, 1990, p. B1.

[3]Ibid.

[4]H. Gilgoff, "Home Center Ad Campaigns Heat Up with Latest Arrival," *Newsday,* November 28, 1989, p. B33.

This case was prepared by Professor Robert F. Bruner. This case was written as a basis for class discussion rather than to illustrate effective or ineffective handling of an administrative situation. Copyright © 1991 by the University of Virginia Darden School Foundation, Charlottesville, VA. All rights reserved. *No part of this publication may be reproduced, stored in a retrieval system, used in a spreadsheet, or transmitted in any form or by any means—electronic, mechanical, photocopying, recording, or otherwise—without the permission of the Darden Foundation. For inquiries, please send an e-mail to dardencases@virginia.edu.* Revised 6/98. Version 1.5.

FIGURE 1 The Home Depot Stock Prices, 1981–91

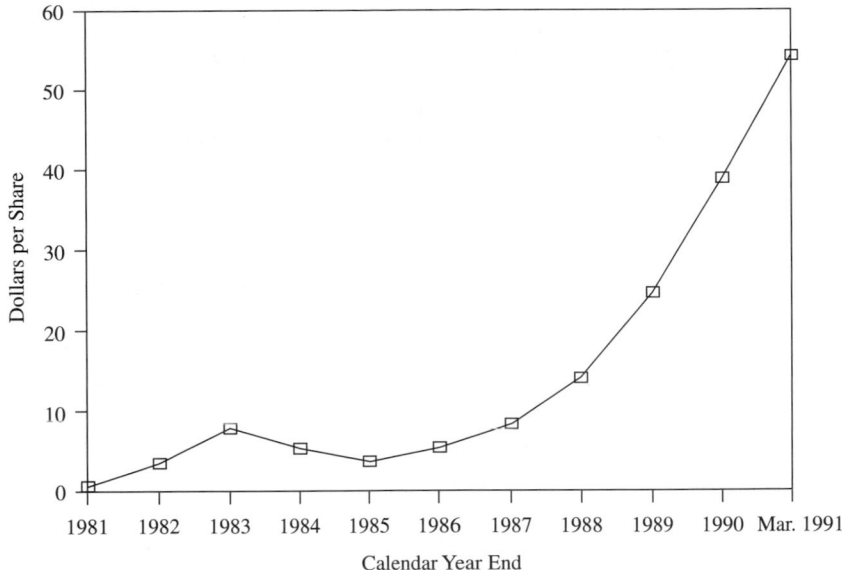

In March 1991, Bernard Marcus, chief executive officer and chairman of The Home Depot (HD), reaffirmed that the firm's annual targeted growth rate in store space would be 25 percent for 1991 and beyond. The firm's sales had grown rapidly, from $22 million in 1980 to $3.8 billion in 1990. Return on average equity had exceeded 20 percent in each of the previous five years. As Figure 1 shows, over the same period the stock price had risen from $0.75 per share to close recently at $54.00 per share, a 53 percent annual compound rate of growth. The stock was currently priced at 40 times trailing earnings per share, over 12 times book value. Securities analysts explained the firm's phenomenal stock-price performance in terms of the firm's aggressive growth strategy.

The company's aggressive expansion strategy suggested that HD would need $1.46 billion in external financing over the next four years, which raised questions about the firm's capital financing policies. Was the firm's historical financing strategy appropriate? Were there better financing strategies that would enhance shareholder value, competitive position, or managerial flexibility? What action should management take now to obtain the capital needed to open 35 new stores in 1991 and 43 stores in 1992?

THE COMPANY

In its 1991 annual report, The Home Depot described itself this way:

> Founded in 1978 in Atlanta, Georgia, The Home Depot is now America's largest home-center retailer and is one of the fastest-growing retailers in the United States. At the close of fiscal 1990, the Company was operating 145 warehouse-style stores in 12 states. The average Home Depot store is approximately 92,000 square feet, with an additional 10,000 to 20,000 square feet of

outside selling area. The stores stock approximately 30,000 different kinds of building materials, home-improvement supplies, and lawn and garden products, a large proportion of which are sold to do-it-yourselfers as well as home-remodeling and building-maintenance professionals. The Company has been credited with being a leading innovator in the home-center retail industry by combining the economies of scale inherent in a warehouse format with a level of customer service unprecedented among warehouse-style retailers. The Home Depot is ranked by *Fortune* magazine as one of the nation's 50 largest retailers and by *Business Month* as one of America's fastest-growing companies in terms of sales, profits, and return on investment.

Home Depot's warehouse-retailing concept was based on several key elements. First, the company provided a wide range of products at competitive, "low, everyday" prices. HD aimed for pricing that was 20 to 30 percent lower than "traditional home centers."[5] Virtually each day in every community, professional shoppers for HD checked prices at the outlets of its major competitors to ensure that HD's prices were competitive within its markets. Second, careful cost management and superior productivity provided an operating margin of 6.7 percent and sales per store at least twice as large as HD's nearest competitor. Third, the store format permitted the firm to eliminate intermediary warehouses: Goods were distributed directly to each store. Fourth, in accordance with a philosophy of "one-on-one service," the stores employed well-trained and service-oriented personnel to assist and help educate the customer. HD sponsored educational seminars and clinics and employed tradespeople in sales. Fifth, HD aggressively advertised prices and special offerings. In 1990, HD raised its TV advertising budget almost nine times, to $15 million in a year, whereas advertising by home centers and hardware stores rose only 6 percent: The clustering of stores permitted the firm to exploit economies of scale in advertising. Compared with its competitors, however, HD's advertising budget was not large.

Implementation of this retailing concept required an unusual culture oriented to innovation, cost control, and customer service. The company innovated relentlessly with new concepts and merchandise and invited customers and employees to contribute their ideas. Out of this innovation process grew decorator centers, delivery services, bulk packaging for commodities, and The Home Depot Television Network, which broadcast and produced training programs. HD's 1991 annual report stated, "We have never subscribed to the idea that if it's not broken, you don't need to fix it. To stay on the leading edge of our industry means fixing things before they break." The emphasis on cost control and service was reinforced by a rigid, promote-from-within, management-development policy and by quarterly question-and-answer rallies, beamed live by satellite, between senior management and the firm's 20,000 employees.

High-volume sales gave HD bargaining power on price and product quality in the company's negotiations with its suppliers. For instance, it pressured manufacturers to rewrite instructions deemed incomprehensible and to put bar codes on bulky items like wood to speed up checkout.

Central to the company's strategy was its commitment to growth. Management's publicly stated growth goals were to expand the number of stores at not more than 25 percent per year and to become the largest home-repair chain in the United States, with $10 bil-

---

[5]H. Jordan "Competition Is Heating Up for Do-It-Yourself Dollars," *New Hampshire Business Review,* September 7, 1990.

lion in sales from more than 350 stores by the end of 1994.[6] The total investment per new store would be approximately $10.65 million.[7] Exhibit 1 summarizes the history of the firm's store expansion and shows the geographical distribution of the stores.[8]

The trend of expansion took two directions. The first was a conscious strategy of "cannibalization" (i.e., opening stores near existing HD stores). HD reasoned that this would relieve congestion and personnel shortages in existing stores. The second direction was an expansion into new territory, out of the Sunbelt of the United States and into the Middle Atlantic and Northeast regions. The move northward began in January 1989, when HD opened a store in East Hanover, New Jersey. The company subsequently opened stores in New Jersey, Connecticut, and New York, and hoped to open as many as 75 stores in the northeastern United States within five years.[9] Regarding the expansion into the Northeast, Bernard Marcus said,

> It costs more there, but the volume per store is incredible. And people can't believe the service. We opened one store in Connecticut and they asked us if we were a religious cult, some sort of love group. They are so used to prepackaged hardware and blank stares or rudeness if they ever ask a question.[10]

HD showed pugnacity in choosing store locations. For instance, HD entered Baltimore in 1990 with one store and announced that three others would be opened by 1993, despite the fact that Baltimore was dominated by 13 Hechinger home centers and was the location of Hechinger's corporate headquarters. Regarding the entry into Baltimore, the *Washington Post* reported,

> Hechinger executives had no comment about the arrival of Home Depot so close to the company's home territory, where Hechinger reigns as undisputed champion of the do-it-yourself retailers and virtually overwhelms area competitors like Builder's Square and Channel. But Bernard Marcus, Home Depot's chairman and chief executive officer, said he was looking forward to the imminent face-off. "We think the market is underserved and expect to do well there," said Marcus. "We think of Hechinger as a fine operation . . . but competition is healthy for everybody and with us coming, Hechinger will be a better business and the consumer will be the winner."[11]

In 1990, HD also entered Long Island, the home base of Grossman's, a competitor, and began an aggressive campaign of price-comparison advertising. In response, Grossman's filed a complaint with the state fair-trade commission.

HD's senior management showed little inclination to expand by acquisition. On December 11, 1984, HD bought nine stores in the Dallas, Texas, area that were previously owned by the Bowater home-improvement chain. The total payment was $40 million: $26 million in cash and $14 million in 9 percent convertible notes. While the purchase gave HD critical mass in the Texas

---

[6]C. Hawkins, "Will Home Depot Be 'The Wal-Mart of the '90s'?" *Business Week,* March 19, 1990, pp. 124, 126.

[7]This estimate reflected preopening expenses ($550,000), fixtures ($900,000), land ($3.5 million), store construction ($3.9 million), and inventory ($3.5 million) net of vendor financing ($1.7 million).

[8]Of 146 stores in operation in March 1991, 86 were leased and 60 were owned (land and buildings). The leases were long term, expiring between 2007 and 2067. HD preferred, however, to buy rather than lease.

[9]*Value Line Investment Survey,* April 27, 1990, p. 898.

[10]Quote from: A. Thurber, "Firing Launched Success; 125 Home Depots Is Proof," *Arizona Republic,* May 23, 1990, Sec. C, p. 1.

[11]K. Swisher, "Home Depot Plans Entry into the Baltimore Area," *Washington Post,* December 20, 1990, Sec. E, p. 1. © 1990, The *Washington Post,* Reprinted with permission.

market, the move proved to be a disaster. The Bowater workers who were retained could not adapt to the HD culture, and the subsequent recession in Texas worsened the performance of HD's Dallas stores. As a result, the whole company's financial performance suffered badly in 1985: Earnings per share fell to $.10 from $.17 a year earlier; average return on equity fell to 9.7 percent from 19.3 percent; and gross margin fell to 25.9 percent. Marcus commented that "he had seriously disadvantaged the shareholders and that it would not happen again."[12]

MANAGEMENT

The Home Depot was founded in 1978 by Bernard Marcus, Arthur Blank, and Kenneth Langone. Langone, who was now the chief executive officer of Invemed Associates, was a director of HD and was not engaged in its daily management. Invemed was a small securities dealer, however, and had comanaged several of HD's securities offerings.

Bernard Marcus, age 62, had received a bachelor of science degree from Rutgers University in 1954, and had begun his career as a registered pharmacist. He entered discount retailing when he was asked to run the pharmacy and cosmetics department of a discount chain in New Jersey. Gradually, he rose to the position of chairman and chief executive officer of Handy Dan, a subsidiary of the Daylin division of W. R. Grace. Handy Dan was a home-improvement chain that had a standard hardware-store retailing strategy. When Marcus and the president of Handy Dan, Arthur Blank,[13] experimented with price discounting, they were fired. Marcus and Blank found financial backing with the assistance of Kenneth Langone and opened their first Home Depot store in Georgia in 1979; the first 16 warehouse stores were concentrated in Georgia, Florida, and Louisiana; the next five were in Arizona, which was a test region for going even farther west into California. Home Depot's expansion into California contributed to the demise of the Handy Dan chain: "Handy Dan is gone now," said Marcus with a smile.[14]

At the end of 1990, Marcus held about 5 percent of HD's common shares outstanding. Officers and directors held a total of 9 percent. Exhibit 2 summarizes the equity ownership of Home Depot and reveals that institutional investors held about 74 percent of the firm's common stock. A leveraged employee stock ownership plan (ESOP) was organized in 1988; by early 1991, the ESOP owned about 2 percent of outstanding shares. Marcus's salary and bonus for 1990 was $1,585,982; Blank's compensation was $1,362,965. The next most senior executives (including the chief financial officer) received $369,492.

THE HOME-IMPROVEMENT RETAILING INDUSTRY

The industry in which Home Depot competed had aggregate sales of $100 billion per year,[15] which implied that HD had approximately 4 percent share of market. Competition

---

[12]A. Zipser, "Down-Home Attitude," *Barron's,* October 1, 1990, p. 44.

[13]In March 1991, Arthur Blank was 47 years old.

[14]Thurber, "Firing Launched Success."

[15]M. J. McCarthy, "Home Depot's Do-It-Yourself Powerhouse," quoting results of analysis by the Home Improvement Research Institute.

was highly fragmented and localized. In 1989, the 10 largest retailers accounted for 1,704 stores and 15 percent of the total market sales. Taking local and regional firms into account, about 350 home-center retailers operated 5,479 stores by 1991.[16] Nevertheless, the trend in the previous 10 years had been toward larger establishments of 50,000 square feet or more in space that offered service or competitive prices. These establishments accounted for most of the industry's sales growth over the past 10 years, and were gradually displacing local hardware stores.

Two merchandising strategies had emerged out of the rivalry among the largest competitors. The "home-center" strategy used large stores, offered competitive (not discount) prices, and catered to both the professional tradesperson and the do-it-yourselfer. Examples of the home-center retailers were Lowe's, Grossman's, Pergament, Channel Home Centers, Rickles, and True Value.

The "warehouse" strategy, by contrast, also used large stores but displayed merchandise on pallets, offered discount prices, and catered to the do-it-yourselfer. The Home Depot introduced this strategy to the home-improvement retailing industry (it had previously been used among other specialty retailers in food, home furnishings, and office supplies). HD was referred to as a "category killer"[17] or "power retailer,"[18] a retailer that offered enormous selection in one particular specialty and did it extremely well, as opposed to the general merchandisers' one-stop-shopping theme.

The emergence of the warehouse strategy was part of a larger trend of competition in retailing. *Fortune* magazine summarized the fundamental trends this way:

> Home Depot, Inc., The Limited, Toys "R" Us, Wal-Mart, Dillard, The Gap, J. C. Penney, and Nordstrom are emerging as the new champions of retailing. They are succeeding by developing exciting merchandising programs, finding innovative uses for technology, and expanding smartly and aggressively. . . They have not forgotten the lesson of staying faithfully focused on their businesses. Respect for the downside of debt has given these companies some of the healthiest balance sheets in retailing. Once the champion retailers have customers sold on attractive merchandise and great-looking stores, they fortify their operations with technological might.[19]

The importance of Home Depot's innovation was not lost on its competitors.

- *Hechinger Company,* with sales of $1.39 billion, operated a chain of 116 specialty-retail, do-it-yourself, home-center stores in the Middle Atlantic region of the United States. The firm pursued a strategy of "clustering" store locations in an effort to build market share. Most of Hechinger's stores were in the older home-center format, although the firm had recently purchased Home Quarters and Triangle Building Centers, retailers with a format identical to HD's, and the company had announced plans for aggressive growth into the Northeast. The company openly acknowledged that its Home Quarters subsidiary would be its main growth vehicle. In early 1991, Hechinger had 27 stores in the warehouse segment and aimed to increase to 36 stores by the end of 1991. The firm stated that its "major expansion thrust will be the Boston market," where plans called for

---

[16]"Home Improvement Retailers," *Investext Report,* 1990, p. 45.

[17]H. Jordan, "Will Granite Staters Take to Warehouse Style Shopping?" *New Hampshire Business Review,* January 11, 1991, p. 2.

[18]P. Demery, "Power Retailers Move to Center Aisle," *LI Business News,* December 24, 1990, p. 19.

[19]S. Caminiti, "The New Champs of Retailing," *Fortune* Magazine, September 24, 1990, p. 85.

15 stores.[20] Hechinger also announced that it would convert all its stores in North Carolina to the warehouse format. Finally, in March 1991, the company announced that it would convert five Baltimore home-center stores to the new warehouse format; observers connected this to Home Depot's aggressive entry into the Baltimore market. In the fiscal year ended February 1991, the company reported a 35 percent decrease in net income—the second year in a row of a large earnings decline.

- *Kmart Corporation,* with sales of $32.1 billion, was the second largest multifaceted retailer in the United States. It offered general-merchandise stores as well as discount department stores, variety stores, and limited-line stores. The company had several warehouse-format retailing operations, including PACE Membership Warehouse (general merchandise), Sports Giant (sporting goods), Office Square (office supplies), American Fare (food), and Builders Square (home improvement). Builders Square had 145 units and aimed to open 15–20 units annually through 1995, for a total of 225 stores. Kmart had overall U.S. advertising expenditures of $561.4 million in 1989.

- *Lowe's Companies, Incorporated,* operated 306 stores, located primarily in the southeastern United States. Its sales in 1990 were $2.8 billion. Since the mid-1980s the firm had devoted itself to expanding the warehouse format. Analysts expected that, by the end of 1991, over half of Lowe's projected 9 million square feet of store space would consist of 45 warehouse outlets.

- *Waban, Incorporated,* operated 59 warehouse "Home Club" home-improvement stores in 10 western and southeastern states. It also operated 23 BJ's Wholesale Club stores, which offered food and general merchandise in a warehouse format. Waban's sales for the previous 12 months had been approximately $2.4 billion. Waban had expanded aggressively, and the company reported sales increases of 24, 32, and 38 percent for each of the last three fiscal years.

- *Wolohan Lumber Company* operated 51 building-supply centers in the Upper Midwest and was expected to add five stores in 1991. Its 1990 sales were $296 million.

- *Grossman's, Incorporated,* operated 158 home-improvement stores, mainly in the northeastern region of the United States. The firm's sales in 1989 were $1.05 billion. In 1990, declining financial performance prompted a group of dissident shareholders to initiate a proxy contest, which ultimately failed. The chief executive officer resigned, however, and McKinsey & Company was retained to help develop a plan for building stockholder value.

Observers agreed that HD's competitors would not stand still while HD grew. Kmart, Hechinger, and Lowe's were plainly copying HD's warehouse format in their subsidiaries. Lowe's was also pursuing sales to small contractors, an important clientele. Smaller chains were adopting a convenience-store orientation. Still other chains were offering installation services. Virtually all major chains were expanding rapidly. Exhibit 3 compares operating and financial information about HD's principal competitors. Exhibit 4 presents excerpts from Standard & Poor's credit bulletins on HD, Lowe's, Hechinger, and Kmart and gives a summary of financial ratios associated with each rating category.

---

[20]*Annual Report,* Hechinger Company, February 1990.

The total size of the future market in do-it-yourself, home-improvement, warehouse-format retailing was difficult to forecast, but one analyst estimated that the United States could support 600 warehouse-style home centers with sales of up to $15 billion (in constant dollars).[21] In early 1991, HD accounted for 146 of the 336 warehouse-style home centers in operation. HD had demonstrated the ability to garner up to 30 percent of the local do-it-yourself market in its more mature locations.

FINANCING

Exhibits 5, 6, and 7 present HD's financial statements and associated analytical ratios for the previous three years. The historical statements reveal a rising though still moderate use of debt, large and rising returns on equity, and modest but rising dividends. The company had made little use of senior bank debt or long-term debt; rather, its pattern was to issue convertible subordinated debentures (see Exhibit 8 for a history of HD's securities issuance). The exact features of securities currently outstanding are detailed in Exhibit 9. The company had a $300 million revolving credit line, which it had not used.

In early 1991, management indicated that it would call its 6.75 percent convertible debentures on May 31, 1991. This security was deep "in the money" against its exercise price of $21.78 and would likely add 12 million shares to the company's outstanding stock.

Exhibits 5, 6, and 7 also forecast HD's financial performance based on management's target of 25 percent rate of store growth, maintenance of its traditional gross margins, and continuation of other average levels of performance. In general, the forecast assumptions listed in Exhibit 7 are consistent with reports issued on Home Depot in early 1991 by various securities analysts. Important assumptions in the model are: *gross margin* (line 1) at 27.5 percent; *operating expense to sales* (line 2) at 21 percent; and *days inventory outstanding* (line 14) at 67.5 days. These three assumptions are consistent with recent performance of the firm.

Other key forecast assumptions were the subject of debate among analysts in 1991: *number of new stores opened each year* (line 26) was consistent with management's 25 percent growth-rate target; *average square feet per store* (line 30) showed a rising trend from 94,000 to 100,000, consistent with an increase in store size in the warehouse segment of the industry; *sales per square feet* (line 31) also showed a gradual increase reflecting a 4 percent rate of inflation; and *land and fixtures per store* (line 35) increased as a result of management's continuing process of store upgrading.

The forecast indicates that the firm would require cumulative external financing of about $1.46 billion over the subsequent four years. Earnings per share (EPS) would rise steadily at a 27.5 percent rate or greater, except for 1992, when it was assumed that dilution from converting the 6.75 percent convertible debentures would slow EPS growth.

---

[21]S. Helm, William Blair & Company, November 20, 1990.

VALUATION

An issue related to The Home Depot's financing plans was the appropriateness of its current stock price of $54 per share. Any analysis on this point would influence management's appetite for issuing stock, convertible securities, debt, or other securities. Several analysts had evaluated Home Depot's stock; their opinions are summarized in Exhibit 10.

Exhibit 11 presents a graph of the weekly closing prices of The Home Depot, Hechinger, and Kmart common shares for the 52 weeks up to the end of March 1991. The graph attests to the high volatility of HD's share prices and their buoyancy relative to the two other retailers' share prices. The prices of all three stocks had been hit hard when Iraq invaded Kuwait on August 6, 1990; prices then lifted at the onset of the air war on January 15, 1991, and at the termination of the war in February. Bernard Marcus expressed puzzlement at the sensitivity of his firm's shares to these events: He argued that in recessions and times of national crisis, the purchase of new homes might decline, although home repair and do-it-yourself projects should increase. The actual financial earnings results for the fiscal year ended February 3, 1991, seemed to support his arguments.

CONCLUSION

HD management's distinctively aggressive expansion strategy created a large external-financing requirement over the medium term. Was this need best filled using the firm's traditional financing approach? What were the weaknesses, if any, of the traditional approach? Was there a better approach? Exhibit 12 presents information on capital market conditions in late March 1991.

EXHIBIT 1 Store Openings by Home Depot by State and Year

Fiscal Year	State												Stores Opened
	TN	GA	FL	AZ	LA	TX	AL	CA	NJ	NY	CT	SC	
Before 1981	4												4
1981			4										4
1982		2											2
1983			4	3	3								10
1984			1	2	1	6	1						11
1985		1	6	1		5		6					19
1986		1	2		1	1		5					10
1987		1	5		1		6						15
1988		2	4	1		1	1	9	1				21
1989	2	1	4	2		2		7		2	2	2	22
1990	1	4	5	1		1		8	3	3	1		27
Jan.–March 1991								1					1
Total	5	16	35	10	5	17	2	42	4	5	3	2	146

EXHIBIT 2 Equity Ownership Profile for Selected Major Home-Improvement Retailers

	Home Depot	Kmart	Hechinger's	Lowe's	Waban	Wolohan
Total shares outstanding (000s)	117,002	199,828	21,939	36,528	28,604	6,476
Where listed	NYSE	NYSE	OTC	NYSE	NYSE	OTC
Average value of holdings	$707,184	$117,178	$33,086	$124,620	$61,978	$43,245
Number of stockholders	4,900	69,917	4,500	6,360	NAv	1,350
Percent insider ownership	9% directors and management 2% ESOP	<1%	See "Special equity positions" below	24.5%	NAv	56%
Percent institutional ownership	74%	84%	56%	55%	46%	36%
Institutional holdings						
Mutual funds	7.7%	8.4%	12.8%	9.3%	3.7%	4.0%
Advisers	45.8%	54.8%	28.3%	29.0%	33.4%	25.9%
Comm'l. banks	13.0%	17.8%	13.2%	9.3%	7.8%	5.7%
Insurance companies	4.5%	3.8%	0.9%	7.4%	1.4%	0.3%
Number of institutional holders	372	486	82	157	84	43
Significant equity positions	Bkrs Tr (1.9m) Citicorp (1.8m) CREF (1.2m) Equitbl (1.1m)	Mellon (8.6m) FMR Corp (7m) Barrow (3.6m) Wells F (3.6m)	Templtn (1.6m) Morgan (1.8m) Nicholas (.7m) Fidelity (.6m)	Mellon (1.2m) CREF (1.1m) Ohio (1.0m) FMR (.9m)	Forstmn (1.98m) FMR (1.89m) Chase (1.77m) Wells F (.63m)	Sunamer (29m) Nicholas (.2m) Ohio (.27m) Wells F (.17m)
Special equity positions			Equity shares are classified into A and B shares. A shares trade publicly and carry one vote each. B shares are held by Hechinger and England families and carry 10 votes each. B shares account for 71 percent of total votes.			

Sources: O'Neil Database and *Value Line Investment Survey.*

EXHIBIT 3   Comparative Operating and Financial Information on Major Home-Improvement Retailers

	Home Depot	Lowe's	Builders Square	Hechinger	Home Club	Grossman's
Unit growth, 1988–89	23%	3%	7%	16%	26%	−36%
1989 sales per store ($ mm)	23	9	13	11	18	5
Average store size (sq. ft.)	88,000	20,324	80,000	60,000	100,000	31,900
Sales per square foot	$266	$426	$158	$192	$185	$160
Stock-keeping units	30,000	18,500	15,000	40,000	25,000	18,000
Stock-keeping units per square foot	0.34	0.91	0.33	0.67	0.25	0.56
Parent	None	None	Kmart	None	Waban	None
1991 standing						
Beta	1.40	1.35	1.15	1.00	2.72	1.40
P/E ratio	43	12.9	10.4	9.2	10	8
Dividend yield	.4%	2.2%	5.1%	2.3%	0	0
1989 results						
Gross margin	28.6%	24.4%	27.9%	27.6%		28.2%
Net margin	4.1%	2.4%	2.5%	2.5%		1.3%
Return on equity	21.9%	11.6%	15%	7.8%		11.6%
Dividend payout	7.0%	24%	42%	10%		0
Long-term debt to net worth	.59	.259	.744	.421		.744
Expected annual growth rates to 1993–95						
Sales	23.0%	9.0%	8.5%	14.5%		0
Earnings	23.5%	11.0%	9.0%	2.5%		2.5%
Dividends	31.5%	11.0%	10.5%	7.5%		0
Expected results, 1993–95						
Gross margin	28.5%	24.5%	28.0%	27.5%		28.0%
Net margin	4.1%	2.9%	2.7%	2.0%		1.4%
Return on equity	17.5%	12.0%	16.0%	8.0%		9.0%
Dividend payout	10.0%	21.0%	41.0%	19.0%		0
Long-term debt to net worth	.28	.244	.40	.576		.394

Sources: Investext and *Value Line Investment Survey.*

EXHIBIT 4   Excerpts of Ratings Comments on Major Warehouse Retailers

---

Home Depot (Rating of convertible, subordinated debt: BBB)

"Home Depot's effectiveness, largely due to its wide selection of competitively priced merchandise and highly trained sales force, has forced more traditional competitors to modify their merchandising practices. However, an ambitious expansion program, adding stores at the rate of 25% a year, continues to pose some risks. Also, financial leverage is aggressive, largely due to lease financing for new stores, with adjusted debt to capital at about 65%. Upgrade potential will demand a continuation of present operating trends and conversion of the outstanding convertible debentures. *Outlook: Positive.*"[a]

Lowe's Companies, Inc. (Rating of senior debt: A)

"The [A] rating reflects Lowe's solid business position and exceptional financial conservatism. The largest specialty retailer of building materials and products for the do-it-yourself and home-construction markets, Lowe's is experiencing a sharp and apparently sustainable recovery from its mediocre 1987 performance . . . Lease-adjusted debt leverage presently is below 30%, and no material change in Lowe's conservative capital structure is expected. *Outlook: Stable*"[b]

"Despite a solid operating record, management has acknowledged a threat to its future growth posed by do-it-yourself retailers operating warehouse formats . . . Lowe's will need to sustain the greater profitability of the larger stores to maintain its competitive position, though business risk associated with this growth is mitigated by confining expansion to existing markets. *Outlook: Stable.*"[c]

Hechinger Company (Rating of senior debt: A−. Rating of subordinated debt: BBB)

" . . . risks associated with the company's aggressive growth . . . Leverage adjusted for capitalization of operating leases, remains in the mid-50% historical range . . . sustained weakness in the business environment or in Hechinger's operating performance, particularly as Hechinger enters new markets, could erode credit quality, resulting in a downgrade in the next couple of years. *Outlook: Negative.*"[d]

Kmart Corporation (Rating of senior debt: A)

" . . . strong competitive position . . . solid business profile . . . The current rating anticipates continuation of Kmart's somewhat conservative financial policy along with an improvement in operating performance resulting from the refurbishing program. *Outlook: Stable.*"[e]

Key Industrial Median Financial Ratios (1987–89)

"These ratios are among those employed by S&P analysts in their quantitative analysis of credit strength . . . Ratio medians do not reflect the many analytical adjustments that S&P common makes in calculating the ratios used in the rating process. For example, they do not incorporate operating lease adjustments or S&P's captive finance company rating methodology. As a proxy for the operating lease adjustment, ratio medians are given for interest coverage, including rents and total debt to capital, including eight times rents as debt."[f]

	AAA	*AA*	*A*	*BBB*	*BB*	*B*	*CCC*
Pretax interest coverage ($\times$)	12.02	9.13	5.54	3.62	2.29	0.99	0.75
Pretax interest coverage incl. rents ($\times$)	4.79	5.04	3.30	2.22	1.76	1.01	0.73
Pretax funds flow interest coverage ($\times$)	14.85	11.36	7.72	5.26	3.42	1.70	1.66
Funds from operations/total debt (%)	89.1	79.2	48.7	35.7	18.6	6.4	5.2
Free operating cash flow/total debt (%)	26.1	16.7	9.1	3.9	(1.8)	(2.5)	(2.8)
Pretax return on permanent capital employed (%)	26.2	21.0	17.5	14.9	12.8	8.8	5.1
Operating income/sales (%)	21.3	16.2	13.4	12.1	13.2	9.5	9.7
Long-term debt/capitalization (%)	15.6	19.2	30.4	37.2	53.0	76.6	74.9
Total debt/capitalization incl. short-term debt (%)	23.3	28.0	35.2	40.8	54.5	77.8	77.6
Total debt/capitalization incl. short-term debt (incl. 8 times rents)(%)	35.3	39.1	48.7	55.5	65.5	81.5	81.0

[a]"The Home Depot, Inc., Excerpts of Ratings Comments on Major Warehouse Retailers," *CreditWeek,* June 25, 1990, p. 67.
[b]Ibid., February 26, 1990, p. 25.
[c]Ibid., July 2, 1990, p. 65.
[d]Ibid., February 26, 1990, p. 23.
[e]Ibid., August 6, 1990, p. 30.
[f]Ibid., November 19, 1990, pp. 30–31.

EXHIBIT 5 Historical and Projected Income Statements (in thousands of dollars)

	Actual					Projected		
	Jan. 29, 1989	Jan. 28, 1990	Feb. 3, 1991	Jan. 1992	Jan. 1993	Jan. 1994	Jan. 1995	Jan. 1996
Net sales	$1,999,514	$2,758,535	$3,815,356	$5,056,338	$6,653,424	$8,841,445	$11,694,730	$15,452,237
Cost of mdse. sold	1,459,862	1,991,777	2,751,085	3,665,845	4,823,732	6,410,048	8,478,679	11,202,872
Gross profit	539,652	766,758	1,064,271	1,390,493	1,829,692	2,431,397	3,216,051	4,249,365
Operating expenses:								
Selling and store op'g.	356,831	504,363	693,657	—	—	—	—	—
Preopening	7,552	9,845	13,315	—	—	—	—	—
General and administrative	48,485	67,901	91,664	—	—	—	—	—
Total operating expenses	412,868	582,109	798,636	1,061,831	1,397,219	1,856,704	2,455,893	3,244,970
Operating income	126,784	184,649	265,635	328,662	432,473	574,694	760,157	1,004,395
Interest income	751	13,320	17,579	12,388	16,301	21,662	28,652	37,858
Interest expense	(1,702)	(15,954)	(23,386)	(49,238)	(76,789)	(110,657)	(152,172)	(155,574)
Net interest expense	(951)	(2,634)	(5,807)	(36,850)	(60,488)	(88,996)	(123,520)	(117,716)
Earnings before taxes	125,833	182,015	259,828	291,812	371,985	485,698	636,638	886,679
Income taxes	49,080	70,061	96,400	109,430	139,494	182,137	238,739	332,505
Net earnings	$ 76,753	$ 111,954	$ 163,428	$ 182,383	$ 232,491	$ 303,561	$ 397,899	$ 554,174
Common shares & equivalents	115,325	118,470	120,835	132,835	132,835	132,835	132,835	132,835
EPS (fully diluted)	$0.67	$0.95	$1.35	$1.37	$1.75	$2.29	$3.00	$4.17
EPS (primary)	N/A	$0.97	$1.38	$1.40	$1.79	$2.33	$3.06	$4.26
Primary no. shares	N/A	115,176	118,066	130,066	130,066	130,066	130,066	130,066
Dividends per share	$0.05	$0.07	$0.11	$0.11	$0.14	$0.19	$0.24	$0.34

Sources: Company annual reports and casewriter analysis.

EXHIBIT 6 Historical and Projected Balance Sheets (in thousands of dollars)

	Actual					Projected		
	Jan. 29, 1989	Jan. 28, 1990	Feb. 3, 1991	Jan. 1992	Jan. 1993	Jan. 1994	Jan. 1995	Jan. 1996
Assets								
1. Cash	$ 15,853	$ 69,525	$ 107,895	$ 176,972	$ 232,870	$ 309,451	$ 409,316	$ 540,828
2. Short-term investments	0	65,856	29,401	—	—	—	—	—
3. Accounts receivable	17,614	38,933	49,325	65,109	85,674	113,849	150,590	198,974
4. Merchandise inventories	294,274	381,452	509,022	677,930	892,060	1,185,420	1,567,975	2,071,764
5. Other current assets	9,201	10,474	17,931	25,661	33,766	44,870	59,351	78,420
6. Total current assets	336,942	566,240	713,574	945,672	1,244,370	1,653,589	2,187,231	2,889,986
7. Land	85,303	128,265	262,560	—	—	—	—	—
8. Buildings	111,350	171,323	272,095	—	—	—	—	—
9. Furniture, fixtures, and equip't.	82,373	125,044	186,025	—	—	—	—	—
10. Leasehold improvements	58,707	94,641	160,760	—	—	—	—	—
11. Land, bldgs., and improv'ts.				1,220,201	1,589,744	2,052,649	2,637,258	3,349,872
12. Construction in progress	30,043	49,417	82,179	122,463	197,530	280,902	378,274	0
13. Gross property and equipment	367,776	568,690	963,619	1,342,664	1,787,274	2,333,551	3,015,532	3,349,872
14. Accumulated depreciation	35,360	54,250	84,889	127,854	185,047	259,721	356,218	463,414
15. Net property and equipment	332,416	514,440	878,730	1,214,810	1,602,227	2,073,830	2,659,314	2,886,459
16. Goodwill	22,664	22,032	21,400	20,000	19,000	18,000	17,000	16,000
17. Other assets	7,157	14,822	25,799	32,993	43,414	57,690	76,308	100,826
18. Total assets	$699,179	$1,117,534	$1,639,503	$2,213,475	$2,909,011	$3,803,110	$4,939,853	$5,893,271
19. Accounts payable	$126,431	$172,876	$235,267	$311,346	$409,687	$544,415	$720,107	$951,477

20. Accrued salaries	22,027	46,253	63,547	—	—	—	—	—
21. Sales taxes payable	0	17,507	26,806	—	—	—	—	—
22. Other accrued expenses	43,378	54,306	76,381	—	—	—	—	—
23. Income taxes payable	2,067	0	8,800	—	—	—	—	—
24. Accruals and other payables	—	—	—	227,535	299,404	397,865	526,263	695,351
25. Current portion, LT debt	233	1,447	1,906	—	—	—	—	—
26. Total current liabilities	194,136	292,389	412,707	538,881	709,091	942,280	1,246,370	1,646,827
27. New external fin'g. req'd.	—	—	—	274,311	580,432	956,751	1,418,023	1,455,828
28. Long-term debt	107,508	302,901	530,774	272,774	272,774	272,774	272,774	272,774
29. Other long-term liabilities	637	601	4,415	5,000	5,000	5,000	5,000	5,000
30. Deferred income taxes	13,960	9,512	8,205	8,000	8,000	8,000	8,000	8,000
31. Common stock	3,767	5,759	5,903	6,503	6,503	6,503	6,503	6,503
32. Paid-in capital	213,562	231,538	264,301	521,701	521,701	521,701	521,701	521,701
33. Retained earnings	185,609	289,177	439,770	607,562	821,453	1,100,730	1,466,797	1,976,637
34. Less notes recvble from ESOP	(20,000)	(26,572)	(26,572)	(21,258)	(15,943)	(10,629)	(5,314)	0
35. Total stockholders' equity	382,938	512,129	683,402	1,114,508	1,333,714	1,618,305	1,989,686	2,504,841
36. Total liabs. & stkhldrs' eq.	$699,179	$1,117,534	$1,639,503	$2,213,475	$2,909,011	$3,803,110	$4,939,853	$5,893,271
Memo								
37. Dividends	—	$8,062	$12,987	$14,591	$18,599	$24,285	$31,832	$44,334
38. Capital expenditures	—	200,914	394,929	379,045	444,610	546,276	681,981	334,340
39. Depreciation expense	—	18,890	30,639	42,965	57,193	74,674	96,497	107,196
40. Additions to net wkg cap.	—	131,045	27,016	105,924	128,488	176,030	229,552	302,298
41. Incr. new external fin'g.	—	—	—	274,311	306,121	376,319	461,272	37,805

Sources: Company annual reports and casewriter analysis.

EXHIBIT 7 Ratio Analyses of Historical and Projected Financial Statements

	Actual					Projected		
	Jan. 29, 1989	Jan. 28, 1990	Feb. 3, 1991	Jan. 1992	Jan. 1993	Jan. 1994	Jan. 1995	Jan. 1996
1. Gross margin (%)	27.0%	27.8%	27.9%	27.5%	27.5%	27.5%	27.5%	27.5%
2. Opg expenses to sales (%)	20.6%	21.1%	20.9%	21.0%	21.0%	21.0%	21.0%	21.0%
3. Operating profit margin (%)	6.3%	6.7%	7.0%	6.5%	6.5%	6.5%	6.5%	6.5%
4. Average tax rate (%)	39.0%	38.5%	37.1%	37.5%	37.5%	37.5%	37.5%	37.5%
5. Return on sales (%)	3.8%	4.1%	4.3%	3.6%	3.5%	3.4%	3.4%	3.6%
6. Return on equity (%)	20.0%	21.9%	23.9%	16.4%	17.4%	18.8%	20.0%	22.1%
7. Return on assets (%)	11.0%	10.0%	10.0%	8.2%	8.0%	8.0%	8.1%	9.4%
8. Debt/equity ratio (%)	28.1%	59.1%	77.7%	49.1%	64.0%	76.0%	85.0%	69.0%
9. Debt/total capital (%)	21.9%	37.2%	43.7%	32.9%	39.0%	43.2%	45.9%	40.8%
10. EBIT/interest (×)	133.3	70.1	45.7	8.9	7.1	6.5	6.2	8.5
11. Cash & invest. to sales (%)	0.8%	4.9%	3.6%	3.5%	3.5%	3.5%	3.5%	3.5%
12. Days in receivables	3.2	5.2	4.7	4.7	4.7	4.7	4.7	4.7
13. Days in payables	31.6	31.7	31.2	31.0	31.0	31.0	31.0	31.0
14. Days in inventory	73.6	69.9	67.5	67.5	67.5	67.5	67.5	67.5
15. Other curr. assets/sales	0.6%	0.5%	0.7%	0.7%	0.7%	0.7%	0.7%	0.7%
16. Other curr. liabs./sales	3.4%	4.3%	4.6%	4.5%	4.5%	4.5%	4.5%	4.5%
17. Other assets/sales	0.5%	0.7%	0.9%	0.9%	0.9%	0.9%	0.9%	0.9%
18. Quick ratio	0.17	0.60	0.45	0.45	0.45	0.45	0.45	0.45
19. Current ratio	1.74	1.94	1.73	1.75	1.75	1.75	1.75	1.75
20. Primary earnings per share	N/A	$0.97	$1.38	$1.40	$1.79	$2.33	$3.06	$4.26
21. Change in EPS (%)	34.0%	41.8%	42.1%	1.7%	27.5%	30.6%	31.1%	39.3%
22. Dividends per share	$0.05	$0.07	$0.11	$0.11	$0.14	$0.19	$0.24	$0.34
23. Dividends to net income (%)	—	7.2%	7.9%	8.0%	8.0%	8.0%	8.0%	8.0%
24. Sales growth rate (%)	37.6%	38.0%	38.3%	32.5%	31.6%	32.9%	32.3%	32.1%
25. Ending number of stores	96	118	145	180	223	282	355	442
26. New stores added	21	22	27	35	43	59	73	87
27. Unit growth (%)	28.0%	23.0%	23.0%	24.1%	23.9%	26.5%	25.9%	24.5%
28. Ending square footage (000)	8,216	10,424	13,278	16,920	21,408	27,354	34,790	44,200
29. Change in square footage (%)	33.4%	26.9%	27.4%	27.4%	26.5%	27.8%	27.2%	27.0%
30. Avg. sq. ft./store (000)	86	88	92	94	96	97	98	100
31. Avg. sales per square foot	$243	$265	$287	$299	$311	$323	$336	$350
32. Avg. sales per store ($ mil.)	20.8	23.4	26	28.1	29.8	31.4	32.9	35.0
33. Same store sales incrs (%)	13.4%	12.9%	10.0%	8.0%	6.2%	5.1%	5.1%	6.1%
34. Advertising expense/sales	1.5%	1.1%	0.9%	N/A	N/A	N/A	N/A	N/A
35. Land, bldg, & fixtures/store	$3,518	$4,401	$6,079	$6,779	$7,129	$7,279	$7,429	$7,579
36. Construction/next new stores	$1,366	$1,830	$2,348	$2,848	$3,348	$3,848	$4,348	$4,848
37. Annual deprecn/gross P&E	—	3.3%	3.2%	3.2%	3.2%	3.2%	3.2%	3.2%

Source: Casewriter analysis.

EXHIBIT 8 Pattern of Financings (in millions of dollars)

	1990	1989	1988	1987	1986	1985	1984
Senior bank debt		(71)	36	(53)	88		
Unsecured debt							
7.95% note due 1995 (ESOP)			20				
Industrial revenue bonds							
6.49% due 2011					5.8		4.2
Convertible subordinated debt							
9s due 1999					(14)	14	
8.50s due 2009					(75)	75	
6.75s due 2014		258					
6s due 1997	230						
Common stock							
Conversions of bonds					89		
New sales of shares				44.2			
Sale of shares to ESOP			20				

Sources: Company annual reports and Moody's *Industrial Manual.*

EXHIBIT 9   Terms of Securities Outstanding

---

1. Bank notes payable

Outstandings:	0
Agreements:	Revolving line of credit agreement for a maximum of $300 million through September 1994 with annual options to extend beyond 1994. Annual facility fee of .125%.
Covenants:	(*a*) Minimum tangible net worth of $270 million plus 65% of consolidated net earnings for periods beginning after January 29, 1989; (*b*) ratio of earnings before income taxes, interest, operating lease expense, and amortization of intangible assets to net interest expense of not less than 1.75 to 1; (*c*) ratio of debt to tangible net worth of no more than 2 to 1.
Agent bank:	Security Pacific

2. 7.95% unsecured note, due 1995 (incurred in connection with the establishment of a leveraged ESOP)

Issued:	1988
Outstandings:	$20,000,000
Covenants:	Debt shall not exceed 66.66% of consolidated assets, net of goodwill and current liabilities.
Maturity:	September 1, 1995

3. 6.75% convertible subordinated debentures, due 2014

Issued:	May 1, 1989
Outstanding:	$258,750,000
Maturity date:	May 15, 2014
Rated:	A2
Callability:	Yes
Conversion terms:	Into common stock at $21.78 per share
Sinking fund:	Annually 1999–2013 sufficient to redeem 66.6% of bonds prior to maturity
Listing:	New York Stock Exchange
Lead manager of offering:	First Boston and Invemed Associates
Bond trustee:	First National Bank of Atlanta

4. 6.00% convertible subordinated debentures, due 1997

Issued:	June 15, 1990
Outstanding:	$230,000,000
Maturity date:	June 15, 1997
Rated:	A2
Callability:	Yes
Conversion terms:	Into common stock at $48.17 per share
Sinking fund:	None
Listing:	None
Lead manager of offering:	First Boston and Invemed Associates
Bond trustee:	First National Bank of Atlanta

5. Leases (mainly operating leases on retail facilities)

Future minimum payments:	1991, $74.8m; 1992, $86.8m; 1993, $85.7m; 1994, $81m; 1995, $80m.
Total undiscounted future payments:	$1,372,195,000

6. Common stock

Issued:	September 22, 1981 (600,000 shares at $.75)
	October 16, 1986 (2,600,000 shares at $4.00)
Outstanding:	118,066,000 shares
Listing:	New York Stock Exchange
Lead manager of offering:	1981, Bear Stearns
	1986, Merrill Lynch
Dividends:	Stock dividends: January 1982 (50%)
	April 1982 (25%)
	December 1982 (100%)
	June 1983 (100%)
	Cash dividends: paid continuously since 1987
Stock splits:	Split 3-for-2 September 1987 and again June 1989

Sources: Company annual reports and Moody's *Industrial Manual.*

EXHIBIT 10   Analysts' Opinions of the Home Depot's Stock

Analyst	Valuation	Analysis Based on	Home Depot Stock Price	S&P 500 Index
W. N. Smith, Smith, Barney, March 12, 1991	$66 per share is target price over next 12–18 months.	P/E multiples	$52.00	370
K. K. Walin, Shearson, Lehman, February 26, 1991	"Selling at a discount . . . Prospects remain outstanding."	P/E multiples	$49.00	363
W. Haad, Prudential-Bache, February 1, 1991	$46 per share over next 12 months.	P/E multiples	$43.25	343
B. Sharav, Value Line Investment, January 25, 1991	$40–56 price range during 1993–95. "The high P/E makes us view the stock with some caution."	Cash flow	$39.00	336
D. Wewer, Robinson-Humphrey, November 28, 1990	"Unusually attractive buying opportunity at $43."	P/E multiples	$36.00	318
S. Helm, William Blair, November 20, 1990	HD is "widening its lead" over competitors. It can achieve 25% annual earnings growth over next 3–5 years.	P/E miltiples	$35.875	315
J. G. Dennis, J. C. Bradford & Co., November 15, 1990	"This was one of the most successful public offerings of the 1980s. The party has not ended yet."	EPS	$34.50	317

EXHIBIT 11   Comparative Stock Prices, Leading Warehouse Retailers

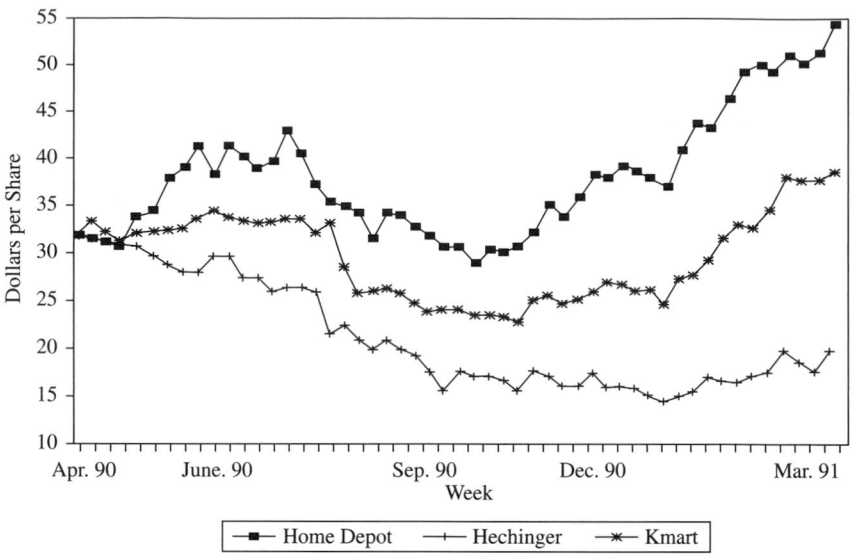

EXHIBIT 12   Current Capital Market Rates and Indexes, March 31, 1991

U.S. Treasury Securities		*Other Interest Rates*	
1 month	5.89%	Prime	8.75–9%
2 months	5.82	Federal funds	6.125
3 months	5.73	Commercial paper	
6 months	6.12	1 month	6.2
1 year	6.49	3 months	6.1
2 years	7.01	LIBOR	
3 years	7.28	3 months	6.375
4 years	7.60	12 months	7.0
5 years	7.80	Eurodollars	6.35%
10 years	8.08		
30 years	8.23%		

Corporate Bonds

Rating	Yield
AAA	8.95%
AA	9.25
A	9.70
BBB	10.33
BB	11.98
B	16.44%

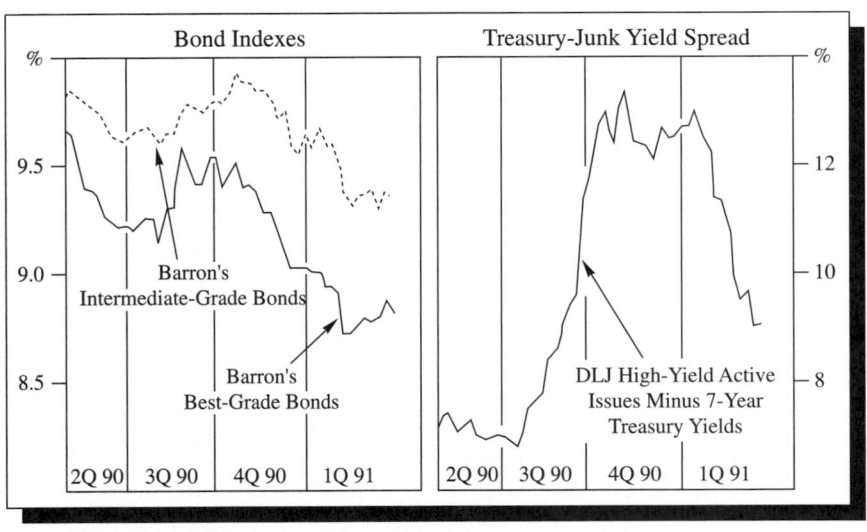

Sources: Reprinted by permission from Barron's (c) 1991 Dow Jones & Company, Inc. All Rights Reserved Worldwide.

United Telecommunications, Inc.

The year 1989 was . . . when we linked the human and technological capabilities of the corporation to become a significant force in the domestic and international communications industries. Our mission is straightforward—to be the best telecommunications company in the world—to rise above the competition and become the standard against which all others in the industry are measured . . . Reflecting the importance of US Sprint to the success of our company, we will ask shareholders to approve changing our name from United Telecom to Sprint Corporation when we exercise our option to purchase the remaining 19.9 percent interest in US Sprint from GTE. We believe all of our companies will benefit from association with the widely recognized and respected Sprint name . . . We're further leveraging our strengths by combining our leadership positions in voice and data to create a wide array of services demanded by the domestic and international consumer. Our domestic fiber routes serve as the backbone of an emerging global, digital highway . . . We don't intend to be just another one of many global participants. We intend to play a leading role in demonstrating how innovation, quality and customer service can, in fact, redefine the basis for competition . . . Our leadership in applying innovative, service-oriented technologies will accelerate the impact of change on our industry . . . At United Telecom, quality is more than just words. It's a way of working, a way of doing business, a way of life. Quite simply, we're moving to become the easiest company in the world with which to do business. Our goal is to exceed the expectations of our customers in everything we do . . . United Telecom's quality also is reflected in its shareholders, who have demonstrated patience and trust as we've overcome great obstacles to reach our current level of achievement. We're grateful for your support. Your company and all of its employees are committed to producing even greater rewards in the years ahead.

Letter to shareholders from Chief Executive Officer William Esrey,
1989 annual report, issued Spring 1990

This case was written as a basis for class discussion rather than to illustrate effective or ineffective handling of an administrative situation. Copyright © 1991 by the University of Virginia Darden School Foundation, Charlottesville, VA. All rights reserved. *No part of this publication may be reproduced, stored in a retrieval*

In November 1990, the senior managers of United Telecommunications, Inc. (UT), faced a serious test of commitment to their corporate vision as expressed in the annual report the previous spring. Only six months earlier, the firm's stock had traded at up to $46.00 per share. Quarterly performance, however, had lagged expectations in July 1990, triggering a 50 percent drop in stock price from the 1990 peak. Now, in an uncertain capital market environment, UT's senior managers had to reconsider the financing plans necessary to support the corporate vision. They were uncertain to what extent the firm could generate funds internally to finance the purchase of the minority interest in Sprint, selected acquisitions, strategic alliances and joint ventures, and a new headquarters complex in Kansas City, Missouri.

Were the firm's financing policies appropriate? If not, what action should management take? What would be the impact of those actions both on symptomatic problems in the short run and on deeper challenges in the long run? Analysts estimated that the firm would have to raise $1.6 billion in new external capital in the next two years. How should this be done?

THE COMPANY

United Telecommunications was founded in 1938 as United Utilities, a holding company for gas-transmission and telephone public utilities. It sold its gas-transmission properties in the 1960s and began a program to acquire local, independent telephone companies: 2 acquisitions in 1965, 7 in 1966, 11 in 1967, 9 in 1968, and 2 in 1969. Fourteen local telephone companies were acquired in the 1970s, and two large, local telephone interests were acquired in the 1980s (most notably a 9.8 percent equity interest in Southern New England Telephone in 1984). Fourteen computer timesharing or software firms were acquired between 1970 and 1985. Virtually all acquisitions had been consummated with an exchange of shares rather than payment in cash. Through start-ups and small acquisitions in the 1980s, UT entered a range of complementary businesses such as directory publishing, telephone-equipment manufacturing, telemarketing, long-distance telephone service, and business databases. For UT the most significant event in recent years had been the formation of the US Sprint Communications Company joint venture in July 1986 between UT and GTE Corporation. In August 1989, Sprint acquired, for $295 million, Private Transatlantic Telecommunications Systems, Inc., which owned a 50 percent interest in PTAT[1] (Cable and Wireless, a U.K. firm, owned the other 50 percent). In October 1989, Sprint acquired Long Distance/USA for $271 million; it provided long-distance communications services with an emphasis on the hospitality industry. Both acquisitions were accounted for as purchases. Exhibits 1 and 2 present historical income statements and balance sheets for UT.

By the fall of 1990, UT was the *only* major player in *both* local and long-distance telephone service: It was the second largest independent, local telephone system after GTE (the

system, used in a spreadsheet, or transmitted in any form or by any means—electronic, mechanical, photocopying, recording, or otherwise—without the permission of the Darden School Foundation. For inquiries, please send an e-mail to dardencases@virginia.edu. Revised 1/98. Version 1.4.

[1]PTAT was the world's first privately owned, transatlantic, fiber-optic undersea-cable system. Alone, this cable could carry more volume than all other transatlantic cables combined.

ninth largest relative to the "Baby Bells" or regional Bell operating companies) and the third largest long-distance company after AT&T and MCI by virtue of its 80 percent equity interest in US Sprint. UT also engaged in various complementary businesses such as directory publishing and the manufacture of telecommunications equipment. Of the three elements in UT's business portfolio, Sprint dominated the reported performance of the company and had driven the firm's stock price in recent years. Exhibit 3 lists certain financial ratios for UT and its competitors in both the local and long-distance segments. The changes in UT's asset portfolio over the last few years are indicated in the following table.

	1989	1988	1987	1986	1985
Consolidated results					
Revenues	7,549.0	6,493.0	2,935.1	3,012.7	3,083.8
Operating income	910.0	252.8	679.3	588.4	157.5
Intercompany revenues	(173.7)	(120.7)	(81.8)	(66.7)	(18.0)
Long-distance communications			(Sprint		
Revenues	4,323.6	3,405.4	not	212.4	342.6
Operating income	266.6	(386.1)	reported)	(109.8)	(494.9)
Local communications					
Revenues	2,637.0	2,509.7	2,388.9	2,311.4	2,302.3
Operating income	636.6	596.8	636.6	667.8	642.4
Complementary businesses					
Revenues	762.1	698.6	628.0	555.6	456.9
Operating income	47.7	42.1	42.7	30.4	10.0

Note: All amounts in $ millions.

The business challenges in UT's two telecommunications segments differed dramatically. The local telephone companies were nearly monopolies, low-growth businesses, and steady cash generators. In contrast, the long-distance business was fiercely competitive, growing rapidly, and extremely price sensitive.

UT's Local Telephone Companies

Exhibit 4 presents a map indicating the market coverage of UT's local telephone operations; they consisted of 16 regulated telephone companies in 17 states and boasted 3.8 million access lines (1 million in Florida alone). Operations in three states—Florida, Ohio, and North Carolina—accounted for 58 percent of the segment revenues. Revenue growth rates hovered between 4.0 and 4.5 percent, at or just above the industry average. The operations ranked among the most efficient and profitable in the industry.

One of UT's goals for this segment was to consolidate the operations in 10 to 12 states in order to exploit operating efficiencies—a widely dispersed set of local companies required great expense for monitoring and control and prevented implementation of operating economies. Another goal was to exploit both technological change and potential deregulation in order to enter new local markets such as cable transmission. UT had dabbled in cellular telecommunications at one time, and was considering reentering this segment by the mid-1990s.[2]

Complementary Businesses

Through DirectoriesAmerica, UT published nearly 270 telephone directories in 21 states. The subsidiary North Supply Company not only distributed telecommunications products from more than 700 manufacturers but also supplied alarm equipment to the security industry.

US SPRINT

As the third largest long-distance telecommunications company, Sprint commanded a 9 percent share of market and revenues of $4.6 billion. Sprint had the only nationwide, 100 percent digital fiber-optic network, which gave it both quality and efficiency advantages over its larger rivals—indeed, quality differentiation was the key element in UT's strategy to increase market share. Sprint was a so-called full-line provider of long-distance services, including voice, video, private line, 800, 900, and international.

When Sprint was formed in July 1986 as a joint venture between UT and GTE Corporation, UT had already been at work since 1984 building an all-digital, all-fiber network. Because the capital requirements were so much bigger than anticipated, UT concluded that a joint venture would be a more appropriate basis for building the network. At formation of the venture, both firms held an equal share. In 1988, UT assumed management control of US Sprint. In its early years Sprint sustained massive losses because of foul-ups in its computerized billing system[3] and construction-related problems in its high-tech fiber network. In January 1989, UT purchased a 30.1 additional percent interest in Sprint from GTE for $585 million in cash, raising its total equity interest to 80.1 percent and leaving GTE with 19.9 percent. UT also held an option to purchase the remaining GTE interest at net book value (currently about $550 million) at any time up to December 31, 1995. Conversely, GTE held a put option allowing it to require UT to purchase the remaining interest any time between December 31, 1991, and December 31, 1995, at the net book value of the interest.

In the meantime, UT would determine whether and to what extent additional capital contributions from the two partners would be required: GTE would be required to contribute

---

[2]In October 1988, UT sold its cellular-telephone and paging-services subsidiary for approximately $775 million, recording a gain of $367 million.

[3]When GTE and UT merged their long-distance operations in 1986, they had to combine different management information systems, which proved challenging and resulted in widespread double billing (and/or lack of billing) of customers. These difficulties coincided with the addition of 2 million new customers in the first six months of operation.

its proportionate share, subject to a cumulative upper limit of $300 million; at the end of 1989, GTE had contributed $65 million under the agreement. As recently as June 1990, William Esrey, UT's chief executive officer, had said that UT would purchase GTE's remaining interest in Sprint in 1990; but with the onset of adverse conditions, Esrey stated in the fall that the purchase would be deferred until 1991. In exercising its option early, UT's goal was to simplify the management structure and control of Sprint.

UT's strategic objectives with Sprint were to expand internationally via joint ventures,[4] add niche acquisitions (such as Long Distance/USA), lower its cost basis, and increase market share. The marketing plan called for service enhancement (e.g., an improved billing system), a fully competitive, high-quality product offering, and retention of a pricing advantage versus AT&T and MCI. With UT's nationwide network largely complete, its goal was to utilize capacity more fully.

COMPETITION IN THE LONG-DISTANCE TELEPHONE INDUSTRY

The long-distance segment was dominated by AT&T, which held a 68 percent share of market and fielded considerable financial and operational clout—in short, it was a multi-tier industry. The second tier consisted of MCI, with 14 percent of the market, and Sprint, with 9 percent. The industry included several other tiers, many of which were tiny players and resellers of services. Unlike other regulated industries, the competitors in the long-distance telephone industry did not compete like a stable oligopoly. Given the capital intensity in the industry, its resulting high operating leverage, and growing excess capacity, fierce competition was to be expected.

The competition for market share was based on several factors. Although price had been the most significant factor, quality of service (e.g., fiber-optic cables) and service customization (e.g., special packages for small businesses) were increasingly important factors in building customer loyalty. Spending on technological improvements was crucial, as was the advertising necessary to broadcast those improvements. Analysts estimated AT&T's advertising budget for 1990 at over $450 million as compared with $125 million for all other long-distance companies *combined*.

Two major technological advances were revolutionizing the telecommunications industry: fiber-optic cables and digital switching, both of which significantly increased the carrying capacity of telecommunications networks.[5] The rapid rate of technological change often rendered obsolete equipment that was otherwise viable, as UT discovered in 1987 when it wrote off $260 million for its analog-microwave network, made redundant by the earlier-than-expected transition of traffic to its new fiber-optic network.

In 1990, revenues in the long-distance telephone industry aggregated about $50 billion and were expected to grow faster than the economy for at least five years, reflecting the

---

[4]UT's 1989 annual report stated: "We don't intend to be just *a* player in making the world a smaller place. In the most creative respects, we can be *the* player."

[5]Quite simply, a fiber-optic cable transmitted signals in the form of light rather than electric pulses, enabling a single cable to carry much more volume than an ordinary copper cable. Digital switching enabled the cable to be packed even fuller: under the old analog technology, the sine-wave signal left considerable unused capacity in the cable, whereas the digital technology packed the cable virtually full.

expected quality improvements and price reductions that would increase demand. Value Line predicted that composite industry revenues (i.e., both local and long-distance segments) would grow at 6 percent per year for the next five years. The composite forecast, however, masked widely differing projected growth rates for individual firms: UT's revenues were expected to grow at 12 percent per year, as compared with 15 percent for MCI and 3.5 percent for AT&T. Exhibit 5 presents comparative expected financial-performance figures for the major players in the industry.

The key trends in the industry were consolidation (purchase of small companies by large companies), stable or declining unit prices in the face of rising competition, and product/ service proliferation. The three major players faced the prospects of rising marketing costs, entry by local telephone companies, revenue erosion from price competition, and the uncertainty attending the Federal Communications Commission's regulation of AT&T (price changes, entries permitted, etc.).

Many observers believed that the survivors in the industry would be large, offering geographical reach and a full product line; would be especially effective marketers and cost controllers; and would exploit a range of strategic alliances from joint ventures to partial and full acquisitions. Given its size, capital resources, and name recognition, AT&T already showed these characteristics. MCI had effectively segmented the market and established a reputation for service among price-sensitive customers. Sprint had the most advantageous pricing of the three, as well as a technological lead; and its state-of-the-art billing system was expected to appeal to customers such as businesses and government agencies with specialized information requirements.

WILLIAM ESREY

Gradually, a new breed of senior manager was taking charge in the telecommunications industry. Before federal Judge Harold Greene approved the breakup of AT&T into one long-distance and several regional companies in 1983, senior managers of telecommunications companies had typically come up through the ranks on the operational side, as engineers. This tendency reflected the focus on operating economies dictated by tight regulation of monopolies. After the breakup, however, a new emphasis was clearly required: Marketers, strategic planners, and financial officers gained more influence in the executive suites.

William Esrey joined United Telecommunications in 1980 as executive vice president of Corporate Planning and was named chief financial officer in January 1984. He became president and chief executive officer in April 1985. Prior to joining UT, Esrey was managing director of Dillon, Reed and Company from 1970 to 1979; earlier he had held management positions with AT&T, New York Telephone Company, and Empire City Subway Company Ltd. He had earned a bachelor's degree in economics from Denison University and a master's degree from Harvard Business School.

Esrey's vision of the future of the telecommunications industry was summarized in the concept *infonics,* his term for the technological infrastructure he believed would "probably reshape the world." A UT press release noted:

> Esrey may be best known as an architect. His own building blocks are fiber-optic cable and digital switches. His most acclaimed structure is arguably the most advanced long-distance network

in the United States . . . He is now leading the company's strategic thrust into worldwide markets, where he sees advancements in the telecommunications industry giving consumers unprecedented opportunities to demand new services from their long-distance carriers.[6]

FINANCING REQUIREMENTS

UT's most prominent investment was its planned purchase of GTE's minority interest in Sprint for approximately $550 million, which would complete and simplify UT's control of Sprint. Although UT had initially intended to purchase the remaining interest in mid-1990, the adverse quarterly performance reported in July had forced the company to delay the purchase until 1991. The effect of any delay would be to share pro rata any ongoing profits or losses in Sprint. GTE had the right to put its interest to UT from December 31, 1991, to December 31, 1995.

UT's internal capital expenditures for 1990 would approximate $1 billion.[7] Observers believed that much of the internal spending was related to installation of digital switches and fiber-optic cable in the local telephone companies and that internal capital expenditures would amount to $1.3 billion[8] in 1991 and a minimum of $1 billion[9] annually thereafter for the foreseeable future. These amounts compared with historical expenditures in the long-distance segment of $705 million in 1989 and $735 million in 1988, both of which were substantially driven by construction costs for the domestic fiber-optic network. The local-telephone segment required capital expenditures of $659 million and $676 million in 1989 and 1988, respectively. The relatively high rate of capital expenditures at the local level reflected the growth of access lines (i.e., customers) and the conversion from analog to digital switching. The diffusion of digital technology to UT's local operations was slow but steady—62 percent of local switching capacity was digital at the end of 1987, as compared with 81 percent at the end of 1989.

A third major capital expenditure was the planned construction of a new office complex adding 2.6 million square feet of space in a campus of 21 modular office buildings ranging from 4 to 15 stories and connected by walkways.[10] The complex would consolidate the headquarters staff, currently spread over 24 buildings in the Kansas City area. A rough estimate of the expenditure for the new complex was $500 million[11] and did not include $50

---

[6]"United Telecom/US Sprint Chairman Esrey Cites Fundamental Changes in Global Communications," September 4, 1990.

[7]UT's 1989 annual report stated that capital expenditures for 1990 would approximate $1.6 billion, which included the purchase of GTE's interest in Sprint. Netting that out would leave internal expenditures of about $1 billion.

[8]Jack R. Grubman, "United Telecom—Company Report," PaineWebber, September 17, 1990.

[9]Edward Greenberg of Morgan Stanley believed that UT's capital expenditures would exceed $1 billion annually at least through 1995. Specifically, he forecasted the following expenditure rates from 1991 through 1996 (in $ billions): 1.73, 1.18, 1.2, 1.33, 1.47, and 1.58.

[10]The company total would rise to 3.3 million square feet of space. UT currently had 2.63 million square feet of space in the metropolitan area. Of that footage, 1.5 million was leased and the rest was owned by United Telecom or Sprint. (Steven Wolcott, "United Telecom Imparting Mixed Signals about Move," *Kansas City Business Journal,* May 7, 1990.)

[11]Casewriter's estimate, based on an assumed cost per square foot of about $200.

million already spent to purchase the land. The timing of the expenditure was open to question: Construction had been expected to begin early in 1990, but with the adverse quarterly report, the ground-breaking had been delayed. Now, in November 1990, analysts expected construction to be deferred at least through 1991.

Financing might also be required in future years to support acquisitions by UT. Observers believed UT would reenter the cellular-telephone market by the mid-1990s, a move that might require between $500 million and $1 billion.[12] Other strategic acquisitions might be made in complementary businesses, international telecommunications, and small, domestic long-distance telephone companies. Observers generally agreed that being able to provide a full product line was essential to survival in the industry.

A final imponderable was the extra spending necessary to build the Sprint brand name and maintain it in the face of opposing efforts by AT&T and MCI. In the fall of 1990, AT&T initiated a massive telemarketing campaign in which it would telephone *every one* of MCI's and Sprint's customers to persuade them to switch to AT&T. One analyst said, "This is going to be a long drawn-out war . . . Sprint may be the biggest casualty of a protracted marketing battle . . . and . . . may not be able to afford the escalating marketing wars."[13] Another observer noted:

> The big trouble is spelled AT&T. After years of letting its share of the long-distance market slip, American Telephone & Telegraph has been fighting back with a vengeance, using tough ads and a telephone marketing campaign that includes ringing up an estimated 6 million of rivals' customers a month, asking them to switch . . . the slug-out is costly.[14]

Forecast of Financing Requirements

Exhibits 6, 7, and 8 present forecasted financial statements for UT on a consolidated basis. The forecasts assume no major acquisitions (other than the minority interest in Sprint in 1991) and no sustained price war or adverse competitive developments for Sprint. The headquarters construction expense is not reflected in the forecasts. The large additions to gross property, plant, and equipment over the forecast period assume expenditures to sustain the firm only at its present scope.

The apparent *incremental* external financing need (Exhibit 7, line 23) is about $600 million in 1990, $1 billion in 1991, and $70 million in 1992—all compared with $750 million of borrowing capacity available under the firm's most restrictive debt covenants.[15] Thereafter, incremental external needs are negative, because, under this forecast, Sprint

---

[12]Casewriter's estimate, based on the sale price of UT's own cellular operation, US TeleSpectrum, in 1988 for $775 million.

[13]Jack R. Grubman (PaineWebber), "AT&T's Long-Distance Marketing Blitz Has MCI, Sprint Scrambling to Keep Up," *The Wall Street Journal,* November 19, 1990.

[14]Reprinted by permission of *The Wall Street Journal,* © 1990 Dow Jones & Company, Inc. All Rights Reserved Worldwide.

[15]This estimate, drawn from UT's 10-Q Statement of June 1990, contrasts with the $631 million in unused revolving bank-credit facilities indicated in its 1989 annual report and in Exhibit 13 of this case. For analytic purposes, one should work with the more recent figure of $750 million.

would begin to throw off a large flow of cash beginning in 1992. The large external financing need has been driven mainly by UT's huge internal capital expenditures, and by its high rate of debt refinancing. The future could differ dramatically from this forecast with relatively minor changes in operating assumptions for Sprint.

CORPORATE FINANCING[16]

Exhibit 9 presents a graph of leverage and capitalization ratios for UT over time. Dividend payout peaked at over 100 percent of earnings in 1986 and 1987. Although dividends per share held steady at $0.96 from 1985 to 1988, earnings per share dropped precipitously as the firm absorbed large losses from its fledgling US Sprint joint venture. The decline in dividend payout since 1988 resulted from slow dividend increases relative to earnings. Debt as a percentage of capital varied between 50 and 65 percent, with the last few periods at the high end of that range. UT incurred debt at the parent and subsidiary levels as indicated in the following table:

Financing Entity and Debt	*Dollar Volume of Debt ($ millions)*	*Percentage of Debt*	*Ratings*
UTI (parent)			
Short-term	194	10.0	A2/P2
Senior long-term	1,427	73.4	BBB/Baa3
Subordinated long-term	324	16.6	BBB-/Ba1
Total	1,945	100.0	
Local communications services			
Short-term	11	0.7	A1/P1
Mortgage bonds	1,144	81.5	AA,A/A
Debentures/other	249	17.8	A/A
Total	1,404	100.0	
Long-distance communications services			
Vendor finance	405	66.6	Not rated
GTE advances*	187	30.8	
Other	16	2.6	
Total	608	100.0	

*Advances by UT and other funding for Sprint are included at the parent level.

Definitions of Standard & Poor's rating categories are given in Exhibit 10. Exhibit 11 presents S&P's rationale for UT's debt ratings and a summary of the financial-ratio benchmarks UT used in rating securities.

Exhibit 12 gives further detail on UT's debt structure, and Exhibit 13 describes the securities in more detail. In addition to the items listed, UT used up to $300 million of receiv-

---

[16]The comments presented in this section refer to UT's *consolidated* statements.

ables financing from Citibank and had $750 million of unused borrowing capacity available under the most restrictive debt covenants. On April 27, 1990, UT shelf-registered an issue of $500 million in debt securities; S&P rated the registration BBB. Exhibit 14 presents the long-term pattern of debt additions. A schedule of forthcoming debt maturities and payments under operating leases is given in Exhibit 15. Finally, Exhibit 16 summarizes public information concerning the ownership of UT's common stock and that of AT&T and MCI.

CAPITAL-MARKET CONDITIONS

Exhibit 17 gives the current term structure of interest rates in U.S. Treasuries as well as current yields to maturity on corporate bonds. Although observers believed the U.S. economy was slipping into a recession (one prominent economist declared the economy had gone into a "free fall"),[17] they also believed it would be short-lived and that the economy would start to rebound in mid-1991. One commentator expected the federal funds rate to fall from 7.75 percent to 6.75 percent by mid-1991, because she expected the Federal Reserve Board to ease interest rates in support of the economy; the 30-year Treasury bond yield was expected to fall from 8.75 to 8.375 percent by midyear, but then rise as the economy rebounded.[18] Exhibit 18 presents forecasts of interest and exchange rates through 1991.

STOCK PRICE

Some of the pressure that management felt in November 1990 was attributable to UT's sagging stock price. The price had reached $46 per share the preceding spring, but then, on July 17, it dropped 10 points in response to an unexpectedly poor earnings report. Exhibit 19 illustrates that the dramatic change in market valuation was not directly attributable to general marketwide movements, although the trend in the broad market indexes was negative from early August. Both MCI and AT&T experienced a slump in stock price of about a third over the same period, which suggested that industry factors were driving the downward revaluation of stock prices.

Exhibit 20 provides a detailed profile of the stock market and pricing of UT stock in mid-November 1990. At a trading price of $22.50 per share, the stock had a price/earnings (P/E) ratio of 14 times, about equivalent to that of AT&T (13✕) and the broader market indexes. Only MCI, with a P/E ratio of 20 times, stood out. UT's dividend yield of 4.7 percent slightly exceeded the telecommunications industry average of 4.3 percent.

Analysts were divided on whether UT's stock was fairly valued in the low $20s. The following table summarizes recent assessments of UT's stock price by prominent securities analysts.

---

[17]H. Erich Heinemann, "Free Fall," *CreditWeek,* Standard & Poor's Corporation, November 26, 1990.

[18]Evelina Tainer, "Economic Outlook," *First Forecasts,* The First National Bank of Chicago, November 15, 1990.

Analyst	Recommendation	Value of Local Telephone Operations	Value of Sprint	Value of UT
Edward Greenberg, Morgan Stanley, August 8, 1990	Buy	$18–$24	$21–$23	$39–$47
Joel Gross, Donaldson, Lufkin & Jenrette, October 15, 1990	Buy	NAv	$10+	$35–$45 (Min. $32)
Jack Grubman, Paine Webber, September 17, 1990	"Attractive"	$20	$15	$35
C. W. Shelke, Smith, Barney, July 24, 1990	Buy	$23	$7	$30
R. L. Altman, Altman, Brenner & Wasserman, August 30, 1990	Sell	NAv	NAv	Max. $23
K. M. Leon, Bear Stearns, July 20, 1990	Drops "buy" recommendation	NAv	NAv	NAv

Some analysts believed a stock price in the low $20s was virtually the value of the local-telephone segment *alone* and gave no regard to any value in Sprint. One analyst observed that, at a stock price in the low $20s, Sprint was valued at 17 percent of sales, 1.4 times cash flow, and 40 percent of book value or 4 times earnings.[19] Whatever the view, UT seemed to be a focus for strong feeling, as suggested by the following comments:

> The intense emotion surrounding United Telecom has driven the stock price down to levels bearing no relationship to underlying value—regardless of the perceived quality of management.[20]
> . . . We believe that the stock selling at current levels represents an excellent opportunity to raise cash. Given present macro- and microeconomic factors, the probabilities of US Sprint turning around . . . are very small, and US Sprint must work for United Telecommunications to be attractive. The question which remains now is whether US Sprint will ever be financially viable.[21]

---

[19]Jack Grubman, "United Telecom: Doing the Right Things—Finally," *Company Report,* PaineWebber, Inc., September 17, 1990.

[20]Edward M. Greenberg, "United Telecom: Resisting Emotion," *Morgan Stanley Investment Research,* August 8, 1990.

[21]R. L. Altman, "United Telecommunications—Company Report," Altman, Brenner & Wasserman, Inc., August 30, 1990.

Sprint was indeed the focus of both optimism and disdain, as illustrated in the following table, which summarizes Edward Greenberg's discounted-cash-flow analysis of the Sprint and non-Sprint segments of UT.[22]

	US Sprint	Non-Sprint Businesses
Discount rate	15.08%	14%
Perpetual growth rate	7.0%	5%
Cash flow ($ millions)		
1990E	113	208
1991E	302	311
1992E	434	385
1993E	561	444
1994E	592	497
1995E	583	531
1996E	611	573
Terminal value ($ millions)	7,132.8	7,593.6
Present value of equity ($ millions)	4,690.3	5,028.7
DCF value per share	**$21.92**	**$23.51**

As apparent in Greenberg's analysis, the key driver of value was the growth rate of Sprint's cash flows over the 1990–96 period: While the non-Sprint cash flows were projected to grow 2.75 times, the Sprint cash flows were projected to grow *5.4 times.* Analyses, such as Greenberg's, rapidly focused investors' eyes on the determinants of Sprint's future cash-flow growth: not only the aggressiveness of capital spending but, more important, the ability to build volume throughput in what was a largely completed network. Because of the economics of high operating leverage, small increases in volume would create proportionally large increases in operating profits. In short, any assessment of Sprint's value was a bet on UT's ability to seize and defend market share.

CONCLUSION

The financing issues facing UT's senior management in November 1990 could be summarized in a few questions: To what extent was UT's corporate financing policy an *instrument* of its corporate vision and competitive strategy? If financing difficulties were allowed to constrain investment or operations, the company might not survive the growing competitive battle. All observers noted that Esrey's vision for UT was expansive: He was not a caretaker.

---

[22]Greenberg's results are reproduced as published in his report, "United Telecom: Resisting Emotion," *Morgan Stanley Investment Research,* August 8, 1990. The exact conclusions of his analysis cannot be reproduced with a handheld calculator, although the qualitative conclusions remain the same. Greenberg probably omitted presenting other assumptions that affect the exact results.

Did a financing policy exist that would assist the creation of both shareholder wealth and competitive advantage? What changes, if any, were required in the current policy? In considering alternative policies, where were the key tradeoffs? What actions taken today would create or foreclose financing options in the future? On what timetable should any policy changes and financing tactics be implemented? Specifically, how should the firm externally raise $1.6 billion in new capital in the next 18 months?

EXHIBIT 1   Consolidated Statements of Income ($ millions)

	1989	1988
Net operating revenues		
Long-distance communications	$4,323.6	$3,405.4
Local communications	2,637.0	2,509.7
Complementary businesses	762.1	698.6
Intercompany revenues	(173.7)	(120.7)
Total net operating revenues	7,549.0	6,493.0
Operating expenses		
Long-distance	4,097.0	3,791.5
Local	2,001.3	1,912.9
Complementary	714.4	656.5
Intercompany	(173.7)	(120.7)
Total operating expenses	6,639.0	6,240.2
Operating income	910.0	252.8
Other (income) expense, net	(11.5)	7.1
Interest charges, net of capitalization	359.8	320.4
Minority interest in Sprint	33.4	(223.4)
Income (loss) from continuing operations before income taxes	528.3	148.7
Income tax provision (benefit)	165.4	6.9
Discontinued operations	0.0	367.1
Net income (loss)	362.9	508.9
Preferred stock dividends	3.0	3.3
Earnings applicable to common stock	$ 359.9	$ 506.6
Earnings (loss) per share		
From continuing operations	$ 1.72	$ 0.68
From discontinued operations		1.80
Total	$ 1.72	$ 2.48
Weighted-average number of common shares outstanding	209.1	204.4

Source: UT's 1989 annual report.

EXHIBIT 2 Consolidated Balance Sheets ($ millions)

	1989	*1988*
Assets		
Cash and temporary investments	114.8	617.1
Accounts receivable	998.7	850.3
Notes receivable	84.4	330.6
Inventories	124.7	131.3
Deferred income taxes	33.5	44.7
Prepayments	153.1	151.0
Total current assets	1,509.2	2,125.0
Property, plant, and equipment		
Long-distance communications services	4,281.4	3,493.0
Local communications services	7,213.9	6,900.8
Complementary and other	259.6	275.4
Less: accumulated depreciation	(3,870.0)	(3,339.4)
Net property, plant, and equipment	7,884.9	7,329.8
Intangible assets, net of amortization	122.4	124.3
Other assets	304.8	237.8
Total assets	9,821.3	9,816.9
Liabilities and shareholders' equity		
Current maturities of long-term debt	384.3	148.5
Accounts payable	738.7	716.9
Accrued local interconnection and leases	318.5	292.1
Advance billings	67.5	63.3
Accrued taxes	237.9	313.2
Accrued interest	107.0	100.8
Other	424.9	514.1
Total current liabilities	2,278.8	2,148.9
Long-term debt	3,747.0	3,674.8
Deferred income taxes	934.2	792.1
Deferred investment tax credits	156.7	188.8
Deferred other credits	126.0	137.3
Minority interest in Sprint	464.8	958.9
Redeemable preferred stock	36.9	38.9
Common stock (250 million shares auth'd)	517.8	256.6
Employees' stock purchase installment	22.3	7.3
Nonredeemable convertible preferred stock	4.0	2.4
Capital in excess of par value	650.0	882.5
Retained earnings	882.8	728.4
Total shareholders' equity	2,076.9	1,877.2
Total liabilities and shareholders' equity	9,821.3	9,816.9

Source: UT's 1989 annual report.

EXHIBIT 3   Comparative Financial Information, 1989

	Net Profit Margin	P/E	Dividend Payout	Beta	Debt Rating	Long-term Debt to Capital	ROE
United Telecom	4.8%	17.2×	56.4%	.95*	A2/P3 BBB/Baa3 (Parent) A1/P1 AA, A/A (Locals)	62.0%	17.5%
Long-Distance Competitors							
AT&T	7.6%	12.7×	48.0%	.90	A1/P1 AA/A	39.0%	21.2%
MCI	9.7%	14.0×	4.0%	1.15	A2/P2 BBB/Baa2	52.9%	26.5%
Local Telephone Companies							
Ameritech	12.1%	13.29×	69%	.90		39.7%	16.0%
Bell Atlantic	11.5	16.87	65	.90		47.3	15.3
Bell South	11.9	14.21	71	1.00		35.0	12.7
Nynex	8.6	17.89	74	.90		40.8	12.1
Pacific Telesis	12.9	15.10	61	.95		40.1	15.7
Southwestern Bell	12.5	14.61	71	.95		39.5	13.1
US West	11.5	11.85	61	.95		47.3	13.8
Cincinnati Bell	10.5	13.75	43	.95		38.6	17.4
GTE	8.1	12.44	66	.95		52.8	17.3
Rochester	9.2	14.31	71	.80		44.8	12.7
Southern New England	10.2	10.81×	58	.85		42.2	14.1
Average	10.8%	14.10×	65%	.92		42.6%	14.5%

*UT's sigma (i.e., annualized standard deviation of common-stock returns) was .40.

Sources: *Value Line Investment Survey* and *Standard & Poor's Bond Guide*.

EXHIBIT 4   Map Indicating Market Presence of UT Local Communications Services

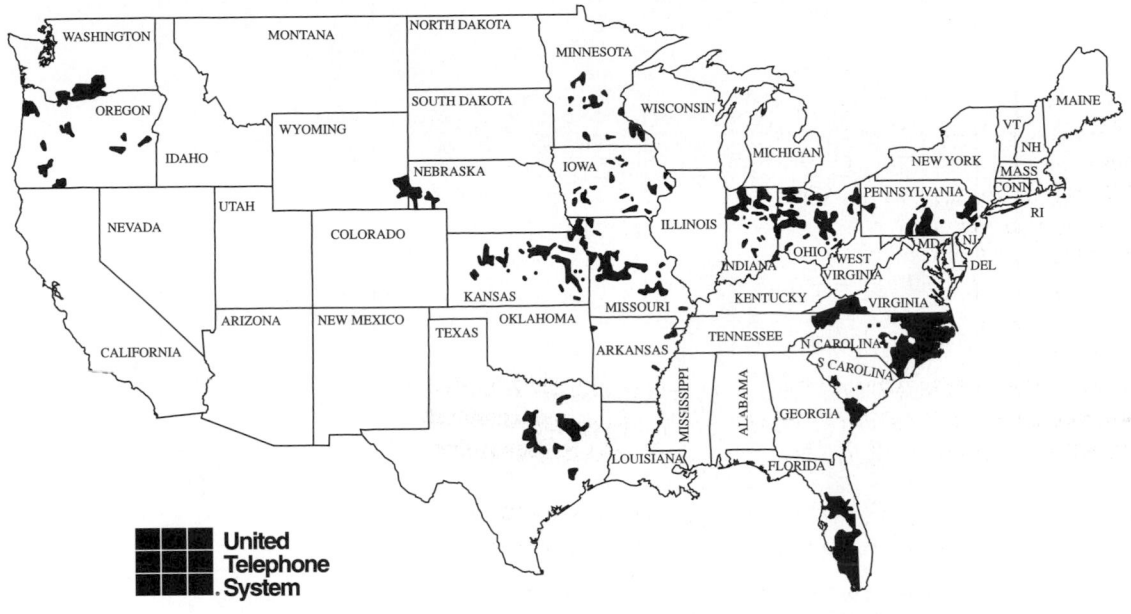

Source: *Moody's Public Utilities Manual*, 1990.

EXHIBIT 5   Comparative Projected Financial Ratios in Long-Distance Telecommunications Industry (projected through 1995)

	AT&T	MCI	UT
Projected annual growth rates			
Revenues	3.5%	15.0%	12.0%
"Cash flow"	5.5	17.5	12.5
Earnings	10.0	21.5	27.0
Dividends	7.0	NMF	9.0
Book value	9.0	30.0	11.5
Expected dividend-payout ratio	47.0%	8.0%	40.0%
Projected LT debt to capital	29.5%	21.8%	52.0%
Projected return on total capital	14.5%	15.0%	22.5%
Projected net profit margin	9.5%	9.0%	7.2%
Projected price/earnings ratio (in 1995)	14×	15×	15×

Source: *Value Line Investment Survey*, 1990.

EXHIBIT 6 Projected Income Statements ($ millions)

	1988	1989	1990e	1991e	1992e	1993e	1994e
1. Revenue: long distance	3,405.0	4,324.0	4,989.9	5,553.8	6,325.7	7,110.1	7,927.8
2. Revenue: local Telcos	2,510.0	2,637.0	2,755.7	2,879.7	3,009.3	3,144.7	3,286.2
3. Revenue: complementary	699.0	762.0	857.3	964.4	1,085.0	1,220.6	1,373.1
4. Total revenue	6,614.0	7,723.0	8,602.8	9,397.8	10,419.9	11,475.4	12,587.1
(Revenues w/o intercompany)							
5. Op. expense: long distance	3,792.0	4,097.0	4,740.4	5,109.5	5,762.7	6,434.7	7,182.6
6. Op. expense: local Telcos	1,912.0	2,001.0	2,066.7	2,159.8	2,256.9	2,358.5	2,464.6
7. Op. expense: complementary	657.0	714.0	801.5	901.7	1,014.4	1,141.2	1,283.9
8. Operating expense	6,361.0	6,812.0	7,608.7	8,170.9	9,034.1	9,934.4	10,931.1
(Op. exp. w/o intercompany)							
9. Gross profit	253.0	911.0	994.1	1,226.9	1,385.8	1,541.0	1,656.0
10. Interest income	(7.0)	11.0	0.0	0.0	0.0	0.0	0.0
11. Total short-term int. exp.	0.0	0.0	42.3	45.3	48.2	44.6	36.6
12. Total int. on sched. debt.	320.4	359.8	315.0	283.3	237.6	195.3	160.6
13. Interest expense: "plug" debt	0.0	0.0	30.8	104.6	154.0	154.0	131.5
14. Total interest expense	327.4	348.8	388.1	433.1	439.7	393.8	328.6
15. Minority interest	(223.0)	34.0	(53.0)	0.0	0.0	0.0	0.0
16. One-time charge (Sprint)	0.0	0.0	72.0	0.0	0.0	0.0	0.0
17. Earnings before taxes	148.6	528.2	587.0	793.8	946.1	1,147.1	1,327.4
18. Provision for income taxes	7.0	165.0	176.2	261.9	312.2	378.5	438.0
19. Earnings from discont'd op.	367.1						
20. Income after taxes	286.0	397.0	357.8	531.8	633.9	768.6	889.3
21. Net income	508.7	363.2	410.8	531.8	633.9	768.6	889.3
22. Dividends	201.0	203.0	213.0	223.0	233.0	243.0	253.0

Source: Casewriter's analysis, consistent with assumptions drawn from leading securities analysts and historical company performance.

EXHIBIT 7 Projected Balance Sheets ($ millions)

	1988	1989	1990e	1991e	1992e	1993e	1994e
Assets							
1. Cash	100.0	115.0	100.0	100.0	100.0	100.0	100.0
2. Marketable securities	517.0	0.0	0.0	0.0	0.0	0.0	0.0
3. Accounts receivable	850.0	999.0	1,104.6	1,200.0	1,322.6	1,449.3	1,582.7
4. Inventories	131.0	125.0	138.2	150.1	165.5	181.3	198.0
5. Notes receivable	331.0	84.0	52.0	52.0	52.0	52.0	52.0
6. Other current assets	196.0	186.0	217.0	248.0	277.0	311.0	349.0
7. Total current assets	2,125.0	1,509.0	1,611.8	1,750.1	1,917.1	2,093.6	2,281.7
8. Gross prop., plant, and equip.	10,669.0	11,755.0	13,255.0	14,755.0	16,105.0	17,455.0	18,805.0
9. Accum. depreciation	3,339.0	3,870.0	4,928.0	6,129.9	7,466.9	8,925.3	10,505.3
10. Net property, plant, and equip.	7,330.0	7,885.0	8,327.0	8,625.1	8,638.1	8,529.7	8,299.7
11. Other intangibles	124.0	122.0	119.0	116.0	113.0	110.0	107.0
12. Other assets	238.0	305.0	317.0	331.0	346.0	362.0	378.0
13. Total assets	9,817.0	9,821.0	10,374.8	10,822.2	11,014.2	11,095.3	11,066.4
Liabilities and shareholders' equity							
14. Accounts payable	717.0	738.0	777.6	813.4	859.4	906.9	956.9
15. Current portion long-term debt	149.0	385.0	478.0	446.0	537.0	373.0	373.0
16. Income taxes payable	313.0	238.0	44.1	65.5	78.1	94.6	109.5
17. Accrued interconnect charges	292.0	318.0	424.1	472.1	537.7	604.4	673.9
18. Advanced billings	63.0	68.0	68.9	72.0	75.2	78.6	82.2
19. Accrued interest	101.0	107.0	118.8	128.1	142.9	145.1	130.0
20. Other current liabilities	514.0	425.0	450.0	475.0	500.0	525.0	525.0
21. Total current liabilities	2,149.0	2,279.0	2,361.5	2,472.0	2,730.3	2,727.6	2,850.4
22. Long-term debt: scheduled	3,675.0	3,747.0	3,269.0	2,823.0	2,286.0	1,913.0	1,540.0
23. Financing need	**0.0**	**0.0**	**628.5**	**1,620.6**	**1,690.4**	**1,621.6**	**1,206.6**
24. Total long-term debt	3,675.0	3,747.0	3,897.5	4,443.6	3,976.4	3,534.6	2,746.6
25. Other deferrals	326.0	282.0	282.0	282.0	282.0	282.0	282.0
26. Deferred income taxes	792.0	934.0	934.0	934.0	934.0	934.0	934.0
27. Minority interest	959.0	465.0	518.0	0.0	0.0	0.0	0.0
28. Total liabilities	7,901.0	7,707.0	7,993.0	8,131.6	7,922.7	7,478.2	6,812.9
29. Common stock and paid-in capital	1,186.0	1,231.0	1,301.0	1,301.0	1,301.0	1,301.0	1,301.0
30. Retained earnings	730.0	883.0	1,080.8	1,389.6	1,790.5	2,316.1	2,952.5
31. Common equity	1,916.0	2,114.0	2,381.8	2,690.6	3,091.5	3,617.1	4,253.5
32. Total liabilities and equity	9,817.0	9,821.0	10,374.8	10,822.2	11,014.2	11,095.3	11,066.4

Source: Casewriter's analysis, consistent with assumptions drawn from leading securities analysts and historical company performance.

EXHIBIT 8 Historical and Projected Financial Ratios

	1988	1989	1990e	1991e	1992e	1993e	1994e
1. Oper. profit margin (P) (%)	3.83	11.80	11.56	13.06	13.30	13.43	13.16
2. Return on sales (%)	7.70	4.70	4.78	5.66	6.08	6.70	7.07
3. Return on equity (%)	26.57	17.17	17.25	19.77	20.50	21.25	20.91
4. Return on assets or inv. (%)	5.06	6.50	5.92	7.56	8.39	9.27	10.00
5. Return on net assets (%)	6.48	8.46	7.66	9.79	11.16	12.29	13.46
6. Debt/equity ratio (%)	199.58	195.46	183.71	181.73	145.99	108.03	73.34
7. Debt/total capital (%)	66.62	66.15	64.75	64.50	59.35	51.93	42.31
8. Equity ratio (%)	19.52	21.53	22.96	24.86	28.07	32.60	38.44
9. Times interest earned (×)	1.92	2.56	2.38	2.83	3.15	3.91	5.04
10. Op. earnings cash int. cvg.	NAv	NAv	2.56	2.83	3.15	3.91	5.04
11. Op. cash flow cash int. cvg.	NAv	NAv	4.14	4.67	5.14	6.28	7.98
12. Days in receivables (avg.)	NAv	43.69	44.63	44.75	44.18	44.08	43.96
13. Days in payables (avg.)	NAv	38.98	36.35	35.53	33.79	32.45	31.12
14. Inventory turnover (avg.)	NAv	53.22	57.82	56.68	57.25	57.30	57.65
15. Fixed asset turnover	NAv	0.98	1.03	1.09	1.21	1.35	1.52
16. Total asset turnover	NAv	0.79	0.83	0.87	0.95	1.03	1.14
17. Days in receivables	46.91	47.21	46.86	46.61	46.33	46.10	45.89
18. Days in payables	41.14	39.54	37.30	36.33	34.72	33.32	31.95
19. Inventory turnover	48.56	54.50	55.06	54.43	54.60	54.80	55.22
20. Quick ratio	0.68	0.49	0.51	0.53	0.52	0.57	0.59
21. Current ratio	0.99	0.66	0.68	0.71	0.70	0.77	0.80
22. Primary earnings per share	4.99	1.72	1.97	2.55	3.05	3.70	4.28
23. Dividends per share	0.95	0.96	1.01	1.06	1.11	1.16	1.21
24. Cash flow per share	NAv	0.81	0.53	2.55	4.42	5.43	6.15
25. Book value per share	18.67	10.21	11.51	13.00	14.94	17.47	20.55
26. Change in EPS (%)	NAv	(65.45)	14.38	29.67	19.30	21.34	15.78
27. Sales growth rate (G) (%)	NAv	16.77	11.39	9.24	10.88	10.13	9.69
28. Inc. fixed cap. inv. (F) (%)	NAv	92.97	50.24	37.49	1.28	(10.28)	(20.68)
29. Inc. work. cap. inv. (W) (%)	NAv	0.63	12.88	(0.52)	(0.03)	1.44	5.87
30. Cash income tax rate (Tc) (%)	NAv	15.17	33.46	33.35	33.32	33.26	33.20

Source: Casewriter's analysis.

EXHIBIT 9   Capitalization and Payout Ratios over Time

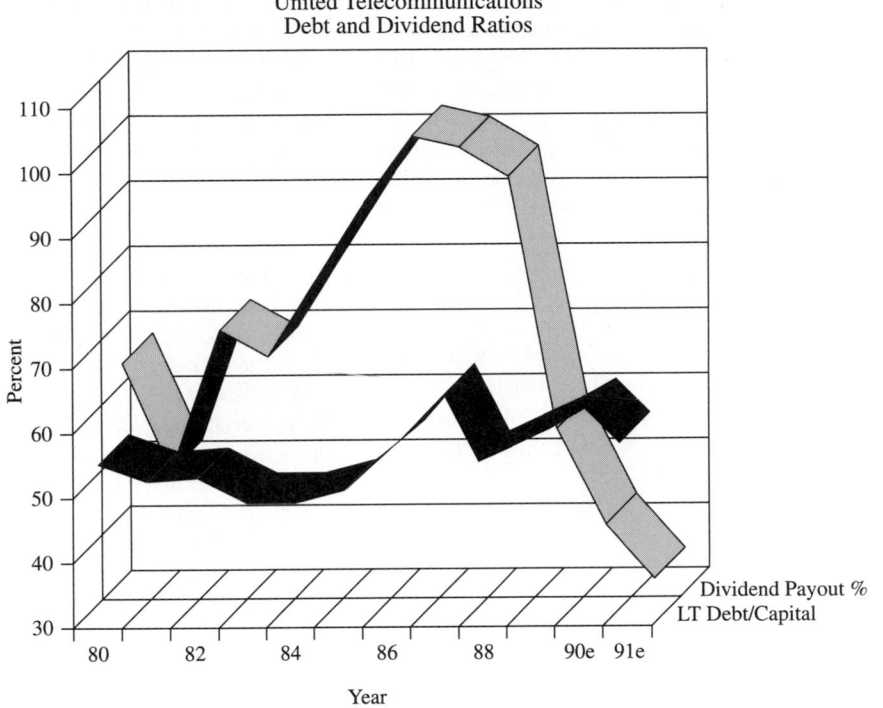

United Telecommunications
Debt and Dividend Ratios

Casewriter's graph. Source of data: *Value Line Investment Survey*, 1990.

EXHIBIT 10   Rating Definitions, Standard & Poor's Corporation

---

A Standard & Poor's corporate or municipal debt rating is a current assessment of the creditworthiness of an obligor with respect to a specific obligation. This assessment may take into consideration obligors such as guarantors, insurers, or lessees.

The debt rating is not a recommendation to purchase, sell, or hold a security, inasmuch as it does not comment as to market price or suitability for particular investor.

The ratings are based on current information furnished by the issuer or obtained by S&P from other sources it considers reliable. S&P does not perform an audit in connection with any rating and may, on occasion, rely on unaudited financial information. The ratings may be changed, suspended, or withdrawn as a result of changes in, or unavailability of, such information, or for other circumstances.

The ratings are based, in varying degrees, on the following considerations:

1. Likelihood of default—capacity and willingness of the obligor as to the timely payment of interest and repayment of principal in accordance with the terms of the obligation;
2. Nature of and provisions of the obligation;
3. Protection afforded by, and relative position of, the obligation in the event of bankruptcy, reorganization, or other arrangement under the laws of bankruptcy and other laws affecting creditors' rights.

Investment grade
AAA   Debt rated 'AAA' has the highest rating assigned by Standard & Poor's. Capacity to pay interest and repay principal is extremely strong.

AA   Debt rated 'AA' has a very strong capacity to pay interest and repay principal and differs from the highest rated issues only in small degree.

A   Debt rated 'A' has a strong capacity to pay interest and repay principal although it is somewhat more susceptible to the adverse effects of changes in circum-

stances and economic conditions than debt in higher rated categories.

BBB   Debt rated 'BBB' is regarded as having an adequate capacity to pay interest and repay principal. Whereas it normally exhibits adequate protection parameters, adverse economic conditions or changing circumstances are more likely to lead to a weakened capacity to pay interest and repay principal for debt in this category than in higher rated categories.

Speculative grade
Debt rated 'BB,' 'B,' 'CCC,' 'CC,' and 'C' is regarded as having predominantly speculative characteristics with respect to capacity to pay interest and repay principal. 'BB' indicates the least degree of speculation and 'C' the highest. While such debt will likely have some quality and protective characteristics, these are outweighed by large uncertainties or major exposures to adverse conditions.

BB   Debt rated 'BB' has less near-term vulnerability to default than other speculative issues. However, it faces major ongoing uncertainties or exposure to adverse business, financial, or economic conditions which could lead to inadequate capacity to meet timely interest and principal payments. The 'BB' rating category is also used for debt subordinated to senior debt that is assigned an actual implied 'BBB−' rating.

B   Debt rated 'B' has a greater vulnerability to default but currently has the capacity to meet interest payments and principal repayments. Adverse business, financial, or economic conditions will likely impair capacity or willingness to pay interest and repay principal. The 'B' rating category is also used for debt subordinated to senior debt that is assigned an actual or implied 'BB' or 'BB−' rating.

CCC   Debt rated 'CCC' has a currently identifiable vulnerability to default, and is dependent upon favorable business, financial, and economic conditions to meet timely payment of interest and repayment of principal. In the event of adverse business, financial, or

---

Source: Standard & Poor's *CreditWeek*.

EXHIBIT 10   *(concluded)*

economic conditions, it is not likely to have the capacity to pay interest and repay principal. The 'CCC' rating category is also used for debt subordinated to senior debt that is assigned an actual or implied 'B' or 'B−' rating.

CC   The rating 'CC' typically is applied to debt subordinated to senior debt that is assigned an actual or implied 'CCC' rating.

C   The rating 'C' typically is applied to debt subordinated to senior debt which is assigned an actual or implied 'CCC−' debt rating. The 'C' rating may be used to cover a situation where a bankruptcy petition has been filed, but debt service payments are continued.

C1   The rating 'C1' is reserved for income bonds on which no interest is being paid.

D   Debt rated 'D' is in payment default. The 'D' rating category is used when interest payments or principal payments are not made on the date due even if the applicable grace period has not expired, unless S&P believes that such payments will be made during such grace period. The 'D' rating also will be used upon the filing of a bankruptcy petition if debt service payments are jeopardized.

Plus (+) or minus (−)   The ratings from 'AA' to 'CCC' may be modified by the addition of a plus or minus sign to show relative standing within the major rating categories.

p   The letter 'p' indicates that the rating is provisional. A provisional rating assumes the successful completion of the project being financed by the debt being rated and indicates that payment of debt service requirements is largely or entirely dependent upon the successful and timely completion of the project. This rating, however, while addressing credit quality subsequent to completion of the project, makes no comment on the likelihood of, or the risk of default upon failure of, such completion. The investor should exercise his own judgment with respect to such likelihood and risk.

i   The letter 'i' indicates the rating is implicit. Such ratings are assigned only to governments that have not requested explicit ratings for specific debt issues, implicit ratings represent the sovereign ceiling or upper limit for ratings on specific debt issues of entities domiciled in the country.

L   The letter 'L' indicates the rating pertains to the principal amount of those bonds to the extent that the underlying deposit collateral is insured by the Federal Savings & Loan Insurance Corp. or the Federal Deposit Insurance Corp. and interest is adequately collateralized. In the case of certificates of deposit, the letter 'L' indicates that the deposit, combined with other deposits being held in the same right and capacity, will be honored for principal and accrued pre-default interest up to the federal insurance limits within 30 days after closing of the insured institution or, in the event that the deposit is assumed by a successor insured institution, upon maturity.

* Continuance of the rating is contingent upon S&P's receipt of an executed copy of the escrow agreement or closing documentation confirming investments and cash flows.

N.R.   Indicates no public rating has been requested, that there is insufficient information on which to base a rating, or that S&P does not rate a particular type of obligation as a matter of policy.

Debt obligations of issuers outside the U.S. and its territories are rated on the same basis as domestic corporate and municipal issues. The ratings measure the creditworthiness of the obligor but do not take into account currency exchange and related uncertainties.

Bond investment quality standards   Under present commercial bank regulations issued by the Comptroller of the Currency, bonds rated in the top four categories ('AAA,' 'AA,' 'A,' 'BBB,' commonly known as "investment grade" ratings) generally are regarded as eligible for bank investment. Also, the laws of various states governing legal investments impose certain rating or other standards for obligations eligible for investment by savings banks, trust companies, insurance companies, and fiduciaries generally.

EXHIBIT 11   S&P Rating of United Telecommunications and Rating Benchmarks

Current Ratings		*Senior Debt History*	
Implied senior debt	—	1989	BBB
Senior secured debt	—	1988	BBB
Senior unsecured debt	BBB	1987	BBB
Subordinated debt	BBB−	1986	BBB
Preferred stock	BBB	1985	BBB
Preference stock	—	1984	BBB+
Commercial paper	A-2	1983	BBB+

Rationale: Credit quality of United Telecommunications Inc. is derived from its very strong and relatively low risk local telephone operations, which make up some 45% of assets, offset by a growing investment in the much riskier long distance carrier US Sprint which amounts to 35% of assets. Outstanding securities total $3.8 billion. Expansion of its share of US Sprint to 80% from 50% in early 1989, and the likelihood that it will ultimately own 100% of the firm, sharply raises business risk. The debt-funded investment results in a weak consolidated financial position. Debt leverage exceeds 60% and pretax interest coverage is in the low to mid-2 times range. Telephone units serve some 3.7 million access lines in 17 states. The mainly rural and suburban properties enjoy strong growth with little bypass risk. They upstream nearly all of the cash necessary to meet United Telecom's interest on $2.5 billion of nontelephone debt and dividend needs that total about $500 million a year. While US Sprint's results seem on the mend, additional external capital may be required in the short run. Ratings anticipate that sufficient cash flow will be generated from US Sprint in nearby years to begin meaningful repayment of the huge debt burden incurred by United Telecom. Ratings may be lowered if US Sprint is not successful in increasing cash flow to levels sufficient to allow meaningful and significant reduction in United Telecom's huge debt load.

Outlook: Negative.

United Telecommunications, Inc., Financial Statistics

	Year ended Dec. 31				
	1989	*1988*	*1987*	*1986*	*1985*
Total capital (bill. $)	6.72	6.71	4.74	4.58	3.85
Short-term debt (%)	5.7	2.2	2.6	1.9	3.4
Long-term debt (%)	55.7	54.8	64.3	58.6	50.6
Preferred stock (%)	0.8	0.8	0.9	1.5	1.9
Common equity (%)	37.8	42.2	32.2	37.9	44.2
Pretax interest coverage (×)	2.33	1.32	1.61	2.24	2.34
Preferred div. coverage (×)	2.30	1.30	1.58	2.12	2.19
Income tax rate (%)	31.3	(5.1)	68.6	21.6	167.1
Ret. on avg. equity (%)	12.6	5.2	N.M.	13.0	10.8
Common div. payout (%)	55.6	140.8	N.M.	101.7	798.1
Net cash flow (NCF) (bill. $)	1.26	0.91	0.25	0.67	0.65
Capital expenditures (Capex) (bill. $)	1.39	1.44	0.70	0.95	1.06
Capex / avg. capital (%)	20.7	25.1	14.9	22.4	27.9
NCF / Capex (%)	91.0	63.4	36.6	70.4	61.3
NCF / avg. capital (%)	18.8	15.9	5.5	15.8	17.1
NCF / long-term debt (%)	34.0	27.1	8.9	28.8	34.3

N.M. = Not meaningful

EXHIBIT 11   *(concluded)*

Financial Benchmarks

Financial benchmarks are guidelines to be used in conjunction with business risk assessments when evaluating credit quality. Local exchange telephone companies are classified as either low-risk or high-risk companies based on S&P's perception of their business risk (*see below*).

	Low-risk	*High-risk*
Total debt/total capital (%)		
AA	Under 47	Under 42
A	45–57	40–52
BBB	55–65	50–62
Pretax interest coverage ($\times$)		
AA	Above 4.0	Above 4.5
A	3.0–4.5	3.5–5.5
BBB	2.3–3.4	2.7–4.0
Net cash flow/average long-term debt (%)		
AA	Above 25	Above 30
A	20–30	25–35
BBB	15–25	20–30

Financial ratios defined

Total debt/total capital—The sum of notes payable and other short-term obligations (including current maturities of long-term debt and capital lease obligations), plus long-term debt (including capital lease obligations), divided by the sum of total capital. Total capital is the sum of all short-term debt, long-term debt, preferred stock (including subsidiary preferred), minority interest, and common equity.

Pretax interest coverage—Income from continuing operations adjusted for nonrecurring items (before taxes), plus minority interest, income taxes, and interest expense, all divided by interest incurred. Capitalized interest is excluded from interest expense but included in interest incurred.

Net cash flow/average long-term debt—Funds from operations (cash flow from operations before working capital changes) less preferred and common dividends paid, divided by average long-term debt.

Source: Standard & Poor's *CreditWeek,* June 4, 1990.

EXHIBIT 12   Long-Term Debt as of December 31, 1989

		Maturing	*Balance ($ millions)*
Corporate			
Senior notes	7.50%	1990	200.0
	8.42 to 9.50%	1991	225.0
	8.10 to 8.25%	1992	215.0
	9.75%	1993	100.0
	8.60 to 9.71%	1994	225.0
	9.40 to 10.45%	1995 to 1997	410.0
Debentures	9.40 to 11.00%	1999 to 2000	52.3
Subordinated debs.	5.00%	1993	2.3
	9.75%	2010	104.9
Subordinated notes	8.90%	1993	200.0
Commercial paper and bank notes	8.33 to 9.13%	1993	193.5
Other	6.13 to 14.63%	1990 to 2007	17.0
Long-Distance Communications Services			
Vendor financing	8.00 to 10.18%	1990 to 2001	405.2
Advances	NAv	NAv	186.8
Other debt	6.41 to 15.00%	1990 to 1993	15.9
Local Communications Services			
First mortgage bonds	4.50 to 7.25%	1990 to 1994	58.6
	2.00 to 11.00%	1995 to 1999	192.0
	5.63 to 12.75%	2000 to 2004	303.0
	4.00 to 10.38%	2005 to 2009	244.0
	7.50 to 13.75%	2010 to 2014	48.7
	8.00 to 14.45%	2015 to 2019	297.6
Debentures	4.35 to 12.00%	1990 to 2016	232.4
Commercial paper and bank notes	9.01 to 10.00%	1993	11.3
Other debt	2.00 to 13.88%	1990 to 2016	17.2
Complementary Businesses			
Senior note	11.70%	2000	40.0
Vendor financing	10.18%	2001	116.9
Other debt	6.20% to 10.70%	1991 to 1993	16.7
Total			4,131.3
Less current maturities			384.3
Total long-term debt, excluding maturities			3,747.0

Source: UT's 1989 annual report.

EXHIBIT 13 Details Regarding Securities Issues Currently Outstanding

---

1. Bank notes payable and commercial paper

Outstanding:	$204,800,000 ($10.9 million of bank notes at 9.62% interest, 42.1 million of master-trust notes at 9.32% interest, and $151.8 million of commercial paper at 9.34% interest)
Agreements:	*Master Trust Note Agreement:* an agreement with the trust division of a bank to borrow funds on demand. The borrowings' rate was set to yield interest equivalent to the most favorable discount rate paid on 180-day commercial paper.
	Agreement in support of commercial paper: two banks provided an $80 million letter of credit and long-term revolving-credit agreement to support commercial paper issued by UT. The agreement was due to expire July 31, 1992.
	Bank commitments: at the end of 1989, UT and its subsidiaries had a total of $984 million of credit available. This included the agreement in support of commercial paper and a $700 million revolving-credit agreement. Total unused lines of credit were $823 million, of which $631 million was available on a long-term basis under the revolver. The 10-Q statement of June 1990 reported that the firm had $750 million of unused borrowing capacity under the most restrictive of its debt covenants.
Key covenants:	UT had to maintain a consolidated tangible net worth of $1.55 billion. At December 31, 1989, $610 million of United's retained earnings was restricted from payment of dividends. Subsidiary financing agreements restricted the payment of dividends to UT (parent): At December 31, 1989, $709 million of the related subsidiaries' $1.4 billion total retained earnings was restricted. The flow of cash, in the form of advances between UT and its subsidiaries, was not restricted.
Agent bank:	Chase Manhattan N.A.

2. United Telecommunications, Inc., sinking-fund debenture 9.40% notes due 1999

Outstanding:	$24,839,000
Rated:	Baa3
Issue date:	April 15, 1974
Maturity date:	April 15, 1999
Callability:	Yes, at various premiums (102% in 1991 falling to 100% in 1994).
Sinking fund:	Yes, between $5 and $2.5 million annually. Designed to retire 90 percent of the issue before maturity.
Security:	Not secured.
Key covenants:	Limits asset dispositions and dividends.
Listed:	New York Stock Exchange
Lead manager of offering:	Kidder Peabody
Trustee:	Irving Trust Co.

3. United Telecommunications, Inc., sinking-fund debenture 11% notes due 2000

Outstanding:	$22,500,000
Rated:	Baa3
Issue date:	April 15, 1975
Maturity date:	April 15, 2000
Callability:	Yes, at various premiums (2.75% in 1991 falling to 100% in 1995).
Sinking fund:	Yes, between $5 and $2.5 million annually. Designed to retire 95 percent of the issue before maturity.
Key covenants:	Certain limitation on creation of additional debt.
Listed:	New York Stock Exchange

EXHIBIT 13   *(continued)*

Lead manager
   of offering: Kidder Peabody
Trustee: Irving Trust Co.

4. United Telecommunications, Inc., 8.25% notes due 1992
   Outstanding: $200,000,000
   Rated: Baa3
   Issue date: April 1, 1986
   Maturity date: August 15, 1992
   Callability: Not callable
   Security: Not secured
   Sinking fund: None
   Lead manager
      of offering: Kidder Peabody

5. United Telecommunications, Inc., 9.75% notes due 2000
   Outstanding: $250,000,000
   Rated: Baa3
   Issue date: April 1, 1990
   Maturity date: April 1, 2000
   Callability: Not callable
   Security: Not secured
   Sinking fund: None
   Lead managers
      of offering: Dillon Read, Goldman Sachs, and Smith Barney

6. United Telecommunications, Inc., convertible subordinated debenture 5% notes due 1993
   Outstanding: $2,242,000
   Issue date: April 1, 1968 ($50 million offered)
   Maturity date: April 1, 1993
   Rated: Ba1
   Callability: Yes
   Convertibility: Yes; into 162,854 shares at $14 per share
   Sinking fund: Yes, $2.5 million per year. Designed to retire 70 percent of the issue before maturity.
   Listed: New York Stock Exchange
   Lead manager
      of offering: Kidder Peabody

7. United Telecommunications, Inc., subordinated exchangeable debenture 9.75% notes due 2010
   Outstanding: $104,880,000
   Issue date: September 1, 1985
   Maturity date: September 1, 2010
   Rated: Ba1
   Callability: Yes, at premiums ranging from 104.9% in 1991 to 100% in 1995.
   Sinking fund: Yes, $7 million per year. Designed to retire 70 percent of the issue before maturity.
   Exchange rights: Exchangeable at the option of UT for 4,248,330 common shares of Southern New England Telephone Company (SNET), acquired at a cost of $63 million (market value of $191 million at Dec. 31, 1989).* UT may, at its option, pay cash in an amount equal to the market value of the SNET common stock in lieu of exchanging the SNET stock.
   Listed: New York Stock Exchange
   Lead managers
      of offering: Dillon Read and Kidder Peabody

EXHIBIT 13   *(concluded)*

8. United Telecommunications, Inc., other debt unspecified
   Parent company
      debt outstanding: $1,191,602,000
   Subsidiary long-
      term debt outstanding: $2,200,937,000 (consisting mainly of mortgages and leases)

9. United Telecommunications, Inc., convertible preferred stock (two series)
Outstanding:	625 thousand shares
Issue date:	1968, 1969
Maturity date:	Perpetual
Callability:	None
Sinking fund:	None
Listed:	New York Stock Exchange
Dividend:	$1.50 per share, first series. $1.25 per share, second series.
Conversion:	Each share first series convertible into 3 shares of common stock. Each share second series convertible into 2 shares of common stock.

10. United Telecommunications, Inc., 7.75% redeemable preferred stock
Outstanding:	25.6 thousand shares
Maturity:	2007
Callability:	Yes, at premiums from 103.33% in 1991, declining to 100% in 2003
Sinking fund:	Yes, to redeem 12,000 shares annually, or $1.2 million per year

11. United Telecommunications, Inc., common stock
Outstanding:	207,100,810 shares
Issue date:	Offerings in 1967, 1969, 1970, 1971, 1974, 1975, and 1985
Listed:	New York Stock Exchange and Midwest and Pacific Exchanges
Lead managers of offering:	Kidder Peabody sole-managed all issues except in 1985, when it comanaged the issue with First Boston and Shearson, Lehman.
Dividends:	Paid continuously since 1939
Shares under option:	2,882,934 at exercise prices ranging from $8.00 to $39.31. Aggregate exercise amount under these options is $48.3 million.
Poison pill:	Yes, new plan adopted September 8, 1989, due to expire September 8, 1999, on preferred-stock purchase right granted per common share. The right would be exercisable upon the occurrence of certain takeover events and would entitle shareholders to buy participating preferred stock or common stock.

*SNET's stock price in late 1990 varied between $28 and $30 per share. Total shares outstanding were 61,965,025 in late 1990. For the years 1993 to 1995, *Value Line* forecasted a target price range for SNET shares between $35 and $40 per share. SNET's beta was .85 and its sigma (i.e., annualized standard deviation of returns) was .40.

Source: "United Telecommunications, Inc., Details Regarding Issues Currently Outstanding." *Moody's Public Utilities Manual,* 1990.

EXHIBIT 14   Significant Changes in Long-Term Debt Outstandings by Year ($ millions)

	1989	1988	1987	1986
Corporate Debt				
Commercial paper and bank notes				
Classified as long term				
Debt 8.33–9.13%	141.9	(138.6)	123.9	109.0
9.75% senior notes due 1993		100.0		
8.54% senior notes			375.0	
7.5% senior notes due 1990				200.0
8.25% senior notes due 1992				200.0
Other senior notes				150.0
Subordinated notes due 1993				200.0
Long-Distance Communications Services				
Vendor financing agreements 8–10.18%*	83.9	321.3		286.0
Minority interest advances†	16.3	170.5		
Other debt		13.1		126.5
Local Communications Services				
First mortgage bonds	164.9	(23.0)	(27.0)	(17.0)
Commercial paper	(19.2)	(32.2)	17.6	45.0
Carolina Tel. & Tel. 9% due 2016				50.0
United Tel. of Fla. 9.25% due 2016				60.0
United Tel. of Fla. 9.875% due 2017			65.0	

*GTE had guaranteed $144 million of US Sprint's borrowings at December 31, 1989.
†Advances by GTE to US Sprint under the joint venture agreement. The remaining portion of these advances is due to be repaid in 1999. The average interest rates on advances from GTE were 9.1 and 8.9 percent for 1989 and 1988.

Source: UT's 1990 annual report.

EXHIBIT 15   Maturities of Long-Term Debt and Minimum Payments under Operating Leases ($ millions)

Year	Debt Maturities	Payments for Operating Leases
1990	384.3	213.3
1991	478.3	164.9
1992	445.9	111.4
1993	537.2	52.7
1994	373.3	38.9
Thereafter		114.4

Source: UT's 1989 annual report.

EXHIBIT 16   Profile of Equity Ownership as of September 30, 1990

	UT	*AT&T*	*MCI*
Institutional ownership (percentage of total shares outstanding)			
Mutual funds	8%	1%	10%
Investment advisers	35	12	43
Commercial banks	17	8	12
Insurance companies	6	2	4
Total	66%	23%	69%
Number of institutional holders			
Mutual funds	109	105	167
Investment advisers	210	291	231
Commercial banks	133	211	119
Insurance companies	22	38	22
Total	474	645	539
Percentage insider equity ownership	Insignificant	Insignificant	2%
Average dollar amount owned by an investor	$66,346	$12,810	$83,944
Number of stockholders	74,700	2,600,000	61,250
Total shares outstanding (000) (September 30, 1990)	214,328	1,089,111	252,878
Other significant equity positions (shares held)	Lehman (5.5m)	Wells Fargo (16.4m)	Wells Fargo (4.4m)
	Prudential (4.5m)	CREF (11.3m)	Bankers Trust (4.1m)
	Eagle (3.5m)	NYState (8.3)	Michigan State (3.4m)
	Wells Fargo (3.3m)	CalPERs (6.9m)	Loo, Inc. (3.2m)
	CREF (3m)	U of Cal (6.2m)	NY State (2.9m)
	JP Morgan (3m)	Barrow (5.5m)	Miller (2.9m)
Special equity positions			IBM owns 100% of the outstanding preferred stock and controls 9.8% of votes.

The *percentage* figures cited are not necessarily exact. There is most likely some duplication of shares owned due to the multiple funds, advisers, and sometimes banks and insurance companies *all* having to file ownership reports with the SEC.

Source: William O'Neil + Co., Incorporated. Los Angeles, CA.

EXHIBIT 17   Current Capital Market Rates and Yields, November 19, 1990

U.S. Treasury Securities		*Corporate Bond Yields*		
		Rating Category	*Industrials*	*Utilities*
1 month	6.46%	AAA	9.35%	—
2 months	6.59	AA	9.68	9.70%
3 months	6.98	A	10.11	9.88
6 months	7.27	BBB	11.36	10.14%
1 year	7.30	BB	13.51	—
2 years	7.56	B	19.85%	—
3 years	7.97			
4 years	8.08			
5 years	8.18			
10 years	8.39			
20 years	8.62			
30 years	8.44%			

Other Interest Rates	
Commercial paper	
30–89 days	7.75%
90–119 days	7.67
120–270 days	7.45
LIBOR	
3 months	8.125
6 months	8.0
12 months	8.0
Bank prime rates	
United States	10.0
Germany	10.5
Japan	8.0
Switzerland	10.5
United Kingdom	14.0%

Source: Reprinted by permission of *The Wall Street Journal,* © 1990 Dow Jones & Company, Inc. All Rights Reserved Worldwide.

EXHIBIT 18   Forecasts of Interest Rates and Foreign Exchange Rates

	1990	*1991*	*1991*	*1991*	*1991*
Quarter	IV	I	II	III	IV
Economic Forecast (% change in data)					
Real gross national product	−0.7	−0.9	1.3	3.2	2.7
Consumer price index	10.0	9.0	−1.6	2.4	4.1
After-tax profits (annualized)	18.5	10.6	−3.3	−16.2	−18.1
Interest-Rate Forecast					
Federal funds	7.75%	6.875%	6.75%	6.75%	6.875%
90-day Treasury bill	6.875	6.125	5.875	5.875	6.25
30-year Treasury bond	8.875	8.75	8.375	8.50	8.75
Corporate base rate	9.75%	8.875%	8.625%	8.50%	8.875%
Foreign-Exchange-Rate Forecast					
Yen/dollar	127	123	122	125	127
DM/dollar	1.51	1.47	1.45	1.49	1.51

Source: *First Forecasts,* First National Bank of Chicago, November 15, 1990.

EXHIBIT 19   Stock Prices, April through September 1990

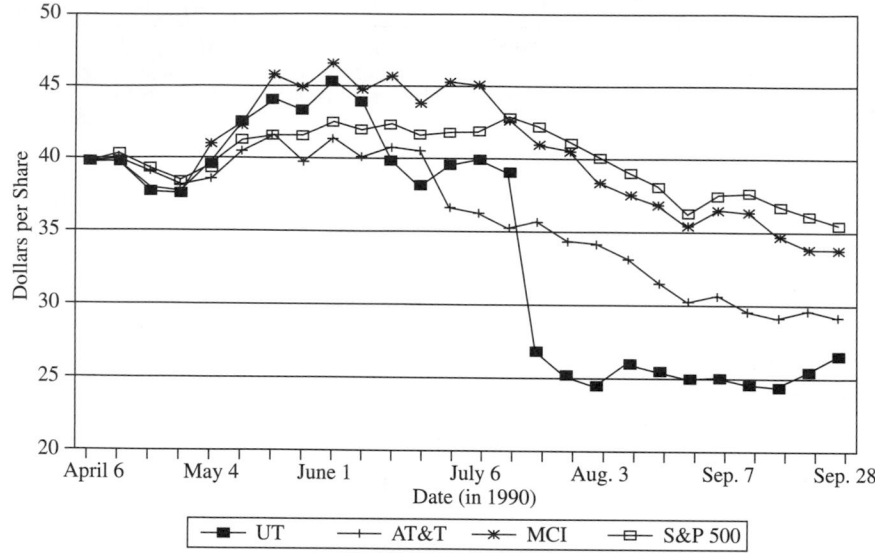

Note: Prices for AT&T, MCI, and the S&P 500 index have been indexed to the price of UT's stock on April 6, 1990. The UT time series reflects the actual prices for UT stock.

EXHIBIT 20   Stock Prices and Indexes as of November 19, 1990

	Price	P/E	Dividend Yield	Earnings Yield	Market-to-Book
United Telecommunications	$22.50	14×	4.7%		
MCI Communications	22.625	20	0.5		
AT&T	$32.00	13	4.8		
Dow Jones industrial average		13.1	4.01	7.51%	199.83%
Dow Jones utilities average		13.9	6.82	7.17	134.63
S&P 500 index		14.6×	3.88%	6.84%	215.35%

Case 53
_____

Rhône-Poulenc S.A.

_____

Rhône-Poulenc is strategically committed to ranking, in each of its businesses, among the world's five leading chemical groups and the 10 largest pharmaceutical companies. By implementing this strategy, the Group is pursuing three key business objectives: achieve an operating margin of 15 percent, generate a 15 percent return on invested capital, and ensure average per share earnings growth of 15 percent per year.

Rhône-Poulenc annual report, 1990

[These objectives will be achieved] by globalizing a strategically related base of high value-added businesses with little cyclical exposure . . . In recent years, these goals have led Rhône-Poulenc to acquire a number of companies and operations to reach critical mass and strengthen its positions in the global marketplace. At the same time, it has refocused on its mainstream businesses and divested underperforming or nonstrategic assets in ways that achieved optimum results for the people and businesses involved.

Rhône-Poulenc press release, 1990

The globalization of competition has gradually whittled down the number of market contenders in each of our business areas. Worldwide critical mass is thus indispensable to amortize the rising R&D costs, increasing capital expenditures, and higher marketing outlays required by accelerated technological developments and tougher standards in quality, safety, and environmental protection.

Chairman Jean-René Fourtou, 1989 annual report

_____

This case study was prepared by Robert F. Bruner from public information as the basis for classroom discussion while the author was a visiting professor at INSEAD, Fontainebleau, France. Copyright © 1991 by the University of Virginia Darden School Foundation, Charlottesville, VA. All rights reserved. *No part of this publication may be reproduced, stored in a retrieval system, used in a spreadsheet, or transmitted in any form or by any means—electronic, mechanical, photocopying, recording, or otherwise—without the permission of the Darden Foundation. For inquiries, please send an e-mail to dardencases@virginia.edu.* Revised 6/98. Version 1.6.

In September 1991, Rhône-Poulenc's corporate vision of high performance and growth to world-class standing faced its stiffest test. Year-to-date performance of the firm had fallen to a third of the firm's peak performance in 1989. Investment opinion was divided on the appropriateness of the firm's current share price of (French francs) FF427; some believed the price was low and that shares should be bought aggressively; others were cautious. The pace of technological innovation and industry consolidation commanded rising amounts of capital. One independent estimate suggested that the firm would need as much as FF38 billion of new external funds over the next five years, but where this capital was to be obtained was unclear. The firm was more heavily indebted than its competitors and had apparently saturated investor demand for its nonvoting equity. In addition, the French government, owner of all the firm's voting common stock, was fighting a large budget deficit and would not provide the needed capital; in fact, many analysts believed Rhône-Poulenc would be privatized within the next three years.

Were the firm's strategic and financial policies appropriate? If not, what action should management take? What would be the impact of those actions on both symptomatic problems in the short run and on deeper challenges in the long run? How should the firm's large requirement for external capital be met?

THE CHEMICALS INDUSTRY

Rhône-Poulenc's historical field of competition, the worldwide chemicals industry, was highly competitive and dominated by several large multinational corporations. The following table lists the 14 largest firms, ranked on the basis of 1990 revenues (U.S. dollars):

Company	Country (Headquarters)	Revenues ($ Millions)	Profits ($ Millions)	Number of Employees (Thousands)
Du Pont	United States	40,047	2,310	143.9
BASF Group	Germany	28,856	685	134.1
Hoechst Group	Germany	27,766	927	172.9
Bayer Group	Germany	25,773	1,164	171.0
ICI	United Kingdom	23,034	1,101	132.1
Dow Chemicals	United States	19,773	1,384	62.1
Rhône-Poulenc	**France**	**14,473**	**356**	**91.6**
Ciba-Geigy	Switzerland	14,183	744	94.1
Montedison	Italy	13,971	207	44.6
Akzo	Holland	9,491	364	70.5
Asahi Chemicals	Japan	9,202	302	25.9
Monsanto	United States	8,995	490	41.1
Solvay Group	Belgium	7,638	501	45.7
Union Carbide	United States	7,621	314	37.8

This industry had several distinctive characteristics: (1) pervasiveness in Western economies; (2) high level of international trade and production; (3) the use of capital-intensive, continuous production processes; (4) an oligopolistic competitive structure that tended toward cartels; and (5) high government involvement because of the economic importance of the industry and because of its health and environmental side effects. Although this industry accounted for no more than 3 or 4 percent of gross national product (GNP) in the typical Western country, it had a strategic impact on as much as 40 percent of the economies of those countries. Many macroeconomic and industry-specific forces influenced the financial performance of the worldwide chemicals industry: volatility in upstream commodities prices (especially oil), GNP growth, inflation, technological innovation, merger and consolidation among competitors,[1] and changing attitudes toward safety and pollution.

Observers characterized the industry as having two main segments, commodity chemicals (having relatively low margins and highly cyclical demand) and specialty chemicals (with higher margins, and less cyclical demand). Over the past 10 years, almost all the major competitors in this industry had dramatically restructured their commodity chemicals segments in pursuit of higher margins and had emphasized investment in the specialty chemicals segment. Ironically, in the late 1980s, the commodity segment actually performed better for most of these firms, because of the restructuring, than did the specialty sector. Even more ironic was the fact that the specialty sector, which was supposed to be the relatively less cyclical, suffered as badly in the recession of 1990–91 as did the commodity-chemicals sector.

THE COMPANY

At the beginning of 1991, Rhône-Poulenc ("the Group" or RP) was probably the seventh largest competitor in the worldwide chemicals industry, with 1990 sales of FF78 billion (about U.S.$15 billion). It had attained this scale through an aggressive program of acquisition and restructuring and now contained five major sectors: health products (e.g., human and animal pharmaceuticals); agrochemicals (e.g., insecticides and herbicides); organic and inorganic intermediates (i.e., chemicals used in the production of other products); fibers and polymers (e.g., nylon yarn); and specialty chemicals (e.g., surfactants). Exhibit 1 presents a breakdown of sales, operating margin, assets, and capital spending by sector.

In 1991, analysts expected about half the firm's sales and profits to come from health products because of rapid internal growth and acquisitions in pharmaceuticals and because of a severe slump in the firm's four other chemicals-related business sectors. The pharmaceuticals sector had optimistic prospects for growth and profits; the large uncertainty in the firm's future stemmed from its chemicals components.

---

[1]The industry leaders were not immune to hostile-takeover threats. In May 1991, Hanson Trust, a well-known corporate raider, announced that it had acquired 2.8 percent of the shares of Imperial Chemicals of the United Kingdom. By September, ICI had undertaken a restructuring in an effort to evade Hanson, but as of the time of this case, Hanson had not withdrawn.

SENIOR MANAGEMENT

Outside analysts characterized the senior management of Rhône-Poulenc as relatively young, ambitious, and bright. None of the top seven executives was older than 53. The presidents of the chemicals and agro sectors had doctorates in chemical engineering. Two other sector presidents (specialty chemicals and health) had master's degrees in business and economics. Most of the sector presidents had served with the company for the bulk of their careers.

Jean-René Fourtou, chairman of the Group, was 51 years old. After graduating from Ecole Polytechnique,[2] he began his career as a consultant in 1963 with Groupe Bossard, a leading French general-management consulting firm. Nine years later, he rose to *directeur-général* and, during 1979–86, was *président* and *directeur-général* of Bossard. Exhibit 2 gives a summary of Fourtou's business approach written by him when he was president of Bossard. In 1986, Fourtou was appointed *président* and *directeur-général* of Rhône-Poulenc, at a time when that company had sustained a decline in both its earnings and sales. As of September 1991, he served on the boards of directors of IBM France and Société Générale, the third largest bank in France. Fourtou cited his membership in the Racing Club de France as his major pastime.

RP's chief financial officer was Jean-Pierre Tirouflet, age 41. After studying economics and politics in college and graduate school,[3] he worked for the French government for eight years. By 1991, he had served with Rhône-Poulenc for nine years. Outside observers regarded Tirouflet's corporate finance group to be one of the sharpest and most innovative in Europe. The group had pioneered the design of several varieties of nonvoting equity securities and of unusual acquisition terms.

STRATEGY

Management pursued RP's goals (see quotations at the beginning of this case) with a five-point strategy calling for "rigorous management," competitive research and development, a high level of capital expenditures (at 9 percent of sales), the use of acquisitions to seize shares of market, and improvements in the qualifications and teamwork of employees. In early 1991, management declared its intention of reducing the firm's debt/equity ratio from 0.9 × at the end of 1990 to 0.5 × by the end of 1993, selling about FF8 billion of nonstrategic assets by the end of 1992, and laying the groundwork for partial privatization by 1994.[4]

Management's concern over cyclicality had spurred a heavy investment in life sciences, a sector that was less capital intensive and less cyclical than basic chemicals, or even than the French and U.S. economies. The company maintained,

---

[2]Ecole Polytechnique, widely regarded as the elite institution of higher education in France, dominated in the ranks of corporate and government leaders in France.

[3]Tirouflet's degrees included the Diplôme de L'Institute d'Etudes Politiques de Paris and the Diplôme d'Etudes Supérieurs de Sciences Economiques.

[4]S. Bridges, "Rhône-Poulenc Company Report," Merrill Lynch Capital Markets, July 10, 1991.

When [the Life Sciences sector is] combined with the Group's other strategic family—composed of the organic and inorganic intermediates, the high-value-added specialty chemicals, and the fibers and polymers sectors—they create a closely related group of highly integrated industrial companies, capable of weathering the cyclical fluctuations in a particular area.[5]

The strategy also sought to broaden the geographical base. Before 1982 the company was highly dependent on operations in two countries, France and Brazil. Because of recent acquisitions, the Group in 1991 generated nearly 25 percent of its revenue from the United States and had strengthened its presence in Europe and Asia, thereby reducing the influence of Brazil. Exhibit 3 summarizes the firm's financial performance by region.

The assessment by outside analysts of management's unfolding strategy was at best mixed. One journalist described Fourtou's program as trying to "turn a perennial loser into a global giant."[6] One securities analyst opined that the sales and market-share goals of the company seemed inconsistent with programs of asset sales and debt reduction; in all likelihood, the goals would be gained only by continued aggressive acquisition.[7]

GOVERNMENT OWNERSHIP AND POLICY TOWARD RHÔNE-POULENC

The French government controlled 100 percent of the shareholder voting rights in the Group. Capital stock was divided into common stock class A (held entirely by the French government) and class B, which was divided into nonvoting investment certificates (CIPs) and voting certificates; the French government also held the voting certificates. The general public held the CIPs and could trade them on the Paris Bourse and the New York Stock Exchange (NYSE). On December 31, 1990, the book value of capital stock consisted of the following:

Common shares, class A		79.4%
French government	56.9%	
Crédit Lyonnais (state owned)	9.4%	
Assurances Générales		
de France (state owned)	6.8%	
Other, state owned	6.3%	
Preferred investment certificates (CIPs), class B		20.6%

The French government nationalized Rhône-Poulenc (along with other large firms) on February 11, 1982, and in doing so snatched the firm nearly from the jaws of bankruptcy. François Mitterrand had been elected President of France, and the Socialist Party swept into power in May 1981 after 23 years of dominance of national politics by the political Right. Between 1981 and 1985, the combined losses of the French state-owned enterprises grew by FF90.8 billion. These enterprises badly needed restructuring, but the national budget could not afford the heavy investment. The election of an opposition majority (the

---

[5]1990 annual report, Rhône-Poulenc, p. 7.
[6]S. Siwolop, "Rhône-Poulenc: Gallic Grandeur," *Financial World,* July 24, 1990, pp. 23–25.
[7]Bridges, "Rhône-Poulenc Company Report."

"Right") to the National Assembly in 1986 prompted legislation providing for the privatization of 60 state-owned enterprises. Public stock offerings privatized a number of prominent firms, but the stock-market crash in 1987 and the return to power of the Socialists in 1988 arrested the privatization program.

The French government had intervened directly and indirectly in the French chemicals industry since the 1920s in pursuit of, often conflicting, goals to (1) achieve national self-sufficiency in chemicals, (2) strengthen French firms' abilities to compete in world markets (i.e., create "national champions"), (3) (re)industrialize France, (4) control the internationalization of the French economy, (5) reduce unemployment, and (6) diversify the industrial base of the country. The Socialist Party program contained an explicit industrial policy that divided all chemicals production among three major enterprises: Atochem in base chemicals and plastics, CdF Chimie in petrochemicals and fertilizers, and Rhône-Poulenc in specialty areas such as pharmaceuticals, agrochemicals, fine chemicals, and synthetic fibers.

The government's ninth five-year plan (1984–88) specifically identified fine chemicals and pharmaceuticals as strategic focuses for investment and expansion. It also identified the need to convert production away from basic chemicals, in which competition was intense.

In pursuit of national policies, French state-owned enterprises had been active buyers of foreign businesses since the late 1980s. One journalist commented:

> France's state-owned industry today bears a passing resemblance to a large drifting jellyfish. It constantly changes shape in response to the currents around it, sometimes shedding bits of itself and sometimes stretching out a tentacle to scoop up a tasty corporate morsel that drifts by.[8]

From 1988 to 1990, Rhône-Poulenc had made eight major acquisitions and many small ones and had executed major programs to divest operations in the media and textiles sectors. The most notable acquisition was the purchase of Rorer Group, Inc., in 1990, because of both its size and its novel terms. The acquisition dramatically increased the scale of RP's pharmaceuticals business, raising sector 1989 sales by 34 percent to U.S.$3.1 billion. Part of the acquisition terms called for Rhône-Poulenc to make up any shortfall in Rhône-Poulenc Rorer's (R-P Rorer) stock price should it fall below a specified level by 1993. The Group estimated that, at the end of 1990, the maximum liability under these contingent value rights (CVRs) was FF4.96 billion. Exhibit 4 gives details on the CVRs. Fourtou said that this acquisition would be Rhône-Poulenc's last big one for some time and that the company planned more than a dozen sales of assets to pay the acquisition costs.

On September 11, 1991, Mitterrand announced that he had authorized the government to sell off minority stakes in state-owned companies, but he insisted that the state would remain the majority shareholder (with 50.1 percent of voting rights) wherever it held a majority. He justified this change in policy on the grounds that many state firms needed fresh capital to cut their crippling levels of debt, that other sources of finance for nationalized companies were drying up, and that the move would improve relationships with the European Commission in Brussels, which opposed state aid to industry. Many observers cited Rhône-Poulenc as a likely candidate for partial privatization. The timing and amount

---

[8]William Dawkins, "Breakdown of the Old Frontiers," *Financial Times,* July 23, 1991.

of privatization were, however, uncertain. Analysts speculated that full privatization was likely after the next French legislative elections in 1993, when the Socialist Party could lose its legislative majority. If the French government were to privatize the company, the government would sell off both its own (voting) shares and voting rights to accompany the nonvoting common stock.

Because of competing budgetary demands, the French government was unwilling to make additional cash investments in the common stock of the company, but indirectly the government supported the company's need for equity infusions. First, in 1989 the government exchanged a 35 percent interest in a diversified pharmaceuticals company, Roussel-UCLAF,[9] in return for new shares of Rhône-Poulenc common stock. This move increased the company's equity base and permitted additional borrowings.

Second, the government encouraged the company to innovate in issuing quasi-equity securities (i.e., securities that would represent pecuniary equity interests in the company but would not dilute the government's voting control). These exotic securities had the qualities of both debt and equity, a characteristic pioneered by Rhône-Poulenc. Examples included participating preferred stock, called *titres participatifs* (for which the dividend varied in relation to the firm's performance), warrants on the participating preferred stock, issuance of the participating preferred to American investors as American depositary shares, and issuance of subordinated perpetual debt. Exhibit 4 describes these various securities in detail.

A challenge facing Rhône-Poulenc management in the 1991 capital-market environment was that investor demand for these kinds of securities was low. To stimulate interest in such securities would require a high dividend. One commentator also noted, "RP's nationalized status has been a handicap to its access to funding."[10]

FINANCIAL PERFORMANCE

Exhibit 5 contains a summary of key RP financial measures for recent years and reveals that performance in 1990 punctured a string of steady annual improvements. Exhibit 6 gives a comparison of Rhône-Poulenc's financial results with a sample of competitors. Exhibit 7 provides forecasts of financial performance by industry sector.

One analyst opined that 1990 "was a disastrous year for the group with nothing going in its favor . . . the year's results [are] dreadful."[11] Although sales rose from FF73 billion to FF78 billion, net profits fell by 54 percent, from FF4.1 to FF1.9 billion. If one were to strip out capital gains and restructuring provisions from the analysis, profits would have slipped 66 percent. Accordingly, in January 1991, the Group's board of directors cut the firm's dividend on its preferred stock by 39 percent.

---

[9]Roussel-UCLAF had 1990 sales of FF13.05 billion derived from human pharmaceuticals, nutrition products, and veterinary pharmaceuticals. The German chemicals company Hoechst owned a majority interest in Roussel's shares.

[10]D. Hunter and D. Jackson, "Rhône-Poulenc: Hey Big Spender," *Chemical Week,* March 14, 1990, p. 42.

[11]P. Tattersall, "Rhône-Poulenc—Net Loss in 90Q3, but This Should Represent Bottom," *Barclays de Zoete Wedd,* December 4, 1990.

The slump of 1990 resulted largely from (1) increased interest expense associated with funds raised to finance the acquisition of Rorer, (2) unfavorable currency movements, (3) continued deepening of the Brazilian recession, (4) a drop in capital gains from asset sales, (5) a full-blown recession in Europe and the United States, (6) growing overcapacity in many product lines, leading to intensified price competition, and (7) a weakening export market to the Far East, where massive investments by Western chemical companies were starting to meet that region's demand. The dilution resulting from Rhône-Poulenc's swap of shares for the French government's interest in Roussel-UCLAF worsened the decline in performance on a per share basis.

In the first half of 1991, Rhône-Poulenc's performance was even worse than the year before. Profits were 54 percent lower because of the same factors that drove the slump in 1990. Management insisted, however, that the second half of 1991 would show a marked improvement as the chemical industry began a cyclical rebound.

STOCK-MARKET RESPONSE

Exhibit 8 presents two graphs regarding the Group's performance in the capital markets. The first graph gives the share price of Rhône-Poulenc's publicly traded CIPs since 1985 and reveals that the CIPs were a much more volatile investment than the CAC-General, a large index of shares listed on the Paris Bourse. The first graph also reveals that the CIP price underperformed the market over the five years.

The second graph in Exhibit 8 plots the cumulative excess returns[12] on the Group's stock to both private investors and the French government. By August 1991, the cumulative excess return on the CIPs was +6 percent; for the French government, it was −11 percent. The difference in returns between these two equity groups arose from a FF5 higher dividend received by the private investors and from special tax benefits on those dividends.

Over the past year, analysts had been divided on the appropriateness of the firm's share price.[13] The following table presents highlights of analysts' opinions:

---

[12]The excess return is the difference between Rhône-Poulenc's actual monthly investment return (reflecting stock-price changes and dividends) and a hypothetical *expected* return estimated by multiplying a beta of 1.30 times the return on the CAC index. The beta was derived from relevering the average asset beta of other chemicals companies. The return on the French government shares assumes that, if these shares had been traded in a competitive capital market, they would have been priced identically with the CIPs.

[13]Rhône-Poulenc's CIPs were traded on the NYSE as American depositary shares (ADSs). One ADS had a claim to .50 of a CIP. The ADS was increasingly used by non-American corporations as a way of accessing the U.S. equity markets without having to comply completely with the stringent American financial-disclosure requirements. A trust owned the underlying Rhône-Poulenc CIPs and, in turn, issued claims against its securities portfolio, in the form of ADSs. The company's preferred participating A shares (PSSA) were also traded in the United States as ADSs, where one ADS would have a claim to .25 of a PSSA share.

Analyst and Date	Share Price	Stock Market Index	Comment
M. Glen, Lehman Brothers August 13, 1990	CIP = FF310 ADS = $14.65 U.S.$1 = FF5.28	CAC = 474.95 S&P 500 = 339	The bad news outweighs the potential good news at the moment for the stock.
P. Tattersall Barclays de Zoete Wedd, March 1, 1991	CIP = FF295.4	CAC = 465	The outlook for the chemicals activities continues to be somewhat clouded as a result of the economic implications of the gulf crisis . . . [but] sharp appreciation of the £ or a sharp fall in interest rates would lead to a substantial upwards revision of this forecast. We believe that the recent outperformance by the shares has more than discounted the likely good news in the shorter term.
J. Wilbur, Smith Barney, April 12, 1991	CIP = FF365 ADS = US$17 U.S.$1 = FF5.65	CAC = 488 S&P 500 = 379	BUY: Annual growth of 25 percent at Rhône-Poulenc Rorer will cause Rhône-Poulenc itself to grow at rates above 15 percent. . . Undervalued stock based on highly valued pharmaceutical subsidiary. . . The chemical part of R-P, representing sales of $11 billion, is valued in the market at negative $12.00 per share. . . There is considerable appreciation potential . . . trends to lower interest rates in France will stimulate that market, resulting in an upward P/E adjustment. On the negative side, the major ownership position of the French government in Rhône-Poulenc makes it likely that the stock will trade at a lower P/E than if it were a completely public company.
S. Bridges, Merrill Lynch July 10, 1991	CIP = FF332.9 ADS = US$14.50 U.S.$1 = FF6.15	CAC = 463 S&P 500 = 377	Speculative Investment/Long-Term Buy: Considering the potential for earnings recovery [the shares] are speculatively attractive.
Allan Campbell, Value Line Sept. 6, 1991	CIP = 406.8 ADS =$16.00 U.S.$1 = FF5.91	CAC = 492 S&P 500 = 389	Recent bottom-line results don't give a true indication of Rhône-Poulenc's earnings power. Last year, earnings per share . . . would have fallen to near breakeven had it not been for gains on asset sales. This year, reported earnings are likely to slip lower, primarily because gains on divestitures will be down and interest expense up. . . Next year we look for operating results to be up across the board as economic growth accelerates again in Europe . . . Rhône's strengths are in pharmaceuticals and agrochemicals. . . The company has a relatively small exposure to commodity chemicals. Nonetheless, Rhône's chemical earnings are down sharply in the current industry downturn as demand and prices have fallen for specialty, as well as for commodity, chemicals. The dividend could be cut again in 1992, if our earnings estimate is on target.

Since January 1991, Rhône-Poulenc's shares had outperformed the market, rising by over 50 percent. Trading volume was also up: the daily float was about .5 percent, more than double the preceding year. In September 1991, the median P/E ratio on the Paris Bourse was about 11×.

FINANCIAL FORECAST

Exhibits 9–12 provide a forecast of financial performance. This forecast assumes no financial effects from possible privatization after 1993 and no payment under the contingent value rights (CVR) in 1994. Analysts focused on two key drivers of financial performance, sales growth and operating margin as a percentage of sales. Recognizing that Rhône-Poulenc consisted of two main businesses, the model breaks out the growth and margin assumptions for the life-sciences business (pharmaceuticals, which were dominated by Rorer) and the chemical businesses. Exhibit 9 summarizes specific assumptions used in the forecast. These assumptions are consistent with forecasts presented by leading securities analysts.

The forecasted balance sheet in Exhibit 11 reveals that Rhône-Poulenc would require almost FF19 billion in new external funds within the next 18 months; the cumulative external need would rise to about FF38 billion by 1996. Capital spending net of depreciation, additions to net working capital, and refinancing of maturing debt cause the need. Exhibit 13 contains information summarizing current capital-market conditions.

CONCLUSION

The strategic and financing issues facing RP's senior management in September 1991 could be summarized in a few questions. First, how appropriate were management's goals for enlarging the firm? Second, were these growth goals consistent with other goals for profitability and payment of dividends? Third, were these goals attainable, and were they consistent with past performance? If not, why would a departure from past experience be justified? Fourth, whose interests did the goals and strategy serve: management, the French government, public investors, the company in general? Fifth, did a better strategy and financing policy exist that would (1) sustain management's vision for the company, (2) create competitive advantage for the company, and (3) create shareholder wealth? What were the key trade-offs in considering any alternative policies? Sixth, when should changes in policy and financing tactics be implemented? Seventh, was the company fairly valued at the present CIP price of FF427? What constraints or opportunities did this price level imply? Finally, how should the firm raise the FF38 billion in new capital externally over the next five years?

EXHIBIT 1 Financial Performance by Business Segment (FF millions)

	Basic Chemicals (organic and inorganic intermediates)	Specialty Chemicals	Fibers and Polymers	Health	Agro	Others	Intergroup Adjustment	Total
1987								
Net sales	26,892	Combined	8,877	14,243	8,574	1,817	(4,244)	56,159
Depreciation	(1,446)	with	(661)	(587)	(316)	(154)	—	(3,164)
Operating margin	2,909	Basic	(305)	1,324	477	(826)	(33)	3,546
Identifiable assets	21,908	Chemicals	7,247	12,991	8,881	5,329	(252)	56,104
Capital expenditures	2,184		768	2,184	433	56	—	4,991
1988								
Net sales	18,861	8,009	13,957	15,671	9,733	2,016	(2,733)	65,334
Depreciation	(1,050)	(467)	(1,124)	(669)	(357)	(151)	—	(3,818)
Operating margin	2,767	384	1,115	1,567	779	(714)	(18)	5,880
Identifiable assets	15,039	7,030	12,017	15,787	9,570	6,063	(475)	65,031
Capital expenditures	1,894	860	1,164	1,259	512	212	—	5,901
1989								
Net sales	19,673	10,167	15,857	17,766	10,527	1,761	(2,683)	73,068
Depreciation	(1,259)	(626)	(1,161)	(781)	(399)	(139)	—	(4,365)
Operating margin	2,862	512	1,174	1,874	1,202	(526)	(35)	7,063
Identifiable assets	16,771	12,548	12,351	21,030	9,263	7,037	(468)	78,532
Capital expenditures	1,845	1,884	1,191	1,262	560	274	—	7,016
1990								
Net sales	18,040	14,086	14,132	23,869	10,168	1,383	(2,868)	78,810
Depreciation	(1,367)	(870)	(1,111)	(1,014)	(435)	(136)	—	(4,933)
Operating margin	1,573	(63)	340	2,465	1,321	(235)	17	5,418
Identifiable assets	16,551	17,020	12,103	37,181	9,943	11,088	(66)	103,820
Capital expenditures	2,214	1,394	1,206	1,908	567	249	—	7,538

Source: Company annual reports.

EXHIBIT 2   Summary of Jean-René Fourtou's Business Approach

Opening up to outside markets, reconverting a business, inventing new structures, discovering new ways of boosting productivity, gearing society to computerization, letting the people take charge of their own affairs, ensuring job satisfaction by making work relevant to people's cultural background and social outlook . . . This is change, and we are all agreed as to the vital need of controlling and adapting ourselves to it.

First-hand experience of the workings of administrative bodies and large companies indicates, more often than not, the urgent need for change, for it is evident that the scope of freedom is becoming progressively restricted, while stagnation prevails.

As may be seen, there is no lack of studies, ideas, new directions, even ready-made solutions; however, the adoption and enforcement of decisions is constantly thwarted by the increasing complexity of systems, and by the inherent resistance to change in each structure and in the struggles for influence and power.

Bringing about change is, clearly, a subtle art, the success of which is governed by three cardinal principles:

- Clear-cut policy decisions (i.e., management's unshakable determination to follow its action through to the end).
- Accurate assessment of the time factor: At the project development stage, this means having ambitious concepts tempered by reason, and at the implementation stage it implies maintaining a fine balance between the company's capacity for absorption and the work tempo, which will, nevertheless, be dictated by any action undertaken.
- Involvement of the full energies of a specialist task force, which remains as independent as possible from the issues of daily management, while maintaining constant and direct contact with the decision makers.

For effective change to be made, the appropriate methods must be used, in conjunction with the skills and abilities of qualified experts.

These principles and methods are well known to consultants, and particularly to organization consultants. Their professional know-how derives from their broad and varied experience of changes they have been called upon to introduce in highly different situations and companies.

J.-R. Fourtou

Source: "Brossard Consultants," a pamphlet about the firm published in 1985.

EXHIBIT 3   Financial Performance by Geographical Area (FF millions)

	France	Other Countries in Europe	United States and Canada	Brazil	Others	Eliminations	Consolidated
1987							
Net sales	36,450	19,802	5,582	5,015	1,662	(12,352)	56,159
Operating margin	2,290	564	453	295	161	(217)	3,546
Identifiable assets	30,154	12,464	4,495	8,164	1,188	(361)	56,104
1988							
Net sales	39,336	22,555	8,484	6,481	2,240	(13,762)	65,334
Operating margin	3,343	1,029	714	789	84	(79)	5,880
Identifiable assets	34,839	13,617	10,972	4,708	1,334	(439)	65,031
1989							
Net sales	42,569	25,016	10,498	7,854	2,627	(15,496)	73,068
Operating margin	4,322	1,001	936	650	98	56	7,063
Identifiable assets	36,339	17,319	14,275	4,894	6,087	(382)	78,532
1990							
Net sales	41,053	27,714	16,697	4,953	3,598	(15,205)	78,810
Operating margin	2,342	1,682	1,472	(229)	90	61	5,418
Identifiable assets	42,272	20,019	34,231	5,116	2,052	(320)	103,820

Source: Company annual reports.

EXHIBIT 4   Description of Securities

---

1. Long-term debt

Outstanding: FF6,962 million bank debentures
                      FF13,374 million bank borrowings
                      FF 20,336 million total
                      Unused multicurrency lines of credit totaled FF5.991 billion.

Currency: French francs, 54 percent; U.S. dollars, 29 percent; deutsche marks (DM), 6 percent;
                      British pounds, 4 percent; Dutch guilders, 3 percent; other, 4 percent.

Lease financing: Included in bank borrowings were capitalized lease obligations.

Repayment:

	Debentures	*Borrowings*	*Leases*	*Total*
1992	1,243	718	232	2,193
1993	882	1,128	193	2,203
1994	1,804	1,554	168	3,526
1995	1,465	1,697	128	3,290
1996+	1,568	7,161	395	9,124
Total	6,962	12,258	1,374	20,336

Rate: Weighted-average interest rate on December 31, 1990, was 9.9 percent per year.

Options: Debentures included an amount of FF1,000 million carrying subscription rights to
                      participating shares. This specific issue included 500,000 debentures issued at 2,000
                      francs nominal value and repayable at par in 1994.

Exotica: Debentures included a U.S.$50 million Eurobond issue whose reimbursement value was
                      tied to the $/DM parity.

Swaps: Total interest-rate swaps and foreign-exchange swaps covered notional amounts of
                      FF1.552 billion. Debt balances reflect the effects of these swaps.

2. Participating loans

Description: These loans receive both a fixed rate of interest and a supplemental payment. The exact
                     formula for the supplemental payment varies with each loan and lender. For instance,
                     in the case of the Caisse des Dépôts et Consignations, the supplement is based on
                     dividends distributed by Rhône-Poulenc.

Rate: After giving effect to supplemental payments, the weighted-average rate of interest on
                     all participating loans was 14.4 percent.

Maturity: The participating loans are due as follows:

Lender	*Issued*	*Due*	*Amount*
Pool of banks	1982	1997	FF200 million
Pool of banks	1983	1998	147
Crédit National	1983	1991–98	390
Caisse des Dépôts	1983	1991–2013	93
Total outstanding			FF830 million

3. Amortizable preferred securities

Currency: U.S. dollars.

Outstanding: $1,200 million (nominal amount). Rhône-Poulenc actually received only U.S.$891.3
                     million after issuance costs of U.S.$17.9 million.

Rate: 9.19 percent. For the first 15 years, periodic payments to vary at a slight premium to
                     LIBOR (London interbank borrowing rate). Thereafter, payments to be at a nominal
                     rate into perpetuity.

EXHIBIT 4 *(continued)*

Pay-in-kind provision:	If the payment of cash interest would imperil the Group's financial condition, the company could pay the interest with similar securities, also having no due date, but with a higher rate of interest.
Subordination:	Subordinated to the complete payment of creditors.
Date of issue:	July 13, 1988 (private placement).
Date of maturity:	No stated due date or maturity. Rhône-Poulenc had no obligation to redeem the securities except that, if a dividend was paid to any other shareholder of the group, but not to holders of these securities, the entire issue would become due and payable.
Trust and option:	Upon issuance of these securities, an independent trust was established by the investment banker. This trust, which was legally protected from invasion by the Group, invested in U.S. Treasury zero-coupon notes. At the end of 15 years, the holders of the securities had the option of exchanging their securities for the assets in the trust. The Group had the right, but not the obligation, to purchase these securities from the trust at their then fair market value.
Amortization:	The company amortized the par value of these securities against the gain in the underlying zero-coupon notes. As the value of the underlying notes accreted, the principal amount of the preferred was, in essence, repaid. The notes accreted, and the preferred amortized, as follows (French francs): 1991, 187 mm; 1992, 216 mm; 1993, 233 mm; 1994, 251 mm; 1995, 270 mm; after 1995, 3,082 mm.
Company comment:	The Group has determined that these securities are in substance equivalent to equity instruments. However, in accordance with the SEC rules requiring presentation of temporary equity apart from stockholders' equity, the Group has classified the proceeds of the issue outside stockholders' equity under the caption "Amortizable Preferred Securities."

4. Contingent value rights

Amount:	20,900,663 contingent value rights.
Investors:	Minority shareholders in Rorer Group, Inc.
Issuance:	In connection with the August 1990 acquisition of a majority interest in Rorer Group, Inc.
Description:	Entitled the holder to the right in 1993 (or 1994 at the option of Rhône-Poulenc) to a cash payment equal to U.S.$49.13 (or U.S.$53.06 if payment was in 1994), less the higher of the value of the Rhône-Poulenc Rorer share at that date and U.S.$26.00. If the value of the Rhône-Poulenc Rorer share was equal to or greater than $49.13 (or $53.06), no payment would be made.
Listing:	American Stock Exchange in New York.
Liability:	At date of issuance, the market value of the rights was FF1,306 million, and the Group's maximum liability was FF5,165 million. At the end of 1990, the market value of the rights was FF844 million, and the Group's maximum liability was FF4,960 million. The foreign-exchange risk of the maximum liability was hedged.

5. Participating shares *(titres participatifs)*

Outstanding:	781,308 shares, par value FF782 million.
Rate:	Minimum of 10 percent consisting of 7 percent fixed component and 3 percent variable component indexed to consolidated sales. Paid on October 1 of each year. Rate paid in 1990 was 11.4 percent.
Redemption:	Not mandatorily redeemable, except in the case of liquidation.

EXHIBIT 4   (*continued*)

Call provision:	The Group had the option of redeeming the shares between 1995 and 2003 at prices varying between FF3,000 per share (1995) to FF5,000 (2003).
Issuance:	620,000 shares in 1983. In October 1988, some debenture holders exercised an option for 161,308 shares.
Listing:	Paris Bourse.

6. Capital equity notes

Outstanding:	U.S.$300 million (FF1,997 million).
Issued:	December 16, 1986. On the Eurodollar market.
Rate:	Semiannual payments at a rate slightly higher than LIBOR. Last payment in 1990 was at the annual rate of 8.1875 percent.
Pay-in-kind provision:	If cash interest payment would imperil the Group's financial condition, the Group could satisfy the obligation with similar securities, but paying a higher interest rate.
Maturity:	No fixed due date.
Subordination:	Subordinated in payment to the Group's creditors and to payments on participating shares.

7. Preferred participating nonvoting shares, series A (PSSA)

Outstanding:	4,025,000 shares.
Issued:	November 1989, at a price of FF465, in an international offering. Total amount was U.S.$300 million. Simultaneous offerings in the United States, Europe, and Japan.
Warrants:	Issued in units with detachable warrants to purchase an additional 16,100,000 shares. Four warrants permitted the purchase of one PSSA at an exercise price of FF535. The warrants would expire on the earlier of December 31, 1992, and the date the company ceased to be a "public sector company." The warrants were listed for trading on the SEAQ International market in London.
Maturity:	No fixed maturity date.
Dividend:	Paid annually on August 15. Equal to the sum of a fixed portion (FF7.50 per PSSA) plus a variable portion equal to 150 percent of the greater of:

1. the dividend approved on ordinary A shares or
2. $A \times B/C \times D/E$, where:

$A = 0.5484$ percent of the FF465 par value of the PSSA

$B =$ Latest year's net income

$C =$ Net income for 1988

$D =$ Sales for 1988

$E =$ Sales for latest year

EXHIBIT 4 (*concluded*)

	The dividend could not reduce the net income available to common shareholders to below FF1 million. The fixed portion of the annual payment was cumulative. The variable portion was not.
Listed:	SEAQ International (London, where it was traded as international depositary shares) and NYSE (traded in the form of American depositary shares where 1 ADS = .25 PSSA).

8. Common stock and preferred investment certificates (CIPs)

Description:	Capital stock was divided into common stock ordinary shares A and preferred stock class B. Preferred shares B were split into nonvoting preferred shares (preferred investment certificates B) and voting certificates. The voting certificates had no par value, and no compensation was paid to the Group upon their issuance. The French state held 77.52 percent of the voting rights; nationalized financial institutions held 22.48 percent of the voting rights.
Outstanding:	Common stock: 45,183,250 shares (FF100 par). CIPs: 11,720,676 shares (FF100 par).
CIP yield:	A fixed dividend of 5 percent of their par value (5 francs), plus a variable dividend of an amount equal to the dividend on ordinary shares A. The fixed dividend was paid if the net income of the Group was positive, and it was not cumulative.
CIP listing:	Paris Bourse since 1989; MONEP (Marché, des Options Négotiables) since 1989; NASDAQ, New York, since 1987 (quoted as American depositary shares, where 1 ADS = .5 CIP); NYSE since 1989. Rhône-Poulenc was the first French company to be quoted on the NYSE.
CIP issuance:	5,671,658 CIPs issued in March 1987 in France and the United States. International units offered in November 1989. One unit = 1 ADS + 1 warrant to buy 1 ADS.
Lead underwriters:	Société Générale, Merrill Lynch, Shearson Lehman Hutton (international offering); Merrill Lynch, Drexel Burnham Lambert, Sogen Securities (American offering).
Transfer agents:	SICOVAM (France), Bank of New York (United States).
Custodian:	Banque Worms (for ADS).

Sources: Company 1990 annual report, Standard & Poor's *NYSE Stock Reports,* and Standard & Poor's *Standard Corporation Record.*

EXHIBIT 5 Historical Financial Performance (FF millions)

	1983	1984	1985	1986	1987	1988	1989	1990
Net sales	43,115	51,207	54,712	51,642	56,159	65,334	73,068	78,810
Income before priority dividend	98	1,820	2,127	2,008	2,360	3,457	4,112	1,942
Preferred remunerations	(30)	(65)	(69)	(96)	(167)	(579)	(1,076)	(845)
Net income available to common	68	1,755	2,058	1,912	2,193	2,878	3,036	1,097
Total assets	39,009	43,312	45,288	53,726	60,069	67,688	83,182	109,147
Common equity	4,601	6,444	8,712	12,358	16,108	18,807	21,272	21,047
Contingent value rights	—	—	—	—	—	—	—	4,960
Preferred securities	—	—	—	—	—	5,400	4,974	4,239
Preferred equity in subsidiaries	—	—	—	968	801	909	868	769
Minority interests	—	960	968	1,086	1,448	1,331	2,624	6,021
Equity plus other funds	4,601	7,404	9,680	14,412	18,357	26,447	29,738	37,036
Nonvoting preferred shares	—	541,667	610,000	3,660,000	10,041,368	11,720,675	11,720,675	11,720,675
Voting common shares	34,643,378	34,643,378	34,643,378	36,643,378	36,643,378	36,643,378	36,643,378	40,169,310
Return on net assets*	8.5%	11.4%	10.2%	5.0%	4.9%	8.0%	8.4%	5.1%
Return on total capital†	9.8%	13.1%	16.2%	7.7%	6.8%	11.8%	12.1%	8.1%
Growth of sales (percent)	—	7.6%	40.8%	10.5%	27.7%	2.2%	17.3%	22.4%
New long-term (LT) borrowings	3,630	3,443	3,234	4,809	1,615	1,967	4,111	7,930
Repayment of LT borrowings	(1,623)	(3,673)	(2,827)	(2,679)	(2,237)	(1,626)	(2,144)	(6,854)
Increase (decr.) in short-term (ST) borrowing	—	—	—	(585)	1,380	(2,177)	5,523	6,458
Issuance of ordinary A shares	—	—	—	—	2,439	—	—	4,685
Issuance of participating shares	1,000	300	1,135	193	132	279	1,712	—
Issuance of capital equity notes	—	—	—	1,984	—	—	—	—
Issuance (amortization) of preferred shares	—	—	—	968	—	—	700	(187)
Dividends paid: Class A	0	(88)	(470)	(470)	(408)	(614)	(787)	(905)
Preferred remunerations paid	(30)	(65)	(69)	(88)	(270)	(300)	(933)	(916)
Total financing activities	2,977	(83)	1,003	4,132	2,651	2,948	8,182	10,211
French government LT bond yield	13.63 %	12.54 %	10.94 %	8.44 %	9.43 %	9.06 %	8.79 %	9.34 %
French corporate lending rate	18.95 %	18.85 %	17.77 %	16.28 %	15.82 %	15.65 %	16.01 %	13.00 %
Net profits/sales	0.2 %	3.6 %	3.9 %	3.9 %	4.2 %	5.3 %	5.6 %	2.5 %
Sales/assets	1.11	1.18	1.21	0.96	0.93	0.97	0.88	0.72
Assets/common equity	8.48	6.72	5.20	4.35	3.73	3.60	3.91	5.19
Return on common equity	1.9 %	28.6 %	24.5 %	16.3 %	14.6 %	18.4 %	19.3 %	9.2 %

*Net assets are defined as total assets less current liabilities.

†Total capital is defined as long-term debt plus all preferred stock plus common equity.

Sources: Company annual reports; International Monetary Fund; *Value Line Investment Survey.*

EXHIBIT 6 Comparative Financial Data for Selected Diversified Chemicals Companies, 1990 Results

	Rhône-Poulenc (France)	Akzo (Holland)	Imperial Chemicals (U.K.)	Montedison (Italy)	Dow (U.S.)	Du Pont (U.S.)	Monsanto (U.S.)
1990 sales (U.S.$ billions)	14.47	9.47	23.1	13.97	19.8	40.0	8.99
Operating margin							
(w/o deprec.; percent)							
1985–90 average	13.7	12.4	13.3	13.3	22.9	18.7	18.2
1991 estimate	14.0	12.5	11.0	12.0	19.0	18.5	20.5
1992 estimate	15.5	13.5	12.5	12.5	20.0	19.0	21.5
1994–96 estimate	17.0	14.0	15.0	13.0	21.0	21.0	20.0
Net margin (percent)							
1985–90 average	4.0	4.6	6.0	2.8	9.3	5.8	5.6
1991 estimate	2.1	3.9	4.5	0.2	5.0	5.6	7.0
1992 estimate	3.2	4.8	5.7	1.3	5.2	6.3	7.8
1994–96 estimate	4.7	6.2	7.1	2.5	6.4	6.6	7.1
Return on capital (percent)							
1985–90 average	9.3	11.5	13.0	7.6	15.1	11.1	9.6
1991 estimate	6.0	8.0	8.5	3.0	8.0	10.5	13.0
1992 estimate	8.0	9.5	10.0	4.5	8.5	11.0	15.0
1994–96 estimate	11.0	12.0	11.0	7.0	11.5	12.5	16.0
Dividend payout (percent)							
1985–90 average	39	33	42	32	42	48	53
1991 estimate	84	45	69	NMF	75	52	39
1992 estimate	62	31	55	67	66	48	36
1994–96 estimate	65	31	47	35	54	50	37
Sales growth rate (percent)							
Past 10 years	NA	1.0	5.0	NA	7.5	6.5	5.0
Past 5 years	8.0	9.0	9.5	NA	12.5	2.5	9.5
1988–96 estimate	3.0	3.0	2.0	5.5	7.0	6.0	10.0
Capitalization (percent)							
Debt	45	19	25	52	35	27	29
Preferred stock	17	0	0	8	1	1	0
Common stock	38	81	75	40	64	72	71
Average tax rate (percent), 1991 estimate	28	34	35	NMF	35	45	33
Statutory tax rate (percent)	37	35	35	36	34	34	34
Beta	NAv.	.95	.90	.75	1.25	1.10	1.15

Source: *Value Line Investment Survey*, 1991; *Country Profiles*, 1991 (Economist Intelligence Unit).

EXHIBIT 7   Forecasted Financial Performance for Selected Industries

	Change in Operating Margin (%)	Average Annual Sales Growth Rate (%)	Return on Total Capital (%)	Dividend Payout Ratio (%)
Basic chemicals				
1991 estimate	−0.5	−3.0	10.0	59
1992 estimate	+1.0	+5.0	11.5	53
1994–96 estimate	+1.5	+7.0	13.5	47
Specialty chemicals				
1991 estimate	+0.2	+1.0	12.0	34
1992 estimate	+0.5	+10.0	12.5	34
1994–96 estimate	+0.5	+11.5	13.0	33
Diversified chemicals				
1991 estimate	−0.6	−0.5	10.5	55
1992 estimate	−0.5	+5.0	10.5	46
1994–96 estimate	+1.5	+8.4	13.0	40
Pharmaceuticals				
1991 estimate	+0.6	+10.4	+30.0	+49
1992 estimate	+1.0	+8.7	+26.5	+48
1994–96 estimate	−0.5	+28.3	+28.0	+47

Source: *Value Line Investment Survey*, 1991.

EXHIBIT 8 Rhône-Poulenc Stock Prices and Cumulative Market-Adjusted Investor Returns Since January 1986

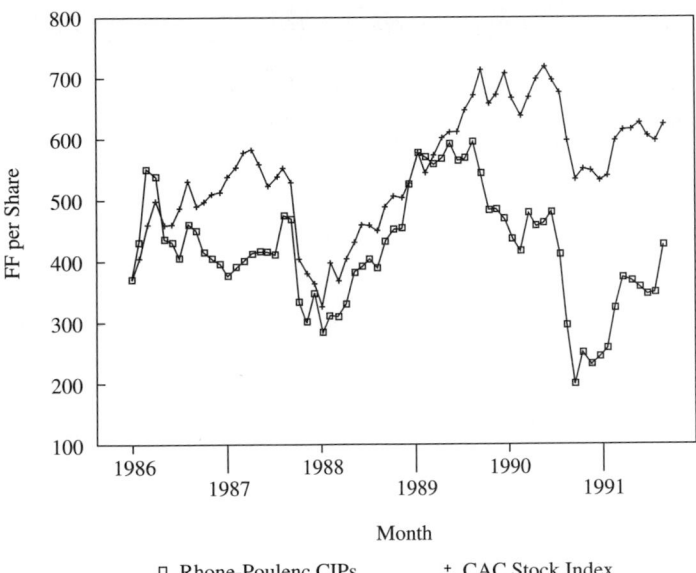

Rhône-Poulenc Stock Price
Compared to Paris Bourse Index

□ Rhone-Poulenc CIPs   + CAC Stock Index

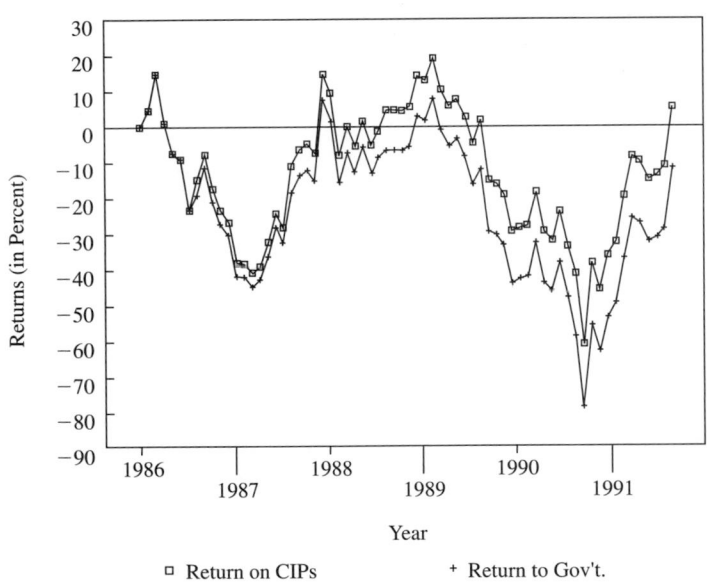

Cumulative Excess Returns
On Rhône-Poulenc Common Equity

□ Return on CIPs   + Return to Gov't.

Source of underlying data: Datastream, Inc.

EXHIBIT 9   Summary of Forecast Assumptions (percentages)

	All Years	Projected					
		1991	*1992*	*1993*	*1994*	*1995*	*1996*
Sales growth: Health sector		0.17	0.125	0.125	0.125	0.125	0.125
Sales growth: Chemical sectors		0.001	0.089	0.07	0.07	0.07	0.07
Operating margin: Health		0.14	0.13	0.15	0.15	0.15	0.15
Operating margin: Chemicals		0.05	0.06	0.06	0.06	0.06	0.06
Capital expenditures/sales	0.09						
Depreciation to gross property, plant, and equipment (PP&E)	0.073						
Dividend payout	0.3						
Melded interest rate	0.1						
Average tax rate	0.24						
Cash and investments to sales	0.07						
Days receivables outstanding	50.0						
Payables to sales	0.11						
Inventories to sales	0.19						
Other current assets to sales	0.1						
Other current liabilities to sales	0.18						
Tax deferrals as percentage of tax expense	0.37						
Market/book value, asset sales	1.25						

Source: Casewriter's estimates, drawing on assumptions of securities analysts.

EXHIBIT 10 Forecasted Income Statements (FF millions; fiscal year ended December 31)

| | Actual | | | | Projected | | | | |
	1988	1989	1990	1991	1992	1993	1994	1995	1996
1. Sales: R-P Rorer	—	—	17,269	20,204	22,730	25,571	28,767	32,363	36,409
2. Sales: R-P other	—	—	61,541	61,603	67,086	71,782	76,806	82,183	87,935
3. Net sales	65,334	73,068	78,810	81,807	89,815	97,353	105,574	114,546	124,344
Operating expenses									
4. Production costs and exp.	42,634	46,621	49,900						
5. Admin. and selling exp.	12,385	14,521	17,605						
6. Depreciation	3,818	4,365	4,933						
7. Restruc. provision	617	498	954						
8. Total operating exp.	(59,454)	(66,005)	(73,392)						
9. Operating margin	5,880	7,063	5,418	5,909	6,980	8,143	8,923	9,785	10,737
Other income (expenses)									
10. Interest expense	(1,557)	(2,125)	(3,488)	(3,500)	(3,637)	(3,915)	(4,329)	(4,609)	(4,881)
11. Gains on asset sales	51	122	1,840	1,500	500	0	0	0	0
12. Amort. of intang. assets	(204)	(422)	(719)	(854)	(854)	(854)	(854)	(854)	(854)
13. Other income (expenses)	(65)	505	543	500	500	500	500	500	500
14. Affiliates' earnings	471	306	164	350	410	410	410	410	410
15. Earnings before taxes	4,576	5,449	3,758	3,905	3,899	4,284	4,651	5,233	5,913
16. Income taxes	(686)	(1,052)	(1,010)	(937)	(936)	(1,028)	(1,116)	(1,256)	(1,419)
17. Minority interests	(239)	(285)	(806)	(1,600)	(1,700)	(1,800)	(1,900)	(2,000)	(2,100)
18. Change in accounting	(194)	0	0	0	0	0	0	0	0
19. Net earnings	3,457	4,112	1,942	1,368	1,263	1,456	1,635	1,977	2,394

(continued)

927

EXHIBIT 10 (*concluded*)

Dividends on									
20. Pfd. equity in subs.	(55)	(73)	(54)	(50)	(60)	(70)	(75)	(75)	(75)
21. Amortizable pfd.	(254)	(561)	(428)	(496)	(496)	(496)	(496)	(496)	(496)
22. Participating shares	(95)	(110)	(115)	(123)	(135)	(146)	(158)	(172)	(187)
23. Capital equity notes	(175)	(196)	(154)	(154)	(154)	(154)	(154)	(154)	(154)
24. Pfd. particip. ser. A	—	(136)	(94)	(44)	(40)	(46)	(51)	(61)	(73)
25. Total pfd. stock divs.	(579)	(1,076)	(845)	(867)	(885)	(912)	(934)	(958)	(985)
26. Earnings to common	2,878	3,016	1,097	501	378	544	701	1,020	1,409
27. Divs. to class A shares	(550)	(641)	(422)	(105)	(76)	(116)	(153)	(229)	(322)
28. Dividends to CIP shares	(234)	(264)	(182)	(86)	(78)	(89)	(98)	(118)	(142)
29. Dividends to all common	(784)	(905)	(603)	(191)	(154)	(204)	(251)	(347)	(464)
30. Retentions of earnings	2,094	2,111	494	309	224	340	449	673	946
31. Number of A shares (average)	36.643	36.643	45.180	45.180	45.180	45.180	45.180	45.180	45.180
32. Number of CIP shares	11.721	11.721	11.721	11.721	11.721	11.721	11.721	11.721	11.721
Results per share of common stock									
33. Earnings per share (EPS), class A	58.29	61.15	20.15	7.77	5.61	8.53	11.28	16.89	23.74
34. EPS, CIP	63.29	66.15	25.15	12.77	10.61	13.53	16.28	21.89	28.74
35. Dividends per class A share	15.00	17.50	10.50	2.33	1.68	2.56	3.38	5.07	7.12
36. Dividends per CIP share	20.00	22.50	15.50	7.33	6.68	7.56	8.38	10.07	12.12

Source: Casewriter's estimates, drawing on assumptions of securities analysts.

EXHIBIT 11 Historical and Projected Balance Sheets (FF millions; fiscal year ended December 31)

	Actual			Projected					
	1988	1989	1990	1991	1992	1993	1994	1995	1996
Assets									
1. Cash	851	1,298	909	5,727	6,287	6,815	7,390	8,018	8,704
2. ST investments	1,806	3,352	4,418	—	—	—	—	—	—
3. Accounts receivable	11,719	9,980	11,156	11,206	12,303	13,336	14,462	15,691	17,033
4. Inventories	11,802	13,938	15,801	15,543	17,065	18,497	20,059	21,764	23,625
5. Other current assets	4,242	7,271	8,826	8,181	8,982	9,735	10,557	11,455	12,434
6. Total current assets	30,420	35,839	41,110	40,657	44,637	48,383	52,469	56,928	61,797
7. Investments and other	5,400	6,456	11,000	11,000	11,000	11,000	11,000	11,000	11,000
8. Gross PP&E	53,148	59,690	67,161	69,724	76,207	84,969	94,470	104,780	115,971
9. Accum. depreciation	(26,578)	(29,505)	(33,099)	(38,189)	(43,752)	(49,955)	(56,851)	(64,500)	(72,966)
10. Net PP&E	26,570	30,185	34,062	31,535	32,455	35,014	37,619	40,280	43,005
11. Intang. assets, gross	5,998	11,495	24,394	24,394	24,394	24,394	24,394	24,394	24,394
12. Accum. amortization	(700)	(793)	(1,419)	(2,273)	(3,127)	(3,980)	(4,834)	(5,688)	(6,542)
13. Intangible assets, net	5,298	10,702	22,975	22,121	21,267	20,414	19,560	18,706	17,852
14. Total assets	67,688	83,182	109,147	105,313	109,360	114,811	120,648	126,914	133,654
15. Bank overdrafts	1,826	2,987	2,647	2,647	2,647	2,647	2,647	2,647	2,647
16. Accounts payable	7,340	7,771	7,864	8,999	9,880	10,709	11,613	12,600	13,678
17. Currently due LT debt	1,051	1,077	2,447	2,071	2,011	2,060	3,408	3,212	3,050
18. Short-term borrowings	1,373	5,737	13,056	—	—	—	—	—	—
19. Restruct. provision	768	0	0	—	—	—	—	—	—
20. Other current liabs.	9,312	12,777	15,847	14,725	16,167	17,523	19,003	20,618	22,382
21. Total current liabs.	21,670	30,349	41,861	28,443	30,705	32,940	36,672	39,078	41,757

(continued)

EXHIBIT 11 *(concluded)*

930

	Actual			Projected					
	1988	1989	1990	1991	1992	1993	1994	1995	1996
22. **New external financing**	**0**	**0**	**0**	**11,127**	**14,618**	**20,755**	**26,757**	**32,297**	**38,228**
23. LT debt: Debentures	6,044	6,403	6,962	5,719	4,837	3,033	1,568	768	268
24. LT debt: Banks	5,658	8,179	13,374	12,656	11,528	9,974	8,277	6,580	4,080
25. Participating loans	1,003	911	830	780	729	679	628	578	527
26. Deferred income taxes	1,364	1,694	2,080	2,427	2,773	3,153	3,566	4,031	4,556
27. Pensions and restruc.	5,502	5,908	7,004	7,004	7,004	7,004	7,004	7,004	7,004
28. Minority ints. in subs.	1,331	2,624	6,021	6,021	6,021	6,021	6,021	6,021	6,021
29. Pfd. equity in subs.	909	868	769	769	769	769	769	769	769
30. Amortizable pfd. secur.	5,400	4,974	4,239	4,052	3,836	3,603	3,352	3,082	2,792
31. CVRs	0	0	4,960	4,960	4,960	4,960	0	0	0
Stockholders' equity									
32. Participating shares	994	994	994	994	994	994	994	994	994
33. Capital equity notes	1,997	1,997	1,997	1,997	1,997	1,997	1,997	1,997	1,997
34. Particip. shs., ser. A	0	1,815	1,815	1,815	1,815	1,815	1,815	1,815	1,815
35. Pfd. inv. certif. B	1,172	1,172	1,172	1,172	1,172	1,172	1,172	1,172	1,172
36. Common stock class A	3,664	3,664	4,518	4,518	4,518	4,518	4,518	4,518	4,518
37. Paid-in capital	5,051	4,948	8,838	8,838	8,838	8,838	8,838	8,838	8,838
38. CVRs' valuation adjust.	0	0	(3,664)	(3,664)	(3,664)	(3,664)	0	0	0
39. Retained earnings	5,194	7,420	7,910	8,218	8,441	8,780	9,228	9,898	10,840
40. Translation reserve	735	(738)	(2,533)	(2,533)	(2,533)	(2,533)	(2,533)	(2,533)	(2,533)
41. Total stockholders' equity	18,807	21,272	21,047	21,356	21,580	21,920	26,033	26,706	27,651
42. Liabs. and equity	67,688	83,182	109,147	105,313	109,360	114,811	120,648	126,914	133,654
Memo									
43. Dividends to all common shs.	784	905	603	191	154	204	251	347	464
44. Invest. in PP&E	(5,901)	(7,016)	(7,538)	(7,363)	(8,083)	(8,762)	(9,502)	(10,309)	(11,191)
45. Other cap. expends.	(1,636)	(2,708)	(5,022)	0	—	—	—	—	—
46. Purchase of companies	(2,048)	(9,270)	(9,562)	0	0	0	0	0	0
47. Asset sales	694	648	4,541	6,000	2,000	0	0	0	0
48. Depreciation expense	3,818	4,365	4,933	5,090	5,563	6,203	6,896	7,649	8,466
49. Addns. to net wkg. cap.	8,744	(3,260)	(6,241)	12,966	1,718	1,511	354	2,053	2,190
50. Incr. new external fin.	—	—	—	11,127	3,491	6,138	6,002	5,540	5,931

Source: Casewriter's estimates, drawing on assumptions of securities analysts.

EXHIBIT 12   Ratio Analyses of Historical and Projected Financial Statements (fiscal year ended December 31)

	Actual				Projected				
	1988	1989	1990	1991	1992	1993	1994	1995	1996
Measures of profitability (%)									
1. Operating profit margin	9.0	9.7	6.9	7.2	7.8	8.4	8.5	8.5	8.6
2. Average tax rate	15.0	19.3	26.9	24.0	24.0	24.0	24.0	24.0	24.0
3. Taxes defd./tax exp.	81.0	31.4	38.2	37.0	37.0	37.0	37.0	37.0	37.0
4. Return on sales	5.3	5.6	2.5	1.7	1.4	1.5	1.5	1.7	1.9
5. Return on equity*	18.4	19.3	9.2	6.4	5.9	6.6	6.3	7.4	8.7
6. Return on total capital	11.8	12.1	8.1	7.2	8.3	9.1	8.9	9.2	9.6
7. Return on net assets	8.0	8.4	5.1	4.8	5.6	6.3	6.7	7.0	7.4
8. Return on assets	5.1	4.9	1.8	1.3	1.2	1.3	1.4	1.6	1.8
Measures of financial leverage									
9. Debt/equity ratio	70.0	96.4	155.5	137.8	143.1	153.4	147.3	154.7	160.3
10. Debt/total capital	41.2	49.1	60.9	57.9	58.9	60.5	59.6	60.7	61.6
11. EBIT/interest (×)†	3.8	3.3	1.6	1.7	1.9	2.1	2.1	2.1	2.2
Measures of asset utilization									
12. Sales/assets	0.97	0.88	0.72	0.78	0.82	0.85	0.88	0.90	0.93
13. Sales growth rate	16.3	11.8	7.9	3.8	9.8	8.4	8.4	8.5	8.6
14. Assets growth rate	12.7	22.9	31.2	−3.5	3.8	5.0	5.1	5.2	5.3
15. Cash and invest./sales	4.1	6.4	6.8	7.0	7.0	7.0	7.0	7.0	7.0
16. Days in receivables	65.5	49.9	51.7	50.0	50.0	50.0	50.0	50.0	50.0
17. Payables to sales (%)	11.2	10.6	10.0	11.0	11.0	11.0	11.0	11.0	11.0
18. Inventories to sales (%)	18.1	19.1	20.0	19.0	19.0	19.0	19.0	19.0	19.0
19. Other curr. assets/sales (%)	6.5	10.0	11.2	10.0	10.0	10.0	10.0	10.0	10.0
20. Other curr. liabs./sales (%)	14.3	17.5	20.1	18.0	18.0	18.0	18.0	18.0	18.0
21. Annual deprec./gross PP&E (%)	7.2	7.3	7.3	7.3	7.3	7.3	7.3	7.3	7.3
22. Amort./gross intangibles (%)	3.4	3.7	2.9	3.5	3.5	3.5	3.5	3.5	3.5
23. Changes in PP&E to sales (%)	13.2	9.0	9.5	3.1	7.2	9.0	9.0	9.0	9.0
Measures of liquidity									
24. Quick ratio	0.66	0.48	0.39	0.60	0.61	0.61	0.60	0.61	0.62
25. Current ratio	1.40	1.18	0.98	1.43	1.45	1.47	1.43	1.46	1.48
Miscellaneous performance measures									
26. EPS growth A shares (%)	28.7	4.9	−67.0	−61.5	−27.7	51.9	32.3	49.7	40.6
27. EPS growth B shares (%)	2.8	4.5	−62.0	−49.2	−16.9	27.5	20.4	34.4	31.3
28. Dividends/net income (%)	27.2	30.0	55.0	38.2	40.9	37.6	35.9	34.0	32.9

*In this calculation, *equity* includes participating shares, capital equity notes, participating preferred shares A, the CIPs, and the common A shares.
†EBIT = earnings before interest and taxes.

Source: Casewriter's analyses of Exhibits 10 and 11.

EXHIBIT 13   Current Capital Market Information (as of September 18, 1991)

	Six-Month Interbank	One-Year Eurocurrency	Bank Prime
Short-term funds (less than 1 year)			
France	9.375 %	9.25 %	10.0 %
United Kingdom	10.125	10.125	11.0
Germany	9.35 %	9.3 %	10.5
United States	—	—	8.0 %

	Domestic	Eurocurrency	
Intermediate-term bonds			
German (DM)	8.59 %	8.99 %	
U.S. ($)	7.30	7.95	
French (FF)	8.88 %	8.65	
European currency unit	—	8.98 %	
Long-term government bonds			
Canada	9.66 %		
Germany	8.47		
France	8.52		
United Kingdom	8.79		
United States	7.92 %		
Exchange rates			
$1/Brazil cruzeiro	433.90		
$1/FF	5.69		
U.S. financial markets			
Median price/earnings ratio of stocks (S&P 500)	21×		
91-day Treasury-bill rate	5.16 %		
30-year Treasury-bond rate	7.92		
Moody's Aaa-rated corporate-bond yield	8.70		
Moody's A-rated corporate-bond yield	9.25		
Moody's A-rated preferred-stocks yield	9.00		
Geometric-mean equity risk premium	5.60		
Arithmetic-mean equity risk premium	8.40 %		

	1991	1992
Forecasted inflation rates		
France	2.9 %	3.1 %
United States	4.0	3.6
All OECD*	4.4	3.8
European Community	5.0 %	4.5 %

*Organization for Economic Cooperation and Development.

Sources: *The Wall Street Journal Europe; Le Monde; Financial Times; OECD Economic Outlook,* July 1991; *1990 Yearbook,* Ibbottson Associates.

Massive Power Design Corporation

In August 1994, Andrew Rand and James Rhodes surveyed the dramatic recovery of Massive Power Design Corporation (MPDC) and contemplated the business and financial challenges that lay ahead. Chief among these was the design of a financing program that would support the expansion of the company.

Rand and Rhodes acquired MPDC in a hostile takeover in 1988, through their private holding company, Kensington Holdings, for $256 million. The acquisition was financed in part with $216 million in debt. Asset sales and operational restructuring had significantly transformed MPDC. But unusual financial and nonoperating demands on the firm triggered a technical default under the firm's borrowing agreements. In 1991, the firm's senior lender negotiated a general restructuring of the firm's debt. This financial restructuring gave management the leeway to continue with its program of operational restructuring. Throughout this period, the firm's operating earnings remained robust.

The firm's senior credit agreement was to expire in 1995. Sinking fund payments on subordinated debt would begin in 1995 and retire the debt in 1998. In addition, a sizable capital investment program would need to be financed—included in this were some important projects deferred from the difficult 1989–93 period. Finally, Rand and Rhodes hoped to undertake an acquisition program through which to expand the firm. These factors called for artful acquisition of capital—without further asset sales or the dilution of Kensington's 100 percent equity ownership of MPDC. James Rhodes said,

This case was written by Professor Robert F. Bruner as a basis for class discussion rather than to illustrate effective or ineffective handling of an administrative situation. The case was prepared with the cooperation of persons and companies who prefer to remain anonymous. All names and company-specific financial information have been disguised. Copyright © 1994 by the University of Virginia Darden School Foundation, Charlotttesville, VA. All rights reserved. *No part of this publication may be reproduced, stored in a retrieval system, used in a spreadsheet, or transmitted in any form or by any means—electronic, mechanical, photocopying, recording, or otherwise—without the permission of the Darden School Foundation. For inquiries, please send an e-mail to dardencases@virginia.edu.* Revised 1/98. Version 2.0.

We would really prefer to finance growth without an equity issue. Look at Lord Hanson of Hanson Industries: He started from nothing and built a huge corporation. But because he sold equity along the way, he now holds a small percentage. We would rather run something smaller and own it completely.

Rand and Rhodes wondered how much and what kind of nonequity capital the firm could sustain given its cash flow and asset base.

THE COMPANY IN 1994

Massive Power Design Corporation, a conglomerate, consisted of 10 autonomous business units, which are summarized in Exhibit 1. These businesses included a wide range of products such as variable-speed drives for large electric motors, plastic medical tubing, electronic and signal connectors, and instrumentation for scientific and industrial uses (for instance, engine monitoring and humidity management). All these businesses had leading or significant market shares in their respective industries. In addition, many of the businesses operated in markets too small to attract major competitors and were sufficiently specialized or customized to exclude foreign competition. These businesses were not R&D or capital intensive, nor were they subject to rapid technological obsolescence. Rand and Rhodes believed that because of the multiple lines of business, MPDC was not dependent on any industry or technology, and that diversification would continue to be essential to MPDC's future financing and growth strategy.

Sales and net income for fiscal year 1994 were $241 million and $2 million, respectively. Exhibits 2 through 5 give the historical income statement, balance sheets, cash-flow statement, and analytical ratios for the period of Kensington Holdings' ownership of MPDC (1989 to 1994).

MPDC was organized as a holding company, in which the business units operated as discrete organizations. Andrew Rand served as chairman of the board, and James Rhodes as chief executive officer. Serving as chief operating officer was Henry Grolier. Grolier had been recruited to the position in 1992 from General Electric, where he had served for 17 years, most recently as group executive. Explaining the organizational structure, Rhodes said,

> We call the senior level the holding company, not the corporate office. When you have a "corporate" office, the division managers assume that's where the decisions get made. Such an idea is anathema to us. We want the division managers to operate autonomously, and to know that "corporate" won't pull them out of trouble.

The holding company allocated capital, performed human resource functions, and implemented total quality management and productivity improvement programs. Rhodes was proud of the holding company's ability to stimulate significant performance improvements within the business units:

> Andrew and I were part of the business school generation that learned that conglomerates are bad—they shield underperformers from capital market discipline—and carried a misguided notion of synergy. Our businesses are completely autonomous. We do not pretend that there exists a synergy. We want diversification to smooth the effects of the business cycle so that we can cover principal and interest payments. By working with these discrete businesses, we have tightened their operations and helped them improve their competitive positions. In this, we synthesize the

lesson of Jack Welch at GE and apply it toward middle-market manufacturing businesses. The middle market is the engine of economic and export growth. It is the part of the economy that is agile and quick in its response to market changes. We want to avoid businesses where scale is important to success. By assuming the capital allocation and financing tasks at the holding company level, we free the business managers to focus on what they know best.

Exhibit 6 gives MPDC's mission statement. Rhodes elaborated on it:

> Our mission is to be the best in any individual business in which we compete. And we know what it takes to be best: implementation and speed. Technology costs you nothing. The big question is, How sophisticated are you in using it? Andrew and I are afraid of "creeping incrementalism" as an attitude toward performance. Instead, we want to see step function gains in performance. For instance, we, like most of our competitors in coaxial connectors, used to take 14–16 weeks to fulfill an order. We looked at the order-fulfillment process and found a way to reduce it to 4–6 weeks. Our orders doubled in what was a declining product segment. We aim to get the order lead time down to two weeks. Our associates, the people who run the manufacturing equipment, must understand the need for step-function gains. Adam Smith is dead. Simple and mindless division of labor is not the solution to business success. Taking personal responsibility and team-based management are the ways to obtain step-function gains. Now that we have invented an approach for squeezing step-function gains out of middle-market businesses, we want to apply it to other businesses. We need a way to finance that expansion.

Rhodes contemplated future growth by acquisition. The size target of such acquisitions could be in the $10 to $20 million range.

COMPANY HISTORY

Massive Power Design Corporation was founded in 1947 by Lazlo Planck, a distinguished professor of physics at the Institute for Advanced Studies of Princeton University. The firm was subsequently listed on the New York Stock Exchange. The original products of the company were van de Graaf generators and other nuclear physics research equipment. Starting in the early 1970s, MPDC began to acquire a diversified portfolio of industrial manufacturing businesses, in some cases straying considerably from the initial focus of the firm's activities. By 1988 the firm had grown to a collection of 19 different business entities grouped into three segments: plastics, industrial instruments, and electrical components. MPDC concentrated on niche markets that, for the most part, were too small to warrant major investment by larger competitors. The businesses were generally characterized by slowly changing technology, low capital investment requirements, and modest R&D requirements. Managerial inattention and investor confusion about the prospects for this small conglomerate caused MPDC's shares to trade at multiples below its peers, and well below restructuring or liquidation values.

In early 1988, Kensington Holdings commenced a hostile tender offer for the shares of MPDC. Surmounting a poison-pill defense and a Connecticut antitakeover statute, Rand and Rhodes successfully acquired the firm for $256 million, or a multiple of nine times trailing operating income. They had secured financial backing from a German company, Humboldt A.G., which had an interest in investing in U.S. takeovers. Humboldt took a 50 percent interest in Kensington Holdings, leaving the remaining 50 percent for Rand and Rhodes to split. The takeover was financed as follows:

Source	Amount
Senior debt from Gotham Bank	$166 million
Senior subordinated debt from Eagle American BankCapital	20
Junior subordinated debt from Canarsie Savings Bank	30
Bridge preferred stock from Humboldt A.G.	28
Common stock, 100% from Kensington	12
Total	$256 million

MPDC performed extremely well during its first year under new management. Rand and Rhodes sold eight businesses, generating almost $100 million, instead of the $46.8 million they had originally projected. As a result, the company reduced the senior bank debt dramatically in its first six months.

At this point, Eagle American BankCapital, a venture-capital affiliate of Eagle American Bank, introduced the bank to Rand and Rhodes with the intent of having Eagle American unseat Gotham as senior creditor. In April 1989, Eagle American proposed a $110 million replacement for the original $166 million reducing revolver. The proceeds were to be used to:

1. Repay the $28 million of bridge preferred supplied by Humboldt, including accumulated dividends.
2. Provide $40 million for the acquisition of Tiber, the main competitor of MPDC's Arno subsidiary.
3. Provide working capital to fund the growth of the retained businesses.

Although the refinancing included a $60 million planned overadvance, Eagle American took comfort in Kensington's ability to get additional capital from Humboldt and sell any of the 10 remaining businesses should they need additional cash. The bank planned to syndicate the loan.

Shortly after winning the deal, the situation began to deteriorate. MPDC fell within the definition of a highly leveraged transaction, which to Eagle American Bank and U.S. bank regulators brought the lending relationship under close scrutiny. Then, the company was hit with a $140 million lawsuit when it was discovered that the land under the former headquarters, which had been sold in 1984, had been contaminated with a toxic solvent. MPDC began incurring significant legal expenses and was forced to take a reserve for damages and the cost of cleanup. Exhibit 7 summarizes the status of MPDC's litigation and environmental liability as of 1994. Aggressive amortization of intangibles and the loss of earnings from the divestiture of the Unibase division reduced earnings significantly and wiped out the firm's equity on a book-value basis. As of the fiscal year-end (April 30) of 1990, total net worth was −$36 million. This triggered a technical default of the bank-loan covenants, and brought the loan under closer regulatory scrutiny.

The recession of 1990 began to affect the sales and margins at several businesses; the Grimm, Arno, Tiber, and Forte Connector businesses were the hardest hit. Together they accounted for nearly half of the fiscal 1990 gross profits. These difficulties notwithstanding, MPDC sales and operating income for 1990 rose by 32 and 78 percent, respectively. Nevertheless, in January 1991 the senior-bank loan was transferred to Eagle American Bank's Loan Workout Department, which negotiated a restructuring of MPDC's capital as follows:

1. Real estate was mortgaged.
2. Canarsie Savings Bank agreed to reduce the coupon on its junior subordinated debt from base + 6 percent to a flat 7.5 percent, and receive cash payments only if certain cash flow and other financial tests were met. Canarsie also received a "contingent interest payment" security that would give an additional one-time payment of interest from MPDC to Canarsie equal to 13 percent of the appraised equity value of MPDC.
3. Eagle American BankCapital agreed to accept half of its 15 percent coupon payment on a pay-in-kind (PIK) basis for four years. BankCapital also received a "contingent interest payment" security worth 11 percent of the appraised equity value of MPDC.
4. Eagle American Bank restructured the senior debt revolver to provide for tighter covenants, rates that varied depending on the exposure, excess cash flow recapture, and deeper subordination terms.

Humboldt A.G. itself had fallen into financial difficulty stemming from some spectacular investment failures of its own. In response, it was forced to sell operations and investment positions. Rand and Rhodes purchased Humboldt's investment stake in Kensington for $2 million.

The situation began to improve by the end of fiscal 1992. Despite reduced operating earnings, cash flow coverage improved as interest rates moved lower and the balance on the revolver declined. The reductions were largely a result of asset sales, modest insurance recoveries from the lawsuits MPDC had filed against its two insurers, and continued postponement of capital expenditures. In fact, the extraordinary gains motivated MPDC to defer some sales and income, take an early charge for the planned consolidation of Tiber and Arno, and write down inventory. All of this was to offset nonoperating gains in order to avoid triggering certain cash payment provisions on the restructured junior subordinated debt.

Some difficult issues remained. Orders at the flagship Tiber/Arno division were beginning to pick up but were not expected to show up in operating profits for some time. Grimm had lost patent protection on some major products and discovered its monopoly position had allowed the company to gravitate toward a high-cost position and lose customer orientation. Global Adaptor suffered from overcapacity in the industry and deteriorating market share from a legacy of arrogance in its customer relations. The Tiber Division was the lone bright spot, having garnered a very profitable contract that added $4 million to revenues and $2 million to EBIT; but management hardly expected Tiber to repeat the large growth gains in the subsequent year. The company managed to report a pretax profit in fiscal 1993 for the first time since the 1988 buyout, but registered a net loss because of overseas taxes.

RAND AND RHODES

Andrew Rand and James Rhodes grew up three miles apart from each other in Sydney, Australia, but had never met until they entered the MBA program at Harvard Business School (HBS), where they were roommates. Rand received a bachelors of accountancy degree from Melbourne University and worked as an accountant with Arthur Andersen. Rhodes graduated from Oxford University in England and had worked as a movie producer in Los Angeles. Both became fascinated with finance in their MBA studies.

Rand and Rhodes graduated from HBS in 1981. Rand was a Baker Scholar at HBS and was employed by McKinsey & Company as an associate consultant from 1981 to 1986.

Rhodes received the Loeb Fellowship for Excellence in Finance at HBS, and joined Goldman, Sachs in 1981 to work in its Mergers and Acquisitions Department.

In 1986 Rand and Rhodes left McKinsey and Goldman to form Kensington Holdings to acquire companies. "Those were the heady days of M&A in the mid-1980s," recounted Rhodes. Kensington initiated two unsuccessful hostile tender offers. One offer was for a company in the Midwest with a large overfunded pension fund. The target company evaded takeover by redeploying its excess pension assets and recapitalizing. Kensington's investment doubled. The second target had been spun off by a parent company and was trading at a depressed multiple. With Kensington's advances, the target company's stock tripled in value. Massive Power Design Corp. was the third, and ultimately successful, attempt to acquire.

In 1994, Kensington's sole investment was MPDC, from which it received an annual management fee of $5 million. This was recognized in MPDC's selling, general and administrative expense. Though set much higher in 1988, the fee had been reduced as part of the financial restructuring of 1991.

Rand and Rhodes explained their interest in investing in middle-market companies as follows:

> Small businesses are playing an unprecedented role in transforming the manufacturing sector of the U.S. economy. Many studies have documented the improvements in American manufacturing competitiveness and efficiency during the 1980s, yet the nation's industrial might is rarely equated with its vast network of small and medium-sized manufacturers. Small manufacturers (those with fewer than 500 employees) account for 98 percent of the nation's 358,000 manufacturing firms and employ nearly 8 million workers—roughly 40 percent of the total manufacturing workforce. Approximately 90 percent of these companies employ fewer than 100 people . . . Small and medium-sized manufacturers will account for 90 percent of new job growth in the nation. By contrast, since 1980, the Fortune 500 have lost 4 million jobs . . . MPDC is committed to increasing its portfolio of midlevel industrial manufacturing businesses in order to participate in the higher-growth segments of the American industrial economy. As a holding company, MPDC is developing a management system specialized in achieving superior financial performance from middle-market size businesses.

CURRENT CAPITAL STRUCTURE

Exhibit 8 summarizes the detailed terms of MPDC's debt and preferred stock financing. MPDC's capital structure offered several interesting challenges to Rand and Rhodes as they contemplated building on the firm's recovery, and its future expansion. The $69.5 million of senior revolving credit with Eagle American Bank would mature on June 30, 1995, less than a year hence. The senior subordinated debt with Eagle American BankCapital would begin amortizing on August 1, 1995, and be completely repaid on August 1, 1997. The junior subordinated debt with Canarsie Savings Bank would mature on September 1, 1997. Half the redeemable preferred stock would mature in 1998. Refinancing these issues and/or replacing them with alternate forms of capital would be a high priority.

Of particular note was the firm's negative book value of common equity. This was largely the result of cumulative losses in net income of $88,564,000 over the 1988–94 period. James Rhodes acknowledged the materiality of the negative equity but argued that this masked the robustness of the firm's underlying operating income. In addition, he broke down the accumulated net losses by certain categories. The analysis showed that these losses were driven largely by nonoperating events, such as the restatement of the firm's

Analysis of Net Income (Losses) Since Acquisition,
March 1988–April 1994 ($ in thousands)

Continuing operations	$124,572
Premerger write-offs	(4,640)
Discontinued ops./disposals	(6,370)
Arno/Tiber consolidation	(1,633)
Sale of divisions	4,262
Foreign currency translations	(4,642)
Division of acquisition expenses	(23,950)
Environmental/litigation	(1,392)
Interest expenses/refinancing	(101,894)
Management/transaction fees	(10,248)
Amortization/depreciation (APB16)	(41,260)
Income tax provisions	$(21,176)
Total net losses	$(88,564)

amortization and depreciation to bring them into conformity with APB16. Accordingly Rhodes said, "The current and future capital structure must be assessed considering the firm's current and future cash flow and operating earnings, rather than in terms of capitalization ratios. On this basis, I think it is reasonable for us to get senior credit in an amount roughly equal to three times EBIT." He compared MPDC to other issuers of high-yield debt (see Exhibit 9) and concluded that MPDC would warrant a debt rating of B.

Rhodes also believed that MPDC compared well to a peer group of seven publicly listed conglomerates with specialization in the instrumentation and controls fields. Exhibit 10 presents financial and valuation data on those comparable companies. The graph in Exhibit 11 compares an investment of $100 in an equally weighted portfolio of these seven companies versus an investment in the S&P 500 index.

OUTLOOK

Exhibits 12, 13, and 14 present a forecast of MPDC's financial performance for the years 1995–2000. Assumptions underlying the forecast are summarized in Exhibit 15. This forecast reflects the projection of existing operations; it does not include the effects of any acquisitions. The financing needed to support growth and to replace existing sources of capital was calculated as a simple plug figure, and appears in the balance sheet item "Financing Needed."

Rand and Rhodes looked to current trends in the economy and the capital markets for clues to the future. The bank prime rate, having fallen to a 30-year low of 6 percent in 1992, had risen in four successive jumps in the summer of 1994 to 7.75 percent (see Exhibit 16). The index of leading economic indicators remained depressed following the recession of 1991, and suggested no dramatic upturn in economic activity.

WEFA Group, a private consulting firm, published forecasts of interest rates and economic activity based on three scenarios: low growth, high growth, and cyclical growth. Exhibit 17 presents a forecast of the bank prime rate of interest under these three scenarios. Exhibit 18 gives a forecast of the growth rate in real gross domestic product.

Exhibit 19 presents information about the current conditions in the U.S. capital markets as of late August 1994.

EXHIBIT 1   The Business Units of MPDC

Division	Product Lines	FY 1994 Revenues	FY 1994 Operating Profit	FY 1994 Operating Margin
Tiber/Arno	Heating and regulating SCR power controls; power systems; precision drives for DC Motors; AC variable frequency drives	$71,422,000	$5,178,000	7.3%
NATVAR	Medical grade tubing; medical subassemblies; electrical sleeving and tubing	$27,896,000	$4,526,000	16.2%
Grimm	Battery-motive connectors; DC explosion-proof mining connectors; marine ship-to-shore connectors; railroad AC power and communication components; distribution equipment; aircraft AC and DC ground power connectors; battery capacity meters; battery diagnostic instrumentation	$33,046,000	$3,940,000	11.9%
NATCO	Electrical and mechanical gauges; sender units; hour meters	$33,950,000	$1,772,000	8.2%
Forte Connector	Radio frequency connectors and related microwave components	$24,484,000	$ 200,000	0.8%
Global Adaptor	Instrumentation for the measurement of humidity	$19,930,000	$2,496,000	12.5%
Showlid	Ion Accelerator Systems; research ion implanters; power supply components; systems for spectoscopy, and X-ray/gamma-ray research	$12,016,000	$1,092,000	9.1%
Barnoloc	Custom injection molding of thermoplastics; clean room molding	$ 9,756,000	$ 806,000	8.3%
Farmer	Hand levels; transit/dumpy levels; instrument tripods; leveling rods	$ 9,054,000	$ (956,000)	NM
Roesh	Physical testing systems and instruments such as durometers; resiliometers; scleroscopes	$ 3,396,000	$1,232,000	36.3%

Source: Company documents.

EXHIBIT 2   Historical Income Statements (in thousands of dollars)

	1989	1990	1991	1992	1993	1994
Sales/Revenue	$180,260	$237,932	$247,152	$224,622	$232,978	$241,130
Cost of sales, net of depreciation	127,658	147,176	159,940	147,676	155,882	156,014
Depreciation in cost of sales	4,628	5,248	6,028	7,840	7,700	7,518
Total cost of sales	132,286	152,424	165,968	155,516	163,582	163,532
Gross profit	47,974	85,508	81,184	69,106	69,396	77,598
Total SG&A expenses	27,432	50,070	57,578	52,470	50,918	53,428
Lease/Rent expense	2,282	1,738	1,684	1,834	1,914	2,252
Amortization	14,102	8,246	7,632	8,284	2,942	1,990
R&D expense	3,064	2,838	3,196	5,704	5,830	7,266
Pension expense	420	932	1,046	0	184	590
Total operating expense	47,300	63,824	71,136	68,292	61,788	65,526
Net operating profit	674	21,684	10,048	814	7,608	12,072
Interest expense	17,428	17,476	19,924	16,434	13,158	13,318
Other income	14,024	120	0	6,876	816	0
Litigation expense	0	16,982	2,758	(2,164)	(4,934)	(13,450)
Other expense	28,764	0	618	2,310	0	430
Consolidation charge	0	0	0	0	0	976
Management fees	1,200	1,330	0	0	0	0
Total other income (expense)	(33,368)	(35,668)	(23,300)	(9,704)	(7,408)	(1,274)
Profit before taxes	(32,694)	(13,984)	(13,252)	(8,890)	200	10,798
Current income tax	(1,618)	8,822	1,608	(1,204)	3,080	766
Deferred income tax	688	926	1,258	(136)	(250)	7,948
Total income tax expense	(930)	9,748	2,866	(1,340)	2,830	8,714
Profit before extraordinary items	(31,764)	(23,732)	(16,118)	(7,550)	(2,630)	2,084
Extraordinary gains	0	678	0	0	712	0
Extraordinary charges	5,604	0	0	0	0	0
Net profit	(37,368)	(23,054)	(16,118)	(7,550)	(1,918)	2,084
Dividends, preferred	$ (3,864)	$ (1,410)	$ (614)	$ (658)	$ (728)	$ (768)

Source: Company annual reports (data disguised).

EXHIBIT 3   Historical Balance Sheets (in thousands of dollars)

	1989	1990	1991	1992	1993	1994
Assets						
Current assets						
Cash	$ 3,392	$ 1,342	$ 7,064	$ 12,100	$ 3,946	$ 2,892
Short-term investments	33,272	0	0	0	0	0
Gross receivables, trade	29,388	38,426	38,864	34,070	39,066	48,364
Allowance for bad debts	252	504	1,122	1,560	1,622	1,812
Total accounts receivable, net	29,136	37,922	37,742	32,510	37,444	46,552
Income tax refund	0	1,550	816	0	0	0
Raw materials	12,060	25,664	22,824	20,462	19,672	18,824
Work in process	14,108	16,460	14,836	15,660	10,370	10,644
Finished goods	11,284	8,568	6,166	6,458	9,672	7,364
Total inventory	37,452	50,692	43,826	42,580	39,714	36,832
Total current assets	103,252	91,506	89,448	87,190	81,104	86,276
Noncurrent assets:						
Gross fixed assets	62,150	80,078	87,342	88,978	87,010	93,594
Accumulated depreciation	4,708	8,824	14,520	22,176	27,132	31,058
Total fixed assets, net	57,442	71,254	72,822	66,802	59,878	62,536
Investments/Advances in						
affiliates & subsidiaries	4,400	4,038	3,972	0	0	0
Prepaids/Deferreds, LTP	6,418	1,804	1,726	5,224	5,918	6,564
Other assets	1,224	4,266	3,836	4,248	3,160	2,406
Assets held for sale	14,572	1,000	400	0	0	0
Intangibles, goodwill	26,628	12,652	5,782	23,464	22,708	22,050
Intangibles, other	9,596	35,514	35,050	7,090	5,798	4,748
Total assets	$223,532	$222,034	$213,036	$194,018	$178,566	$184,580
Liabilities and Shareholders' Equity						
Current portion of long-term						
debt	$ 17,636	$ 846	$ 710	$ 964	$ 1,036	$ 1,564
Accounts payable, trade	44,436	52,072	51,744	40,194	35,082	37,314
Income taxes payable	28,426	26,350	2,466	7,396	12,456	1,556
Customer advance payment	4,168	5,556	5,274	10,670	4,572	3,602
Net liability, disc ops	1,478	0	0	0	0	0
Total current liabilities	96,144	84,824	60,194	59,224	53,146	44,036
Noncurrent liabilities:						
Long-term debt	15,794	68,168	93,838	85,352	78,742	69,504
Capital lease obligation	19,018	20,200	20,056	19,574	19,158	22,042
Deferred compensation/						
revenue	0	0	1,324	0	0	0
Other liabilities	17,618	15,130	16,594	12,286	8,886	12,846
Environmental cleanup	5,920	0	0	0	0	0
Reserves and credits	782	0	0	0	0	0
Deferred taxes	1,270	2,268	3,418	3,394	3,144	16,544
Total unsubordinated liabilities	156,546	190,590	195,424	179,830	163,076	164,972
Subordinated debt	50,000	50,000	53,362	57,418	61,110	63,270
Redeemable preferred stock	11,168	17,500	18,114	18,772	19,500	20,268
Total liabilities	217,714	258,090	266,900	256,020	243,686	248,510
Minority interest, liabilities	18,846	0	0	0	0	0
Net worth:						
Capital-common stock	2	2	2	2	2	2
Paid-in capital	39,536	34,832	34,652	34,652	34,652	34,652
Pension liab. adjustment	0	0	0	0	(88)	(148)
Translation adjustment	(6,694)	(554)	(1,450)	(1,380)	(1,764)	(1,830)
Retained earnings	(45,872)	(70,336)	(87,068)	(95,276)	(97,922)	(96,606)
Total net worth	(13,028)	(36,056)	(53,864)	(62,002)	(65,120)	(63,930)
Total liabilities and net worth	$223,532	$222,034	$213,036	$194,018	$178,566	$184,580

Source: Company annual reports (data disguised).

EXHIBIT 4 Historical Statement of Change in Cash (in thousands of dollars)

	1990	1991	1992	1993	1994
Net to be financed	(85,020)	(23,696)	8,984	(5,768)	1,636
Long-term debt	54,402	26,236	(8,004)	(5,990)	(4,790)
Subordinated debt	0	3,362	4,056	3,692	2,160
Stock issued	(4,704)	(180)	0	(88)	(60)
Short-term investment	33,272	0	0	0	0
Change in cash	(2,050)	5,722	5,036	(8,154)	(1,054)

Source: Company annual reports (data disguised).

EXHIBIT 5   Analytical Ratios Based on Historical Financial Statements

	1989	*1990*	*1991*	*1992*	*1993*	*1994*
Liquidity						
Working capital	3,554	3,341	14,627	13,983	13,979	21,120
Quick ratio	0.68	0.46	0.74	0.75	0.78	1.12
Current ratio	1.07	1.08	1.49	1.47	1.53	1.96
Leverage/coverage						
Total liabilities/net worth	(16.71)	(7.16)	(4.96)	(4.13)	(3.74)	(3.89)
Tot. liabs–sub. debt/ tang. net worth and sub. debt.	249.41	(6.08)	(5.17)	(5.65)	(5.61)	(6.75)
Total liabilities/Total assets	0.97	1.16	1.25	1.32	1.36	1.35
Senior debt/EBITDA	2.70	2.54	4.83	6.25	5.42	4.31
OFC/Total interest	—	1.00	(0.28)	1.36	1.26	0.57
Profitability						
Return on assets	(16.72)	(10.38)	(7.57)	(3.89)	(1.07)	1.13
Return on equity	286.83	63.94	29.92	12.18	2.95	(3.26)
Gross profit to sales	26.61	35.94	32.85	30.77	29.79	32.18
Operating profit to sales	0.37	9.11	4.07	0.36	3.27	5.01
Net profit to sales	(20.73)	(9.69)	(6.52)	(3.36)	(0.82)	0.86
Dividend payout rate	(10.34)	(6.12)	(3.81)	(8.72)	(37.96)	36.85
Effective tax rate	2.84	(69.71)	(21.63)	15.07	1,415.00	80.70
Activity						
Net receivables days on hand	59.00	58.17	55.74	52.83	58.66	70.47
% Raw materials to total inv.	32.20	50.63	52.08	48.06	49.53	51.11
% Work in process to total inv.	37.67	32.47	33.85	36.78	26.11	28.90
% Finished goods to total inv.	30.13	16.90	14.07	15.17	24.35	19.99
Inventory days on hand	103.34	121.39	96.38	99.94	88.61	82.21
Payables days on hand	122.61	124.69	113.80	94.34	78.28	83.28
Net sales/Working capital	25.36	35.61	8.45	8.03	8.33	5.71
Net sales/Net fixed assets	3.14	3.34	3.39	3.36	3.89	3.86
Profit before taxes/Assets	(0.15)	(0.06)	(0.06)	(0.05)	0.00	0.06
Z—Score	0.21	0.52	0.64	0.55	0.74	1.06
Growth Rates						
Total assets growth (%)		(0.67)	(4.05)	(8.93)	(7.96)	3.37
Total liabilities growth (%)		18.55	3.41	(4.08)	(4.82)	1.98
Net worth growth (%)		NMF	NMF	NMF	NMF	NMF
Net sales growth (%)		31.99	3.88	(9.12)	3.72	3.50
Operating profit growth (%)		3,177.21	(53.66)	(91.90)	834.64	58.68
Net profit growth (%)		NMF	NMF	NMF	NMF	NMF
Sustainable growth (%)	170.94	29.44	16.66	8.07	2.43	(1.22)
Bank Risk Rating Ratios						
TD/TNW	(4.42)	(3.06)	(2.82)	(2.77)	(2.60)	(2.74)
TD/(TD+TNW)	1.29	1.48	1.55	1.57	1.62	1.58
EBIT/Interest	0.04	1.24	0.50	0.05	0.58	0.91
OCF/Total debt service	NMF	0.50	(0.27)	1.30	1.18	0.53
NIBT/Sales %	(18.14)	(5.88)	(5.36)	(3.96)	0.09	4.48
TD/EBITDA	11.22	7.34	11.26	15.12	13.35	11.52

NMF indicates data are not meaningful.

Source: Company annual reports (data disguised).

EXHIBIT 6   Mission Statement

Our vision:	Massive Power Design Corporation is determined to be the *best* in all of our businesses.
Our commitment:	We are dedicated to every aspect of the total quality process and to the following values:
Our values:	Our highest priority is to satisfy our customers.
	We expect our associates (employees) to achieve their maximum potential as individuals and as empowered team members.
	We focus on speed for competitive advantage by simplifying processes and compressing cycle times.
	We demand the highest level of integrity and ethical standards.
	We encourage high expectations, set ambitious goals, and meet our financial commitments.
	We share technologies and best practices and team with our suppliers.

Source: Company documents.

EXHIBIT 7   Summary of Environmental Problem and Related Litigation

---

Background

In March 1984, North American Land Company (NALC) purchased a parcel of land from MPDC in Connecticut, containing a building which was the former MPDC headquarters. NALC paid $37 million for the real estate, $12.5 million in cash, and $24.5 million in a note to MPDC. Prior to closing, NALC and its environmental consultants examined the property for hazardous-waste contamination. They toured the facility and conducted environmental tests. Unfortunately, the tour did not include areas ultimately identified as contaminated. Subsequently, NALC conducted further tests and found contamination beneath a degreaser unit which used highly toxic cleaning solvents.

Under the terms of sale, MPDC did not indemnify NALC against potential environmental risks. However the then-president of MPDC did write a letter stating that the company did not commit any act that was a violation of the Connecticut environmental code. In April 1988, MPDC agreed with the State of Connecticut that it would assess and remediate the site, and provided financial assurances of $4 million to do so.

In September 1988, NALC sued MPDC for violation of the Connecticut environmental code, and for misrepresentation, breach of warranty, and unfair and deceptive acts, based on MPDC's failure to disclose contamination of the property. NALC sought $60 million in damages, and hoped to prove fraud, in which case, a judgment would have been as high as $140 million. MPDC filed a counterclaim and made demand on the $24.5 million promissory note.

To date, MPDC had incurred legal fees totaling almost $20 million in connection with the litigation.* The total cleanup costs for the property were estimated to be $14 million, which were to be paid out over a number of years. Also, the company wrote off the full amount of the promissory note and accrued interest (about $15 million) soon after the suit was filed.

Current Situation

In 1991 MPDC and NALC negotiated a settlement with these key terms: (1) MPDC will remediate the site, (2) the $24.5 million note would convert into a 25 percent profit participation in development of the site, and (3) MPDC would pay $3.6 million in cash to NALC.

*This is the gross obligation of litigation expense shown in the historical statements (Exhibit 2) for years 1991–92. Insurance recoveries against this expense were realized in the years 1992–94. The net obligation for environmental litigation was $808,000. The corporation also incurred a net environmental litigation obligation of $1,382,000; this figure is slightly higher because it includes environmental litigation expense in 1988.

EXHIBIT 8   Detailed Terms of Sources of Long-Term Debt and Preferred Stock

---

Revolving credit agreement. This agreement between MPDC and Eagle American Bank provided a facility equal to
$110 million, less outstanding letters of credit in excess of $6 million, and less $26,356,000 in contractual
reductions in connection with fiscal 1994 and prior year environmental insurance recoveries, permitted asset
sales, and the reduction in the bank's commitment to make funds available. At April 30, 1994, the total amount
used was $69,504,000, and the amount unused and available under this agreement was $8,140,000. Interest was
computed on two possible bases: *(a)* the Eurodollar rate (4⁵⁄₁₆ percent at April 30, 1994) plus 3 to 4 percent; or *(b)*
the bank's base borrowing rate (6¾ percent at April 30, 1994) plus 1½ to 2½ percent. The bank's commitment to
make funds available would be reduced by $1.5 million per quarter starting in July 1994 through maturity at
June 30, 1995. MPDC was required to pay a commitment fee ranging from ⅜ percent to ¾ percent of the
available funds. The Agreement provided for liens on substantially all of the firm's assets. In addition to
covenants restricting the payment of common stock dividends, additional borrowings, the refinancing of existing
borrowings, or the acquisition of material subsidiaries, the Agreement required the company to maintain a
minimum level of capital funds. These funds included the consolidated stockholder's deficiency (excluding
foreign currency translation adjustments), plus redeemable preferred stock and junior and senior subordinated
debt. The capital minimums were to increase quarterly from $18 million to $21 million at April 29, 1995.
Furthermore, senior liabilities could not exceed a multiple of 9 times capital funds at April 30, 1994, or 8 times
capital funds at April 29, 1995, and thereafter. Finally, the company had to maintain a minimum working capital
(current assets less current liabilities excluding current debt maturities) of $27 million at April 30, 1994, and $28
million at April 29, 1995.

Senior subordinated note. MPDC executed this note due to Eagle American BankCapital in a total principal
amount of $26,808,680. This note carried a coupon of 15 percent, payable quarterly, half in cash and half in pay-
in-kind (PIK) interest, through July 1, 1995. Thereafter, the interest was payable in cash. This note was to begin
amortization on August 1, 1995, and to mature on August 1, 1997. The amount outstanding in excess of $20
million represented accrued PIK interest. The $6,808,680 could be prepaid without penalty. The remaining
balance was to be repaid as follows: $10 million in FY 1996, $6,666,000 in FY 1997, and $3,334,000 in 1998.*
In connection with this note, MPDC entered into a contingent interest payment (CIP) agreement with
BankCapital which provided for a one-time additional interest payment, equal to 11 percent of the fair market
value of the equity of MPDC. This CIP could be paid by MPDC (or called by BankCapital) anytime during the
debt amortization period, 1996–98.

Junior subordinated note. MPDC executed this note due to Canarsie Savings Bank in a total principal amount of
$36,460,980. This note carried a coupon of 7.25 percent, payable semiannually in cash. The note would mature
on September 1, 1997. In connection with this note, MPDC entered into a CIP agreement which provided for a
one-time payment calculated as 13 percent of the fair market value of MPDC. The CIP could be paid by MPDC
(or called by Canarsie) anytime before maturity of the loan. This note agreement called for a 3 percent
prepayment penalty upon the sale of assets or capital stock of MPDC to a third party.

Mortgage notes payable. These notes were to mature in January 2003, and June 2004, and bore interest at 8⅜
percent and 9¾ percent, respectively. The notes were collateralized by buildings with a net book value of
$3,989,000 at April 30, 1994.

Redeemable preferred stock. The preferred stock was held half by Canarsie Savings Bank and half by Kensington
Holdings. The preferred stock owned by Canarsie had a mandatory redemption date of June 1, 1998, and carried
a dividend rate of 7.6 percent of par value per year, to be paid in kind (PIK) to maturity. The preferred stock held
by Kensington had a mandatory redemption date of August 16, 2009, and carried a dividend rate of 17½ percent,
also to be paid in kind. Dividend and redemption payments to Canarsie were senior to Kensington.

*Note that maturities in August of each year would fall within the fiscal year ending the following May.

Source: 1994 Company annual report.

EXHIBIT 9 Debt Ratings and Financial Ratios for a Sample of Companies with High-Yield Debt

	Jordan Industries	Chatwins Group	IDEX Corp.	Eagle Industries	Mark IV Industries	Average of Five Peers	MPDC 1995 Pro Forma Results
Rating (S&P/Moody's)	B3/B+	NA/B−	Ba3/B+	B2/B−	B1/B+	NMF	Not rated
EBITDA/Interest	1.3×	1.8×	5.3×	1.6×	3.3×	2.66×	2.42×*
EBITDA/Cash interest	1.7	1.8	5.3	2.2	3.3	2.86	3.47†
(EBITDA-Capex)/Interest	1.0	1.6	4.6	1.2	2.7	2.22	0.93
Senior debt/EBITDA	5.1	4.5	2.0	5.8	1.0	3.68	2.14
Total LT debt/EBITDA	6.6	5.0	2.0	5.9	3.1	4.52	4.11
LT debt/Book capitalization	133%	110.3%	58.4%	87.4%	62%	90%	187%

*EBITDA/Interest = ($20,976 + 11,359)/13,340.
†EBITDA/Cash Interest = ($20,976 + 11,359)/(13,340 − 4,021). This calculation adjusts for PIK interest on the senior subordinated debt.

Source of data: Company documents.

EXHIBIT 10   Information on Comparable Companies (Dollars in thousands except per share price)

Company	Current Price (8/26/94)	Market Cap.	Beta (vs. SPX)	Unlev. Beta (t=.38)	P/E (1995EPS)	*Multiples of Value			
						Price/ Book	Price/ Sales	Debt + Equity to:	
								EBITDA	EBIT
Amtrol Inc.	17¼	$128,740	NA	NA	10.27	2.33	0.41	5.40	6.70
Computer Products	3⅜	68,120	1.36	0.72	12.05	2.07	0.57	7.20	12.20
Core Industries Inc.	10½	102,920	0.88	0.61	10.71	1.45	0.50	5.60	6.90
Dynatech	21½	199,890	0.70	0.61	21.50	1.40	0.44	3.20	5.60
Esterline Technol.	9⅞	64,320	0.59	0.32	22.44	1.16	0.23	4.60	16.10
Genlyte Group Inc.	5	63,660	0.76	0.38	20.00	1.05	0.15	5.20	11.20
Moorco Inte. Inc.	15⅛	$180,670	0.53	0.52	12.20	1.96	0.94	6.00	10.50
Mean*		$115,474	0.80	0.53	15.60	1.63	0.46	5.31	9.89
Median*		102,920	0.73	0.56	12.20	1.45	0.44	5.40	10.50

*Of those with data.

Book D/E	Market D/E	Effective Tax Rate	Historical 5-Yr Sales Growth	Projected 5-Yr EPS Growth	EBIT/ Interest Expense	Current Ratio	Gross Margin	Latest Year ROA	% Shares Held by Institutions	Approx Short Int. Ratio
58%	25%	NA	NA	NA	NA	2.42	NA	NA	NA	NA
141%	68%	NA	3.20%	12%	1.27	2.33	39%	1%	47%	0.00%
70%	48%	35%	−1.90%	11%	3.61	3.85	28%	6%	42%	0.00%
25%	18%	NA	5.50%	15%	NA	1.87	52%	-9%	46%	2.50%
135%	116%	NA	-0.60%	12%	NA	1.10	38%	-12%	45%	0.00%
165%	157%	44%	−2.70%	8%	1.74	2.22	30%	1%	44%	0.00%
3%	1%	36%	NA	12%	35.64	2.41	28%	9%	51%	0.25%
85%	62%	39%	1%	12%	10.57	2.31	36%	−1%	46%	0.46%
70%	48%	36%	−1%	12%	2.68	2.33	34%	1%	46%	0.00%

Company Descriptions

Amtrol Inc. — Designs and markets products used in flow control, storage, heating, and other treatment of fluids in water systems and heating, ventilating, and air conditioning. The company's products include well-water tanks, hot-water expansion tanks, and nonreturnable, pressurized chemical tanks.

Computer Products Inc. — Designs, develops, and manufactures power supplies and measurement and control systems for business, industrial, and government customers worldwide. Customers consist of Hewlett-Packard, Northern Telecom, Westinghouse, Asea Brown Boveri, General Electric, and Texas Instruments.

Core Industries Inc. — Manufactures specialty products for electronics, fluid controls, construction, farm equipment, and industrial markets. Products include power supplies, computer components, pipeline valves, steel doors, hinges, feeders, hydraulic wagons, plows, fork lifts, molded plastics, and metal stampings. The company markets its products internationally.

Dynatech — Through its subsidiaries, designs, manufactures, and sells a diversified line of proprietary electronic and microprocessor-based equipment, instruments and systems for measurement, analysis, and control. These products serve users in the communications, scientific, diagnostic, medical, and governmental agency markets.

Esterline Technol. Corp. — Manufactures automation, aerospace/defense, and instrumentation products. The automation equipment is used to produce printed circuit boards and equipment used in sheet metal. Aerospace/defense products consist of combustible ammunition components and air navigation systems. Instrumentation products include monitoring instruments and electrical power devices.

Genlyte Group Inc. — Manufactures lighting fixtures for indoor and outdoor use. The company's products use incandescent, fluorescent, and high-intensity discharge lights. Genlyte's fixtures are sold to residential, commercial, and industrial markets throughout the United States and Canada.

Moorco International Inc. — Designs, manufactures, and sells fluid measurement and pressure control products for the petroleum, industrial process, and electric power generation industries. The company also provides related design, engineering, and repair services.

Source of data: Bloomberg Data Services, Zach's, Nelson's.

EXHIBIT 11   Average Return on Seven Comparable Companies versus the S&P 500, 1990–94.

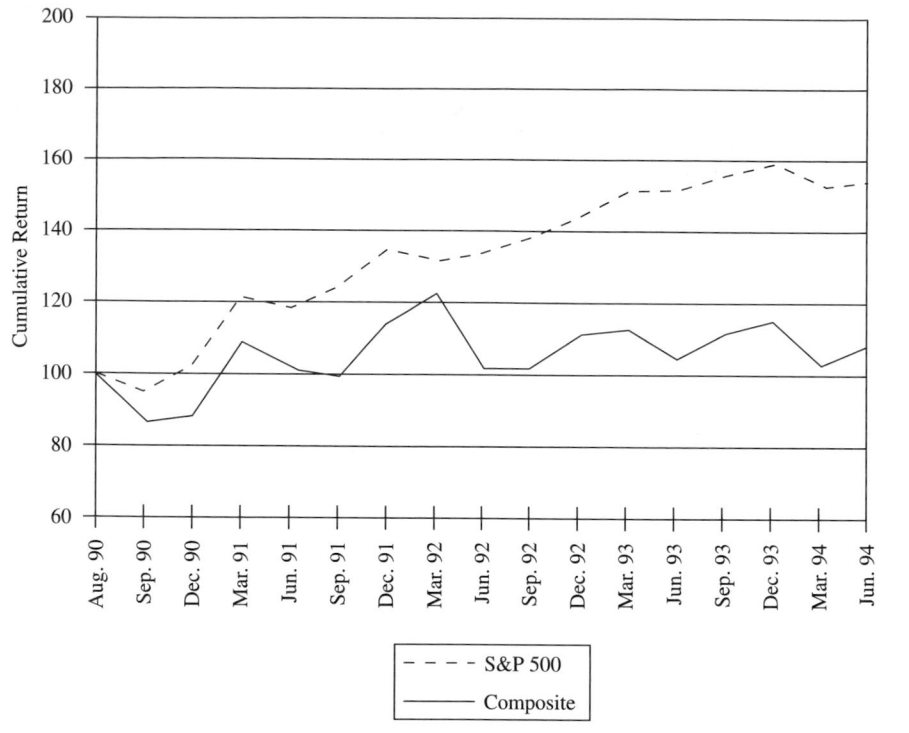

Source of data: Bloomberg Data Services.

EXHIBIT 12 Forecasted Income Statement (in thousands of dollars, at April 30, fiscal year-ends)

	1995	1996	1997	1998	1999	2000
Net sales	$258,990	$279,124	$301,941	$327,940	$357,727	$392,042
Production costs and expenses	173,572	187,698	203,808	222,280	243,579	268,270
Total admin. and selling expenses	64,814	69,858	75,566	82,059	89,483	98,015
Total operating expenses	(238,386)	(257,556)	(279,374)	(304,339)	(333,061)	(366,286)
Total income from operations	20,976	22,087	23,257	24,486	25,775	27,120
Interest expense	(13,340)	(13,567)	(13,794)	(14,038)	(14,320)	(14,667)
Other income (expenses)	0	0	0	0	0	0
Earnings before taxes	7,636	8,521	9,463	10,448	11,455	12,454
Income taxes	(3,054)	(3,408)	(3,785)	(4,179)	(4,582)	(4,981)
Extraordinary items	0	0	0	0	0	0
Net earnings	$ 4,582	$ 5,112	$ 5,678	$ 6,269	$ 6,873	$ 7,472
Earnings available to equity	4,582	5,112	5,678	6,269	6,873	7,472
Preferred dividends	2,327	865	901	937	976	1,016
Change in retained earnings	$ 2,255	$ 4,247	$ 4,777	$ 5,332	$ 5,897	$ 6,456

Source: Casewriter estimate.

EXHIBIT 13   Forecasted Balance Sheets (in thousands of dollars, at April 30, fiscal year-ends)

	1995	1996	1997	1998	1999	2000
Assets						
Cash and equivalents	$ 7,252	$ 7,815	$ 8,454	$ 9,182	$ 10,016	$ 10,977
Accounts receivable (net)	41,297	44,507	48,145	52,291	57,040	62,512
Inventories	44,287	47,730	51,632	56,078	61,171	67,039
Other current assets	4,403	4,745	5,133	5,575	6,081	6,665
Total current assets	97,238	104,798	113,364	123,126	134,309	147,193
Gross property, plant, and equipment	113,594	126,852	141,195	156,772	173,764	192,386
Accumulated depreciation	(42,417)	(55,103)	(69,222)	(84,899)	(102,276)	(121,514)
Net property, plant, and equipment	71,177	71,750	71,972	71,872	71,488	70,872
Other assets	39,411	42,474	45,946	49,903	54,435	59,657
Total assets	$207,826	$219,022	$231,283	$244,901	$260,233	$277,722
Liabilities and stockholders' equity						
Accounts payable	$ 41,697	$ 44,939	$ 48,612	$ 52,798	$ 57,594	$ 63,119
Current portion, LT debt (scheduled)	10,000	6,666	49,247	0	0	0
Taxes payable	778	778	778	778	778	778
Deferred income taxes	4,672	4,672	4,672	4,672	4,672	4,672
Advance payments by customers	6,993	7,536	8,152	8,854	9,659	10,585
Total current liabilities	64,140	64,591	111,462	67,103	72,703	79,154
Financing required (Plug)	**7,612**	**89,681**	**98,925**	**150,934**	**154,114**	**158,019**
Existing (August 1994) revolving credit	69,504	0	0	0	0	0
Senior subordinated note	16,810	10,144	0	0	0	0
Junior subordinated note	39,103	39,103	0	0	0	0
Mortgage notes payable	4,418	4,367	4,317	4,266	4,216	4,165
Environmental cleanup costs	14,008	14,008	14,008	14,008	14,008	14,008
Deferred income taxes	7,200	7,200	7,200	7,200	7,200	7,200
Accrued pension obligation	1,538	1,538	1,538	1,538	1,538	1,538
Other	24,069	23,853	23,620	23,369	23,099	22,809
Total liabilities	248,402	254,486	261,069	268,418	276,877	286,894
Redeemable preferred stock	21,099	21,964	22,865	23,802	24,778	25,794
Stockholders' deficiency or equity						
Common stock	2	2	2	2	2	2
Paid-in capital	34,652	34,652	34,652	34,652	34,652	34,652
Pension liability adjustment	(148)	(148)	(148)	(148)	(148)	(148)
Accumulated deficit	(94,351)	(90,104)	(85,327)	(79,995)	(74,098)	(67,642)
Translation reserve	(1,830)	(1,830)	(1,830)	(1,830)	(1,830)	(1,830)
Total stockholders' equity	(61,675)	(57,428)	(52,651)	(47,319)	(41,422)	(34,966)
Total liabilities and stockholders' equity	$207,826	$219,022	$231,283	$244,901	$260,233	$277,722
Memo						
Purchases of property, plant, and equipment	($ 20,000)	($ 13,258)	($ 14,342)	($ 15,577)	($ 16,992)	($ 18,622)
Other capital expenditures	0	0	0	0	0	0
Proceeds from asset sales	0	0	0	0	0	0
Depreciation expense	11,359	12,685	14,119	15,677	17,376	19,239
Additions to net working capital	(938)	3,774	4,277	4,874	5,584	6,432
Incremental new external financing	**7,612**	**82,069**	**9,244**	**52,009**	**3,180**	**3,906**

Source: Casewriter estimate.

EXHIBIT 14 Analytical Ratios of Financial Forecast (as of fiscal year-ends, April 30)

	1995	*1996*	*1997*	*1998*	*1999*	*2000*
Profitability						
Operating profit margin (%)	8.1%	7.9%	7.7%	7.5%	7.2%	6.9%
Return on sales (%)	1.8%	1.8%	1.9%	1.9%	1.9%	1.9%
Return on equity (%)	−7.4%	−8.9%	−10.8%	−13.2%	−16.6%	−21.4%
Return on total capital (%)	18.5%	17.1%	31.7%	14.9%	14.4%	13.9%
Return on net assets (%)	9.2%	9.0%	12.2%	8.7%	8.7%	8.6%
Return on assets (%)	2.2%	2.3%	2.5%	2.6%	2.6%	2.7%
Leverage						
Debt/Equity ratio (%)	−394.1%	−449.0%	−527.9%	−651.3%	−868.3%	−1340.5%
Debt/Total capital (%)	134.0%	128.7%	123.4%	118.1%	113.0%	108.1%
EBIT/Interest (×)	1.6	1.6	1.7	1.7	1.8	1.8
Asset Utilization						
Sales/Assets	1.25	1.27	1.31	1.34	1.37	1.41
Sales growth rate (%)	7.4%	7.8%	8.2%	8.6%	9.1%	9.6%
Assets growth rate (%)	12.6%	5.4%	5.6%	5.9%	6.3%	6.7%
Cash and invest. to sales (%)	2.8%	2.8%	2.8%	2.8%	2.8%	2.8%
Days in receivables	58.2	58.2	58.2	58.2	58.2	58.2
Payables to sales	16.1%	16.1%	16.1%	16.1%	16.1%	16.1%
Inventories to sales	17.1%	17.1%	17.1%	17.1%	17.1%	17.1%
Other current assets/Sales	1.7%	1.7%	1.7%	1.7%	1.7%	1.7%
Other current liabilities/Sales	2.7%	2.7%	2.7%	2.7%	2.7%	2.7%
Annual depreciation/Gross P&E	10.0%	10.0%	10.0%	10.0%	10.0%	10.0%
Liquidity						
Quick ratio	0.76	0.81	0.51	0.92	0.92	0.93
Current ratio	1.52	1.62	1.02	1.83	1.85	1.86

Source: Casewriter estimate.

EXHIBIT 15 Summary of Forecast Assumptions

	Sales Growth (%)	COGS-to-Sales (%)	Admin. and Selling Exp. to Sales (%)
	Performance by Division		
Tiber/Arno	3.5%	68.0%	15.0%
Natco	11.0	63.0	23.0
Showlid	0.1	66.0	31.8
Farmer	9.0	83.0	20.0
Roesch	0.0	45.0	19.0
Global Adaptor	6.0	48.0	35.0
Grimm	6.0	70.0	19.0
Forte Connector	24.0	78.0	18.0
NATVAR	7.0	66.0	11.0
Barnoloc	1.9%	77.3%	15.1%

		Firm-Level Assumptions	
Cap. expenditures in 1995 (000s)	$20,000	Days receivables outstanding	58.2
Cap. expends./Sales (1996–2000)	4.75%	Payables to sales	16.1%
Depreciation to gross PPE	10.0%	Inventories to sales	17.1%
Dividend payout (common)	0.0%	Other current assets to sales	1.7%
Dividend payout (PIK preferred)	4.10%	Other current liabs. to sales	2.7%
Melded interest rate	9.0%	Tax deferrals as % of tax exp.	0%
Average tax rate	40.0%	Mkt/Book value, asset sales	100.0%
Cash and investments to sales	2.8%		

Source: Casewriter estimate.

EXHIBIT 16   Historical Trend of Bank Prime Rate of Interest

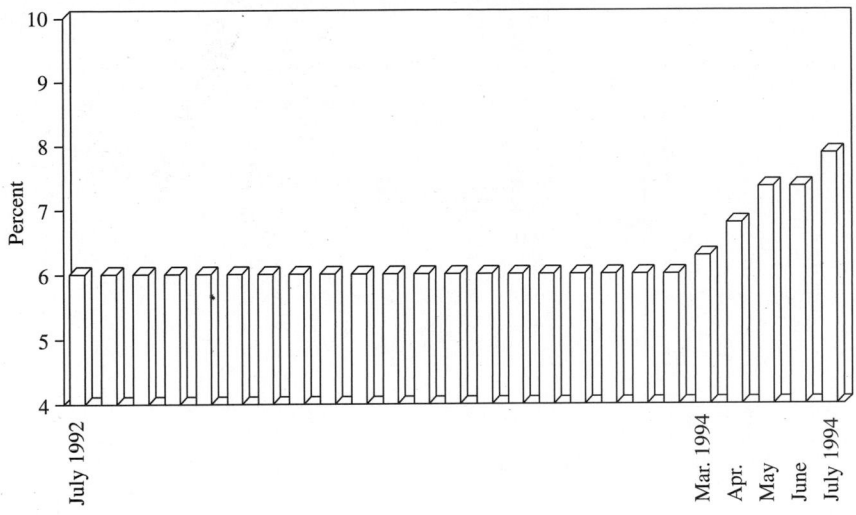

Source of graph: Casewriter analysis.
Source of data: *Current Statistics,* Standard & Poor's Statistical Service.

EXHIBIT 17   Forecast of Bank Prime Rate of Interest under Three Economic Scenarios

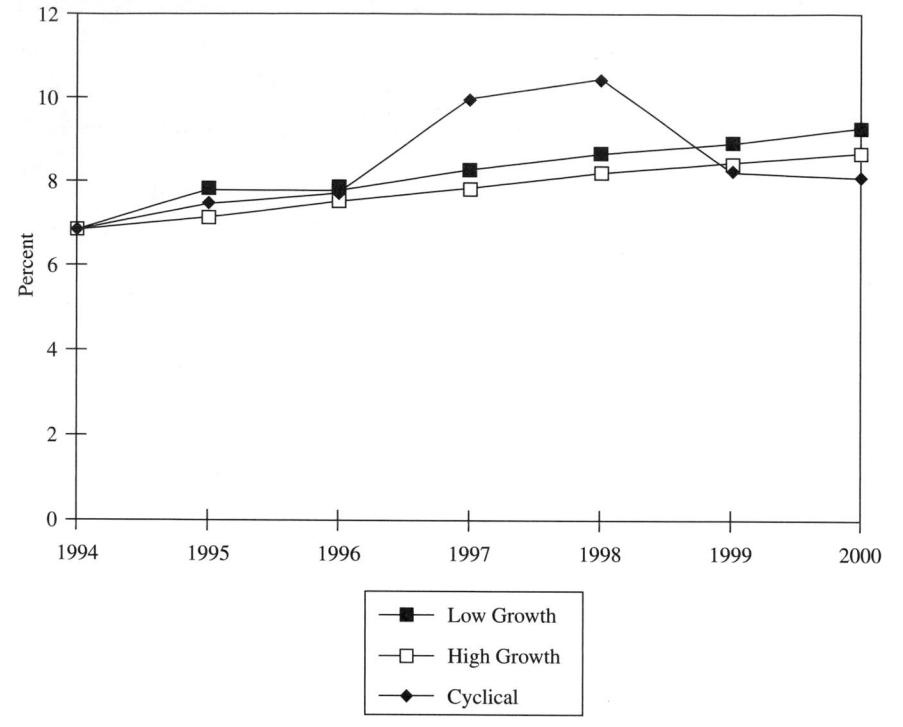

Source of graph: Casewriter analysis.
Source of data: *U.S. Long-Term Economic Outlook,* The WEFA Group, Second Quarter 1994.

EXHIBIT 18   Forecast of Real Growth Rate of Gross Domestic Product

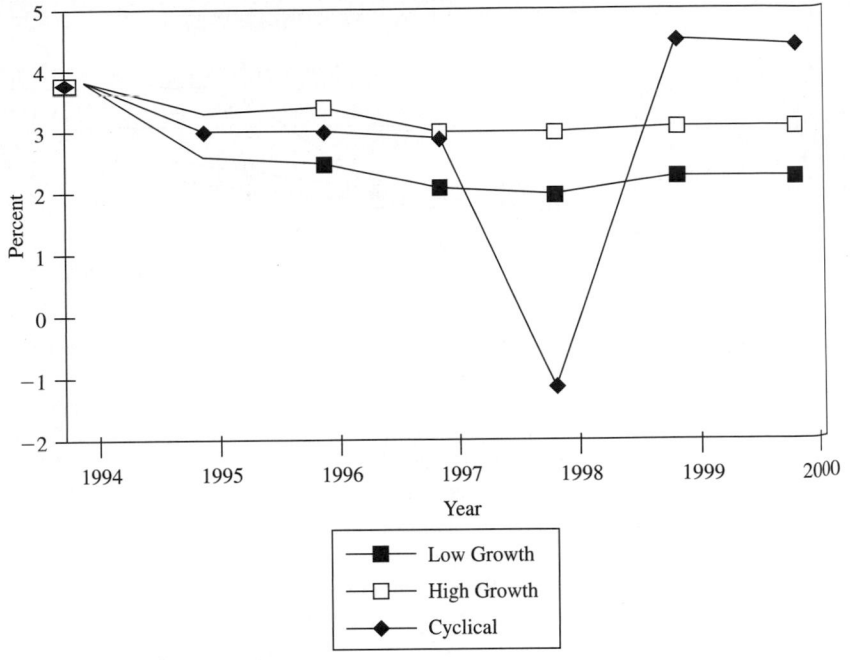

Source of graph: Casewriter analysis.
Source of data: *U.S. Long-Term Economic Outlook,* The WEFA Group, Second Quarter 1994.

EXHIBIT 19   Current Capital Market Conditions, Late August 1994

Stock Market Values

	Price/Earnings Ratios		Market/Book Value Ratios	
	Current	*Year Ago*	*Current*	*Year Ago*
Dow Jones industrials	19.9	43.9	3.47	2.78
S&P 500 index	18.8	23.8	4.08	1.57

Rates of Interest

	Rate/YTM
Treasuries	
90-day bills	4.65%
1-year notes	5.51
5-year notes	6.82
10-year bonds	7.21
20-year bonds	7.57
30-year bonds	7.58
Floating corporate rates	
Prime rate	7.75%
LIBOR (6-month)	5-⁵⁄₁₆
Commercial paper (3 month)	4.89
Fixed corporate rates (industrials)	
AAA	6.84%
AA	7.39
A	7.91
BBB	8.58
BB	9.14
B	10.60
Equity market premiums (1926–93)	
Arithmetic average (stocks-bills)	8.60%
Geometric average (stocks-bonds)	5.40%

Sources of data: Bloomberg Data Services, Ibbotson Associates, *Barron's, Current Statistics* (S&P Statistical Service, August 1994).